IMPORTANT

HERE IS YOUR REGISTRATION CODE TO ACCESS MCGRAW-HILL
PREMIUM CONTENT AND MCGRAW-HILL ONLINE RESOURCES

To obtain 30-day trial access to premium online resources for both students and instructors, you need THIS CODE. Once the code is entered, you will be able to use the web resources.

Access is provided for examination purposes only to assist faculty in making textbook adoption decisions.

If the registration code is missing from this examination copy, please contact your local McGraw-Hill representative for access information.

If you have adopted this textbook for your course, contact your local representative for permanent access

To gain access to these online resources

1. USE your web browser to go to: **www.mhhe.com/crusius**

2. CLICK on "First Time User"

3. ENTER the Registration Code printed on the tear-off bookmark on the right

4. After you have entered your registration code, click on "Register"

5. FOLLOW the instructions to setup your personal UserID and Password

6. WRITE your UserID and Password down for future reference. Keep it in a safe place.

If your course uses WebCT or Blackboard, you'll be able to use this code to access the McGraw-Hill content within your online course. Contact your system administrator for details.

The McGraw-Hill Companies

 Higher Education

Thank you, and welcome to your McGraw-Hill Online Resources.

0-07-320931-7 T/A CRUSIUS: AIMS OF ARGUMENT, 5/E EXAM COPIES BOTH BIG AND BRIEF

REGISTRATION CODE

ZHNZ-5X2B-LSU4-D3JA-JGYN

REGISTRATION CODE

The McGraw-Hill Companies
Mc Graw Hill **Higher Education**

The Aims of Argument

FIFTH EDITION

The Aims of Argument

A TEXT AND READER

Timothy W. Crusius

Southern Methodist University

Carolyn E. Channell

Southern Methodist University

Boston   Burr Ridge, IL   Dubuque, IA   Madison, WI   New York   San Francisco   St. Louis
Bangkok   Bogotá   Caracas   Kuala Lumpur   Lisbon   London   Madrid   Mexico City
Milan   Montreal   New Delhi   Santiago   Seoul   Singapore   Sydney   Taipei   Toronto

Higher Education

Published by McGraw-Hill, an imprint of The McGraw-Hill Companies, Inc., 1221 Avenue of the Americas, New York, NY 10020. Copyright © 2006, 2003, 2000, 1998, 1995 by The McGraw-Hill Companies, Inc. All rights reserved. No part of this publication may be reproduced or distributed in any form or by any means, or stored in a database or retrieval system, without the prior written consent of The McGraw-Hill Companies, Inc., including, but not limited to, in any network or other electronic storage or transmission, or broadcast for distance learning.

This book is printed on acid-free paper.

1 2 3 4 5 6 7 8 9 0 DOC DOC 0 9 8 7 6 5

ISBN: 0-07-296077-9

Cover image: *Whirl,* © Kenneth Noland/Licensed by VAGA, New York, NY. Purchased with funds from the Coffin Fine Arts Trust; Nathan Emory Coffin Collection of the Des Moines Art Center, 1974.79.

Vice president and Editor-in-chief: *Emily G. Barrosse*
Publisher: *Lisa Moore*
Director of development: *Carla Kay Samodulski*
Sponsoring editor: *Christopher Bennem*
Developmental editor: *Joshua Feldman*
Marketing manager: *Lori DeShazo*
Production editor: *Fairplay Publishing Service*
Lead production supervisor: *Randy Hurst*
Art director: *Jeanne M. Schreiber*
Design manager: *Cassandra Chu*
Interior designers: *Ellen Pettengell and Maureen McCutcheon*
Cover designer: *Maureen McCutcheon*
Photo research coordinator: *Natalia Peschiera*
Photo researcher: *Judy Mason*
Compositor: *G&S Typesetters*
Typeface: 10.25/12 *Giovanni Book*
Printer and binder: *RR Donnelley, Crawfordsville*

Text and photo credits appear on pages C1–C5 at the back of the book and constitute an extension of the copyright page.

LIBRARY OF CONGRESS CATALOGING-IN-PUBLICATION DATA

Crusius, Timothy W.
   The aims of argument : a text and reader / Timothy W. Crusius,
Carolyn E. Channell.—5th ed.
     p. cm.
   Includes index.
   ISBN 0-07-296077-9
   1. English language—Rhetoric—Handbooks, manuals, etc.   2. Persuasion (Rhetoric)—Handbooks, manuals, etc.   3. Report writing—Handbooks, manuals, etc.   I. Channell, Carolyn E.   II. Title.

   PE1431.C778 2005
   808'.042—dc22   2005041642

www.mhhe.com

For W. Ross Winterowd

Preface

As its first four editions were, the fifth edition of *The Aims of Argument* is different from other argumentation texts because it remains the only one that focuses on the aims, or purposes, of argument. That this book's popularity increases from edition to edition tells us that our approach does in fact satisfy the previously unmet need that moved us to become textbook authors. We're gratified that our approach has proven useful.

NOTES ON THIS TEXT'S ORIGINS

With over thirty years of teaching experience between us, we had tried most argument books. Many of them were good and we learned from them. However, we found ourselves adopting a text not so much out of genuine enthusiasm but because it had fewer liabilities than the others. We wondered why we were so lukewarm about even the best argumentation textbooks. We boiled our dissatisfaction down to a few major criticisms:

- Most treatments were too formalistic and prescriptive.
- Most failed to integrate class discussion and individual inquiry with written argumentation.
- Apart from moving from simple concepts and assignments to more complicated ones, no book offered a learning sequence.
- Despite the fact that argument, like narrative, is clearly a mode or means of discourse, not a purpose for writing, no book offered a well-developed view of the aims or purposes of argument.

We thought that these shortcomings had undesirable consequences in the classroom, including the following:

- The overemphasis on form confused students with too much terminology, made them doubt their instincts, and drained away energy from inventing and discovering good arguments. Informal argumentation is not formal logic but open-ended and creative.

- The separation of class discussion from composing created a hiatus between oral and written argument. Students had difficulty seeing the relation between the two and using insights from each to improve the other.
- The lack of a learning sequence—of assignments that build on each other—meant that courses in argumentation were less coherent and meaningful than they could be. Students did not understand why they were doing what they were doing and could not envision what might come next.
- Finally, inattention to what people actually use argument to accomplish resulted in too narrow a view of argument and in unclear purposes for writing. Because instruction was mainly limited to what we call arguing to convince, students took argument only as monologues of advocacy. They ignored inquiry.

We set out to solve these problems. The result is a book different from any other argument text because it focuses on four aims of argument:

Arguing to inquire, questioning opinions
Arguing to convince, making cases
Arguing to persuade, appealing to the whole person
Arguing to mediate, finding common ground between conflicting positions

COMMON QUESTIONS ABOUT THE AIMS OF ARGUMENT

Instructors have certain questions about these aims, especially how they relate to one another. Here are some of the most frequently asked questions:

1. *What is the relative value of the four aims? Because mediation comes last, is it the best or most valued?* No aim is "better" than any other aim. Given needs for writing and certain audiences, one aim can be more appropriate than another for the task at hand. Mediation comes last because it integrates inquiry, convincing, and persuading.

2. *Must inquiry be taught as a separate aim?* No. It *may* be taught as a separate aim, but we do not intend this "may" as a "must." Teaching inquiry as a distinct aim has certain advantages. Students need to learn how to engage in constructive dialogue, which is more disciplined and more focused than class discussion usually is. Once they see how it is done, students enjoy dialogue with one another and with texts. Dialogue helps students think through their arguments and imagine reader reaction to what they say, both of which are crucial to convincing and persuading. Finally, as with mediation, inquiry offers avenues for assignments other than the standard argumentative essay.

3. *Should inquiry come first?* For a number of reasons, inquiry has priority over the other aims. Most teachers are likely to approach inquiry as prewriting, preparatory to convincing or persuading. And commonly, we return to inquiry when we find something wrong with a case we are trying to construct, so the relationship between inquiry and the other aims is also recursive.

   Moreover, inquiry has psychological, moral, and practical claims to priority. When we are unfamiliar with an issue, inquiry comes first psychologically, as a felt need to explore existing opinion. Regardless of what happens in the "real world," convincing or persuading without an open, honest, and earnest search for the truth is, in our view, immoral. Finally, inquiry goes hand-in-hand with research, which requires questioning the opinions encountered.

4. *Isn't the difference between convincing and persuading more a matter of degree than kind?* Sharp distinctions can be drawn between inquiry and mediation and between both these two aims and the monologues of advocacy, convincing and persuading. But convincing and persuading do shade into one another so that the difference is clearest at the extremes, with carefully chosen examples. Furthermore, the "purest" appeal to reason—a legal brief, a philosophical or scientific argument—appeals in ways beyond the sheer cogency of the case. Persuasive techniques are submerged but not absent in arguing to convince.

   Our motivation for separating convincing from persuading is not theoretical but pedagogical. Case-making is complex enough that attention to logical appeal by itself is justified. Making students conscious of the appeals to character, emotion, and style while they are learning to cope with case-making can overburden them to the point of paralysis.

   Regardless, then, of how sound the traditional distinction between convincing and persuading may be, we think it best to take up convincing first and then persuasion, especially because what students learn in the former can be carried over intact into the latter. And because one cannot make a case without unconscious appeal to character, emotional commitments (such as values), and style, teaching persuasion is a matter of exposing and developing what is already there in arguing to convince.

Here are the central tenets of an approach based on aims of argument:

- *Argumentation is a mode or means of discourse, not an aim or purpose for writing;* consequently, we need to teach the aims of argument.
- *The aims of argument are linked in a learning sequence so that convincing builds on inquiry, persuasion on convincing, and all three contribute to mediation;* consequently, we offer a learning sequence for conceiving a course or courses in argumentation.

We believe in the sequence as much as the aims. We think that many will come to prefer it over any other approach.

Of course, textbooks are used selectively, as teachers and programs need them in achieving their own goals. As with any other text, this one can be used selectively, ignoring some parts, playing up others, designing other sequences, and so on. If you want to work with our learning sequence, it's there for creative adaptation. If not, the text is flexible enough for almost any course structure or teaching method.

A NOTE ABOUT THE READINGS

You will discover that the issues around which this text's essays are organized involve students in race, class, and gender difference. This slant does not reflect a hidden agenda on our part. Rather, students can come to feel more engaged by issues of this sort than they do by others we have tried. Class debates are livelier, maybe because such issues hit closer to home.

Such issues work because they expose something obvious about argumentation: People differ because they are different, and not just on the basis of race, class, and gender. Without confrontation with difference, students miss the social and cultural roots of argument and fail to understand why people think in such varied ways about homosexuality, feminism, and other issues that obviously turn on difference, as well as issues such as genetic manipulation, which may seem at first to have nothing to do with difference.

We have avoided the "great authors, classic essays" approach (with the exception of Martin Luther King, Jr.'s "Letter from Birmingham Jail"). We tried instead to find bright, contemporary people arguing well from diverse viewpoints—articles and chapters similar to those that can be found in our better journals and trade books, the sort of publications students should read most in doing research. We have not presented any issue in simple pro-and-con fashion, as if there were only two sides.

Included in the range of perspectives are arguments made with both words and images. We include a full instructional chapter examining visual arguments such as editorial cartoons, advertisements, public sculpture, and photographs.

A FINAL WORD ABOUT THE APPROACH

Some reviewers have called our approach innovative. But is it better? Will students learn more? Will instructors find the book more satisfying and more helpful than what they currently use? Our experience—both in using the book ourselves and in listening to the responses of those who have read it or tested it in the classroom or used it for years—is that they will. Students complain less about having to read this book than about having to read others used in our program. They do seem to learn more. Teachers claim to find the text stimulating, something to work with rather than around. We hope your experience is as positive as ours has been. We invite your comments and will use them in the perpetual revision that constitutes the life of a text and our lives as writing teachers.

NEW TO THE FIFTH EDITION

Here are the important changes for this edition:

- We completely overhauled Chapter 9, now "Resolving Conflict: Arguing to Mediate." It had not changed much in previous editions and needed updating. For purposes of illustration, we discarded the topic of abortion and replaced it with a recurrent topic that changes with every new wave of immigrants: the melting pot versus the quilt metaphor-model for American culture. Finally, as the new title indicates, negotiation has largely been subsumed by mediation, partly because it makes far more sense to essay mediation than to attempt negotiation in prose. The chapter is now more coherent, better written, and easier to use—and reflects our continuing experimentation with this complex and fascinating aim.
- We also added more material on plagiarism, always a problem but aggravated by increasing student reliance on the Internet.
- We brought both casebooks up-to-date with many new selections. We also refocused them. The terrorism casebook has moved away from 9/11 and its immediate aftermath to a greater emphasis on the ongoing war on terror. As its new title, "Sex, Relationships, and Maybe Even Marriage," implies, the second casebook concentrates on the lives of young adults, many of whom are not dating in the traditional sense, are postponing marriage, and are starting families later in life.
- As always, some readings in the anthology chapters fell out to make room for fresh ones. The biggest change in Part Four is the deletion of "News and Ethics." Chapter 14 is now "Genetics and Enhancement: Better Than Human?" a topic having perhaps greater intrinsic interest and, with each advance in biotechnology, greater urgency. Note also the new titles in the feminism and the race and class chapters.
- Finally, as with people as they get older, textbooks with each edition tend to pick up a little in the waistline. We're happy to say that *Aims* has lost weight in this incarnation, not by reckless, last-minute slashing of any one section or chapter, but by careful, general slimming down.

Revised Online Learning Center

In addition to the many changes the fifth edition offers in the text itself, this edition of *Aims* is accompanied by a newly revised Online Learning Center, accessible at www.mhhe.com/crusius. The bind-in card at the front of the text gives you access to this powerful resource, which now features all the tools of Catalyst 2.0, McGraw-Hill's award-winning writing and research Web site. You will find integrated references throughout the text, pointing you to additional online coverage of the topic at hand.

Online Course Delivery and Distance Learning

In addition to the Web site, McGraw-Hill offers the following technology products for composition classes. The online content of *The Aims of Argument* is supported by WebCT, Blackboard, eCollege.com, and most other course systems. Additionally, McGraw-Hill's PageOut service is available to get you and your course up and running online in a matter of hours—at no cost! To find out more, contact your local McGraw-Hill representative or visit <http://www.pageout.net>.

PageOut

McGraw-Hill's widely used click-and-build Web site program offers a series of templates and many design options, requires no knowledge of HTML, and is intuitive and easy to use. With PageOut, anyone can produce a professionally designed course Web site in very little time.

AllWrite! 2.1

Available online or on CD-ROM, *AllWrite!* 2.1 offers over 3,000 exercises for practice in basic grammar, usage, punctuation, context spelling, and techniques for effective writing. The popular program is richly illustrated with graphics, animations, video, and Help screens.

Teaching Composition Faculty Listserv at <www.mhhe.com/tcomp>

Moderated by Chris Anson at North Carolina State University and offered by McGraw-Hill as a service to the composition community, this listserv brings together senior members of the college composition community with newer members—junior faculty, adjuncts, and teaching assistants—in an online newsletter and accompanying discussion group to address issues of pedagogy, in both theory and in practice.

ACKNOWLEDGMENTS

We have learned a great deal from the comments of both teachers and students who have used this book, so please continue to share your thoughts with us.

We wish to acknowledge the work of the following reviewers who guided our work on the first, second, third, and fourth editions: Linda Bensel-Meyers, University of Tennessee, Knoxville; Elizabeth Howard Borczon, University of Kansas; Joel R. Brouwer, Montcalm Community College; Lisa Canella, DePaul University; Mary F. Chen-Johnson, Tacoma Community College; Matilda Cox, University of Maryland–College Park; Margaret Cullen, Ohio Northern University; Dr. Charles Watterson Davis, Kansas State University; Amy Cashulette Flagg, Colorado State University; Richard Fulkerson, Texas A&M University–Commerce; Lynee Lewis Gaillet, Georgia State University; Cynthia Haynes, University of Texas at Dallas; Matthew Hearn, Valdosta State University; Peggy B. Jolly, University of Alabama at Birmingham; James L. Kastely, University of Houston; William Keith, Oregon State University; Lisa J. McClure, Southern Illinois University, Carbondale; Rolf Norgaard, University of Colorado at Boulder; Julie Robinson, Colorado State University; Gardner Rogers, University of Illinois, Urbana-Champaign; Judith Gold Stitzel, West Virginia University; Cara-Lynn Ungar, Portland Community College; N. Renuka Uthappa, Eastern Michigan University; and Anne Williams, Indiana University-Purdue University Indianapolis.

We also thank the reviewers of the fifth edition: John F. Barber, University of Texas, Dallas; Claudia Becker, Loyola University; Kathleen Bell, University of Central Florida; Richard Fantina, Florida International University; Lynne Graft, Saginaw Valley State University; Peggy Jolly, University of Alabama at Birmingham; Beth Madison, West Virginia University; Patricia Medeiros, Scottsdale Community College; Christine Miller, California State University, Sacramento; Sarah R. Morrison, Morehead State University; Angela Rhoe, University of Cincinnati; James Sodon, St. Louis Community College; Mary Torio, University of Toledo; Julie Wakeman-Linn, Montgomery College; Sandra Zapp, Paradise Valley Community College; and Tom Zimmerman, Washtenaw Community College.

April Wells-Hayes of Fairplay Publishing Service, our production editor, and Margaret Moore, our copyeditor, went far beyond the call of duty in helping us refine and complete the revised manuscript. At McGraw-Hill, Marty Granahan's work with permissions and Natalia Peschiera's photo research also deserve special recognition and our deepest gratitude. Finally, Christopher Bennem and Joshua Feldman, our editors, showed their usual brilliance and lent their unflagging energy throughout the process that led to this new edition of *Aims*.

Timothy Crusius
Carolyn Channell
Dallas, Texas

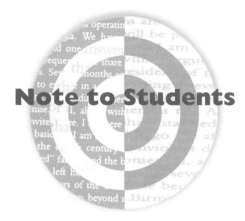

Note to Students

Our goal in this book is not just to show you how to construct an argument but also to make you more aware of why people argue and what purposes argument serves. Consequently, Part Two of this book introduces four specific aims that people have in mind when they argue: to inquire, to convince, to persuade, and to mediate. Part One precedes the aims of argument and focuses on understanding argumentation in general, reading and analyzing arguments, doing research, and working with forms of visual persuasion such as advertising.

The selections in Parts One and Two offer something to emulate. All writers learn from studying the strategies of other writers. The object is not to imitate what a more experienced writer does but to understand the range of strategies you can use in your own way for your own purposes.

Included are arguments made with words and images. We have examples of editorial cartoons, advertisements, and photographs.

The additional readings in Parts Three and Four serve another function. To learn argument, we have to argue; to argue, we must have something to argue about. So we have grouped essays and images around central issues of current public discussion. Part Three's two casebooks offer expanded treatment of two subjects we think you'll find especially interesting: terrorism, and sex and relationships. We selected the essays of Part Four rather than others for two main reasons. One is that the included essays have worked better than those we tried and rejected. The other is that most of the topics of these essays deal centrally with difference, which causes people to disagree with one another in the first place.

People argue with one another because they do not see the world the same way, and they do not see the world the same way because of different backgrounds. Therefore, in dealing with how people differ, a book about argument must deal with what makes people different, with the sources of disagreement itself—including gender, race/ethnicity, class, sexual orientation, and religion. Rather than ignoring or glossing over difference, the readings in Parts Three and Four will help you better understand it.

This book concludes with an appendix on editing, the art of polishing and refining prose, and finding common errors. Consult this reference often as you work through the text's assignments.

Arguing well is difficult for anyone. We have tried to write a text no more complicated than it has to be. We welcome your comments to improve future editions. Write us at

> The Rhetoric Program
> Dallas Hall
> Southern Methodist University
> Dallas, Texas 75275

or e-mail your comments to

> cchannel@mail.smu.edu

About the Authors

Timothy W. Crusius is professor of English at Southern Methodist University, where he teaches beginning and advanced composition. He's the author of books on discourse theory, philosophical hermeneutics, and Kenneth Burke. He resides in Dallas with his wife, Elizabeth, and their children, Micah and Rachel.

Carolyn E. Channell taught high school and community college students before coming to Southern Methodist University, where she is now a senior lecturer and specialist in first-year writing courses. She resides in Richardson, Texas, with her husband, David, and "child," a boxer named Gretel.

Contents

Part Four   Readings: Issues and Arguments

Chapter 12   Feminism: Evaluating the Effects of Gender Roles   567

BOXES BY TYPE

Part One Resources for Reading and Writing Arguments

Part One Resources for Reading and Writing Arguments

Chapter I

Understanding Argument

The *Aims of Argument* is based on two key concepts: argument and rhetoric. These days, unfortunately, the terms *argument* and *rhetoric* have acquired bad reputations. The popular meaning of *argument* is *disagreement;* we think of raised voices, hurt feelings, winners and losers. Most people think of *rhetoric,* too, in a negative sense—as language that sounds good but evades or hides the truth. In this sense, rhetoric is the language we hear from the politician who says anything to win votes, the public relations person who puts "positive spin" on dishonest business practices, the buck-passing bureaucrat who blames the foul-up on someone else, the clever lawyer who counterfeits passion to plead for the acquittal of a guilty client.

The words *argument* and *rhetoric,* then, are commonly applied to the darker side of human acts and motives. This darker side is real—arguments are often pointless and silly, ugly and destructive; all too often, rhetoric is empty words contrived to mislead or to disguise the desire to exert power. But this book is not about that kind of argument or that kind of rhetoric. Here we develop the meanings of *argument* and *rhetoric* in an older, fuller, and far more positive sense—as the language and art of mature reasoning.

WHAT IS ARGUMENT?

In this book, **argument** means *mature reasoning.* By *mature,* we mean an attitude and approach to argument, not an age group. Some older adults are incapable of mature reasoning, whereas some young people reason very well. And all of us, regardless of age, sometimes fall short of mature reasoning. What is "mature" about the kind of argument we have in mind? One meaning of *mature* is "worked out fully by the mind" or "considered" (*American Heritage Dictionary*). Mature decisions, for example, are thoughtful ones, reached slowly after full consideration of all the consequences. And this is true also of mature reasoning.

The second term in this definition of argument also needs comment: *reasoning*. If we study logic in depth, we find many definitions of reasoning, but for practical purposes, *reasoning* here means *an opinion plus a reason (or reasons) for holding that opinion*. As we will see in detail later in this chapter, good arguments require more than this; to be convincing, reasons must be developed with evidence like specific facts and examples. However, understanding the basic form of "opinion-plus-a-reason" is the place to begin when considering your own and other people's arguments.

One way to understand argument as mature reasoning is to contrast it with *debate*. In debate, opponents take a predetermined, usually assigned, side and attempt to defend it, in much the same way that an army or a football team must hold its ground. The point is to win, to best one's opponent. In contrast, rather than starting with a position to defend, mature reasoners work toward a position. If they have an opinion to start with, mature reasoners think it through and evaluate it rather than rush to its defense. To win is not to defeat an opponent but rather to gain insight into the topic at hand. The struggle is with the problem, question, or issue we confront. Rather than seeking the favorable decision of the judges, as in debate, we are after a sound opinion in which we can believe—an opinion consistent with the facts and that other people will respect and take seriously.

Of course, having arrived at an opinion that seems sound to us, we still must *make our case*—argue in the sense of providing good reasons and adequate evidence in support of them. But whereas debaters must hold their positions at all costs, mature reasoners may not. The very process of making a case will often show us that what we thought was sound really isn't. We try to defend our opinion and find that we can't—or at least, not very well. And so we rethink our position until we arrive at one for which we *can* make a good case. From beginning to end, therefore, mature reasoning is a process of discovery.

WHAT IS RHETORIC?

Over time, the meanings of most words in most languages change—sometimes only a little, sometimes a lot. The word *rhetoric* is a good example of a big change. As indicated already, the popular meaning of *rhetoric* is empty verbiage—the art of sounding impressive while saying little—or the art of verbal deception. This meaning of *rhetoric* confers a judgment, and not a positive one.

In contrast, in ancient Greece, where rhetoric was invented about 2,500 years ago, *rhetoric* referred to the art of public speaking. The Greeks

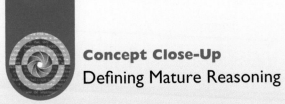
Argument as mature reasoning means:

- Defending *not the first position* you might take on an issue *but the best position*, determined through open-minded inquiry
- Providing reasons for holding that position that can earn the respect of an opposing audience

recognized that rhetoric could be abused, but, for their culture in general, it was not a negative term. They had a goddess of persuasion (see Figure 1.1), and they respected the power of the spoken word to move people. It dominated their law courts, their governments, and their public ceremonies and events. As an art, the spoken word was an object of study. People

Figure 1.1   Peitho, the goddess of Persuasion, was often involved in seductions and love affairs. On this piece (a detail from a terracota kylix, c. 410 BC), Peitho, the figure on the left, gives advice to a dejected-looking woman, identified as Demonassa. To the right, Eros, the god of Love, stands with his hands on Demonassa's shoulder, suggesting the nature of this advice.

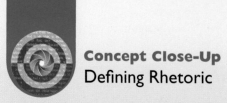
Rhetoric is the art of argument as mature reasoning. The study of rhetoric develops self-conscious awareness of the principles and practices of mature reasoning and effective arguing.

enrolled in schools of rhetoric to become effective public speakers. Further, the ancient rhetoricians put a high value on good character. Not just sounding ethical but being ethical contributed to a speaker's persuasive power.

This old, highly valued meaning of rhetoric as oratory survived well into the nineteenth century. In Abraham Lincoln's day, Americans assembled by the thousands to hear speeches that went on for hours. For them, a good speech held the same level of interest as a big sporting event does for people today.

In this book, we are interested primarily in various ways of using *written* argument, but the rhetorical tradition informs our understanding of mature reasoning. Mature reasoning has nothing to do with the current definition of rhetoric as speech that merely sounds good or deceives people. The ancient meaning of *rhetoric* is more relevant, but we update it here to connect it directly with mature reasoning.

If argument is mature reasoning, then rhetoric is its *art*—that is, how we go about arguing with some degree of success. Just as there is an art of painting or sculpture, so is there an art of mature reasoning. Since the time of Aristotle, teachers of rhetoric have taught their students *self-conscious* ways of reasoning well and arguing successfully. The study of rhetoric, therefore, includes both what we have already defined as reasoning *and* ways of appealing to an audience. These include efforts to project oneself as a good and intelligent person as well as efforts to connect with the audience through humor, passion, and image.

AN EXAMPLE OF ARGUMENT

So far, we've been talking about argument in the abstract—definitions and explanations. To really understand argument, especially as we define it here, we need a concrete example. One thing mature reasoning does is to challenge unexamined belief, the stances people take out of habit without much thought. The following argument by a syndicated columnist would have us consider more carefully our notion of "free speech."

6

You Also Have the Right
to Tell a Bigot What You Think
Leonard Pitts

For the record, I have no idea who let the dogs out. I didn't even know the gate was open.

We Americans get hooked on saying some pretty silly things, you know? "Where's the beef?" "Make my day."

Generally, it is pretty harmless stuff. Granted, after the fifteenth time someone avows that he feels your pain, you probably are ready to inflict some of your own. But overall, yeah — pretty harmless.

There is, however, one expression that never fails to make me nuts. Truth be told, it is less a catchphrase than a cop-out, a meaningless thing people say — usually when accusations of racism, sexism, anti-Semitism or homophobia have been leveled and they are being asked to defend the indefensible.

"Entitled to my opinion," they say. Or "entitled to his opinion," as the case may be. The sense of it is the same even when the words vary: People clamber atop the First Amendment and remind us that it allows them or someone they decline to criticize to say or believe whatever they wish.   5

It happened again just the other day, on the eve of the Grammys. One of the entertainment news programs did an informal poll of musicians, asking them to comment on the rapper Eminem's violently homophobic and misogynistic music. You would have sworn they all were reading from the same script: "He is entitled to say what he feels," they said.

In that, they echoed the folks who thought John Rocker was unfairly maligned for his bigotry: "He is entitled to his opinion," the ballplayer's defenders told us. And that, in turn, was an echo of what happened in 1993 when a reporter asked a student at City University of New York about Dr. Leonard Jeffries' claim of a Jewish conspiracy against black people. "He had a right to say whatever he chooses to say," the student replied.

As I said, it makes me crazy — not because the observation isn't correct, but because it is beside the point.

Anybody who is a more ardent supporter of the First Amendment than I probably ought to be on medication. I believe the liberties it grants are meaningless unless extended as far as possible into the ideological hinterlands. Only in this way can you preserve and defend those liberties for the rest of us. So, as far as I am concerned, every sexist, homophobe, communist, flag burner, Jew baiter, Arab hater and racist must be protected in the peaceful expression of his or her beliefs.

But after acknowledging the right of the hateful to be hateful and the   10
vile to be vile, it seems to me that the least I can do is use my own right of
free speech to call those people what they are. It seems to me, in fact, that I
have a moral obligation to do so. But many people embrace moral cow-
ardice instead and blame it on the First Amendment.

It is a specious claim. The First Amendment is violated when the government seeks to censor expression. That didn't happen to Eminem. That
didn't happen to John Rocker, either. What did happen was that the media
and private citizens criticized them and demanded that some price—public
condemnation or professional demotion—be extracted as a penalty for the
stupid things they said.

Friends and neighbors, that isn't a violation of free speech. That *is* free
speech. And if some folks confuse the issue, well, that is because too many
of us believe freedom of speech means freedom from censure, the unfettered right to say whatever you please without anyone being allowed to
complain. Worse, many of us accept that stricture for fear of seeming "judgmental." These days, of course, "judgmental" is a four-letter word.

I make no argument for being closed-minded. People ought to open
themselves to the widest possible variety of ideas and expressions. But that
doesn't mean losing your ability to discern or abdicating your responsibility
to question, criticize . . . *think*. All ideas aren't created equal. To pretend
otherwise is to create a rush from judgment—to free a bigot from taking
responsibility for his beliefs and allow him a facade of moral validity to
hide behind.

So I could happily live the rest of my life without being reminded that
this fool or that has the right to say what he thinks. Sure, he does. But you
know what? We all do.

Discussion of "You Also Have the Right . . ."

Leonard Pitts's argument is an example of a certain type or *genre* of written argument, the opinion column we find in the editorial section of newspapers.
Arguments of this genre are usually brief and about some issue of general
public concern, often an issue prominent in recent news stories. Most arguments written for college assignments are longer and deal with academic topics, but if we want to grasp the basics of mature reasoning, it's good to begin
with the concise and readable arguments of professional columnists. Let's
consider both the argument Pitts makes and his rhetoric—the art he uses to
make his argument appealing to readers.

Pitts's Reasoning

In defining argument as mature reasoning, we stressed the process of arriving
at an opinion as much as defending it. Arriving at an opinion is part of the
aim of argument we call **inquiry**, and it's clearly very important for college

writers who must deal with complex subjects and digest much information. Unfortunately, we can't see how authors arrived at their opinions by reading their finished work. As readers, we "come in" at the point where the writer states and argues for a position; we can't "go behind" it to appreciate how he or she got there. Consequently, all we can do with a published essay is discover how it works.

Let's ask the first question we must ask of any argument we're analyzing: What is Pitts's opinion, or claim? If a piece of writing is indeed an argument, we should be able to see that the author has a clear position or opinion. We can call this the **claim** of the argument. It is what the author wants the audience to believe or to do.

All statements of opinion are answers to questions, usually **implied questions** because the question itself is too obvious to need spelling out. But when we study an argument, we must be willing to be obvious and spell it out anyway to see precisely what's going on. The question behind Pitts's argument is: What should we do when we hear someone making clearly bigoted remarks? His answer: We have the right and even the moral obligation to "call those people what they are." That is his claim.

What reasons does Pitts give his readers to convince them of his claim? He tells them that the common definition of freedom of speech is mistaken. Freedom of speech does not give everyone the right to say whatever he or she wants without fear of consequences, without even the expectation of being criticized. He thinks people use this definition as an excuse not to speak up when they hear or read bigotry.

In developing his reason, Pitts explains that this common definition is beside the point because no one is suggesting that people aren't entitled to their opinions. Of course they are, even if they are uninformed and full of hatred for some person or group of people. But freedom of speech is not the right to say anything without suffering consequences; rather, as Pitts says, it's a protection against government censorship, what's known in law as *prior restraint.* In other words, if a government authority prevents you from saying or printing something, that is censorship and a violation of the First Amendment in most cases. We should not feel that someone's rights have been taken away if a high price—for instance, "public condemnation or professional demotion" (paragraph 11)—must be paid for saying stupid things. The First Amendment does not protect us from the social or economic consequences of what we say or write. "All ideas aren't created equal," as Pitts maintains. Some deserve the condemnation they receive.

Now that we understand what Pitts is arguing, we can ask another question: What makes Pitts's argument mature, an example of the kind of reasoning worth learning how to do? First, it's mature in contrast to the opinion about free speech he criticizes, which clearly does not result from a close examination of what free speech means. Second, it's mature because it assumes civic responsibility. It's not a cop-out. It argues for doing the difficult thing because it is right and good for our society. It shows mature reasoning when it says: "People ought to open themselves to the widest possible variety of ideas and expressions. But that doesn't mean losing your responsibility to question, criticize . . . *think.*" Finally, it's mature in contrast to another common response to bigotry that Pitts doesn't discuss — the view that "someone ought to shut that guy up" followed by violence or the threat of violence directed at the offending person. Such an attitude is neither different from nor better than the attitude of a playground bully, and the mature mind does not accept it.

In recognizing the maturity of Pitts's argument, we should not be overly respectful of it. Ultimately, the point of laying out an argument is to respond to it maturely ourselves, and that means asking our own questions. For instance, we might ask:

> When we say, "He's entitled to his opinion," are we *always* copping out, or is such a response justified in some circumstances?
> Does it do any good to call a bigot a bigot? Is it wiser sometimes to just ignore hate speech?
> How big a price is too big for stating a foolish opinion? Does it matter if a bigot later retracts his opinion, admits he was wrong, and apologizes?

One of the good things about mature arguments is that we can pursue them at length and learn a lot from discussing them.

 Following Through

Select an opinion column on a topic of interest to your class from your local city or campus newspaper. Choose an argument that you think exemplifies mature reasoning. Discuss its reasoning as we have here with Pitts's essay. Can you identify the claim or statement of the author's opinion? The claim or opinion is what the author wants his or her readers to believe or to do. If you can find no exact sentence to quote, can you nevertheless agree on what it is he or she wants the readers to believe or to do? Can you find in the argument one or more reasons for doing so?

Other Appeals in Pitts's Argument

Finally, we ask, what makes Pitts's argument effective? That is, what makes it succeed with his readers? We have said that reasoning isn't enough when it comes to making a good argument. A writer, like a public speaker, must employ more than reason and make a conscious effort to project personality, to connect with his or her readers. Most readers seem to like Leonard Pitts because of his T-shirt-and-shorts informality and his conversational style, which includes remarks like "it makes me crazy" and sentence fragments like "But overall, yeah — pretty harmless."

We can't help forming impressions of people from reading what they write, and often these impressions correspond closely to how authors want us to perceive them anyway. Projecting good character goes all the way back to the advice of the ancient rhetoric teachers. Showing intelligence, fairness, and other signs of maturity will help you make an argument effectively.

Pitts also makes a conscious effort to appeal to his readers (that is, to gain their support) by appealing to their feelings and acknowledging their attitudes. Appreciating Pitts's efforts here requires first that we think for a moment about who these people probably are. Pitts writes for the *Miami Herald*, but his column appears in many local papers across the United States. It's safe to say that the general public are his readers. Because he is writing an argument, we assume he envisions them as not already seeing the situation as he sees it. They might be "guilty" of saying, "Everyone's entitled to an opinion." But he is not angry with them. He just wants to correct their misperception. Note that he addresses them as "friends and neighbors" in paragraph 12.

He does speak as a friend and neighbor, opening with some small talk, alluding to a popular song that made "Who let the dogs out" into a catchphrase. Humor done well is subtle, as here, and it tells the readers he knows they are as tired of this phrase as he is. Pitts is getting ready to announce his serious objection to one particular catchphrase, and he wants to project himself as a man with a life, an ordinary guy with common sense, not some neurotic member of the language police about to get worked up over nothing. Even though he shifts to a serious tone in the fourth paragraph, he doesn't completely abandon this casual and humorous personality—for example, in paragraph 9, where he jokes about his "ardent" support of the First Amendment.

But Pitts also projects a dead serious tone in making his point and in presenting his perspective as morally superior. One choice that conveys this attitude is his comment about people in the "ideological hinterlands": "every sexist, homophobe, communist, flag burner, Jew baiter, Arab hater and racist must be protected in the peaceful expression of his or her beliefs."

 Following Through

For class discussion: What else in Pitts's argument strikes you as particularly good, conscious choices? What choices convey his seriousness of purpose? Pay special attention to paragraphs 9 and 13. Why are they there? How do they show audience awareness? Which of Pitts's strategies or choices seem particularly appropriate for op-ed writing? Which might not be appropriate in an academic essay? One reason for noticing the choices professional writers make in their arguments is to learn some of their strategies, which you can use when writing your own arguments.

FOUR CRITERIA OF MATURE REASONING

Students often ask, "What does my professor want?" Although you will be writing many different kinds of papers in response to the assignments in this textbook, your professor will most likely look for evidence of mature reasoning. When we evaluate student work, we look for four criteria that we consider marks of mature reasoning.

Mature Reasoners Are Well Informed

Your opinions must develop from knowledge and be supported by reliable and current evidence. If the reader feels that the writer "doesn't know his or her stuff," the argument loses all weight and force.

You may have noticed that people have opinions about all sorts of things, including subjects they know little or nothing about. The general human tendency is to have the strongest opinions on matters about which we know the least. Ignorance and inflexibility go together because it's easy to form an opinion when few or none of the facts get in the way and we can just assert our prejudices. Conversely, the more we know about most topics, the harder it is to be dogmatic. We find ourselves changing or at least refining our opinions more or less continuously as we gain more knowledge.

Mature Reasoners Are Self-Critical and Open to Constructive Criticism from Others

We have opinions about all sorts of things that don't matter much to us, casual opinions we've picked up somehow and may not even bother to defend if challenged. But we also have opinions in which we are heavily invested, sometimes to the point that our whole sense of reality, right and wrong, good and bad—our very sense of ourselves—is tied up in them. These opinions we defend passionately.

On this count, popular argumentation and mature reasoning are alike. Mature reasoners are often passionate about their convictions, as committed to them as the fanatic on the street corner is to his or her cause. A crucial difference, however, separates the fanatic from the mature reasoner. The fanatic is all passion; the mature reasoner is able and willing to step back and examine even deeply held convictions. "I may have believed this for as long as I can remember," the mature reasoner says to him- or herself, "but is this conviction really justified? Do the facts support it? When I think it through, does it really make sense? Can I make a coherent and consistent argument for it?" These are questions that don't concern the fanatic and are seldom posed in the popular argumentation we hear on talk radio.

In practical terms, being self-critical and open to well-intended criticism boils down to this: Mature reasoners can and do change their minds when they have good reasons to do so. In popular argumentation, changing one's mind can be taken as a weakness, as "wishy-washy," and so people tend to go on advocating what they believe, regardless of what anyone else says. But there's nothing wishy-washy about, for example, confronting the facts, about realizing that what we thought is not supported by the available evidence. In such a case, changing one's mind is a sign of intelligence and the very maturity mature reason values. Nor is it a weakness to recognize a good point made against one's own argument. If we don't listen and take seriously what others say, they won't listen to us.

Mature Reasoners Argue with Their Audiences or Readers in Mind

Nothing drains energy from argument more than the feeling that it will accomplish nothing. As one student put it, "Why bother? People just go on thinking what they want to." This attitude is understandable. Popular, undisciplined argument often does seem futile: minds aren't changed; no progress is made; it's doubtful that anyone learned anything. Sometimes the opposing positions only harden, and the people involved are more at odds than before.

Why does this happen so often? One reason we've already mentioned — nobody's really listening to anyone else. We tend to hear only our own voices and see only from our own points of view. But there's another reason: The people making the arguments have made no effort to reach their audience. This is the other side of the coin of not listening — when we don't take other points of view seriously, we can't make our points of view appealing to those who don't already share them.

To have a chance of working, arguments must be *other-directed*, attuned to the people they want to reach. This may seem obvious, but it's also commonly ignored and not easy to do. We have to imagine the other guy. We have to care about other points of view, not just see them as obstacles to our own. We have to present and develop our arguments in ways that won't turn off the very people for whom we're writing. In many ways, *adapting to the audience* is the biggest challenge of argument.

www.mhhe.com/**crusius**

For practice identifying audience, go to: Argument Exercises > Understanding Audience

Mature Reasoners Know Their Arguments' Contexts

All arguments are part of an ongoing conversation. We think of arguments as something individuals make. We think of our opinions as *ours*, almost like private property. But arguments and opinions have pasts: Other people argued about more or less the same issues and problems before — often long before — we came on the scene. They have a present: Who's arguing what now, the current state of the argument. And they have a future: What people will be arguing about tomorrow, in different circumstances, with knowledge we don't have now.

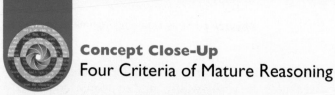

Concept Close-Up
Four Criteria of Mature Reasoning

Mature Reasoners Are Well Informed
Their opinions develop out of knowledge and are supported by reliable and current evidence.

Mature Reasoners Are Self-Critical and Open to Constructive Criticism
They balance their passionate attachment to their opinions with willingness to evaluate and test them against differing opinions, acknowledge when good points are made against their opinions, and even, when presented with good reasons for doing so, change their minds.

Mature Reasoners Argue with Their Audience or Readers in Mind
They make a sincere effort to understand and connect with other people and other points of view because they do not see differences of opinion as obstacles to their own points of view.

Mature Reasoners Know Their Arguments' Contexts
They recognize that what we argue about now was argued about in the past and will be argued about in the future, that our contributions to these ongoing conversations are influenced by who we are, what made us who we are, where we are, what's going on around us.

So most arguments are not the isolated events they seem to be. Part of being well informed is knowing something about the history of an argument. By understanding an argument's past, we learn about patterns that will help us develop our own position. To some extent, we must know what's going on now and what other people are saying to make our own reasoning relevant. And although we can't know the future, we can imagine the drift of the argument, where it might be heading. In other words, there's a larger context we need to join — a big conversation of many voices to which our few belong.

WHAT ARE THE AIMS OF ARGUMENT?

The heart of this book is the section entitled "The Aims of Argument." In conceiving this book, we worked from one basic premise: Mature reasoners do not argue just to argue; rather, they use argument to accomplish something: *to inquire* into a question, problem, or issue (commonly part of the research process); *to convince* their readers to assent to an opinion, or claim; *to persuade* readers to take action, such as buying a product or voting for a candidate; and *to mediate* conflict, as in labor disputes, divorce proceedings, and so on.

Let's look at each of these aims in more detail.

Arguing to Inquire

Arguing to **inquire** is using reasoning to determine the best position on an issue. We open the "Aims" section with inquiry because mature reasoning is not a matter of defending what we already believe but of questioning it. Arguing to inquire helps us form opinions, question opinions we already have, and reason our way through conflicts or contradictions in other people's arguments on a topic. Inquiry is open minded, and it requires that we make an effort to find out what people who disagree think and why.

The ancient Greeks called argument as inquiry **dialectic;** today we might think of it as dialogue or serious conversation. There is nothing confrontational about such conversations. We have them with friends, family, and colleagues, even with ourselves. We have these conversations in writing, too, as we make notations in the margins of the arguments we read. Listserv groups engage in inquiry about subjects of mutual interest.

Inquiry centers on questions and involves some intellectual legwork to answer them—finding the facts, doing research. This is true whether you are inquiring into what car to buy, what major to choose in college, what candidate to vote for, or what policy our government should pursue on any given issue.

Arguing to Convince

We've seen that the goal of inquiry is to reach some kind of conclusion on an issue. Let's call this conclusion a **conviction** and define it as "an earned opinion, achieved through careful thought, research, and discussion." Once we arrive at a conviction, we usually want others to share it. The aim of further argument is to secure the assent of people who do not share our conviction (or who do not share it fully).

Argument to **convince** centers on making a case, which means offering reasons and evidence in support of our opinion. Arguments to convince are all around us. In college, we find them in scholarly and professional writing. In everyday life, we find arguments to convince in editorials, courtrooms, and political speeches. Whenever we encounter an opinion supported by reasons and asking us to agree, we are dealing with argument to convince.

Arguing to Persuade

Like convincing, persuasion attempts to earn agreement, but it wants more. **Persuasion** attempts to influence not just thinking but also behavior. An advertisement for Mercedes-Benz aims to convince us not only that the company makes a high-quality car but also that we should go out and buy one. A Sunday sermon asks for more than agreement with some interpretation of a biblical passage; the minister wants the congregation to live according to its message. Persuasion asks us to do something—spend money, give money,

Concept Close-Up
Comparing the Aims of Argument

The aims of argument have much in common. For example, besides sharing argument, they all tend to draw on sources of knowledge (research) and to deal with controversial issues. But the aims also differ from one another, mainly in terms of purpose, audience, situation, and method, as summarized here and on the inside front cover.

	Purpose	Audience	Situation	Method
Inquiry	Seeks truth	Oneself, friends, and colleagues	Informal; a dialogue	Questions
Convincing	Seeks assent to a thesis	Less intimate; wants careful reasoning	More formal; a monologue	Case-making
Persuading	Seeks action	More broadly public, less academic	Pressing need for a decision	Appeals to reason and emotions
Mediating	Seeks consensus	Polarized by differences	Need to cooperate, preserve relations	"Give-and-take"

We offer this chart as a general guide to the aims of argument. Think of it as the "big picture" you can always return to as you work your way through Part Two, which deals with each of the aims in detail.

join a demonstration, recycle, vote, enlist, acquit. Because we don't always act on our convictions, persuasion cannot rely on reasoning alone. It must appeal in broader, deeper ways.

Persuasion appeals to readers' emotions. It tells stories about individual cases of hardship that move us to pity. It often uses photographs, as when charities confront us with pictures of poverty or suffering. Persuasion uses many of the devices of poetry, such as patterns of sound, repetitions, metaphors, and similes to arouse a desired emotion in the audience.

Persuasion also relies on the personality of the writer to an even greater degree than does convincing. The persuasive writer attempts to represent something "higher" or "larger" than him- or herself—some ideal with which the reader would like to be associated. For example, a war veteran and hero like John McCain naturally brings patriotism to the table when he makes a speech.

Arguing to Mediate

By the time we find ourselves in a situation where our aim is to **mediate**, we will have already attempted to convince an opponent to settle a conflict or dispute our way. Our opponent will have done the same. Yet neither side has secured the assent of the other, and "agreeing to disagree" is not a practical solution because the participants must decide what to do.

In most instances of mediation, the parties involved try to work out the conflict themselves because they have some relationship they wish to preserve—as employer and employee, business partners, family members, neighbors, even coauthors of an argument textbook. Common differences requiring mediation include the amount of a raise or the terms of a contract. In private life, mediation helps roommates live together and families decide on everything from budgets to vacation destinations.

Just like other aims of argument, arguing to mediate requires sound logic and the clear presentation of positions and reasons. However, mediation challenges our interpersonal skills more than do the other aims. Each side must listen closely to understand not just the other's case but also the emotional commitments and underlying values. When mediation works, the opposing sides begin to converge. Exchanging viewpoints and information and building empathy enable all parties to make concessions, to loosen their hold on their original positions, and finally to reach consensus—or at least a resolution that all participants find satisfactory.

A GOOD TOOL FOR UNDERSTANDING AND WRITING ARGUMENTS: THE WRITER'S NOTEBOOK

Argumentation places unique demands on readers and writers. One of the most helpful tools that you can use to meet these demands is a writer's notebook.

The main function of a writer's notebook is to help you sort out what you read, learn, accomplish, and think as you go through the stages of creating a finished piece of writing. A writer's notebook contains the writing you do before you write; it's a place to sketch out ideas, assess research, order what you have to say, and determine strategies and goals for writing.

Why Keep a Notebook?

Some projects require extensive research and consultation, which involve compiling and assessing large amounts of data and working through complex chains of reasoning. Under such conditions, even the best memory will fail without the aid of a notebook. Given life's distractions, we often forget too much and imprecisely recall what we do manage to remember. With a writer's notebook, we can preserve the ideas that come to us as we walk across campus or stare into space over our morning coffee. Often, a writer's notebook even provides sections of writing that can be incorporated into your papers and so can help you save time.

In the chapters that follow, we refer frequently to your writer's notebook. We hope you'll use this excellent tool.

Any entry that you may want to use for future reference is appropriate to add to your writer's notebook. It's for private exploration, so don't worry about organization, spelling, or grammar. Following are some specific possibilities.

To Explore Issues You Encounter in and out of Class

Bring your notebook to class each day. Use it to respond to ideas presented in class and in every reading assignment. When you're assigned a topic, write down your first impressions and opinions about it. When you're to choose your own topic, use the notebook to respond to controversial issues in the news or on campus. Your notebook then becomes a source of ideas for your essays.

To Record and Analyze Assignments

Staple your instructor's handouts to a notebook page, or write the assignment down word for word. Take notes as your instructor explains the assignment. Later, look it over more carefully, circling and checking key words, underlining due dates and other requirements. Record your questions, ask your instructor as soon as possible, and jot down the answers.

To Work Out Timetables for Completing Assignments

To avoid procrastination, schedule. Divide the task into blocks—preparing and researching, writing a first draft, revising, editing, final typing and proofreading—and work out how many days you can devote to each. Your schedule may change, but making one and attempting to stick to it helps avoid last-minute scrambling.

To Make Notes As You Research

Record ideas, questions, and preliminary conclusions that occur to you as you read, discuss your ideas with others, conduct experiments, compile surveys and questionnaires, and consult with experts. Keep your notebook handy at all times; write down ideas as soon as possible and assess their value later.

To Respond to Arguments You Hear or Read

To augment the notes you make in the margins of books, jot down extended responses in your notebook. Evaluate the strengths and weaknesses of texts, compare an argument with other arguments; make notes on how to use what you read to build your own arguments. Note page numbers to make it easier to use this information later.

To Write a Rhetorical Prospectus

A *prospectus* details a plan for proposed work. In your notebook, explore

> *Your thesis:* What are you claiming?
> *Your aim:* What do you want to accomplish?
> *Your audience:* Who should read this? Why? What are these people like?

Your persona: What is your relationship to the audience? How do you want them to perceive you?

Your subject matter: What does your thesis obligate you to discuss? What do you need to learn more about? How do you plan to get the information?

Your organizational plan: What should you talk about first? Where might that lead? What might you end with?

To Record Useful Feedback

Points in the writing process when it is useful to seek feedback from other students and the instructor include

When your *initial ideas* have taken shape, to discover how well you can explain your ideas to others and how they respond

After you and other students have *completed research* on similar topics, to share information and compare evaluations of sources

Upon completion of a *first draft,* to uncover what you need to do in a second draft to accommodate readers' needs, objections, and questions

At the end of the *revising process,* to correct surface problems such as awkward sentences, usage errors, misspellings, and typos

Prepare specific questions to ask others, and use your notebook to jot them down; leave room to sum up the comments you receive.

To Assess a Graded Paper

Look over your instructor's comments carefully, and write down anything useful for future reference. For example, what did you do well? What might you carry over to the next assignment? Is there a pattern in the shortcomings your instructor has pointed out?

Chapter 2

Reading an Argument

In a course in argumentation, you will read many arguments. Our book contains a wide range of argumentative essays, some by students, some by established professionals. In addition, you may find arguments on your own in books, newspapers, and magazines, or on the Internet. You'll read them to develop your understanding of argument. That means you will analyze and evaluate these texts—known as **critical reading.** Critical reading involves special skills and habits that are not essential when you read a book for information or entertainment. This chapter discusses those skills and habits.

By the time most students get to high school, reading is no longer taught. While there's plenty to read, any advice on *how to read* is usually about increasing vocabulary or reading speed, not reading critically. This is too bad, because in college you are called on to read more critically than ever.

Have patience with yourself and with the texts you work with in this book. Reading will involve going through a text more than once, no matter how careful that single reading may be. You will go back to a text several times, asking new questions with each reading. That takes time, but it's time well spent. Just as when you see a film a second time, you notice new details, so each reading increases your knowledge of a text.

Before we start, a bit of advice: Attempt critical reading only when your mind is fresh. Find a place conducive to concentration—such as a table in the library. Critical reading requires an alert, active response.

THE FIRST ENCOUNTER: SEEING THE TEXT IN CONTEXT

Critical reading begins not with a line-by-line reading but with a fast overview of the whole text, followed by some thinking about how the text fits into a bigger picture, or *context*, which we describe shortly.

We first **sample** a text rather than read it through. Look at the headings and subdivisions. They will give a sense of how the text is organized. Note what parts look interesting and/or hard to understand. Note any information about the author provided before or after the text itself, as well as any publication information (where and when the piece was originally published). Look at the opening and closing paragraphs to discern the author's main point or view.

Reading comprehension depends less on a large vocabulary than on the ability to see how the text fits into contexts. Sampling will help you consider the text in two contexts that are particularly important:

1. *The general climate of opinion* surrounding the topic of the text. This includes debate on the topic both before and since the text's publication.
2. *The rhetorical context* of the text. This includes facts about the author, the intended audience, and the setting in which the argument took place.

Considering the Climate of Opinion

Familiarity with the climate of opinion will help you view any argument critically, recognize a writer's biases and assumptions, and spot gaps or errors in the information. Your own perspective, too, will affect your interpretation of the text. So think about what you know, how you know it, what your opinion is, and what might have led to its formation. You can then interact with a text, rather than just read it passively.

 Following Through

An argument on the topic of body decoration (tattoos and piercing) appears later in this chapter. "On Teenagers and Tattoos" is about motives for decorating the body. As practice in identifying the climate of opinion surrounding a topic, think about what people say about tattooing. Have you heard people argue that it is "low-class"? a rebellion against middle-class conformity? immoral? an artistic expression? a fad? an affront to school or parental authority? an expression of individuality? If you would not want a tattoo, why not? If you have a tattoo, why did you get it? In your writer's notebook, jot down some positions you have heard debated, and state your own viewpoint.

Considering the Rhetorical Context

Critical readers also are aware of the **rhetorical context** of an argument. They do not see the text merely as words on a page but as a contribution to some debate among interested people. Rhetorical context includes the

To determine an argument's rhetorical context, answer the following questions:

Who wrote this argument, and what are his or her occupation, personal background, and political leanings?

To whom do you think the author is writing? Arguments are rarely aimed at "the general public" but rather at a definite target audience, such as "entertainment industry moguls," "drivers in Dallas," or "parents of teenagers."

Where does the article appear? If it is reprinted, where did it appear originally? What do you know about the publication?

When was the argument written? If not recently, what do you know about the time during which it appeared?

Why was the article written? What prompted its creation, and what purpose does the author have for writing?

author, the intended audience, and the date and place of publication. The reader who knows something about the author's politics or affiliations will have an advantage over the reader who does not. Also, knowing if a periodical is liberal, like *The Nation*, or conservative, like *National Review*, helps.

An understanding of rhetorical context comes from both external and internal clues — information outside the text and information you gather as you read and reread it. You can glean information about rhetorical context from external evidence such as publishers' notes about the author or about a magazine's editorial board or sponsoring foundation. You can find this information in any issue of a periodical or by following an information link on the home page of an online publication.

You may also have prior knowledge of rhetorical context — for example, you may have heard of the author. Or you can look in a database such as *InfoTrac* (see pages 95, 100–103) to see what else the author has written. Later, when you read the argument more thoroughly, you will enlarge your understanding of rhetorical context as you discover what the text itself reveals about the author's bias, character, and purpose for writing.

In sum, the first encounter with a text is preliminary to a careful, close reading. It prepares you to get the most out of the second encounter. If you are researching a topic and looking for good sources of information and viewpoints about it, the first encounter with any text will help you decide whether you want to read it at all. A first encounter can be a time-saving last encounter if the text does not seem appropriate or credible.

Following Through

Note the following information about "On Teenagers and Tattoos."

When published: In 1997, reprinted fall 2000.
Where published: In the *Journal of Child and Adolescent Psychiatry*, published by the American Academy of Child and Adolescent Psychiatry, then reprinted in *Reclaiming Children and Youth*.
Written by *whom*: Andres Martin, MD. Martin is an assistant professor of child psychiatry at the Yale Child Study Center in New Haven, CT.

Then do a fast sampling of the text itself. In your writer's notebook, make some notes about what you expect to find in this argument. What do you think the author's perspective will be, and why? How might it differ from that of a teen, a parent, a teacher? Do the subheadings give you any idea of the main point? Do you notice at the opening or closing any repeated ideas that might give a clue to the author's claim? To whom do you imagine the author was writing, and what might be the purpose of an essay in a journal such as the one that published his argument?

AN ARGUMENT FOR CRITICAL READING

On Teenagers and Tattoos
Andres Martin

The skeleton dimensions I shall now proceed to set down are copied verbatim from my right arm, where I had them tattooed: as in my wild wanderings at that period, there was no other secure way of preserving such valuable statistics.

—Melville, *Moby Dick*

Tattoos and piercing have become a part of our everyday landscape. They are ubiquitous, having entered the circles of glamour and the mainstream of fashion, and they have even become an increasingly common feature of our urban youth. Legislation in most states restricts professional tattooing to adults older than 18 years of age, so "high end" tattooing is rare in children and adolescents, but such tattoos are occasionally seen in older teenagers. Piercings, by comparison, as well as self-made or "jailhouse" type tattoos, are not at all rare among adolescents or even among school-age children. Like hairdo, makeup, or baggy jeans, tattoos and piercings can be subject to fad influence or peer pressure in an effort toward group affiliation. As with any other fashion statement, they can be construed as bodily aids in the inner struggle toward identity consolidation, serving as adjuncts to the

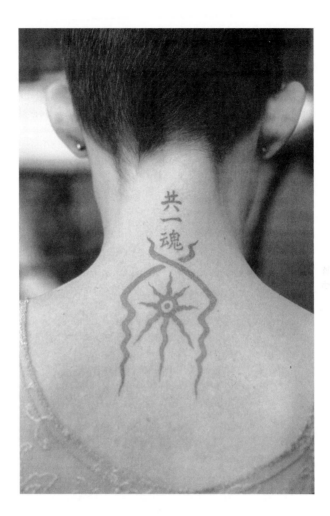

defining and sculpting of the self by means of external manipulations. But unlike most other body decorations, tattoos and piercings are set apart by their irreversible and permanent nature, a quality at the core of their magnetic appeal to adolescents.

Adolescents and their parents are often at odds over the acquisition of bodily decorations. For the adolescent, piercing or tattoos may be seen as personal and beautifying statements, while parents may construe them as oppositional and enraging affronts to their authority. Distinguishing bodily adornment from self-mutilation may indeed prove challenging, particularly when a family is in disagreement over a teenager's motivations and a clinician is summoned as the final arbiter. At such times it may be most important to realize jointly that the skin can all too readily become but another battleground for the tensions of the age, arguments having less to do with tattoos and piercings than with core issues such as separation from the family matrix. Exploring the motivations and significance [underlying] tattoos (Grumet, 1983) and piercings can go a long way toward resolving such differences and can become a novel and additional way of getting to know teenagers. An interested and nonjudgmental appreciation of teenagers' surface presentations may become a way of making contact not only in their terms but on their turfs: quite literally on the territory of their skins.

The following three sections exemplify some of the complex psychological underpinnings of youth tattooing.

IDENTITY AND THE ADOLESCENT'S BODY

Tattoos and piercing can offer a concrete and readily available solution for many of the identity crises and conflicts normative to adolescent development. In using such decorations, and by marking out their bodily territories, adolescents can support their efforts at autonomy, privacy, and insulation. Seeking individuation, tattooed adolescents can become unambiguously demarcated from others and singled out as unique. The intense and often disturbing reactions that are mobilized in viewers can help to effectively keep them at bay, becoming tantamount to the proverbial "Keep Out" sign hanging from a teenager's door.

Alternatively, feeling prey to a rapidly evolving body over which they have no say, self-made and openly visible decorations may restore adolescents' sense of normalcy and control, a way of turning a passive experience into an active identity. By indelibly marking their bodies, adolescents can strive to reclaim their bearings within an environment experienced as alien, estranged, or suffocating or to lay claim over their evolving and increasingly unrecognizable bodies. In either case, the net outcome can be a resolution to unwelcome impositions: external, familial, or societal in one case; internal and hormonal in the other. In the words of a 16-year-old girl with several facial piercings, and who could have been referring to her body just as well as to the position within her family: "If I don't fit in, it is because I say so."

INCORPORATION AND OWNERSHIP

Imagery of a religious, deathly, or skeletal nature, the likenesses of fierce animals or imagined creatures, and the simple inscription of names are some of the time-tested favorite contents for tattoos. In all instances, marks become not only memorials or recipients for dearly held persons or concepts: they strive for incorporation, with images and abstract symbols gaining substance on becoming a permanent part of the individual's skin. Thickly embedded in personally meaningful representations and object relations, tattoos can become not only the ongoing memento of a relationship, but at times even the only evidence that there ever was such a bond. They can quite literally become the relationship itself. The turbulence and impulsivity of early attachments and infatuations may become grounded, effectively bridging oblivion through the visible reality to tattoos.

Case Vignette: "A," a 13-year-old boy, proudly showed me his tattooed deltoid. The coarsely depicted roll of the dice marked the day and month of his birth. Rather disappointed, he then uncovered an immaculate back, going on to draw for me the great "piece" he envisioned for it. A menacing figure held a hand of cards: two aces, two eights, and a card with two sets of dates. "A's" father had belonged to Dead Man's Hand, a motorcycle gang named after the set of cards (aces and eights) that the legendary Wild Bill Hickock had held in the 1890s when shot dead over a poker table in Deadwood, South Dakota. "A" had only the vaguest memory of and sketchiest information about his father, but he knew he had died in a motorcycle accident: The fifth card marked the dates of his birth and death.

The case vignette also serves to illustrate how tattoos are often the culmination of a long process of imagination, fantasy, and planning that can start at an early age. Limited markings, or relatively reversible ones such as piercings, can at a later time scaffold toward the more radical commitment of a permanent tattoo.

THE QUEST OF PERMANENCE

The popularity of the anchor as a tattoo motif may historically have had to do less with guild identification among sailors than with an intense longing for rootedness and stability. In a similar vein, the recent increase in the popularity and acceptance of tattoos may be understood as an antidote or counterpoint to our urban and nomadic lifestyles. Within an increasingly mobile society, in which relationships are so often transient—as attested by the frequencies of divorce, abandonment, foster placement, and repeated moves, for example—tattoos can be a readily available source of grounding. Tattoos, unlike many relationships, can promise permanence and stability. A sense of constancy can be derived from unchanging marks that can be carried along no matter what the physical, temporal, or geographical vicissitudes at hand. Tattoos stay, while all else may change.

Case Vignette: A proud father at 17, "B" had had the smiling face of his 4-month-old baby girl tattooed on his chest. As we talked at a tattoo convention, he proudly introduced her to me, explaining how he would "always know how beautiful she is today" when years from then he saw her semblance etched on himself. 10

The quest for permanence may at other times prove misleading and offer premature closure to unresolved conflicts. At a time of normative uncertainties, adolescents may maladaptively and all too readily commit to a tattoo and its indefinite presence. A wish to hold on to a current certainty may lead the adolescent to lay down in ink what is valued and cherished one day but may not necessarily be in the future. The frequency of self-made tattoos among hospitalized, incarcerated, or gang-affiliated youths suggests such motivations: A sense of stability may be a particularly dire need under temporary, turbulent, or volatile conditions. In addition, through their designs teenagers may assert a sense of bonding and allegiance to a group larger than themselves. Tattoos may attest to powerful experiences, such as adolescence itself, lived and even survived together. As with Moby Dick's protagonist, Ishmael, they may bear witness to the "valuable statistics" of one's "wild wandering(s)": those of adolescent exhilaration and excitement on the one hand; of growing pains, shared misfortune, or even incarceration on the other.

Adolescents' bodily decorations, at times radical and dramatic in their presentation, can be seen in terms of figuration rather than disfigurement, of the natural body being through them transformed into a personalized body (Brain, 1979). They can often be understood as self-constructive and adorning efforts, rather than prematurely subsumed as mutilatory and destructive acts. If we bear all of this in mind, we may not only arrive at a position to pass more reasoned clinical judgment, but become sensitized through our patients' skins to another level of their internal reality.

References

Brain, R. (1979). *The decorated body.* New York: Harper & Row.
Grumet, G. W. (1983). Psychodynamic implications of tattoos. *American Journal of Orthopsychiatry, 53,* 482–92.

THE SECOND ENCOUNTER: READING AND ANALYZING THE TEXT

We turn now to suggestions for reading and analyzing. These are our own "best practices," what we do when we prepare to discuss or write about a written text. Remember, when you read critically, your purpose goes beyond merely finding out what an argument says. The critical reader is different from the target audience. As a critical reader, you are more like the food critic who dines not merely to eat but to evaluate the chef's efforts.

To see the difference, consider the different perspectives that an ant and a bird would have when looking at the same suburban lawn. The ant is down among the blades of grass, climbing one and then the next. It's a close look, but the view is limited. The bird in the sky above looks down, noticing the size and shape of the yard, the brown patches, the difference between the grass in this yard and the grass in the surrounding yards. The bird has the big picture, the ant the close-up. Critical readers move back and forth between the perspective of the ant and the perspective of the bird, each perspective enriching the other. The big picture helps one notice the patterns, even as the details offer clues to the big picture.

Because critical reading means interacting with the text, be ready with pencil or pen to mark up the text. Highlighting or underlining is not enough. Write comments in the margin.

Wrestling with Difficult Passages

Because one goal of the second encounter is to understand the argument fully, you will need to determine the meanings of unfamiliar words and difficult passages. In college reading, you may encounter new words. You may find allusions or references to other books or authors that you have not read. You may encounter metaphors and irony. The author may speak ironically or for another person. The author may assume that readers have lived through all that he or she has or share the same political viewpoint. All of this can make reading harder. Following are common features that often make reading difficult.

Unfamiliar Contexts

If the author and his or her intended audience are removed from your own experience, you will find the text difficult. Texts from a distant culture or time will include concepts familiar to the writer and original readers but not to you. This is true also of contemporary writing intended for specialists. College increases your store of specialized knowledge and introduces you to new (and old) perspectives. Accepting the challenge of difficult texts is part of college. Look up concepts you don't know. Your instructors can also help you to bridge the gap between your world and the text's.

Contrasting Voices and Views

Authors may state viewpoints that contradict their own. They may concede that part of an opposing argument is true, or they may put in an opposing view to refute it. These voices and viewpoints may come as direct quotations or paraphrases. To avoid misreading these views as the author's, be alert to words that signal contrast. The most common are *but* and *however.*

Allusions

Allusions are brief references to things outside the text—to people, works of art, songs, events in the news—anything in the culture that the author assumes he or she shares knowledge of with readers. Allusions are one way for an author to form a bond with readers—provided the readers' and authors' opinions are the same about what is alluded to. Allusions influence readers. They are persuasive devices that can provide positive associations with the author's viewpoint.

In "On Teenagers and Tattoos," the epigraph (the quotation that appears under the title of the essay) is an allusion to the classic novel *Moby Dick.*

Martin alludes to the novel again in paragraph 11. He assumes that his readers know the work—not just its title but also its characters, in particular, the narrator, Ishmael. And he assumes his readers would know that the "skeleton dimensions" of a great whale were important and that readers would therefore understand the value of preserving these statistics. The allusion predisposes readers to see that there are valid reasons for permanently marking the body.

Specialized Vocabulary

If an argument is aimed at an audience of specialists, it will undoubtedly contain vocabulary peculiar to that group or profession. Martin's essay contains social science terminology: "family matrix" and "surface presentations" (paragraph 2), "individuation" (paragraph 4), "grounded" (paragraph 6), "sense of constancy" (paragraph 9), and "normative uncertainties" (paragraph 11).

The text surrounding these terms provides enough help for most lay readers to get a fair understanding. For example, the text surrounding *individuation* suggests that the person would stand out as a separate physical presence; this is not quite the same as *individuality*, which refers more to one's character. Likewise, the text around *family matrix* points to something the single word *family* does not: it emphasizes the family as the surroundings in which one develops.

If you need to look up a term and a dictionary does not seem to offer an appropriate definition, go to one of the specialized dictionaries available on the library reference shelves. (See pages 98–103 for more on these.)

If you encounter an argument with more jargon than you can handle, you may have to accept that you are not an appropriate reader for it. Some readings are aimed at people with highly specialized graduate degrees or training. Without advanced courses, no one could read these articles with full comprehension, much less critique their arguments.

 Following Through

> Find other words in Martin's essay that sound specific to the field of psychology. Use the surrounding text to come up with laymen's terms for these concepts.

Missing Persons

A common difficulty with scientific writing is that it can sound disembodied and abstract. You won't find a lot of people doing things in it. Sentences are easiest to read when they take a "who-does-what" form. However, these can be rare in scientific writing. Many of Martin's sentences have abstract subjects and nonaction verbs like *be* and *become:*

> *An interested and nonjudgmental appreciation of teenagers' surface presentations* may become a way of making contact not only in their terms but on their turfs. . . .

In at least one other sentence, Martin goes so far in leaving people out that his sentence is grammatically incorrect. Note the dangling modifier:

www.mhhe. com/**crusius**

For more coverage of dangling modifiers, go to: Editing > Dangling Modifiers

> Alternatively, *feeling prey to a rapidly evolving body over which they have no say*, self-made and openly visible decorations may restore adolescents' sense of normalcy and control, a way of turning passive experience into active identity.

The italicized phrase describes adolescents, not decorations. If you have trouble reading passages like this, take comfort in the fact that the difficulty is not your fault. Recasting the idea into who-does-what can clear things up:

> Teens may feel like helpless victims of the changes taking place in their bodies. They may mark themselves with highly visible tattoos and piercings to regain a sense of control over their lives.

Passive Voice

Passive voice is another common form of the missing-person problem. In an active-voice sentence, we see our predictable who-does-what pattern:

www.mhhe. com/**crusius**

For more information on verbs and voice, go to: Editing > Verbs

> *Active voice:* The rat ate the cheese.

In passive-voice sentences, the subject of the verb is not an agent; it does not act.

> *Passive voice:* The cheese was eaten by the rat.

At least in this sentence, we know who the agent is. But scientists often leave out any mention of agents. Thus, in Martin's essay we have sentences like this one:

> Adolescents' bodily decorations . . . *can be seen* in terms of figuration rather than disfigurement. . . .

Who can see them? Martin means that *psychiatrists should see tattoos* as figuration rather than disfiguration. But that would sound too committed, not scientific. Passive-voice sentences are common in the sciences, part of an effort to sound objective.

If you learn to recognize passive voice, you can often mentally convert the troublesome passage into active voice, making it clearer. Passive voice takes this pattern:

> A helping verb in some form of the verb *to be: Is, was, were, has been, will be, will have been, could have been,* and so forth.

Followed by a main verb, a past participle: Past participles end in *ed, en, g, k,* or *t.*

Some examples:

The car *was being driven* by my roommate when we had the wreck.

Infections *are spread* by bacteria.

The refrain *is sung* three times.

Following Through

Convert the following sentences into active voice. We have put the passive-voice verbs in bold type, but you may need to look at the surrounding text to figure out who the agents are.

A sense of constancy *can be derived* from unchanging marks that *can be carried* along no matter what the physical, temporal, or geographical vicissitudes at hand. (paragraph 9) To edit this one, ask *who* can derive what and *who* can carry what.

The intense and often disturbing reactions that *are mobilized* in viewers can help to effectively keep them at bay, becoming tantamount to the proverbial "Keep Out" sign hanging from a teenager's door. (paragraph 4) To edit, ask *what* mobilizes the reactions in other people.

Using Paraphrase to Aid Comprehension

As we all know, explaining something to someone else is the best way to make it clear to ourselves. Putting an author's ideas into your own words, **paraphrasing** them, is like explaining the author to yourself. For more on paraphrasing, see Chapter 5, pages 111–114.

Paraphrase is often longer than the original because it loosens up what is dense. In paraphrasing, try to make both the language and the syntax (word order) simpler. Paraphrase may require two sentences where there was one. It looks for plainer, more everyday language, converts passive voice to active voice, and makes the subjects concrete.

Analyzing the Reasoning of an Argument

As part of your second encounter with the text, pick out its reasoning. The reasoning is the author's case, which consists of the *claim* (what the author wants the readers to believe or do) and the *reasons* and *evidence* offered in support of it. State the case in your own words and describe what else is going on in the argument, such as the inclusion of opposing views or background information.

- Use your own words, but don't strain to find a different word for every single one in the original. Some of the author's plain words are fine.
- If you take a phrase from the original, enclose it in quotation marks.
- Use a simpler sentence pattern than the original, even if it means making several short sentences. Aim for clarity.
- Check the surrounding sentences to make sure you understand the passage in context. You may want to add an idea from the context.
- Try for who-does-what sentences.

If a text is an argument, we can state what the author wants the readers to believe or do, and just as importantly, *why*. We should look for evidence presented to make the reasons seem believable. Note claims, reasons, and evidence in the margins as you read.

Reading Martin's Essay

Complex arguments require critical reading. Two critical-reading skills will help you: **subdividing the text** and **considering contexts**.

Finding Parts

Critical readers break texts down into parts. By *parts*, we mean groups of paragraphs that work together to perform some role in the essay. Examples of such roles are to introduce, to provide background, to give an opposing view, to conclude, and so on.

Discovering the parts of a text can be simple. Authors often make them obvious with subheadings and blank space. Even without these, transitional expressions and clear statements of intention make subdividing a text almost as easy as breaking a Hershey bar into its already well-defined segments. However, some arguments are more loosely constructed, their subdivisions less readily discernible. Even so, close inspection will usually reveal subdivisions and you should be able to see the roles played by the various chunks.

We have placed numbers next to every fifth paragraph in the essays reprinted in our text. Numbering makes it easier to refer to specific passages and to discuss parts.

Martin helps us see the parts of his essay by announcing early on, in paragraph 3, that it will have three sections, each "[exemplifying] some of the complex psychological underpinnings of youth tattooing." Martin's essay can thus be subdivided as follows:

1. Epigraph
2. Paragraphs 1, 2, and 3: the introduction

3. Paragraphs 4 and 5: an example
4. Paragaphs 6, 7, and 8: another example
5. Paragraphs 9, 10, and 11: a third example
6. Paragraph 12: the conclusion

Using Context

Taking the larger view again, we can use context to help pick out the reasoning. While a quick reading might suggest that Martin is arguing that teens have good reasons for decorating their bodies, we need to recall that the essay appeared in a journal for psychiatrists—doctors, not parents or teachers. Martin is writing to other psychiatrists and psychologists, clinicians who work with families. Reading carefully, we learn that his audience is an even smaller portion of this group: clinicians who have been "summoned as the final arbiter" in family disputes involving tattoos and other body decoration (paragraph 2). Because journals such as the *Journal of Child and Adolescent Psychiatry* are aimed at improving the practice of medicine, we want to note sentences that tell these readers what they ought to do and how it will make them better doctors.

Identifying the Claim and Reasons

The claim: Martin is very clear about his claim, repeating it three times, using just slightly different wording:

> His readers should "[explore] **the motivations and significance [underlying] tattoos and piercings. . . .**" (paragraph 2)

> His readers should have "**[a]n interested and nonjudgmental appreciation of teenagers' surface presentations. . . .**" (paragraph 2)

> His readers should see "**[a]dolescents' bodily decorations . . . in terms of figuration rather than disfigurement. . . .**" (paragraph 12)

Asked to identify Martin's claim, you could choose any one of these statements.

The reason: The reason is the "because" part of the argument. Why should the readers believe or do as Martin suggests? We can find the answer in paragraph 2, in the same sentences with his claim:

> Because doing so "**can go a long way toward resolving . . . differences and can become a novel and additional way of getting to know teenagers.**"

> Because doing so "**may become a way of making contact not only in their terms but on their turfs. . . .**"

And the final sentence of Martin's essay offers a third version of the same reason:

> Because "**we may not only arrive at a position to pass more reasoned clinical judgment, but become sensitized through our patients' skins to another level of their internal reality.**"

Again, we could choose any one of these sentences as the stated reason or paraphrase his reason. Using paraphrase, we can begin to outline the case structure of Martin's argument:

Claim: Rather than dismissing tattoos as disfigurement, mental health professionals should take a serious interest in the meaning of and motivation behind the tattoos.

Reason: Exploring their patients' body decorations can help them gain insight and make contact with teenagers on teenagers' own terms.

Where is Martin's evidence? Martin tells us that the three subsections will "exemplify some of the complex psychological underpinnings of youth tattooing." In each, he offers a case, or vignette, as evidence.

Example and Evidence (paragraphs 4 and 5): Tattoos are a way of working out identity problems when teens need either to mark themselves off from others or to regain a sense of control of a changing body or an imposing environment. The sixteen-year-old-girl who chose not to fit in.

Example and Evidence (paragraphs 6, 7, and 8): Tattoos can be an attempt to make the intangible a tangible part of one's body. The thirteen-year-old boy remembering his father.

Example and Evidence (paragraphs 9, 10, and 11): Tattoos are an "antidote" to a society that is on the run. The seventeen-year-old father.

THE THIRD ENCOUNTER: RESPONDING CRITICALLY TO AN ARGUMENT

Once you feel confident that you have the argument figured out, you are ready to respond to it, which means evaluating and comparing it with other perspectives, including your own. Only by *writing words* can you respond critically. As the reading expert Mortimer Adler says in *How to Read a Book*,

Reading, if it is active, is thinking, and thinking tends to express itself in words, spoken or written. The person who says he knows what he thinks but cannot express it in words usually does not know what he thinks. (49)

Annotation Is Key

We suggest that you annotate heavily. **Annotation** simply means making a note. Use the margins, and/or writer's notebook, for these notes of critical response. Many writers keep reading journals to practice active interaction with what they read and to preserve the experience of reading a text they want to remember.

What should you write about? Think of questions you would ask the author if he or she were in the room with you. Think of your own experience with the subject. Note similarities and contrasts with other arguments you have read or experiences of your own that confirm or contradict what the author is saying. Write about anything you notice that seems interesting, unusual, brilliant, or wrong. *Comment, question*— the more you actually write on the page, the more the essay becomes your own. And you will write more confidently about a text you own than one you are just borrowing.

The list on the next page will give you more ideas for annotations.

A concluding comment about responses: Even if you agree with an argument, think about who might oppose it and what their objections might be. Challenge the views you find most sympathetic.

We offer below an example of annotation for part of Martin's argument.

Sample Annotations

How is he defining "solution"? Do tattoos solve a problem or just indicate one?

Tattoos and piercing can offer a concrete and readily available <u>solution</u> for many of the identity crises and conflicts normative to adolescent development. In using such decorations, and by marking out their bodily territories, adolescents can support their efforts at autonomy, privacy, and insulation. Seeking individuation, tattooed adolescents can become unambiguously demarcated from

It seems like there are more mature ways to do this.

others and singled out as unique. The intense and often disturbing reactions that are mobilized in viewers can

Or would it cause parents to pay attention to them rather than leave them alone?

help to effectively <u>keep them at bay</u>, becoming tantamount to the proverbial "Keep Out" sign hanging from a teenager's door.

Alternatively, feeling prey to a rapidly evolving body over which they have no say, self-made and openly visible decorations may restore adolescents' sense of <u>normalcy</u> and control, a way of turning a passive experience into an

What is normal?

Is he implying that the indelible mark is one they will not outgrow? What if they do?

active identity. By <u>indelibly marking their bodies</u>, adolescents can strive to reclaim their bearings within an environment experienced as alien, estranged, or suffocating or to lay claim over their evolving and increasingly unrecognizable bodies. In either case, the net outcome <u>can be a resolution to unwelcome impositions: external, familial, or societal</u> in one case, internal and hormonal in the other. In the words of a 16-year-old girl with several facial piercings, and who could have been referring to her body just as well as to the position within her family: "If I don't fit in, it is because I say so."

Would he say the same about anorexia?

5

Does he assume this family needs counseling—or will not need it? He says the problem is "resolved."

- Paraphrase the claim and reasons next to where you find them stated.
- Consider: Does the author support his or her reasons with evidence? Is the evidence sufficient in terms of both quantity and quality?
- Circle the key terms. Note how the author defines or fails to define them.
- Ask: What does the author assume? Behind every argument, there are assumptions. For example, a baseball fan wrote to our local paper arguing that the policy of fouls after the second strike needs to be changed. His reason was that the fans would not be subjected to such a long game. The author assumed that a fast game of hits and outs is more interesting than a slow game of strategy between batters and hitters. Not every baseball fan shares that assumption.
- Note any contradictions you see, either within the text itself or with anything else you've read or learned.
- Consider the implications of the argument. If we believe and/or do what the author argues, what is likely to happen?
- Think of someone who would disagree with this argument, and say what that person might object to.
- If you see any opposing views in the argument, question the author's fairness in presenting them. Consider whether the author has represented opposing views fairly or has set them up to be easily knocked down.
- Ask: What is the author overlooking or leaving out?
- Consider: Where does the argument connect with anything else you have read?
- Consider: Does the argument exemplify mature reasoning as explained in Chapter 1, "Understanding Argument"?
- Ask: What aim does the argument seem to pursue? One of the four in the box on page 16, or some combination of them?
- Ask: What kind of person does the author sound like? Mark places where you hear the author's voice. Describe the tone. How does the author establish credibility — or fail to?
- Note the author's values and biases, places where the author sounds liberal or conservative, religious or materialistic, and so on.
- Note places where you see clues about the intended audience of the argument, such as appeals to their interests, values, tastes, and so on.

WRITING ASSIGNMENT: A CRITICAL RESPONSE TO A SINGLE ARGUMENT

www.mhhe.
com/crusius

For general help on getting started writing, go to:
Writing

This assignment asks you to write an essay about your critical reading of an argument. Writing about your encounters with a text will make you more conscious about your critical thinking, exposing your habits and practices.

Here, write for your classmates. The goal of your paper is to help your classmates better comprehend and criticize an essay you have all read.

In Part One

The project has two parts. In Part One, explain the rhetorical context, including who the author is and his or her point of view, as well as the intended audience as you infer it from clues outside and inside the text. Describe what you see as the claim and reason. Comment on the organization, referring to groups of paragraphs and the role they play in the argument. Tell about your experience of reading the essay—whether you found it easy, difficult, or confusing, and why. Be specific, and refer to actual passages.

In Part Two

In Part Two, evaluate the argument. How effective might it have been for its target audience? Focus on the text of the argument, but talk about its strengths and weaknesses. Your point is not simply to agree or disagree with the author; instead, show your understanding of the qualities of mature argumentation. In developing Part Two, use the suggestions for annotation on pages 35–37 as well as the criteria for mature reasoning on pages 12–14. Although your responses may be critical in the sense of negative, we use the term here to mean "a careful and exact evaluation and judgment" (*American Heritage Dictionary*).

Other Advice for Both Parts

- Refer to paragraphs in the text by number.
- Quote exactly and use quotation marks. Indicate in parentheses the paragraph they come from.
- Use paraphrase when talking about key ideas in the essay, and cite the paragraph in which the idea appeared.
- Use first person.
- Refer to the author by full name on first mention and by last name only after.

STUDENT SAMPLE ESSAY: CRITICAL RESPONSE TO A SINGLE ARGUMENT

Here we have reproduced another argument on the topic of tattoos and body decorations. Following it is one student's critical response to this essay, which follows the structure laid out above.

The Decorated Body

France Borel

Nothing goes as deep as dress nor as far as the skin; ornaments have the dimensions of the world.

—MICHEL SERRES, *The Five Senses*

Human nakedness, according to social custom, is unacceptable, unbearable, and dangerous. From the moment of birth, society takes charge, managing, dressing, forming, and deforming the child—sometimes even with a certain degree of violence. Aside from the most elementary caretaking concerns—the very diversity of which shows how subjective the motivation is—an unfathomably deep and universal tendency pushes families, clans, and tribes to rapidly modify a person's physical appearance.

One's genuine physical makeup, one's given anatomy, is always felt to be unacceptable. Flesh, in its raw state, seems both intolerable and threatening. In its naked state, body and skin have no possible existence. The organism is acceptable only when it is transformed, covered with signs. The body only speaks if it is dressed in artifice.

For millennia, in the four quarters of the globe, mothers have molded the shape of their newborn babies' skulls to give them silhouettes conforming to prevalent criteria of beauty. In the nineteenth century, western children were tightly swaddled to keep their limbs straight. In the so-called primitive world, children were scarred or tattooed at a very early age in rituals which were repeated at all the most important steps of their lives. At a very young age, children were fitted with belts, necklaces, or bracelets; their lips, ears, or noses were pierced or stretched.

Some cultures have designed sophisticated appliances to alter physical structure and appearance. American Indian cradleboards crushed the skull to flatten it; the Mangbetus of Africa wrapped knotted rope made of bark around the child's head to elongate it into a sugar-loaf shape, which was considered to be aesthetically pleasing. The feet of very young Chinese girls were bound and spliced, intentionally and irreversibly deforming them, because this was seen to guarantee the girls' eventual amorous and matrimonial success.[1]

Claude Lévi-Strauss said about the Caduveo of Brazil: "In order to be a man, one had to be painted; whoever remained in a natural state was no different from the beasts."[2] In Polynesia, unless a girl was tattooed, she would not find a husband. An unornamented hand could not cook, nor dip into the communal food bowl. Pink lips were despicable and ugly. Anyone who refused the test of the tattoo was seen to be marginal and suspect.

5

Among the Tivs of Nigeria, women called attention to their legs by means of elaborate scarification and the use of pearl leg bands; the best decorated calves were known for miles around. Tribal incisions behind the ears of Chad men rendered the skin "as smooth and stretched as that of a drum." The women would laugh at any man lacking these incisions, and they would never accept him as a husband. Men would subject themselves willingly to this custom, hoping for scars deep enough to leave marks on their skulls after death.

At the beginning of the eighteenth century, Father Laurent de Lucques noted that any young girl of the Congo who was not able to bear the pain of scarification and who cried so loudly that the operation had to be stopped was considered "good for nothing."[3] That is why, before marriage, men would check to see if the pattern traced on the belly of their intended bride was beautiful and well-detailed.

The fact that such motivations and pretexts depend on aesthetic, erotic, hygienic, or even medical considerations has no influence on the result, which is always in the direction of transforming the appearance of the body. Such a transformation is wished for, whether or not it is effective.

The body is a supple, malleable, and transformable prime material, a kind of modeling clay, easily molded by social will and wish. Human skin is an ideal subject for inscription, a surface for all sorts of marks which make it possible to differentiate the human from the animal. The physical body offers itself willingly for tattooing or scarring so that, visibly and recognizably, it becomes a social entity.

The absolutely naked body is considered as brutish, reduced to the level of nature where no distinction is made between man and beast. The decorated body, on the other hand, dressed (if even only in a belt), tattooed, or mutilated, publicly exhibits humanity and membership in an established group. As Theophile Gautier said, "The ideal disturbs even the roughest nature, and the taste for ornamentation distinguishes the intelligent being from the beast more exactly than anything else. Indeed, dogs have never dreamed of putting on earrings." 10

So, it is by their categorical refusal of nakedness that human beings are distinguished from nature. The "mark makes unremarkable"—it creates an interval between what is biologically and brutally given in the animal realm and what is won in the cultural realm. The body is tamed continuously; social custom demands, at any price—including pain, constraint, or discomfort—that wildness be abandoned.

Each civilization chooses—through a network of elective relationships which are difficult to determine—which areas of the body deserve transformation. These areas are as difficult to define and as shifting as those of eroticism or modesty. An individual alone eludes bodily modifications; they are the expression of a homogeneous collectivity which, at a chosen moment, comes to a tacit agreement to attack one or another part of the anatomy.

Whatever the choices, options, or differences may be, that which remains constant is the transformation of appearance. In spite of our contemporary western belief that the body is perfect as it is, we are constantly changing it: clothing it in musculature, suntan, or makeup; dying its head hair or pulling out its bodily hair. The seemingly most innocent gestures for taking care of the body very often hide a persistent and disguised tendency to make it adhere to the strictest of norms, reclothing it in a veil of civilization. The total nudity offered at birth does not exist in any region of the world. Man puts his stamp on man. The body is not a product of nature, but of culture.

Notes

1. Of course, there are also many different sexual mutilations, including excisions and circumcisions, which we will not go into at this time as they constitute a whole study in themselves.
2. C. Lévi-Strauss, <u>Tristes Tropiques</u> (Paris: Plon, 1955), p. 214.
3. J. Cuvelier, <u>Relations sur le Congo du Père Laurent de Lucques</u> (Brussels: Institut royal colonial belge, 1953), p. 144.

From France Borel, *Le Vêtement incarné: Les Métamorphoses du corps* (Paris: Calmann-Lévy, 1992), pp. 15–18. Copyright © Calmann-Lévy, 1992. Translated by Ellen Dooling Draper with the permission of the publisher.

A SAMPLE STUDENT RESPONSE

ANALYSIS OF "THE DECORATED BODY"
Katie Lahey

Part One

"The Decorated Body" by France Borel addresses the idea of external body manipulation not only as an issue prevalent to our own culture and time but also as a timeless concept that exists beyond cultural boundaries. It was published in *Parabola*, a magazine supported by the Society for the Study of Myth and Tradition. Borel discusses the ways in which various cultures both ancient and modern modify the natural body. Borel, who has written books on clothing and on art, writes with a style that is less a critique than an observation of his populations. This style suggests an anthropological approach rather than a psychological one, focusing on the motivations of people as a whole and less on the specific individuals within the societies. It seems, therefore, that he may be targeting an academic audience of professional anthropologists or other readers who are interested in the similarities of both "primitive" and "modern" cultures and the whole idea of what it means to be human.

Borel makes the claim that "social custom" dictates that all humans manipulate their bodies to brand themselves as humans. He says in the first paragraph that "an unfathomably deep and universal tendency pushes families, clans, and tribes to rapidly modify a person's physical appearance." He restates the idea in paragraph 2: The body "is acceptable only when it is transformed, covered with signs." He believes that in all cultures this type of branding or decorating is essential to distinguish oneself as legitimate within a civilization. Man has evolved from his original body; he has defied nature. We are no longer subject to what we are born with; rather, we create our bodies and identities as we see fit.

Borel reasons that this claim is true simply because all cultures conform to this idea and do so in such diverse ways. As he says, "the very diversity . . . shows how subjective the motivation is . . ." (paragraph 1). He provides ample evidence to support this reasoning in paragraphs 3 through 7, citing various cultures and examples of how they choose to decorate the body.

Part Two

However, Borel does not provide a solid explanation as to why the human race finds these bodily changes necessary to distinguish itself as human. It serves his argument to state that the various specific motivations behind these changes are irrelevant. All he is interested in proving is that humans must change their bodies, and he repeats this concept continually throughout the essay, first saying that a man remaining "in a natural state was no different from the beasts" in paragraph 5 and again in paragraphs 9 and 10. Maybe some readers would think this reiteration makes his point stronger, but I was unsatisfied.

I found myself trying to provide my own reasons why humans have this need to change their bodies. What makes this essay so unsatisfying to me is that, once I thought about it, it does in fact matter why cultures participate in body decoration. For example, why did the Chinese find it necessary to bind the feet of their young girls, a tradition so painful and unhealthy and yet so enduring? In such traditions, it becomes obvious that ulterior motives lie beneath the surface. The binding of the feet is not simply a tradition that follows the idea of making oneself human. In fact, it methodically attempts to put women below men. By binding the feet, a culture disables the young women not only physically but emotionally as well. It teaches them that they do not deserve the same everyday comforts as men and belittles them far beyond simply having smaller feet. Borel, however, fails to discuss any of these deeper motives. He avoids supplying his own opinion because he does not want to get into the politics of the practices he describes. He wants to speak in generalizations

5

about body modification as a mark of being human, even though people in modern Western culture might see some of these activities as violations of human rights.

Borel barely touches on modern Western civilization. He really only addresses our culture in the final paragraph, where he alleges that everyday things we do to change ourselves, whether it be shaving, tanning, toning, dying, or even applying makeup, are evidence that we have the same need to mark ourselves as human. He challenges our belief that "the body is perfect as it is" by showing that "we are constantly changing it" (paragraph 13). But many people today, especially women, *do* doubt that their individual bodies are perfect and would concede that they are constantly trying to "improve" them. What does Borel mean by "perfect as it is?" Is he talking about an ideal we would like to achieve?

His placement of this paragraph is interesting. I wondered why he leaves this discussion of our own culture until the very end of the essay so that his ideas of European and American culture appear as an afterthought. He spends the majority of the essay discussing other, more "primitive cultures" that yield many more examples of customs, such as the American Indian cradleboards, that clearly mark one as a member of a tribe. Perhaps Borel tends to discuss primitive cultures as opposed to our modern Western culture because primitive cultures generally back up his thesis, whereas American culture, in particular, veers from his claim that people decorate themselves in order to demonstrate what they have in common.

Borel ignores any controversy over tattoos and piercing, which people in Western culture might do to mark themselves as different from other people in their culture. In America, we value individualism, where everyone tries to be unique, even if in some small way. Other authors like Andres Martin, who wrote "On Teenagers and Tattoos," look at American culture and claim that we use body decoration as a means to show and celebrate our individuality. Martin says one good reason for teens to tattoo themselves is for "individuation"—to mark themselves as distinct from their peers and their families. This goes completely opposite from Borel's claim that "[a]n individual alone eludes bodily modifications; they are the expression of a homogeneous collectivity . . ." (paragraph 12).

Borel makes a sound argument for his claim that human existence is something more complex or more unnatural than simply being alive. But we know this already through humans' use of speech, social organization, and technology. Before I read his argument and even after the first time I read it, I wasn't swayed by Borel. I was looking for something more specific than what he is saying. In fact, all he is showing is that we decorate to symbolize our humanity. He does support this claim with good evidence. In this sense, the argument holds. But I cannot help but prefer to think about the other, more specific things we symbolize through our body decorations.

Chapter 3

Analyzing Arguments: A Simplified Toulmin Method

In Chapter 2, we discussed the importance of reading arguments critically: breaking them down into their parts to see how they are put together, noting in the margins key terms that are not defined, and raising questions about the writer's claims or evidence. Although these general techniques are sufficient for analyzing many arguments, sometimes—especially with intricate arguments and with arguments we sense are faulty but whose weaknesses we are unable to specify—we need a more systematic technique.

In this chapter, we explain and illustrate such a technique based on the work of Stephen Toulmin, a contemporary philosopher who has contributed a great deal to our understanding of argumentation. This method will allow you to analyze the logic of any argument; you will also find it useful in examining the logic of your own arguments as you draft and revise them. Keep in mind, however, that because it is limited to the analysis of logic, the Toulmin method is not sufficient by itself. It is also important to question an argument through dialogue (see Chapter 6) and to look at the appeals of character, emotion, and style (see Chapter 8).

www.mhhe.
com/crusius

For an interactive
exercise dealing
with the Toulmin
method, go to:

Argument
Exercises >
Toulmin Model
of Argument

A PRELIMINARY CRITICAL READING

Before we consider Toulmin, let's first explore the following argument carefully. Use the general process for critical reading we described in Chapter 2.

Rising to the Occasion of Our Death
William F. May

William F. May (b. 1927) is a distinguished professor of ethics at Southern Methodist University. The following essay appeared originally in The Christian Century *(1990).*

For many parents, a Volkswagen van is associated with putting children to sleep on a camping trip. Jack Kevorkian, a Detroit pathologist, has now linked the van with the veterinarian's meaning of "putting to sleep." Kevorkian conducted a dinner interview with Janet Elaine Adkins, a 54-year-old Alzheimer's patient, and her husband and then agreed to help her commit suicide in his VW van. Kevorkian pressed beyond the more generally accepted practice of passive euthanasia (allowing a patient to die by withholding or withdrawing treatment) to active euthanasia (killing for mercy).

Kevorkian, moreover, did not comply with the strict regulations that govern active euthanasia in, for example, the Netherlands. Holland requires that death be imminent (Adkins had beaten her son in tennis just a few days earlier); it demands a more professional review of the medical evidence and the patient's resolution than a dinner interview with a physician (who is a stranger and who does not treat patients) permits; and it calls for the final, endorsing signatures of two doctors.

So Kevorkian-bashing is easy. But the question remains: Should we develop a judicious, regulated social policy permitting voluntary euthanasia for the terminally ill? Some moralists argue that the distinction between allowing to die and killing for mercy is petty quibbling over technique. Since the patient in any event dies—whether by acts of omission or commission—the route to death doesn't really matter. The way modern procedures have made dying at the hands of the experts and their machines such a prolonged and painful business has further fueled the euthanasia movement, which asserts not simply the right to die but the right to be killed.

But other moralists believe that there is an important moral distinction between allowing to die and mercy killing. The euthanasia movement, these critics contend, wants to engineer death rather than face dying. Euthanasia would bypass dying to make one dead as quickly as possible. It aims to relieve suffering by knocking out the interval between life and death. It solves the problem of suffering by eliminating the sufferer.

The impulse behind the euthanasia movement is understandable in an age when dying has become such an inhumanly endless business. But the movement may fail to appreciate our human capacity to rise to the occasion of our death. The best death is not always the sudden death. Those forewarned of death and given time to prepare for it have time to engage in acts of reconciliation. Also, advanced grieving by those about to be bereaved may ease some of their pain. Psychiatrists have observed that those who lose a loved one accidentally have a more difficult time recovering from the loss than those who have suffered through an extended period of illness before the death. Those who have lost a close relative by accident are more likely to experience what Geoffrey Gorer has called limitless grief. The community, moreover, may need its aged and dependent, its sick and its dying, and the virtues which they sometimes evince—the virtues of hu-

5

mility, courage, and patience—just as much as the community needs the virtues of justice and love manifest in the agents of care.

On the whole, our social policy should allow terminal patients to die, but it should not regularize killing for mercy. Such a policy would recognize and respect that moment in illness when it no longer makes sense to bend every effort to cure or to prolong life and when one must allow patients to do their own dying. This policy seems most consonant with the obligations of the community to care and of the patient to finish his or her course.

Advocates of active euthanasia appeal to the principle of patient autonomy—as the use of the phrase "voluntary euthanasia" indicates. But emphasis on the patient's right to determine his or her destiny often harbors an extremely naïve view of the uncoerced nature of the decision. Patients who plead to be put to death hardly make unforced decisions if the terms and conditions under which they receive care already nudge them in the direction of the exit. If the elderly have stumbled around in their apartments, alone and frightened for years, or if they have spent years warehoused in geriatrics barracks, then the decision to be killed for mercy hardly reflects an uncoerced decision. The alternative may be so wretched as to push patients toward this escape. It is a huge irony and, in some cases, hypocrisy to talk suddenly about a compassionate killing when the aging and dying may have been starved for compassion for many years. To put it bluntly, a country has not earned the moral right to kill for mercy unless it has already sustained and supported life mercifully. Otherwise we kill for compassion only to reduce the demands on our compassion. This statement does not charge a given doctor or family member with impure motives. I am concerned here not with the individual case but with the cumulative impact of a social policy.

I can, to be sure, imagine rare circumstances in which I hope I would have the courage to kill for mercy—when the patient is utterly beyond human care, terminal, and in excruciating pain. A neurosurgeon once showed a group of physicians and an ethicist the picture of a Vietnam casualty who had lost all four limbs in a landmine explosion. The catastrophe had reduced the soldier to a trunk with his face transfixed in horror. On the battlefield I would hope that I would have the courage to kill the sufferer with mercy.

But hard cases do not always make good laws or wise social policies. Regularized mercy killings would too quickly relieve the community of its obligation to provide good care. Further, we should not always expect the law to provide us with full protection and coverage for what, in rare circumstances, we may morally need to do. Sometimes the moral life calls us out into a no-man's-land where we cannot expect total security and protection under the law. But no one said that the moral life is easy.

A STEP-BY-STEP DEMONSTRATION OF THE TOULMIN METHOD

The Toulmin method requires an analysis of the claim, the reasons offered to support the claim, and the evidence offered to support the reasons, along with an analysis of any refutations offered.

Analyzing the Claim

Logical analysis begins with identifying the *claim*, the thesis or central contention, along with any specific qualifications or exceptions.

Identify the Claim

First, ask yourself, *What statement is the author defending?* In "Rising to the Occasion of Our Death," for example, William F. May spells out his claim in paragraph 6:

> [O]ur social policy should allow terminal patients to die, but it should not regularize killing for mercy.

In his claim, May supports passive euthanasia (letting someone die by withholding or discontinuing treatment) but opposes "regularizing" (making legal or customary) active euthanasia (administering, say, an overdose of morphine to cause a patient's death).

Much popular argumentation is sometimes careless about what exactly is being claimed: Untrained arguers too often content themselves with merely taking sides ("Euthanasia is wrong"). Note that May, a student of ethics trained in philosophical argumentation, makes a claim that is both specific and detailed. Whenever an argument does not include an explicit statement of its claim, you should begin your analysis by stating the writer's claim yourself. Try to state it in sentence form, as May's claim is stated.

Look for Qualifiers

Next, ask, *How is the claim qualified?* Is it absolute, or does it include words or phrases to indicate that it may not hold true in every situation or set of circumstances?

May qualifies his claim in paragraph 6 with the phrase "On the whole," indicating that he recognizes possible exceptions. Other qualifiers include "typically," "usually," and "most of the time." Careful arguers are wary of making absolute claims. Qualifying words or phrases are used to restrict a claim and improve its defensibility.

Find the Exceptions

Finally, ask, *In what cases or circumstances would the writer not press his or her claim?* Look for any explicit exceptions the writer offers.

May, for example, is quite clear in paragraph 8 about when he would not press his claim:

> I hope I would have the courage to kill for mercy—when the patient is utterly beyond human care, terminal, and in excruciating pain.

Once he has specified these abstract conditions, he offers a chilling example of a case in which mercy killing would be appropriate. Nevertheless, he insists that such exceptions are rare and thus do not justify making active euthanasia legal or allowing it to become common policy.

Critical readers respond to unqualified claims skeptically—by hunting for exceptions. With qualified claims, they look to see what specific exceptions the writer will admit and what considerations make restrictions necessary or desirable.

Summarize the Claim

At this point it is a good idea to write out in your writer's notebook the claim, its qualifiers, and its exceptions so that you can see all of them clearly. For May, they look like this:

(qualifier)	"On the whole"
(claim)	"our social policy should allow terminal patients to die, but it should not regularize killing for mercy"
(exception)	"when the patient is utterly beyond human care, terminal, and in excruciating pain"

Analyzing the Reasons

Once you have analyzed the claim, you should next identify and evaluate the reasons offered for the claim.

List the Reasons

Begin by asking yourself, *Why is the writer advancing this claim?* Look for any statement or statements that are used to justify the thesis. May groups all of his reasons in paragraph 5:

> The dying should have time to prepare for death and to reconcile with relatives and friends.
>
> Those close to the dying should have time to come to terms with the impending loss of a loved one.
>
> The community needs examples of dependent but patient and courageous people who sometimes do die with dignity.
>
> The community needs the virtues ("justice and love") of those who care for the sick and dying.

When you list reasons, you need not preserve the exact words of the arguer; often, doing so is impossible because reasons are not always explicit but may have to be inferred. Be very careful, however, to adhere as closely as possible to the writer's language. Otherwise, your analysis can easily go astray, imposing a reason of your own that the writer did not have in mind.

Note that reasons, like claims, can be qualified. May does not say, for instance, that "the aged and dependent" *always* show "the virtues of humility, courage, and patience." He implicitly admits that they can be ornery and cowardly as well. But for May's purposes it is enough that they sometimes manifest the virtues he admires.

Use your writer's notebook to list the reasons following your summary of the claim, qualifiers, and exceptions. One possibility is to list them beneath the summary of the claim in the form of a tree diagram (see the model diagram in the Concept Close-Up box on page 52).

Examine the Reasons

There are two questions to ask as you examine the reasons. First, ask, *Are they really good reasons?* A reason is only as good as the values it invokes or implies. A value is something we think is good — that is, worth pursuing for its own sake or because it leads to attaining other goods. For each reason, specify the values involved and then determine whether you accept those values as generally binding.

Second, ask, *Is the reason relevant to the thesis?* In other words, does the relationship between the claim and the reason hold up to examination? For example, the claim "You should buy a new car from Fred Freed" cannot be supported by the reason "Fred is a family man with three cute kids."

Be careful as you examine whether reasons are good and whether they are relevant. No other step is as important in assessing the logic of an argument, and no other can be quite as tricky.

To illustrate, consider May's first reason: Those who know they are about to die should have time to prepare for death and to seek reconciliation with people from whom they have become estranged. Is this a good reason? Yes, because we value the chance to prepare for death and to reconcile with estranged friends or family members.

But is the reason relevant? May seems to rule out the possibility that a dying person seeking active euthanasia would be able to prepare for death and reconcile with others. But this is obviously not the case. Terminally ill people who decide to arrange for their own deaths may make any number of preparations beforehand, so the connection between this reason and May's claim is really quite weak. To accept a connection, we would have to assume that active euthanasia necessarily amounts to a sudden death without adequate preparation. We are entitled to question the relevance of the reason, no matter how good it might be in itself.

Following Through

Now examine May's second, third, and fourth reasons on your own, as we have just examined the first one. Make notes about each reason, evaluating how good each is in itself and how relevant it is to the thesis. In your writer's notebook, create your own diagram based on the model on page 52.

Analyzing the Evidence

Once you have finished your analysis of the reasons, the next step is to consider the evidence offered to support any of those reasons.

List the Evidence

Ask, *What kinds of evidence (data, anecdotes, case studies, citations from authority, and so forth) are offered as support for each reason?* Some arguments advance little in the way of evidence. May's argument is a good example of a moral argument about principles; such an argument does not require much evidence. Lack of evidence, then, is not always a fault. For one of his reasons, however, May does offer some evidence: After stating his second reason in paragraph 5 — the chance to grieve before a loved one dies — he invokes authorities who agree with him about the value of advanced grieving.

Examine the Evidence

Two questions apply. First, ask, *Is the evidence good?* That is, is it sufficient, accurate, and credible? Second, ask, *Is it relevant to the reason it supports?* The evidence May offers in paragraph 5 is sufficient. We assume his citations are accurate and credible as well. We would also accept them as relevant because, apart from our own experience with grieving, we have to rely on expert opinion. (See Chapter 5 for a fuller discussion of estimating the adequacy and relevance of evidence.)

Noting Refutations

A final step is to assess an arguer's refutations. In a refutation, a writer anticipates potential objections to his or her position and tries to show why they do not undermine the basic argument. A skilled arguer uses them to deal with any obvious objections a reader is likely to have.

First, ask, *What refutations does the writer offer?* Summarize them. Then, ask, *How does the writer approach each objection?* May's refutation occupies paragraph 7. He recognizes that the value of free choice lends weight to the proeuthanasia position, and so he relates this value to the question of "voluntary euthanasia." Because in our culture individual freedom is so strong a value, May doesn't question the value itself; rather, he leads us to question

Concept Close-Up
Model Toulmin Diagram for Analyzing Arguments

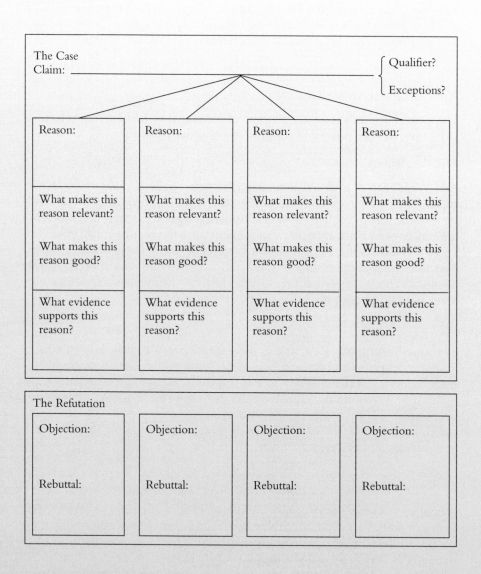

The Case
Claim: _____

Qualifier?

Exceptions?

Reason:	Reason:	Reason:	Reason:
What makes this reason relevant? What makes this reason good?	What makes this reason relevant? What makes this reason good?	What makes this reason relevant? What makes this reason good?	What makes this reason relevant? What makes this reason good?
What evidence supports this reason?	What evidence supports this reason?	What evidence supports this reason?	What evidence supports this reason?

The Refutation

Objection:	Objection:	Objection:	Objection:
Rebuttal:	Rebuttal:	Rebuttal:	Rebuttal:

A. Analyze the Claim

1. **Find the claim.** In many arguments, the claim is never explicitly stated. When it isn't, try to make the implied claim explicit by stating it in your own words. (Note: If, after careful analysis, you aren't sure *exactly* what the writer is claiming, you've found a serious fault in the argument.)

2. **Look for qualifiers.** Is the claim absolute? Or is it qualified by some word or phrase like *usually* or *all things being equal*? If the claim is absolute, can you think of circumstances in which it might not apply? If the claim is qualified, why is it not absolute? That is, is there any real thought or content in the qualifier — good reasons for qualifying the claim?

3. **Look for explicit exceptions to the claim.** If the writer has pointed out conditions in which he or she would *not* assert the claim, note them carefully.

Summarize steps 1–3. See the diagram on page 52.

B. Analyze the Reasons

1. **Find the reason or reasons advanced to justify the claim.** All statements of reason will answer the question, "Why are you claiming what you've claimed?" They can be linked to the claim with *because*. As with claims, reasons may be implied. Dig them out and state them in your own words. (Note: If, after careful analysis, you discover that the reasons aren't clear or relevant to the claim, you should conclude that the argument is either defective and in need of revision or invalid and therefore unacceptable.)

2. **Ponder each reason advanced.** Is the reason good in itself? Is the reason relevant to the thesis? Note any problems.

List the reasons underneath the claim. See the diagram on page 52.

C. Analyze the Evidence

1. **For each reason, locate all evidence offered to back it up.** Evidence is not limited to hard data. Anecdotes, case studies, and citations from authorities also count as evidence. (Note: Not all reasons require extensive evidence. But we should be suspicious of reasons without evidence, especially when it seems that evidence ought to be available. Unsupported reasons are often a sign of bad reasoning.)

2. **Ponder each piece of evidence.** Is it good? That is, is it accurate and believable? Is it relevant to the reason it supports? Note any problems.

List the evidence underneath the claim. See the diagram on page 52.

D. Examine the Refutations

If there are refutations — efforts to refute objections to the case — examine them. If not, consider what objections you think the writer should have addressed.

whether voluntary euthanasia is actually a matter of free choice. He suggests that unwanted people may be coerced into "choosing" death or may be so isolated and neglected that death becomes preferable. Thus, he responds to the objection that dying people should have freedom of choice where death is concerned.

Summarizing Your Analysis

Once you have completed your analysis, it is a good idea to summarize the results in a paragraph or two. Be sure to set aside your own position on the issue, confining your summary to the argument the writer makes.

Although May's logic is strong, it doesn't seem fully compelling. He qualifies his argument and uses exceptions effectively, and his single use of refutation is skillful. However, he fails to acknowledge that active euthanasia need not be a sudden decision leading to sudden death. Consequently, his reasons for supporting passive euthanasia can be used to support at least some cases of active euthanasia as well. It is here—in the linkage between reasons and claim—that May's argument falls short. Furthermore, we may question whether the circumstances under which May would permit active euthanasia are in fact as rare as he suggests. Many people are beyond human care, terminal, and in pain, and many others suffer acute anguish for which they might legitimately seek the relief of death.

 Following Through

Following is a student-written argument on capital punishment. Read it through once, and then use the Toulmin method as described in this chapter to analyze its logic systematically.

STUDENT SAMPLE: *An Argument for Analysis*

CAPITAL PUNISHMENT: SOCIETY'S SELF-DEFENSE

Amber Young

www.mhhe.
com/crusius

For additional
information on
writing analysis
essays, go to:
Writing >
Writing Tutors >
Interpretive
Analysis and
Writing about
Literature

Just after 1:00 a.m. on a warm night in early June, Georgeann, a pretty college student, left through the back door of a fraternity house to walk the ninety feet down a well-lighted alley to the back door of her sorority house. Lively and vivacious, Georgeann had been an honor student, a cheerleader, and Daffodil Princess in high school, and now she was in the middle of finals week, trying to maintain her straight A record. That evening, several people saw Georgeann walk to within about forty feet of the door of her sorority house. She never arrived. Somewhere in that last forty feet, she met a tall, handsome young man on crutches, his leg in a cast, struggling with a briefcase. The young man asked Georgeann if she could help him get to his car, which was parked nearby. She consented. Then, a housemother sleeping by an open window in a nearby fraternity house was awakened by a high-pitched, terrified scream that suddenly stopped. That was the last anyone ever heard or saw of Georgeann Hawkins. Her bashed skull and broken body were dumped on a hillside many miles away, along with the bodies of several other young female victims who had also been lured to their deaths by the good-looking, clean-cut, courteous, intelligent, and charming Ted Bundy.

By the time Ted Bundy was caught in Utah with his bashing bar and other homemade tools of torture, he had bludgeoned and strangled to death at least thirty-two young women, raping and savaging many of them in the process. His "hunting" trips had extended into at least five Western states, including Washington, Oregon, Idaho, Utah, and Colorado.

Bundy was ultimately convicted of the attempted kidnapping of Carol DeRonche and imprisoned. For this charge he probably would have been paroled within eighteen months. However, before parole could be approved, Bundy was transferred to a jail in Colorado to stand trial for the murder of Caryn Campbell. With Bundy in jail, no one else died. Young women could go about their lives normally, "safe" and separated from Ted Bundy by prison walls. Yet any number of things could have occurred to set him free—an acquittal, some sympathetic judge or parole board, a psychiatrist pronouncing him rehabilitated and safe, a state legislature passing shorter sentencing or earlier parole laws, inadequate prison space, a federal court ruling abolishing life in prison without any possibility for parole, or an escape.

In Bundy's case, it was escape—twice—from Colorado jails. The first time, he was immediately caught and brought back. The second time, Bundy made it to Florida, where fifteen days after his escape he bludgeoned and strangled Margaret Bowman, Lisa Levy, Karen Chandler, and Kathy Kleiner in their Tallahassee sorority house, tearing chunks out of Lisa Levy's breast and buttock with his teeth. Ann Rule, a noted crime writer who became Bundy's confidant while writing her book *The Stranger Beside Me,* described Bundy's attack on Lisa Levy as like that of a rabid animal. On the same night at a different location, Bundy sneaked through an open window and so savagely attacked Cheryl Thomas in her bed that a woman in the apartment next door described the clubbing as seeming to reverberate through the whole house. Then, three weeks later, less than forty days after his escape from the Colorado jail, Bundy went hunting again. He missed his chance at one quarry, junior high school student Leslie Ann Parmenter, when her brother showed up and thwarted her abduction. But Bundy succeeded the next day in Lake City, where he abducted and killed twelve-year-old Kimberly Diane Leach and dumped her strangled, broken body in an abandoned pig barn.

The criminal justice system did not keep Margaret Bowman, Lisa   5
Levy, Karen Chandler, Kathy Kleiner, Cheryl Thomas, Leslie Ann Parmenter, or little Kimberly Leach safe from Ted Bundy. The state of Florida,
however, with its death penalty, has made every other young woman safe
from Ted Bundy forever. Capital punishment is society's means of self-
defense. Just as a person is justified in using deadly force in defending
herself against a killer, so society also has a right to execute those who
kill whenever the opportunity and the urge arise.

However, while everyone wants a safe society, some people would
say that capital punishment is too strong a means of ensuring it. Contemporary social critic Hendrick Hertzberg attacks the death penalty, using
arguments that are familiar, but not compelling, to those who do not share
his absolute value-of-life position. For example, in one article he paints a
graphic picture of how horrible and painful even lethal injection is to the
prisoner ("Premeditated"). Elsewhere he dismisses the deterrence argument as "specious," since "[n]o one has ever been able to show that capital punishment lowers the murder rate" ("Burning" 4). But the Florida
death penalty has, in fact, made certain that Ted Bundy will never kill
again. A needle prick in the arm is hardly cruel and unusual. Thousands
of good people with cancer and other diseases or injuries endure much
greater pain every day.

Of course, the possibility of executing an innocent person is a serious
concern. However, our entire criminal justice system is tilted heavily toward the accused, who is protected from the start to the end of the criminal justice procedure by strong individual-rights guarantees in the Fourth,
Fifth, Sixth, and Seventh Amendments of the U.S. Constitution. The burden of proof in a criminal case is on the government, and guilt must be
proved beyond a reasonable doubt. The chances of a guilty person going
free in our system are many times greater than those of an innocent person being convicted.

If, however, a mistake occurs despite all the safeguards, such an
innocent death would be tragic, just as each of the nearly 50,000 deaths
of innocent people each year on our highways is tragic. As much as we
value human life, we inevitably weigh that value against social costs and
benefits, whether we like to admit it or not. If the possibility that an innocent person might be executed is bad enough to require abolition of capital punishment, then why don't we also demand the abolition of automobiles as well? We don't because we accept the thousands of automobile
deaths per year to keep our cars. It is interesting to note that opponents
of capital punishment like Hertzberg do not demand abolition of the
automobile. So preservation of life must not be the highest value in all
cases.

Just as society has decided that the need for automobiles outweighs
their threat to innocent life, so capital punishment is necessary for the
safety and well-being of the general populace. The strongest reason for

capital punishment is not retribution or deterrence, but simply self-defense. We have a right to demand that government remove forever first-degree murderers, like Bundy, who hunt and kill their victims with premeditation and malice.

There are only two alternatives—life in prison or death. We base our approval or disapproval of capital punishment on fundamental values relating to life itself, rather than on statistics or factual evidence. Few in our society go so far as to believe that we must preserve life above all else. Our founding fathers wrote in the Declaration of Independence that all men are endowed by their Creator with unalienable rights, including "life, liberty, and the pursuit of happiness." However, there is no indication that life was more sacred to them than liberty. In fact, Patrick Henry, who would later be instrumental in the adoption of the Bill of Rights to the U.S. Constitution, is most famous for his defiant American Revolutionary declaration, "I know not what course others may take, but as for me, give me liberty or give me death!"

The sentiment that some things are worse than death remains. Millions of soldiers have put themselves in harm's way and lost their lives to preserve and defend freedom. Many people will admit to their willingness to use deadly force to protect themselves or their families from a murderer. The preservation of life, any life, regardless of everything else, is not an absolute value for most people.

In fact, many prisoners would prefer to die than to languish in prison. Bundy himself, in his letters from prison to Ann Rule, declared, "My world is a cage," as he tried to describe "the cruel metamorphosis that occurs in captivity" (qtd. in Rule 148). After his sentencing in Utah, Bundy described his attempts to prepare mentally for the "living hell of prison" (qtd. in Rule 191). Thus, some condemned prisoners, including Gary Gilmore, the first person to be executed after the U.S. Supreme Court found that Utah's death penalty law met Constitutional requirements, refused to participate in the appeals attempting to convert his death sentence to life in prison because he preferred death. In our society, founded on the principle that liberty is more important than life, the argument that it is somehow less cruel and more civilized to deprive someone of liberty for the rest of his or her life than to end the life sounds hollow. The Fifth Amendment of the U.S. Constitution prohibits the taking of either life or liberty without due process of law, but it does not place one at a higher value than the other.

The overriding concerns of the Constitution, however, are safety and self-defense. The chance of a future court ruling, a release on parole, a pardon, a commutation of sentence, or an escape—any of which could turn the murderer loose to prey again on society—creates a risk that society should not have to bear. Lisa Levy, Margaret Bowman, Karen Chandler, Kathy Kleiner, Cheryl Thomas, and Kimberly Leach were not protected from Bundy by the courts and jails in Utah and Colorado, but other

10

young women who were potential victims are now safe from Bundy thanks to the Florida death penalty.

Capital punishment carries with it the risk that an innocent person will be executed; however, it is more important to protect innocent, would-be victims of convicted murderers. On balance, society was not demeaned by the execution of Bundy in Florida, as Hertzberg claimed ("Burning" 49). On the contrary, society is better off with Ted Bundy and others like him gone.

Works Cited

Hertzberg, Hendrick. "Burning Question." <u>The New Republic</u> 20 Feb. 1989: 4+.

---. "Premeditated Execution." <u>Time</u> 18 May 1992: 49.

Rule, Ann. <u>The Stranger Beside Me.</u> New York: Penguin, 1989.

A FINAL NOTE ABOUT LOGICAL ANALYSIS

No method for analyzing arguments is perfect, and no method can guarantee that everyone using it will assess an argument the same way. Uniform results are not especially desirable anyway. What would be left to talk about? The point of argumentative analysis is to step back and examine an argument carefully, to detect how it is structured, to assess the cogency and power of its logic. The Toulmin method helps us move beyond a hit-or-miss approach to logical analysis, but it cannot yield a conclusion as compelling as mathematical proof.

Convincing and persuading always involve more than logic, and, therefore, logical analysis alone is never enough to assess the strength of an argument. For example, William May's argument attempts to discredit those like Dr. Jack Kevorkian who assist patients wishing to take their own lives. May depicts Kevorkian as offering assistance without sufficient consultation with the patient. Is his depiction accurate? Clearly, we can answer this question only by finding out more about how Kevorkian and others like him work. Because such questions are not a part of logical analysis, they have not been of concern to us in this chapter. But any adequate and thorough analysis of an argument must also address questions of fact and the interpretation of data.

Chapter 4

Reading and Writing about Visual Arguments

We live in a world awash in pictures. We turn on the TV and see not just performers, advertisers, and talking heads but also dramatic footage of events from around the world, commercials as visually creative as works of art, and video images to accompany popular music. We boot up our computers and surf the Net; many of the waves we ride are visual swells, enticing images created or enhanced by the very machines that take us out to sea. We drive our cars through a gallery of street art—on billboards and buildings and on the sides of buses and trucks. We go to movies, video stores, arcades, and malls and window-shop, entertained by the images of fantasy fulfillment each retailer offers. Print media are full of images; in our newspapers, for instance, photos, drawings, and computer graphics appear in color and vie with print for space. Even college textbooks, once mostly blocks of uninterrupted prose with an occasional black-and-white drawing or photo, now often have colorful graphics and elaborate transparency overlays.

If a picture is indeed worth a thousand words, then perhaps our image-saturated world is all to the good. Or perhaps, as some argue, all this rapid-fire, reality-manipulating technology yields jaded people with short attention spans who haven't the patience for the slower thought needed to understand words in print. But no matter how we assess it, the technology rolls on, continually extending its range and reach, filling our minds and, more importantly, *forming* them. Visual images are not just "out there" clamoring for our attention but also "in here," part of how we attend to and judge experience. Like language, visual images are rhetorical. They persuade us in obvious and not-so-obvious ways. And so we need some perspective on visual rhetoric; we need to understand its power and how to use it effectively and responsibly.

UNDERSTANDING VISUAL ARGUMENTS

Visual rhetoric is *the use of images, sometimes coupled with sound or appeals to the other senses, to make an argument or persuade us to act as the image-maker would have us act.* Probably the clearest examples are advertisements and political cartoons, a few of which we will examine shortly. But visual rhetoric is everywhere. We do not ordinarily think, say, of a car's body style as "rhetoric," but clearly it is, because people are persuaded to pay tens of thousands of dollars for the sleekest new body style when they could spend a few thousand for an older car that would get them from home to work or school just as well. Consider also the billions of dollars we spend on clothes, hairstyles, cosmetics, diets, and exercise programs—all part of the rhetoric of making the right "visual statement" in a world that too often judges us solely by how we look. We spend so much because our self-images depend in part on others' responses to our cars, bodies, offices, homes—to whatever represents "us." No doubt we all want to be liked and loved for our true selves, but distinguishing this "inside" from the "outside" we show the world has never been easy. Because we tend to become the image we cultivate, the claim that "image is everything" may not be as superficial as it sounds.

We might assume that visual rhetoric is modern—that without photography, computers, and Madison Avenue it wouldn't amount to much. But we would be mistaken. The pharaohs of ancient Egypt didn't build the pyramids merely to have a place to be buried; these immense structures "proclaim" the power and status of the rulers who had them built, as well as the civilization and empire they symbolize, and they "argue" against a view of human existence as merely transitory. Even now, millennia after ancient Egypt's decline, we can only stand before the pyramids in awe and wonder. The impact of visual rhetoric is not always as fleeting as the clever new commercial on television.

As old as the pyramids are, visual rhetoric is still older. We will never find its origins, for it began with natural places that prehistoric people invested with sacred power, with the earliest drawings and paintings, with natural and sculpted objects used in religious rites and festivals.

Although there is much that we cannot know about visual rhetoric, we can learn to appreciate the art that goes into making potent images. We can learn how to interpret and evaluate them. We can create visual rhetoric ourselves, images that stand alone or visuals combined with text. This chapter analyzes some common forms of visual rhetoric. The assignments will give you practice in analyzing images and creating visual rhetoric of your own.

"READING" IMAGES

Rhetorical analysis of visual rhetoric involves examining images to see how they attempt to convince or persuade an audience. We must first recognize that "reading" an image demands interpretive skills no less than reading a written text does. Images do not merely capture reality, not even in the case of photographs. Pictures are symbols that must be read, just as language is read; this becomes clear when we look at art from different cultures. The bodies in Egyptian paintings seem distorted to us, flattened to combine frontal and profile views, but the Egyptians understood these figures as representing the timeless and ideal. Visual symbols gain meaning from culture—the color white, for example, suggests purity in one culture, death in another. To read an argument made through images, a critic must be able to recognize allusions to popular culture. For example, Americans knew that the white mustaches on the celebrities in the milk commericals referred to the way children drink milk; more recently, the milk mustache symbolizes the ad campaign itself, now part of our culture.

As with inquiry into any argument, we ought to begin with questions about rhetorical context: When was the visual argument created and by whom? To what audience was it originally aimed and with what purpose? Then we can ask what claim a visual argument makes and what reasons it offers in support of that claim. Then, as with verbal texts that make a case, we can examine visual arguments for evidence, assumptions, and bias, and we can ask what values they favor and what the implications of accepting their argument are—for instance, if we buy the Jaguar, what kind of debt will we incur?

Although it is possible to make a claim and support it with no words at all, most visual arguments use words as well. Some of the reasoning will appear in these words. Either way, if we see that an argument is offered, we can inquire into it as we have done with written texts: What is the claim? the reason(s)? the evidence? the assumptions? the bias? the implications? What values are being promoted? We cannot, however, expect a visual argument to make a fully developed argument.

Many visuals do not even attempt reasoning; they rely instead on emotional appeals. Such appeals are most obvious in advertising, where the aim is to move a target audience to buy a service or product. In many advertisements, especially for products like beer, cigarettes, and perfume, where the differences are subjective, emotional appeal is all there is. Most emotional appeals work by promising to reward our desires for love, status, peace of mind, or escape from everyday responsibilities.

Advertisements also use ethical appeals, associating their claim with values the audience approves of and wants to identify with—such as images that show nature being preserved, races living in harmony, families staying in touch, and people attaining the American dream of upward mobility.

In evaluating the ethics of visual rhetoric, we need to consider whether the argument is at least reasonable: Does the image demonstrate reasoning, or does it oversimplify and mislead? We will want to look at the emotional and ethical appeals to decide if they pander to audience weaknesses and prejudices or manipulate fantasies and fears.

ANALYSIS: FIVE COMMON TYPES OF VISUAL ARGUMENT

We analyze below some visual arguments in various genres: advertisements, editorial cartoons, public sculpture, and news photographs. We show how "reading" visual texts requires interpretive skills and how interpretive skills, in turn, depend on the critic's knowledge of cultural context.

Advertisements

Advertisements usually make clear claims. And because target audiences are carefully selected, we can readily see the strategy in choosing ethical and emotional appeals.

An advertisement for Pentax (see Figure C-1 in the color section) appeared originally in *Sierra*, a magazine published by the environmentalist Sierra Club. *Sierra*'s readership is primarily middle-class adults who love nature and are concerned about preserving the environment. Most of the ads and articles are of interest to parents planning family trips and wanting to ensure that wilderness will be around for their children and grandchildren to enjoy.

The logical appeal of the ad is obvious. It argues that readers should buy a Pentax IQZoom 140M because it is a convenient, light camera with features that will help them take great pictures. The features of the camera are the reasons for buying it, and these are clearly indicated by the large photo of the camera itself and the text in red print. The small, tacked-on snapshot of the boys is evidence in support of the reasons. Rather than letting the argument rest entirely on the camera's features, the advertisers depend heavily on ethical and emotional appeals.

The ad features the image of a stock character: the soccer mom—in this case, a Badger den mother. The strategy is to employ a wholesome, friendly young mother who reaches out—literally—and "testifies" to how successfully she uses the camera. The advertiser expects *Sierra* readers would trust such a character and admire her values. Her affectionate descriptions of the "scrappy champions" and her reference to the "box of bandages" show that she is loving and nurturing. The Band-Aid on her right knee shows that she is a participant in the action. She is energetic and cheerful in her bright yellow uniform as she smiles up at the readers. They would find nothing in this ad to challenge traditional gender roles for women and boys. In short, she confirms conventional middle-class American values.

None of what we have said so far addresses the deeper appeal of the ad, however. The advertisers wanted to amuse the audience, and the eye-catching image of the woman does that with photographic effects. The image distorts "reality," providing ridiculous relationships in size—for example, between the woman's head and the cap that should fit it. The camera and the woman's hand seem grossly out of proportion compared to her tiny hiking boots. These distortions are funny, not threatening or disorienting, as images in photographic art can be.

The direct, friendly relationship between the viewer and the woman in the ad is supported by the angle of the camera that took her photograph. The camera angle puts the viewers above her in a reassuring position of power.

You may not think of postage as advertising, but the stamp in Figure C-2 has raised over $22.3 million for breast cancer research since it was first issued in 1998. Its fundraising success indicates its power as visual rhetoric, despite its actual size. Called a "semi-postal" stamp, because a percentage of its sale price is donated to fund the cause it represents, it and other stamps in the U.S. Postal Service's "social awareness" category rely on all of the appeals — logical, ethical, emotional, stylistic.

That you can buy an attractive stamp *and* contribute to a good cause is a good reason to purchase it. But the breast cancer stamp also persuades people to buy it because all postage stamps confer honor on the subjects they represent. Malcolm X got a stamp; the Sonoran Desert got a stamp. That they did confirms their importance and worthiness. Every time we buy such stamps, we reconfirm the subject's value, participate in our country's shared values, and reinforce the federal government's authority, since it decides who or what gets a stamp.

Is it, however, just government recognition that has sold more than 377.2 million copies of this stamp? Its success also has a lot to do with how its image works. Designed by breast cancer survivor Ethel Kessler of Bethesda, Maryland, and illustrated by Whitney Sherman of Baltimore, the stamp depicts a goddess. While we may not consciously recognize the female figure as a goddess, we do recognize the image's combination of femaleness and strength: Non-angular lines dominate, suggesting softness, traditionally a female attribute; however, the stamp's colors are bold — suggesting vitality and even triumph — and exclude the traditionally feminine color pink. The stamp's minimal main text, "Fund the Fight. Find a Cure," furthers its rhetorical effectiveness by beginning at the left edge of the image, moving in a straight line, and then curving down sharply to encircle the area where the figure's right breast would be. The visual effect highlights the important point.

As the postage stamp shows, visuals with little or no accompanying text can be powerfully persuasive by implying an argument rather than stating it explicitly. Consider the poster reproduced as Figure C-3, created by an advertising agency for the Southampton Anti-Bias Task Force. It shows a line of five sharp new crayons, each labeled "flesh." On one level, a viewer may see the poster as an eye-catching message for racial tolerance. However, anyone old enough to recall a now-discontinued Crayola called "flesh" that was the color of the center crayon will see a more complicated argument. Such viewers will read the image as an argument against the cultural bias that allowed millions of children to grow up thinking that "flesh" was white, all other skin colors being deviations from the norm. Children of other races or mixed races knew that "flesh" was not their flesh.

Because an image invites interpretation rather than stating a message, it opens a space for contemplation, just as we may contemplate the implied message of any work of art—fiction, film, poetry, painting. Studying visual rhetoric reminds us how much the reader contributes to the meaning of any text, visual or verbal.

 Following Through

1. Although the advertisement for the Volkswagen Beetle in Figure C-4 features an image of the product, customary with car ads, the lack of background, the size of the image relative to the white space surrounding it, and the unusual wording of the text all contribute to making this an unconventional piece of visual rhetoric. Consider these elements and any other aspect of the ad as you discuss how it might appeal to a specific audience of car buyers.

2. An advertisement for Comstock, Inc., a company that rents out photographs for commercial purposes, promotes its service with a striking example of its own product. The company wishes to persuade potential clients that it can supply a visual image for any idea. Discuss how the image of the goldfish bowl (Figure C-5) conveys the feeling of being "stuck." Do you find the image and accompanying text persuasive?

3. The Adidas advertisement in Figure C-7 shows the creative effects possible with photographic techniques. How do you "read" the image of the man in relation to the image of the shadow? How does the entire picture convey the idea of speed? Why do you think the advertisers chose to identify the celebrity athlete in fine print?

Editorial Cartoons

Editorial cartoons comment on events and issues in the news. They are funny but offer concise arguments too. Many political cartoons rely on captions and on dialogue spoken by characters in the picture to make their argument, so they combine the visual and verbal. Like advertisements, editorial cartoons are not ambiguous in their purpose; their arguments are easily inferred. However, as they age, editorial cartoons may become harder to "read" because they usually allude to current events. But some cartoons have longer lifespans, like the one by Mike Keefe (Figure 4.1, page 65) that comments on how computers affect the idea of knowledge.

This cartoon illustrates how "reading" a visual argument depends on shared cultural knowledge of symbols and metaphors. The image of a thirsty man crawling on hands and knees through a desert stands for any environment that denies humans something they need. What's needed could be anything from love to religion to the music of Mozart. The cartoon takes our common metaphor for the Internet, the "information superhighway," and depicts it graphically. The man is on the Internet, desperate for wisdom. To read the

My Pentax IQZoom 140M

My Photo

How I captured my little Badgers, after they emerged victorious from "Capture the Flag."

This is the print format switch. I chose to get a panorama print of all my scrappy champions.

This is the compact, lightweight design. Smaller to carry than your average box of bandages.

This is the six-segment multi-pattern metering system that shed a winning light on the whole bunch, from persistent Pete to wild William.

This is the 38-140mm power zoom lens. A handy zoom to have when your subjects are wielding live snakes or suspicious bugs.

Aren't your pictures worth a PENTAX ?

Pentax Corporation
35 Inverness Drive East
Englewood, CO 80112
www.pentax.com

Figure C-1

Figure C-2

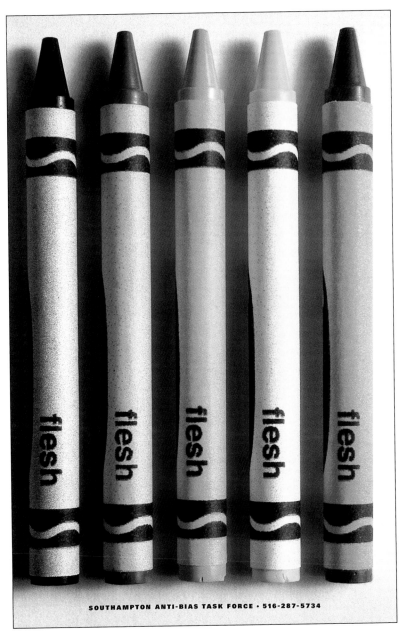

Figure C-3

Figure C-4

Figure C-5

Figure C-6

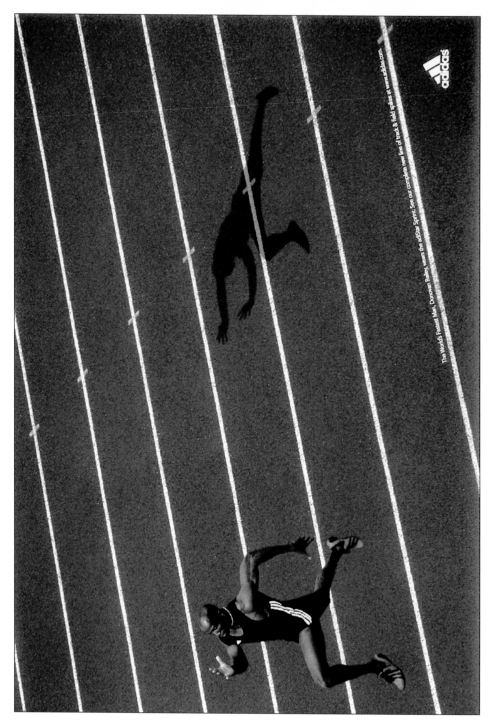

Figure C-7

Figure 4.1   Mike Keefe, dePIXion studios. Reprinted with permission.

argument of the cartoon and appreciate its humor, the viewer has to know about the overwhelming glut of information on the Internet, suggested by the size of the letters on the road. The cartoon "argues" that relying on the Internet for knowledge will deprive a civilization of the wisdom it needs to sustain itself.

How convincing are political cartoons? Can they change people's views? Anthony Blair, a critic of visual arguments, says that "visual arguments tend to be one-dimensional; they present the case for one side only, without including arguments against it. . . . [They] must always be suspect . . . and their power countered by a degree of skepticism and a range of critical questions: 'Is that the whole story?' 'Are there other points of view?' 'Is the real picture so black and white?'"

Cartoons also may fail to change people's minds because their humor comes at the expense of the side they oppose — they satirize by exaggerating the opposition's view. Political cartoons usually "preach to the choir." Believers will applaud having their position cleverly portrayed, while nonbelievers will be annoyed or offended. Consider the two cartoons in Figure 4.2 (page 66), which ridicule what the cartoonists see as misplaced priorities in the pro-life and pro-choice movements.

The McCloskey cartoon (page 66, top) argues that the pro-choice demonstrators are hypocrites in protesting murdered doctors, for they ignore the dead fetus. The lower half of the drawing emphasizes the fetus by giving it wings to symbolize its soul. This half of the cartoon stands in stark contrast to the "noisy" upper half, in which the protesters look deranged. In the Luckovich cartoon (page 66, bottom), the contrast is between the shapeless fetus and the more fully depicted corpse of the doctor, both preserved in specimen

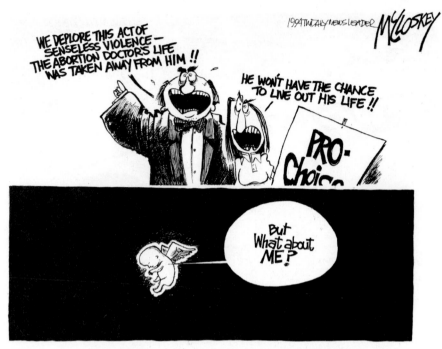

Jim McCloskey, *The News Leader*, Staunton, Virginia. Reprinted by permission.

Figure 4.2   By permission of Mike Lukovich and Creators Syndicate, Inc.

Figure 4.3   Gary Varvel. Courtesy of Creators Syndicate, Inc.

bottles. One is a person; the other clearly is not. Viewers on either side of this issue would argue that these portraits misrepresent their positions through oversimplification.

 Following Through

1. The cartoon by Gary Varvel (Figure 4.3) comments on attempts in Oregon to legalize doctor-assisted suicide. This is not a funny topic, but Varvel makes a humorous comment on it by exploiting a stock situation—the ledge-jumper and the would-be rescuer. How does the humor work to poke fun at the idea of doctor-assisted suicide? What aspects of the larger issue does the cartoon leave out?
2. Find a recent editorial cartoon on an issue of interest to you. Bring it to class, and be prepared to elaborate on its argument and explain its persuasive tactics. Do you agree or disagree with the cartoonist's perspective? Discuss the fairness of the cartoon. Does it minimize the complexity of the issue it addresses?

Public Sculpture

Public sculptures, such as war memorials, aim to teach an audience about a nation's past and to honor the values for which its citizens were willing to die. An example of a public sculpture that can be read as an argument is the

Figure 4.4

Marine Corps Memorial (better known as the Iwo Jima Memorial), which was erected in 1954 on the Mall in Washington, D.C. (see Figure 4.4, the photograph above). The memorial honors all Marines who gave their lives for their country through a depiction of one specific act of bravery, the planting of the American flag on Iwo Jima, a Pacific island that the United States captured from the Japanese in 1945. The claim that the sculpture makes to American audiences is clear: Honor your country. The image of the soldiers straining every muscle to raise the American flag gives the reason: "These men made extreme sacrifices to preserve the values symbolized by this flag." Interpreting the memorial is not difficult for Americans who know about the flag in the fierce Iwo Jima battle. The sculpture also communicates through details like the wind-whipped flag and the angles of the men's arms and legs, suggesting supreme struggle.

The Iwo Jima sculpture is a traditional war memorial, glorifying a victory on enemy soil. We might therefore compare it with the very different Vietnam War Memorial, dedicated in Washington in November 1982. Maya Lin designed what has come to be known as "the Wall" while she was an undergraduate student at Yale. Her design was controversial because the monument was so unconventional (see Figures 4.5 and 4.6, opposite) and anti-war. Its low, black granite slates are etched with the names of war dead; it honors the individuals who died in a war that tore the nation apart.

Figure 4.5

Figure 4.6

Figure 4.7

News Photographs

While some news photographs seem merely to record an event, the camera is not objective. The photographer makes many "editorial" decisions — whether to snap a picture, when to snap it, what to include and exclude from the image — and decisions about light, depth of field, and so on. Figure 4.7 (above), a photograph that appeared in the *New York Times,* shows a scene photographer Bruce Young encountered covering a snowstorm that hit Washington, D.C., in January 1994. The storm was severe enough to shut down the city and most government offices. Without the caption supplied by the *New York Times,* readers might not recognize the objects in the foreground as human beings, homeless people huddled on benches, covered by undisturbed snow.

The picture depicts homelessness in America as a national disgrace, a problem that must be addressed. Its composition supports the claim. The White House in the background is our nation's "home," a grand and lavishly decorated residence symbolic of national wealth. In juxtaposition with the foreground, the homeless people look like bags of garbage, marring the beautiful picture of the snow-covered landscape. No blame attaches to the homeless for their condition; they are too pathetic, captured under their blankets of snow. True, there is no in-depth argument taking into account causes of the problem, such as unemployment or mental illness, or solutions such as shelters. The picture shows the homeless as a fact of life in our cities, tarnishing the idealized image of our nation.

Following Through

1. The Vietnam War Memorial invites interpretation and analysis. Because it does not portray a realistic scene as the Iwo Jima Memorial does, readings of it vary considerably—part of the controversy surrounding it. If you have visited the Wall, try to recall your reaction to it. What specific details led to your interpretation? Could you characterize the Wall as having logical, ethical, and emotional appeals?
2. Find public sculpture or monuments to visit and analyze. Alone or with some classmates, take notes and photographs. Then develop your interpretation of the sculpture's argument, specifying how visual details contribute to the case, and present your analysis to the class. Compare your interpretation with those of your classmates.

Following Through

1. A color news photograph of the October 1998 launch of the space shuttle *Discovery* is reproduced as Figure C-6. This was the flight that carried John Glenn into space for the second time. Photographer Gregg Newton captured this image well into the launch, when the plume of smoke was all that was visible. Although some Americans were skeptical that Glenn's flight was merely a public relations ploy by NASA, most people celebrated Glenn's accomplishment. Media images such as this contributed to Americans' perspective on the launch. How do you "read" the photo's argument?
2. In a recent newspaper or news magazine, find a photograph related to an issue in the news, something people may have differing opinions about. What perspective or point of view does the photograph offer? Explain your "reading" of the photograph through an analysis of the content, composition, and any details that contribute to your interpretation.

Graphics

Visual supplements to a longer text such as an essay, article, or manual are known as **graphics.** Given the ubiquity of visual appeals in almost everything we read and the widespread use of them in business and industry, it is odd how few school writing assignments require graphics. When students want to use photos, drawings, graphs, and the like in a paper, they tend to ask permission, as if they fear violating some unspoken rule. We believe that the

www.mhhe.
com/crusius

If you want
information on
using PowerPoint
to create graphics,
go to:
Writing >
PowerPoint
Tutorial

pictorial should not be out of bounds in English papers or other under-graduate writing. Many texts could be more effective with visual supplements, and we encourage you to use them whenever they are appropriate and helpful.

Most graphics fall into one of the following categories:

Tables and charts (typically an arrangement of data in columns and
   rows that summarizes the results of research)
Graphs (including bar, line, and pie graphs)
Photographs
Drawings (including maps and cartoons)

Although charts and tables are not images, they present data in visual form rather than prose. Tables are used to display data economically in one place so that readers can assess the information easily as they read and find it af-terward if they want to refer to it again. Consider Figure 4.8, which combines a table with bar graphs. It comes from a study of poverty in the United States. Note how much information is packed into this single visual and how easy it is to read, moving top to bottom and left to right through the categories. Consider how many long and boring paragraphs it would take to say the same thing in prose.

Graphs are usually no more than tables transformed into visuals we can interpret more easily. Bar graphs, for example, allow us to compare subcate-gories within major categories almost at a glance. Making the comparisons would be much more difficult if we had only the percentages listed in a table. Bar graphs are best at showing comparisons at some single point in time. In contrast, line graphs reveal trends—for example, the performance of the stock market. Pie graphs highlight relative proportions well. When newspa-pers want to show us how the federal budget is spent, for example, they typ-ically use pie graphs with the pieces labeled in some way to represent cate-gories such as national defense, welfare, entitlement programs, and the like. What gets the biggest pieces of the pie becomes instantly clear and easy to re-member—the two major purposes all graphs try to achieve. Graphs don't make arguments, but they are powerful deliverers of evidence and therefore are part of visual rhetoric.

As graphics, photographs represent people, objects, and scenes realisti-cally and concretely. For instance, owner's manuals for cars often have a shot of the engine compartment that shows where fluid reservoirs are located. Clearly, such photos serve highly practical purposes, such as helping us locate the dipstick. But they're also used, for example, in biographies; we get a bet-ter sense of, say, Abraham Lincoln's life and times when pictures of him, his family, his home, and so on are included. But photographs can do much more than merely inform. They can also be highly dramatic and powerfully emotional in ways that only the best writers can manage with prose. Photos are powerful persuaders.

But photographs are not analytical—by their nature, they give us the sur-face, only what the camera can "see." A different type of graphic, drawings, is

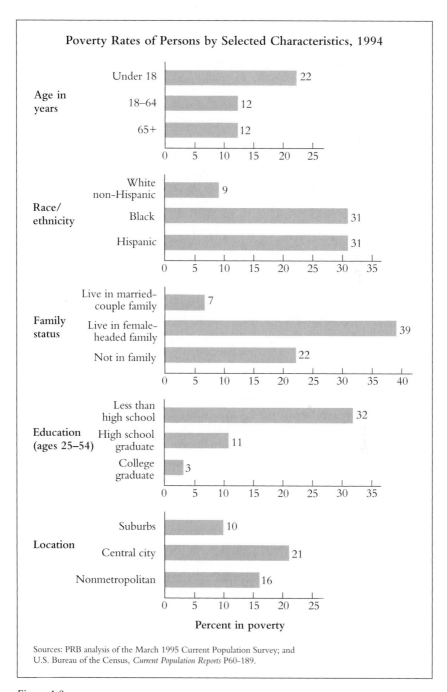

Poverty Rates of Persons by Selected Characteristics, 1994

Figure 4.8

preferable when we want to depict how something is put together or structured. For instance, instructions for assembling and installing a ceiling fan or a light fixture usually have many diagrams—a large one showing how all the parts fit together and smaller ones that depict steps in the process in more detail. Corporate publications often include diagrams of the company's organizational hierarchy. Scientific articles and textbooks are full of drawings or illustrations created with computer graphics; these publications use drawings because science writers want us to understand structures, particularly internal structures, impossible to capture on film. For example, our sense of DNA's double-helical structure comes entirely from diagrams.

The following article illustrates how a variety of graphics can contribute to the effectiveness of a written text. Attention-deficit hyperactivity disorder (ADHD) afflicts millions of people, most in their youth, during the years of formal education. You probably have friends whose intense struggle for self-control and focus makes coping with college especially difficult. This article both informs us about ADHD and argues two theses about it: (1) that self-control is the primary problem and (2) that the disorder is genetic, related to smaller-than-usual structures in the brain that regulate attention. As you read, notice how the graphics support the author's informative and argumentative purposes. (In our textbook's reproduction of the article, the original page layout has been changed. You may wish to access it via the Net at <www.sciam.com>.)

Attention-Deficit Hyperactivity Disorder
Russell A. Barkley

This article appeared in the September 1998 issue of Scientific American; *its author, Russell Barkley, is a professor of psychiatry and neurology at the University of Massachusetts Medical Center in Worcester and an internationally recognized expert on ADHD.*

As I watched five-year-old Keith in the waiting room of my office, I could see why his parents said he was having such a tough time in kindergarten. He hopped from chair to chair, swinging his arms and legs restlessly, and then began to fiddle with the light switches, turning the lights on and off again to everyone's annoyance—all the while talking nonstop. When his mother encouraged him to join a group of other children busy in the playroom, Keith butted into a game that was already in progress and took over, causing the other children to complain of his bossiness and drift away to other activities. Even when Keith had the toys to himself, he fidgeted aimlessly with them and seemed unable to entertain himself quietly. Once I

Children with ADHD cannot control their responses to their environment. This lack of control makes them hyperactive, inattentive, and impulsive.

examined him more fully, my initial suspicions were confirmed: Keith had attention-deficit hyperactivity disorder (ADHD).

Since the 1940s, psychiatrists have applied various labels to children who are hyperactive and inordinately inattentive and impulsive. Such youngsters have been considered to have "minimal brain dysfunction," "brain-injured child syndrome," "hyperkinetic reaction of childhood," "hyperactive child syndrome" and, most recently, "attention-deficit disorder." The frequent name changes reflect how uncertain researchers have been about the underlying causes of, and even the precise diagnostic criteria for, the disorder.

Within the past several years, however, those of us who study ADHD have begun to clarify its symptoms and causes and have found that it may have a genetic underpinning. Today's view of the basis of the condition is strikingly different from that of just a few years ago. We are finding that ADHD is not a disorder of attention per se, as had long been assumed. Rather it arises as a developmental failure in the brain circuitry that underlies inhibition and self-control. This loss of self-control in turn impairs other important brain functions crucial for maintaining attention, including the ability to defer immediate rewards for later, greater gain.

ADHD involves two sets of symptoms: inattention and a combination of hyperactive and impulsive behaviors (see table on page 77). Most children are more active, distractible and impulsive than adults. And they are more inconsistent, affected by momentary events and dominated by objects in their immediate environment. The younger the children, the less able they are to be aware of time or to give priority to future events over more immediate wants. Such behaviors are signs of a problem, however, when children display them significantly more than their peers do.

Boys are at least three times as likely as girls to develop the disorder; indeed, some studies have found that boys with ADHD outnumber girls with the condition by nine to one, possibly because boys are genetically more prone to disorders of the nervous system. The behavior patterns that typify ADHD usually arise between the ages of three and five. Even so, the age of onset can vary widely: some children do not develop symptoms until late childhood or even early adolescence. Why their symptoms are delayed remains unclear.

Huge numbers of people are affected. Many studies estimate that between 2 and 9.5 percent of all school-age children worldwide have ADHD; researchers have identified it in every nation and culture they have studied. What is more, the condition, which was once thought to ease with age, can persist into adulthood. For example, roughly two thirds of 158 children with ADHD my colleagues and I evaluated in the 1970s still had the disorder in their twenties. And many of those who no longer fit the clinical description of ADHD were still having significant adjustment problems at work, in school or in other social settings.

To help children (and adults) with ADHD, psychiatrists and psychologists must better understand the causes of the disorder. Because researchers have traditionally viewed ADHD as a problem in the realm of attention, some have suggested that it stems from an inability of the brain to filter competing sensory inputs, such as sights and sounds. But recently scientists led by Joseph A. Sergeant of the University of Amsterdam have shown that children with ADHD do not have difficulty in that area; instead they cannot inhibit their impulsive motor responses to such input. Other researchers have found that children with ADHD are less capable of preparing motor responses in anticipation of events and are insensitive to feedback about errors made in those responses. For example, in a commonly used test of reaction time, children with ADHD are less able than other children to ready themselves to press one of several keys when they see a warning light. They also do not slow down after making mistakes in such tests in order to improve their accuracy.

Diagnosing ADHD

Psychiatrists diagnose attention-deficit hyperactivity disorder (ADHD) if the individual displays six or more of the following symptoms of inattention or six or more symptoms of hyperactivity and impulsivity. The signs must occur often and be present for at least six months to a degree that is maladaptive and inconsistent with the person's developmental level. In addition, some of the symptoms must have caused impairment before the age of seven and must now be causing impairment in two or more settings. Some must also be leading to significant impairment in social, academic or occupational functioning; none should occur exclusively as part of another disorder.

Inattention	Hyperactivity and Impulsivity
Fails to give close attention to details or makes careless mistakes in schoolwork, work or other activities	Fidgets with hands or feet or squirms in seat
Has difficulty sustaining attention in tasks or play activities	Leaves seat in classroom or in other situations in which remaining seated is expected
Does not seem to listen when spoken to directly	Runs about or climbs excessively in situations in which it is inappropriate (in adolescents or adults, subjective feelings of restlessness)
Does not follow through on instructions and fails to finish schoolwork, chores or duties in the workplace	
Has difficulty organizing tasks and activities	Has difficulty playing or engaging in leisure activities quietly
Avoids, dislikes or is reluctant to engage in tasks that require sustained mental effort (such as schoolwork)	Is "on the go" or acts as if "driven by a motor"
Loses things necessary for tasks or activities (such as toys, school assignments, pencils, books or tools)	Talks excessively
	Blurts out answers before questions have been completed
Is easily distracted by extraneous stimuli	Has difficulty awaiting turns
Is forgetful in daily activities	Interrupts or intrudes on others

Source: Reprinted with permission from the *Diagnostic and Statistical Manual of Mental Disorders, Fourth Edition, Text Revision.* Copyright © 2000, American Psychiatric Association.

THE SEARCH FOR A CAUSE

No one knows the direct and immediate causes of the difficulties experienced by children with ADHD, although advances in neurological imaging techniques and genetics promise to clarify this issue over the next five years. Already they have yielded clues, albeit ones that do not yet fit together into a coherent picture.

Imaging studies over the past decade have indicated which brain regions might malfunction in patients with ADHD and thus account for the symptoms of the condition. That work suggests the involvement of the prefrontal cortex, part of the cerebellum, and at least two of the clusters of nerve cells deep in the brain that are collectively known as the basal ganglia (see illustration opposite). In a 1996 study F. Xavier Castellanos, Judith L. Rapoport and their colleagues at the National Institute of Mental Health found that the right prefrontal cortex and two basal ganglia called the caudate nucleus and the globus pallidus are significantly smaller than normal in children with ADHD. Earlier this year Castellanos's group found that the vermis region of the cerebellum is also smaller in ADHD children.

The imaging findings make sense because the brain areas that are reduced in size in children with ADHD are the very ones that regulate attention. The right prefrontal cortex, for example, is involved in "editing" one's behavior, resisting distractions and developing an awareness of self and time. The caudate nucleus and the globus pallidus help to switch off automatic responses to allow more careful deliberation by the cortex and to coordinate neurological input among various regions of the cortex. The exact role of the cerebellar vermis is unclear, but early studies suggest it may play a role in regulating motivation.

10

What causes the structures to shrink in the brains of those with ADHD? No one knows, but many studies have suggested that mutations in several genes that are normally very active in the prefrontal cortex and basal ganglia might play a role. Most researchers now believe that ADHD is a polygenic disorder—that is, that more than one gene contributes to it.

Early tips that faulty genetics underlie ADHD came from studies of the relatives of children with the disorder. For instance, the siblings of children with ADHD are between five and seven times more likely to develop the syndrome than children from unaffected families. And the children of a parent who has ADHD have up to a 50 percent chance of experiencing the same difficulties.

The most conclusive evidence that genetics can contribute to ADHD, however, comes from studies of twins. Jacquelyn J. Gillis, then at the University of Colorado, and her colleagues reported in 1992 that the ADHD risk of a child whose identical twin has the disorder is between 11 and 18 times greater than that of a nontwin sibling of a child with ADHD; between 55 and 92 percent of the identical twins of children with ADHD eventually develop the condition.

One of the largest twin studies of ADHD was conducted by Helene Gjone and Jon M. Sundet of the University of Oslo with Jim Stevenson of the University of Southampton in England. It involved 526 identical twins, who inherit exactly the same genes, and 389 fraternal twins, who are no more alike genetically than siblings born years apart. The team found that ADHD has a heritability approaching 80 percent, meaning that up to 80 percent of the differences in attention, hyperactivity and impulsivity

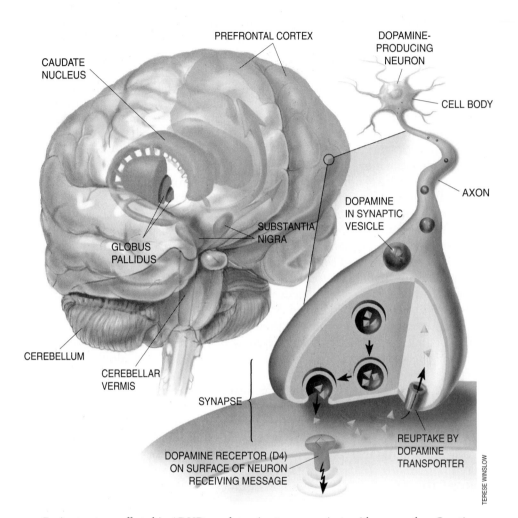

Brain structures affected in ADHD use dopamine to communicate with one another. Genetic studies suggest that people with ADHD might have alterations in genes encoding either the D4 dopamine receptor, which receives incoming signals, or the dopamine transporter, which scavenges released dopamine for reuse. The substantia nigra, where the death of dopamine-producing neurons causes Parkinson's disease, is not affected in ADHD.

between people with ADHD and those without the disorder can be explained by genetic factors.

    Nongenetic factors that have been linked to ADHD include premature birth, maternal alcohol and tobacco use, exposure to high levels of lead in early childhood and brain injuries — especially those that involve the

15

prefrontal cortex. But even together, these factors can account for only between 20 and 30 percent of ADHD cases among boys; among girls, they account for an even smaller percentage. (Contrary to popular belief, neither dietary factors, such as the amount of sugar a child consumes, nor poor child-rearing methods have been consistently shown to contribute to ADHD.)

Which genes are defective? Perhaps those that dictate the way in which the brain uses dopamine, one of the chemicals known as neurotransmitters that convey messages from one nerve cell, or neuron, to another. Dopamine is secreted by neurons in specific parts of the brain to inhibit or modulate the activity of other neurons, particularly those involved in emotion and movement. The movement disorders of Parkinson's disease, for example, are caused by the death of dopamine-secreting neurons in a region of the brain underneath the basal ganglia called the substantia nigra.

Some impressive studies specifically implicate genes that encode, or serve as the blueprint for, dopamine receptors and transporters; these genes are very active in the prefrontal cortex and basal ganglia. Dopamine receptors sit on the surface of certain neurons. Dopamine delivers its message to those neurons by binding to the receptors. Dopamine transporters protrude from neurons that secrete the neurotransmitter; they take up unused dopamine so that it can be used again. Mutations in the dopamine receptor gene can render receptors less sensitive to dopamine. Conversely, mutations in the dopamine transporter gene can yield overly effective transporters that scavenge secreted dopamine before it has a chance to bind to dopamine receptors on a neighboring neuron.

In 1995 Edwin H. Cook and his colleagues at the University of Chicago reported that children with ADHD were more likely than others to have a particular variation in the dopamine transporter gene *DAT1*. Similarly, in 1996 Gerald J. LaHoste of the University of California at Irvine and his co-workers found that a variant of the dopamine receptor gene *D4* is more common among children with ADHD. But each of these studies involved 40 or 50 children—a relatively small number—so their findings are now being confirmed in larger studies.

FROM GENES TO BEHAVIOR

How do the brain-structure and genetic defects observed in children with ADHD lead to the characteristic behaviors of the disorder? Ultimately, they might be found to underlie impaired behavioral inhibition and self-control, which I have concluded are the central deficits in ADHD.

Self-control—or the capacity to inhibit or delay one's initial motor (and perhaps emotional) responses to an event—is a critical foundation for the performance of any task. As most children grow up, they gain the ability to engage in mental activities, known as executive functions, that

20

help them deflect distractions, recall goals and take the steps needed to reach them. To achieve a goal in work or play, for instance, people need to be able to remember their aim (use hindsight), prompt themselves about what they need to do to reach that goal (use forethought), keep their emotions reined in and motivate themselves. Unless a person can inhibit interfering thoughts and impulses, none of these functions can be carried out successfully.

In the early years, the executive functions are performed externally: children might talk out loud to themselves while remembering a task or puzzling out a problem. As children mature, they internalize, or make private, such executive functions, which prevents others from knowing their thoughts. Children with ADHD, in contrast, seem to lack the restraint needed to inhibit the public performance of these executive functions.

The executive functions can be grouped into four mental activities. One is the operation of working memory—holding information in the mind while working on a task, even if the original stimulus that provided the information is gone. Such remembering is crucial to timeliness and goal-directed behavior: it provides the means for hindsight, forethought, preparation and the ability to imitate the complex, novel behavior of others—all of which are impaired in people with ADHD.

The internalization of self-directed speech is another executive function. Before the age of six, most children speak out loud to themselves frequently, reminding themselves how to perform a particular task or trying to cope with a problem, for example. ("Where did I put that book? Oh, I left it under the desk.") In elementary school, such private speech evolves into inaudible muttering; it usually disappears by age 10 [see "Why Children Talk to Themselves," by Laura E. Berk; *Scientific American*, November 1994]. Internalized, self-directed speech allows one to reflect to oneself, to follow rules and instructions, to use self-questioning as a form of problem solving and to construct "meta-rules," the basis for understanding the rules for using rules—all quickly and without tipping one's hand to others. Laura E. Berk and her colleagues at Illinois State University reported in 1991 that the internalization of self-directed speech is delayed in boys with ADHD.

A third executive mental function consists of controlling emotions, motivation and state of arousal. Such control helps individuals achieve goals by enabling them to delay or alter potentially distracting emotional reactions to a particular event and to generate private emotions and motivation. Those who rein in their immediate passions can also behave in more socially acceptable ways.

The final executive function, reconstitution, actually encompasses two separate processes: breaking down observed behaviors and combining the parts into new actions not previously learned from experience. The capacity for reconstitution gives humans a great degree of fluency, flexibility and creativity; it allows individuals to propel themselves toward a goal without having to learn all the needed steps by rote. It permits children as they

25

A Psychological Model of ADHD

A loss of behavioral inhibition and self-control leads to the following disruptions in brain functioning:

Impaired Function	Consequence	Example
Nonverbal working memory	Diminished sense of time Inability to hold events in mind Defective hindsight Defective forethought	Nine-year-old Jeff routinely forgets important responsibilities, such as deadlines for book reports or an after-school appointment with the principal
Internalization of self-directed speech	Deficient rule-governed behavior Poor self-guidance and self-questioning	Five-year-old Audrey talks too much and cannot give herself useful directions silently on how to perform a task
Self-regulation of mood, motivation and level of arousal	Displays all emotions publicly; cannot censor them Diminished self-regulation of drive and motivation	Eight-year-old Adam cannot maintain the persistent effort required to read a story appropriate for his age level and is quick to display his anger when frustrated by assigned schoolwork
Reconstitution (ability to break down observed behaviors into component parts that can be recombined into new behaviors in pursuit of a goal)	Limited ability to analyze behaviors and synthesize new behaviors Inability to solve problems	Fourteen-year-old Ben stops doing a homework assignment when he realizes that he has only two of the five assigned questions; he does not think of a way to solve the problem, such as calling a friend to get the other three questions

Source: Lisa Burnett

mature to direct their behavior across increasingly longer intervals by combining behaviors into ever longer chains to attain a goal. Initial studies imply that children with ADHD are less capable of reconstitution than are other children.

I suggest that like self-directed speech, the other three executive functions become internalized during typical neural development in early childhood. Such privatization is essential for creating visual imagery and verbal thought. As children grow up, they develop the capacity to behave covertly, to mask some of their behaviors or feelings from others. Perhaps because of faulty genetics or embryonic development, children with ADHD have not attained this ability and therefore display too much public behavior and

Psychological tests used in ADHD research include the four depicted here. The tower-building test (upper left), in which the subject is asked to assemble balls into a tower to mimic an illustration, measures forethought, planning and persistence. The math test (upper right) assesses working memory and problem-solving ability. In the auditory attention test (lower left), the subject must select the appropriate colored tile according to taped instructions, despite distracting words. The time estimation test (lower right) measures visual attention and subjective sense of time intervals. The subject is asked to hold down a key to illuminate a lightbulb on a computer screen for the same length of time that another bulb was illuminated previously.

speech. It is my assertion that the inattention, hyperactivity and impulsivity of children with ADHD are caused by their failure to be guided by internal instructions and by their inability to curb their own inappropriate behaviors.

PRESCRIBING SELF-CONTROL

If, as I have outlined, ADHD is a failure of behavioral inhibition that delays the ability to privatize and execute the four executive mental functions I have described, the finding supports the theory that children with ADHD might be helped by a more structured environment. Greater structure can be an important complement to any drug therapy the children might receive. Currently children (and adults) with ADHD often receive drugs such as Ritalin that boost their capacity to inhibit and regulate impulsive behaviors. These drugs act by inhibiting the dopamine transporter, increasing the time that dopamine has to bind to its receptors on other neurons.

Such compounds (which, despite their inhibitory effects, are known as psychostimulants) have been found to improve the behavior of between 70 and 90 percent of children with ADHD older than five years. Children with ADHD who take such medication not only are less impulsive, restless and distractible but are also better able to hold important information in mind, to be more productive academically, and to have more internalized speech and better self-control. As a result, they tend to be liked better by other children and to experience less punishment for their actions, which improves their self-image.

My model suggests that in addition to psychostimulants — and perhaps antidepressants, for some children — treatment for ADHD should include training parents and teachers in specific and more effective methods for managing the behavioral problems of children with the disorder. Such methods involve making the consequences of a child's actions more frequent and immediate and increasing the external use of prompts and cues about rules and time intervals. Parents and teachers must aid children with ADHD by anticipating events for them, breaking future tasks down into smaller and more immediate steps, and using artificial immediate rewards. All these steps serve to externalize time, rules and consequences as a replacement for the weak internal forms of information, rules and motivation of children with ADHD.

In some instances, the problems of ADHD children may be severe   30
enough to warrant their placement in special education programs. Although such programs are not intended as a cure for the child's difficulties, they typically do provide a smaller, less competitive and more supportive environment in which the child can receive individual instruction. The hope is that once children learn techniques to overcome their deficits in self-control, they will be able to function outside such programs.

There is no cure for ADHD, but much more is now known about effectively coping with and managing this persistent and troubling developmental disorder. The day is not far off when genetic testing for ADHD may become available and more specialized medications may be designed to counter the specific genetic deficits of the children who suffer from it.

Analyzing Barkley's Graphics

Barkley's article contains the following graphics, listed in order of appearance:

A cartoon depicting the whirling, chaotic world of the ADHD sufferer
A chart of the symptoms of the disorder entitled "Diagnosing ADHD"

> A computer-generated, three-dimensional graphic depicting the brain
>   and processes having to do with neural activity
> Another chart entitled "A Psychological Model of ADHD"
> A set of photographs showing tests used in ADHD research

Thus, in a relatively short article, we have a wide range of graphics, each one of which we could comment on at greater length than we do here. The following comments are designed to stimulate thinking about how graphics function rhetorically.

Turning to the first graphic on page 75, we should notice what it "says" about the intended audience. *Scientific American's* readership is mixed; it is not limited to scientists but includes scientists who enjoy reading about the work of scientists in other fields. Thus, the articles must be "real science" but also have broad appeal. The cartoonlike image we first encounter would almost certainly not appear in a "hard-core" science journal written by specialists for specialists. We might also consider how well the graphic works to "predict" the content of the article and to represent the problem of ADHD.

Compare the opening graphic with the drawing of the brain on page 79. Clearly, the cartoon is intended for the more "pop" side of *Scientific American's* readership, whereas the drawing targets those who want a more detailed understanding of the "hard science" involved in ADHD research. The article itself moves from knowledge that can be widely shared to information more specialized and harder to grasp, returning at the end to its broader audience's interests. The movement from the cartoon to the drawing reflects the text's development. The drawing assists Barkley in presenting essential information about the disorder itself.

The four photos near the end of the article (page 83) depict a humanistic concern for the welfare of ADHD children. The role of these photographs is less informative than persuasive. Although less controversial than it once was, when even its existence was in dispute, ADHD remains a disputed topic. Some contend that the syndrome is diagnosed too often and too easily, perhaps in part at the urging of parents who know that laws mandate special treatment for ADHD cases in schools, such as more time to complete tests. Others argue that the disorder is more environmental than genetic and trace its source to a chaotic family life, too much TV, bad eating habits, and factors other than (or in addition to) brain abnormalities. Finally, among other doubts and criticism are questions raised by teachers: When a child is properly treated for ADHD, just how impaired is he or she? Is special consideration really warranted? up to what age?

Barkley's article hardly alludes to the controversies surrounding ADHD, probably because the view he develops represents an emerging consensus among researchers. But if we read the article with its unspoken context in mind, we see much is intended to refute skeptics. Clearly, the genetic hypothesis is advanced by both text and graphics, and the concluding four photos claim, in effect, that actual and reliable testing is part of the diagnostic process.

We turn now to another graphic, the charts. Surely the chart entitled "Diagnosing ADHD" on page 77 confirms the existence of definite criteria for diagnosis and to insist that diagnosis should be neither hasty nor uncertain. Note especially the sentence "The signs must occur often and be present for at least six months to a degree that is maladaptive and inconsistent with the person's developmental level." A similar implicit argument can be found in the second chart, "A Psychological Model of ADHD." It "says" that the disorder is thoroughly conceived, that we know much about it, and that we can be concrete about the symptoms. These charts, then, although they may appear to be merely information, are actually arguments—claims about the solid, objective reality of ADHD.

Following Through

1. Discuss the first graphic in the article as an introduction to the article's topic and argument. What function does this graphic serve? What message is conveyed by the assortment of items swirling around the child? Into what categories do the items fall? Why is the child male? How would you characterize his expression? What attitude about his plight does this image convey?

2. Consider these questions as you examine the drawing of the brain on page 79 and the enlarged drawing of the connections between nerve cells, or neurons: What purposes do these visuals serve? For what part of the audience are they intended? Do they help you understand the physiology of the disorder? Can you explain how perspective comes into play in the drawing of the two neurons? Without these graphics, how much would you understand about the complex brain and neural processes discussed?

3. Discuss the four concluding photographs in the article as persuasion. How much information about psychological testing is conveyed by the photos themselves? Why are the adult figures women? How are they dressed? (Suppose they were men in white lab coats. What different impression would this create?) How would you characterize the office or clinical environment in which the child performs the tests? What messages are sent by the child's gender, age, race, clothes, hair, and cast on his left arm? by his body language and facial expressions? What might the persuasive intent be? If there is an implicit argument, what would it be, and why is it necessary?

4. Discuss why Barkley decided to present the material in the two charts in this tabulated form rather than incorporating it into the body of the article.

5. As an exercise in considering the role of graphics, bring to class a paper you have written recently for a college or high school assignment. If you didn't use graphics, ask yourself the following questions: Could the

paper be improved with graphic support? If so, given your audience and purpose(s), what graphic types would you use and why? How would you go about securing or creating the graphics? If you did use graphics, be prepared to discuss them—what you did and why, how you went about creating the visuals, and so on. If you now see ways to improve the graphics, discuss your revision strategies as well.

WRITING ASSIGNMENTS

Assignment 1: Analyzing an Advertisement or Editorial Cartoon

Choose an ad or cartoon from a current magazine or newspaper. First, inquire into its rhetorical context: What situation prompted its creation? What purpose does it aim to achieve? Where did it originally appear? Who is its intended audience? What would they know or believe about the product or issue? Then inquire into the argument being made. To do this, you should consult the questions for inquiry on pages 159–160 to the extent that they apply to visual rhetoric. You should also consider some of the points we have made in this chapter: What visual metaphors or allusions appear in the ad or cartoon? What prior cultural knowledge and experiences would the audience need to "read" the image? Consider how the visual argument might limit the scope of the issue or how it might play to the audience's biases, stereotypes, or fears. After thorough inquiry, reach some conclusion about the effectiveness and ethics of this particular visual argument. Write your conclusion as a thesis or claim. Write your analysis as an argument to convince, using the evidence gathered during the inquiry to support and develop your claim.

STUDENT SAMPLE: *Analysis of Visual Rhetoric*

The following student essay is an example of Assignment 1. Before you begin your own essay, read it and discuss the conclusions reached about an advertisement for Eagle Brand condensed milk. We were unable to obtain permission to reprint the advertisement under discussion but the descriptions of it should make the analysis easy to follow.

A MOTHER'S TREAT

Kelly Williams

Advertisements are effective only if they connect with their audiences. Advertisers study the group of people they hope to reach and know what the group values and what images they have of themselves. Often these images come from social expectations that tell businessmen, mothers, fathers, teens that they should look or act a certain way. Most people adhere to the norms because they give social status. Advertisers tend to look to these norms as a way to sell their products. For example, an ad depicts a man in an expensive suit driving a luxury car, and readers assume he is a lawyer, physician, or business executive. Such people will buy this car because they associate it with the status they want to project. Likewise, some advertisements manipulate women with children by associating a product with the ideal maternal image.

An advertisement for Eagle Brand condensed milk typifies this effort. The advertisement appeared in magazines aimed at home-makers and in *People* magazine's "Best and Worst Dressed" issue of September 1998. The readers are predominantly young women; those with children may be second-income producers or single mothers. They are struggling to raise a family and have many demands on their time. They feel enormous pressure to fulfill ideal work and domestic roles.

The advertisement creates a strong connection with a maternal audience. The black-and-white photograph depicts a young girl about kindergarten age. The little girl's facial expression connotes hesitation and sadness. In the background is a school yard. Other children are walking toward the school, their heads facing down, creating a feeling of gloom. All readers will recognize the situation. The little girl is about to attend her first day of school. One could easily guess that she is looking back at her mother with a sense of abandonment, pleading for support.

The wording of the text adds some comic relief. The ad is not intended to make the readers sad. The words seem to come from the mind of the child's mother: "For not insisting on bunny slippers for shoes, for leaving Blankie behind, for actually getting out of the car. . . ." These words show that the mother is a good mother, very empathetic. Even the print type is part of the marketing strategy. It mimics a "proper" mother's handwriting. There are no sharp edges, implying softness and gentleness.

The intent is to persuade mothers that if they buy Eagle Brand milk   5
and make the chocolate bar treat, they will be good mothers like the speaker in the ad. It tells women that cooking such treats helps alleviate stressful situations in everyday family life. The little girl reminds mothers of their duty to comfort their kids. She evokes the "feminine" qualities of compassion, empathy, and protectiveness.

The ad also suggests that good mothers reward good behavior. As the ad says, "It's time for a treat." But good mothers would also know that "Welcome Home Chocolate Bars" are rich, so this mother has to say, "I'll risk spoiling your dinner." The invisible mother in the ad is ideal because she does care about her child's nutrition, but more about the emotional state of her child.

In many ways this ad is unethical. While the ad looks harmless and cute, it actually reinforces social pressures on women to be "perfect" mothers. If you don't bake a treat to welcome your child back home after school, you are failing as a mother. The recipe includes preparation time, showing that the treat can be made with minimal effort. It gives mothers no excuse for not making it. Moreover, the advertisement obviously exploits children to sell their product.

Desserts do not have much nutritional value. It would be hard to make a logical case for Welcome Home Bars, so Eagle Brand appeals to emotion. There's nothing wrong with a treat once in a while, but it is wrong to use guilt and social pressure to persuade mothers to buy a product.

Assignment 2: Using Visual Rhetoric to Promote Your School

Colleges and universities compete fiercely for students and are therefore as concerned about their image as any corporation or politician. As a class project, collect images your school uses to promote itself, including brochures for prospective students, catalogs, class lists, and Web home pages. Choose three or four of the best ones, and in class discussions analyze them. Then, working in groups of three or four students or individually, do one or all of the following:

1. Find an aspect of your college or university overlooked in the publications that you believe is a strong selling point. Employing photographs, drawings, paintings, or some other visual medium, create an image appropriate for one of the school publications. Compose an appealing text to go with it. Then, in a page or two, explain why you think your promotional image would work well.
2. If someone in the class has the computer knowledge, create an alternative to your school's home page, or make changes that would make it more appealing to prospective students and their parents.
3. Imagine that for purposes of parody or protest you wanted to call attention to aspects of your school that the official images deliberately omit. Proceed as in item 1. In a short statement, explain why you chose the image you did and what purpose(s) you want it to serve.
4. Select a school organization (a fraternity or sorority, a club, etc.) whose image you think could be improved. Create a promotional image for it either for the Web or for some other existing publication.
5. As in item 3, create a visual parody of the official image of a school organization, perhaps as an inside joke intended for other members of the organization.

Assignment 3: Analyzing Your Own Visual Rhetoric

Study all the images your class created as argument and/or persuasion in the previous assignment. Select an image to analyze in depth. Write an essay that addresses these questions:

What audience does the image intend to reach?
What goal did the creator of the image seek to accomplish?

If something is being argued, ask:

What thesis is advanced by the image or accompanying text?
Do aspects of the image or text function as reasons for holding the thesis?

If an image persuades more than it argues, attempt to discover and understand its major source of appeal. Persuasion appeals to the whole person in an effort to create **identification,** a strong linking of the reader's interests and values with the image that represents something desired. Hence, we can ask

How do the images your class created appeal to the audience's interests and values?
Do the images embody emotional appeals? How?

Assignment 4: Writing to Convince

Newspapers have been criticized for printing pictures that used to be considered too gruesome for publication. Highly respected newspapers like the *New York Times* have offered defenses of graphic photos. Look into what publishers, readers, and critics have to say on this topic. What issues and questions come up in these debates? Draw a conclusion of your own, and write an essay supporting it.

Assignment 5: Using Graphics to Supplement Your Own Writing or Other Texts

Select an essay that could be improved either by adding graphics or by revising the graphics used. Working alone or collaboratively with a writing group, revise it. For help with using graphics effectively in your writing, see the Best Practices box opposite, "Guidelines for Using Visuals." You have many revision options: Besides adding visuals, you can cut unneeded ones, redesign existing ones, change media (for example, from a photo to a drawing), change image types (for example, from a table to a graph), and so on. Revising graphics always means reworking the text as well. Expect changes in one to require changes in the other.

Graphics come in a variety of useful forms: as tables to display numerical data economically, as graphs to depict data in a way that permits easy comparison of proportions or trends, as photographs to convey realism and drama, and as drawings to depict structures. Whatever graphics you use, be sure to do the following:

- Make sure every graphic has a definite function. Graphics are not decorative and should never be "thrown" into an essay.
- Choose the kind or form of visual best suited to convey the point you are trying to make.
- Design graphics so that they are easy to interpret. That is, keep them simple, make them large enough to be read without strain, and use clear labeling.
- Place graphics as close as possible to the text they explain or illustrate. Remember, graphics should be easier to understand than the text they supplement.
- Refer to all your graphics in the text. Readers usually need both the graphic and a text discussion for full understanding.
- Acknowledge the creator or source of each graphic next to the graphic itself. As long as you acknowledge the source or creator, you can borrow freely, just as you can with quotations from texts. Of course, if you wish to publish an essay that includes borrowed graphics, you must obtain written permission.

Chapter 5

Writing Research-Based Arguments

www.mhhe.
com/crusius

For a wealth
of research
resources, go to:
Research

Research, which simply means "careful study," is essential to serious inquiry and most well-constructed cases. Before you write, you need to investigate the ongoing conversation about your issue. As you construct your argument, you will need specific evidence and the support of authorities to make a convincing case.

The distinction between researched and nonresearched writing does not usually apply to argumentation. An argument with no research behind it is generally weak. Many of the arguments you read may not appear to have been researched because the writers have not cited sources—most likely because they were writing for the general public rather than for an academic audience. In college, however, students are usually required to document all sources of ideas. Documentation is important for two main reasons: (1) It allows readers to look up source material, and (2) it protects the writer of the paper from **plagiarism,** the presenting of another's ideas or words as one's own. (See the Concept Close-Up box on page 94.)

www.mhhe.
com/crusius

For more
information
on plagiarism,
go to:
Research >
Plagiarism

Research for argumentation should begin as inquiry into the issue chosen or assigned. Your task is to discover information about the issue and, more importantly, to find arguments that address the issue to familiarize yourself with the range of opinion. Use the critical-reading skills developed in Chapter 2.

Sometimes, however, research must begin at an earlier stage—for example, when your instructor asks you to select an issue to write about. So we begin with suggestions for finding an issue.

FINDING AN ISSUE

Let's say you have been assigned an essay on any issue of current public concern, ranging from local to international affairs. If you have no idea what to write about, what should you do?

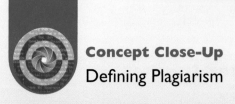

Concept Close-Up
Defining Plagiarism

Plagiarism: From the Latin *plagiarius,* a plunderer, kidnapper, literary thief.

> Appropriating and putting forth as one's own the ideas, language, or designs of another.—*New Grolier Webster International Dictionary*

> Act or instance of taking and passing off as one's own someone else's work or ideas.—*Scribner Dictionary*

Plagiarism is not limited to copying a source or having someone else write a paper for you. These are just the worst cases. It also includes taking an idea from a source without acknowledgment or using a source's actual words without quotation marks. All are serious violations of academic honesty.

Understand That an Issue Is More Than Just a Topic

You must look for a subject about which people genuinely disagree. For example, homelessness is a **topic:** you could report on many different aspects of it—from the number of homeless people in our country to profiles of individual homeless people. But a topic is not an issue. Once you start considering solutions for homelessness, you are dealing with an **issue,** because people will disagree about how to solve the problem.

Keep Abreast of Current Events and Research the News

Develop the habit of reading newspapers and magazines in print or online. Many newspapers are available online. Here are several:

> *Chicago Tribune* <http://www.chicagotribune.com>
> *Los Angeles Times* <http://www.latimes.com>
> *New York Times* <http://www.nytimes.com>
> *Wall Street Journal* <http://www.wsj.com>
> *Washington Post* <http://www.washingtonpost.com>

In addition to newspapers, such magazines as *Time, Newsweek,* and *U.S. News & World Report* cover current events; and others, such as *Harper's, Atlantic Monthly, New Republic, National Review,* and *Utne Reader,* offer essays, articles, and arguments on important current issues. Many of these are available online.

In your writer's notebook, record your responses to your reading so that you have a readily available source of ideas.

Research Your Library's Periodicals Indexes

Indexes are lists of articles in specific publications or groups of publications. Your school's library has a number of periodicals indexes in print, online, or in other electronic formats. You may be familiar with the *Readers' Guide to*

Periodical Literature. (For names of other indexes, see the section "Finding Sources," which begins on this page.) If you have a vague subject in mind, such as gender discrimination, consulting an index for articles and arguments on the topic can help you narrow your focus. However, if you don't have an issue in mind, looking through the *Readers' Guide* won't be very helpful, so we offer some suggestions for using indexes more efficiently.

You can look, for example, in a newspaper index (some are printed and bound; others are computerized) under "editorial" for a list of topics on which the editors have stated positions, or you can look under the name of a columnist—such as William F. Buckley, Anna Quindlen, or A. M. Rosenthal—whose views on current issues regularly appear in that paper. The bonus for using a newspaper index in this way is that it will lead you directly to arguments on an issue.

Another resource for finding arguments is *InfoTrac,* a computerized index to magazines, journals, and selected current articles in the *New York Times.* After you type in an appropriate subject word, *InfoTrac* allows you to narrow your search further. If you type in the key word of your subject followed by "and editorial" or "and opinion," only argumentative columns and editorials will appear on your screen. *InfoTrac* includes many full texts of articles.

A further possibility is to browse through an index dedicated solely to periodicals that specialize in social-issues topics, such as the *Journal of Social Issues* and *Vital Speeches of the Day.*

Inquire into the Issue

Once you have chosen an issue, you can begin your inquiry into positions. You may already hold one of your own, but during inquiry be open to the full range of viewpoints. Inquiry is central to mature reasoning. Inquiring into an issue also involves evaluating sources (see pages 106–109). The more care you take now, the more time you'll save in overall preparation of your paper.

Before you read further, take a moment to read the Concept Close-Up box, "Understanding the Ethics of Plagiarism," on page 96. In all writing, but especially in research writing, a grasp of the full importance of plagiarism is crucial.

FINDING SOURCES

Sources for developing an argument can be found through several kinds of research. Library and Internet research will lead you to abundant sources, but don't overlook what social scientists call *field research.*

Field Research

Research "in the field" means studying the world directly through observations, questionnaires, and interviews.

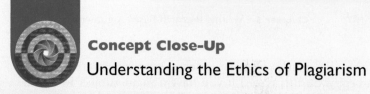

Concept Close-Up
Understanding the Ethics of Plagiarism

A student who plagiarizes faces severe penalties: a failing grade on a paper, perhaps failure in a course, even expulsion from the university and an ethics violation recorded on his or her permanent record. Outside of academe, in the professional world, someone who plagiarizes may face public humiliation, loss of a degree, rank, or job, perhaps even a lawsuit. Why is plagiarism such a serious offense?

Plagiarism is theft. If someone takes our money or our car, we rightly think that person should be punished. Stealing ideas or the words used to express them is no less an act of theft. That's why we have laws that protect *intellectual property* such as books and essays.

Plagiarism is a breach of ethics. In our writing, we are *morally obligated* to distinguish between our ideas, information, and language and somebody else's ideas, information, and language. If we don't, it's like taking someone else's identity, pretending to be what we're not. Human society cannot function without trust and integrity—hence the strong condemnation of plagiarism.

Plagiarism amounts to taking an unearned and unfair advantage. You worked hard to get that "B" on the big paper in your political science class. How would you feel if you knew that another student had simply purchased an "A" paper, thereby avoiding the same effort? At the very least, you'd resent it. We hope you'd report the plagiarism. For plagiarism is not just a moral failure with potentially devastating consequences for an individual. *Plagiarism, like any form of dishonesty intended to gain an unfair advantage, damages human society and hurts everyone.*

Observations

Do not discount the value of your own personal experiences as evidence in making a case. You will notice that many writers of arguments offer as evidence what they themselves have seen, heard, and done.

Alternatively, you may seek out a specific personal experience as you inquire into your topic. For example, one student writing about homelessness in Dallas decided to visit a shelter. She called ahead to get permission and schedule the visit. Her paper was memorable because she was able to include the stories and physical descriptions of several homeless women, with details of their conversations.

Questionnaires and Surveys

You may be able to get information on some topics, especially if they are campus related, by doing surveys or questionnaires. This can be done very efficiently in electronic versions (Web-based or e-mail). Be forewarned, however, that it is very difficult to conduct a reliable survey.

First, there is the problem of designing a clear and unbiased survey instrument. If you have ever filled out an evaluation form for an instructor or a course, you will know what we mean about the problem of clarity. For example, one evaluation might ask whether an instructor returns papers "in a reasonable length of time"; what is "reasonable" to some students may be too long for others. As for bias, consider the question "Have you ever had trouble getting assistance from the library's reference desk?" To get a fair response, this questionnaire had better also ask how many requests for help were handled promptly and well. If you do decide to draft a questionnaire, we suggest you do it as a class project so that students on all sides of the issue can contribute and troubleshoot for ambiguity.

Second, there is the problem of getting a representative response. For the same reasons we doubt the results of certain magazine-sponsored surveys of people's sex lives, we should be skeptical about the statistical accuracy of surveys targeting a group that may not be representative of the whole. For example, it would be impossible generalize about all first-year college students in the United States based on a survey of only your English class — or even the entire first-year class at your college.

Surveys can be useful, but design, administer, and interpret them carefully.

Interviews

You can get a great deal of current information by talking to experts. As with any kind of research, the first step in conducting an interview is to decide exactly what you want to find out. Write down your questions.

The next step is to find the right person to interview. As you read about an issue, note the names (and possible biases) of any organizations mentioned; these may have local offices, the telephone numbers of which you could easily find. In addition, institutions such as hospitals, universities, and large corporations have public relations offices whose staffs provide information. An excellent source of over 30,000 names and phone numbers of experts in almost any field is a book by Matthew Lesko, *Lesko's Info-Power*. Finally, do not overlook the expertise available from faculty members at your own school.

Once you have determined possible sources for interviews, you must begin a patient and courteous round of telephone calls, continuing until you connect with the right person; according to Lesko, this can take as many as seven calls. If you have a subject's e-mail address, you might write to introduce yourself and request an appointment for a telephone interview.

Whether your interview is face to face or over the telephone, begin by acknowledging that the interviewee's time is valuable. Tell the person something about the project you are working on, but withhold your own position on any controversial matters. Sound neutral and be specific about what you want to know. Take notes, and include the title and background of the person being interviewed and the date of the interview, which you will need to cite this source. If you want to tape the interview, ask permission first. Finally, if you have the individual's mailing address, send a thank-you note after the interview.

If everyone in your class is researching the same topic and more than one person wants to contact the same expert, avoid flooding that person with requests. One or two students could do the interview and report to the class, or the expert could visit the class.

Library and Online Research

www.mhhe.
com/**crusius**
For further
information on
research in the
library, go to:
Research >
Using the Library

University libraries are complicated repositories of information. Consult with professional librarians. Even college faculty discover new sources by talking with librarians about their current research.

The Internet and the World Wide Web offer immediate access to millions of documents on almost any subject. The Internet offers currency and convenience, but not the reliability of print. The Internet is not a shortcut to the research process. We begin with a discussion of the resources available in your library or through its online network.

Library of Congress Subject Headings

Finding library sources will involve using computerized catalogs, reference books, and indexes to periodicals. Before using these, however, it makes sense first to look through a set of books every library locates near its catalog — the *Library of Congress Subject Headings*. This multivolume set will help you know what terms to look under when you move on to catalogs and indexes. The Library of Congress catalog is also available on the Internet at <http://catalog.loc.gov>. (See Figure 5.1.) Consulting these subject headings

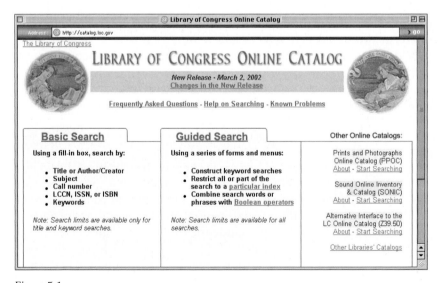

Figure 5.1

first will save you time in the long run: It will allow you to narrow your search and keep you from overlooking potentially good sources, because it also suggests related terms under which to look. For example, "mercy killing" will direct you to to "euthanasia," where you can find the following helpful information:

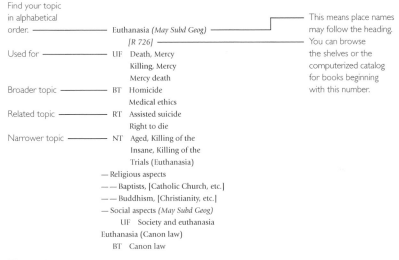

Figure 5.2

Your Library's Catalog

Use your library's catalog primarily to find books or government documents. (For arguments and information on current issues, keep in mind that the library catalog is not ideal because books take years to write and publish and therefore quickly become outdated.) Library catalogs list all holdings and are referenced according to author, title, and subject. With a computerized catalog, it is also possible to find works according to key words and by Library of Congress number. Look under the subject headings you find in the *Library of Congress Subject Headings.* Moreover, because the Library of Congress system groups books according to subject matter, you may want to browse in the catalog (or on the shelves) for other books in the same range of call numbers.

Typically, the library's catalog card or screen will appear as illustrated in Figure 5.3 (page 100).

www.mhhe.
com/**crusius**

For an extensive listing of sources in the library and on the Internet, go to: Research > Discipline-Specific Resources in the Library and on the Internet

Indexes to Periodicals

Libraries contain many indexes that list articles in newspapers, magazines, and journals. Some of these are printed and bound; others are online and on CD-ROM. Once again, the *Library of Congress Subject Headings* can help you determine the best words to search in these indexes.

```
Search Request: A=FALUDI SUSAN
BOOK - Record 2 of 3 Entries Found                          Brief View
---------------------------- Screen 1 of 1 -----------------------------
        TITLE:  Backlash : the undeclared war against American women
      EDITION:  1st ed.
       AUTHOR:  Faludi, Susan.

    PUBLISHER:  New York : Crown, c1991.
  DESCRIPTION:  xxiii, 552 p. : 25 cm.

     SUBJECTS:  Feminism--United States.
               Women--United States--Social conditions.
               Women--Psychology.
---------------------------------------------------------------------
       LOCATION:          CALL NUMBER:                STATUS:
 1. Fondren Browsing      HQ1426 .F35 1991         Charged, Due: 04/02/93
    Coll.

---------------------------------------------------------------------
 COMMANDS:           LO Long View        I Index
                     N  Next Record       H Help
 O  Other Options    P  Previous Record

 NEXT COMMAND:
```

Figure 5.3

Newspaper Indexes   The *New York Times Index* is printed and bound in volumes. Each volume indexes articles for one year, grouped according to subject and listed according to the month and day of publication. The subject headings in the *New York Times Index* are very general. For example, we could not find the heading "euthanasia," the term for mercy killing used in the *Library of Congress Subject Headings.* We had to think of a more general term, so we tried "medicine." There we found the information in Figure 5.4, opposite. We decided the entry "death" on this list seemed most likely to lead us to articles on euthanasia, and we were correct. Figure 5.5 (page 102) shows a small selection of what we found.

You will also find a limited number of *New York Times* articles listed in the computerized periodicals index known as *InfoTrac.* To search for *New York Times* articles and opinion columns on issues of interest to college students, go to <http://www.nytimes.com/college>. Better yet, search the major newspapers' online archives. Another excellent source of online articles is *Lexis-Nexis.*

Other printed and bound newspaper indexes carried by most libraries are the *Christian Science Monitor Index,* the *Times Index* (to the London *Times,* a good source for international issues), the *Wall Street Journal Index,* and the *Washington Post Index* (good for federal government issues).

Newsbank offers computerized indexes of hundreds of local and state newspapers. Your library is likely to subscribe to *Newsbank* for indexes of only one or two regional papers in your area. *Newsbank*'s CD-ROMs contain the entire text of each article indexed.

Indexes to Magazines, Journals, and Other Materials   Many libraries have CD-ROM databases indexing journals in business and academic fields. *Info-Trac,* one such database, indexes current articles from the *New York Times* and

MEDICINE AND HEALTH. See also
Abortion
Accidents and Safety
Acupuncture
Aged
Anatomy and Physiology
Anesthesia and Anesthetics
Antibiotics
Autopsies
Bacteria
Birth Control and Family Planning
Birth Defects
Blood
Death ————————————————— The subject
Environment   heading most
Epidemics   likely to lead
Exercise   to articles on
Faith Healers   euthanasia
First Aid
Food Contamination and Poisoning
Handicapped
Hormones
Immunization and Immunity
Implants
Industrial and Occupational Hazards
Malpractice Insurance
Mental Health and Disorders
Nursing Homes
Pesticides and Pests
Population
Radiation
Smoking
Spas
Surgery and Surgeons
Teeth and Dentistry
Transplants
Vaccination and Vaccines
Veterinary Medicine
Viruses
Vitamins
Water Pollution
Workmen's Compensation Insurance
X-Rays

Figure 5.4

many other periodicals, so you may want to begin your search here rather than with the printed and bound indexes. Be aware, however, that *InfoTrac* is very selective, far less comprehensive than the printed ones, which also go back further in time. In addition, *InfoTrac* will not include many articles that can be found in the specialized indexes that follow.

1. General interest indexes:

    Essay and General Literature Index
    Public Affairs Information Service (PAIS)
    Readers' Guide to Periodical Literature
    Speech Index

Topic headings
are listed in
alphabetical
order.

Each entry
contains an
abstract.

(S), (M), or (L)
before the date
indicates whether
an article is short,
medium, or long.

DEATH. See also

Deaths

Several laws enacted in New York State in 1990 are set to take effect, including measure that will allow New Yorkers to designate another person to make health-care decisions on their behalf if they become unable to do so (M). Ja 1.1.32:1

Another right-to-die case emerges in Missouri, where Christine Busalacchi had been in persistent vegetative state as result of auto accident on May 29, 1987, when she was 17-year-old high school junior; her father, Pete Busalacchi, who has been seeking unsuccessfully to have his daughter transferred to Minnesota, where feeding tube may possibly be removed, says that Christine never discussed matters of life or death; Nancy Cruzan case recalled; photo (M). Ja 2.A.12:1

Missouri state court dismisses order preventing Pete Busalacchi from moving his comatose daughter Christine to another state where less strict rules might allow removal of feeding tube (S). Ja S.A.16:1

In a case that medical ethicists and legal experts say is apparently a first, Minneapolis-based Hennapin County Medical Center plans to go to court for permission to turn off 37-year-old Helga Wanglie's life support system against her family's wishes; photos (L). Ja 10.A.1:1

Probate Judge Louis Kohn of St. Louis County rules that Pete Busalacchi may move his daughter, Christine, from Missouri hospital where she has lain for more than three years with severe brain damage and take her to Minnesota where law might allow removal of her feeding tube (S). Ja 17.3.5:1

People wishing to avoid heroic medical treatment in event they become hopelessly ill and unable to speak for themselves are often poorly served by so-called "living wills" to achieve that end; many health care experts recommend a newer document, health care proxy, in which patients designate surrogate who has legal authority to make medical decisions if they are too sick to offer an opinion; others recommend combining living will with health care proxy; drawing (M). Ja 17.3.9:1

Missouri Judge Louis Kohn rules Pete Busalacchi had right to determine medical care of his daughter Christine, who has been severely brain-damaged for more than three years; gives him authority to have feeding tube removed (S). Ja 18.A.16:4

Missouri appeals court bars Pete Busalacchi from moving his comatose 20-year-old daughter Christine to Minnesota where laws governing removal of life-support systems are less restrictive (S). Ja 19.1.17:2

Editorial Notebook commentary by Fred M. Hechinger says his 94-year-old mother's last days were fiilled with needless suffering and fear because doctors ignored her, and her family's wish that no heroic efforts be taken to prolong her life; says inhumane legal restrictions have made doctors accomplices in torture, and medical profession has shown little courage in fighting them (M). Ja 24.A.22:1

Articles
are listed in
chronological
order.

Each entry
concludes
with the
month, day,
section, page,
and column.

Figure 5.5

2. Arts and humanities indexes:

Art Index
Film Literature Index
Humanities Index
Music Index
Philosopher's Index
Popular Music Periodical Index

3. Social science, business, and law indexes:

> *Business Periodicals Index*
> *Criminology Index*
> *Education Index*
> *Index to Legal Periodicals*
> *Psychological Abstracts*
> *Social Sciences Index*
> *Sociological Abstracts*
> *Women's Studies Abstracts*

4. Science and engineering indexes:

> *Applied Science and Technology Index*
> *Biological and Agricultural Index*
> *Current Contents*
> *Environmental Index*
> *General Science Index*

Reference Books

Students often overlook many helpful reference books because they don't know about them. You may find reference books useful early in the research process and also for locating supporting evidence as you develop your own argument. The following are some reference books you might find helpful:

> *First Stop: The Master Index to Subject Encyclopedias* (a subject index to 430 specialized encyclopedias — a good source of general background information)
> *Demographic Yearbook*
> *Facts on File*
> *Guide to American Law* (a reference work that explains legal principles and concepts in plain English)
> *Statistical Abstract of the United States*
> *World Almanac and Book of Facts*

Bibliographies

Books and articles sometimes include works-cited lists or bibliographies, which list numerous additional sources. Library catalog entries and many indexes indicate whether a book or article contains a bibliography.

Internet Research

The Internet is a valuable research tool because it provides access to information in the computers of educational institutions, businesses, government bureaus, and nonprofit organizations all over the world. Most people now

www.mhhe.
com/**crusius**

For further
advice on using
the Internet to
conduct research,
go to:
Research >
Using the
Internet

use the World Wide Web for access to the Internet. The Web is that portion of the Internet that uses HTML (hypertext mark-up language) to present information on Web sites with individual Web pages. E-mail and online discussion groups are also valuable resources for Internet research.

Just as we advise you to seek help from a librarian when beginning your library research, so we also suggest that you begin electronic or online research by consulting librarians at your school. Because the Internet is large and complex and perpetually changing, we will offer only general advice about what Internet resources would be most useful for undergraduate research on contemporary public issues. One of the best online sources for help with the Internet is the Library of Congress Resource Page, at <http://lcweb.loc.gov/global/search.html>. Once you are connected to this page, you can link to the following resources.

The World Wide Web

Of all the networks on the Internet, the *World Wide Web* is the friendliest and the most fun because it links files from various "host" computers around the world; from one site on the Web, you can click on highlighted words known as *hypertext links* that will take you to other sites where related information is stored. For example, an online article on euthanasia may highlight the words "Hippocratic oath"; clicking on the highlighted words will allow you to read a copy of the oath.

Finding useful sites is not always as easy as finding books and articles in the library because there is no system that neatly catalogs all the information as material is posted. However, technology to help users navigate the Internet is constantly improving. The Web does support a number of *search engines,* which index existing and newly posted information through the use of key words. Once you connect to your school's Internet browser (such as Netscape or Microsoft Internet Explorer), you can type in the address of one of these engines, or you may be able to load it by simply clicking on an icon. Addresses on the Internet are known as *uniform resource locators (URLs).* The following lists the names and URLs of search engines and metasearch engines that are recommended by the Librarians' Index to the Internet <http://www.lii.org>. World Wide Web URLs begin with "http," which stands for "hypertext transfer protocol."

Search Engines Recommended by Librarians

Google <http://www.google.com>
AllTheWeb <http://www.alltheweb.com>
AltaVista <http://www.altavista.com>
Excite <http://www.excite.com>
HotBot <http://www.hotbot.lycos.com>
NorthernLight <http://www.northernlight.com>

Recommended Metasearch Engines

Ixquick <http://www.ixquick.com>
MetaCrawler <http://www.metacrawler.com>

Once you access the search engine, enter key words describing the information you want. For example, by typing in "search engine," you can find the addresses of other search engines. We recommend that you try this because new search engines are being created all the time.

Surfing the Web, however, is not always a quick and easy way to do research. Be prepared to spend time trying a variety of search engines and metasearch engines. Web searches can in fact take more time than library research because you will encounter so much irrelevant information. You will also find much information that is not suitable for academic writing. Because anyone can post a document on the Web, you need to check the author's credentials carefully. (See "Evaluating Sources," pages 106–109.) The Internet is valuable but will not replace the library as your primary research venue.

Listservs and Usenet Newsgroups

The Internet allows groups of people to communicate on topics of common interest; observing and participating in such groups is another way to learn about a topic and find out what issues are being debated. *Listservs* are like electronic bulletin boards or discussion groups, where people with a shared interest can post or ask for information and simply converse. Listservs are supported by e-mail, so if you have an e-mail account, it will cost you nothing to join a group. You may find an appropriate listserv group by e-mailing <listserv@listserve.net> with a message specifying your area of interest, such as "list environmentalism" or "list euthanasia." You can also find listserv groups on the World Wide Web at <http://tile.net/lists>. *Usenet newsgroups* also act like electronic bulletin boards, which your college's system administrator may or may not make available on your school's server. To find lists of active newsgroups, type in "newsgroups" as a search term in one of the Web search engines, such as Yahoo!

Newsgroups and listservs are often composed of highly specialized professionals who expect other participants to have followed their discussions for weeks and months before participating. They even post lists of *frequently asked questions (FAQs)* to avoid having to cover the same topics repeatedly. Finding the exact information you need in the transcripts of their discussions is like looking for the proverbial needle in a haystack, so Usenet is not likely to be as useful as the Web as a general research tool. However, while searching the Web, you may encounter links to some discussions relevant to your topic that have been archived on the Web. You may want to cite information gathered from these groups, but you need to be very careful about what you use because anyone can join in, regardless of credentials and expertise. Most correspondents who have professional affiliations list them along with their name and "snail mail" (U.S. Postal Service) address. In addition to credentials, be sure to note the name of the group, the name of the individual post-ing the message, the date and time it was posted, and the URL if you have found it on the Web. (See "Creating Works-Cited and Reference Lists" on pages 126–132 for more information on citing electronic sources.)

EVALUATING SOURCES

www.mhhe.com/**crusius**

For a tutorial on evaluating sources, go to:
Research >
Source Evaluation
Tutor: CARS

Before beginning to read and evaluate your sources, you may need to reeval-uate your issue. If you have been unable to find many sources that address the question you are raising, consider changing the focus of your argument.

For example, one student, Michelle, had the choice of any issue under the broad category of the relationship between humans and other animals. Michelle decided to focus on the mistreatment of circus animals, based on claims made in leaflets handed out at the circus by animal-rights protestors. Even with a librarian's help, however, Michelle could find no subject head-ings that led to even one source in her university's library. She then called and visited animal-rights activists in her city, who provided her with more mate-rials written and published by the animal-rights movement. She realized, however, that researching the truth of their claims was more than she could undertake, so she had to acknowledge that her entire argument was based on heavily biased sources.

Once you have reevaluated your topic, use the following method to record and evaluate sources.

Eliminate Inappropriate Sources

You may find that some books and articles are intended for audiences with more specialized knowledge than you have. If you have trouble using a source, put it aside, at least temporarily.

Also, carefully review any electronic sources you are using. While search engines make it easy to find material on the Web, online documents often have met no professional standards for scholarship. Material can be "pub-lished" electronically without review by experts, scholars, and editors that must occur in traditional publishing. Nevertheless, you will find legitimate scholarship on the Internet—news reports, encyclopedias, government doc-uments, and even scholarly journals appear online. While the freedom of electronic publishing creates an exciting and democratic arena, it also puts a much heavier burden on students and researchers to ensure that the sources they use are worthy of readers' respect.

Carefully Record Complete Bibliographic Information

For every source you consider using, be sure to record full bibliographic in-formation. Take this information from the source itself, not from an index, which may be incomplete or inaccurate. If you make a record of this information immediately, you will not have to go back later to fill in omissions. We recommend that you use a separate index card for each source, but whatever you use, record the following:

1. For a book:

> Author's full name (or names)
> Title of book
> City where published
> Name of publisher
> Year published

For an article or essay in a book, record all of the information for the book, including the name(s) of the book's author or editor and the title and the author(s) of the article; also record the inclusive page numbers of the article or chapter (for example, "pp. 100–150").

2. For a periodical:

> Author's full name (or names)
> Title of the article
> Title of the periodical
> Date of the issue
> Volume number, if given
> Inclusive page numbers

3. For a document found on the World Wide Web:

> Author's full name (or names)
> Title of the work
> Original print publication data, if applicable
> Title of the database or Web site
> Full URL
> Date you accessed the document

4. For material found through listservs and Usenet newsgroups:

> Author's full name (or names)
> Author's e-mail address
> Subject line from the posting
> Date of the posting
> Address of the listserv or newsgroup
> Date you accessed the document

Read the Source Critically

As discussed in Chapter 2, critical reading depends on having some prior knowledge of the subject and the ability to see a text in context. As you research a topic, your knowledge naturally becomes deeper with each article you read. But your sources are not simply windows, giving you a clear view;

whether argumentative or informative, they have bias. Before looking through them, you must look *at* your sources. Therefore, devote conscious attention to the rhetorical context of each source. Keep these questions in mind.

Who Is the Writer, and What Is His or Her Bias?

Is there a note that tells about the writer's professional title or institutional affiliation? If not, search the Internet for the writer's personal home page or university Web site. Or look in the *Dictionary of American Biographies,* or the *Biography and Genealogy Master Index,* which will send you to numerous specialized biographical sketches.

How Reliable Is the Source?

Again, checking for credibility is particularly important when you are working with electronic sources. For example, one student found two sites on the Web, both through a key word search on "euthanasia." One, entitled "Stop the Epidemic of Assisted Suicide," was posted by a person identified only by name, the letters MD, and the affiliation "Association for Control of Assisted Suicide." There was no biographical information, and the "snail mail" address was a post office box. The other Web site, "Ethics Update: Euthanasia," was posted by a professor of philosophy at the University of San Diego whose home page included a complete professional biography detailing his education, titles, and the publishers of his many books and articles. The author gave his address at USD in the Department of Philosophy. The student decided that, although the first source had some interesting information—including examples of individual patients who were living with pain rather than choosing suicide—it was not a source that skeptical readers would find credible. Search engines often land you deep within a Web site, and you have to visit the site's home page to get any background information about the source and its author. Be suspicious of sites that do not contain adequate source information; they probably aren't reliable.

When Was This Source Written?

If you are researching a current issue, decide what sources are too old. Arguments on current issues often benefit from earlier perspectives.

Where Did This Source Appear?

If you are using an article from a periodical, be aware of the periodical's readership and editorial bias. For example, *National Review* is conservative, *The Nation* liberal. An article in the *Journal of the American Medical Association* will usually defend the medical profession. Looking at the table of contents and scanning editorial statements will give you a feel for the periodical's politics. Also look at the page that lists the publisher and editorial board. You will find, for example, that *New American* is published by the ultra-right-wing

1. Look at the last segment of the domain name, which will tell you who developed the site. The most reliable ones are developed by colleges and universities (.edu) or by the government (.gov). Of course, commercial sites (.com, .biz) are profit-minded.
2. Check whether the name of the creator of the Web page or its Webmaster appears, complete with an e-mail address and the date of the last update, near either the top or the bottom of the page.
3. Check whether the source includes a bibliography, a sign of scholarly work.
4. Ask yourself if the links are credible.
5. A tilde (˜) indicates a personal page; these pages must be evaluated with special care.

John Birch Society. If you need help determining bias, ask a librarian. A reference book that lists periodicals by subject matter and explains their bias is *Magazines for Libraries*.

Why Was the Book or Article Written?

Although some articles are occasioned by news events, most books and arguments are written as part of an ongoing conversation among scholars or journalists. Being aware of the issues and the participants in this conversation is essential, as you will be joining it with your own researched argument. You can check *Book Review Index* to find where a book has been reviewed, and then consult some reviews to see how the book was received.

What Is the Author's Aim?

First, determine whether the source informs or argues. Both are useful and both will have some bias. When your source is an argument, note whether it aims primarily to inquire, to convince, to persuade, or to mediate.

How Is the Source Organized?

If the writer doesn't use subheadings or chapter titles, break the text into parts yourself and note what function each part plays in the whole.

Inquire into the Source

Because we devote so much attention to inquiry in Chapters 5 and 6, we will not go into detail here. However, look especially closely at arguments that support your own position; seeing weaknesses can change your outlook on an issue. The box "Additional Guidelines for Evaluating Internet Sources" will help you evaluate Web sources.

Avoid plagiarism by *distinguishing sharply* between quoting and paraphrasing. Anytime you take exact words from a source, even if it is only a phrase or a significant word, you are quoting. You must use quotation marks and documentation. If you make any change at all in the wording of a quotation, you must indicate the change with square brackets. If you remove any words from a direct quotation, use ellipses (three spaced dots) to indicate the deletion. If you use your own words to summarize or paraphrase portions of a source, name that source in your text and document it. Be careful to use your own words when paraphrasing and summarizing.

1. Use an attributive tag such as "According to . . ." to introduce quotations both direct and indirect. Don't just drop them in.
2. Name the person whose words or idea you are using. Provide the full name on first mention.
3. Identify the author(s) of your source by profession or affiliation so that readers will understand the significance of what he or she has to say. Omit this if the speaker is someone readers are familiar with.
4. Use transitions into quotations to link the ideas they express to whatever point you are making.
5. If your lead-in to a quotation is a phrase, follow it with a comma. But if your lead-in can stand alone as a sentence, follow it with a colon.
6. Place the period at the end of a quotation or paraphrase, after the parenthetical citation, except with block quotations. (See page 124 for treatment of block quotations.)

Consider How You Might Use the Source

If you are fortunate, your research will uncover many authoritative and well-crafted arguments. The challenge is to work out a way to use them in your own argument, built on your own structure and strategy, suited to your own aim and audience.

A good argument results from synthesizing research results. Your sources should help you come up with reasons and evidence as well as ideas about opposing views. But your reasons should not all come from one source, nor do you want to create an argument that reads like a patchwork of other people's ideas. Thus, you must organize your sources according to your own argument and integrate material from a variety of sources.

Consult Chapter 7, where we discuss developing and refining a thesis (or claim) and constructing a brief (pages 201–215). As you make your brief, identify those sources that will help you with reasons or support, such as expert opinion or specific data.

1. Note your source. Use the author's last name or an abbreviated title.
2. Note the exact page or pages where the information or quotation appears.
3. When you quote, *be exact,* and put quotation marks around the writer's words.
4. Prefer paraphrase and summary; reserve quotations for passages in which the writer's words are memorable and/or for passages you plan to comment on.

USING SOURCES

How you use a source depends on function. After you have drafted an argument, you may simply need to consult an almanac for additional evidence or, say, look up John F. Kennedy's inaugural address to find a quotation. But at earlier stages of the writing process, you may be unsure of your own position and in need of general background information. What follows is some advice for these early stages. Remember to write down all bibliographical information for every source you might use.

Taking Notes

Just as you can check out books from the library, so you can photocopy entire articles for use away from the library. Likewise, with electronic sources, you can print out the entire text of many online documents. These various methods of gathering materials are helpful, but using the sources requires note-taking, paraphrasing, and summarizing to avoid plagiarism.

Write down—preferably on a large notecard—anything that strikes you as important. Taking notes will help you find the idea you thought would work two weeks ago. The box "Guidelines for Taking Notes" summarizes the process.

Paraphrasing

Paraphrasing, which means restating a passage in your own words, improves reading comprehension. You are actually explaining the passage to yourself. When you have a firm grasp of it, you can write more confidently. The box "Guidelines for Paraphrasing" on page 112 summarizes the technique.

We illustrate paraphrasing with an excerpt from a source selected by a student, Patrick Pugh, who was researching the topic of euthanasia and planning to defend active euthanasia, or assisted suicide. In the university library, Patrick found an essay collection, *Suicide and Euthanasia: The Rights of*

1. Use a dictionary if any words in the original are not familiar.
2. Work with whole ideas—remember paraphrasing does not mean keeping the original word order and plugging in synonyms. Your paraphrase can be longer than the original. Break a complex sentence into several simpler ones of your own; take apart a difficult idea and rebuild it, step by step. Don't just echo the original passage.
3. Don't be a slave to the thesaurus. Read the passage until you think you understand it. Then write your version without looking back at it.
4. Don't strain to find substitutes for words that are essential to the meaning of a passage.

Personhood. He read an essay, "In Defense of Suicide," by Joseph Fletcher, a former professor at the Episcopal Divinity School and president of the Society for the Right to Die. Before taking notes on Fletcher's essay, Patrick made a bibliography card recording all the necessary information about this source:

> Fletcher, Joseph. "In Defense of Suicide." In <u>Suicide</u> <u>and</u> <u>Euthanasia</u> : <u>The</u> <u>Rights</u> <u>of</u> <u>Personhood</u>. Eds. Samuel E. Wallace and Albin Eser. Knoxville : U of Tennessee P 1981
>
> Fletcher's article : pp. 38—50.

The following passage from Fletcher's essay offers a crucial definition; it is the kind of passage that a researcher should paraphrase rather than write down word for word.

> We must begin with the postulate that no action is intrinsically right or wrong, that nothing is inherently good or evil. Right and wrong, good and evil, desirable and undesirable—all are ethical terms and all are predicates, not

properties. The moral "value" of any human act is always contingent, depending on the shape of the action in the situation. . . . The variables and factors in each set of circumstances are the determinants of what ought to be done—not prefabricated generalizations or prescriptive rules. . . . No "law" of conduct is always obliging; what we ought to do is whatever maximizes human well-being.

—JOSEPH FLETCHER, "In Defense of Suicide"

Patrick paraphrased this passage on the following notecard. Note that he names the author of the essay, the editors of the book, and the exact pages on which the idea was found.

Fletcher's definition of ethical action:

The ethical value of any human action is not a quality inherent in the act itself. It is a judgment that we make about the act after examining the entire situation in which it takes place. Rather than relying on general rules about what is moral and immoral, we should make our decision on the basis of what is best for human well-being in any given set of circumstances.

Fletcher, pp. 38-39, in Wallace/Eser.

Following Through

Write a paraphrase of the following paragraph, also from Joseph Fletcher's "In Defense of Suicide." Or select a passage of similar length and complexity from your own research.

What is called positive euthanasia—doing something to shorten or end life deliberately—is the form [of euthanasia] in which suicide is the question, as a voluntary, direct choice of death. For a long time the Christian moralists have distinguished between negative or indirectly willed suicide, like not taking a place in one of the *Titanic*'s lifeboats, and positive or directly willed suicide, like jumping out of a lifeboat to make room for a fellow victim of

1. Read and reread the original text until you have identified the claim and the main supporting points. You ought to be able to write an outline of the case, using your own words. Depending on your purpose for summarizing and the amount of space you can devote to the summary, decide how much, if any, of the evidence to include.
2. Make it clear at the start whose ideas you are summarizing.
3. If you are summarizing a long passage, break it down into subsections and work on summarizing one at a time.
4. As with paraphrasing, work from memory. Go back to the text to check your version for accuracy.
5. Maintain the original order of points, with this exception: If the author delayed presenting the thesis, refer to it earlier in your summary.
6. Use your own words.
7. Avoid quoting entire sentences. If you want to quote key words and phrases, incorporate them into sentences of your own, using quotation marks around the borrowed words.

a shipwreck. The moralists mean that we may choose to allow an evil by acts of omission but not to do an evil by acts of comission. The moralists contend that since all suicide is evil, we may only "allow" it; we may not "do" it. (47)

Summarizing

Whereas a paraphrase may be longer or shorter than the original passage, a summary is always shorter. It ought to be at least one-third the length of the original or less: you may, for example, reduce an entire article to one or two paragraphs.

A summary must contain the main idea or claim and the main points of support. The amount of evidence and detail you include depends on your purpose: If you merely want to give your audience the gist, a bare-bones summary is enough; but if you plan to use the summary in making your case, include the original's evidence as well. The box "Guidelines for Summarizing" outlines the process.

For an example of using a summary as part of an argument, we return to Patrick Pugh's investigation of euthanasia. In another book, *The End of Life: Euthanasia and Morality* by James Rachels, Patrick found what Rachels describes as the chief religious objections to euthanasia, with Rachels's rebuttals for each. Patrick decided to include this material in a summary. First read the passage from Rachels's book, then read Patrick's summarized version.

The End of Life*
James Rachels

RELIGIOUS ARGUMENTS

Social observers are fond of remarking that we live in a secular age, and there is surely something in this. The power of religious conceptions was due, in some considerable measure, to their usefulness in explaining things. In earlier times, religious ideas were used to explain everything from the origins of the universe to the nature of human beings. So long as we had no other way of understanding the world, the hold of religion on us was powerful indeed. Now, however, these explanatory functions have largely been taken over by the sciences: physics, chemistry, and their allies explain physical nature, while evolutionary biology and psychology combine to tell us about ourselves. As there is less and less work for religious hypotheses to do, the grip of religious ideas on us weakens, and appeals to theological conceptions are heard only on Sunday mornings. Hence, the "secular age."

However, most people continue to hold religious beliefs, and they especially appeal to those beliefs when morality is at issue. Any discussion of mercy killing quickly leads to objections based on theological grounds, and "secular" arguments for euthanasia are rejected because they leave out the crucial element of God's directions on the matter.

Considering the traditional religious opposition to euthanasia, it is tempting to say: If one is not a Christian (or if one does not have some similar religious orientation), then perhaps euthanasia is an option; but for people who do have such a religious orientation, euthanasia cannot be acceptable. And the discussion might be ended there. But this is too quick a conclusion; for it is possible that the religious arguments against euthanasia are not valid *even for religious people.* Perhaps a religious perspective, even a conventional Christian one, does *not* lead automatically to the rejection of mercy killing. With this possibility in mind, let us examine three variations of the religious objection.

What God Commands

It is sometimes said that euthanasia is not permissible simply because God forbids it, and we know that God forbids it by the authority of either scripture or Church tradition. Thus, one eighteenth-century minister,

---

*James Rachels, "The End of Life" from *The End of Life: Euthanasia and Morality* by James Rachels. © James Rachels 1986. By permission of Oxford University Press.

Humphrey Primatt, wrote ironically that, in the case of aged and infirm animals,

> God, the Father of Mercies, hath ordained Beasts and Birds of Prey to do that distressed creature the kindness to relieve him his misery, by putting him to death. A kindness which *We* dare not show to our own species. If thy father, thy brother, or thy child should suffer the utmost pains of a long and agonizing sickness, though his groans should pierce through thy heart, and with strong crying and tears he should beg thy relief, yet thou must be deaf unto him; he must wait his appointed time till his charge cometh, till he sinks and is crushed with the weight of his own misery.

When this argument is advanced, it is usually advanced with great con-   5
fidence, as though it were *obvious* what God requires. Yet we may well wonder whether such confidence is justified. The sixth commandment does not
say, literally, "Thou shalt not *kill*"—that is a bad translation. A better translation is "Thou shalt not commit *murder*," which is different, and which
does not obviously prohibit mercy killing. Murder is by definition *wrongful* killing; so, if you do not think that a given kind of killing is wrong, you
will not call it murder. That is why the sixth commandment is not normally
taken to forbid killing in a just war; since such killing is (allegedly) justified,
it is not called murder. Similarly, if euthanasia is justified, it is not murder,
and so it is not prohibited by the commandment. At the very least, it is
clear that we cannot infer that euthanasia is wrong *because* it is prohibited
by the commandment.

If we look elsewhere in the Christian Bible for a condemnation of euthanasia, we cannot find it. These scriptures are silent on the question. We
do find numerous affirmations of the sanctity of human life and the father-
hood of God, and some theologians have tried to infer a prohibition on
euthanasia from these general precepts. (The persistence of the attempts,
in the face of logical difficulties, is a reminder that people insist on reading their moral prejudices *into* religious texts much more often than they derive their moral views *from* the texts.) But we also find exhortations to kindness and mercy, and the Golden Rule proclaimed as the sum of all morality;
and these principles, as we have seen, support euthanasia rather than condemn it.

We *do* find a clear condemnation of euthanasia in Church tradition. Regardless of whether there is scriptural authority for it, the Church has historically opposed mercy killing. It should be emphasized, however, that
this is a matter of history. Today, many religious leaders favour euthanasia
and think the historical position of the Church has been mistaken. It was
an Episcopal minister, Joseph Fletcher, who in his book *Morals and Medicine* formulated the classic modern defence of euthanasia. Fletcher does not
stand alone among his fellow churchmen. The Euthanasia Society of America, which he heads, includes many other religious leaders; and the recent
"Plea for Beneficent Euthanasia," sponsored by the American Humanist As-

sociation, was signed by more religious leaders than people in any other category. So it certainly cannot be claimed that *contemporary* religious forces stand uniformly opposed to euthanasia.

It is noteworthy that even Roman Catholic thinkers are today reassessing the Church's traditional ban on mercy killing. The Catholic philosopher Daniel Maguire has written one of the best books on the subject, *Death by Choice*. Maguire maintains that "it may be moral and should be legal to accelerate the death process by taking direct action, such as overdosing with morphine or injecting potassium"; and moreover, he proposes to demonstrate that this view is *"compatible with historical Catholic ethical theory,"* contrary to what most opponents of euthanasia assume. Historical Catholic ethical theory, he says, grants individuals permission to act on views that are supported by "good and serious reasons," even when a different view is supported by a majority of authorities. Since the morality of euthanasia *is* supported by "good and serious reasons," Maguire concludes that Catholics are permitted to accept that morality and act on it.

Thus, the positions of both scripture and Church authorities are (at least) ambiguous enough so that the believer is not bound, on these grounds, to reject mercy killing. The argument from "what God commands" should be inconclusive, even for the staunchest believer.

The Idea of God's Dominion

Our second theological argument starts from the principle that "The life of man is solely under the dominion of God." It is for God alone to decide when a person shall live and when he shall die; we have no right to "play God" and arrogate this decision unto ourselves. So euthanasia is forbidden.   10

This is perhaps the most familiar of all the theological objections to euthanasia; one hears it constantly when the matter is discussed. However, it is remarkable that people still advance this argument today, considering that it was decisively refuted over 200 years ago, when Hume made the simple but devastating point that *if it is for God alone to decide when we shall live and when we shall die, then we "play God" just as much when we cure people as when we kill them.* Suppose a person is sick and we have the means to cure him or her. If we do so, then we are interfering with God's "right to decide" how long the life shall last! Hume put it this way:

> Were the disposal of human life so much reserved as the peculiar providence of the Almighty that it were an encroachment on his right, for men to dispose of their own lives; it would be equally criminal to act for the preservation of life as for its destruction. If I turn aside a stone which is falling upon my head, I disturb this course of nature, and I invade the peculiar providence of the Almighty by lengthening out my life beyond the period which by the general laws of matter and motion he had assigned it.

We alter the length of a person's life when we save it just as much as when we take it. Therefore, if the taking of life is to be forbidden on the grounds that only God has the right to determine how long a person shall live, then the saving of life should be prohibited on the same grounds. We would then have to abolish the practice of medicine. But everyone (except, perhaps, Christian Scientists) concedes that this would be absurd. Therefore, we may *not* prohibit euthanasia on the grounds that only God has the right to determine how long a life shall last. This seems to be a complete refutation of this argument, and if refuted arguments were decently discarded, as they should be, we would hear no more of it.

Suffering and God's Plan

The last religious argument we shall consider is based on the idea that suffering is a part of God's plan for us. God has ordained that people should suffer; he never intended that life should be continually pleasurable. (If he had intended this, presumably he would have created a very different world.) Therefore, if we were to kill people to "put them out of their misery," we would be interfering with God's plan. Bishop Joseph Sullivan, a prominent Catholic opponent of euthanasia, expresses the argument in a passage from his essay "The Immorality of Euthanasia":

> If the suffering patient is of sound mind and capable of making an act of divine resignation, then his sufferings become a great means of merit whereby he can gain reward for himself and also win great favors for the souls in Purgatory, perhaps even release them from their suffering. Likewise the sufferer may give good example to his family and friends and teach them how to bear a heavy cross in a Christlike manner.
>
> As regard those that must live in the same house with the incurable sufferer, they have a great opportunity to practice Christian charity. They can learn to see Christ in the sufferer and win the reward promised in the Beatitudes. This opportunity for charity would hold true even when the incurable sufferer is deprived of the use of reason. It may well be that the incurable sufferer in a particular case may be of greater value to society than when he was of some material value to himself and his community.

This argument may strike some readers as simply grotesque. Can we imagine this being said, seriously, in the presence of suffering such as that experienced by Stewart Alsop's roommate? "We know it hurts, Jack, and that your wife is being torn apart just having to watch it, but think what a good opportunity this is for you to set an example. You can give us a lesson in how to bear it." In addition, some might think that euthanasia is exactly what *is* required by the "charity" that bystanders have the opportunity to practice.

But, these reactions aside, there is a more fundamental difficulty with the argument. For if the argument were sound, it would lead not only to

15

the condemnation of euthanasia but of *any* measures to reduce suffering. If God decrees that we suffer, why aren't we obstructing God's plan when we give drugs to relieve pain? A girl breaks her arm; if only God knows how much pain is right for her, who are we to mend it? The point is similar to Hume's refutation of the previous argument. This argument, like the previous one, cannot be right because it leads to consequences that no one, not even the most conservative religious thinker, is willing to accept.

We have now looked at three arguments that depend on religious assumptions. They are all unsound, but I have *not* criticized them simply by rejecting their religious presuppositions. Instead, I have criticized them on their own terms, showing that these arguments should not be accepted even by religious people. As Daniel Maguire emphasizes, the ethics of theists, like the ethics of all responsible people, should be determined by "good and serious reasons," and these arguments are not good no matter what world-view one has.

The upshot is that religious people are in the same position as everyone else. There is nothing in religious belief in general, or in Christian belief in particular, to preclude the acceptance of mercy killing as a humane response to some awful situations. So, as far as these arguments are concerned, it appears that Christians may be free, after all, to accept the Golden Rule.

STUDENT SAMPLE: *A Summary*

In the following paper, the numbers in parentheses indicate the original pages where material appeared. We explain this method of documentation later in this chapter.

SUMMARY OF EXCERPT FROM *THE END OF LIFE*
Patrick Pugh

According to James Rachels, despite living in a secular age, many objections to active euthanasia are religious, specifically Christian. However, even religious people ought to be able to see that these arguments may not be valid. For example, one of the most often-stated objections is that in the Ten Commandments God forbids killing. Rachels counters by pointing out that the Sixth Commandment is more accurately translated as "Thou shalt not commit murder." Because we define murder as "wrongful killing," we will not call some killing murder if we do not see it as wrong. Thus, the Sixth Commandment "is not normally taken to forbid killing in a just war; since such killing is (allegedly) justified" (161–62). Rachels points out that although the scriptures do not mention euthanasia and affirm the "sanctity of human life," one also finds "exhortations to kindness and mercy" for fellow humans, principles that "support active euthanasia rather than condemn it" (162).

To those who claim that "[i]t is for God alone to decide when a person shall live and when he shall die," Rachels responds that "if it is for God alone to decide when we shall live and when we shall die, then we 'play God' just as much when we cure people as when we kill them" (163). He notes that philosopher David Hume made this argument more than two hundred years ago.

A third common argument is that because suffering is a part of God's plan for humans, we should not interrupt it by euthanasia. Rachels responds to this with the question, How can we then justify the use of any pain-relieving drugs and procedures? (165). He concludes that "[t]here is nothing in religious belief in general, or in Christian belief in particular, to preclude the acceptance of mercy killing as a humane response to some awful situations" (165).

 Following Through

Write a summary of the argument opposing euthanasia entitled "Rising to the Occasion of Our Death" by William F. May, on pages 45–47. Or summarize any other argument that you are considering using as a source for a project you are currently working on.

Creating an Annotated Bibliography

To get an overview of the sources they have compiled, many writers find it useful to create an annotated bibliography. A **bibliography** is simply a list of works on a particular topic; it can include any kind of source—newspaper articles, books, government documents, and so on. Information in a bibliography is identical to a works-cited list: it includes author, title, publisher, date, and, in the case of articles, periodical name, volume, and page numbers. (See the section "Creating Works-Cited and Reference Lists" for examples.) Like a works-cited list, a bibliography is arranged in alphabetical order, based on each author's last name.

To **annotate** a bibliography means to include critical commentary about each work listed, usually in one short paragraph. Each annotation should contain the following:

- A sentence or two about the rhetorical context. Is it an informative news article? an opinion column? a scholarly essay? Is it intended for lawyers? the public? students? the elderly? What is the bias?
- A capsule summary of the content.
- A note about why this source seems valuable and how you might use it.

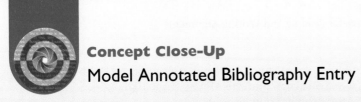

Concept Close-Up
Model Annotated Bibliography Entry

Ames, Katrine. "Last Rights." <u>Newsweek</u> 26 Aug. 1991: 40–41.

This is a news article for the general public about the popularity of a book called <u>Final Exit,</u> about how to commit suicide. Ames explains the interest in the book as resulting from people's perception that doctors, technology, and hospital bureaucrats are making it harder and harder to die with dignity. The article documents with statistics the direction of public opinion on this topic and also outlines some options, besides suicide, that are becoming available to ensure the right to die. Ames shows a bias against prolonging life through technology, but she includes quotations from authorities on both sides.

Following Through

Write an annotated bibliography of the sources you are using for a researched argument of your own. Use the model above as a guide.

INCORPORATING AND DOCUMENTING SOURCE MATERIAL IN THE TEXT OF YOUR ARGUMENT

We turn now to the more technical matter of how to incorporate source material in your own writing and how to document it. You incorporate material through direct quotation or through summary or paraphrase; you document material by naming the writer and providing full publication details of the source—a two-step process. In academic writing, documenting sources is essential, with one exception: You do not need to document your source for factual information that could easily be found in common references, such as an encyclopedia or atlas.

Different Styles of Documentation

Different disciplines have specific conventions for documentation. In the humanities, the most common style is the Modern Language Association (MLA). In the physical, natural, and social sciences, the American Psychological Association (APA) style is most often used. We will illustrate both in the examples that follow. Both MLA and APA use parenthetical citations in the text and simple, alphabetical bibliographies at the end, making revision and typing

www.mhhe.
com/crusius

For Web sites
with information
on documentation
styles, go to:
Research >
Annotated Links
to Documentation
Sites

much easier. (For a detailed explanation of these two styles, visit the Web sites for the MLA at <http://www.mla.org> and the APA at <http://apa.org>.)

In both MLA and APA formats, you provide some information in the body of your paper and the rest of the information under the heading "Works Cited" (MLA) or "References" (APA) at the end of your paper. The following summarizes the essentials of both systems.

Instructions for Using MLA and APA Styles

MLA Style

www.mhhe.
com/**crusius**

For a student
sample of a
paper in MLA
format, go to:
Research >
Sample Paper
in MLA Style

1. In parentheses at the end of both direct and indirect quotations, supply the last name of the author of the source and the exact page number(s) where the quoted or paraphrased words appear. If the name of the author appears in your sentence that leads into the quotation, omit it in the parentheses.

   > A San Jose State University professor argues that affirmative action "does not teach skills, or educate, or instill motivation" (Steele 121).

   > Shelby Steele, a professor of English at San Jose State University, argues that the disadvantages of affirmative action for blacks are greater than the advantages (117).

2. In a works-cited list at the end of the paper, provide complete bibliographical information in MLA style (explained and illustrated later).

APA Style

www.mhhe.
com/**crusius**

For a student
sample of a
paper in APA
format, go to:
Research >
Sample Paper
in APA Style

1. In parentheses at the end of direct or indirect quotations, place the author's last name, the date published, and the page number(s) where the cited material appears. If the author's name appears in the sentence, the date of publication should follow it in parentheses; the page number still comes at the end of the sentence. Unlike MLA, the APA style uses commas between the parts of the citation and "p." or "pp." before the page numbers.

   > A San Jose State University professor argues that affirmative action "does not teach skills, or educate, or instill motivation" (Steele, 1990, p. 121).

Shelby Steele (1990), a professor of English at San Jose State University, argues that the disadvantages of affirmative action for blacks are greater than the advantages (p. 117).

2. In a reference list at the end of the paper, provide complete bibliographical information in APA style (explained and illustrated later).

Direct Quotations

Direct quotations are exact words taken from a source. The simplest direct quotations are whole sentences worked into your text, as illustrated in the following excerpt.

MLA Style

In a passage that echos Seneca, <u>Newsweek</u> writer Katrine Ames describes the modern viewpoint: "Most of us have some choices in how we live, certainly in how we conduct our lives" (40).

This source is listed in the works-cited list as follows:

Ames, Katrine. "Last Rights." <u>Newsweek</u> 26 Aug. 1991: 40–41.

APA Style

In a passage that echos Seneca, *Newsweek* writer Katrine Ames (1991) describes the modern viewpoint: "Most of us have some choices in how we live, certainly in how we conduct our lives" (p. 40).

This source is listed in the reference list as follows:

Ames, K. (1991, August 26). Last rights. *Newsweek*, pp. 40–41.

Altering Direct Quotations with Ellipses and Square Brackets

Although there is nothing wrong with quoting whole sentences, it is often more economical to quote some words or parts of sentences from the original in your own sentences. When you do this, use *ellipses* (three evenly spaced periods) to signify the omission of words from the original; use square *brackets* to substitute words, to add words for purposes of clarification, and to change the wording of a quotation so that it fits gracefully into your own sentence. (If ellipses already appear in the material you are quoting and you are omitting additional material, place your ellipses in square brackets to distinguish them.)

The following passage illustrates quoted words integrated into the sentence, using ellipses and square brackets. The citation is in MLA style.

Robert Wennberg, a philosopher and Presbyterian minister, explains that "euthanasia is not an exclusively modern development, for it was widely endorsed in the ancient world. [It was] approved by such respected ancients as . . . Plato, Sophocles, . . . and Cicero" (1).

The source appears in the works-cited list as follows:

> Wennberg, Robert N. Terminal Choices: Euthanasia, Suicide, and the Right to Die. Grand Rapids: Eerdmans, 1989.

Using Block Quotations

If a quoted passage runs to four or more lines of text in your essay, indent it one inch (ten spaces of type) from the left margin, double-space it as with the rest of your text, and omit quotation marks. In block quotations, a period is placed at the end of the final sentence, followed by one space and the parenthetical citation.

The idea of death as release from suffering was expressed by Seneca, a Stoic philosopher of Rome, who lived during the first century CE:

> Against all the injuries of life, I have the refuge of death. If I can choose between a death of torture and one that is simple and easy, why should I not select the latter? As I chose the ship in which I sail and the house which I inhabit, so will I choose the death by which I leave life. . . . Why should I endure the agonies of disease . . . when I can emancipate myself from all my torments? (qtd. in Wennberg 42–43)

Note that the source of the Seneca quotation is the book by Wennberg. In the parenthetical citation, "qtd." is an abbreviation for "quoted." The entry on the works-cited page would be the same as for the previous example.

Indirect Quotations

Indirect quotations are paraphrases or summaries of a source. The Concept Close-Up box on page 125 gives an example of a direct quotation on a student notecard.

Here is how this quotation might be incorporated in a paper as an indirect quotation. Note that the author of the book is the same as the person indirectly quoted, so it is not necessary to repeat his name in parentheses.

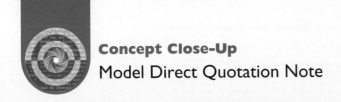

> *Expert's opinion — pro:*
>
> "It is time to rethink many of our attitudes toward death and dying.... I feel that society is ready to take a giant step toward a better understanding of the dignity of death, and in the attainment of that dignity, if necessary, through the acceptance of euthanasia."
>
> — *Barnard in Barnard, p.8*

MLA Style

> One cannot help but agree with pioneer heart-transplant surgeon Christiaan Barnard that death should involve dignity and that society may have to accept the practice of euthanasia as a means to death with dignity (8).

The entry on the works-cited list would appear as follows:

> Barnard, Christiaan. Good Life, Good Death. Englewood Cliffs: Prentice, 1980.

APA Style

> One cannot help but agree with pioneer heart-transplant surgeon Christiaan Barnard (1980) that death should involve dignity and that society may have to accept the practice of euthanasia as a means to death with dignity (p. 8).

The entry in the reference list would appear as follows.

> Barnard, C. (1980). *Good life, good death.* Englewood Cliffs, NJ: Prentice-Hall.

In-Text References to Electronic Sources

The conventions just described apply to print sources. Adapt the examples to Internet and other electronic sources. Because you must include the electronic sources in your works-cited or reference list, your in-text citations should connect the material quoted or paraphrased in your text to the matching work or posting on the list. Therefore, your in-text citation should begin with the author's name or, lacking that, the title of the work or posting. The APA format requires that you also include the posting date.

CREATING WORKS-CITED AND REFERENCE LISTS

www.mhhe. com/**crusius**

For an electronic tool that helps create properly formatted works-cited pages, go to: Research > Bibliomaker

At the end of your paper, include a bibliography of all sources that you quoted, paraphrased, or summarized. If you are using MLA style, your heading for this list will be *Works Cited*; if you are using APA style, it will be *References*. In either case, the list is in alphabetical order based on either the author's (or editor's) last name or — in the case of unidentified authors — the first word of the title, not counting the articles *a, an, the.* The entire list is double-spaced both within and between entries. See the works-cited page of the sample student paper at the end of this chapter for the correct indentation and spacing. Note that MLA format requires that the first line of each entry be typed flush with the left margin; subsequent lines of each entry are indented half an inch (five spaces on a typewriter). The APA recommends the same indentation.

The following examples illustrate the correct MLA and APA style for the types of sources you will most commonly use.

Books

Book by One Author

MLA: Crusius, Timothy W. <u>Discourse: A Critique & Synthesis of Major Theories</u>. New York: MLA, 1989.

APA: Crusius, T. W. (1989). *Discourse: A critique & synthesis of major theories.* New York: Modern Language Association.

(Note that APA uses initials rather than the author's first name and capitalizes only the first word and proper nouns in titles and subtitles.)

Two or More Works by the Same Author

MLA: Crusius, Timothy W. <u>Discourse: A Critique & Synthesis of Major Theories</u>. New York: MLA, 1989.

    ---. <u>A Teacher's Introduction to Philosophical Hermeneutics</u>. Urbana: NCTE, 1991.

(Note that MLA arranges works alphabetically by title and uses three hyphens to show that the name is the same as the one directly above.)

APA: Crusius, T. W. (1989). *Discourse: A critique & synthesis of major theories.* New York: Modern Language Association.

Crusius, T. W. (1991). *A teacher's introduction to philosophical hermeneutics.* Urbana, IL: National Council of Teachers of English.

(Note that APA repeats the author's name and arranges works in chronological order.)

Book by Two or Three Authors

MLA: Deleuze, Gilles, and Felix Guattari. <u>Anti-Oedipus: Capitalism and Schizophrenia</u>. New York: Viking, 1977.

APA: Deleuze, G., & Guattari, F. (1977). *Anti-Oedipus: Capitalism and schizophrenia.* New York: Viking.

(Note that MLA style inverts only the first author's name. APA style, however, inverts both authors' names and uses an ampersand [&] between authors instead of the word "and.")

Book by Four or More Authors

MLA: Bellah, Robert N., et al. <u>Habits of the Heart: Individualism and Commitment in American Life</u>. New York: Harper, 1985.

(Note that the Latin abbreviation *et al.,* meaning "and others," stands in for all subsequent authors' names. MLA style also accepts spelling out all authors' names instead of using *et al.*)

APA: Bellah, R., Madsen, R., Sullivan, W., Swidler, A., & Tipton, S. (1985). *Habits of the heart: Individualism and commitment in American life.* New York: Harper & Row.

(Note that APA uses *et al.* only for more than six authors.)

Book Prepared by an Editor or Editors

MLA: Connors, Robert J., ed. <u>Selected Essays of Edward P. J. Corbett</u>. Dallas: Southern Methodist UP, 1989.

APA: Connors, R. J. (Ed.). (1989). *Selected essays of Edward P. J. Corbett.* Dallas: Southern Methodist University Press.

Work in an Edited Collection

MLA: Jackson, Jesse. "Common Ground: Speech to the Democratic National Convention." The American Reader. Ed. Diane Ravitch. New York: Harper, 1991. 367–71.

APA: Jackson, J. (1991). Common ground: Speech to the Democratic National Convention. In D. Ravitch (Ed.), *The American reader* (pp. 367–371). New York: HarperCollins.

Translated Book

MLA: Vattimo, Gianni. The End of Modernity: Nihilism and Hermeneutics in Postmodern Culture. Trans. Jon R. Snyder. Baltimore: Johns Hopkins UP, 1988.

APA: Vattimo, G. (1988). *The end of modernity: Nihilism and hermeneutics in postmodern culture.* (J. R. Snyder, Trans.). Baltimore: Johns Hopkins University Press.

Periodicals

Article in a Journal with Continuous Pagination

MLA: Herron, Jerry. "Writing for My Father." College English 54 (1992): 928–37.

APA: Herron, J. (1992). Writing for my father. *College English, 54,* 928–937.

(Note that in APA style the article title is not fully capitalized, but the journal title is. Note also that the volume number is italicized in APA style.)

Article in a Journal Paginated by Issue

MLA: McConnell, Margaret Liu. "Living with Roe v. Wade." Commentary 90.5 (1990): 34–38.

APA: McConnell, M. L. (1990). Living with *Roe v. Wade. Commentary, 90*(5), 34–38.

(In both examples, "90" is the volume number and "5" is the number of the issue.)

Article in a Magazine

MLA: D'Souza, Dinesh. "Illiberal Education." <u>Atlantic</u> Mar. 1990: 51+.

(Note that the plus sign indicates that the article runs on nonconsecutive pages.)

APA: D'Souza, D. (1990, March). Illiberal education. *Atlantic,* pp. 51–58, 62–65, 67, 70–74, 76, 78–79.

(Note that APA requires all page numbers to be listed.)

Anonymous Article in a Newspaper

MLA: "Clinton Warns of Sacrifice." <u>Dallas Morning News</u> 7 Feb. 1993: A4.

APA: Clinton warns of sacrifice. (1993, February 7). *The Dallas Morning News,* p. A4.

(In both examples, the "A" refers to the newspaper section in which the article appeared.)

Editorial in a Newspaper

MLA: Lewis, Flora. "Civil Society, the Police and Abortion." Editorial. <u>New York Times</u> 12 Sept. 1992, late ed.: A14.

APA: Lewis, F. (1992, September 12). Civil society, the police and abortion [Editorial]. *The New York Times,* p. A14.

(Note that in MLA style the edition of the newspaper must be specified.)

Nonprint Sources

Interview

MLA: May, William. Personal interview. 24 Apr. 1990.

(Note that APA style documents personal interviews only parenthetically within the text: "According to W. May [personal interview, April 24, 1990], ..." Personal interviews are not included on the reference list.)

Sound Recording

MLA: Glass, Philip. Glassworks. CBS Sony, MK 37265, 1982.

APA: Glass, P. (1982). *Glassworks* [CD Recording No. MK 37265]. Tokyo:
   CBS Sony.

Film (on video—for DVD, substitute "DVD" for "videocassette")

MLA: Scott, Ridley, dir. Thelma and Louise. Perf. Susan Sarandon, Geena
   Davis, and Harvey Keitel. 1991. Videocassette. MGM/UA
   Home Video, 1996.

APA: Scott, R. (Director). (1991). *Thelma and Louise* [Motion picture].
   Culver City, CA: MGM/UA Home Video.

(Note that with nonprint media, APA asks you to identify the medium — CD, cassette, film, and so forth. MLA includes the principal actors, but APA does not. APA specifies the place of production, but MLA does not.)

Electronic Sources

Although the documentation requirements for MLA and APA citations of electronic sources contain much of the same information, there are also differences. Use the following lists as general guides when you cite Internet sources.

MLA Style: Citing Internet Sources

1. Author's or editor's name, followed by a period
2. Title of the article or short work (such as a short story or poem) followed by a period and enclosed by quotation marks
3. Name of the book, journal, or other longer work underlined
4. Publication information, followed by a period:

> City, publisher, and date for books
> Volume and year for journals
> Date for magazines
> Date for and description of government documents

5. Date on which you accessed the information (no period)
6. URL, placed inside angle brackets, followed by a period

APA Style: Citing Internet Sources

1. Author's or editor's last name, followed by a comma and the initials

2. Year of publication, followed by a comma, with the month and day for magazine and newspaper articles, within parentheses and followed by a period
3. Title of the article, book, or journal (follow APA conventions for titles of works)
4. Volume number
5. Page numbers
6. The words "Retrieved from," followed by the date of access, followed by the source (such as the World Wide Web) and a colon
7. URL, without a period

An Online Book

MLA: Strunk, William. The Elements of Style. 1st ed. Geneva: Humphrey, 1918. May 1995. Columbia U Academic Information Systems, Bartleby Lib. 12 Apr. 1999 <http://www.Columbia.edu/acis/ bartleby/strunk/strunk100.html>.

APA: Strunk, W. (1918). *The elements of style* (1st ed.). [Online]. Retrieved April 12, 1999, from http://www.Columbia.edu/ acis/bartleby/strunk/strunk100.html

(Note that MLA requires that the original publication data be included if it is available for works that originally appeared in print. The APA, however, requires only an online availability statement.)

World Wide Web Site

MLA: Victorian Women Writers Project. Ed. Perry Willett. Apr. 1999. Indiana U. 12 Apr. 1999 <http://www.indiana.edu/ ˜letrs/vwwp>.

APA: Willett, P. (1999, April). *Victorian women writers project* [Web page]. Retrieved April 12, 1999, from http://www.indiana .edu/˜letrs/vwwp

Article in an Electronic Journal

MLA: Harnack, Andrew, and Gene Kleppinger. "Beyond the MLA Handbook: Documenting Sources on the Internet." Kairos 1.2 (Summer 1996). 7 Jan. 1997 <http://english.ttu.edu/ Kairos/1.2/index.html>.

APA: Harnack, A., & Kleppinger, G. (1996). Beyond the *MLA Handbook:*
        Documenting sources on the Internet. *Kairos* [Online], *1*(2).
        Retrieved January 7, 1997, from http://english.ttu.edu/
        Kairos/1.2/index.html

Encyclopedia Article on CD-ROM

MLA: Duckworth, George. "Rhetoric." Microsoft Encarta '95. CD-ROM.
        Redmond: Microsoft, 1995.

APA: Duckworth. G. (1995). Rhetoric. In *Microsoft encarta '95* [CD-ROM].
        Redmond, WA: Microsoft.

Encyclopedia Article Online

MLA: "Toni Morrison." Encyclopaedia Britannica Online. 1994–
        1999. Encyclopaedia Britannica. 4 Mar. 1999 <http://
        members.eb.com/bol/topic?eu=55183&sctn=#s_top>.

APA: (1994–1999). Toni Morrison. In *Encyclopaedia Britannica Online*
        [Online]. Retrieved March 4, 1999, from http://members
        .eb.com/bol/topic?eu=55183&sctn=#s_top

E-Mail, Listserv, and Newsgroup Citations

For MLA, give in this order the author's name, the title of the document (in quotation marks), followed by the description *Online posting,* the date when the material was posted, the name of the forum (if known), the date of access, and in angle brackets the online address of the list's Internet site or, if unknown, the e-mail address of the list's moderator.

MLA: Stockwell, Stephen. "Rhetoric and Democracy." Online posting. 13
        Jan. 1997. 22 Jan. 1997 <H-Rhetor@msu.edu>.

For APA, the custom is not to include e-mail, listservs, and newsgroups in a reference list but rather to give a detailed in-text citation as follows: (S. Stockwell, posting to H-Rhetor@msu.edu, January 13, 1997).

However, if the content of the message is scholarly, many researchers do include messages in the references:

APA: Stockwell, S. (1997, January 13). Rhetoric and democracy. Re-
        trieved January 22, 1997, from e-mail: H-Rhetor@msu.edu

STUDENT SAMPLE: *A Research Paper (MLA Style)*

www.mhhe.
com/crusius

For another
model essay
in MLA format,
go to:
Research >
Sample Paper
in MLA Style

Following is student Patrick Pugh's research paper in MLA style.

Pugh 1

*Last name, page
number on each
page*

Patrick Pugh

Professor Smith

English 1302

October 21, 2004

*Standard
heading*

Legalizing Euthanasia: A Means

to a More Comfortable Dying Process

*Title centered;
skip no lines
between heading
and first
paragraph*

All people are linked by one indisputable fact: Every
human being dies. For some, death comes early, seeming to
cut off life before many of its mysteries have even begun to
unfold. For others, death is the conclusion to a lengthy and
experience-filled existence. Death is life's one absolute
certainty.

*Announces
theme*

*Paragraphs
indented
5 character
spaces or 1/2"*

At issue, however, is the desire by some men and
women, many of the most vocal of whom are in the medical
profession, to intervene in what they describe as a heartless
extension of the dying process. The term euthanasia, a Greek
word whose literal translation is "good death," has been
adopted by those who advocate legalizing certain measures to
ensure a transition from life to death that is as comfortable and

Poses issue

*No word breaks
at ends of lines*

dignified as possible. One cannot help but agree with pioneer
heart-transplant surgeon Dr. Christiaan Barnard that death
should involve dignity and that society may have to accept the
practice of euthanasia as a means to death with dignity (8).

Takes stance

*Parenthetical
page number
only because
author's name
mentioned in
text. Note: Page
number goes
before period.*

To me, having watched both my grandfather and
my aunt spend months dying slow, torturous deaths
from incurable lung cancer, there can be little doubt that
euthanasia would have provided a far more humane close
to their lives than the painful and prolonged dying that the

*Ties stance to
personal
experience*

Pugh 2

ultimately futile regimens of chemotherapy and radiation caused them to suffer. My family members' experiences were far too common, for "80 percent of Americans who die in hospitals are likely to meet their end . . . in a sedated or comatose state; betubed nasally, abdominally, and intravenously, far more like manipulated objects than moral subjects" (Minow 124).

Advocates of euthanasia can turn to history for support of their arguments. Robert Wennberg, a philosopher and Presbyterian minister, explains that "euthanasia is not an exclusively modern development, for it was widely endorsed in the ancient world. [It was] approved by such respected ancients as . . . Plato, Sophocles, . . . and Cicero" (1). The idea that we have a right to choose death was expressed by Seneca, a Stoic philosopher of Rome, who lived in the first century CE:

> Against all the injuries of life, I have the refuge of death. If I can choose between a death of torture and one that is simple and easy, why should I not select the latter? As I chose the ship in which I sail and the house which I inhabit, so will I choose the death by which I leave life. In no matter more than death should we act according to our desire. . . . Why should I endure the agonies of disease . . . when I can emancipate myself from all my torments? (qtd. in Wennberg 42–43)

In a passage that echos Seneca, <u>Newsweek</u> writer Katrine Ames describes the modern viewpoint: "Most of us have some choices in how we live, certainly in how we conduct our lives. How we die is an equally profound choice, and, in the exhilarating and terrifying new world of medical technology, perhaps almost as important" (40).

"Run in" quotation; use for shorter citations.

Both author and page number used because author not mentioned in sentence

Identifies source unknown to audience; establishes authority of source

Block quotation; use for longer citations. *Note:* No quotation marks; indented 10 character spaces or 1".

Note parenthetical citation. No end punctuation after block quote; contrast with "run in" quotation.

Pugh 3

Regardless of historical precedents and humane implications, euthanasia in both of its forms remains a controversial issue for many. In the first kind, known as passive or indirect euthanasia, death results from such measures as withholding or withdrawing life-support systems or life-sustaining medications. Passive euthanasia is often equated with simply "letting someone die," in contrast to the far more controversial active or direct euthanasia, in which life is ended by direct intervention, such as giving a patient a lethal dose of a drug or assisting a patient in his or her suicide.

Makes important distinction

During the past two decades, the so-called Right to Die movement has made great strides in the promotion of passive euthanasia as an acceptable alternative to the extension of impending death.

> There seems to be a clear consensus that the competent adult has the right to refuse treatments. . . . This legal recognition of the right to reject medical treatment is grounded in a respect for the bodily integrity of the individual, for the right of each person to determine when bodily invasions will take place. (Wennberg 116)

End of sentence plus omission from text; a period plus three spaced periods used.

Passive euthanasia, as an extension of the stated wishes of the dying patient, has become a widely accepted practice, a fact confirmed by medical ethicist and theologian Joseph Fletcher:

> What is called passive euthanasia, letting the patient die . . . is a daily event in hospitals. Hundreds of thousands of Living Wills have been recorded, appealing to doctors, families, pastors, and lawyers to stop treatment at some balance point of the pro-life, pro-death assessment. (47)

Three periods; omission from cited text

Pugh 4

The case for passive euthanasia has withstood, for the most part, the arguments of those who claim that life must be preserved and extended at all costs.

The euthanasia debate that is currently being waged focuses on active or direct euthanasia, where another person, notably a physician, assists a terminally ill patient in dying by lethal injection or provides the dying patient with the means to commit suicide. The case for active euthanasia is strong. For example, active euthanasia is preferable to passive euthanasia in cases of chronic and incurable diseases that promise the patient pain and suffering for the duration of his or her life. As Robert K. Landers explains, with the advance of AIDS and diseases such as Alzheimer's affecting our aging population, Americans are paying more attention to the idea of "giving death a hand" (555). Surely, many terminally ill patients whose only hope for release from agonizing pain or humiliating helplessness is death would welcome the more comfortable and dignified death that physician-assisted suicide can bring.

Restates stance, now focused on active euthanasia only

Still, there are those who argue that although passive euthanasia is moral, the active type is not. Ethically, is there a difference between passive and active euthanasia? Christiaan Barnard thinks not:

> Passive euthanasia is accepted in general by the medical profession, the major religions, and society at large. Therefore, when it is permissible for treatment to be stopped or not instituted in order to allow the patient to die, it makes for small mercy and less sense when the logical step of actively terminating life, and hence suffering, is not taken. Why, at that point, can life not be brought to an end, instead of extending the suffering of the patient by

Pugh 5

hours or days, or even weeks? . . . Procedurally,
there is a difference between direct and indirect
euthanasia, but ethically, they are the same. (68–69)

Argues that
active
euthanasia is
ethical

Barnard's ethics are supported by Joseph Fletcher's definition
of ethical action, which holds that the ethical value of any
human action is not a quality inherent in the act itself but
rather a judgment that we make about the act after
examining the entire situation in which it takes place. We
should decide what is moral and immoral on the basis of
what is best for human well-being in any given set of
circumstances (38–39).

*Defines ethics
in situational
terms*

Although Fletcher is an Episcopal theologian,
many other Christians do make arguments against active
euthanasia on religious grounds. However, according to
ethicist James Rachels, even religious people ought to be
able to see that these arguments may not be valid. For
example, one of the most often-stated objections is that
in the Ten Commandments God forbids killing. Rachels
counters by pointing out that the Sixth Commandment is
more accurately translated as "Thou shalt not commit
murder." Because we define murder as "wrongful killing,"
we will not call some killing murder if we do not see it as
wrong. Thus, the Sixth Commandment "is not normally
taken to forbid killing in a just war; since such killing is
(allegedly) justified" (161–62). Rachels points out that
although the scriptures do not mention euthanasia and
in fact affirm the "sanctity of human life," one also finds
"exhortations to kindness and mercy" for fellow humans,
principles that "support active euthanasia rather than condemn it" (162).

Takes up major
objection;
refutes the
notion that
mercy killing is
murder

To those who claim that "[i]t is for God alone to decide
when a person shall live and when he shall die," Rachels
responds that "if it is for God alone to decide when we shall

Pugh 6

live and when we shall die, then we 'play God' just as much when we cure people as when we kill them" (163). He notes that philosopher David Hume made this argument over two hundred years ago.

Transitional
sentences signal
change of focus,
allow smooth
movement from
paragraph to
paragraph

————A third common Christian argument is that because suffering is a part of God's plan for humans, we should not interrupt it by euthanasia. Rachels responds to this with the question, How can we then justify the use of any pain-relieving drugs and procedures? (165). He concludes that "[t]here is nothing in religious belief in general, or in Christian belief in particular, to preclude the acceptance of mercy killing as a humane response to some awful situations" (165).

In fact, the American public supports active euthanasia, specifically physician-assisted euthanasia, as an alternative to a lingering death for terminal patients. Polls show support running as high as 70 percent (ERGO). Support for assisted suicide may have leveled off recently, but polls still indicate that more Americans favor assisted suicide than oppose it (American Life League). Fifty percent of doctors also support it, with about 15 percent actually practicing it when a patient's dire situation warrants (ERGO).

Public support, however, has not translated into significant changes in the law. Only Oregon permits assisted suicides (ERGO). Maine rejected a measure similar to the Oregon law in the 2000 election ("Assisted Suicide"), and Attorney General John Ashcroft, reversing the stance of his predecessor, Janet Reno, has recently taken action to block implementation of Oregon's law (Vicini). Furthermore, the Supreme Court has ruled in two cases that the Constitution does not provide a right to die and therefore has upheld state laws against assisted suicide ("Physician"; Vacco v. Quill).

Pugh 7

At this point, then, the law seems unresponsive to public opinion. There is no way to predict whether active euthanasia will be legalized in the near future. One thing is reasonably certain, however: Any compassionate person who has sat by helplessly as a fellow human being has spent his or her final days thrashing around on a sweat-soaked bed or who has observed a once-alert mind that has become darkened by the agony of inescapable pain will consider the eventual fate that awaits him or her. In times like these, frightened humans are united in the universal prayer, "God, spare me from this when my time comes," and even the most stubborn anti-euthanasia minds are opened to the option of an easier journey between life and death, an option that can be made a reality by the legalization of physician-assisted euthanasia.

Forceful conclusion; avoids saying "in conclusion"

Pugh 8

Works Cited

American Life League, Inc. Legislative Guide to End-
   of-Life Issues. 11 Dec. 2001 <http://www.all.org/
   legislat/guide01.htm>.

Ames, Katrine. "Last Rights." Newsweek 26 Aug. 1991:
   40–41.

"Assisted Suicide, Gay Rights, Lose in Maine." USA Today
   Network. 8 Nov. 2000. 11 Dec 2001 <http://www.
   usatoday.com/news/vote2000/me/main.htm>.

Barnard, Christiaan. Good Life, Good Death. Englewood
   Cliffs: Prentice, 1980.

ERGO (Euthanasia Research & Guidance Organization).
   "Frequently Asked Questions." Euthanasia
   World Directory. 11 Dec. 2001 <http://
   www.finalexit.org>.

Fletcher, Joseph. "In Defense of Suicide." Suicide and Eu-
   thanasia: The Rights of Personhood. Ed. Samuel
   E. Wallace and Albin Eser. Knoxville: U of Tennessee
   P, 1981. 38–50.

Landers, Robert. "Right to Die: Medical, Legal, and Moral
   Issues." Editorial Research Reports 1.36 (1990):
   554–64.

Minow, Newton. "Communications in Medicine." Vital
   Speeches of the Day. 1 Dec. 1990: 121–25.

"Physician-Assisted Suicide: Vacco v. Quill; Washington
   v. Glucksberg." Supreme Court—Key Cases
   1996–1997. Washington Post database. 11 Dec. 2001
   <http://www.washingtonpost.com/
   wp-dyn/politics>.

Rachels, James. The End of Life. Oxford: Oxford UP,
   1987.

Sources listed
in alphabetical
order

Author's last
name first

Pugh 9

Vacco v. Quill. 95-1858. U.S. Supreme Ct. 1997. FindLaw
    Resources legal database. 11 Dec. 2001
    <http://caselaw.lp.findlaw.com/us/000/
    95-1858.html>.

Vicini, James. "Doctor-Assisted Suicide Policy Reversed."
    Excite Canada. 6 Nov. 2001. 11 December 2001
    <http://www.excite.com>.

Wennberg, Robert N. Terminal Choices: Euthanasia, Sui-
    cide, and the Right to Die. Grand Rapids: Eerdmans,
    1989.

Part Two The Aims of Argument

Part Two The Aims of Argument

Chapter 6

Looking for Some Truth: Arguing to Inquire

To inquire is to look into something. Inquiry can be a police investigation or a doctor's effort to diagnose a patient's illness, a scientist's experiment or an artist's attempt to see the world differently. According to singer and songwriter Lucinda Williams, one of the joys of life in this "sweet old world" is "looking for some truth."

It is satisfying to be able to say, "This is true." If we are religious, we find truth in the doctrines of our faith. But in our daily lives, we often must discern for ourselves what is true. We look for truth in messages from family and friends and lovers, in nature, and in art, music, and literature. Often we have to work to decide what to believe, for newspapers and textbooks offer differing versions of fact. The search for truth, then, is closely allied to the question "What is knowledge?" The pursuit of both is inquiry.

INQUIRY AND INTERPRETATION IN ACADEMIC WRITING

Inquiry is an important part of college learning because college is where we learn that one "true" body of knowledge or facts about the world does not exist. Take, for example, something usually considered fact:

Columbus discovered America in 1492.

If this statement were on a true/false test, would your answer be "true," "false," or "that depends"? With hardly any inquiry at all, we see that this "fact" depends on

- the calendar you use to mark time on this Earth
- your definition of the word "discover"
- your definition of "America"
- whether your ancestors were here before Columbus
- whether you know anything about Vikings and other early explorers

So what we accept as fact, as truth, is *an interpretation*. Most significant claims to truth are *efforts to understand and/or explain*; as such, they are interpretations that need defending. Later in this chapter, you will read several arguments, each claiming to know the truth about whether violence on television causes children to act out violently. All offer data to prove their claims, but data are meaningless without interpretation. And interpretations are open to inquiry.

The current state of knowledge on any given topic depends on who is doing the interpreting and whether the data are of interest to people in a particular culture. Some facts remain unknown for centuries because no one thought they mattered. What one considers knowledge or truth, then, depends on the perspective of the interpreters, which in turn depends on the interpreters' social class, politics, religion, and a host of other factors that make up who they are and how they see the world.

Like the high school research paper, college writing requires research. Unlike the high school paper, which typically requires only that you obtain information, organize it, and restate it in your own words, most college assignments will require *inquiry* into sources.

It's important to gather information and viewpoints. But research itself is not the goal of inquiry. The most important part of inquiry is the thinking you do before and after gathering sources. The quality of your paper will depend on your initial thinking as well as on your sources and your understanding of them. Nothing is more vital to writing well than learning how to inquire well.

As we begin to inquire, it is important not to try to "prove" anything. Argument as inquiry is not confrontational; rather, it is conversational. It is conversation with friends, family, and colleagues. We can have these kinds of conversations with ourselves, too, asking and answering questions about the arguments we read.

To inquire well, we must question our initial viewpoints instead of holding on to them. We need to ask hard questions, even if the answers threaten our preconceptions and beliefs. Before Copernicus, "common sense" held that the Earth was stationary and religious beliefs reinforced this "truth." To question our truths makes us uncomfortable. But inquiry requires holding a question open. The scientist whose theory wins respect from other scientists must test its truth rather than protect it from further inquiry. Likewise, a college student needs to test received wisdom from his or her past to grow intellectually. After inquiry, you may still hold the same belief, but because you have tested it, your belief will be a claim to truth that you have earned, not just been told.

This chapter offers guidelines for inquiring and shows how writing plays a part in it. The writing project is the exploratory essay, through which the following pages will guide you.

THE WRITING PROJECT: PART 1

The exploratory essay is an account of inquiry. Your goal is to share the experience of questioning your opinions and the arguments of others on your chosen topic. The paper will be a journey with a starting point, a tour of viewpoints on the issue, and a destination, a claim you can defend. The essay has three parts, one written before inquiry, the other two written after. In this informal paper, you will refer to yourself and your own thoughts and experiences. Write in first person.

Here is an overview of the paper:

In Part 1, you will tell what question or issue interests you most about a given topic and express your initial opinion.

Part 2 will be the exploration itself. The point is to open the question and keep it open, testing your opinions and exploring the issue through conversations and research that connect you to a range of expert opinions. You are not trying to support your initial opinion but to test it. You'll write about readings that confirm and contradict your thinking and evaluate these arguments fairly.

Part 3, the conclusion, will be a statement of your thinking after inquiry, an explanation of the truth as you now see it. Think of exploration as the process of *arriving* at a claim.

Your instructor may follow this paper with Chapter 7, "Making Your Case: Arguing to Convince," and an assignment to convince others to assent to your claim. But in this paper you'll explore, not make a case.

We illustrate inquiry and the steps of writing the exploratory essay by exploring violence in the media and its relation to violence in society. We show some students' initial thinking about this issue and take you through their exploration of it.

Step 1: Choosing a Topic for Inquiry

If your instructor has not assigned a topic, begin by looking at newspapers. Current events offer good topics that need interpretation. If you are familiar with a news topic, you probably already have an opinion, and that is a good place to begin inquiry. We came upon our violence in the media topic by noticing an op-ed column in the *New York Times*, but yours could come from a front-page story or an item on television news.

Once you have selected a topic, consider what you already know about it and consider narrowing the focus. Violence in the media is a huge subject. There's staged or *pretend violence*—the quarrels, muggings, rapes, and so on of television and movie dramas. There's *virtual violence* in computer games. And there's *actual violence*, the staple of broadcast news. "If it bleeds, it leads": Local TV news programs often start with an account of a brutal murder or a big traffic accident.

www.mhhe.com/crusius

For more sources of a potential topic, go to:
Research >
Discipline-Specific Resources in the Library and on the Internet

The more you narrow your topic, the easier it will be to find issues to argue about and sources that converse with each other. For example, narrowing media violence to video games or music lyrics is a good strategy.

Step 2: Finding an Issue

An issue is a controversial question. With the example topic, such questions include: Why do people find violence so engrossing, so entertaining? Why do we like to see it in sports like football, hockey, and auto racing? Why do we go to movies that feature violence? Is it our nature or our culture? How is it related to gender?

All are worthwhile questions, but we need to identify a central or primary issue. In this instance, that issue is whether pretend violence can be connected to aggressive acts. It's central because most articles about the topic address it and because our answer determines what the other issues are.

Inquiry looks for order or hierarchy among issues; that is, our answer to one question leads to the next. *If* there is a link between fantasy violence and actual violence, *then* the next question is, How significant is the connection? We can't ask the second question until we answer the first. *If* we decide that pretend violence is a major contributor to actual aggression, *then* we must decide what action should be taken — and this leads to issues of censorship. For media violence, then, we can list this hierarchy of issues:

- Is there a link between fantasy violence and real-world violence? If so, what is it exactly?
- How strong is the link? Does media violence make people more aggressive and less sensitive to the suffering of others? Does it contribute to murders and assaults?
- If the contribution is significant, should we consider censorship, or does the Constitution prohibit taking this kind of action?
- If we can't censor, what other action(s) can we suggest to reduce the negative effect?

Locating the issues is usually not difficult. Often we can supply them from general knowledge and experience. We need only ask, What have we heard people arguing about when this topic came up? What have we ourselves argued about it? If we can't identify the issues before research, sources will reveal them. Once you begin reading what others have said about your topic, you may discover an issue more interesting than ones you thought of beforehand.

 Following Through

In preparation for writing your exploratory paper, select a topic of current interest. What do you see as the main issue that people debate? With answers to that question, draw up a chain of questions that follow one another. Which interests you most?

Following Through

Read an argument on the topic you intend to explore. What issue does this argument primarily address? What is the author's answer to this question — in other words, what is the author's claim? Restate it in your own words. What other issues are raised in the argument? What *other* issues do you know about?

Step 3: Stating Your Initial Opinions

In this step, you will write Part 1 of your exploratory essay, where you state your initial ideas before inquiry. Write this part of your paper before doing any serious research. Begin by introducing your topic and the issue or issues you intend to consider. State your opinions on those issues now and explain your reasoning. Include some explanation of what, in your own experiences or observations, has contributed to your opinions.

Below is an example on the media violence topic.

STUDENT SAMPLE: *Exploratory Essay, Part 1—Lauren's Initial Opinions*

I have to admit that I am somewhat biased when it comes to the topic of the relation between entertainment and violence in children. I have been involved in several life-altering experiences before this assignment that made me feel very strongly that virtual violence and aggressive behavior in children are causally related. When I was in high school, a group of kids I grew up with got mixed up in the whole "gangster" scene. They listened to rap music about murder and drugs. Ultimately, these boys took the life of a fellow student at the McDonald's down the street from my school. They used a shotgun to murder him in a drug deal gone bad. Because I knew these kids when they were younger, I can say that when they were in the seventh grade they were incapable of committing such a crime. Did the rap music influence them? They had to get the idea from somewhere, and I cannot think of another reasonable explanation.

Even though music may not plant evil in a child's mind, it can lead to problems. Throughout my senior year, I did volunteer work at the Salvation Army recreation center. It's located in the so-called ghetto of Lincoln, Nebraska and intended for children to walk to after school when their parents are still working. Working here opened my eyes to how the future of America is growing up.

My first encounter was with a six-year-old boy who called me profane names. Not only was I verbally abused, but also pushed, shoved, and kicked. Later, after discussing the situation with the boy in time-out,

I found out that he had heard these names in an Eminem song that bashes women.

Because of these experiences, my negative opinion about media violence is strong.

 Following Through

Draft Part 1 of your paper. In the opening paragraph or two, state what your opinions were before you researched the topic. Describe and explain experiences that influenced your outlook. Refer to specific films or music or news broadcasts. If you've read or heard about the topic before or discussed it in school or elsewhere, recall both context and content and share them with your readers. Edit for clarity and correctness.

Step 4: Exploring an Issue

Once you have written Part 1, concentrate on exploring—reading and talking about your topic. Because you will eventually write about these experiences in Part 2, use your writer's notebook and make good annotations in the margins of what you read, to record your thoughts. These notes are the raw material from which you will eventually write the account of your exploration.

CONVERSATION AND DIALOGUE IN INQUIRY

A good way to begin inquiry is to talk through your position in serious conversation with a friend, family member, classmate, or teacher. Inquiry often takes the form of discussion or conversation. And conversation is a big part of higher education. Many college classes are devoted to discussion rather than lecture; even lecturers encourage classes to discuss controversial questions. Out of class, students can talk with professors and each other.

As you know from watching talk shows, conversation is not always a search for truth. There's an art to productive conversation. In Chapter 2, we noted that critical reading depends on developing certain practices and habits. Conversation aimed at finding some truth also depends on good practices and habits. Participants need to move beyond ordinary conversation, often just an exchange of opinions, to *dialogue*, a *questioning* of opinions.

Let's begin by looking at a conversation about violence in entertainment.

An Example Conversation

The conversation that follows took place shortly after the Columbine High School killings. It was recorded and transcribed, and an excerpt of it appeared in the May 17, 1999, issue of *Newsweek*. The conversation is neither especially good nor especially bad but rather typical, the sort of thing we encounter routinely in media-arranged talk. Read it carefully. Comments follow explaining what we can learn from it.

Moving beyond the Blame Game
Jonathan Alter, Moderator

A month after the Littleton tragedy, the conversation continues — in schools, in homes and at this week's White House conference on youth violence. The theories of why Eric Harris and Dylan Klebold went on their rampage have given way to a broader discussion of the deeper sources of the problem and where to go from here. Obviously, there are no quick fixes; everything from more values [in] education to better supervision of anti-depressant medication has been introduced into the debate. But Americans have singled out a few issues for special attention. According to the new *Newsweek* Poll, about half of all Americans want to see the movie industry, the TV industry, computer-game makers, Internet services and gun manufacturers and the NRA make major policy changes to help reduce teen violence. Slightly fewer want the music industry to change fundamentally. Younger Americans are less concerned about media violence than their elders are. On guns, there's a racial gap, with 72 percent of nonwhites and 41 percent of whites seeking major changes.

To further the conversation, *Newsweek* assembled a panel last week to explore the complexities. One after another, the people who actually make heavily violent movies, records and games declined to participate, just as they did when the White House called. This could be a sign that they are feeling the heat — or perhaps just avoiding it. Those who did take part in the *Newsweek* forum include Wayne LaPierre, executive director of the NRA; Jack Valenti, president of the Motion Picture Association of America; Hillary Rosen, president of the Recording Industry Association of America; Doug Lowenstein, president of the Interactive Digital Software Association; Marshall Herskovitz, TV and movie producer and director; and Jonah Green, a 15-year-old New York high-school student. *Newsweek*'s Jonathan Alter moderated the discussion.

Excerpts:

Alter: Youth shall be served, so I want to start with Jonah. You seem to think that there's [a] lot of scapegoating going on.

Green: Well, I have to say that America is very confused and scared. There's no one simple answer to teen violence. It's understandable because we're seeking answers, but right now people are focusing too much on putting the blame somewhere. We should be focusing on solutions.

Alter: Ok, Wayne, wouldn't making guns less easily accessible be at least a 5 partial solution?

LaPierre: You can't talk about easy access to guns by people we all don't want to have guns without talking about the shameful secret that really hasn't been reported. Which is the complete collapse of enforcement of the existing firearm laws on the books by the Department of Justice [in] the last six years. The proof is in the statistics. Six thousand kids illegally brought guns to school the last two years. We've only had 13 [federal] prosecutions. And only 11 prosecutions for illegally transferring guns to juveniles.

Alter: Do you think that if an 11-year-old brings his father's gun to school, the child should be prosecuted?

LaPierre: Yes, I do. They did not prosecute Kip Kinkel out in Oregon after he was blowing up cats, threatening people. He walks into school with a gun. They do nothing to him except send him home. And he comes back to the school two days later with a gun and shoots those kids. I mean, the fact is we're either serious about this situation or we're not.

Alter: How about Clinton's gun-limit proposal? Why does anyone need to buy more than one gun a month?

LaPierre: That's just a sound bite. 10

Alter: Doug, some of your industry's games are a long way from Pac-Man, right?

Lowenstein: Oh, absolutely. There are some very violent videogames, although they represent only a small fraction of the market. There's a critical parental role here: It costs over $1,000 to own a computer. A hundred dollars plus to own a videogame machine. There's a very conscious choice involved in bringing this kind of entertainment into your home. And the parent needs the tools to make an informed choice.

Alter: You don't think it desensitizes kids to violence to play games over and over?

Green: Personally, I think some kids use videogames, especially the violent ones, just as some violent movies, as a vent. You know, they like to live vicariously and vent their anger through that. And Doug was right that we can't really map out everything a kid has and how they use it and what makes them able to kill somebody.

Alter: Hillary, MTV is doing a stop-the-violence campaign, but then they 15 air—and you supported—something like Eminem's song about stuffing a woman into the trunk of a car. Don't you see a contradiction here?

Rosen: Young people are so much smarter than anybody—the media or politicians or most adults, in fact—may give them credit for being. They understand the difference between fantasy and reality, and that's why giving them concrete steps to take when they face personal conflict or when they face a gang conflict or school bullying, or those sorts of things, are much more productive means for giving them tools to be nonviolent in their lives than taking away their culture.

Alter: Do you think that a music-rating system just makes it forbidden fruit and makes kids want to play or see it more?

Rosen: We've done surveys that show it doesn't encourage young people to buy artists. People buy music that they connect with, that they like, that has a good beat, that sounds good. The label is there for parents and for retailers.

Green: I actually think artists like Eminem are very sarcastic. It is more playful than hard core. I find rap being a little more human than it used to be. Gangsta rap isn't as big anymore, and now sampling is.

Rosen: It's true.   20

Green: Edgar Allan Poe talked about death—he was dark, but he was a celebrated poet. It's about having an edge, a hook. That can be violence.

Alter: You don't have any problem with Marilyn Manson naming himself after a serial killer?

Green: I think it's in bad taste. It was just stupid and controversial.

Alter: Hillary, how about you?

Rosen: Well, I agree with Jonah that it's bad taste, but that's the point. Mari-   25
lyn Manson is an act. It's an act that's sort of designed to create a persona of empowering the geek. Unfortunately, Charles Manson was a real person. People don't have to make up horrible tragedies in this world.

Green: Entertainment and the media were never really for getting across good, moral messages like "I love my school and my mother." People rarely feel they need to express bland feelings like that.

Rosen: But it is on some level, because Britney Spears sells more records than Marilyn Manson. You know there's been a resurgence of young pop music. B*Witched and the Dixie Chicks and Britney Spears and 'N Sync. I mean, these artists are selling a hell of a lot more records than Marilyn Manson.

Alter: Do you think that kids have kind of gotten that message and are less interested in gratuitously violent lyrics than they used to be? Because they've seen so much death, either in their own neighborhoods or on TV?

Rosen: Well, there's no question that what used to be known as gangsta rap is definitely played out. Rap is much more light-hearted. It's about getting money and getting women. The music has evolved.

Alter: Why is that?   30

Rosen: Well, this might be controversial, but I'm actually one of those people who believes that young people are a lot more positive about the world today than most of the media is giving them credit for in the last couple of weeks. Surveys have shown that young people are more optimistic about their future, they're more positive, they're more connected to their parents than they have been in generations. And these all speak to really good, positive things.

Alter: Marshall, what do you think are some of Hollywood's responsibilities in this area?

Herskovitz: I think we now have virtual reality available to people that is nihilistic, anarchic and violent. And it is possible for a person to so completely live in that virtual reality that they come to confuse it for the real world around them.

Alter: But you know from firsthand experience that violence sells.

Herskovitz: "Legends of the Fall" was a very violent movie. I think violence   35
has a potentially strong part in any artistic venture. It's not something I would ever want to talk about legislatively. I would like to talk about it in terms of individual responsibility, yes.

Alter: So where should the thoughtful consumer of all of this draw the line between gratuitous violence and necessary violence for dramatic purposes?

Herskovitz: Oh, I think that's the point. The thoughtful consumers feel it in their gut. I think the problem in this culture is that thoughtful consumers are not particularly influencing their children.

Alter: But isn't it a little too easy to just say it's all the parent's responsibility?

Valenti: Well, I don't think the movie industry can stand *in loco parentis.* Over 30 years ago I put in place a movie-rating system, voluntary, which gives advanced cautionary warnings to parents so that parents can make their own judgments about what movies they want their children to see.

Alter: I think what a lot of parents wonder is, why is it that NC-17 is not   40
applied to gratuitously violent movies?

Valenti: Well, it's because the definition of "gratuitous" is shrouded in subjectivity. There is no way to write down rules. I think Marshall can tell you that creative people can shoot a violent scene a hundred different ways. Sex and language are different, because there are few ways that you can couple on the screen that—there's only a few. And language is language. It's there or it isn't. But violence is far more difficult to pin down. It's like picking up mercury with a fork.

Alter: A movie director told me recently that he went to see "The Matrix," and there was a 5-year-old at the film with his mother. Isn't that a form of child abuse?

Valenti: If a parent says he wants his 5-year-old to be with him, who is to tell this parent he can't do it? Who is to tell him?

Alter: But if it was NC-17, that 5-year-old wouldn't be allowed to go, right?

Valenti: Well, that's right.   45

Alter: So why allow them in when it's R?

Valenti: Because the way our system is defined, we think there's a dividing line.

Alter: When parents aren't doing their job properly, where does the responsibility of everybody else begin?

LaPierre: I was talking with John Douglas, the FBI's criminal profiler. And he said, "Wayne, never underestimate the fact that there are some people that are just evil." And that includes young people. We go searching for solutions, and yet some people are just plain bad apples. You look around the country—the cities that are making progress across the board are really combining prevention and working with young people when you get the first warning signs. And making sure they find mentors. Making sure they're put into programs. And they're combining that with very, very tough enforcement of things like the gun laws.

Herskovitz: I have a fear that modern society, and in particular television,   50
may be beyond the ability of parents to really control. I think movies are different, because the kid has to go out of the house and go there. TV is a particular problem because it's in the house.

Alter: But Marshall, maybe that's because the values that are being propagated by the media, broadly speaking, are so much more powerful that parents can't compete as easily as they used to.

Herskovitz: I don't believe that. I accept a lot of responsibility for the picture the media create of the world. But I don't think there's a conflict between that and the responsibility of parents to simply sit down and talk with their children. Most violent crime is committed by males. Young men are not being educated in the values of masculinity by their fathers.

Alter: So why then let all of these boys see scenes of gratuitous violence that don't convey human values to them?

Valenti: There are only three places where a child learns what Marshall was talking about, values. You learn them in the church. You learn them in school. And you learn them at home. And if you don't have these moral shields built in you by the time you're 10 or 12 years old, forget it.

Alter: I'm not sure that people in Hollywood are thinking, "Is what we do   55
part of the solution on this values question, or does it just contribute to the problem?"

Herskovitz: The answer is the people who aren't contributing to the problem are thinking about it a lot, and the people who are contributing to the problem are not thinking about it.

Valenti: Well, how does *Newsweek* then condone its putting on the cover of your magazine Monica Lewinsky? What kind of a value system does that convey?

Alter: Well, that's a separate discussion.

Valenti: Oh, I don't think it is.

Alter: Well, let me say this. We very explicitly did not put Dylan Klebold   60
and Eric Harris on our cover the first week. We're wrong in these judgments sometimes, but we do at least try to think about the consequences of what we put out there, instead of just saying it's up to the parents. That seems to me a cop-out.

Lowenstein: What you're looking for is an elimination of any problematic content.

Alter: No, I'm not. I'm looking for a sense of shame and a sense of responsibility. I'm wondering where it is in all of the industries that we have represented here today.

Herskovitz: Most people, especially in electronic journalism, don't think at all about this, and their role is incredibly destructive, just like most people in the movie and television business don't think at all about this. And their role is destructive. I think there's a great need for shame. Most people I know and speak to are very ashamed, but unfortunately they're not the people who make violent movies.

Analysis of "Moving beyond the Blame Game"

It's obvious that the *Newsweek* excerpts are not part of a natural, spontaneous conversation, the sort of thing we might have with friends around a campfire or at a bar after work. It's been *arranged*. The participants didn't just happen to come together some place and start talking; they were invited. Furthermore, they knew why they were invited — each represents a group or industry implicated in teen violence. Even Jonah Green, the fifteen-year-old, is cast (that's the right word) as "youth," as if one young person could stand for all young people. Each participant knew his or her role in advance, then, and what was at stake. Except perhaps for Jonah Green, each had an agenda and an interest in protecting their reputations and the public image of their businesses and organizations. Therefore, unlike the conversations in which we ask you to engage, theirs from the start was something less than an open-minded search for truth. In a genuine dialogue, people do not attack each other or become defensive.

In addition to its adversarial tone, this discussion falls short of good inquiry because it lacks depth. It is an extreme example of what tends to go wrong with *all* discussions, including class discussions. In the classroom, the teacher plays Alter's role, trying to get students to talk. When a question is greeted by silence from the class, sometimes teachers do what Alter does: solicit opinions by addressing questions to individuals, who then have no choice but to answer. Often the instructor is happy to get any opinion just to get things going. Once the ice is broken, students usually join in. It can be stimulating just to hear what everybody else is thinking. Before long, we're caught up in the discussion and don't perceive what it is: a superficial exchange of opinions, like the *Newsweek* example. Much is said, but almost nothing is *examined, pursued, genuinely explored.*

Exactly what do we mean? Look at the first few exchanges in the *Newsweek* example. Alter addresses Jonah Green, the fifteen-year-old high school student, who had apparently talked enough previously to reveal an opinion. Alter summarizes that opinion: "There's a lot of scapegoating going on." Green himself immediately offers two more intelligent observations, better than anything we get from the adult participants: "There's no one simple answer to teen violence" and "we should be focusing on solutions" rather than on blame.

These statements merit attention. But what happens? Alter must get the others into the discussion, so he turns to LaPierre and asks if better gun control might be part of the solution. *The secret of a good discussion is not to allow intelligent comments to go unquestioned.* Imagine, for example, what the following line of questioning might lead to. ("Q" stands for "questioner," who could be anyone involved in the discussion.)

> Green: There's a lot of scapegoating going on.
>
> Q: What do you mean by "scapegoating"?
>
> Green: A scapegoat is someone who gets blamed or punished for doing something everyone is guilty of or responsible for.
>
> Q: So you're saying that youth violence is a collective problem that everyone contributes to in one way or another. Is that right?
>
> Green: Yes.

Now that we know what Green's assertion actually means, we can really discuss it, look for whatever truth it may convey. Are we *all* really implicated in youth violence? How exactly? If we are, what can each of us do?

We handle Green's comment about looking for solutions the same way. All we need to ask is, What might be part of the solution? It would be interesting to hear Jonathan's ideas. Maybe he has an idea how high schools could build more community or how parents could get involved. But no—the conversation moves in a new direction.

Our intent is not to put down conversation. Exchanging opinions is one of the great pleasures of social life. For inquiry, however, we need genuine dialogue.

To help your conversations become dialogue, we offer "Questions for Inquiry" on pages 159–160. These same questions will help you inquire into

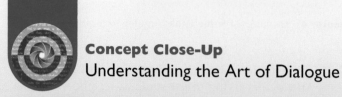

Concept Close-Up
Understanding the Art of Dialogue

To be useful for inquiry, conversations must become dialogues. They become dialogues when someone questions, in a nonhostile way, what someone else has said. Only then are we really discussing something, not just stating our opinion and talking for talking's sake.

written texts, such as the sources encountered in research. Most of the questions on this list can be traced to the origins of dialogue in ancient Greece and have demonstrated their value for about 2,500 years. Commit the list to memory, and practice asking these questions until they become second nature.

Following Through

Mark up the *Newsweek* dialogue. Use the "Questions for Inquiry" to probe the participants' comments. For example, one question suggests that you inquire about analogies and comparisons. You might ask Jonah if Edgar Allen Poe's "darkness" is truly comparable to the creations of Marilyn Manson. Aren't there some significant differences in the context in which these art forms present violence? Be ready to point out places where the discussants failed to answer questions directly or where you would have posed a good question if you had been there. Note places where the discussion moved toward dialogue and where it moved toward mere venting of opinion. Does Alter do a good job as moderator, or is he mainly concerned with going broader rather than deeper? Be ready to discuss your annotations in class.

Step 5: Engaging in a Dialogue about Your Initial Opinions

Earlier, you wrote Part 1 of your exploratory essay, a statement of your initial opinions. A good way to begin exploration is with what you said in Part 1. Exchanging these initial statements with a classmate and then asking each other questions will get you thinking more deeply about what you already believe.

Read the example on p. 160, which shows one student's first thoughts and the dialogue that he and another student had. These students used a software program that allowed them to record their conversation, and what follows is a transcript of a real-time chat. They had printouts of each other's initial opinions in front of them as they took turns being each other's friendly questioner. First, read Matt's initial thoughts and then the dialogue he had with Lauren, whose own first thoughts we reproduced earlier. Note where the dialogue seems to be a conversation and where Lauren attempts to make it an inquiry. Where does it succeed as inquiry, and where does it not?

1. *Ask if you have understood the arguer's position on the issue.* The best way to do this is to restate, paraphrase, or summarize the thesis. (Face-to-face, you might say, "I believe that you are saying . . . Am I understanding you?") Be sure to note how strongly the claim is made. If you are inquiring into your own argument, ask if you have stated your own position clearly. Do you need to qualify it in any way?

2. *Ask about the meaning of any words central to the argument.* You can do this at any point in a conversation and as often as it seems necessary. When dealing with a written text, try to discern the meaning from the context. For instance, if an author's case depends on the fairness of a proposed solution, you'll need to ask what "fair" means, because the word has a range of possible applications. You might ask, "Fair to whom?"

3. *Ask what reasons support the thesis.* Paraphrasing reasons is a good way to open up a conversation to further questions about assumptions, values, and definitions.

4. *Ask about the assumptions on which the thesis and reasons are based.* Most arguments are based on one or more unstated assumptions. For example, if a college recruiter argues that the school he or she represents is superior to most others (thesis) because its ratio of students to teachers is low (reason), the unstated assumptions are (1) that students there will get more attention and (2) that more attention results in a better education. As you inquire into an argument, note the assumptions, and ask if they are reasonable.

5. *Ask about the values expressed or implied by the argument.* For example, if you argue that closing a forest to logging operations is essential even at the cost of dozens of jobs, you are valuing environmental preservation over the livelihoods of the workers who must search for other jobs.

6. *Ask how well the reasons are supported.* Are they offered as opinions only, or are they supported with evidence? Is the evidence recent? sufficient? What kind of testimony is offered? Who are the authorities cited? What are their credentials and biases?

7. *Consider analogies and comparisons.* If the author makes an argument by analogy, does the comparison hold up? For example, advocates of animal rights draw an analogy with civil rights when they claim that just as we have come to recognize the immorality of exploiting human beings, so we should recognize the immorality of exploiting other species. But is this analogy sound?

8. *Ask about the arguer's biases and background.* What past experiences might have led the arguer to take this position? What does the holder

(continues)

of this position stand to gain? What might someone gain by challenging it?

9. *Ask about implications.* Where would the argument ultimately lead if we accept what the speaker advocates? For example, if someone contends that abortion is murder, asking about implications would lead to the question, Are you willing to put women who get abortions on trial for murder and, if they are convicted, to punish them as murderers are usually punished?

10. *Ask whether the argument takes opposing views into account.* If it does, are they presented fairly and clearly or with mockery and distortion? Does the author take them seriously or dismiss them? Are they effectively refuted?

STUDENT SAMPLE: *Example Dialogue for Analysis—Matt's Initial Opinions*

I think the issue of violence in the media is overdone. I believe that violence is a conscious act by people who are evil, not people motivated by what they have seen or heard in the media. Some people are violent, and they cannot be stopped from committing their crimes simply by censoring media violence. Violence is natural, an instinct all humans have, yet most restrain themselves from acting on their impulse. Though I have seen and heard my share of violence in the media, I am not a violent person. Sure, sometimes after watching a violent movie, I think about what it would be like to do some of that stuff, but I am not stupid enough to act out my curiosity.

STUDENT SAMPLE: *Example Dialogue between Matt and Lauren*

Lauren: You don't think there is any relation between violence and the entertainment industry?

Matt: Not really. I don't see how music could influence someone to the point of violence.

Lauren: I kind of agree with you, but I don't know. I think that sometimes it gives a person the mentality to do that kind of stuff when their friends are—when people are impressionable like that, they will do a lot of stupid things. When I was in high school, a group of kids I grew up with started getting into the whole "gangster" scene. They listened to rap talking about murder, drugs, and destruction. They murdered a fellow student at the McDonalds down the street from the school. Did the music make them do this? We'll never know, but they had to get the idea from somewhere.

Matt: What happened to the guys that killed that person?

Lauren: They are all in jail now. Only one has gone to trial.

Matt: That's crazy. I listened to all kinds of music, and I am not violent.

Lauren: You can't assume everyone is like you. How do you explain kids doing the kind of stuff they are doing?

Matt: There are just some violent, evil people. They just aren't right, if you know what I mean.

Lauren: Do you mean they are crazy?

Matt: Yes, they're crazy.

Lauren: I think you said violence is an act of nature. Does that mean we are born violent? Is it normal to be violent?

Matt: I think everyone has a violent side, but they act on it in different ways. I go play sports or work out to get rid of the aggression.

Lauren: But is violence the same thing as evil? Or aggression? Those kids at my school were evil, not natural. I think you need to think more about what you mean by violent when you say it's natural. Maybe it's natural for animals to have aggression and to attack and kill to stay alive, but is that evil? When you say people are "just not right," do you mean that they are natural or not natural?

Matt: Okay, I think we are born violent, but some of us are also born evil.

Lauren: So, are you saying that nothing good could change these people for the better, like having a good family or going to church? Are they just how they were born?

Matt: I'd have to think about that. They could maybe be taught.

Lauren: Well, I'm just saying, if they can be influenced for the better, why not for the worse—that the media could influence them to be worse?

Matt: I don't know.

Lauren: What about real life? When the media pays too much attention to one issue, like the school shooting in Columbine, do you think it makes other people want to do the same thing?

Matt: I don't know. A good friend of mine got kicked out of school for calling in a bomb threat. He probably wouldn't have done that if all that hadn't been on the news.

Following Through

Look at Matt's initial opinion statement on page 160. Use the "Questions for Inquiry" (pages 159–160) to suggest questions you would have asked him if you had been his partner.

Following Through

Writing should be a rhythm between "drawing in"—the solo act of composing—and "reaching out" through dialogues during every phase of the composing process.

Exchange initial opinion statements with a classmate. Take turns asking each other questions based on the "Questions for Inquiry" on pages 159–160. Explore one person's thinking at a time. After twenty minutes, trade roles. If you do not have a software program that allows you to make a transcript of the discussion, tape it, or simply take notes after each questioning session. Be ready to report on how the dialogue clarified or modified your thinking. What did the dialogue make you realize you need to think and read about more?

We should never think of dialogue as something unrelated to writing. Dialogue can help us write better. The notes and written records of dialogues will provide material for your paper, so save them as we turn to the next step, reading about the topic.

Step 6: Engaging in Dialogue with a Reading

Inquiry into a text begins with a critical reading of it, including attention to its rhetorical context, as discussed in Chapter 2 (pages 22–23). Sample the text quickly to see if it is worth your attention. If it is, read it thoroughly and mark it up, noting its subdivisions and case structure—that is, mark claims and note evidence.

What we have just discussed about turning conversation into dialogue also applies to reading, but obviously conversations and written arguments can't be approached the same way.

In conversations, we mostly encounter simple statements of opinion. People say what they think without much explanation or support unless someone asks for it. In contrast, writers *argue* their opinions. That is, a written piece typically contains a *thesis* or *claim*. That claim is *explained* and justified or defended with reasons backed up by evidence. A text must stand on its own—a writer cannot respond to a reader's questions. Instead, *the writer must anticipate the questions an alert, critical reader will have and answer them in advance.*

Consequently, whereas in conversation we can question simple statements of opinion as they occur, with written arguments we question *entire cases*. We need to use "Questions for Inquiry" (pages 159–160), which lead us to question all parts of a case. We should also note whether opposing views appear in the argument and how the author handles them.

Example Dialogue with a Reading

As an example of how to engage in dialogue with a written text, let's work with "Hollow Claims about Fantasy Violence," by Richard Rhodes, which appeared September 17, 2000, in the *New York Times*. Rhodes has won awards for his books on the making of the atomic and hydrogen bombs. This essay appeared after the publication of *Why They Kill*, based on interviews with convicted murderers.

Hollow Claims about Fantasy Violence
Richard Rhodes

The moral entrepreneurs are at it again, pounding the entertainment industry for advertising its Grand Guignolesque confections to children. If exposure to this mock violence contributes to the development of violent behavior, then our political leadership is justified in its indignation at what the Federal Trade Commission has reported about the marketing of violent fare to children. Senators John McCain and Joseph Lieberman have been especially quick to fasten on the F.T.C. report as they make an issue of violent offerings to children.

But is there really a link between entertainment and violent behavior?

The American Medical Association, the American Psychological Association, the American Academy of Pediatrics and the National Institute of Mental Health all say yes. They base their claims on social science research that has been sharply criticized and disputed within the social science profession, especially outside the United States. In fact, no direct, causal link between exposure to mock violence in the media and subsequent violent behavior has ever been demonstrated, and the few claims of modest correlation have been contradicted by other findings, sometimes in the same studies.

History alone should call such a link into question. Private violence has been declining in the West since the media-barren late Middle Ages, when homicide rates are estimated to have been 10 times what they are in Western nations today. Historians attribute the decline to improving social controls over violence—police forces and common access to courts of law—and to a shift away from brutal physical punishment in child-rearing (a practice that still appears as a common factor in the background of violent criminals today).

The American Medical Association has based its endorsement of the   5
media violence theory in major part on the studies of Brandon Centerwall,
a psychiatrist in Seattle. Dr. Centerwall compared the murder rates for
whites in three countries from 1945 to 1974 with numbers for television
set ownership. Until 1975, television broadcasting was banned in South
Africa, and "white homicide rates remained stable" there, Dr. Centerwall
found, while corresponding rates in Canada and the United States doubled
after television was introduced.

A spectacular finding, but it is meaningless. As Franklin E. Zimring and
Gordon Hawkins of the University of California at Berkeley subsequently
pointed out, homicide rates in France, Germany, Italy and Japan either
failed to change with increasing television ownership in the same period or
actually declined, and American homicide rates have more recently been
sharply declining despite a proliferation of popular media outlets—not
only movies and television, but also video games and the Internet.

Other social science that supposedly undergirds the theory, too, is marginal and problematic. Laboratory studies that expose children to selected
incidents of televised mock violence and then assess changes in the children's behavior have sometimes found more "aggressive" behavior after the
exposure—usually verbal, occasionally physical.

But sometimes the control group, shown incidents judged not to be
violent, behaves more aggressively afterward than the test group; sometimes
comedy produces the more aggressive behavior; and sometimes there's no
change. The only obvious conclusion is that sitting and watching television
stimulates subsequent physical activity. Any kid could tell you that.

As for those who claim that entertainment promotes violent behavior
by desensitizing people to violence, the British scholar Martin Barker offers
this critique: "Their claim is that the materials they judge to be harmful can
only influence us by trying to make us be the same as them. So horrible
things will make us horrible—not horrified. Terrifying things will make us
terrifying—not terrified. To see something aggressive makes us feel aggressive—not aggressed against. This idea is so odd, it is hard to know where to
begin in challenging it."

Even more influential on national policy has been a 22-year study by   10
two University of Michigan psychologists, Leonard D. Eron and L. Rowell
Huesmann, of boys exposed to so-called violent media. The Telecommunications Act of 1996, which mandated the television V-chip, allowing
parents to screen out unwanted programming, invoked these findings,
asserting, "Studies have shown that children exposed to violent video programming at a young age have a higher tendency for violent and aggressive
behavior later in life than children not so exposed."

Well, not exactly. Following 875 children in upstate New York from
third grade through high school, the psychologists found a correlation between a preference for violent television at age 8 and aggressiveness at age
18. The correlation—0.31—would mean television accounted for about

10 percent of the influences that led to this behavior. But the correlation only turned up in one of three measures of aggression: the assessment of students by their peers. It didn't show up in students' reports about themselves or in psychological testing. And for girls, there was no correlation at all.

Despite the lack of evidence, politicians can't resist blaming the media for violence. They can stake out the moral high ground confident that the First Amendment will protect them from having to actually write legislation that would be likely to alienate the entertainment industry. Some use the issue as a smokescreen to avoid having to confront gun control.

But violence isn't learned from mock violence. There is good evidence—causal evidence, not correlational—that it's learned in personal violent encounters, beginning with the brutalization of children by their parents or their peers.

The money spent on all the social science research I've described was diverted from the National Institute of Mental Health budget by reducing support for the construction of community mental health centers. To this day there is no standardized reporting system for emergency-room findings of physical child abuse. Violence is on the decline in America, but if we want to reduce it even further, protecting children from real violence in their real lives—not the pale shadow of mock violence—is the place to begin.

Inquiring into sources presents a special challenge: to overcome the authority the source projects. When ideas are in print, we tend to accept them uncritically, especially when they support our own opinion. If the argument appears in a leading newspaper like the *New York Times*, the piece can seem to have such authority that people just quote it and don't bother to assess it critically, especially when the author is as respected as Rhodes. We think, Who am I to question what he says? After all, I've gone to him to find out about fantasy violence. Shouldn't I just accept what he says, at least until I read other sources that oppose his view?

Our earlier chapters on reading and analyzing an argument show how we can overcome this natural tendency to be passive when we encounter an authoritative text. It's true that we are only inquirers, not experts, and so we cannot question Rhodes as another expert might. But we are hardly powerless. We can put into practice the critical-reading habits and skills discussed in Chapter 2. And we can use the "Questions for Inquiry" on pages 159–160 to open an argument to scrutiny.

A Dialogue with Rhodes

Looking at the "Questions for Inquiry," note that some seem perfect entry points into Rhodes's argument. We have no problems understanding his claim, but we might ask about the second item on our list, "the meaning of any words central to the argument." How does Rhodes define "violence"?

In the fourth, fifth, and sixth paragraphs, he refers to declining homicide rates despite proliferating media violence. But when we think of violence today, we think not only of homicide but also of date rape, domestic violence, bullying, and even road rage.

Following Through

After sampling Rhodes's essay and reading it through, mark it up. What are the introduction and the conclusion? Are there any other subsections besides the presentation of the reasoning? Do you see the claim, reasons, and evidence? (See Chapter 3, "Analyzing Arguments," pages 45–58.) Mark and annotate them. How does Rhodes handle opposing views? Finally, use the "Questions for Inquiry" on pages 159–160. Make marginal annotations in response to Rhodes, and compare them with our discussion of the argument's strengths and weaknesses, pages 165–167.

Following Through

If you are working on a different topic, find an argument that addresses one of the topic's central issues. Do it as we have done it with Rhodes.

We could also question the thinking of one of Rhodes's sources, Martin Barker, who says it is "odd" to assume that watching "horrible things will make us horrible—not horrified." There are many depictions of violent acts shown in the media, and some glorify violence or make it seem funny. Barker's language oversimplifies the problem.

We might also ask the sixth question for inquiry, about evidence. In the third paragraph, Rhodes acknowledges that the American Medical Association, the American Psychological Association, the American Academy of Pediatrics, and the National Institute of Mental Health all affirm "a link between entertainment and violent behavior." Much of the rest of the article is an effort to undermine the science that claims to establish such a link. Is it likely that the AMA, APA, and the other institutions mentioned are *all* wrong? Is it likely that the AMA based its opinion "in major part" on only *one* study of fantasy violence, as Rhodes claims in paragraph 5? Neither seems very likely. We should be suspicious enough to visit one of the Web sites for these organizations to find out more about the basis of their opinion.

And we might question an assumption Rhodes makes, using question 4 as our inspiration. When he says that the rates of television ownership rose in France, Germany, Italy, and Japan while homicide rates did not change, is he assuming that the same shows were broadcast in these countries as in the United States and Canada, where homicide rates doubled? He seems to assume that the technology rather than the programs is an appropriate basis for comparison.

Finally, we might question Rhodes's assumption that if one thing is not necessary for another thing to happen, it therefore cannot be a factor at all. For example, cell phone use is not necessary for a car wreck to occur. However, cell phone use does *contribute* to automobile accidents. Rhodes claims that "violence isn't learned from mock violence. There is good evidence — causal evidence, not correlational — that it's learned in personal violent encounters, beginning with the brutalization of children by their parents or their peers." Does anyone doubt that real violence in children's lives contributes more than fantasy violence to aggressive behavior? Of course not. But that doesn't mean that fantasy violence contributes *nothing*. We can't dismiss something altogether just because something else contributes more.

Following Through

If you are inquiring into a topic of your own, use the "Questions for Inquiry" to open it up, as we have with Rhodes's essay. Do not try to pose all possible questions; find those that point to areas of weakness in the argument.

Another Example of Dialogue with a Reading

Let's also examine a book on violent entertainment, Sissela Bok's *Mayhem* (1998). Following is a chapter in which Bok assesses various ways to resist the effects of media violence. The chapter is especially interesting because it focuses on what children can do "to think for themselves and to become discriminating viewers."

Sissela Bok is professor of philosophy at Brandeis University.

Media Literacy
Sissela Bok

How can children learn to take a more active and self-protective part in evaluating what they see? For an example of such learning, consider a class of second-graders in Oregon that Peter Jennings introduced on ABC's evening news in March 1995. With the help of their teacher, these children had arranged to study the role that television violence played in their lives: now they were presenting their "Declaration of Independence from Violence" to the rest of the student body. Their assignment had been to watch half an hour of television at home for several days running and to count the incidents of violence in each one — kicking, shooting, bombarding, killing. To their amazement, they had found nearly one such incident a minute in the programs they watched. The media mayhem they had taken for granted as part of their daily lives was suddenly put in question. One girl acknowledged that "before, I didn't even know what violence was."

The children then discussed the role of media violence in their own lives and concluded that what they saw on TV did affect them. Together, they considered different types of responses, often also discussing these choices in their homes. In their "Declaration of Independence from Violence," they addressed not only their school but the county board of education and community service organizations. Some pledged to limit their intake of violent programming and to refuse to watch certain shows; others wrote letters to television stations; a few organized a boycott of the products advertised on the programs they considered most violent.

These children were learning the rudiments of critical judgment and experiencing the pleasure of thinking for themselves about the messages beamed at them by advertisers and programmers. They were beginning to draw distinctions with respect to types of violence and their effects and to consider what might lie in their power to do in response. Throughout, they were learning to make active use of the media, including having their own initiative beamed to millions via the Jennings broadcast.

In so doing, the second-graders were participating in what has come to be called "media literacy education."[1] The media literacy movement, begun in Australia in the 1980s, views all media as offering scope for participants to learn not to submit passively to whatever comes along, but instead to examine offerings critically while recognizing the financial stakes of programmers and sponsors, to make informed personal and group choices, and to balance their own TV intake with participation in other activities. The hope is that children who become able to take such an approach will be more self-reliant, more informed, and correspondingly less fearful and passive, when it comes to their use of modern media. And since few adults have acquired critical viewing skills, such education is important at all ages.

Maturing, learning how to understand and deal with violence, coping   5
better with its presence on the screen as in the world, knowing its effects, and countering them to the extent possible involves exploring distinctions such as the following:

- between physical violence and psychological and other forms of violence
- between actual and threatened violence
- between direct and indirect violence
- between active violence and violence made possible by neglect or inaction
- between unwanted violence and, say, surgery, performed with consent
- between violence done to oneself and that done to others
- between seeing real violence and witnessing it on the screen

- between portrayals of "real" and fictional violence
- between violence conveyed as information and as entertainment
- between levels of violence in the media and in real life
- between oneself as viewer and as advertising or programming target
- between gratuitous portrayals of violence and others
- between violence glamorized or not

Learning to deal with violence involves sorting out such distinctions and categories and seeking to perceive when they overlap and interact and shade into one another. It is as inaccurate to view all these distinctions as utterly blurred as to imagine each category in a watertight compartment. Exploring these distinctions and their interactions is facilitated by talking them over with others and by seeing them illuminated, first in the simplest stories and pictures, later in literature and works of art.

Because the approach must be gradual and attuned to children's developmental stage, a film such as Steven Spielberg's *Schindler's List,* which offers searing insight into most of the distinctions listed above, is inappropriate for small children, who have not learned to make the necessary distinctions.[2] If they are exposed to such a film before they have learned to draw even rudimentary distinctions with respect to violence, they can respond with terror, numbing, sometimes even misplaced glee. As far as they are concerned, it is beside the point whether the horrors the film conveys are gratuitous or not, real or fictional, or meant as entertainment or not. They cannot tell the difference and should not be exposed to such material before they can do so. The film can be misunderstood, too, by those who would ordinarily be old enough to perceive such distinctions but whose capacity to respond to them has been thwarted or numbed, through personal experience, perhaps from violence in the home, or through overexposure to entertainment violence. The half-embarrassed, half-riotous laughter with which some high school audiences greeted the film troubled many: it was as if these students had lost their ability to make even the most basic distinctions.

A number of these distinctions are hard even for the most experienced media critics to pin down. Take the concept of "gratuitous" violence, violence not needed for purposes of the story being told but added for its shock or entertainment value. Some regard it as a characterization primarily in the eye of the beholder, while others insist that it can be clearly identified in particular films and television programs. Whatever the answer, there are borderline cases of violence where it is hard for anyone to be sure whether it is gratuitous or not. Works such as Spielberg's *Schindler's List* show instances of extreme cruelty that are necessary to convey the horror and inhumanity of the work's subject, and are thus not gratuitous in their own right; yet that film also explores how gratuitous violence is inflicted, even enjoyed, by its perpetrators. The film is about gratuitous violence, then, without in any sense exploiting it or representing an instance of it; and it is emphatically not meant as entertainment violence. Perhaps this is part of what Spielberg meant in saying that he made the film "thinking that if it did entertain, then I would have failed. It was important to me not to set out to please. Because I always had."[3]

Long before callous or uncomprehending ways of responding become ingrained, children can learn, much as the second-graders in the Jennings program were learning, to play a greater part in sorting out the distinctions regarding violence and media violence and to consider how they wish to respond. They can learn to think for themselves and to become discriminating viewers and active participants, rather than passive consumers of the entertainment violence beamed at them daily. Such learning helps, in turn, with the larger goal of achieving resilience — the ability to bounce back, to resist and overcome adversity.

Just as "Buyer beware" is an indispensable motto in today's media environment but far from sufficient, so is a fuller understanding of the role of violence in public entertainment. Individuals, families, and schools can do a great deal; but unless they can join in broader endeavors devoted to enhancing collective resilience, the many admirable personal efforts now under way will not begin to suffice. When neither families nor schools, churches, and neighborhoods can cope alone, what is the larger social responsibility? 10

Notes

1. See Neil Anderson, *Media Works* (Oxford: Oxford University Press, 1989); and Madeline Levine, *Viewing Violence* (New York: Doubleday, 1996).

2. When *Schindler's List* was about to be broadcast on television, Spielberg was quoted as saying that the film was not, in his opinion, one that should be shown to the very young. His own children, of elementary school age, had not seen it in 1997; but he would want them to once they were of high school age. See Caryn James, "Bringing Home the Horror of the Holocaust," *New York Times*, February 23, 1997, p. 36 H.

3. Steven Spielberg, quoted by Stephen Schiff in "Seriously Spielberg," *New Yorker*, March 21, 1994, p. 101.

Possibilities for Dialogue with "Media Literacy"

There's no one right way to have a dialogue, just as there's no magic question that will always unlock the text in front of us. But it's a good idea to begin with the question *What exactly is the arguer's position?* It's clear that Bok favors "media literacy education." She advocates it, but as only part of the solution to children's exposure to media violence. Her last paragraph implies that we will need other measures as well. And so we might ask, "Why is media education not the only solution?" or "Why isn't media education enough?" Can we tell what she thinks the limitations are?

Having begun with the position question, where we go from there *depends on the nature of the text*. In this case, we need to ask question 2, *What do certain key terms mean?* Paragraph 5 is about the kind of distinctions necessary to a mature understanding of violence. But are we sure about the distinctions? What is "psychological violence"? Bok doesn't say. How would we answer? If there are both physical and psychological forms of violence, what other forms are there? Again, Bok provides no explanation or examples. Can we? It's far from clear what she means. We must figure this out ourselves or work through these distinctions in class discussion.

We should also ask about assumptions and implications. Bok admits that "[a] number of these distinctions are hard even for the most experienced media critics to pin down" (paragraph 8). As adults and college students, we're certainly having our troubles with them; how can we assume that the second-graders referred to in the first paragraph can make them? Do they really understand whatever distinctions their teacher is helping them to make?

Once we question what the argument assumes—that young children (about seven or eight years old) can make meaningful distinctions and understand them—we begin to wonder about implications as well. For instance, the students present what they call a "Declaration of Independence from Violence" to "the rest of the student body." Does the declaration imply that violence is *not* part of the human condition? Are we ignoring reality or learning how to cope with it? More broadly, Bok's discussion implies that media education must continue as students grow up. Is this practical? realistic? Is it something our schools can or should undertake?

 ## Following Through

In class discussion, continue the dialogue with "Media Literacy." What other questions are relevant from our list of "Questions for Inquiry"? What questions can we ask that do not appear on the list? Be sure to consider the rather unusual case of *Schindler's List*. Why might high school students laugh at it? Is the *only* explanation the one that Bok offers, that the students didn't understand the horror of Nazi violence? Does a movie like *Schindler's List*, when audiences understand and react appropriately to it, help us in "achieving resilience—the ability to bounce back, to resist and overcome adversity"?

 ## Following Through

As prewriting for Part 2 of your exploratory essay, read one substantial argument on the topic. Write a brief summary of the argument, noting its claim and reasons. Then write a few paragraphs of response to it, as we have done with Rhodes's essay and Bok's chapter, showing how the "Questions for Inquiry" opened up that argument to closer inspection. How did the argument compare with your own initial opinions? Was your thinking changed in any way? Why or why not?

INQUIRY AGAIN: DIGGING DEEPER

Inquiry can always lead to more inquiry. For example, if, after reading Bok, we doubt that media literacy can work, we can find out more about it, including what went on in Australia in the 1980s. If we question what second-graders can understand about media violence, we can research the cognitive development of young children. If we aren't sure about the impact of *Schindler's List,* we can watch it ourselves and/or read about Spielberg's making of the film and the popular and critical reception of it. There's nothing important in "Media Literacy" that can't be researched and explored further. Digging deeper means getting more information. But mere quantity is not the goal. Moving deeper also means moving closer to genuine expertise. For example, Richard Rhodes is a journalist, not a social scientist. He consulted social scientists to write his argument. To evaluate Rhodes's claims we need to do the same. Digging deeper should take us closer to people who ought to know the most.

Digging deeper also means sharpening the focus of inquiry. As we said earlier, the narrow but deep inquiry will produce a better argument than a broad survey. Look for arguments and informative sources that address the same aspect of a topic. You may find two or more arguments that debate each other.

To find good sources, read the sections on finding and evaluating sources, pages 95–110. There are always resources for digging deeper into a question. Reference librarians can help. They are experts at finding the experts.

When should you stop digging deeper? You can tell when you're near the end of inquiry. You'll be reading but not finding much you haven't seen already. That's the time to stop—or find another avenue for further research.

Most important, *seek out some sources with points of view that differ from your own.* The whole point of inquiry is to seek the new and challenging. *Remember: We are not defending what we think but putting it to the test.*

 Following Through

> Read pages 95–110 on finding and evaluating sources. Using the library and electronic indexes available, find at least five good articles and arguments about your chosen issue. Be sure to find sources that contain a variety of opinions but that address the same issues. Read each carefully, and write notes and annotations based on the "Questions for Inquiry."

When the Experts Disagree

A professor once advised his classes, "If you want to think you know something about a subject, read one book, because reading a second will just confuse you." Some confusion is unavoidable in inquiry. Digging deeply will reveal sources that conflict. Instead of avoiding conflicting sources (the professor was mocking those who do), seek out conflict and analyze it. Decide which sources to accept, which to reject. We illustrate some strategies for dealing with conflict in the following exploration of two articles that assess the research linking fantasy violence to actual violence.

An Example of Experts Disagreeing

When we left Richard Rhodes, we still wondered, Does violent entertainment contribute to violence in our society? He made a good case against such a link, but we can't ignore all the experts he mentions who do take it seriously. Nor can we put aside the results of our own inquiry into the article, which gave us good reason to doubt his position. So we went to the social scientists themselves to see how they interpret the research. We located the following exchange from the *Harvard Mental Health Letter* (1996). Jonathan L. Freedman, a professor of psychology at the University of Toronto, argues much as Rhodes did—that there's no proof linking fantasy violence to actual violence. L. Rowell Huesmann, a professor of psychology at the University of Michigan, and his graduate assistant, Jessica Moise, defend the link, based in part on their own research.

Now we have conflicting arguments. Read the following articles and assess them on your own. Ask yourself, Who makes the better case?

Violence in the Mass Media and Violence in Society: The Link Is Unproven*

Jonathan L. Freedman

Imagine that the Food and Drug Administration (FDA) is presented with a series of studies testing the effectiveness of a new drug. There are some laboratory tests that produce fairly consistent positive effects, but the drug does not always work as expected and no attempt has been made to discover why. Most of the clinical tests are negative; there are also a few weak positive results and a few results suggesting that the drug is less effective than a placebo. Obviously the FDA would reject this application, yet the widely accepted evidence that watching television violence causes aggression is no more adequate.

In laboratory tests of this thesis, some children are shown violent programs, others are shown nonviolent programs, and their aggressiveness

---

*Jonathan L. Freedman, "Violence in the Mass Media and Violence in Society: The Link Is Unproven." Excerpted from the *Harvard Mental Health Letter*, May 1996, © 1996, President and Fellows of Harvard College. www.health.harvard.edu.

is measured immediately afterward. The results, although far from consistent, generally show some increase in aggression after a child watches a violent program. Like most laboratory studies of real-world conditions, however, these findings have limited value. In the first place, most of the studies have used dubious measures of aggression. In one experiment, for example, children were asked, "If I had a balloon, would you want me to prick it?" Other measures have been more plausible, but none is unimpeachable. Second, there is the problem of distinguishing effects of violence from effects of interest and excitement. In general, the violent films in these experiments are more arousing than the neutral films. Anyone who is aroused will display more of almost any behavior; there is nothing special about aggression in this respect. Finally and most important, these experiments are seriously contaminated by what psychologists call demand characteristics of the situation: the familiar fact that people try to do what the experimenter wants. Since the children know the experimenter has chosen the violent film, they may assume that they are being given permission to be aggressive.

PUTTING IT TO THE TEST

The simplest way to conduct a real-world study is to find out whether children who watch more violent television are also more aggressive. They are, but the correlations are small, accounting for only 1% to 10% of individual differences in children's aggressiveness. In any case, correlations do not prove causality. Boys watch more TV football than girls, and they play more football than girls, but no one, so far as I know, believes that television is what makes boys more interested in football. Probably personality characteristics that make children more aggressive also make them prefer violent television programs.

To control for the child's initial aggressiveness, some studies have measured children's TV viewing and their aggression at intervals of several years, using statistical techniques to judge the effect of early television viewing on later aggression. One such study found evidence of an effect, but most have found none.

For practical reasons, there have been only a few truly controlled experiments in which some children in a real-world environment are assigned to watch violent programs for a certain period of time and others are assigned to watch nonviolent programs. Two or three of these experiments indicated slight, short-lived effects of TV violence on aggression; one found a strong effect in the opposite of the expected direction, and most found no effect. All the positive results were obtained by a single research group, which conducted studies with very small numbers of children and used inappropriate statistics.

5

SCRUTINIZING THE EVIDENCE

An account of two studies will give some idea of how weak the research results are and how seriously they have been misinterpreted.

A study published by Lynette Friedrichs and Aletha Stein is often described (for example, in reports by the National Institute of Mental Health
and the American Psychological Association) as having found that children
who watched violent programs became more aggressive. What the study actually showed was quite different. In a first analysis the authors found that
TV violence had no effect on physical aggression, verbal aggression, aggressive fantasy, or object aggression (competition for a toy or other object).
Next they computed indexes statistically combining various kinds of aggression, a technique that greatly increases the likelihood of connections appearing purely by chance. Still they found nothing.

They then divided the children into two groups—those who were already aggressive and those who were not. They found that children originally lower in aggression seemed to become more aggressive and children
originally higher in aggression seemed to become less aggressive no matter
which type of program they watched. This is a well-known statistical artifact
called regression toward the mean, and it has no substantive significance.
Furthermore, the less aggressive children actually became more aggressive
after watching the neutral program than after watching the violent program.
The only comfort for the experimenters was that the level of aggression in
highly aggressive children fell more when they watched a neutral program
than when they watched a violent program. Somehow that was sufficient
for the study to be widely cited as strong evidence that TV violence causes
aggression.

An ambitious cross-national study was conducted by a team led by
Rowell Huesmann and Leonard Eron and reported in 1986. In this widely
cited research the effect of watching violent television on aggressiveness at a
later age was observed in seven groups of boys and seven groups of girls in
six countries. After controlling for initial aggressiveness, the researchers
found no statistically significant effect for either sex in Australia, Finland,
the Netherlands, Poland, or kibbutz children in Israel. The effect sought by
the investigators was found only in the United States and among urban Israeli children, and the latter effect was so large, so far beyond the normal
range for this kind of research and so incongruous with the results in other
countries, that it must be regarded with suspicion. Nevertheless, the senior
authors concluded that the pattern of results supported their position. The
Netherlands researchers disagreed; they acknowledged that they had not
been able to link TV violence to aggression, and they criticized the methods
used by some of the other groups. The senior authors refused to include
their chapter in the book that came out of the study, and they had to publish a separate report.

A SECOND LOOK

If the evidence is so inadequate, why have so many committees evaluating   10
it concluded that the link exists? In the first place, these committees have
been composed largely of people chosen with the expectation of reaching
that conclusion. Furthermore, committee members who were not already
familiar with the research could not possibly have read it all themselves,
and must have relied on what they were told by experts who were often biased. The reports of these committees are often seriously inadequate. The
National Institute of Mental Health, for example, conducted a huge study
but solicited only one review of the literature, from a strong advocate of the
view that television violence causes aggression. The review was sketchy—it
left out many important studies—and deeply flawed.

The belief that TV violence causes aggression has seemed plausible because it is intuitively obvious that this powerful medium has effects on children. After all, children imitate and learn from what they see. The question,
however, is what they see on television and what they learn. We know that
children tend to imitate actions that are rewarded and avoid actions that
are punished. In most violent television programs villains start the fight
and are punished. The programs also show heroes using violence to fight
violence, but the heroes almost always have special legal or moral authority; they are police, other government agents, or protectors of society like
Batman and the Power Rangers. If children are learning anything from
these programs, it is that the forces of good will overcome evil assailants
who are the first to use violence. That may be overoptimistic, but it hardly
encourages the children themselves to initiate aggression.

TELLING THE DIFFERENCE

Furthermore, these programs are fiction, and children know it as early as
the age of five. Children watching Power Rangers do not think they can
beam up to the command center, and children watching "Aladdin" do not
believe in flying carpets. Similarly, children watching the retaliatory violence of the heroes in these programs do not come to believe they themselves could successfully act in the same way. (Researchers concerned about
mass media violence should be more interested in the fights that occur during hockey and football games, which are real and therefore may be imi-
tated by children who play those sports.)

Recently I testified before a Senate committee, and one Senator told me
he knew TV made children aggressive because his own son had met him at
the door with a karate kick after watching the Power Rangers. The Senator
was confusing aggression with rough play, and imitation of specific actions
with learning to be aggressive. Children do imitate what they see on television; this has strong effects on the way they play, and it may also influence

the forms their real-life aggression takes. Children who watch the Ninja Turtles or Power Rangers may practice martial arts, just as years ago they might have been wielding toy guns, and long before that, wrestling or dueling with wooden swords. If there had been no television, the Senator's son might have butted him in the stomach or poked him in the ribs with a gun. The question is not whether the boy learned his karate kick from TV, but whether TV has made him more aggressive than he would have been otherwise.

Television is an easy target for the concern about violence in our society but a misleading one. We should no longer waste time worrying about this subject. Instead let us turn our attention to the obvious major causes of violence, which include poverty, racial conflict, drug abuse, and poor parenting.

Media Violence: A Demonstrated Public Health Threat to Children*

L. Rowell Huesmann and Jessica Moise

Imagine that the Surgeon General is presented with a series of studies on a widely distributed product. For 30 years well-controlled experiments have been showing that use of the product causes symptoms of a particular affliction. Many field surveys have shown that this affliction is always more common among people who use the product regularly. A smaller number of studies have examined the long-term effects of the product in different environments, and most have shown at least some evidence of harm, although it is difficult to disentangle effects of the product itself from the effects of factors that lead people to use it. Over all, the studies suggest that if a person with a 50% risk for the affliction uses the product, the risk rises to 60% or 70%. Furthermore, we have a fairly good understanding of how use of the product contributes to the affliction, which is persistent, difficult to cure, and sometimes lethal. The product is economically important, and its manufacturers spend large sums trying to disparage the scientific research. A few scientists who have never done any empirical work in the field regularly point out supposed flaws in the research and belittle its conclusions. The incidence of the affliction has increased dramatically since the product was first introduced. What should the Surgeon General do?

This description applies to the relationship between lung cancer and cigarettes. It also applies to the relationship between aggression and children's viewing of mass media violence. The Surgeon General has rightly come to the same conclusion in both cases and has issued similar warnings.

*L. Rowell Huesmann and Jessica Moise, "Media Violence: A Demonstrated Public Health Threat to Children." Excerpted from the *Harvard Mental Health Letter*, June 1996. Copyright © 1996 President and Fellows of Harvard College. www.health.harvard.edu.

CAUSE AND EFFECT

Dr. Freedman's highly selective reading of the research minimizes over-whelming evidence. First, there are the carefully controlled laboratory stud-ies in which children are exposed to violent film clips and short-term changes in their behavior are observed. More than 100 such studies over the last 40 years have shown that at least some children exposed to visual depictions of dramatic violence behave more aggressively afterward both toward inanimate objects and toward other children. These results have been found in many countries among boys and girls of all social classes, races, ages, and levels of intelligence.

Freedman claims that these studies use "dubious measures of aggres-sion." He cites only one example: asking children whether they would want the researcher to prick a balloon. But this measure is not at all representa-tive. Most studies have used such evidence as physical attacks on other chil-dren and dolls. In one typical study Kaj Bjorkqvist exposed five- and six-year-old Finnish children to either violent or non-violent films. Observers who did not know which kind of film each child had seen then watched them play together. Children who had just seen a violent film were more likely to hit other children, scream at them, threaten them, and intention-ally destroy their toys.

Freedman claims that these experiments confuse the effects of arousal 5
with the effects of violence. He argues that "anyone who is aroused will dis-play more of almost any behavior." But most studies have shown that pro-social behavior decreases after children view an aggressive film. Finally, Freedman says the experiments are contaminated by demand characteris-tics. In other words, the children are only doing what they think the re-searchers want them to do. That conclusion is extremely implausible, con-sidering the wide variety of experiments conducted in different countries by researchers with different points of view.

LARGE BODY OF EVIDENCE

More than 50 field studies over the last 20 years have also shown that chil-dren who habitually watch more media violence behave more aggressively and accept aggression more readily as a way to solve problems. The rela-tionship usually persists when researchers control for age, sex, social class, and previous level of aggression. Disbelievers often suggest that the correla-tion is statistically small. According to Freedman, it accounts for "only 1% to 10% of individual differences in children's aggressiveness." But an in-crease of that size (a more accurate figure would be 2% to 16%) has real so-cial significance. No single factor has been found to explain more than 16% of individual differences in aggression.

Of course, correlations do not prove causality. That is the purpose of laboratory experiments. The two approaches are complementary.

Experiments establish causal relationship, and field studies show that the relationship holds in a wide variety of real-world situations. The causal relationship is further confirmed by the finding that children who view TV violence at an early age are more likely to commit aggressive acts at a later age. In 1982 Eron and Huesmann found that boys who spent the most time viewing violent television shows at age eight were most likely to have criminal convictions at age 30. Most other long-term studies have come to similar conclusions, even after controlling for children's initial aggressiveness, social class, and education. A few studies have found no effect on some measures of violence, but almost all have found a significant effect on some measures.

Freedman singles out for criticism a study by Huesmann and his colleagues that was concluded in the late 1970s. He says we found "no statistically significant effect for either sex in Australia, Finland, the Netherlands, Poland, or kibbutz children in Israel." That is not true. We found that the television viewing habits of children [as] young as six or seven predicted subsequent increases in childhood aggression among boys in Finland and among both sexes in the United States, in Poland, and in Israeli cities. In Australia and on Israeli kibbutzim, television viewing habits were correlated with simultaneous aggression. Freedman also suggests that another study conducted in the Netherlands came to conclusions so different from ours that we banned it from a book we were writing. In fact, the results of that study were remarkably similar to our own, and we did not refuse to publish it. The Dutch researchers themselves chose to publish separately in a different format.

CULTURAL DIFFERENCES

Freedman argues that the strongest results reported in the study, such as those for Israeli city children, are so incongruous that they arouse suspicion. He is wrong. Given the influence of culture and social learning on aggressive behavior, different results in different cultures are to be expected. In fact, the similarity of the findings in different countries is remarkable here. One reason we found no connection between television violence viewing and aggression among children on [kib]butzim is the strong cultural prohibition against intra-group aggression in those communities. Another reason is that kibbutz children usually watched television in a group and discussed the shows with an adult caretaker afterward.

Two recently published meta-analyses summarize the findings of many   10
studies conducted over the past 30 years. In an analysis of 217 experiments and field studies, Paik and Comstock concluded that the association between exposure to television violence and aggressive behavior is extremely strong, especially in the data accumulated over the last 15 years. In the other meta-analysis, Wood, Wong, and Chachere came to the same conclusion after combined analysis of 23 studies of unstructured social interaction.

We now have well-validated theoretical explanations of these results. Exposure to media violence leads to aggression in at least five ways. The first is imitation, or observational learning. Children imitate the actions of their parents, other children, and media heroes, especially when the action is rewarded and the child admires and identifies with the model. When generalized, this process creates what are sometimes called cognitive scripts for complex social problem-solving: internalized programs that guide everyday social behavior in an automatic way and are highly resistant to change.

TURNING OFF

Second, media violence stimulates aggression by desensitizing children to the effects of violence. The more televised violence a child watches, the more acceptable aggressive behavior becomes for that child. Furthermore, children who watch violent television become suspicious and expect others to act violently—an attributional bias that promotes aggressive behavior.

Justification is a third process by which media violence stimulates aggression. A child who has behaved aggressively watches violent television shows to relieve guilt and justify the aggression. The child then feels less inhibited about aggressing again.

A fourth process is cognitive priming or cueing—the activation of existing aggressive thoughts, feelings, and behavior. This explains why children observe one kind of aggression on television and commit another kind of aggressive act afterward. Even an innocuous object that has been associated with aggression may later stimulate violence. Josephson demonstrated this . . . in a study of schoolboy hockey players. She subjected the boys to frustration and then showed them either a violent or a non-violent television program. The aggressor in the violent program carried a walkie-talkie. Later, when the referee in a hockey game carried a similar walkie-talkie, the boys who had seen the violent film were more likely to start fights during the game.

A NUMBING EFFECT

The fifth process by which media violence induces aggression is physiological arousal and desensitization. Boys who are heavy television watchers show lower than average physiological arousal in response to new scenes of violence. Similar short-term effects are found in laboratory studies. The arousal stimulated by viewing violence is unpleasant at first, but children who constantly watch violent television become habituated, and their emotional and physiological responses decline. Meanwhile the propensity to aggression is heightened by any pleasurable arousal, such as sexual feeling, that is associated with media violence.

15

Freedman argues that in violent TV shows, villains start the fight and are punished and the heroes "almost always have special legal or moral authority." Therefore, he concludes, children are learning from these programs that "the forces of good will overcome evil assailants." On the contrary, it is precisely because media heroes are admired and have special authority that children are likely to imitate their behavior and learn that aggression is an acceptable solution to conflict. Freedman also claims that media violence has little effect because children can distinguish real life from fiction. But children under 11 do not make this distinction very well. Studies have shown that many of them think cartoons and other fantasy shows depict life as it really is.

The studies are conclusive. The evidence leaves no room for doubt that exposure to media violence stimulates aggression. It is time to move on and consider how best to inoculate our children against this insidious threat.

Commentary on the Experts' Disagreement

When experts disagree, the rest of us can respond in only a few ways. We can throw up our hands and say, "Who knows?" But this response doesn't work because expert disagreement is so common. We'd have to give up on most issues. Another response is to take seriously only those experts who endorse the opinion we favor and ignore the rest, a common tactic in debate, legal pleadings, business, and politics whenever truth gives way to self-interest. We can also "go with our gut," opting for the opinion that "feels right." But gut feelings amount to little more than our prejudices talking. And so we are left with the only response appropriate to inquiry: *rational assessment of the competing arguments.* We should take as true the better or best case.

How can we decide which of two or several arguments is better or best?

In this instance, let's recognize that Huesmann and Moise have an advantage simply because they wrote second, after Freedman, who has no opportunity to respond to what they've said. Huesmann and Moise can *both* refute Freedman *and* make their own case without the possibility of rebuttal. Granting this it's still hard to find Freedman's case more convincing. Why?

We'll offer only a few reasons for assenting to the Huesmann–Moise argument. You and your class can take the analysis further—it's a good opportunity to practice critical reading and thinking.

Both articles begin with an analogy. Freedman compares the research on violent TV programs with the research required to approve a drug. Huesmann and Moise compare the research linking cigarettes to lung cancer with the research linking violent TV to aggressive behavior in children. The second comparison is better because the two instances of research compared are more nearly alike. Furthermore, the fact that the Surgeon General has issued warnings both for cigarettes and for violent entertainment's effect on children shows how seriously research on the latter is taken by qualified authorities. In fact, one of the more convincing aspects of the Huesmann–Moise case is the amount of support they claim for their position. They are specific about the numbers: "50 field studies over the last 20 years" (paragraph 6); "an analysis of 217 experiments and field studies" (paragraph 10)—all confirm their conclusion. If Freedman has evidence to rival this, he does not cite it. We must assume he doesn't because he doesn't have it.

Another strength of the Huesmann–Moise article is that they go beyond linking TV violence to aggression by offering five *explanations* for the negative impact of fantasy violence (paragraphs 11–15). We come away not only convinced that the link exists but also understanding why it exists. Freedman has no well-developed explanation to support his position. What he offers, such as the assertion that children know the difference between pretend and real violence, is refuted by Huesmann and Moise.

If you are thinking that the better or best case isn't always so easy to discern, you're right. Comparative assessment will not always yield a clearly superior case. We will sometimes argue with ourselves and others over whose case merits our support. Nonetheless, when we encounter opposing positions, we should set aside our prejudices and study the arguments made. We should resolve the conflict by taking the better or best case as the closest thing we have to the truth.

In most cases, the better or best argument will emerge as you think your way through the arguments, comparing their strengths and weaknesses. What's hard is to let go of a position we're attracted to when another one has the better case. *The real challenge of inquiry is to change or revise our own opinions as we encounter arguments stronger than our own.*

 Following Through

Even if they do not speak directly to each other, as our examples here do, find two sources that present conflicting data or information or conflicting interpretations of the same information. Write an evaluation of these arguments, telling which one has the better case. Explain why you think so. Did you find that comparing these arguments influenced your own thinking? If so, how?

THE WRITING PROJECT: PART 2

By now you have many notes that you can use as raw material for writing Part 2 of your essay. You have had a serious dialogue with at least one other person about your ideas. You should have notes about this dialogue and maybe a recording or transcript of it. Look over this material, and make more notes about how this conversation modified your ideas—by clarifying them, by presenting you with a new idea, or by solidifying a belief you already held.

You have also read several printed arguments. You have written evaluations of these arguments and marked them up. Now note places where they touch upon the same points. Use highlighters to color-code passages that connect across the readings. Draft paragraphs about what different experts have to say on the same question, including an estimate of how sound their points are and how they increased your own knowledge. Which viewpoints seemed most persuasive, and why?

You are ready to draft the body of your paper. It should contain at least four well-developed paragraphs that describe your inquiry. Discuss the conversations you had and the materials you read, and show how these lines of inquiry influenced your thinking. Assess the arguments you read, consider their rhetorical context, include the names of the authors and the biases they might have. Talk about why an author's argument was sound or not sound, why it influenced your initial opinion or why it did not.

Part 2 could be organized around a discussion of initial opinions strengthened by your research versus those reconsidered because of it. Did a source offer new information that caused you to reconsider what you thought? Tell what the information was, and explain why it's changed your outlook. Did you encounter a well-developed argument defending a position different from your own? How did you react? What aspects of the argument do you take seriously enough to modify or change your own opinion? Explain why. If you found sources who disagreed, which side did you find more convincing, and why?

Some paragraphs could be devoted to a single source. Others could compare an idea across two or more sources; you could point out ways in which they agree or disagree, showing how each contributed to changing your opinion.

No matter how you organize your paper, *be specific about what you have read.* You will need to quote and paraphrase; when you refer to sources, do so very specifically. See our advice about using sources on pages 111–114.

Don't merely summarize your sources or use them to support and illustrate your own argument. *You are evaluating the thinking expressed in the sources,* not making your own case.

Rhetorical context is vital and it should be part of your consideration of each source. *Be selective.* Your readers don't want to get bogged down in needless detail; they want the information that altered your understanding of the topic and the arguments that opened up new considerations. *The point is to show how your research-inquiry refined, modified, or changed your initial opinions and to explain why.* Anything that doesn't do this should be cut from the final draft of your paper.

THE WRITING PROJECT: PART 3

In preparation for writing the conclusion of your essay, reread Part 1, the overview of your exploration. Have you arrived at a claim you could defend in an essay to convince or persuade an audience? If so, what is it? Perhaps you're still unsure—what then? One option is to conclude your paper by explaining what you are unsure of and why, and what you'd like to learn from further research. An inconclusive but honest ending is better than a forced one making a claim you don't really believe.

Draft a conclusion in which you honestly discuss the results of your exploration, whatever they were. This section is about *where you stand now*, but it needn't be final or conclusive. If you have doubts, state them and indicate how you might resolve them through further research and inquiry.

AFTER DRAFTING YOUR ESSAY

Revise your draft to make sure each paragraph is unified around one point and to remove any unnecessary summarizing. Check your work against the guidelines for incorporating source material in your own writing (pages 111–114).

Edit your paper for wordiness, repetition, and excessive passive voice. See the suggestions for editing in the appendix (pages A1–A13).

Proofread your paper. Read it aloud to catch omissions and errors of grammar and punctuation.

STUDENT SAMPLE: *An Exploratory Essay*

EXPLORATORY ESSAY

Sydney Owens

Part 1

I think that the relationship between violence and the media is hard to define. There is definitely some relation between them, but to what extent it is hard to say. Media itself is only one word, but it includes television, radio, CDs, video games, papers, books, the Internet, and more. It's hard to say what each contributes. Also, you have to look at what kind of violence you are talking about. Do media influence extreme aggressive behavior, such as killing? Lastly, a child's environment, personality, and parents also have to be considered. It is difficult to say why people do anything, including acts of violence.

Each human is unique so that it's hard to say that media violence makes people more violent. One person could watch gruesome violence every day and remain caring and loving, whereas another individual might see minimal violent media and go out and kill. How do you explain the difference? You have to define a norm. But that norm only defines "normal" people's reactions to media violence. A person outside of the norm may still commit acts of violence.

When I see or hear violence in the media, I know that I am not inclined to do anything more violent than if I had not. Granted, a high-action movie thriller has given me that feeling of kick-ass satisfaction and exposure to rap has caused me to use strong language. But feelings and slang are not acts of violence. These examples do show that there is a connection between the media and people's behavior.

Part 2

When I read "Violence in the Mass Media and Violence in Society: The Link Is Unproven," I began to think that there really is not much evidence indicating that media violence leads to violent behavior. The author, Jonathan Freedman, argued that you could not prove the link because the "studies . . . used dubious measures of aggression," they could not "distinguish effects of violence from effects of interest and excitement," and the studies were "seriously contaminated by . . . demand characteristics of the situation." All of this made sense to me. I especially agreed with the contamination of the demand characteristics because I had just learned about this in my psychology class. I was taught that experimenters have to take into account that subjects alter their own behavior to meet what they think the experimenter wants.

Freedman also gave an example that stuck in my mind as proof that there is not a strong enough link to prove anything. He said to imagine that the FDA was testing the effectiveness of a new drug. The results came out negative, even less effective than a placebo. He said that obviously the FDA would reject this drug and that, similarly, media should be rejected as having a significant effect on violence. This made perfect sense until I compared it to "Media Violence: A Demonstrated Public Health Threat to Children," an article by L. Rowell Huesmann and Jessica Moise that counters Freedman's position. The FDA analogy that had sounded so good now looked faulty compared with Huesmann's Surgeon General analogy. In Huesmann's analogy, he points out that if something has shown even the slightest negative effect, it can't be dismissed. Freedman was right to say that we cannot prove for certain that media violence leads to violent behavior, but what he failed to acknowledge is that we should still warn about negative effects. After contrasting these two articles, I had changed my mind and decided that media violence does play a role in violent behavior.

With this new state of mind, I read several other articles that reinforced the claim that media violence promotes violent behavior. In the article "We Are Training Our Kids to Kill," Dave Grossman claims that "the desensitizing techniques used for training soldiers are being replicated in contemporary mass media movies, television, and video games, giving rise to the alarming rate of homicide and violence in our schools and

5

communities." Not only was this article interesting, but it also made sense. Grossmann, who travels the world training medical, law enforcement, and U.S. military personnel about the realities of warfare, supported his claim by showing how classical and operant conditioning used in the military parallel the effects of violent media on young children. Grossman's article was simple and straightforward. I followed his argument and agreed that the desensitizing effects of media train our kids to kill.

To be sure that his argument was true, I tried looking for some evidence that would prove that desensitizing did not have an effect. The only text I could find was the article by Richard Rhodes, "Hollow Claims about Fantasy Violence." In this article, there is one short and very confusing paragraph (paragraph 9) in which Rhodes offers "a British scholar's" critique of the desensitization argument:

> [T]heir claim is that the materials they judge to be harmful can only influence us by trying to makes us be the same as them. So horrible things will make us horrible—not horrified. . . . This idea is so odd, it is hard to know where to begin in challenging it.

After reading this, I felt like saying the same thing to Rhodes. His paragraph was so confusing I had a hard time knowing where to begin in challenging it. In reality, it is not really an argument at all because Rhodes offers only a quote without explanation. The quote lumps all forms of violence together and ignores the different ways violence is depicted. I stuck with my new view that desensitization does promote violent behavior.

Part 3

After reading all of these articles and deciding that I do think that media contributes to violent behavior, I began thinking about my own personal experiences again. I thought about that "kick-ass feeling" I get when I watch certain action movies, and I began feeling somewhat ashamed. As film producers Edward Zwick and Marshall Herskovitz pointed out in their *New York Times* column "When the Bodies Are Real," written after 9/11, "perhaps what this event has revealed, with its real bodies blown to bits and real explosions bringing down buildings, is the true darkness behind so much of the product coming out of Hollywood today."

Annotated Bibliography

Freedman, Jonathan L. "Violence in the Mass Media and Violence in Society: The Link Is Unproven." <u>Harvard Mental Health Letter</u> May 1996: 4–6.
    This article claims that there is not solid proof that mass media leads to violence. The author, Jonathan Freedman, proves his claim by showing that the studies have used dubious measures of aggression, by showing that it is hard to distinguish effects of violence from effects of excitement, and to separate either from the effects of

demand characteristics. This would be a good article to use to prove that media does not influence aggressive behavior; however, I used the article's weak points to prove that media does lead to aggressive behavior.

Grossman, Dave. "We Are Training Our Kids to Kill." Saturday Evening
Post July/Aug 1999: 64–70.
This article explains the killings committed by America's youth as a result of media violence. First the author discusses how killing is unnatural. He then goes on to show how several military techniques for training soldiers resemble the ways the media interact with children. This article gives logical support to the claim that media influences violent behavior.

Herskovitz, Marshall, and Edward Zwick. "When the Bodies Are Real."
Editorial. New York Times.
This is a short article written in response to the horrible tragedy of 9/11. It is written for the general public but focuses specifically on how the media community will respond to this tragedy. The authors, Marshall Herskovitz and Edward Zwick, are producers, directors, and writers. They point out how 9/11 has caused Hollywood, and all of us, to reexamine violence.

Huesmann, L. Rowell, and Jessica Moise. "Media Violence: A Demonstrated Public Health Threat to Children." Harvard Mental Health
Letter June 1996: 5–7.
This article responds to Jonathan Freedman's article, "Violence in the Mass Media and Violence in Society: The Link Is Unproven." The authors refute most of Freedman's article with research. The article offers good support for the link between media and real violence.

Rhodes, Richard. "Hollow Claims about Fantasy Violence." Editorial. New
York Times 17 Sept. 2000.
This essay attempts to prove that there is not enough evidence to claim that media violence leads to real violence. The author says that people (in particular, politicians) use media as a scapegoat for not looking at the real problems behind violence.

Note: For a discussion of how to create an annotated bibliography, see Chapter 5, pages 120–121.

INQUIRY: SUMMING UP THE AIM

In this chapter, we've introduced you to college-level inquiry. Here are the key points:

- In college, we don't just ransack sources for information and quotes. *We interact with them.* "Interact" means be critical of sources and allow them to influence, even change, our point of view.

- Informal conversation is a valuable medium of inquiry. But it becomes more valuable when we turn conversation into dialogue. *Assert opinions less, and question opinions more.* When a good question elicits a good response, pursue it with more questions.
- The best and most stimulating sources need dialogue. *Think of texts as something to "talk with."* Such dialogues will uncover more research possibilities. Pursue these, and you'll approach the depth of inquiry valued in college work and beyond, in graduate school and the workplace.

Inquiry is learning. Inquiry is finding what we really think and have to say. It's the most creative part of the writing process. Invest in it. It will repay your best efforts.

Chapter 7

Making Your Case:
Arguing to Convince

The last chapter ended where inquiry ends—with the attempt to formulate a position, an opinion that we can assert with some confidence. Once our aim shifts from inquiring to convincing, everything changes.

The most significant change is in audience. In inquiry, our audience consists of our fellow inquirers—friends, classmates, and teachers we can talk with face to face. We seek assurance that our position is at least plausible and defensible, a claim to truth that can be respected whether or not the audience agrees with it. In convincing, however, our audience consists of readers whose positions differ from our own or who have no position at all. The audience changes from a small, inside group that helps us develop our argument to a larger, public audience who will either accept or reject it.

As the audience changes, so does the situation or need for argument. Inquiry is a cooperative use of argument; it cannot take place unless people are willing to work together. Conversely, convincing is competitive. We pit our case against the case(s) of others to win the assent of readers who will compare the various arguments and ask, Who makes the best case? With whom should I agree? Our arguments now compete for "best or better" status, just as do the disagreeing arguments of experts.

Because of the change in audience and situation, our thinking also changes, becomes more strategic and calculated to influence readers. In inquiry, we make a case we can believe in; in convincing, we make a case readers can believe in. What we find compelling in inquiry will sometimes also convince our readers, but *in convincing we must adapt our reasoning to appeal to their beliefs, values, and self-interest*. We will also likely offer reasons that did not occur to us at all in inquiry but come as we attempt to imagine the people we hope to convince. Convincing, however, does not mean abandoning the work of inquiry. Our version of the truth, our convictions, gained through inquiry, are what we argue for.

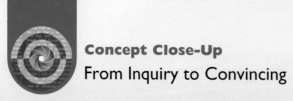

Concept Close-Up
From Inquiry to Convincing

Inquiry ⟶ Convincing

Inquiry	Convincing
Intimate audience	Public readership
Cooperative	Competitive
Earns a conviction	Argues a thesis
Seeks a case convincing *to us*	Makes a case convincing *to them*, the readers

We take the position we discovered through inquiry and turn it into a thesis supported by a case designed to gain the assent of a specific group of readers.

In this chapter, we look first at the structure and strategy of complete essays that aim to convince. Then we provide a step-by-step analysis of the kind of thinking necessary to produce such an essay.

THE NATURE OF CONVINCING: STRUCTURE AND STRATEGY

An argument is an assertion supported by a reason. To convince an audience, writers need to expand on this structure. They usually must offer more than one reason and support all reasons with evidence. We use **case structure** to describe a flexible plan for making *any argument to any audience* who expects sound reasoning. We use **case strategy** to describe the reader-centered moves writers make *to shape a particular argument*— selecting reasons, ordering them, developing evidence, and linking the sections of the argument together for maximum impact.

Case Structure

All cases have at least three levels of assertion. The first level is the thesis, or central claim, which everything else in the case supports. The second level is the reason or reasons the arguer advances for holding the thesis. The third level is the evidence offered to support each reason, typically drawn from some authoritative source.

In the abstract, then, cases look like this:

Figure 7.1

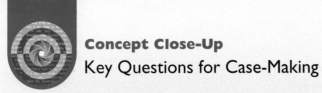

Concept Close-Up

Key Questions for Case-Making

1. Who is your **target audience?**
2. What **preconceptions** and **biases** might they hold about your topic?
3. What **claim** do you want your readers to accept?
4. What **reasons** are likely to appeal to this audience?
5. How should you **arrange** these reasons for **maximum impact** on your target audience?
6. How might you **introduce** your case?
7. How might you **conclude** it?
8. How can you gain the **trust** and **respect** of your audience?

Convincing is audience centered. Every choice we make must be made with the target audience in mind.

Our diagram shows three reasons, but good cases can be built with only one reason or with more than three.

Case Strategy

In Chapter 2, we explain that you can read an argument with greater comprehension if you have a sense of the rhetorical context in which the writer worked. Likewise, in preparing to write an argument, consider your own context by using the "Key Questions for Case-Making" above.

By working out answers to these questions in your writer's notebook, you'll create a **rhetorical prospectus** that will help you envision a context within which to write and a tentative plan to follow.

To demonstrate case strategy, we'll look at "Arrested Development: The Conservative Case against Racial Profiling." The author, James Forman, Jr., is an educator and fellow at the New American Foundation in Washington, D.C. His article was published in *The New Republic*, September 10, 2001.

Thinking about Audience

To make an effective case for his position, Forman envisions an audience who favors racial profiling, and his strategy is to use reasons and evidence to convince readers who will resist his thesis. Therefore, he had to consider their likely responses. He posed questions like these:

- Who will my readers be?
- How will they be predisposed to view racial profiling?
- What will they have on their minds as soon as they see that my argument is against it?

Based on these questions, Forman assumes something like the following about the intended audience:

> My conservative audience supports the police and approves of or at least tolerates racial profiling as a tactic for apprehending criminals. I want to show them not only that profiling doesn't work but also, more importantly, that it violates fundamental conservative principles.

Strategy, then, must begin with thoughts about the audience, its values and preconceptions. Next, we examine how Forman shapes the elements of case structure — thesis, reasons, and evidence — to appeal to his readers.

Formulating the Thesis

Your thesis may not be explicitly stated but it must be *strongly implied,* clear to you and your reader. It must be clear to you because you must build a case around it. It must be clear to your readers so that they know what you're claiming and what to expect from your case. Forman's thesis is implied and can be stated as follows: *Political conservatives, most of whom now support racial profiling, ought to oppose it.*

Choosing Reasons

Forman constructs his case around four reasons, all designed to appeal to his audience and undercut their support of racial profiling.

> *Thesis:* Political conservatives, most of whom now support racial profiling, ought to oppose it.
>
> *Reason 1:* Racial profiling is ineffective — it doesn't reliably identify criminals. (Strategy: Forman wants to take away the major justification for profiling, that it helps the police catch lawbreakers.)
>
> *Reason 2:* Racial profiling harasses law-abiding blacks just because they are black. (Strategy: Forman wants his readers, most of whom have not been stopped and frisked by the police, to appreciate how discriminatory profiling is and the damage it does to people's respect for authority.)
>
> *Reason 3:* Racial profiling violates the conservative principle that equates equal rights with equal responsibilities. (Strategy: Forman wants his readers to see that racial profiling contradicts his audience's values — in this instance, the relationship of individual achievement to full, equal participation in the community.)
>
> *Reason 4:* Racial profiling violates the conservative ideal of a color-blind society. (Strategy: Forman wants his audience to see that their reasons for opposing affirmative action apply with equal force to racial profiling.)

As you read Forman's argument, note how he arranges his reasons; the order of presentation matters. Note also his strategies for developing reasons, especially his use of evidence.

Figure 7.2   Hulbert Waldroup, the artist who painted the controversial mural of Amadou Diallo in the Bronx near where Diallo was shot, signs his initials to his latest work, a painting on racial profiling, after unveiling it in New York's Times Square, Tuesday, July 24, 2001. Waldroup says his work portrays racial profiling "through the eyes of a cop—what he sees, what he thinks, the stereotypes we are all responsible for." (AP Photo/Kathy Willens)

Arrested Development:
The Conservative Case against Racial Profiling
James Forman, Jr.

The Maya Angelou Public Charter School in Washington, D.C., is the kind of institution conservatives love—a place that offers opportunity but demands responsibility. Students are in school ten and a half hours per day, all year long, mostly studying core subjects like reading, writing, math, and history. When not in class, they work in student-run businesses, where they earn money and learn job skills. Those who achieve academically are held in high esteem not only by their teachers but by their peers. Those who disrupt class or otherwise violate the rules are subject to punishment, including expulsion, as determined by a panel of students and teachers.

The results have been impressive. Most Maya Angelou students had academic difficulty at their previous schools. In fact, more than one-half had stopped even attending school on a regular basis before they came to Maya

Angelou, while more than one-third had been in the juvenile court system. Yet more than 90 percent of its graduates go on to college, compared with a citywide rate of just 50 percent. This success stems in part from the school's small classes, innovative curriculum, and dedicated staff. But it is also due to its fundamentally conservative ethos: If you work hard and don't make excuses, society will give you a chance, no matter what your background is.

I can speak to this with some authority because I helped establish the school four years ago and still teach an elective there today. But, for all the school's accomplishments, we keep running up against one particularly debilitating problem. It's awfully hard to convince poor, African American kids that discrimination isn't an obstacle, that authority must be respected, and that individual identity matters more than racial identity when experiences beyond school walls repeatedly contradict it. And that's precisely what's happening today, thanks to a policy many conservatives condone: Racial profiling by the police.

The prevalence of racial profiling is no secret. Numerous statistical studies have shown that being black substantially raises the odds of a person being stopped and searched by the police—even though blacks who are stopped are no more likely than whites to be carrying drugs. As David Cole and John Lamberth recently pointed out in *The New York Times*, in Maryland "73 percent of those stopped and searched on a section of Interstate 95 were black, yet state police reported that equal percentages of the whites and blacks who were searched, statewide, had drugs or other contraband." Blacks were actually far less likely than whites to be found carrying drugs in New Jersey, a state whose police force has acknowledged the use of racial profiling. According to Cole and Lamberth, consensual searches "yielded contraband, mostly drugs, on 25 percent of whites, 13 percent of blacks and only 5 percent of Latinos."

Behind these statistics are hundreds if not thousands of well-chronicled anecdotes, some from America's most prominent black citizens. Erroll McDonald, vice president and executive editor of Pantheon publishing, was driving a rented Jaguar in New Orleans when he was stopped—simply "to show cause why I shouldn't be deemed a problematic Negro in a possibly stolen car." . . .

Even off-duty black police frequently tell of being harassed by their unsuspecting white colleagues. Consider the case of Robert Byrd, an eleven-year veteran of the D.C. police, who was off duty and out of uniform when he tried to stop a carjacking and robbery in Southeast Washington last March. After witnessing the crime, Byrd used his police radio to alert a police dispatcher, then followed the stolen van in his own. Byrd got out of his van as marked police vehicles arrived. According to Byrd, white officers then began beating him in the belief that he was the African American suspect. The real perpetrators were caught later that night.

None of these stories would surprise the students at Maya Angelou. Almost weekly this past spring, officers arrived at the corner of 9th and

T Streets NW (in front of our school), threw our students against the wall, and searched them. As you might imagine, these are not polite encounters. They are an aggressive show of force in which children are required to "assume the position": legs spread, face against the wall or squad car, hands behind the head. Police officers then search them, feeling every area of their bodies. Last spring, a police officer chased one male student into the school, wrestled him to the ground, then drew his gun. Another time, when a student refused a police request to leave the corner in front of our school (where the student was taking a short break between classes, in complete compliance with school rules and D.C. law), the officer grabbed him, cuffed him, and started putting him into a police van, before a school official intervened. These students committed no crime other than standing outside a school in a high-drug-use neighborhood. Indeed, despite the numerous searches, no drugs have ever been discovered, and no student has ever been found in violation of the law.

Liberals generally decry such incidents; conservatives generally deny that they take place. "[T]he racial profiling we're all supposed to be outraged about doesn't actually happen very much," explained Jonah Goldberg in his *National Review Online* column last spring. And even those conservatives who admit the practice's frequency often still insist it does more good than harm. "The evidence suggests," William Tucker wrote in a recent issue of *The Weekly Standard*, "that racial profiling is an effective law enforcement tool, though it undeniably visits indignity on the innocent."

In other words, liberals—who are generally more concerned about individual rights and institutionalized racism—believe racial profiling contradicts their principles. Conservatives, on the other hand—who tolerate greater invasions of privacy in the name of law and order—consider racial profiling to be generally consistent with theirs. But conservatives are wrong—racial profiling profoundly violates core conservative principles.

It is conservatives, after all, who remind us that government policy doesn't affect only resources; it affects values, which in turn affect people's behavior. This argument was at the heart of the conservative critique of welfare policy. For years, conservatives (along with some liberals) argued that welfare policies—like subsidizing unmarried, unemployed women with children—fostered a culture of dependency. Only by demanding that citizens take responsibility for their own fates, the argument went, could government effectively combat poverty. 10

But if sending out welfare checks with no strings attached sends the wrong message, so does racial profiling. For the conservative ethos about work and responsibility to resonate, black citizens must believe they are treated the same way as white citizens—that with equal responsibilities go equal rights. In *The Dream and the Nightmare*, which President Bush cites as one of the most influential books he has ever read, the conservative theorist Myron Magnet writes: "[W]hat underclass kids need most . . . is an authoritative link to traditional values of work, study, and self-improvement, and the assurance that these values can permit them to claim full membership in the larger community." Magnet quotes Eugene Lange, a businessman who promised scholarships to inner-city kids who graduated from high school: "It's important that [inner-city kids] grow up to recognize that they are not perpetuating a life of the pariah, but that the resources of the community are legitimately theirs to take advantage of and contribute to and be a part of."

Magnet is right. But random and degrading police searches radically undermine this message. They tell black kids that they are indeed pariahs — that, no matter how hard they study, they remain suspects. As one Maya Angelou first-year student explained to me: "We can be perfect, perfect, doing everything right, and they still treat us like dogs. No, worse than dogs, because criminals are treated worse than dogs." Or, as a junior asked me, noting the discrepancy between the message delivered by the school and the message delivered by the police: "How can you tell us we can be anything if they treat us like we're nothing?"

Indeed, people like myself — teachers, counselors, parents — try desperately to convince these often jaded kids that hard work really will pay off. In so doing, we are quite consciously pursuing an educational approach that conservatives have long advocated. We are addressing what conservative criminologist James Q. Wilson calls "intangible problems — problems of 'values,'" the problems that sometimes make "blacks less likely to take advantage of opportunities." But we are constantly fighting other people in the neighborhood who tell kids that bourgeois norms of work, family, and sexuality are irrelevant and impossible. Since the state will forever treat you as an outlaw, they say, you might as well act like one. Every time police single out a young black man for harassment, those other people sound more credible — and we sound like dupes.

Then there's that other vaunted conservative ideal: color-blindness. In recent years, conservatives have argued relentlessly for placing less emphasis on race. Since discrimination is on the wane, they suggest, government itself must stop making race an issue — i.e., no more affirmative action in admissions, no more set-asides in contracting, no more tailoring of government programs to favor particular racial or ethnic groups. In the words of affirmative action critics Abigail and Stephen Thernstrom, it's essential to fight the "politics of racial grievance" and counter the "suspicion that nothing fundamental [has] changed." Society, says Magnet, "needs to tell [blacks] that they can do it — not that, because of past victimization, they cannot."

But it's hard to tell young black men that they are not victims because of their race when police routinely make them victims because of their race. Students at Maya Angelou are acutely aware that the police do not treat young people the same way at Sidwell Friends and St. Albans, schools for Washington's overwhelmingly white elite. As another Maya Angelou first-year told me, "You think they would try that stuff with white kids? Never." Such knowledge makes them highly suspicious of the conservative

15

assertion that blacks should forego certain benefits—such as racial preferences in admissions—because of the moral value of color-blindness. Why,
they wonder, aren't white people concerned about that principle when it
hurts blacks as well as when it benefits them? And racial profiling makes
them cynical about the conservative demand that blacks not see the world
in racialized, group-identity terms. Why, they wonder, don't white people
demand the same of the police?

Most conservatives who support racial profiling are not racist; they simply consider the practice an essential ingredient of effective law enforcement. But it isn't. Indeed, the great irony of conservative support for racial
profiling is that conservative principles themselves explain why racial
profiling actually makes law enforcement less effective.

. . . [D]iscriminatory police practices create unnecessary and unproductive hostility between police and the communities they serve. Imagine that
you are 17, standing outside your school during a break from class, talking
to friends, laughing, playing, and just relaxing. Imagine that squad cars pull
up; officers jump out, shouting, guns drawn; and you are thrown against
the wall, elbowed in the back, legs kicked apart, and violently searched.
Your books are strewn on the ground. You ask what's going on, and you are
told to "shut the fuck up" or you will be taken downtown. When it finally
ends, the officers leave, giving no apology, no explanation, and you are left
to fix your clothes, pick up your books, and gather your pride. Imagine that
this is not the first time this has happened to you, that it has happened
repeatedly, in one form or another, throughout your adolescence. Now
imagine that, the day after the search, there is a crime in your neighborhood about which you hear a rumor. You know the police are looking for
information, and you see one of the officers who searched you yesterday
(or indeed any officer) asking questions about the crime. How likely are
you to help? . . .

Arranging Reasons

Conservative support for racial profiling depends on belief in its effectiveness, especially in combating illegal drugs. Forman therefore challenges this
belief first. If he can show that profiling doesn't produce the results claimed
for it, his readers should then be more receptive to his other reasons, all of
which establish its negative impact.

His second reason has force because no law-abiding citizen wants to be
treated as if she or he were suspected of criminal activity. No matter who you
are, however, and no matter what you are doing, you can be so treated if you
fit the profile. Such harassment would not be tolerated by the conservative,
mostly white audience Forman is trying to reach and so should not be con-
doned by that audience when directed toward other racial and ethnic groups.
It's a matter of fairness.

Forman's first two reasons engage relatively concrete and easily grasped issues: Does racial profiling work? Are innocent people harassed when it's used? His third and fourth reasons are more abstract and depend on the reader's recognition of contradiction. If we oppose welfare because it encourages dependency and lack of personal responsibility, shouldn't we oppose racial profiling because it "tell[s] black kids that they are indeed pariahs — that, no matter how hard they study, they remain suspects"? Similarly, if we oppose affirmative action because it favors people because of race, shouldn't we also oppose profiling because it also singles out race? Rational people want to be consistent; Forman shows his readers that they haven't been — a powerful strategy after showing that profiling doesn't work and harasses innocent people.

Using Evidence

How well does Forman use the third level of case structure, the supporting evidence for each reason?

Note that he uses different *kinds* of evidence appropriately. To support his contention that racial profiling doesn't work, he cites *data* — in this case, statistics — showing that blacks are less likely, than whites or Latinos to be caught with contraband (paragraph 4). Profiling blacks, therefore, makes no sense. Next, he uses *individual examples* to confirm that innocent people, including police officers, are treated as suspects simply because they're black. These individual examples may have more impact than statistics because they personalize the problem. Used together, individual examples and statistics complement each other.

Then, in paragraph 7, Forman draws on *personal experience* as evidence, what he himself has observed. He's seen police shake down students at the school where he teaches. He wants his readers to *feel* the sense of violation involved and so offers a graphic description. Clearly, personal experience can be a powerful source of evidence.

Finally, to back up his last two reasons, Forman cites *well-known authorities*, prominent conservatives such as Myron Magnet and Abigail and Stephen Thernstrom (paragraphs 11 and 14). He cites these sources, obviously, because his audience considers them representative of their own viewpoint and respects them. Forman combines these authorities with the voices of his own students, who gain additional credibility simply by being cited along with the experts.

Forman's essay merits close study for its use of evidence alone. He employs different kinds of evidence, combines different types well, and never forgets that evidence must appeal to his audience.

Introducing and Concluding the Argument

We have analyzed Forman's strategies for using the three levels of case structure — thesis, reasons, and evidence — to build a convincing argument. Arguing to convince also requires a writer to think about effective ways to open and close the case.

The Introduction   When you read Forman's essay the first time, you may have thought that somehow we had attached the wrong title to an essay about school reform. Not until the end of the third paragraph does the author announce his actual subject, racial profiling. Why this long introduction about the Maya Angelou Public Charter School?

The introduction accomplishes at least the following key purposes. Conservatives are strong supporters of alternatives to public schools. One of these is the charter school, and the author uses his story about a highly successful one to confirm conservative policy. Note how he emphasizes the seriousness of the curriculum and other school activities. He also points to the strict rules and discipline and how the Maya Angelou school has turned around standard public school failures, including kids headed for serious trouble with the law. All of this is likely to sound especially good to conservatives.

The story also establishes the author's authority as someone who makes conservative ideas work. Later on, when he cites his students' words to confirm his points, we do not doubt their authenticity. We can see, then, how crucial the introduction is to setting up the case.

Finally, the introduction anticipates the contradictions he'll address later, especially in reasons 3 and 4. The Maya Angelou school has succeeded in educating the kind of student that other schools often don't reach. Kids who could be a public danger now and adult criminals later are apparently becoming good citizens instead. But everything the school has accomplished can be undone by racial profiling. Thus, conservative educational reform clashes with conservative law enforcement policy. They don't fit together, and clearly the former is more important than the latter because the school is creating students who will stay on the right side of the law. Forman is already implying that racial profiling must go, which is the whole point of his essay.

The point for us is that introductions shouldn't be dashed off carelessly, thrown together just because we know we need one. Our introductions must prepare the way for our case.

The Conclusion   Paragraphs 16 and 17 conclude his argument. What do they achieve?

Paragraph 16 states that most conservatives are not racists, that they just have been misled into thinking profiling works. In effect, these assertions release conservatives from the common accusation that they don't care about blacks and support policies that discriminate against them. Forman also reminds his readers that he has used *conservative principles* to explain why racial profiling diminishes police effectiveness.

Paragraph 17 explains in a concrete and memorable way how police tactics like profiling can interfere with law enforcement. Forman wants his readers to remember the harshness of the procedures and that the experience makes minorities suspicious of and uncooperative with police. We see the damage profiling does from the inside, and we cannot help but appreciate its negative consequences. The implied message is: If you value law and order, be against racial profiling. In this way, Forman advances his major point from another conservative value—support for the police.

Like introductions, conclusions are not throwaways, not merely hasty summaries. Like introductions, they should do something, not just repeat what we've said already. *The conclusion must clinch our case by ending it forcefully and memorably.*

Following Through

A successful essay has smooth transitions between its opening and its first reason and between its last reason and its conclusion, as well as between each reason in the body of the essay. In your writer's notebook, describe how Forman (1) announces that he is moving from his introduction to the first reason, from the first reason to the second, and so on and (2) at the same time links each section to what has come before.

WRITING A CONVINCING ARGUMENT

www.mhhe.
com/**crusius**

For some
electronic
guidance on
writing
arguments, go to:
Writing >
Writing Tutors >
Argument

Few people draft an essay sequentially, beginning with the first sentence of the first paragraph and ending with the last sentence of the last paragraph. But the final version of any essay must read as if it had been written sequentially, with the writer fully in control.

A well-written essay is like a series of moves in a chess game, in which each move is part of an overall plan. In the case of convincing, the purpose is to gain the agreement of the reader.

Although readers may not be fully aware of the "moves" that make up a convincing argument, the writer probably made most of them consciously. As we have seen in this chapter, we can learn much about how to convince by studying finished essays. However, it is one thing to understand how something works and quite another to make it work ourselves. Part of the difficulty is that we cannot see in the final product everything that went into making it work so well. Just as a movie audience typically cannot imagine all the rehearsals, the many takes, and the editing that make a scene powerful, so it is hard for us to imagine all the research and thinking, the many drafts, and the process of editing and proofreading that Forman must have gone through to make "Arrested Development" effective. Yet it's precisely this process you must understand and immerse yourself in to produce convincing arguments of your own.

The following discussion of the composing process assumes that the work of research (Chapter 5) and inquiry (Chapter 6) has already been done. It also assumes that you have worked out a rhetorical prospectus (see Chapter 1, pages 18–19) to guide you in combining structure with strategy.

1. Your thesis can be stated or implied, but **you and your readers must have no doubt about what you're contending.**
2. **Begin with your most important reason.** (For example, if your audience supports racial profiling because they think it works, begin your case against profiling by showing them that it doesn't.)
3. In general, **provide the kind of evidence each reason requires.** (For example, if you contend that helmet laws will reduce head injuries in motorcycle accidents, such a reason requires *data* for support. In contrast, if you contend that helmet laws do not seriously intrude upon personal freedom, data won't help—you must show that helmet laws are no more restrictive than other laws we accept as justified, such as seat belt or maximum speed laws.)
4. Use the **full range** of evidence available (data, individual examples, personal experience, expert opinion, etc.). When possible and appropriate, **mix different kinds of evidence to support a single reason.**
5. **Devote serious effort to introductions and conclusions.** They should accomplish definite tasks, such as generating interest at the beginning and leaving your reader with something memorable at the end. Avoid "throwaway," high school introductions that begin with "In this essay, I will discuss . . ." or "In conclusion . . ." conclusions.

Preparing a Brief

Before you begin to draft, it is a good idea to prepare a **brief,** which shows the thesis and reasons you plan to use and gives some indication of how you will support each reason with evidence. The brief ought to arrange the reasons in order, but the order may change as you draft and revise.

Working toward a Position

First, we need to distinguish a position from a thesis. A **position** (or a stance or opinion) amounts to an overall, summarizing attitude or judgment about some issue. "Universities often exploit student athletes" is an example of a position. A **thesis** is not only more specific and precise but also more strategic, designed to appeal to readers and be consistent with available evidence. For example, "Student athletes in revenue-generating sports ought to be paid for their services" is one possible thesis representing the preceding position, perhaps for an audience of college students. We cannot construct a case without a thesis. But without a position, we cannot experiment with various thesis formulations. Positions precede theses.

Finding a position can be a significant challenge in itself. What often happens is that we begin with a strong opinion, find it failing under scrutiny, discover other positions that do not fully satisfy us, and so emerge from inquiry uncertain about what we do think. Another common path is to start with no opinion at all, find ourselves attracted to parts of several conflicting positions, and so wind up unsure, confused, even vexed because we can't decide what to think.

In such situations, resolve to be patient with yourself. The best, most mature positions typically come only after a struggle. Second, take out your writer's notebook and start making lists. Look over your research materials, especially the notecards on which you have recorded positions and evidence from your sources. Make lists in response to these questions:

What positions have you encountered in research and class discussion?

What seems strongest and weakest in each position? What modifications might be made to eliminate or minimize the weak points? Are there other possible positions? What are their strong and weak points?

What evidence impressed you? What does each piece of evidence imply or suggest? What connections can you draw among the pieces of evidence given in various sources? If there is conflict in the implications of the evidence, what is that conflict?

While all this list-making may seem only doodling, you'll begin to sort things out.

Bear in mind that, although emotional commitment to ideas and values is important, it can impede clear thought. Sometimes we find our stance by relinquishing a strongly held opinion—perhaps for lack of compelling reasons or evidence. The more emotional the issue—abortion or pornography, for instance—the more likely we are to cling to a position that is difficult to defend. When we sense deep conflict, when we want to argue a position even in the face of strong contradictory evidence, it's time to consider changing our minds.

Finally, if you find yourself holding out for the "perfect" position, all strength and no weakness, give up. Controversial issues are controversial precisely because no single stance convinces everyone, because there is always room for counterargument and for other positions that have their own power to convince.

Student Sample: Working toward a Position   Justin Spidel's class began by reading many arguments about homosexuality and discussing issues related to gay rights. Justin decided to investigate whether same-sex marriage should be legal. His initial position was that same-sex marriage ought to be legal because gays and lesbians should be treated like everyone else. Research revealed that a majority of Americans oppose same-sex marriage because they believe its legalization would change the definition of marriage and alter its sacred bond. Justin read articles opposing gay marriage by such well-known public figures as William Bennett, but he also read many in favor. He found especially convincing the arguments by gays and lesbians who were in stable, loving, monogamous relationships but barred from marrying. Justin's initial round of research led him to the position "Gays and lesbians should be able to marry."

During the inquiry stage, Justin discussed his position with his classmates and instructor. Knowing that gays and lesbians do sometimes get married in churches, Justin's classmates asked him to clarify "able to marry." Justin explained that he meant *legal recognition* of same-sex marriages by all state governments. When asked if other countries recognize same-sex marriage, Justin said that some do. He thought that the United States should be among the leaders in valuing equality and individual rights. He was asked about the implications of his position: Would granting legal status to same-sex marriage devalue the institution? He said that the people fighting for legalization have the deepest respect for marriage and that marriage is about love and commitment, not sexual orientation.

 Following Through

> Formulate a tentative position on a topic that you have researched and into which you have inquired. Write it up with a brief explanation of why you support this stand. Be prepared to defend your position in class or with a peer in a one-on-one exchange of position statements.

Analyzing the Audience

Before you decide on a thesis, give some thought to the rhetorical context of your argument. Who needs to hear it? What are their values? What common ground might you share with them? How might you have to qualify your position to influence their opinions?

To provoke thought, people occasionally make cases for theses that they know have little chance of winning assent. One example is the argument for legalizing all drug use; although a reasonably good case can be made, most Americans find it too radical. If you want to convince rather than provoke, formulate a thesis that *both* represents your position *and* creates as little resistance in your readers as possible. Instead of arguing for legalizing all drug use, for example, you might argue that much of the staggering amount spent on the war on drugs should be diverted to rehabilitation and dealing with social problems connected with drug abuse. Because positions allow for many possible theses, you should analyze your audience before settling on one.

Student Sample: Analyzing the Audience Justin knew that many people would view same-sex marriage as radical. Some audiences, such as conservative Christians, would never assent to it. So Justin targeted an audience he had some chance of convincing—people who opposed same-sex marriage but were tolerant of homosexuals. Justin wrote the following audience profile:

> My audience would be heterosexual adults who accept that some people are homosexual or lesbian; they know people who are. They would be among the nearly 47 percent of Americans who do not object to same-sex relationships between consenting adults. They may be fairly well educated and could belong to any age group. They are not likely to have strong religious objections, so my argument will not focus on whether homosexuality is a sin. However, these readers oppose legalizing marriage between gays and lesbians because they think it would threaten the traditional role of marriage as the basis of family life. They think that marriage is troubled enough by divorce, and they want to preserve its meaning. Their practical position is that, if same-sex couples want to live together and act like they're married, there's nothing to stop them—so leave things as they are. They believe in the value of heterosexual marriage; I can appeal to that. They also hold basic American principles of equal rights and the right to the "pursuit of happiness." But mainly I want to show my readers that gays and lesbians are missing out on basic civil rights and that permitting marriage would benefit everyone.

 Following Through

> Write a profile of the audience you hope to reach through an argument you want to make. Be as specific as possible; include any information—age, gender, economic status, and so forth—that may contribute to your audience's outlook and attitudes. What interests, beliefs, and values might they hold? How might you have to phrase your thesis to give your argument a chance of succeeding? What reasons might they be willing to consider? What would you have to rule out?

Developing a Thesis

A good thesis grows out of many factors: your position, your research, your exploration of reasons to support your position, and your understanding of the audience. During drafting, you may refine the thesis by phrasing it more precisely, but for now concentrate on stating a thesis that represents your position clearly and directly.

Your thesis should present only the claim. Save the reasons for the body of the paper.

Student Sample: Developing a Thesis   Justin's original statement, "Gays and lesbians should be able to marry," expresses a position, but it could be more precise and better directed toward the readers Justin defined in his audience profile. He refined his position to the following:

A couple's right to marry should not be restricted because of sexual orientation.

This version emphasized that marriage is a right everyone should enjoy, but it did not clarify why readers should recognize it as a right. Justin tried again:

Every couple who wishes to commit to each other in marriage should have the right to do so, regardless of sexual preference.

Justin was fairly satisfied with this version because it appealed to a basic value — commitment.

He then started thinking about how committed relationships benefit society, an argument that would appeal to his readers. He wanted to portray the thesis not just as an issue of rights for homosexuals but also as a benefit for everyone, broadening its appeal. He tried one more time and settled on the following thesis:

Everyone, gay and straight, will benefit from extending the basic human right of marriage to all couples, regardless of sexual preference.

 Following Through

1. Refine your thesis as Justin did for the essay on which you are currently working. Why did you settle on one way of stating it?
2. As we saw in analyzing William May's case against assisted suicide (Chapter 3), sometimes a thesis needs to be qualified and exceptions to the thesis stated and clarified. Now is a good time to think about qualifications and exceptions.

You can handle qualifications and exceptions in two ways. First, you can add a phrase to your thesis that limits it, as William May did in his argument on assisted suicide: "*On the whole*, our social policy . . . should not regularize killing for mercy." May admits that a few extreme cases of suffering justify helping someone die. The other method is to word the thesis in such a way that exceptions or qualifications are implied rather than spelled out. For example, "Life sentences with no parole are justifiable for all sane people found guilty of first-degree murder." Here the exceptions would be "those who are found insane" and "those tried on lesser charges."

Using your best thesis statement, decide whether qualifications and exceptions are needed. If so, decide how best to handle them.

Analyzing the Thesis

Once you have a thesis, *unpack* it to determine what you must argue. To do this, put yourself in the place of your readers. To be won over, what must they find in your argument? Answering that question requires looking very closely at both what the thesis says and what it implies. It also requires thinking about the position and attitudes of your readers as you described them earlier in your audience profile.

Many thesis sentences appear simple, but analysis shows they are complex. Let's consider a thesis on the topic of whether Mark Twain's *Huckleberry Finn* should be taught in public schools. Some people have argued that Twain's classic novel should be removed from reading lists because some readers, especially African-Americans, find its subject matter and language offensive. In some schools the novel is not assigned, whereas in others it's optional. In our example thesis, the writer supports teaching the novel: "Mark Twain's *Huckleberry Finn* should be required reading for all high school students in the United States."

Unpacking this thesis, we see that the writer must first argue for *Huckleberry Finn* as *required* reading—not merely a good book but an indispensable one. The writer must also argue that the book should be required at the high school level rather than in middle school or college. Finally, the author must defend the novel from charges of racism, even though the thesis does not explicitly state, "*Huckleberry Finn* is not a racist book." Otherwise, these charges stand by default; to ignore them is to ignore the context of the issue.

Student Sample: Analyzing the Thesis By analyzing his thesis—"Everyone, gay and straight, will benefit from extending the basic human right of marriage to all couples, regardless of sexual preference"—Justin realized that his main task was to explain specific benefits that would follow from allowing gays to marry. He knew that his readers would agree that marriage is a "basic human right" for heterosexual adults, but could not assume that they would see it that way for homosexual couples. Therefore, he had to lead them to see that same-sex couples have the same needs as other couples. He also wanted his readers to understand that he was arguing only that *the law* should recognize such marriages. Churches would not have to sanctify them.

 Following Through

Unpack a thesis of your own or one that your instructor gives you to see what key words and phrases an argument based on that thesis must address. Also consider what an audience would expect you to argue given the current context of the dispute.

Finding Reasons

For the most part, no special effort goes into finding reasons to support a thesis. They come to us as we attempt to justify our opinions, as we listen to the arguments of our classmates, as we encounter written arguments in research, and as we think about how to reach the readers we hope to convince. Given good writing preparation, we seldom formulate a thesis without already having some idea of the reasons we will use to defend it. Our problem, rather, is usually selection — picking out the best reasons and shaping and stating them in a way that appeals to our readers. When we do find ourselves searching for reasons, however, it helps to be aware of their common sources.

The Audience's Belief System Ask yourself, What notions of the real, the good, and the possible will my readers entertain? Readers will find any reason unconvincing if it is not consistent with their understanding of reality. For example, based on their particular culture's notions about disease, people will accept or reject arguments about how to treat illness. Likewise, people have differing notions of what is good. Some people think it is good to exploit natural resources so that we can live with more conveniences; others see more good in preserving the environment. Finally, people disagree about what is possible. Those who believe that some aspects of human nature can't be changed will not accept arguments that certain types of criminals can be rehabilitated.

Special Rules or Principles Good reasons can also be found in a community's accepted rules and principles. For example, we believe that a person is innocent until proven guilty. We apply this principle in even nonlegal situations when someone is accused of misconduct.

The law is only one source of special rules or principles. We also find them in politics ("one person, one vote"), in business (the principle of seniority, which gives preference to employees who have been on the job longest), and even in the home, where each family formulates its own house rules. In other words, all human settings and activities have norms and we can draw on them.

Expert Opinion and Hard Evidence We rely on expert opinion when we lack direct experience with a particular subject. Most readers respect the opinion of trained professionals with advanced degrees and prestige in their fields. Especially when you can show that most experts agree, you have a good basis for a reason.

Hard evidence can also yield good reasons. Research shows, for example, that wearing a bicycle helmet significantly reduces the incidence of head injuries in accidents. Therefore, we can support the thesis "Laws should require bicycle riders to wear helmets" with the reason "because statistics show that fewer serious head injuries occurred in bicycle accidents when the riders were wearing helmets."

Tradition   We can sometimes strengthen a position by citing or alluding to well-known sources that are part of our audience's cultural tradition — for example, the Bible and the sayings or writings of people our readers recognize and respect. Although reasons drawn from tradition may lose force if audience members identify with different cultures or resist tradition itself, they will be effective when readers revere the source.

Comparison   A reason based on similarity argues that what is true in one instance should be true in another. For example, we could make a case for legalizing marijuana by showing that it is similar in effect to alcohol, which is legal — and also a drug. The argument might look like this:

> *Thesis:* Marijuana use should be decriminalized.
>
> *Reason:* Marijuana is no more harmful than alcohol.

Many comparison arguments attempt to show that present situations are similar to past ones. For example, many who argue for the civil rights of gays and lesbians say that discrimination based on sexual preference should not be tolerated today just as discrimination based on race, common thirty-five years ago, is no longer tolerated.

A special kind of argument based on similarity is *analogy*, which attempts to explain one thing, usually abstract, in terms of something else, usually more concrete. For example, in an argument opposing sharing the world's limited resources, philosopher Garrett Hardin reasons that requiring the wealthy nations of the world to feed the starving ones is like requiring the occupants of a lifeboat filled to capacity to take on those still in the water until the lifeboat sinks and everyone perishes.

Arguments of comparison can also assert difference, showing how two things are not the same. For example, some Americans supported participation in the 1991 Persian Gulf War by arguing that, unlike the disastrous conflict in Vietnam, this war was winnable. The argument went as follows:

> *Thesis:* America can defeat Iraq's military.
>
> *Reason:* Warfare in the deserts of Kuwait and Iraq is very different from warfare in the jungles of Vietnam.

The Probable or Likely   All reasoning about controversial issues relies on making a viewpoint seem probable or likely, but specific reasons drawn from the probable or likely come into play when we want to defend one account of events over another or when we want to attack or support a proposed policy. For example, in 1991 defenders of Supreme Court nominee Clarence Thomas attempted to discredit Anita Hill's accusations of sexual harassment in a number of ways, all related to probability: Is it likely, they asked, that she would remember so clearly and in such detail events that happened as long as ten years ago? Is it probable that a woman who had been harassed would follow Thomas from one job to another, as Hill did?

Cause and Effect   People think that most circumstances result from causes and that most changes in circumstances result in new effects. Belief in cause-and-effect relationships can provide reasons for certain arguments. For example, environmentalists have successfully argued for reductions in the world's output of hydrofluorocarbons by showing that the chemicals damage the Earth's ozone layer.

Cause-and-effect arguments are difficult to prove; witness the fact that cigarette manufacturers argued for years that the connection between smoking and lung disease cannot be demonstrated. Responsible arguments from cause and effect depend on credible and adequate hard evidence and expert opinion. And they must always acknowledge the possible existence of hidden factors; smoking and lung disease, for example, may be influenced by genetic predisposition.

Definition   Arguments often require definitions for clarification. However, a definition can also provide a reason in support of a thesis. If we define a term by placing it in a category, we are saying that whatever is true for the category is true for the term we are defining. For example, Elizabeth Cady Stanton's landmark 1892 argument for women's rights ("The Solitude of Self") was based on the definition "women are individuals":

> *Thesis:* Women must have suffrage, access to higher education, and sovereignty over their own minds and bodies.
>
> *Reason:* Women are individuals.

Stanton's audience, the American Congress, believed that all individuals are endowed with certain inalienable rights. Stanton's definition reminded them that women belong in the category "individual" as much as men and deserve the same rights.

Most good reasons come from one or a combination of these eight sources. However, simply knowing the sources will not automatically provide you with good reasons. Nothing can substitute for research and thoughtful inquiry.

Also, do not feel that quantity is crucial in finding good reasons. Be selective: focus on those reasons that appeal most to your audience and that you can develop thoroughly. A good argument is often based on one or two good reasons.

Student Sample: Finding Reasons   Justin used five of the eight sources listed in this section to help find some of his reasons. Here are the possible reasons he found; note that each reason is stated as a complete sentence.

From the audience's belief system:
Marriage is primarily about love and commitment, not sex.
Marriage is a stabilizing influence in society.

From rules or principles the audience would hold:
Everyone has an equal right to life, liberty, and the pursuit of happiness.

From expert opinion (in this case, a lawyer and some noted authors on gay rights):
Denying gays and lesbians the right to marry is discrimination.
Allowing gays and lesbians to marry will promote family values such as
    monogamy and the two-parent family.

From comparison or analogy:
Just as many people once thought marriage between blacks and whites
    should be illegal, now a majority think same-sex marriage should
    be illegal.
Gay and lesbian couples can love each other just as devotedly as
    heterosexual couples.

From cause and effect:
Marriage is a way for people to take care of each other rather than being
    a burden on society should they become ill or unemployed.

Justin now had far more reasons for his case than he needed. He now had
to evaluate his list.

 Following Through

> Here is one way to brainstorm for reasons. First, list the eight sources for
> finding reasons discussed on pages 209–210 in your writer's notebook, per-
> haps on the inside front cover or on the first or last page—someplace where
> you can easily find them. Practice using these sources by writing your current
> thesis at the top of another page and going through the list, writing down
> reasons as they occur to you.

Selecting and Ordering Reasons

Selecting reasons depends on two considerations: your thesis and your readers. Any thesis demands a certain line of reasoning. For example, the writer
contending that *Huckleberry Finn* should be required reading in high school
must offer a compelling reason for accepting no substitute—not even another novel by Mark Twain. Such a reason might be, "Because many critics
and novelists see *Huckleberry Finn* as the inspiration for much subsequent
American fiction, we cannot understand the American novel if we are not familiar with *Huckleberry Finn*." A reason of this kind should appeal to teachers or school administrators.

It is often difficult to see how to order reasons prior to drafting. Because we can easily reorder reasons as we rewrite, in developing our case we need only attempt an order that seems right. The writer advocating *Huckleberry Finn,* for example, might first defend the novel from the racism charge. Readers unaware of the controversy will want to know why the book needs defending, and well-informed readers will expect an immediate response to the book's critics who want to remove it from the classroom. Once racism has been disposed of, readers will be prepared to hear the reasons for keeping the book on required-reading lists.

Besides thinking about what your readers need and expect and how one reason may gain force by following another one, keep in mind a simple fact about memory: We recall best what we read last; next best, what we read first. A good rule of thumb, therefore, is to begin and end your defense of a thesis with your strongest reasons. A strong beginning also helps keep the reader reading; a strong conclusion avoids a sense of anticlimax.

Student Sample: Selecting and Ordering Reasons   Justin generated eight possible reasons to support his position on gay and lesbian marriage. To help decide which ones to use, he looked again at his audience profile. What had he said about the concerns of people who oppose same-sex marriage? Which of his potential reasons would best address these concerns?

Because his audience did not believe that the ban on same-sex marriage was a great loss to gays and lesbians, Justin decided to use the lawyer's point that the ban is discriminatory. The audience's other main concern was with the potential effect of gay marriage on the rest of society, particularly traditional marriage and family. Therefore, Justin decided to use the reasons about the benefits of same-sex marriage to society: that family values would be reinforced and that marriage keeps people from burdening society if they become unable to support themselves.

Justin noticed that some of his reasons overlapped. For example, the point that marriage is stabilizing was better expressed in combination with his more specific reasons about economic benefits and family values. And discrimination overlapped with his point about "life, liberty, and the pursuit of happiness." Overlap is common and requires some consolidation of reasons.

What is the best strategy for arranging the reasons? Initially, Justin wanted to begin with the point about discrimination, but then he decided to appeal to his audience's interests by listing the advantages of same-sex marriage first. Saving discrimination until the second half of his essay would let him end more strongly with an appeal to the readers' sense of fairness.

Then Justin rechecked his thesis to confirm that the reasons really supported it. He decided that his readers might not accept that marriage is a "basic human right" for those of the same sex, so he decided to add one more reason to support the similarities between heterosexuals and homosexuals.

Justin outlined his argument:

> *Thesis:* Everyone, gay and straight, will benefit from extending the basic human right of marriage to all couples, regardless of sexual preference.
>
> > *Reason:* It would reinforce family values such as monogamy and the two-parent family.
> >
> > *Reason:* It would help keep people from burdening society.
> >
> > *Reason:* Denying people the right to marry is discrimination.
> >
> > *Reason:* The love homosexuals have for each other is no different from love between heterosexuals.

Following Through

We call case structure flexible because as long as you maintain the three-level structure of thesis, reasons, and evidence, you can change everything else: throw out one thesis for another or alter its wording, add or take away reasons or evidence, or reorder both to achieve the desired impact. Order your reasons based on these questions:

What will my audience need or expect to read first?
Will one reason help set up another?
Which of my reasons are stronger? Can I begin and conclude my argument with the better reasons I have?

To a thesis you have already refined, now add the second level of your brief, the reason or reasons. Be ready to explain your decisions about selection and arrangement. Final decisions about ordering may come late in drafting—in a second or third writing. Spending a little time now thinking about orderings can save time later and make composing less difficult.

Using Evidence

The skillful use of evidence involves many judgments. Let's begin with some basic questions.

What Counts as Evidence? Because science and technology rely on the hard data of quantified evidence—especially statistics—some people assume that hard data are the only really good form of evidence. Such a view, however, is far too narrow. Besides hard data, evidence includes

- Quotation from authorities: expert opinion and traditional authorities such as respected political leaders, philosophers, and well-known authors. Besides printed sources, you can gather quotations from interviews and electronic sources.

- Constitutions, statutes, court rulings, organizational bylaws, company policy statements, and the like
- Examples and case histories (that is, extended narratives about an individual's or an organization's experience)
- The results of questionnaires that you devise and administer
- Personal experience

In short, evidence includes anything that confirms a good reason or that might increase your readers' acceptance of a reason.

What Kind of Evidence Is Best?   It depends on the particular reason. To argue for bicycle helmet legislation, we need facts and figures—hard data—to back up our claim that wearing helmets reduces the number of serious head injuries. To defend *Huckleberry Finn* by saying that it indicts racism will require quoted passages from the novel itself, statements from respected interpreters, and so forth.

When you have many pieces of evidence to choose from, select based on the quality of the evidence itself and its likely impact on readers. In general the best evidence is the most recent. The more trusted and prestigious the source, the more authority it will have. Arguments about AIDS in the United States, for example, often use data from the Centers for Disease Control in Atlanta, a research facility that specializes in the study of epidemics.

Finally, always look for evidence that will give you an edge in winning reader assent. For example, given the charge that *Huckleberry Finn* is offensive to blacks, its defense by an African-American literary scholar would carry more weight than its defense by a white scholar.

How Much Evidence Is Needed?   The amount of evidence required depends on two judgments: (1) how crucial a reason is to your case and (2) how much resistance readers are likely to have. Most cases have a pivotal reason, one point on which the whole case is built and therefore either stands or falls. Forman's case against racial profiling turns on accepting its unreliability. Such a reason needs much evidence; about one-fourth of Forman's essay supports this reason alone.

Of course, the pivotal reason may also be one which readers will resist. For instance, many arguments supporting women's right to abortion depend on a fetus not being considered fully human until it reaches a certain stage of development. This reason is obviously both pivotal and likely to be resisted, so devoting much space to evidence would be justified.

Student Sample: Using Evidence   Justin took the brief showing his case so far and on a table laid out all of his notecards and the material he had photocopied and marked up during research. He needed to select the expert opinions, quotations, statistics, dates, and other evidence to support his reasons. Doing this before drafting reveals where evidence is lacking or thin and what further research is necessary. To handle many sources, use different-colored markers to indicate which passages will work with which reasons. Justin then added evidence to his case structure, including noting the sources and page numbers.

> *Thesis:* Everyone, gay and straight, will benefit from extending the basic human right of marriage to all couples, regardless of sexual preference.
>
> > *Reason:* It would reinforce family values such as monogamy and the two-parent family.
> > *Evidence:* Marriage stabilizes relationships. (Sources: Rauch 23; Dean 114)
> > *Evidence:* Children of gays and lesbians should not be denied having two parents. (Sources: Dean 114; Sullivan; Salholz)
> > *Evidence:* If gays can have and adopt children, they should be able to marry. (Source: Salholz)
> >
> > *Reason:* It would provide a means of keeping people from burdening society.
> > *Evidence:* Spouses take care of each other. (Source: Rauch)
> >
> > *Reason:* Denying gays and lesbians the right to marry is discriminatory.
> > *Evidence:* Marriage includes rights to legal benefits. (Source: Dean 112)
> > *Evidence:* Domestic partnerships fail to provide these rights. (Sources: Dean 112; Salholz)
> > *Evidence:* Barring these marriages violates many democratic principles. (Sources: "Declaration"; Dean 113; Salholz)
> >
> > *Reason:* The love homosexuals have for each other is no different from love between heterosexuals.
> > *Evidence:* Many gays and lesbians are in monogamous relationships. (Source: Ayers 5)
> > *Evidence:* They have the same need to make a public, legal commitment. (Source: Sullivan)

 **Following Through**

Prepare a complete brief for an argument. Include both reasons and evidence and note sources. Remember that a brief is flexible, not engraved in stone. It can change as you draft and revise.

From Brief to Draft

Turning a brief into a paper is never easy. You will have to create parts of the essay that are not represented in the brief, such as an effective introduction and conclusion. You may also need paragraphs that provide background on

1. A position or general outlook on a topic is not a thesis. A thesis is a carefully worded **claim** that your entire essay backs up with reasons and evidence. **Experiment with various ways of stating your thesis** until it says *exactly* what you want it to say and creates the least resistance in your readers.

2. Be willing to give up or modify significantly a thesis you find you cannot support with good reasons and strong evidence that appeal *to your readers.* **We must argue a thesis that fits the available evidence,** which may differ a little or a lot from what we really believe.

3. Take the time to create a specific **audience profile.** What are the age, gender, and economic status of your target audience? What interests, beliefs, and values might they bring to your topic and thesis? Remember: There is no such thing as a "general audience." **We are always trying to convince some definite group of possible readers.**

4. **Unpack your thesis** to discover what you must argue. If you say, for instance, that *Huckleberry Finn* should be *required* reading in high school, you must show why *this particular novel* should be an experience shared by all American high school students. It won't be enough to argue that it's a good book.

5. Select your reasons based on what you must argue to defend your thesis combined with what you should say **given your audience's prior knowledge, preconceptions, prejudices, and interests.**

6. Be prepared to **try out different ways of ordering your reasons.** The order that seemed best in your brief might not work best as you draft and redraft your essay.

your topic, clarify or define an important term, or present and rebut an opposing argument. Following are suggestions and examples that should help.

The Introduction

Introductions are among the hardest things to write well. *Remember that an introduction need not be one paragraph;* it is often two or even three short ones. A good introduction (1) meets the needs of the audience by setting up the topic with just enough background information and (2) goes right to the heart of the issue as it relates to the audience's concerns.

Should the introduction end with the thesis statement? Such placement can work well in offering a transition to the reasons. However, the thesis need not be the last sentence in the introduction; it need not appear until much later — or at all, provided that readers can tell what it is from the title or from reading the essay.

Student Sample: The Introduction   Justin had to consider whether he should refer to the history of marriage and why people feel strongly about its value. Because his readers oppose same-sex marriage, presumably they were familiar with the traditions underpinning the institution. What would these readers need in the introduction? That the gay and lesbian rights movement calls for extending to same-sex couples the legal right to marry and that Justin's argument supports its position.

If Justin had opened with "The current intolerant attitudes toward homosexuality are excluding a whole class of citizens from exercising the right to marry," he would have been assuming that no valid reasons exist for denying same-sex marriage. Such a statement would offend his target audience members, who are not homophobic and would resent the implication that their view is based on prejudice. Justin's introduction attempts to establish some common ground with his readers:

> When two people fall deeply in love, they want to share every part of their lives with each other. For some, that could mean making a commitment, living together, and having children. But most people want more than that; they want to make their commitment public and legal through marriage, a tradition thousands of years old that has been part of almost every culture.
>
> But not everyone has the right to make that commitment. In this country and in most others, gays and lesbians are denied the right to marry. According to many Americans, allowing them to marry would destroy the institution and threaten traditional family values. Nevertheless, "advances in gay and lesbian civil rights [are] bringing awareness and newfound determination to many," and hundreds of same-sex couples are celebrating their commitment in religious ceremonies (Ayers 6). These couples would like to make their unions legal, and we should not prohibit them. Everyone, gay and straight, will benefit from extending the basic human right of marriage to all couples, regardless of sexual orientation.

Justin's first paragraph builds common ground by offering an overview of marriage that his readers are likely to share. In the second paragraph, he goes on to introduce the conflict, showing his awareness of the main objections to same-sex marriage. Note the tone: he's presenting himself as fair and responsible. Finally, Justin builds common ground by showing gays and lesbians positively, as people who love and commit to each other just as heterosexuals do.

A good introduction gains reader interest. To do this, writers use a number of techniques. They may open with the story of a person whose experience illustrates some aspect of the topic. Or they may begin with a surprising fact or opinion, as Jonathan Rauch, one of Justin's sources, did when he began his essay with this: "Whatever else marriage may or may not be, it is certainly falling apart." Usually, dictionary definitions are dull openers, but a *Newsweek* writer used one effectively to start her article on gay marriage: "Marry. 1 a) to join as husband and wife; unite in wedlock, b) to join (a man) to a woman as her husband, or (a woman) to a man as his wife." All of these are fairly dramatic techniques, but the best advice about openings is that *specifics work better than generalizations*. The *Newsweek* article just mentioned had this statement: "Say marriage and the mind turns to three-tiered cakes, bridal gowns, baby carriages."

How you open depends on your audience. Popular periodicals like *Newsweek* are more appropriate for dramatics than academic journals and college papers, but readers appreciate a memorable opening.

The Body: Presenting Reasons and Evidence

We now turn to drafting the body paragraphs. Although it's possible for one paragraph to develop a reason, *avoid thinking in terms of only one paragraph per reason*. Multiple paragraphs are the norm.

Paragraphs perform some function in presenting the case. You ought to be able to say what the function of a given paragraph is—and your readers ought to be able to sense it. Does it introduce a reason? Does it define a term? Does it support a reason by setting up an analogy? Does another paragraph support the same reason by offering examples or data or an illustrative case?

Not all paragraphs need topic sentences. Try instead to open each paragraph with hints that allow readers to see its function. For example, a transitional word or phrase announces that you are turning from one reason to a new one. When you introduce a new reason, be sure that readers can see how it relates to the thesis.

Student Sample: Presenting Reasons and Evidence   Let's look at how Justin developed his first reason. Recall that he decided to put the two reasons about benefits to society ahead of his reasons against discrimination. Of the two benefits he planned to cite, strengthening family values seemed the stronger one, so he led with it. Note how Justin's transitional phrase connects his first reason to the introduction, which had mentioned opposing views. Observe how he *develops his reason over a number of paragraphs*, drawing upon multiple sources, using both paraphrase and direct quotation.

In contrast to the critics, allowing gays and lesbians to marry promotes family values because it encourages monogamy and two-parent homes. As Jonathan Rauch, a gay writer, explains, marriage stabilizes relationships:

> One of the main benefits of publicly recognized marriage is that it binds couples together not only in their own eyes but also in the eyes of society at large. Around the partners is woven a web of expectations that they will spend nights together, go to parties together, take out mortgages together, buy furniture . . . together, and so on—all of which helps tie them together and keep them off the streets and at home. (23)

Some people would say that gays and lesbians can have these things without marriage by living together, but if marriage is not necessary for gays, it's not necessary for heterosexuals either. If it's immoral to live together outside marriage, then gays and lesbians should marry too. Craig Dean, a Washington, D.C., lawyer and gay-marriage activist, says that it is "paradoxical that mainstream America stereotypes Gays and Lesbians as unable to maintain long-term relationships, while at the same time denying them the very institutions to stabilize such relationships" (114).

Furthermore, many homosexual couples have children from previous marriages or by adoption. According to a study by the American Bar Association, gay and lesbian families with children make up six percent of all families in the United States (Dean 114). A secure environment is important for raising children, and allowing same-sex couples to marry would help. It would also send children the positive message that marriage is the foundation for family life. As Andrew Sullivan, a senior editor of *The New Republic,* says, why should gays be denied the very same family values that many politicians are arguing everyone else should have? Why should their children be denied these values? *Newsweek* writer Eloise Salholz describes the problem: If "more and more homosexual pairs are becoming parents . . . but cannot marry, what kind of bastardized definition of family is society imposing on their offspring?"

At this point, Justin is ready to take up his next reason: Marriage provides a system by which people take care of each other, lessening the burden on society. Justin's entire essay appears on pages 222–225. Look it over carefully before you draft your essay. Note which paragraphs bring in the remaining reasons and which paragraphs present and rebut opposing views.

The Conclusion

Once you have presented your case, what else is there to say? Short papers don't need summaries. And the conclusion is not a place for new points.

Strategically, in your conclusion you want to imply, "Case made!" Here are some suggestions for doing so:

1. Look back at your introduction. Perhaps a question you posed there has an answer, a problem a solution.
2. Think about larger contexts for your argument. For example, the *Huckleberry Finn* case could end by pointing out that education becomes diluted and artificial when the curriculum avoids controversy.
3. If you end with a memorable quotation, comment on it as you would whenever you quote.
4. Be aware that many conclusions should be shorter. If you are dissatisfied with yours, lop off the last sentence or so. You may uncover the real ending.

5. Pay attention to style, especially in the last sentence. An awkwardly worded sentence will not have a sound of finality, but one with some rhythmic punch or consciously repeated sounds can wrap up an essay neatly.

Student Sample: The Conclusion   Following is Justin's conclusion.

It's only natural for people in love to want to commit to each other; this desire is the same for homosexuals and lesbians as it is for heterosexuals. One recent survey showed that "over half of all lesbians and almost 40% of gay men" live in committed relationships and share a home together (Ayers 5). As Sullivan, who is gay, explains, "At some point in our lives, some of us are lucky enough to meet the person we truly love. And we want to commit to that person in front of family and country for the rest of our lives. It's the most simple, the most natural, the most human instinct in the world. How could anyone seek to oppose that?" And what does anyone gain when that right is denied? That's a question that everyone needs to ask themselves.

 Following Through

Using your brief as a guide, write a draft version of your argument to convince. In addition to the advice in this chapter, refer to Chapter 5, which covers paraphrasing, summarizing, quoting, incorporating, and documenting source material.

Revising the Draft

Too often, revising is confused with editing. Revising makes large changes in content and organization, not sentence-level corrections or stylistic changes, which are part of editing.

To get a sense of what is involved in revising, you should know that the brief of Justin Spidel's essay on page 214 is actually a revised version. Justin had originally written a draft with his reasons presented in a different order and without three of the sources that now appear in his paper. When Justin exchanged drafts with another classmate who was writing on the same topic, he discovered that some of her sources would also help him. The following paragraph was the original third paragraph of Justin's draft, immediately following the thesis. Compare it to the revised essay, printed on pages 222–225. Justin improved this part of his argument by developing the point more thoroughly in two paragraphs and by placing them toward the end of the paper.

Not to allow same-sex marriage is clearly discriminatory. The Human Rights Act of 1977 in the District of Columbia "prohibits discrimination based on sexual orientation. According to the Act, 'every individual shall have an equal opportunity to participate in the economic, cultural, and intellectual life of the District and have an *equal opportunity to participate in all aspects of life*'" (Dean 112). If politicians are going to make such laws, they need to recognize all their implications and follow them. Not allowing homosexuals to marry is denying the right to "participate" in an aspect of life that is important to every couple that has found love in each other. Also, the Constitution guarantees equality to every man and woman; that means nondiscrimination, something that is not happening for gays and lesbians in the present.

Reading Your Own Writing Critically

Chapter 2 discussed critical or analytical reading. Apply what you learned to reading your own writing.

Read for Structure   Remember, different parts of an argument perform different jobs. Read to see if you can divide your draft easily into its strategic parts and can identify the role each group of paragraphs plays in the paper. If you have trouble identifying the parts and how they fit together, you need to see where you repeat yourself or separate connected points. This may be the time for scissors and tape, or electronic cutting and pasting.

Read for Rhetorical Context   You may need to revise to make the rhetorical context clearer: Why are you writing and to whom? You establish this reader awareness in the introduction, and you need to think about your readers' values and beliefs that underlie their position on the issue. You may need to revise your introduction to engage your readers better. The more specific you can make your opening, the more likely you are to succeed.

Inquire into Your Own Writing   Have a dialogue with yourself about it. Some of the questions listed on pages 159–160 are relevant:

1. Ask what you mean by the words that are central to the argument. Have you provided definitions as needed?
2. Find the reasons, and ask about their relation to the thesis. State the connection with the word "because."
3. Explore the assumptions behind your thesis and your reasons. Ask yourself, What's not said that someone has to believe? Be sure your audience will share the assumption. If not, state the assumption and argue for it.
4. Look at your comparisons and analogies. Are they plausible?

1. Be sure you understand the writer's intended audience, by either discussing it with the writer or reading any notes the writer has provided. Read the entire draft. Number the paragraphs so that you can refer to them later.
2. If you can find an explicit statement of the author's thesis, underline or highlight it. If you cannot find one, ask yourself whether it is necessary. If the thesis is easily inferred, restate it in your own words at the top of the first page.
3. Think about how the thesis could be improved. Is it offensive, vague, too general? Does it have a single focus? Is it clearly stated?
4. Circle the words most central to the thesis. Could there be disagreement about the meaning of any of them? If so, has the author clarified what he or she means?
5. Look for the argument's structure and strategy. Underline the sentences that present the reasons. If you can't identify the reasons, let the author know. Also think about the order of the reasons. Suggest improvements if you can.
6. Identify the author's best reason. How would it appeal to the audience? Has the author placed it in a good position for emphasizing it?
7. What reasons need more or better support? Indicate what factual information seems lacking, what sources don't seem solid or credible, what statements sound too general, or what reasoning — such as analogies — seems shaky.
8. Ask whether the author shows awareness of opposing arguments. If not, should this be added? What are the best challenges you can make to anything the author has said?
9. Evaluate the introduction and conclusion.

5. Look at your evidence. Have you offered facts, expert opinion, illustrations, and so on? Have you presented these in a way that would not raise doubts but eliminate them?
6. Consider your own bias. What do you stand to gain from advocating the position you take? Is your argument self-serving or truth-serving?

Getting Feedback from Other Readers

Because it's hard to be objective about our own work, getting feedback from a friend, classmate, or teacher is a good way to see where revision would help. Ask your readers to use a revision checklist, such as the one above.

Following Through

1. After you have written a draft of your own argument, revise it using the suggestions in the preceding section. Then exchange your revised draft for a classmate's, and use the "Reader's Checklist for Revision" on page 221 to guide you in making suggestions for each other's drafts.
2. Read the final version of Justin Spidel's argument, following. Then apply the questions for inquiry listed on pages 159–160 to assess his argument.
3. If you were assigned to suggest ways to improve Justin's argument, what would you advise? Reread his audience profile (page 204), and use the "Reader's Checklist for Revision" (page 221) to help you decide.

www.mhhe.
com/crusius

For help editing
your essay,
go to:
Editing

Editing and Proofreading

The final steps of writing any argument are editing and proofreading, which we discuss in the appendix.

STUDENT SAMPLE: *An Essay Arguing to Convince*

www.mhhe.
com/crusius

For other
student-written
arguments,
go to:
Writing >
Sample
Argument
Papers

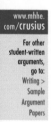

WHO SHOULD HAVE THE RIGHT TO MARRY?

Justin Spidel

When two people fall deeply in love, they want to share their lives. For some, that could mean making a commitment, living together, and maybe having children. But most people in love want more: they want to make their commitment public and legal through marriage, a tradition thousands of years old and part of almost every culture.

But not everyone has the opportunity to make that commitment. In this country and most others, gays and lesbians are denied the right to marry. According to many citizens and politicians, allowing them that right would destroy the institution and threaten traditional family values. Nevertheless, "advances in gay and lesbian civil rights [are] bringing awareness and newfound determination to many," and hundreds of same-sex couples are celebrating their commitment to each other in religious ceremonies (Ayers 6). These couples would like to make their unions legal, and we should not prohibit them. Everyone, gay and straight, will benefit from extending marriage to all couples, regardless of sexual orientation.

In contrast to the critics, allowing gays and lesbians to marry promotes family values because it encourages monogamy and two-parent homes. As Jonathan Rauch, a gay writer, explains, marriage stabilizes relationships:

> One of the main benefits of publicly recognized marriage is that it binds couples together not only in their own eyes but also in the eyes of society at large. Around the partners is woven a web of expectations that they will spend nights together, go to parties together, take out mortgages together, buy furniture . . . together, and so on—all of which helps tie them together and keep them off the streets and at home. (23)

Some people would say that gays and lesbians can have these things without marriage by living together, but if marriage is not necessary for gays, it's not necessary for heterosexuals either. If it's immoral to live together outside of marriage, then gays and lesbians should marry too. Craig Dean, a Washington, D.C., lawyer and gay-marriage activist, says that it is "paradoxical that mainstream America stereotypes Gays and Lesbians as unable to maintain long-term relationships, while at the same time denying them the very institutions to stabilize such relationships" (114).

Furthermore, many homosexual couples have children from previous marriages or by adoption. According to a study by the American Bar Association, gay and lesbian families with children make up six percent of all families in the United States (Dean 114). A secure environment is important for raising children, and allowing same-sex couples to marry would help. It would also send children the positive message that marriage is the foundation for family life. As Andrew Sullivan, a senior editor of *The New Republic,* asks, why should gays be denied the very same family values that many politicians are arguing everyone else should have? Why should their children be denied these values? *Newsweek* writer Eloise Salholz describes the problem: If "more and more homosexual pairs are becoming parents . . . but cannot marry, what kind of bastardized definition of family is society imposing on their offspring?"

Binding people together in marriage also benefits society because marriage encourages people to take care of each other. Marriage means that individuals are not a complete burden on society when they become sick, injured, old, or unemployed. Jonathan Rauch argues, "If marriage has any meaning at all, it is that when you collapse from a stroke, there will be at least one other person whose 'job' it is to drop everything and come to your aid" (22). This benefit of marriage may be even more important for homosexuals because their relationships with parents and other relatives may be strained. Same-sex couples already show such devotion to each other; recognition of legal marriage would strengthen that devotion. 5

In spite of the benefits, some say that same-sex marriage would upset our society's conventional idea of marriage. According to William Bennett, letting people of the same sex marry "would obscure marriage's enormously consequential function—procreation and childrearing."

Procreation may be a consequence of marriage, but it is not the main reason people get married. Today "even for heterosexuals, marriage is becoming an emotional union and commitment rather than an arrangement to produce . . . children" ("Marriage" 770). And what about sterile heterosexual couples? No one would say they should not be allowed to marry. If the right to marry is based on the potential to have children, "then a postmenopausal woman who applies for a marriage license should be turned away at the courthouse door" (Rauch 22). No one expects couples who get married to prove that they can have children and intend to do so.

In the same way, to outlaw same-sex marriage is clearly discriminatory. According to Craig Dean, "Marriage is an important civil right because it gives societal recognition and legal protection to a relationship and confers numerous benefits to spouses" (112). Denying same-sex marriage means that gays and lesbians cannot enjoy such benefits as health insurance through a spouse's employer, life insurance benefits, tax preferences, leaves for bereavement, and inheritance. In some states, laws about domestic partnership give same-sex couples some of these rights, but they are not as secure as they would be if the couple were legally next of kin. Thomas Stoddard, a lawyer, says that domestic partnership is the equivalent of "second-class citizenship" (qtd. in Salholz).

Aside from these concrete forms of discrimination, denying same-sex marriage keeps gay and lesbian citizens from enjoying the basic human right to "life, liberty, and the pursuit of happiness." The Human Rights Act of 1977 in the District of Columbia makes one of the strongest stands against discrimination based on sexual orientation. According to the Act, "every individual shall have an equal opportunity to participate in the economic, cultural, and intellectual life of the District and have an equal opportunity to participate in all aspects of life" (qtd. in Dean 113). Not allowing homosexuals to marry does deny them the right to participate in an aspect of life important to almost every loving couple.

Of course, some churches will never agree to perform same-sex marriages because they believe that homosexuality is a sin. The separation of church and state allows all churches to follow their own doctrines; many things that are legal in this country are opposed by some churches. The government should not deny the *legal* right to marry because some churches oppose it.

It's only natural for people in love to want to commit to each other; 10
this desire is the same for homosexuals and lesbians as it is for heterosexuals. One recent survey showed that "over half of all lesbians and almost 40% of gay men" live in committed relationships and share a house together (Ayers 5). As Sullivan explains, "At some point in our lives, some of us are lucky enough to meet the person we truly love. And we want to commit to that person in front of family and country for the rest of our lives. It's the most simple, the most natural, the most human instinct in the world. How could anyone seek to oppose that?" And what does

anyone gain when the right is denied? That's a question that everyone needs to ask themselves.

Works Cited

Ayers, Tess, and Paul Brown. The Essential Guide to Lesbian and Gay Weddings. San Francisco: Harper, 1994.

Bennett, William, "Leave Marriage Alone." Newsweek 3 June 1996: 27.

Dean, Craig R. "Gay Marriage: A Civil Right." The Journal of Homosexuality 27.3–4 (1994): 111–15.

"Marriage." The Encyclopedia of Homosexuality. Ed. Wayne R. Dynes. New York: Garland, 1990.

Rauch, Jonathan. "For Better or Worse?" The New Republic 6 May 1996: 18–23.

Salholz, Eloise. "For Better or For Worse." Newsweek 24 May 1993: 69.

Sullivan, Andrew. "Let Gays Marry." Newsweek 3 June 1996: 26.

www.mhhe.
com/crusius

For an electronic tool that helps create properly formatted works-cited pages, go to:
Research >
Bibliomaker

Chapter 8

Motivating Action: Arguing to Persuade

In Chapter 1, we defined persuasion as "convincing *plus*" because, in addition to reason, three other forms of appeal come into play: (1) appeal to the writer's character, (2) appeal to the emotions of the audience, and (3) appeal to style, the artful use of language itself. Building on what you learned about making cases in Chapter 7, this chapter's goal is to help you understand and control persuasion's wider range of appeals.

But shouldn't reason be enough? Perhaps it would be if human beings were completely rational. But we are only sometimes rational—and then imperfectly. We often agree with an argument but lack the courage or motivation to translate assent into action.

Persuasion, then, aims to close the gap between assent and action. Because persuasion seeks a deeper and stronger commitment, it appeals to the whole person, to our full humanity, not just to the mind. It offers reasons because people respond to them. But it also wants the reader to identify with the writer, to like and trust the arguer. The persuader also wants to stir the reader's emotions because strong feelings prompt the will to act; persuasion works on the heart too. Finally, style matters in persuasion because favorable response to what is said depends on how well it is said. (See the Concept Close-Up box on page 228.)

WHEN TO CONVINCE AND WHEN TO PERSUADE: A MATTER OF EMPHASIS

When should you aim to persuade rather than convince? Always notice what an assignment calls for because the full range of persuasive appeal is not always appropriate in college. In general, the more academic the audience or the more purely intellectual the issue, the less appropriate the full resources of persuasion are. Philosophy or science papers require you to convince, but seldom to persuade. Good reasons and evidence are all that matters.

Concept Close-Up
The Four Forms of Appeal

Form	Function	Presence in Text
Reason	Logical cogency	Your case; any supported contention
Character	Personal appeal	Indications of author's status and values
Emotion	Appeals to feelings	Concrete descriptions, moving images
Style	Appeals through language	Word choice, sentence structure, metaphor

Essentially, persuasion differs from convincing in seeking action, not just agreement; it integrates rational appeal with other ways to influence people. We'll look more closely at the various forms of appeal later in the chapter.

When you are working with public issues, matters of policy or questions of right and wrong, persuasion's fuller range of appeal is usually appropriate. Arguments in these areas affect not just how we think but also how we act; the heightened urgency of persuasion sparks action or change.

Convincing requires control over case-making. In persuasion we must also (1) gain our readers' confidence and respect, (2) touch our readers' emotions, and (3) focus on language itself. We want an essay that integrates all appeals so that they work together.

As with convincing, writing a persuasive argument begins with inquiry and research. However, you must think more about the audience you seek to persuade from the outset.

ANALYZING YOUR READERS

Persuasion begins with difference and ends with identity; our readers will differ from us in beliefs, attitudes, and desires. Successful persuasion brings readers and writer together, creating a sense of connection between people previously separated by viewpoint. What can we do to overcome difference and create identity? First, we need to understand our readers' frame of mind.

Who Is the Audience, and How Do They View the Topic?

Good persuaders are able to empathize and sympathize with other people, building solidarity. To aid audience analysis, ask these questions:

- Who are my readers? How do I define them in terms of age, economic and social class, gender, education, and so forth?
- What typical attitudes or stances toward my topic do they have?
- What in their background or daily experiences helps explain their point of view?

- What are they likely to know about my topic?
- How might they be uninformed or misinformed about it?
- How would they like to see the problem, question, or issue resolved, answered, or handled? Why? That is, what *personal stake* do they have in the topic?
- In what larger framework—religious, ethical, political, economic— do they see my topic? That is, what general beliefs and values are involved?

What Are Our Differences?

Audience analysis isn't complete until you specify exactly what divides you from your readers. These questions can help:

- Is the difference a matter of assumptions? If so, how can I shake my readers' confidence in their assumptions and offer others favorable to my position?
- Is the difference a matter of principle, the application of general rules to specific cases? If so, should I dispute the principle itself and offer a competing one the audience also values? Or should I show why the principle does not apply to my subject?
- Is the difference a matter of a hierarchy of values—that is, do we value the same things but in a different order of priority? If so, how might I restructure my readers' values?
- Is the difference a matter of ends or of means? If ends, how can I show that my vision of what ought to be is better or that realizing my ends will also secure the ends of my readers? If a difference of means, how can I show that my methods are justified and effective, preferable to others?
- Is the difference a matter of interpretation? If so, how can I show that my interpretation is better, accounting more adequately for the facts?
- Is the difference a matter of implications or consequences? If so, how can I convince my readers that what they fear may happen will not happen, or that the outcome will not be as bad as they think, or that any negatives will be outweighed by positives?

What Do We Have in Common?

In seeking common ground with your readers, remember that, no matter how sharply you and your readers disagree, resources for identification always exist. Ask

- Do we have a shared local identity—as members of the same organization or as students at the same university?
- Do we share a more abstract, collective identity—citizens of the same region or nation, worshippers in the same religion, and so forth?

- Do we share a common cause—such as preventing child abuse or overcoming racial prejudice?
- Is there a shared experience or human activity—raising children, caring for aging parents, helping a friend in distress, struggling to make ends meet?
- Can we connect through a well-known event or cultural happening—a popular movie, a best-selling book, something in the news of interest to both you and your readers?
- Is there a historical event, person, or document we both respect?

READING A PERSUASIVE ESSAY

To illustrate the importance of audience analysis, we turn to a classic persuasive essay of the twentieth century, Martin Luther King's "Letter from Birmingham Jail." As we will see, King masterfully analyzed his audience and used the full range of appeals for his readership.

Background

To appreciate King's persuasive powers, we must first understand the events that led to the "Letter" and the actions King wanted his readers to take. In 1963, as president of the Southern Christian Leadership Conference, King had been organizing and participating in civil rights demonstrations in Birmingham, Alabama. He was arrested, and while he was in jail, eight white Alabama clergymen of various denominations issued a public statement critical of his activities. Published in a local newspaper, the statement deplored the demonstrations as "unwise and untimely":

> We the undersigned clergymen are among those who, in January, issued "An Appeal for Law and Order and Common Sense," in dealing with racial problems in Alabama. We expressed understanding that honest convictions in racial matters could properly be pursued in the courts, but urged that decisions of those courts should in the meantime be peacefully obeyed.
>
> Since that time there had been some evidence of increased forbearance and a willingness to face facts. Responsible citizens have undertaken to work on various problems which cause racial friction and unrest. In Birmingham, recent public events have given indication that we all have opportunity for a new constructive and realistic approach to racial problems.
>
> However, we are now confronted by a series of demonstrations by some of our Negro citizens, directed and led in part by outsiders. We recognize the natural impatience of people who feel that their hopes are slow in being realized. But we are convinced that these demonstrations are unwise and untimely.
>
> We agree rather with certain local Negro leadership which has called for honest and open negotiation of racial issues in our area. And we believe this

Concept Close-Up
Audience Analysis

To understand any audience we hope to persuade, we must know *both* what separates us from them *and* what common ground we share.

We may **differ** from our audience in:

Kind of Difference	Example
Assumptions	Western writers assume that separation of church and state is normal; some Muslim audiences do not make the distinction.
Principles	Most conservative writers believe in the principle of the open market; labor audiences often believe in protecting American jobs from foreign competition.
Value rankings	Some writers value personal freedom over duty and obligation; some audiences place duty and obligation above personal freedom.
Ends and means	Writer and audience may agree about purpose (for example, making America safe from terrorism) but disagree about what policies will best accomplish this end.
Interpretation	Some writers understood the September 11, 2001, attacks as acts of war; some audiences saw them as criminal acts that demanded legal rather than military measures.
Consequences	Some writers think making divorce harder would keep more couples together; some audiences think it would only promote individual unhappiness.

We may **share** with our audience:

Kind of Identification	Example
Local identity	Students and teachers at the same university
Collective identity	Citizens of the same state or the same nation
Common cause	Improving the environment
Common experience	Pride in the success of American Olympic athletes
Common history	Respect for soldiers who have died defending the United States

Essentially, we must understand differences to discover how we need to argue; we must use the resources of identification to overcome differences separating us from our readers.

---

kind of facing of issues can best be accomplished by citizens of our own metropolitan area, white and Negro, meeting with their knowledge and experience of the local situation. All of us need to face that responsibility and find proper channels for its accomplishment.

Just as we formerly pointed out that "hatred and violence have no sanction in our religious and political traditions," we also point out that such actions as

Figure 8.1   Rosa Parks, whose refusal to move to the back of a bus touched off the Mont-gomery bus boycott and the beginning of the civil rights movement, is fingerprinted by Deputy Sheriff D. H. Lackey in Montgomery, Alabama, February 22, 1956. She was among some 100 people charged with violating segregation laws. (AP Photo/Gene Herrick)

incite to hatred and violence, however technically peaceful those actions may be, have not contributed to the resolution of our local problems. We do not be-lieve that these days of new hope are days when extreme measures are justified in Birmingham.

We commend the community as a whole, and the local news media and law enforcement officials in particular, on the calm manner in which these demon-strations have been handled. We urge the public to continue to show restraint should the demonstrations continue, and the law enforcement officials to re-main calm and continue to protect our city from violence.

We further strongly urge our own Negro community to withdraw support from these demonstrations, and to unite locally in working peacefully for a better Birmingham. When rights are consistently denied, a cause should be pressed in the courts and in negotiations among local leaders, and not in the streets. We appeal to both our white and Negro citizenry to observe the principles of law and order and common sense.

Signed by:
C. C. J. Carpenter, D.D., LL.D., *Bishop of Alabama*
Joseph A. Durick, D.D., *Auxiliary Bishop, Diocese of Mobile, Birmingham*
     Rabbi Milton L. Grafman, *Temple Emanu-El, Birmingham, Alabama*
Bishop Paul Hardin, *Bishop of the Alabama-West Florida Conference of the*
     Methodist Church
Bishop Nolan B. Harmon, *Bishop of the North Alabama Conference of the*
     Methodist Church
George M. Murray, D.D., LL.D., *Bishop Coadjutor, Episcopal Diocese of Alabama*
Edward V. Ramage, *Moderator, Synod of the Alabama Presbyterian Church in the*
     United States
Earl Stallings, *Pastor, First Baptist Church, Birmingham, Alabama*

In his cell, King began his letter on the margins of that newspaper page, addressing it specifically to the eight clergymen, hoping to move them from disapproval to support, to recognizing the need for demonstrations. King knew that his letter would reach a larger audience, including the demonstrators themselves, who were energized by its message when 50,000 copies were later distributed. King's letter has since reached a global audience with its argument for nonviolent protest in the service of moral law.

The Basic Message

Before turning to King's "Letter from Birmingham Jail," read the following summary, which differs from King's prose as a nursery song differs from a Beethoven symphony.

> Because I am the leader of an organization that fights injustice, it is most appropriate for me to be in Birmingham, where human rights are being violated. Our campaign of nonviolent civil disobedience was not rash and unpremeditated but the result of a history of failed negotiations and broken promises. We aim to increase tensions here until the city leaders realize that dialogue must occur. Our actions are not untimely but long overdue, given that blacks have been denied their civil rights in this country for over 340 years.
>
> While we advocate breaking some laws, we distinguish between moral laws and immoral laws that degrade the human personality. The former must be obeyed, the latter disobeyed openly and lovingly. We may seem extreme, but people who accomplish great things are often so labeled, and our nonviolent protests are preferable to inaction.
>
> In failing to support us, white Southern religious leaders fail to meet the challenges of social injustice. You should not praise the police for breaking up the demonstrations but rather the demonstrators for standing up for human dignity.

Letter from Birmingham Jail
Martin Luther King, Jr.

April 16, 1963

My Dear Fellow Clergymen:

While confined here in the Birmingham city jail, I came across your recent statement calling my present activities "unwise and untimely." Seldom do I pause to answer criticism of my work and ideas. If I sought to answer all the criticisms that cross my desk, my secretaries would have little time for anything other than such correspondence in the course of the day, and I would have no time for constructive work. But since I feel that you are men of genuine good will and that your criticisms are sincerely set forth, I want to try to answer your statement in what I hope will be patient and reasonable terms.

I think I should indicate why I am here in Birmingham, since you have been influenced by the view which argues against "outsiders coming in." I have the honor of serving as president of the Southern Christian Leadership Conference, an organization operating in every southern state, with headquarters in Atlanta, Georgia. We have some eighty-five affiliated organizations across the South, and one of them is the Alabama Christian Movement for Human Rights. Frequently we share staff, educational, and financial resources with our affiliates. Several months ago the affiliate here in Birmingham asked us to be on call to engage in a nonviolent direct-action program if such were deemed necessary. We readily consented, and when the hour came we lived up to our promise. So I, along with several members of my staff, am here because I was invited here. I am here because I have organizational ties here.

But more basically, I am in Birmingham because injustice is here. Just as the prophets of the eighth century BC left their villages and carried their "thus saith the Lord" far beyond the boundaries of their home towns, and just as the Apostle Paul left his village of Tarsus and carried the gospel of Jesus Christ to the far corners of the Greco-Roman world, so am I compelled to carry the gospel of freedom beyond my own home town. Like Paul, I must constantly respond to the Macedonian call for aid.

Moreover, I am cognizant of the interrelatedness of all communities and states. I cannot sit idly by in Atlanta and not be concerned about what happens in Birmingham. Injustice anywhere is a threat to justice everywhere. We are caught in an inescapable network of mutuality, tied in a single garment of destiny. Whatever affects one directly, affects all indirectly. Never again can we afford to live with the narrow, provincial "outside agitator" idea. Anyone who lives inside the United States can never be considered an outsider anywhere within its bounds.

You deplore the demonstrations taking place in Birmingham. But your   5
statement, I am sorry to say, fails to express a similar concern for the conditions that brought about the demonstrations. I am sure that none of you
would want to rest content with the superficial kind of social analysis that
deals merely with effects and does not grapple with underlying causes. It is
unfortunate that demonstrations are taking place in Birmingham, but it is
even more unfortunate that the city's white power structure left the Negro
community with no alternative.

In any nonviolent campaign there are four basic steps: collection of the
facts to determine whether injustices exist; negotiation; self-purification;
and direct action. We have gone through all these steps in Birmingham.
There can be no gainsaying the fact that racial injustice engulfs this community. Birmingham is probably the most thoroughly segregated city in the
United States. Its ugly record of brutality is widely known. Negroes have experienced grossly unjust treatment in the courts. There have been more un-
solved bombings of Negro homes and churches in Birmingham than in
any other city in the nation. These are the hard, brutal facts of the case.
On the basis of these conditions, Negro leaders sought to negotiate with
the city fathers. But the latter consistently refused to engage in good-faith
negotiation.

Then, last September, came the opportunity to talk with leaders of
Birmingham's economic community. In the course of the negotiations, certain promises were made by the merchants — for example, to remove the
stores' humiliating racial signs. On the basis of these promises, the Reverend Fred Shuttlesworth and the leaders of the Alabama Christian Movement for Human Rights agreed to a moratorium on all demonstrations.
As the weeks and months went by, we realized that we were the victims
of a broken promise. A few signs, briefly removed, returned; the others
remained.

As in so many past experiences, our hopes had been blasted, and the
shadow of deep disappointment settled upon us. We had no alternative except to prepare for direct action, whereby we would present our very bodies
as a means of laying our case before the conscience of the local and the national community. Mindful of the difficulties involved, we decided to undertake a process of self-purification. We began a series of workshops on
nonviolence, and we repeatedly asked ourselves: "Are you able to accept
blows without retaliating?" "Are you able to endure the ordeal of jail?" We
decided to schedule our direct-action program for the Easter season, realizing that except for Christmas, this is the main shopping period of the year.
Knowing that a strong economic-withdrawal program would be the by-
product of direct action, we felt that this would be the best time to bring
pressure to bear on the merchants for the needed change.

Then it occurred to us that Birmingham's mayoral election was coming
up in March, and we speedily decided to postpone action until after election day. When we discovered that the Commissioner of Public Safety,
Eugene "Bull" Connor, had piled up enough votes to be in the run-off, we

decided again to postpone action until the day after the run-off so that the demonstrations could not be used to cloud the issues. Like many others, we waited to see Mr. Connor defeated, and to this end we endured postponement after postponement. Having aided in this community need, we felt that our direct-action program could be delayed no longer.

You may well ask: "Why direct action? Why sit-ins, marches and so   10
forth? Isn't negotiation a better path?" You are quite right in calling for negotiation. Indeed, this is the very purpose of direct action. Nonviolent direct action seeks to create such a crisis and foster such a tension that a community which has constantly refused to negotiate is forced to confront the issue. It seeks so to dramatize the issue that it can no longer be ignored. My citing the creation of tension as part of the work of the nonviolent-resister may sound rather shocking. But I must confess that I am not afraid of the word "tension." I have earnestly opposed violent tension, but there is a type of constructive, nonviolent tension which is necessary for growth. Just as Socrates felt that it was necessary to create a tension in the mind so that individuals could rise from the bondage of myths and half-truths to the unfettered realm of creative analysis and objective appraisal, so must we see the need for nonviolent gadflies to create the kind of tension in society that will help men rise from the dark depths of prejudice and racism to the majestic heights of understanding and brotherhood.

The purpose of our direct-action program is to create a situation so crisis-packed that it will inevitably open the door to negotiation. I therefore concur with you in your call for negotiation. Too long has our beloved Southland been bogged down in a tragic effort to live in monologue rather than dialogue.

One of the basic points in your statement is that the action that I and my associates have taken in Birmingham is untimely. Some have asked: "Why didn't you give the new city administration time to act?" The only answer that I can give to this query is that the new Birmingham administration must be prodded about as much as the outgoing one, before it will act. We are sadly mistaken if we feel that the election of Albert Boutwell as mayor will bring the millennium to Birmingham. While Mr. Boutwell is a much more gentle person than Mr. Connor, they are both segregationists, dedicated to maintenance of the status quo. I have hope that Mr. Boutwell will be reasonable enough to see the futility of massive resistance to desegregation. But he will not see this without pressure from devotees of civil rights. My friends, I must say to you that we have not made a single gain in civil rights without determined legal and nonviolent pressure. Lamentably, it is an historical fact that privileged groups seldom give up their privileges voluntarily. Individuals may see the moral light and voluntarily give up their unjust posture; but, as Reinhold Niebuhr has reminded us, groups tend to be more immoral than individuals.

We know through painful experience that freedom is never voluntarily given by the oppressor; it must be demanded by the oppressed. Frankly,

I have yet to engage in a direct-action campaign that was "well timed" in the view of those who have not suffered unduly from the disease of segregation. For years now I have heard the word "Wait!" It rings in the ear of every Negro with piercing familiarity. This "Wait" has almost always meant "Never." We must come to see, with one of our distinguished jurists, that "justice too long delayed is justice denied."

We have waited for more than 340 years for our constitutional God-given rights. The nations of Asia and Africa are moving with jetlike speed toward gaining political independence, but we still creep at horse-and-buggy pace toward gaining a cup of coffee at a lunch counter. Perhaps it is easy for those who have never felt the stinging darts of segregation to say, "Wait." But when you have seen vicious mobs lynch your mothers and fathers at will and drown your sisters and brothers at whim; when you have seen hate-filled policemen curse, kick, and even kill your black brothers and sisters; when you see the vast majority of your twenty million Negro brothers smothering in an airtight cage of poverty in the midst of an affluent society; when you suddenly find your tongue twisted and your speech stammering as you seek to explain to your six-year-old daughter why she can't go to the public amusement park that has just been advertised on television, and see tears welling up in her eyes when she is told that Funtown is closed to colored children, and see ominous clouds of inferiority beginning to form in her little mental sky, and see her beginning to distort her personality by developing an unconscious bitterness toward white people; when you have to concoct an answer for a five-year-old son who is asking: "Daddy, why do white people treat colored people so mean?"; when you take a cross-country drive and find it necessary to sleep night after night in the uncomfortable corners of your automobile because no motel will accept you; when you are humiliated day in and day out by nagging signs reading "white" and "colored"; when your first name becomes "nigger," your middle name becomes "boy" (however old you are), and your last name becomes "John," and your wife and mother are never given the respected title "Mrs."; when you are harried by day and haunted by night by the fact that you are a Negro, living constantly at tiptoe stance, never quite knowing what to expect next, and are plagued with inner fears and outer resentments; when you are forever fighting a degenerating sense of "nobodiness"—then you will understand why we find it difficult to wait. There comes a time when the cup of endurance runs over, and men are no longer willing to be plunged into the abyss of despair. I hope, sirs, you can understand our legitimate and unavoidable impatience.

You express a great deal of anxiety over our willingness to break laws. 15
This is certainly a legitimate concern. Since we so diligently urge people to obey the Supreme Court's decision of 1954 outlawing segregation in the public schools, at first glance it may seem rather paradoxical for us consciously to break laws. One may well ask: "How can you advocate breaking some laws and obeying others?" The answer lies in the fact that there are

two types of laws: just and unjust. I would be the first to advocate obeying just laws. One has not only a legal but a moral responsibility to obey just laws. Conversely, one has a moral responsibility to disobey unjust laws. I would agree with St. Augustine that "an unjust law is no law at all."

Now, what is the difference between the two? How does one determine whether a law is just or unjust? A just law is a man-made code that squares with the moral law or the law of God. An unjust law is a code that is out of harmony with the moral law. To put it in the terms of St. Thomas Aquinas: An unjust law is a human law that is not rooted in eternal law and natural law. Any law that uplifts human personality is just. Any law that degrades human personality is unjust. All segregation statutes are unjust because segregation distorts the soul and damages the personality. It gives the segregator a false sense of superiority and the segregated a false sense of inferiority. Segregation, to use the terminology of the Jewish philosopher Martin Buber, substitutes an "I–it" relationship for an "I–thou" relationship and ends up relegating persons to the status of things. Hence, segregation is not only politically, economically, and sociologically unsound, it is morally wrong and sinful. Paul Tillich has said that sin is separation. Is not segregation an existential expression of man's tragic separation, his awful estrangement, his terrible sinfulness? Thus it is that I can urge men to obey the 1954 decision of the Supreme Court, for it is morally right; and I can urge them to disobey segregation ordinances, for they are morally wrong.

Let us consider a more concrete example of just and unjust laws. An unjust law is a code that a numerical or power majority group compels a minority group to obey but does not make binding on itself. This is *difference* made legal. By the same token, a just law is a code that a majority compels a minority to follow and that it is willing to follow itself. This is *sameness* made legal.

Let me give another explanation. A law is unjust if it is inflicted on a minority that, as a result of being denied the right to vote, had no part in enacting or devising the law. Who can say that the legislature of Alabama which set up that state's segregation laws was democratically elected? Throughout Alabama all sorts of devious methods are used to prevent Negroes from becoming registered voters, and there are some counties in which, even though Negroes constitute a majority of the population, not a single Negro is registered. Can any law enacted under such circumstances be considered democratically structured?

Sometimes a law is just on its face and unjust in its application. For instance, I have been arrested on a charge of parading without a permit. Now, there is nothing wrong in having an ordinance which requires a permit for a parade. But such an ordinance becomes unjust when it is used to maintain segregation and to deny citizens the First-Amendment privilege of peaceful assembly and protest.

I hope you are able to see the distinction I am trying to point out. In no   20
sense do I advocate evading or defying the law, as would the rabid segrega-

tionist. That would lead to anarchy. One who breaks an unjust law must do so openly, lovingly, and with a willingness to accept the penalty. I submit that an individual who breaks a law that conscience tells him is unjust, and who willingly accepts the penalty of imprisonment in order to arouse the conscience of the community over its injustice, is in reality expressing the highest respect for law.

Of course, there is nothing new about this kind of civil disobedience. It was evidenced sublimely in the refusal of Shadrach, Meshach, and Abednego to obey the laws of Nebuchadnezzar, on the ground that a higher moral law was at stake. It was practiced superbly by the early Christians, who were willing to face hungry lions and the excruciating pain of chopping blocks rather than submit to certain unjust laws of the Roman Empire. To a degree, academic freedom is a reality today because Socrates practiced civil disobedience. In our own nation, the Boston Tea Party represented a massive act of civil disobedience.

We should never forget that everything Adolf Hitler did in Germany was "legal" and everything the Hungarian freedom fighters did in Hungary was "illegal." It was "illegal" to aid and comfort a Jew in Hitler's Germany. Even so, I am sure that, had I lived in Germany at the time, I would have aided and comforted my Jewish brothers. If today I lived in a Communist country where certain principles dear to the Christian faith are suppressed, I would openly advocate disobeying that country's antireligious laws.

I must make two honest confessions to you, my Christian and Jewish brothers. First, I must confess that over the past few years I have been gravely disappointed with the white moderate. I have almost reached the regrettable conclusion that the Negro's great stumbling block in his stride toward freedom is not the White Citizen's Counciler or the Ku Klux Klanner, but the white moderate, who is more devoted to "order" than to justice; who prefers a negative peace which is the presence of tension to a positive peace which is the presence of justice; who constantly says: "I agree with you in the goal you seek, but I cannot agree with your methods of direct action"; who paternalistically believes he can set the timetable for another man's freedom; who lives by a mythical concept of time and who constantly advises the Negro to wait for a "more convenient season." Shallow understanding from people of good will is more frustrating than absolute misunderstanding from people of ill will. Lukewarm acceptance is much more bewildering than outright rejection.

I had hoped that the white moderate would understand that law and order exist for the purpose of establishing justice and that when they fail in this purpose they become the dangerously structured dams that block the flow of social progress. I had hoped that the white moderate would understand that the present tension in the South is a necessary phase of the transition from an obnoxious negative peace, in which the Negro passively accepted his unjust plight, to a substantive and positive peace, in which all men will respect the dignity and worth of human personality. Actually, we who engage in nonviolent direct action are not the creators of tension. We merely bring to the surface the hidden tension that is already alive. We bring it out in the open, where it can be seen and dealt with. Like a boil that can never be cured so long as it is covered up but must be opened with all its ugliness to the natural medicines of air and light, injustice must be exposed, with all the tension its exposure creates, to the light of human conscience and the air of national opinion before it can be cured.

In your statement you assert that our actions, even though peaceful, **25** must be condemned because they precipitate violence. But is this a logical assertion? Isn't this like condemning a robbed man because his possession of money precipitated the evil act of robbery? Isn't this like condemning Socrates because his unswerving commitment to truth and his philosophical inquiries precipitated the act by the misguided populace in which they made him drink hemlock? Isn't this like condemning Jesus because his unique God-consciousness and never-ceasing devotion to God's will precipitated the evil act of crucifixion? We must come to see that, as the federal courts have consistently affirmed, it is wrong to urge an individual to cease his efforts to gain his basic constitutional rights because the quest may precipitate violence. Society must protect the robbed and punish the robber.

I had also hoped that the white moderate would reject the myth concerning time in relation to the struggle for freedom. I have just received a letter from a white brother in Texas. He writes: "All Christians know that the colored people will receive equal rights eventually, but it is possible that you are in too great a religious hurry. It has taken Christianity almost two thousand years to accomplish what it has. The teachings of Christ take time to come to earth." Such an attitude stems from a tragic misconception of time, from the strangely irrational notion that there is something in the very flow of time that will inevitably cure all ills. Actually, time itself is neutral; it can be used either destructively or constructively. More and more I feel that the people of ill will have used time much more effectively than have the people of good will. We will have to repent in this generation not merely for the hateful words and actions of the bad people but for the appalling silence of the good people. Human progress never rolls in on wheels of inevitability; it comes through the tireless efforts of men willing to be coworkers with God, and without this hard work, time itself becomes an ally of the forces of social stagnation. We must use time creatively, in the knowledge that the time is always ripe to do right. Now is the time to make real the promise of democracy and transform our pending national elegy into a creative psalm of brotherhood. Now is the time to lift our national policy from the quicksand of racial injustice to the solid rock of human dignity.

You speak of our activity in Birmingham as extreme. At first I was rather disappointed that fellow clergymen would see my nonviolent efforts as those of an extremist. I began thinking about the fact that I stand in the middle of two opposing forces in the Negro community. One is a force of complacency, made up in part of Negroes who, as a result of long years of oppression, are so drained of self-respect and a sense of "somebodiness" that they have adjusted to segregation; and in part of a few middle-class Negroes who, because of a degree of academic and economic security and because in some ways they profit by segregation, have become insensitive to the problems of the masses. The other force is one of bitterness and hatred, and it comes perilously close to advocating violence. It is expressed in the various black nationalist groups that are springing up across the nation, the largest and best-known being Elijah Muhammad's Muslim movement. Nourished by the Negro's frustration over the continued existence of racial discrimination, this movement is made up of people who have lost faith in America, who have absolutely repudiated Christianity, and who have concluded that the white man is an incorrigible "devil."

I have tried to stand between these two forces, saying that we need emulate neither the "do-nothingism" of the complacent nor the hatred and despair of the black nationalist. For there is the more excellent way of love and nonviolent protest. I am grateful to God that, through the influence of the Negro church, the way of nonviolence became an integral part of our struggle.

If this philosophy had not emerged, by now many streets of the South would, I am convinced, be flowing with blood. And I am further convinced that if our white brothers dismiss as "rabble-rousers" and "outside agitators" those of us who employ nonviolent direct action, and if they refuse to support our nonviolent efforts, millions of the Negroes will, out of frustration and despair, seek solace and security in black-nationalist ideologies — a development that would inevitably lead to a frightening racial nightmare.

Oppressed people cannot remain oppressed forever. The yearning for freedom eventually manifests itself, and that is what has happened to the American Negro. Something within has reminded him of his birthright of freedom, and something without has reminded him that it can be gained. Consciously or unconsciously, he has been caught up by the *Zeitgeist*, and with his black brothers of Africa and his brown and yellow brothers of Asia, South America, and the Caribbean, the United States Negro is moving with a sense of great urgency toward the promised land of racial justice. If one recognizes this vital urge that has engulfed the Negro community, one should readily understand why public demonstrations are taking place. The Negro has many pent-up resentments and latent frustrations, and he must release them. So let him march; let him make prayer pilgrimages to the city hall; let him go on freedom rides — and try to understand why he must do so. If his repressed emotions are not released in nonviolent ways, they will seek expression through violence; this is not a threat but a fact of history. So I have not said to my people: "Get rid of your discontent." Rather, I have tried to say that this normal and healthy discontent can be channeled into the creative outlet of nonviolent direct action. And now this approach is being termed extremist.

30

But though I was initially disappointed at being categorized as an extremist, as I continued to think about the matter I gradually gained a measure of satisfaction from the label. Was not Jesus an extremist for love: "Love your enemies, bless them that curse you, do good to them that hate you, and pray for them which despitefully use you, and persecute you." Was not Amos an extremist for justice: "Let justice roll down like waters and righteousness like an ever-flowing stream." Was not Paul an extremist for the Christian gospel: "I bear in my body the marks of the Lord Jesus." Was not Martin Luther an extremist: "Here I stand; I cannot do otherwise, so help me God." And John Bunyan: "I will stay in jail to the end of my days before I make a butchery of my conscience." And Abraham Lincoln: "This nation cannot survive half slave and half free." And Thomas Jefferson: "We hold these truths to be self-evident, that all men are created equal. . . ." So the question is not whether we will be extremists, but what kind of extremists we will be. Will we be extremists for hate or for love? Will we be extremists for the preservation of injustice or for the extension of justice? In that dramatic scene on Calvary's hill three men were crucified. We must never forget that all three were crucified for the same crime—the crime of extremism. Two were extremists for immorality, and thus fell below their environment. The other, Jesus Christ, was an extremist for love, truth and goodness, and thereby rose above his environment. Perhaps the South, the nation and the world are in dire need of creative extremists.

I had hoped that the white moderate would see this need. Perhaps I was too optimistic; perhaps I expected too much. I suppose I should have realized that few members of the oppressor race can understand the deep groans and passionate yearnings of the oppressed race, and still fewer have the vision to see that injustice must be rooted out by strong, persistent, and determined action. I am thankful, however, that some of our white brothers in the South have grasped the meaning of this social revolution and committed themselves to it. They are still all too few in quantity, but they are big in quality. Some—such as Ralph McGill, Lillian Smith, Harry Golden, James McBride Dabbs, Ann Braden, and Sarah Patton Boyle—have written about our struggle in eloquent and prophetic terms. Others have marched with us down nameless streets of the South. They have languished in filthy, roach-infested jails, suffering the abuse and brutality of policemen who view them as "dirty nigger-lovers." Unlike so many of their moderate brothers and sisters, they have recognized the urgency of the moment and sensed the need for powerful "action" antidotes to combat the disease of segregation.

Let me take note of my other major disappointment. I have been so greatly disappointed with the white church and its leadership. Of course, there are some notable exceptions. I am not unmindful of the fact that each of you has taken some significant stands on this issue. I commend you, Reverend Stallings, for your Christian stand on this past Sunday, in welcoming Negroes to your worship service on a nonsegregated basis. I commend the Catholic leaders of this state for integrating Spring Hill College several years ago.

But despite these notable exceptions, I must honestly reiterate that I have been disappointed with the church. I do not say this as one of those negative critics who can always find something wrong with the church. I say this as a minister of the gospel, who loves the church; who was nurtured in its bosom; who has been sustained by its spiritual blessings and who will remain true to it as long as the cord of life shall lengthen.

When I was suddenly catapulted into the leadership of the bus protest 35 in Montgomery, Alabama, a few years ago, I felt we would be supported by the white church. I felt that the white ministers, priests, and rabbis of the South would be among our strongest allies. Instead, some have been outright opponents, refusing to understand the freedom movement and misrepresenting its leaders; all too many others have been more cautious than courageous and have remained silent behind the anesthetizing security of stained-glass windows.

In spite of my shattered dreams, I came to Birmingham with the hope that the white religious leadership of this community would see the justice of our cause and, with deep moral concern, would serve as the channel through which our just grievances could reach the power structure. I had hoped that each of you would understand. But again I have been disappointed.

I have heard numerous southern religious leaders admonish their worshipers to comply with a desegregation decision because it is the law, but I have longed to hear white ministers declare: "Follow this decree because integration is morally right and because the Negro is your brother." In the midst of blatant injustices inflicted upon the Negro, I have watched white churchmen stand on the sideline and mouth pious irrelevancies and sanctimonious trivialities. In the midst of a mighty struggle to rid our nation of racial and economic injustice, I have heard many ministers say: "Those are social issues, with which the gospel has no real concern." And I have watched many churches commit themselves to a completely otherworldly religion which makes a strange, un-Biblical distinction between body and soul, between the sacred and the secular.

I have traveled the length and breadth of Alabama, Mississippi, and all the other southern states. On sweltering summer days and crisp autumn mornings I have looked at the South's beautiful churches with their lofty spires pointing heavenward. I have beheld the impressive outlines of her massive religious-education buildings. Over and over I have found myself asking: "What kind of people worship here? Who is their God? Where were their voices when the lips of Governor Barnett dripped with words of interposition and nullification? Where were they when Governor Wallace gave a clarion call for defiance and hatred? Where were their voices of support when bruised and weary Negro men and women decided to rise from the dark dungeons of complacency to the bright hills of creative protest?"

Yes, these questions are still in my mind. In deep disappointment I have wept over the laxity of the church. But be assured that my tears have been tears of love. There can be no deep disappointment where there is not deep love. Yes, I love the church. How could I do otherwise? I am in the rather unique position of being the son, the grandson, and the great-grandson of preachers. Yes, I see the church as the body of Christ. But, oh! How we have blemished and scarred that body through social neglect and through fear of being nonconformists.

There was a time when the church was very powerful—in the time when the early Christians rejoiced at being deemed worthy to suffer for what they believed. In those days the church was not merely a thermometer that recorded the ideas and principles of popular opinion; it was a thermostat that transformed the mores of society. Whenever the early Christians entered a town, the people in power became disturbed and immediately sought to convict the Christians for being "disturbers of the peace" and "outside agitators." But the Christians pressed on, in the conviction that they were "a colony of heaven," called to obey God rather than man. Small in number, they were big in commitment. They were too God-intoxicated to be "astronomically intimidated." By their effort and example they brought an end to such ancient evils as infanticide and gladiatorial contests.

40

Things are different now. So often the contemporary church is a weak, ineffectual voice with an uncertain sound. So often it is an archdefender of the status quo. Far from being disturbed by the presence of the church, the power structure of the average community is consoled by the church's silent—and often even vocal—sanction of things as they are.

But the judgment of God is upon the church as never before. If today's church does not recapture the sacrificial spirit of the early church, it will lose its authenticity, forfeit the loyalty of millions, and be dismissed as an irrelevant social club with no meaning for the twentieth century. Every day I meet young people whose disappointment with the church has turned into outright disgust.

Perhaps I have once again been too optimistic. Is organized religion too inextricably bound to the status quo to save our nation and the world? Perhaps I must turn my faith to the inner spiritual church, the church within the church, as the true *ekklesia* and the hope of the world. But again I am thankful to God that some noble souls from the ranks of organized religion have broken loose from the paralyzing chains of conformity and joined us as active partners in the struggle for freedom. They have left their secure congregations and walked the streets of Albany, Georgia, with us. They have gone down the highways of the South on tortuous rides for freedom. Yes, they have gone to jail with us. Some have been dismissed from their churches, have lost the support of their bishops and fellow ministers. But they have acted in the faith that right defeated is stronger than evil triumphant. Their witness has been the spiritual salt that has preserved the true meaning of the gospel in these troubled times. They have carved a tunnel of hope through the dark mountain of disappointment.

I hope the church as a whole will meet the challenge of this decisive hour. But even if the church does not come to the aid of justice, I have no despair about the future. I have no fear about the outcome of our struggle in Birmingham, even if our motives are at present misunderstood. We will reach the goal of freedom in Birmingham and all over the nation, because the goal of America is freedom. Abused and scorned though we may be, our destiny is tied up with America's destiny. Before the pilgrims landed at Plymouth, we were here. Before the pen of Jefferson etched the majestic words of the Declaration of Independence across the pages of history, we were here. For more than two centuries our forebears labored in this country without wages; they made cotton king; they built the homes of their masters while suffering gross injustice and shameful humiliation—and yet out of a bottomless vitality they continued to thrive and develop. If the inexpressible cruelties of slavery could not stop us, the opposition we now face will surely fail. We will win our freedom because the sacred heritage of our nation and the eternal will of God are embodied in our echoing demands.

Before closing I feel impelled to mention one other point in your statement that has troubled me profoundly. You warmly commended the Birmingham police force for keeping "order" and "preventing violence." I doubt that you would have so warmly commended the police force if you had seen its dogs sinking their teeth into unarmed, nonviolent Negroes. I doubt that you would so quickly commend the policemen if you were to observe their ugly and inhumane treatment of Negroes here in the city jail; if you were to watch them push and curse old Negro women and young Negro girls; if you were to see them slap and kick old Negro men and young boys; if you were to observe them, as they did on two occasions, refuse to give us food because we wanted to sing our grace together. I cannot join you in your praise of the Birmingham police department.   45

It is true that police have exercised a degree of discipline in handling the demonstrators. In this sense they have conducted themselves rather "nonviolently" in public. But for what purpose? To preserve the evil system of segregation. Over the past few years I have consistently preached that nonviolence demands that the means we use must be as pure as the ends we seek. I have tried to make clear that it is wrong to use immoral means to attain moral ends. But now I must affirm that it is just as wrong, or perhaps even more so, to use moral means to preserve immoral ends. Perhaps Mr. Connor and his policemen have been rather nonviolent in public, as was Chief Pritchett in Albany, Georgia, but they have used the moral means of nonviolence to maintain the immoral end of racial injustice. As T. S. Eliot has said: "The last temptation is the greatest treason: To do the right deed for the wrong reason."

I wish you had commended the Negro sit-inners and demonstrators of Birmingham for their sublime courage, their willingness to suffer and their amazing discipline in the midst of great provocation. One day the South will recognize its real heroes. They will be the James Merediths, with the noble sense of purpose that enables them to face jeering and hostile mobs, and with the agonizing loneliness that characterizes the life of the pioneer. They will be old, oppressed, battered Negro women, symbolized in a seventy-two-year-old woman in Montgomery, Alabama, who rose up with a sense of dignity and with her people decided not to ride segregated buses, and who responded with ungrammatical profundity to one who inquired about her weariness: "My feets is tired, but my soul is at rest." They will be the young high school and college students, the young ministers of the gospel and a host of their elders, courageously and nonviolently sitting in at lunch counters and willingly going to jail for conscience's sake. One day the South will know that when these disinherited children of God sat down at lunch counters, they were in reality standing up for what is best in the American dream and for the most sacred values in our Judaeo-Christian heritage, thereby bringing our nation back to those great wells of democracy which were dug deep by the founding fathers in their formulation of the Constitution and the Declaration of Independence.

Never before have I written so long a letter. I'm afraid it is much too long to take your precious time. I can assure you that it would have been much shorter if I had been writing from a comfortable desk, but what else can one do when he is alone in a narrow jail cell, other than write long letters, think long thoughts, and pray long prayers?

If I have said anything in this letter that overstates the truth and indicates an unreasonable impatience, I beg you to forgive me. If I have said anything that understates the truth and indicates my having a patience that allows me to settle for anything less than brotherhood, I beg God to forgive me.

I hope this letter finds you strong in faith. I also hope that circumstances will soon make it possible for me to meet each of you, not as an integrationist or a civil-rights leader but as a fellow clergyman and a Christian brother. Let us all hope that the dark clouds of racial prejudice will soon pass away and the deep fog of misunderstanding will be lifted from our fear-drenched communities, and in some not too distant tomorrow the radiant stars of love and brotherhood will shine over our great nation with all their scintillating beauty.

50

Yours for the cause of Peace and Brotherhood
MARTIN LUTHER KING, JR.

King's Analysis of His Audience:
Identification and Overcoming Difference

King's letter is worth studying for the resources of identification alone. For example, he appeals in his salutation to "My Dear Fellow Clergymen," which emphasizes at the outset that he and his readers share a role. Elsewhere he calls them "my friends" (paragraph 12) and "my Christian and Jewish brothers" (paragraph 23). In many other places, King alludes to the Bible and to other religious figures; these references put him on common ground with his readers.

King's letter also deals with that which separates him from his readers.

Assumptions

King's readers assumed that if black people waited long enough, their situation would inevitably grow better. They argued for patience. King, in paragraph 26, questions "the strangely irrational notion that . . . the very flow of time . . . will inevitably cure all ills." Against this common assumption that "time heals," King offers the view that "time itself is neutral," something that "can be used either destructively or constructively."

Principles

King's readers believed in always obeying the law, a principle blind to intent and application. King substitutes another principle: Obey just laws, but disobey, openly and lovingly, unjust laws (paragraphs 15–22).

Hierarchy of Values

King's readers elevated the value of reducing racial tension over the value of securing racial justice. In paragraph 10, King's strategy is to talk about "constructive, nonviolent tension," clearly an effort to get his readers to see tension as not necessarily a bad thing.

Ends and Means

King's audience seems to disagree with him not about the ends for which he was working but about the means. King focuses not on justifying civil rights but on justifying civil disobedience.

Interpretation

King's audience interpreted extremism as always negative, never justifiable. King counters by showing, first, that he is actually a moderate, neither a "do-nothing" nor a militant (paragraph 28). But then he redefines extremism, arguing that extremism for good causes is justified and citing historical examples to support his point (paragraph 31).

Implications or Consequences

King's readers doubtless feared the consequences of supporting civil rights too strongly—losing the support of conservative members of their congregations. But as King warns, "If today's church does not recapture the sacrificial spirit of the early church, it will . . . be dismissed as an irrelevant social club" (paragraph 42). King's strategy is to emphasize long-term consequences—the church's loss of vitality and relevance.

Following Through

As a class, look closely at one of the essays from an earlier chapter, and do an audience analysis. What audience did the writer attempt to reach? How did the writer connect or fail to connect with the audience's experience, knowledge, and concerns? What exactly divides the author from his or her audience, and how did the writer attempt to overcome the division? How effective were the writer's strategies for achieving identification? What can you suggest that might have worked better?

USING THE FORMS OF APPEAL

We turn now to the forms of appeal in persuasion, noting how King used them. For a summary of the forms, see the Close-Up box on page 228.

The Appeal to Reason

Persuasion uses the same appeal to reason as convincing. King, however, chose to respond to the clergymen's statement with a personal letter, organized around their criticisms. Most of King's letter amounts to self-defense and belongs to the genre called *apologia*, from which our word "apology" derives. An **apologia** is an effort to explain and justify what one has done, or chosen not to do, in the face of disapproval or misunderstanding.

Rather than making a single case, King uses a series of short arguments, occupying from one to as many as eight paragraphs, to respond to the criticisms. These are the more important ones:

Refutation of the "outside agitator" concept (paragraphs 2–4)
Defense of nonviolent civil disobedience (paragraphs 5–11)
Definitions of "just" versus "unjust" laws (paragraphs 15–22)
Refutation and defense of the label "extremist" (paragraphs 27–31)
Rejection of the ministers' praise for the conduct of the police during
    the Birmingham demonstration (paragraphs 45–47)

In addition to defending himself and his cause, King advances his own criticisms, most notably of the "white moderate" (paragraphs 23–26) and the "white church and its leadership" (paragraphs 33–44). This concentration on rational appeal is both effective and appropriate: It confirms King's character as a man of reason, and it appeals to an audience of well-educated professionals.

King also cites evidence that his readers must respect. In paragraph 16, for example, he cites the words of St. Thomas Aquinas, Martin Buber, and

Paul Tillich—representing, respectively, the Catholic, Jewish, and Protestant traditions—to defend his position on just and unjust laws. He has chosen these authorities so that each of his eight accusers has someone from his own tradition with whom to identify.

Following Through

1. Look at paragraphs 2–4 of King's letter. What reasons does he give to justify being in Birmingham? How does he support each reason? Do his reasons and evidence indicate a strategy aimed at his clergy audience?
2. King's argument for civil disobedience (paragraphs 15–22) is based on one main reason. What is it, and how does he support it?
3. What are the two reasons King gives to refute his audience's charge of extremism (paragraphs 27–31)?
4. Think about a time in your life when you did (or did not do) something for which you were unfairly criticized. Choose one or two of the criticisms, and defend yourself in a short case of your own. Remember to persuade *your accusers,* not yourself. Ask, as King did, How can I appeal to them? What will they find reasonable?

The Appeal to Character

In Chapter 7, our concern was how to make a good case. We did not discuss self-presentation there, but when you make a good case you are also creating a positive impression of good character. A good argument will always reveal the writer's values, intelligence, and knowledge. We respect and trust a person who reasons well, even when we do not agree with him or her.

The appeal to character in persuasion differs from convincing only in degree. In convincing, the appeal is implicit, and diffused throughout the argument; in persuading, the appeal is often explicit and concentrated in a specific section of the essay. The effect on readers is consequently different: In convincing, we are seldom aware of the writer's character; in persuading, the writer's character assumes a major role in how we respond.

Perception of character was a special problem for King when he wrote his letter. He was not a national hero in 1963 but rather a controversial civil rights leader whom many viewed as a troublemaker. Furthermore, he wrote this now celebrated document while in jail—hardly a condition that inspires respect and trust. Self-presentation, then, was very significant for King, something he concentrated on, especially at the beginning and end.

In his opening paragraph, King acknowledges that he is currently in jail. But he goes on to establish himself as a professional person like his readers, with secretaries, correspondence, and important work to do.

Just prior to his conclusion, King offers a strongly worded critique of the white moderate and the mainstream white church, taking the offensive in a way that his readers are certain to perceive as an attack. In paragraph 48, however, he suddenly becomes self-deprecating: "Never before have I written so long a letter." As unexpected as it is, this sudden shift of tone disarms the reader. Then, with gentle irony (the letter, he says, would have been shorter "if I had been writing from a comfortable desk"), King explains the length of his letter as the result of his having no other outlet for action. What can one do in jail but "write long letters, think long thoughts, and pray long prayers?" King turns the negative of jail into a positive, an opportunity rather than a limitation.

His next move is equally surprising, especially after the assertive tone of his critique of the church. He begs forgiveness—from his readers if he has overstated his case, from God if he has understated it. This daring, dramatic move is just the right touch, the perfect gesture of reconciliation. Because he asks so humbly, his readers *must* forgive him. What else can they do? The subordination of his own will to God's is the stance of the sufferer and martyr in both Jewish and Christian traditions.

Finally, King sets aside that which divides him from his readers—integration and civil rights—in favor of that which unifies them: All are men of God, brothers in faith. Like an Old Testament prophet, he envisions a time when the current conflicts will be over, when "the radiant stars of love and brotherhood will shine over our great nation." In other words, King holds out the possibility for transcendence, for rising above racial prejudice to a new age. In the end, his readers are encouraged to soar with him into hope for the future.

Here King enlists the power of identification to overcome the differences, invoking his status as a "fellow clergyman and a Christian brother." *The key to identification is to reach beyond the individual self, associating one's character with something larger*—the Christian community, the history of the struggle for freedom, national values, "spaceship Earth," or any appropriate cause or movement in which readers can also participate.

 Following Through

Look at the list of questions for creating audience identification on pages 229–230. Other than in the conclusion, find some examples in King's letter in which he employs some of these resources of identification. What methods does King use that any persuader might use?

The Appeal to Emotion

Educated people aware of the techniques of persuasion are often deeply suspicious of emotional appeal. Among college professors this prejudice can be especially strong because all fields of academic study claim to value reason, dispassionate inquiry, and critical analysis. Many think of emotional appeal as the opposite of sound thinking and associate it with politicians who prey on fears, dictators and demagogues who exploit prejudices, and advertisers and televangelists who claim to satisfy dreams and prayers.

We can all cite examples of the destructive power of emotional appeal. But to condemn it wholesale, without qualification, exhibits lack of self-awareness. Most scientists will concede, for instance, that they are passionately committed to their methods, and mathematicians say that they are moved by the elegance of certain equations. All human activity has some emotional dimension, a strongly felt adherence to a common set of values.

Moreover, we ought to have strong feelings about certain things: revulsion at the horrors of the Holocaust, pity and anger over the abuse of children, happiness when a war is concluded or when those kidnapped by terrorists are released, and so on. We cease to be human if we are not responsive to emotional appeal.

Clearly, then, we must distinguish between legitimate and illegitimate emotional appeals. Distinguishing the two is not always easy, but answering certain questions can help:

Do the emotional appeals substitute for knowledge and reason?
Do they employ stereotypes and pit one group against another?
Do they offer a simple, unthinking reaction to a complex situation?

Whenever the answer is yes, our suspicions should be aroused.

Perhaps an even better test is to ask yourself, If I act on the basis of how I feel, who will benefit and who will suffer? You may be saddened, for example, to see animals used in medical experiments, but an appeal showing only the animals and ignoring the benefits for humans panders to emotions.

In contrast, legitimate emotional appeal *supplements* argument, drawing on knowledge and often firsthand experience. At its best, it can bring alienated groups together and create empathy or sympathy. Many examples could be cited from King's letter, but the most effective passage is surely paragraph 14:

> We have waited for more than 340 years for our constitutional God-given rights. The nations of Asia and Africa are moving with jetlike speed toward gaining political independence, but we still creep at horse-and-buggy pace toward gaining a cup of coffee at a lunch counter. Perhaps it is easy for those who have never felt the stinging darts of segregation to say, "Wait." But when you have seen vicious mobs lynch your mothers and fathers at will and drown your sisters and brothers at whim; when you have seen hate-filled policemen curse, kick, and even kill your black brothers and sisters; when you see the vast majority of your twenty million Negro brothers smothering in an airtight cage

of poverty in the midst of an affluent society; when you suddenly find your tongue twisted and your speech stammering as you seek to explain to your six-year-old daughter why she can't go to the public amusement park that has just been advertised on television, and see tears welling up in her eyes when she is told that Funtown is closed to colored children, and see ominous clouds of inferiority beginning to form in her little mental sky, and see her beginning to distort her personality by developing an unconscious bitterness toward white people; when you have to concoct an answer for a five-year-old son who is asking: "Daddy, why do white people treat colored people so mean?"; when you take a cross-country drive and find it necessary to sleep night after night in the uncomfortable corners of your automobile because no motel will accept you; when you are humiliated day in and day out by nagging signs reading "white" and "colored"; when your first name becomes "nigger," your middle name becomes "boy" (however old you are), and your last name becomes "John," and your wife and mother are never given the respected title "Mrs."; when you are harried by day and haunted by night by the fact that you are a Negro, living constantly at tiptoe stance, never quite knowing what to expect next, and are plagued with inner fears and outer resentments; when you are forever fighting a degenerating sense of "nobodiness"—then you will understand why we find it difficult to wait. There comes a time when the cup of endurance runs over, and men are no longer willing to be plunged into the abyss of despair. I hope, sirs, you can understand our legitimate and unavoidable impatience.

Just prior to this paragraph, King has concluded an argument justifying the use of direct action to dramatize social inequities and to demand rights and justice denied to oppressed people. Direct-action programs are necessary, he says, because "freedom is never voluntarily given by the oppressor; it must be demanded by the oppressed." It is easy for those not oppressed to urge an underclass to wait. But "[t]his 'Wait' has almost always meant 'Never.'"

At this point, King deliberately sets out to create in his readers a feeling of outrage. Having ended paragraph 13 by equating "wait" with "never," King next refers to a tragic historical fact: For 340 years, since the beginning of slavery in the American colonies, black people have been waiting for their freedom. He sharply contrasts the "jetlike speed" with which Africa is overcoming colonialism with the "horse-and-buggy pace" of integration in the United States. In African homelands, black people are gaining their political independence; but here, in the land of the free, they are denied even "a cup of coffee at a lunch counter." Clearly, this is legitimate emotional appeal, based on fact and reinforcing reason.

In the long and rhythmical sentence that takes up most of the rest of the paragraph, King unleashes the full force of emotional appeal in a series of concrete images designed to make his privileged white readers feel the anger, frustration, and humiliation of the oppressed. In rapid succession, King alludes to mob violence, police brutality, and economic discrimination—the more public evils of racial discrimination—and then moves to the personal, everyday experience of segregation, concentrating especially on what it does to innocent children. For any reader with even the least capacity for sympathy, these images strike home, creating identification with the suffering of the oppressed and impatience with the evil system that perpetuates it. In sum, through the use of telling detail drawn from his own experience, King succeeds in getting his audience to feel what he feels.

What have we learned from King about the available means of emotional appeal? Instead of telling his audience what they should feel, he has evoked that emotion using five specific rhetorical techniques:

Concrete examples
Personal experiences
Metaphors and similes
Sharp contrasts and comparisons
Sentence rhythm, particularly the use of intentional repetition

We next consider how style contributes to persuasion.

 Following Through

1. Emotional appeals need to be both legitimate and appropriate — honest and suitable for the subject matter and the audience. Find examples of arguments from books, newspapers, magazines, and professional journals and discuss the use or avoidance of emotional appeal in each. On the basis of this study, generalize about what subjects and audiences allow direct emotional appeal.
2. Write an essay analyzing the tactics of emotional appeal in editorials in your campus or local newspaper. Compare the strategies with those used by King. Evaluate the appeals. How effective are they? How well do they reinforce the reasoning offered? Be sure to discuss their legitimacy and appropriateness.

The Appeal through Style

Style refers to the choices a writer makes at the level of words, phrases, and sentences. Style is not merely a final touch, a "dressing up" of an argument. Ideas and arguments do not get expressed apart from style, and all the appeals involve stylistic choices. You are concerned with style when you consider what words will state a thesis precisely or provide your reader with a compelling image. Style works hand-in-hand with reason, character, and emotion.

Furthermore, style makes what we say memorable. Because persuasive impact depends largely on what readers remember, style matters as much as any of the other appeals.

Style means choice from options. One choice involves the degree of formality. King strikes a formal and professional tone through most of his letter, choosing words like *cognizant* (paragraph 4) rather than the more common *aware*. Writers also choose words based on **connotation** (what a word implies or what we associate with it) as much as on **denotation** (a word's literal meaning). For example, King opens his letter with "While confined here in the Birmingham city jail." The word *confined* denotes the same condition as *incarcerated* but has more favorable connotations, because people can be *confined* in ways that evoke sympathy.

Memorable writing often appeals to sight and sound. Concrete words paint a picture; in paragraph 45, for example, King tells about "dogs sinking their teeth" into nonviolent demonstrators. Writers may also evoke images through metaphor and simile. King's "the stinging darts of segregation" (paragraph 14) is an example of metaphor. In this same paragraph, King refers to the "airtight cage of poverty," the "clouds of inferiority" forming in his young daughter's "mental sky," and the "cup of endurance" that has run over for his people—each a powerful metaphor.

Even when read silently, language has sound. Style also includes variety in sentence length and rhythms. For example, a writer may emphasize a short, simple sentence by placing it at the end of a series of long ones, as King does in paragraph 14. Or she may repeat certain phrases to emphasize a point. In the fourth sentence of paragraph 14, King repeats "when you" a number of times, piling up examples of racial discrimination and creating a powerful rhythm that carries readers through this unusually long sentence. Another common rhythmic pattern is parallelism. Note the following phrases, again from the fourth sentence of paragraph 14:

"lynch your mothers and fathers at will"

"drown your sisters and brothers at whim"

Here King uses similar words in the same places, even the same number of syllables in each phrase. The parallelism is further emphasized by *alliteration*, repetition of consonant sounds. In yet another passage from paragraph 14, King suggests violence when he describes police who "curse, kick, and even kill" black citizens. Repetition of the hard *k* sound, especially in one-syllable words, makes the violence sound urgent and brutal.

 Following Through

1. Analyze King's style in paragraphs 6, 8, 23, 24, 31, and 47. Compare what King does in these paragraphs with paragraph 14. How are they similar? How are they different? Why?

2. To some extent, style is a gift or talent. But it is also learned by imitating authors we admire. Use your writer's notebook to increase your stylistic options; whenever you hear or read something stated

well, copy it down and analyze why it's effective. Make up a sentence of your own using the same techniques with different subject matter. In this way, you can begin to use analogy, metaphor, repetition, alliteration, parallelism, and other stylistic devices. Begin by imitating six or so sentences or phrases that you especially liked in King's letter.
3. Write an essay analyzing your own style in a previous essay. What would you do differently now? Why?

DRAFTING A PERSUASIVE ESSAY

Outside the classroom, persuasion meets real needs to move people to act. In the classroom, you create need. Begin by thinking about what action you want your readers to take and how to move them to take it.

Conceiving a Readership

Finding and analyzing your readership is your first concern. Because instructors evaluate the writing of their students, it's understandable that college writers write for their instructors. However, real persuasion has a genuine readership, some definite group of people with a stake in the question or issue addressed. Whatever you say must be adapted for this audience.

How do you conceive a readership? First, throw out the notion of writing to the "general public." Such a "group" is a nearly meaningless abstraction. Suppose, for example, you are arguing that sex education in public schools must include a moral dimension as well as the clinical facts. Are you addressing students, who may not want the moral lectures; school administrators, who may not want the added responsibility and curriculum changes; or parents, who may not want the schools to take over what they see as the responsibility of family or church?

Second, given the issue and your position, ask who you would want to persuade. On the one hand, don't persuade those who already agree; on the other, don't target those so committed to other positions that nothing you could say would make any difference. An argument against logging in old-growth forests, for example, would not address staunch environmentalists nor timber industry workers but rather a readership between these extremes — say, people concerned about the environment but not focused specifically on the threat to mature forests.

Third, when you have a degree of choice among possible readerships, select your target audience based on two criteria. First, seek above all to influence those readers best able to influence events. Second, when this group includes a range of readers, consider which group you know the most about and can therefore appeal to best.

The following list summarizes pages 255–261, "Drafting a Persuasive Essay."

1. Choose a **specific** audience whose characteristics you **know well** and who have some capacity for **taking action** or **influencing events.**
2. Identify your audience early in the process.
3. In your case, show **need** and emphasize **urgency.**
4. Your readers must feel that you are **well-informed, confident, fair, honest,** and have their **interests** and **values** in mind. Avoid ridicule of other positions. Recognize and respond to the main objections your readers are likely to have to your proposal.
5. Arouse emotions you genuinely feel. Concentrate on those feelings your audience may lack or not feel strongly enough. Use emotional appeal sparingly.
6. Favor a **middle style** for persuasion, conversational without being too familiar or informal.

Essentially, you are making a case, just as you do when convincing. To this, add attention to the impression you make on your audience, especially at the beginning of the essay. Add descriptive and narrative detail designed to arouse favorable emotions. Finally, work hard on style, especially in second and third drafts.

Following Through

For a persuasive argument you are about to write, determine your audience; that is, decide who can make a difference with respect to this issue and what they can do to make a difference. Be sure that you go beyond the requirements of convincing when you make these decisions. For example, you may be able to make a good case that just as heterosexuals do not "choose" their attraction to the opposite sex, so homosexuality is also not voluntary. Based on this point, you could argue to a local readership of moderate-to-liberal voters that they should press state legislators to support a bill extending full citizens' rights to homosexuals. But with such a desire for action in mind, you would have to think even more about who your audience is and why they might resist such a measure or not care enough to support it strongly.

In your writer's notebook, respond to the questions "Who is my audience?" and "What are our differences?" (refer to the lists of questions on pages 228–229 to help formulate answers). Use your responses to write an audience profile that is more detailed than the one you wrote for an argument to convince.

Because all appeals are addressed to an audience, identify your reader early in the process. You can change your mind later, but doing so will require rewriting. Devoting time at the outset to thinking carefully about your intended audience will save time and effort.

Discovering the Resources of Appeal

With audience in mind, you are ready to think about how to appeal to them. Before and during the drafting stage, you will be making choices about

> How to formulate a case and support it with research
> How to present yourself
> How to arouse your readers' emotions
> How to make the style of your writing contribute to the argument's effectiveness

All these decisions will be influenced by your readers' needs and interests.

Appealing through Reason

What you learned in Chapter 7 about case-making applies here as well, so review that chapter. Of course, research (Chapter 5) and inquiry into the truth (Chapter 6) are just as relevant.

One difference between convincing and persuading, however, is that in persuasion you devote your argument to defending a course of action. The steps here are common sense:

1. Show that there is a need for action.
2. If your audience, like King's, inclines to inactivity, show urgency as well—we must act and act now.
3. Satisfy the need, showing that your proposal meets it or will solve the problem. Compare your course of action with other possibilities, indicating why yours is best.

Sometimes your goal will be to persuade your audience *not* to act because what they want to do is wrong or inappropriate. Need is still the issue. The difference, obviously, is to show that no need exists or that awaiting further developments will enable a proposed action to work better.

 Following Through

Prepare a brief of your argument (see Chapter 7). Be ready to present an overview of your audience and to defend your brief, either before the class or in small groups. Pay special attention to how well the argument establishes a need for your defined audience to act (or shows that there is no need to act). If action is called for, assess the solution in the context of other proposals: Will the proposed action meet the need? Is it realistic—that is, can it be done?

Appealing through Character

A reader who finishes your essay should have the following impressions:

The author is well-informed.
The author is confident, honest, and sincere.
The author is fair and balanced in dealing with other positions.
The author understands my concerns and objections and has dealt
  with them.
The author values what I value; his or her heart is in the right place.

What can you do to communicate these impressions? You must earn them, just as you must earn a good argument. There are no shortcuts. Educated readers are seldom fooled.

To *seem* well informed, you must *be* well informed. This requires digging into the topic, thinking about it carefully, researching it thoroughly and taking good notes, discussing the topic and your research with other students, consulting campus experts, and so on. This work will provide you with the signs of being well informed:

The ability to make passing references to events and people connected
  with the issue now or recently
The ability to create a context or provide background information,
  which may include comments on the history of the question or issue
The ability to produce sufficient high-quality evidence to back up
  contentions

Just as digging in will make you well informed, so inquiry (struggling to find the truth) and convincing (making a case for your conviction about the truth) will lend your argument sincerity and confidence. Draw upon personal experience when it has played a role in determining your position, and don't be reluctant to reveal your own stake in the issue. Make your case boldly, qualifying it as little as possible. If you have prepared yourself with good research, genuine inquiry, and careful case-making, you have earned authority; what remains is to claim it.

Represent other positions accurately and fairly; then present evidence that refutes those positions or show that the reasoning is inadequate or inconsistent. Don't be reluctant to agree with parts of other opinions when they are consistent with your own. Partial agreements can play a major role in overcoming reader resistance.

Don't subject other positions to ridicule. Some of your readers will take offense. Even readers gratified by your attack may feel that you have gone too far. *Concentrate on the merits of your own case,* not the faults of others.

Coping with your readers' concerns and objections should present no special problems, assuming that you have thought seriously about both the common ground you share and the way their outlook differs from yours. You can handle concerns and objections in one of two ways: (1) by adjusting your case—your thesis and supporting reasons—so that the concerns or objections do not arise or (2) by taking up the more significant objections one by one and responding to them in a way that reduces reader doubts. Doing one does not preclude doing the other: You can both adjust your case and answer whatever objections remain. What matters is that you not ignore likely and weighty objections to your case.

Responding to objections will also help with the most important impression that readers must have of you—that you value what they value. Sensitivity to the moral and emotional commitments of others is crucial.

Persuading doesn't happen without trust, so honesty is essential. Honesty requires (1) reporting evidence accurately and with regard for the original context; (2) acknowledging significant counterevidence and explaining why it does not defeat your argument; and (3) pointing out areas of doubt and uncertainty that remain.

 Following Through

The "Following Through" assignment on page 256 asked you to prepare an audience profile and explore your key areas of difference. Now use the results to think through how you can appeal to these readers. Use the questions on pages 229–230 to help establish commonality.

Appealing to Emotion

As in King's essay, argument is the center, the framework, while emotional appeal plays a supporting role, taking center stage only occasionally. Consequently, your decisions are these:

What emotions to arouse and by what means
How frequent and intense the emotional appeals should be
Where to include them

The first of these decisions is usually the easiest. Arouse emotions that you genuinely feel; what moved you should move your readers. If your emotions come from direct experience, use it for concrete descriptive detail, as King did. (The best strategy for arousing emotions is to avoid emotionalism yourself. Let the descriptive detail, the concrete examples, do the work, just as King did.)

Deciding how often, at what length, and how intensely to make emotional appeals presents a greater challenge. Much depends on the topic, the audience, and your own range and intensity of feeling. Estimate as best you can what will be appropriate, but the following suggestions may help.

As always in persuasion, the primary consideration is audience. What attitudes and feelings do they have already? Which of these lend support to your case? Which work against it? Emphasize those feelings consistent with your position, and show why any others are understandable but inappropriate.

Then ask a further question: What does my audience not feel or not feel strongly enough? King decided that his readers' greatest emotional deficit was their inability to feel what victims of racial discrimination feel—hence paragraph 14, the most intense emotional appeal in the letter.

The questions of how often and where to include emotional appeals are both worth careful consideration. Take your shots sparingly, getting as much as you can each time. Positioning emotional appeals depends on pacing: Use them to lead into or clinch a key point. So positioned, they temporarily relieve the audience of the intellectual effort required to follow an argument.

It's not a good idea to begin an essay with your most intense emotional appeal; you'll peak too early. Besides that, in your introduction you need to concentrate on establishing your tone and authority, providing needed background information, and clearly and forcefully stating your thesis. The conclusion can be an effective position because your audience is left with something memorable to carry away from the reading. Otherwise, concentrate emotional appeals from the middle to near the end of an essay.

 Following Through

> After you have a first draft of your essay, reread it with an eye to emotional appeal. Highlight the places where you have sought to arouse the audience's emotions.
>
> Decide if you need more attention to emotional appeal through additional concrete examples, direct quotations, or something else. Consider how you could make each appeal more effective and intense and whether each appeal is located well.

Appealing through Style

The style of your argument evolves with every choice you make. Stylistic choices are part of drafting, but refining them belongs to revision.

In the first draft, set an appropriate level of formality. Most persuasive writing is neither familiar nor stiff. Rather, persuasive prose is dignified conversation—the way people talk when they respect one another but do not know each other well. We can see some of the hallmarks of persuasive prose in King's letter:

- It uses *I, you,* and *we.*
- It avoids both technical jargon and slang.

- It inclines toward strong action verbs.
- It chooses examples and images familiar to the reader.
- It connects sentence to sentence and paragraph to paragraph with transitional words and phrases like *however, moreover,* and *for instance.*

These and other features characterize the **middle style** of most persuasive writing.

As we discovered in King's letter, this middle style can cover a range of choices. King varies his style from section to section, depending on his purpose. Notice how King sounds formal in his introduction (paragraphs 1–5), where he wants to establish authority, but plainspoken when he narrates the difficulties he and other black leaders had in their efforts to negotiate with city leaders (paragraphs 6–9). Notice as well how his sentences and paragraphs shorten, on average, in the passage comparing just and unjust laws (paragraphs 15–22).

Just as King matches style with function, so you need to vary your style based on what each part of your essay is doing. This variation creates *pacing,* the sense of overall rhythm. Readers need places where they can relax a bit between points of high intensity such as lengthy arguments and passionate pleas.

As you write your first draft, concern yourself with matching style to purpose from section to section, depending on whether you are providing background information, telling a story, developing a reason in your case, mounting an emotional appeal, and so on. Save detailed attention to style for later in the process while editing a second or third draft.

Following Through

Once you have completed the first draft of an argument to persuade, select one paragraph in which you have consciously made stylistic choices to create images, connotations, sound patterns, and so on. Share the paragraph with your class, describing your choices as we have done with passages from King's letter.

Following Through

Read the student argument that begins on page 263 and be ready to discuss its effectiveness as persuasion. Build your evaluation around the suggestions listed in the "Reader's Checklist for Revising a Persuasive Essay" on page 262.

The following list will direct you to specific features of a good persuasive essay. You and a peer may want to exchange drafts; having someone else give your paper a critical reading often helps identify weaknesses you may have overlooked. After you have revised your draft, use the suggestions in the appendix to edit for style and check for errors at the sentence level.

☐ Read the audience profile. Then read the draft through, taking the role of the target audience. After reading the draft, mark the essay's divisions. You may also want to number paragraphs so that you can refer to them easily.

☐ Recall that persuasive arguments must be based on inquiry and case-making. Inspect the case first. Underline the thesis and mark the reasons. Circle words that need definition. Note any reasons that need more evidence or other support, such as illustrations.

☐ Evaluate the plan. Are the reasons presented in a compelling order? Does the argument build to a strong conclusion? Can you envision a better arrangement? Make suggestions, referring to paragraphs by number.

☐ Persuasion requires the writer to present him- or herself as worthy of the reader's trust and respect. Reread the draft, marking specific places where the writer has sought identification from the target audience. Has the writer made an effort to find common ground with readers by using any of the ideas listed on pages 229–230? Suggest improvements.

☐ Persuasion also requires emotional support through concrete examples and imagery, analogies and metaphors, first-person reporting, quotations, and so on. Locate the emotional appeals. Are they successful? What improvements can you suggest?

☐ Look to see if the draft exhibits the middle style. Mark any instances of
   Poor transitions between sentences or paragraphs
   Wordy passages, especially those containing the passive voice (see "Editing for Clarity and Conciseness" in the appendix)
   Awkward sentences
   Poor diction—that is, the use of incorrect or inappropriate words

☐ Note any examples of effective style—good use of metaphor, repetition, or parallelism, for example.

☐ Describe the tone. Does it change from section to section? How appropriate and effective is tone in specific sections of the essay?

☐ After studying the argument, ask whether you are sure what action the writer wants or expects from the audience. Has he or she succeeded in persuading the audience? Why or why not?

STUDENT SAMPLE: *An Essay to Persuade*

Charity Miller wrote the following essay in a first-year composition course. The intended audience was relatively well-off white students. She's writing in the context of negative public opinion about affirmative action and recent court rulings tending to undermine it. She argues that affirmative action is just, helps to create fairness, and has not yet outlived its value as a corrective to past discrimination.

WHEN WILL RACE LOSE THE RACE?

Charity Miller

www.mhhe.com/**crusius**

For many additional examples of student writing, go to:
Writing

It is Tuesday, September 23, 2003, and I am thrilled to see a bake sale as I walk out of the West bridge exit of the Hughes-Trigg Student Center. Spotting Rice Krispies bars, my favorite, on the table, I excitedly skip over because I suffer from what I like to call "college-student-starvation around-11am-syndrome." But I stop midway as I read a red-lettered poster taped to the front of the table: "Affirmative Action Is Racist." Initially, the sign does not deter my determination to purchase my Rice Krispie. *We all are entitled to our own opinions,* I privately resolve. Then I see another poster that allocates prices for the goodies according to race and gender: White males, $1, White females, $0.75, Hispanics, $0.50, and Blacks, $0.25. The radical poster pricks my interest, so I ask the student vendor, "What is this about?"

He says that it is a "practical example to show that Affirmative Action is unfair." I must admit the vendor has a point; Affirmative Action is not "fair." Yet in the same manner, it is not fair that a gallon of water costs $1.79 at The Market and only $0.79 at Kroger. It is an appalling injustice that some students have to pay a whopping $31,979 to attend SMU, while other students receive healthy refund checks because of excess financial aid. It is certainly a major bias that students may enroll in schools solely based on their parents' political and/or financial status. Furthermore, it is insanely unfair that all minorities together make up only 19.9% of students and 13.8% of faculty at Southern Methodist University ("Facts about SMU" 3). Perhaps the author of the cliché "Life isn't fair" should win the Nobel Peace Prize for his or her wisdom.

People across the globe recognize and then refuse to accept the injustices of life. Our government, our schools, and even our families implement laws and procedures to resolve life's inequalities. For example, a mother with two sons may give her ill son two tasty Flintstone vitamins but give her well son only one. She "unfairly" gives the sickly son two vitamins to maintain a healthy level of nutrition in both of her children. In the same manner, some tactics that appear biased are intended to make up for the biases of life. This paradoxical statement is the foundation of justice, as we know it in the United States. Many laws, policies, and commissions, such as the Civil Rights Act of 1964 and the Equal Employment Opportunity Commission, are established to promote justice of education, employment, gender, and religion (Sykes 1). For instance, destitute families receive welfare to help pay the cost of living until their income is stable. Technically, it is not *fair* that only poor families receive government money, but it is *just* because poor families need it and more affluent families do not. Therefore, justice does not equal fairness. Rather, justice creates fairness.

Likewise, Affirmative Action is not fair, but it is just. It meets the needs of minorities and also accommodates for disadvantages such as language differences, substandard schooling, financial deficiency, handicaps, and other setbacks for all victims of inequality. Affirmative Action is an idealistic endeavor, but is not intended to achieve perfection. While total equality will never exist because "life isn't fair," it is imperative for us to strive to lessen injustices. Therefore, Affirmative Action is necessary in colleges and universities to create diversity, limit discrimination, and eventually create a state of fairness in which this policy can become obsolete.

Many schools use Affirmative Action to admit a diverse student body. Originally, when segregation was more prominent, Affirmative Action introduced policies that integrated races and genders and remedied the unsuccessful "separate but equal" court rule. Today, Affirmative Action continues to graciously level the playing field of college admission by providing opportunities to disadvantaged students. Minorities competing for college admission are outnumbered like ten red gumballs in a machine of fifty blue ones. Therefore, some schools use race as an admissions factor to ensure that a ration of minority students is selected. Admitting students of wide geographic representation and a variety of cultures, languages, religions, and talents yields a more knowledgeable and culturally balanced student body. Race does not substitute for merit; it is simply another factor in the admissions process to create diversity.

Furthermore, Affirmative Action solidifies the playing field, replacing the quicksand of discrimination. In concurrence with the 14th amendment, the government mandated Affirmative Action in the mid-twentieth century to ensure equal protection for people of socioeconomic, ethnic, or gender differences. Hence, prejudiced school officials were pressed to end illegal and blatant discrimination against minority students. My father is a product of mandatory Affirmative Action. Despite his excellent grades in high school, he could not afford college, and as a minority, he was not eligible for admission into the college of his choice because it was a "white school." However, in 1970, Affirmative Action stepped in like Superman to save the day. The government threatened to suspend funding for the school if it did not admit and support minority students. My dad accepted this measure of grace and worked hard in school to become a successful lawyer and pastor. Not only did Affirmative Action allow my dad to

5

achieve his dreams, but it also gave him a chance to disprove negative ethnic stereotypes. Many people accept stereotypes that classify minorities as poor and uneducated because minorities have been excluded from education and wealth throughout this country's history. Affirmative Action eliminates discrimination and enables minorities to kick down stereotypical barriers and reach their greatest potential through higher education.

Today, racist discrimination in colleges is less conspicuous than it was years ago. Apparently, Affirmative Action is fulfilling its purpose. However, just as fashion styles come and go seasonally, Affirmative Action will eventually become outdated. If it outlives its purpose, it will generate a counterproductive effect. If the government continues to aid minorities when schools have become more diverse, equal opportunities more available, and discrimination less tolerated, then Affirmative Action will unjustly discriminate against Whites. Affirmative Action should serve only temporarily to resolve inequalities. For example, there was a time when Black women could not enter beauty contests because of their ethnicity. Hence, Blacks created their own beauty contest as a kind of Affirmative Action to publicly say, "Black is beautiful, too." Presently, race is no longer an obstacle in national beauty contests. In fact, Miss America of 2004 is an African American from Florida. Although ethnic contests still exist today, the black beauty contest served its purpose and is no longer needed.

Has Affirmative Action outlived its purpose in all colleges and universities? Has Affirmative Action become racist? According to the minority enrollment statistics on college campuses, the best answer is "No, not yet." Minorities are still underrepresented. However, some schools, such as SMU, no longer adhere to Affirmative Action policies, and minority percentages are still increasing. The 2003 incoming class at SMU is one of its most diverse ever (Wertheimer 6b). This proves that Affirmative Action has impacted some schools and is becoming less necessary. Soon, all citizens will receive more equal opportunities for higher education. Once we have achieved this new "fairness," then signs that read, "Affirmative Action Is Racist" will uphold justice. I believe this day is approaching, but until it comes, I will gratefully buy my Rice Krispies treat for $0.25.

Works Cited

"Facts about SMU." Southern Methodist University. 2003. 30 Sept. 2003
    <http://smu.edu/facts/facts.asp>.
Sykes, Marquita. "The Origins of Affirmative Action." National
    Organization for Women. 2003. 30 Sept. 2003 <http://www.org/
    nnt/08-95/affimhs.html>.
Wertheimer, Linda K. "SMU Halts Race-Based Bake Sale." Dallas Morning
    News 25 Sept. 2003: B1+.

Work Consulted

Trimble, Ryan. "The Cookie Crumbles." Daily Campus 26 Sept. 2003: 1+.

www.mhhe.
com/crusius

For an electronic
tool that helps
create properly
formatted works-
cited pages,
go to:
Research >
Bibliomaker

Chapter 9

Resolving Conflict: Arguing to Mediate

Private citizens can avoid the big conflicts that concern politicians and activist groups: debates over gay marriage, abortion, taxes, foreign policy, and so on. However, we cannot hide from all conflict. Family members have different preferences about budgeting, major purchases, where to go on vacation, and much else. Furthermore, if you care about what goes on beyond your front door, you will find conflict close to home. The school down the street, for example, wants to expand its athletic stadium. Some parents support the decision because their children play sports at the school. Others oppose it because they think the expansion will bring more traffic, noise, and bright lights to the neighborhood.

One way to resolve conflict is through reasoned arguments. The chapters on convincing and persuading show how appeals to logic and emotion can change minds. But what if we cannot change someone's mind and can't impose our will in other ways?

Some conflicts don't have to be resolved. The Republican husband can live happily with the Democratic wife. Other conflicts are resolved by compromise. We can go to the mountains this year, the seashore the next. Compromise is better than shouting matches, but it does not result in a common understanding.

This chapter presents mediation as argument whose aim is to resolve conflict by thinking more critically about it. People too often see disputes uncritically by simplifying them to their extreme positions, pro and con. The news media does little to help us see conflicts as complex and many-sided, with related issues and shades of gray. *Mediation aims to move disputants beyond the polarized thinking that makes conflicts impossible to resolve.*

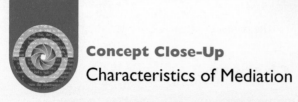

Concept Close-Up

Characteristics of Mediation

1. Aims to **resolve conflict** between opposing and usually **hardened** positions, often because action of some kind must be taken.
2. Aims to reduce hostility and promote understanding between or among conflicting parties; **preserving human relationships and promoting communication** are paramount.
3. Like inquiry, mediation **involves dialogue** and requires that one understand all positions and strive for an **open mind.**
4. Like convincing, mediation involves making a case that **appeals to all parties in the controversy.**
5. Like persuasion, mediation depends on the **good character** of the negotiator and on sharing **values and feelings.**
6. Mediation depends on conflicting parties' desire to **find solutions to overcome counterproductive stalemates.**

Essentially, mediation comes into play when convincing and persuading have resulted in sharply differing viewpoints. The task is first to understand the positions of all parties involved and second to uncover a mediating position capable of producing consensus and a reduction in hostility.

MEDIATION AND THE OTHER AIMS OF ARGUMENT

Mediation uses the other three aims of argument: inquiry, convincing, and persuading. Like inquiry, it open-mindedly examines the range of positions on an issue. Mediation requires knowledge of case structure. The mediator must scrutinize the arguments offered by all sides. A mediatory essay must also present a well-reasoned case of its own. Finally, like persuasion, mediation considers the values, beliefs, and assumptions of the people who hold the conflicting positions. Mediators must appeal to all sides and project a character all sides will trust and find attractive.

In short, mediation requires the mediator to rise above a dispute, including his or her own preferences, to see what is reasonable and right in conflicting positions. The mediator's best asset is wisdom.

THE PROCESS OF MEDIATION

Mediation takes place more often in conversation, through dialogue with the opposing sides, than in writing. But essays can mediate by attempting to argue for middle ground in a conflict. Whether it eventually takes the form of an essay or a dialogue, mediation begins where all arguments should—with inquiry.

A Conflict to Mediate

The United States is a nation of immigrants, but recently the immigrant population includes a wider array of races, ethnicities, religions, and cultures than in the past. The result is a population less white and less Protestant. Should we become a multicultural nation or maintain a single culture based on the original northern European settlers?

Some people argue that the influx of diverse people should have no impact on the traditional Eurocentric identity of America. According to this position, America has a distinctive and superior culture, traceable to the Puritan settlers and based more broadly on Western civilization. This culture is the source of our nation's strength. To keep it strong, newcomers need to assimilate, adopting its values and beliefs. In other words, people holding this position advocate the melting-pot metaphor. Because they believe cultural differences should dissolve as new immigrants become "true Americans," they oppose multiculturalism. We have chosen a recent essay by Roger Kimball, an art critic and editor at the conservative journal *The New Criterion*, to represent the assimilationist position.

Opponents argue that newcomers should preserve their distinctive cultures, taking pride in being Mexican, Chinese, African, and so on. Their metaphor is the mosaic, with each culture remaining distinct but contributing to the whole, like the tiles in a mosaic. We have chosen an essay by Elizabeth Martínez to represent the multiculturalist perspective. Martínez is a Chicana writer and an activist on issues of social justice, including racism and women's rights.

Understanding the Positions

Any attempt to mediate positions requires an understanding of opposing cases. Printed below are the two arguments, followed by our analyses.

Institutionalizing Our Demise: America vs. Multiculturalism
Roger Kimball

The following abridged article appeared in The New Criterion *(June 2004). Roger Kimball's recent books include* The Long March: How the Cultural Revolution of the 1960s Changed America *(Encounter, 2000) and* Tenured Radicals: How Politics Has Corrupted Our Higher Education *(HarperCollins, 1990).*

There is no room in this country for hyphenated Americanism. When I refer to hyphenated Americans, I do not refer to naturalized Americans. Some of the very best Americans I have ever known were naturalized Americans, Americans born abroad.

But a hyphenated American is not an American at all. This is just as true of the man who puts "native" before the hyphen as of the man who puts German or Irish or English or French before the hyphen.

—THEODORE ROOSEVELT, *1915*

It is often said that the terrorist attacks of September 11 precipitated a new resolve throughout the nation. There is some truth to that. Certainly, the extraordinary bravery of the firefighters and other rescue personnel in New York and Washington, D.C., provided an invigorating spectacle—as did Todd "Let's roll" Beamer and his fellow passengers on United Airlines Flight 93. Having learned from their cell phones what had happened at the World Trade Center and the Pentagon, Beamer and his fellows rushed and overpowered the terrorists who had hijacked their plane. As a result, the plane crashed on a remote Pennsylvania farm instead of on Pennsylvania Avenue. Who knows how many lives their sacrifice saved?

The widespread sense of condign outrage—of horror leavened by anger and elevated by resolve—testified to a renewed sense of national purpose and identity after 9/11. Attacked, many Americans suddenly (if temporarily) rediscovered the virtue of patriotism. At the beginning of his remarkable book *Who Are We? The Challenges to America's National Identity* (2004), the Harvard political scientist Samuel Huntington recalls a certain block on Charles Street in Boston. At one time, American flags flew in front of a U.S. Post Office and a liquor store. Then the Post Office stopped displaying the flag, so on September 11, 2001, the flag was flying only in front of the liquor store. Within two weeks, seventeen American flags decorated that block of Charles Street, in addition to a huge flag suspended over the street close by. "With their country under attack," Huntington notes, "Charles Street denizens rediscovered their nation and identified themselves with it."

Was that rediscovery anything more than a momentary passion? Huntington reports that within a few months, the flags on Charles Street began to disappear. By the time the first anniversary rolled around in September 2002, only four were left flying. True, that is four times more than were there on September 10, 2001, but it is less than a quarter of the number that populated Charles Street at the end of September 2001.

There are similar anecdotes from around the country—an access of flag-waving followed by a relapse into indifference. Does it mean that the sudden upsurge of patriotism in the weeks following 9/11 was only, as it were, skin deep? Or perhaps it merely testifies to the fact that a sense of permanent emergency is difficult to maintain, especially in the absence of fresh attacks. Is our sense of ourselves as Americans patent only when challenged? "Does it," Huntington asks, "take an Osama bin Laden . . . to make us realize that we are Americans? If we do not experience recurring destructive attacks, will we return to the fragmentation and eroded Americanism before September 11?"

One hopes that the answer is No. . . . But I fear that for every school-   5
child standing at attention for the National Anthem, there is a teacher or
lawyer or judge or politician or ACLU employee militating against the hegemony of the dominant culture, the insupportable intrusion of white, Christian, "Eurocentric" values into the curriculum, the school pageant, the town
green, etc., etc. . . .

The threat shows itself in many ways, from culpable complacency to the
corrosive imperatives of "multiculturalism" and political correctness. . . . In
essence, as Huntington notes, multiculturalism is "anti-European civilization. . . . It is basically an anti-Western ideology." . . . [W]herever the imperatives of multiculturalism have touched the curriculum, they have left broad
swaths of anti-Western attitudinizing competing for attention with quite
astonishing historical blindness. Courses on minorities, women's issues,
the Third World proliferate; the teaching of mainstream history slides into
oblivion. "The mood," Arthur Schlesinger wrote in *The Disuniting of America*
(1992), his excellent book on the depredations of multiculturalism, "is
one of divesting Americans of the sinful European inheritance and seeking
redemptive infusions from non-Western cultures."

A profound ignorance of the milestones of American culture is one predictable result of this mood. The statistics have become proverbial. Huntington quotes one poll from the 1990s showing that while 90 percent of Ivy
League students could identify Rosa Parks, only 25 percent could identify the
author of the words "government of the people, by the people, for the people." (Yes, it's the Gettysburg Address.) In a 1999 survey, 40 percent of seniors
at fifty-five top colleges could not say within half a century when the Civil
War was fought. Another study found that more high school students knew
who Harriet Tubman was than knew that Washington commanded the
American army in the revolution or that Abraham Lincoln wrote the Emancipation Proclamation. Doubtless you have your own favorite horror story.

But multiculturalism is not only an academic phenomenon. The attitudes it fosters have profound social as well as intellectual consequences.
One consequence has been a sharp rise in the phenomenon of immigration
without—or with only partial—assimilation: a dangerous demographic
trend that threatens American identity in the most basic way. These various
agents of dissolution are also elements in a wider culture war: the contest
to define how we live and what counts as the good in the good life. Anti-
Americanism occupies such a prominent place on the agenda of the culture
wars precisely because the traditional values of American identity—
articulated by the Founders and grounded in a commitment to individual
liberty and public virtue—are deeply at odds with the radical, de-civilizing
tenets of the "multiculturalist" enterprise.

To get a sense of what has happened to the institution of American
identity, compare Robert Frost's performance at John F. Kennedy's inaugura-
tion in 1961 with Maya Angelou's performance thirty-two years later.

As Huntington reminds us, Frost spoke of the "heroic deeds" of America's founding, an event, he said, that with "God's approval" ushered in "a new order of the ages." By contrast, Maya Angelou never mentioned the words "America" or "American." Instead, she identified twenty-seven ethnic or religious groups that had suffered repression because of America's "armed struggles for profit," "cynicism," and "brutishness." . . .

A favorite weapon in the armory of multiculturalism is the lowly   10
hyphen. When we speak of an African-American or Mexican-American or Asian-American these days, the aim is not descriptive but deconstructive. There is a polemical edge to it, a provocation. The hyphen does not mean "American, but hailing at some point in the past from someplace else." It means "only provisionally American: my allegiance is divided at best." . . . The multicultural passion for hyphenation is not simply a fondness for syntactical novelty. It also bespeaks a commitment to the centrifugal force of anti-American tribalism. The division marked by the hyphen in African-American (say) denotes a political stand. It goes hand-in-hand with other items on the index of liberal desiderata — the redistributive impulse behind efforts at "affirmative action," for example. . . .

Multiculturalism and "affirmative action" are allies in the assault on the institution of American identity. As such, they oppose the traditional understanding of what it means to be an American — an understanding hinted at in 1782 by the French-born American farmer J. Hector St. John de Crèvecoeur in his famous image of America as a country in which "individuals of all nations are melted into a new race of men." This crucible of American identity, this "melting pot," has two aspects. The negative aspect involves disassociating oneself from the cultural imperatives of one's country of origin. One sheds a previous identity before assuming a new one. One might preserve certain local habits and tastes, but they are essentially window-dressing. In essence one has left the past behind in order to become an American citizen.

The positive aspect of advancing the melting pot involves embracing the substance of American culture. The 1795 code for citizenship lays out some of the formal requirements.

> I do solemnly swear (1) to support the Constitution of the United States; (2) to renounce and abjure absolutely and entirely all allegiance and fidelity to any foreign prince, potentate, state, or sovereignty of whom or which the applicant was before a subject or citizen; (3) to support and defend the Constitution and the laws of the United States against all enemies, foreign and domestic; (4) to bear true faith and allegiance to the same; and (5) (A) to bear arms on behalf of the United States when required by law, or (B) to perform noncombatant service in the Armed Forces of the United States when required by law. . . .

For over two hundred years, this oath had been required of those wishing to become citizens. In 2003, Huntington tells us, federal bureaucrats launched a campaign to rewrite and weaken it.

I shall say more about what constitutes the substance of American identity in a moment. For now, I want to underscore the fact that this project of Americanization has been an abiding concern since the time of the Founders. "We must see our people more Americanized," John Jay declared in the 1780s. Jefferson concurred. Teddy Roosevelt repeatedly championed the idea that American culture, the "crucible in which all the new types are melted into one," was "shaped from 1776 to 1789, and our nationality was definitely fixed in all its essentials by the men of Washington's day."

It is often said that America is a nation of immigrants. In fact, as Huntington points out, America is a country that was initially a country of *settlers*. Settlers precede immigrants and make their immigration possible. The culture of those mostly English-speaking, predominantly Anglo-Protestant settlers defined American culture. Their efforts came to fruition with the generation of Franklin, Washington, Jefferson, Hamilton, and Madison. The Founders are so denominated because they founded, they inaugurated a state. Immigrants were those who came later, who came from elsewhere, and who became American by embracing the Anglophone culture of the original settlers. The English language, the rule of law, respect for individual rights, the industriousness and piety that flowed from the Protestant work ethic—these were central elements in the culture disseminated by the Founders. And these were among the qualities embraced by immigrants when they became Americans. "Throughout American history," Huntington notes, "people who were not white Anglo-Saxon Protestants have become Americans by adopting America's Anglo-Protestant culture and political values. This benefited them and the country."

Justice Louis Brandeis outlined the pattern in 1919. Americanization, he said, means that the immigrant "adopts the clothes, the manners, and the customs generally prevailing here . . . substitutes for his mother tongue the English language" and comes "into complete harmony with our ideals and aspirations and cooperate[s] with us for their attainment." Until the 1960s, the Brandeis model mostly prevailed. Protestant, Catholic, and Jewish groups, understanding that assimilation was the best ticket to stability and social and economic success, eagerly aided in the task of integrating their charges into American society.

The story is very different today. In America, there is a dangerous new tide of immigration from Asia, a variety of Muslim countries, and Latin America, especially from Mexico. The tide is new not only chronologically but also in substance. First, there is the sheer matter of numbers. More than 2,200,000 legal immigrants came to the U.S. from Mexico in the 1990s alone. The number of illegal Mexican immigrants is staggering. So is their birth rate. Altogether there are more than 8 million Mexicans in the U.S. Some parts of the Southwest are well on their way to becoming what Victor Davis Hanson calls "Mexifornia," "the strange society that is emerging as the result of a demographic and cultural revolution like no other in our times." A professor of Chicano Studies at the University of New Mexico

15

gleefully predicts that by 2080 parts of the Southwest United States and Northern Mexico will join to form a new country, "La Republica del Norte."

The problem is not only one of numbers, though. Earlier immigrants made—and were helped and goaded by the ambient culture to make—concerted efforts to assimilate. Important pockets of these new immigrants are not assimilating, not learning English, not becoming or thinking of themselves primarily as Americans. The effect of these developments on American identity is disastrous and potentially irreversible.

Such developments are abetted by the left-wing political and educational elites of this country, whose dominant theme is the perfidy of traditional American values. Hence the passion for multiculturalism and the ideal of ethnic hyphenation that goes with it. This has done immense damage in schools and colleges as well as in the population at large. By removing the obligation to master English, multiculturalism condemns whole subpopulations to the status of permanent second-class citizens. . . .

As if in revenge for this injustice, however, multiculturalism also weakens the social bonds of the community at large. The price of imperfect assimilation is imperfect loyalty. Take the movement for bilingualism. Whatever it intended in theory, in practice it means *not* mastering English. It has notoriously left its supposed beneficiaries essentially monolingual, often semi-lingual. The only *bi* involved is a passion for bifurcation, which is fed by the accumulated resentments instilled by the anti-American multicultural orthodoxy. Every time you call directory assistance or some large corporation and are told "Press One for English" and "Para español oprime el numero dos" it is another small setback for American identity. . . .

We stand at a crossroads. The future of America hangs in the balance.   20
Huntington outlines several possible courses that the country might take, from the loss of our core culture to an attempt to revive the "discarded and discredited racial and ethnic concepts" that, in part, defined pre-mid-twentieth century America. Huntington argues for another alternative. If we are to preserve our identity as a nation we need to preserve the core values that defined that identity. This is a point that the political philosopher Patrick, Lord Devlin made in his book *The Enforcement of Morals* (1965):

> [S]ociety means a community of ideas; without shared ideas on politics, morals, and ethics no society can exist. Each one of us has ideas about what is good and what is evil; they cannot be kept private from the society in which we live. If men and women try to create a society in which there is no fundamental agreement about good and evil they will fail; if having based it upon a common set of core values, they surrender those values, it will disintegrate. For society is not something that can be kept together physically; it is held by the invisible but fragile bonds of common beliefs and values. . . . A common mo-

rality is part of the bondage of a good society, and that bondage is part of the price of society which mankind must pay.

What are those beliefs and values? They embrace several things, including religion. You wouldn't know it from watching CNN or reading *The New York Times*, but there is a huge religious revival taking place now, affecting just about every part of the globe except Western Europe, which slouches towards godlessness almost as fast as it slouches towards bankruptcy and demographic collapse. (Neither Spain nor Italy are producing enough children to replace their existing populations, while the Muslim birthrate in France continues to soar).

Things look different in America. For if America is a vigorously secular country—which it certainly is—it is also a deeply religious one. It always has been. Tocqueville was simply minuting the reality he saw around him when he noted that "[o]n my arrival in the United States the religious aspect of the country was the first thing that struck my attention." As G. K. Chesterton put it a century after Tocqueville, America is "a nation with the soul of a church." Even today, America is a country where an astonishing 92 percent of the population says it believes in God and 80 to 85 percent of the population identifies itself as Christian. Hence Huntington's call for a return to America's core values is also a call to embrace the religious principles upon which the country was founded, "a recommitment to America as a deeply religious and primarily Christian country, encompassing several religious minorities adhering to Anglo-Protestant values, speaking English, maintaining its cultural heritage, and committed to the principles" of political liberty as articulated by the Founders. . . . Huntington is careful to stress that what he offers is an "argument for the importance of Anglo-Protestant culture, not for the importance of Anglo-Protestant people." That is, he argues not on behalf of a particular ethnic group but on behalf of a culture and set of values that "for three and a half centuries have been embraced by Americans of all races, ethnicities, and religions and that have been the source of their liberty, unity, power, prosperity, and moral leadership."

American identity was originally founded on four things: ethnicity, race, ideology, and culture. By the mid-twentieth century, ethnicity and race had sharply receded in importance. Indeed, one of America's greatest achievements is having eliminated the racial and ethnic components that historically were central to its identity. Ideology—the package of Enlightened liberal values championed by the Founders—[is] crucial but too thin for the task of forging or preserving national identity by themselves. ("A nation defined only by political ideology," Huntington notes, "is a fragile nation.") Which is why Huntington, like virtually all of the Founders, explicitly grounded American identity in religion.

. . . Opponents of religion in the public square never tire of reminding us that there is no mention of God in the Constitution. This is true. Neither is the word "virtue" mentioned. But both are presupposed. For the

American Founders, as the historian Gertrude Himmelfarb points out, virtue, grounded in religion, was presumed "to be rooted in the very nature of man and as such . . . reflected in the *moeurs* of the people and in the traditions and informal institutions of society." It is also worth mentioning that if the Constitution is silent on religion, the Declaration of Independence is voluble, speaking of "nature's God," the "Creator," "the supreme judge of the world," and "divine Providence." . . . Benjamin Rush, one of the signers of the Declaration of Independence, summed up the common attitude of the Founders toward religion when he insisted that "[t]he only foundation for a useful education in a republic is to be laid in religion. Without it there can be no virtue, and without virtue there can be no liberty, and liberty is the object of all republican governments." George Washington concurred: "Reason and experience both forbid us to expect that national morality can prevail in exclusion of religious principles."

No nation lasts forever. An external enemy may eventually overrun and subdue it; internal forces of dissolution and decadence may someday undermine it, leaving it prey to more vigorous competitors. Sooner or later it succumbs. The United States is the most powerful nation the world has ever seen. Its astonishing military might, economic productivity, and political vigor are unprecedented. But someday, as Huntington reminds us, it too will fade or perish as Athens, Rome, and other great civilizations have faded or perished. Is the end, or the beginning of the end, at hand?

So far, the West — or at least the United States — has disappointed its self-appointed undertakers. How do we stand now, at the dawn of the twenty-first century? It is worth remembering that besieged nations do not always succumb to the forces, external or internal, that threaten them. Sometimes, they muster the resolve to fight back successfully, to renew themselves. Today, America faces a new external enemy in the form of militant Islam and global terrorism. That minatory force, though murderous, will fail in proportion to our resolve to defeat it. Do we still possess that resolve? Inseparable from resolve is self-confidence, faith in the essential nobility of one's regime and one's way of life. To what extent do we still possess, still practice that faith?

25

Reinventing "America": Call for a New National Identity
Elizabeth Martínez

Elizabeth Martínez has written six books, including one on Chicano history. This essay comes from her 1998 book, De Colores Means All of Us: Latina Views for a Multi-Colored Century.

For some 15 years, starting in 1940, 85 percent of all U.S. elementary schools used the Dick and Jane series to teach children how to read.

The series starred Dick, Jane, their white middle-class parents, their dog Spot and their life together in a home with a white picket fence.

"Look, Jane, look! See Spot run!" chirped the two kids. It was a house full of glorious family values, where Mom cooked while Daddy went to work in a suit and mowed the lawn on weekends. The Dick and Jane books also taught that you should do your job and help others. All this affirmed an equation of middle-class with whiteness with virtue.

In the mid-1990s, museums, libraries and 80 Public Broadcasting Service (PBS) stations across the country had exhibits and programs commemorating the series. At one museum, an attendant commented, "When you hear someone crying, you know they are looking at the Dick and Jane books." It seems nostalgia runs rampant among many Euro-Americans: a nostalgia for the days of unchallenged White Supremacy—both moral and material—when life was "simple."

We've seen that nostalgia before in the nation's history. But today it signifies a problem reaching a new intensity. It suggests a national identity crisis that promises to bring in its wake an unprecedented nervous breakdown for the dominant society's psyche.

Nowhere is this more apparent than in California, which has long been on the cutting edge of the nation's present and future reality. Warning sirens have sounded repeatedly in the 1990s, such as the fierce battle over new history textbooks for public schools, Proposition 187's ugly denial of human rights to immigrants, the 1996 assault on affirmative action that culminated in Proposition 209, and the 1997 move to abolish bilingual education. Attempts to copycat these reactionary measures have been seen in other states.

The attack on affirmative action isn't really about affirmative action. Essentially it is another tactic in today's war on the gains of the 1960s, a tactic rooted in Anglo resentment and fear. A major source of that fear: the fact that California will almost surely have a majority of people of color in 20 to 30 years at most, with the nation as a whole not far behind.

Check out the February 3, 1992, issue of *Sports Illustrated* with its double-spread ad for *Time* magazine. The ad showed hundreds of newborn babies in their hospital cribs, all of them Black or brown except for a rare white face here and there. The headline says, "Hey, whitey! It's your turn at the back of the bus!" The ad then tells you, read *Time* magazine to keep up with today's hot issues. That manipulative image could have been published today; its implication of shifting power appears to be the recurrent nightmare of too many potential Anglo allies.

Euro-American anxiety often focuses on the sense of a vanishing national identity. Behind the attacks on immigrants, affirmative action and multiculturalism, behind the demand for "English Only" laws and the rejection of bilingual education, lies the question: with all these new people, languages and cultures, what will it mean to be an American? If that question once seemed, to many people, to have an obvious, universally applicable answer, today new definitions must be found. But too often Americans, with supposed scholars in the lead, refuse to face that need and instead nurse a nostalgia for some bygone clarity. They remain trapped in denial.

An array of such ostriches, heads in the sand, began flapping their feathers noisily with the publication of Allan Bloom's 1987 best-selling book, *The Closing of the American Mind.* Bloom bemoaned the decline of our "common values" as a society, meaning the decline of Euro-American cultural centricity (shall we just call it cultural imperialism?). Since then we have seen constant sniping at "diversity" goals across the land. The assault has often focused on how U.S. history is taught. And with reason, for this country's identity rests on a particular narrative about the historical origins of the United States as a nation.

THE GREAT WHITE ORIGIN MYTH

Every society has an origin narrative that explains that society to itself and the world with a set of stories and symbols. The origin myth, as scholar-activist Roxanne Dunbar Ortiz has termed it, defines how a society understands its place in the world and its history. The myth provides the basis for a nation's self-defined identity. Most origin narratives can be called myths because they usually present only the most flattering view of a nation's history; they are not distinguished by honesty.

Ours begins with Columbus "discovering" a hemisphere where some 80 million people already lived but didn't really count (in what became the United States, they were just buffalo-chasing "savages" with no grasp of real estate values and therefore doomed to perish). It continues with the brave Pilgrims, a revolution by independence-loving colonists against a decadent English aristocracy and the birth of an energetic young republic that promised democracy and equality (that is, to white male landowners). In the 1840s, the new nation expanded its size by almost one-third, thanks to a victory over that backward land of little brown people called Mexico. Such has been the basic account of how the nation called the United States of America came into being as presently configured.

The myth's omissions are grotesque. It ignores three major pillars of our nationhood: genocide, enslavement and imperialist expansion (such nasty words, who wants to hear them?—but that's the problem). The massive extermination of indigenous peoples provided our land base; the enslavement of African labor made our economic growth possible; and the seizure of half of Mexico by war (or threat of renewed war) extended this nation's boundaries north to the Pacific and south to the Rio Grande. Such are the foundation stones of the United States, within an economic system that made this country the first in world history to be born capitalist.

Those three pillars were, of course, supplemented by great numbers of dirt-cheap workers from Mexico, China, the Philippines, Puerto Rico and other countries, all of them kept in their place by White Supremacy.

10

In history they stand alongside millions of less-than-supreme white workers and sharecroppers.

Any attempt to modify the present origin myth provokes angry efforts to
repel such sacrilege. In the case of Native Americans, scholars will insist that
they died from disease or wars among themselves, or that "not so many
really did die." At worst it was a "tragedy," but never deliberate genocide,
never a pillar of our nationhood. As for slavery, it was an embarrassment,
of course, but do remember that Africa also had slavery and anyway enlightened white folk finally did end the practice here.

In the case of Mexico, reputable U.S. scholars still insist on blaming   15
that country for the 1846–48 war. Yet even former U.S. President Ulysses
Grant wrote in his memoirs that "[w]e were sent to provoke a fight [by moving troops into a disputed border area] but it was essential that Mexico
should commence it [by fighting back]." (*Mr. Lincoln's General: Ulysses S.
Grant, an illustrated autobiography.*) President James Polk's 1846 diary records
that he told his cabinet his purpose in declaring war as "acquiring California, New Mexico, and perhaps other Mexican lands." (*Diary of James K. Polk
1845–49.*) To justify what could be called a territorial drive-by, the Mexican
people were declared inferior; the U.S. had a "Manifest Destiny" to bring
them progress and democracy.

Even when revisionist voices expose particular evils of Indian policy, slavery or the war on Mexico, they remain little more than unpleasant footnotes;
the core of the dominant myth stands intact. PBS's eight-part documentary
series of 1996 titled "The West" is a case in point. It devoted more than the
usual attention to the devastation of Native Americans, but still centered on
Anglos and gave little attention to why their domination evolved as it did.
The West thus remained the physically gorgeous backdrop for an ugly, unal-
tered origin myth.

In fact, "The West" series strengthens that myth. White Supremacy needs
the brave but inevitably doomed Indians to silhouette its own inevitable conquest. It needs the Indian-as-devil to sustain its own holy mission. Remember
Timothy Wight, who served as pastor to Congress in the late 1700s and wrote
that, under the Indians, "Satan ruled unchallenged in America" until "our
chosen race eternal justice sent." With that self-declared moral authority, the
"winning of the West" metamorphosed from a brutal, bloody invasion into a
crusade of brave Christians marching across a lonely, dangerous landscape.

RACISM AS LINCHPIN OF THE U.S. NATIONAL IDENTITY

A crucial embellishment of the origin myth and key element of the national
identity has been the myth of the frontier, analyzed in Richard Slotkin's *Gun-
fighter Nation,* the last volume of a fascinating trilogy. He describes Theodore Roosevelt's belief that the West was won thanks to American arms,
"the means by which progress and nationality will be achieved." That success, Roosevelt continued, "depends on the heroism of men who impose

on the course of events the latent virtues of their 'race.'" Roosevelt saw conflict on the frontier producing a species of virile "fighters and breeders" who
would eventually generate a new leadership class. Militarism thus went
hand in hand with the racialization of history's protagonists.

No slouch as an imperialist, Roosevelt soon took the frontier myth
abroad, seeing Asians as Apaches and the Philippines as Sam Houston's
Texas in the process of being seized from Mexico. For Roosevelt, Slotkin
writes, "racial violence [was] the principle around which both individual
character and social organization develop." Such ideas have not remained
totally unchallenged by U.S. historians, nor was the frontier myth always
applied in totally simplistic ways by Hollywood and other media. (The outlaw, for example, is a complicated figure, both good and bad.) Still, the frontier myth traditionally spins together virtue and violence, morality and war,
in a convoluted, Calvinist web. That tortured embrace defines an essence of
the so-called American character — the national identity — to this day.

The frontier myth embodied the nineteenth-century concept of Manifest   20
Destiny, a doctrine that served to justify expansionist violence by means of
intrinsic racial superiority. Manifest Destiny saw Yankee conquest as the inevitable result of a confrontation between enterprise and progress (white)
versus passivity and backwardness (Indian, Mexican). "Manifest" meant
"God-given," and the whole doctrine is profoundly rooted in religious conviction going back to the earliest colonial times. In his short, powerful book
Manifest Destiny: American Expansion and the Empire of Right, Professor An-
ders Stephanson tells how the Puritans reinvented the Jewish notion of cho-
senness and applied it to this hemisphere so that territorial expansion became God's will. . . .

MANIFEST DESTINY DIES HARD

The concept of Manifest Destiny, with its assertion of racial superiority sustained by military power, has defined U.S. identity for 150 years. Only the
Vietnam War brought a serious challenge to that concept of almightiness.
Bitter debate, moral anguish, images of My Lai and the prospect of military
defeat for the first time in U.S. history all suggested that the long-standing
marriage of virtue and violence might soon be on the rocks. In the final
years of the war the words leaped to mind one day: this country is having
a national nervous breakdown.

Perhaps this is why the Vietnam War continues to arouse passions today. Some who are willing to call the war "a mistake" still shy away from
recognizing its immorality or even accepting it as a defeat. A few Americans
have the courage to conclude from the Vietnam War that we should abandon the idea that our identity rests on being the world's richest, most powerful and indeed *best* nation. Is it possible that the so-called Vietnam syndrome might signal liberation from a crippling self-definition? Is it possible

the long-standing belief that "American exceptionalism" had made freedom possible might be rejected someday?

The Vietnam syndrome is partly rooted in the fact that, although other societies have also been based on colonialism and slavery, ours seems to have an insatiable need to be the "good guys" on the world stage. That need must lie at least partially in a Protestant dualism that defines existence in terms of opposites, so that if you are not "good" you are bad, if not "white" then Black, and so on. Whatever the cause, the need to be seen as virtuous, compared to someone else's evil, haunts U.S. domestic and foreign policy. Where on earth would we be without Saddam Hussein, Qaddafi, and that all-time favorite of gringo demonizers, Fidel Castro? Gee whiz, how would we know what an American really is?

Today's origin myth and the resulting concept of national identity make for an intellectual prison where it is dangerous to ask big questions about this society's superiority. When otherwise decent people are trapped in such a powerful desire not to feel guilty, self-deception becomes unavoidable. To cease our present falsification of collective memory should, and could, open the doors of that prison. When together we cease equating whiteness with Americanness, a new day can dawn. As David Roediger, the social historian, has said, "[Whiteness] is the empty and therefore terrifying attempt to build an identity on what one isn't, and on whom one can hold back."

Redefining the U.S. origin narrative, and with it this country's national identity, could prove liberating for our collective psyche. It does not mean Euro-Americans should wallow individually in guilt. It does mean accepting collective responsibility to deal with the implications of our real origin. A few apologies, for example, might be a step in the right direction. In 1997, the idea was floated in Congress to apologize for slavery; it encountered opposition from all sides. But to reject the notion because corrective action, not an apology, is needed misses the point. Having defined itself as the all-time best country in the world, the United States fiercely denies the need to make a serious, official apology for anything. . . . To press for any serious, official apology does imply a new origin narrative, a new self-image, an ideological sea change.

Accepting the implications of a different narrative could also shed light on today's struggles. In the affirmative-action struggle, for example, opponents have said that that policy is no longer needed because racism ended with the Civil Rights Movement. But if we look at slavery as a fundamental pillar of this nation, going back centuries, it becomes obvious that racism could not have been ended by 30 years of mild reforms. If we see how the myth of the frontier idealized the white male adventurer as the central hero of national history, with the woman as sunbonneted helpmate, then we might better understand the dehumanized ways in which women have continued to be treated. A more truthful origin narrative could also help break down divisions among peoples of color by revealing common experiences and histories of cooperation.

A new origin narrative and national identity could help pave the way to a more livable society for us all. A society based on cooperation rather than competition, on the idea that all living creatures are interdependent and that humanity's goal should be balance. Such were the values of many original Americans, deemed "savages." Similar gifts are waiting from other despised peoples and traditions. We might well start by recognizing that "America" is the name of an entire hemisphere, rich in a stunning variety of histories, cultures and peoples—not just one country.

The choice seems clear, if not easy. We can go on living in a state of massive denial, affirming this nation's superiority and virtue simply because we need to believe in it. We can choose to believe the destiny of the United States is still manifest: global domination. Or we can seek a transformative vision that carries us forward, not backward. We can seek an origin narrative that lays the groundwork for a multicultural, multinational identity centered on the goals of social equity and democracy. We do have choices.

There is little time for nostalgia. Dick and Jane never were "America," they were only one part of one community in one part of one country in one part of one continent. Yet we have let their image define our entire society and its values. Will the future be marked by ongoing denial or by steps toward a new vision in which White Supremacy no longer determines reality? When on earth will we transcend the assumptions that imprison our minds?

At times you can hear the clock ticking.   30

Analysis of the Writers' Positions

The first step in resolving conflict is to understand what the parties are claiming and why. Below is our paraphrase of Kimball's and Martínez's arguments.

Kimball's Position   He opposes multiculturalism and wants to preserve an American identity based in Anglo-Protestant culture.

> *Thesis:* Multiculturalism weakens America by keeping people of different cultures from assimilating to the core values of America's Anglo-Protestant identity.
>
>> *Reason:* Educational multiculturalism degrades traditional American values and ignores mainstream history and culture.
>>> *Evidence:* Opinions of Samuel Huntington and Arthur Schlesinger, Jr. Examples of college students' ignorance about history. Maya Angelou's speech at Clinton's inauguration.
>>
>> *Reason:* Multiculturalism "weakens the social bond" by denying that immigrants need to assimilate to the language and values of the dominant culture.
>>> *Evidence:* Rise of hyphenization. Rise of non-English-speaking communities. Calls for affirmative action, which violates the idea of success based on merit.

> *Reason:* America should be defined by one culture and nationality, not many.
>
>> *Evidence:* Quotations from de Crèvecoeur on the "new race of men." Quotations from Theodore Roosevelt, John Jay, Thomas Jefferson, Benjamin Franklin. The 1795 oath of allegiance for citizenship.
>
> *Reason:* The single, unifying identity of America should be based in Anglo-Saxon Protestant Christianity.
>
>> *Evidence:* Religious beliefs of original settlers. Historian Himmelfarb on American virtue as deeply rooted in religion. Quotes from Founding Fathers on relation of virtue to religion. Huntington on the need for national identity based in religion.

Martínez's Position   She wants to replace traditional Anglo-American identity with a multicultural one.

> *Thesis:* The United States needs to discard its "white supremacist" identity.
>
> *Reason:* It's based on racism, genocide, and imperialist expansion.
>
>> *Evidence:* The "origin myth" in common accounts of U.S. history. The historical record of slavery, takeover of Native American land, wars of expansion. Primary sources such as Presidents Grant and Polk. Theodore Roosevelt's statements about racial superiority. Historian Richard Slotkin's analysis of frontier myth.
>
> *Reason:* It's based on a false sense of moral superiority and favor in the eyes of God.
>
>> *Evidence:* Professor Anders Stephanson on the concept of Manifest Destiny. Protestant moral dualism—seeing the world in terms of good and evil. Social historian David Roediger on the Anglo sense of superiority.
>
> *Reason:* America will be a more fair and democratic country if we revise our identity to acknowledge Anglo faults and adopt the values of non-Anglo cultures.
>
>> *Evidence:* Racism and sexism not eliminated. The valuable gifts of other cultures, such as cooperation over competition.

 Following Through

If you and some of your classmates have written arguments taking opposing views on the same issue, prepare briefs of your respective positions to share with one another. (You might also create briefs of your opponents' positions to see how well you have understood one another's written arguments.)

Alternatively write briefs summarizing the opposing positions offered in several published arguments as a first step toward mediating these viewpoints.

Locating the Areas of Agreement and Disagreement

Differences over Facts

Most conflicts result from interpreting facts differently rather than disagreement about the facts themselves. For example, in the arguments of Kimball and Martínez, we see agreement on many factual points:

- that whites are becoming the minority in some parts of the United States
- that assimilation has meant conformity to a culture defined by Anglo-Protestant values
- that Christianity has played a large role in America's sense of identity

If a mediator finds disagreement over facts, he or she needs to look into it and provide evidence from credible sources that would resolve these details. Or the problem might be that one or both sides are arguing without enough information. The mediator can help here by doing the needed research or advising the parties to find out more about what they are arguing over. If they know each other personally, doing the research jointly is a good idea.

 Following Through

> For the arguments you are mediating, make a list of facts that the authors both accept. Note facts offered by one side but denied or not considered by the other. Where your authors don't agree on the facts, do research to decide how valid the facts cited on both sides are. Explain the discrepancies. If your class is mediating the same conflict, compare your findings.

Differences over Interests, Values, and Interpretations

Facts alone cannot resolve entrenched disputes such as the debate over multiculturalism. For example, a history lesson about white settlers' treatment of Native Americans would not change Kimball's mind. Nor would a lesson in Enlightenment philosophy alter what Martínez thinks. When we attempt to mediate, *we have to look into what causes people to hold the positions they do.* Like persuasion, mediation looks at the contexts of a dispute.

To identify these differences, we can ask questions similar to those that are useful in persuasion for identifying what divides us from our audience (see "Questions for Understanding Difference," page 286). We apply below the questions about difference to Kimball's and Martínez's positions.

Is the Difference a Matter of Assumptions? Every argument has assumptions—unstated assertions that the audience must share to find the reasoning valid and persuasive. Kimball assumes that Anglo-Protestant culture is moral; therefore, he does not show how Christianity has made America a moral nation. Martínez disputes the very assumption that America is moral. But she also makes assumptions. She assumes that the "origin narrative" of the white man's conquest and exploitation is the sole basis for the nation's past and present identity. This assumption allows her to argue that the culture of the United States is simply white supremacist.

These two assumptions show polarized thinking—one assumes that Anglo-Protestant values are all good, the other that Anglo-Protestant values are all evil. Such polarized assumptions are common in disputes because, as philosopher of ethics Anthony Weston explains, we polarize not just to simplify but to justify: "We polarize . . . to be able to picture ourselves as totally justified, totally right, and the 'other side' as totally unjustified and wrong."[1] It's precisely this tactic that mediation must resist and overcome.

Is the Difference a Matter of Principle?   By principles, we mean informal rules that guide our actions, like the "rule" in sales: "The customer is always right." Kimball's principle is patriotism, that Americans should be undivided in loyalty and allegiance to the United States. Martínez's principle is fairness and justice for all, which means rewriting the origin narrative, admitting past mistakes, and recognizing the richness and morality of all the cultures that make up America. A mediator might ask: Can we be patriotic *and* self-critical? Do we have to repudiate the past entirely to fashion a new national identity?

Is the Difference a Matter of Values or Priorities?   The principles just discussed reflect differing priorities. In the post-9/11 world, Kimball is concerned with America's strength on the world stage, whereas Martínez concentrates more on America's compassion in its domestic policies. This is a significant difference because Martínez supports programs like affirmative action and multicultural education, the very policies Kimball claims weaken our social bonds (paragraph 10). Once we see this difference, we can see the dispute in the context of liberal and conservative opinion in general. Kimball is arguing for a national identity acceptable to conservatives, Martínez for one acceptable to liberals. But what we need, obviously, is something that can cross this divide and appeal to all or most Americans.

Is the Difference a Matter of Ends or Means?   Martínez and Kimball have different ends in mind, so they also have different means to achieve the ends. For Martínez, a multicultural identity is the means to a more fair and livable society for all. For Kimball, a common identity in Anglo-Protestant culture is the means to remaining "the most powerful nation the world has ever seen." A mediator could reasonably ask: Couldn't we have both? Couldn't the United States be a powerful nation that is also fair and livable for all its citizens?

Is the Difference a Matter of Implications or Consequences?   The mediator has to consider what each side fears will happen if the other side prevails. Kimball fears that multiculturalism will lead Americans to self-doubt, loss of

[1] Anthony Weston, *A Practical Companion to Ethics* (New York: Oxford) 50.

1. Is the difference a matter of *assumptions?* As we discussed in Chapter 3 on the Toulmin method of analysis and in Chapter 6 on inquiry, all arguments are based on some assumptions.
2. Is the difference a matter of *principle?* Are some parties to the dispute following different principles, or general rules, from others?
3. Is the difference a matter of *values* or a matter of having the same values but giving them different *priorities?*
4. Is the difference a matter of *ends* or *means?* That is, do people want to achieve different goals, or do they have the same goals in mind but disagree on the means to achieve them?
5. Is the difference a matter of *interpretation?*
6. Is the difference a matter of *implications* or *consequences?*
7. Is the difference a result of *personal background, basic human needs,* or *emotions?*

To our list of questions about difference in persuasive writing, we add this last question because mediators must look not just at the arguments but also at the disputants as people with histories and feelings. It is not realistic to think that human problems can be solved without taking human factors into consideration. Mediators must take into account such basic human needs as personal security, economic well-being, and a sense of belonging, recognition, and people's control over their own lives. If you are mediating among printed texts, you must use the texts themselves as evidence of these human factors.

confidence. He also forecasts a large population of "permanent second-class citizens" if subgroups of the population do not assimilate. Martínez fears continuing oppression of minorities if our national self-conception doesn't change to fit our country's actual diversity. The mediator must acknowledge the fears of both sides while not permitting either to go unquestioned. Fear is a powerful motivator that must be confronted squarely.

Is the Difference a Matter of Interpretation?   A major disagreement here is over how to interpret the values of Anglo-Protestant culture. To Kimball, these values are "individual liberty and public virtue" (paragraph 8), "the rule of law" (paragraph 14), "respect for individual rights" (paragraph 14), devotion to God and a strong work ethic (paragraph 14). In contrast, Martínez interprets Anglo-Protestant values as a belief in whites' moral superiority and favor in the eyes of God (paragraph 20) that enabled them to see their own acts of "genocide, enslavement, and imperialist expansion" (paragraph 12) as morally acceptable and even heroic (paragraph 19). These interpretations stem from the different backgrounds of the writers, which we consider next.

Is the Difference a Matter of Personal Background, Basic Human Needs, or Emotions? When mediating between positions in written arguments such as these, it's a good idea to go to the library or an online source for biographical information about the authors. It will pay off with insight into why they disagree.

Kimball and Martínez obviously come from very different backgrounds that are representative of others who hold the same positions they do. For example, as a white male with the financial means to have attended Yale, Kimball represents the group that has benefited most from the traditional national identity. His conservative views have pitted him against liberal academics and social activists.

Martínez identifies herself as a Chicana, an American woman of Mexican descent (her father was an immigrant). She is an activist for social justice and heads the Institute for MultiRacial Justice in San Francisco and has taught women's studies and ethnic studies in the California State University system. She knows the burden of discrimination from personal experience and from her work and research. As a proponent of bilingual and multicultural education, she sees people like Kimball as the opposition.

Following Through

If you are mediating among printed arguments, write an analysis based on applying the questions in the Best Practices box on page 286 to two or more arguments. You could write out your analysis in list form, as we did in analyzing the differences between Kimball and Martínez, or you could treat it as an exploratory essay.

As a creative variation for your analysis, write a dialogue with yourself as mediator, posing questions to each of the opposing parties. Have each side respond to your questions just as we demonstrated in our sample dialogue on pages 160–161.

Finding Creative Solutions: Exploring Common Ground

Using critical thinking to mediate means looking closely at what people want and why they want it. It also means seeing the dispute in larger contexts. For example, the dispute over national identity is part of a larger debate between liberals and conservatives over politics, social policy, and education.

Mediation won't and shouldn't try to reach everyone. Some people hold extreme views that reason cannot touch. An example would be the professor Kimball cites who predicts that the southwestern United States and northern Mexico will eventually become a new and separate country. Mediation between this person and Kimball is about as likely as President Bush and Osama bin Laden having dinner together. But mediators can bring reasonable people closer together by trying to arrive at creative solutions that appeal to some of the interests and values of all parties.

Taking a simple example of conflicting interests, consider the family divided about their vacation destination, mountains or seashore. If the seashore lovers go for swimming and sunbathing and the mountain enthusiasts hiking and mountain biking, why not look for places that have both — mountains *and* seashore?

In complex conflicts, such as the one over multiculturalism and national identity, creative solutions are possible if people can move beyond polarized to cooperative thinking. The ethicist Anthony Weston suggests trying to see conflict in terms of what each side is right about. He says, "If both sides (or all sides) are to some extent right, then we need to try to honor what is right in each of them."[2]

Weston points to the debate over saving owls in old-growth forests versus logging interests that employ people. Preserving the environment and endangered species is good, but so is saving jobs. If jobs could be created that use wood in craft-based ways, people could make a living without destroying massive amounts of timber. This solution is possible if the parties cooperate — but not if greedy corporations are deadlocked with radical environmentalists, neither willing to concede anything or give an inch.

Mediators should aim for "win-win" solutions, which resolve conflict by dissolving it. The challenge for the mediator is keeping the high ground and looking for the good and reasonable in what each side wants. Perfect neutrality isn't necessary and mediators do have to expose bad thinking or factual errors, but they must not fall into advocating one side over the other.

Exploring Common Ground in the Debate over National Identity

To find integrative solutions for the national identity – multiculturalism dispute, we analyzed our list of questions for understanding difference to find interests and values Kimball and Martínez might share or be persuaded to share. Here's what we found.

Both want Americans to know their history. Kimball is right. It's a disgrace that college students can't recognize a famous phrase from the Gettysburg Address. But they need to know that *and* the relevance of Harriet

---

[2] Weston, *Practical Companion* 56.

Tubman to those words. Martínez is right also that history should not be propaganda for one view of events. The history of all nations is a mix of good and bad.

Neither Kimball nor Martínez wants a large population of second-class citizens, living in isolated poverty, not speaking English, not seeing themselves as Americans, and not having a say in the democratic process. Martínez's multiculturalism would "break down divisions among peoples of color by revealing common experiences and histories of cooperation" with the goal of "social equity and democracy." She would be more likely, however, to achieve her goal if she considered white men and women *as participants* in this multicultural discussion. To exclude whites keeps people of color where they too often are — on the margins, left out. Kimball needs to be reminded that failure to assimilate is not typically a choice. First-generation immigrants usually learn little English partly because they work several jobs to survive. Living in segregated neighborhoods with others like them provides security and support and can make success easier for their children. Studies show that children who assimilate to the culture of America's poor neighborhoods do less well in school than those whose parents raise them in traditional ways. As in the past, assimilation works only when educational and economic opportunities exist. Kimball needs to look into solutions to the problem of poverty among immigrants.

There is agreement too on the need for a national identity. Martínez calls for "a new identity," implying that we need something deep to define us as Americans. But asking what culture should provide it is the wrong question. Concentrating on the values themselves will help everyone see that most values are shared across races and cultures. For example, Martínez takes Anglo-Protestant culture as competitive, not cooperative. While competition drives capitalism, we need to recall that early Protestant settlers also valued community. The Puritans tried to establish utopian communities devoted to charity; John Winthrop almost went bankrupt making himself an example of generosity to his neighbors. Kimball's "Protestant" work ethic can be found in every ethnic group — for example, in the predominantly Catholic Mexican laborers who do backbreaking work in agriculture and construction. Instead of getting hung up on which religion or ethnic group provided the values, those arguing for a strong American identity can agree on the values themselves: justice, equality, democracy, productivity, charity toward one another, respect for human rights, and love of country.

Finally, what agreement could be reached about assimilation? What does it mean to become "Americanized"? Kimball suggests that immigrants follow Justice Louis Brandeis's advice — adopting "the clothes, the manners, and the customs generally prevailing here." But would such advice mean that what "prevails" here is based in Protestantism and Anglo-Saxon culture? A more realistic idea of "Americanization" comes from our third writer, Bharati Mukherjee, who suggests in her mediatory essay that "assimilation" is a two-way transformation, with immigrants and mainstream culture interacting, influencing each other. Such a conception *requires* both the preservation of tradition Kimball wants and the respect for diversity Martínez wants.

Mediating any controversy involves opening up the thinking of all parties by questioning assumptions, checking facts, and searching for what pulls together rather than tears apart.

Following Through

Either in list form or as an informal exploratory essay, explore possible areas of agreement between the various positions you have been analyzing. End your list or essay with a summary of a position that all sides might be willing to acknowledge has some validity.

THE MEDIATORY ESSAY

The natural human tendency in argument is to polarize—to see conflict as simply "us" versus "them," like children choosing up sides in a game. Modern media, often striving only for ratings by playing up the dramatic and the sensational, can make matters worse by featuring representatives of extreme positions locked in verbal combat. The result is rarely arguments intended to persuade but rather arguments aimed at solidifying the support of those already in agreement with one or the other sides.

That's why mediation is necessary and matters so much as a way of moving beyond polarized thinking. An example of mediation in the multiculturalism debate appears below. The essay's author is the novelist Bharati Mukherjee. She was born into a wealthy family in Calcutta but became an American citizen. She is now Distinguished Professor of English at the University of California at Berkeley.

She has been faulted by some Indians and other South Asians for depicting India and its culture too harshly in her fiction; her characters are immigrants who embrace, rather than resist, American culture. These critics, whom Mukherjee denounces near the end of her essay, are part of the academic multiculturalists Kimball describes as anti-American. Obviously, Mukherjee is not writing to them nor to "rabid Eurocentrists" on the other side, people she mentions who want to close our borders and stop even legal immigration. She's writing to people who accept either Kimball's position— preserve the Euro-Protestant "core" of American identity—or Martínez's— create a new national identity based on the multicultural mosaic.

There's no single model for a mediatory essay. In this case, Mukherjee's essay mediates by making a case against both radical extremes, one way of seeking to bring people together on the remaining middle ground.

Beyond Multiculturalism:
A Two-Way Transformation
Bharati Mukherjee

The United States exists as a sovereign nation with its officially stated Constitution, its economic and foreign policies, its demarcated, patrolled boundaries. "America," however, exists as image or idea, as dream or nightmare, as romance or plague, constructed by discrete individual fantasies, and shaded by collective paranoias and mythologies.

I am a naturalized U.S. citizen with a certificate of citizenship; more importantly, I am an American for whom "America" is the stage for the drama of self-transformation. I see American culture as a culture of dreamers, who believe material shape (which is not the same as materialism) can be given to dreams. They believe that one's station in life—poverty, education, family background—does not determine one's fate. They believe in the reversal of omens; early failures do not spell inevitable disaster. Outsiders can triumph on merit. All of this happens against the backdrop of the familiar vicissitudes of American life.

I first came to the United States—to the state of Iowa, to be precise—on a late summer evening nearly thirty-three years ago. I flew into a placid, verdant airport in Iowa City on a commercial airliner, ready to fulfill the goals written out in a large, lined notebook for me by my guiltlessly patriarchal father. Those goals were unambiguous: I was to spend two years studying Creative Writing at Paul Engle's unique Writers Workshop; then I was to marry the perfect Bengali bridegroom selected by my father and live out the rest of a contented, predictable life in the city of my birth, Calcutta. In 1961, I was a shy, pliant, well-mannered, dutiful young daughter from a very privileged, traditional, mainstream Hindu family that believed women should be protected and provided for by their fathers, husbands, sons, and it did not once occur to me that I might have goals of my own, quite distinct from those specified for me by my father. I certainly did not anticipate then that, over the next three decades, Iowans—who seemed to me so racially and culturally homogeneous—would be forced to shudder through the violent paroxysms of a collective identity in crisis.

When I was growing up in Calcutta in the fifties, I heard no talk of "identity crisis"—communal or individual. The concept itself—of a person not knowing who she or he was—was unimaginable in a hierarchical, classification-obsessed society. One's identity was absolutely fixed, derived from religion, caste, patrimony, and mother tongue. A Hindu Indian's last name was designed to announce his or her forefathers' caste and place of origin. A Mukherjee could *only* be a Brahmin from Bengal. Indian tradition forbade inter-caste, inter-language, inter-ethnic marriages. Bengali tradition discouraged even emigration; to remove oneself from Bengal was to "pollute" true culture.

Until the age of eight, I lived in a house crowded with forty or fifty   5
relatives. We lived together because we were "family," bonded by kinship, though kinship was interpreted in flexible enough terms to include, when necessary, men, women, children who came from the same *desh*— which is the Bengali word for "homeland"—as had my father and grand-father. I was who I was because I was Dr. Sudhir Lal Mukherjee's daughter, because I was a Hindu Brahmin, because I was Bengali-speaking, and be-cause my *desh* was an East Bengal village called Faridpur. I was encouraged to think of myself as indistinguishable from my dozen girl cousins. Identity was viscerally connected with ancestral soil and family origins. I was first a Mukherjee, then a Bengali Brahmin, and only then an Indian.

Deep down I knew, of course, that I was not quite like my girl cousins. Deeper down, I was sure that pride in the purity of one's culture has a sinis-ter underside. As a child I had witnessed bloody religious riots between Muslims and Hindus, and violent language riots between Bengalis and Biharis. People kill for culture, and die of hunger. Language, race, religion, blood, myth, history, national codes, and manners have all been used, in India, in the United States, are being used in Bosnia and Rwanda even today, to enforce terror, to "otherize," to murder.

I do not know what compelled my strong-willed and overprotective father to risk sending us, his three daughters, to school in the United States, a country he had not visited. In Calcutta, he had insisted on sheltering us from danger and temptation by sending us to girls-only schools, and by providing us with chaperones, chauffeurs, and bodyguards.

The Writers Workshop in a quonset hut in Iowa City was my first expe-rience of coeducation. And after not too long, I fell in love with a fellow student named Clark Blaise, an American of Canadian origin, and impul-sively married him during a lunch break in a lawyer's office above a coffeeshop.

That impulsive act cut me off forever from the rules and ways of upper-middle-class life in Bengal, and hurled me precipitously into a New World life of scary improvisations and heady explorations. Until my lunchtime wedding, I had seen myself as an Indian foreign student, a transient in the United States. The five-minute ceremony in the lawyer's office had changed me into a permanent transient.

Over the last three decades the important lesson that I have learned is   10
that in this era of massive diasporic movements, honorable survival re-quires resilience, curiosity, and compassion, a letting go of rigid ideals about the purity of inherited culture.

The first ten years into marriage, years spent mostly in my husband's *desh* of Canada, I thought myself an expatriate Bengali permanently stranded in North America because of a power surge of destiny or of desire. My first novel, *The Tiger's Daughter,* embodies the loneliness I felt but could

not acknowledge, even to myself, as I negotiated the no-man's-land between the country of my past and the continent of my present. Shaped by
memory, textured with nostalgia for a class and culture I had abandoned,
this novel quite naturally became my expression of the *expatriate
consciousness.*

It took me a decade of painful introspection to put the smothering
tyranny of nostalgia into perspective, and to make the transition from expatriate to immigrant. I have found my way back to the United States after a
fourteen-year stay in Canada. The transition from foreign student to U.S.
citizen, from detached onlooker to committed immigrant, has not
been easy.

The years in Canada were particularly harsh. Canada is a country that
officially—and proudly—resists the policy and process of cultural fusion.
For all its smug rhetoric about "cultural mosaic," Canada refuses to reno-
vate its national self-image to include its changing complexion. It is a New
World country with Old World concepts of a fixed, exclusivist national
identity. And all through the seventies when I lived there, it was a country
without a Bill of Rights or its own Constitution. Canadian official rhetoric
designated me, as a citizen of non-European origin, one of the "visible
minority" who, even though I spoke the Canadian national languages of
English and French, was straining "the absorptive capacity" of Canada.
Canadians of color were routinely treated as "not real" Canadians. In fact,
when a terrorist bomb, planted in an Air India jet on Canadian soil, blew
up after leaving Montreal, killing 329 passengers, 90 percent of whom were
Canadians of Indian origin, the prime minister of Canada at the time, Brian
Mulroney, cabled the Indian prime minister to offer Canada's condolences
for India's loss, exposing the Eurocentricity of the "mosaic" policy of
immigration.

In private conversations, some Canadian ambassadors and External
Affairs officials have admitted to me that the creation of the Ministry of
Multiculturism in the seventies was less an instrument for cultural tolerance, and more a vote-getting strategy to pacify ethnic European constituents who were alienated by the rise of Quebec separatism and the simultaneous increase of non-white immigrants.

The years of race-related harassments in a Canada without a Constitu-   15
tion have politicized me, and deepened my love of the ideals embedded in
the American Bill of Rights.

I take my American citizenship very seriously. I am a voluntary immigrant. I am not an economic refugee, and not a seeker of political asylum.
I am an American by choice, and not by the simple accident of birth. I have
made emotional, social, and political commitments to this country. I have
earned the right to think of myself as an American.

But in this blood-splattered decade, questions such as who is an American and what is American culture are being posed with belligerence and being answered with violence. We are witnessing an increase in physical, too

often fatal, assaults on Asian Americans. An increase in systematic "dot-busting" of Indo-Americans in New Jersey, xenophobic immigrant-baiting in California, minority-on-minority violence during the south-central Los Angeles revolution.

America's complexion is browning daily. Journalists' surveys have established that whites are losing their clear majority status in some states, and have already lost it in New York and California. A recent *Time* magazine poll indicated that 60 percent of Americans favor limiting *legal* immigration. Eighty percent of Americans polled favor curbing the entry of undocumented aliens. U.S. borders are too extensive and too porous to be adequately policed. Immigration, by documented and undocumented aliens, is less affected by the U.S. Immigration and Naturalization Service, and more by wars, ethnic genocides, famines in the emigrant's own country.

Every sovereign nation has a right to formulate its immigration policy. In this decade of continual, large-scale diasporic movements, it is imperative that we come to some agreement about who "we" are now that the community includes old-timers, newcomers, many races, languages, and religions; about what our expectations of happiness and strategies for its pursuit are; and what our goals are for the nation.

Scapegoating of immigrants has been the politicians' easy instant remedy. Hate speeches fill auditoria, and bring in megabucks for those demagogues willing to profit from stirring up racial animosity. [20]

The hysteria against newcomers is only minimally generated by the downturn in our economy. The panic, I suspect, is unleashed by a fear of the "other," the fear of what Daniel Stein, executive director of the Federation for American Immigration Reform, and a champion of closed borders, is quoted as having termed "cultural transmogrification."

The debate about American culture has to date been monopolized by rabid Eurocentrists and ethnocentrists; the rhetoric has been flamboyantly divisive, pitting a phantom "us" against a demonized "them." I am here to launch a new discourse, to reconstitute the hostile, biology-derived "us" versus "them" communities into a new *consensual* community of "we."

All countries view themselves by their ideals. Indians idealize, as well they should, the cultural continuum, the inherent value system of India, and are properly incensed when foreigners see nothing but poverty, intolerance, ignorance, strife, and injustice. Americans see themselves as the embodiments of liberty, openness, and individualism, even when the world judges them for drugs, crime, violence, bigotry, militarism, and homelessness. I was in Singapore when the media was very vocal about the case of an American teenager sentenced to caning for having allegedly vandalized cars. The overwhelming local sentiment was that caning Michael Fay would deter local youths from being tempted into "Americanization," meaning into gleefully breaking the law.

Conversely, in Tavares, Florida, an ardently patriotic school board has legislated that middle school teachers be required to instruct their students that American culture—meaning European-American culture—is inherently "superior to other foreign or historic cultures." The sinister, or at least misguided, implication is that American culture has not been affected by the American Indian, African American, Latin American, and Asian American segments of its population.

The idea of "America" as a nation has been set up in opposition to the tenet that a nation is a collection of like-looking, like-speaking, like-worshiping people. Our nation is unique in human history. We have seen very recently, in a Germany plagued by anti-foreigner frenzy, how violently destabilizing the traditional concept of nation can be. In Europe, each country is, in a sense, a tribal homeland. Therefore, the primary criterion for nationhood in Europe is homogeneity of culture, and race, and religion. And that has contributed to blood-soaked balkanization in the former Yugoslavia and the former Soviet Union. [25]

All European Americans, or their pioneering ancestors, gave up an easy homogeneity in their original countries for a new idea of Utopia. What we have going for us in the 1990s is the exciting chance to share in the making of a new American culture, rather than the coerced acceptance of either the failed nineteenth-century model of "melting pot" or the Canadian model of the "multicultural mosaic."

The "mosaic" implies a contiguity of self-sufficient, utterly distinct culture. "Multiculturism" has come to imply the existence of a central culture, ringed by peripheral cultures. The sinister fallout of official multiculturism and of professional multiculturists is the establishment of one culture as the norm and the rest as aberrations. Multiculturism emphasizes the differences between racial heritages. This emphasis on the differences has too often led to the dehumanization of the different. Dehumanization leads to discrimination. And discrimination can ultimately lead to genocide.

We need to alert ourselves to the limitations and the dangers of those discourses that reinforce an "us" versus "them" mentality. We need to protest any official rhetoric or demagoguery that marginalizes on a race-related and/or religion-related basis any segment of our society. I want to discourage the retention of cultural memory if the aim of that retention is cultural balkanization. I want to sensitize you to think of culture and nationhood *not* as an uneasy aggregate of antagonistic "them" and "us," but as a constantly re-forming, transmogrifying "we."

In this diasporic age, one's biological identity may not be the only one. Erosions and accretions come with the act of emigration. The experiences of violent unhousing from a biological "homeland" and rehousing in an adopted "homeland" that is not always welcoming to its dark-complected citizens have tested me as a person, and made me the writer I am today.

I choose to describe myself on my own terms, that is, as an American without hyphens. It is to sabotage the politics of hate and the campaigns of [30] revenge spawned by Eurocentric patriots on the one hand and the professional multiculturists on the other, that I describe myself as an "American" rather than as an "Asian-American." Why is it that hyphenization is imposed only on non-white Americans? And why is it that only non-white citizens are "problematized" if they choose to describe themselves on their own terms? My outspoken rejection of hyphenization is my lonely campaign to obliterate categorizing the cultural landscape into a "center" and its "peripheries." To reject hyphenization is to demand that the nation deliver the promises of the American Dream and the American Constitution to *all* its citizens. I want nothing less than to invent a new vocabulary that demands, and obtains, an equitable power-sharing for all members of the American community.

But my self-empowering refusal to be "otherized" and "objectified" has come at tremendous cost. My rejection of hyphenization has been deliberately misrepresented as "race treachery" by some India-born, urban, upper-middle-class Marxist "green card holders" with lucrative chairs on U.S. campuses. These academics strategically position themselves as self-appointed spokespersons for their ethnic communities, and as guardians of the "purity" of ethnic cultures. At the same time, though they reside permanently in the United States and participate in the capitalist economy of this nation, they publicly denounce American ideals and institutions.

They direct their rage at me because, as a U.S. citizen, I have invested in the present and the future rather than in the expatriate's imagined homeland. They condemn me because I acknowledge erosion of memory as a natural result of emigration; because I count that erosion as net gain rather than as loss; and because I celebrate racial and cultural "mongrelization." I have no respect for these expatriate fence-straddlers who, even while competing fiercely for tenure and promotion within the U.S. academic system, glibly equate all evil in the world with the United States, capitalism, colonialism, and corporate and military expansionism. I regard the artificial retentions of "pure race" and "pure culture" as dangerous, reactionary illusions fostered by the Eurocentric and the ethnocentric empire builders within the academy. I fear still more the politics of revenge preached from pulpits by some minority demagogues. . . .

As a writer, my literary agenda begins by acknowledging that America has transformed *me*. It does not end until I show that I (and the hundreds of thousands of recent immigrants like me) am minute by minute transforming America. The transformation is a two-way process; it affects both the individual and the national cultural identity. The end result of immigration, then, is this two-way transformation: that's my heartfelt message.

Others often talk of diaspora, of arrival as the end of the process. They talk of arrival in the context of loss, the loss of communal memory and the erosion of an intact ethnic culture. They use words like "erosion" and "loss" in alarmist ways. I want to talk of arrival as gain. . . .

What excites me is that we have the chance to retain those values we   35
treasure from our original cultures, but we also acknowledge that the outer
forms of those values are likely to change. In the Indian American community, I see a great deal of guilt about the inability to hang on to "pure culture." Parents express rage or despair at their U.S.-born children's forget-
ting of, or indifference to, some aspects of Indian culture. Of those parents,
I would ask: What is it we have lost if our children are acculturating into
the culture in which we are living? Is it so terrible that our children are discovering or inventing homelands for themselves? Some first-generation
Indo-Americans, embittered by overt anti-Asian racism and by unofficial
"glass ceilings," construct a phantom more-Indian-than-Indians-in-India
identity as defense against marginalization. Of them I would ask: Why
not get actively involved in fighting discrimination through protests and
lawsuits?

I prefer that we forge a national identity that is born of our acknowledgment of the steady de-Europeanization of the U.S. population; that constantly synthesizes—fuses—the disparate cultures of our country's resi-
dents; and that provides a new, sustaining, and unifying national creed.

Analyzing Mukherjee's Essay

Let's see what we can learn about how to appeal to audiences in mediatory
essay. We'll look at *ethos* (how she projects good character), *pathos* (how she
arouses emotions favorable to her case), and *logos* (how she wins assent
through good reasoning).

Ethos: Earning the Respect of Both Sides

Mediatory essays are not typically as personal as this one. But the author is in
an unusual position, which makes the personal relevant. By speaking in the
first person and telling her story, Mukherjee seeks the goodwill of people on
both sides. She presents herself as patriotic, a foreigner who has assimilated
to American ways, clearly appealing to those on Kimball's side. But she is also
a "person of color," who's been "tested" by racial prejudices in the United
States, clearly appealing to Martínez's side. She creates negative ethos for the
radical extremists in the identity debate, depicting them as lacking morality
and/or honesty. That's why she cites the violence committed by both whites
and minorities, the scapegoating by politicians pandering to voter fears, the
hypocrisy of professors who live well in America while denouncing its values. She associates her own position with words like *commitment, compassion,
consensus, equality* and *unity.*

By including her own experiences in India and Canada and her references to Bosnia, Rwanda, Germany, and the former Soviet Union, Mukherjee
is able to place this American debate in a larger context—parts of the world
in which national identity incites war and human rights violations.

Pathos: Using Emotion to Appeal to Both Sides

Appealing to the right emotions can help to move parties in conflict to the higher ground of consensus. Mukherjee displays a range of emotions, including pride, anger, and compassion. In condemning the extremes on both sides, her tone becomes heated. She uses highly charged words like *rabid, demagogues, scapegoaters, fence-straddlers,* and *reactionaries* to describe them. Her goal is to distance the members of her audience who are reasonable from those who aren't, so her word choice is appropriate and effective.

Patriotism is obviously emotional. Mukherjee's repeated declaration of devotion to her adopted country stirs audience pride. So does the contrast with India and Canada and the celebrating of individual freedom in the United States.

Her own story of arrival, nostalgia, and transformation arouses compassion and respect because it shows that assimilation is not easy. She understands the reluctance of Indian parents to let their children change. This shows her ability to empathize.

Finally, she appeals through hope and optimism. Twice she describes the consensus she proposes as *exciting*—and also fresh, new, vital, alive—in contrast to the rigid and inflexible ethnic purists.

Logos: Integrating Values of Both Sides

Mukherjee's thesis is that the opposing sides in the national identity debate are two sides of the wrong coin: the mistaken regard for ethnic purity. Making an issue of one's ethnicity, whether it be Anglo, Chicano, Indian-American, or whatever, is not a means to harmony and equality. Instead, America needs a unifying national identity that blends the ever-changing mix of races and cultures that make up our population.

Mukherjee offers reasons to oppose ethnic "purity":

Violence and wars result when people divide according to ethnic and religious differences. It creates an "us" versus "them" mentality.

The multicultural Canadian program created second-class, marginal populations.

Hyphenization in America makes a problem out of non-whites in the population.

We said that mediation looks for the good in each side and tries to show what they have in common. Mukherjee shows that her solution offers gains for both sides, a "win-win" situation. She concedes that her solution would mean some loss of "cultural memory" for immigrants, but these losses are offset by the following gains:

The United States would be closer to the strong and unified nation that Kimball wants because *everyone's* contributions would be appreciated.

The cultural barriers between minorities would break down, as Martínez wants. This would entail speaking to each other in English, but being free to maintain diverse cultures at home.

The barriers between "Americans" and hyphenated Americans would break down, as both Kimball and Martínez want. In other words, there would be assimilation, as Kimball wants, but not assimilation to one culture, which Martínez strongly resists.

By removing the need to prove one's own culture superior, we could all recognize the faults in our past as well as the good things. We would have no schools teaching either the superiority or the inferiority of any culture.

Emphasizing citizenship instead of ethnicity is a way of standing up for and demanding equal rights and equal opportunity, helping to bring about the social justice and equality Martínez seeks.

The new identity would be "sustaining," avoiding future conflicts because it would adapt to change.

Mukherjee's essay mediates by showing that a definition of America based on either one ethnic culture or many ethnic cultures is not satisfactory. By dropping ethnicity as a prime concern, both sides can be better off and freer in pursuit of happiness and success.

 Following Through

Look over the essays by Elizabeth Martínez and Roger Kimball. Do you think either of them would find Bharati Mukherjee's essay persuasive? What does Mukherjee say that might cause either of them to relax their positions about American identity? Do you think any further information might help to bring either side to Mukherjee's consensus position? For example, Kimball mentions the "Letter from an American Farmer" by de Crèvecoeur, who describes Americans as a new "race" of blended nationalities, leaving behind their ties and allegiances to former lands. How is Crèvecouer's idea of the "new race" similar to Mukherjee's?

Writing a Mediatory Essay

Prewriting

If you have been mediating the positions of two or more groups of classmates or two or more authors of published arguments, you may be assigned to write a mediatory essay in which you argue for a compromise position, appealing to an audience of people on all sides. In preparing to write such an essay, you should work through the steps of mediation as described on pages 284–287. In your writer's notebook, prepare briefs of the various conflicting positions, and note areas of disagreement; think hard about the differing interests of the conflicting parties, and respond to the questions about difference on page 286.

If possible, give some thought to each party's background — age, race, gender, and so forth — and how it might contribute to his or her viewpoint on the issue. For example, in a debate about whether *Huckleberry Finn* should be taught and read aloud in U.S. high schools, an African-American parent whose child is the only minority student in her English class might well have a different perspective from that of a white teacher. Can the white teacher be made to understand the embarrassment that a sole black child might feel when the white characters speak with derision about "niggers"?

In your writer's notebook, describe the conflict in its full complexity, not just its polar opposites. For example, considering the controversy over *Huckleberry Finn*, you might find some arguments in favor of teaching it anytime, others opposed to teaching it at all, others suggesting that it be an optional text for reading outside of class, and still others proposing that it be taught only in twelfth grade, when students are mature enough to understand Twain's satire. Try to find the good values in each position: a desire to teach the classics of American literature for what they tell us about the human condition and our country's history and values; a desire to promote respect for African-American students; a desire to ensure a comfortable learning climate for all students; and so on. You may be able to see that people's real interests are not as far apart as they might seem. You may be able to find common ground. For example, those who advocate teaching *Huckleberry Finn* and those who are opposed may both have in mind the goal of eliminating racial prejudice.

At this point in the prewriting process, think of some solutions that would satisfy at least some of the interests on all sides. It might be necessary for you to do some additional research. What do you think any of the opposing parties might want to know more about in order to accept your solution?

Finally, write up a clear statement of your solution. Can you explain how your solution appeals to the interests of all sides? In the *Huckleberry Finn* debate, we might propose that the novel be taught at any grade level provided that it is presented as part of a curriculum to educate students about the African-American experience with the involvement of African-American faculty or visiting lecturers.

Drafting

There is no set form for the mediatory essay. In fact, it is an unusual, even somewhat experimental, form of writing. As with any argument, the important thing is to have a plan for arranging your points and to provide clear signals to your readers. One logical way to organize a mediatory essay is in three parts:

> *Overview of the conflict.* Describe the conflict and the opposing positions in the introductory paragraphs.

Discussion of differences underlying the conflict. Here your goal is to make all sides more sympathetic to one another and to sort out the important real interests that must be addressed by the solution.

Proposed solution. Here you make a case for your compromise position, giving reasons why it should be acceptable to all—that is, showing that it does serve at least some of their interests.

Revising

When revising a mediatory essay, you should look for the usual problems of organization and development that you would be looking for in any essay to convince or persuade. Be sure that you have inquired carefully and fairly into the conflict and that you have clearly presented the cases for all sides, including your proposed solution. At this point, you also need to consider how well you have used the persuasive appeals:

The appeal to character. Think about what kind of character you have projected as a mediator. Have you maintained neutrality? Do you model open-mindedness and genuine concern for the sensitivities of all sides?

The appeal to emotions. To arouse sympathy and empathy, which are needed in negotiation, you should take into account the emotional appeals discussed on pages 251–253. Your mediatory essay should be a moving argument for understanding and overcoming difference.

The appeal through style. As in persuasion, you should put the power of language to work. Pay attention to concrete word choice, striking metaphors, and phrases that stand out because of repeated sounds and rhythms.

For suggestions about editing and proofreading, see the appendix.

www.mhhe. com/crusius

For help editing your essay, go to: Editing

STUDENT SAMPLE: *An Essay Arguing to Mediate*

The following mediatory essay was written by Angi Grellhesl, a first-year student at Southern Methodist University. Her essay examines opposing written views on the institution of speech codes at various U.S. colleges and its effect on freedom of speech.

MEDIATING THE SPEECH CODE CONTROVERSY
Angi Grellhesl

The right to free speech has raised many controversies over the years. Explicit lyrics in rap music and marches by the Ku Klux Klan are just some examples that test the power of the First Amendment. Now, students and administrators are questioning if, in fact, free speech ought to be limited on university campuses. Many schools have instituted speech codes to protect specified groups from harassing speech.

www.mhhe. com/crusius

For many additional examples of student writing, go to: Writing

Both sides in the debate, the speech code advocates and the free speech advocates, have presented their cases in recent books and articles. Columnist Nat Hentoff argues strongly against the speech codes, his main reason being that the codes violate students' First Amendment rights. Hentoff links the right to free speech with the values of higher education. In support, he quotes Yale president Benno Schmidt, who says, "Freedom of thought must be Yale's central commitment. . . . [U]niversities cannot censor or suppress speech, no matter how obnoxious in content, without violating their justification for existence . . ." (qtd. in Hentoff 223). Another reason Hentoff offers against speech codes is that universities must teach students to defend themselves in preparation for the real world, where such codes cannot shield them. Finally, he suggests that most codes are too vaguely worded; students may not even know they are violating the codes (216).

Two writers in favor of speech codes are Richard Perry and Patricia Williams. They see speech codes as a necessary and fair limitation on free speech. Perry and Williams argue that speech codes promote multicultural awareness, making students more sensitive to the differences that are out there in the real world. These authors do not think that the codes violate First Amendment rights, and they are suspicious of the motives of those who say they do. As Perry and Williams put it, those who feel free speech rights are being threatened "are apparently unable to distinguish between a liberty interest on the one hand and, on the other, a quite specific interest in being able to spout racist, sexist, and homophobic epithets completely unchallenged—without, in other words, the terrible inconvenience of feeling bad about it" (228).

Perhaps if both sides trusted each other a little more, they could see that their goals are not contradictory. Everyone agrees that students' rights should be protected. Hentoff wishes to ensure that students have the right to speak their minds. He and others on his side are concerned about freedom. Defenders of the codes argue that students have the right not to be harassed, especially while they are getting an education. They are concerned about opportunity. Would either side really deny that the other's goal had value?

Also, both sides want to create the best possible educational environment. Here the difference rests on the interpretation of what benefits the students. Is the best environment one most like the real world, where prejudice and harassment occur? Or does the university have an obligation to provide an atmosphere where potential victims can thrive and participate freely without intimidation?

I think it is possible to reach a solution that everyone can agree on. Most citizens want to protect constitutional rights; but they also agree that those rights have limitations, the ultimate limit being when one person infringes on the rights of others to live in peace. All sides should agree that a person ought to be able to speak out about his or her convictions, values, and beliefs. And most people can see a difference between that

5

protected speech and the kind that is intended to harass and intimidate. For example, there is a clear difference between expressing one's view that Jews are mistaken in not accepting Christ as the son of God, on the one hand, and yelling anti-Jewish threats at a particular person in the middle of the night, on the other. Could a code not be worded in such a way as to distinguish between these two kinds of speech?

Also, I don't believe either side would want the university to be an artificial world. Codes should not attempt to ensure that no one is criticized or even offended. Students should not be afraid to say controversial things. But universities do help to shape the future of the real world, so shouldn't they at least take a stand against harassment? Can a code be worded that would protect free speech and prevent harassment?

The current speech code at Southern Methodist University is a compromise that ought to satisfy free speech advocates and speech code advocates. It prohibits hate speech at the same time that it protects an individual's First Amendment rights.

First, it upholds the First Amendment by including a section that reads, "[D]ue to the University's commitment to freedom of speech and expression, harassment is more than mere insensitivity or offensive conduct which creates an uncomfortable situation for certain members of the community" (*Peruna* 92). The code therefore should satisfy those, like Hentoff, who place a high value on the basic rights our nation was built upon. Secondly, whether or not there is a need for protection, the current code protects potential victims from hate speech or "any words or acts deliberately designed to disregard the safety or rights of another, and which intimidate, degrade, demean, threaten, haze, or otherwise interfere with another person's rightful action" (*Peruna* 92). This part of the code should satisfy those who recognize that some hurts cannot be overcome. Finally, the current code outlines specific acts that constitute harassment: "Physical, psychological, verbal and/or written acts directed toward an individual or group of individuals which rise to the level of 'fighting words' are prohibited" (*Peruna* 92).

The SMU code protects our citizens from hurt and from unconstitutional censorship. Those merely taking a position can express it, even if it hurts. On the other hand, those who are spreading hatred will be limited as to what harm they may inflict. Therefore, all sides should respect the code as a safeguard for those who use free speech but a limitation for those who abuse it.

10

Works Cited

Hentoff, Nat. "Speech Codes on the Campus and Problems of Free Speech." <u>Debating P.C.</u> Ed. Paul Berman. New York: Bantam, 1992. 215–24.

Perry, Richard, and Patricia Williams. "Freedom of Speech." <u>Debating P.C.</u> Ed. Paul Berman. New York: Bantam, 1992. 225–30.

<u>Peruna Express 1993–1994</u>. Dallas: Southern Methodist U, 1993.

www.mhhe.
com/crusius

For an electronic
tool that helps
create properly
formatted works-
cited pages,
go to:
Research >
Bibliomaker

Two
Casebooks
for
Argument

Part Three   Two Casebooks for Argument

Chapter 10

Casebook: After 9/11: Understanding Terrorism, Assessing the Response

GENERAL INTRODUCTION: THREE YEARS LATER

By the time you read this introduction, the third anniversary of the 9/11 attack will have come and gone—we hope without any terrorist acts to rival its magnitude, horror, and grief. We need to remember the 3,000 people who lost their lives, either in the attack itself or in trying to help the victims. We must not forget they were human beings, not statistics, who had families and friends whose suffering is still not over. The gash in the Pentagon building has been repaired and the rubble from the Twin Towers hauled away, with plans selected to replace it with another structure—but thousands of lives whose potential we can't imagine are beyond recovery.

The first version of this casebook, pieced together immediately after 9/11, focused much attention on the event itself. As the title of this version promises, the focus now goes elsewhere, on what's happened since. Because so much has occurred, we can't do more than touch on most matters. For example, a controversial bill was passed shortly after 9/11 called the USA Patriot Act, which, in granting additional power to federal authorities to combat terrorism, some argue also violated the Constitution, especially the First and Fourth Amendments, parts of the Bill of Rights. The Patriot Act could be a casebook unto itself. Almost as controversial was the formation of a new cabinet-level ministry, the Department of Homeland Security, whose task it is to coordinate all the many departments and agencies playing a role in counterterrorism. Many experts doubt that creating yet another huge and unwieldy bureaucracy will make us any safer. Domestically, two major questions have come to the fore: Are we safer now? Have we given up too much liberty to gain whatever additional security we have?

Foreign affairs, though, have taken on as much importance as domestic issues, perhaps more. The somber mood immediately after 9/11 gave way rapidly to a strong public demand for action against the terrorists. The first target was Afghanistan, understandably because the Taliban-led government was allied with Osama bin Laden and his associates and had provided them sanctuary, a headquarters for Al Qaeda's worldwide terrorist network, and a place to indoctrinate and train new recruits. The Afghan government collapsed under the combined pressure of U.S. airpower and ground forces from northern Afghanistan, who had long resisted Taliban rule. In the process, many Al Qaeda operatives were killed or captured, some of them high up in the organization. However, bin Laden and his inner circle of closest associates eluded capture. The United States "degraded" Al Qaeda, to use the terminology of the military and intelligence community, but hardly put it out of business. Furthermore, although the United States can claim the major role in liberating Afghanistan from an extreme and repressive regime, the fate of the country is still in doubt and American troops are still deployed there. At best, then, the Afghan affair qualifies as a partial success that bears watching—the consequences are still unfolding.

Iraq was next. World opinion by and large favored American action in Afghanistan. Iraq was another story. Many of the United States' oldest and traditional allies opposed an invasion and continue to criticize American policies for rebuilding Iraq. Why? What made Iraq so different from Afghanistan?

First, terrorism experts question the connection between Saddam Hussein, Iraq's leader, and Al Qaeda. Although Hussein liked to present himself to the Iraqi masses as an observant Muslim, his rule was secular, far from the theocracy bin Laden wants for all Muslim countries. Bin Laden and Hussein may have shared a common goal—weakening U.S. influence in the Middle East—but they were hardly directly allied, as bin Laden was with the Taliban before our intervention there.

Second, the U.S. government and our closest ally, Great Britain, justified attacking Iraq based mainly on the alleged presence of weapons of mass destruction (WMDs)—biological, nuclear, and chemical devices. So far no such weapons have been found—only perhaps facilities in which they could be made. Sources within our government have argued over the level of doubt that existed prior to the invasion about the existence of WMD's in Iraq. Whatever went on before our troops went in, the fact remains that a prime reason for removing Hussein from power now seems unwarranted.

Finally, our action in Iraq was an application of the "Bush doctrine," or what the administration calls "preemptive war." The basic idea is that 9/11 taught us that the nation cannot wait for the terrorist enemy to attack before responding—the United States must instead attack first in an effort to prevent more 9/11's or something worse. It sounds like good common sense but raises a number of difficult questions. Can it be invoked to attack any regime, whether it sponsors terrorism or otherwise poses an immediate threat to our country? Does the doctrine square with international law? How about the reaction of allies, especially in Europe, who are also targets of terrorism? Will it strengthen the U.S. position among moderate Muslims, whose support is indispensable for reducing Al Qaeda's influence? Finally, how long can the United States sustain the enormous expense of using the military as it has in Afghanistan and Iraq? Even the world's only superpower has limited resources.

These and other controversial questions connected with foreign policy since 9/11 dominate current discussion. At bottom, however, two closely related questions go to the heart of the terrorism issue: How does terrorism work? Given how it operates, how can it best be countered? In other words, our understanding of terrorism largely dictates what we think we ought to do. The old maxim "Know your enemy" certainly applies here. But the still older maxim "Know yourself" applies also, maybe with greater force. This casebook is centrally concerned with both principles and with the ongoing struggle to decide how to cope with a new form of terrorism for which the past is not an adequate guide.

SECTION 1: BACKGROUND INFORMATION

Overview

To understate the obvious, terrorism is a complex topic. Nearly everything one might say about it is contested. Yet we need some factual basis for discussing it. This section offers a bare minimum of such knowledge, to which we add a warning: Any aspect of terrorism you take up seriously will require more information than we can provide here.

We begin with how the media created the popular perception of terrorism immediately after 9/11 and how its depictions conditioned the public to accept uncritically the notion of a "war on terrorism." Eileen Berrington is writing about the press in England, but what she says applies to American news sources with at least equal force. We must never forget that our first exposure to world events is almost always through media predisposed to view what's happening a certain way—one way among many possible ways of interpreting reality—and that, for the most part, our sense of things remains heavily dependent on media representations.

Nevertheless, facts exist. We need a considerable store of them to discuss terrorism and counterterrorism intelligently. We need to know what motivates terrorism and how terrorists understand what success means; we need to know why the United States and Americans are targets of terrorism as well as why other nations and their people are more often victims than we are; we need to grasp something of the complexity of the Middle East; we need some background on the Jewish-Palestinian question; we need an understanding of the weapons available to terrorists and how they might use them. These concerns and more are addressed in the following selections.

Representations of Terror in the Legitimation of War
Eileen Berrington

Eileen Berrington is a criminologist at Edge Hill University College in the United Kingdom. The following selection appeared in Beyond September 11: An Anthology of Dissent *(2002).*

Initial reports of major disasters and their tragic circumstances powerfully define the key issues, shaping understanding and constructing a collective memory. Flying hijacked passenger airliners into each of the World Trade Center (WTC) towers and, almost simultaneously, the Pentagon, constituted acts beyond imagination. Happening, as they did, in the heart of the

From *Beyond September 11: An Anthology of Dissent.* Phil Scraton, ed. London: Pluto Press, 2002.

most advanced telecommunications system in the world, these unfolding disasters were covered internationally via live broadcasts. [. . .]

Inevitably the images published in the press reflected the intensity of the disasters, the horror of survivors and the distress of victims' families. Given the instantly recognisable Manhattan skyline, the collapsed buildings of the WTC, plumes of smoke and the intensity of the flames became the focus of attention. As if to emphasise the significance of the WTC at the economic heart of global capitalism, the *Sun* proclaimed September 11 as the DAY THAT CHANGED THE WORLD. The full-page photograph showed the WTC in flames shortly after the second aircraft exploded. The *Daily Star* used a similar picture, the image cropped, bringing the flames and smoke into close-up. The paper offered its readers a SPECIAL EDITION ON THE WORST TERRORIST OUTRAGE IN HISTORY. IS THIS THE END OF THE WORLD? asked the front page, adding, BIG APPLE HORROR PUTS US ON THE BRINK OF WAR.

The *Daily Mail* led with a distance shot across the Hudson River, depicting the volumes of smoke but no flames. The headline was stark: APOCALYPSE NEW YORK. SEPTEMBER 11, 2001. The *Daily Express* promised THE MOST COMPLETE AND UP-TO-DATE COVERAGE. Its front page used a close-up of the WTC engulfed in flames and smoke, adding a white overlay: DECLARATION OF WAR. The *Guardian, Independent* and *The Times* used the same image — black smoke rising from the towers, flames and falling debris. The newspapers' respective headlines were A DECLARATION OF WAR; DOOMSDAY AMERICA THOUSANDS KILLED AFTER HIJACKED AIRLINERS DESTROY WORLD TRADE CENTER AND SMASH INTO PENTAGON and WAR COMES TO AMERICA. [. . .]

Early the following week, when the military action promised in the immediate aftermath by President Bush had not yet materialised, Osama bin Laden's image appeared on front pages. I WANT HIS HEAD ON A PLATTER, declared the US vice-president, Dick Cheney (*Mirror,* September 17). The *Daily Star* issued a warning to Afghanistan: GIVE HIM UP OR WE BOMB YOU, as BUSH AND BLAIR UNITE TO FIGHT. A simulation of a "Wild West" poster appeared the following day with a picture of Osama bin Laden, WANTED DEAD OR ALIVE (*Mirror,* September 18). President Bush's picture was incorporated into the paper's masthead. The *Daily Star* used the same headline, adding that there was a FIVE MILLION DOLLAR REWARD. Bin Laden was "in the sights" of Britain's élite military force: SAS WE'LL TAKE HIM OUT (*Daily Express*). The *Sun* took a very different approach, using a colour picture of a vigil in Las Vegas. A photogenic four-year-old was on her father's shoulders, with "Tears in her eyes" and "the Star-Spangled Banner in her hand." GOD BLESS AMERICA, proclaimed the headline, asking readers to FLY THE FLAG and observe three minutes' silence at 11 A.M.

The imagery, tone and style of reporting provided only one context and outcome: "terrorism" and "war." An attack of such magnitude on the United States would have global repercussions. Even in a largely secular society there was an assumption that people would understand the biblical references and ideological associations. While they might not have the degree of religious significance they once had, such imagery is embedded in popular culture, through films, drama and fiction. The difference now was that this was reality and that on September 11 there was no all-American hero saving the day.

Yet even at this early stage in the reporting process there was sensationalism, dramatisation and exaggeration of events that were in themselves so horrific that they needed no embellishment. The same processes were discernible in official statements by President Bush, senior officials and a range of (Western) world leaders, notably the UK prime minister, Tony Blair. This was "an attack," "terrorism"; it was "unprovoked." Therefore the US was justified, even compelled, to respond with aggression. That this could be interpreted as retaliatory action for any number of instances of Western, but particularly US, military or political intervention or oppression around the world did not figure in political, popular or populist discourses. Events on September 11 were firmly categorised within the context of war atrocities. In terms of media coverage, therefore, there was recourse primarily to the conventions and templates relating to war reporting rather than those typically associated with reporting disaster or tragedy.

Reporting war and conflict follows particular, general patterns, depending on who is depicted as "victim" or "aggressor." So in the West, events involving Western aggression or military intervention are typically represented as regrettable but necessary to preserve or restore some greater good. Armed conflict is seen as a last resort, as an obligation on the part of powerful Western democracies to support the powerless and oppressed, to protect or restore freedom and democratic processes. The "other side," therefore, becomes automatically aligned with injustice, "wrong" and "evil." There are expectations that the domestic media will adopt a "patriotic" stance. Accounts of civilian deaths or injuries caused by Western military action are denied if possible, or recontextualised where denial becomes unsustainable. Phrases like "collateral damage" dehumanise and depersonalise, particularly when placed alongside the personal biographies of "our" casualties — servicemen (and, occasionally, women) and their families. [. . .]

Journalists [. . .] became caught up in jingoism and nationalism. Increasingly, many found themselves identifying with their "comrades" — the military personnel with whom they travelled, lived and on whom their survival depended. As David Morrison has commented, journalists in such situations are "not removed from the pressures and forces of the drama that is going on around them." So some journalists become, or see themselves as, participants in rather than detached observers of conflict. Self-censorship is a feature of reporting, creating additional opportunities for sanitised news representations through informal means, while further limiting the representation of alternative views.

In addition, there are some news events where, even without such strictures and difficulties, it is difficult to express "alternative" views without appearing callous or insensitive. Reporting that appears to "side with the enemy" leads to accusations that journalists, publications or programmes are apologists for the inexcusable; supporters of terrorism and unpatriotic. [. . . D]iscussion of September 11 in a special edition of BBC1's *Question Time* led to an apology to the former US ambassador to Britain by the BBC director-general. Expression of anti-American views by some members of the audience was "regrettable." Live transmission was "inappropriate" and the programme should have been recorded and edited before screening to prevent offence.

It is significant that despite the uniqueness of September 11, newspaper reports fit easily into the established frames and templates of journalism. In addition to the conventions of war reporting, the use of ideological cues and the invocation of folk devils and moral panics are immediately apparent. Certain words, phrases and images, through repetition, conjure up a range of emotions and associations. They become a form of mental shorthand and, quite literally, word association. Right from the start particular key themes were foregrounded. "Middle Eastern" terrorists are popular folk devils who feature in news, current affairs and foreign policy, but are also the subject of cultural transmission. "Us" against "them," "good" *versus* "evil," democracy intervening to free the enslaved — all are popular themes in film and TV entertainment. Given Western, globalised media ownership and control, it is of little surprise that the "good guys" are overwhelmingly white and/or American; that the "bad guys" are typically depicted as visibly "foreign," by appearance, accent or through stereotyped "cultural" characteristics. Audiences have come to expect that the "good guy," because he is invariably a man, no matter how heavily outnumbered and lacking in firepower, will prevail and will, through force, restore "order" and rescue the helpless.

Media reporting is quick to personalise stories. In relation to crime there are individuals whose behaviour attracts such widespread condemnation that "folk devil" is too benign a label to apply. [. . .] After September 11 there were new monsters, whose names, Osama bin Laden and the al-Qaida network, were very quickly on every presenter's lips and in newspapers across the world. There was now a direct, focused target for blame and retribution; vague "Middle Eastern terrorism" was supplanted as the US military gaze and the world's attention became firmly fixed on Afghanistan. Bin Laden's image became instantly familiar and recognisable; his name tripped increasingly easily off the tongue both in the US and in Britain.

What is omitted from news representations, however, is as significant as what is highlighted. Early accounts failed to inform audiences that bin Laden's training camps, where it was alleged the September 11 atrocities had been nurtured if not actually planned, owed their existence to US political intervention. While Afghanistan was under Soviet occupation, the CIA actively encouraged and financially supported "freedom fighters" in their struggles against their oppressor. The film *Rocky 3*, starring Sylvester Stallone, arguably one of the most easily identifiable symbols of American military muscle, is dedicated to the "brave people" of Afghanistan. Britain also played its part in creating bin Laden the "monster," with the SAS providing specialised training for his followers.

10

Political alliances change when former "brothers-in-arms" become powerful and no longer reliant on outside intervention or support. They develop new allegiances; enemies become friends and vice versa. Decontextualised news reports blur the history and origins of conflict [. . .]. No explanation is offered or, initially, at least, demanded, other than that Osama bin Laden and the "extremist" Islamic Taliban rulers of Afghanistan are to blame. Bin Laden and his associates must be hunted down and "brought to justice." There is an immediate call for alignment—those governments who support bin Laden, however marginally, become equally culpable. They too are enemies of the US state. They become potential targets of retributive justice in whatever form the US decides it will be administered. First news reports included discussion and debate over which world leaders had and, more significantly, had not, aligned themselves with the US. Expressions of sympathy were no longer sufficient; battle lines were being drawn. [. . .]

As the weeks passed there was a gradual, albeit limited, emergence of alternative views within mainstream media reporting. This offered a degree of challenge to initial one-dimensional, simplistic, unsophisticated accounts that offered one explanation alone, assuming a unanimous response from audiences. What happened on September 11 was exceptional and horrific. Such actions cannot be justified. The difficulty lies in locating what happened in its wider context, not to be disrespectful or lacking in sympathy, but in terms of understanding. Simplistic depictions of "good" and "evil" provided the US with the legitimacy to invade and attack. Rational, considered analysis offers scope for alternative ways of seeing and responding. Was military action to exact retribution, revenge or "justice" the only viable response?

At the time of writing, there is a dawning awareness that the show of force by the US and its close allies has not achieved its promised objective. Osama bin Laden has been neither captured nor killed, despite the defeat of Afghanistan's Taliban rulers. Instead, the outcomes of the military assault are civilian casualties, further division, hostility and resentment. This creates or exacerbates the conditions within which the kind of views that underpinned what happened on September 11 will flourish. In any conflict, each side has its own victims, martyrs and sense of grievance. No single nation-state has the monopoly on nationalism, patriotism or self-sacrifice.

15

Why Terrorism?
Philip Jenkins

Philip Jenkins teaches at Penn State University, where he is Distinguished Professor of History and Religious Studies. This selection comes from Images of Terror: What We Can and Can't Know about Terrorism *(2003).*

WHY TERRORISM?

In order to understand the goals of terrorism, let us begin with a specific incident that is relatively straightforward—the 2002 bus attack in Jerusalem by Muhammad al-Ghoul. In this case, we know the identity of the offender, the group, and the cause for which he was prepared to kill and die.

Since the Palestinian cause is so often cited as a factor in contemporary terrorism, some political background is necessary here (Sayigh 1999). During the early twentieth century, the land of Palestine was mainly inhabited by Arabs, who were predominantly Muslim with a sizable Christian minority. However, Jews in Europe and elsewhere wished to establish a national home in that same land, from which they had been expelled centuries earlier, and they began to immigrate in large numbers. Violent conflicts resulted. In 1948, the land was partitioned between a Jewish state of Israel, and the remaining territories under the control of Arab states. During this and subsequent wars, millions of Palestinian Arabs were expelled from their family homes, and many were forced to live in refugee camps on the West Bank of the Jordan, in the Gaza Strip, or in neighboring Arab countries. They saw little chance of escaping from this situation, since repeatedly, Arab states like Egypt and Syria failed to defeat the powerful Israeli armed forces.

As Palestinian despair deepened after the Arab-Israeli war of 1967, there emerged a variety of radical and revolutionary movements pledged to expel the Israelis, and to force the return of Arab lands. Since conventional armed forces could not defeat Israel, Palestinians turned to irregular forces and methods, to guerrilla and terrorist warfare. This decision led to the wave of attacks through the 1970s and 1980s: first the hijackings, later the bombings of airliners and attacks on airports and embassies around the globe. From the late 1980s, the most active and effective guerrilla groups were those preaching Islamic fundamentalism, like Hamas and Palestinian Islamic Jihad (Sivan and Friedman 1990; Miller 1996). In 2000, a new wave of violence broke out, and the fundamentalists began a campaign of suicide bombings (Anti-Defamation League of B'nai B'rith 2002). As of 2002, there were serious concerns that Hamas was seeking to escalate its activities into the realm of "megaterrorism," trying to kill very large numbers of Jews by mass poisoning, or by bringing down skyscrapers (Katzenell 2002).

What did al-Ghoul and the other bombers want to achieve? In trying to explain this, I am not for a moment justifying their acts, but rather seeking to understand what might otherwise seem to be incomprehensible behavior. In essence, Hamas and its followers have the same goals of any nation fighting a war, namely to inflict the maximum possible damage on an enemy, in order to force the other side to surrender or withdraw. To that extent, al-Ghoul's motives were the same as any soldier prepared to kill for his country or his people, who would echo the bomber's remark that he did not want to "kill for the sake of killing but so that others might have life, to kill and be killed for the lives of the coming generation." In his suicide note, he declared, "I am happy that my body will be the response for the attacks conducted by the Israelis, and that my body will turn into an explosive shred mill against the Israelis." In other circumstances, he would perhaps have picked up a rifle to confront the enemy, but given the overwhelming Israeli military superiority, this was not an option. He chose clandestine means, which the Israelis could not prevent. Since he could not fight soldiers, he targeted civilians (Beaumont 2002; Rubin 2002).

Strange as it may appear, al-Ghoul and his kind would have presented   5
their actions in terms of self-defense, or retaliation for previous offenses committed by the Israelis. Of course, he would not have believed that specific individuals on the bus he attacked had done any personal harm to himself or his community, but like other terrorists before or since, he would have justified the violence in terms of acts previously committed by the authorities or the enemy nation. The argument is, "you started it," by occupying our country or by persecuting other activists. Such a moral claim is important for religious activists, who try to justify acts through religious thought and language, but it is also commonplace for secular radicals. Among other things, the idea helps defuse the associations of the word terrorism. Although we are committing a violent act, the rhetoric claims, it is justified as retribution for what has previously been done to us. As Leon Trotsky (1909) wrote, "The most important psychological source of terrorism is always the feeling of revenge in search of an outlet" (Compare Rapoport and Alexander eds 1989; Wright 1991). Oklahoma City bomber Timothy McVeigh explained his action in these words: "Foremost, the bombing was a retaliatory strike; a counterattack, for the cumulative raids (and subsequent violence and damage) that federal agents had participated in over the preceding years (including, but not limited to, Waco)" (Quoted in http://www.backwoodshome.com/columns/duffy010501.html).

Clearly, al-Ghoul did not believe that in setting off his bomb he would end what he saw as the injustices imposed on his people, any more than a soldier in action believes that he single-handedly will destroy an enemy nation. But we can think of several goals of an action like this. Significantly, the terrorists and those who sent them are trying to demonstrate the weakness of the state—in this case, the nation of Israel—and its inability to protect its citizens. They are showing that the state does not have a monopoly of violence. This has the dual effect of encouraging the enemies of the state, realizing that Israel is not as invulnerable as it may appear, while forcing the Israelis to realize that even their military might can be challenged. This was all the more effective at that point in time because the Jerusalem bus bombing occurred just a month after the Israelis had launched a major invasion of the West Bank that was intended to root out terrorism. The intention was to teach Israelis that in order to stop future bombings, they would have to negotiate or make concessions.

Terrorism serves to show that Palestinian issues cannot simply be ignored, in Israel or overseas. When buses and shopping centers are blown up regularly, when death can strike at any moment, it is simply impossible for the state and regular society to continue business as usual. When many people feel that a government can no longer protect the lives of its citizens, that sense obviously has a devastating effect on everyday life. Ideally, the continued violence would provoke a catastrophic social breakdown, out of which the new revolutionary order will emerge. In 2002, Salah Sh'hadeh, leader of Hamas' fighting organization, remarked on the soaring number of candidates willing to undertake suicide missions, with or without official approval, and what that meant for his movement: "If some of the youths do not follow the military apparatus's instructions, and [set out on operations on their own] without being linked officially to this apparatus, this proves that the [entire] nation has become a nation of Jihad on the threshold of liberation, and that it rejects humiliation and submission" ("Interview with Salah Sh'hadeh" 2002). In the years before the great French revolution of the eighteenth century, the queen Marie Antoinette warned, "After us, the deluge." Modern terrorists would rather say, "After the deluge, us." Put another way, the worse the better.

In addition, a movement like Hamas is trying to improve its own political position. The more effective any group is in provoking this kind of disorder, the more it will attract followers and supporters, and probably the financial support of outside governments. And the more a government attacks a group as evil and dangerous, the better the publicity, since it shows that they are having a major effect, and alarming the regime. Once a group is labeled as Public Enemy Number One, it can serve as a focus of dissent and discontent within the larger society. In Palestinian communities, the popular cult of the *shahid,* the martyr-bomber, reflects directly on the movement for which these individuals fight.

WINNING AND LOSING

In all these respects, we can see the suicide bombings as rational, however ruthless and cynical they appear. The point should also be made about another predictable effect of terrorist violence, which is that they incite further repression and violence. Looking at a situation like the Israel-Palestine conflict, Americans are likely to react with puzzlement when they see ever more violent and provocative acts that target innocent civilians. We are tempted to ask: do the terrorists not realize that they will enrage the Israelis, and drive them to new acts of repression? The answer of course is that they know this very well, and this is exactly what they want. From our normal point of view, this seems incomprehensible. If we are doing something wrong, we do not want to invite the police to come in and try and stop us, especially if repression will result in the deaths or imprisonment of many of our followers. In a terrorist war, however, repression is often valuable because it escalates the growing war, and forces people to choose between the government and the terrorists. The terror/repression cycle makes it virtually impossible for anyone to remain a moderate. By increasing polarization within a society, terrorism makes the continuation of the existing order impossible.

Once again, let us take the suicide bombing example. After each new   10
incident, Israeli authorities tightened restrictions on Palestinian communities, arrested new suspects, and undertook retaliatory strikes. As the crisis escalated, they occupied or reoccupied Palestinian cities, destroying Palestinian infrastructure. The result, naturally, was massive Palestinian hostility and anger, which made further attacks more likely in the future. The violence made it more difficult for moderate leaders on both sides to negotiate. In the long term, the continuing confrontation makes it more likely that ever more extreme leaders will be chosen on each side, pledged not to negotiate with the enemy. The process of polarization is all the more probable when terrorists deliberately choose targets that they know will cause outrage and revulsion, such as attacks on cherished national symbols, on civilians, and even children. [. . .]

Far from being a deterrent, arrest and imprisonment are among the most valuable weapons for a terrorist movement. The courtroom can be used as a theater for political statements and media spectaculars, while jailed terrorists can serve as martyrs who are used to inspire new generations of fighters (Hayden 1970). In the Arab nations as well as countless other conflicts, prisoners serve as the focus for potent sympathy campaigns. Many people who would not give money to support overt armed terrorism might well give to a charity that claimed to be helping the families of imprisoned political prisoners—even though in reality, the money would still find its way to buying guns and explosives. During the Troubles in Northern Ireland, the most successful means of fund-raising for the IRA involved requesting donations for "the men behind the wire," the imprisoned guerrillas and their families. Money flowed freely into the organization's coffers when authorities were charged with maltreating the prisoners, and reached a peak in the early 1980s when prisoners died during hunger strike protests (Taylor 1980; Beresford 1997). Even in the United States, a left-wing guerrilla movement that was thoroughly isolated by the mid-1980s won new sympathizers through campaigns on behalf of political prisoners, through films like *Through the Wire*. And imprisonment gives the terrorists other advantages. Terrorists in prison can recruit other inmates to their cause, people who would previously have been non-political criminal offenders. Jailing hundreds or thousands of terrorists will not of itself end an antigovernment campaign, but might conceivably keep the flames burning (Page 1998).

The Israeli response to terrorism is also valuable for the terrorists in global publicity terms, since the international media attack Israel for its repression of civilians. Hamas military commander Salah Sh'hadeh, quoted earlier, was killed in an Israeli raid on Gaza in 2002, an act which by any normal standards of warfare would represent a major Israeli victory. In this case, though, the killing provoked ferocious criticism of Israel by the U.S. and western Europe, and made Israel's diplomatic situation much more difficult. In short, a terrorist attack itself may or may not attract widespread publicity, but the official response to it very likely will. In saying this, I am not suggesting that governments should not respond to terrorism, or that retaliation is in any sense morally comparable to the original attacks. Many historical examples show that terrorism can be uprooted and defeated, and military action is often an essential part of the official response. But terrorism operates on a logic quite different from that of most conventional politics and law enforcement, and concepts like defeat and victory must be understood quite differently from in a regular war.

Works Cited

Anti-Defamation League of B'nai B'rith. *Countering Suicide Terrorism.* New York: iUniverse, Incorporated, 2002.

Beaumont, Peter. "It Is Nice to Be Killed While Killing." *Guardian* (London) 20 June 2002.

Beresford, David. *Ten Men Dead.* New York: Atlantic Monthly Press, 1997.

Hayden, Tom. *Trial.* New York: Holt, Rinehart and Winston, 1970.

Interview with Salah Sh'hadeh. 2002. Interview with Salah Sh'hadeh. <http://www.memri.org/bin/latestnews.cgi?ID=SD40302>.

Katzenell, Jack. "Palestinian Accused of Planning Mass Cyanide Poisonings of Israelis." (Associated Press) *Boston Globe* 1 August 2002.

Miller, Judith. *God Has Ninety-Nine Names.* New York: Simon and Schuster, 1996.

Page, Michael Von Tangen. *Prisons, Peace, and Terrorism.* New York: St. Martin's Press, 1998.

Rapaport, David, and Yonah Alexander. *Morality of Terrorism.* 2nd ed. New York: Columbia University Press, 1989.

Rubin, Elizabeth. The Most Wanted Palestinian. *New York Times Magazine* 30 June 2002.

Sayigh, Yazid. *Armed Struggle and the Search for State.* New York: Oxford University Press, 1999.

Sivan, Emmanuel, and Menachem Friedman, eds. *Religious Radicalism and Politics in the Middle East.* Albany: State U of New York P, 1990.

Taylor, Peter. *Beating the Terrorists.* London: Penguin, 1980.

Trotsky, Leon. *Why Marxists Oppose Individual Terrorism.* 1909. <http://www.marxists.org/archive/trotsky/works/1909/tia09.htm>.

Wright, Joanne. *Terrorist Propaganda: The Red Army Faction and the Provisional IRA, 1968–86.* New York: St. Martin's Press, 1991.

Ten Things to Know about the Middle East
Stephen Zunes

Stephen Zunes is a professor of political science and chair of the Peace and Justice Studies Program at the University of San Francisco. His article was posted on AlterNet, October 1, 2001.

1. WHO ARE THE ARABS?

Arab peoples range from the Atlantic coast in northwest Africa to the Arabian peninsula and north to Syria. They are united by a common language and culture. Though the vast majority are Muslim, there are also sizable Christian Arab minorities in Egypt, Lebanon, Iraq, Syria and Palestine. Originally the inhabitants of the Arabian peninsula, the Arabs spread their language and culture to the north and west with the expansion of Islam in the 7th century. There are also Arab minorities in the Sahel and parts of east Africa, as well as in Iran and Israel. The Arabs were responsible for great advances in mathematics, astronomy and other scientific disciplines while Europe was still mired in the Dark Ages.

Though there is great diversity in skin pigmentation, spoken dialect and certain customs, there is a common identity that unites Arab people, which has sometimes been reflected in pan-Arab nationalist movements. Despite substantial political and other differences, many Arabs share a sense that they are one nation, which has been artificially divided through the machinations of Western imperialism and which came to dominate the region with the decline of the Ottoman Empire in the 19th and early 20th century. There is also a growing Arab diaspora in Europe, North America, Latin America, West Africa and Australia.

2. WHO ARE THE MUSLIMS?

The Islamic faith originated in the Arabian peninsula, based on what Muslims believe to be divine revelations by God to the prophet Mohammed. Muslims worship the same God as do Jews and Christians, and share many of the same prophets and ethical traditions, including respect for innocent life. Approximately 90 percent of Muslims are of the orthodox or Sunni tradition; most of the remainder are of the Shi'ite tradition, which dominates Iran but also has substantial numbers in Iraq, Bahrain, Yemen and Lebanon. Sunni Islam is nonhierarchical in structure. There is not a tradition of separation between the faith and state institutions as there is in the West, though there is enormous diversity in various Islamic legal traditions and the degree to which governments of predominantly Muslim countries rely on religious bases for their rule.

Political movements based on Islam have ranged from left to right, from nonviolent to violent, from tolerant to chauvinistic. Generally, the more moderate Islamic movements have developed in countries where there is a degree of political pluralism in which they could operate openly. There is a strong tradition of social justice in Islam, which has often led to conflicts with regimes that are seen to be unjust or unethical. The more radical movements have tended to arise in countries that have suffered great social dislocation due to war or inappropriate economic policies and/or are under autocratic rule.

Most of the world's Muslims are not Arabs. The world's largest Muslim country, for example, is Indonesia. Other important non-Arab Muslim countries include Malaysia, Bangladesh, Pakistan, Afghanistan, Iran, Turkey and the five former Soviet republics of Central Asia, as well as Nigeria and several other black African states. Islam is one of the fastest growing religions in the world and scores of countries have substantial Muslim minorities. There are approximately five million Muslims in the United States.

5

3. WHY IS THERE SO MUCH VIOLENCE AND POLITICAL INSTABILITY IN THE MIDDLE EAST?

For most of the past 500 years, the Middle East actually saw less violence and warfare and more political stability than Europe or most other regions of the world. It has only been in the last century that the region has seen such widespread conflict. The roots of the conflict are similar to those elsewhere in the Third World, and have to do with the legacy of colonialism, such as artificial political boundaries, autocratic regimes, militarization, economic inequality and economies based on the export of raw materials for finished goods. Indeed, the Middle East has more autocratic regimes, militarization, economic inequality and the greatest ratio of exports to domestic consumption than any region in the world.

At the crossroads of three continents and sitting on much of the world's oil reserves, the region has been subjected to repeated interventions and conquests by outside powers, resulting in a high level of xenophobia and suspicion regarding the intentions of Western powers going back as far as the Crusades. There is nothing in Arab or Islamic culture that promotes violence or discord; indeed, there is a strong cultural preference for stability, order and respect for authority. However, adherence to authority is based on a kind of social contract that assumes a level of justice which — if broken by the ruler — gives the people a right to challenge it. The word *jihad*, often translated as "holy war," actually means "holy struggle," which can sometimes mean an armed struggle (*qital*), but also can mean nonviolent action and political work within the established system. *Jihad* also can mean a struggle for the moral good of the Muslim community, or even a personal spiritual struggle.

Terrorism is not primarily a Middle Eastern phenomenon. In terms of civilian lives lost, Africa has experienced far more terrorism in recent decades than has the Middle East. [. . .]

4. WHY HAS THE MIDDLE EAST BEEN THE FOCUS OF U.S. CONCERN ABOUT INTERNATIONAL TERRORISM?

There has been a long history of terrorism—generally defined as "violence by irregular forces against civilian targets"—in the Middle East. During Israel's independence struggle in the 1940s, Israeli terrorists killed hundreds of Palestinian and British civilians; two of the most notorious terrorist leaders of that period—Menachem Begin and Yitzhak Shamir—later became Israeli prime ministers whose governments received strong financial, diplomatic and military support from the United States. Algeria's independence struggle from France in the 1950s included widespread terrorist attacks against French colonists. Palestine's ongoing struggle for independence has also included widespread terrorism against Israeli civilians, during the 1970s through some of the armed militias of the Palestine Liberation Organization and, more recently, through radical underground Islamic groups. Terrorism has also played a role in Algeria's current civil strife, in Lebanon's civil war and foreign occupations during the 1980s, and for many years in the Kurdish struggle for independence. Some Middle Eastern governments—notably Libya, Syria, Sudan, Iraq and Iran—have in the past had close links with terrorist organizations. In more recent years, the Al Qaeda movement—a decentralized network of terrorist cells supported by Saudi exile Osama bin Laden—has become the major terrorist threat [. . .].

The vast majority of the people in the Middle East deplore terrorism, yet point out that violence against civilians by governments has generally surpassed that of terrorists. For example, the Israelis have killed far more Arab civilians over the decades through using U.S.-supplied equipment and ordinance than have Arab terrorists killed Israeli civilians. Similarly, the U.S.-supplied Turkish armed forces have killed far more Kurdish civilians than have such radical Kurdish groups like the PKK (the Kurdish acronym for the Kurdistan Workers' Party). Also, in the eyes of many Middle Easterners, U.S. support for terrorist groups like the Nicaraguan contras and various right-wing Cuban exile organizations in recent decades, as well as U.S. air strikes and the U.S.-led sanctions against Iraq in more recent years, have made the U.S. an unlikely leader in the war against terrorism.

10

5. WHAT KIND OF POLITICAL SYSTEMS AND ALLIANCES EXIST IN THE MIDDLE EAST?

There are a variety of political systems in the Middle East. Saudi Arabia, Oman, Bahrain, Kuwait, United Arab Emirates, Qatar, Morocco and Jordan are all conservative monarchies (in approximate order of absolute rule). Syria and Libya are left-leaning dictatorships [. . .]. Egypt and Tunisia are conservative autocratic republics. Iran is an Islamic republic with an uneven trend in recent years towards greater political openness. Sudan and Algeria are under military rulers facing major insurrections.

Lebanon, Turkey and Yemen are republics with repressive aspects but some degree of political pluralism. The only Middle Eastern country with a strong tradition of parliamentary democracy is Israel, though the benefits of this political freedom [are] largely restricted to its Jewish citizens (the Palestinian Arab minority is generally treated as second-class citizens and Palestinians in the occupied territories are subjected to military rule and human rights abuses). The largely autocratic Palestinian Authority has been granted limited autonomy in a series of noncontiguous enclaves in the West Bank and Gaza Strip surrounded by Israeli occupation forces.

All Arab states, including the Palestinian Authority, belong to the League of Arab States, which acts as a regional body similar to the Organization of African Union or the Organization of American States, which work together on issues of common concern. However, there are enormous political divisions within Arab countries and other Middle Eastern states. Turkey is a member of the NATO alliance, [which is] closely aligned with the West and hopes to eventually become part of the European Union. The six conservative monarchies of the Persian Gulf region have formed the Gulf Cooperation Council (GCC), from where they pursue joint strategic and economic interests and promote close ties with the West, particularly Great Britain (which dominated the smaller sheikdoms in the late 19th and early 20th centuries) and, more recently, the United States.

Often a country's alliances are not a reflection of its internal politics. For example, Saudi Arabia is often referred [to] in the U.S. media as a "moderate" Arab state, though it is the most oppressive fundamentalist theocracy in the world today [. . .]; "moderate," in this case, simply means that it has close strategic and economic relations with the United States.

Jordan and Egypt are pro-Western, but have been willing to challenge   15
U.S. policy on occasion. Israel identifies most strongly with the West: most of its leaders are European-born or have been of European heritage, and it has diplomatic relations with only a handful of Middle Eastern countries. Iran alienated most of its neighbors with its threat to expand its brand of revolutionary Islam to the Arab world, though its increasingly moderate orientation in recent years has led to some cautious rapprochement. Syria, a former Soviet ally, has been cautiously reaching out to more conservative Arab governments and to the West; it currently exerts enormous political

influence over Lebanon. [. . .] Libya under Muammar Qaddafi and Sudan under their military junta remain isolated from most other Middle Eastern countries due to a series of provocative policies, though many of these same countries oppose the punitive sanctions and air strikes the United States has inflicted against these countries in recent years.

6. WHAT IS THE IMPACT OF OIL IN THE MIDDLE EAST?

The major oil producers of the Middle East include Saudi Arabia, Kuwait, United Arab Emirates, Qatar, Bahrain, Iraq, Iran, Libya and Algeria. Egypt, Syria, Oman and Yemen have smaller reserves. Most of the major oil producers of the Middle East are part of the Organization of Petroleum Exporting Countries, or OPEC. (Non-Middle Eastern OPEC members include Indonesia, Venezuela, Nigeria and other countries.) Much of the world's oil wealth exists along the Persian Gulf, with particularly large reserves in Saudi Arabia, Kuwait and the United Arab Emirates. About one-quarter of U.S. oil imports come from the Persian Gulf region; the Gulf supplies European states and Japan with an even higher percentage of those countries' energy needs. The imposition of higher fuel efficiency standards and other conservation measures, along with the increased use of renewable energy resources for which technologies are already available, could eliminate U.S. dependence on Middle Eastern oil in a relatively short period of time.

The Arab members of OPEC instigated a boycott against the United States in the fall of 1973 in protest of U.S. support for Israel during the October Arab-Israeli war, creating the first in a series of energy shortages. The cartel has had periods of high and low costs for oil, resulting in great economic instability. Most governments have historically used their oil wealth to promote social welfare, particularly countries like Algeria, Libya and Iraq, which professed to a more socialist orientation. Yet all countries have squandered their wealth for arms purchases and prestige projects. In general, the influx of petrodollars has created enormous economic inequality both within oil-producing states and between oil-rich and oil-poor states as well as widespread corruption and questionable economic priorities.

7. WHAT IS THE ISRAELI-PALESTINIAN CONFLICT ABOUT?

The Israeli-Palestinian conflict is essentially over land, with two peoples claiming historic rights to the geographic Palestine, a small country in the eastern Mediterranean about the size of New Jersey. The creation of modern Israel in 1948 was a fulfillment of the goal of the Jewish nationalist movement, known as Zionism, as large numbers of Jews migrated to their faith's ancestral homeland from Europe, North Africa and elsewhere throughout the 20th century. They came into conflict with the indigenous Palestinian

Arab population, which also was struggling for independence. The 1947 partition plan, which divided the country approximately in half, resulted in a war that ended with Israel seizing control of 78 percent of the territory within a year. Most of the Palestinian population became refugees, in some cases through fleeing the fighting and in other cases through being forcibly expelled. The remaining Palestinian areas—the West Bank and Gaza Strip—came under control of the neighboring Arab states of Jordan and Egypt, though these areas were also seized by Israel in the 1967 war.

Israel has been colonizing parts of these occupied territories with Jewish settlers in violation of the Geneva Conventions and UN Security Council resolutions. Historically, both sides have failed to recognize the legitimacy of the others' nationalist aspirations, though the Palestinian leadership finally formally recognized Israel in 1993. The peace process since then has been over the fate of the West Bank (including Arab East Jerusalem) and the Gaza Strip, which is the remaining 22 percent of Palestine, occupied by Israel since 1967. The United States plays the dual role of chief mediator of the conflict as well as the chief financial, military and diplomatic supporter of Israel. The Palestinians want their own independent state in these territories and to allow Palestinian refugees the right to return. [. . .]

Most Arabs feel a strong sense of solidarity with the Palestinian strug-   20
gle, though their governments have tended to manipulate their plight for their own political gain. Neighboring Arab states have fought several wars with Israel, though Egypt and Jordan now have peace agreements and full diplomatic relations with the Jewish state. [. . .]

8. WHAT HAS BEEN THE LEGACY OF THE GULF WAR?

Virtually every Middle Eastern state opposed the Iraqi invasion and occupation of Kuwait in 1990, though they were badly divided on the appropriateness of the U.S.-led Gulf War that followed. Even among countries that supported the armed liberation of Kuwait, there was widespread opposition to the deliberate destruction by the United States of much of Iraq's civilian infrastructure during the war. Even more controversial has been the enormous humanitarian consequences of the U.S.-led international sanctions against Iraq in place since the war, which have resulted in the deaths of hundreds of thousands of Iraqis, mostly children, from malnutrition and preventable diseases.

The periodic U.S. air strikes against Iraq also have been controversial, as has the ongoing U.S. military presence in Saudi Arabia, other Gulf states and in the Persian Gulf and Arabian Sea. Since Iraq's offensive military capability was largely destroyed during the Gulf War and during the subsequent inspections regime, many observers believe that U.S. fears about Iraq's current military potential are exaggerated [. . .].

9. HOW HAS THE POLITICAL SITUATION IN AFGHANISTAN EVOLVED AND HOW IS IT CONNECTED TO THE MIDDLE EAST?

Afghanistan, an impoverished, landlocked, mountainous country, has traditionally been identified more with Central and South Asia than with the Middle East. A 1978 coup by communist military officers resulted in a series of radical social reforms, which were imposed in an autocratic matter and which resulted in a popular rebellion by a number of armed Islamic movements. The Soviet Union installed a more compliant communist regime at the end of 1979, sending in tens of thousands of troops and instigating a major bombing campaign, resulting in large-scale civilian casualties and refugee flows. The war lasted for much of the next decade. The United States sent arms to the Islamic resistance, known as the *mujahadin,* largely through neighboring Pakistan, then under the rule of an ultra-conservative Islamic military dictatorship. Most of the U.S. aid went to the most radical of the eight different *mujahadin* factions on the belief that they would be least likely to reach a negotiated settlement with the Soviet-backed government and would therefore drag the Soviet forces down. Volunteers from throughout the Islamic world, including the young Saudi businessman Osama bin Laden, joined the struggle. The CIA trained many of these recruits, including bin Laden and many of his followers.

When the Soviets and Afghanistan's communist government were defeated in 1992, a vicious and bloody civil war broke out between the various *mujahadin* factions, war lords and ethnic militias. Out of this chaos emerged the Taliban movement, led by young seminary students from the refugee camps in Pakistan who were educated in ultra-conservative Saudi-funded schools. The Taliban took over 85 percent of the country by 1996 and imposed long-awaited order and stability, but established a brutal totalitarian theocracy based on a virulently reactionary and misogynist interpretation of Islam. The Northern Alliance, consisting of the remnants of various factions from the civil war in the 1990s, control a small part of the northeast corner of the country.

10. HOW HAVE MOST MIDDLE EASTERN GOVERNMENTS REACTED TO THE SEPTEMBER 11 TERRORIST ATTACKS AND THEIR AFTERMATH?

Virtually every government and the vast majority of their populations reacted with the same horror and revulsion as did people in the United States, Europe and elsewhere. Despite scenes shown repeatedly on U.S. television of some Palestinians celebrating the attacks, the vast majority of Palestinians also shared in the world's condemnation. If the United States, in conjunction with local governments, limits its military response to commando-style operations against suspected terrorist cells, the U.S. should receive the

25

cooperation and support of most Middle Eastern countries. If the response is more widespread, based more on retaliation than self-defense, and ends up killing large numbers of Muslim civilians, it could create a major anti-American reaction that would increase support for the terrorists and lessen the likelihood for the needed cooperation to break up the Al Qaeda network, which operates in several Middle Eastern countries. [. . .]

Bin Laden Allies Want Islamic Unity
Jim Landers

Jim Landers is an investigative journalist for the Dallas Morning News.

Mustafa Kemal Attaturk, the founder of modern Turkey, abolished the caliphate of the Islamic world in 1924 in a deliberate turn toward Western law and politics.

Osama bin Laden is among the Muslim fundamentalists who say this was the biggest calamity of the modern era and the start of a continuing war on Islam.

The caliph — commander of the faithful — was the unifying figure of mosque and palace, the leader who could give spiritual as well as political direction to Muslims worldwide.

It has been the life mission of men such as Mr. bin Laden to bring that unity back, to drive off colonial and occupying powers, to restore *sharia* — divinely inspired Islamic law — and to maintain Islamic cultural identity.

Mr. bin Laden's ideas and organizing methods owe much to the Muslim Brotherhood, a disciplined political force begun in Egypt in 1928 to restore Islamic lands, law, and values.

His method — "death to all Americans" — is widely condemned by Islamic clerics and laity. The few who embrace it can wreak terrifying violence. U.S. officials say the suicide hijackers [. . .] on Sept. 11 were part of Mr. bin Laden's al-Qaeda network. Others with al-Qaeda or another fundamentalist terrorist group, or those simply goaded by fiery sermons have raged against "infidels and nonbelievers" from Southeast Asia to West Africa.

Nigerian and Sudanese Muslims war with Christians to assert religious and political dominance. Filipino Muslim terrorists decapitate hostages when their demands for Islamic self-rule go unanswered. Kashmiri militants trained in Afghanistan kill Hindus and tourists to liberate the Muslim majority from Indian rule.

Mr. bin Laden and other al-Qaeda leaders justify all of these groups with the argument that the restoration of the Islamic nation makes their actions righteous.

Terrorism is the choice of only a few. Thousands of others sympathize with Mr. bin Laden's message, if not his methods.

"I don't think theologically he has a leg to stand on," said Michael   10
Hudson, director of contemporary Arab studies at Georgetown University. "But I must say he's very effective. He's going over the heads of the Islamic establishment to say, 'We have an enemy in our midst called the United States of America, invading our space, corrupting our values and killing our people, and we have to do a jihad against it.'

"What should be very worrying to the U.S. government is this message seems to be surprisingly widely accepted," Dr. Hudson said. [. . .]

AMERICANS AS TARGETS

Religious radicals have made Americans their targets since at least 1979, when scores of U.S. diplomats and embassy workers were held hostage for more than a year by Iranian revolutionaries.

Hundreds of American soldiers and diplomats died at the hands of Islamic extremists in the 1980s. Those suicide assaults came from Shiite Muslims inspired by Iran's revolutionary guard who formed Hezbollah, or Party of God.

The 1979 Iranian revolution restored a Shiite vision of religion and politics united in the Ayatollah Ruhollah Khomeini. Shiites split from the dominant Sunni branch of Islam more than 1,300 years ago over their belief in hereditary rule through the family of the Prophet Muhammad. Shiite mullahs have more titles and authority than Sunni imams.

Iran's revolutionaries hated America out of a belief that it was coloniz-   15
ing the Islamic world. U.S. support for Israel made America synonymous with the Jewish state. The United States was accused of creating puppet regimes in Iran, then in Iraq, Egypt, and Saudi Arabia, to protect its access to oil.

Dissenters against these regimes were intimidated into silence, imprisoned, or exiled. The popular media were encouraged to voice outrage against Israel and the United States but censored for any criticisms of the government at home.

The anger of being voiceless was often matched by the despair of poverty. Despite the fabled wealth of a few oil producers, the Middle East is poorer than all regions of the world except sub-Saharan Africa. Average annual incomes in Latin America ($1,880 per person) are almost three times as large as incomes in the Middle East ($640).

Politically mute and poor, much of the Muslim world is also young. Most are disappointed when opportunities for education, jobs, or advancement are scarce.

The Arab world has gone through a decade-long population explosion. Thirty-five percent of Egyptians are under 15, as are 40 percent of Saudis.

More than half the Palestinians in the West Bank and Gaza Strip are younger than 15.

Islamic countries such as Indonesia and Malaysia have educated their people to the point that more than 85 percent can read and write. But other Muslim countries have suffered in the provision of education. The literacy rate in Bangladesh is 39 percent. In Pakistan it is 41 percent, and it is less than 53 percent in Egypt.

Poverty, disappointment, and youth form a potent mix for revolt. So it was a shock to some analysts that the suicide hijackers who slammed planes into the World Trade Center and the Pentagon had middle-class origins. Many were college graduates.

WESTERN CULTURE

"These are people trying to make sense of a complicated world out there," said Ahmet Karamustafa, a professor of Islamic history at Washington University in St. Louis. "They had a moment to pause and ponder and come up with an explanation, and, tragically, that tends to be an extremely dangerous and faulty scheme.

"No single Muslim should presume the power and authority to turn into almost divine judges of the human condition."

The middle-class, educated backgrounds of the hijackers are much like that of their ancestors in the Muslim Brotherhood, however, said Joseph Kechichian, a Los Angeles consultant and author of two books on Saudi Arabia.

Another aspect of this anti-Americanism is cultural. U.S. culture has spread the allure of change around the world. Anthony Giddens, director of the London School of Economics, writes that "fundamentalism is beleaguered tradition." It seems an apt description of much of Islam's anti-Americanism.

"Muslims the world over are asking, can Islam have a rapprochement with the American-led modern world?" Dr. Hudson said. "It's a world of everything from McDonald's to blue jeans to the notion that religion has no place in the political sphere." [. . .]

ROLE OF WOMEN

As Dr. Giddens writes in *Runaway World,* nowhere is the clash of ideas more explosive than in family relations and the role of women. Western values are a direct threat to the sexual apartheid practiced in Saudi Arabia and Afghanistan, and to a lesser extent in Iran.

"Equality of the sexes, and the sexual freedom of women, which are incompatible with the traditional family, are anathema to fundamentalist groups," Dr. Giddens wrote. "Opposition to them, indeed, is one of the defining features of religious fundamentalism across the world."

MUSLIM BROTHERHOOD

Secular Egyptian governments have fought radical Islamic militants since the Muslim Brotherhood was banned in 1949. Today the militants are with al-Gama'a al-Islamiyya, or the Islamic Group; and Egyptian Islamic Jihad. Both owe much of their teachings and discipline to the Muslim Brotherhood.

Al-Gama'a and Islamic Jihad merged with Mr. bin Laden's al-Qaeda in the mid-1990s.

Al-Qaeda has cells spread through as many as 60 countries. The Muslim Brotherhood overlaps with al-Qaeda in many of those same countries.

Al-Qaeda "has structural parallels with the Muslim Brotherhood, but what's new is they have been released from nationalism and have created for themselves a transnational type of force, thanks to direct nurturing by Saudi Arabia and Pakistan," said Dr. Karamustafa. "It is no longer dissidents against a particular nation state."

The Brotherhood started with an emphasis on rigorous scholarship, physical fitness, and an ascetic lifestyle honed in desert camps. Soon it was overtly political. Members were indoctrinated within a "family" or five-man cell.

After World War II, the Brotherhood spread widely in the Muslim world. Volunteers fought in Palestine in 1948 against the creation of Israel. Yasser Arafat and other founding members of the Palestine Liberation Organization were once members of the Muslim Brotherhood.

Persecution in Egypt sent many Muslim Brothers to Saudi Arabia and other countries of the Gulf in the 1960s, where some became teachers. The Brotherhood started Medina University, which was the wellspring of the 1979 attempted coup in Saudi Arabia by university students who seized the Grand Mosque in Mecca and proclaimed one of their members the Mahdi, or messiah.

The Muslim Brotherhood in Syria staged a war against the secular regime of President Hafez al-Assad from 1980 to 1982, but Mr. Assad crushed the revolt by destroying Hamas, a Syrian stronghold of the Brotherhood, killing more than 10,000 people in the process.

The war against the Soviet Union brought thousands of Muslim Brotherhood volunteers from throughout the Islamic world together in Afghanistan, where the brotherhood's discipline and teachings were bonded with Mr. bin Laden's personal wealth and connections to other rich Saudis.

Muslim Brotherhood leaders in Pakistan and Sudan inspired and tutored Mr. bin Laden, and helped shape his philosophies.

BIN LADEN'S MENTOR

Abdullah Azzam, a Palestinian professor of Islamic law, was Mr. bin Laden's mentor in Pakistan. He was fired from his teaching position at Amman University in Jordan in 1980 for criticizing the government. He went to Pakistan to organize a recruiting campaign for Muslim volunteers to fight the Soviet occupation of Afghanistan.

Dr. Azzam, who was killed in a Peshawar car bombing in 1989, also   40
played a leading role in transforming the Muslim Brotherhood of Palestinians into Hamas, which has conducted many suicide bombings against Israelis.

Mr. bin Laden offered to organize an army of Afghan war veterans to repel Iraq's 1990 invasion of Kuwait. But the Saudi royal family turned to the United States for help instead, and in the process made an enemy of Mr. bin Laden.

Mr. bin Laden went to Sudan at the invitation of Hasan al-Turabi, former dean of the law school at Khartoum University and another of the leading thinkers of the Muslim Brotherhood. Mr. al-Turabi is considered the intellectual author of the 1989 coup that brought an Islamic government to power in Khartoum. [. . .]

Mr. bin Laden set about organizing al-Qaeda while living in Sudan, U.S. officials say. There, he worked with veterans of the war in Afghanistan to organize an effort to free Islam from the corrupting influences of the outside world. [. . .]

SAUDI ARABIA ISSUES

Mr. bin Laden's greatest complaint is close to home. One of the traditions of Islamic fundamentalism is a supposed deathbed statement from the Prophet Muhammad: "Do not let the unbelievers live in the land of Arabia."

Tens of thousands of non-Muslims have worked and lived in Saudi Arabia since the oil price spike of 1973 set the kingdom on the road to   45
riches. Mr. bin Laden, however, is most disturbed by the presence of U.S. military forces.

The Saudi government bars non-Muslims from the city limits of Mecca and from entering the Prophet's Mosque in Medina, where Muhammad is buried.

Mr. bin Laden wants them out of Saudi Arabia entirely. But that won't be the end of it, said Dr. Karamustafa.

"I think his task clearly would be incomplete from his perspective if the current Saudi Arabian regime were to stay in power," he said.

To Mr. bin Laden, much of the Saudi royal family is corrupt and apostate. To restore the caliphate, such rulers must be overthrown.

Israel through the Years

1947–1948

Mediterranean Sea

Dead Sea

ISRAEL

Sinai Peninsula

JORDAN

Gulf of Suez

Gulf of Aqabah

0   50m
0   80km

EGYPT

SAUDI ARABIA

| | U.N. partition plans 1947 | | Territory added in 1948 |

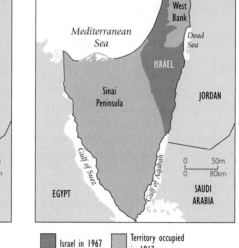

1967

Golan Heights

West Bank

Mediterranean Sea

Dead Sea

ISRAEL

Sinai Peninsula

JORDAN

Gulf of Suez

Gulf of Aqabah

0   50m
0   80km

EGYPT

SAUDI ARABIA

| | Israel in 1967 | | Territory occupied in 1967 |

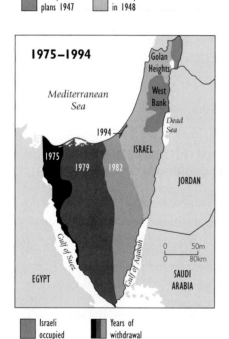

1975–1994

Golan Heights

Mediterranean Sea

West Bank

1994

Dead Sea

ISRAEL

1975

1979   1982

JORDAN

Gulf of Suez

Gulf of Aqabah

0   50m
0   80km

EGYPT

SAUDI ARABIA

| | Israeli occupied | | Years of withdrawal |

TODAY

Golan Heights

West Bank

Mediterranean Sea

Dead Sea

ISRAEL

JORDAN

EGYPT

Gulf of Suez

Gulf of Aqabah

0   50m
0   80km

SAUDI ARABIA

1917—Britain issues the Balfour Declaration, expressing its support for a Jewish homeland in Palestine.

1920—The League of Nations grants Britain a mandate to govern Palestine.

1947—The United Nations divides Palestine into a Jewish state and an Arab state.

1948–1949—David Ben-Gurion and other Jewish leaders proclaim the establishment of the state of Israel on May 14. Egypt, Syria,

Lebanon, Iraq and Jordan attack Israel the next day. Israel wins the war, gaining about half the territory the U.N. had set aside for a new Arab state.

1967—Israel defeats Egypt, Jordan and Syria in the Six-Day War, gaining control of the Gaza Strip, Sinai Peninsula, West Bank and Golan Heights, as well as the rest—the eastern part—of Jerusalem.

1973—Egyptian president Anwar Sadat leads Egypt and Syria in another war against Israel. Arab gains are neutralized by U.S. support of Israel, and Arab oil producers put an embargo on sales to the United States.

1978—Israel and Egypt, with U.S. mediation, reach the Camp David Accords, which would end their dispute and restore the Sinai to its pre-1967 borders.

1981—Islamic extremists assassinate Sadat, largely because he made peace.

1982—Israel invades Lebanon in an attempt to crush the Palestine Liberation Organization.

U.S. intervention allows the PLO to retreat to Tunisia.

1988—The PLO recognizes Israel's right to exist, making the United States willing to negotiate.

1993—Israeli Prime Minister Yitzak Rabin leads Israel into negotiations with the PLO under the auspices of Norway, and then of the United States. He and PLO leader Yasser Arafat shake hands at the White House. The Palestinian Authority is created to provide limited rule over Gaza and growing portions of the West Bank.

1995—A Jewish extremist assassinates Rabin because of the Oslo accords.

2000—Mr. Arafat, Israeli prime minister Ehud Barak and President Bill Clinton fail in an attempt to negotiate a peace agreement.

Sources: *Dallas Morning News* research; World Book Encyclopedia; *New York Times*; Associated Press

---

A World Made More Dangerous as Terrorism Spreads
Don Van Natta, Jr.

Every day—some days, it seems, nearly every hour—a terrorist alarm is sounded somewhere in the world. Each new threat has immediate consequences. Flights may be canceled, a few embassies closed. And it almost always stokes fears that another terrorist attack is imminent.

Is the world more dangerous today than it was a year ago, or on Sept. 10, 2001, or even since the end of the cold war?

Yes, say many terrorism experts, for a number of reasons: the American-led occupation of Iraq, which has become a rallying cry for hundreds, perhaps thousands, of Islamic militants; the campaigns by a growing number of groups to obtain weapons of mass destruction; and the prolific violence of local terrorist groups.

Since being routed from Afghanistan in late 2001, Al Qaeda has again proved its protean nature by morphing into a baseless, rootless organization with potent alliances. Although two-thirds of its core leadership has been killed or captured, Al Qaeda has managed to export its violent, anti-Western militancy to dozens of like-minded regional terrorist groups.

"Al Qaeda has been replaced by Qaeda-ism," a top counterterrorism official based in Europe said recently.

5

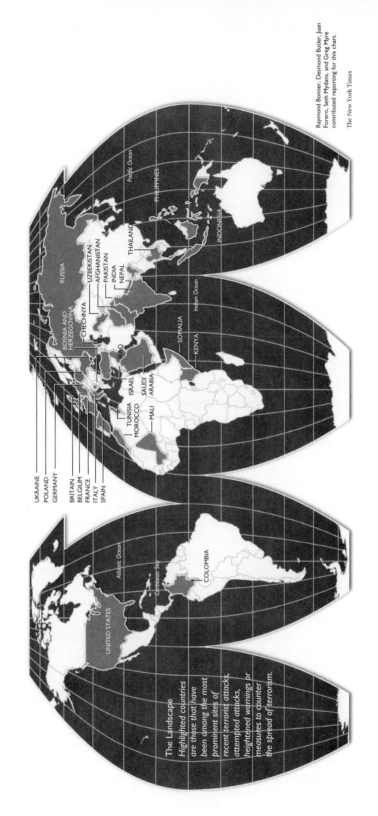

The Landscape
Highlighted countries are those that have been among the most prominent sites of recent terrorist attacks, attempted attacks, heightened warnings or measures to counter the spread of terrorism.

Atlantic Ocean

Caribbean Sea

UNITED STATES

COLOMBIA

Pacific Ocean

PHILIPPINES

INDONESIA

THAILAND

RUSSIA

UZBEKISTAN

AFGHANISTAN
PAKISTAN
INDIA
NEPAL

BOSNIA AND
HERZEGOVINA

CHECHNYA

IRAQ

ISRAEL

SAUDI
ARABIA

TUNISIA
MOROCCO

MALI

SOMALIA

KENYA

Indian Ocean

UKRAINE
POLAND
GERMANY

BRITAIN
BELGIUM
FRANCE
ITALY
SPAIN

Raymond Bonner, Desmond Butler, Juan Forero, Seth Mydans, and Greg Myre contributed reporting for this chart.

The New York Times

This Qaeda-ism accounts for some but hardly all of the world's terrorist activities. There are dozens of other groups with locally motivated reasons for murder and mayhem, from Maoist guerrillas in Nepal to right-wing paramilitary groups in Colombia.

A worldwide map [opposite, page 340] of the hotbeds of terrorist activity shows a daunting array of distinct and interconnected motives. With so many groups declaring the United States their principal enemy, the map also illustrates why even the most optimistic counterterrorism officials predict that the war on terrorism will last generations.

THE AMERICAS

While the United States focuses on Al Qaeda, Colombia offers proof that some of the bloodiest terrorism has no links to Islamic fundamentalism. There are hundreds of violent incidents each year, from car bombings to kidnappings, mass killings in isolated villages and assassinations of human rights advocates and journalists. The culprits are Marxist insurgencies and a right-wing paramilitary group linked in the past to Colombia's army.

EUROPE

The Madrid bombings last month confirmed Europe's fears that it is a Qaeda target. Analysts say Al Qaeda and its affiliates are more deeply entrenched in Europe than in North America. Investigators have thwarted suspected plots in Britain, France, Belgium, Spain and Germany, and terrorist groups may view Eastern Europe as the new soft spot for entry and hiding.

AFRICA

In Morocco, now both a target and operating base for bin Laden followers, more than 30 people died in a suicide bombing in Casablanca last May. Most of the suspects arrested in the Madrid bombings were Moroccan, the suspected mastermind a Tunisian. America and France have reportedly been trying to assist Mali, where members of an Algerian terrorist group affiliated with Al Qaeda have taken refuge.

THE MIDDLE EAST

Since the American-led invasion of Iraq, coalition troops there as well as Shiite clerics, foreign aid workers and U.N. staff members have been targets of bombings, killings and kidnappings, most by Iraqis, although American officials say there is some foreign involvement. Israel, where hijackings and bombings long predate Al Qaeda, remains a frequent target of Palestinian suicide bombers. In Saudi Arabia, Al Qaeda has been linked to attacks whose ultimate target is the royal establishment that Osama bin Laden hates.

CENTRAL AND SOUTH ASIA

Afghanistan's government remains threatened by Al Qaeda and the Taliban, while in Pakistan, more attempts on the life of President Pervez Musharraf are expected. Meanwhile, Islamic militants stage attacks weekly in the Indian-controlled part of Kashmir and mingle among Chechnya's rebels. Suicide bombers linked to Al Qaeda have attacked in Uzbekistan. In Nepal, Maoist insurgents have been blamed for several bombings.

SOUTHEAST ASIA

Indonesia, where a Bali nightclub was bombed two years ago, and the Philippines, where the Abu Sayyaf rebellion continues, were identified early as places where Qaeda affiliates operated. The Philippine rebels now help train the Indonesian group. Malaysia was a meeting place for Qaeda operatives before Sept. 11. Now militant Islam, with apparent Qaeda connections, has flared in southern Thailand, and Cambodia has responded to the spread of militant Wahhabi madrassas.

Analysis of Terrorist Weapons and the Liberal State Response
Paul Wilkinson

An internationally recognized expert on terrorism, Wilkinson is a professor of international relations and the director of the Centre for the Study of Terrorism and Political Violence at the University of St. Andrews in Scotland. The following selection comes from Terrorism Versus Democracy: The Liberal State Response *(2000).*

NUCLEAR TERRORISM

Many analysts have endorsed the somewhat sanguine assessment of an American writer that "the threat of nuclear action by terrorists appears to be exaggerated."[1] In support of this optimistic view it has been argued that terrorists are not really interested in mass murder, but in gaining publicity and using propaganda to influence people. Of course publicity and propaganda are generally key tactical objectives. But in many cases the terrorists' cardinal aim is to create a climate of fear and collapse, essentially by terrifying and demoralising their targets into capitulation. And what more potent weapon of psychological coercion can be conceived in the modern age than the threat to explode a nuclear device or to release lethal levels of radioactivity into the atmosphere, perhaps rendering an entire area of a city uninhabitable.

It would be extraordinarily foolish to assume that all terrorist groups shared the same perceptions of rationality, humanity and prudence that inform the consciences of most of humanity. In the strange transcendental logic of the fanatical political terrorist, as I have earlier observed, the end is held to justify any means. If any individual life is expendable in the cause of "revolutionary justice" or "liberation" so many hundreds, even thousands, of lives may have to be "sacrificed." [. . .] Hence, although still a low probability, nuclear terrorism is potentially so high a consequence that we must have contingency plans to prevent such an attack and to deal with the possible consequences should it happen, in order to minimise loss of life. [. . .]

VULNERABLE TARGETS

There are extremely grave dangers involved in the diffusion of civil nuclear facilities and technologies in many states. These processes involve the use of substances which could be employed to make a nuclear explosive device. Plutonium, which is used for incorporation into reactor fuel, has to be shipped and in some cases transported by road. It is clearly vulnerable to theft by terrorists while it is in transit. Still more dangerous is the practice which has developed in the nuclear power industry of transporting plutonium nitrate in liquid form by road. This is a hazardous process. Plutonium transported as a pure compound, even in small quantities, is a particularly tempting target for terrorist theft or hijack because of the material's obvious value in constructing a nuclear weapon. And, because of its extreme toxicity, it could also be used by terrorists as a weapon of radiological extortion. Reports by scientific experts have underlined both these dangers, but this does not appear to have influenced the policy of the EU member states' authorities regarding the transportation of nuclear fuels. Plutonium is also present in spent reactor fuel. It then has to be stored because there is to date no commercially viable system for reprocessing it. And in the special case of the liquid metal fast-breeder reactor, more plutonium is produced than is actually consumed, so that the problem of disposal is especially acute.

Terrorists, therefore, might seek by various means, including infiltration of the nuclear industry workforce, to obtain regular small supplies of nuclear materials. The particularly vulnerable points for nuclear theft include storage facilities for spent fuel, fuel reprocessing plants, and fabrication and uranium enrichment plants. There is little doubt that sufficient quantities of enriched uranium and plutonium could be obtained to make possible the manufacture of a primitive device. Recent firm evidence of the smuggling of nuclear materials from Russian installations underlines the growing seriousness of this threat. Even more worrying is the strong possibility that disaffected scientists and engineers from the Former Soviet Union's nuclear weapons programme have been lured into the employ of rogue states or terrorist groups. It is certainly credible that a group of competent and qualified scientists and engineers could be recruited for the special purpose of building an atomic weapon or advising the group on techniques of nuclear sabotage and extortion. A team of five or six could probably accomplish this within the space of five or six weeks without incurring any serious risk to their personal health or safety. Estimates of the financial costs involved vary. [. . .]

CHEMICAL AND BIOLOGICAL WEAPONS

Most specialists in the study of terrorism have been as sceptical about the possibility of terrorists using chemical or biological weapons as they have about the prospect of nuclear terrorism. Dr Richard Clutterbuck in his *Terrorism in an Unstable World* concluded:

> Clearly we should not be complacent about nuclear, biological and chemical weapons, both because of the need to evaluate hoax calls . . . and because all of them would be feasible for a group which was both desperate and suicidal. But the threat is far less, and would in many ways be easier to handle because of its lack of credibility, than the terrorist actions to which we are accustomed.[2]

The tragic attack on the Tokyo underground system with the nerve gas Sarin, which killed 12 and injured many more, has made it vital to reconsider the conventional wisdom. It is unlikely that there are more than a tiny number of groups willing to commit such acts. It is still a low-probability threat. But the fact that it has been attempted and that it clearly could have caused a large number of deaths if the Sarin had been used in a purer form, may tempt another group to emulate the Aum group's action.

The methods for making nerve gases and biological pathogens have been known for decades. The formula for making Sarin is on the Internet. The materials and equipment for making crude chemical and biological weapons are cheap and easily obtained and the weapons could be made by a person with only basic scientific training.[3] [. . .]

TERRORIST TACTICS AND THE USE OF CONVENTIONAL WEAPONS

In a recently published symposium edited by myself, a number of experts rightly stressed that the most likely trend in terrorist weaponry and tactics was further refinement and adaptation, and deployment of what is already widely available and affordable. Why go to the trouble of acquiring more hazardous and costly weapons when so much death and destruction can be achieved by traditional means? It is worth bearing in mind that the bomb used in [. . .] Oklahoma, which killed 169, comprised ammonium nitrate and fuel oil; the same bomb is also one of the most effective conventional weapons used by the IRA. The IRA provides us with the outstanding example of an experienced terrorist group improvising and adapting traditional weaponry, for example in its development of the drogue grenade, home-made mortars and booby-trap devices. There are reports that they have recently been developing a remote control device to guide a driverless car containing a bomb to its target. When terrorist groups are able to achieve "successes" using such improvisations, they are less likely to feel the need to experiment with entirely new weapons that carry a high risk of death or injury to their own operatives. We are likely to see more developments of this kind in a constant battle to keep ahead of the technology available to the counter-terrorist agencies.[4]

One important source of innovations or switches in tactics and weaponry is the introduction by the authorities of more effective counter-measures against certain types of attack. For example, as the civil aviation system's measures to improve protection against the sabotage bombing of airliners become more efficient, we are likely to see a greater use of alternative means of terrorist attack against aviation, such as surface-to-air missiles. There are clear signs that this was already happening in the 1990s. There have been at least 25 attacks using man-portable SAMs since November 1990, and in 15 of these incidents an aircraft was shot down causing an estimated 300 deaths. So far most of the aircraft involved have been military. However, in view of the clear evidence that terrorist groups in many parts of the world have managed to obtain SAMs, the security authorities in the European democracies should be urgently concerting efforts to combat this growing threat.[5]

COUNTERING INTERNATIONAL TERRORISM: THE DEMOCRATIC RESPONSE

In countering international terrorism, the democratic state confronts an inescapable dilemma. It has to deal effectively with the terrorist threat to citizens and to vulnerable potential targets, such as civil aviation, diplomatic and commercial premises, without at the same time destroying basic civil rights, the democratic process and the rule of law. On the one hand, the democratic government and its agencies of law enforcement must avoid the heavy-handed overreaction which many terrorist groups deliberately seek to provoke: such a response would only help to alienate the public from the government and could ultimately destroy democracy more swiftly and completely than any small terrorist group ever could. On the other hand, if government, judiciary and police prove incapable of upholding the law

10

and protecting life and property, then their whole credibility and authority will be undermined.

If this balance is to be maintained, the liberal state should seek at all times to combat terrorism using its criminal justice and law-enforcement mechanisms. However, it is clearly the case that some terrorist groups attain a level of fire-power that outstrips even the capabilities of elite squads of armed police. It has been proven time and again that in certain circumstances of high emergency, such as the hijacking to Entebbe in 1976 and the Iranian embassy siege of 1980, it may be essential to deploy a highly trained military rescue commando force to save hostages. Military, naval or air forces may be invaluable in interdicting a major terrorist assault, as has been seen in the case of Israel's measures against terrorist groups attacking its borders from land and sea. But in the more normal conditions enjoyed by the democratic states in Western Europe, the occasions when military deployment to tackle international terrorists is required will be very rare.

A number of dangers need to be constantly borne in mind when deploying the army in a major internal terrorist emergency role. First, an unnecessarily high military profile may serve to escalate the level of violence by polarising pro- and anti-government elements in the community. Second, there is a constant risk that a repressive overreaction or a minor error in judgment by the military may trigger further civil violence. Internal security duties inevitably impose considerable strains on the soldiers, who are made well aware of the hostility of certain sections of the community towards them. Third, anti-terrorist and internal security duties absorb considerable manpower and involve diverting highly trained military technicians from their primary NATO and external defence roles. Fourth, there is a risk that the civil power may become overdependent on the army's presence and there may be a consequent lack of urgency in preparing the civil police for gradually reassuming the internal security responsibility. Finally, in the event of an international terrorist attack, a military operation to punish a state sponsor or to strike at alleged terrorist bases may trigger an international conflict worse than the act of terrorism one is seeking to oppose.

High-quality intelligence is at the heart of the proactive counter-terrorism strategy. It has been used with notable success against many terrorist groups. By gaining advanced warning of terrorists' planned operations, their weaponry, personnel, financial assets and fund-raising, tactics, communications systems and so on, it becomes feasible to preempt terrorist attacks, and ultimately to crack open the terrorist cell structure and bring its members to trial. Impressive examples of this proactive intelligence-led counter-terrorism strategy are frequently ignored or forgotten by the public, but this should not deceive us into underestimating their value. At the international level, the most impressive example has been the brilliant intelligence cooperation among the Allies to thwart Saddam Hussein's much-vaunted campaign of "holy terror" during operations Desert Shield and Desert Storm. Sadly, such high levels of international cooperation against terrorism are hard to find. Just as the lack of intelligence sharing between uniformed and nonuniformed security agencies often damages national counter-terrorism responses, so international mistrust and reluctance to share information often vitiates an effective international response. The most useful enhancements of policy to combat terrorism at the international level need to be made in intelligence gathering, by every means available, intelligence sharing, intelligence analysis and threat assessment. This is my key recommendation, and it is my hope that there will be a fuller debate on refining a better proactive strategy for America and G8 and EU friends and allies, and the newly democratised states of Eastern Europe. [. . .]

It would be a grave error to assume that even the most sophisticated intelligence and security measures are going to be sufficient to eradicate or even contain the most dangerous forms of international terrorism. In situations where there is a deep-seated ethnic or ethnoreligious conflict involved, as in the case of the relationship between Israel and the Palestinians, much will depend on the will and ability of the political leaders involved to address the underlying causes of the conflict by imaginative political and socioeconomic measures and a generous spirit of compromise. [. . .]

Notes

1. Brian Jenkins, "International Terrorism: Trends and Potentialities: A Summary of Conclusions," unpublished mimeographed paper, March 1976, 3.

2. Richard Clutterbuck, *Terrorism in an Unstable World* (London: Macmillan, 1994) 54.

3. The threat is discussed by R. H. Kupperman and D. M. Trent in their pioneering study of potential terrorist weaponry, tactics and targets, *Terrorism, Threat, Reality, Response* (Stanford: Hoover Institute Press, 1979).

4. This is a recurrent theme in the contributions to Paul Wilkinson (ed.), *Technology and Terrorism* (London: Frank Cass, 1993).

5. See Thomas B. Hunter, "The Proliferation of Manportable SAMs," *Counter-Terrorism and Security Report* 6.2 (July/August 1997): 2–5.

Questions for Discussion

1. "Initial reports of major disasters and their tragic circumstances," Berrington claims, "powerfully define the key issues, shaping understanding and constructing a collective memory." Try to recall your outlook in the weeks following 9/11. How much of your understanding remains what it was then? How much has changed?

2. In "Why Terrorism?" Jenkins tries to explain what the terrorists are trying to achieve. Summarize his explanation. In a memorable play on Marie Antoinette's famous statement, Jenkins says that the terrorist motto should be "After the deluge, us." What does he mean?

3. We tend to associate the Middle East with terrorism. What evidence does Zunes cite to show that this association is not accurate?
4. How does Zunes explain the civil unrest, violence, and terrorism in the recent history of the Middle East?
5. According to Wilkinson, what are the dangers in using the military for counterterrorism? Are any of the dangers evident in the deployment of our forces in Afghanistan and Iraq?
6. Read carefully the Van Natta article and ponder the map included with it and its associated information on pages 341–342. What conclusions about terrorism *as a worldwide phenomenon* can you draw out of it? Where does the threat to us, to Americans and the United States, fit within this big picture?

Suggestions for Writing

For Research and Collaborative Writing

At least five million Muslims live in the United States. Worldwide Islam is second only to Christianity in number of adherents and is growing faster than any other faith. Yet most Americans know little or nothing about the religion that began on the Arabian peninsula more than thirteen centuries ago. As a class, research the history and present condition of Islam. Share and discuss the information you find. Compose as a class an article you might call "Ten Things to Know about Islam," using Zunes's piece as a model. Post it on an appropriate Web site.

For Convincing

Probably no knowledge is more important than an understanding of the Arab world and Islamic culture and religion. Write a brief op-ed piece arguing for a mandatory course in these two subjects for undergraduates in American universities. Try to get it published in your local campus or city newspaper.

For Mediation

There's no denying the seriousness of the threat posed by terrorism — especially if a terrorist group should acquire and use, for example, an atom bomb or a "dirty bomb," a conventional device that would scatter high levels of radioactive material over a large area. At the same time, as individuals we are far more likely to die from a heart attack or in an automobile accident. We are pouring billions of dollars into counterterrorism, more than we devote to any single more immediate threat to American lives. How can we mediate the conflicting imperatives of protecting ourselves from terrorist attacks versus research needed to reduce deaths from heart attacks, cancer, and car accidents? Write an essay making a case for a reasonable balance between resources used to combat terrorism as against other risks we face daily.

For Research and Convincing

As events in Afghanistan and Iraq clearly show, U.S. military power has no rival. But experts claim that we are losing the propaganda war, the struggle to win the hearts and minds of the Muslim masses in the Middle East and elsewhere. Find out what you can about the propaganda side of our struggle against terrorism. Write an essay advocating whatever measures you think we ought to take to enhance our appeal in the Muslim world. Be sure to assess our current efforts as part of your own proposal.

SECTION 2: VIEWS OF TERRORISM

Overview

If you can say what terrorism is and distinguish it from other forms of violence, and if you can explain what motivates it, perhaps you think you understand it—and you have, at one level. But this level is too abstract, not specific enough to address a particular kind of terrorism. What we need is a more specific interpretation, one designed to account for militant Islam.

Each of the writers in this section offers a different "take" on this kind of terrorism. Samuel Huntington sees it as part of a new world alignment, essentially the clash of civilizations rather than nations. Edward Said attempts to cast doubt on Huntington's highly influential view, arguing instead that the conflict is based on cultural mixture and interdependence rather than the West versus Islam. Charles Krauthammer's view is similar to Said's in not taking Islam as the enemy—rather, for him the problem is an irrational and destructive philosophy, nihilism, not peculiar to Islamic extremists nor typical of most Muslims. Yonah Alexander differs from Huntington and Said in seeing the motivations as primarily religious, a view Krauthammer would endorse, but Alexander's view does not imply that Islam isn't part of the problem—quite the contrary, "the complete surrender of religion to Arab political needs" *is* the problem as Alexander sees it. In sharp contrast, Chalmers Johnson looks to U.S. foreign policy to account for our being the target of terrorist activity. In his view, we are reaping what we have sown—as, for example, when we used bin Laden and his supporters to counter the invasion of Afghanistan by the USSR during the Cold War era. Finally, Leo Braudy takes a stance radically different from all but a few feminist interpreters: Terrorism is rooted in the long tradition of the male as warrior and is therefore inseparable from how the West and Arab culture construct masculinity.

What can/should we do with all of these views of terrorism, each one focused on interpreting militant Islam specifically?

First, probably one of the views will satisfy you or catch your imagination the most. That's fine, but do not ignore the others. For instance, if you see masculinity as the heart of the problem, you needn't exclude the contribution of U.S. foreign policy to terrorist motivation, especially since our foreign policy is largely conceived and carried out by men. Seeing terrorism predominantly from one point of view does not require denying the contributions of other points of view.

However, second, it's also true that some decisions about how to interpret militant Islam do require "this, not that" choices. For instance, if you accept Alexander's religious reading, you can't release Islam from *some* responsibility for terrorism, as you can if you adopt Krauthammer's viewpoint. The important thing is to see *what each view implies*. For instance, although Huntington grants that conflict between civilizations need not be violent conflict, his view does imply that *some kind of* conflict between the West and Islam is unavoidable and that ultimately the cultural emphases of one or the other must prevail. In other words, the Huntington view supports the use of power—military, economic, and otherwise—to continue Western control over the Middle East, a policy that goes back at least as far as World War I.

Third, and most important, of all the implications of a particular way of interpreting militant Islam, what counts the most is *what sort of action* it tends to find reasonable to combat terrorism. For Said and Johnson, for instance, U.S. foreign policy must change fundamentally. For Huntington and Krauthammer, what the Bush administration has done makes sense—indeed, may not have gone far enough in aggressive action against Islamic extremist groups. In contrast, Braudy's view must see foreign policy as a relatively superficial concern—nothing will change fundamentally until men learn to behave differently.

It's worth repeating: *How we interpret militant Islam will largely determine what we do to counter it.* A faulty interpretation will lead to measures that will be ineffective at best, at worst ways to nurture terrorism rather than defeat it. Interpretation, then, matters more than anything else in confronting terrorism successfully.

The Clash of Civilizations?
Samuel P. Huntington

Probably the most influential theorist on foreign policy among conservatives, Huntington is a distinguished professor at Harvard and director of the John M. Olin Institute for Strategic Studies. The following article first appeared in Foreign Policy *(Summer 1993).*

THE NEXT PATTERN OF CONFLICT

World politics is entering a new phase, and intellectuals have not hesitated to proliferate visions of what it will be—the end of history, the return of traditional rivalries between nation states, and the decline of the nation state from the conflicting pulls of tribalism and globalism, among others. Each of these visions catches aspects of the emerging reality. Yet they all miss a crucial, indeed a central, aspect of what global politics is likely to be in the coming years.

It is my hypothesis that the fundamental source of conflict in this new world will not be primarily ideological or primarily economic. The great divisions among humankind and the dominating source of conflict will be cultural. Nation states will remain the most powerful actors in world affairs, but the principal conflicts of global politics will occur between nations and groups of different civilizations. The clash of civilizations will dominate global politics. The fault lines between civilizations will be the battle lines of the future. [. . .]

THE NATURE OF CIVILIZATIONS

During the Cold War the world was divided into the First, Second and Third Worlds. Those divisions are no longer relevant. It is far more meaningful now to group countries not in terms of their political or economic systems or in terms of their level of economic development but rather in terms of their culture and civilization.

What do we mean when we talk of a civilization? A civilization is a cultural entity. Villages, regions, ethnic groups, nationalities, religious groups, all have distinct cultures at different levels of cultural heterogeneity. The culture of a village in southern Italy may be different from that of a village in northern Italy, but both will share in a common Italian culture that distinguishes them from German villages. European communities, in turn, will share cultural features that distinguish them from Arab or Chinese communities. Arabs, Chinese and Westerners, however, are not part of any broader cultural entity. They constitute civilizations. A civilization is thus the highest cultural grouping of people and the broadest level of cultural identity people have short of that which distinguishes humans from other species. It is defined both by common objective elements, such as language, history, religion, customs, institutions, and by the subjective self-identification of people. People have levels of identity: a resident of Rome may define himself with varying degrees of intensity as a Roman, an Italian, a Catholic, a Christian, a European, a Westerner. The civilization to which he belongs is the broadest level of identification with which he intensely identifies. People can and do redefine their identities and, as a result, the composition and boundaries of civilizations change. [. . .]

WHY CIVILIZATIONS WILL CLASH

Civilization identity will be increasingly important in the future, and the world will be shaped in large measure by the interactions among seven or eight major civilizations. These include Western, Confucian, Japanese,

Islamic, Hindu, Slavic-Orthodox, Latin American and possibly African civilization. The most important conflicts of the future will occur along the cultural fault lines separating these civilizations from one another.

Why will this be the case?

First, differences among civilizations are not only real; they are basic. Civilizations are differentiated from each other by history, language, culture, tradition and, most important, religion. The people of different civilizations have different views on the relations between God and man, the individual and the group, the citizen and the state, parents and children, husband and wife, as well as differing views of the relative importance of rights and responsibilities, liberty and authority, equality and hierarchy. These differences are the product of centuries. They will not soon disappear. They are far more fundamental than differences among political ideologies and political regimes. Differences do not necessarily mean conflict, and conflict does not necessarily mean violence. Over the centuries, however, differences among civilizations have generated the most prolonged and the most violent conflicts.

Second, the world is becoming a smaller place. The interactions between peoples of different civilizations are increasing; these increasing interactions intensify civilization consciousness and awareness of differences between civilizations and commonalities within civilizations. North African immigration to France generates hostility among Frenchmen and at the same time increased receptivity to immigration by "good" European Catholic Poles. Americans react far more negatively to Japanese investment than to larger investments from Canada and European countries. Similarly, as Donald Horowitz has pointed out, "An Ibo may be . . . an Owerri Ibo or an Onitsha Ibo in what was the Eastern region of Nigeria. In Lagos, he is simply an Ibo. In London, he is a Nigerian. In New York, he is an African." The interactions among peoples of different civilizations enhance the civilization-consciousness of people that, in turn, invigorates differences and animosities stretching or thought to stretch back deep into history.

Third, the processes of economic modernization and social change throughout the world are separating people from longstanding local identities. They also weaken the nation state as a source of identity. In much of the world religion has moved in to fill this gap, often in the form of movements that are labeled "fundamentalist." Such movements are found in Western Christianity, Judaism, Buddhism and Hinduism, as well as in Islam. In most countries and most religions the people active in fundamentalist movements are young, college-educated, middle-class technicians, professionals and business persons. The "unsecularization of the world," George Weigel has remarked, "is one of the dominant social facts of life in the late twentieth century." The revival of religion, "la revanche de Dieu," as Gilles Kepel labeled it, provides a basis for identity and commitment that transcends national boundaries and unites civilizations.

Fourth, the growth of civilization-consciousness is enhanced by the dual role of the West. On the one hand, the West is at a peak of power. At the same time, however, and perhaps as a result, a return to the roots phenomenon is occurring among non-Western civilizations. Increasingly one hears references to trends toward a turning inward and "Asianization" in Japan, the end of the Nehru legacy and the "Hinduization" of India, the failure of Western ideas of socialism and nationalism and hence "re-Islamization" of the Middle East, and now a debate over Westernization versus Russianization in [Russia]. A West at the peak of its power confronts non-Wests that increasingly have the desire, the will and the resources to shape the world in non-Western ways. [. . .]

Fifth, cultural characteristics and differences are less mutable and hence less easily compromised and resolved than political and economic ones. In the former Soviet Union, communists can become democrats, the rich can become poor and the poor rich, but Russians cannot become Estonians and Azeris cannot become Armenians. In class and ideological conflicts, the key question was "Which side are you on?" and people could and did choose sides and change sides. In conflicts between civilizations, the question is "What are you?" That is a given that cannot be changed. And as we know, from Bosnia to the Caucasus to the Sudan, the wrong answer to that question can mean a bullet in the head. Even more than ethnicity, religion discriminates sharply and exclusively among people. A person can be half-French and half-Arab and simultaneously even a citizen of two countries. It is more difficult to be half-Catholic and half-Muslim. [. . .]

THE FAULT LINES BETWEEN CIVILIZATIONS

The fault lines between civilizations are replacing the political and ideological boundaries of the Cold War as the flash points for crisis and bloodshed. The Cold War began when the Iron Curtain divided Europe politically and ideologically. The Cold War ended with the end of the Iron Curtain. As the ideological division of Europe has disappeared, the cultural division of Europe between Western Christianity, on the one hand, and Orthodox Christianity and Islam, on the other, has reemerged. [. . .]

Conflict along the fault line between Western and Islamic civilizations has been going on for 1,300 years. After the founding of Islam, the Arab and Moorish surge west and north only ended at Tours in 732. From the eleventh to the thirteenth century the Crusaders attempted with temporary success to bring Christianity and Christian rule to the Holy Land. From the fourteenth to the seventeenth century, the Ottoman Turks reversed the balance, extended their sway over the Middle East and the Balkans, captured Constantinople, and twice laid siege to Vienna. In the nineteenth and early twentieth centuries as Ottoman power declined Britain, France, and Italy established Western control over most of North Africa and the Middle East.

After World War II, the West, in turn, began to retreat; the colonial empires disappeared; first Arab nationalism and then Islamic fundamentalism manifested themselves; the West became heavily dependent on the Persian Gulf countries for its energy; the oil-rich Muslim countries became money-rich and, when they wished to, weapons-rich. Several wars occurred between Arabs and Israel (created by the West). France fought a bloody and ruthless war in Algeria for most of the 1950s; British and French forces invaded Egypt in 1956; American forces went into Lebanon in 1958; subsequently American forces returned to Lebanon, attacked Libya, and engaged in various military encounters with Iran; Arab and Islamic terrorists, supported by at least three Middle Eastern governments, employed the weapon of the weak and bombed Western planes and installations and seized Western hostages. This warfare between Arabs and the West culminated in 1990, when the United States sent a massive army to the Persian Gulf to defend some Arab countries against aggression by another. In its aftermath NATO planning is increasingly directed to potential threats and instability along its "southern tier."

This centuries-old military interaction between the West and Islam is unlikely to decline. It could become more virulent. The [first] Gulf War left some Arabs feeling proud that Saddam Hussein had attacked Israel and stood up to the West. It also left many feeling humiliated and resentful of the West's military presence in the Persian Gulf, the West's overwhelming military dominance, and their apparent inability to shape their own destiny. Many Arab countries, in addition to the oil exporters, are reaching levels of economic and social development where autocratic forms of government become inappropriate and efforts to introduce democracy become stronger. Some openings in Arab political systems have already occurred. The principal beneficiaries of these openings have been Islamist movements. In the Arab world, in short, Western democracy strengthens anti-Western political forces. This may be a passing phenomenon, but it surely complicates relations between Islamic countries and the West.

15

Those relations are also complicated by demography. The spectacular population growth in Arab countries, particularly in North Africa, has led to increased migration to Western Europe. The movement within Western Europe toward minimizing internal boundaries has sharpened political sensitivities with respect to this development. In Italy, France and Germany, racism is increasingly open, and political reactions and violence against Arab and Turkish migrants have become more intense and more widespread since 1990.

On both sides the interaction between Islam and the West is seen as a clash of civilizations. The West's "next confrontation," observes M. J. Akbar, an Indian Muslim author, "is definitely going to come from the Muslim world. It is in the sweep of the Islamic nations from the Maghreb to

Pakistan that the struggle for a new world order will begin." Bernard Lewis comes to a similar conclusion:

> We are facing a mood and a movement far transcending the level of issues and policies and the governments that pursue them. This is no less than a clash of civilizations—the perhaps irrational but surely historic reaction of an ancient rival against our Judeo-Christian heritage, our secular present, and the world wide expansion of both.[1] . . .

The Clash of Ignorance
Edward W. Said

Said (1935–2003) was University Professor of English and Comparative Literature at Columbia University. The following article appeared first in The Nation *(October 22, 2001).*

Samuel Huntington's article "The Clash of Civilizations?" appeared in the Summer 1993 issue of *Foreign Affairs,* where it immediately attracted a surprising amount of attention and reaction. Because the article was intended to supply Americans with an original thesis about "a new phase" in world politics after the end of the cold war, Huntington's terms of argument seemed compellingly large, bold, even visionary. He very clearly had his eye on rivals in the policy-making ranks, theorists such as Francis Fukuyama and his "end of history" ideas, as well as the legions who had celebrated the onset of globalism, tribalism and the dissipation of the state. But they, he allowed, had understood only some aspects of this new period. He was about to announce the "crucial, indeed a central, aspect" of what "global politics is likely to be in the coming years." Unhesitatingly he pressed on:

"It is my hypothesis that the fundamental source of conflict in this new world will not be primarily ideological or primarily economic. The great divisions among humankind and the dominating source of conflict will be cultural. Nation states will remain the most powerful actors in world affairs, but the principal conflicts of global politics will occur between nations and groups of different civilizations. The clash of civilizations will dominate global politics. The fault lines between civilizations will be the battle lines of the future."

Most of the argument in the pages that followed relied on a vague notion of something Huntington called "civilization identity" and "the interactions among seven or eight [*sic*] major civilizations," of which the conflict between two of them, Islam and the West, gets the lion's share of his attention. In this belligerent kind of thought, he relies heavily on a 1990 article by the veteran Orientalist Bernard Lewis, whose ideological colors are manifest in its title, "The Roots of Muslim Rage." In both articles, the personification

---

[1] Bernard Lewis, "The Roots of Muslim Rage," *The Atlantic Monthly,* vol. 266, September 1990, p. 60; *Time,* June 15, 1992, pp. 24–28.

of enormous entities called "the West" and "Islam" is recklessly affirmed, as if hugely complicated matters like identity and culture existed in a cartoon-like world where Popeye and Bluto bash each other mercilessly, with one always more virtuous pugilist getting the upper hand over his adversary. Certainly neither Huntington nor Lewis has much time to spare for the internal dynamics and plurality of every civilization, or for the fact that the major contest in most modern cultures concerns the definition or interpretation of each culture, or for the unattractive possibility that a great deal of demagogy and downright ignorance is involved in presuming to speak for a whole religion or civilization. No, the West is the West, and Islam Islam.

The challenge for Western policy-makers, says Huntington, is to make sure that the West gets stronger and fends off all the others, Islam in particular. More troubling is Huntington's assumption that his perspective, which is to survey the entire world from a perch outside all ordinary attachments and hidden loyalties, is the correct one, as if everyone else were scurrying around looking for the answers that he has already found. In fact, Huntington is an ideologist, someone who wants to make "civilizations" and "identities" into what they are not: shut-down, sealed-off entities that have been purged of the myriad currents and countercurrents that animate human history, and that over centuries have made it possible for that history not only to contain wars of religion and imperial conquest but also to be one of exchange, cross-fertilization and sharing. This far less visible history is ignored in the rush to highlight the ludicrously compressed and constricted warfare that "the clash of civilizations" argues is the reality. [. . .]

This is the problem with unedifying labels like Islam and the West: They mislead and confuse the mind, which is trying to make sense of a disorderly reality that won't be pigeonholed or strapped down as easily as all that. I remember interrupting a man who, after a lecture I had given at a West Bank university in 1994, rose from the audience and started to attack my ideas as "Western," as opposed to the strict Islamic ones he espoused. "Why are you wearing a suit and tie?" was the first retort that came to mind. "They're Western too." He sat down with an embarrassed smile on his face, but I recalled the incident when information on the September 11 terrorists started to come in: how they had mastered all the technical details required to inflict their homicidal evil on the World Trade Center, the Pentagon and the aircraft they had commandeered. Where does one draw the line between "Western" technology and [. . .] "Islam's" inability to be a part of "modernity"?

One cannot easily do so, of course. How finally inadequate are the labels, generalizations and cultural assertions. [. . .]

In a remarkable series of three articles published between January and March 1999 in *Dawn*, Pakistan's most respected weekly, the late Eqbal Ahmad, writing for a Muslim audience, analyzed what he called the roots of the religious right, coming down very harshly on the mutilations of

Islam by absolutists and fanatical tyrants whose obsession with regulating personal behavior promotes "an Islamic order reduced to a penal code, stripped of its humanism, aesthetics, intellectual quests, and spiritual devotion." And this "entails an absolute assertion of one, generally decontextualized, aspect of religion and a total disregard of another. The phenomenon distorts religion, debases tradition, and twists the political process wherever it unfolds." As a timely instance of this debasement, Ahmad proceeds first to present the rich, complex, pluralist meaning of the word *jihad* and then goes on to show that in the word's current confinement to indiscriminate war against presumed enemies, it is impossible "to recognize the Islamic—religion, society, culture, history or politics—as lived and experienced by Muslims through the ages." The modern Islamists, Ahmad concludes, are "concerned with power, not with the soul; with the mobilization of people for political purposes rather than with sharing and alleviating their sufferings and aspirations. Theirs is a very limited and time-bound political agenda." What has made matters worse is that similar distortions and zealotry occur in the "Jewish" and "Christian" universes of discourse. [. . .]

[T]here are closer ties between apparently warring civilizations than most of us would like to believe; both Freud and Nietzsche showed how the traffic across carefully maintained, even policed boundaries moves with often terrifying ease. But then such fluid ideas, full of ambiguity and skepticism about notions that we hold on to, scarcely furnish us with suitable, practical guidelines for situations such as the one we face now. Hence the altogether more reassuring battle orders (a crusade, good versus evil, freedom against fear, etc.) drawn out of Huntington's alleged opposition between Islam and the West, from which official discourse drew its vocabulary in the first days after the September 11 attacks. There's since been a noticeable deescalation in that discourse, but to judge from the steady amount of hate speech and actions, plus reports of law enforcement efforts directed against Arabs, Muslims and Indians all over the country, the paradigm stays on.

One further reason for its persistence is the increased presence of Muslims all over Europe and the United States. Think of the populations today of France, Italy, Germany, Spain, Britain, America, even Sweden, and you must concede that Islam is no longer on the fringes of the West but at its center. [. . .]

Then there is the persisting legacy of monotheism itself, the Abrahamic   10
religions, as Louis Massignon aptly called them. Beginning with Judaism and Christianity, each is a successor haunted by what came before; for Muslims, Islam fulfills and ends the line of prophecy. There is still no decent history or demystification of the many-sided contest among these three followers—not one of them by any means a monolithic, unified camp—of the most jealous of all gods, even though the bloody modern convergence on Palestine furnishes a rich secular instance of what has been so tragically irreconcilable about them. Not surprisingly, then, Muslims and Christians

speak readily of crusades and *jihads*, both of them eliding the Judaic presence with often sublime insouciance. Such an agenda, says Eqbal Ahmad, is "very reassuring to the men and women who are stranded in the middle of the ford, between the deep waters of tradition and modernity."

But we are all swimming in those waters, Westerners and Muslims and others alike. And since the waters are part of the ocean of history, trying to plow or divide them with barriers is futile. These are tense times, but it is better to think in terms of powerful and powerless communities, the secular politics of reason and ignorance, and universal principles of justice and injustice, than to wander off in search of vast abstractions that may give momentary satisfaction but little self-knowledge or informed analysis. "The Clash of Civilizations" thesis is a gimmick like "The War of the Worlds," better for reinforcing defensive self-pride than for critical understanding of the bewildering interdependence of our time.

The Enemy Is Not Islam: It Is Nihilism
Charles Krauthammer

A distinguished columnist and public intellectual, Krauthammer has influence in the Bush administration, where he serves on the President's Council for Bioethics. Nihilism means "total rejection of all existing political and social institutions and traditional religious and moral values" (Scribner's Dictionary).

Europe's great religious wars ended in 1648. Three and a half centuries is a long time, too long for us in the West to truly believe that people still slaughter others to vindicate the faith.

Thus in the face of radical Islamic terrorism that murders [3,000] innocents in a day, we find it almost impossible to accept at face value the reason offered by the murderers. Yet Osama bin Laden could not be clearer. Jihad has been declared against the infidel, whose power and influence thwart the triumph of Islam, and whose success and example—indeed, whose very existence—are an affront to the true faith. As a leader of Hamas declared at a rally three days after the World Trade Center attack, "[T]he only solution is for Bush to convert to Islam."

To Americans, who are taught religious tolerance from the cradle, who visit each other's churches for interdenominational succor and solidarity, this seems simply bizarre. On September 25, bin Laden issues a warning to his people that Bush is coming "under the banner of the cross." Two weeks later, in his pre-taped post-attack video, he scorns Bush as "head of the infidels."

Can he be serious? This idea is so alien that our learned commentators, Western and secular, have gone rummaging through their ideological attics to find more familiar terms to explain why we were so savagely attacked: poverty and destitution in the Islamic world; grievances against the West, America, Israel; the "wretched of the earth"—Frantz Fanon's 1960s apotheosis of anti-colonialism—rising against their oppressors.

Reading conventional notions of class struggle and anti-colonialism   5
into bin Laden, the Taliban, and radical Islam is not just solipsistic. It is nonsense. If poverty and destitution, colonialism and capitalism are animating radical Islam, explain this: In March, the Taliban went to the Afghan desert where stood great monuments of human culture, two massive Buddhas carved out of a cliff. At first, Taliban soldiers tried artillery. The 1,500-year-old masterpieces proved too hardy. The Taliban had to resort to dynamite. They blew the statues to bits, then slaughtered 100 cows in atonement—for having taken so long to finish the job.

Buddhism is hardly a representative of the West. It is hardly a cause of poverty and destitution. It is hardly a symbol of colonialism. No. The statues represented two things: an alternative faith and a great work of civilization. To the Taliban, the presence of both was intolerable.

The distinguished Indian writer and now Nobel Prize winner V. S. Naipaul, who has chronicled the Islamic world in two books (*Among the Believers* and *Beyond Belief*), recently warned (in a public talk in Melbourne before the World Trade Center attack), "We are within reach of great nihilistic forces that have undone civilization." In places like Afghanistan, "religion has been turned by some into a kind of nihilism, where people wish to destroy themselves and destroy their past and their culture . . . to be pure. They are enraged about the world and they wish to pull it down." This kind of fury and fanaticism is unappeasable. It knows no social, economic, or political solution. "You cannot converge with this [position] because it holds that your life is worthless and your beliefs are criminal and should be extirpated."

This insight offers a needed window on the new enemy. It turns out that the enemy does have recognizable analogues in the Western experience. He is, as President Bush averred in his address to the nation, heir to the malignant ideologies of the 20th century. In its nihilism, its will to power, its celebration of blood and death, its craving for the cleansing purity that comes only from eradicating life and culture, radical Islam is heir, above all, to Nazism. The destruction of the World Trade Center was meant not only to wreak terror. Like the smashing of the Bamiyan Buddhas, it was meant to obliterate greatness and beauty, elegance and grace. These artifacts represented civilization embodied in stone or steel. They had to be destroyed.

This worship of death and destruction is a nihilism of a ferocity unlike any since the Nazis burned books, then art, then whole peoples. Goebbels would have marvelled at the recruitment tape for al Qaeda, a two-hour orgy of blood and death: image after image of brutalized Muslims shown in various poses of victimization, followed by glorious images of desecration of the infidel—mutilated American soldiers in Somalia, the destruction of the USS *Cole,* mangled bodies at the American embassies in Kenya and Tanzania. Throughout, the soundtrack endlessly repeats the refrain "with blood, with blood, with blood." Bin Laden appears on the tape to counsel that "the love of this world is wrong. You should love the other world . . . die in the right cause and go to the other world." In his October 9 taped message, al Qaeda spokesman Sulaiman abu Ghaith gloried in the "thousands of young people who look forward to death, like the Americans look forward to living."

Once again, the world is faced with a transcendent conflict between   10
those who love life and those who love death both for themselves and their enemies. Which is why we tremble. Upon witnessing the first atomic bomb explode at the Trinity site at Alamogordo, J. Robert Oppenheimer recited a verse from the Hindu scripture *Bhagavad Gita:* "Now I am become death, the destroyer of worlds." We tremble because for the first time in history, nihilism will soon be armed with the ultimate weapons of annihilation. For the first time in history, the nihilist will have the means to match his ends. Which is why the war declared upon us on September 11 is the most urgent not only of our lives, but in the life of civilization itself.

Terrorism in the Name of God
Yonah Alexander

An internationally recognized expert on terrorism, Alexander directs the Inter-University Center for Terrorism Studies in Arlington, Virginia. His article appeared in World and I *(October 2002).*

History is filled with evidence that religions contain many elements of ha-tred and antagonism toward other religions. Consequently, fighting between enemy camps in the name of faith has not been unusual. Similarly, terror-ism, as a cost-effective tool of low-intensity conflict that projects psychologi-cal intimidation and physical force in violation of law, has ancient roots.

Examples are attacks mounted by Jewish religious extremists, known as the Zealot Sicarii, against the Romans in occupied Judaea, as well as the martyrdom missions of the Assassins, targeting the Crusaders in the Middle East. The former were active for 70 years in the first century, and the latter lasted some 200 years from the eleventh to the thirteenth centuries.

Present-day terrorists nourished by theological roots have introduced a new scale of violence. Their threats and responses make it clear that we have entered an age of terrorism, with serious implications for national, re-gional, and global security concerns. Perhaps the most significant dangers are those relating to the safety, welfare, and rights of ordinary people; the stability of the state system; the health of economic development; the ex-pansion of democracy; and possibly the survival of civilization itself. [. . .]

This article focuses on two major theological Arab terrorist groups, Hamas and Palestinian Islamic Jihad (PIJ), which pose a serious challenge to the security interests of the United States and its allies. These movements are members of the al Qaeda international framework currently operating in some 80 countries around the world.

PALESTINIAN THEOLOGICAL TERRORISM

"Holy" terrorism in the name of higher Islamic imperatives is the leading spoiler of Middle Eastern peace. Clearly, the spread of "sacred" Islamic violence is rapidly becoming one of the most serious challenges to regional and global stability. This threat does not come from traditional Islam or even fundamentalist Islam, which is dedicated to the search for social and political organization on the basis of Islamic values. The true threat comes from radical movements that use terrorism to achieve their goals and justify their barbaric actions on the basis of misinterpretation of Islam.

The Islamic Resistance Movement—Hamas—was officially founded in 1978, shortly after the outbreak of the first Palestinian intifada (uprising). The movement's roots can be traced to the 1940s as an extension of the Muslim Brotherhood. During the first intifada, the leaders of the Muslim Brotherhood realized that the time was ripe to add a military component to their organization. The group took active measures against Israel, educating youth against its existence.

A large part of Hamas' success is due to its influence in the Gaza Strip. The socioeconomic hardships of refugees in Gaza and the fact that other nationalist parties were not dominant at the time enabled Hamas to increase its following. The PLO center of activity in the late 1970s and '80s was in Tunisia—a factor that contributed to the development of local Palestinian leadership. Hamas was also successful in forming a social system, providing an alternative to the PLO.

In August 1988, Hamas published its ideological doctrine, the Islamic Covenant. The covenant challenges both Israel and the PLO and claims that Hamas is the sole legitimate representative of the Palestinian people. Hamas' participation in street violence during the intifada contributed to that organization's central role in the uprising and increased its popularity and growth.

After the Gulf War, Hamas became the leading terrorist entity in the occupied territories and the single most powerful group, after Fatah, headed by Yasser Arafat. In 1991, Ziccaria Walid Akhel established the Izz al-Din al-Qassam Battalions, which kidnapped and executed suspected collaborators with Israel.

The deportation of 415 Hamas and Islamic Jihad activists from Israel by the Yitzhak Rabin government in 1992 marked a changing point in policy. Hamas decided to adopt Hezbollah terrorist methods and began using car bombs, suicide bombers, and kidnappings against Israeli civilians and military personnel.

The 1993 Oslo Accords and the signing of the Declaration of Principles between Israel and the Palestinian Authority (PA) changed the strategic situation. The agreement put an end to the intifada, and the PLO's agreement to curtail violence in the territories threatened Hamas' military abilities and freedom of action. The Hamas leadership nevertheless decided to continue the jihad against Israel, while preserving unity within the Palestinian ranks. Hamas escalated the violence through suicide bombings, which thwarted the peace process and at times threatened to stop it completely.

Since the establishment of the PA in 1994, Hamas' civic activities have focused on maintaining a strong opposition to the PA, in the short term, and then creating a possible alternative to it. The PA views Hamas as a serious challenge to its power.

In an attempt to limit the organization's activity following the February–March 1996 terrorism attacks on Israeli citizens, the PA took steps against Hamas' financial base by closing down several charitable organizations and confiscating funds and equipment. These actions, along with Israel's crackdown on the Islamic movement in Um al-Fahem and Nazareth (two cities in Israel), significantly hindered Hamas' activities and financial resources.

Hamas maintains charitable institutions in Jerusalem, the West Bank, the Gaza Strip, the United States, Saudi Arabia, the Gulf States, Iran, and elsewhere. Those networks focus on providing aid to the families of terrorists who committed suicide bombings, or to prisoners and their families. It also provides funding for Hamas' military operations.

The outbreak of the second intifada was seen as a strategic opportunity   15
to continue the resistance to Israel's occupation and boost Palestinian national unity. From September 2000 to March 2002, Hamas took responsibility for approximately 40 suicide bombing incidents, taking the lives of over 400 Israeli citizens.

In sum, Hamas [. . .] has five major objectives. First is a commitment to Islam as a way of life. Second, the destruction of the "Zionist Entity" [Israel] is seen as the only solution to the Arab-Israeli conflict. The movement contends that the third goal, creation of a Palestinian Arab state replacing Israel, is vital because Israel is located on Islamic sacred land. Thus, any concessions that would leave part of the land in Israel's hands constitute treason to the Palestinian-Arab cause and signify heresy. The fourth and fifth goals are the synthesis of pan-Islamic religious ideals and Palestinian nationalism and violent opposition to the Israel-Palestinian peace process.

PALESTINIAN ISLAMIC JIHAD

In recent years, the PIJ has become the most prominent Palestinian terrorist group to adopt the jihadist ideology. It views Israel as the main enemy of Muslims and a target for destruction. Thus, it calls for an Islamic armed struggle in order to liberate all of Palestine.

The desired tactic is the use of guerrilla groups, led by a revolutionary vanguard, to carry out terrorist attacks aimed at weakening Israel. PIJ militants see themselves as laying the groundwork for the day when a great Islamic army will destroy Israel in a military confrontation. The faction launched some of the deadliest terrorist suicide attacks carried out in Israel from 1995 to 2000.

Palestinian students in Egypt who had split from the Muslim Brotherhood in the Gaza Strip founded the PIJ in 1979–1980. The founders were influenced by the Islamic revolution in Iran and also by the radicalization and militancy of student organizations in Egypt.

[They] were concerned that the Muslim Brotherhood movement was neglecting the Palestinian question and the establishment of a Palestinian state. They proposed an alternative ideology, which became the basis for the new organization. Their central claim is that the unity of the Islamic world is not a precondition to the liberation of Palestine; rather, the liberation was a key to the unification of the Islamic world. They believe that jihad by Islamic groups will liberate Palestine and reconstruct a greater and unified Islamic state.

The PIJ evolved as an umbrella organization comprising several fundamentalist Muslim groups. These factors operate separately but share an allegiance to the Islamic regime in Iran and its goal of putting the region under Islamic law. The PIJ has been characterized as one of the most radical and violent Islamic organizations in the Middle East.

The PIJ attempted to capitalize on the intifada soon after it erupted in December 1987. It was the first radical organization to issue a call for general strikes. The attempt to lead the popular violent movement ended in failure after the arrest and subsequent deportation of its leaders and the arrest of their replacements in Gaza in mid-1988.

Reports state that the Islamic Jihad is used by Syrian intelligence agencies to carry out terrorist operations. Items in the Lebanese news media have linked the PIJ to the Lebanon-based and Iranian-backed Hezbollah. It is believed that the organizations have coordinated training exercises and terrorist attacks.

The PIJ has maintained a more radical position than that of Hamas, but it has also been willing to negotiate with the PLO. A PIJ leader stated in January 1993 his group could possibly join the PLO, if the latter group underwent a fundamental transformation of its ideological and strategic policies. Yet it refused to do so when Israel deported more than 100 of its members, along with several hundred Hamas activists, to southern Lebanon in December 1993.

Following the Oslo Accords between Israel and the PLO, Shqaqi expanded the political connection. The PIJ became a member of the new Syrian-influenced Rejection Front, a coalition of terror groups opposed to the Israeli-PLO accord.

The PIJ and Hamas were considered rivals in the Gaza Strip until after the establishment of the PA in 1994. Since then, there has been operational

20

25

cooperation between the two organizations in carrying out terror attacks. [. . .]

After Hamas switched to suicide bombings in the late 1980s, the two groups developed some operational cooperation in carrying out the terrorist attacks. America's strong support for Israel has made it a PIJ target, as well. In July 2000, the PIJ threatened to attack U.S. interests if the American embassy were moved to Jerusalem from Tel Aviv.

Since the outbreak of the second intifada, the PIJ has been collaborating with Hamas on a number of suicide bombings. In April 2002, during Operation Defensive Wall, Israel's latest attempt to break down Palestinian terrorist networks in the West Bank and the Gaza Strip, new light was shed on the connection between the PA and Palestinian religious terrorist groups.

The Israeli Defense Forces discovered documents revealing cooperation between the PA and both the Hamas and PIJ movements. The cooperation includes executing large-scale suicide attacks in Israel. [. . .]

In sum, the PIJ's ideology is based on three fundamental objectives: 30 first, the destruction of the state of Israel through violent means, which is the primary objective of the jihad; second, the overthrow of Arab governments that do not uphold Islamic law; and third, harsh criticism of the PLO because of its involvement in the peace process with Israel. According to the PIJ, such cooperation threatens the continuation and further escalation of the Palestinian uprising.

CONCLUSION

In July 2000, a Middle East peace summit was hosted at Camp David by President Clinton. Unfortunately, PA Chairman Yasser Arafat rejected the American-initiated plan for peace. He decided to achieve through violence what he could not realize through negotiations. Two years after the outbreak of the current intifada, the wave of terrorist attacks supported by the PA continues and is likely to grow. A major element in the expansion of terrorism is the destructive role played by Islamic-oriented groups like Hamas and the PIJ. In August, the latest major attack by Hamas at the Hebrew University campus in Jerusalem killed 7 (including 5 U.S. citizens) and wounded 86, once again underscoring the challenge to regional and global stability.

The Islamic-based rationalization of terrorism is illustrated by a communication emerging from a religious convention held in Beirut in January 2002. Attended by representatives of Hamas and PIJ, it was hosted by Hezbollah's "Party of God." The conference also attracted Muslim clerics from Lebanon, the PA, Sudan, the United Arab Emirates, Morocco, Algeria, and Jordan. The participants issued an official declaration in support of suicide bombings against Israel, stating that the "suicide attacks against Israel are legitimate according to the Qur'an." Suicide attacks, they said, are a "strategic weapon which enable us to regain the strategic balance with the Zionist enemy."

The complete surrender of religion to Arab political needs is the most alarming threat to peace in the Middle East. That is, Hamas and the PIJ have carefully, systematically, and continuously tailored their messages to specific audiences, at home and abroad, with a theological jargon that produces an extreme, self-righteous form of nationalism. Through the spoken and written word, including graphics, these groups drew upon those components of Islam that helped them to severely damage the credibility of Israel's case while fostering their own on unassailable terms.

Their interpretation of jihad, which regards any deviation as a "shameful sin against religion" and a "renunciation of Islam," must be treated in relation to the secular Arab pledge for Israel's annihilation. The identification of both religious and political obligations of Arab resistance to the Jewish state has played a key role in molding Islamic "Israelphobia," particularly among more observant Muslims.

The vehement campaigns of Hamas and the PIJ are generating more acts of terrorism, destroying regional peace efforts, and encouraging anti-Semitism throughout the world. The war against terrorism, led by the United States, must therefore continue in the Middle East and elsewhere.   35

Blowback
Chalmers Johnson

A frequent contributor to the Los Angeles Times *and* The Nation, *Johnson is the author of many books on East Asia and political violence. This article is based on his book* Blowback: The Costs and Consequences of American Empire.

For Americans who can bear to think about it, those tragic pictures from New York of women holding up photos of their husbands, sons and daughters and asking if anyone knows anything about them look familiar. They are similar to scenes we have seen from Buenos Aires and Santiago. There, too, starting in the 1970s, women held up photos of their loved ones, asking for information. Since it was far too dangerous then to say aloud what they thought had happened to them—that they had been tortured and murdered by US-backed military juntas—the women coined a new word for them, *los desaparecidos*—"the disappeareds." Our government has never been honest about its own role in the 1973 overthrow of the elected government of Salvador Allende in Chile or its backing, through "Operation Condor," of what the State Department has recently called "extrajudicial killings" in Argentina, Paraguay, Brazil and elsewhere in Latin America. But we now have several thousand of our own disappeareds, and we are badly mistaken if we think that we in the United States are entirely blameless for what happened to them.

The suicidal assassins of September 11, 2001, did not "attack America," as our political leaders and the news media like to maintain; they attacked American foreign policy. Employing the strategy of the weak, they killed innocent bystanders who then became enemies only because they had already become victims. Terrorism by definition strikes at the innocent in order to draw attention to the sins of the invulnerable. The United States deploys such overwhelming military force globally that for its militarized opponents only an "asymmetric strategy," in the jargon of the Pentagon, has any chance of success. When it does succeed, as it did spectacularly on September 11, it renders our massive military machine worthless: The terrorists offer it no targets. On the day of the disaster, President George W. Bush told the American people that we were attacked because we are "a beacon for freedom" and because the attackers were "evil." In his address to Congress on September 20, he said, "This is civilization's fight." This attempt to define difficult-to-grasp events as only a conflict over abstract values — as a "clash of civilizations," in current post–cold war American jargon — is not only disingenuous but also a way of evading responsibility for the "blowback" that America's imperial projects have generated.

"Blowback" is a CIA term first used in March 1954 in a recently declassified report on the 1953 operation to overthrow the government of Mohammed Mossadegh in Iran. It is a metaphor for the unintended consequences of the US government's international activities that have been kept secret from the American people. The CIA's fears that there might ultimately be some blowback from its egregious interference in the affairs of Iran were well founded. Installing the Shah in power brought twenty-five years of tyranny and repression to the Iranian people and elicited the Ayatollah Khomeini's revolution. The staff of the American embassy in Teheran was held hostage for more than a year. This misguided "covert operation" of the US government helped convince many capable people throughout the Islamic world that the United States was an implacable enemy.

The pattern has become all too familiar. Osama bin Laden, the leading suspect as mastermind behind the carnage of September 11, is no more (or less) "evil" than his fellow creations of our CIA: Manuel Noriega, former commander of the Panama Defense Forces until George Bush pere in late 1989 invaded his country and kidnapped him, or Iraq's Saddam Hussein, whom we armed and backed so long as he was at war with Khomeini's Iran and whose people we have bombed and starved for a decade in an incompetent effort to get rid of him. These men were once listed as "assets" of our clandestine services organization.

Osama bin Laden joined our call for resistance to the Soviet Union's   5
1979 invasion of Afghanistan and accepted our military training and equipment along with countless other mujahedeen "freedom fighters." It was only after the Russians bombed Afghanistan back into the stone age and

suffered a Vietnam-like defeat, and we turned our backs on the death and destruction we had helped cause, that he turned against us. The last straw as far as bin Laden was concerned was that, after the Gulf War, we based "infidel" American troops in Saudi Arabia to prop up its decadent, fiercely authoritarian regime. Ever since, bin Laden has been attempting to bring the things the CIA taught him home to the teachers. On September 11, he appears to have returned to his deadly project with a vengeance.

There are today, ten years after the demise of the Soviet Union, some 800 Defense Department installations located in other countries. The people of the United States make up perhaps 4 percent of the world's population but consume 40 percent of its resources. They exercise hegemony over the world directly through overwhelming military might and indirectly through secretive organizations like the World Bank, the International Monetary Fund and the World Trade Organization. Though largely dominated by the US government, these are formally international organizations and therefore beyond Congressional oversight.

As the American-inspired process of "globalization" inexorably enlarges the gap between the rich and the poor, a popular movement against it has gained strength, advancing from its first demonstrations in Seattle in 1999 through protests in Washington, DC; Melbourne; Prague; Seoul; Nice; Barcelona; Quebec City; Goteborg; and on to its violent confrontations in Genoa earlier this year. Ironically, though American leaders are deaf to the desires of the protesters, the Defense Department has actually adopted the movement's main premise—that current global economic arrangements mean more wealth for the "West" and more misery for the "rest"—as a reason why the United States should place weapons in space. The US Space Command's pamphlet "Vision for 2020" argues that "the globalization of the world economy will also continue, with a widening between the 'haves' and the 'have-nots'," and that we have a mission to "dominate the space dimension of military operations to protect US interests and investments" in an increasingly dangerous and implicitly anti-American world. Unfortunately, while the eyes of military planners were firmly focused on the "control and domination" of space and "denying other countries access to space," a very different kind of space was suddenly occupied.

On the day after the September 11 attack, Democratic Senator Zell Miller of Georgia declared, "I say, bomb the hell out of them. If there's collateral damage, so be it." "Collateral damage" is another of those hateful euphemisms invented by our military to prettify its killing of the defenseless. It is the term Pentagon spokesmen use to refer to the Serb and Iraqi civilians who were killed or maimed by bombs from high-flying American warplanes in our campaigns against Slobodan Milosevic and Saddam Hussein. It is the kind of word our new ambassador to the United Nations, John Negroponte, might have used in the 1980s to explain the slaughter of peasants, Indians and church workers by American-backed right-wing death squads in E1 Salvador, Guatemala, Honduras and Nicaragua while he was ambassador to Honduras. These activities made the Reagan years the worst decade for Central America since the Spanish conquest.

Massive military retaliation with its inevitable "collateral damage" will, of course, create more desperate and embittered childless parents and parentless children, and so recruit more maddened people to the terrorists' cause. In fact, mindless bombing is surely one of the responses their grisly strategy hopes to elicit. Moreover, a major crisis in the Middle East will inescapably cause a rise in global oil prices, with, from the assassins' point of view, desirable destabilizing effects on all the economies of the advanced industrial nations.

What should we do? The following is a start on what, in a better world, we might modestly think about doing. But let me concede at the outset that none of this is going to happen. The people in Washington who run our government believe that they can now get all the things they wanted before the trade towers came down: more money for the military, ballistic missile defenses, more freedom for the intelligence services and removal of the last modest restrictions (no assassinations, less domestic snooping, fewer lists given to "friendly" foreign police of people we want executed) that the Vietnam era placed on our leaders. An inevitable consequence of big "blowback" events like this one is that, the causes having been largely kept from American eyes (if not Islamic or Latin American ones), people cannot make the necessary connections for an explanation. Popular support for Washington is thus, at least for a while, staggeringly high. [. . .]

More difficult than [. . .] fairly simple reforms would be to bring our rampant militarism under control. From George Washington's "farewell address" to Dwight Eisenhower's invention of the phrase "military-industrial complex," American leaders have warned about the dangers of a bloated, permanent, expensive military establishment that has lost its relationship to the country because service in it is no longer an obligation of citizenship. Our military operates the biggest arms sales operation on earth; it rapes girls, women and schoolchildren in Okinawa; it cuts ski-lift cables in Italy, killing twenty vacationers, and dismisses what its insubordinate pilots have done as a "training accident"; it allows its nuclear attack submarines to be used for joy rides for wealthy civilian supporters and then covers up the negligence that caused the sinking of a Japanese high school training ship; it propagandizes the nation with Hollywood films glorifying military service (Pearl Harbor); and it manipulates the political process to get more carrier task forces, antimissile missiles, nuclear weapons, stealth bombers and other expensive gadgets for which we have no conceivable use. Two of the most influential federal institutions are not in Washington but on the south side of the Potomac River—the Defense Department and the Central Intelligence Agency. Given their influence today, one must conclude that [what] the government outlined in the Constitution of 1787 no longer bears much relationship to the government that actually rules from

10

Washington. Until that is corrected, we should probably stop talking about "democracy" and "human rights." [. . .]

If we do these things, the crisis will recede. If we play into the hands of the terrorists, we will see more collateral damage among our own citizens. Ten years ago, the other so-called superpower, the former Soviet Union, disappeared almost overnight because of internal contradictions, imperial overstretch and an inability to reform. We have always been richer, so it might well take longer for similar contradictions to afflict our society. But it is nowhere written that the United States, in its guise as an empire dominating the world, must go on forever.

Terrorism as a Gender War
Leo Braudy

Braudy is a distinguished professor at the University of Southern California. The following article is an abridged version of the last chapter of his celebrated book, From Chivalry to Terrorism: War and the Changing Notion of Masculinity *(Knopf, 2003).*

As a history comes closer and closer to the present, the broad outlines of many trends become more confused and various. The events of September 11, 2001, and the subsequent war in Afghanistan against the Taliban and Al Qaeda thus cast an intriguing light on many of the issues [about masculinity and war] considered in these pages.

One central issue has been the many threats to the legitimacy of the nation-state, especially as it was defined in Europe over the last few hundred years to be the unquestioned summum bonum of human political organization. The United Nations and whatever submission of national sovereignty to the world good it implies is one kind of threat; religiously based terrorism and its hostility to secular societies is another. Since its birth in the sixteenth century, the European nation-state had stepped into the gap between individual male values and their military embodiment by taking to itself the awarding of honor and the waging of war. But by the end of the twentieth century the state was losing that function, or at least its mythic connections, especially in the industrialized world. Nations might have armies, but armies were often no longer the sole or even primary repository of "real men."

Yet even with global economic, cultural, and political connections increasing, the state persists as a prime form of human organization. Globalism has modified, and will continue to modify, some of its structures but will hardly usher it out of existence. [. . .]

[. . .] Modern terrorism first came onto the world stage as the political aggression of the disenfranchised, either in the name of alternate na-

tionalisms (as in Algeria, Northern Ireland, and Israel), or in the attacks
against world capitalism made by radical groups in Europe and Japan in
the 1960s and 1970s. It was preeminently a politics of individuals and
small groups, and as it developed, it came to represent the dark side of
global interconnections, relying for its capital on a system of worldwide
finance that also protected the finances of multinational corporations from
scrutiny [. . .].

Like the guerrilla warfare of the past, which usually focused on attacks   5
by natives against the foreign occupiers of their country, early terrorism was
the weapon of small cultures fighting for autonomy and, above all, for publicity on the world stage. Since it first came to worldwide notice with the attacks on Israeli athletes at the 1972 Olympics, terrorism, even more than
guerrilla warfare, has been primarily symbolic and propagandistic: the
weapon of the weak against the strong, meant to galvanize opinion, focus energies, and create solidarity for one's side rather than win decisively.
[. . . G]uerrilla tactics of harassment, sabotage, and, above all, avoidance of
pitched battle emphasize a war of attrition, and the need for technologically
superior professional forces to climb down out of their electronic control
rooms and fight on the ground, or else to leave.

Terrorist tactics in general try to imply that all the high technology in the
world cannot stop a determined enemy, even one armed only with primitive
weapons, especially if it is psychologically bent on self-sacrifice. But the tactics of suicide bombers oddly resemble the changes in other more conventional national armies in that they rely on small professional forces, in which
semi-independent groups are the most effective combatants. The soldier is
no longer a member of an actual army but of, at most, a small group [. . .].

The September 11 attacks, however, show how the previously nationalistic and quasi-political goals of terrorism have changed into something
more apocalyptic, summoning the imagery of Armaggedon if not the actu-
ality and making those groups, even the most militant Palestinians, who
are actually fighting for a state with its own sovereignty, seem by contrast
rational and part of the world community.

Commentators have often been puzzled by the new fundamentalisms
in the world, Christian, Jewish, Islamic, Hindu—in virtually all traditional
religions. But I would say that this is a neglected aspect of the general drift
of the world toward more global structures of relationship and away from
the nation-states that have dominated political life since the Renaissance.
Not all globalization can be comprehended in the rise of multinational corporations, the appearance of American fast-food companies on the street
corners of Asia and Africa, or the ability to recognize the face of Muhammad Ali or Michael Jackson.

The challenge of Osama bin Laden and Islamic fundamentalism [. . .] is
that they want to establish a global definition of both civilization and masculinity based on their particular beliefs and even their biochemistry. Other
fundamentalisms are still working within the nationalistic framework.

However much they might want to change their own country into a holier place, it is still their country that they are changing. But Islam, unlike Christianity, developed without a military, imperialist Rome to play its own beliefs against. As a result, in some versions it has retained a more male and warrior-oriented aspect than has Christianity, which even in its most militant periods has had an alternate, even pacifist tradition that could be appealed to.[1]

Faced with a movement that dispensed with national boundaries, the United States turned the terrorist attack against New York and Washington into a conventional war by targeting the nation-state most clearly associated with those who launched the attacks. But terrorism of the bin Laden sort seeks no battle so keenly as the battle of the spirit. Suicide fighters of the past, like the kamikaze pilots of World War II, represented one strategy (a last-ditch one at that) among many. They also drew upon many of the same emotions that recruiters excited in the suicide bombers: the commitment to religion along with the promise of glory [. . .].

In a sense, then, modern terrorism resembles assassination more than it does war. Focusing upon individuals and symbolic places, what could its tangible gains be? The Brigada Rossa terrorist wanted to bring down the Italian government, the Algerian terrorist to free his country from France, the Stern Gang terrorist to get the British out of Palestine, the Palestinian terrorist to win recognition for a Palestinian state. What gains were expected if the attacks of September 11 were "successful" in any long-range sense? [. . .] Most of the political demands Osama bin Laden outlined before September 11, like the withdrawal of U.S. troops from Saudi Arabia, call for America to pull back from its intervention in the rest of the world, just as Japanese military planners sought to get the United States not to interfere in Japan's expansion into East Asia and the Pacific. Here is another analogy between Pearl Harbor and September 11: both seem to have been meant to warn the United States away from an area of the world, to make American politicians realize that they didn't want to risk soldiers in such battles—but both succeeded only in provoking further military commitment.

So far as political goals go, then, the Al Qaeda network is hardly interested in defeating the United States and taking over the country. They want instead to frighten Americans away from Muslim countries and convince audiences that Al Qaeda should have political power there, not in the United States. They seek to bring down the great Satan, capitalism, America, whiteness, Christianity, the West—whatever it is—and thereby enhance themselves. The attacks are not about nationhood but about masculine tribal self-esteem.

---

[1] Christianity also absorbed more of the matriarchal traditions that preceded it. There is no equivalent in Islam to the figure of Mary, and therefore little alternative to male clerical authority.

The paradox of the attacks is thus that, whatever the devastation and loss of life they wreak, they ultimately fail as warfare on other than the psychological level. Just as before the September 11 attacks, American military power, along with the support it can summon especially from its European allies, is unprecedented in world history. Even more importantly, as the war in Afghanistan demonstrated, lessons about the relation between bombing and ground troops, trying to win hearts and minds as well as defeat the enemy, and quitting while you are ahead instead of seeking absolute victory have begun to be learned, however falteringly and inconsistently. After some gross missteps (like George W. Bush's use of the word "crusade"), the American government tried to present an ecumenical image to the world, responding with a message of inclusiveness to bin Laden's insistence on the rhetoric of absolute difference. Bush in his early statements presented himself as more like Shane, the patient man pushed beyond all endurance, than like John Wayne, the berserker plunging into the heat of battle. It was later, after what appeared to be American victories, that the more bellicose rhetoric took over, including the effort to expand the war to the "axis of evil"—an obvious attempt to apply the language and the emotional associations of World War II to the perceived new threat.

Is it possible to separate the rhetoric of heroism, honor, and masculinity from the specific arena of warfare and weapons? The idea of the military hero as the man on whom all other men must pattern themselves infects the tangled nexus of war, masculine honor, and sexuality as well. [. . . C]ultural beliefs do have life cycles. Some move forward; others are rooted in the past until they become outmoded, even though some individuals might cling to them for their own reasons: the belief that the past was better, that an absolute truth exists somewhere on earth, that there are firm boundaries, not just physical or genetic but also psychological and social, between the sexes.

The United States and Europe, the villains in the fundamentalist   15
equation, are also the places where over the last century the definition of masculinity has most separated from its military embodiment. Here is where the psychological attack especially comes into play, for the enemies of Western technological and cultural power are also the enemies of a Western idea of gender that has slowly but perceptibly over the last century changed from the assumption that male and female are polarities to the belief that they are a continuum. As it was for the neowarrior societies of Nazi Germany and militarist Japan, the result for the radical Islamic world represented by bin Laden is that American men are no better than women, that secularism is debilitating, and that diversity means weakness. As bin Laden said in an interview in 1998:

> Our brothers who fought in Somalia saw wonders about the weakness, feebleness, and cowardliness of the U.S. soldier. . . . We believe that we are men, Muslim men who have the honor of defending [Mecca]. We do not want American women soldiers defending [it]. . . . The rulers in that region have been deprived of their manhood. And they think that the people are women.

By God, Muslim women refuse to be defended by these American and Jewish prostitutes. (Judt, 4)

Such comments point out how paradoxical is the combat between the "pure" (and masculine) warrior society and the "impure" (and feminine) commercial society. Although the warrior group reaches back to tribal roots and professes to emphasize the brotherhood of the group, it actually fosters a frequently maniacal separatism and localism, while the mercantile culture of the West with its individualist ethic actually cultivates an affinity with the group, out of patriotism, practicality, or some combination of both. The crucial question is how the group is defined: in its exclusive connections with one another against the rest of the world with a Führer or holy warrior at its head, or as an inclusive, ever-expanding camaraderie where authority is, at least in principle, constantly open to challenge.

The possibility that male and female may be connected rather than eternally separate is a special threat to traditional societies that are still emerging from an agricultural into an industrial world, where a strict division of male versus female work seems necessary to the stability of life itself. Given the high ratio of men to women and the difficulties of subsisting on the family farm, there are large numbers of young men for whom domestic life is a dim possibility. In medieval Europe, they might have gone either to war or into the church. With bin Laden's brand of Islamic fundamentalism, they can do both.

In such societies, the seamless identification of the warrior image with general masculinity thus preserves a sense of male uniqueness, as does polygamous marriage and the requirement that women show virtually nothing of their bodies or faces. The result is an overcompensation familiar in warrior societies, where the combined fear of women (as weakeners of male sexuality) and disdain for them (as representing the softer virtues of domestic life) results in the need for a sexual subordination that reestablishes male honor at the top of the ladder of being.

None of these attitudes or customs are unfamiliar in Western history. They are based on a polarized idea of male and female that simultaneously asserts masculine power even as it covertly admits that the male sense of honor and selfhood is so flimsy that the slightest exposure of the female body may shatter it. The remarkable irony of history is that just at the time that, in the wake of World War II, such attitudes have been open to the most widespread criticism, at a time when women have achieved more structural equality than ever before, when homosexual behavior is no longer so officially stigmatized, the West is faced with an enemy emerging from the ancient lands of the Aryan warriors, whose own canons of sexuality attempt to reestablish a past from which the West has been distancing itself.

Instead of the monolithic states of interwar fascism, the world has in the last half century moved toward a greater number of multicultural states, whose diverse makeup reflects the new waves of immigration for economic interests that followed World War II. More than ever before, the populations

20

of the industrialized countries represent not racial purity but a rainbow of the rest of the world, and the conflict is not so much between nations as it is between the forces of commonality and the forces of exclusion. But this diversity, which has nurtured the acceptance of racial, religious, and ethnic difference, has become the enemy for the most militant groups. In a changing world, not changing becomes the mark of virtue. Rigid styles of masculinity that have evolved for cultural situations that no longer exist and for reasons that are no longer functional are brought back as the ideological core of a refusal to engage with the present. Arising from tribal pockets, such essentially local masculinities now take the world stage because of the availability of weapons, the ease of transportation, and the permeability of borders, putting an advanced technology intended to bring people together into the hands of those who want to avoid the future at any cost. Thus, whatever bin Laden's specific complaints about American foreign policy, the energy of his attacks on the West comes instead from a much more fundamental response to the modern world, including its Islamic nations.

Once again, this is a phenomenon that has its parallels in the West. The fundamentalist branches of other religions, as well as less institutionalized spiritual practices, have grown over the past few decades in part because of a shared sense that they have been both exploited and left behind by an increasingly commercialized and mercantile world. But whatever the affinities of their critique of modernity, few have scapegoated the West as thoroughly as militant Islam, which bases its nostalgia for a past religious purity so firmly on a particular style of warrior masculinity. [. . .]

[. . .] The heroicizing of the aggressive warrior in militia movements, along with the justification of violence in the name of the unborn among some antiabortion activists and other vigilante groups, reflects how since the 1980s the United States itself has gone through similar spasms of wondering what the role of traditional masculinity is in the modern world. Little of this uncertainty has found its way into literature except for the fictions of survivalism and racial superiority. But it has become the matter of popular films. As so many action movies of the past two decades show, at a time when technology lets any nondescript, physically uninspiring person have the power to annihilate many, there is some nostalgic satisfaction in seeing a correlation between body and violence, action and personal will, where the hero — Sylvester Stallone, Arnold Schwarzenegger, Jean Claude Van Damme — has access to both the most advanced technology and his own cuirasslike bare chest and muscled arms. Like paintball wars, extreme sports, and battlefield reenactments, their stories are filled with artificially pumped-up excitement and jeopardy. Many of these films are mythic efforts to synthesize technology and personal physical prowess in the same spirit as the army's 2001 advertising campaign: "An Army of One."

Since the end of the Vietnam War, American films have been filled with characters in whom the line between the human and the technological is ambiguous. *RoboCop* represents one sort, the remanufactured man; the androids of films like *Blade Runner* and *Aliens* another, apparent human beings who are actually robots. Indirectly commenting on the use of overwhelming firepower in Vietnam and later wars, such characters raise the question of whether superweaponry is enough. Despite all the "smart bombs," the answer seems to be no. Some recourse to the individual and the primitive is necessary in order to ground the otherwise abstract technology: Rambo emerges from the swamp with his bow and arrows to defeat his enemies [. . .]. Although sometimes cloaked in Cold War politics, action films are at root about questions of personal honor — the violence of righteous revenge that is beyond the law, like the justifications of dueling that began in the sixteenth century, when the state was assuming the monopoly of violence. The difference now is that the honor dramatized in most action films is not aristocratic but democratic, heroes without family name, whose only resource is themselves. Ironically enough, with September 11, at a time when the United States was indulging in widespread nostalgia about World War II and its citizen soldiers, a full-fledged enemy appears who targets civilians and makes heroes of the policemen and firemen who protect them. At least for the moment, the heroic on the Western side, in the images of the World Trade Center, is defined by the normal person doing his or her job.

Films may still rely on the solitary hero, but the political propaganda of the warrior who will set the corrupt world right by violence now no longer comes out of either official Europe or official Japan but from thwarted and marginalized small groups around the world. Most prominently in the Middle East, it is the revenge of the nomad against the settled, or of the religion of the desert against the values of the city. [. . .]

Work Cited

Judt, Tony. "America and the War." *New York Review of Books* 15 Nov. 2001: 4–6.

Questions for Discussion

1. "Blowback" is one of many metaphors used to characterize 9/11 and other terrorist attacks on Americans and the United States abroad. What evidence does Chalmers offer that such attacks were one of the many "unintended consequences of the U.S. government's international activities"? Is his evidence convincing? Why or why not?

2. On the one hand, Huntington says that "people can and do redefine their identities" so that "the composition and boundaries of civilizations change." On the other, he also says that "cultural characteristics and differences are less mutable . . . than political and economic ones," that "in the former Soviet Union, communists can become

democrats . . . but Russians cannot become Estonians." Are these statements contradictory? Are some aspects of identity more resistant to change than others? If so, why? If not, why not?

3. Like "blowback," Huntington's use of "fault lines" between civilizations is a metaphor that creates a certain mental image. Describe it. What does it imply? Does 9/11 call this metaphor into question, since the attack took place in the United States, far from the fault zones in the Middle and Far East?

4. What does Said mean by the "pluralism of civilizations"? Has our government's response to 9/11 taken American pluralism into account? Does Huntington show any awareness of the pluralism Said refers to?

5. "We are all swimming in these waters," Said claims in his last paragraph, giving us yet another metaphor for our situation, one quite different from the geological "fault lines." Which metaphor do you find the more attractive? Why?

6. Krauthammer provides much support for the contention that liberal democracy is fundamentally incompatible with militant Islam's creeds and goals. Study his evidence for this contention. If true, how does it fit with Huntington's theory about the clash of civilizations? How does it fit with Alexander's description of the goals and attitudes of Hamas and Palestinian Islamic Jihad? Is the destruction of militant Islam our only option?

7. "The complete surrender of religion to Arab political needs is the most alarming threat to peace in the Middle East," Alexander claims. Suppose he's right. What might we do to pry religion and politics apart in the Muslim world? How could we enlist religion to combat terrorism? What role do you see religion playing in U.S. counter-terrorist policies and actions?

8. "The possibility that male and female may be connected rather than eternally separate is a special threat to traditional societies that are still emerging from an agricultural into an industrial world," Braudy asserts, going on to point out that the treatment of women in militant Islam is consistent with warrior societies in general. In other words, what we are fighting against is a certain construction of masculinity from which, as Braudy says, "the West has been distancing itself." If his view has merit as an explanation for significant aspects of Al Qaeda's behavior, is there anything we can do except wait for a more modern view of masculinity to develop in the still very traditional societies characteristic of the Middle and Far East?

9. At the end of his chapter, Braudy refers to action films popular in the West and connects them with threats to masculine identity and power in the West. What is his point? Do you see these films as largely harmless, fantasy compensation for insecure men? Or do you see the appeal of these films as something we should worry about,

as a serious reaction to the breakdown of traditional masculine identity as women have gained more rights and power?

Suggestions for Writing

For Collaborative Inquiry and Mediation

Huntington's "clash of civilizations" viewpoint has received much commentary—it's by far the best known and most influential view of what's going on in the world. As a class, collect about a dozen responses and, from this group, select what you consider the six best, being sure to include a diversity of opinion. After discussing the six articles in class, write an essay that mediates between Huntington's theory and the objections raised against it, including Said's. That is: Hold on to the basic idea of Huntington's viewpoint, but modify or reformulate the theory to address as many of the differing views as possible.

For Analysis and Convincing

Find out more about nihilism as both a concept and an historical phenomenon. A good place to start is the *Encyclopedia of Philosophy*. Then, based on what you know about militant Islam, assess Krauthammer's identification of it with nihilism. Make a case supporting Krauthammer, or refuting him, or partly agreeing, partly disagreeing.

For Persuasion

No nation has more impact on the world in every way than the United States does. Even so, much that happens "out there" is not our doing nor easily affected by what we chose to do or to leave undone. Militant Islam, for instance, developed for all sorts of reasons that have little or nothing to do with U.S. foreign policy. Conceding this at the outset, write an essay that advocates certain changes in U.S. policy you think will make Americans and our government less of a target for militant Islamic groups. That is: What *can* we do that might reduce the threat significantly without abandoning our vital interests abroad?

For Inquiry

Women have played major roles in terrorism, past and present. Sometimes females have even acted as "suicide bombers." Nevertheless, terrorism, like most forms of violence, is disproportionately dominated by males. Do research on the relation between masculinity and violence, being sure to explore both physiological and cultural factors. Discuss the results of your research in class. Then write a paper exploring your view of the relation between being male, being masculine, and violence. Connect your exploration with terrorism specifically. Conclude your paper with what you think must change to reduce the common masculine resort to violence to solve problems.

SECTION 3: ASSESSING THE WAR ON TERROR

Overview

There's a story that an aging and revered leader of an Asian country was asked not long ago what he thought about the French Revolution. He paused for a moment and said, "It's too early to tell." We may smile at the thought that a more than 200-year-old event is still too recent to assess, but there may be more than a little wisdom in withholding judgment. The consequences of the French Revolution are still with us—especially in its justification of force from within to topple corrupt and oppressive regimes. Who knows what the ultimate impact of such a belief, echoed in the rationale for our own American revolution, might be? Perhaps some future historian will trace a coming global catastrophe we can't imagine to the kind of thinking that led first to the Reign of Terror and then to the megalomania of Napoleon.

One thing we can say about the present war on terror without fear of contradiction: It's only a little over three years old. We are fighting it now, caught up in the middle of it too much to see it coolly and with the perspective only distance from an era can provide. It's way too early to tell.

And yet we cannot afford to say simply, "Give it time." Too much is at stake. Recognizing that we could well be wrong no matter what position we take, we still must take an informed and well-reasoned stance—no responsible citizen should retreat to either mindless patriotism or contemptuous rejection of current foreign policy.

What can we safely assume? And what must we decide?

We can assume that Al Qaeda will remain an implacable enemy. Perhaps America can become a smaller target and certainly a harder one to strike at, but the government cannot negotiate peace with people who believe it is their religious duty to kill. Besides that, in almost every respect liberal democracy is at odds with militant Islam. Where would common ground be found?

What we must decide is, first, what are we after? What is our goal or goals? And second, how can we best go about realizing it/them?

Is it realistic to imagine rooting out Al Qaeda, destroying it as the Allies destroyed Nazi Germany and imperial Japan? Or is the only hope to contain the threat, doing what is possible to thwart terrorist ambitions and to create a world that will hasten Al Qaeda's collapse? Is it realistic to imagine Western-style liberal democracies replacing the largely autocratic regimes in predominantly Muslim countries? Or can the West only hope for more or less peaceful coexistence and perhaps small, hesitant steps toward democracy and well-developed modern economies?

Once we decide what we're after, then we can mull over possible routes for getting there. As we do, we can assume at least two things. First, if a policy has an up side, it will also have a down side. No way of dealing with terrorism is all positive. Second, regardless of how it is waged, the fight will be a long one, probably a matter of decades at least, and the outcome will almost certainly not be entirely to our liking.

There was a time when war meant nations fighting nations, when victory was simply a matter of one side surrendering. That time is over. The challenge is to think in new ways and to be swift in adjusting to ever-changing circumstances.

The Al Qaeda Threat and the International Response

Rohan Gunaratna

An authority on Islamic terrorist groups, especially bin Laden's, Gunaratna speaks frequently on counterterrorism at seminars around the globe. The following is from his book, Inside Al Qaeda: Global Network of Terror *(Columbia University Press, 2002).*

Our next victory, God willing, is going to be in Hejaz and Najd. We will make America suffer a defeat worse than she suffered in Lebanon and Vietnam.
> —Commentary from an Al Qaeda recruitment video seized by police in London in the aftermath of 9/11

THE CONTEXT

The global fight against Al Qaeda will be the defining conflict of the early 21st century. Osama bin Laden has built an organisation that functions both operationally and ideologically at local, national, regional and global levels. Defeating Al Qaeda and its associate groups will be the single biggest challenge confronting the international security and intelligence community, law enforcement authorities and national militaries in the foreseeable future. [. . .]

As long as its operational and support infrastructure remains intact, Al Qaeda will threaten both the Muslim and the Western world. Al Qaeda is not invincible, nor is it infallible. Through understanding its operational and ideological techniques, counter-measures can be developed to disrupt, degrade and destroy it. By painstakingly detecting its worldwide physical infrastructure and human network, the organisation can be dismantled and its leadership neutralised.

UNDERSTANDING THE THREAT

In the past Islamist organisations fizzled out because of a lack of battle-hardened and tested structures. They relied on village, clan and tribe and built organisations based on traditional loyalties. As such, they lacked a modern, robust and resilient organisation. By adapting and seamlessly grafting pre-existing models, Al Qaeda has built an Islamist organisation full of vitality. Its politically clandestine structure is built on the idea of internationalism. [. . .] Al Qaeda is self-reproducing and therefore hard to defeat.

Because there is no historical precedent for Al Qaeda, the past offers very little guidance. The success and failure of the US-led anti-terrorist campaign will depend on the ability and willingness of America, its allies and its coalition partners to learn as they progress. In an ever-changing, fluid and dynamic environment, only by minimising failures and maximising successes can they prevail against a determined enemy willing to kill and die.

Although heavy bombing detected, disrupted and degraded the physical infrastructure of Al Qaeda and the Taliban in Afghanistan, their fighting cadres are intact. The Muslim territorial and migrant communities from Australia to the Middle East and Canada will continue to provide recruits and finance. Al Qaeda's future survival will depend on the continuing appeal of its radical ideology that sustains a fledgling global support network. In the virtual absence of counter-propaganda, many literate and illiterate Muslims view its ideology as compatible with Islamic theology. To counter its non-military capability and capacity, the anti-terrorist coalition needs both a strategic vision and tactical direction. There is no opposite number in the anti-terrorist coalition to counter Al Qaeda's broad strategy as formulated by Dr Ayman Al-Zawahiri, Osama's principal strategist. [. . .]

AL QAEDA'S STRATEGY

[. . .] In his post-9/11 book, *Knights Under the Prophet's Banner—Meditations on the Jihadist Movement*, al-Zawahiri justifies an escalation of terrorist techniques and tactics:

1. The need to inflict the maximum casualties against the opponent, for this is the language understood by the West, no matter how much time and effort such operations take.
2. The need to concentrate on the method of martyrdom operations as the most successful way of inflicting damage against the opponent and the least costly to the *mujahidin* in terms of casualties.
3. The targets as well as the type and method of weapons used must be chosen to have an impact on the structure of the enemy and deter it enough to stop its brutality, arrogance and disregard for all taboos and customs. [. . .]
4. To re-emphasise what we have already explained, we reiterate that focusing on the domestic enemy alone will not be feasible at this stage.[1]

Considering the limitations imposed on Al Qaeda, its post-Taliban exhortations have urged other Islamist groups to engage in mass casualty terrorism. [. . .] As most Islamist groups are territorially bound, they are unlikely to follow Al Qaeda's request. Nonetheless, Al Qaeda's sleeper cells in Europe and the US, its newly-formed cells and its pre-existing cells introduced from overseas are likely to strike targets on Western soil. As a priority, Al Qaeda has called for the campaign to focus on the continental US. The state of alertness of European and North American countries will not deter it from mounting an operation to strike the West. Nor will conventional methods of deterrence—capture, arrest, trial, imprisonment, or humiliation, injury or death—protect the West from suicide terrorism. [. . .]

Given the increased threat to Islamist terrorist groups [after 9/11], Al Qaeda is enlisting the support of underground groups as well as legitimate political parties. Instead of Islamist terrorist groups shouldering the burden of politicising, radicalising and mobilising Muslims, Al Qaeda has called upon Islamist political parties to shoulder the duties of propaganda, recruitment and fundraising, thus freeing Islamist terrorist groups to concentrate on planning, preparing and conducting attacks. [. . .] Among Muslim migrant communities in North America, Europe, and Australia, preventing Islamists from advancing their political aims and objectives non-violently is well nigh impossible. To operate amid tight security and vigilance, Al Qaeda's post 9/11 strategy is designed for Islamist parties hiding behind the political veil to produce a generation of recruits and supporters to sustain the fight in Afghanistan and elsewhere. Until favourable conditions emerge, Al Qaeda will operate through mosques, [. . .] community centres and, as best it can, charities in Western Europe and North America. [. . .]

AL QAEDA'S MINDSET

Al Qaeda did not anticipate the US induction of ground troops to Afghanistan in the wake of 9/11. Its thinking was influenced by the withdrawal of US troops from three theatres: Beirut after the Hezbollah bombings in October 1983; Aden after the Al Qaeda bombings in December 1992; and Somalia after the Al Qaeda-trained Al-Ittihad attacks in October 1993. When Osama—accompanied by his sons Hamza, Muhammad, Khaled and Laden—visited the site where the first US helicopter crashed in Afghanistan, one of his sons remarked to an Al Qaeda member: "You see? They are commandos. They are a superpower only in Hollywood and in films. Their heroes are only mythical like Rambo and they won't come to Afghanistan. And if they do come here, they will end up in pieces like this." [2]

Al Qaeda's leadership, membership and supporters firmly believe that everything happens according to God's will. [. . .] The message "You are carrying out God's wish" makes an Al Qaeda member relentlessly pursue *jihad*. Thus the state of mind of an average Al Qaeda member prepares him psychologically and physically to struggle against all odds, suffer heavy losses yet continue fighting to the death. All Islamic and Islamist movements, including Al Qaeda, think and plan for years, if not for decades. In the mindset of an Al Qaeda member or supporter, whether in Afghanistan, Palestine, Iraq, or elsewhere, the fight is between God's warriors — the *mujahidin* — and Satanic forces — the US troops. As a Muslim's duty is *jihad*, all Muslims are expected to participate, if not support, the *mujahidin* fighting the US.

Will Al Qaeda, like some Islamist groups in the past that compromised   10 with their opponents, be prepared to give and take? No. Al Qaeda was founded on the premise that it will not compromise, however long it takes, however hard the fight and whatever the losses it suffers. As long as Osama is Emir General and al-Zawahiri is the principal strategist, it will not compromise. Post-Osama, its psyche will commit its members to his dream and al-Zawahiri's strategy — until or unless Osama's legacy fades away. [. . .]

THREAT TRAJECTORY

Al Qaeda's trajectory is no different from that of most terrorist groups. [. . .] In the first wave, Al Qaeda and its associate groups attacked secular and moderate Muslim countries like Egypt, Saudi Arabia, Jordan and Pakistan. The brutal response of the Middle Eastern and Asian security services led Al Qaeda and its associate members, collaborators and supporters to be detained, tortured and killed and their safe houses, vehicles and finances seized. As a result of these setbacks, Al Qaeda decided to target its distant enemy — the West — that was supporting the near enemy: friendly Muslim rulers and their regimes.

There has been an underestimation of the Islamist threat by the West because until recently it was largely directed at Muslim rulers, regimes and populations. [. . .] As long as Islamists did not target the West, liberal democracies tacitly permitted Al Qaeda and its associate groups to operate — to disseminate propaganda, recruit, raise funds and procure and ship goods. Even today, liberal democracies are against regulating terrorist propaganda, including the internet, a favoured Al Qaeda tool. Al Qaeda and its associate groups raised more funds from liberal democracies than they received from their state sponsors. When the time was ripe, it used Europe, its forward operational base, to strike the US. Moreover, the Western intelligence community, suffering from the Cold War legacy of "monitoring spies" as opposed to disrupting terrorist support operations, had little knowledge of what went on in their backyards. They failed to understand that watching post–Cold War terrorists was different from monitoring Cold War spies. As such, the intelligence community failed miserably to deter Al Qaeda from mounting operations from the West. Until some 2,900 American and other lives were lost on 9/11, Western governments and their security services were reticent about sharing intelligence, and judicial authorities rarely entertained requests for extradition from the rest of the world.

Liberal democracies have limited experience in managing the Islamist threat, but Al Qaeda poses a more serious threat to Muslims. [. . .] Unlike Western countries that have been physically and psychologically affected by its terrorist attacks, Muslim territorial and migrant communities are susceptible to its ideological penetration. Upon successful penetration, some of their number serve as an extended arm of Al Qaeda, first as sympathisers, then as supporters, thereafter as collaborators, and finally as members. [. . .]

As long as Al Qaeda and its associate groups can appeal to Muslims worldwide to share its ideals, aims and objectives, its support and operational cells will regenerate and multiply. [. . .] [S]anctions and penalties must be imposed on their sponsors and hosts, whether governments or, more importantly, organisations; a relentless global, regional and national hunt and harsh sentences for Al Qaeda leaders, members, collaborators and supporters; irresistible incentives for Al Qaeda defectors; and attractive rewards for information leading to the arrest of Al Qaeda operatives or disruption of Al Qaeda plans and preparations. But of equal importance are resolving Kashmir, Palestine, and other international conflicts where Muslims are affected; redressing grievances and meeting the legitimate aspiration of Muslims; and helping Arab and Muslim states to improve the quality of life of their citizens. Above all, Al Qaeda's ideology must be countered, in order to deflect and lessen its appeal to serving members, fresh recruits and actual or potential supporters.

As Islamist groups have repeatedly demonstrated in the recent past, a military solution is only one part of a wider strategy of implementing socio-economic and political reforms. Otherwise, the threat will diminish in the short term but re-emerge in the midterm. [. . .] Instead of addressing the threat at a tactical level, the West and other countries must develop a strategic framework for managing the Islamist threat.   15

Although Al Qaeda threatens both Western and Muslim countries, the West—primarily the US—has the diplomatic, political, economic and military means to set the agenda against terrorism. [. . .] The West must work with the Muslim world—governments *and* people; working only with governments is not enough. Sharing intelligence with Muslim rulers and regimes that proves that Al Qaeda was responsible for 9/11 did little to convince Muslim societies. Therefore, public diplomacy should be an integral feature in the campaign against terrorism.

Active measures [. . .] should include the military and non-military [options]. Military methods will provide the security and political conditions to implement the far reaching socio-economic, welfare and political programs that will have a lasting impact. [. . .]

LONG-TERM RESPONSE

Al Qaeda's new trajectory of targeting the West won it significant support among the Muslim masses. Leaving aside the Muslim elite, ordinary

Muslims worldwide view the West through the prism of anti-Americanism. 61% of Muslims polled in nine countries—Indonesia, Iran, Jordan, Kuwait, Lebanon, Morocco, Pakistan, Saudi Arabia and Turkey—denied that Arabs were involved in the September 11 attacks.[3] The corresponding statistics were 89% in Kuwait, 86% in Pakistan, 74% in Indonesia, 59% in Iran, 58% in Lebanon, and 43% in Turkey.[4] Only 18% of those polled in six Islamic countries said they believed Arabs carried out the attacks and just 9% said they thought US military action in Afghanistan was morally justified.[5] In Kuwait, a country liberated by the US from Iraqi aggression in 1991, 36% said that the 9/11 attacks were justifiable.[6] Just 7% said Western nations are fair in their perceptions of Muslim countries.[7] In perception and in reality there are two worlds, the Western and the Muslim. When President George W. Bush said, "You are either with us, or with the terrorists," Al Qaeda interpreted it as an American admission of the existence of two worlds,[8] and to build further support it misinterpreted Bush's infamous phrase "waging a crusade against terrorism" as "a crusade against Islam."[9] Clearly the US has no public support from the Muslim world either to fight terrorism or to remain in Afghanistan. However, the US, its allies and its coalition partners would be taking an incalculable risk if they withdrew from Afghanistan without creating the security, socio-economic and political conditions for a modern system of government to function.

Every terrorist group has a lifespan. Al Qaeda's lifespan will be determined by the ability and the willingness of the anti-terrorist coalition to destroy its leadership, counter its ideology, marginalise its support and disrupt its recruitment. [. . .] Although the West can help Muslim rulers and regimes to fight Al Qaeda on the military plane, there is little it can actually do to isolate it politically and win over its support base. As Al Qaeda poses a durable long-term threat to Muslims worldwide, it is the Muslim elite who must stand up and fight the threat it represents. The West can help, but it is a battle that can best be fought and won by Muslims against Muslims.

Islamists are resilient. They move rapidly in search of new opportunities. To influence, control and build support, they step in wherever there is a space. Arab, Muslim and other countries that host Muslim territorial and migrant populations have neglected their welfare for decades, and Islamist parties and groups have filled the vacuum by establishing socio-economic and welfare organisations. The interaction with Muslim communities has given these organisations an opportunity to politicise and radicalise the Muslim masses into supporting their aims and objectives. By their selfless actions and intense ideological indoctrination, the Islamic movements actively recruit members and increase support. Their projects and plans appear much better and worthier of support than the corrupt, unjust and unholy governments that attempt to rule them.

In addition to providing welfare, Islamists formed non-governmental organisations (NGOs) to provide employment and Islamic education. They have mobilised the poor, the illiterate and the needy. Until Muslim rulers and regimes compete with these Islamist-infiltrated NGOs and provide an alternative, groups like Al Qaeda and its associates will always find recruits and financial backers. [. . .] To build anti-Western support, Islamists selectively retrieve and present a mixture of fact and fiction as truth. Arguing convincingly that it is only a question of time before the West is overwhelmed, they record that the Western population has declined relatively from 25% of the world total at the beginning of the 20th century to 15% a century later. With the Koran in one hand and a Kalashnikov in the other, the [. . .] Islamist lives a life of anger and hope. Western governments and NGOs should seek to work with Muslim regimes and societies and help build schools and community centres that impart a modern education and instill humane, non-sectarian values. Among the priorities of the international community should be, as well as reforming education, fostering truly independent media and building criminal justice and prison systems that are truly just. [. . .]

Notes

1. Ayman al-Zawahiri, *Knights Under the Prophet's Banner—Meditations on the Jihadist Movement,* London, *Al-Sharq al-Awsat* (in Arabic), December 2, 2001.

2. "The Wills of the New York and Washington Battle Martyrs." This is the Al Qaeda video in which al-Zawahiri took credit for the 9/11 attacks. It includes footage of Ahmed Ibrahim al-Haznawi (*alias* Alghamdi), one of the hijackers of UA93 that crashed in Pennsylvania, pleading with God to accept him as a martyr, the background being a montage of a burning WTC. The film was released by al-Jazeera satellite television station, Qatar, to Western networks, on April 15, 2002. The entire film was broadcast on Al Jazeera on April 18, 2002.

3. Andrea Stone, "In Poll, Islamic World Says Arabs Not Involved in 9/11," *USA Today,* February 27, 2002, p. 1.

4. Ibid.

5. Ibid.

6. Ibid.

7. Ibid.

8. Tayseer Allouni [the Kabul correspondent of Al-Jazeera], transcript of an interview with Osama Bin Laden, October 21, 2001, translated from Arabic by the Institute for Islamic Studies and Research (www.alneda.com).

9. Ibid.

The Terror Trap
Gershom Gorenberg

Gorenberg's essay is important for at least two reasons: he sees what we are doing in the context of Israeli counterterrorism, and he traces the lineage of modern terrorism back to a main source, Russian anarchism. His essay appeared in the

January 2004 issue of The American Prospect, *a respected liberal journal, for which Gorenberg is a senior correspondent.*

The four men, veterans of a grim business, had only grim words. Former heads of the Shin Bet, the Israeli security service entrusted with righting terrorism, they gathered to tell Israel's largest newspaper that the Sharon government was failing completely in its war on terrorism.

The problem, said Ami Ayalon, who headed the elite, secretive agency in the late 1990s, is, "We have built a strategy of immediate prevention"— of stopping the next attack—while ignoring causes. His colleagues echoed that evaluation in a mid-November joint interview. "We must, once and for all, admit that there is an other side, that it has feelings and that it is suffering," said Avraham Shalom, who held the agency's top post in the early '80s.

Insisting that Israel needs to end the occupation, the four seized attention at home and abroad. Yet for all the headlines, their message deserves a closer reading than it got, as it contains a lesson for the U.S. war on terrorism as well. In effect, they argued that fighting terrorism with military and intelligence efforts alone is likely to boomerang, creating the fury and despair that drive people to support suicide bombers.

Perhaps that should be obvious. But both Israeli and American policies, with their focus on military and intelligence responses, indicate it's not. I'd suggest that the problem begins with the way terrorism is usually described: as a behavior rather than as a political doctrine, an "ism." The U.S. Department of State definition is typical: It says terrorism is "premeditated, politically motivated violence perpetrated against noncombatant targets by subnational groups . . . usually intended to influence an audience." The Israeli army uses a similar definition. Those descriptions fail to explain just how terrorism is meant to influence an audience. They ignore strategy.

In fact, terrorism is rooted in an intellectual tradition that's at least 120 years old, according to University of California, Los Angeles, political scientist David Rapoport, editor of the *Journal of Terrorism and Political Violence.* The strategy was first proposed by late-19th-century Russian anarchists in response to public apathy, after older revolutionary efforts, including pamphlets and meetings, had failed to awaken the masses. Terrorists, the new theory went, would seize public attention through their willingness to violate conventions and take risks. More important, they'd engage in political judo: By breaking accepted rules on the use of force, they'd provoke the government to break its own rules and polarize society. The apathetic masses would discover that moderation and fence-sitting were impossible. Terrorism, says Rapoport, was designed to "command the masses' attention, arouse latent political tensions and provoke government to respond indiscriminately, undermining in the process its own credibility and legitimacy."

Frantz Fanon, the Martinique-born psychoanalyst and social philosopher who joined the Algerian revolution, took the notion to new heights. His 1961 treatise on decolonialization, "The Wretched of the Earth," with

5

its breathless preface by Jean-Paul Sartre, inspired a generation of Western leftists and Third World revolutionaries. Fanon anointed "absolute violence" as the only means of ending colonial rule. "If the last shall be first," he wrote, borrowing Jesus' words, it would require "murderous and decisive struggle." Violence "is a cleansing force." It forges the nation, which embodies truth. The dead are instruments of liberation, not shattered human beings.

Fanon makes killing a therapy for the oppressed. But he also gives unbridled violence a strategic purpose: It will eliminate the middle ground. Violence by the oppressed will call forth "mass slaughter" by the regime.[. . .] Responding to brutality with greater brutality, the regime recruits the apathetic to the side of the revolutionaries.

Fanon provided the inspiration for the Palestinian terrorist groups, especially Yasir Arafat's Fatah organization. Israeli researcher Ely Karmon notes that "the third Fatah leaflet, entitled 'Revolution and Violence, the Path to Victory' . . . was little more than a collection of quotations from . . . 'The Wretched of the Earth.'"[. . .]

The secular Fanon also helped kindle the Islamic revolution in Iran. As French scholar Gilles Kepel writes in his book *Jihad: The Trail of Political Islam*, Fanon was translated into Persian by Ali Shariati, one of the intellectual fathers of the Iranian revolution. In the process, Shariati translated Fanon into Islam, using religious terms for words such as "oppressed." [. . .]

But the terrorist philosophy also entered Islamic thinking in less explicit ways. Arab recruits to Islamic movements of the 1980s came from a milieu saturated with adulation of armed struggle. Rejecting secular movements as failures, they were also shaped by them. Some experts on Islamic terrorism insist that Islamicists had no need of Western influence to choose terrorism, that they were simply returning to a traditional concept of jihad. But that classical concept, Rapoport stresses, "is not an insurrectional strategy. The Islamic tradition is antagonistic toward internal violence." Yet a central target of jihad in the last generation has been "unbelieving" regimes within the Muslim world—in Afghanistan, Algeria, Egypt and even Saudi Arabia. The strategy for insurrection, Rapoport argues, has been drawn from the West, where an intellectual tradition rooted in the French Revolution "recognizes the legitimacy of violence within the system." One part of this move has been importing the doctrine of terrorism and dressing it in tradition.

Osama bin Laden is a case in point. As Kepel points out, bin Laden's attack on America came when Islamic radicalism was at "a political impasse." Afghan-trained rebels had failed in Algeria, Egypt and Bosnia during the '90s. The attacks on America—like the efforts of leftist terrorists of the 1970s after the left had lost its appeal in the West—were a bid to revive mass support "through a cycle of provocation, repression and solidarity."

This doesn't mean that every terrorist follows the traditional strategy, or that the strategy necessarily works. But the essential conclusion remains: A campaign against terrorism that drives moderates to support terrorists isn't just a failure. It fulfills terrorist goals. A long-term strategy against terrorism should drive a wedge between terrorists and the public they'd like to recruit. It should show moderates that they can progress better without extremists than with them.

Initially, the Oslo process was a successful example. It offered Palestinians in the West Bank and Gaza Strip an end to Israeli occupation—and not an Islamic state in Israel's place. Pollster Khalil Shikaki, of the Palestinian Center for Policy and Survey Research, documented the effect: In January 1994, soon after the Oslo Accords were signed, only 51 percent of Palestinians backed negotiations with Israel; by early 1996, after Israeli pullouts from West Bank cities, that had risen to 78 percent. Between late 1994 and early 1996, support for violence against Israeli civilians slid from nearly three-fifths of Palestinians to just one-fifth. The shift, says Israeli political scientist Menachem Klein of Bar-Ilan University, gave Palestinian Authority security chiefs the mandate they needed to crack down on Hamas, and Israelis enjoyed relative calm.

But by 2000, Klein says, the pendulum had swung. Israeli settlements kept growing. Palestinian moderates put high hopes on then-Israeli Prime Minister Ehud Barak and were frustrated by delays in achieving independence. When negotiations stalled, the intifada erupted with a wave of terrorism against Israeli civilians. Israeli responses, from roadblocks to invasions of Palestinian towns, are perceived as a war against the entire population. Palestinian support for violence and for Islamic groups has since climbed.

For Israel the implication is clear: Renewing dialogue with Palestinian   15
moderates and moving toward a peace deal can't wait until the fight against terrorism ends. It's the only way to push terrorists back to the margins.

And the lessons for the United States? The first is to avoid a "clash of civilizations," which is what bin Laden seeks to ignite. Shortly after September 11, Bush spoke of the war on terrorism as a "crusade"—which for Muslims means a Christian assault on Islam. His attack on Iraq underscored that point: While the Afghan invasion took away bin Laden's base, the Iraqi invasion convinced many moderates that the United States is at war with the Muslim world as such. The highly publicized affair of Lt. Gen. William Boykin, who declared Allah "an idol" and America a "Christian nation" at war with Satan, risks deepening that impression. So does Bush's support for Israeli Prime Minister Ariel Sharon.

Military measures alone won't defeat Islamic terrorism. The United States should be looking for ways to address moderate Muslim aspirations. A quick turnover of power in Iraq could be a step forward, as would be real American pressure on pro-U.S. Muslim regimes to liberalize. And decisively pushing for Israeli-Palestinian peace would help America while serving Israel's interests as well. The problem is that both Bush and Sharon appear much more comfortable using might alone. That's just what terrorists want them to do.

The Velvet Hegemon: How Soft Power Can Help Defeat Terrorism
Joseph S. Nye, Jr.

Joseph S. Nye, Jr., is dean of the John F. Kennedy School of Government at Harvard University. The following article appeared in Foreign Policy, *the May-June issue, 2003.*

When George Carey, former archbishop of Canterbury, stood up at the 2003 World Economic Forum in Davos, Switzerland, in January and asked U.S. Secretary of State Colin Powell why the United States seems to focus only on its hard power rather than its soft power, I was gratified and bemused. Gratified that a concept I had proposed in *Foreign Policy* in 1990 has gained wide currency; bemused at how often that concept is misunderstood.

Power is the ability to produce the outcomes you want. When someone does something he would otherwise not do but for force or inducement, that's hard power—the use of sticks and carrots. Soft power is the ability to secure those outcomes through attraction rather than coercion. It is the ability to shape what others want. Hard and soft power sometimes reinforce and sometimes substitute for each other. If you can produce the right outcomes by attracting others to want what you want, you can afford to spend less on carrots and sticks.

Hard and soft power can also limit each other. That may explain why some of the unilateralists in the Pentagon now seem to neglect soft power. Unfortunately, that neglect may have dangerous consequences for the successful prosecution of both the war on terrorism and a conflict with Iraq.

Soft power can rest on the attractiveness of one's culture, political ideals, and policies, or on one's ability to manipulate other countries' political agendas. But many people confuse the resources that can generate soft power with the essence of soft power itself. Writing in *Foreign Policy* ("Think Again: Power," January/February 2003), the distinguished historian Niall Ferguson describes soft power as "nontraditional forces such as cultural and commercial goods" and then dismisses it on the grounds "that it's, well, soft." Of course, Coke and Big Macs do not necessarily encourage people in the Islamic world to love the United States. And Hollywood films that make the United States attractive in China or Latin America may have the opposite effect and actually diminish U.S. soft power in Saudi Arabia or Pakistan. Ferguson concludes that real power depends on "having credibility and legitimacy." Exactly! "Credibility and legitimacy" are what soft power is all about.

The attractiveness of the United States rests on resources such as its culture (sometimes), its political values of democracy and human rights (when it lives up to them), and its policies (when they are framed with

5

some humility and awareness of others' interests). At Davos, Secretary Powell correctly replied to George Carey that the United States needed hard power to win World War II but followed up with the Marshall Plan and support for democracy. By providing tangible economic incentives and making the United States more attractive, the Marshall Plan was a source of both hard and soft power. And, of course, soft power was crucial to the U.S. victory in the Cold War. After all, the Soviet Union was still attractive in many parts of Western Europe after World War II, but it squandered its soft power with repressive policies at home and the invasions of Hungary and Czechoslovakia.

Some hard-line skeptics in the Bush administration might say that whatever the merits of soft power, it has little role to play in the current war on terrorism. Osama bin Laden and his followers are repelled, not attracted, by U.S. culture, values, and policies. Military power was essential in defeating the Taliban regime in Afghanistan; soft power will never convert fanatics. True, but the skeptics mistake half the answer for the whole answer.

Look again at Afghanistan. Precision bombing and U.S. Special Forces may have subdued the Taliban, but so far, U.S. agents have captured only a fraction of al Qaeda operatives, who form a transnational network with cells in 60 countries. The United States cannot bomb al Qaeda cells in Hamburg, Kuala Lumpur, or Detroit. Success against this network depends on close civilian cooperation across borders, whether that means sharing intelligence, coordinating police work across borders, or tracking global financial flows. U.S. allies and partners collaborate partly out of self-interest, but the inherent attractiveness of U.S. policies influences the degree of such collaboration. Equally important, the current war on terrorism is not a clash of civilizations but a struggle whose outcome is closely tied to a civil war between moderates and extremists within Islamic civilization. The United States will win only if moderate Muslims win, and the United States' ability to attract moderates is critical to victory. The United States must adopt policies that appeal to moderates and must use public diplomacy more effectively to explain common interests to would-be allies in the Muslim world.

How would a war in Iraq affect our soft power vis-à-vis moderate Muslims around the world? Hawks reply that the successful exercise of hard power can also attract, pointing to the rise of American prestige in the Middle East after the first Gulf War. But that war was fought by a broad coalition with the United Nations' blessing. The strength of U.S. soft power depends in part on the breadth of U.S. coalitions. For example, a multinational force and administration in Iraq may be less efficient than a U.S. force, but what the United States loses in efficiency it more than gains in legitimacy and in the protection of its soft power.

U.S. economic policies not directly linked to the war on terrorism also affect soft power. Skeptics correctly argue that development assistance cannot remove the roots of terrorism because most of the terrorists who have struck the United States and other targets are not poor. Yes, but terrorist movements are often led by people who claim to act in the name of the poor and then recruit them to violent causes. The United States can reduce such appeal and enhance its soft power by aligning its policies with the aspirations of ordinary citizens in poor countries. U.S. President George W. Bush's commitment to increase development assistance and to spend an additional $10 billion to combat AIDS in Africa and the Caribbean is not only right for humanitarian reasons—it is also a wise investment in U.S. soft power. [. . .]

Nearly five centuries ago, Niccolò Machiavelli advised princes in Italy that it was more important to be feared than to be loved. In today's world, it is best to be both. To defeat terrorism, the United States must learn to combine soft and hard power more effectively.

The Bush Revolution
Ivo H. Daalder and James M. Lindsay

Daalder and Lindsay were both prominent members of the Clinton administration, so their far-from-negative view of Bush's foreign policy has special interest. It's common to take Bush's policies as hawkish conservative, Clinton's as dovish liberal, but as these authors show, the policies are arguably different sides of one movement, American internationalism, with Bush stressing the "free hand" position of American interventionism, Clinton the strengthening of international law. The following is from the first chapter of their book, America Unbound: The Bush Revolution in Foreign Policy *(Brookings Institution Press, 2003).*

George W. Bush had reason to be pleased as he peered down at Baghdad from the window of Air Force One in early June 2003. He had just completed a successful visit to Europe and the Middle East. The trip began in Warsaw, where he had the opportunity to personally thank Poland for being one of just two European countries to contribute troops to the Iraq War effort. He then traveled to Russia to celebrate the three hundredth birthday of St. Petersburg and to sign the papers formally ratifying a treaty committing Moscow and Washington to slash their nuclear arsenals. He flew on to Évian, a city in the French Alps, to attend a summit meeting of the heads of the world's major economies. He next stopped in Sharm el-Sheik, Egypt, for a meeting with moderate Arab leaders, before heading to Aqaba, Jordan, on the shore of the Red Sea to discuss the road map for peace with the Israeli and Palestinian prime ministers. He made his final stop in Doha, Qatar, where troops at U.S. Central Command greeted him with thunderous applause. Now Bush looked down on the city that American troops had seized only weeks before. As he pointed out landmarks below to his advisers, the pilot dipped Air Force One's wings in a gesture of triumph.

Bush's seven-day, six-nation trip was in many ways a victory lap to celebrate America's win in the Iraq War—a war that many of the leaders Bush
met on his trip had opposed. But in a larger sense he and his advisers saw it
as a vindication of his leadership. The man from Midland had been mocked
throughout the 2000 presidential campaign as a know-nothing. He had
been denounced early in his presidency for turning his back on time-tested
diplomatic practices and ignoring the advice of America's friends and allies.
Yet here he was traveling through Europe and the Middle East, not as a pen-
itent making amends but as a leader commanding respect. [. . .]

Nevertheless, good beginnings do not always come to good endings.
Even as Bush peered out the window of Air Force One to look at Baghdad,
there were troubling signs of things to come. American troops in Iraq found
themselves embroiled in what had all the makings of guerrilla war. Anger
had swelled overseas at what was seen as an arrogant and hypocritical America. Several close allies spoke openly about how to constrain America rather
than how best to work with it. As the president's plane flew home, Washington was beginning to confront a new question: Were the costs of the
Bush revolution about to swamp the benefits?

The question of how the United States should engage the world is an
old one in American history. The framers confronted the question only four
years after ratifying the Constitution when England went to war with France.
President George Washington ultimately opted for neutrality, disappointing
partisans on both sides. The hero of Valley Forge calculated that the small
and fragile experiment in republican government would likely be crushed
if it joined a battle between the world's two greatest powers.

America's relationship with Europe remained an issue throughout   5
Washington's presidency. He discussed the topic at length in his magiste-
rial address announcing his decision to retire to his beloved Mount Vernon.
He encouraged his countrymen to pursue peace and commercial relations.
"Harmony, liberal intercourse with all nations are recommended by policy,
humanity, and interest." But he discouraged them from tying their political fate to the decisions of others. "It is our true policy," Washington coun-
seled, "to steer clear of permanent alliances with any portion of the foreign
world."[1] [. . .]

[. . .] John Quincy Adams eloquently summarized this sentiment and
gave it an idealistic twist in an address he made before the House of Representatives on July 4, 1821. America applauds those who fight for liberty
and independence, he argued, "but she goes not abroad, in search of monsters to destroy. She is the well-wisher to the freedom and independence of
all. She is the champion and vindicator only of her own."[2] [. . .]

However, even liberal, democratic spirits can be tempted by changed
circumstances. When Adams spoke, the United States was an inconse-
quential agrarian country of twenty-three states, only one of which—
Louisiana—was west of the Mississippi. By the end of the nineteenth

century, it was an industrial colossus that spanned a continent. Its new status as a leading economic power brought with it growing demands from within to pursue imperial ambitions. [. . .]

The opportunity that imperialists had waited for came with the Spanish-American War. The windfall from that "splendid little war," as its supporters took to calling it, was an empire that stretched from Puerto Rico in the Caribbean to the Philippines in the Pacific. With victory safely in hand, concerns that America would lose its soul if it went abroad quickly faded. [. . .]

With the Spanish-American War [. . .], internationalists for the first time triumphed over isolationists in the struggle to define the national interest. However, the imperialist cause would soon begin to struggle. Part of the problem was the cost of empire. America's new subjects did not always take easily to Washington's rule. In the Philippines, the United States found itself bloodily suppressing a rebellion. American occupations of several Caribbean countries failed to produce the stability that Roosevelt had promised. By then, the imperialists were confronted by another, more serious challenge. This one came not from isolationists, but from within the internationalist camp itself.

Woodrow Wilson took office in 1913 determined to concentrate on domestic concerns. Shortly before taking the oath of office, he told an old colleague: "It would be the irony of fate if my administration had to deal chiefly with foreign affairs." [3] Yet fate had precisely that destiny for Wilson. His domestic policies are long forgotten; his foreign policy legacy is historic. Wilson's importance rests not on his achievements—he ultimately failed to see his proposal for a new world order enacted—but on his vision of America's role in the world. It was a vision that would dominate American politics after World War II.

Wilson shared with all his predecessors an unwavering belief in American exceptionalism. "It was as if in the Providence of God a continent had been kept unused and waiting for a peaceful people who loved liberty and the rights of men more than they loved anything else, to come and set up an unselfish commonwealth." [4] But whereas that claim had always been used to argue that America would lose its soul if it went abroad in search of monsters to destroy, Wilson turned it on its head. America would lose its soul if it did not go abroad. His liberal internationalism set forth a moral argument for broad American engagement in world affairs.

"We insist," Wilson told Congress in 1916, "upon security in prosecuting our self-chosen lines of national development. We do more than that. We demand it also for others. We do not confine our enthusiasm for individual liberty and free national development to the incidents and movements of affairs which affect only ourselves. We feel it wherever there is a people that tries to walk in these difficult paths of independence and right." [5] Not surprisingly, when Wilson requested a declaration of war against Germany—thereby doing the unthinkable, plunging the United States into a European war—he did not argue that war was necessary because Germany endangered American interests. Rather, the United States must fight because "the world must be made safe for democracy."[6]

Wilson's commitment to a world in which democracy could flourish was by itself revolutionary. Equally revolutionary was the second component of his vision —the belief that the key to creating that world lay in extending the reach of international law and building international institutions. [. . .]

The idea of the League of Nations was also revolutionary for American politics. Wilson was asking Americans to do more than just cast away their aversion to entangling alliances. The United States, after all, had fought World War I as an "associated" power and not an "allied" one in deference to the traditional reluctance to become tied militarily to other countries. He was asking them to spearhead an international organization that would seek to protect the security of its members, however far they might be from American shores. That would prove the rub.

The Senate's rejection of the Treaty of Versailles is usually recounted as a triumph of traditional isolationism. [. . . However,] many of the Senate's most ardent internationalists and imperialists also opposed the treaty. What bothered them was not that Wilson wanted to involve the United States in affairs beyond its borders. They were all for that. They simply opposed the way Wilson intended to engage the world. These anti-League internationalists, who included most Republicans and a few Democrats, believed that the United States had to preserve a free hand to act abroad, not tie its fate to the whims and interests of others. [. . .] The leader of the anti-League internationalists, Republican Senator Henry Cabot Lodge of Massachusetts, went to the heart of the matter when he asked his colleagues: "Are you willing to put your soldiers and your sailors at the disposition of other nations?"[7] [. . .]

15

The foreign policy questions Americans faced at the end of World War II had little to do with what the United States *could* do abroad. By every measure, America dominated the world as no nation had ever done before. All the other major powers, whether victor or vanquished, were devastated. The United States, in contrast, emerged from the war not only unscathed, but far stronger than it was when it entered the hostilities. Its economy was by far the world's largest. It possessed the world's strongest navy and most powerful air force. And it alone held the secret to the world's most terrifying weapon: the atomic bomb.

The foreign policy questions facing Americans dealt much more with what the United States *should* do abroad. Some Americans wanted to "bring the boys back home" from Europe and the Pacific and to return to a "normal" life. Others warned against a return to isolationism. But internationalists themselves disagreed on important questions. Should the United States define its interests regionally or globally? What were the threats to U.S. security? How should the United States respond to these threats? [. . .]

The task of answering these questions fell to President Harry Truman, a man who in many ways was ill prepared for it. [. . .] Whatever Truman lacked in experience he more than made up for with a commitment to pursuing Woodrow Wilson's aims without making his mistakes. During his seven years as president, Truman remade American foreign policy. In March 1947 [he] went before a joint session of Congress and declared what became known as the Truman Doctrine: "It must be the policy of the United States to support free peoples who are resisting attempted subjugation by armed minorities or by outside pressures."[8] Three months later his secretary of state, George C. Marshall, unveiled the Marshall Plan in a commencement address at Harvard, claiming a major role for the United States in rebuilding a war-torn Europe. Two years later, Truman signed the treaty creating the North Atlantic Treaty Organization (NATO). With the stroke of his pen, he cast off America's traditional aversion to entangling alliances and formally declared that Washington saw its security interests as inextricably linked with those of Western Europe.

The hallmark of Truman's foreign policy revolution was its blend of power and cooperation. Truman was willing to exercise America's great power to remake world affairs, both to serve American interests and to advance American values. However, he and his advisers calculated that U.S. power could more easily be sustained, with less chance of engendering resentment, if it were embedded in multilateral institutions. During his presidency, Truman oversaw the creation of much of the infrastructure of the international order: the United Nations, the International Monetary Fund, the World Bank, the General Agreement on Tariffs and Trade, and the Organization of American States among other multilateral organizations. In creating these institutions, he set a precedent: Even though the United States had the power to act as it saw fit, it accepted, at least notionally, that its right to act should be constrained by international law. In marked contrast to the epic League of Nations debate, the Senate overwhelmingly endorsed this multilateral approach. [. . .]

Eisenhower's embrace of Truman's foreign policy blueprint solidified America's basic approach to world affairs for the next half century. Even with the debacle in Vietnam, a basic foreign policy consensus held. The United States had extensive interests overseas that it must be prepared to defend. Washington actively cultivated friends and allies because in a world with a superpower adversary it was dangerous to be without them. International organizations, and especially military alliances, were a key instrument of foreign policy.

At the same time, however, the ever-present Soviet threat muffled the continuing disagreement between the intellectual descendants of Woodrow Wilson and those of Henry Cabot Lodge. Those in the Wilson school cherished the contribution of international law to world stability and prosperity. They took pride in the fact that Washington had championed

20

the creation of international organizations such as NATO and the United Nations and that by doing so the United States was laying the groundwork for the gradual expansion of the rule of law in international affairs. Those in the Lodge school longed for the policy of the free hand but were comforted by the fact that America's great wealth and military might enabled it to dominate international organizations. In NATO, for example, the United States was not simply Italy with more people. It was the superpower that provided the alliance's ultimate security guarantee, and as a result it had a disproportionate say over alliance policy. When multilateral organizations refused to heed American wishes, the United States could—and frequently did—act alone. [. . .]

The foreign-policy debates of the 1990s were at first mistakenly seen as a replay of the debates between isolationists and internationalists of the 1930s. [. . .] The real debate in the 1990s was not over *whether*, but *how* the United States should engage the world. Bill Clinton's presidency in most ways represented a continuation of the traditional Wilsonian approach of building a world order based on the rule of law. Clinton and his advisers argued that globalization was increasing economic, political, and social ties among nations and that this growing interconnectedness made fulfillment of Wilson's vision all the more important. In keeping with this thinking, the Clinton administration pursued traditional arms control agreements such as the Comprehensive Test Ban Treaty and a strengthening of the Biological Weapons Convention. It also sought to create new international arrangements such as the Kyoto Protocol and the International Criminal Court to deal with a new set of policy challenges.

Clinton's opponents criticized his decisions on numerous grounds, but one in particular stood out: He had failed to recognize that, with the demise of the Soviet Union, the United States now had the freedom to act as it saw fit. [. . .] As the columnist Charles Krauthammer put it, "An unprecedentedly dominant United States . . . is in the unique position of being able to fashion its own foreign policy. After a decade of Prometheus playing pygmy, the first task of the new [Bush] administration is precisely to reassert American freedom of action."[9] America, in short, could and should be unbound.

George W. Bush delivered the revolution that Krauthammer urged. It was not a revolution that started, as many later have suggested, on September 11, 2001. The worldview that drove it existed long before jet planes plowed into the Twin Towers and the Pentagon. Bush outlined its main ideas while he was on the campaign trail, and he began implementing parts of it as soon as he took the oath of office. What September 11 provided was the rationale and the opportunity to carry out his revolution.

But what precisely was the Bush revolution in foreign policy? At its broadest level, it rested on two beliefs. The first was that in a dangerous world the best—if not the only—way to ensure America's security was to shed the constraints imposed by friends, allies, and international

25

institutions. Maximizing America's freedom to act was essential because the unique position of the United States made it the most likely target for any country or group hostile to the West. Americans could not count on others to protect them; countries inevitably ignored threats that did not involve them. Moreover, formal arrangements would inevitably constrain the ability of the United States to make the most of its primacy. Gulliver must shed the constraints that he helped the Lilliputians weave.

The second belief was that an America unbound should use its strength to change the status quo in the world. Bush's foreign policy did not propose that the United States keep its powder dry while it waited for dangers to gather. The Bush philosophy instead turned John Quincy Adams on his head and argued that the United States should aggressively go abroad searching for monsters to destroy. That was the logic behind the Iraq War, and it animated the administration's efforts to deal with other rogue states.

These fundamental beliefs had important consequences for the practice of American foreign policy. One was a decided preference for unilateral action. Unilateralism was appealing because it was often easier and more efficient, at least in the short term, than multilateralism. [. . .] This is not to say that Bush flatly ruled out working with others. Rather, his preferred form of multilateralism [. . .] involved building ad hoc coalitions of the willing, or what Richard Haass, an adviser to Colin Powell, called "a la carte multilateralism." [10]

Second, preemption was no longer a last resort of American foreign policy. In a world in which weapons of mass destruction were spreading and terrorists and rogue states were readying to attack in unconventional ways, Bush argued that "the United States can no longer solely rely on a reactive posture as we have in the past. . . . We cannot let our enemies strike first." [11] Indeed, the United States should be prepared to act not just preemptively against imminent threats, but also preventively against potential threats. Vice President Dick Cheney was emphatic on this point in justifying the overthrow of Saddam Hussein on the eve of the Iraq War. "There's no question about who is going to prevail if there is military action. And there's no question but what it is going to be cheaper and less costly to do now than it will be to wait a year or two years or three years until he's developed even more deadly weapons, perhaps nuclear weapons." [12]

Third, the United States should use its unprecedented power to produce regime change in rogue states. The idea of regime change was not new to American foreign policy. The Eisenhower administration engineered the overthrow of Iranian Prime Minister Mohammed Mossadegh; the CIA trained Cuban exiles in a botched bid to oust Fidel Castro; Ronald Reagan channeled aid to the Nicaraguan contras to overthrow the Sandinistas; and Bill Clinton helped Serb opposition forces get rid of Slobodan Milosevic. What was different in the Bush presidency was the willingness, even in the absence of a direct attack on the United States, to use U.S. military forces for the express purpose of toppling other governments. This was the gist of both the Afghanistan and the Iraq wars. Unlike proponents of rollback, who never succeeded in overcoming the argument that their policies would produce World War III, Bush based his policy on the belief that nobody could push back. [. . .]

Notes

1. *The Writings of George Washington,* vol. 35, ed. John C. Fitzpatrick (Government Printing Office, 1940) 234.

2. John Quincy Adams, "Address of July 4, 1821," *John Quincy Adams and American Continental Empire: Letters, Papers, and Speeches,* ed. Walter LaFeber (Chicago: Quadrangle Books, 1965) 45, emphasis in original.

3. Quoted in Graham Evans, "The Vision Thing: In Search of the Clinton Doctrine," *World Today* 53 (August/September 1997): 216.

4. *The Papers of Woodrow Wilson,* vol. 37, ed. Arthur S. Link (Princeton UP, 1981) 213–14.

5. Woodrow Wilson, "Annual Address to Congress," *Congressional Record* 7 Dec. 1915: 96.

6. Woodrow Wilson, "Address to Congress," *Congressional Record* 2 April 1917: 120.

7. Quoted in Thomas G. Paterson, J. Garry Clifford, and Kenneth J. Hagan, *American Foreign Relations: A History since 1895,* vol. 2, 4th ed. (Lexington: D. C. Heath, 1995) 112.

8. *Public Papers of the Presidents of the United States: Harry S. Truman, 1947* (Government Printing Office, 1963) 178–79.

9. Charles Krauthammer, "The New Unilateralism," *Washington Post* 8 June 2001: A29.

10. Quoted in Thom Shanker, "White House Says the U.S. Is Not a Loner, Just Choosy," *New York Times,* 31 July 2001: A1.

11. *The National Security Strategy of the United States,* Washington, D.C., September 2002, accessed July 2003 <http://www.whitehouse.gov/nsc/nss.pdf>

12. Dick Cheney, NBC's *Meet the Press,* Washington, D.C., 16 March 2003, accessed July 2003 <http://www.mtholyoke.edu/acad/intrel/bush/cheneymeetthepress.htm>

One Man's World
Noam Chomsky

A great linguist and prominent leftist intellectual, Chomsky is a distinguished professor at the Massachusetts Institute of Technology. The following article appeared in New Statesman *(1996), November 17, 2003.*

High on the global agenda by autumn 2002 was the declared intention of the most powerful state in history to maintain its hegemony through the threat or use of military force, the dimension of power in which it reigns supreme. In the official rhetoric of the National Security Strategy, released in September 2002: "Our forces will be strong enough to dissuade potential adversaries from pursuing a military build-up in hopes of surpassing, or equaling, the power of the United States."

One well-known international affairs specialist, John Ikenberry, has described the declaration as a "grand strategy [that] begins with a fundamental commitment to maintaining a unipolar world in which the United States has no peer competitor," a condition that is to be "permanent [so] that no state or coalition could ever challenge [the US] as global leader, protector and enforcer." The "approach renders international norms of self-defense—enshrined by Article 51 of the UN Charter—almost meaningless."

The imperial grand strategy asserts the right of the US to undertake "preventive war" at will. Preventive, please note, not pre-emptive. Pre-emptive war might fall within the framework of international law. Thus, if the US had detected Russian bombers approaching from Grenada in 1983, with the clear intent to bomb, then, under a reasonable interpretation of the UN Charter, a pre-emptive attack destroying the planes and perhaps their Grenadian base would have been justifiable. [. . .] But the justifications for pre-emptive war do not hold for preventive war, particularly as that idea is interpreted by its current enthusiasts: the use of military force to eliminate an imagined or invented threat, so that even the term preventive is too charitable.

As Arthur Schlesinger, the former adviser to President Kennedy, observed, George W. Bush's "policy of 'anticipatory self-defense' [against Iraq] is alarmingly similar to the policy that imperial Japan employed at Pearl Harbor, on a date which, as an earlier American president said it would, lives in infamy . . . today, it is we Americans who live in infamy." Schlesinger added that even in friendly countries the public regards Bush "as a greater threat to peace than Saddam Hussein."

Some defenders of the strategy recognize that it runs roughshod over international law but see no problem in that. The whole framework of international law is just "hot air," the legal scholar Michael Glennon writes. "The grand attempt to subject the rule of force to the rule of law," he argues, should be deposited in the dustbin of history. How so? According to Glennon, Washington "made it clear that it intends to do all it can to maintain its pre-eminence," then announced that it would ignore the UN Security Council over Iraq and declared more broadly that "it would no longer be bound by the [UN] Charter's rules governing the use of force." QED. Accordingly, the rules have "collapsed" and "the entire edifice came crashing down."

The enlightened leader is also free to change the rules at will. When the military forces that now occupy Iraq failed to discover weapons of mass destruction, the administration's stance shifted from "absolute certainty" that Iraq possessed WMDs on a scale that required immediate military action to the assertion that American accusations had been "justified by the discovery of equipment that potentially could be used to produce weapons." Senior officials suggested a refinement in the controversial concept of a "preventive war" so that, as writers for the *Financial Times* have put it, the US can "act against a hostile regime that has nothing more than the intent and ability to develop [WMDs]." Since virtually any country has the potential and ability to produce WMDs, the refined version of the grand strategy grants Washington, in effect, the right of arbitrary aggression. [. . .]

The declaration of the grand strategy was rightly understood to be an ominous step in world affairs. It is not enough, however, for a great power to declare an official policy. It must go on to establish the policy as a new norm of international law by carrying out exemplary actions. The target of preventive war must have several characteristics. It must be virtually defenseless; it must be important enough to be worth the trouble; it must be possible to portray it as the ultimate evil and an imminent threat to our survival. Iraq qualified on all counts: the first two obviously, the third by virtue of the impassioned orations of George Bush and Tony Blair.

As the time approached to demonstrate the new norm of preventive war in September 2002, Condoleezza Rice, the national security adviser, warned that the next evidence of Saddam Hussein's intentions might be a mushroom cloud—presumably in New York. [. . .]

Within weeks of the claims in 2002, around 60 percent of Americans came to regard Saddam Hussein as "an immediate threat to the US." By March, almost half believed that he was personally involved in the 11 September attacks. Support for the war was strongly correlated with such beliefs. Diplomacy may have failed overseas, but it worked at home. The political analyst Anatol Lieven commented that most Americans had been duped "by a propaganda programme which for systematic mendacity has few parallels in peacetime democracies." In October, Congress granted the president authority to go to war "to defend the national security of the United States against the continuing threat posed by Iraq." [. . .]

The brilliant success of public diplomacy on the domestic front was revealed once again when the president, at the end of the war in Iraq in May 2003, stood on the deck of the aircraft carrier *Abraham Lincoln.* He was free to declare that he had won a "victory in a war on terror" by having "removed an ally of al-Qaeda." It was immaterial that the alleged link between Saddam Hussein and Osama bin Laden (his bitter enemy, in fact) was based on no credible evidence. Also immaterial was the only known connection between the Iraq invasion and the threat of terror: that the invasion enhanced the threat, as had been widely predicted, by sharply increasing al-Qaeda recruitment. [. . .]

After the invasion of Iraq was declared a success, it was publicly recognized that one motive for the war had been to establish the imperial grand strategy as a new norm: "Publication of the [National Security Strategy] was the signal that Iraq would be the first test, not the last," the

10

New York Times reported. "Iraq became the Petri dish in which this experiment in pre-emptive policy grew." The message, according to Roger Owen, a historian of the Middle East at Harvard University, was that peoples and regimes would have to change the way they see the world "from a view based on the United Nations and international law to one based on an identification" with Washington's agenda. [. . .]

The fundamental assumption that lies behind the imperial grand strategy is the guiding principle of Woodrow Wilson's idealism: we are good, even noble. Hence our interventions are necessarily righteous in intent, if occasionally clumsy in execution. In the words of President Wilson, we have "elevated ideals" and are dedicated to "stability and righteousness," and it is natural, as he wrote of the conquest of the Philippines, that "our interest must march forward, altruists though we are; other nations must see to it that they stand off, and do not seek to stay us."

"History," writes one commentator in our own time, "has a discernible direction and destination. Uniquely among all the nations of the world, the United States comprehends and manifests history's purpose." Accordingly, what US hegemony achieves is for the common good, so that empirical evaluation is unnecessary, if not faintly ridiculous. The primary principle of foreign policy, rooted in Wilsonian idealism and carried over from Bill Clinton to George Bush, is "the imperative of America's mission as the vanguard of history, transforming the global order and, in doing so, perpetuating its own dominance," guided by "the imperative of military supremacy, maintained in perpetuity and projected globally." Thus America is entitled, indeed obligated, to act as its leaders determine to be best, for the good of all, whether others understand or not. [. . .]

But there is rarely any shortage of elevated ideals to accompany the resort to violence. In 1990, Saddam Hussein assured the world that he wanted not "permanent fighting, but permanent peace . . . and a dignified life." In 1938, President Roosevelt's close confidant Sumner Welles praised the Munich agreement with the Nazis and felt that it might lead to a "new world order based upon justice and upon law." When Hitler occupied Czechoslovakia, he explained his earnest desire "to serve the true interests of the peoples dwelling in this area, to safeguard the national individuality of the German and Czech peoples, and to further the peace and social welfare of all." What could be more moving than Japan's "exalted responsibility" to establish a "New Order" in 1938 to "insure the permanent stability of East Asia" based on the "mutual aid" of Japan, Manchuria and China "in political, economic and cultural fields"?

After the war, interventions were routinely declared to be "humanitarian" or in self-defense and therefore in accord with the UN Charter. For example, Russia's murderous invasion of Hungary in 1956 was justified by Soviet lawyers on the grounds that it was undertaken at the invitation of the Hungarian government as a "defensive response to foreign funding of subversive activities." With comparable plausibility, the US attack against

15

South Vietnam a few years later was undertaken in "collective self-defense" against "internal aggression." [. . .]

As these few examples illustrate, even the harshest and most shameful measures are regularly accompanied by profession of noble intent. An honest look would only generalize Thomas Jefferson's observation on the world situation of his day: "We believe no more in Bonaparte's fighting merely for the liberties of the seas, than in Great Britain's fighting for the liberties of mankind. The object is the same, to draw to themselves the power, the wealth and the resources of other nations."

A century later, Robert Lansing, Woodrow Wilson's secretary of state (who also appears to have had few illusions about Wilsonian idealism), commented scornfully on "how willing the British, French or Italians are to accept a mandate" from the League of Nations, as long as "there are mines, oil fields, rich grain fields or railroads" that will "make it a profitable undertaking."

One may choose to have selective faith in one's domestic political leadership, adopting the stance that Hans Morgenthau, one of the founders of modern international relations theory, condemned as "our conformist subservience to those in power," the usual stance of most intellectuals throughout history. But it is important to recognize that profession of noble intent is predictable, and therefore carries no information [. . .]. Those who are seriously interested in understanding the world will adopt the same standards whether they are evaluating their own political and intellectual elites or those of official enemies. [. . .]

Where We Stand: The Situation in Iraq, and How to Go Forward
John O'Sullivan

O'Sullivan is editor-in-chief of United Press International and a frequent contributor to conservative magazines. The following article appeared in the National Review, *September 29, 2003.*

What the Bush administration most needs in its Iraqi policy is not greater U.N. involvement, or more soldiers, or even an infusion of $87 billion—but steady nerves. For it is in danger of being panicked into foolish new initiatives by [. . .] exaggerated claims and false arguments. [. . . T]hus far it is not responding to these challenges with firmness, persuasiveness, or indeed any very clear perception of what exactly is at stake. One crucial exception to that criticism must be made: In his September 7 television address, President Bush himself very clearly argued that Iraq is now the central front in the war against terrorism; his administration should heed his words.

The terrorists have made Iraq the main battleground by sneaking into the country, linking up with well-financed Baathist remnants, and embarking on a classic guerrilla-cum-terrorist campaign against Coalition forces and Iraqi patriots cooperating with them. [. . .] They believe, though perhaps with fading certainty, that the U.S. is vulnerable to guerrilla attacks because the American people cannot accept even a moderate number of casualties in foreign wars. That belief happens to be false. As Lawrence Kaplan establishes with a wealth of survey evidence in a recent *New Republic* article, it is not the people but the elites who shrink from casualties. What ordinary Americans rightly oppose is a war conducted without any clear aim or prospect of victory. And as yet opinion polls show an overwhelming majority of Americans believe the war in Iraq to be just, necessary, and winnable. But the terrorists' faith in America's lack of resolve helps to sustain their campaign.

It was imperative, therefore, that the president firmly declare that whatever the terrorists throw at us, the U.S. will stay in Iraq until the Iraqi people can operate and defend their own democratic government—which he did, with admirable clarity, on September 7. On less clear-cut issues, however, the administration's case is not being advanced effectively. Let me briskly summarize the arguments of the anti-Coalition coalition.

One: The war is being lost. According to a British Foreign Office document, self-evidently written to be leaked and thus to increase the pressure for U.N. involvement, the Coalition faces "strategic defeat" in Iraq. In the less flamboyant rhetoric of a *Washington Post* report, Iraq is "engulfed in guerrilla violence." In fact, virtually every reporter who actually travels outside Baghdad points out that most of Iraq is relatively peaceful; serious violence is largely confined to the "Sunni Triangle" between Baghdad and Tikrit, the long-predicted Shiite violence against Coalition forces seems not to have materialized, and the number of Coalition casualties is militarily insignificant. That last sentence will strike many readers, especially those with family members serving in Iraq, as harsh and callous. I appreciate that, and acknowledge that every death is a tragedy for some family somewhere. But the blunt truth is that the U.S. can withstand the death of one soldier a day—or fewer than 4,000 soldiers a decade—indefinitely, provided that the American people believe that the deaths are in a decent and winnable cause. And the sooner that fact is generally appreciated, the quicker the terrorists will lose the battle in Iraq and lose heart across the world. If, on the other hand, the U.S. loses heart and scuttles, then Iraq will become the headquarters and training ground for terrorist violence committed not in Iraq against soldiers but in American and West European cities against civilians. Take your choice.

Two: We need more troops on the ground—and that means troops from currently reluctant allies. Other things being equal, it would naturally be pleasant to have more troops in Iraq. But as several anti-terrorism

5

experts have pointed out, increasing the number of troops is not as important as improving the intelligence those troops are provided. And the intelligence-gathering process is indeed paying off: 39 of the top 55 officials on the playing-card list of senior Saddamites have been arrested or killed. If additional troops are genuinely needed for military reasons, then the U.S. would do well to seek them from those national armed forces that have real military clout and experience in working with U.S. forces—namely, Britain, Canada, Australia, New Zealand, and some NATO allies in Europe. Simply adding a bunch of U.N. peacekeepers is likely to complicate and weaken the Coalition effort. Some of those advocating it do so in order to strengthen the U.N.'s claims over Iraq rather than to defeat terrorism more expeditiously.

Three: We need a greater U.N. role in Iraq in order to provide legitimacy for the Coalition. But legitimacy with whom? Not with the terrorists, since—as the bombing of the U.N. headquarters in Iraq amply demonstrated—the Islamists regard the U.N. as just another instrument of a corrupt and godless West. With the Iraqi people? But they will remember that the U.N. ran a "food for oil" program that benefited the U.N. far more than the Iraqi people. With reluctant allies such as France and Germany? But they favor multilateralism not as means of achieving joint objectives but as a mechanism for frustrating U.S. policy. [. . .]

These dubious arguments hold general sway in the public debate, while developments that would tend to support U.S. policy tend to be overlooked. Little attention has been paid to the evidence, outlined by Amir Taheri in the *New York Post*, that Syria is already responding to the "demonstration effect" of Iraqi freedom by modest steps toward liberalization and the ending of the one-party state. But this merely underscores the need for the U.S. to argue its case better, and to stay the course in Iraq.

Are there then no valid criticisms of administration policy? Certainly there are. The "swagger" element in the Bush foreign policy has been grossly overdone; a firm policy can still be advanced in soothing diplomatic terms. The vulgar undifferentiated attacks on "the Europeans" have distorted the reality of strong support for the U.S. in many European nations and alienated potential supporters across the Continent. At the same time, the failure to develop a serious long-term policy that would prevent France and Germany from conscripting the "New Europe" into an anti-American coalition will weaken the U.S. [. . .]

The U.S. has quietly acquiesced over the years in the construction of a set of transnational rules, practices, and organizations that are hostile in principle to an international system based on nation-states and thus to the U.S. as the single most important state in that system. It is then unreasonably surprised when, in a crisis like Iraq, these transnational forces object to America's pursuing its interests without due deference to the new structures. [. . .]

Rights to Remember
Harold Hongju Koh

Koh is a professor of international law at Harvard. The following essay comes from the 2003 John Galway Foster lecture, London, October 21, 2003.

I would argue that September 11th ended the euphoria brought on by the fall of the Berlin Wall, the belief that American-led global co-operation could solve global problems. The American administration responded to the twin-towers tragedy with a sweeping new global strategy: an emerging "Bush doctrine," if you will.

One element of this doctrine is what I call "Achilles and his heel." September 11th brought upon America, as once upon Achilles, a schizophrenic sense of both exceptional power and exceptional vulnerability. Never has a superpower seemed so powerful and so vulnerable at the same time. The Bush doctrine asked: "How can we use our superpower resources to protect our vulnerability?"

The administration's answer has been "homeland security." To preserve American power and prevent future attack, the government has asserted a novel right under international law to disarm through "pre-emptive self-defence" any country that poses a threat. At home it has instituted sweeping strategies of immigration control, security detention, governmental secrecy, and information awareness.

The administration has also radically shifted its emphasis on human rights. In 1941, Franklin Delano Roosevelt called the allies to arms by painting a vision of the world we were trying to make: a post-war world of four fundamental freedoms: freedom of speech, freedom of religion, freedom from want, freedom from fear.

This framework foreshadowed the post-war human-rights construct—   5
embedded in the Universal Declaration of Human Rights and subsequent international convenants—that emphasised comprehensive protection of civil and political rights (freedom of speech and religion), economic, social and cultural rights (freedom from want), and freedom from gross violations and persecution (the Refugee Convention, the Genocide Convention and the Torture Convention). But Bush administration officials have now reprioritised "freedom from fear" as the number-one freedom we need to preserve. Freedom from fear has become the obsessive watchword of America's human-rights policy.

Witness five faces of a human-rights policy fixated on freedom from fear. First, closed government and invasions of privacy. Second, scapegoating immigrants and refugees. Third, creating extra-legal zones, most prominently at the naval base at Guantanamo Bay in Cuba. Fourth, creating extra-legal persons, particularly the detainees of American citizenship labelled "enemy combatants." Fifth, a reduced American human-rights presence through the rest of the globe.

The following vignettes illustrate this transformation of human rights.

Closed government and invasions of privacy. Two core tenets of a post-Watergate world had been that our government does not spy on its citizens, and that American citizens should see what our government is doing. But since September 11th, classification of government documents has risen to new heights.

The Patriot Act, passed almost without dissent after September 11th, authorises the Defence Department to develop a project to promote something called "total information awareness." Under this programme, the government may gather huge amounts of information about citizens without proving they have done anything wrong. They can access a citizen's records—whether telephone, financial, rental, internet, medical, educational or library—without showing any involvement with terrorism. Internet service providers may be forced to produce records based solely on FBI declarations that the information is for an anti-terrorism investigation.

Many absurdities follow: the Lawyers Committee for Human Rights, in a study published in September (www.lchr.org), reports that 20 American peace activists, including nuns and high-school students, were recently flagged as security threats and detained for saying that they were travelling to a rally to protest against military aid to Colombia. The entire high-school wrestling team of Juneau, Alaska, was held up at airports seven times just because one member was the son of a retired Coast Guard officer on the FBI watch-list.

Scapegoating immigrants. After September 11th, 1,200 immigrants were detained, more than 750 on charges based solely on civil immigration violations. The Justice Department's own inspector-general called the attorney-general's enforcement of immigration laws "indiscriminate and haphazard." The Immigration and Naturalisation Service, which formerly had a mandate for humanitarian relief as well as for border protection, has been converted into an arm of the Department of Homeland Security.

The impact on particular groups has been devastating. The number of refugees resettled in America declined from 90,000 a year before September 11th to less than a third that number, 27,000, this year. The Pakistani population of Atlantic County, New Jersey, has fallen by half.

The creation of extra-legal zones. Some 660 prisoners from 42 countries are being held in Guantanamo Bay, some for nearly two years. Three children are apparently being detained, including a 13-year-old, several of the detainees are aged over 70, and one claims to be over 100. Courtrooms are being built to try six detainees, including two British subjects who have been declared eligible for trial by military commission. There have been 32 reported suicide attempts. Yet the administration is literally pouring concrete around its detention policy, spending another $25m on buildings in Guantanamo that will increase the detention capacity to 1,100.

The creation of extra-legal persons. In two cases that are quickly working their way to the Supreme Court, Yasser Hamdi and Jose Padilla are two American citizens on American soil who have been designated as "enemy combatants," and who have been accorded no legal channels to assert their rights.

The racial disparities in the use of the "enemy combatant" label are glaring. Contrast, for example, the treatment of Mr Hamdi, from Louisiana but of Saudi Arabian ancestry, with that of John Walker Lindh, the famous "American Taliban," who is a white American from a comfortable family in the San Francisco Bay area. Both are American citizens; both were captured in Afghanistan in late 2001 by the Northern Alliance; both were handed over to American forces, who eventually brought them to the United States. But federal prosecutors brought criminal charges against Mr Lindh, who got an expensive lawyer and eventually plea-bargained to a prison term. Meanwhile, Mr Hamdi has remained in incommunicado detention, without a lawyer, in a South Carolina military brig for the past 16 months.

The effect on the rest of the world. America's anti-terrorist activities have given cover to many foreign governments who want to use "anti-terrorism" to justify their own crackdowns on human rights. Examples abound. In Indonesia, the army has cited America's use of Guantanamo to propose building an offshore prison camp on Nasi Island to hold suspected terrorists from Aceh. In Australia, Parliament passed laws mandating the forcible transfer of refugees seeking entry to detention facilities in Nauru, where children as young as three years old are being held, so that Australia does not (in the words of its defence minister) become a "pipeline for terrorists."

In China, Wang Bingzhang, the founder of the pro-democracy magazine *China Spring,* was recently sentenced to life imprisonment for "organising and leading a terrorist group," the first time, apparently, that the Chinese government has charged a democracy activist with terrorism. In Russia, Vladimir Putin on September 12th 2001 declared that America and Russia "have a common foe" because Osama bin Laden's people are connected to events in Chechnya. Within months the American government had added three Chechen groups to its list of foreign terrorist organisations.

In Egypt, the government extended for another three years its emergency law, which allows it to detain suspected national-security threats almost indefinitely without charge, to ban public demonstrations, and to try citizens before military tribunals. President Hosni Mubarak announced that America's parallel policies proved that "we were right from the beginning in using all means, including military tribunals, to combat terrorism."

What's wrong with this picture? Each prong of the Bush doctrine places America in the position of promoting double standards, one for itself, and another for the rest of the world. The emerging doctrine has placed startling pressure upon the structure of human-rights and international law that the

15

United States itself designed and supported since 1948. In a remarkably
short time, the United States has moved from being the principal supporter
of that system to its most visible outlier.

Around the globe, America's human-rights policy has visibly softened,   20
subsumed under the all-encompassing banner of the "war against terrorism." And at home, the Patriot Act, military commissions, Guantanamo
and the indefinite detention of American citizens have placed America in
the odd position of condoning deep intrusions by law, even while creating
zones and persons outside the law.

At this point, you are surely asking: "Why did this happen?" and "What
can we do about it?" People living outside America sometimes suggest that
the reason is rooted in the American national culture of unilateralism,
parochialism and an obsession with power. With respect, let me urge you
to see it differently. The Bush doctrine, I believe, is less a broad manifestation of American national character than of shortsighted decisions made by
a particularly extreme American administration.

Many, if not most, Americans would have supported dealing with September 11th in a different way. Imagine, for example, the Bush administration dealing with the atrocity through the then prevailing multilateralist
strategy of using global co-operation to solve global problems. On the day
after the attack, George Bush could have flown to New York to stand in solidarity with the world's ambassadors in front of the United Nations.

He could have supported the International Criminal Court as a way of
bringing the Osama bin Ladens and Saddam Husseins of the world to justice. He could have refrained from invading Iraq without a second UN resolution, and he could have maintained a host of human-rights treaties to
signal the need for even greater global solidarity in a time of terror. I am
convinced that the American people would have supported him in all those
efforts.

So to those who would blame American culture for America's unilateralism, let me remind you that not every American is equally well-placed
to promote American unilateralism. In recent years, such individuals as
Mr. Bush, Donald Rumsfeld, John Bolton, Jesse Helms and Justice Antonin
Scalia have held particularly strategic positions that enabled them to promote this sea-change in human-rights policy.

But if particular politicians and judges are part of the problem, they   25
are also part of the solution. For, in recent months, American human-rights
lawyers have launched multiple efforts to counter these trends, particularly
through lawsuits seeking to persuade judges to construe American law in
light of universal human-rights principles.

What are the signs of this trend? With each passing day, I see growing
resistance to these policies among ordinary Americans. Some promising
examples:

- Career bureaucrats have started to challenge the administration's
  policies for undoing years of hard work.

- Military judges and former federal prosecutors have expressed dismay over military commissions.
- A group of former federal judges filed a brief in the Padilla case challenging the president's detention of American citizens without express congressional authorisation. They were joined in those efforts by two conservative libertarian groups: the Cato Institute and the Rutherford Institute.
- Career diplomats have told me of early retirements by those who refuse to implement what they view as discriminatory visa policies.
- A group of former American diplomats and former American prisoners-of-war have challenged the administration's flouting of the Geneva Conventions before the Supreme Court.
- Librarians and booksellers have joined a bipartisan group of 133 congressional representatives to press for a law, called the Freedom to Read Protection Act, that would shield library and bookstore records from government surveillance.

These grassroots efforts are finally reaching the political actors. The public outcry following the leak of a proposed second Patriot Act has put that legislation on hold. Resolutions opposing the first Patriot Act have passed in three states and 162 municipalities. The House of Representatives has refused to provide funding for the part of the Patriot Act that allows so-called "sneak and peek" searches of private property without prompt notice to the resident. A battle is brewing in Congress over whether parts of the current act should be eliminated in 2005. [. . .]

In 1759, Benjamin Franklin wrote: "They that can give up essential liberty to obtain a little temporary safety deserve neither." In the months ahead, I believe, we can both obtain our security and preserve our essential liberty, but only so long as we have courage from our courts, commitment from our citizens, and pressure from our foreign allies. Even after September 11th, America can still stand for human rights, but we can get there only with a little help from our friends.

Mr. President, Stop the Torture!
Dianna Ortiz

Ortiz directs the Torture Abolition and Survivors Support Coalition in Washington, D.C. She received the 2003 U.S. Catholic Award for Furthering the Cause of Women in the Church. Her article appeared in U.S. Catholic *(July 2004).*

After Abu Ghraib, it is no longer possible to say, "We didn't know." One would have to avoid television and newspapers completely not to know that the U.S. has been involved in the torture of Iraqi detainees. Of course, officials still insist on using the term abuse, even though, in fact, it is torture they are talking about. They may be squeamish about using the latter term, but historically our government has not been shy about its involvement with torture.

It is interesting to those of us who are torture survivors that at the very time when new investigations are being started, congressional hearings being held, and atrocious visual evidence still being released, senior U.S. officials have already pronounced that such "un-American" activity is the product of a relatively few low-ranking individuals. No investigation has concluded this, thus far. And I should also note that the very officials who make this judgment might still be found responsible themselves when the investigations are finally complete.

There are times when I find it difficult to listen to the public discourse about torture. Academics from a Harvard law professor to a University of Pennsylvania ethicist to a Georgetown University priest-philosopher, among others, continue to advertise the virtues of torture for the benefit of our society. At such times I can't help but think back to my own torture and wonder what unfathomable benefit it carried for either Guatemalan or U.S. society.

Of course, these scholars and others are advocating that only "really dangerous" people be tortured. Apparently my being a nun teaching Mayan children in Guatemala was thought sufficiently dangerous that I should be burned, raped, and otherwise brutalized. And if they mean that only the U.S. should have the right to employ torture, I point to the American who had a role in what was done to me. One difference between these pundits and me, of course, is that they are speaking in the abstract while I experienced torture in body and mind.

Most disconcerting of all, however, is that the revelation about the torture at Abu Ghraib is being treated as a unique event. While it is true that throughout the years successive administrations have sought to maintain secrecy, enough is known to disabuse us of any idea that this is our government's first brush with torture.

In the plainest of language, the United States government, its leaders, and those who have done their bidding have countenanced torture, watched torture as it was being practiced, taught torture, and practiced torture on the innocent and the helpless. Witness Greece in the 1940s and Iran in the '50s. Consider as well the U.S. involvement over the years in torture in Uruguay, Brazil, Bolivia, Guatemala, Honduras, El Salvador, Argentina, and other countries.

There is one question that I—a torture survivor, a Catholic, a nun—wish to ask. In *Torture and Eucharist* (Blackwell), William Cavanaugh writes, "The true body of Christ is the suffering body, the destitute body, the body which is tortured and sacrificed." If Cavanaugh is indeed correct about torture relating so integrally to our faith, then why are the Christian churches not in the forefront of this confrontation with such a crime against humanity?

Cavanaugh recounts a conversation reported in 1987 in the German newsmagazine *Der Spiegel* between the Chilean dictator president General Augusto Pinochet and then-West German labor minister Norbert Blum. Blum told Pinochet that he accepted that one should not interfere in the internal affairs of another nation, but he went on to note an exception to that principle: human rights. "Here interference is an obligation," he said. "Mr. President, stop torturing."

During our government's long, sorry history of involvement with torture, was there no church leader, Catholic or other, who would say, "Mr. President, stop torturing"?

Today, by our actions, survivors of torture say this every day to every leader of the more than 150 governments that torture: "Stop torturing!"

10

Is it not our Christian, moral responsibility to demand this of the world's leaders? If it is, then will you join with us in our efforts to denounce torture wherever and whenever it occurs and create a torture-free world?

Questions for Discussion

1. Gunaratna claims that, after 9/11, Al Qaeda has relied "on Islamic parties hiding behind the political veil to produce a generation of recruits and supporters," adding that it "will operate through mosques . . . community centers and . . . charities in Western Europe and North America." Liberal democracies regard freedom of religion as fundamental; what, then, if anything, can we do about the Islamic parties Gunaratna points to as a key source of Al Qaeda's support?

2. According to Gunaratna, what led Al Qaeda to reduce its targeting of moderate and secular Muslim countries? What did the West do and fail to do to head off the terrorist threat? What do these lessons from before 9/11 imply about what we should be doing now?

3. Why, according to Gunaratna, does Al Qaeda pose a greater threat to Muslim countries than to European or North American countries? If he's right, what does this imply about winning the war against terror long term?

4. Gorenberg's view on countering terrorism boils down to this: "drive a wedge between terrorists and the public they'd like to recruit." Gunaratna clearly agrees that isolating terrorists groups must be part of the counterterrorism picture. What can the United States and other liberal democracies do to drive the wedge?

5. According to Nye, "when someone does something he would otherwise not do but for force or inducement, that's hard power"; in contrast, "soft power is the ability to secure [desired] outcomes through attraction rather than coercion." *"It is the ability to shape what others want"* (our emphasis). Have you seen

indications that the Muslim masses are attracted to at least *some* of what the West in general and the United States in particular has to offer? That is, are the conditions right for exercising more soft power in the Middle East and elsewhere where terrorism flourishes?

6. In important ways, recent American foreign policy, whether pursued by Republican or Democratic administrations, derives from the revolution in foreign policy envisioned by Woodrow Wilson around the time of World War I. Using Daalder and Lindsay's account, explain what Wilson did and tried to do and why his vision marks a turning point in American foreign policy. According to this same account, which chief executive succeeded in realizing most of Wilson's intentions?

7. Daalder and Lindsay call Bush's foreign policy revolutionary. In their view, what features make it so? What conditions both within the United States and across the globe permitted such policies full expression?

8. Chomsky strongly rejects Wilsonian idealism, the view of America as embodying the best hope for humanity, as being "the vanguard of history." He's critical of such views because they mask policies driven by economic advantage and the desire for power rather than humanitarian goals. Do you see what we have done since 9/11 as pure self-interest? Do you dismiss the idea entirely that the United States represents, in some ways at least, what much of the world needs?

9. O'Sullivan defends our actions in Iraq against widespread assertions that the enterprise is in trouble, on the verge of failure. What assertions does O'Sullivan address? What evidence does he offer that they are false or exaggerated? What criticisms does he have of Bush administration foreign policy?

10. Koh cites Benjamin Franklin's often-quoted statement: "They that give up essential liberty to obtain a little temporary safety deserve neither." Koh plainly believes that, following 9/11, we have given up essential liberty. Do you find his argument persuasive? If so, how do you propose to deal with the "Islamic parties" Al Qaeda is said to rely on for support in Europe and North America? How can their efforts be frustrated without violating freedom of speech, association, and religion?

11. The exposure of torture and abuse at Abu Ghraib prison has not only spurred public recognition of human rights abuses by our own government but also done incalculable damage to the image of the United States in the Muslim world, an image already extremely negative. Ortiz makes an eloquent plea for ending all torture on moral and religious grounds. How else can we argue against it?

Suggestions for Writing

For Research, Analysis, and Convincing

One feature of the Bush administration's approach to foreign policy is not to wait for change in a regime unfavorable to the United States but, rather, to use military force to remove it from power. That's what happened in both Afghanistan and Iraq. Choose one or the other country, and assess regime change by force as a foreign policy measure. First, collect up-to-date information on the situation in the country you've chosen. Read a variety of experts who assess the outcome from different points of view. Then write an essay taking a stance on whether regime change by force is worth the money and the casualties. If you think it is or can be, specify the circumstances within which you think the measure ought to be used.

For Research and Persuasion

Recently much attention has gone to our prison facilities at Guantanamo Bay in Cuba, a U.S. military outpost housed on land rented from the Cuban government long before Castro came to power. We have placed prisoners there acquired during the Afghan and Iraq campaigns—about 600 when this assignment was written. Find out everything you can about Guantanamo. Pay careful attention to the legal reasons it was chosen as a place for prisoners who may have been or collaborated with terrorists. Then write an essay defending our use of Guantanamo or arguing for some other way of dealing with suspected terrorists. Conceive your essay as a letter to your senator or representative in the U.S. Congress.

For Mediation

There are Al Qaeda "sleeper cells" in the United States and Islamic groups working through mosques and community centers to further the goals of militant Islamic groups abroad. So we are told by terrorist experts like Rohan Gunaratna. In our system of law, we can do nothing about groups that entertain ideas we don't like or who speak in favor of ideas we'd like to see suppressed. Nor can we prevent such groups from raising money that could wind up supporting Al Qaeda directly or indirectly, except by temporary measures used during times of war. Unless and until such groups break the law, commit a criminal act, what they do is protected as free speech, freedom of association, and freedom of religion.

Traditionally we've guarded such rights based on a sharp contrast between ideas, protected by free speech, and acts, which in some cases constitute a violation of the law. But now we face a threat we've never faced before located in an international terrorist organization dependent on sources of support all over the world. An autocratic government, such as Iraq under Hussein, handles such internal threats by simply rounding up and killing as many adherents as they can find. We can't do this. However, it would be foolish and naïve to simply ignore sleeper cells or Islamic groups sympathetic to

Al Qaeda. How, then, can we be effective in combating terrorism within our borders without ceasing to be "the land of the free"? Write an essay justifying some middle course between the traditional way and the measures used by the Bush administration after 9/11. Think of what you're proposing as long-term policy, not something based in the extraordinary executive powers that exist in wartime.

For Research, Discussion, and Convincing

You might imagine that no moral person could support torture in any form for any reason. But as Ortiz points out, torture is defended by even some ethicists and philosophers, well-educated people who cannot be easily accused of either ignorance of or insensitivity to human suffering.

Find three or four good examples of their arguments. Summarize them in class discussion and ponder what they say carefully. Read or reread Ortiz's argument against torture and discuss how well it holds up against those who advocate it in certain circumstances.

Write an essay stating and defending your own position on torture. State your claim precisely. Defend your position with reasons designed to appeal to as broad a range of readers as you can. Consider publishing your article in your school's newspaper or on a suitable Web site.

FOR FURTHER READING AND RESEARCH

Gupta, Suman. *The Replication of Violence: Thoughts on International Terrorism after September 11th 2001.* London: Pluto Press, 2002.

Harmon, Christopher C. *Terrorism Today.* London: Frank Cass, 2000.

Jenkins, Philip. *Images of Terror: What We Can and Can't Know about Terrorism.* New York: Aldine de Gruyter, 2003.

Maxwell, Bruce. *Terrorism: A Documentary History.* Washington: CQ Press, 2003.

Miller, Judith. *God Has Ninety-Nine Names: Reporting from a Militant Middle East.* New York: Simon and Schuster, 1996.

Reich, Walter, ed. *Origins of Terrorism: Psychologies, Ideologies, Theologies, States of Mind.* Cambridge: Cambridge UP, 1990.

Scraton, Phil, ed. *Beyond September 11: An Anthology of Dissent.* London: Pluto Press, 2002.

Talbott, Strobe, and Nayan Chanda, eds. *The Age of Terror: America and the World after September 11.* New York: Basic Books, 2001.

Wilkinson, Paul. *Terrorism versus Democracy: The Liberal State Response.* London: Frank Cass, 2000.

Chapter 11

Casebook on Personal Relationships: Sex, Love, and Maybe Even Marriage

"I don't care if she is a tape dispenser. I love her."

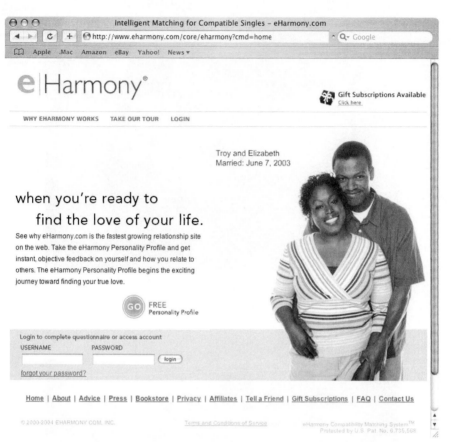

Reprinted with permission.

"And do you, Rebecca, promise to make love only to Richard, month after month, year after year, and decade after decade, until one of you is dead?"

Questions for Discussion

1. The love-struck snail on page 417 knows that the object of his affection is a tape dispenser but believes, like many people, that the only thing that matters is love. In Section Two of this casebook, David Buss writes about what brings lovers together, noting that people with similar interests and backgrounds are more likely to be compatible lovers. Discuss the idea that the power of love can overcome significant differences between partners.

2. In the 1950s, the most popular venue for dating was the soda shop, and a standard "couple" photo showed them drinking ice cream sodas, often with their heads together, as in the picture on page 418. In contrast, media images today often show the couple in a bar, drinking cosmopolitans, as in the scene from the popular show *Sex and the City* immediately below it. What messages about love or "romance" do these two images send, according to your interpretation?

3. The bottom photograph on page 419, titled "Kiss at the Hotel de Ville," was taken by Robert Doisneau in Paris in 1950. Doisneau was shooting a pseudo-documentary series for *Life* magazine on young lovers in the spring. He used models and posed them in various locations around Paris. The photograph became an iconic image of love, ubiquitous as a poster in the 1980s. In Section 1 of the readings in this casebook, both Diane Ackerman and Chrys Ingraham discuss the effects of art, literature, and film on a culture's understanding of love. What message about love does this art photograph convey? Does knowing that it was posed affect your interpretation of it? What does it say about love?

4. Officials in California and other states have married same-sex couples in defiance of state laws forbidding such marriages. The top photograph on page 419 shows Joy Galloway and Keltie Jones's ceremony in San Francisco's City Hall in February 2004. In our original image, their dresses are pastels—one aqua and the other violet. After reading Chrys Ingraham's description of "white weddings" as shown through the film industry (pages 453–463), discuss the ways in which same-sex wedding ceremonies are similar to and different from the standard heterosexual wedding.

5. Computer dating services claim that by studying the personalities and tastes of clients, they can find good matches more effectively and efficiently than people can find for themselves through ads, friends, and the more traditional ways of finding a partner. After reading "Who Wants to Marry a Soul Mate?" (pages 497–505), discuss the eHarmony ad (page 420) and the service itself. (You may want to log in and take the free personality profile.) How do the ad and service appeal to people looking for a soul mate? Do some research on the success of marriages between couples who met through dating services such as eHarmony.

6. The cartoon by Tom Cheney on page 421 gets its humor from its re-wording of the standard wedding vows—and the expressions of the couple at the altar, who have apparently never thought of their life-long monogamous commitment as the preacher's words describe it. Read Laura Kipnis's essay "Against Love" (pages 544–551), and dis-cuss the connections between Cheney's joke and Kipnis's view of "mature love."

GENERAL INTRODUCTION: LOVE TODAY

As we enter the twenty-first century, there appears to be no decline in the pat-terns and habits of life that make us less connected as a society: families see each other less because of the demands of school and jobs; neighbors move in and out without our knowing much about them; marriages continue to break up at the rate of about 50%; more and more people are living alone; and our churches and high schools are so large that individuals may feel like just another number. The pursuit of individual happiness, however we define it, means that we go our own ways rather than adhering to traditional insti-tutions that once connected us to family, friends, and neighbors. But one connection persists and may in fact have become more important to us—the personal relationship based in love. Our love lives are perhaps the defining factor in personal happiness today.

Whether you call the person a husband or wife, girlfriend or boyfriend, partner, significant other, or something else, we Americans seem highly in-vested in finding someone to love and to love us. Surveys of college freshmen show that interest in marriage and raising a family is among their highest goals; surveys of young adults indicate the desire to find a soul mate and stay married for life. While some people resist conventional marriage, the major-ity still seek lifelong commitment.

And yet none of this comes easily for most individuals. While mar-riage is still a stated goal, the percentage of unmarried people is at an all-time high. The process of finding a mate, making a commitment to marry, and re-maining married is more and more defined in terms of work, not pleasure. Books, magazines, reality TV, Dr. Phil, E. Jean, Dear Abby, therapists and counselors—all offer advice about how to obtain, maintain, and recover from personal relationships. In spite of its importance, the personal rela-tionship seems a source of insecurity and anxiety. Why are Americans hav-ing so much trouble with the personal relationships they claim to value so much?

The writers who appear in this casebook describe Americans trying to navigate in a sea of conflicting ideas and social pressures:

1. We have unrealistic ideas about what love is. Popular culture depicts love as romantic infatuation, even obsession, between beautiful

people, usually young. We don't see many portrayals of love as long-term attachment between real-life, mature couples.

2. We have high expectations for what we want in a mate. According to evolutionary psychologists, nature made us fussy. We look for a partner with good genes and reproductive potential. But our culture exaggerates the youth, beauty, wealth, and status that an ideal mate should possess. Other expectations are just as high. Whoever invented the term "soul mate" hit a chord with people's needs today; both sexes want deep emotional intimacy with their partner. We want mates who will anticipate and satisfy all our needs.

3. We want intimacy, and yet we fear it. According to one essay in our chapter on liberal education (Chapter 15), college students go out in groups because they want to protect themselves from intimacy. But avoiding personal relationships for years makes the search for the right partner more serious than fun. Dating services and publishers of advice books feed off of people's anxiety about finding the right partner and women's fears that it will not happen in time for them to bear children.

4. Marriage has gone from a public institution to a private one. Family and community used to be more involved when marriages were arranged, or at least when courtship took place in the family home; when marriages were seen as the joining of two families, not just two individuals. Economic factors also make us more independent than when women depended on a husband for financial support and when men depended on a wife for domestic services. These factors have made personal relationships less stable.

SECTION 1: DEFINING LOVE

Overview

The human race needs sex to survive, but what about love? Is romantic love a natural occurrence or a cultural invention? Imagine people living in a society with no books, poems, movies, or songs about love. Would they still fall in love?

The anthropologists say we would. Romantic love is universal. People the world over who claim to be in love report the same feelings of obsession, infatuation, increased energy, ecstasy, and despair, mixed with sexual desire. In her book *Why We Love: The Nature and Chemistry of Romantic Love*, Helen Fisher offers examples of ancient texts from Hebrew, Arabic, Indian, Chinese, and other civilizations expressing the ecstasy and agony of passion. For example, the love-obsessed lines "How can I not think of you?" and "My longing has no time when it ceases" come from poets in fourth-century China and eighth-century Japan (8).

Fisher used technology to find if romantic love exists in some tangible way in the human brain. She and neuroscientists at Albert Einstein College of Medicine used fMRI (functional magnetic resonance imaging) to scan the brains of love-struck volunteers as they gazed at pictures of their sweethearts. Her conclusion is that what we call romantic love is a drive embedded in the structure of the brain, visible in areas of the brain that release dopamine and other chemicals that cause the symptoms of falling in love: speeded up heartbeat, butterflies, exhilaration, concentration on the beloved, high energy, sleeplessness (Fisher 69–72). So, why do fools fall in love? Because it's literally addictive.

But the "high" of infatuation is not the only kind of love that Fisher and others have found evidence of in their brain scans and surveys. In an excerpt published here from Fisher's book, she describes an array of chemicals found in the brains of people experiencing lust, romantic love, and the more stable and enduring kind of love found in long-term relationships, which she calls *attachment*. Fisher's essay raises some questions about Western culture's expectation that love needs to be romantic and passionate. Keeping the dopamine flowing for decades with the same mate may not be possible, biologically. Why does it matter so much that we keep romance alive?

This question takes us back to where we began: Is love a natural occurrence or a cultural invention? While love may be universal, the two writers who conclude this section argue that the meaning of love is a product of social, economic, and cultural forces. As a social creation, love can be an instrument of change or an effort to resist change. Diane Ackerman, in her selection on the history of romantic love, shows that love as a passionate uniting of two human souls was a revolutionary idea that emerged out of medieval songs and poems. Chrys Ingraham analyzes two recent films to show that modern popular culture defines romantic love in ways that maintain patriarchal, heterosexual, and middle-class consumer values.

Web of Love: Lust, Romance, and Attachment
Helen Fisher

Helen Fisher, Ph.D., is a research professor in anthropology at Rutgers University. She has written several books on love and sex, including The First Sex *(2000),* Anatomy of Love *(1994), and* Why We Love: The Nature and Chemistry of Romantic Love *(2004), from which this reading comes.*

Love is "as sweet and musical / As bright Apollo's lute, strung with his hair. / And when Love speaks, the voices of all the gods / Makes heaven drowsy with the harmony."[1] Love is a harmony, as Shakespeare wrote, sometimes even a cacophony of sensations. Exuberance, tenderness, compassion, possessiveness, rapture, adoration, longing, despair: romance is a kaleidoscopic pattern of shifting needs and feelings all tethered to a celestial being on whose slightest word or smile one dangles, spinning with hope and joy and craving. Complexity, thy name is love.

Yet with time and circumstance, nature has built a few major chords within this symphony. Romantic love is deeply entwined with two other mating drives: *lust*—the craving for sexual gratification; and *attachment*—the feelings of calm, security, and union with a long-term partner.[2]

Each of these basic mating drives travels along different pathways in the brain. Each produces different behaviors, hopes, and dreams. And each is associated with different neurochemicals. Lust is associated primarily with the hormone testosterone in both men and women. Romantic love is linked with the natural stimulant dopamine and perhaps norepinephrine and serotonin. And feelings of male-female attachment are produced primarily by the hormones oxytocin and vasopressin.

Moreover, each brain system evolved to direct a different aspect of reproduction. Lust evolved to motivate individuals to seek sexual union with almost *any* semi-appropriate partner. Romantic love emerged to drive men and women to focus their mating attention on a preferred individual, thereby conserving invaluable courtship time and energy. And the brain circuitry for male-female attachment developed to enable our ancestors to live with this mate at least long enough to rear a single child through infancy together.[3]

All three of these brain networks—lust, romantic attraction, and attachment—are multipurpose systems. In addition to its reproductive purpose, the sex drive serves to make and keep friends, provide pleasure and adventure, tone muscles, and relax the mind. Romantic love can stimulate you to sustain a loving partnership or drive you to fall in love with a new person and initiate divorce. And feelings of attachment enable us to express genuine affection for children, family, and friends, as well as a beloved.

Nature is conservative. When she has a good design, she sticks with it, expanding its uses to suit many situations. But the primary purpose of these interlocking drives is to motivate us to seek an array of sexual partners, choose one to dote upon, then remain emotionally engaged with "him" or "her" at least long enough to rear a child together—the basics of the mating game.

To understand how romantic passion affects the sex drive and feelings of long-term attachment, I embarked on a research project with Jonathan Stieglitz, then a student at Rutgers University. We mined MedLine, PubMed, and other search engines on the Internet for academic articles illustrating how the chemistry of these three mating drives—lust, romantic attraction, and attachment—affect one another.

Indeed, romantic love weaves its way through these other brain networks in ways that both enrich and tear the fabric of our lives.

ON LUST

"What arms and shoulders did I touch and see, / How apt her breasts were to be pressed by me, / How smooth a belly under her waist saw I, / How large a leg, and what a lusty thigh. / To leave the rest, all liked me passing well; / I clinged her naked body, down she fell; / Judge you the rest, being tired she bade me kiss; / Jove send me more such afternoons as this!"[4] Ovid, the Roman poet, was one of countless millions who have savored lust.

Lust is a primordial human feeling. It is unpredictable, too. The craving for sexual fulfillment can pop up in your mind as you are driving in your car, watching a movie on TV, reading in the office, or daydreaming on the beach. And this urge is very different from the feeling of romantic love. In fact, few people in Western societies confuse the elation of romance with the longing for sexual release.[5]

People in far different cultures also easily distinguish between these feelings.[6] On the Polynesian island of Mangaia, "real love" is called *inangaro kino*, a state of romantic passion quite distinct from one's sexual desires. In their native language, the Taita of Kenya call lust *ashiki* while they refer to love as *pendo*.[7] And in Caruaru, a town in northeast Brazil, locals say, "*Amor* is when you feel a desire to always be with her, you breathe her, eat her, drink her, you are always thinking of her, you don't manage to live without her."[8] *Paixao*, on the other hand, is "horniness" and *tesao* is "a very strong sexual attraction for a person."[9]

These people are correct to regard these feelings as distinct. Scientists have recently established that lust and romantic love are associated with different constellations of brain regions.[10] In one study, researchers scanned the brains of a group of young heterosexual men using the fMRI brain scanner. The men were shown three types of videos: some were erotic, some relaxing, some related to sports.[11] Each volunteer wore a custom-built pneumatic pressure cuff around his penis to record firmness. The pattern of brain activity was quite different from the one we found among the lovesick subjects in our brain scanning project.

Lust and romantic love are not the same.

And just as people everywhere have concocted love potions to spur romance, they have tried all sorts of potions to trigger lust—what an Italian proverb calls "the oldest lion of them all."

THE HORMONE OF DESIRE

"Candy is dandy, but liquor is quicker," quipped Ogden Nash. Everywhere humankind has used what they hoped was an aphrodisiac to trigger lust. When the tomato first crossed the Atlantic from the Americas, the Europeans thought this juicy red fruit would spark the sexual appetite; they called it the "love apple." Shark's fins, bird's nest soup, powdered rhinoceros horn, curry, chutney, mandrake root, chocolate, hyena eyes, caviar, clams, oysters, lobsters, dove brains, goose tongues, apples, bananas, cherries, dates, figs, peaches, pomegranates, asparagus, garlic, beer, perspiration: scents and tastes and ointments of dazzling variety have been employed to charm reluctant partners into bed.

The Elizabethans served free prunes in brothels because they were convinced this spurred lust. In past centuries Arabs tried to lure hesitant women into sampling a bit of camel hump to pique their sexual desire. Pliny wrote that hippopotamus snouts would do the trick. The Aztecs saw sexual magic in goat and rabbit parts because these animals were fast breeders. Sea slugs caught the fancy of the Chinese, largely because these strange animals enlarge when touched. And Europeans historically pulverized a certain type of beetle found in southern Europe to incite sexual desire; they called it Spanish fly.[12]

Eating increases blood pressure and the pulse rate, raises body temperature, and sometimes makes us sweat, physiological changes that also occur with sex. Perhaps this is why men and women have long associated different foods with sexual excitement. But nature has made only one true substance to stimulate sexual desire in men and women — testosterone, and to a lesser degree, its kin, the other male sex hormones.

This is well established. Men and women who have higher circulating levels of testosterone tend to engage in more sexual activity.[13] Male athletes who inject testosterone to elevate their strength and stamina have more sexual thoughts, more morning erections, more sexual encounters, and more orgasms. And women who take testosterone in middle age boost their sexual desire. The male libido peaks in the early twenties, when levels of testosterone are highest. And many women feel more sexual desire around ovulation, when levels of testosterone increase.[14]

As elevated levels of testosterone stimulate the sex drive, declining levels dampen it. Both sexes have fewer sexual fantasies, masturbate less regularly, and engage in less intercourse as they age.[15] Poor health, unhappiness, overwork, lack of opportunity, laziness, and boredom undoubtedly contribute to this waning lust. But with age, levels of testosterone decline, often depressing sex desire.

Some two-thirds of middle-aged women do not experience any decline in libido, however.[16] This, too, may be due to testosterone. As the estrogens decline with menopause, levels of testosterone and the other androgens become unmasked: these potent hormones can finally express themselves more fully. Indeed, they do. In one study of middle-aged women, almost 40 percent complained that they were not having enough sex.[17]

When it comes to sexual desire, people vary, in part because levels of testosterone are inherited.[18] Levels also fluctuate according to the day, the week, the year, and the life cycle. Moreover, the balance of testosterone,

20

estrogen, and other bodily ingredients, as well as social circumstances and a host of other factors, all play a role in when, where, and how often we feel lust.[19] Nevertheless, testosterone is central to this appetite. And this primordial chemical can swamp the thinking brain. As poet Tony Hoagland said of lust, "As long as there is desire, we are not safe."[20]

Men and women are often sexually stimulated by different things, however. Men like to look. They are sexually turned on by visual stimuli. Even when men fantasize, they conjure up vivid images of body parts and copulation.[21] This lascivious peering probably boosts levels of testosterone. When male monkeys see a sexually available female or watch a companion copulate with a female, their levels of testosterone soar.[22] So the men who go to strip bars or look at "girlie" magazines are probably boosting levels of testosterone and triggering lust.

Women are generally more turned on by romantic words, images, and themes in films and stories. Women's sexual fantasies also include more affection, commitment, and sex with familiar partners.[23] And women like to yield. About 70 percent of American men and women fantasize while making love.[24] But as conquest is at the core of most men's mental plots, active surrender is prevalent in women's sexual reveries.[25]

These tastes for conquest and surrender have nothing to do with rape. Less than half of 1 percent of men enjoy forcing a woman into coitus; and less than half of 1 percent of women want to be coerced into copulation.[26] Still, American women are twice as likely as men to actively fantasize about being "done to" as opposed to "doing."[27]

Danger, novelty, particular smells and sounds, love letters, candy, endearing conversations, sexy clothes, swaying music, elegant dinners: many cues can trigger that "eternal thirst," as poet Pablo Neruda called the sex drive. How do feelings of romantic love affect this primordial brain circuit, lust?

ROMANCE TRIGGERS LUST

Surely you have noticed that when you fall in love, your ardor stimulates the sex drive. Novelists, dramatists, poets, and songwriters all rhapsodize about this urge to kiss, cuddle, and make love to someone you adore.

Why do we feel lust when we fall in love?

Because dopamine, the liquor of romance, can stimulate the release of testosterone, the hormone of sexual desire.[28]

This relationship between elevated levels of dopamine and sexual arousal, frequency of intercourse, and positive sexual function is common in animals.[29] When dopamine is injected into a male rat's bloodstream, for example, it stimulates copulatory behaviors.[30] Moreover, when a male laboratory rat is placed in an adjacent cage where he can see or smell an estrous female, he becomes sexually excited; with this, levels of dopamine also rise.[31] And when the barrier is removed and he is allowed to copulate, levels of dopamine rise even higher.[32]

Dopamine can also stimulate lust in humans.[33] When men and women   30
who are depressed take drugs that elevate levels of dopamine in the brain, their sex drive regularly improves.[34]

A friend of mine in her thirties told me a remarkable story regarding this. She had been mildly depressed for several years, so recently she began to take one of the newer antidepressants (one without negative sexual side effects) that elevates levels of dopamine in the brain. A month after starting this drug she not only thought more about sex, but she had also begun to have multiple orgasms with her boyfriend. I suspect her sudden change in sexual desire and sexual function occurred because the pill she was taking daily to enhance dopamine triggered the release of testosterone as well.

This positive relationship between dopamine and testosterone may also explain why people feel so sexy when they go on vacation, try some new trick in the bedroom, or make love to a new partner. Novel experiences drive up levels of dopamine in the brain—hence they can also trigger the brain chemistry of lust.

Norepinephrine, another stimulant that probably plays a role in romantic love, also stimulates the sex drive. Addicts who take amphetamines, known as "uppers" or "speed," say their sex drive can be constant. This lustiness probably stems from the same biological equation: amphetamines largely boost norepinephrine (as well as dopamine). And norepinephrine can stimulate the production of testosterone.[35]

Once again some caveats: the dosage of all these chemicals, as well as the timing of their release in the brain, makes a difference. None of these interactions are direct or simple. But generally speaking, dopamine and norepinephrine spark sexual desire,[36] most likely by elevating levels of testosterone. No wonder new lovers stay up all night caressing. The chemistry of romance ignites the most powerful urge of nature: the drive to copulate.

This chemical connection between romantic love and lust makes   35
evolutionary sense. After all, if romantic love evolved to stimulate mating with a "special" other, it *should* trigger the drive to have sex with this beloved, too.

DOES LUST TRIGGER ROMANCE?

But is the reverse true? Can lust stimulate amour? Can you climb in bed with "just a friend" or even a stranger, then suddenly fall in love with him or her?

Ovid, a man who had many love affairs, believed that a strong sexual attraction could often provoke a person to fall in love.[37] But lust does not always trigger romantic ardor, as many people know. Most sexually liberated contemporary adults have had sex with someone they were not in love with. Many have even copulated with this "friend" regularly. But, alas, they never felt the exhilaration of romantic passion for this bed partner. Lust does not necessarily lead to the passion and obsession of romantic love.

In fact, there is a great deal of data to the contrary. Athletes who inject synthetic androgens to build muscles don't fall in love as they take their drugs. When middle-aged men and women inject testosterone or apply testosterone cream to various body parts to stimulate their sex drive, their sexual thoughts and fantasies increase.[38] But they don't fall in love either. The brain circuitry of lust does not necessarily ignite the furnace of romance.

This is not to say that lust never triggers romantic love. It can. A middle-aged friend of mine is a good example. She had been having sex with "just a friend" for almost three years. These were sporadic events, she told me; she and her friend had sex no more than two or three times annually. Then one summer evening, about five minutes after coupling with him, she fell profoundly in love with him. At that moment the obsessive thinking, the pining, and the rapture started. In the weeks and months that followed, she told me, she lay awake at night and thought of him constantly, waited by the phone to hear his voice, dressed attractively to win him, and fantasized about a life together. Fortunately he loved her, too.

"Naso pasyo, maya basyo." Women in rural western Nepal use this off-color saying to express the same phenomenon. It means, "The penis entered and love arrived."[39]

I think biology contributes to this spontaneous love for a sex partner. Sexual activity can increase brain levels of dopamine and norepinephrine in male rats.[40] Even without sexual activity, increasing levels of testosterone can elevate levels of dopamine[41] and norepinephrine[42] as well as suppress levels of serotonin.[43] In short, the hormone of sexual desire can trigger the release of the brain's elixirs for romantic passion. As my friend cuddled and copulated with "just a friend," I think she triggered her brain circuit for romance and fell in love.

That "ol' black magic" is a fickle force. The chemistry of romantic love can trigger the chemistry of sexual desire and the fuel of sexual desire can trigger the fuel of romance. This is why it is dangerous to copulate with someone with whom you don't wish to become involved. Although you intend to have casual sex, you might just fall in love.

Romantic passion also has a special relationship with feelings of attachment.

ON ATTACHMENT

"Who ordered that their longing's fire / Should be, as soon as kindled, cooled?"[44] Poet Matthew Arnold mourned the passing of romantic love.

Love changes over time. It becomes deeper, calmer. No longer do cou-   45
ples talk all day or dance till dawn. The mad passion, the ecstasy, the longing, the obsessive thinking, the heightened energy: all dissolve. But if you
are fortunate, this magic transforms itself into new feelings of security, comfort, calm, and union with your partner. Psychologist Elaine Hatfield calls
this feeling "companionate love," a feeling of happy togetherness with
someone whose life has become deeply entwined with yours.[45] I call this
complex feeling "attachment."

And just as men and women intuitively distinguish between the feelings of romantic love and those of lust, people just as easily distinguish
between feelings of romance and attachment.

Nisa, a !Kung Bushman woman of the Kalahari Desert of Botswana, explained this feeling of man-woman attachment succinctly to anthropologist
Marjorie Shostak. "When two people are first together," Nisa said, "their
hearts are on fire and their passion is very great. After a while, the fire cools
and that's how it stays. They continue to love each other, but it's in a
different way—warm and dependable."[46]

The Taita of Kenya would agree. They say that love comes in two forms,
an irresistible longing, a "kind of sickness," and a deep enduring affection
for another.[47] Brazilians have a poetic proverb that distinguishes between
these two feelings, saying, "Love is born in a glance and matures in a
smile."[48] And for the Koreans, "*sarang*" is a word close to the Western concept of romantic love, while "*chong*" is more like feelings of long-term
attachment. But perhaps Abigail Adams, the wife of America's second
president, said it best, writing to John in 1793, "Years subdue the ardor of
passion, but in lieu thereof friendship and affection deep-rooted subsists,
which defies the ravages of time, and whilst the vital flame exists."[49]

THE CHEMISTRY OF ATTACHMENT

Scientists began to examine this brain system, attachment, decades ago
when British psychiatrist John Bowlby proposed that humans have
evolved an innate attachment system consisting of specific behaviors and
physiological responses.[50] Only recently, however, have researchers begun
to understand which brain chemicals produce this feeling of fusion with a
long-term mate. Most now believe that vasopressin and oxytocin, closely
related hormones made largely in the hypothalamus and the gonads,
produce many of the behaviors associated with attachment.

But to grasp how these hormones generate the sensation of union   50
with a sweetheart, I must [introduce] you to the American [midwestern]
prairie voles. [. . . T]hese brown-gray, mouselike rodents form pair-bonds to
rear their young; some 90 percent mate for life with a single partner. A few
years ago neuroscientists Sue Carter, Tom Insel, and others pinpointed the

cause of this attachment in males. As the male prairie vole ejaculates, levels of vasopressin increase in the brain, triggering his spousal and parenting zeal.[51]

Is vasopressin nature's cocktail for male attachment?

To investigate this hypothesis, scientists then injected vasopressin into the brains of *virgin* male prairie voles raised in the lab. These males immediately began to defend the space around them from other males, an aspect of pair formation in prairie voles. And when each was introduced to a female, he became instantaneously possessive of her.[52] Moreover, when these same scientists blocked the production of vasopressin in the brain, male prairie voles acted like cads instead—copulating with a female, then abandoning her for another mating opportunity.

Nature has given male mammals a chemical to feel the paternal instinct: vasopressin.

OXYTOCIN: ANOTHER COCKTAIL FOR DEVOTION?

"So we grew together, / Like to a double cherry, / seeming parted, / But yet a union in partition; / Two lovely berries moulded on one stem."[53] Few poets write about the durable feeling of attachment, perhaps because this drive rarely compels one to compose passionate verse in the dead of night. These lines by Shakespeare are an exception. Yet the feeling of attachment must be a common sensation among all birds and mammals, because it is associated not only with vasopressin but also with oxytocin—a related hormone that is ubiquitous in nature.[54]

Like vasopressin, oxytocin is made in the hypothalamus, as well as in the ovaries and testes. Unlike vasopressin, oxytocin is released in all female mammals (including women) during the birthing process.[55] It initiates contractions of the uterus and stimulates the mammary glands to produce milk. But scientists have now established that oxytocin also stimulates bonding between a mother and her infant.

More important, many now believe that oxytocin is also involved in the feelings of adult male-female attachment.[56]

You have undoubtedly felt the power of these two "satisfaction hormones," as vasopressin and oxytocin are sometimes called. We secrete them at two poignant moments during sexual intercourse: during stimulation of the genitals and/or nipples[57] and during orgasm. At orgasm, levels of vasopressin dramatically increase in men and levels of oxytocin rise in women.[58] These "cuddle chemicals" undoubtedly contribute to that sense of fusion, closeness, and attachment you can feel after sweet sex with a beloved.

How does the chemistry of attachment affect feelings of lust and romantic love?

DOES LUST DAMPEN ATTACHMENT?

The chemical components of attachment have complex effects on both the sex drive and feelings of romantic passion.

Under some circumstances, testosterone can elevate levels of vaso-pressin [59] and oxytocin [60] in animals, increasing attachment behaviors such as mutual grooming, scent marking, and defending a nesting site.[61] The reverse can also happen: oxytocin and vasopressin can increase testoster-one production under some conditions.[62] In short, the chemistry of attach-ment can trigger lust and the chemistry of lust can trigger expressions of attachment.

But all these hormones can also have negative effects on one another. Increasing levels of testosterone can sometimes *drive down* levels of vaso-pressin (and oxytocin) and elevated levels of vasopressin can *decrease* levels of testosterone.[63] This inverse relationship between lust and attachment is "dose-dependent"; it varies depending on the quantities, timing, and inter-actions among several hormones.[64] But high levels of testosterone can re-duce attachment. And there is a great deal of evidence that this happens to people regularly — sometimes with disastrous effects.

Men with high baseline levels of testosterone marry less frequently, have more adulterous affairs, commit more spousal abuse, and divorce more often. As a man's marriage becomes less stable, his levels of tes-tosterone rise. With divorce, his testosterone levels rise even more. And single men tend to have higher levels of testosterone than mar-ried men.[65]

The reverse can also happen: as a man becomes more and more at-tached to his family, levels of testosterone can decline. In fact, at the birth of a child, expectant fathers experience a significant decline in levels of testosterone.[66] Even when a man holds a baby, levels of testosterone decrease.

This negative relationship between testosterone and attachment is also seen in other creatures. Male cardinals and blue jays flit from one female to the next; they never stick around to parent their young. These profligate fa-thers have high levels of testosterone. Males of species that form monoga-mous pair-bonds and remain with this mate to father infants, however, have much lower levels of testosterone during the parenting phase of the breeding season.[67] And when scientists surgically pumped testosterone into monogamous male sparrows, these faithful fathers abandoned their nests, their young, and their "wives" to court other females.[68]

As I have said, the interactions between these chemical systems for lust and attachment are complex and variable. But there is data to suggest that as people grow like "two lovely berries moulded on one stem," the chemistry of attachment can dampen lust. This is probably why men and women in long stable marriages tend to spend less time in their bedroom making love.

But what about romance? How does dopamine, the fuel of romantic love, affect levels of vasopressin and oxytocin, the brain's intoxicants for attachment? Do deep feelings of union and attachment enhance or stifle romantic passion?

ROMANCE *AND* ATTACHMENT?

Nature isn't tidy. She likes options. And there is no definite relationship between the neurotransmitters of romance and the hormones of attachment. As should be said of all these chemical interactions: it depends.

Under some circumstances, dopamine and norepinephrine can stimulate the release of oxytocin and vasopressin[69]—and contribute to one's growing feelings of attachment. But increasing levels of oxytocin (found in both men and women) can also interfere with dopamine and norepinephrine pathways in the brain, *decreasing* the impact of these excitatory substances.[70] Hence the chemistry of attachment can quell the chemistry of romance.

There is a great deal of anecdotal evidence for this negative chemical relationship between attachment and romantic love. People around the world say the exhilaration of romance wanes as their marriage or partnership becomes increasingly stable, comfortable, and secure. Some even go to psychiatrists or marriage counselors to try to renew romantic passion in their relationship. Some seek romance outside their marriage instead. Some divorce. And many settle into a long-term partnership devoid of romantic bliss.

I have mixed feelings about this fate nature has decreed. First, many of us would die of sexual exhaustion if romantic love flourished endlessly in a relationship. We wouldn't get to work on time or concentrate on anything except "him" or "her." Moreover, as romantic love matures, it often expands into hundreds of complex and fulfilling feelings of attachment that produce an enormously intricate, interesting, and emotionally rewarding union with another living soul.

At the same time, I think you can keep the primal flame of romantic ecstasy alive in a long-term comfortable relationship [. . .].

But to maintain that magic you have to play a few tricks on the brain. Why? Because romantic love did not evolve to help us maintain a stable, enduring partnership. It evolved for different purposes: to drive ancestral men and women to prefer, choose, and pursue specific mating partners, then start the mating process and remain sexually faithful to "him" or "her" long enough to conceive a child. After the child is born, however, parents need a new set of chemicals and brain networks to rear their infant as a team—the chemistry of attachment. As a result, feelings of attachment often dampen the ecstasy of romance, replacing it with a deep sense of union with a mate.

70

THE TRELLIS OF LOVE

In spite of this evolutionary trajectory of loving, in which romantic passion gradually transforms into feelings of deep attachment, these three brain circuits—lust, romantic love, and attachment—can ignite in any combination.

In the traditional Western course of events, you meet a man or woman. You talk and laugh and begin to "date." Rapidly or gradually you fall in love. As the camaraderie escalates to bliss, your sex drive surges into higher action. Then after months or years of joyous times together, your raging romantic passion and raw sexual hunger begin to wane, replaced by what Theodor Reik called that warm "afterglow,"[71] attachment. In this scenario, romantic love has triggered lust; then with time, these raw feelings of passion and desire have settled into a sinew of emotional union and commitment—attachment.

Lust, romance, and attachment can visit you in other sequences, however. You may begin a liaison with someone for whom you feel only sexual desire. For a few months you have sex irregularly. Then one day you begin to feel possessive. Soon you fall in love with "him" or "her." And over time you become deeply emotionally entwined. In this case, lust has preceded romance, which then led to attachment.

Then there are couples who actually begin their relationship with feelings of attachment. They quickly achieve emotional union in the college dorm, at the office, or in their social circle. They become fast friends. With time, this attachment metamorphoses into romantic passion—which finally triggers lust.

Alas, many of us also have periods in our lives when these three mating drives—lust, romantic love, and attachment—do not focus on the same person. It seems to be the density of humankind that we are *neurologically* able to love more than one person at a time. You can feel profound attachment for a long-term spouse, *while* you feel romantic passion for someone in the office or your social circle, *while* you feel the sex drive as you read a book, watch a movie, or do something else unrelated to either partner. You can even swing from one feeling to another.

In fact, as you lie in the dark at night you can become engulfed by feelings of attachment to your spouse; then seconds later you feel crazy romantic passion for someone you just met; then you become aware of sexual craving as an unrelated image sweeps into mind. As these three brain circuits fire interactively, yet independently, you feel as if you are having a committee meeting in your head.

"Wild is love," as the song goes. Lust, romantic love, and deep attachment can visit you in such different and unexpected combinations that many people have come to believe the mixture of sensations that draws you to another is mysterious, elusive, perhaps even heaven-sent. But once you begin to envisage lust, romantic love, and attachment as three specific

75

mating drives, each producing many gradations of feeling that endlessly combine and recombine in countless different ways, love takes on tangibility. [. . .]

Notes

1. Shakespeare 1936, *Love's Labors Lost,* act IV, scene iii, line 341.
2. H. Fisher 1998; H. Fisher et al. 2002a; H. Fisher et al. 2002b.
3. H. Fisher 1989, 1992, 1998, 1999.
4. Hamill 1996, p. 32.
5. Tennov 1979; Hatfield and Rapson 1996.
6. Jankowiak 1995.
7. Bell 1995.
8. Rebhun 1995, p. 253.
9. Rebhun 1995, p. 254.
10. Animal studies indicate that several brain structures are associated with the sex drive and sexual expression, including the medial amygdala, medial preoptic area, paraventricular nucleus, and the periaqueductal gray (Heaton 2000). Using fMRI, Arnow and colleagues report that when male subjects look at erotic video material, they show strong activations in the right subinsular region including the claustrum, left caudate and putamen, right middle occipital/middle temporal gyri, bilateral cingulate gyrus, and right sensorimotor and premotor regions, whereas lesser activation occurs in the right hypothalamus (Arnow et al. 2002). Beauregard and colleagues also measured brain activation (using fMRI) in men as they viewed erotic film excerpts (Beauregard et al. 2001). Activations occurred in limbic and paralimbic structures, including the right amygdala, right anterior temporal pole, and hypothalamus. Using fMRI, Karama and colleagues recorded brain activity while men and women viewed erotic film excerpts (Karama et al. 2002). The blood oxygen level dependent (BOLD) signal increased in the anterior cingulate, medial prefrontal cortex, orbitofrontal cortex, insula and occipitotemporal cortices, as well as in the amygdala and the ventral striatum. Men also showed activation in the thalamus and significantly greater activation than women in the hypothalamus, specifically in a sexually dimorphic area associated with sexual arousal and behavior. In another experiment, researchers measured brain activity among eight men as these subjects experienced orgasm. Blood flow *decreased* in all regions of the cortex except one region of the prefrontal cortex, where it dramatically increased (Tiihonen et al. 1994). Perhaps this decreased activity explains why one becomes almost totally unconscious of the world at large during orgasm.
11. Arnow et al. 2002.
12. Farb and Armelagos 1983.
13. Edwards and Booth 1994; Sherwin 1994.
14. Van Goozen et al. 1997.
15. Edwards and Booth 1994.

16. Hâllström and Samuelsson 1990.
17. Tavris and Sadd 1977.
18. Meikle et al. 1988.
19. Nyborg 1994.
20. Hoagland 1998.
21. Ellis and Symons 1990.
22. Blum 1997.
23. Ellis and Symons 1990.
24. Reinisch and Beasley 1990, p. 92.
25. Laumann et al. 1994; Ellis and Symons 1990. Because this gender difference also exists in Japan and Great Britain (Barash and Lipton 1997; Wilson and Land 1981), some scientists believe these variations may be inherited. This makes sense. Female birds and mammals must remain still and cooperative for coitus to occur. And males must display some assertiveness to mate successfully. So signs of surrender by the female in conjunction with cues of dominance by the male are important mating signals (Eibl-Eibesfeldt 1989). In fact, ethologist Ireneus Eibl-Eibesfeldt proposes that these leitmotifs of human sexuality, male dominance and female surrender, arise from primitive brain regions where they evolved to ensure mating success in all reptiles, birds, and mammals.
26. Laumann et al. 1994.
27. Ellis and Symons 1990; Barash and Lipton 1997.
28. Hull et al. 1995; Hull et al. 1997; Kawashima and Takagi 1994.
29. Liu et al. 1998; Herbert 1996.
30. Ferrari and Giuliani 1995.
31. Hull et al. 1995; Wenkstern et al. 1993; West et al. 1992.
32. Hull et al. 1995.
33. Clayton et al. 2000; Walker et al. 1993; Heaton 2000.
34. Walker et al. 1993; Coleman et al. 1999; Ascher et al. 1995.
35. Mayerhofer et al. 1992; Fernandez et al. 1975; Cardinali et al. 1975.
36. Fabre-Nys 1998.
37. Hopkins 1994, p. 14.
38. Sherwin et al. 1985; Sherwin and Gelfand 1987.
39. Ahearn 1998.
40. Damsma et al. 1992; Pleim et al. 1990; Yang et al. 1996.
41. Hull et al. 1999.
42. T. J. Jones et al. 1998.
43. Netter et al. 1998; Sundblad and Eriksson 1997; Gonzalez et al. 1994.
44. Matthew Arnold, "To Marguerite." In Quiller-Couch 1919.
45. Hatfield 1988, p. 191.
46. Shostak 1981, p. 268.
47. Bell 1995, p. 158.
48. Rebhun 1995, p. 252.
49. McCullough 2001.
50. Bowlby 1969, 1973, 1980.

51. Carter et al. 1997; Young, Wang, and Insel 1998; Young et al. 1999; Wang, Ferris, and DeVries 1994; Pitkow et al. 2001.

52. Wang, Ferris, and DeVries 1994.

53. Shakespeare 1936, *A Midsummer Night's Dream,* act III, scene iii, lines 217–20.

54. Pedersen et al. 1992; Carter, DeVries, and Getz 1995.

55. Pedersen et al. 1992.

56. Young, Wang, and Insel 1998; Williams et al. 1994.

57. Damasio 1994, p. 122.

58. Young, Wang, Insel 1998; Carmichael et al. 1987.

59. Villalba, Auger, and DeVries 1999; Delville, Mansour, and Ferris 1996; Wang and DeVries 1995; Wang et al. 1994.

60. Arsenijevic and Tribollet 1998; Johnson et al. 1991.

61. Winslow and Insel 1991a; Winslow and Insel 1991b.

62. Sirotkin and Nitray 1992; Homeida and Khalafalla 1990. When a male prairie vole cohabits with a female mate, levels of vasopressin and testosterone increase (Wang et al. 1994). The vasopressin seems to elicit expressions of attachment, scent marking, and grooming behaviors (Winslow and Insel 1991b) while the testosterone probably enables the male to aggressively defend the nest from interlopers.

63. Thomas, Kim, and Amico 1996a; Thomas, Kim, and Amico 1996b.

64. Delville and Ferris 1995.

65. Booth and Dabbs 1993.

66. Berg and Wynne-Edwards 2001.

67. De Ridder, Pinxten, and Eens 2000; Raouf et al. 1997.

68. Wingfield 1994.

69. Galfi et al. 2001; Ginsberg et al. 1994.

70. Kovacs et al. 1990; Schwarzberg et al. 1981; Van de Kar et al. 1998.

71. Reik 1964.

References

Ahearn, L. M. 1998. "Love keeps afflicting me": Agentive discourse in Nepali love letters. Paper presented at the annual meeting of the American Anthropological Association, Washington, D.C.

Arnow, B. A., J. E. Desmond, L. L. Banner, G. H. Glover, A. Solomon, M. L. Polan, T. F. Lue, S. W. Atlas. 2002. Brain activation and sexual arousal in healthy, heterosexual males. *Brain* 125 (pt 5):1014–23.

Arsenijevic, Y., and E. Tribollet. 1998. Region-specific effect of testosterone on oxytocin receptor binding in the brain of the aged rat. *Brain Research* 785(1):167–70.

Ascher, J. A., J. O. Cole, J. N. Colin, J. P. Feighner, R. M. Ferris, H. C. Fibiger, R. N. Golden, P. Martin, W. Z. Potter, E. Richelson, and F. Sulser. 1995. Bupropion: A review of its mechanism of antidepressant activity. *Journal of Clinical Psychiatry* 56(9):396–402.

Barash, D. P., and J. E. Lipton. 1997. *Making Sense of Sex: How Genes and Gender Influence Our Relationships.* Washington, D.C.: Island Press.

Beauregard, M., J. Levesque, and P. Bourgouin. 2001. Neural correlates of conscious self-regulation of emotion. *Journal of Neuroscience* 21(18): RC165.

Bell, J. 1995. Notions of love and romance among the Taita of Kenya. In *Romantic Passion: A Universal Experience?*, ed. W. Jankowiak. New York: Columbia University Press.

Berg, S. J., and K. E. Wynne-Edwards. 2001. Changes in testosterone, cortisol, and estradiol levels in men becoming fathers. *Mayo Clinic Proceedings* 76(6): 582–92.

Blum, D. 1997. *Sex on the Brain: The Biological Differences between Men and Women.* New York: Viking.

Booth, A., and J. M. Dabbs. 1993. Testosterone and men's marriages. *Social Forces* 72(2):463–77.

Bowlby, J. 1969. *Attachment and Loss: Attachment* (vol. 1). New York: Basic Books.

———. 1973. *Attachment and Loss: Separation* (vol. 2). New York: Basic Books.

———. 1980. *Attachment and Loss: Loss* (vol. 3). New York: Basic Books.

Cardinali, D. P., C. A. Nagle, E. Gomez, and J. M. Rosner. 1975. Norepinephrine turnover in the rat pineal gland. Acceleration by estradiol and testosterone. *Life Science* 16(11):1717–24.

Carmichael, M. S., R. Humbert, J. Dixen, G. Palmisano, W. Greenleaf, and J. M. Davidson. 1987. Plasma oxytocin increases in the human sexual response. *Journal of Clinical Endocrinology and Metabolism* 64(1): 27–31.

Carter, C. S., A. C. DeVries, and L. L. Getz. 1995. Physiological substrates of mammalian monogamy: The prairie vole model. *Neuroscience and Biobehavioral Reviews* 19(2):303–14.

Carter, C. S., A. DeVries, S. E. Taymans, R. L. Roberts, J. R. Williams, and L. L. Getz. 1997. Peptides, Steroids, and Pair Bonding. In *The Integrative Neurobiology of Affiliation*, ed. C. S. Carter, I. I. Lederhendler, and B. Kirkpatrick. Annals of the New York Academy of Sciences, 807:260–72. New York: The New York Academy of Sciences.

Clayton, A. H., E. D. McGarvey, J. Warnock, et al. 2000. Bupropion as an antidote to SSRI-induced sexual dysfunction. Poster presented at the New Clinical Drug Evaluation Unit Program (NCDEU), Boca Raton, Fla.

Coleman, C. C., L. A. Cunningham, V. J. Foster, S. R. Batey, R. M. J. Donahue, T. L. Houser, and J. A. Ascher. 1999. Sexual dysfunction associated with the treatment of depression: A placebo-controlled comparison of bupropion sustained release and sertraline treatment. *Annals of Clinical Psychiatry* 11(4):205–15.

Damasio, A. R. 1994. *Descartes' Error: Emotion, Reason, and the Human Brain.* New York: G. P. Putnam's Sons.

Damsma, G., J. G. Pfaus, D. G. Wenkstern, A. G. Phillips, and H. C. Fibiger. 1992. Sexual behavior increased dopamine transmission in the nucleus accumbens and striatum of male rats: Comparison with novelty and locomotion. *Behavioral Neuroscience* 106:181–91.

Delville, Y., and C. F. Ferris. 1995. Sexual differences in vasopressin receptor binding within the ventrolateral hypothalamus in golden hamsters. *Brain Research* 68(1):91–96.

Delville, Y., K. M. Mansour, and C. F. Ferris. 1996. Testosterone facilitates aggression by modulating vasopressin receptors in the hypothalamus. *Physiology and Behavior* 60(1):25–29.

De Ridder, E., R. Pinxten, and M. Eens. 2000. Experimental evidence of a testosterone-induced shift from paternal to mating behavior in a facultatively polygynous songbird. *Behavioral Ecology and Sociobiology* 49(1): 24–30.

Edwards, J. N., and A. Booth. 1994. Sexuality, Marriage, and Well-Being: The Middle Years. In *Sexuality across the Life Course*, ed. A. S. Rossi. Chicago: University of Chicago Press.

Eibl-Eibesfeldt, I. 1989. *Human Ethology.* New York: Aldine de Gruyter.

Ellis, B. J., and D. Symons. 1990. Sex differences in sexual fantasy: An evolutionary psychological approach. *Journal of Sex Research* 27:527–55.

Fabre-Nys, C. 1998. Steroid control of monoamines in relation to sexual behavior. *Reviews of Reproduction* 3(1):31–41.

Farb, P., and G. Armelagos. 1983. *Consuming Passion: The Anthropology of Eating.* New York: Pocket Books.

Fernandez, B. E., N. A. Vidal, and A. E. Dominguez. 1975. Action of the sexual hormones on the endogenous norepinephrine of the central nervous system. *Revista Española de Fisiologia* 31(4):305–7.

Ferrari, F., and D. Giuliani. 1995. Sexual attraction and copulation in male rats: Effects of the dopamine agonist SND 919. *Pharmacology, Biochemistry, and Behavior* 50(1):29–34.

Fisher, H. 1989. Evolution of serial pairbonding. *American Journal of Physical Anthropology* 78:331–54.

———. 1992. *Anatomy of Love: A Natural History of Mating, Marriage, and Why We Stray.* New York: W. W. Norton.

———. 1998. Lust, attraction, and attachment in mammalian reproduction. *Human Nature* 9(1):23–52.

———. 1999. *The First Sex: The Natural Talents of Women and How They Are Changing the World.* New York: Random House.

Fisher, H. 2002a. Defining the brain systems of lust, romantic attraction and attachment. *Archives of Sexual Behavior* 31(5):413–19.

———. 2002b. The neural mechanisms of mate choice: A hypothesis. *Neuroendocrinology Letters* 23 (suppl 4):92–97.

Galfi, M., T. Janaky, R. Toth, G. Prohaszka, A. Juhasz, C. Varga, and F. A. Laszlo. 2001. Effects of dopamine and dopamine-active compounds on oxytocin and vasopressin production in rat neurohypophyseal tissue cultures. *Regulatory Peptides* 98(1–2):49–54.

Ginsberg, S. D., P. R. Hof, W. G. Young, and J. H. Morrison. 1994. Noradrenergic innervation of vasopressin- and oxytocin-containing neurons in the hypothalamic paraventricular nucleus of the macaque monkey: Quantitative analysis using double-label immunohistochemistry and confocal laser microscopy. *Journal of Comparative Neurology* 341(4):476–91.

Gonzalez, M. I., F. Farabollini, E. Albonetti, and C. A. Wilson. 1994. Interactions between 5-hydroxytryptamine (5-HT) and testosterone in the control of sexual and nonsexual behaviour in male and female rats. *Pharmacology Biochemistry and Behavior* 47(3):591–601.

Hållström, T., and S. Samuelsson. 1990. Changes in women's sexual desire in middle life: The longitudinal study of women in Gothenburg. *Archives of Sexual Behavior* 19(3):259–68.

Hamill, S. 1996. *The Erotic Spirit: An Anthology of Poems of Sensuality, Love and Longing.* Boston: Shambhala.

Hatfield, E. 1988. Passionate and companionate love. In *The Psychology of Love,* ed. R. J. Sternberg and M. L. Barnes. New Haven: Yale University Press.

Hatfield, E., and R. Rapson. 1996. *Love and Sex: Cross-Cultural Perspectives.* Needham Heights, Mass.: Allyn and Bacon.

Heaton, J. P. 2000. Central neuropharmacological agents and mechanisms in erectile dysfunction: the role of dopamine. *Neuroscience and Biobehavioral Reviews* 24(5):561–69.

Herbert, J. 1996. Sexuality, stress, and the chemical architecture of the brain. *Annual Review of Sex Research* 7:1–44.

Hoagland, T. 1998. *Donkey Gospel: Poems.* St. Paul, Minn.: Graywolf Press.

Homeida, A. M., and A. E. Khalafalla. 1990. Effects of oxytocin and an oxytocin antagonist on testosterone secretion during the oestrous cycle of the goat (*Capra hircus*). *Journal of Reproduction and Fertility* 89(1):347–50.

Hopkins, A. 1994. *The Book of Courtly Love: The Passionate Code of the Troubadours.* San Francisco: HarperSanFrancisco.

Hull, E. M., J. Du, D. S. Lorrain, and L. Matuszewich. 1995. Extracellular dopamine in the medial preoptic area: Implications for sexual motivation and hormonal control of copulation. *Journal of Neuroscience* 15(11): 7465–71.

———. 1997. Testosterone, preoptic dopamine, and copulation in male rats. *Brain Research Bulletin* 44(4):327–33.

Hull, E. M., D. S. Lorrain, J. Du, L. Matuszewich, L. A. Lumley, S. K. Putnam, and J. Moses. 1999. Hormone-neurotransmitter interactions in the control of sexual behavior. *Behavioural Brain Research* 105(1):105–16.

Jankowiak, W. 1995. Introduction. In *Romantic Passion: A Universal Experience?,* ed. W. Jankowiak. New York: Columbia University Press.

Johnson, A. E., H. Coirine, T. R. Insel, and B. S. McEwen. 1991. The regulation of oxytocin receptor binding in the ventromedial hypothalamic nucleus by testosterone and its metabolites. *Endocrinology* 128(2):891–96.

Jones, T. J., G. Dunphy, A. Milsted, and D. Ely. 1998. Testosterone effects on renal norepinephrine content and release in rats with different Y chromosomes. *Hypertension* 32(5):880–85.

Karama, S., A. R. Lecours, P. Bourgouin, G. Beaudoin, S. Joubert, and M. Beauregard. 2002. Areas of brain activation in males and females during viewing of erotic film excerpts. *Human Brain Mapping* 16(1):1–13.

Kawashima, S., and K. Takagi. 1994. Role of sex steroids on the survival, neuritic outgrowth of neurons, and dopamine neurons in cultured preoptic area and hypothalamus. *Hormones and Behavior* 28(4):305–12.

Kovacs, G. L., Z. Sarnyai, E. Barbarczi, G. Szabo, and G. Telegdy. 1990. The role of oxytocin-dopamine interactions in cocaine-induced locomotor hyperactivity. *Neuropharmacology* 29(4):365–68.

Laumann, E. O., J. H. Gagnon, R. T. Michael, and S. Michaels. 1994. *The Social Organization of Sexuality: Sexual Practices in the United States.* Chicago: University of Chicago Press.

Liu, Y.-C., B. D. Sachs, and J. D. Salamone. 1998. Sexual behavior in male rats after radiofrequency or dopamine-depleting lesions in nucleus accumbens. *Pharmacology Biochemistry and Behavior* 60(1):585–92.

Mayerhofer, A., R. W. Steger, G. Gow, and A. Bartke. 1992. Catecholamines stimulate testicular testosterone release of the immature golden hamster via interaction with alpha- and beta-adrenergic receptors. *Acta Endocrinologia* 127(6):526–30.

McCullough, D. 2001. *John Adams.* New York: Simon and Schuster.

Meikle, A., J. Stringham, D. Bishop, and D. West. 1988. Quantitating genetic and nongenetic factors influencing androgen production and clearance rates in men. *Journal of Clinical Endocrinology Metabolism* 67:104–9.

Netter, P., J. Hennig, B. Meier, and S. Rohrmann. 1998. Testosterone as an indicator of altered 5-HT responsivity in aggressive subjects. *European Psychiatry* 13(4):181s.

Nyborg, H. 1994. *Hormones, Sex and Society.* Westport, Conn.: Praeger.

Pedersen, C. A., J. D. Caldwell, G. F. Jirikowsk, and T. R. Insel, eds. 1992. *Oxytocin in Maternal, Sexual and Social Behaviors.* New York: New York Academy of Sciences.

Pitkow, L. J., C. A. Sharer, X. Ren, T. R. Insel, E. F. Terwilliger, and L. J. Young. 2001. Facilitation of affiliation and pair-bond formation by vasopressin receptor gene transfer into the ventral forebrain of a monogamous vole. *Journal of Neuroscience* 21(18):7392–96.

Pleim, E. T., J. A. Matochik, R. J. Barfield, and S. B. Auerbach. 1990. Correlation of dopamine release in the nucleus accumbens with masculine sexual behavior in rats. *Brain Research* 524:160–63.

Quiller-Couch, Arthur, ed. 1919. *The Oxford Book of English Verse: 1250–1900.* Oxford, Eng.: Oxford University Press.

Raouf, S. A., P. G. Parker, E. D. Ketterson, V. Nolan, Jr., and C. Ziegenfus. 1997. Testosterone affects reproductive success by influencing extra-pair fertilizations in male dark-eyed juncos (*Aves: Junco hyemalis*). *Proceedings of the Royal Society of London—Series B, Biological Sciences* 264(1388):1599–1603.

Rebhun, L. A. 1995. Language of love in northeast Brazil. In *Romantic Passion: A Universal Experience?*, ed. W. Jankowiak. New York: Columbia University Press.

Reik, T. 1964. *The Need to Be Loved.* New York: Bantam.

Reinisch, J. M., and R. Beasley. 1990. *The Kinsey Institute New Report on Sex.* New York: St. Martin's Press.

Schwarzberg, H., G. L. Kovacs, G. Szabo, and G. Telegdy. 1981. Intraventricular administration of vasopressin and oxytocin affects the steady-state levels of serotonin, dopamine and norepinephrine in rat brain. *Endocrinologia Experimentalis* 15(2):75–80.

Shakespeare, W. 1936. *The Complete Works of William Shakespeare: The Cambridge Edition Text,* ed. W. A. Wright. New York: Doubleday.

Sherwin, B. B. 1994. Sex hormones and psychological functioning in post-menopausal women. *Experimental Gerontology* 29(3/4):423–30.

Sherwin, B. B., and M. M. Gelfand. 1987. The role of androgen in the maintenance of sexual functioning in oophorectomized women. *Psychosomatic Medicine* 49:397.

Sherwin, B. B., M. M. Gelfand, and W. Brender. 1985. Androgen enhances sexual motivation in females. *Psychosomatic Medicine* 47:339–51.

Shostak, M. 1981. *Nisa: The Life and Words of a !Kung Woman.* Cambridge, Mass.: Harvard University Press.

Sirotkin, A. V., and J. Nitray. 1992. The influence of oxytocin, vasopressin and their analogues on progesterone and testosterone production by porcine granulosa cells in vitro. *Annales d'endocrinologie* (Paris) 53(1): 32–36.

Sundblad, C., and E. Eriksson. 1997. Reduced extracellular levels of serotonin in the amygdala of androgenized female rats. *European Neuropsychopharmacology* 7(4):253–59.

Tavris, C., and S. Sadd. 1977. *The Redbook Report on Female Sexuality.* New York: Delacorte.

Tennov, D. 1979. *Love and Limerence: The Experience of Being in Love.* New York: Stein and Day.

Thomas, A., N. B. Kim, and J. A. Amico. 1996a. Differential regulation of oxytocin and vasopressin messenger ribonucleic acid levels by gonadal steroids in postpartum rats. *Brain Research* 738(1):48–52.

———. 1996b. Sequential exposure to estrogen and testosterone (T) and subsequent withdrawal of T increases the level of arginine vasopressin messenger ribonucleic acid in the hypothalamic paraventricular nucleus of the female rat. *Journal of Neuroendocrinology* 8(10):793–800.

Tiihonen, J., J. Kuikka, J. Kupila, K. Partanen, P. Vainio, J. Airaksinen, M. Eronen, T. Hallikainen, J. Paanila, I. Kinnunen, and J. Huttunen. 1994. Increase in cerebral blood flow of right prefrontal cortex in men during orgasm. *Neuroscience Letters* 170:241–43.

Van de Kar, L. D., A. D. Levy, Q. Li, and M. S. Brownfield, 1998. A comparison of the oxytocin and vasopressin responses to the 5-HT1A agonist and potential anxiolytic drug alnespirone (S-20499). *Pharmacology, Biochemistry, and Behavior* 60(3):677–83.

Van Goozen, S., V. M. Wiegant, E. Endert, F. A. Helmond, and N. E. Van de Poll. 1997. Psychoendocrinological assessment of the menstrual cycle: The relationship between hormones, sexuality, and mood. *Archives of Sexual Behavior* 26(4): 359–82.

Villalba D., C. J. Auger, and G. J. De Vries. 1999. Antrostenedione effects on the vasopressin innervation of the rat brain. *Endocrinology* 140(7):3383–86.

Walker, P. W., J. O. Cole, E. A. Gardner, et al. 1993. Improvement in fluoxetine-associated sexual dysfunction in patients switched to bupropion. *Journal of Clinical Psychiatry* 54:459–65.

Wang, Z., and G. J. De Vries. 1995. Androgen and estrogen effects on vasopressin messenger RNA expression in the medial amygdaloid nucleus in male and female rats. *Journal of Neuroendocrinology* 7(1):827–31.

Wang, Z. Z., C. F. Ferris, and G. J. De Vries. 1994. The role of septal vasopressin innervation in paternal behavior in prairie voles (*Microtus ochrogaster*). *Proceedings of the National Academy of Sciences (USA)* 91:400–404.

Wang, Z., W. Smith, D. E. Major, and G. J. De Vries. 1994. Sex and species differences in the effects of cohabitation on vasopressin messenger RNA expression in the bed nucleus of the stria terminalis in prairie voles (*Microtus ochrogaster*) and meadow voles (*Microtus pennsylvanicus*). *Brain Research* 650(2):212–18.

Wenkstern, D., J. G. Pfaus, and H. C. Fibiger. 1993. Dopamine transmission increases in the nucleus accumbens of male rats during their first exposure to sexually receptive female rats. *Brain Research* 618:41–46.

West, C. H. K., A. N. Clancy, and R. P. Michael. 1992. Enhanced responses of nucleus accumbens neurons in male rats to novel odors associated with sexually receptive females. *Brain Research* 585:49–55.

Williams, J. R., T. R. Insel, C. R. Harbaugh, and C. S. Carter. 1994. Oxytocin administered centrally facilitates formation of a partner preference in female prairie voles (*Microtus ochrogaster*). *Journal of Neuroendocrinology* 6(3):247–50.

Wilson, G. D., and R. J. Land. 1981. Sex differences in sexual fantasy patterns. *Personality and Individual Differences* 2:343–46.

Wingfield, J. C. 1994. Hormone-behavior interactions and mating systems in male and female birds. In *The Differences between the Sexes*, ed. R. V. Short and E. Balaban. New York: Cambridge University Press.

Winslow, J. T., and T. R. Insel. 1991a. Social status in pairs of male squirrel monkeys determines the behavioral response to central oxytocin administration. *The Journal of Neuroscience* 11(7):203–8.

———. 1991b. Vasopressin modulates male squirrel monkeys' behavior during social separation. *European Journal of Pharmacology* 200(1):95–101.

Yang, S. P., K. Y. F. Pau, D. L. Hess, and H. G. Spies. 1996. Sexual dimorphism in secretion of hypothalamic gonadotropin-releasing hormone and norepinephrine after coitus in rabbits. *Endocrinology* 137(7):2683–93.

Young, L. J., Z. Wang, and T. R. Insel. 1998. Neuroendocrine bases of monogamy. *Trends in Neurosciences* 21(2):71–75.

Young, L. J., R. Nilsen, K. G. Waymire, G. R. MacGregor, and T. R. Insel. 1999. Increased affiliative response to vasopressin in mice expressing the V1a receptor from a monogamous vole. *Nature* 400:766–68.

The Medieval Contribution to Love
Diane Ackerman

*Diane Ackerman writes poetry, novels, and natural history. Her best-known nonfiction
is* A Natural History of the Senses *(1990) and* A Natural History of Love *(1994),
from which this selection has been excerpted.*

[In Europe, prior to the Middle Ages, m]ost ideas about love came from
reading the pagan or Christian thinkers. Books were rare, but students
could find some in the libraries of monasteries and cathedrals. There they
might read a smattering of Greek and Roman authors, some of whom were
just being translated. Plato was popular because he renounced the material
world and abandoned the delights of the flesh. Distrust of the body, while
seeking the spiritual, fit neatly into Christian teachings. Plato and Cicero
both celebrated lofty, nonerotic love between men, and that appealed to
the celibate clergy. From Virgil's Dido and Aeneas, students learned of love
as a demented passion, a mix of bliss and raw danger. People could die
from love, so surely it was an affliction, a deadly humour, a plague. Ovid's
smart-alecky *Art of Love* introduced them to the frank country joys of lust,
where every lover was a soldier in the trenches. But in Ovid's writings, they
also found descriptions of the tender love he felt for women. The myth of
Orpheus and Eurydice taught them about the heroics of love, which led
deep into the Underworld and out again.

They learned from the Christian writers of a loving and merciful God,
an idea we now take for granted; but to the ancients it was a startling
thought. The pagan gods didn't waste affection on human beings, whom
they often toyed with as rather peevish pets. Gigantic, alien, and magically
endowed, the gods were nonetheless all too human in their sadism,
whimsy, and churlishness. In contrast, the Old Testament God, obsessed
with love, commands his people first and foremost to "love the lord your
God with all your heart, and with all your soul, and with all your might." It
is one's moral duty to feel love. This continues into the New Testament,
where we learn that "God is love," that "God so loved the world that he
gave his only Son," and that one must love one's neighbor as oneself. With
what poignancy St. Paul describes this new importance of love:

> If I speak in the tongues of men and of angels, but have not love, I am a noisy
> gong or a clanging cymbal. And if I have prophetic powers and understand all
> mysteries and all knowledge, and if I have all faith, so as to remove mountains,
> but have not love, I am nothing. If I give away all I have, and if I deliver my
> body to be burned, but have not love, I gain nothing. . . . So faith, hope, love
> abide, these three; but the greatest of these is love.

The Bible teaches that God's love is unconditional, a gift given by a
doting parent. It needn't be won, and it doesn't go only to those who deserve

it. Altruism appears as a moral good, even if loving one's neighbor does have a missionary zeal to it. No one can be saved who doesn't convert to Christianity, so converting a neighbor is the greatest gift you can give him.

Heterosexual love in the Old Testament is sometimes down to earth, very material, and deliciously sensual, as when Solomon tells his future bride:

> You are stately as a palm tree,
>   and your breasts are like its clusters.
> I say I will climb the palm tree
>   and lay hold of its branches.
> Oh, may your breasts be like
>   clusters of the vine,
>   and the scent of your breath like apples,
> And your kisses like the best wine
>   that goes down smoothly,
>   gliding over lips and teeth . . .

But, in the New Testament, sex becomes nonerotic and full of self-denial.[1] Paul advises that "It is well for a man not to touch a woman," but he concedes that marriage is a last resort for those who can't be celibate. Because pent-up desires can lead to fornication or adultery, "each man should have his own wife and each woman her own husband." Their duty is to use sex as a safety valve and to produce children. Divorce is forbidden. "To the unmarried and the widows," Paul warns, "I say that it is well for them to remain single as I do. But if they cannot exercise self-control, they should marry. For it is better to marry than to burn." And better to marry than to burn with desire, which he depicts as a private hell in which sin walks one's nerves as if they were so many tightropes. In this mix of traditions, Plato's call for sublimating one's desires blended neatly with Christianity's, and at times celibacy seems to be enjoyed as a reverse erotics all its own. St. Augustine describes his vow of abstinence like this: "Now was my soul free from the biting cares of canvassing and getting, and weltering in filth, and scratching off the itch of lust." That's rather spirited self-sacrifice.[2] Then something happened that would change the course of love in the western world.

When he returned from a spotty career in the Crusades, William IX, duke of Aquitaine (1071–1127), began composing songs of love and

---

[1] The word *testament* comes from the Indo-European root *tre*, having to do with triads (two deal makers and a witness). A testament was a pledge, and it concealed the idea of castration. When a man swore something was true, giving *testimony*, he put his hands on his testicles. In effect, he was saying: *You can cut off my balls if I'm lying.* In time, law courts decided that asking a man to put his hands on the Bible might be more decorous.

[2] Compare this with a confidence offered by a twentieth-century Arabian woman, who said that wearing a veil gave her a profound sense of relief, because it freed her from being sexually attractive to men, a feeling that had dominated her thoughts and bedeviled her self-esteem.

yearning, which we now recognize as the first troubadour love songs. He may well have been inspired by Moorish writers, who sang of love as an ennobling force and women as transcendent goddesses. Arabia and Spain regularly exchanged artists as well as ambassadors, and their culture spread into southern France. Best known was the Andalusian poet Ibn-Hazm, who wrote in his classic *The Ring of the Dove* (1022) that "the union of souls is a thousand times more beautiful than that of bodies." His attitude was deeply Platonic as well as Muslim, especially when he spoke about the need to become one with the beloved. It was a natural need, common as sand but powerful as radium, because love is the reunion of souls that, before creation, were made from the same primordial stuffs that became divided later in the physical universe. "The lover's soul," he says, "is ever seeking for the other, striving after it, searching it out, yearning to encounter it again, drawing it to itself it might be as a magnet draws the iron."

Beauty is the lure. The soul is beautiful and it feels drawn to physical beauty. But if sex is the only appeal, then the soul can't grasp the beautiful object long enough for love to take shape; it needs the glue of finding a kindred spirit. Arguing that lust is a vulgar emotion, though reveling in the other's senses is magnificent, he depicts the lover as his mistress's slave, who should address her either as *sayyidi* ("my lord") or *mawlaya* ("my master"). He cautions the lover against actually possessing his beloved, details the torment of lovesickness, and even offers this guide to help read love's facial semaphores:

> To make a signal with the corner of the eye is to forbid the lover something; to droop the eye is an indication of consent; to prolong the gaze is a sign of suffering and distress; to break off the gaze is a mark of relief; to make signs of closing the eyes is an indicated threat. To turn the pupil of the eye in a certain direction and then to turn it back swiftly, calls attention to the presence of a person so indicated. A clandestine signal with the corner of both eyes is a question; to turn the pupil rapidly from the middle of the eye to the interior angle is a demonstration of refusal; to flutter the pupils of both eyes this way and that is a general prohibition. The rest of these signals can only be understood by actually seeing them demonstrated.

Ibn-Hazm's lovers become transformed by love, growing strong and brave, dignified and generous. His countrymen wrote love stories with similar concerns, steeped in the senses; they relied heavily on natural imagery, and were usually accompanied by musical instruments. The sensuous world of the East would have been as welcome as perfume in French society, at a time when the upper class was becoming richer and idler. [. . .]

Most of the troubadours were commoners, the medieval equivalent of traveling folksingers who played other people's songs along with some of their own. If they were talented and lucky, and could find a hospitable lord or lady with money, they performed regularly at a castle. That small world could get smaller by the hour in idle moments. There were no novels of romance, no gossip magazines, no thrillers to watch at the cinema. A clever singer, full of soap-operalike stories and bloodcurdling adventures, was a welcome guest. Thanks to the troubadours, affairs of the heart became a favorite theme of poetic sagas, and so the love story first entered European literature. The compass of heroism widened, and the idea of "the couple"— two people served by a single verb—began to tantalize society.

One of the great changes of the Middle Ages was a shift from unilateral love to mutual love. That love could be shared, that two people could feel passionate concern and desire for each other, was at first an avant-garde and dangerous idea. Because the Church taught that love was appropriate only for God, it found the idea of mutual love simply impossible. After all, one was to love God without ransom, expecting nothing in return. To the churchman's mind, love was not a collaboration of hearts, not a pas de deux, not a two-way street, not an exchange of goods and services, but a solitary state.

I don't think the troubadours believed they were being subversive by saying that the lightning of love could flow between two people, not just toward heaven. Nonetheless, by making love available on earth, between mortals, they could be charged with encouraging the worship of false idols. They introduced the image of the lovers, a society of two, as something noble and valuable. They honored pairs who felt passionate love for each other. Until then, love between men and women was thought to be sinful and vulgar. As often as not, it led to madness. And it was always degrading. To portray love as majestic, an ideal to be searched for, was truly shocking. To accept that sexual desire might be a natural part of love, but that the total feeling was more spiritual, an intense oneness, didn't jibe with classical teachings. After all, in Greek tragedy, love was an affliction, a horror that led to cruelty and death. For theologians, human love was a poor reflection of the real thing, which could be found only in spiritual rapture. Insisting that women were equal participants in love, even ennobled by it, seemed outlandish because it tampered with the natural order of feudal life, where men served their lords, and women were faithful to their men. If one's lover deserved one's total dedication, where did one's feudal master fit into the equation?

As courtly love bewitched society, the grip of the Church weakened and power began to sift from the hands of the nobles. This new concept of love radically altered how people defined themselves and sought fulfillment. Most revolutionary of all, perhaps, it introduced the idea of personal choice. In a world where hierarchy ruled, one owed one's fealty first to God and next to the lord of the manor. Choosing whom to love—expressing a preference—was an act of outright rebellion, a revolt against the morality of the age, which denied the individual. Yet this coup d'état found its leaders in the highest ranks of government.

It was in the court of Queen Eleanor of Aquitaine (William's granddaughter), and her daughter, Marie, that the tournament of love really

10

flourished. There, troubadours wrote some of their most daring and exquisite songs, often combining love stories with tales of adventure, such as the Celtic myth of King Arthur and his knights of the Round Table. The ladies of the songs bore such names as "Beautiful Glance," "Pure Joy," and "Beautiful Hope." And the troubadours tossed them bouquets of praise and adoration. They crafted an art form from music, poetry, and pure desire. "Courtly love" it came to be called,[3] a phrase intentionally ambiguous. A courtship developed at court, but it was also very much a game played on a court. Just as sports are played in the confines of an arena, courtly love was played inside the small world of a castle. Its strict rules were known by all, often rehearsed in public, and viewed by many. One game that became popular was the Court of Love, which was as much a debate as a litigation. Everyone would gather in a central hall, and some love problem would be offered for consideration. Each player chose a position and had to defend it. The question might be: "Who is easier to win over, the wife of an impotent man or the wife of a jealous man?"; or "What do you prefer, warm clothing in winter or a courtly mistress in summer?"; or "If your lady gives herself to you on the condition of her spending a night with a toothless old man, would you prefer she fulfill this condition before or afterward?" Clearly no one expected solutions to these predicaments, only witty banter and the chance to enjoy love talk in public. In one such game, Queen Eleanor was asked to decide which she would rather have as a lover—a young man of no virtue or an old man of much virtue. She picked the old man, because in courtly love virtue was paramount. In the revolving worlds of court, the players knew one another, if only in passing, or by reputation. But beyond their magic circle, courtly love followed a purer path. [. . .]

What fascinated the troubadours were the first stages of love, whose flickering emotions they chronicled, the trembling moments at the beginning of an affair when two lovers were transfixed by one another, absorbed into each other's version of reality, but quivering with uncertainty. Sexual intercourse put an end to such a story, and conjugal love didn't interest them at all. It was too dull. They preferred the lying awake at night, the devoured glances, the secret codes, the fetishes and tokens, the steamy fantasizing, the moaning to one's pillow, the fear of discovery, the agony of separation, the torrents of bliss followed by desperate hours. [. . .]

Why did such stylized love evolve at this point in history? [. . .] One thing is certain: during the Crusades, knights discovered a more elastic sense of society, and savored cultures that had a greater respect for women. Widening their horizons made them more receptive to the social changes already taking place in France while they were away. In Byzantium, they

---

[3] Because we use the word *love* in so many ways, we find "courtly love" a useful term. However, the phrase originated in the late nineteenth century, when a French medievalist, Gaston Paris, referred to the *amour courtois* of twelfth-century France.

encountered the cult of worshiping the Virgin Mary. This stood in stark contrast to the age-old teaching of the Church, which held that Eve's wickedness doomed all of us. Out of Oedipal feelings, perhaps, the profane idea of "the noble Lady" and the sacred idea of the Virgin Mary eventually became interchangeable to the point where, at one time, the worship or love of Mary surpassed the love or worship of Jesus. Churches were christened "Our Lady" (as in Notre Dame de Paris). Knights didn't serve women, they served "ladies," the elite form of the female.

However, the momentous change was the notion that women could be the objects of love. This was by no means an attitude that all of society shared. Medieval thinkers habitually depicted women as inferior beings unfit for education. They were still a land to be tilled, as they had been to the Greeks and Romans. Thomas Aquinas's explanation for such a state of affairs is that by nature

15

> woman is defective and misbegotten, for the active force in the male seed tends to the production of a perfect likeness in the masculine sex, while the production of woman comes from a defect in the active force or from some external change, such as that of a south wind, which is moist, as the Philosopher observes. On the other hand, in relation to the universal nature, woman is not misbegotten, but is included in nature's intention as ordered to the work of generation.

After three thousand years of subjugation, women certainly didn't mind being elevated above valiant knights. They enjoyed their higher status, and knights enjoyed the purification and nobility courtly love bestowed. In a coarse, crude society, where it was difficult to advance oneself, knights liked being part of a moral aristocracy, an elite that could be achieved by men of any class.

The seeds of courtly love were imported in part from the Arab countries, the style and sentiment of whose poetry delighted troubadours in southern France. However, there was one important way in which Frenchwomen differed from the idealized and longed-for women of the harem—Frenchwomen were available. One could bump into them in the marketplace, castles, at tournaments, or at court. This took away some of the challenge, and much of the mystery. In converting Islamic love to the freer European world, obstacles somehow had to be replaced. According to Tannahill, "Virtue was the attribute that, by elevating woman to some immaculate plane, cleansed their love of all taint of carnality and left it free to soar into the realm of the spirit. Virtue became the European harem." Notice that it's the woman's *virtue*, not her personality, that is so winning. Her reality as a down-to-earth, full-bodied woman, one with talents and troubles, allergies and brains, doesn't figure in the quest. What the knight seeks is the conquest of virtue by virtue. His lady is only a memory aid so that, on the battlefield, when weakening, he can remember what virtue is, can spell it with his pulse, embody it in his mind. She makes possible his spiritual awakening, and her reward is an improved image of herself. Later in the Middle Ages, the engagement between knight and lady became more abstract, and though knights rode to battle with talismans from their ladies, they might equally well have been fighting for colors or country. [. . .]

With many men away at war much of the time, women dominated court life. So there were many influential married women, thirsty for intrigue and starved for love, whose favor could be won through flirtation and flattery. This would not have been a circumstance shared by their husbands, who could bed women wherever they wished. It didn't matter if the husband fooled around, but if the wife did the husband might end up supporting a child he hadn't sired. So, naturally, husbands didn't approve of erotic love, nor troubadours think highly of husbands. Their songs often refer to a husband showing up at an inopportune moment to spoil things for the lovers, and they endorse a blatant double standard—jealousy is depicted as noble when felt by lovers, despicable when felt by husbands.

One must keep in mind that a knight's lady was a complete stranger, a pretty face encountered on his travels. The Church didn't allow marriages between even distant kin, so knights had to leave their homes and search for a mate. But it was also possible to be an unattached (or "free-lance") knight, someone who owned no land and answered to no feudal lord. Such knights defined themselves through acts of valor, and prized a good reputation, that small theater district of self-regard. Their goal was to romance other men's wives with a gusto and tenderness that contrasted sharply with the dreariness of a loveless marriage. Danger was a tonic.

Passionate devotion was possible because the lovers were abstract objects of desire, whose love was forbidden, a taboo and a novelty. Intimacy between lovers, a fairly recent idea, was not any part of the medieval mood, but it gradually arose from the pressure on lovers to be secretive. Wallowing in each other's eyes, speaking through gestures, exchanging notes and signs, they learned to be a secret society complete with passwords and ceremonies and a holy crusade, a religion of two.

So many of our novels, poems, operas, and songs are about love that we take it for granted. What else, it's assumed, should authors write about? But that fashion began in eleventh-century France. One day it is likely to change, as fashions do, into a mass obsession with something else. But, in the meantime, we still practice somewhat medieval codes of chivalry and etiquette—men opening doors for women, helping them on with coats, and so on—along with our understanding of love as a noble passion, and our taste for romance. No small change. As C. S. Lewis says so well, 20

> French poets, in the eleventh century, discovered or invented, or were the first to express, that romantic species of passion which English poets were still writing about in the nineteenth. They effected a change which has left no corner of our ethics, our imagination, or our daily life untouched, and they erected impassable barriers between us and the classical past or the Oriental present. Compared with this revolution, the Renaissance is a mere ripple. . . .

In the late twentieth century, while gangs riot in the ghettos, countries are craven for power, and sirens wail through the steep canyons of the inner cities and sprawling suburbs, we talk dreamily about courtly love. The twentieth-century Swiss thinker Denis de Rougemont railed against it and dismissed it out of hand as a plague, a bother, and a downright bad mistake. He despised the way it gave emotion mastery over reason. Sensible people longed for sound judgment, and romantic love left one feeling helplessly out of control. He asked: "Why does Western Man wish to suffer this passion which lacerates him and which all his common sense rejects?" He felt it made human relationships far too intense and unsettling, and he didn't like the way suffering was openly sought and enjoyed, or how it ruined one's chance for a happy marriage, which certainly couldn't compete with the remembered succulence of love. More than that, it pandered to an instinct subterranean, dangerous, and unspoken—a yearning for death. People secretly felt this attraction but could not risk acknowledging the phenomenon. It was all so chaotic and plural out there, all such a battle to stay orderly. Struggling every second of one's life against odds that would defeat one in the end, in fatigue heavy as a glacier, one secretly longed for annihilation. No one said so, but all this organized suffering and torment, wishing to die or be struck blind by the mere sight of the beloved—it felt too close to giving in to the seductiveness of death itself.

Perhaps de Rougemont was right. On the other hand, courtly love did help to raise the status of women and of many knights, granted individuals the right to make certain choices about their fate, encouraged mutual affection, and urged lovers to feel tenderness and respect for each other. As gentle-hearted friends, flushed with intimacy and regard, lovers tried to improve their character and talents, and so become worthy of love. No wonder it had such a powerful appeal.

What Wedding Films Tell Us about Love
Chrys Ingraham

Chrys Ingraham, an associate professor of sociology at Russell Sage College, writes on gender and class. She is co-editor of Materialist Feminism: A Reader in Class, Difference, and Women's Lives *(1997).*

Howard's mother, on hearing that he might be gay: "Howard, we want you to know, you're our son and we'll always love you—gay/straight, red/green, if you rob a bank, if you kill someone. . . ."

Howard's father: "If you get drunk, climb a clock tower and take out the town. . . ."

> Howard's mother: "As long as you get married. I need that wedding. I need some beauty and some music and some place cards before I die. It's like heroin. Do you hear me, Howard?"
>
> *In & Out*

In the quote above, Howard Brackett's mother has just learned, by way of an Oscar acceptance speech from her son's former student, Cameron Drake, that Howard may be gay. With Howard's wedding just three days away, this revelation comes as a shock to Mr. and Mrs. Brackett, who make it very clear to their son that even if he is gay, he *will* get married whether he wants to or not. At one point, Mrs. Brackett asks, "I can understand that he's gay, but why wouldn't he want a wedding?" Of course, this line is intended to be humorous, but the humor depends upon certain assumptions about the audience. The filmmakers expect the viewer to think this is absurd, laughable. Why would anyone think it's understandable to be gay? At the same time, they expect the audience to find it unimaginable that anyone wouldn't want a wedding. The combination of these two assumptions works to naturalize both institutionalized heterosexuality and its organizing rituals, exemplifying one of the dominant themes in wedding-oriented movies and television shows.

The foundational assumptions in this quote illustrate how some of these ideologies circulate. First, by the string of associations she lays out, Howard's mother asserts her "unconditional" love for her son, indicating that she will love him regardless of how bad or awful he might be. Using the dominant way of thinking about difference, she associates "gay" with color, crime, violence, and murder and places "gay" in a string of descriptors that signify criminal, ugly, unnatural, and deviant. The race theme also surfaces here in her reference to color. While it is somewhat subverted by mentioning red/green as opposed to black/white, the invocation of the color code has the same consequence. According to this passage, to be "of color" is to be "out of the ordinary."

Second, she asserts the primacy of the wedding with her emphasis on the "need" to marry. In her mind, weddings and marriage are natural and compulsory, not optional and certainly not something to take lightly.

Third, she tells us what a wedding means. It is about beauty and order and the desire to escape the real world. The message about heroin is very important here. It is the defining signifier of this passage, making it clear that the wedding is much more than a ritual. It is addictive, compulsory, a "have-to-have." It is the heterosexual imaginary at work, the moment for creating the illusion of happiness, order, well-being, and plenitude. It is the event that allows us to feel comfortable with the dominant social order, conceal any of its contradictions, and anesthetize ourselves against an everyday "state of affairs which needs illusions." [1] Weddings are ritual, drugged, and "feel-good" experiences. Mom needs a fix! [. . .]

"AND WE'LL NEVER BE LONELY ANY MORE . . ."

The visual media constitutes the most affective site in the wedding-industrial and -ideological complexes. By providing compelling images, popular film and television commodify weddings and create the market, the desire, and the demand for the white wedding. Watching our favorite actors achieve happiness or love allows us to live vicariously through the experiences of characters with whom we identify and grow to love and appreciate. The visual simulation of the wedding story is a powerful means for suturing an audience to the interests represented in a film or television show. Even though most of us are able to separate fantasy from reality, we still experience these stories and the emotions they evoke on the level of both the conscious and the unconscious. It's possible to be both critically aware of this medium while simultaneously crying or laughing with the characters. The romantic illusions created by media weddings construct desire to such an extent that, without realizing it, we place these illusions above reality. When the average bride spending $823 on a wedding gown, $19,000 on a wedding, and incurring a wedding debt far beyond her means, it appears the wedding-ideological complex is succeeding.

Messages from these films make their way into the cultural real—the culturally constructed world as opposed to the real world—in very powerful ways. Consider, for example, the now legendary attack on single motherhood by former Vice President Dan Quayle, who assailed the fictional character Murphy Brown for her irresponsibility in having a child out of wedlock. Touchstone Pictures' *Father of the Bride* and *Father of the Bride II* was so successful in capturing the imaginations of the American public that Disney, the parent company for Touchstone, developed their own Fairy Tale Wedding Pavilion complete with wedding consultants and spaces modeled on the film. In a recent commercial advertising the upcoming wedding of *The Nanny,* cast members talked about what a beautiful wedding it was, as

[1] The reference to illusion in this analysis comes from a passage by Karl Marx in the introduction to *Contribution to the Critique of Hegel's Philosophy of Law* (1844). With the elegance of a poet, Marx argues that religion is the "sigh of an oppressed people," who need the illusion of well-being rather than confront the source of their oppression and create "real" happiness. "To abolish religion as the illusory happiness of the people is to demand their real happiness. The demand to give up illusions about the existing state of affairs is the demand to give up a state of affairs which needs illusions. The criticism of religion is therefore in embryo the criticism of the vale of tears, the halo of which is religion. Criticism has torn up the imaginary flowers from the chain not so that man shall wear the unadorned, bleak chain but so that he will shake off the chain and pluck the living flower." This metaphor applies to all those sites that we use to numb us to the our real conditions of existence. One could substitute the word romance for religion and the meaning of this passage would still hold.

though an actual wedding had occurred. These instances are indicative of the influential role popular film and television have on how we think about ourselves, other people, and our values and on how we should behave in the real world. But more than that, they support a wedding-industrial complex that needs the romance fantasy in order to keep weddings and marriage desirable and profitable. Using the heterosexual imaginary, the visual media are highly effective in communicating how to imagine weddings, romance, marriage, and heterosexuality. Consent to the wedding industry, the dominant class, and the capitalist patriarchal social order is assured by the popularity of these images.

Films and television are well liked in part because the tales they present are intelligible to us. The comprehensibility they produce is a product of dominant ideologies about marriage combined with utopian notions of love and community, a dash of male resistance, and a hint of alternatives, circulating in the culture-at-large as well as in the guise of entertainment and escape. These media tales make use of the romance-novel, fairy-tale formula made familiar to many — especially women — since early childhood. [. . .]

One of the central objectives of the mass media is to provide the images necessary to reproduce the ruling order. As Douglas Kellner points out in his essay "Cultural Studies, Multiculturalism and Media Culture,"

> Media images help shape our view of the world and our deepest values: what we consider good or bad, positive or negative, moral or evil. Media stories provide the symbols, myths and resources through which we constitute a common culture. . . . Media spectacles demonstrate who has the power and who is powerless. . . . They dramatize and legitimate the power of the forces that be and show the powerless that they must stay in their places or be destroyed. . . . Ideologies make inequalities and subordination appear natural and just and thus induce consent to relations of domination. (1995, 5)

Consistent with Kellner's argument, weddings in popular culture are powerful sites for the enactment of dominant messages about society-at-large. Film and television industries know just how to use weddings to reflect and reproduce the kinds of messages necessary to ensure compliance with the dominant social order as they secure their own interests and markets.

In the presentation of wedding stories in popular film and television, the heterosexual imaginary makes the social order appear more manageable and comfortable. Using the power celebrities hold as the embodiment of fantasy to authorize particular social behaviors and beliefs, the visual media demonstrate where the margin of acceptability begins and ends. By making visible the consequences of operating outside the norm or the constructed "natural," the film industry legitimizes ruling interests and gains our compliance with practices that keep power in place. For example, the consumption of tales of romance, while profit-making for the producers of soap operas, romance novels, romantic comedies, and media weddings, prevents us from seeing the underlying material consequences these images and practices allow. They promote the "structured invisibility" of whiteness, numb us to excess, and police the boundaries of social acceptability around categories of race, class, sexuality, and even beauty.

In concert with some of the other components of the wedding-ideological complex [. . .], weddings in popular film and television contribute to the *creation of many taken-for-granted beliefs, values, and assumptions about weddings.* This wedding-ideological complex works to naturalize romance, weddings, marriage, and heterosexuality rather than present them as the result of meaning-making systems that organize what may or may not be the "natural" world. For example, in *all* of the film and television weddings studied [here], the following references were made by or about the bride:

> "It's my wedding day!"
> "I've been planning for this day all my life (or since I was . . .)"
> "I want a storybook wedding."
> "It's the most important day of my life."
> "I've waited my whole life for this day."
> "Everything has to be (is) perfect."
> "This will be the perfect wedding with the perfect guy."
> "This is the happiest day of my life."
> "I have to have the perfect wedding dress."

The pervasiveness of these messages is a sign of the intense socialization effort that the wedding-ideological complex has undertaken in constructing femininity, heterosexuality, and the importance of weddings to a woman's identity. What does it mean that the most important day of a woman's life is her wedding day? Why go on living after it's over? These messages are so powerful that even when characters in films and television weddings—not to mention women in real life—acknowledge the artificiality of these messages, it is still in the context of "Oh, well, I still want a wedding" or "I guess I'm just old-fashioned." Recently a friend of mine confessed, "I tried on my old wedding dress, and I hate to tell you this, but it felt great!" While many women comply with the dominant messages about femininity, heterosexuality, and weddings, some participate in the white wedding mill for other reasons. Weddings can represent a form of resistance among women who must face the social pressures of the workplace and other responsibilities. They can claim the romantic illusion of guarantees, kept promises, and well-being created by the wedding as a way to escape the strain of the real conditions of existence. Regardless of the motivation, the naturalization of the white wedding has been enormously successful. [. . .]

"WHAT'S LOVE GOT TO DO WITH IT?"

[. . .] The increased prevalence of weddings in popular film and television in the 1990s provides an important opportunity to examine and make visible what the culture "permits" us to believe about romance, weddings, marriage, and heterosexuality. [. . .]

"HERE COMES THE BRIDE, ALL DRESSED IN WHITE . . ."

[. . .] Romance, most often expressed as the illusion of well-being, is central to the selling of media weddings. Romance represents the utopian promise of love, joy, happiness, well-being, belonging, and community. Ultimately, romance is ideology at work in the creation of illusion. It is not about the real but is, instead, about the fantasy, fairy-tale, or utopian vision of the real. Applied to weddings and the institution of heterosexuality, romance works in the service of the heterosexual imaginary. Embedded within the film romance are messages about the value of weddings and marriage. In the heterogendered division of labor, romance is primarily the domain of women, or the emotive side of labor. It is the work of women within heterogendered social arrangements to do the work of feeling and caring as well as the work of providing an affective environment and of eliciting emotion from her partner. [. . .]

[. . .R]omance plays a pivotal role in setting up the subordinate position of women in relation to men. Over and over again we get the message that romance and wedding planning is the separate sphere of women or women's work. *Father of the Bride* revolves around the commiseration of Dad, who complains, scowls, and is mystified by how his wife and daughter spend "his" money in the name of a beautiful romantic white wedding. The image created in this movie is of two women sparing no expense to make sure this is the "wedding of a lifetime," one that is befitting the great love the bride-to-be Annie Banks (Kimberly Williams) has found with the groom-to-be Bryan MacKenzie (George Newbern).

The success of this film depends upon the intersection of several ideological frames: prevailing beliefs about romance and the heterogendered division of labor, and their link to class and accumulation interests. For example, in the opening scene of the movie we are greeted by George Banks (Steve Martin), the father of the bride, owner of a successful shoe factory, immediately after the wedding of his daughter Annie Banks-MacKenzie. The father of the bride confides to the audience: "I'll tell you a secret. This wedding cost more than this house when we bought it seventeen years ago. I'm told I'll look back on this day with affection and nostalgia. I hope so." This whole scene lasts for several minutes, as Banks recounts for the audience — and particularly fathers — what they should expect to encounter when their daughters marry. With a mixture of nostalgia for the little girl who once sat on his lap and called him "her hero" combined with complaints about expenses, this opening monologue teaches the audience that weddings are the irrational and expensive domain of women — the irrational and spendthrift sex.

The film makes use of the heterogender stereotype of women as consumers and as hopeless romantics spending excessively to provide something men find both painful and unintelligible unless, of course, they happen to be Franck Eggelhoffer (Martin Short), the effeminate wedding

15

coordinator. The ideological work of this film is to delineate the heterogen-dered division of labor portraying Dad as successful factory owner and Mom and daughter as women who spend his money frivolously. What is interesting about this film is how it both trivializes and elevates women's interest in weddings in an effort to secure both a female and male audience and preserve patriarchal heterosexuality and the heterogendered division of labor.

With refrains of "A wedding's a big deal!" and "We have to have a wed-ding coordinator" and "Welcome to the '90s, George!" from Nina Banks (Diane Keaton), the mother of the bride and George's wife, combined with the father's romance with his daughter, an estimated expenditure of about $45,000 is legitimized, twice the cost of the average American wedding. To convey to the viewer a "Father Knows Best" middle-America backdrop to this wedding, the filmmakers use two devices. First, they provide small-town, Main Street images of Dad coming home from work as he narrates how he's not "big on change," "loves this small town," and enjoys every facet of parenting. The first time we see Dad with his daughter is when she returns from a semester in Italy. He hurries home to see her, telling us how much he loves his big white colonial house with the white picket fence and how the best part of this house is the family life it's made possible. He's greeted at the door by his wife and young son and is warned that his daughter, Annie, has changed. Annie greets him by sliding down the banis-ter into his arms, calling up images of what she's probably done since she was a small child, and reassuring him that she hasn't changed that much.

Ideological notions of middle-class, middle-American, traditional fam-ily values are securely established in the first ten minutes of this film. This depiction of the white middle-class marriage and family makes use of a number of images already firmly in place in the collective imagination. By calling up themes from *Father Knows Best, Leave it to Beaver,* or *The Donna Reed Show, Father of the Bride* naturalizes notions of the traditional, nuclear, middle-class family and removes from view the reality that such media con-structions are historical and serve particular socioeconomic interests.

Later in the movie, we have the opportunity to see "real," big-city wealth when the Banks are invited to visit with the groom's family, the MacKenzies of Los Angeles. They live in a gated community in Bel Air and own "the biggest house on the street." While they present themselves as everyday, nice people, their wealth and privilege is made visible in a variety of ways. As George moves through their house, his thoughts are revealed to the viewer: "All I could think about was the size of this place. I could have parked our whole house in the foyer." When George asks where the bath-room is, Mrs. MacKenzie directs him to the "seventh door on the left" on the second floor, signaling to the audience the enormity of this house and the MacKenzies' wealth. The contrasts between upper-class and middle-class trappings work to suture the viewer to the class "plight" of the Banks. Even though Mr. and Mrs. Banks are both business owners, the audience is invited to sympathize with their "lack," or relative poverty. The film attempts to conceal the class privilege of the Banks by accentuating the excesses of MacKenzies.

As the story progresses and we watch George's frustration with the excesses of the wedding preparations and the wealthiness of the MacKenzies, the film works to comfort the white middle-class viewer with complaints about consumer rip-offs and feelings of economic inadequacy. The story line of this film depends upon the viewing audience identifying with the Bankses and appreciating the contrasts and discomforts between small town and big city, middle-class income and upper-class wealth. Significant in these contrasts is the way they also legitimize the $45,000 wedding for the middle class as well as the interests of the owning class. The expense of this wedding is justified as an expression of the love of the parents for their daughter and as "affordable" for the middle-class family, which may have to give up some things but puts the interests of their child's "special day" ahead of any practicality or notion of excess. [. . .]

"IT'S A NICE DAY FOR A WHITE WEDDING . . ."

The Wedding Singer is a campy romantic comedy full of garish colors and unusual-looking people. This film makes use of dominant notions of difference to legitimize romantic love, a heterogendered division of labor, and marriage. Robbie Hart (Adam Sandler) is the wedding singer, performing at working-class to lower-middle-class weddings in a small town where all of the receptions are held at the same banquet hall. Portrayed as a very sweet, considerate guy, Robbie meets Julia (Drew Barrymore), one of the waitresses where he's singing. In their first conversation they tell each other about their engagements and wedding plans. Robbie tells Julia he is getting married next week, and Julia tells Robbie that her boyfriend, Glen, won't set a date.

In the next scene, we watch as Robbie is stood up at the altar, when Linda changes her mind about marrying Robbie and doesn't appear for their formal white wedding. Humiliated in front of half the town, Robbie finds out from Linda that she decided she didn't want to be married to a wedding singer and stay in Ridgefield for the rest of her life. At this point in the film, we learn that Robbie is a nice, small-town guy who cares about kids, old ladies, and being romantic.

Julia, a small, big-eyed blond, who dresses sweetly and is kind to everyone, is engaged to Glen (Matthew Glave), a smooth-talking, handsome financial analyst who loves to womanize, talk big, and bully gentle guys like Robbie. In a sense, this film works more like a cartoon than a movie, setting Glen and Linda up as the "bad guys" and Robbie and Julia — a '90s Romeo and Juliet — as the "good guys," who are obviously meant to be

20

together because they have so much in common. Before we reach the predictable romantic happy ending, in which Robbie defeats Glen for Julia's love, we learn through constructions of difference what makes people worthy of marriage.

Robbie's band is made up of three performers. His backup singer is a Boy George lookalike named George. Whenever he's left to fill in for Robbie he sings Boy George's song "Do You Really Want to Hurt Me?" In each instance we watch as the wedding guests get more and more abusive and disgusted by this cross-dressing, gender-bending guy. The humor at this point depends on the audience finding this Boy George "wannabe," coded as stereotypically gay, repulsive and laughable, and the violence of the wedding guests understandable. At several points throughout the movie there are mocking references to gays or homoerotic behaviors. Even Robbie is constructed as having gay behaviors. In several scenes between Robbie and Glen, "the bully," Glen, makes reference to Robbie as "limp-wristed" or effeminate because he's considerate and gentle.

In his first public appearance following his "jilting," Robbie is consumed with emotion and enraged at the prospect that he's not going to marry. It doesn't really matter that he's lost Linda. What's really important is that he believes no one else will want him, that he's not worthy of marriage. To make his point he sings the song "Love Stinks" and invites another marriage reject, a fat man, to sing the song with him. During this sequence Robbie identifies for the audience which people will never marry:

> Some of us will never ever find true love. Take for instance . . . me! And take, for instance, that guy right there. And that lady with the sideburns and, basically, everybody at table 9. And the interesting thing is . . . me, fatty, the lady with the sideburns, and the mutants at table 9 will never ever find a way to better our situation, because apparently we have absolutely nothing to offer the opposite sex.

In this amazing scene, Robbie identifies all the unfit people in the room and declares that neither he nor any of them are marriageable. No one would want anyone that ugly, useless, and undesirable. This is designed to be one of the most humorous segments in the film, inviting the audience to join Robbie in agreeing that these people are undesirable. In the climax of this scene Robbie moves around the reception inviting each of the "mutants" to join him in singing "Love Stinks." For the first time during the wedding reception, they smile and become excited. The scene ends with the father of the bride punching Robbie.

These constructions of difference act as social control mechanisms, elevating the institution of heterosexuality and weddings by coding those who don't marry as deviant, ugly, unworthy, and resentful. By contrast, those who marry and have the traditional white wedding are constructed as superior. Their joy in singing "Love Stinks" only reinforces the pattern that anyone

25

who doesn't enjoy a wedding or who acknowledges the pain of so-called love relationships is predictably bitter and resentful because they're unfit. The blame for being without a partner or without love is placed firmly on the shoulders of the individual who's not worthy rather than on a culture that sets up these social arrangements and their corresponding social controls.

A similar pattern occurs in the *Lois & Clark* television wedding where Superman marries Lois Lane. A villain called the "wedding destroyer" attempts to murder Lois at the altar to force Clark to live with the type of pain she's had to endure since her groom-to-be died on his way to their wedding. Ideologically, these messages work to demonstrate that anyone who dislikes weddings is either disfigured or hostile.

The boundaries of acceptability are clearly demarcated in both of these examples, establishing what counts as beautiful, attractive, desirable, and worthy of love and marriage by making visible what typifies the opposite of these things as well as the consequences of occupying these marginalized positions.

In addition to ideologies of difference, *The Wedding Singer* also establishes that weddings and wedding preparations are the space of the feminine and the domain of women, that dreams are made of finding true love, and that happiness can be found by a woman surrendering her identity to the right man. As Julia prepares for her wedding, she tries on her white wedding gown and stands in front of the mirror and rehearses what she will say in the receiving line.

> Hi, nice to meet you. I'm Mrs. Glen Gulia. I'm Julia Gulia.
>
> It's nice to meet you, I'm Mrs. Julia Gulia [she sobs].
>
> Hi, I'm Mrs. Robbie Hart. Robbie and I are so pleased you could come to our wedding [she beams].

In this moment Julia realizes she loves Robbie but believes she has to go through with the wedding because she thinks Robbie is back with Linda. Robbie finds out Julia and Glen are on their way to Las Vegas to get married and follows her there. Much to his surprise, he realizes they're on the same plane. He finds her while Glen is in the bathroom, sings a romantic song he wrote for her, and they declare their love for each other. Boy meets girl, boy gets girl . . . and the scene ends with a kiss in front of everyone on the plane as they applaud. The conclusion of the film is—you guessed it!—a big white wedding. The ideology of romantic love overcomes all obstacles except those it keeps in place to preserve the interests of patriarchal capitalism and the institution of heterosexuality. [. . .]

These themes are pervasive in popular culture, signaling a disturbing trend among the white middle class—the nearly exclusive obsession of young white women with romance and weddings. Without exception, it appears that this is all women think or care about. The consequence to women can be profound, manifesting in a form of anti-intellectualism where women are concerned, reducing their expectations in life to one moment of spectacle, rendering their talents and desires to the domestic sphere, trivializing their interests in the world around them, and situating them as the standard-bearers of traditional femininity and the heterogendered division of labor.

The heterogendered division of labor and heterosexual supremacy are   30
well preserved in television and popular film, inviting us to laugh and cry while we celebrate the setbacks and triumphs of characters who appear real to us. As we do, we become complicit in the ways of thinking that allow for racial, class, gender, and sexual hierarchies, varying kinds of sexual/gender violence, a patriarchal heterogendered division of labor, and subservience to a class/accumulation model for personal relations. The heterosexual imaginary circulating in popular film and television works to obscure these consequences by cloaking them in humor and romance. And it discourages any critical analysis of the consequences of how we've organized and regulated heterosexuality as an institution. In the end, we're left to wonder who it is, exactly, who lives "happily ever after."

Work Cited

Kellner, Douglas. "Cultural Studies, Multiculturalism, and Media Culture." *Media Culture*. Ed. Douglas Kellner. New York: Routledge, 1995.

Questions for Discussion

1. In "Web of Love," Fisher describes the chemicals active in the brain during three different kinds of love. According to her theory, what would explain the situation of a person who was "in love" with one person and yet wanting to have sex with another? What seems to be her attitude toward the contradictory directions that love can pull us in?

2. Later readings in this chapter describe young people seeking sexual relationships with no emotional commitment (see "Hook-Up Culture," pages 514–516, and "Dinner and a Movie? No Thanks on College Campuses," pages 510–514). What do Fisher's scientific findings indicate about the possibility of success in trying to have a "no strings" sexual relationship?

3. How realistic is it to expect "romantic love" to last through a lifetime marriage, according to Fisher's study of the brain activity of long-term lovers? What evidence does she give for saying that keeping romantic love alive is an uphill battle against the natural brain chemistry of love?

4. From Ackerman's description, what were some of the features of courtly love that made it revolutionary? Which of these do you see evidence of in today's ideas about lovers' relationships?

5. The actual white wedding gown tradition began with Queen Victoria's wedding to Prince Albert in 1840; however, other elements of the ritual have deeper roots. Given what you have learned from the selection by Ackerman, what does the modern idea of the white wedding owe to the tradition of courtly love? In what ways is it different from courtly love?

6. Ingraham argues that both *Father of the Bride* and *The Wedding Singer* present romantic love as a regressive rather than progressive cultural institution. According to her analysis of the films, what do they tell us about love and lovers? What evidence does she offer from the films to make her point? If you have seen the films yourself, discuss whether you agree or disagree with her interpretation. If you have seen other, more recent, wedding films, discuss whether they suggest the same set of ideas or different ones.

Suggestions for Writing

For Persuasion

Read again the arguments by Denis de Rougemont against romantic love (paragraph 21 in Ackerman's essay). Do you see any validity to his reasons for denouncing it? If so, make your own case against "romance," adding your own evidence to support any of his reasons you agree with and adding any other reasons and evidence that come to mind. It would be impossible to persuade someone not to fall in love, but you can make a case against the idea of romantic love as a desirable state for anyone to be in.

For Inquiry

Ackerman explains how the songs of the troubadours offered a view of love that influenced people at the time, revolutionizing Western civilization's ideas of love. Are there singers today whose songs offer interpretations of love that might be influencing people's view of love now? What songs have influenced your views? What evidence can you find that the music you describe has any effect on real people's attitudes?

For Research and Convincing

Do research on the amounts of time and money spent on the average wedding ceremony today. If you can, try to find if "perfect weddings" correlate with stronger marriages. You may want to consult friends and family members who have recently gotten married in the traditional way—with the formal wedding ceremony and reception. Draw some conclusions about the value of these expenditures. To what extent do they contribute to the institution of marriage in American culture?

SECTION 2: CHOOSING PARTNERS

Overview

The readings in this section address the question of how lovers choose each other. Just as biology and culture influence the experience of love, the readings in this section suggest that both nature and nurture are involved in sexual attraction. Evolution programmed men and women to prefer mates that would increase their chances of reproducing and raising healthy offspring. However, as the two selections by David Buss reveal, these preferences differ significantly by sex. We might like to say we have evolved to a point where men would look for more than just youth and beauty (signs of health and fertility) in a woman, and women would look for more than wealth and status (signs of ability to protect them and the babies) in a man, but the fact is, even today, college males say physical attractiveness is the main criterion in deciding to have sexual intercourse, while women consider social and economic resources when deciding to have sex with a man. (See Knox 2001 in "For Further Reading and Research," page 564.) Even women who are doctors and lawyers want men with more money and status than they have (Fisher 114).

Still, all is not bad news for those without glamour and wealth. According to evolutionary psychologist Geoffrey Miller, other criteria matter too. We humans are highly evolved creatures, interested in things like art, jazz, and humor. Miller argues here that intellectual and creative qualities developed in humans of both sexes as a means to impress potential mates. So brains and personality make us attractive too.

And so does our ability to love and care for others. When the Rutgers Marriage Project surveyed both men and women about what they want in a mate, the dominant answer from both sexes is emotional and spiritual compatibility. As religious influences diminish, the spiritual component reenters the marriage in this secular way—through the personal bond between two souls. However, the search for a soul mate is problematic. As the reading by John Armstrong shows, it is likely to lead one to believe that finding a partner is essential and that without a partner one is not "complete."

What Women Want

David Buss

David Buss is an evolutionary psychologist who taught at Harvard and the University of Michigan before joining the faculty at the University of Texas at Austin in 1996. In addition to human mating strategies, other areas of interest he researches are conflict between the sexes, jealousy, status, and the emotion of jealousy. In 2000, he won the

Robert W. Hamilton Book Award for Evolutionary Psychology: The New Science of the Mind *(Allyn & Bacon, 1999).*

We are walking archives of ancestral wisdom.
—Helena Cronin, *The Ant and the Peacock*

What women actually want in a mate has puzzled male scientists and other men for centuries, for good reason. It is not androcentric to propose that women's preferences in a partner are more complex and enigmatic than the mate preferences of either sex of any other species. Discovering the evolutionary roots of women's desires requires going far back in time, before humans evolved as a species, before primates emerged from their mammalian ancestors, back to the origins of sexual reproduction itself.

One reason women exert choice about mates stems from the most basic fact of reproductive biology—the definition of sex. It is a remarkable circumstance that what defines biological sex is simply the size of the sex cells. Males are defined as the ones with the small sex cells, females as the ones with the large sex cells. The large female gametes remain reasonably stationary and come loaded with nutrients. The small male gametes are endowed with mobility and swimming speed.[1] Along with differences in the size and mobility of sex cells comes a difference between the sexes in quantity. Men, for example, produce millions of sperm, which are replenished at a rate of roughly twelve million per hour, while women produce a fixed and unreplenishable lifetime supply of approximately four hundred ova.

Women's greater initial investment does not end with the egg. Fertilization and gestation, key components of human parental investment, occur internally within women. One act of sexual intercourse, which requires minimal male investment, can produce an obligatory and energy-consuming nine-month investment by the woman that forecloses other mating opportunities. Women then bear the exclusive burden of lactation, an investment that may last as long as three or four years. [. . .]

The great initial parental investment of women makes them a valuable, but limited, resource.[2] Gestating, bearing, nursing, nurturing, and protecting a child are exceptional reproductive resources that cannot be allocated indiscriminately. Nor can one woman dispense them to many men.

Those who hold valuable resources do not give them away cheaply or unselectively. Because women in our evolutionary past risked enormous investment as a consequence of having sex, evolution favored women who were highly selective about their mates. Ancestral women suffered severe costs if they were indiscriminate—they experienced lower reproductive success, and fewer of their children survived to reproductive age. A man in human evolutionary history could walk away from a casual coupling having lost only a few hours of time. His reproductive success was not seriously compromised. A woman in evolutionary history could also walk away from

5

a casual encounter, but if she got pregnant as a result, she bore the costs of that decision for months, years, and even decades afterward. [. . .]

Evolution has favored women who prefer men who possess attributes that confer benefits and who dislike men who possess attributes that impose costs. Each separate attribute constitutes one component of a man's value to a woman as a mate. Each of her preferences tracks one component. [. . .]

ECONOMIC CAPACITY

The evolution of the female preference for males who offer resources may be the most ancient and pervasive basis for female choice in the animal kingdom. Consider the gray shrike, a bird that lives in the Negev Desert of Israel.[3] Just before the start of the breeding season, male shrikes begin amassing caches of edible prey, such as snails, and other useful objects, such as feathers and pieces of cloth, in numbers ranging from 90 to 120. They impale these items on thorns and other pointed projections within their territory. Females look over the available males and prefer to mate with those having the largest caches. When the biologist Reuven Yosef arbitrarily removed portions of some males' caches and added edible objects to others, females shifted to the males with the larger bounties. Females avoided entirely males without resources, consigning them to bachelorhood. Wherever females show a mating preference, the male's resources are often the key criterion.

Among humans, the evolution of women's preference for a permanent mate with resources would have required three preconditions. First, resources would have had to be accruable, defensible, and controllable by men during human evolutionary history. Second, men would have had to differ from each other in their holdings and their willingness to invest those holdings in a woman and her children — if all men possessed the same resources and showed an equal willingness to commit them, there would be no need for women to develop the preference for them. Constants do not count in mating decisions. And third, the advantages of being with one man would have to outweigh the advantages of being with several men.

Among humans, these conditions are easily met. Territory and tools, to name just two resources, are acquired, defended, monopolized, and controlled by men worldwide. Men vary tremendously in the quantity of resources they command — from the poverty of the street bum to the riches of Trumps and Rockefellers. Men also differ widely in how willing they are to invest their time and resources in long-term mateships. Some men are cads, preferring to mate with many women while investing little in each. Other men are dads, channeling all of their resources to one woman and her children.[4] [. . .]

The premium that women place on economic resources has been   10
revealed in many contexts. The psychologist Douglas Kenrick and his colleagues devised a useful method for revealing how much people value
different attributes in a marriage partner; they asked men and women to
indicate the "minimum percentiles" of each characteristic that they would
find acceptable.[5] The percentile concept was explained with such examples
as: "A person at the 50th percentile would be above 50% of the other people on earning capacity, and below 49% of the people on this dimension."
American college women indicate that their minimum acceptable percentile for a husband on earning capacity is the 70th percentile, or above
70 percent of all other men, whereas men's minimum acceptable percentile
for a wife's earning capacity is only the 40th.

Personal ads in newspapers and magazines confirm that women who
are actually in the marriage market desire financial resources. A study of
1,111 personal ads found that female advertisers seek financial resources
roughly eleven times as often as male advertisers do.[6] In short, sex differences in a preference for resources are not limited to college students and
are not bound by the method of inquiry. [. . .]

Henry Kissinger once remarked that power is the most potent aphrodisiac. Women desire men who command a high position in society because social status is a universal cue to the control of resources. Along with
status come better food, more abundant territory, and superior health care.
Greater social status bestows on children social opportunities missed by the
children of lower-ranked males. For male children worldwide, access to
more mates and better quality mates typically accompanies families of
higher social status. In one study of 186 societies ranging from the Mbuti
Pygmies of Africa to the Aleut Eskimos, high-status men invariably had
greater wealth, better nourishment for children, and more wives.[7]

Women in the United States do not hesitate to express a preference for
mates who have high social status or a high-status profession, qualities that
are viewed as only slightly less important than good financial prospects.[8]
Using a rating scale from irrelevant or unimportant to indispensable, American women from Massachusetts, Michigan, Texas, and California rate social status as between important and indispensable, whereas men rate it as
merely desirable but not very important. In one study of 5,000 college
students, women list status, prestige, rank, position, power, standing,
station, and high place as important considerably more frequently than
men do.[9] [. . .]

American women also place great value on education and professional
degrees in mates — characteristics that are strongly linked with social status.
The same study found that women rate lack of education as highly undesirable in a potential husband. The cliché that women prefer to marry doctors,
lawyers, professors, and other professionals seems to correspond with reality. Women shun men who are easily dominated by other men or who fail
to command the respect of the group. [. . .]

AGE

The age of a man also provides an important cue to his access to resources.   15
Just as young male baboons must mature before they can enter the upper
ranks in the baboon social hierarchy, human adolescents and young men
rarely command the respect, status, or position of more mature older men.
This tendency reaches an extreme among the Tiwi tribe, a gerontocracy in
which the very old men wield most of the power and prestige and control
the mating system through complex networks of alliances. Even in American culture, status and wealth tend to accumulate with increasing age.

In all thirty-seven cultures included in the international study on
choosing a mate, women prefer men who are older than they are.[10] Averaged over all cultures, women prefer men who are roughly three and a half
years older. The smallest preferred age difference is seen in French Canadian women, who seek husbands who are not quite two years older, and
the largest is found among Iranian women, who seek husbands who are
more than five years older. The worldwide average age difference between
actual brides and grooms is three years, suggesting that women's marriage
decisions often match their mating preferences.

To understand why women value older mates, we must turn to the
things that change with age. One of the most consistent changes is access to
resources. In contemporary Western societies, income generally increases
with age.[11] American men who are thirty years old, for example, make fourteen thousand dollars more than men who are twenty; men who are forty
make seven thousand dollars more than men who are thirty. These trends
are not limited to the Western world. Among traditional nonmodernized
societies, older men have more social status. Among the Tiwi tribe, men are
typically at least thirty years of age before they acquire enough social status
to acquire a first wife.[12] Rarely does a Tiwi man under the age of forty attain
enough status to acquire more than one wife. Older age, resources, and status are coupled across cultures. [. . .]

Women may prefer older men for reasons other than tangible resources. Older men are likely to be more mature, more stable, and more
reliable in their provisioning. Within the United States, for example, men
become somewhat more emotionally stable, more conscientious, and more
dependable as they grow older, at least up through the age of thirty.[13] In a
study of women's mate preferences, one woman noted that "older men
[are] better looking because you [can] talk to them about serious concerns;
younger men [are] silly and not very serious about life."[14] The status potential of men becomes clearer with increasing age. Women who prefer older
men are in a better position to gauge how high they are likely to rise. [. . .]

[. . .E]xceptions occur among women who already have high status and
plentiful resources of their own and then take up with much younger men.
Cher and Joan Collins are striking celebrity examples; they became involved with men who were two decades younger. But these cases are rare,

because most women with resources prefer to mate with men at least as rich in resources as they are, and preferably more so.[15] Women may mate temporarily with a younger man, but typically they seek an older man when they decide to settle down in marriage. Neither Cher's nor Joan Collins's romance with a younger man proved to be stable over time. [. . .]

DEPENDABILITY AND STABILITY

Among the eighteen characteristics rated in the worldwide study on choosing a mate, the second and third most highly valued characteristics, after love, are a dependable character and emotional stability or maturity. In twenty-one out of thirty-seven cultures, men and women have the same preference for dependability in a partner. Of the sixteen cultures where there is a sex difference, women in fifteen of the cultures value dependability more than men. Averaged across all thirty-seven cultures, women rate dependable character 2.69 where a 3.00 signifies indispensable; men rate it nearly as important, with an average of 2.50. In the case of emotional stability or maturity, the sexes differ more. Women in twenty-three cultures value this quality significantly more than men do; in the remaining fourteen cultures, men and women value emotional stability equally. Averaging across all cultures, women give this quality a 2.68, whereas men give it a 2.47. In all cultures, in effect, women place a tremendous value on these characteristics, judging them to be anywhere from important to indispensable in a potential spouse.

20

These characteristics may possess such a great value worldwide because they are reliable signals that resources will be provided consistently over time. Undependable people, in contrast, provide erratically and inflict heavy costs on their mates. In a study of newlyweds, my colleagues and I contacted 104 couples at random from the public records of all marriages that had been licensed in a large county in Michigan during a six-month period. These couples completed a six-hour battery of personality tests and self-evaluations of their marital relationship, and evaluations of their spouse's character, and they were each interviewed by both a male and a female interviewer. Among these tests was an instrument that asked the participants to indicate which among 147 possible costs their partner had inflicted on them over the past year. Emotionally unstable men—as defined by themselves, their spouses, and their interviewers—are especially costly to women. First, they tend to be self-centered and monopolize shared resources. Furthermore, they tend to be possessive, monopolizing much of the time of their wives. They show higher than average sexual jealousy, becoming enraged when their wives even talk with someone else. They show dependency, insisting that their mates provide for all of their needs. They tend to be abusive both verbally and physically. They display inconsiderateness, such as by failing to show up on time. And they are moodier than their more stable counterparts, often crying for no apparent reason. They have more affairs than average, which suggests a further diversion of time and resources.[16] All of these costs indicate that such spouses will absorb their partner's time and resources, divert their own time and resources elsewhere, and fail to channel resources consistently over time. Dependability and stability are personal qualities that signal increased likelihood that a woman's resources will not be drained by the man. [. . .]

INTELLIGENCE

Dependability, emotional stability, industriousness, and ambition are not the only personal qualities that signal the acquisition and steadiness of resources. The ephemeral quality of intelligence provides another important cue. No one knows for sure what intelligence tests measure, but there is clear evidence of what high scorers can do. Intelligence is a good predictor of the possession of economic resources within the United States.[17] People who test high go to better schools, get more years of education, and ultimately get higher paying jobs. Even within particular professions, such as construction and carpentry, intelligence predicts who will advance more rapidly to positions of power and who will command higher incomes. In tribal societies, the head men or leaders are almost invariably among the more intelligent members of the group.[18] [. . .]

The quality of intelligence signals many potential benefits. These are likely to include good parenting skills, capacity for cultural knowledge, and adeptness at parenting.[19] In addition, intelligence is linked with oral fluency, ability to influence other members of a group, prescience in forecasting danger, and judgment in applying health remedies. Beyond these specific qualities, intelligence conveys the ability to solve problems. Women who select more intelligent mates are more likely to become the beneficiaries of all of these critical resources. [. . .]

COMPATIBILITY

Successful long-term mating requires a sustained cooperative alliance with another person for mutually beneficial goals. Relationships riddled with conflict impede the attainment of those goals. Compatibility between mates entails a complex mesh between two different kinds of characteristics. One kind involves complementary traits, or a mate's possession of resources and skills that differ from one's own, in a kind of division of labor between the sexes. Both persons benefit through this specialization and division.

The other kinds of traits crucial to compatibility with a mate, however, are those that are most likely to mesh cooperatively with one's own

25

particular personal characteristics and thus are most similar to one's own. Discrepancies between the values, interests and personalities of the members of a couple produce strife and conflict. The psychologist Zick Rubin and his colleagues studied 202 dating couples over several years to see which ones stayed together and which broke up.[20] They found that couples who were mismatched in these regards tend to break up more readily than their matched counterparts. The 103 couples who broke up had more dissimilar values on sex roles, attitudes toward sex among acquaintances, romanticism, and religious beliefs than did the 99 couples who stayed together.

One solution to the problem of compatibility is thus to search for the similar in a mate. Both in the United States and worldwide, men and women who are similar to each other on a wide variety of characteristics tend to get married. The tendency for like people to mate shows up most obviously in the areas of values, intelligence, and group membership.[21] People seek mates with similar political and social values, such as their views on abortion or capital punishment, for which couples are correlated +.50. Mismatches on these values are likely to lead to conflict. People also desire mates who are similar in race, ethnicity, and religion. Couples desire and marry mates of similar intelligence, on which spouses correlate +.40. In addition, similarity matters in personality characteristics such as extraversion, agreeableness, and conscientiousness, which show correlations between spouses of +.25. People like mates who share their inclination toward parties if they are extraverted and toward quiet evenings at home if they are introverted. People who are characteristically open to experience prefer mates who share their interest in fine wines, art, literature, and exotic foods. Conscientious people prefer mates who share their interest in paying bills on time and saving for the future. Less conscientious people prefer mates who share their interest in living for the moment. [. . .]

SIZE AND STRENGTH

When the great basketball player Magic Johnson revealed that he had slept with thousands of women, he inadvertently revealed women's preference for mates who display physical and athletic prowess. The numbers may be shocking, but the preference is not. Physical characteristics, such as athleticism, size, and strength, convey important information that women use in making a mating decision. [. . .]

[. . .O]ne benefit to women of permanent mating is the physical protection a man can offer. A man's size, strength, and physical prowess are cues to solutions to the problem of protection. The evidence shows that women's preferences in a mate embody these cues. In the study of temporary and permanent mating, American women rated the desirability or undesirability of a series of physical traits. Women judge short men to be undesirable as a permanent mate.[22] In contrast, they find it very desirable for a potential permanent mate to be tall, physically strong, and athletic. Another group of American women consistently indicates a preference for men of average or greater than average height, roughly five feet and eleven inches, as their ideal marriage partner. Tall men are consistently seen as more desirable dates and mates than men who are short or of average height.[23] Furthermore, the two studies of personal ads described earlier revealed that, among women who mention height, 80 percent want a man who is six feet or taller. Perhaps even more telling is the finding that ads placed by taller men receive more responses from women than those placed by shorter men. Tall men date more often than short men and have a larger pool of potential mates. Women solve the problem of protection from aggressive men at least in part by preferring a mate who has the size, strength, and physical prowess to protect them.

Tall men tend to have a higher status in nearly all cultures. "Big men" in hunter-gatherer societies—men high in status—are literally big men physically.[24] In Western cultures, tall men make more money, advance in their professions more rapidly, and receive more and earlier promotions. Few American presidents have been less than six feet tall. Politicians are keenly aware of voters' preference. Following the televised presidential debate in 1988, George Bush made a point of standing very close to his shorter competitor, Michael Dukakis, in a strategy of highlighting their disparity in size. As the evolutionary psychologist Bruce Ellis notes:

> Height constitutes a reliable cue to dominance in social interactions . . . shorter policemen are likely to be assaulted more than taller policemen . . . suggesting that the latter command more fear and respect from adversaries . . . taller men are more sought after in women's personal advertisements, receive more responses to their own personal advertisements, and tend to have prettier girlfriends than do shorter men.[25] [. . .]

Attributes such as size, strength, and athletic prowess are not the only physical attributes that signal high mating value. Another physical quality critical for survival is good health.

30

GOOD HEALTH

Women worldwide prefer mates who are healthy.[26] In all thirty-seven cultures included in the international study on choosing a mate, women judge good health to be anywhere from important to indispensable in a marriage partner. In another study on American women, poor physical conditions, ranging from bad grooming habits to a venereal disease, are regarded as extremely undesirable characteristics in a mate. The biologists Clelland Ford and Frank Beach found that signs of ill health, such as open sores, lesions, and unusual pallor, are universally regarded as unattractive.[27]

In humans, good health may be signaled by behavior as well as by physical appearance. A lively mood, high energy level, and sprightly gait, for example, may be attractive precisely because they are calorically costly and can be displayed only by people brimming with good health. [. . .]

LOVE AND COMMITMENT

A man's possession of such assets as health, status, and resources, however, still does not guarantee his willingness to commit them to a particular woman and her children. Indeed, some men show a tremendous reluctance to marry, preferring to play the field and to seek a series of temporary sex partners. Women deride men for this hesitancy, calling them "commitment dodgers," "commitment phobics," "paranoid about commitment," and "fearful of the M word."[28] And women's anger is reasonable. Given the tremendous costs women incur because of sex, pregnancy, and childbirth, it is reasonable for them to require commitment from a man in return. [. . .]

Women past and present face the adaptive problem of choosing men who not only have the necessary resources but also show a willingness to commit those resources to them and their children. This problem may be more difficult than it seems at first. Although resources can often be directly observed, commitment cannot be. Instead, gauging commitment requires looking for cues that signal the likelihood of fidelity in the channeling of resources. Love is one of the most important cues to commitment.

Feelings and acts of love are not recent products of particular Western views. Love is universal. Thoughts, emotions, and actions of love are experienced by people in all cultures worldwide—from the Zulu in the southern tip of Africa to the Eskimos in the north of Alaska. In a survey of 168 diverse cultures from around the world, the anthropologist William Jankowiak found strong evidence for the presence of romantic love in nearly 90 percent of them. For the remaining 10 percent, the anthropological records were too sketchy to definitely verify the presence of love. When the sociologist Sue Sprecher and her colleagues interviewed 1,667 men and women in Russia, Japan, and the United States, they found that 61 percent of the Russian men and 73 percent of the Russian women were currently in love. Comparable figures for the Japanese were 41 percent of the men and 63 percent of the women. Among Americans, 53 percent of the men and 63 percent of the women acknowledged being in love. Clearly, love is not a phenomenon limited to Western cultures.[29]

To identify precisely what love is and how it is linked to commitment, I initiated a study of acts of love.[30] First, I asked fifty women and fifty men from the University of California and the University of Michigan to think of people they knew who were currently in love and to describe actions performed by those people that reflect or exemplify their love. A different group of forty college men and women evaluated each of the 115 acts

35

named for how typical it was of love in their estimation. Acts of commitment top the women's and men's lists, being viewed as most central to love. Such acts include giving up romantic relations with others, talking of marriage, and expressing a desire to have children with the person. When performed by a man, these acts of love signal the intention to commit resources to one woman and her children.

Commitment, however, has many facets. One major component of commitment is fidelity, exemplified by the act of remaining faithful to a partner when they are separated. Fidelity signals the exclusive commitment of sexual resources to a single partner. Another aspect of commitment is the channeling of resources to the loved one, such as buying her an expensive gift or ring. Acts such as this signal a serious intention to commit economic resources to a long-term relationship. Emotional support is yet another facet of commitment, revealed by such behavior as being available in times of trouble and listening to the partner's problems. Commitment entails a channeling of time, energy, and effort to the partner's needs at the expense of fulfilling one's own personal goals. Acts of reproduction also represent a direct commitment to one's partner's genes. All these acts, which are viewed as central to love, signal the commitment of sexual, economic, emotional, and genetic resources to one person. [. . .]

Two additional personal characteristics, kindness and sincerity, are critical to securing long-term commitment. In one study of 800 personal advertisements, sincerity was the single most frequently listed characteristic sought by women.[31] Another analysis of 1,111 personal advertisements again showed that sincerity is the quality most frequently sought by women — indeed, women advertisers seek sincerity nearly four times as often as men advertisers.[32] Sincerity in personal advertisements is a code word for commitment, used by women to screen out men seeking casual sex without any commitment.

People worldwide depend on kindness from their mates. As shown by the international study on choosing a mate, women have a strong preference for mates who are kind and understanding. In thirty-two out of the thirty-seven cultures, in fact, sexes are identical in valuing kindness as one of the three most important qualities out of a possible thirteen in a mate. Only in Japan and Taiwan do men give greater emphasis than women to kindness. And only in Nigeria, Israel, and France do women give greater emphasis than men to kindness. In no culture, for either sex, however, is kindness in a mate ranked lower than third out of thirteen.

Kindness is an enduring personality characteristic that has many components, but at the core of all of them is the commitment of resources. The trait signals an empathy toward children, a willingness to put a mate's needs before one's own, and a willingness to channel energy and effort toward a mate's goals rather than exclusively and selfishly to one's own goals.[33] Kindness, in other words, signals the ability and willingness of a potential mate to commit energy and resources selflessly to a partner.

40

The lack of kindness signals selfishness, an inability or unwillingness to commit, and a high likelihood that costs will be inflicted on a spouse. The study of newlyweds, for example, identified unkind men on the basis of their self-assessment, their wives' assessment, and the judgment of male and female interviewers, and then examined the wives' complaints about these husbands. Women married to unkind men complain that their spouses abuse them both verbally and physically by hitting, slapping, or spitting at them. Unkind men tend to be condescending, putting down their wife's opinions as stupid or inferior. They are selfish, monopolizing shared resources. They are inconsiderate, failing to do any housework. They are neglectful, failing to show up as promised. Finally, they have more extramarital affairs, suggesting that these men are unable or unwilling to commit to a monogamous relationship.[34] Unkind men look out for themselves, and have trouble committing to anything much beyond that.

Because sex is one of the most valuable reproductive resources women can offer, they have evolved psychological mechanisms that cause them to resist giving it away indiscriminately. Requiring love, sincerity, and kindness is a way of securing a commitment of resources commensurate with the value of the resource that women give to men. Requiring love and kindness helps women to solve the critical adaptive mating problem of securing the commitment of resources from a man that can aid in the survival and reproduction of her offspring. [. . .]

Notes

1. Trivers 1972; Williams 1975.
2. Trivers 1972.
3. Yosef 1991.
4. Draper and Harpending 1982; Belsky, Steinberg, and Draper 1991.
5. Kenrick, Sadalla, Groth, and Trost 1990.
6. Wiederman, in press.
7. Betzig 1986.
8. Hill 1945; Langhorne and Secord 1955; McGinnis 1958; Hudson and Henze 1969; Buss and Barnes 1986.
9. Langhorne and Secord 1955.
10. Buss 1989a.
11. Jencks 1979.
12. Hart and Pilling 1960.
13. McCrae and Costa 1990; Gough 1980.
14. Jankowiak, Hill, and Donovan 1992.
15. Townsend 1989; Townsend and Levy 1990; Wiederman and Allgeier 1992; Buss 1989.
16. Buss 1991.
17. Jencks 1979.
18. Herrnstein 1989; Brown 1991; Brown and Chai-yun, n.d.
19. Barkow 1989.

20. Hill, Rubin, and Peplau 1976.
21. Buss 1984, 1985, n.d.
22. Buss and Schmitt 1993.
23. Jackson 1992.
24. Brown and Chai-yun n.d.
25. Ellis 1992, 279–81.
26. Buss et al. 1990.
27. Ford and Beach 1951.
28. Farrell 1986, 50.
29. Jankowiak and Fisher 1992; Sprecher, Aron, Hatfield, Cortese, Potapova, and Levitskaya 1992.
30. Buss 1988.
31. Harrison and Saeed 1977.
32. Wiederman, in press.
33. Buss 1991.
34. Buss 1991.

References

Barkow, J. (1989). *Darwin, sex, and status.* Toronto: University of Toronto Press.

Belsky, J., Steinberg, L., & Draper, P. (1991). Childhood experience, interpersonal development, and reproductive strategy: An evolutionary theory of socialization. *Child Development, 62,* 647–670.

Betzig, L. (1986). *Despotism and differential reproduction: A Darwinian view of history.* Hawthorne, NY: Aldine de Gruyter.

Brown, D. E. (1991). *Human universals.* Philadelphia: Temple University Press.

Brown, D. E., & Chai-yun, Y. (n.d.). *"Big Man:" Its distribution, meaning and origin.* Unpublished manuscript, Department of Anthropology, University of California, Santa Barbara.

Buss, D. M. (1984). Toward a psychology of person-environment (PE) correlation: The role of spouse selection. *Journal of Personality and Social Psychology, 47,* 361–377.

Buss, D. M. (1985). Human mate selection. *American Scientist, 73,* 47–51.

Buss, D. M. (1988). Love acts: The evolutionary biology of love. In R. J. Sternberg & M. L. Barnes (Eds.), *The psychology of love* (pp. 100–118). New Haven, CT: Yale University Press.

Buss, D. M. (1989). Sex differences in human mate preferences: Evolutionary hypotheses tested in 37 cultures. *Behavioral and Brain Sciences, 12,* 1–49.

Buss, D. M. (1991). Conflict in married couples: Personality predictors of anger and upset. *Journal of Personality, 59,* 663–688.

Buss, D. M. (n.d.). *Contemporary worldviews: Spousal assortment or convergence?* Department of Psychology, University of Michigan, Ann Arbor.

Buss, D. M., Abbott, M., Angleitner, A., Asherian, A., Biaggio, A., Blanco-VillaSeñor, A., Bruchon-Schweitzer, M., Ch'u, Hai-yuan, Czapinski, J., DeRaad, B., Ekehammar, B., Fioravanti, M., Georgas, J., Gjerde, P., Guttman, R., Hazan, F., Iwawaki, S., Janakiramaiah, N., Khosroshani, F., Kreitler, S., K. Lachenicht, L.,

Lee, M., Liik, K., Little, B., Lohamy, N., Makim, S., Mika, S., Moadel-Shahid, M., Moane, G., Montero, M., Mundy-Castle, A. C., Little, B., Niit, T., Nsenduluka, E., Peltzer, K., Pienkowski, R., Pirttila-Backman, A., Ponce De Leon, J., Rousseau, J., Runco, M. A., Safir, M. P., Samuels, C., Sanitioso, R., Schweitzer, B., Serpell, R., Smid, N., Spencer, C., Tadinac, M., Todorova, E. N., Troland, K., Van den Brande, L., Van Heck, G., Van Langenhove, L., & Yang, Kuo-Shu. (1990). International preferences in selecting mates: A study of 37 cultures. *Journal of Cross-Cultural Psychology, 21,* 5–47.

Buss, D. M., & Barnes, M. F. (1986). Preferences in human mate selection. *Journal of Personality and Social Psychology, 50,* 559–570.

Buss, D. M., & Schmitt, D. P. (1993). Sexual strategies theory: An evolutionary perspective on human mating. *Psychological Review, 100,* 204–232.

Draper, P., & Harpending, H. (1982). Father absence and reproductive strategy: An evolutionary perspective. *Journal of Anthropological Research, 38,* 255–273.

Ellis, B. J. (1992). The evolution of sexual attraction: Evaluative mechanisms in women. In J. Barkow, L. Cosmides, & J. Tooby (Eds.), *The adapted mind: Evolutionary psychology and the generation of culture* (pp. 267–288). New York: Oxford University Press.

Farrell, W. (1986). *Why men are the way they are.* New York: Berkley Books.

Ford, C. S., & Beach, F. A. (1951). *Patterns of sexual behavior.* New York: Harper & Row.

Gough, H. G. (1980). *Manual for the California Psychological Inventory.* Palo Alto, CA: Consulting Psychologists Press.

Harrison, A. A., & Saeed, L. (1977). Let's make a deal: An analysis of revelations and stipulations in lonely hearts' advertisements. *Journal of Personality and Social Psychology, 35,* 257–264.

Hart, C. W., & Pilling, A. R. (1960). *The Tiwi of North Australia.* New York: Holt, Rinehart & Winston.

Herrnstein, R. (1989, May). IQ and falling birth rates. *Atlantic Monthly,* pp. 73–79.

Hill, C. T., Rubin, Z., & Peplau, L. A. (1976). Breakups before marriage: The end of 103 affairs. *Journal of Social Issues, 32,* 147–168.

Hill, R. (1945). Campus values in mate selection. *Journal of Home Economics, 37,* 554–558.

Hudson, J. W., & Henze, L. F. (1969). Campus values in mate selection: A replication. *Journal of Marriage and the Family, 31,* 772–775.

Hunt, M. (1974). Sexual behavior in the 70's. Chicago: Playboy Press.

Jackson, L. A. (1992). *Physical appearance and gender: Sociobiological and sociocultural perspectives.* Albany: State University of New York Press.

Jankowiak, W. R., & Fisher, E. F. (1992). A cross-cultural perspective on romantic love. *Ethnology, 31,* 149–155.

Jankowiak, W. R., Hill, E. M., & Donovan, J. M. (1992). The effects of sex and sexual orientation on attractiveness judgments: An evolutionary interpretation.

Ethology and Sociobiology, 13, 73–85.

Jencks, C. (1979). *Who gets ahead? The determinants of economic success in America.* New York: Basic Books.

Kenrick, D. T., Sadalla, E. K., Groth, G., & Trost, M. R. (1990). Evolution, traits, and the stages of human courtship: Qualifying the parental investment model. *Journal of Personality, 58,* 97–116.

Langhorne, M. C., & Secord, P. F. (1955). Variations in marital needs with age, sex, marital status, and regional composition. *Journal of Social Psychology, 41,* 19–37.

McCrae, R. R., & Costa, P. T., Jr. (1990). *Personality in adulthood.* New York: Guilford Press.

McGinnis, R. (1958). Campus values in mate selection. *Social Forces, 35,* 368–373.

Sprecher, S., Aron, A., Hatfield, E., Cortese, A., Potapova, E., & Levitskaya, A. (1992). *Love: American style, Russian style, and Japanese style.* Paper presented at the Sixth International Conference on Personal Relationships, Orono, Maine.

Townsend, J. M. (1989). Mate selection criteria: A pilot study. *Ethology and Sociobiology, 10,* 241–253.

Townsend, J. M., & Levy, G. D. (1990). Effects of potential partners' physical attractiveness and socioeconomic status on sexuality and partner selection. *Archives of Sexual Behavior, 371,* 149–164.

Trivers, R. (1972). Parental investment and sexual selection. In B. Campbell (Ed.), *Sexual selection and the descent of man* (pp. 136–179). New York: Aldine de Gruyter.

Wiederman, M. W. (in press). Evolved gender differences in mate preferences: Evidence from personal advertisements. *Ethology and Sociobiology.*

Wiederman, M. W., & Allgeier, E. R. (1992). Gender differences in mate selection criteria: Sociobiological or socioeconomic explanation? *Ethology and Sociobiology, 13,* 115–124.

Williams, G. C. (1975). *Sex and evolution.* Princeton, NJ: Princeton University Press.

Yosef, R. (1991, June). Females seek males with ready cache. *Natural History,* p. 37.

Men Want Something Else

David Buss

David Buss also wrote the preceding selection. Read the headnote on page 465 for more about his work.

Beauty is in the adaptations of the beholder.
—Donald Symons, "What Do Men Want?"

Why men marry poses a puzzle. Since all an ancestral man needed to do to reproduce was to impregnate a woman, casual sex without commitment would have sufficed for him. For evolution to have produced men who desire marriage and who are willing to commit years of investment to a woman, there must have been powerful adaptive advantages, at least under some circumstances, to that state over seeking casual sex partners.

One solution to the puzzle comes from the ground rules set by women. Since it is clear that many ancestral women required reliable signs of male commitment before consenting to sex, men who failed to commit would have suffered selectively on the mating market. Men who failed to fulfill women's standards typically would have failed to attract the most desirable women and perhaps even failed to attract any women at all. Women's requirements for consenting to sex made it costly for most men to pursue a short-term mating strategy exclusively. In the economics of reproductive effort, the costs of not pursuing a permanent mate may have been prohibitively high for most men.

A further cost of failing to seek marriage was impairment of the survival and reproductive success of the man's children. In human ancestral environments, it is likely that infants and young children were more likely to die without prolonged investment from two parents or related kin.[1] Even today, among the Ache Indians of Paraguay, when a man dies in a club fight, the other villagers often make a mutual decision to kill his children, even when the children have a living mother. In one case reported by the anthropologist Kim Hill, a boy of thirteen was killed after his father had died in a club fight. Overall, Ache children whose fathers die suffer a death rate more than 10 percent higher than children whose fathers remain alive. Such are the hostile forces of nature among the Ache.

Over human evolutionary history, even children who did survive without the father's investment would have suffered from the absence of his teaching and political alliances, since both of these assets help to solve mating problems later in life. Fathers in many cultures past and present have a strong hand in arranging beneficial marriages for their sons and daughters. The absence of these benefits hurts children without fathers. These evolutionary pressures, operating over thousands of generations, gave an advantage to men who married.

Another benefit of marriage is an increase in the quality of the mate a man is able to attract. The economics of the mating marketplace typically produce an asymmetry between the sexes in their ability to obtain a desirable mate in a committed as opposed to a temporary relationship.[2] Most men can obtain a much more desirable mate if they are willing to commit to a long-term relationship. The reason is that women typically desire a lasting commitment, and highly desirable women are in the best position to get what they want. In contrast, most women can obtain a much more desirable temporary mate by offering sex without requiring commitment, since high-status men are willing to relax their standards and have sex with

5

a variety of women if the relationship is only short-term and carries no commitment. Men of high status typically insist on more stringent standards for a spouse than most women are able to meet.

The puzzle remains as to precisely what characteristics were desired by ancestral men when they sought a long-term mate. To be reproductively successful, ancestral men had to marry women with the capacity to bear children. A woman with the capacity to bear many children was more valuable in reproductive currencies than a woman who was capable of bearing few or none. Men needed some basis, however, on which to judge a woman's reproductive capacity.

The solution to this problem is more difficult than it first might appear. Ancestral men had few obvious aids for figuring out which women possessed the highest reproductive value. The number of children a woman is likely to bear in her lifetime is not stamped on her forehead. It is not imbued in her social reputation. Her family is clueless. Even women themselves lack direct knowledge of their reproductive value.

A preference nevertheless evolved for this quality that cannot be discerned directly. Ancestral men evolved mechanisms to sense cues to a woman's underlying reproductive value. These cues involve observable features of females. Two obvious cues are youth and health.[3] Old or unhealthy women clearly could not reproduce as much as young, healthy women. Ancestral men solved the problem of finding reproductively valuable women in part by preferring those who are young and healthy.

YOUTH

Youth is a critical cue, since women's reproductive value declines steadily with increasing age after twenty. By the age of forty, a woman's reproductive capacity is low, and by fifty it is close to zero. Thus, women's capacity for reproduction is compressed into a fraction of their lives.

Men's preferences capitalize on this cue. Within the United States men uniformly express a desire for mates who are younger than they are. Among college students surveyed from 1939 through 1988 on campuses coast to coast, the preferred age difference hovers around 2.5 years.[4] Men who are 21 years old prefer, on average, women who are 18.5 years old.

Men's preoccupation with a woman's youth is not limited to Western cultures. When the anthropologist Napoleon Chagnon was asked which females are most sexually attractive to Yanomamö Indian men of the Amazon, he replied without hesitation, "Females who are *moko dude*."[5] The word *moko*, when used with respect to fruit, means that the fruit is harvestable, and when used with respect to a woman, it means that the woman is fertile. Thus, *moko dude*, when referring to fruit, means that the fruit is perfectly ripe and, when referring to a woman, means that she is postpubescent but has not yet borne her first child, or about fifteen to eighteen years of age. Comparative information on other tribal peoples suggests that the Yanomamö men are not atypical in their preference.

Nigerian, Indonesian, Iranian, and Indian men are similarly inclined. Without exception, in every one of the thirty-seven societies examined in the international study on choosing a mate, men prefer wives who are younger than themselves. Nigerian men who are 23.5 years old, for example, express a preference for wives who are six and a half years younger, or just over 17 years old. Yugoslavian men who are 21.5 years old express a desire for wives who are approximately 19 years old. Chinese, Canadian, and Colombian men share with their Nigerian and Yugoslavian brethren a powerful desire for younger women. On average, men from the thirty-seven cultures express a desire for wives approximately 2.5 years younger than themselves. [. . .]

A comparison of the statistics derived from personal advertisements in newspapers reveals that a man's age has a strong effect on his preferences. As men get older, they prefer as mates women who are increasingly younger than they are. Men in their thirties prefer women who are roughly five years younger, whereas men in their fifties prefer women ten to twenty years younger.[6] [. . .]

STANDARDS OF PHYSICAL BEAUTY

A preference for youth, however, is merely the most obvious of men's preferences linked to a woman's reproductive capacity. Evolutionary logic leads to an even more powerful set of expectations for universal standards of beauty. Just as our standards for attractive landscapes embody cues such as water, game, and refuge, mimicking our ancestors' savanna habitat, so our standards for female beauty embody cues to women's reproductive capacity.[7] Beauty may be in the eyes of the beholder, but those eyes and the minds behind the eyes have been shaped by millions of years of human evolution.

Our ancestors had access to two types of observable evidence of a woman's health and youth: features of physical appearance, such as full lips, clear skin, smooth skin, clear eyes, lustrous hair, and good muscle tone, and features of behavior, such as a bouncy, youthful gait, an animated facial expression, and a high energy level. These physical cues to youth and health, and hence to reproductive capacity, constitute the ingredients of male standards of female beauty.

Because physical and behavioral cues provide the most powerful observable evidence of a woman's reproductive value, ancestral men evolved a preference for women who displayed these cues. Men who failed to prefer qualities that signal high reproductive value—men who preferred to marry gray-haired women lacking in smooth skin and firm muscle tone—would have left fewer offspring, and their line would have died out.

Clelland Ford and Frank Beach discovered several universal cues that correspond precisely with this evolutionary theory of beauty.[8] Signs of youth, such as clear skin and smooth skin, and signs of health, such as the absence of sores and lesions, are universally regarded as attractive. Any cues to ill health or older age are seen as less attractive. Poor complexion is always considered sexually repulsive. Pimples, ringworm, facial disfigurement, and filthiness are universally repugnant. Cleanliness and freedom from disease are universally attractive. [. . .]

Cues to youth are also paramount in the aesthetics of women's attractiveness. When men and women rate a series of photographs of women differing in age, judgments of facial attractiveness decline with the increasing age of the woman.[9] The decline in ratings of beauty occurs regardless of the age or sex of the judge. The value that men attach to women's faces, however, declines more rapidly than do women's ratings of other women's faces as the age of the woman depicted in the photograph increases, highlighting the importance to men of age as a cue to reproductive capacity.

Most traditional psychological theories of attraction have assumed that standards of attractiveness are learned gradually through cultural transmission, and therefore do not emerge clearly until a child is at least three or four years old. The psychologist Judith Langlois and her colleagues have overturned this conventional wisdom by studying infants' social responses to faces.[10] Adults evaluated color slides of white and black female faces for their attractiveness. Then infants of two to three months of age and six to eight months of age were shown pairs of these faces that differed in their degree of attractiveness. Both younger and older infants looked longer at the more attractive faces, suggesting that standards of beauty apparently emerge quite early in life. In a second study, Langlois and her colleagues found that twelve-month-old infants showed more observable pleasure, more play involvement, less distress, and less withdrawal when interacting with strangers who wore attractive masks than when interacting with strangers who wore unattractive masks.[11] In a third study, they found that twelve-month-old infants played significantly longer with attractive dolls than with unattractive dolls. No training seems necessary for these standards to emerge. This evidence challenges the common view that the idea of attractiveness is learned through gradual exposure to current cultural standards.

The constituents of beauty are neither arbitrary nor culture bound. When the psychologist Michael Cunningham asked people of different races to judge the facial attractiveness of photographs of women of various races, he found great consensus about who is and is not good looking.[12] Asian and American men, for example, agree with each other on which Asian and American women are most and least attractive. Consensus has also been found among the Chinese, Indian, and English; between South Africans and Americans; and between black and white Americans.[13] [. . .]

20

BODY SHAPE

Facial beauty is only part of the picture. Features of the rest of the body provide an abundance of cues to a woman's reproductive capacity. Standards for female bodily attractiveness vary from culture to culture, along such dimensions as a plump versus slim body build or light versus dark skin. Emphasis on particular physical features, such as eyes, ears, or genitals, also varies by culture. Some cultures, such as the Nama, a branch of Hottentots residing in Southwest Africa, consider an elongated labia majora to be sexually attractive, and they work at pulling and manipulating the vulvar lips to enhance attractiveness. Men in many cultures prefer large, firm breasts, but in a few, such as the Azande of Eastern Sudan and the Ganda of Uganda, men view long, pendulous breasts as the more attractive.[14]

The most culturally variable standard of beauty seems to be in the preference for a slim versus plump body build. This variation is linked with the social status that body build conveys. In cultures where food is scarce, such as among the Bushmen of Australia, plumpness signals wealth, health, and adequate nutrition during development.[15] In cultures where food is relatively abundant, such as the United States and many western European countries, the relationship between plumpness and status is reversed, and the rich distinguish themselves through thinness.[16] Men apparently do not have an evolved preference for a particular amount of body fat per se. Rather, they have an evolved preference for whatever features are linked with status, which vary in predictable ways from culture to culture. Clearly such a preference does not require conscious calculation or awareness.

Studies by the psychologist Paul Rozin and his colleagues reveal a disturbing aspect of women's and men's perceptions of the desirability of plump versus thin body types.[17] American men and women viewed nine female figures that varied from very thin to very plump. The women were asked to indicate their ideal for themselves, as well as their perception of what men's ideal female figure was. In both cases, women selected a figure slimmer than average. When men were asked to select which female figure they preferred, however, they selected the figure of average body size. American women erroneously believe that men desire thinner women than is the case. These findings refute the belief that men desire women who are emaciated.

While men's preferences for a particular body size vary, the psychologist Devendra Singh has discovered one preference for body shape that is invariant—the preference for a particular ratio of waist size to hip size.[18] Before puberty, boys and girls show a similar fat distribution. At puberty, however, a dramatic change occurs. Boys lose fat from their buttocks and thighs, while the release of estrogen in pubertal girls causes them to deposit fat in their lower trunk, primarily on their hips and upper thighs. Indeed, the volume of body fat in this region is 40 percent greater for women than for men.

The waist-to-hip ratio is thus similar for the sexes before puberty. After 25 puberty, however, women's hip fat deposits cause their waist-to-hip ratio to become significantly lower than men's. Healthy, reproductively capable women have a waist-to-hip ratio between 0.67 and 0.80, while healthy men have a ratio in the range of 0.85 to 0.95. Abundant evidence now shows that the waist-to-hip ratio is an accurate indicator of women's reproductive status. Women with a lower ratio show earlier pubertal endocrine activity. Married women with a higher ratio have more difficulty becoming pregnant, and those who do become pregnant do so at a later age than women with a lower ratio. The waist-to-hip ratio is also an accurate indication of long-term health status. Diseases such as diabetes, hypertension, heart problems, previous stroke, and gallbladder disorders have been shown to be linked with the distribution of fat, as reflected by the ratio, rather than with the total proportion of body fat. The link between the waist-to-hip ratio and both health and reproductive status makes it a reliable cue for ancestral men's preferences in a mate.

Singh discovered that waist-to-hip ratio is a powerful cue to women's attractiveness. In a dozen studies conducted by Singh, men rated the attractiveness of female figures, which varied in both their waist-to-hip ratio and their total amount of fat. Men find the average figure to be more attractive than a thin or fat figure. Regardless of the total amount of fat, however, men find women with a low waist-to-hip ratio to be the most attractive. Women with a ratio 0.70 are seen as more attractive than women with a ratio of 0.80, who in turn are seen as more attractive than women with a ratio of 0.90. Studies with line drawings and with computer-generated photographic images produced the same results. Finally, Singh's analysis of *Playboy* centerfolds and winners of beauty contests within the United States over the past thirty years confirmed the invariance of this cue. Although both centerfolds and beauty contest winners got thinner over that period, their waist-to-hip ratio remained exactly the same at 0.70.

There is one more possible reason for the importance of waist-to-hip ratio in men's evolved preferences. Pregnancy alters this ratio dramatically. A higher ratio mimics pregnancy and therefore may render women less attractive as mates or sexual partners. A lower ratio, in turn, signals health, reproductive capacity, and lack of current pregnancy. Men's standards of female attractiveness have evolved over thousands of generations to pick up this reliable cue.

IMPORTANCE OF PHYSICAL APPEARANCE

Because of the many cues conveyed by a woman's physical appearance, and because male standards of beauty have evolved to correspond to these cues, men place a premium on physical appearance and attractiveness in their mate preferences. Within the United States mate preferences for physical attractiveness, physical appearance, good looks, or beauty have been lavishly documented. When five thousand college students were asked in the 1950s to identify the characteristics they wanted in a future husband or wife, what men listed far more often than women was physical attractiveness.[19] The sheer number of terms that men listed betrays their values. They wanted a wife who was pretty, attractive, beautiful, gorgeous, comely, lovely, ravishing, and glamorous. American college women, at that time at least, rarely listed physical appearance as paramount in their ideal husband.

A cross-generational mating study, spanning a fifty-year period within the United States from 1939 to 1989, gauged the value men and women place on different characteristics in a mate. The same eighteen characteristics were measured at roughly one-decade intervals to determine how mating preferences have changed over time within the United States. In all cases, men rate physical attractiveness and good looks as more important and desirable in a potential mate than do women.[20] Men tend to see attractiveness as important, whereas women tend to see it as desirable but not very important. The sex difference in the importance of attractiveness remains constant from one generation to the next. Its size does not vary throughout the entire fifty years. Men's greater preference for physically attractive mates is among the most consistently documented psychological sex differences.[21]

This does not mean that the importance people place on attractiveness   30
is forever fixed by our genes. On the contrary, the importance of attractiveness has increased dramatically within the United States in this century alone.[22] For nearly every decade since 1930, physical appearance has gone up in importance for men and women about equally, corresponding with the rise in television, fashion magazines, advertising, and other media depictions of attractive models. [. . .]

MEDIA EFFECTS ON STANDARDS

Advertisers exploit the universal appeal of beautiful, youthful women. Madison Avenue is sometimes charged with inflicting pain on people by advancing a single, arbitrary standard of beauty that everyone must live up to.[23] Advertisements are thought to convey unnatural images of beauty and to tell people to strive to embody those images. This interpretation is at least partially false. The standards of beauty are not arbitrary but rather embody reliable cues to reproductive value. Advertisers have no special interest in inculcating a particular set of beauty standards and merely want to use whatever sells most easily. Advertisers perch a clear-skinned, regular-featured young woman on the hood of the latest model car because the image exploits men's evolved psychological mechanisms and therefore sells cars, not because they want to promulgate a single standard of beauty.

The media images we are bombarded with daily, however, have a potentially pernicious consequence. In one study, after groups of men looked at photographs of either highly attractive women or women of average attractiveness, they were asked to evaluate their commitment to their current romantic partner.[24] Disturbingly, the men who had viewed pictures of attractive women thereafter judged their actual partner to be less attractive than did the men who had viewed analogous pictures of women who were average in attractiveness. Perhaps more important, the men who had viewed attractive women thereafter rated themselves as less committed, less satisfied, less serious, and less close to their actual partners. Parallel results were obtained in another study in which men viewed physically attractive nude centerfolds — they rated themselves as less attracted to their partners.[25] [. . .]

As a consequence of viewing such images, men become dissatisfied and less committed to their mates. The potential damage inflicted by these images affects women as well, because they create a spiraling and unhealthy competition with other women. Women find themselves competing with each other to embody the images they see daily — images desired by men. The unprecedented rates of anorexia nervosa and radical cosmetic surgery may stem in part from these media images; some women go to extreme lengths to fulfill men's desires. But the images do not cause this unfortunate result by creating standards of beauty that were previously absent. Rather, they work by exploiting men's existing evolved standards of beauty and women's competitive mating mechanisms on an unprecedented and unhealthy scale.

Facial and bodily beauty, as important as they are in men's mating preferences, solve for men only one set of adaptive problems, that of identifying and becoming aroused by women who show signs of high reproductive capacity. Selecting a reproductively valuable woman, however, provides no guarantee that her value will be monopolized exclusively by one man. The next critical adaptive problem is to ensure paternity.

CHASTITY AND FIDELITY

Mammalian females typically enter estrus only at intervals. Vivid visual cues and strong scents often accompany estrus and powerfully attract males. Sexual intercourse occurs primarily in this narrow envelope of time. Women, however, do not have any sort of genital display when they ovulate. Nor is there evidence that women secrete detectable olfactory cues. Indeed, women are rare among primates in possessing the unusual adaptation of concealed or cryptic ovulation.[26] Cryptic female ovulation obscures a woman's reproductive status.

Concealed ovulation dramatically changed the ground rules of human mating. Women became attractive to men not just during ovulation but throughout their ovulatory cycles. Cryptic ovulation created a special adaptive problem for men by decreasing the certainty of their paternity. Consider a primate male who monopolizes a female for the brief period that she is in estrus. In contrast to human males, he can be fairly confident of his paternity. The period during which he must guard her and have sex with her is sharply constrained. Before and after her estrus, he can go about his other business without running the risk of cuckoldry.

Ancestral men did not have this luxury. Our human ancestors never knew when a woman was ovulating. Because mating is not the sole activity that humans require to survive and reproduce, women could not be guarded around the clock. And the more time a man spent in guarding, the less time he had available for grappling with other critical adaptive problems. Ancestral men, therefore, were faced with a unique paternity problem not faced by other primate males—how to be certain of their paternity when ovulation was concealed. [. . .]

Our forebears solved this uniquely male adaptive problem by seeking qualities in a potential mate that might increase the odds of securing their paternity. At least two preferences in a mate could solve the problem for males: the desire for premarital chastity and the quest for postmarital sexual loyalty. Before the use of modern contraceptives, chastity provided a cue to the future certainty of paternity. On the assumption that a woman's proclivities toward chaste behavior would be stable over time, her premarital chastity signaled her likely future fidelity. A man who did not obtain a chaste mate risked becoming involved with a woman who would cuckold him.

In modern times, men value virgin brides more than women value virgin grooms. Within the United States, a cross-generational mating study found that men value chastity in a potential mate more than women do. But the value they place on it has declined over the past half century, coinciding with the increasing availability of birth control and probably as a consequence of this cultural change.[27] In the 1930s, men viewed chastity as close to indispensable, but in the past two decades men have rated it as desirable but not crucial. Among the eighteen characteristics rated, chastity declined from the tenth most valued in 1939 to the seventeenth most valued in the late 1980s. Furthermore, not all American men value chastity equally. Regions differ. College students in Texas, for example, desire a chaste mate more than college students in California, rating it a 1.13 as opposed to 0.73 on a 3.00 scale. Despite the decline in the value of chastity in the twentieth century and despite regional variations, the sex difference remains—men more than women emphasize chastity in a potential committed mateship. [. . .]

Variation in the value people place on chastity may be traceable in part to variability in the economic independence of women and in women's control of their own sexuality. In some cultures, such as Sweden, premarital

40

sex is not discouraged and practically no one is a virgin at marriage. One reason may be that women in Sweden are far less economically reliant on men than women in most other cultures. The legal scholar Richard Posner notes that marriage provides few benefits for Swedish women relative to women in most other cultures.[28] The Swedish social welfare system includes day care for children, long paid maternity leaves, and many other material benefits. The Swedish taxpayers effectively provide what husbands formerly provided, freeing women from their economic dependence on men. Women's economic independence from men lowers the cost to them of a free and active sex life before marriage, or as an alternative to marriage. Thus, practically no Swedish women are virgins at marriage, and hence the value men place on chastity has commensurately declined to a worldwide low of 0.25.[29]

Differences in the economic independence of women, in the benefits provided by husbands, and in the intensity of competition for husbands all drive the critical cultural variation.[30] Where women benefit from marriage and where competition for husbands is fierce, women compete to signal chastity, causing the average amount of premarital sex to go down. Where women control their economic fate, do not require so much of men's investment, and hence need to compete less, women are freer to disregard men's preferences, which causes the average amount of premarital sex to go up. Men everywhere might value chastity if they could get it, but in some cultures they simply cannot demand it of their brides. [. . .]

The sexual revolution of the 1960s and 1970s, with its promises of sexual freedom and lack of possessiveness, apparently has had a limited impact on men's preferences for sexual fidelity. Cues to fidelity still signal that the woman is willing to channel all of her reproductive value exclusively to her husband. A woman's future sexual conduct looms large in men's marriage decisions.

EVOLUTIONARY BASES OF MEN'S DESIRES

[. . .] Men worldwide want physically attractive, young, and sexually loyal wives who will remain faithful to them until death. These preferences cannot be attributed to Western culture, to capitalism, to white Anglo-Saxon bigotry, to the media, or to incessant brainwashing by advertisers. They are universal across cultures and are absent in none. They are deeply ingrained, evolved psychological mechanisms that drive our mating decisions, just as our evolved taste preferences drive our decisions on food consumption.

Homosexual mate preferences, ironically, provide a testament to the depth of these evolved psychological mechanisms. The fact that physical appearance figures centrally in homosexual men's mate preferences, and that youth is a key ingredient in their standards of beauty, suggests that not even variations in sexual orientation alter these fundamental mechanisms.

These circumstances upset some people, because they seem unfair. We   45
can modify our physical attractiveness only in limited ways, and some people are born better looking than others. Beauty is not distributed democratically. A woman cannot alter her age, and a woman's reproductive value declines more sharply with age than a man's; evolution deals women a cruel hand, at least in this regard. Women fight the decline through cosmetics, through plastic surgery, through aerobics classes—an eight billion dollar cosmetics industry has emerged in America to exploit these trends.

After a lecture of mine on the subject of sex differences in mate preferences, one woman suggested that I should suppress my findings because of the distress they would cause women. Women already have it hard enough in this male-dominated world, she felt, without having scientists tell them that their mating problems may be based in men's evolved psychology. Yet suppression of this truth is unlikely to help, just as concealing the fact that people have evolved preferences for succulent, ripe fruit is unlikely to change their preferences. Railing against men for the importance they place on beauty, youth, and fidelity is like railing against meat eaters because they prefer animal protein. Telling men not to become aroused by signs of youth and health is like telling them not to experience sugar as sweet.

Many people hold an idealistic view that standards of beauty are arbitrary, that beauty is only skin deep, that cultures differ dramatically in the importance they place on appearance, and that Western standards stem from brainwashing by the media, parents, culture, or other agents of socialization. But standards of attractiveness are not arbitrary—they reflect cues to youth and health, and hence to reproductive value. Beauty is not merely skin deep. It reflects internal reproductive capabilities. Although fertility technology may grant women greater latitude for reproducing across a wider age span, men's preferences for women who show apparent signs of reproductive capacity continue to operate today, in spite of the fact that they were designed in an ancestral world that may no longer exist. [. . .]

Notes

1. Hill and Hurtado, in press.
2. Symons 1979, 271.
3. Symons 1979; Williams 1975.
4. Hill 1945; McGinnis 1958; Hudson and Henze 1969; Buss 1989.
5. Symons 1989, 34–35.
6. Kenrick and Keefe 1992.
7. Orions and Heerwagen 1992; Symons 1979.
8. Ford and Beach 1951.
9. Jackson 1992.

10. Berscheid and Walster 1974; Langlois, Roggman, Casey, Ritter, Rieser-Danner, and Jenkins 1987.

11. Langlois, Roggman, and Reiser-Danner 1990; Cross and Cross 1971.

12. Cunningham, Roberts, Richards, and Wu 1989.

13. Thakerar and Iwawaki 1979; Morse, Reis, Gruzen, and Wolff 1974; Cross and Cross 1971; Jackson 1992.

14. Ford and Beach 1951.

15. Rosenblatt 1974.

16. Symons 1979.

17. Rozin and Fallon 1988.

18. Singh, 1993, in press a, b.

19. Langhorne and Secord 1955.

20. Hill 1945; McGinnis 1958; Hudson and Henze 1969; Buss 1985, 1989; Buss and Barnes 1986.

21. Buss 1987a.

22. Buss, in preparation.

23. Wolf 1991.

24. Kenrick, Neuberg, Zierk, and Krones, in press.

25. Kenrick, Gutierres, and Goldberg 1989.

26. Alexander and Noonan 1979; Daniels 1983; Strassman 1981.

27. Hill 1945; McGinnis 1958; Hudson and Henze 1969; Buss, in preparation.

28. Posner 1992.

29. Buss 1989.

30. Tooby and Cosmides 1989, 39.

References

Alexander, R. D., & Noonan, K. M. (1979). Concealment of ovulation, parental care, and human social evolution. In N. A. Chagnon & W. Irons (Eds.), *Evolutionary biology and human social behavior: An anthropological perspective* (pp. 402–435). North Scituate, MA: Duxbury Press.

Berscheid, E., & Walster, E. (1974). Physical attractiveness. In L. Berkowitz (Ed.), *Advances in experimental social psychology* (pp. 157–215). New York: Academic Press.

Buss, D. M. (1985). Human mate selection. *American Scientist, 73,* 47–51.

Buss, D. M. (1987). Sex differences in human mate selection criteria: An evolutionary perspective. In C. Crawford, D. Krebs, & M. Smith (Eds.), *Sociobiology and psychology: Ideas, issues, and applications* (pp. 335–352). Hillsdale, NJ: Erlbaum.

Buss, D. M. (1989). Sex differences in human mate preferences: Evolutionary hypotheses tested in 37 cultures. *Behavioral and Brain Sciences, 12,* 1–49.

Buss, D. M. (in preparation). *Cross-generational preferences in mate selection.* Department of Psychology, University of Michigan, Ann Arbor.

Buss, D. M., & Barnes, M. F. (1986). Preferences in human mate selection. *Journal of Personality and Social Psychology, 50,* 559–570.

Cross, J. F., & Cross, J. (1971). Age, sex, race, and the perception of facial beauty. *Developmental Psychology, 5,* 433–439.

Cunningham, M. R., Roberts, T., Richards, T., & Wu, C. (1989). *The facial-metric prediction of physical attractiveness across races, ethnic groups, and cultures.* Unpublished manuscript, Department of Psychology, University of Louisville, Kentucky.

Daniels, D. (1983). The evolution of concealed ovulation and self-deception. *Ethology and Sociobiology, 4,* 69–87.

Ford, C. S., & Beach, F. A. (1951). *Patterns of sexual behavior.* New York: Harper & Row.

Hill, K., & Hurtado, A. M. (in press). *Demographic/life history of Ache foragers.* Hawthorne, NY: Aldine de Gruyter.

Hill, R. (1945). Campus values in mate selection. *Journal of Home Economics, 37,* 554–558.

Hudson, J. W., & Henze, L. F. (1969). Campus values in mate selection: A replication. *Journal of Marriage and the Family, 31,* 772–775.

Hunt, M. (1974). *Sexual behavior in the 70's.* Chicago: Playboy Press.

Jackson, L. A. (1992). *Physical appearance and gender: Sociobiological and socio-cultural perspectives.* Albany: State University of New York Press.

Kenrick, D. T., Gutierres, S. E., & Goldberg, L. (1989). Influence of erotica on ratings of strangers and mates. *Journal of Experimental Social Psychology, 25,* 159–167.

Kenrick, D. T., & Keefe, R. C. (1992). Age preferences in mates reflect sex differences in reproductive strategies. *Behavioral and Brain Sciences, 15,* 75–133.

Kenrick, D. T., Neuberg, S. L., Zierk, K. L., & Krones, J. M. (in press). Contrast effects as a function of sex, dominance, and physical attractiveness. *Personality and Social Psychology Bulletin.*

Langhorne, M. C., & Secord, P. F. (1955). Variations in marital needs with age, sex, marital status, and regional composition. *Journal of Social Psychology, 41,* 19–37.

Langlois, J. H., Roggman, L. A., Casey, R. J., Ritter, J. M., Rieser-Danner, L. A., & Jenkins, V. Y. (1987). Infant preferences for attractive faces: Rudiments of a stereotype. *Developmental Psychology, 23,* 363–369.

Langlois, J. H., Roggman, L. A., & Reiser-Danner, L. A. (1990). Infants' differential social responses to attractive and unattractive faces. *Developmental Psychology, 26,* 153–159.

McGinnis, R. (1958). Campus values in mate selection. *Social Forces, 35,* 368–373.

Morse, S. J., Reis, H. T., Gruzen, J., & Wolff, E. (1974). The "eye of the beholder": Determinants of physical attractiveness judgments in the U.S. and South Africa. *Journal of Personality, 42,* 528–542.

Orions, G. H., & Heerwagen, J. H. (1992). Evolved responses to landscapes. In J. Barkow, L. Cosmides, & J. Tooby (Eds.), *The adapted mind: Evolutionary psychology and the generation of culture* (pp. 555–579). New York: Oxford University Press.

Posner, R. A. (1992). *Sex and reason.* Cambridge, MA: Harvard University Press.

Rosenblatt, P. C. (1974). Cross-cultural perspective on attractiveness. In T. L. Huston (Ed.), *Foundations of interpersonal attraction* (pp. 79–95). New York: Academic Press.

Rozin, P., & Fallon, A. (1988). Body image, attitudes to weight, and misperceptions of figure preferences of the opposite sex: A comparison of men and women in two generations. *Journal of Abnormal Psychology, 97,* 342–345.

Singh, D. (1993). Adaptive significance of waist-to-hip ratio and female physical attractiveness. *Journal of Personality and Social Psychology, 65,* 293–307.

Singh, D. (in press a). Body shape and female attractiveness: Critical role of waist-to-hip ratio. *Human Nature.*

Singh, D. (in press b). Is thin really beautiful and good? Relationship between waist-to-hip ratio and female attractiveness. *Personality and Individual Differences.*

Strassman, B. I. (1981). Sexual selection, parental care, and concealed ovulation in humans. *Ethology and Sociobiology, 2,* 31–40.

Symons, D. (1979). *The evolution of human sexuality.* New York: Oxford University Press.

Symons, D. (1989). The psychology of human mate preferences. *Behavioral and Brain Sciences, 12,* 34–35.

Thakerar, J. N., & Iwawaki, S. (1979). Cross-cultural comparisons of interpersonal attraction of females toward males. *Journal of Social Psychology, 108,* 121–122.

Tooby, J., & Cosmides, L. (1989). The innate versus the manifest. How universal does universal have to be? *Behavioral and Brain Sciences, 12,* 36–37.

Williams, G. C. (1975). *Sex and evolution.* Princeton, NJ: Princeton University Press.

Wolf, N. (1991). *The beauty myth.* New York: William Morrow.

The Gray Matter of Love: An Interview with Geoffrey Miller

Natalie Angier

Geoffrey Miller is an evolutionary biologist at University College, London. This interview appeared in The New York Times *on May 30, 2000.*

Look around a human-wrought landscape like Manhattan, and the term *Homo manipulens* might spring to mind. People are irrepressible toolmakers, slapping down grid systems and trumping up towers, and braking for nothing but the occasional Starbucks. Surely the human mind evolved to wrest from the environment every possible survival advantage, including a cell phone that works in the subway.

But think again about Manhattan, and the things that make it livable: the museums, ballet corps, jazz clubs, comedy acts, drag shows. What good are they, really? More precisely, how can humanity's boundless thirst for the arts be explained in Darwinian terms as the product of natural selection — the evolutionary process most commonly soundbitten as "survival of the fittest"?

Dr. Geoffrey F. Miller, an evolutionary psychologist at University College, London, says it cannot. As Dr. Miller sees it, the most outstanding features of the human mind — its creativity, its consciousness, its moral sense, its artfulness and its love of a good punch line — were shaped not by natural selection but by the other strong evolutionary force called sexual selection.

In this view, which he lays out in his new book, *The Mating Mind* (Doubleday), humans are imaginative, artistic, humorous and relatively amiable for the same reason that peacocks fan their fancy tails and cicadas thrum through the summer: to attract mates and increase their so-called reproductive success.

Born in 1965 in Ohio and educated at Columbia, Dr. Miller has lived in England for seven years, long enough to say things like "cheerio" and to assume the lanky, languid air of British film charmers like Ralph Fiennes or Ben Chaplin. He talked about his book and the underappreciated power of sexual choice, in a recent stop in New York.

Q: Give me a quick-and-dirty explanation of the difference between natural selection and sexual selection.

A: Natural selection is about living long enough to reproduce. Sexual selection is about convincing others to mate with you. It's about animal minds, our ancestors' minds, influencing other minds, which is why it appealed to me as a way of understanding the evolution of the human mind.

Q: So what's wrong with the idea of the mind as problem solver, or of humans as the best of all handymen?

A: When you think of what makes humans unique, you think of art, music, our sense of humor, our creativity. For 140 years, biologists have attempted to explain these traits by means of natural selection, and survival of the fittest, and they have completely failed to make the connection between Darwinism and the humanities. And as I read the standard evolutionary psychology stuff on mate choice, I thought there were several pieces of the puzzle that were missing here. I thought it was quite possible that art and music and creativity have quite a lot to do with somebody's psychological attraction.

Q: One of your premises is the idea that technological innovation was at a standstill during most of our brain evolution, suggesting that the brain was evolving for reasons other than to make better tools. Why do you think that was so?

A: Two million years ago, our ancestors were making and using hand-axes and other stone tools. Their brains tripled in size over the following 1.75 million years. By the time brain size increase stopped, the hand ax and similar tools were still in use around the world. Only in the last 100,000 years have we had all the increase in technological complexity. So you've got brain size increase first, and that stops, and then the tool use increases, very, very recently in evolutionary terms. You couldn't ask for a worse correlation in terms of evolutionary trends. The traditional story that brains are technophilic, tool-producing machines just doesn't match the archaeological evidence.

Q: Let's talk about why early humans focused on the brain and mental traits when selecting their mates.

A: We must bear in mind that brains were already important to great apes generally by the time we started to diverge from chimps five million years ago. There's a consensus now that selection for social intelligence is extremely important in the emergence of great apes compared to other primates, like monkeys. If social intelligence in a general sense was crucial to survival and reproduction among these relatively big-brained primates like proto-chimps, then sexual choice has a powerful incentive to look for evidence of social intelligence when choosing a mate. Second, the bigger and more complex the brain gets, the larger the proportion of genes in the genome are involved in brain development. If you're choosing a mate for his or her genetic quality, what you want to focus on are the traits that give you the best window on the quality of the individual's genome.

Q: But we went further than chimpanzees did in attending to mental traits. Why is that?

A: I'm afraid I'll have to invoke Stephen Jay Gould here, and say there is a strong component of contingency in sexual selection, much more so than in natural selection. I think that most theoretical biologists recognize that sexual selection is evolution's wild card.

Q: Talk about the handicap principle here, which is so important to sexual selection theory, and to your book.

A: I didn't really understand the handicap principle until I read Thorstein Veblen talking about conspicuous consumption in his classic, *Theory of the Leisure Class.* I think there are close analogies between luxury goods that we acquire and sexual ornaments. What makes a good a luxury good is simply the cost. The more something costs, and the more reliably it can say "I'm expensive," then the better an indicator it makes of wealth. Amotz Zahavi reinvented Veblen's principle and applied it to sexual selection. The peacock's tail is not just an arbitrary outcome of sexual selection. It's there because it's costly, which means only those fit, healthy, strong peacocks can afford to carry around those tails.

Q: It's easy to see the handicap principle as applying to the peacock's tail, but to human intelligence?

A: It's important to distinguish between the mental traits that I think really are handicaps from those that aren't. Our brighter ancestors would have survived better and attracted more mates. So the handicap principle doesn't apply to intelligence per se. But I think it does apply to behaviors like art, music and humor, or poetic uses of language, or the production of fictional stories. In those instances, nobody has been able to find any possible survival function. And yet, for the people that do these things, the traits consume enormous amounts of time and energy, not only to produce them, but to learn the skills necessary to produce them.

Q: So creativity becomes a "fitness indicator," a way to strut one's quality, precisely because it is so wasteful and expensive?

A: Once mate choice identifies a trait as informative about something, that trait is going to be under strong selection to amplify its appearance. Those who invest the most energy, the most maintenance time, the most genes, into growing the trait, will attract the most mates. One of the book's main ideas is that the human traits of art, music and creativity are in there by design, as fitness indicators.

Q: You also propose that a father's devotion to his children, and his willingness to care for them, may be an unconscious courtship display, an extension of an ancestral man's willingness to show a woman that he is a kind and gentle guy who will treat her kids well, even if they were fathered by the fellow who came before him. What's the evidence?

A: One valid bit of evidence is simply the behavior of modern fathers across cultures. A typical problem with divorce is that divorced men seriously reduce their investment in their children. If paternal instincts had evolved simply for the good of their children, fathers shouldn't care whether they're sleeping with the mother. These are their kids, they should be supporting them, investing in them, acting like they recognize that the kids are vehicles carrying their genes. But the sad truth is that it's very hard to get a lot of men to pay child support. But I feel a bit humble about making predictions about what's testable in my book and what's not, given the rate of advance in genetics. A good theory should go in advance of the evidence. It shouldn't be circumscribed by the evidence. It should stick its neck out and say, this is how I think the world is, and leave it to other people to test it.

Q: One of the refreshing things about your book is that you discuss mutual mate selection for mental traits, and the idea that the female mind isn't just a consolation prize—that intelligence, wittiness, creativity may have been sexually selected in women just as it was in men.

A: Absolutely. Darwin got almost everything right, except that he did view the human female brain as riding along on the evolutionary coat-tails of the male brain. I think that's wrong. And a lot of my colleagues still have this fixed idea that sexual selection always implies sex differences. They know in their hearts that we're a species with mutual choice, but they tend to ignore it.

Q: What about your own mate choice?

A: She's a television producer, and, as a psychologist, I introspected quite a bit as we were falling in love. I think I was drawn to her because she was very witty and funny and a woman I thought I could learn a lot from. You look for somebody who you feel you could talk to for years without getting bored, and when you find that person it's a very exciting event.

Who Wants to Marry a Soul Mate?
Barbara Dafoe Whitehead and David Popenoe

The Rutgers National Marriage Project, (http://marriage.rutgers.edu/about.htm) headed by Rutgers sociology professors David Popenoe and Barbara Dafoe Whitehead, aims to study the institution of marriage in America and, from a conservative perspective, educate the public about their concerns over the apparent decline of marriage as the foundation for family life. Each year the Project focuses on a different question. In 2001, the Project sociologists surveyed young people on their preferences for choosing a mate. The most recent report, 2004, is titled "The Marrying Kind: Which Men Marry and Why" (http://marriage.rutgers.edu/Publications/SOOU/SOOU2004.pdf).

KEY FINDINGS

Young adults today are searching for a deep emotional and spiritual connection with one person for life. At the same time, the bases for marriage as a religious, economic or parental partnership are receding in importance for many men and women in their twenties. Taken together, the survey findings present a portrait of marriage as emotionally deep and socially shallow.

- An overwhelming majority (94%) of never-married singles agree that "when you marry you want your spouse to be your soul mate, first and foremost."
- Less than half (42%) of single young adults believe that it is important to find a spouse who shares their own religion.
- A large majority of young adults (82%) agree it is unwise for a woman to rely on marriage for financial security.
- A clear majority of young men (62%) agree that while it may not be ideal, it's okay for an adult woman to have a child on her own if she has not found the right man to marry.

- Over 80% of women agree it is more important to them to have a husband who can communicate about his deepest feelings than to have a husband who makes a good living.
- A high percentage of young adults (86%) agree that marriage is hard work and a full-time job.
- Close to nine out of ten (88%) agree that the divorce rate is too high and that the nation would be better off if we could have fewer divorces, with 47% agreeing that the laws should be changed so that divorces are more difficult to get.
- Except for restricting divorce, the majority of young people see little role for government in marriage. Eight out of ten agree that marriage is nobody's business but the two people involved. A substantial proportion (45%) agree that the government should not be involved in licensing marriage.

ABOUT THE SURVEY

This survey represents the second phase of an ongoing investigation into the attitudes and behaviors of young adults toward dating, cohabitation, marriage and parenthood.

For this year's report, we commissioned a national survey to further explore and expand on the earlier qualitative study. The survey, conducted by the Gallup Organization from January to March 2001, is based on a statistically representative national sample of 1,003 young adults, ages 20–29. The sample population includes both married and single men and women and covers a broad range of topics, including dating, living together, marriage, divorce and parenthood.

A majority (61%) of the young adults in this sample were single and never married. Thirty-four percent were married and about 5% were divorced, separated, or widowed. The sample included slightly more women than men (51% v 49%), which is also true of the American population as a whole. Of those who were single, 38% lived with their parents, 22% lived alone, 14% lived with a roommate, 14% cohabited with a boyfriend or girlfriend, and 8% were living with relatives.

Forty-four percent of those surveyed had lived at some time with an opposite sex partner outside of marriage and of those who had done so (slightly more women than men), 46% of the men and 37% of the women had had more than one such living-together relationship.

Young adults in this sample reported a variety of household living arrangements at age 15. Sixty-two percent said they had lived with their married biological parents, 20% with their mother, 4% with their father, 7% with one parent and a stepparent, and 3% with grandparents or other relatives. [. . .]

5

WHO WANTS TO MARRY A SOUL MATE?

Practically all young adults, according to a national survey of men and women conducted for the National Marriage Project by the Gallup Organization—the first large-scale study to look at attitudes about dating and marriage among married and single people, ages 20–29.

Young adults today are searching for a deep emotional and spiritual connection with one person for life. The overwhelming majority (94%) of never-married singles agree that "when you marry you want your spouse to be your soul mate, first and foremost." There is no significant gender gap in this response; similarly high proportions of men and women agree that they want to marry a soul mate. In another measure of the strength of the soul-mate ideal, over 80% of all women, married and single, agree it is more important to them to have a husband who can communicate about his deepest feelings than to have a husband who makes a good living.

Among single men and women, a large majority (88%) also agree that "there is a special person, a soul mate, waiting for you somewhere out there." And never-married singles are highly confident that they will be successful in locating that soul mate; a substantial majority (87%) agree that they will find that special someone when they are ready to get married.

Along with their ambitions for a spouse who meets their needs for emotional closeness and intimacy, these twentysomething singles also aspire to a marriage that lasts a lifetime. Seventy-eight percent agree that a couple should not get married unless they are prepared to stay together for life. In addition, they are reasonably confident that their own future marriages will be long lasting. Only 6% say it is unlikely that they will stay married to the same person for life.

10

Although young adults are confident that they will be successful in achieving a soul-mate marriage for themselves, they are less confident about the state of marriage in general. A substantial majority (68%) agree that it is more difficult to have a good marriage today than in their parents' generation, and slightly more than half (52%) agree that one sees so few good or happy marriages that one questions it as a way of life. Women, and those with a high-school education or less, are more likely than others to agree that there are very few people who have really good or happy marriages.

As one might expect, the generation that grew up in the midst of the divorce revolution also worries about the risks of divorce. Slightly more than half of all single adults (52%)—and an even higher percentage of those in their late twenties (60%)—agree that one of their biggest concerns about getting married is the possibility it will end in divorce.

The high aspirations for a soul mate may be one reason why so many young adults are cohabiting before they take the plunge into marriage.

Among the young adults surveyed, 44% had at some time lived with an opposite sex partner outside of marriage. As we reported in *The State of Our Unions, 2000*, single men and women in their twenties see cohabitation as a way to investigate a prospective partner's character, habits and capacity for fidelity before marriage. Many believe that living together yields more useful information about a partner than simply dating for a period of time. According to this reasoning, if one wants to marry a soul mate, then one has to live with a prospective spouse "24/7" in order to evaluate his or her emotional fitness for this special kind of relationship.

In addition, the widespread fear of divorce among young singles today contributes to the propensity to live together before marriage. Although there is no evidence to support the view that living together improves the chances of staying married, a majority (62%) agree that living together before marriage is a good way to avoid divorce. More than four in ten (43%) agree they would only marry someone who agreed to live together first.

Although most young adults believe that there is a "special someone waiting for them," they also indicate that some relationships are limited to "sex without strings." A large majority—78% overall and 84% of those with a college degree—agree that "it is common these days for people my age to have sex just for fun, and not expect any commitment beyond the sexual encounter itself." For example, more than half of the young singles (54%) agree there are people with whom they would have sex even though they have no interest in marrying them, though men (65%) are more likely to agree than women (41%). Half of young men (50%) agree with the statement that "if two people really like each other, it's all right for them to have sex even if they've known each other for only a very short time," compared to 36% of women. Six out of ten young unmarried women agree that they wish guys would be more interested in them as a person and less as a sex object.

At the same time, young adults seem to distinguish casual sexual relationships from potential soul-mate relationships. About three in four (76%) agree if they meet a person with whom they think they could have a long-term relationship, they will try to postpone sex until they really know each other.

FROM SOCIAL INSTITUTION TO SOUL-MATE RELATIONSHIP

Although young adults express high aspirations for the marital relationship, they see a diminished role for marriage in other domains. Many of the larger social, economic, religious and public purposes once associated with marriage are receding or missing altogether from their portrait of marriage.

Most noteworthy is the weakened link between marriage and child rearing. Only 16% of young adults agree that the main purpose of marriage these days is to have children. The idea that marriage is the principal pathway into parenthood is changing as well. A clear majority of young men (62%) agree that, while it may not be ideal, it's okay for an adult woman to have a child on her own if she has not found the right man to marry. More than four out of ten describe adults who choose to raise a child out of wedlock as "doing their own thing."

The survey also points to some evidence of the declining importance of marriage as an economic institution. Although two-thirds (65%) of singles say that they believe that marriage will improve their economic situation, an even higher percentage say it is extremely important to be economically "set" as individuals before they marry. It is especially noteworthy that young women are as likely as young men to agree that it is important for them to be economically "set" before marriage.

Indeed, this attitude represents a dramatic shift for women. In earlier generations, most women saw marriage as a stepping-stone to achieving economic independence from parents and to gaining economic security. Today, however, women are more likely to look to themselves and to their own educational and career achievements as a source of economic independence and security.

Partly this shift is due to changing patterns of education and work during the young adult years. More women are going on to higher education—now outranking men among college graduates—and also spending more years as working singles before marriage. During this expanded period of early adult singlehood, they acquire credit ratings, debts and assets on their own. For this reason, they tend to think about their economic lives and fortunes in individual terms.

But the shift is also due to fears of the high risk of divorce. Because marriages break up at a high rate, young adults—and especially young women—no longer trust marriage as a reliable economic partnership. A large majority (82%) agree it is unwise for a woman to rely on marriage for financial security. For this reason, young women may prefer to invest in portable assets, like education and career development, rather than to place all their trust and self-investment in marriage. This pattern may also explain why young women say that they are less interested in having a spouse who makes a good living than in having a spouse who is a soul mate.

For young men, the shift away from marriage as an economic partnership is more subtle but nonetheless convergent with women's attitudes. Unlike young women in earlier times, young men have traditionally sought to be economically "set," before marriage. However, they used to pursue this goal as part of their expected role as primary breadwinner in a family household. Now they are likely to pursue the goal of economic independence for the same reasons young women do. They want to stand on their own two feet economically, not because they expect to be financially responsible for a family, but because they expect to be financially responsible for themselves. In other words, both young men and young women are

20

likely to define their economic lives and future in individual terms rather than as part of a marriage partnership.

Along with the diminished importance assigned to marriage as a parental and economic partnership, the role of marriage as a religious institution seems to be fading. Although young adults seek a deep spiritual connection through marriage, they are not necessarily looking to marry someone who shares their own religion. Among singles, less than half (42%) agree that it is important to find a spouse who shares their own religious faith. Indeed, the popular soul-mate ideal may be a substitute for more traditional religious understandings of marriage. In a secular society, where sex has lost its connection to marriage and also its sense of mystery, young people may be attracted to the soul-mate ideal because it endows intimate relationships with a higher spiritual, though not explicitly religious, significance.

Marriage is also losing its standing as a public institution among these 25 young adults. According to the survey, young adults tend to see marriage as a private matter between two consenting adults. Eight out of ten agree that marriage is nobody's business but the two people involved. Further, a substantial proportion (45%) agree that the government should not be involved in licensing marriages. A high percentage also believe that the government should not give special privileges to married couples. Four in ten (43%) agree that government should provide cohabiting couples the same benefits provided to a married couple.

However, when it comes to divorce, young adults tend to see a more pro-marriage role for government. Close to nine out of ten (88%) agree that the divorce rate in this country is too high and the nation would be better off if we could have fewer divorces. A significant proportion (47%) agree that laws need to be changed so that divorces are more difficult to get. Women are more likely than men to hold this opinion.

Taken together, these findings paint a portrait of marriage as emotionally deep but socially shallow. While marriage is losing much of its broad public and institutional character, it is gaining popularity as a SuperRelationship, an intensely private spiritualized union, combining sexual fidelity, romantic love, emotional intimacy and togetherness. Indeed, this intimate couple relationship pretty much defines the sum total of marriage. Other bases for the marital relationship, such as an economic partnership or parental partnership, have receded in importance or disappeared altogether.

SOUL-MATE MARRIAGE IN A HIGH-DIVORCE SOCIETY

There is nothing historically new in the desire for lasting friendship in marriage. Indeed, the notion of combining friendship, romantic love and sexual fidelity in marriage is one of the distinctive features, and perhaps most daring experiments, in the Western marriage tradition. (Most societies, past and present, still prefer marriages arranged by kin or parents, and many adhere to the sexual double standard "she's faithful, he's not.") However, the findings in this survey suggest that today's young adults may be reaching even higher in their expectations for marriage. The centuries-old ideal of friendship in marriage, or what sociologists call companionate marriage, may be evolving into a more exalted and demanding standard of a spiritualized union of souls.

This development is understandable. Amid the dislocations of today's mobile society, dynamic economy, and frantic pace of life, it is difficult to sustain deep and lasting attachments. What's more, the desire for loving and lasting relationships may be especially strong among members of a generation that has come of age during the divorce revolution. It is not surprising, therefore, that young adults look to a soul mate for the steady emotional support and comfort that may be missing in other parts of their life. And, indeed, this is not an unworthy aspiration. For those who achieve it, a soul-mate relationship can be personally rewarding and deeply satisfying.

However, as today's young adults seem to realize, a soul-mate marriage in a high divorce society is difficult to sustain. Perhaps that is why a high percentage (86%) indicate that marriage is hard work and a full-time job. Over eight in ten young adults (86%) agree that one reason for divorce is too much focus on expectations for happiness and not enough hard work needed for a successful marriage. Women and college-educated young adults are more likely than men and those with fewer years of formal education to agree that marriage is hard work.

The notion of "marriage as hard work" is also consistent with the idea of marriage as a private relationship. When marriage is defined as a private couples relationship, one cannot look to larger institutional forces, such as religion, law or social convention, to sustain marriage. Consequently, it is left to individuals to work hard on their own to maintain the quality of the marriage, often in the face of social and cultural trends that are adverse to marriage.

It is quite likely that women will take on primary responsibility for the emotional maintenance of the soul-mate relationship, as they typically have done with marriage in the past. However, given the exacting standards for successful soul-mate relationships, this kind of emotional maintenance will probably require high investments of time, attention and vigilance. This may be one reason why women are more likely than men to say that marriage takes work.

IMPLICATIONS FOR CHILDREN

The emphasis on marriage as an intimate couples relationship rather than as a child-rearing partnership has profound implications for children. For one thing, it means that marriages with children are likely to remain at high risk of breakdown and breakup. The soul-mate ideal intensifies the natural tension between adult desires and children's needs. When children arrive, some couples may find it difficult to make the transition between couple-hood and parenthood and may become disappointed and estranged from one another during the child-rearing years. This is not to say that couples should neglect each other while they are in the intensive child-rearing years, but it is to suggest that the soul-mate ideal of marriage may create unrealistic expectations that, if unfulfilled, may lead to marital discontent and perhaps a search for a new soul mate.

Moreover, the high expectations for marriage as a couples relationship may also cause parents to leave marriages at a lower threshold of unhappiness than in the past. Indeed, in 1994, a nationally representative survey found only 15% of the population agreeing that "when there are children in the family, parents should stay together even if they don't get along." And, according to one recent study, the meaning of "not getting along" is being defined down. It's been estimated that more than half of recent divorces occur, not because of high conflict, but because of "softer" forms of psychological distress and unhappiness. Unfortunately, these are the marriages that might improve over time and with help. As it turns out, people do change their minds about the level of marital contentment. One recent large-scale study indicates that 86% of people who said they were unhappily married in the late 1980s but stayed married, indicated that they were happier when interviewed five years later. Indeed, three-fifths of the formerly unhappily married couples rated their marriages as either "very happy" or "quite happy."

The central importance assigned to the soul-mate relationship also means that unwed parenthood is likely to remain at high levels. As the survey indicates, a high percentage of young adults, who are in the peak years of fertility, tend to separate sex and parenthood, on the one hand, from marriage, on the other. Put another way, people are pickier about the person they choose for a soul-mate relationship than they are about the people they choose as sexual partners, or as biological parents of their children. This is consistent with findings in other recent surveys. For example, a 1994 survey of University of California undergraduates found both men and women agreeing that a man is financially responsible for his child but not responsible to marry his pregnant girlfriend.

However, these speculations could be wrong. Perhaps today's young adults will be able to reconcile their aspirations for emotional closeness with the realities of parenthood and domestic life. Clearly, they are more strongly committed to avoiding parental divorce than the Baby Boom generation. Indeed, while only 15% of adults in the general population agree that parents should stay together for the sake of the children, 40% of young adults in the National Marriage Project survey agree. Moreover, our survey indicates that young adults are not cavalier about marriage or marital permanence. They are committed to lifelong marriage and to the idea that it takes constant effort to sustain a happy marriage. These attitudes may offer some glimmer of hope for their future marriages and for the future of marriage itself.

The Perfect Union
John Armstrong

This selection comes from a short book titled Conditions of Love: The Philosophy of Intimacy *(2002), by John Armstrong, who is a research fellow in the philosophy of art at the University of Melbourne.*

In the beginning—according to the most famous myth of the origin of love—each human being was a "rounded whole" with two faces, two backs, four arms and four legs. These double creatures were of three types depending on the genders of their component halves: male, female and hermaphrodite. "Their strength and vigour made them very formidable, and their pride was overweening; they attacked the gods." To weaken them and put an end to their insolence—but not quite destroy them—Zeus cut them in two. "If this doesn't keep them quiet I'll bisect them again; they can hop on one leg." Love is the yearning of each part to find its original partner and return to the original, complete state. The perfect lovers are those who were originally joined together. If they find each other they wish never to be separated and try to merge completely, to become once more the single being they originally were.

This myth, put into the mouth of Aristophanes, is recounted in Plato's *Symposium*—perhaps the most successful philosophical drama we have (the competition has not been too intense). The play presents speeches at a drinking party supposedly given by a young poet to celebrate his triumph at the Athenian festival. Although the speeches are almost exclusively concerned with homosexual relationships they have been widely influential in the Western vision of love in general.

One major theme of this myth is that there is a "right" person for each of us. If we can only find this person our problems will be over. This is to construe the difficulty of love by analogy with a treasure hunt. Correspondingly, what goes wrong in love always derives from attaching ourselves to the wrong person—or the wrong person getting attached to us. Of course, there is much to be said in favour of this view. Many couples have to separate because they do not see eye to eye on practical matters. One wants to live in a large city, the other longs for the countryside; one likes only antique furniture, the other only modern. In reacting to this, one might seek out a partner whose tastes and aspirations perfectly coincide with one's own. This approach is sensibly respectful of fragility. It recognizes that goodwill can founder on deep-set incompatibility. According to this view, the blindness of romantic love consists precisely in the assumption that love will triumph over practicality—that the excitement you feel in the presence of this special person will overcome the fact that you want to live in different countries. Or eat in different kinds of restaurant.

In *Husbands and Wives*, Woody Allen sympathetically caricatures the kind of longing which may be traced to this good sense. "Spencer was searching for a woman interested in golf, inorganic chemistry, outdoor sex and the music of Bach. In short he was looking for himself, only female." The painful side of the joke is that this attempt to overcome a problem of love leads to an avoidance of love; the other person is no longer someone else. This shouldn't be seen as a way of trying to legitimize a kind of narcissistic dream of self-love. The point, surely, is that the other person, in this scenario, is one's own creation—a person whose characteristics are governed by one's own demands.

This scheme of calculated love comes up against certain difficulties. 5 Firstly, the demand for compatibility is never satisfied. The list we make always leaves room for new demands—and hence new ways in which people can turn out to be incompatible. They may wish to live in the same country, the same city, the same house, but if they want to paint the sitting-room walls differently then they may be heading for divorce. When people agree about almost everything, the few points of difference can still seem— to them—enormous. The attempt to foreclose this possibility by seeking more and more perfect compatibility is self-defeating. In other words, the search for perfect compatibility can be a highly respectable way of not loving. The searcher can say: "I am loving, I am capable of love, only I haven't found the right person yet," but the "right person" is specified so closely that they never will find such a person; they will always be disappointed because whoever they find will fall short in some way, will fail to meet one of their requirements. But, in their own eyes, this is not a shortcoming of their own; it is simply bad luck. And what gives this strategy its power is the fact that it shelters behind a very sensible observation: incompatibility often destroys relationships—therefore perfect compatibility must be the right basis. This may look like good logic but is actually fallacious. It is like convincing yourself that because overeating is bad for you, the perfect meal would be a gulp of air.

Avoidance, in fact, is a key characteristic of the search for the "right person." Attention is diverted away from the seeker. They have no responsibility to be loving; they imagine that when they do find the right person love will be easy, will flower spontaneously and survive of its own accord. [However,] finding a good enough partner is no guarantee at all that love will flourish. We can easily imagine that if Woody Allen's Spencer finds his ideal mate, love will still elude him. The problem is not in finding the person but in finding the resources and capacities in oneself to care for another person—to love them. Searching for the right "object" diverts attention from finding the right attitude.

A second problem with this attempt to find the "right person" is that it does not pay enough attention to the ways in which priorities change through a relationship. A woman who has—as she thinks—no interest in having children may, from within a loving relationship, come to have a different view. And here, the ground of the change is the relationship itself. She may have learned, with her partner, to recognize capacities and concerns she did not know she had. The calculation—the picturing of the perfect partner—presupposes that we can enter a relationship with a clearsighted and complete understanding of our needs and capacities. This is to see a relationship as a kind of garment which merely goes on top of, and does not in any way change, the inner person.

Against this we have to set a comment which is occasionally heard from people who have loved in the long term. In some moods they may be tempted to say that they could have loved someone else. It didn't have to be this person. Perhaps what they have in mind is this: the experience of learning to love someone in the long term involves various adaptations of oneself to the other; it involves dropping certain demands, learning others, changing priorities. But if you are able to do this with one person you would probably have been able to do it with another—at least with some others. Compatibility, on this view, is an achievement of love, not a precondition for love.

So what do we really mean by "compatibility"? It is, after all, one of the leading terms in the modern vocabulary of love. We have to admit two points. On the one hand it is naive to neglect the destructive power of seriously divergent tastes, needs and interests. But on the other hand it is a mistake to infer from this that avoiding such conflict is the same as finding love. On reflection what emerges is this: there is no such thing as perfect compatibility. Therefore all loving relationships must accommodate some degree of incompatibility. [. . .]

Questions for Discussion

1. Women who put wealth high on their list of criteria for a mate have been called "gold diggers" and other unflattering names. Does Buss's essay cause you to see that there is more involved in this preference than mere materialism and status-seeking on the part of these women? Does his evidence convince you that evolution could have programmed women to look for men with resources? What seems strong about his case, and what might make you question it?

2. For men who are not wealthy or tall, other attributes can compensate. What seem to be the best attributes for attracting women? Consider how Miller's argument about the "gray matter of love" connects with the findings reported by Buss. And the study by Popenoe

and Whitehead also suggests that other attributes matter more than money. On what points do these readings concur?

3. The sexual revolution liberalized attitudes about chastity and fidelity and reduced the "double standard" that used to suggest women should be virgins until marriage or at least until they make a commitment. Buss shows that men would still prefer women who are chaste and faithful to them. Summarize Buss's argument (paragraphs 40–41 of "Men Want Something Else") that women's economic independence figures into their freedom to engage in premarital sex.

4. How convincingly does Buss make his case that standards of beauty are not totally determined by culture? To what extent does he show, however, that culture plays a role? What contribution does the media make to men's preferences in mate selection?

5. Buss describes men and women as having different sets of priorities in mate selection. To what extent are these criteria complementary and likely to lead to harmonious long-term relationships? To what extent might they lead to problems in a relationship? For example, the Bureau of Labor Statistics reports that 24% of working wives now earn more than their husbands. Buss's findings indicate that this situation could be a possible source of tension.

6. Buss studied thirty-seven cultures in arriving at his conclusions about the biological basis of mate selection. In an article that appeared in the *New York Times* after he had presented some of these findings, he reports that the findings disturbed people for many reasons. Why might they disturb women who feel that media portraits of young, slender, and curvy women have misled women into thinking they must diet, use cosmetics, and even have cosmetic surgery in order to attract a mate? Before responding to these questions, you should look at a reading in Chapter 12, on feminism: the excerpt from Naomi Wolfe's book *The Beauty Myth*, in which she argues that standards of beauty are culturally imposed (pages 612–621).

7. According to Miller's hypothesis, why is creative talent like the ability to write music or paint pictures an indicator of fitness?

8. The Rutgers study of what young people are looking for in a partner shows some contrast with Buss's "evolutionary" criteria. What are the biggest contrasts, and what remains consistent?

9. Based on Popenoe and Whitehead's study, how would you define the meaning of "soul mate," according to the people who responded to the survey? What is your own definition? For the Rutgers respondents? for you? Do you think that casting the search for a partner in terms of finding one's soul mate is a good idea — or too idealistic? You might want to read the essay by Ethan Watters in the next section (pages 516–518), in which he refers to the search for the soul mate as an "*über*-romantic" idea that keeps people looking for the perfect partner well into their thirties (paragraph 3).

10. Armstrong does not use the term "soul mate." In what ways, however, is his "perfect partner" similar to the idea of the soul mate as described in Whitehead and Popenoe's study? What are his reasons for saying that partners must "accommodate some degree of incompatibility"?

Suggestions for Writing

For Persuasion

Buss points out that money and an impressive physical build are not the only indication that a mate will have the resources to provide for a spouse and children. Thus women have learned to look for other evidence—such as potential to achieve status, willingness to make a commitment, and mental stability. Write to persuade a reader that the less obvious indicators may be the better clues to finding a compatible partner.

For Inquiry

In spite of the old saying that "opposites attract," Buss shows that compatibility is important—the most successful matches are between people who come from similar backgrounds and have similar values and viewpoints. And yet, increasingly, couples marry outside of their religion and ethnic backgrounds. Do research and decide whether these marriages have as good a chance as between people with more in common from their backgrounds.

For Convincing

After reading Armstrong's "The Perfect Union" and Whitehead and Popenoe's "Who Wants to Marry a Soul Mate?" consider the pros and cons of the soul-mate marriage. For example, in paragraph 33, Whitehead and Popenoe point to possible problems when children arrive in a "soul-mate" marriage. Using these two sources and any other field or library research, make a case either for or against the "soul-mate" partnership. Be sure that you clearly define what you mean by "soul mate".

SECTION 3: COURTING, DATING, OR JUST HOOKING UP

Overview

How do lovers find each other in a large and impersonal world? It must have been easier when communities were smaller, and family and friends who knew you well might introduce you to a "likely prospect." Maybe it was more fun before the post–World War II era when dating got serious and emotionally heavy—and couples were expected to "go steady." It might have been less stressful when sex wasn't expected until well into the relationship. At any rate, the articles in this section show that finding partners, especially a partner to marry, involves a lot of stress and expense today.

For one thing, people are postponing making emotional commitments. Our culture's ideal of "romantic love" with a soul mate means holding out until you find that special person. In the meantime, you want to avoid the messy entanglement of "romantic love" with the wrong person. One risks a broken heart or the responsibility for hurting a romantic partner. Many young people are too busy for the emotional costs of romantic involvement.

People may not want a committed relationship until late in their twenties or even their thirties, but let them try to tell that to their sex drives. As the first two selections in this unit show, many young people try to meet their sexual needs in ways where no strings are attached. But this kind of arrangement may itself entail costs, as these readings show. First, it may not be possible to keep love out of a sexual relationship, if not for both partners, then at least for one of them. The culture of casual sex, or hook-ups, may seem liberating to women, but on closer examination, even some of the men say that they are the winners in a system that still employs a double standard to judge the sexually promiscuous. There is also a cost in terms of the quality of the sexual experience itself—if it has no meaning other than physical pleasure.

Once people decide that they do want to settle down, they need to find a partner with whom they want to share the long-awaited emotional commitment. Perhaps avoiding it all along has made them inexperienced, but they seem to need a lot of help. An entire industry has grown up to meet their needs: Internet dating services, speed dating, lunch dating, group dinners, and the latest, simulated dating, offered by a New York City company called First Impressions Consulting. Clients have a practice date with a consultant/psychologist who later clues them in on what they can do to improve their dating behavior. Our final two selections in this section reveal how the dating and matchmaking industry puts pressure on singles, especially women, to see being single as an abnormal state and to turn relationships into commodities to buy, earn, and exploit.

Dinner and a Movie? No Thanks on College Campuses
Bella English

This is a feature article from the Boston Globe, *published on December 11, 2003. The author is a staff writer for the paper.*

Chrissy Herman is a junior at Boston University. She is pretty and smart, and she has a lot going on in her life. But only once in the three years she has been on campus has a guy called her up and asked her out. "It was someone from BC [Boston College], and his sister and my mom set it up," says Herman, who is from Los Angeles.

Her friend Zoe Panama, a sophomore who is also from LA, nods knowingly. She had her first college date last month. He asked her to dinner and a movie. "I said, 'I've never done that before.' The whole time we were together, I kept saying, 'This is so weird.'" Despite that, she had a good time. But she adds: "I don't like that cheesy, cliché thing of 'dating.' I like being more spontaneous, more casual."

It used to be that college students fell in love on campus. Couples dated, lived together, or got engaged. But nowadays the children of those parents have ditched the date. The act of picking up a telephone and asking someone out seems as obsolete as the panty raid. Because of a variety of factors, including changing cultural mores and demographics, the dinner-and-a-movie date is all but dead. Today, as one college senior puts it, campus social life centers around "skimpy outfits and strong drinks."

Two years ago, the Independent Women's Forum, a conservative group, conducted a nationwide survey of 1,000 college women. Only half of the seniors reported being asked out on six or more dates during their entire college career, yet 63 percent said they wanted to meet their future husbands in college. And 91 percent reported "a rampant hookup culture" on campus. "Hooking up," according to college students, can range from kissing to intercourse.

"Hooking up has just become the norm," says Kristen Richardson, campus program manager of the IWF. "For women especially, these uncommitted, purely physical relationships can wreak havoc later on and distort their idea of relationships." In her opinion, the arrangement benefits the guys. "They have it made right now. They don't have to open doors, take a woman to dinner, buy flowers, or even call the next day." Her group has taken out ads in many campus newspapers urging students to "Take Back the Date." With the headline "Free Cupid!" the ad depicts the downcast cherub in chains. "Take someone out to dinner or buy someone flowers," it cajoles.

Ask a couple of Harvard women if they date, and one has an answer reminiscent of Bill Clinton: "It depends on what you mean by dating." Another adds: "Last night, a guy asked me to go to dinner and a movie. I was shocked."

Today, college students hang out in groups, sometimes becoming "friends with benefits." The benefits? Sex without commitment. Students have sex first, and then they may decide to go out. Today, asking someone to have dinner seems to be a bigger deal than asking someone to have sex. "It's kind of like in reverse order," says Becca Mildrew, a Harvard sophomore from California. "It's sad, but hooking up is pretty universal." Mildrew has been at Harvard for a year and a half and had her first real date there last month. "It was refreshing," says Mildrew. "I haven't done that in forever." She adds: "It's hard to have a serious relationship here. That sort of courtship thing doesn't exist anymore."

5

Some students say that both men and women are loath to commit to one another, with guys fearful of being stuck with "a wife" and women fearful of losing their identity and independence. It is this sort of thinking that exasperates those who work with young people. "There's a lot of confusion about how people find each other from a post-feminist kind of place," says Catherine Steiner-Adair, a clinical psychologist and director at the Harvard Eating Disorders Center. "Women want to be self-possessed and independent. . . . That doesn't mean it's a weakness or unhealthy dependence to want a good, romantic relationship."

Steiner-Adair hears constant complaints from women students about the dating scene — or lack thereof. "These kids know about the sexual side of things, but they don't know about the emotional side," she says. "Hooking up is not healthy, whether you're male or female. It requires such emotional distance." Despite the "sexual liberation" of women, the time-honored double standard remains. Even though hooking up is prevalent, young women say they are sometimes called "sluts," while young men are "players." Such so-called liberation, Steiner-Adair says, offers nothing positive to the young woman involved. "Is it progress that both genders can now behave equally awful?" she says.

Dr. Drew Pinsky, host of the national teen call-in show "Loveline," speaks to college students across the country on the subject of dating. He worries aloud to his audience about binge drinking followed by casual sex. Both young men and women tell him they use alcohol for "liquid courage" — and, for the woman, to later excuse her behavior. "I ask the women what they'd want if they could create a fantasy world that suited their needs. They immediately say, 'I wish a guy would just sit down and talk to me.' The guys are like, 'What, talk?' Men at that age are under the influence of an extremely powerful biology. It doesn't mean they're bad guys. They just need to understand what girls need." Hooking up, says Pinsky, is "awful for the girls, though it's politically incorrect to say that."   10

Many students say the group dynamic, with young men and women hanging out as friends and casual partners, is preferable to the "housekeeping" of serious couples. With today's young men and women sharing dorms, apartments, cafeteria tables, eating clubs, and study groups, they have plenty of friendly contact. So, they reason, a formal date isn't as necessary as it was when their parents were in college. Back then, women often waited for the phone to ring. If it didn't, they'd be stuck in the dorm on a Saturday night. That situation has disappeared. What remains is a gap between "hooking up" and "housekeeping."

"There needs to be a process of evaluation," says Pinsky. "Call it dating, call it courtship. [A friend] with benefits is someone you walk over to at the end of the night. It's not a relationship. Both sexes get hurt. Someone develops feelings for the other one, usually the woman." Fear and loafing.

But some college men say it's the women who don't want to date. "To ask a girl out, . . . most would look at you strangely and think you're too formal," says Mike Sands, a Harvard sophomore from Austin, Texas. "Friends with [benefits] wouldn't work for me. I'm looking to connect emotionally. I think people really want that, but because the empty physical relationship is available, it's so much easier to do that."

Sands's friend Andrew Kreicher of New Canaan, Conn., says it's not fair to blame men for the woeful dating scene on campus. The idea of dating, he says, has become so loaded that "it's more challenging and terrifying for a guy than just asking a girl to dance at a party. So one way of avoiding that is hooking up at a party." He does allow: "Guys are also lazy." At Boston College, sophomore Michael Grant of Beverly [Mass.] has had three real dates. He and five of his friends have a "date night" each semester, when they take women out to dinner and then a club. "It's a $120 investment, which is why it only happens once a semester," he says. "Here, you just hang out with peers in groups."

The all-important pull of the group is huge on campus these days. It is the group, rather than the couple, that rules. "There are tons of friends, guys and girls, who live in houses together, so that takes away the need for dating," says Natalie Blazer, a Boston College junior from Fairfax, Va. Sometimes, it can all feel a bit like middle school, says classmate Grace Simmons, "when your friends are trying to set you up." Simmons, a junior from Skaneateles, N.Y., says she knows people who are dating: "But it doesn't last long, because they feel isolated from their friends and the social scene." 15

"It's dangerous to jump to 'girlfriend' or 'boyfriend,'" says Christina Parisi, 20, of Holmdel, N.J. "You don't want to be pegged with that title or the image that you are taken. You want to be free to explore other options as long as you can." At Boston University, sophomore Stacey Meisel of Los Angeles talks about "the group date," in which groups go out and party. She's not a fan of friends-with-benefits relationships, but she concedes that "girls can be just as detached" about it as boys. One of Meisel's friends recently broke up with a boy because she felt she was missing out on a good time.

What women — and men — in college want isn't always clear. "To combine physical and emotional needs is dangerous," says Parisi. "You can get hurt. You have your friends for emotional support." "And then people have friends with benefits for the physical," interjects Blazer. "I know that sounds really crass, but no one wants to put themselves out there emotionally." Blazer says she has found a guy she really likes. "We'll see what happens. But I'm assuming he doesn't want to be tied down."

Unlike their parents, these young women do not expect to meet anyone serious until after college, and they say they won't consider marriage until their 30s. They acknowledge that their male classmates might be intimidated by them. "Women are ambitious, career-driven, and independent," says Simmons, who is chief of academic affairs for the student government at BC. Muses Parisi: "Maybe women don't need men like our mothers' generation did." "I feel guys are really confused," says Lauren Daniel, 20, of Warwick, R.I. "They're caught between two generations."

Obviously there are college students who have more traditional relationships. Thea Daniels, a Harvard junior from Oklahoma City, met her
boyfriend the first day of class. "There is still romance on campus," she
says. But she knows many for whom "hookups are their first introduction
to each other." At Boston College, junior Brian Garrett and senior Matt
Hanlon have settled down with girlfriends. "The thing that happened for
me," says Garrett of Potomac, Md., "was that I was finding random people
and not committing. It was just kind of tiring."

Unlike their fathers, today's college men often find themselves outnum- 20
bered by women. At BC, 52 percent of the student body is female. At BU,
it's 60 percent. Women mention the heated competition with one another
for men's attention. "Girls' standards are definitely lower here, due to the
lack of the male species," says Blair Parsont, a BU sophomore from New
York who says she has gone out on an occasional date. Still, she hopes to
have a serious relationship while in college. So does Meisel, her classmate.
"It would be nice to have a boyfriend," she says, "just so I know what
it's like."

Hook-Up Culture

Jack Grimes

*Jack Grimes was a senior at Tufts when he wrote this opinion column for the school
paper, the Tufts Daily. It appeared March 30, 2004.*

Whatever happened to dating? College students have been asking that question for years. Every once in a while, even a newspaper will pick up the
question and interview a few co-eds. The reporter finds dating's departure
mostly blamed on what is universally called "the hook-up culture." While
there are no (as of yet) proposals for the Senate to take on a Hook-up Culture Rep, I do not think many would deny that the culture is here and thriv-
ing at Tufts. But where did it come from? And is it here to stay?

The hook-up culture is simply an environment that expects casual sexual encounters that do not necessarily lead to anything further. Common
sense would say that people hook-up for basic physical needs. They do not
want to get involved in a relationship, but they do have intense desires for a
sexual partner. In a word, they are horny. So they hook-up—either with a
friend or a stranger. But something makes me think folks hook-up for
something more than just the raging hormones.

What makes me think horniness cannot fully explain the hook-up culture is this question: Would you hook-up with someone who was fast
asleep—totally unresponsive? You could kiss them, touch them, make
them touch you, whatever you would like. But they would remain completely oblivious to you and just lay there dead to the world. Not exactly

appealing, is it? A bit like eating cold oatmeal. All the physical parts are there, all the same sensations, but something is missing—an energy, a spark, a life. There must then be a pleasure that is not strictly physical. What makes a hook-up more desirable than any pornography or anything you could do to yourself is the one pleasure neither of those could ever provide—the consent of a partner.

A lively, animated partner is lively and animated for you and (for the moment at least) you alone. You are special. What your partner does not let the world see, she lets you see. Personal space that is ordinarily walled off from the outside world becomes open to you alone. You are being let in, given privileged access. You become, for a few moments, the center of his attention. The real thrill of a hook-up is not simply what you do with a partner, but the fact that your partner wants to be doing it with you! It is not just "She's so hot," but "She's so hot and she wants me!" Not just "He's so cute," but "He's so cute and he likes me!"

The physical pleasure does not, and cannot, exist by itself. It is inextricably tied up with the emotional. The body and soul are one. To give someone your body is to give them all of yourself. A sexual encounter is in its essence an act of deepest intimacy, and so to be considered worthy of that intimacy is powerfully affirming and very exciting. Everyone wants to be loved that much. Consensual sex is an affirmation so powerful that the porno fiend fabricates it and the rapist steals it. It is a feeling of acceptance so intoxicating that it gets pursued weekend after weekend in frat after frat.

Is it being found there? Well, how could it be? How can you find love and intimacy in a system that presupposes the meaninglessness of sex? If sex is simply handed out to anyone, then sexual intimacy becomes no big deal. Even if it happens to get handed over to you, you are no longer special. You are just a fling. The premise of the hook-up culture is to receive pleasure without commitment. But the pleasure really being sought can only come from commitment, from someone saying "Yes, I want to give my all to you and no one else." But hooking-up is all about holding back, not giving all of one's self, not committing. The more that commitment gets detached from sex, the less sex means anything. The less it means anything, the less enjoyable it becomes, and so the more hook-ups are made to get the old thrill. And on it goes, spiraling down. Trying to find intimate fulfillment by hooking-up is like trying to dig your way out of a hole in the ground.

Some people claim that they are not at all bothered by emotional needs. They get a thrill from the display of independence and sexual virility that serial hook-ups can give. Now this used to be said mostly by men. They do not talk like this much anymore (at least in public), as it seems to hinder their ability to get much play.

Appeals to self-determination and sexual empowerment to support hook-ups are now given by women. And this I find strange. I wonder what is so empowering about being, in essence, an unpaid prostitute. The boys

may politely clap and publicly congratulate the women for liberating their
sexuality and owning their miniskirt and so on, but privately they are having a good laugh and passing the word on who is the easy lay. A woman
who embraces the hook-up culture is simply making it easier for guys to
treat her as a sex object. Is this women's liberation? Both sexes can use a
partner for their own selfish gratification, but more often than not, it is the
woman whose hopes of a relationship get tossed in the trash. The real sexual power a woman has is to refuse to give away sex until the man has
proved his commitment to her.

The hook-up culture is very deceptive. Hooking-up promises to be
liberating and strengthening. Yet people find themselves needing more and
more "liquid courage" to even make the first move. Hooking-up promises
fun and fulfillment and no regrets, but when morning comes it delivers the
"walk of shame." The hook-up culture has tricked us. It has led us to believe
that our emotions are disconnected from our bodies, that love is divorced
from sex.

What can we do about it? Well, a culture only lasts as long as people   10
are willing to live it. If we refuse to believe its false promises, then we can
build a new culture that says sex is just too good to be thrown around.
We can bring back some middle ground between random hook-ups and
being joined-at-the-hip. We can bring dating back to life. Or not. We can
also make the break between love and sex complete and final. We can
become dead to the ache within for intimacy. We can consider ourselves
simply people with assets: he has what she wants, she has what he wants.
Just a mutual exchange. Just business. Cold, soulless, heartless, loveless
business.

In My Tribe
Ethan Watters

Ethan Watters is a writer whose book Urban Tribes *(2003), from which this essay is
excerpted, describes his own life prior to marriage, as part of a circle of good friends
similar to those depicted in television shows like* Seinfeld *and* Friends.

You may be like me: between the ages of 25 and 39, single, a college-
educated city dweller. If so, you may have also had the unpleasant experience
of discovering that you have been identified (by the U.S. Census Bureau,
no less) as one of the fastest-growing groups in America—the "never marrieds." In less than 30 years, the number of never-marrieds has more than
doubled, apparently pushing back the median age of marriage to the oldest
it has been in our country's history—about 25 years for women and 27
for men.

Ethan Watters, center, with his tribe in San Francisco

As if the connotation of "never married" weren't negative enough, the vilification of our group has been swift and shrill. These statistics prove a "titanic loss of family values," according to *The Washington Times*. An article in *Time* magazine asked whether "picky" women were "denying themselves and society the benefits of marriage" and in the process kicking off "an outbreak of 'Sex and the City' promiscuity." In a study on marriage conducted at Rutgers University, researchers say the "social glue" of the family is at stake, adding ominously that "crime rates . . . are highly correlated with a large percentage of unmarried young males."

Although I never planned it, I can tell you how I became a never-married. Thirteen years ago, I moved to San Francisco for what I assumed was a brief transition period between college and marriage. The problem was, I wasn't just looking for an appropriate spouse. To use the language of the Rutgers researchers, I was "soul-mate searching." Like 94 percent of never-marrieds from 20 to 29, I, too, agree with the statement "When you marry, you want your spouse to be your soul mate first and foremost." This *über*-romantic view is something new. In a 1965 survey, fully three out of four college women said they'd marry a man they didn't love if he fit their criteria in every other way. I discovered along with my friends that finding that soul mate wasn't easy. Girlfriends came and went, as did jobs and apartments. The constant in my life—by default, not by plan—became a loose group of friends. After a few years, that group's membership and routines began to solidify. We met weekly for dinner at a neighborhood restaurant. We traveled together, moved one another's furniture, painted one another's apartments, cheered one another on at sporting events and open-mike nights. One day I discovered that the transition period I thought I was living wasn't a transition period at all. Something real and important had grown there. I belonged to an urban tribe.

I use the word "tribe" quite literally here: this is a tight group, with unspoken roles and hierarchies, whose members think of each other as "us" and the rest of the world as "them." This bond is clearest in times of trouble. After earthquakes (or the recent terrorist strikes), my instinct to huddle with and protect my group is no different from what I'd feel for my family.

Once I identified this in my own life, I began to see tribes everywhere   5
I looked: a house of ex-sorority women in Philadelphia, a team of ultimate-frisbee players in Boston and groups of musicians in Austin, Tex. Cities, I've come to believe, aren't emotional wastelands where fragile individuals with arrested development mope around self-indulgently searching for true love. There are rich landscapes filled with urban tribes.

So what does it mean that we've quietly added the tribe years as a developmental stage to adulthood? Because our friends in the tribe hold us responsible for our actions, I doubt it will mean a wild swing toward promiscuity or crime. Tribal behavior does not prove a loss of "family values." It is a fresh expression of them.

It is true, though, that marriage and the tribe are at odds. As many ex-girlfriends will ruefully tell you, loyalty to the tribe can wreak havoc on romantic relationships. Not surprisingly, marriage usually signals the beginning of the end of tribal membership. From inside the group, marriage can seem like a risky gambit. When members of our tribe choose to get married, the rest of us talk about them with grave concern, as if they've joined a religion that requires them to live in a guarded compound.

But we also know that the urban tribe can't exist forever. Those of us who have entered our mid-30's find ourselves feeling vaguely as if we're living in the latter episodes of *Seinfeld* or *Friends*, as if the plot lines of our lives have begun to wear thin.

So, although tribe membership may delay marriage, that is where most of us are still heading. And it turns out there may be some good news when we get there. Divorce rates have leveled off. Tim Heaton, a sociologist at Brigham Young University, says he believes he knows why. In a paper to be published next year, he argues that it is because people are getting married later.

Could it be that we who have been biding our time in happy tribes are   10
now actually grown up enough to understand what we need in a mate? What a fantastic twist—we "never marrieds" may end up revitalizing the very institution we've supposedly been undermining.

And there's another dynamic worth considering. Those of us who find it so hard to leave our tribes will not choose marriage blithely, as if it is the inevitable next step in our lives, the way middle-class high-school kids choose college. When we go to the altar, we will be sacrificing something precious. In that sacrifice, we may begin to learn to treat our marriages with the reverence they need to survive.

Mr. Goodbar Redux: Illusions. Affectation. Lies.[1]

Cristina Nehring

Cristina Nehring is a writer and professor of English literature at the University of California at Los Angeles. She frequently writes book reviews as well. This review of eleven (!) dating manuals appeared in the January 2002 issue of Atlantic Monthly.

Books discussed in this essay:

The Mating Game
by Lyndon McGill
Sundial Press, 207 pages, $12.95

The Rules: Time-Tested Secrets for Capturing the Heart of Mr. Right
by Ellen Fein and Sherrie Schneider
Warner Books, 174 pages, $22.00

How to Make Anyone Fall in Love With You
by Leil Lowndes
McGraw-Hill, 328 pages, $13.95

Date Like a Man
by Myreah Moore and Jodie Gould
HarperCollins, 235 pages, $19.95

Mars and Venus on a Date
by John Gray
HarperCollins, 370 pages, $25.00

How to Meet the Rich: For Business, Friendship, or Romance
by Ginie Sayles
Perennial, 304 pages, $14.00

Dating Secrets of the Ten Commandments
by Shmuley Boteach
Doubleday, 256 pages, $21.00

The Real Rules
by Barbara De Angelis
Bantam Doubleday Dell Publishing, 182 pages, $5.99

What Men Want
by Bradley Gerstman, Christopher Pizzo, and Rich Seldes
Harper Mass Market Paperbacks, 272 pages, $5.99

Do Not Talk to, Touch, Marry, or Otherwise Fiddle With Frogs:
    How to Find Prince Charming by Finding Yourself
by Nailah Shami
Plume, 228 pages, $12.00

How Not to Stay Single
by Nita Tucker
Crown, 157 pages, $12.00

Lyndon McGill wanted to know how people fell in love. So he decided, he confides in *The Mating Game* (1992), "to take a field trip to a farm and observe the animals." He was soon witnessing the copulation of a cow and a bull. "Coupling continued for a few minutes," he reports, "and then, without warning, the cow suddenly pulled away and ran to the opposite side of the corral. . . . I recalled how our family dog had behaved similarly." McGill's conclusion? To keep a man's interest, a woman must rise abruptly after sex and leave the room, the city, or even the country. It rekindles the man's desire. As McGill explains with a flourish, it's "just like taking a bone away from a dog." Such is the state of contemporary dating research in America.

If *The Mating Game* is a particularly unfortunate example of the proliferating genre of dating-advice books, it is not very different in substance from its companions. Its advice to women is that of the *New York Times* best-seller *The Rules: Time-Tested Secrets for Capturing the Heart of Mr. Right* (1995), by Ellen Fein and Sherrie Schneider: Make him miss you! Be mean to him so he'll be nice to you! It is the wisdom of John Gray's stunningly successful *Mars and Venus* series: Man is the pursuer. Make him pursue you. Although perfunctory contempt for such books is taken for granted among America's intelligentsia, guilty fascination with them is equally evident. Dating books are like traffic accidents: everybody says they're awful, and everybody sneaks a look at them.

Little is easier than poking fun at most of these seduction manuals—at their cartoonish view of human nature, their bulleted lists of proven ploys, their quadruple exclamation points, and their sometimes bludgeoningly repetitive self-promotion ("You're not doing The Rules! . . . You have to do The Rules! We suggest you try The Rules for six months before doing anything else. You can't do The Rules and something else . . . Just do The Rules!"). Nothing is easier than laughing at their gimmicks. Dilate your pupils, says *How to Make Anyone Fall in Love With You* (1996), by Leil Lowndes: the "copulatory gaze plays a big role in lovemaking." "Massage your neck with one hand," says *Date Like a Man* (2000), by Myreah Moore and Jodie Gould. "It has the effect of raising the breast . . . which is erotic." Go to the bathroom in a restaurant, says Gray's *Mars and Venus on a Date* (1997): it gives men the chance to see you. "Read the obituaries," says *How to Meet the Rich: For Business, Friendship, or Romance* (1999), by Ginie Sayles.

If the gimmicks range from bizarre to morbid, the contradictions among—and within—these books go from insidious to incapacitating.   5

Never let a man know you're interested, says *The Rules*. Rent a billboard and trumpet your love ("'Bill Thomas, what are you waiting for? Give me a call so I can show you why we are made for each other! Love, Ginnie'"), says *Date Like a Man*. Postpone sex, say *The Rules, Mars and Venus*, and *Dating Secrets of the Ten Commandments* (2000), by Shmuley Boteach. "Men are businessmen," Boteach writes: if they're getting sex without a ring, they won't produce the ring. Unless they happen to be millionaires. "Sex usually begins soon with the rich," declares *How to Meet the Rich*. "Do you really think someone will marry you because he just has to have sex with you?" Ginie Sayles also provides my favorite contradiction of all—coming, as it does, from a book that suggests (among other gambits) that you invent an out-of-town job and fake a move far away to provoke a proposal: Don't play games. "If you play games, you have to be prepared to have someone play them with you."

In fact, no matter how deceitful these books urge you to be, a common denominator among them—and probably a key to American self-image in our moment in history—is that they also urge you to be "true to yourself"; they all tout "self-esteem," not merely as the highest of virtues in general but also as the source and end of their instructions in particular. Thus *The Rules* tells you that to suppress the urge to call your boyfriend constitutes "self-esteem"; its competitor, *The Real Rules* (1997), by Barbara De Angelis, says that "Old Rules" like these "sabotage your self-esteem," and intones that real self-esteem consists precisely in making that call. No matter what game they advocate, they want self-esteem on their team. Self-esteem is to popular psychology what God is to fundamentalism—the banner under which you fight, no matter for what desperate or cruel thing you are fighting.

As a genre these books draw astonishing numbers of readers. Many of these doubtless consider themselves ironic and atypical; but ironic audiences are often the most faithful of all. Nor are they motivated, as one might suppose, mainly by curiosity about all matters erotic. In fact, the assumption in all this literature is that its audience is not pleasure-seeking but desperate; not confident, adventuresome, and looking for tips on how to have a good time, but frightened and looking for hints on how to avoid disaster—how to avoid further time as a single girl. Because, yes, 95 percent of these books are written to women. When men do the writing, they present themselves as avuncular advisers to panicking girls—the few good wolves helping the sheep. Men are bad, they seem to admit: they "use women for sex," declares the smiling threesome Bradley Gerstman, Christopher Pizzo, and Rich Seldes, in *What Men Want* (1998), and "if [they] didn't have to marry, [they] wouldn't." But the larger question that emerges from these books is not so much why men don't want to marry (supposing this were true) as why women want so much to marry. Or why these writers think they should want so much to marry, quickly and at any cost. Face it, say the self-styled "Rules Girls" Ellen Fein and Sherrie Schneider, "most women want to be proposed to yesterday." Most women who begin dating an appealing man "bring up marriage or the future after a couple of weeks." Is this true? If it is, one cannot help thinking that men's much lamented "resistance to commitment" is thoroughly sane. What man could feel, under such circumstances, like anything but a convenient walk-on player in a drama whose substance and staging were established long before his arrival?

One of the most disturbing aspects of these books is, in fact, the extent to which they endeavor to squash women's penchant for pursuit, adventure, and choice. Rather than allow that women need excitement as much as men do (and can enjoy "conquest," and—yes—fear the loss of freedom in marriage), they vigorously pretend that the predator instinct is peculiar to men, and then alternately bewail it (Gerstman et al.) and instruct women to fashion themselves into fit prey for it (Fein and Schneider; Gray). After all, "men . . . thrive on challenge, . . . while women crave security. . . . This has been true since civilization began" (*Rules II*). Not satisfied to trust in "civilization," John Gray goes so far as to say that if a woman happens to bear a closer resemblance to "Mars" than to "Venus" (that is, proves more active than passive, more adventuresome than acquiescent), she must use her "Martian" initiative to cultivate "Venutian" passivity. "Although there is nothing intrinsically wrong with a woman expressing her Martian attributes," Gray offers disingenuously, "it will backfire"—unless she locks those attributes up in the closet when she leaves the office, and dons a Venutian mask at home. "While dating and finding a fulfilling relationship can be more difficult" for women who have learned to make things happen on their own in the workplace, Gray writes, "all successful women have an incredible ability for self-correction. All a woman needs is the complete awareness . . . of the problem, and then she immediately sets out to fix it." In other words, she exploits her "masculine" determination to affect the "feminine" spinelessness that will presumably recommend her to men.

The tragedy here is not only the terrific gender essentialism but also that these books encourage the extinction of a quality that might allow women to feel independent and to take pleasure in their relationships—as opposed to fixing their hearts and egos exclusively on marriage. Women possess no more natural taste for boredom or lost opportunity than men do, and—beyond having to decide whether and when to bear children—they have no greater need for certainty and security. But books like these encourage the worst and weakest in them, playing to every fear. They put overwhelming pressure on women to put overwhelming pressure on men to "commit" at a moment and in a way that nobody really wants. "As a result of [my] experience," Shmuley Boteach tells women in *Dating Secrets of the Ten Commandments,*

> I now know exactly what it means when a man says he is not ready [for marriage]. He is directing it specifically at you and it is an insult. Don't take it from him. Preserve your dignity and break off the relationship. If he wants a plaything, he can buy a life-size blow-up Barbie doll.

Such testimony, coming from the witty and worldly rabbi who brought us
Kosher Sex, is appalling. A confident young woman who may be entirely
content in her relationship with a boyfriend who has not proposed now
has a new way to see things: no proposal is an insult—gee. This we have
from a man whose personal experience in dating seems somewhat modest:
Shmuley (he likes to be addressed familiarly) was engaged at twenty. Such
blithe assumption of superior wisdom is, alas, in no way limited to rabbis.
When Shmuley and the Rules Girls met at a forum in New York in 2000,
the main thing they discovered was how often they agreed. Fein and
Schneider share his pity (and contempt) for women with no rings to show
for their love lives. Indeed, in their books they essentially dismiss every
woman who challenges their tenets by demanding, "If you're so smart, why
aren't you married?" If she is married, the question becomes "How long did
it take you to get married?" If the answer is much over a year, they strike
back with disdain: "Most girls," Fein said to an audience member who admitted to a few years, "don't want to wait that long!"

One of the ironies here is that Fein and Schneider have some extremely   10
gloomy things to say about the marital state. On one hand, they constantly
repeat that "A Rules marriage is forever," and that once you're wed, you can
relax their strictures without fear that the man who fell in love because you
made yourself scarce will get bored when you become available around the
clock—or that the guy who responded so positively to your provocative si-
lences might recoil when you blather on about your daily life (unconvincing reassurances both). On the other hand, they make no bones about the
fact that a Rules marriage frequently involves accepting your husband's lack
of interest. In fact, it "means acting single. . . all over again." It means doing
without the attention and tenderness your courtship led you to expect. But
what the hell, say the Rules Girls, don't despair: "after all"—and here comes
the clincher—" he married you, didn't he?"

It's easy to scoff at the now divorcing Ellen Fein, but it is more important to note that most of her ring-mongering colleagues never harbored
blissful visions of marriage in the first place. John Gray informs us, chas-
teningly, that "Stage Five" of his multiple-stage dating program is vital, because it provides good memories that allow a couple to survive "the stress
of marriage." The memory of this stage, he says, permits a wife to "reach
back and reconnect with the [presumably forgotten] part of her that trusts,
accepts, and appreciates her partner. . . . By remembering the . . . loving
feelings she experienced" in the past, she will be better able to sustain the
unloving present. Is it worth mentioning that John Gray has been through
a divorce?

Illusions. Affectation. Lies by omission. Lies by invention. This is the
legacy of the majority of modern dating books—and it is a violence to human relationships. With the exception of Shmuley's *Dating Secrets* and De
Angelis's *The Real Rules,* which advocate a circumscribed honesty, all the
books I examined supply advice that explodes whatever trust your partner

might feel in you and whatever comfort you might feel with him. Sometimes the suggested deceit is quite flamboyant: an invented expatriation, a fake rival. More often it is a subtle matter of mis- or under-representing yourself in such a way that you end up feeling that if your mate really knew you, he would sicken or tire of you. *The Rules* recommends, for example, that you set a timer so that you can "sweetly" end a phone call with your boyfriend in less than ten minutes and "leave him wanting more"—hardly a morally reprehensible deed, but corrosive in that it forces you to falsify your feelings, to feign a breeziness and busyness that aren't yours. ("Do not affect a breezy manner," wrote Strunk and White, style moguls for generations of college composition students. Better advice this, I say, than *The Rules.*) When you start pretending, however incidentally, to be something you're not (bright and bushy-tailed when you're pensive, cool when you're warm), you build walls between yourself and your partner. You feel at once inferior and superior—inferior because your natural instincts are presumably not good enough to please him, superior because you are pulling the wool over his eyes, and we always feel superior to those we fool. This is not a sound basis for intimacy; it's rather like communicating from different floors of a high-rise.

Worse, you grow dull. That may be the greatest problem with disingenuousness—not that it is unethical but that it is boring. It precludes thinking aloud and thereby precludes conversational discovery. It keeps us from talking about what we know best—our real experience, our present concerns—and instructs us to talk instead about the experience and concerns that we imagine nice people like us should have. If "men were entirely honest," someone once said, "every man's autobiography would be fascinating." Since we're not, even the ten-minute phone chat the Rules Girls recommend is likely to be dreary.

In our compartmentalization-happy culture, we have separated everything: social from professional relationships, therapeutic from social conversations, lovers from friends, friends from therapists. One of the noisome results of such compartmentalization is that relationship "experts" warn us incessantly, "If you have to talk, see a therapist." Maybe call your mom. Don't call your boyfriend. An evening with someone you love is no time for a confidence. You must never "use" your desired mate as a "therapist." We think this with the same misguidedness that prompted Victorian men not to "use" their wives as sexual companions; just as they thought their sexuality sullied their honorable spouses, we think our psychology burdens our healthy partners.

More banal, our dating becomes incredibly arduous. All this putting your best foot forward and never revealing a true or a troubled thought makes dating as one long triple back flip. Dating books admit this—"The Rules are difficult!" one says. Dating is hell, another confesses. The authorities would have one believe that going to a bistro is like heading to boot camp: "Make sure you get a good night's sleep," *Date Like a Man* advises. "Call your home number and fill up your voice mail with compliments,"

15

suggests Nailah Shami, the author of *Do Not Talk to, Touch, Marry, or Other-wise Fiddle With Frogs: How to Find Prince Charming by Finding Yourself* (2001).

"I often take a long bath beforehand and enjoy a glass of wine or a cup of mint tea to calm my nerves," Myreah Moore reveals. "While in the bath, take some deep clarifying breaths and start imagining yourself having a good time. . . . Repeat 'I'm going to have fun.'" "The only people who think dating is fun," Nita Tucker counters in *How Not to Stay Single* (1996), "are married people who haven't done it in years." She herself found it abominable—but worthwhile, since it secured her a husband.

A strange flip-flop has taken place in Western clichés about relation-ships: once upon a time marriage was seen as the arduous obligation and dating (pre- or extra-marital) was seen as the easy, free, and romantic pleas-ure. Look at Casanova, George Sand, La Rochefoucauld—or at Ovid. Not one of the relationships celebrated in his *Art of Love* is between spouses: marriage, to him and to writers for centuries afterward, involved duty and discipline; dating was where the fun and the liberty lay. If Ovid's contempo-raries dismissed marriage, at least they had marvelous visions of affairs. In our day we are moving toward a point where we have positive views of nei-ther—where everything in our love life is grim, everything is work. Dating is hell, we think; but its reward is marriage. Marriage is "stress," but its con-solation is the memory of dating. What with our fear of singlehood, our Puritan work ethic, our endurance of game playing, and our knowledge of the high divorce rate, we have arranged it so that eros in all its manifesta-tions provokes fear and trembling.

Is it any surprise, then, that so many of today's ambitious university students have no time for relationships until these explicitly serve their career-and-life-advancement programs? Is it any surprise that by the time they do cast a tentative look around for potential partners, they no longer know how to start a relationship, sometimes already feel biologically "behind schedule," and—with gender wars seething on college campuses— may have assimilated a severe mistrust of the opposite sex? Such mistrust is abundantly evident, time and again, in the very books presumably designed to reduce it in the name of relationship building. Take Nailah Shami's *Frogs*. Here is a book that proposes to help women find a loving mate but that actually speaks such bitterness against men, and proves so eager to displace them with "teddy bears, a vibrator . . . and girl power records," that it accomplishes precisely the opposite.

Off-putting though it is, this book highlights a problem well: On one hand, women feel that they can and should be responsible for their own "power," both professional and personal; for their own self-esteem; and even for their own sexual satisfaction. On the other, they can't help feeling, somewhere down the line, that vibrators and even good careers and friends are not enough. Is it any surprise, then, that they ultimately funnel the same drive, determination, organizational prowess, and even, to some ex-tent, the same willingness to play by "the rules" into relationships which they previously funneled into educational and professional achievement?

"My success came," writes the high-end career woman Nita Tucker, "when I . . . began thinking of [falling in love] as a project . . . I applied the same skills that had made me successful in other areas of life to finding a relationship." Is it any surprise that, conflicted as they are about men, and disenfranchised as they are in many cases by their lack of romantic experience, young women revert nervously to the "hard-to-get" (but easy-to-follow) ploys of their great-grandmothers?

As women reassess their roles in society; as both sexes work together   20
more and more and trust each other less and less; as everyone brings careerish determination to sentimental accident, there is a space — nay, a cry — for intelligent reappraisals of romantic love. What we have instead is fearful repetition of romantic cliché — tired and retired romantic cliché. The great minds of our moment steer clear of the great questions. Once upon a time it was Ovid and Montaigne, Stendhal and Balzac, Hazlitt and Emerson, who tried their hands at treatises about how to love. Now it's aging, self-congratulatory frat boys like Gerstman, Pizzo, and Seldes; failed farmhands like Lyndon McGill; and peevish spice girls like Nailah Shami who hold the floor and set the tone of the discussion. The dearth of commanding commentary gives audience to idiots.

Turn from them back to the ancients. Love, Ovid wrote, "is no assignment for cowards." Safe sex, fine; but safe love is impossible. Love that manifests itself in considerate questions designed to rule out mates with family problems (as we find in *The Real Rules*) — no. Love as "project," as a kind of postdoc undertaken after our real goals have been attained — no. Let us allow boldness to prevail where rules make cowards of us all. Let us allow magic to reign where we find it, lest we color the world gray.

Note

1. The title of this review/essay is an allusion to a mid-1970s books by Judith Rossner titled *Looking for Mr. Goodbar*. It is about a woman's double life, schoolteacher by day and sexual adventurer by night, cruising the singles bars. The book was made into a movie starring Diane Keaton and Richard Gere.

Just Saying No to the Dating Industry
Kate Zernike

Kate Zernike is a reporter for The New York Times. *This article originally appeared in November 2003.*

By her own admission, Sara Cambridge was "totally cruising." She spent hours trolling online dating sites, sending e-mail messages to potential mates and creating "a real connection," which would invariably sour into deep disappointment within the first five minutes of an actual date. At which point she would return to the sites, send more e-mail, make another connection and suffer another snap disappointment. Finally, there was the left-leaning writer, who took her to a Japanese tea garden and, like so many of the others, seemed so perfect from his résumé. "In the e-mails, he would say, 'Tell me a story,' which I thought was kind of charming," said Ms. Cambridge, 38, a graphic designer in San Francisco. "When we got together it was, 'Tell me stories, tell me stories, tell me stories.' I felt like I was auditioning for a play."

That was it. "I realized I could be starting my own business in the time I was spending looking at these ads and crafting these responses," she said. So instead of going back online, she began taking a Small Business Administration class and designing funky planters.

Ms. Cambridge's tale is one small act of resistance against what might be called the Dating-Industrial Complex, a mighty fortress increasingly hard to ignore. To Match.com and Nerve.com, add DreamMates, The Right Stuff, eHarmony and eCrush (neither to be confused with Etrade, though the general concept is the same). TurboDate, HurryDate, 8minuteDating—or It's Just Lunch.

Reality television shows—*The Bachelorette, Average Joe*—have fed the impression that finding the right mate is as simple as being presented with a room of 10 people and picking one. Bookstores bulge: *Surrendered Single, Find a Husband After 35 Using What I Learned at Harvard Business School, Make Every Girl Want You.* That is just a sampling from the last year; the next two months will bring one manual promising to lure the love of your life in seven weeks, another in a sleeker six.

"There's a fetishization of coupling," said Bella DePaulo, a visiting professor of psychology at the University of California at Santa Barbara, who studies perceptions of singles. "It's made the pressure that's always been there more intense."

5

Yet like Ms. Cambridge, longtime combatants in the dating wars, psychologists and those who study the lives of singles talk about increasing dating fatigue. They say more and more people are taking dating sabbaticals or declaring they will let romance happen by chance, not commerce. Once-obsessive online daters are logging off, clients of speed dating services—which offer dozens of encounters in a roomful of strangers—are slowing down. A book due out in January, "Quirkyalone," offers "a manifesto for uncompromising romantics"—those not opposed to romance but against the compulsory dating encouraged by the barrage of books, Web sites and matchmaking services.

Pottery Barn and Williams-Sonoma report that singles are signing up for housewarming and birthday registries, deciding they do not have to wait for a wedding to request the pastamaker and flatware. Smaller stores report single women registering for china patterns and crystal, without ring, proposal or mate.

On the extreme end of political activism, the American Association for Single People, a kind of AARP for the unmarried, convinced governors in five states to declare Unmarried and Single Americans Week in September. And a small voice in the Web wilderness reassures: Itsokaytobesingle.com.

"I have no doubt that there is a great, committed relationship out there for me," Ms. Cambridge said. "I don't identify at all with people who think, 'I'll never find another person.' I just think the best thing to do is pursue my goals, and whatever unfolds will be a new story."

Barbara Dafoe Whitehead, co-director of the National Marriage Project, who relied on a national survey as well as in-depth interviews and dating histories of 60 women for her 2002 book, *Why There Are No Good Men Left: The Romantic Plight of the New Single Woman,* said this hard-won wisdom is increasingly common. "People are making some kind of private agreement with themselves that they're not going to do this in a panicky, driven way that implicitly buys into the notion that if it doesn't happen to you, you'll be miserable," she said.   10

As Sari Siegal, who surrendered her love life to fate after a dating binge last spring, said, "This Internet stuff makes it seem like there's no excuse for not having someone." "It trivializes it," said Ms. Siegal, a 30-year-old graduate student in New York. "It's like a math equation."

The discontent, Ms. Whitehead said, is not limited to women. Marc Johnson, 33, describes his late 20's and early 30's as a cycle between looking for dates, planning dates, going on dates or deconstructing dates with friends. He submitted to innumerable setups and endured the gentle but persistent nagging of suburban-with-children friends. Every year, the fall scramble — the rush to find someone to cuddle with against the winter chill — gave way to the spring fling, and then a rinse-repeat. It all began to seem a bit small last year when he returned to New York from a trip to Vietnam and was greeted by friends hassling him about when he was going to date various women. "When you're seeing the world and civilizations that are thousands of years old — it seemed so petty to focus on 'meeting the right match,'" he said, his voice mocking the phrase. "You get a bit older, you go through this a couple of times, you start to think that life is short."

Like others, Mr. Johnson now feels you can't hurry love. "It's not a backlash or resenting the whole dating thing," he said. "It's just, you've gotten over it, it's no longer of the utmost importance to go on a set number of dates or be on dates or to meet some specific person. By taking off that pressure you allow yourself to just go through life, enabled to meet people." [. . .]

Sasha Cagen, the author of *Quirkyalone,* wrote her book after being, as she said, "thoroughly messed up by *The Rules,*" the best-seller that advised women to play the old-fashioned game of hard-to-get. "The whole idea that you shouldn't ask someone out, that you're putting yourself out there to be rejected, that's just stupid," she said. "It just reinforces this warped, passive vision of what it means to be a woman." Her manifesto exhorts singles to "resist the tyranny of coupledom." To Bridget Jones's Smug Marrieds, she adds the "Perkytogethers." After she wrote about the concept in her self-published magazine and the story was picked up by the *Utne Reader*, people in four cities held "International Quirkyalone Day" parties as alternatives to Valentine's Day celebrations earlier this year. [. . .]

"I think the era of the pitied single is on the way out," Ms. Cagen said in an interview. "It's about trusting yourself and respecting yourself despite the onslaught of subtle and not-so-subtle messages that there's something wrong with you if you're not dating, that you must have some sort of fear-of-commitment pathology, or you're overly picky or you've become so accustomed to being by yourself that you'll never be able to accommodate another person." Still, the dating industry steamrolls forward, particularly online services, which claim a huge jump in membership in the last two years.

15

While the services love to talk about the success stories, they also admit, more quietly, to the dropouts. Matchmaker.com said its internal surveys show that the No. 1 reason people leave is that they do not find the right person. Just below that is that they have met someone, and men are twice as likely as women to say they met that companion offline, not on. (Women who drop out after meeting someone are twice as likely to cite an online connection.) Tim Sullivan, the president of Match.com, one of the biggest dating sites, said people can't rely on fate alone. "I don't think their chances are as good if they don't take a proactive approach and try to blend the natural fates that exist out there with a proactivity," he said.

Experts say the rise of the Dating-Industrial Complex, and the burnout, is an inevitable result of the increasingly delayed age of marriage and the lengthening of the dating years. Nationwide, the number of single households continues to rise. The technology and advice industry that has developed in response advertises efficiency. In fact, Ms. Whitehead said, it offers anything but. "It requires a whole bunch of energy and time and entrepreneurial drive," she said. "If you do that for a number of years, it begins to be fatiguing and you think, 'There are better things to do with my time,' things with a known payoff like travel or learning a language." "It's like trying out a new diet," she added. "You hear about a new system or a new approach or a new site, and it seems to offer a lot of what you're after. You go through a period of being very high in the initial experience, then it doesn't quite pan out, there's a low, it leads to discouragement, you think, 'Why am I doing this, I can be happy without it.'"

Ethan Watters, the author of *Urban Tribes*, which began with his own exploration of why he had remained single into his 30's said as people delay marriage, they begin to rely more on friends, and see relationships less as the missing piece that will complete their lives. "They realize that a good love affair has as the basis a really good friendship," he said. "They're not becoming cynical, but they're getting more savvy about the ebb and flow of relationships. I think people get a bit more relaxed about this thing as they realize that being single is normal."

Being relaxed, the resisters say, is putting faith in the age-old wisdom: you find the thing you're looking for just as you stop looking. "Not that I'm going to meet someone across a crowded room," Ms. Siegal said. "But I want it to happen in an organic way, where it starts as just friendship or I meet someone at a party. I think people think I'm living a fairy tale, that it's unrealistic, but I don't feel that way. The right person has not walked into my world."

Questions for Discussion

1. Instead of dinner and a movie, college students' social life now involves "skimpy outfits and strong drinks," according to a student quoted in Grimes's article. In paragraph 8, having dinner is described as a "bigger deal" than having sex. If you have read David Buss's articles about what men and women are looking for in partners, how does this shift in dating behavior affect the abilities of both sexes to find what they are looking for?

2. In paragraph 9 of "Dinner and a Movie?" a psychologist mentions the danger of separating sex from emotion. However, Grimes goes into much more detail in explaining this danger. Summarize and discuss his argument against sex without commitment

3. Both English and Grimes raise the point that women who engage in hooking up are acting in a liberated way, and yet may be being exploited. Do you think that calling them exploited is invoking the old double standard?

4. Grimes seems to be asking for a compromise between the old exclusivity of couples "joined-at-the hip" and this new freedom from any commitment. Can you envision what this new form of dating might be like? Would it involve "love"? Read what Helen Fisher has to say about the differences and chemistry of lust, romantic love, and long-term attachment (pages 425–445). Which of these kinds of love might be possible in a mediated new kind of date?

5. Ethan Watters describes his "tribe" as a kind of extended family that takes the place of a spouse and may even compete with potential marriage partners for an individual's allegiance. Consider the description from English's article about college students in Boston. She says, "The all-important pull of the group is huge on campus these days. It is the group, rather than the couple, that rules." In what ways is Watters's "tribe" an extension of the college group?

6. In a world of people apparently looking for soul mates, the dating guides Nehring describes seem designed to eliminate the possibility of ever finding one. Discuss why their advice seems counter to finding a soul mate or at least a caring and emotionally supportive

person. What *does* seem to be the purpose of getting married, according to these guides?

7. Zernike quotes a University of California at Santa Barbara professor who says that our society has made a fetish of the couple (paragraph 5). What is a fetish? What evidence do you see in our culture that her point is true? If you know people in their late twenties and thirties who are not in a relationship (or if you are such a person), discuss whether they feel a stigma about being single.

8. In paragraph 7, Zernike refers to the dating services as the "Dating-Industrial Complex," a spoof on the "military-industrial complex," a term denoting the huge "business" of war. In what sense has dating become a huge business? In what sense has commercializing the search for a partner trivialized love, as Sari Siegal says in paragraph 11?

Suggestions for Writing

For Inquiry

Some people argue that the hook-up culture is more myth than reality. *Time* magazine reported that only 56% of college students living away from home are sexually active (Aug. 18, 2003). From your own observations and inquiry, what can you say about the prevalence of the kind of dating described in Grimes's and English's articles?

For Analysis and Convincing

Consider Watters's argument that postponing marriage and living the tribal life into one's thirties is good preparation for a marriage that will last. Bear in mind that Watters uses the search for the "soul mate" as one reason for postponing commitment. Is he assuming that avoiding commitment until the right partner comes along will make all the difference in whether the marriage succeeds? What other benefits does he claim for the choices he is making? Make a case for or against the tribal life he describes as preparation for married life.

SECTION 4: GETTING MARRIED

Overview

The readings in this section explore a variety of viewpoints on reasons for choosing marriage, delaying marriage, refusing and redefining marriage. Although the right to marry has become a front-page issue for gays and lesbians, the fact is that among heterosexuals, marriage rates are down. In 1999, a group of scholars at Rutgers University formed the National Marriage Project to study the state of marriage in America. In their annual reports to the public, they describe findings that indicate a move away from marriage as the basis for family life. Their concern is that the traditional idea of family, a married couple with children, is losing ground to a view of marriage as an option, even for women who decide to become mothers.

As an indication of the trend away from marriage, the Rutgers report for 2004 reveals that the percentage of all people 15 years and older who were married has declined since 1960. In that year, 69.3% of the men and 65.9% of the women were married, whereas only 57.1% of men and 54% of women were in marriages in 2003. The rate of marriages yearly per 1,000 women 15 and older went from 73.5 in 1960 to 46.5 in 2000. In contrast, the Rutgers group and other census surveys indicate a rise in cohabitation from 439,000 in 1960 to 4,898,000 in 2002.

While the statistics on marriage show it to be in decline, it is hardly a dead institution. There are many reasons for the rise in single people in our country's population: people are living longer as widows and widowers, people are marrying later in their twenties, many divorced people choose not to marry again, and many cohabiting couples plan to marry eventually. Marriage is still the goal of 94% of young single people surveyed by the Rutgers group in 2002 (see "Who Wants to Marry a Soul Mate?" on pages 497–505). The Rutgers group may be right that marriage is no longer the foundation for family life. In fact, the majority of Americans do not see having children as the main purpose for marriage. You can blame it on individualism or on images of romance in popular culture, but the main motivation for marriage today seems to be to share an emotional union with one special person. And defenders of this idea argue that committed love is one of the few ways we can transcend the self in today's world.

Happily Ever After?
Linda J. Waite and Maggie Gallagher

Linda J. Waite is the Lucy Flower Professor in Urban Sociology at the University of Chicago. Maggie Gallagher is a nationally syndicated columnist and Director of the Marriage Program at the Institute of American Values. This selection is excerpted from their book. The Case for Marriage: Why Married People are Happier, Healthier, and Better Off Financially *(Doubleday, 2000).*

In most cultures, marriage marks the end of carefree adolescence and the beginning of serious adult responsibility. Marriage is both the end point of romantic longing but perhaps also, we fear, the end of romantic love.

Most of us carry within us, unresolved, both images of marriage: a source of happiness, satisfaction, and gratification and a source of restriction, frustration, and curtailment.

Thus, in his study of successful men, Robert Weiss reports, "When men who have been married fifteen or twenty years are asked how marriage changed their lives, their first thought is apt to be lost freedom."

"If I weren't married I'd probably have one hell of a time" is Mr. Brewer's first, immediate response. "I'd probably spend my summers in Newport and my winters on the Caribbean." In the next breath, Mr. Brewer offers a different vision of life without the burdens of marriage: "Much as I wouldn't want to admit it, I'd probably be lonesome with life. Because I know quite a few guys that got divorced and what it really comes down to, a lot of them go home at night to a cold home."[1]

Now that women have the same sexual license as men do and more economic opportunity, they, too, voice a similar ambivalence about the relationship between marriage and happiness. Today's young women live with both the fairy tale and its negation, the old yearning for a happily-ever-after and the modern disillusioned "knowledge" that pinning one's hopes for happiness on a husband is a recipe for disaster. Women, experts warn, may be "casualties of a marital subculture that crushes their emerging identities."[2]

These two competing visions of marriage — the wedding as a doorway to happiness and the wedding as an obstacle to individual growth — subsist side by side in contemporary American culture. Each has resonance; each perhaps reflects some hard-won bits of personal truth.

Is there any objective way to sort out the probabilities of these competing points of view? Is marriage generally good for one's mental and emotional health, or is living with one person for the rest of your life enough to drive a sane person bonkers? When people consider getting or staying married, the question often at the forefront of their minds is, Will getting married (or getting a divorce) make me happy?

A MEASURE OF HAPPINESS?

For a social scientist, the first step to answering such a question is defining the terms. For one thing, the line between physical and mental health is nowhere near as sharp and bright as people commonly assume. Emotional distress [. . .] often leads to physical illness, while chronic physical illness frequently results in mental distress, including depression. Moreover, mental disorders such as anxiety or depression often manifest themselves in a series of physical symptoms, such as sleeplessness, fatigue, sweaty palms, racing heartbeats, or a loss of appetite. Separating the mind from the body is not so easy.

And mental health and happiness, though intimately related, are not exactly the same thing either. Researchers have developed various measures to help capture subjective well-being. Psychological well-being consists of feeling hopeful, happy, and good about oneself. Those in good emotional health feel energetic, eager to get going, and connected to others.

Psychological distress, by contrast, comes in a variety of forms, including depression, or feelings of sadness, loneliness, and hopelessness. Psychological distress may also appear as anxiety, tenseness, or restlessness.

Anxiety can also produce other physical symptoms such as acid stomach, sweaty palms, shortness of breath, and hard, rapid beating of the heart in the absence of exercise.[3]

Like physical health, emotional well-being is both a good in itself and a means to other goods, the necessary precondition to functioning effectively in our various roles and fulfilling our diverse ambitions.

How does marriage influence our odds of achieving a sense of emotional well-being or avoiding psychological distress? Does marriage more often make us happy or frustrate our desire for emotional growth? Overall, perhaps surprisingly, the evidence gathered by social science points more in the direction of an older, rosier view than the bleaker modern suspicion. Marriage appears to be an important pathway toward better emotional and mental health.

ESCAPING THE ABYSS

When it comes to avoiding misery, a wedding band helps. Married men and women report less depression, less anxiety, and lower levels of other types of psychological distress than do those who are single, divorced, or widowed.[4]

As one researcher summarized the international data on marriage and mental health, "Numerous studies have shown that the previously married tend to be considerably less happy and more distressed than the married."[5]

One study of the more than eighty thousand suicides in the United States between 1979 and 1981 found that overall, both widowed and divorced persons were about three times as likely to commit suicide as the married were.[6] Although more men than women kill themselves, marriage protects wives as well as husbands. Divorced women are the most likely to commit suicide, following by widowed, never-married, and married (in that order).[7]

When it comes to happiness, the married have a similarly powerful advantage. One survey of fourteen thousand adults over a ten-year period, for example, found that marital status was one of the most important predictors of happiness.[8] According to the latest data, 40 percent of the married said they are very happy with their life in general, compared to just under a quarter of those who were single or who were cohabiting. The separated (15 percent very happy) and the divorced (18 percent very happy) were the least happy groups. The widowed were, perhaps surprisingly, just about as likely to say they are very happy as singles or as cohabitors—22 percent.[9]

On the other end of the scale, married people were also about half as likely as singles or cohabitors to say they are unhappy with their lives. The divorced were two and a half times more likely, and the widowed were almost three times more likely than spouses to confess they are "not too happy." The most miserable were the separated, who at 27 percent were

15

almost four times more likely than the married to say they are "not too happy with life."[10]

DOES MARRIAGE MAKE YOU HAPPY OR DO HAPPY PEOPLE GET MARRIED?

Why are married people so much healthier mentally and happier emotionally than those who are not married? One possibility is that happy, healthy people find it easier to get (and keep) mates. Divorced and widowed people may be unhappier, because the gay divorcées and merry widows disproportionately remarry. The happiness boost from marriage may be more apparent than real, a function of the selection of individuals into and out of the married state.

In recent years, social scientists have extensively investigated this theory, tracking people into and out of the married state to see if marriage really is a cause of mental health and happiness. This powerful new body of research clearly comes down against the cynics: The selection of happy and healthy people into marriage cannot explain the big advantage in mental and emotional health husbands and wives enjoy.

Certainly happily married people do not doubt that the love of their spouses helps them weather the storms and shocks of life. "Before my father died, we went on a vacation together where we talked and talked. We told each other how much we loved each other. . . . Matt was there with me and for me, always, to get through these terrible things, as I was with him when his parents died," said Sara, a slim woman in her early fifties.[11] "[S]he shares and defends my interests," her husband, Matt, an environmental policy analyst, chimes in. "She understands what I do. None of what I do now would have happened without her active support. She encourages me all the time."[12]

20

Economists write a great deal about the economic specialization that takes place in marriage; spouses just as often spontaneously offer stories of emotional specialization, a balancing act that leaves both partners better off. "I've learned I need balance, to be cautious. Otherwise, I'll get into a lot of trouble," notes Helen, the livelier and less emotionally inhibited member of her marriage. "And [Keith] provides that. [He] is not a risk taker. I add spice to his life. I want quick solutions and I tend to jump ahead. He's slower to act and react."[13]

Tina acknowledges the role her tumultuous marriage played even in providing the support she needed to resolve her childhood traumas: "As crazy as he [her husband] was — and he was crazy — I never had to wonder if I was alone," she said. "Sometimes I felt alone, but I knew I wasn't alone. Because I wasn't alone, I could feel how lonely I used to be. I felt safe and protected and loved. And by my midthirties I could finally begin to face that I had been unsafe, unprotected, and unloved throughout my whole childhood. . . ."[14]

When Nicholas, a very successful executive, went to the hospital with an anxiety attack, he credits his wife with knowing just what he needed to help him recover: "During that entire frightening time, she was wonderful. She was calm, sympathetic, reassuring, but never intrusive and certainly never hysterical. Whatever she suffered—and I'm sure she did, we both did—she protected me. She gave me the support and the space that I needed." [15]

Spouses can help in these times of crisis in a way that a friend or lover cannot precisely because of what marriage means: someone who will be there for you, in sickness or in health. Living with someone "until death do us part" provides a particular kind of intimacy—a spouse comforts partly because he or she has the knowledge that comes from long, emotional acquaintance but also because only a spouse can offer the peculiar reassurance that whatever life tosses at you, as Tina put it, at least you won't face it alone.

The most convincing evidence that marriage causes better emotional health comes from studies that follow people's life changes over a number of years, as some marry and stay married, some marry and divorce, and some remain divorced or never marry.   25

Nadine Marks and James Lambert did precisely this kind of work, looking at changes in the psychological health of men and women from the late 1980s to the mid-1990s. They took into account the psychological health of each individual in the year the monitoring began and watched what happened to him or her over the next five years. They measured psychological well-being in amazing detail, along eleven separate dimensions, including many measures that psychologists have used for years, such as depression, happiness with life in general, and self-esteem, as well as other, newer measures: personal mastery (which reflects the feeling that one has control over his or her life and can reach the goals set for oneself); hostility (feeling angry, irritable, or likely to argue); autonomy (being independent of influence by others); positive relations with others (having close personal relations, being a giving person); having a purpose in life (which reflects one's aims in life); self-acceptance (liking oneself); environmental mastery (being able to meet the demands of everyday life); and personal growth, which reflects one's learning, changing, and growing. [16]

When people married, their mental health improved—consistently and substantially. Meanwhile, over the same period, when people separated and divorced, they suffered substantial deterioration in mental and emotional well-being, including increases in depression and declines in reported happiness, compared to the married—even after Marks and Lambert took into account their subjects' mental health at the start of the study. Those who dissolved a marriage also reported less personal mastery, less positive relations with others, less purpose in life, and less self-acceptance than their married peers did.

Divorce, Marks and Lambert found, was especially damaging to women's mental health; divorcing women reported more of an increase in depression, more hostility, more of a decline in self-esteem, less personal growth, and less self-acceptance and environmental mastery than divorcing men.[17]

Because they had measures of people's mental health both before and after marriage, Marks and Lambert were able to rule out selection as the explanation for the mental-health advantage of married people. Instead, they found the act of getting married actually makes people happier and healthier; conversely, getting a divorce reverses these gains—even when we take into account prior measures of mental and emotional health.

In a similarly powerful study aptly titled "Becoming Married and Mental Health," researchers Allan Horwitz, Helen Raskin White, and Sandra Howell-White examined changes in psychological well-being among young adults over a seven-year period. They paid particular attention to those men and women who got married during the study period. The researchers measured the emotional health of each person at the beginning of the study, using that data as their starting point, and looked for changes when certain events occurred, especially marriage. They compared the mental health of those who got married with that of people who stayed single over the entire study. They used two measures of mental health: depression and problems with alcohol.

Once again, marriage made a big difference: Young adults who got married experience sharper drops in levels of both depression and problem drinking than did young adults who stay single. Interestingly, although more of the men than the women were problem drinkers, getting married led to bigger declines in problem drinking for women.[18] By the same token, more of the women were depressed than the men, but getting married reduced depression for the men but not for the women.[19] Horwitz and his colleagues concluded that "adequate statements about the relative advantages of marriage for men and women cannot be based on single mental health outcomes." They also concluded that marriage advantages both men and women, but does it through different mechanisms.[20]

Selection played a surprisingly small role in who marries, at least with regard to depression and alcohol abuse. Horwitz, White, and Howell-White found that alcohol use has no impact on entry into marriage; problem drinkers were just as likely as abstainers to find someone to marry. The same was true of depression, at least for the men; relatively high levels of depression do not preclude marriage or even reduce a person's chances of marrying. More of the depressed women did face increased chances of remaining single. But the strong positive impact of getting married remained even when the researchers took into account initial levels of depression and alcohol abuse for the individuals. Their conclusion? "Selection effects do not account for the lower rates of depression among people who become married, compared to those who remain single."[21]

THE LONELY HEART?

Researchers who first noticed this correlation between mental health and marital status speculated that simply living with other persons—which almost all married persons do—was the source of the emotional-health advantages of the married. Living alone, they theorized, causes distress, and those single men and women who live with others probably are as psychologically healthy as the married.

But social scientists who have tested the idea found, to their surprise, that living arrangements cannot explain the emotional advantages of marriage. Walter R. Gove and Michael Hughes compared mental-health measurements of married adults and unmarried adults who lived alone with those of people who lived with someone else. Even single adults who lived with others were more depressed than the married.[22]

The latest studies confirm these findings. In their joint research, Linda Waite and Mary Elizabeth Hughes examined two different measures of emotional health among adults in their fifties and early sixties. They found that all the single adults, whether living alone, with children, or with others, described their emotional health more negatively than did the married people. Just 17 percent of older wives characterized their emotional health as either fair or poor, compared to 28 percent of the older single women. Similarly, just 14 percent of the husbands versus 27 percent of the single men described their emotional health as fair or poor. At the other end of the happiness spectrum, 50 percent of the wives versus only 38 percent of the unmarried women described their emotional health as either very good or excellent. Meanwhile, 53 percent of the husbands but only 42 percent of the older unmarried guys rated their emotional health so high.

The husbands and wives also reported substantially fewer symptoms of depression than the single adults did, who were more depressed, on average, than the married even when they were living with their children or other people.[23]

To married couples, these results must not have been so surprising. For marriage changes not just people's outward physical arrangement but their inner relation to one another. The tendency among social scientists has been to conceptualize marriage as an external, structural category and to look beneath the piece of paper for the "real" reasons married people appear happier and healthier. But in American society, marriage is not just a label, it remains a transformative act—marriage not only names a relationship but it creates a relationship between two people, one that is acknowledged, not just by the couple itself, but by the couples' kin, friends, religious community, and larger society.

Almost by definition, married people share their lives with each other to a much greater extent than single adults do. Roommates, parents, adult children, friends, even live-in lovers, all have separate lives from those of

35

the people they live with and expect more independence and autonomy from each other than spouses do.

THE LIMITS OF COHABITATION

Indeed, researchers have found that a desire to retain one's autonomy — to keep a life apart — is one of the prime factors that drives individuals toward cohabitation over marriage. Cohabitors, for example, are far more likely to spend leisure time apart from their lovers than spouses are. Cohabitors also place a higher value than do the married on having time for one's own individual leisure activities.[24]

In the short term, cohabitors may gain some (though not nearly all) of the emotional benefits of marriage. But over the long haul, it appears co-habitors may be no better off than singles. Another large study, this time of more than 100,000 Norwegians, found that for both the men and women, "the married have the highest level of subjective well-being, followed by the widowed."

Even the divorced or separated people who cohabited did not seem to be much better off than those who lived alone, with one important excep-tion: Those who moved in with a new partner within one year after divorce or separation reported very high rates of happiness, higher even than those of the married.

This phenomenon may reflect, as the study suggests, a buffering effect that protects an ex-spouse during the strains of divorce. But it may also reflect the likelihood that those who move in with a partner immediately following a divorce began the relationship before the end of the marriage. The glow of happiness these couples report may reflect the underlying social reality: It is far more pleasant to be the one who dumps one's spouse for a new love than to be traded in for a different model. But this newfound happiness of live-in lovers appears to be short-lived (at least among those who do not quickly remarry). "[A]mong those who have remained divorced for three years or more the level of well-being is much lower and very similar for the single and cohabiting," the study concludes.[25]

Cohabitation provides some — but not all — of the same emotional benefits of marriage, yet only for a short time and at a high price. Breaking up with a live-in lover carries many of the same emotional costs as divorce but happens far more frequently. People who are cohabiting are less happy generally than the married and are less satisfied with their sex lives. In America, long-term cohabiting relationships are far rarer than successful marriages.[26]

Of course, marriage can be a source of stress as well as comfort. The strong emotional benefits of marriage come only from relationships that spouses rate as "very happy."[27] Those who describe their marriages as

40

"pretty happy" are somewhat better off than singles, but not as well off as those in "very happy" relationships.[28]

Not surprisingly, the men and women in the relatively small number of "not too happy" marriages show more psychological distress than do singles. Horwitz and his colleagues find that the quality of the marriage is the most consistent determinant of both depression and problem drinking; both husbands and wives who say they have a good relationship with their spouses also report lower levels of depression and fewer problems with alcohol.[29] People who say their relationships are unhappy, that they would like to change many aspects of their relationship and that they often consider leaving their spouses or partners have higher distress levels than people without partners at all.[30]

Fortunately for the mental health of the country, most married people describe their marriages as "very happy." Among the nearly twenty thousand married men and women questioned over the last several decades as part of the General Social Survey, 66 percent of the husbands and 62 percent of the wives give their marriage the highest possible happiness rating. Almost no one—2 percent of the married men and 4 percent of the married women—described their marriage as "not too happy."[31] So the emotional damage from an unhappy marriage is quite a rare occurrence, and the vast majority of married men and women get emotional benefits—usually very large ones—from being married.

Nor do unhappy marriages necessarily stay that way: 86 percent of those who rated their marriage as unhappy in the late eighties and who were still married five years later said their marriages had become happier.[32]

THE MARITAL TRANSFORMATION

New marriage partners together create a shared sense of social reality and meaning—their own little separate world, populated by only the two of them. This shared sense of meaning can be an important foundation for emotional health.[33]

Ordinary, good-enough marriages provide the partners with a sense that what they do matters, that someone cares for, esteems, needs, loves, and values them as a person. No matter what else happens in life, this knowledge makes problems easier to bear.

Over a century ago, sociologist Émile Durkheim found that people who were integrated into society were much less likely to commit suicide than people who were more socially marginal. Life is uncertain and often hard, he argued, but being part of a larger group one loves gives people the strength and will to cling to life in the face of difficulties.[34]

Marriage and family provide the sense of belonging that Durkheim had in mind, the sense of loving and being loved, of being absolutely essential to the life and happiness of others. Believing that one has a purpose in life and a reason for continued existence, that life is worth the effort because one's activities and challenges are worthy comes from having other people depending on you, counting on you, caring about you. Married people have a starring role in the lives of their spouses; their shared universe would cease to exist if something happened to one of them. When the shared universe includes children, the sense of being essential, of having a purpose and a full life, expands as well. Marriage improves emotional well-being in part by giving people a sense that their life has meaning and purpose.[35]

The enhanced sense of meaning and purpose that marriage provides protects each spouse's psychological health. Russell Burton examined reports of psychological distress for a national sample of adults. As other sociologists have, Burton found that multiple social roles seem to protect people's mental health. Men who were employed, married, and parents, for example, were less distressed than other men.[36] Men who were employed and married or married and a parent but not employed also felt that their lives had more meaning and purpose than other men did. Burton found a similar picture for women: Employed single women, employed wives, employed single mothers, married mothers, and employed married mothers were less distressed than women who were single, childless, and not employed. But while having more than one social role can boost one's health, marriage appears to be the key role. Married women — regardless of whether they worked or had children — reported greater purpose and meaning in life, and neither work nor children, in the absence of marriage, increased women's feelings of purpose and meaning. The sense of meaning and purpose marriage creates, concluded Burton, seems to be in itself responsible for the better psychological health of husbands and wives.[37]

Oddly, contemporary experts have often failed to notice the immense transformative power of the marriage act. Perhaps because, in the age of divorce, sensible people naturally place a great deal of emphasis on finding the right partner, experts tend to talk as if a marriage license were only a "piece of paper," as if the relationship were everything and the marriage ceremony merely a public certification of a preexisting condition.

The ideas that happiness is a purely individual rather than an interpersonal achievement, that marriage is simply a sum of the characteristics of the individuals that enter into it, that getting married cannot change an individual's outlook, behavior, or internal feelings are surprisingly influential in contemporary America. Noting that married people say they are lonely less often than do singles, a recent college textbook on marriage and family concludes, "It would be ludicrous to suggest that young adults who experience loneliness and stress should marry to alleviate their problems. Obviously, the same personal characteristics that resulted in their distressful state in singleness would also be reflected in marriage."[38]

As Professor Norval Glenn stated in a critique of textbooks, "[M]ost social scientists who have studied the data believe that marriage itself accounts for a great deal of the difference in average well-being between married and unmarried persons. Indeed, loneliness is probably the negative feeling most likely to be alleviated simply by being married."[39]

The latest research shows the skeptics are wrong: In real life, the public legal commitment represented by that "piece of paper" makes a big difference. The married really are emotionally healthier than their single counterparts because they've chosen to live in this particular type of committed relationship. The commitment married people make to each other is reinforced and supported not only by their own private efforts and emotions, but by the wider community—by the expectations and support of friends, families, bosses, and colleagues who share basic notions about how married people behave.

The emotional support and monitoring of a spouse encourages healthy behavior that in turn affects emotional as well as physical well-being: regular sleep, a healthy diet, moderate drinking. But the key seems to be the marriage bond itself: Having a partner who is committed for better or for worse, in sickness and in health, makes people happier and healthier. The knowledge that someone cares for you and that you have someone who depends on you helps give life meaning and provides a buffer against the inevitable troubles of life.

In contemporary folklore, marriage may represent the end of the period of happy, carefree youth. But science tends to confirm Grandma's wisdom: On the whole, man was not meant to live alone, and neither was woman. Marriage makes people happier.

Notes

1. Robert S. Weiss, *Staying the Course: The Emotional and Social Lives of Men Who Do Well at Work* (New York: Fawcett Columbine, 1990), 113.

2. Christopher Hayes, Deborah Anderson, and Melina Blau, *Our Turn: Women Who Triumph in the Face of Divorce* (New York: Pocket Books, 1993), 70, quoted in Barbara Dafoe Whitehead, *The Divorce Culture: How Divorce Became an Entitlement and How It Is Blighting the Lives of Our Children* (New York: Alfred A. Knopf, 1997), 60.

3. John Mirowsky and Catherine E. Ross, *Social Causes of Psychological Distress* (New York: Aldine De Gruyter, 1989).

4. Ibid., 90–92.

5. Arne Mastekaasa, "The Subjective Well-being of the Previously Married: The Importance of Unmarried Cohabitation and Time Since Widowhood or Divorce," *Social Forces* 73 (1994): 665.

6. Jack C. Smith, Mercy, and Conn, "Marital Status and the Risk," 78–80.

7. Ibid.

8. James A. Davis, "New Money, an Old Man/Lady, and 'Two's Company': Subjective Welfare in the NORC General Social Surveys, 1972–1982," *Social Indicators Research* 15 (1984): 319–50. Davis also found that race and recent financial change predicted happiness.

9. Seven percent of spouses versus 13 percent of singles said they were "not too happy." Twenty percent of the widowed were "not too happy," as were 18 percent of the divorced and 27 percent of the separated. Tabulations by Linda J. Waite from the General Social Survey, 1990–1996 waves.

10. Tabulations by Linda J. Waite from the General Social Survey, 1990–1996 waves.

11. Judith S. Wallerstein and Sandra Blakeslee, *The Good Marriage: How and Why Love Lasts* (Boston: Houghton Mifflin, 1995), 85.

12. Ibid., 45.

13. Ibid., 115.

14. Ibid., 139.

15. Ibid., 219.

16. For a detailed discussion of these measures, see Carol D. Ryff and Corey Lee M. Keyes, "The Structure of Psychological Well-being Revisited," *Journal of Personality and Social Psychology* 69 (1995): 719–27.

17. Nadine F. Marks and James D. Lambert, "Marital Status Continuity and Change among Young and Midlife Adults: Longitudinal Effects on Psychological Well-being," *Journal of Family Issues* 19 (1998): 652–86.

18. Allan V. Horwitz, Helene Raskin White, and Sandra Howell-White, "Becoming Married and Mental Health: A Longitudinal Study of a Cohort of Young Adults," *Journal of Marriage and the Family* 58 (1996): 895–907. Once the authors take into account age, income, and social support, the impact of marriage on problem drinking becomes statistically insignificant for men but remains significant for women.

19. For women, Horwitz et al. ("Becoming Married and Mental Health," 895–907) find that depression in the later year depends *only* on depression at the beginning of the study.

20. Horwitz et al., "Becoming Married and Mental Health," 904.

21. Ibid., 901. See also Marks and Lambert, "Marital Status Continuity," 652–86.

22. Walter R. Gove and Michael Hughes, "Possible Causes of the Apparent Sex Differences in Physical Health: An Empirical Investigation," *American Sociological Review* 44 (1979): 126–46.

23. Tabulations done for this book by Linda J. Waite from the Health and Retirement Survey. See Thomas F. Juster and Richard Suzman, "An Overview of the Health and Retirement Survey," *Journal of Human Resources* 30 (1995): S7–S56. See also Linda J. Waite and Mary Elizabeth Hughes, "At Risk on the Cusp of Old Age: Living Arrangements and Functional Status among Black, White, and Hispanic Adults in the Health and Retirement Survey," *Journal of Gerontology: Social Sciences* 54B (1998): S136–S144.

24. Blumstein and Schwartz, *American Couples*, 186–87; Clarkberg, Stolzenberg, and Waite, "Attitudes, Values and Entrance," 609–34.

25. Mastekaasa, "Subjective Well-being," 682.

26. Bumpass and Sweet, "National Estimates of Cohabitation," 615–25.

27. Horwitz et al., "Becoming Married and Mental Health," 903.

28. Ross, "Reconceptualizing Marital Status," 129–40.

29. Horwitz et al., "Becoming Married and Mental Health," 903.

30. Ross, "Reconceptualizing Marital Status," 137.

31. Linda J. Waite's tabulations from the 1972–1994 General Social Survey. Although we might suspect that many more people are unhappy in their marriage than will admit this to a survey interviewer, responses on marital happiness are closely related to reports of overall happiness. We might also suspect that in an era of easy divorce, unhappily married people divorce, leaving only the happily married. In fact, we see no evidence that this has occurred. See Norval D. Glenn, "Values, Attitudes," 15–33.

32. Linda J. Waite's tabulations from the National Survey of Families and Households, 1987/88 and 1992/94.

33. Peter Berger and Hansfried Kellner, "Marriage and the Construction of Reality: An Exercise in the Microsociology of Knowledge," *Diogenes* 46 (1964): 1–25.

34. Émile Durkheim, *Suicide* (1897; reprint, New York: Free Press, 1951).

35. Russell P. D. Burton, "Global Integrative Meaning as a Mediating Factor in the Relationship between Social Roles and Psychological Distress," *Journal of Health and Social Behavior* 39 (1998): 201–15. See also Mirowsky and Ross, *Social Causes*, 25.

36. Ibid., 209. Burton also found that men who were employed but neither married nor parents were less distressed than the comparison group—men who were unemployed, single, and not parents.

37. Ibid, 210–13.

38. J. Kenneth Davidson, Sr., and Nelwyn B. Moore, *Marriage and Family: Change and Continuity* (Boston: Allyn and Bacon, 1996), 322.

39. Norval Glenn, *Closed Hearts, Closed Minds: The Textbook Story of Marriage* (New York: Institute for American Values 1997), 11.

Against Love
Laura Kipnis

Laura Kipnis, a professor in the School of Communications at Northwestern University, is a cultural theorist and award-winning writer. This essay originally appeared in the New York Times Magazine *in 2001. She has since published a book by the same title,* Against Love: A Polemic *(Pantheon, 2003).*

Love is, as we know, a mysterious and controlling force. It has vast power over our thoughts and life decisions. It demands our loyalty, and we, in turn, freely comply. Saying no to love isn't simply heresy; it is tragedy—the failure to achieve what is most essentially human. So deeply internalized is our obedience to this most capricious despot that artists create passionate odes to its cruelty, and audiences seem never to tire of the most deeply unoriginal mass spectacles devoted to rehearsing the litany of its torments, fixating their very beings on the narrowest glimmer of its fleeting satisfactions.

Yet despite near total compliance, a buzz of social nervousness attends the subject. If a society's lexicon of romantic pathologies reveals its particular anxieties, high on our own list would be diagnoses like "inability to settle down" or "immaturity," leveled at those who stray from the norms of domestic coupledom by either refusing entry in the first place or, once installed, pursuing various escape routes: excess independence, ambivalence, "straying," divorce. For the modern lover, "maturity" isn't a depressing signal of impending decrepitude but a sterling achievement, the sine qua non of a lover's qualifications to love and be loved.

This injunction to achieve maturity — synonymous in contemporary usage with 30-year mortgages, spreading waistlines and monogamy — obviously finds its raison d'être in modern love's central anxiety, that structuring social contradiction the size of the San Andreas Fault: namely, the expectation that romance and sexual attraction can last a lifetime of coupled togetherness despite much hard evidence to the contrary.

Ever optimistic, heady with love's utopianism, most of us eventually pledge ourselves to unions that will, if successful, far outlast the desire that impelled them into being. The prevailing cultural wisdom is that even if sexual desire tends to be a short-lived phenomenon, "mature love" will kick in to save the day when desire flags. The issue that remains unaddressed is whether cutting off other possibilities of romance and sexual attraction for the more muted pleasures of mature love isn't similar to voluntarily amputating a healthy limb: a lot of anesthesia is required and the phantom pain never entirely abates. But if it behooves a society to convince its citizenry that wanting change means personal failure or wanting to start over is shameful or simply wanting more satisfaction than what you have is an illicit thing, clearly grisly acts of self-mutilation will be required.

There hasn't always been quite such optimism about love's longevity. For the Greeks, inventors of democracy and a people not amenable to being pushed around by despots, love was a disordering and thus preferably brief experience. During the reign of courtly love, love was illicit and usually fatal. Passion meant suffering: the happy ending didn't yet exist in the cultural imagination. As far as togetherness as an eternal ideal, the 12th-century advice manual "De Amore et Amor is Remedio" ("On Love and the Remedies of Love") warned that too many opportunities to see or chat with the beloved would certainly decrease love.

The innovation of happy love didn't even enter the vocabulary of romance until the 17th century. Before the 18th century — when the family was primarily an economic unit of production rather than a hothouse of Oedipal tensions — marriages were business arrangements between families; participants had little to say on the matter. Some historians consider romantic love a learned behavior that really only took off in the late 18th century

5

along with the new fashion for reading novels, though even then affection between a husband and wife was considered to be in questionable taste.

Historians disagree, of course. Some tell the story of love as an eternal and unchanging essence; others, as a progress narrative over stifling social conventions. (Sometimes both stories are told at once; consistency isn't required.) But has modern love really set us free? Fond as we are of projecting our own emotional quandaries back through history, construing vivid costume dramas featuring medieval peasants or biblical courtesans sharing their feelings with the post-Freudian savvy of lifelong analysands, our amatory predecessors clearly didn't share all our particular aspirations about their romantic lives.

We, by contrast, feel like failures when love dies. We believe it could be otherwise. Since the cultural expectation is that a state of coupled permanence is achievable, uncoupling is experienced as crisis and inadequacy—even though such failures are more the norm than the exception.

As love has increasingly become the center of all emotional expression in the popular imagination, anxiety about obtaining it in sufficient quantities—and for sufficient duration—suffuses the population. Everyone knows that as the demands and expectations on couples escalated, so did divorce rates. And given the current divorce statistics (roughly 50 percent of all marriages end in divorce), all indications are that whomever you love today—your beacon of hope, the center of all your optimism—has a good chance of becoming your worst nightmare tomorrow. (Of course, that 50 percent are those who actually leave their unhappy marriages and not a particularly good indication of the happiness level or nightmare potential of those who remain.) Lawrence Stone, a historian of marriage, suggests—rather jocularly, you can't help thinking—that today's rising divorce rates are just a modern technique for achieving what was once taken care of far more efficiently by early mortality.

Love may or may not be a universal emotion, but clearly the social forms it takes are infinitely malleable. It is our culture alone that has dedicated itself to allying the turbulence of romance and the rationality of the long-term couple, convinced that both love and sex are obtainable from one person over the course of decades, that desire will manage to sustain itself for 30 or 40 or 50 years and that the supposed fate of social stability is tied to sustaining a fleeting experience beyond its given life span.

10

Of course, the parties involved must "work" at keeping passion alive (and we all know how much fun that is), the presumption being that even after living in close proximity to someone for a historically unprecedented length of time, you will still muster the requisite desire to achieve sexual congress on a regular basis. (Should passion fizzle out, just give up sex. Lack of desire for a mate is never an adequate rationale for "looking elsewhere.") And it is true, many couples do manage to perform enough psychic retooling to reshape the anarchy of desire to the confines of the marriage bed, plugging away at the task year after year (once a week, same time, same position) like diligent assembly-line workers, aided by the occasional fantasy or two to help get the old motor to turn over, or keep running, or complete the trip. And so we have the erotic life of a nation of workaholics: if sex seems like work, clearly you're not working hard enough at it.

But passion must not be allowed to die! The fear—or knowledge—that it does shapes us into particularly conflicted psychological beings, perpetually in search of prescriptions and professional interventions, regardless of cost or consequence. Which does have its economic upside, at least. Whole new sectors of the economy have been spawned, with massive social investment in new technologies from Viagra to couples' porn: capitalism's Lourdes for dying marriages.

There are assorted low-tech solutions to desire's dilemmas too. Take advice. In fact, take more and more advice. Between print, airwaves and the therapy industry, if there were any way to quantify the G.N.P. in romantic counsel, it would be a staggering number. Desperate to be cured of love's temporality, a love-struck populace has molded itself into an advanced race of advice receptacles, like some new form of miracle sponge that can instantly absorb many times its own body weight in wetness.

Inexplicably, however, a rebellious breakaway faction keeps trying to leap over the wall and emancipate themselves, not from love itself—unthinkable!—but from love's domestic confinements: The escape routes are well trodden—love affairs, midlife crises—though strewn with the left-behind luggage of those who encountered unforeseen obstacles along the way (panic, guilt, self-engineered exposures) and beat self-abashed retreats to their domestic gulags, even after pledging body and soul to newfound loves in the balmy utopias of nondomesticated romances. Will all the adulterers in the audience please stand up? You know who you are. Don't be embarrassed! Adulterers aren't just "playing around." These are our homegrown closet social theorists, because adultery is not just a referendum on the sustainability of monogamy; it is a veiled philosophical discussion about the social contract itself. The question on the table is this: "How much renunciation of desire does society demand of us, versus the degree of gratification it provides?" Clearly, the adulterer's answer, following a long line of venerable social critics, would be, "Too much."

But what exactly is it about the actual lived experience of modern domestic love that would make flight such a compelling option for so many? Let us briefly examine those material daily life conditions.

15

Fundamentally, to achieve love and qualify for entry into that realm of salvation and transcendence known as the couple (the secular equivalent of entering a state of divine grace), you must *be* a lovable person. And what precisely does being lovable entail? According to the tenets of modern love, it requires an advanced working knowledge of the intricacies of *mutuality*.

Mutuality means recognizing that your partner has needs and being prepared to meet them. This presumes, of course, that the majority of those needs can and should be met by one person. (Question this, and you question the very foundations of the institution. So don't.) These needs of ours run deep, a tangled underground morass of ancient, gnarled roots, looking to ensnarl any hapless soul who might accidentally trod upon their outer radices.

Still, meeting those needs is the most effective way to become the object of another's desire, thus attaining intimacy, which is required to achieve the state known as psychological maturity. (Despite how closely it reproduces the affective conditions of our childhoods, since trading compliance for love is the earliest social lesson learned; we learn it in our cribs.)

You, in return, will have your own needs met by your partner in matters large and small. In practice, many of these matters turn out to be quite small. Frequently, it is the tensions and disagreements over the minutiae of daily living that stand between couples and their requisite intimacy. Taking out the garbage, tone of voice, a forgotten errand — these are the rocky shoals upon which intimacy so often founders.

Mutuality requires *communication*, since in order to be met, these needs   20
must be expressed. (No one's a mind reader, which is not to say that many of us don't expect this quality in a mate. Who wants to keep having to tell someone what you need?) What you need is for your mate to understand you — your desires, your contradictions, your unique sensitivities, what irks you. (In practice, that means what about your mate irks you.) You, in turn, must learn to understand the mate's needs. This means being willing to hear what about yourself irks your mate. Hearing is not a simple physiological act performed with the ears, as you will learn. You may think you know how to *hear*, but that doesn't mean that you know how to *listen*.

With two individuals required to coexist in enclosed spaces for extended periods of time, domesticity requires substantial quantities of compromise and adaptation simply to avoid mayhem. Yet with the post-Romantic ideal of unconstrained individuality informing our most fundamental ideas of the self, this can prove a perilous process. Both parties must be willing to jettison whatever aspects of individuality might prove irritating while being simultaneously allowed to retain enough individuality to feel their autonomy is not being sacrificed, even as it is being surgically excised.

Having mastered mutuality, you may now proceed to *advanced intimacy*. Advanced intimacy involves inviting your partner "in" to your most interior self. Whatever and wherever our "inside" is, the widespread — if somewhat metaphysical — belief in its existence (and the related belief that whatever is in there is dying to get out) has assumed a quasi-medical status. Leeches once served a similar purpose. Now we "express our feelings" in lieu of our fluids because everyone knows that those who don't are far more prone to cancer, ulcers or various dire ailments.

With love as our culture's patent medicine, prescribed for every ill (now even touted as a necessary precondition for that other great American obsession, longevity), we willingly subject ourselves to any number of arcane procedures in its quest. "Opening up" is required for relationship health, so lovers fashion themselves after doctors wielding long probes to penetrate the tender regions. Try to think of yourself as one big orifice: now stop clenching and relax. If the procedure proves uncomfortable, it just shows you're not open enough. Psychotherapy may be required before sufficient dilation can be achieved: the world's most expensive lubricant.

Needless to say, this opening-up can leave you feeling quite vulnerable, lying there psychically spread-eagled and shivering on the examining table of your relationship. (A favored suspicion is that your partner, knowing exactly where your vulnerabilities are, deliberately kicks you there — one reason this opening-up business may not always feel as pleasant as advertised.) And as anyone who has spent much time in — or just in earshot of — a typical couple knows, the "expression of needs" is often the Trojan horse of intimate warfare, since expressing needs means, by definition, that one's partner has thus far failed to meet them.

In any long-term couple, this lexicon of needs becomes codified over time into a highly evolved private language with its own rules. Let's call this couple grammar. Close observation reveals this as a language composed of one recurring unit of speech: the interdiction — highly nuanced, mutually imposed commands and strictures extending into the most minute areas of household affairs, social life, finances, speech, hygiene, allowable idiosyncrasies and so on. From bathroom to bedroom, car to kitchen, no aspect of coupled life is not subject to scrutiny, negotiation and codes of conduct.

A sample from an inexhaustible list, culled from interviews with numerous members of couples of various ages, races and sexual orientations:

You can't leave the house without saying where you're going. You can't not say what time you'll return. You can't go out when the other person feels like staying at home. You can't be a slob. You can't do less than 50 percent of the work around the house, even if the other person wants to do 100 percent more cleaning than you find necessary or even reasonable. You can't leave the dishes for later, load them the way that seems best to you, drink straight from the carton or make crumbs. You can't leave the bathroom door open — it's offensive. You can't leave the bathroom door closed — your partner needs to get in. You can't not shave your underarms or legs. You can't gain weight. You can't watch soap operas. You can't watch infomercials or the pregame show or Martha Stewart. You can't eat what you want — goodbye Marshmallow Fluff; hello tofu meatballs. You can't spend too much time on the computer. And stay out of those chat rooms. You can't take risks, unless they are agreed-upon risks, which somewhat limits the concept of "risk." You can't make major purchases alone, or spend money on things the other person considers excesses. You can't blow money just because you're in a bad mood, and you can't be in a bad mood without being required to explain it. You can't begin a sentence with "You always . . . ." You can't begin a sentence with "I never . . . ." You can't be simplistic, even when things are simple. You can't say what you really think of that outfit or color combination or cowboy hat. You can't be cynical about things the other person is sincere about. You can't drink without the other person counting your drinks. You can't have the wrong laugh. You can't bum cigarettes when you're out because it embarrasses your mate, even though you've explained the unspoken fraternity between smokers. You can't tailgate, honk or listen to talk radio in the car. And so on. The specifics don't matter. What matters is that the operative word is "can't."

Thus is love obtained.

Certainly, domesticity offers innumerable rewards: companionship, childrearing convenience, reassuring predictability and many other benefits too varied to list. But if love has power over us, domesticity is its enforcement wing: the iron dust mop in the velvet glove. The historian Michel Foucault has argued that modern power made its mark on the world by inventing new types of enclosures and institutions, places like factories, schools, barracks, prisons and asylums, where individuals could be located, supervised, processed and subjected to inspection, order and the clock. What current social institution is more enclosed than modern intimacy? What offers greater regulation of movement and time, or more precise surveillance of body and thought, to a greater number of individuals?

Of course, it is your choice — as if any of us could really choose not to desire love or not to feel like hopeless losers should we fail at it. We moderns are beings yearning to be filled, yearning to be overtaken by love's mysterious power. We prostrate ourselves at love's portals, like social strivers waiting at the rope line outside some exclusive club hoping to gain admission and thereby confirm our essential worth. A life without love lacks an organizing narrative. A life without love seems so barren, and it might almost make you consider how empty the rest of the world is, as if love were vital plasma and everything else just tap water.

Exchanging obedience for love comes naturally — after all, we all were once children whose survival depended on the caprices of love. And there you have the template for future intimacies. If you love me, you'll do what I want — or need, or demand — and I'll love you in return. We all become household dictators, petty tyrants of the private sphere, who are, in our turn, dictated to.

And why has modern love developed in such a way as to maximize submission and minimize freedom, with so little argument about it? No doubt a citizenry schooled in renouncing desire instead of imagining there could be something more would be, in many respects, advantageous. After all, wanting more is the basis for utopian thinking, a path toward dangerous social demands, even toward imagining the possibilities for altogether different social arrangements. But if the most elegant forms of social control are those that came packaged in the guise of individual needs and satisfactions, so wedded to the individual psyche that any opposing impulse registers as the anxiety of unlovability, who needs a soldier on every corner? We are more than happy to police ourselves and those we love and call it living happily ever after. Perhaps a secular society needed another meta-physical entity to subjugate itself to after the death of God, and love was available for the job. But isn't it a little depressing to think we are somehow incapable of inventing forms of emotional life based on anything other than subjugation?

Why Marriage?
Jane Smiley

"Why Marriage?" appeared in a much longer version in Harper's Magazine *in June, 2000. Jane Smiley has written eight novels, winning the Pulitzer Prize in 1992 for one of them,* A Thousand Acres. *She taught for many years in the University of Iowa Writers' Workshop.*

My guinea-pig child, now twenty-one, was home from her senior year in college for Christmas vacation. The last night before [she] went back to college, we had another one of those family dinners—you know, me, my boyfriend, his daughter and son by his second wife, my daughters by my second husband, and my seven-year-old son by my third husband. The topic of conversation was how my son came to walk home from school— more than a mile up a steep, winding road on a very warm day. "What did you do when cars went by?" I asked.

"I stepped to the side of the road!" he answered. He was laughing at the success of his exploit. Not only had he been a very bold boy who had ac-complished something he had been wanting to do; he had been impres-sively disobedient. We all laughed, and my boyfriend and I squeezed each other's hands, pleased and seduced by that happy-family idea, everyone safe and well-fed, getting along, taken care of.

But we are not married, and we have no plans to blend our families. I come to the theory and practice of marriage at the start of the new millen-nium with a decidedly checkered past and an outsider's view. But, I admit, I'm still paying attention, implicated, at least, by the fact that my children assume they will get married. I see the same thing as many others do—the breakdown of the traditional family—but I don't see this as a dark and fear-some eventuality, rather as something interesting to observe, something that I have endured, survived, and actually benefited from, something that will certainly be part of the material from which my children build their lives.

Capitalism has an excellent reputation, among fans of the free market, for disseminating goods and information and molding the lives of con-sumers in the ways that best serve both the system and individuals. If this is indeed the case, then late capitalism has evidently decided that what is best for us and our children is serial monogamy, frequent changes of employ-ment, and a high degree of instability. It has decided that, on balance, it is better for all adults to work rather than for one designated gender to stay home with the children. It has decided that most children will spend at least part of their early childhoods in the care of people outside their families who are hired to care for them, often in institutional settings rather than at home. It has decided that the inherent instability of marriage is to be promoted rather than suppressed. It has decided that the individual's relationship to society will be less and less mediated through the family and more and more experienced directly. Fans of the free market would say—should say, if they dared—that we should embrace rather than resist what capitalism has decided.

Which is not to say that when, sixteen years ago, I parted from the father of my two daughters I wasn't traumatized. The choice of staying or leaving presented itself to me as a choice between suicide and mass murder. For years afterward, I secretly scrutinized the girls for signs of psychological damage, and I read, with sinking heart, every article in the news about the negative impact of divorce upon children. It wasn't until my son came along, the child of my next marriage, that I appreciated this gloriously cruel fact of life: had I not divorced my daughters' father, I would never have borne my son, and how could I do without any of the three of them?

My daughters are twenty-one and seventeen now, and they have spent many years contemplating their own family and the families of their friends, of course comparing and choosing and wishing. They have a network of siblings: a stepsister and stepbrother nearly their own age from their father's second marriage, a foster brother, also from that marriage, and a half brother, my son. Their stepsiblings have stepsiblings of their own, to which my daughters feel somewhat related. All eight of these kids elect to maintain family ties with one another, ties that bind them more closely to one another than to their various stepparents. My daughters like the looseness of this; in fact, most of the time they like the general looseness of our family and compare it favorably with the tightness, and even suspiciousness, of their friends' traditional families, which seem a little suffocating. Both girls have had crushes on the families of friends, tried in some sense to be in those families, but in the end have found those families a little hidebound, a little boring. And I have experienced the input of the stepparents and the stepsiblings as productive and enlightening. What I thought of as mass murder turned out to be freedom—freedom from the particular family pathology that the girls' father and I were monogamously building in our four-bedroom house on that corner lot in that state I now think of as Monogamy Central.

One thing that seems to be evident from history is that marriage as a property relationship is more stable than marriage as a personal relationship. It is not until women emerge from property status that the tension between monogamy and promiscuity is really a problem. It is women with voices and a certain amount of power who force men to choose between possible types of relationships. We can easily imagine a man having a mother, a housekeeper, a wife who has produced his legitimate children, a

5

concubine, a sister, and even a female friend, all living under the same roof. The trouble is, we can't imagine him in America. In America, custom requires that the mother and sister live elsewhere and all of the others be rolled into one, the wife. Wives require it, too. When courtship was about joining properties, then it could be short. Now that marriage is about being everything to one another, courtship takes a long time and can break down at any point. It is difficult to find a mate who is equally good at every function, and it is also difficult to know oneself well enough to know which function you care about more than the others. And then, of course, as the marriage project moves through its stages — householding, child rearing, professional success, aging — the functions you once cared about change or evolve. The great lover who can't manage to get a dirty dish into the dishwasher becomes more annoying than exciting, the wonderful friend who is infertile is a figure of tragedy, the terrific mother who harps about responsibility comes to seem like a nag.

And that tension between monogamy and promiscuity remains, now transformed into a dilemma of character. The trouble with serial monogamy, which I define as being faithfully married to one person until you can't stand it anymore, and then being faithfully married to another person who fits the new standard better, is that each transition in the series comes as a personal defeat. Serial infidelity is even worse, a strange combination of victory and defeat every time the husband cheats on his wife, until he is numb not only to the moral attractions of monogamy but also to the erotic attractions of promiscuity. Everything he said, every promise he made, every way that he knew himself — all were wrong. [. . .]

Infidelity in marriage is a form of inattention. The spouse becomes less interesting than someone new, and the unfaithful party either isn't around much or seems distracted when he or she is. Some years ago, for example, a friend of mine had a breast biopsy. Her husband took her to the clinic on Thursday, stayed with her, brought her home, and tended to her that afternoon and evening. The next morning, when she was to go back for a checkup, he coolly suggested that their sixteen-year-old daughter could handle it and that the wife would be fine for the rest of the day by herself. It later turned out that he had prior plans to spend the day with his twenty-five-year-old girlfriend and didn't want to change them. In the course of their bitter divorce, this callousness seemed particularly monstrous, the wife sitting home alone in pain and fear while the husband was cavorting with a woman twenty-five years his junior. Yes, he was a lout, and no doubt covertly rather than honestly expressing resentment and anger toward his wife that he might have set aside for the time being. But what if he had been able to treat both women with love and compassion and patience and tenderness? What if when he was with the wife he had been fully with her, and when he was with the girlfriend he had been fully with her? Would each have been satisfied? Could he, could anyone, have done that?

When I began seeing my current boyfriend, he had another girlfriend, 10
who was seeing another guy. Since the very thing that broke up my last
marriage was my former husband's infidelity, it seemed to me that I was
putting myself right back into danger, and so for a long time we refrained
from identifying our relationship even as a "relationship." We were friends,
then "all-inclusive friends." A turning point came about six months in,
when the other girlfriend broke up with her other boyfriend and said to
Jack, "Well, I guess it's just you and me again," and he said to her, "Well,
you, me, and Jane." Within a few weeks, she had another boyfriend. Sometimes we would have dinner together, all four of us, but our dinners were,
to say the least, volatile. Even so, all of the relationships, mine with him,
his with her, hers with the other guy, endured, and not without pain and
jealousy on the part of every single one of us. But we had a principle. We
were not married, and, further, we didn't wish to take marriage as our paradigm. Couples in America begin taking marriage as their paradigm almost
as soon as they begin dating: going steady, exchanging rings, or whatever. It
takes real conviction and unusual stubbornness to flout the paradigm, and
I, for one, needed help to do so. More than anything, I wanted another
marriage to close over my head like the surface of a vast sea, preventing the
acquisition of any real understanding of myself, my sexuality, and my ways
of relating to men. The other girlfriend and her very central place in the life
of the man I loved prevented that, and her own refusal to allow her sexual
freedom to be restricted offered a model of an alternative.

Some men and women have the knack of being so delightfully present
that time with them is worthwhile in and of itself, whether or not any
promises about exclusiveness have been made. There are people in whom
freedom is the very essence of their appeal, and those who love them have
to make the choice: Is the desire to possess, in and of itself, more worth
pursuing than the relationship with that delightful person, and if so, why?
Or is that relationship, whatever it entails, the valuable thing?

To be forced to ponder these questions is to be forced to ask yourself
about your own freedom and autonomy, your own ability to be present
with your friend or spouse when he is present with you as well as your ability to be present with yourself when he is not with you.

One thing I have discovered is that I always mistook longing for love.
If I felt enough longing, then that was the sure sign that this was love. The
trouble was that I could feel unassuageable longing for my friend when he
was right there, right in my arms, talking right to me. If I got rid of the longing, then I didn't recognize what was left as love, and in fact it took me a long
time to recognize love when I felt it or saw it. Not getting married was the education in learning not to be oblivious, but instead honest and observant.

Fidelity, more than anything else, is the signifier of marriage. To forswear
fidelity is to open yourself up to other ideas, other thoughts, about what love
is, what desire is, what happiness is, and what commitment is. [. . .]

Since marriage began as a property relationship, its foundations are 15
challenged by the transformation of the property into personhood.

In William Shakespeare's *Winter's Tale*, Leontes' right to kill his wife in a jealous rage is not challenged by law, nor is his right to kill his daughter. He can only be worked on in private, by the nag Paulina, who torments his conscience for sixteen years. Leontes' transformation comes as a result of his recognition of the divine nature of Hermione. She was never his property to begin with. True marriage, or remarriage, begins with the revelation that union between male and female is a divine reconciliation between equals. [. . .]

Leontes' original sin was the sin of jealousy: that is, the sin of trying to corner the market on another person's inner life. The history of speculation shows us that trying to corner the market is always an act of hubris that leads to bankruptcy. The flow of another's feelings is not unlike the flow of a particular asset through the economy. Stopping the flow or attempting to contain it is a misapprehension of what feelings and assets are, which are inherently dynamic, without meaning or value in themselves but gaining meaning and value from their relationship to other feelings, other assets. Leontes' sin and punishment are ones he imposes upon himself, by mis-interpreting a personal relationship as a property relationship and discover-ing that the lost "property" is, indeed, irreplaceable. His misapprehension runs so deep that he can be saved only by what he interprets as a miracle; the recognition of the holy in another person is the one thing that counter-acts the idea that another person is merely an object to be exploited.

If marriage or partnership is for anything in this day and age, then it is for this: learning by experience how to express love. Compassion, tender-ness, patience, responsibility, kindness, and honesty are actions that elicit similar responses from others. These are not bargaining chips; when they are used that way they lose their essence as well as their ability to elicit any-thing from others but suspicion. Moreover, compassion, tenderness, pa-tience, responsibility, kindness, and honesty increase the happiness of the compassionate, tender, patient, responsible, kind, and honest man or woman, no matter what the response of others is, because they remind him or her of his or her own agency. To live in accordance with these qualities is to live by choice and awareness rather than by obliviousness and reactiveness. Who better to practice them with than someone whom you already love and who loves you, with whom you have agreed to seek happiness?

The social redemption of marriage in our time is precisely in intimacy as a countervailing force against the chaotic isolation promoted by free-market capitalism. If we can share with our spouses and understand that we both benefit, then we can share with our children and understand the same thing, and after that we can share with other children, and with our friends, with our communities, and with the larger community that is all around us, now rendered less fearsome by our own choice to approach it with a sense of connection. We can build up a network that reminds us over and over that connection is the very stuff of life, liberty, and the pursuit of happiness.

Am I the Oldest Living Monogamist?
Anne Roiphe

This selection comes from Anne Roiphe's 2002 book, Married: A Fine Predicament. *Roiphe is a novelist, literary critic, and magazine columnist.*

In 1973 as the new sexual freedoms were becoming commonplace, sweeping through middle-class homes such as ours, a sixteen-year-old teenager in my family turned to me in irritation one summer, a summer she was spending on the beach with boys and at late-night parties in the dunes (where what I was worrying about happening was happening), and said (in that tone of voice teenagers can use that produces in the listener the desire to grind the teeth), "You and Dad are the only people on the face of this planet who believe in fidelity anymore. You're so out of date." This stung. I had thought of myself as a revolutionary, a lover of freedom, a rebel against conventional bonds. I had worn black leotards in college long before this became the emblem of the new generation. I had engaged in premarital sex when my mother believed with all her soul that a loss of virginity would make me unmarriageable and condemn me to a life of single misery. I risked it. I had been ahead of my times, never a sheep that followed instructions. Nevertheless this teenager had a point. Now with a family I had become less of an adventurer and it was true I did value fidelity, not in the abstract but in the most particular, mine to him, his to me.

When I met my husband he was already divorced. I was a single mother. So I was surprised that after our first date which was on a Friday night he called and invited me out for the following Friday. I was surprised that after a month of Friday night dates he seemed not to want to come upstairs with me. Perhaps he was gay. Perhaps he was really married and I had been completely fooled. Perhaps he had problems. I had dated enough to know that all of the above could have been true. I knew that sex was not so simple for men as it might seem. I also knew I was listening for his voice, remembering his smile all through the week. Perhaps I should stop seeing him before I became so attached that a break would knock me down, bury me under a mountain of disappointment.

A few weeks later I asked him why he only saw me Friday nights. I was too shy to ask about why he hadn't even begun to approach any further intimate activity, though I could feel him wanting to. I wanted him and I couldn't believe he didn't know that. What he said in response surprised me. He had a relationship with another woman that he knew was not satisfactory. He had wanted to break it off before he had met me and it was gradually ending. He could not have two women at once. He needed to shed his Saturday night date before we could begin. Just as he promised me he did so the following week.

I could not ever violate such a man's trust. I knew he would not harm me. A man who cannot even date two ladies at once without suffering guilt, without feeling dishonorable, who must put it straight with the first before he can begin with the second, will not cheat, betray me behind my back. If this was the way he loved then I would love that way too.

There have been opportunities. I am at lunch with a man who has invited me out to discuss a book project he would like to work on with me. Before the coffee arrives he tells me he wants one more adventure in his life before age binds him to his home. I think he wants to climb a mountain or fly an airplane. It seems he wants to have an affair with me. He is appealing. He smiles at me. "What could be wrong?" he says. "It will be our secret." He offers a little excitement that won't hurt anybody. He takes my hand. I am pleased. When you are a married woman this does not happen very often. My feathers must still be shining. Why not? No one would have to know. I could play. I don't believe that sexual pleasure beyond the marital license is a serious sin. I don't believe in my immortal soul. My mortal soul gives me trouble enough. But then I think of something far worse than sin. I could hurt my husband whom I would never hurt, not for a second, and I would hurt him if for even one afternoon I went with this man and let him touch my body that knows so well my husband's body. I would defile the thing we do with each other in the bed when the children are sleeping. I am not sorry the man has asked me. A woman likes to know that her options are still there. But I am certain I will not accept. I am not afraid my husband will find out. I am afraid that my knowing will slide into my life with him, will destroy some absolute closeness we have achieved, will harm us both in some unknown way. I wonder if I am just conventional, afraid of life, too cautious for a swim in the wide sea. That is possible. But I have known what it is like to be alone in the world and I have known that I could not harm my love or even bring it into dangerous waters. Maybe this is fear. Maybe this is what we mean by love. I would not break his trust in me. After all my trust in him is the cornerstone of my life and all would tumble down without it. I drink my coffee and go home.

Monogamy has its price. But it has its rewards too. Would I be a more interesting person, a better lover to my spouse, a wiser woman had I met this one or that one in this place or that? I will never know. What I do know is that, reasonable or not, to be with another man in the ways I am with my husband is unthinkable, would violate the web of life we have spun together, would jar and tear at the very roots of our trust.

I know there are other ways of looking at this: other women play and consider it play. Other women do as they please, as suits them, other women are in marriages with men who disappoint in some profound ways and feel incomplete without the excitement and additional romance of an affair. I do understand that. There are men whose marriages have dried, who are contending with depressed or rage-filled wives, who are lonely beyond bearing. This is not a matter of sin, it is a matter of circumstance, need, soul. I myself can only be faithful, not because of a sacred vow, not because of the children (who are now grown and what I do is none of their business), but because I have something I do not want to bruise or crumple. I want my love just as it is for as long as fate allows it.

Does this make me a family values crusader in secular clothing? I don't think so. I don't believe that my way is the only way or the moral way to live. I respect the varied decisions people make about fidelity, the solutions they find to the stirring of their hearts and minds. I don't want to condemn anyone or legislate anything. What I do is my choice intended for my life alone. What others do is their own decision. We are all of us seeking to find safe havens, sparkling lights, warm spaces, to preserve the spirit. But how?

Grown-Up Love

Joan Konner

Joan Konner is a professor and dean emerita of the Columbia University Graduate School of Journalism. She has written and produced over fifty documentary films and has received twelve Emmys. This essay appeared originally in O, The Oprah Magazine *in February 2003.*

I have been researching the subject of love all my life. First, unsystematically, as a girl, trying to follow the programmed prescription — seeking "the one" and living happily ever after. Next I divorced and researched love as a woman, more systematically, confronting fantasies and failures, possibilities and disappointments, false starts, and at last, beginning 24 years ago, a love that's enduring and nourishing — at least for the moment (I've learned never to take the gift of love for granted).

Now I am on the case as a professional, a journalist who rebels against almost everything I see, hear, and read about love in the popular media. Every story insults my experience of love. Every story offers a ridiculous scenario that results in half-baked romance and scorched lives. There's the tragic version: Love, Obstacle, Separation, Loss (*Romeo and Juliet, Tristan and Isolde,* Erich Segal's *Love Story*). And there's the fairy-tale version: Love, Obstacle, Triumph, Happily Ever After (*Cinderella, My Big Fat Greek Wedding*). The obstacles — class, clan, race, work, conflicting dreams — provide the dramatic tension.

In America we live in a culture that glorifies passionate, romantic love. Our friends are in love, dreaming or daydreaming of it, waiting and dating to fall into it. Women and men begin new lives in love. Romantic love is our inspiration, our motivation — our reason to be. Romance is a cultural obsession, an imperial ideal. We believe that love can be found, here and now and forever, in an instant, across a crowded room — or tomorrow, just around the corner.

It can—but rarely. In reality, romance is more fleeting and more dangerous than we are told, more complicated than we could have imagined, more elusive than we've been led to believe. Love is a promise made every day only to be broken tomorrow.

As the Jungian analyst Robert Johnson wrote in *We: Understanding the Psychology of Romantic Love,* "The fact that we say 'romance' when we mean 'love' shows us that underneath our language there is a psychological muddle. . . . We are confusing two great psychological systems within us, and this has a devastating effect on our lives and our relationships."

In a documentary I'm researching and developing for television, I want to distinguish love from romance, to explore the ideal of true love, or real love, as Johnson describes it. Talking to Johnson, I told him that it seems to me that love, not romance, is the love we seek, the love we need, the love that enriches life and has the potential to make us happy. That's the story I want to tell, I said—a different story of love—and show its appeal to our deeper desires and nature.

"Good luck!" Johnson said. "In this society, nobody wants to hear about it. Even if it is the truth."

He may be right. Even our language undermines that story[. W]e use words like *settle* and *settle down* when we marry or accept a more stable relationship. We "compromise" for a mate who is flesh and blood if not quite the prince we imagined. Johnson calls the love he's talking about oatmeal love. Isn't there a tastier image? The very vocabulary advertises that the champagne of true love is flat.

If we care or dare to look at what those who have thought deeply about love have written, we could learn that romance is potentially transformational but never lasting. Research conducted by social scientists suggests that "romance" lasts 18 months to three years. (Isolde's love potion worked for three years before it wore off.) We could learn that sexual union is only one expression of transcendent passion and human connection. More often sex is neither. We could learn that although the chemistry of connection can occur in an instant, the passage of time—along with friendship and respect—is a crucial element of grown-up love, what might be called enlightened love.

"The passion of romance is always directed at our own projections, our own expectations, our own fantasies," Johnson writes. "It is a love not of another person, but of ourselves."

On the other hand, "Love is the one power that awakens the ego to the existence of something outside itself, outside its empire, outside its security."

Love, in other words, is transcending the ego to connect with another.

Johnson writes: "The task of salvaging love from the swamps of romance begins with a shift of vision. . . . Real relatedness between two people is experienced in the small tasks they do together: the quiet conversation when the day's upheavals are at rest, the soft word of understanding, the daily companionship, the encouragement offered in a difficult moment, the small gift when least expected, the spontaneous gesture of love."

Enlightened love is the connective tissue of existence—a state of being that exists regardless of our opinions of what it ought to be. We live for this kind of love. We work for this kind of love.

The noted psychoanalyst Ethel Person wrote in *Dreams of Love and Fateful Encounters:* "Love is an act of the imagination." She says, "Most of us are not originators of stories. Most of us pull our ideas of love from the culture, from the poets and artists who bring this form of desire and gratification together into one script, one scenario. Only then does the average individual try to change the imaginary act into a lived life." In other words: Me, Meg Ryan; you, Tom Hanks—even in New Jersey, maybe especially in New Jersey.

So love is a story we tell ourselves. Except the familiar love stories have gone stale. Today Cinderella's sisters hold jobs, and her stepmother has a support group. The prince buys Viagra on the Internet, and the king opens his castle to the public to make ends meet, if he's not trafficking in insider trading. Romance has been degraded into a sexual how-to. We need a new story or a new telling of the old story. We need a *Star Wars* of the heart—an epic, with heroes and heroines, huge challenges and glorious victories.

Here's a personal story:

It was our first vacation together now 24 years ago. We were rafting on the Rio Grande in central Colorado. Just the two of us, in a small rubber raft. No guide, as two inexperienced rafters probably should have had. The gray water was swift and turbulent. Rocks jutted out everywhere, jagged knives, sentries of slime, poised to rip our flimsy float. We twisted and spun in the flow. Now I was in front, then he, then I. Hoarse with fear, I shouted over the roar of the river: Paddle this way! Paddle that! I resurrected strokes from long-gone memories of summer camp. Pull the paddle! Push the paddle! (No time for feathering now.) We traveled like smoke in a breeze, for miles it seemed, when abruptly the river veered right and a tall wall of rock appeared directly in our path. "Back, back," I screamed. "Stroke! Back!" Though he must have heard, he did not heed me. He'd gone to camp, too—Boy Scout camp. He did what he had to do, issued orders of his own—not that I could see or hear beyond myself at that moment. Miraculously, we cleared the wall and headed into a lull in the river. In frustration and fatigue, I announced: "We have conceptual differences!" To which he answered: "Shut up and paddle." Not exactly what I might have dreamed of. But we were safe after all, and in relief and disillusion, we laughed and kept paddling down the canyon.

What is a story if not a metaphor, a myth in the making?

Love is a raft in a swiftly moving river, scant protection against rapids and rocks, a private place of smells and tastes, eloquent looks and intimate

15

20

touch, a cache of common dreams and accumulated history. We seek its secret, but it is as individual as one's own face, hidden even from ourselves. Me, Joan; you, Al. We have conceptual differences. We are conceptual differences. We don't even pull into the driveway the same way. But isn't that where love begins, in the difference — the otherness — that makes love possible, and necessary?

Love is the mystery of union, the distance to be transcended, the fuel to cross an infinity. It's another kind of math. Two times Love equals One. We are One and not One, a paradox in being. And that's only the half of it, maybe only half of the half — my half. We shout and we shut up. We laugh, we paddle. The fuel is a flame that flickers. We give it air, and we trust the flame will not go out. The dramatic tension is internal.

As Robert Heinlein told us in his 1961 novel *Stranger in a Strange Land:* "Love is that condition in which the happiness of another person is essential to your own." So simple — the happiness of the other is essential to our own. Practice it for homework. That's a how-to that bears repeating, on a daily basis. As one wise woman, who outlived three happy husbands, advised: "Find out what he doesn't like, and don't do it."

That's a love story I'd like to report, a story missing in the popular media. As Johnson said: It takes a shift of vision.

Questions for Discussion

1. "Happily Ever After?" is a good example of a case to convince. What evidence do Waite and Gallagher offer to convince readers that married people really are happier than unmarried people? Their argument illustrates the importance of definition (defining happiness), concession (some marriages are not happy), and refutation of an opposing view (that cohabitation is as good as marriage if not better). Discuss how effectively the authors build their argument. Are you convinced? Why or why not?

2. Waite and Gallagher make a strong case for marriage as a "transformative act" that creates a relationship of emotional support unlike anything possible through cohabitation. Interestingly, they steer clear of the gay and lesbian marriage debate. However, Gallagher writes frequently and strongly against gay and lesbian marriage. Gallagher and Waite make their case for marriage here on the grounds of personal happiness. However, Gallagher makes her case against gay marriage on different grounds. In the *Online National Review* of July 14, 2003, Gallagher writes, "Polygamy is not worse than gay marriage, it is better. At least polygamy, for all its ugly

defects, is an attempt to secure stable mother-father families for children. . . . By embracing gay marriage the legal establishment will have declared that the public purposes of marriage no longer include anything to do with making babies, or giving children mothers and fathers" (http://www.nationalreview.com/comment/comment-gallagher071403.asp). How does Gallagher's opposition to gay marriage affect your reading of her ethos in this selection?

3. Kipnis argues against the "tyranny" of "mature love." If you have read Fisher's "Web of Love" (pages 425–445), compare Kipnis's "mature love" with Fisher's "attachment" stage.

4. Since Kipnis doesn't use interviews, surveys, and scholarship as evidence, how does she make her case? How persuasive do you find her case? Evaluate specific parts of the argument that either work for you or don't.

5. Kipnis says that although love may be a universal emotion, our expectations for marriage are based on a "social contradiction the size of the San Andreas Fault: namely, the expectation that romance and sexual attraction can last a lifetime of coupled togetherness despite much hard evidence to the contrary" (paragraph 3). Does she offer any such evidence? If you have read Fisher's discussion of love, lust, and long-term attachment, does she give any evidence that would support Kipnis's point here?

6. Smiley argues that economic forces, capitalism in particular, have led to the destabilization of marriage. What are some of the ways she describes that life in a society like modern America tends to destabilize marriage?

7. Smiley explores the possibility of rejecting sexual exclusivity in oneself and one's partner. What kind of love does she envision, and what would be its advantages over fidelity in monogamy? Do you think it is possible not to feel possessive and jealous when someone you love loves not only you but another person?

8. What is Roiphe's reason for choosing fidelity in marriage? If you have read Smiley's "Why Marriage?" (pages 551–555), consider how her argument agrees and disagrees with Roiphe's.

9. Like so many other writers in this casebook, Konner complains that our idea of love is limited to what sells in popular culture: "passionate, romantic love." She compares romance to love, or grown-up love, which she also calls transcendent or enlightened love. What is "grown-up" about the kind of love she says we should celebrate? What is not grown-up about "romance"?

10. Do you think Robert Johnson was right in telling Konner that no one would want to hear stories about grown-up love? Do you know of any films, songs, or novels that depict the kind of love Konner would like to see more of in popular culture?

Suggestions for Writing

For Inquiry

To what extent do the different views of marriage by Kipnis on the one hand and by Konner and Roiphe on the other come down to a matter of different values and definitions of personal happiness? With which of these arguments do you feel more personal affinity? Why? What in your life experience might make you feel as you do?

For Convincing

Read the article in Section 2 titled "Who Wants to Marry a Soul Mate?" What is it that people are looking for in a soul mate? Review what Kipnis has to say about "mutuality" and "advanced intimacy." Is she describing a marriage based on the soul-mate concept? Do more research, including field research among your married and nonmarried friends. Arrive at your own definition of the soul-mate marriage, and make a case for or against that view of marriage. Some things to consider: Is it too private? Is it realistic?

For Persuasion

Konner quotes psychoanalyst Ethel Person: "Most of us are not originators of stories. Most of us pull our ideas of love from the culture, from the poets and artists who bring this form of desire and gratification together into one script, one scenario" (paragraph 15). If you have read the selections in Section One on the medieval troubadors' influence on the concept of love and on the wedding films' influence today, you will understand that stories tell us how to love. What new stories do Americans need to hear about love? If you know of couples — or even one couple — whose marriage or long-term relationship seems a good story for improving our understanding of love, write a nontraditional "persuasive" essay that tells their story in a way that might influence our understanding of love.

FOR FURTHER READING AND RESEARCH

Ackerman, Diane. *The Natural History of Love.* New York: Random House, 1994.

Batstone, David. "Click Here for Cupid." *Sojourners* Apr. 2004: 31. (About Internet dating.)

Buss, David M. *The Evolution of Desire: Strategies of Human Mating.* New York: Basic Books, 1994.

Fisher, Helen. *Why We Love: The Nature and Chemistry of Romantic Love.* New York: Henry Holt, 2004.

Ghebre-Ab, Rahwa. "Diverse Dating Has Benefits for Students." [U of] *Michigan Daily* 13 Feb. 2003. (About cross-cultural dating.)

Halikman, Ruth. "In Knots." *New Republic* (18 Oct. 1999). (About hassles of wedding planning.)

Ingraham, Chrys. *White Weddings: Romancing Heterosexuality in Popular Culture.* New York and London: Routledge, 1999. (On the wedding industry and its ideology.)

Kinnon, Joy Bennett. "The Shocking State of Black Marriage." *Ebony* Nov. 2003: 192.

Knox, David, et al. "College Student Attitudes toward Sexual Intimacy." *College Student Journal* June 2001.

Lambert, Tracy A., Arnold S. Kahn, and Kevin J. Apple. "Pluralistic Ignorance and Hooking Up." *Journal of Sex Research* May 2003: 129.

Mead, Rebecca. "You're Getting Married." *The New Yorker* 21 Apr. 2003: 76. (On the wedding industry.)

Roffman, Deborah. "What Our Kids Know about Sex: All Mechanics, No Meaning." *The Washington Post* 9 June 2002: B01.

Scruton, Roger. "The Moral Birds and Bees: Sex and Marriage, Properly Understood." *National Review* 15 Sept. 2003.

Whitehead, Barbara Dafoe, and David Popenoe. "Why Men Won't Commit: Exploring Young Men's Attitudes about Sex, Dating, and Marriage." *The State of Our Unions* (Nov. 2002) Rutgers Marriage Project. 26 Sept. 2004 <http://marriage.rutgers.edu/Publications/SOOU/SOOU2002.pdf>. (All past annual reports by the Rutgers Marriage Project are available at <http://marriage.rutgers.edu/>).

Wilding, Raelene. "Romantic Love and 'Getting Married'. Narratives of the Wedding in and out of Cinema Texts." *Journal of Sociology* Dec. 2003: 373.

Part Four Readings: Issues and Arguments

Chapter 12

Feminism: Evaluating the Effects of Gender Roles

In the United States, the women's rights movement dates back to the nineteenth century, when the main issues were full rights of citizenship and access to higher education. The women's movement was highly visible during the early part of the twentieth century, leading up to the achievement of voting rights in 1920. By that time, some women and men had realized that the fight for particular rights must be part of a larger revolution in society's attitudes toward the relationship between the sexes. Those who wanted to eliminate the long-standing, oppressive, and patriarchal attitudes that held women subordinate to men became known as feminists. The classic definition of feminism is simply the doctrine that women should enjoy all the rights—political, social, and economic—that men enjoy.

What became known as the "second wave" of feminism began in the 1960s and received its greatest impetus from the success of Betty Friedan's

1963 book, *The Feminine Mystique.* Friedan argued that a myth prevailed in American society that told women they could be happy and fulfilled only by accepting their "feminine" role as sexually passive, nurturing homemakers, content to live under male protection and domination. Second-wave feminism therefore advocated independence from men, liberation from the sexual double standard, and achievement in the world outside the home.

As the twentieth century moved to a close and the twenty-first century opened, debate increased about the nature of feminism. Some people argue that feminism is dead, that it is no longer needed, that we have entered the "postfeminist" era and the battles are over. In a 2001 study of young women aged 13–20, only 34% said they would call themselves feminists. Yet 97% said women should receive the same pay as men for the same work, and 92% agreed that "a woman's lifestyle choices should not be limited by her gender." In this same study, only 25% of these young women believe "there are still many inequalities between the sexes, and women need to continue to fight for their rights." However, in the 108th Congress, women made up only 14% of the Senate and 14.5% of the House of Representatives, and a study by the AFL-CIO in 2001 found women still earn, on average, 79 cents to every dollar earned by men. Because of statistics like these, Gloria Steinem, Betty Friedan, and other second-wave feminists say that women need to keep fighting for policies and projects that will give them greater equality in the twenty-first century: restructuring the workplace with child care, parental leaves, and flexible hours so that work and parenting are possible for both men and women; instituting a national program of child care as most other industrialized nations have; passing legislation to ensure shelter, adequate nutrition, and health care for children; and changing stereotypical gender roles to make men and women more equal inside the home.

We begin with an overview of the history of the American feminist movement and then turn to a series of arguments about equality and gender roles. Writing to young women today who take for granted the gains made by feminism, Jennifer Baumgardner and Amy Richards remind us all what life would be like for women today if feminism had not happened and the sweeping changes of the 1970s had never occurred. Suzanne Fields, offering an opposing view, describes women who have gone into the workforce and found that it did not offer them the fulfillment they expected.

These arguments address the problems of how women can have what they want from both gender roles: the same political power and professional opportunities that men have and the deeply satisfying role that traditionally belonged to a woman—caring for children and keeping a home. But in her 2000 book, *Unbending Gender,* Joan Williams suggests that this dilemma may result from the wrong assumptions about the goals of feminism. In a chapter from this book, she argues for a "reconstructive" feminism that would change not just women's roles but men's as well in both the home and the workplace.

We also include a classic argument about cultural impairment of opportunity for women in Western culture. Naomi Wolfe's introduction to her 1991 book, *The Beauty Myth: How Images of Beauty Are Used against Women*, argues that despite gains in equality, women continue to be oppressed by traditional images of feminine beauty that undermine their mental and physical health. But such Western concerns need to find their place in a larger context. In recent years, violations of human rights and women's rights in particular have been noted around the globe. In countries affected by war and economic collapse, millions of women and girls have been forced into prostitution, sex slavery, and domestic servitude in foreign lands. In the concluding essay, Katha Pollitt cites these and other abuses such as genital mutilation, forced marriage, AIDS, denial of education, and legalized wife murder as evidence of the need for an international feminist movement. In light of the abuses Pollitt discusses, it is difficult to say that we live in a "postfeminist" world.

What Is Feminism?

Cassandra L. Langer

This selection comes from the first chapter of Cassandra Langer's A Feminist
Critique: How Feminism Has Changed American Society, Culture and How
We Live from the 1940s to the Present *(1996). Here, Langer attempts to define
feminism by showing how events since colonial times have influenced the evolution
of the concept. Her purpose, however, is not merely to present a historical narrative
from a feminist perspective. She believes that reminders of the movement's historical
accomplishments will help modern feminists get beyond the current polarizations
that are weakening the movement.*

Today we are still grappling with Sigmund Freud's question, "What do
women want?" This is a fascinating, poorly understood, time-consuming,
and often disheartening topic to explore.[1] It's hard to make sense of the
ever-shifting points of view and developments within a social movement,
as well as the many academic controversies found in the popular presentations of it. The interests of feminism are varied, and the balancing of rights
against responsibilities still challenges us. The feminist critique is a way of
asking questions and searching for answers based on women's experience.
Although not all women want the same things, feminism has had an
unparalleled influence on American life and culture. [. . .]

The central goal of feminism is to reorganize the world on the basis of
equality between the sexes in all human relations. To advance their cause,
feminists have focused on a variety of problems, including patriarchy, gender modeling, individual freedom, social justice, equal educational opportunity, equal pay for equal work, sexual harassment, and human rights.
Unfortunately, woman's power in shaping governmental policy to her own
needs has been severely limited by the politics of gender. The revolutionary
fathers did not heed Abigail Adams's advice to her husband, John (who was
sitting as a delegate to the Continental Congress in Philadelphia in 1777),
when she wrote:

> In the new code of laws which I suppose will be necessary for you to make, I
> desire you would remember the ladies and be more generous and favorable to
> them than your ancestors. Do not put such unlimited power into the hands of
> the husbands. Remember, all men would be tyrants if they could. If particular
> care and attention is not paid to the ladies, we are determined to foment a
> rebellion, and will not hold ourselves bound by any laws in which we have no
> voice or representation.[2]

Among the mothers of the American Revolution, Abigail Adams is particularly prominent. Her strength of character and her patriotism stood the

severest test, and she realized that she could not simply surrender to the legislative process created by her husband and the Sons of Liberty. Unfortunately, she could not enforce her womanly sentiments, so they went unheeded.

Higher education for women became a primary goal of the reform movement. In the United States change came at a snail's pace. Only as women emerged from the home as public speakers and abolitionists could they effect any meaningful change in their conditions. Only by breaking the bondage of the home and the handicap of silence imposed on them by patriarchy did women begin to transcend their condition. The term *patriarchy* means a system of male authority that oppresses women through its social, political, and economic institutions. In all the historical forms that patriarchal society takes, whether feudal, capitalist, or socialist, a sex-gender system and a system of economic discrimination operate simultaneously. Patriarchy results from men's greater access to, and control of, the resources and rewards of the social system. Furthermore, specifically male values are expressed through a system of sanctions that reward the upholders and punish the transgressors.[3] In the socioeconomic sphere, women are disadvantaged by a system that favors men through legal rights, religion, education, business, and access to sex.

This imbalance led analytic feminists to coin the word *sexism*, a social situation in which men exert a dominant role over women and express in a variety of ways, both private and institutional, the notion that women are inferior to men. The terms *patriarchy* and *sexism* reflect women's rising awareness of the oppression women suffer under this system.[4] The British writer Virginia Woolf showed that she understood the circumstances that gave rise to these terms (long before the 1970s) when she argued that a woman needs financial independence and "a room of her own" to become herself. Woolf's 1929 essay "A Room of One's Own" is applicable today.[5] For the vast majority of women workers, finding a way to obtain better wages and working conditions is still a priority. Although the number of women who were "gainfully employed" increased rapidly during the nineteenth century, they were unable to control their own wages, legally manage their own property, or sign legal papers. The American writer Lydia Maria Child was outraged when she was not allowed to sign her own will; her husband, David, had to do it for her.

For these and other reasons, most feminists agree that poverty is not gender neutral. During the nineteenth century, inequities were worse for working-class women who could be forced to hand over all their earnings to an irresponsible husband, even if they were left with nothing for their own survival or the maintenance of their children. If a woman tried to divorce such a husband, he was legally entitled to sole guardianship of the children. In this system, a woman had no right to her own children, and male lawmakers customarily gave custody of the babies even to an

5

alcoholic father. Women were subordinate to men on the basis of discriminatory legislation, as well as men's exclusive ability to participate in
public life.

Many men, as well as women, rebelled against this unjust system, considering the marriage laws unfair and iniquitous because they gave men
control over the rights of women. Between 1839 and 1850, most states
passed some kind of legislation recognizing the right of married women
to own property. Women continued to struggle against the perception
that they were unfit to participate in government because of their physical
circumstances. Since the founding of our nation, the politics of reproduction has dominated social and economic relations between the sexes.
Because of gender manipulations, it becomes very difficult to see and
understand the realities of women's experience and how it affected
them. [. . .]

Organized feminism [. . .] began with the Seneca Falls Convention of
1848, an event that articulated what some American women wanted in
the mid-nineteenth century.[6] On July 19 and 20 of that year, five women
decided to call a Women's Rights Convention at Seneca Falls, New York, to
discuss the social, civil, and religious rights of women. During this period,
Elizabeth Cady Stanton and Lucretia Mott reviewed the Declaration of
Independence in light of their own experiences and those of other women.
Their Declaration of Principles, which fueled generations of women in their
bid for equality, declared: "The history of mankind is a history of repeated
injuries and usurpations on the part of man toward woman, having in
direct object the establishment of an absolute tyranny over her. To prove
this, let facts be submitted to a candid world."[7]

In a manner similar to the current presentation of facts offered by
the contemporary women's movement, these foremothers and others
introduced a range of issues that implicated men and showed how their
self-serving acts affected woman's status in society. These reforming women
had no illusions about the gender system and knew that their views would
be distorted. The declaration asserted, "In entering upon the great work
before us, we anticipate no small amount of misconception, misrepresenta-
tion, and ridicule; but we shall use every instrumentality within our
power to effect our object."[8]

The struggle was on. Margaret Fuller's brave book, *Woman in the
Nineteenth Century,* put it bluntly:

> We would have every arbitrary barrier thrown down. We would have every path
> laid open to Woman as freely as Man . . . then and then only will mankind
> be ripe for this, when inward and outward freedom for Women as much as for
> Man shall be acknowledged as a *right,* not yielded as a concession. As the friend
> of the Negro assumes that one man cannot by right hold another in bondage,
> so would the friend of Woman assume that Man cannot by right lay even well-
> meant restrictions on Woman.[9]

Indeed, women have been answering Freud's question for a long time. The main problem is that they still are not being heard.

The Civil War of 1861 helped bring women into national politics. After the victory, the intersection of the women's liberation movement and the emancipation of the slaves underscored the issue of enlarging the electorate. Since the blacks were now free citizens, they were entitled to the suffrage rights of citizens. Women saw this development as one that might bring them the vote as well. They were totally unprepared for the opposition of the Republican politicians and the desertion of their cause by the abolitionists, who had been their staunch allies. Appalled at the appearance of the word *male* in the proposed Fourteenth Amendment to the Constitution, Elizabeth Cady Stanton, Susan B. Anthony, and Lucy Stone, leaders of the liberation movement, raised the issue of whether women were actually citizens of the United States. The advocacy of "manhood" suffrage, as Stanton warned, "creates an antagonism between black men and all women that will culminate in fearful outrages on womanhood." [10] Men, including large numbers of white men, were concerned with ensuring the vote for black men, but they were little interested in how such a measure would affect women.

From a historical vantage point, Stanton's misgivings seem prophetic. Racism and the condition of women have continued to be explosive national issues since the Civil War. These twin injustices ignited the revolution of the 1960s and sparked the heated debates surrounding the Anita Hill and Clarence Thomas Senate hearings of the 1990s. [11]

The growing chasm between men and women, regardless of race, was thrown into sharp relief by the Fourteenth Amendment, which was passed in July 1868. Although Senator Cowan of Pennsylvania offered to strike the word *male* from the legislation, and Senator Williams of Oregon argued that the interests of men and women were one, their views were ignored. Williams understood that putting women in an adversarial, rather than a complementary, position in relation to men would eventually create a state of war and "make every home a hell on earth."

On the other side of the divide, Senator Frelinghuysen of New Jersey argued that women had a "holier mission" in the home, which was to assuage the passions of men as "they come in from the battles of life." When all was said and done, the hand that rocked the cradle still had no say in the process.

The beginning of the twentieth century saw American women still fighting for the right to vote. Inequities continued in education, marriage, property rights, legal rights, religion, and the realm of divorce. The years between 1910 and 1915 were a period of confusion and growth, during which a growing number of female workers were providing fresh arguments for women's suffrage. The foundation of the Women's Party in 1916 brought new energy into the political sphere. Twelve states had finally given women the vote, so that women now constituted a new force in the presidential election.

10

By this time, it was clear to all parties that the group that opposed   15
national suffrage for women would lose women's support in twelve states
that controlled nearly a hundred electoral votes. Even though the female
vote did not sway the election of 1916, women were able to win presidential support and reorganize their party. By 1918, after years of dogged effort,
the suffrage amendment passed by a vote of 274 to 136, exactly the two-
thirds majority required to accomplish it. After fifty-three years of progressive effort, women finally had won the right to vote. This was the wedge
women would need in the coming years to force their way past what
Carrie Chapman Catt warned suffragists would be "locked doors."

Women's greatest challenge, however, was not to gain the vote, but to
change patriarchal values. Their efforts were based on two assumptions:
(1) that a man claiming to be sensitive to what women want must first
recognize, as Fuller pointed out, that "Man cannot by right lay even
well-meant restrictions on Woman" and (2) that men who are humanists
can be persuaded to give up their unfair advantages voluntarily. These
assumptions bring forth an underlying assumption that feminism is both
a movement that strives for equal rights for women and an ideology of
social transformation whose aim is to create a better world for women
beyond simple social equity. In fact, feminism urges such men to question
the whole idea that an unfair advantage is really an "advantage." [. . .]

There are many different views and factions within feminism. The
movement encompasses major differences of opinion about how its goals
can best be achieved and how they should be defined. This situation is
not unusual, since in all the major movements in the history of ideas and
social reform, the participants have had such differences. What unites all
feminists, what they all have in common that makes them "feminists," is
the belief that they must question and challenge sexual stereotypes and
that opportunity should not be denied to either men or women on the
grounds of gender. Friedan, who is often called the mother of contemporary feminism, defined it as a conviction "that women are people in the
fullest sense of the word, who must be free to move in society with all the
privileges and opportunities and responsibilities that are their human and
American right." [12] This is a major aspect of "classical feminism." Its mission
is to achieve full equality for women of every race, religion, ethnic group,
age, and sexual orientation. [. . .]

A major premise of feminist theory is that sexual politics supports
patriarchy in its politicization of personal life. In such a system, the majority of men view women first and foremost as child bearers. So the female
body and how it is represented is continually and inevitably caught up in
any discussion of women's liberation. Most men imagine that women's
chief concerns, because of their reproductive biology, center on home and
family. Thus, a patriarchal system locks women into roles that are based
on their bodies' capacity to reproduce. Most men think of the home as the
physical space in which women do their work: housekeeping, cooking,

serving, taking care of the children, and other tasks associated with the domestic sphere. It is in this frame of reference that feminist theorists work.

The "myth of motherhood" and the cult of the nineteenth-century "true woman" persist. They categorize all women as mothers and caregivers even when they do not wish to perform these roles, or as Mary Wollstonecraft put it, "All women are to be levelled, by meekness and docility, into one character of yielding softness and gentle compliance." Under patriarchy, differences between men's and women's "true" natures have been based on a conviction that women have softer emotions than do men and that their job is to marry, produce children, and strengthen family life. According to this implied contract, as long as a woman sticks to the program, she is entitled to certain compensations and privileges. Thus, traditional marriage ensures a wedded woman's use of her husband's name and his protection and financial support. [. . .]

Although the 1950s were seen as a golden age of marriage and domesticity by many, Friedan's groundbreaking study of "The Happy Housewife Heroine" in *The Feminine Mystique* (1963) exposed the frustration of the unhappy, educated, middle-class, mostly white housewives between what they were supposed to feel and what they actually felt. Each one believed that "the problem that has no name" was hers alone—such was women's isolation from each other. At home, these women tried to make themselves beautiful, cultured, and respectable, but they were never really away from their children; they went marketing with their children, changed their children's diapers, talked about their children, and played mahjong or bridge.

"Raising three small children in suburbia," artist and writer Phyllis Rosser explained, "was the most depressing work I've ever done." Surrounded by baby bottles, cereal boxes, and dirty dishes, married women found that child rearing consumed most of their day. This was the "American Dream" that Rosser and millions of other intelligent American women were living, and for many it was a nightmare. Friedan's comparison of housewives' lives to conditions in Nazi concentration camps may seem extreme to many women (although many women viewed their mothers' lives this way), but during the 1960s, it struck a resounding chord for a generation of middle-class white women whose self-respect had been systematically destroyed by their inferior status as unpaid home workers and consumers.

The "mystique of feminine fulfillment" that Friedan chronicled emerged after World War II, when suburban housewives like my mother became the "dream image" of women all over the world. Behind it, as Friedan demonstrated, was anger and mental anguish—even insanity, brought about by the fact that they had no public careers. The loss of identity that came from being relegated to and isolated in the home created the psychic distress that many of these women experienced—"the problem with no name." It contributed to the depression and rage that many middle-class women of that generation felt because their contributions

20

to society were belittled and child rearing was not considered intellectually challenging. Friedan rejected the biological determinism of Freudian theory. Her view of women as a weaker social group led her to argue for a massive self-help program to help women reenter the labor market.

Inspired by Friedan's book, women began to form consciousness-raising groups. In the absence of psychological experts, women's own thoughts and feelings about marriage, motherhood, and their bodies began to emerge. They discovered that women were treated like children. In essence, they felt they had no identity of their own, which led them to sail boldly into the unknown in search of themselves. [. . .]

From the late 1960s to the mid-1980s, feminism was a clear force for progress and against alienation. Feminism's effects on gender issues, business, government, the military, education, religion, families, and dating and sexuality—in short, all aspects of life—was felt throughout the society and culture. But Friedan's book established a framework that was hostile to the traditional nuclear family and conventional female roles, and it seemed to exclude the homemaker from feminism's brave new world. The idea of staying home, raising a family, and doing housework was so negatively portrayed that it left no place for many women who wanted to do so.

During this stage, Kate Millett's *Sexual Politics* became a best-seller, and it was by far the most demanding feminist book of the 1970s. The author charged that throughout history, the interaction between men and women was one of domination and subordination. On the basis of this premise, Millett isolated "patriarchy," a pattern of male domination based on gender, as the chief institution of women's oppression. From this vantage point, it was reasonable to see the nuclear family as a "feudal institution that reduces women to chattel status." In such a system, there is no possibility of an honest disagreement among equals. In Millett's view, patriarchy authorizes the relative dominance of male domains over female ones. This dominance disadvantages women and puts them at the mercy of those who control the resources. In fact, women themselves are resources, like water or pastureland, to be traded among men. If a woman belongs to a man, she is like a slave; for example, a father may marry a daughter off against her will to further his own ambitions. The woman has no rights, and her offspring are her husband's property to do with as he likes. Millett's appraisal simply reiterated the judgments of nineteenth-century feminists, who saw a connection between the sexual division of labor in the home and in the workplace and women's oppression in modern industrial society.

According to Millett's reasoning, marriage is a financial arrangement—an exchange of goods and services in which men benefit and women lose. In this pooling of resources and sharing of responsibilities, one party, the man, retains everything he came into the marriage with, whereas in many cases, the woman brings a dowry with her, contributes free domestic and

25

child care services, and serves her husband and his career. If she has an education and aspirations of her own, they are sacrificed to the needs of her husband and family. [. . .]

Coming out of the first stage of the contemporary women's movement, Millett believed that her main concern was to find an explanatory theory for the subordination of women to men. In the United States, an alliance of conservative women and clergymen insists that woman's role is to be a homemaker and caretaker. Modernism and sexism view gender in terms of occupational specialties: Man is the hardworking provider who has liberated his woman from the burdens of production. Contrary to this model, Millett and many socialist feminists of the period believed that most women would be better off if they did not have to choose between their offspring and meaningful work. They argued for professional care of the young because it would allow women to [. . .] choose both. In short, they were attempting to change the prevailing idea that the domestic sphere was the sole appropriate domain of women. [. . .]

The 1960s and 1970s saw the emergence of many spokespersons for feminism, which led to the establishment of courses that introduced women into history. It was not surprising that with a discipline as new, as unusual, and as speculative as contemporary women's studies, dissension soon emerged. I think dissension arose for two reasons. First, some of the major feminist thinkers, such as Friedan, Millett, and Gloria Steinem, were inflexible about their initial theories—Steinem's notion of women's moral superiority, for example. Many people were put off, especially, by these women's views on the nature of men and women and on women's oppression in marriage, home, and bed. Second, and, in the long run, more important, was the natural growth and continuing outreach of the liberation movement itself. Changes in occupations, day care centers, dual earning capacity, and family leave have all contributed to a more egalitarian and less conventional contemporary lifestyle in the United States.

Despite these factional disputes about the actual conditions of women's lives, despite the hardships that the antifeminist backlash of the 1980s, with its attempts to scare women back into the home, imposed on those struggling for women's liberation, feminism has impelled all types of people to construct and reconstruct their respective roles in this society and culture. The current unrest and mood of apprehension that seems to pervade the women's movement arose from the fact that many people don't really understand the double bind that women are in. Moreover, women generally fail to see their own position within the private and public domains. Caught between their own lives and political ideologies, they are only beginning to gain some insight into how policy decisions are directed at them. The ongoing debates about welfare, for example, demonstrate how laws manage women and children. "Each time we talk about things that can be experienced only in privacy or intimacy," explained political scientist Hannah Arendt, "we bring them out into a sphere where they will assume a kind of reality, which, their intensity notwithstanding, they never could have had before."[13]

Nowhere is this situation more evident than in attempts to deal with women's experience in the world. Foes of feminism argue that contrary to what Friedan said, what happens in the home has an impact on society and the public sphere. Their relatively recent attempts to police the womb in order to protect the life of the unborn have collapsed the private into the public. The medical control of birth has given new meaning to the expression "the personal is the political." But what does this phrase really mean? As author Mary Gordon explained, "We have to examine the definition of the personal. . . . The personal and the private have long been the hiding place of scandals. As long as the personal is defined by men, and until men listen to what women consider the personal, neither side knows what the other is talking about."[14] So it is imperative to examine individual women's experiences to provide a framework of meaning: to understand women's experiences from the standpoint of how we actually live our lives, rather than through theoretical investigations. It is crucial to ask how we arrived at where we are now. This is far more important than knowing the political cataclysms that occurred along the way. Only by striving to transcend the unproductive polarization that has grown out of questions of private and public, identity and value, masculine and feminine, can we move beyond the play of politics and get closer to the true meaning of the movement to liberate women. [. . .]

[. . .] Between 1963 and the present, ideas stemming from the movement to liberate women have permeated psychology, sociology, anthropology, literature, art, and politics, and gained measurable influence over educational theory. Many people now recognize that inequality limits women's participation in public life and perpetuates the social emphasis on male values.

Feminism, for all its faults, has given birth to one of the few compelling visions of our era. It is a vision that attempts to deal compassionately not only with women's inequality, but with the pressing problems in the world.

The struggle for knowledge, for training, and for opportunity was first articulated by American women because of their discontent with women's status. This discontent gave birth to a reform movement on behalf of women. It was women's general belief that they were treated as mere chattel, having no rights whatsoever, existing merely to serve a father, husband, brother, or some other man. Such a picture contains partial truths. The stories of feminist networks, individual courageous acts, and collective pioneering exploits offer touchstones on the long road to answering Freud's question, "What do women want?"

Notes

1. For instance, Gloria Steinem's books make the best-seller list; Susan Faludi's blockbuster *Backlash* exposed an undeclared war against American women; Naomi Wolf's *Fire with Fire* urged women to seize the day; and in *Who Stole Feminism?* Christina Hoff Sommers accused feminist extremists of promoting a dangerous new agenda.

2. *Familiar Letters of John Adams and His Wife Abigail Adams during the Revolution* (New York, 1876) 286–87, letter dated March 31, 1776.

3. Maggie Humm, ed., *Modern Feminisms: Political Literary Cultural* (New York: Columbia UP, 1992) 408.

4. Marilyn French, *The War against Women* (New York: Summit, 1992).

5. Virginia Woolf, *A Room of One's Own* (New York: Harcourt, 1929).

6. For an excellent overview of these women and the events that shaped the women's rights movement, see Eleanor Flexner, *Century of Struggle: The Woman's Rights Movement in the United States* (New York: Atheneum, 1970).

7. Flexner 75.

8. Flexner 75.

9. Flexner 67.

10. Flexner 144.

11. Anna Quindlen, "Apologies to Anita" in the *New York Times* Nov. 1994: Op-Ed 5. See Jane Mayer and Jill Abramson, *Strange Justice* (New York: Houghton, 1994) regarding the many confusions about this historic case of sexual harassment and sexual politics.

12. Betty Friedan, *It Changed My Life: Writings on the Women's Movement* (New York: Random, 1976) 127.

13. Hannah Arendt, *The Human Condition* (Chicago: U of Chicago P, 1958) 50.

14. See "Mary Gordon and Robert Stone Talk about Sexual Harassment," in *Pen Newsletter* 85 (Fall 1994): 27.

For Discussion

1. To what extent were you already familiar with some of the people and events described in this reading? Did you know about the property laws, the contributions of women to the Seneca Falls Convention, or the attitudes of Abigail Adams? If you have been taught about the women's movement, was it part of a women's studies course or part of a course in U.S. history? If you have had little exposure to the subject, can you explain why that might be?

2. From this account, what seems to be the explanation of why black males were able to achieve voting rights before any women did, even though white women had more money and more education?

3. Langer states in paragraph 16 that feminists assume that "men who are humanists can be persuaded to give up their unfair advantages voluntarily." Is this what happened in the case of women gaining the right to vote, to be paid the same as men, or to serve alongside men in the military? Substitute "people" for "men" in this sentence, and discuss whether it holds true in general. Do problems come from the word "unfair"?

4. In paragraph 27, Langer presents Millett's argument that state-supported, professional child care would enable women to choose both raising children and engaging in "meaningful work." Does such language suggest that child rearing is not meaningful work? Does our society as a whole regard it as meaningful work? How does our society reward those in occupations that we respect?

For Research and Analysis

As examples of persuasion, some of the writings and speeches from female abolitionists are outstanding. Angeline Grimke's speech "Bearing Witness against Slavery" is particularly moving. Find one of these speeches or writings, and assess its rhetorical context: speaker, audience, occasion, purpose. Write an essay in which you describe the key persuasive strategies, such as identification, emotional appeals, and stylistic devices.

For Inquiry and Persuasion

Look at two or three contemporary U.S. history textbooks, for either high school or college, and compare their treatment of the women's movement. (Even high school texts are often found in your college library.) You might consider the amount of space allotted to the topic, the types of evidence included (for example, are there primary texts such as the portion of the letter from Abigail Adams?), and the perspective of the authors. Write an essay persuading an audience of teachers to adopt the textbook you think provides the best treatment of the issue, being very clear about what "best" means to you.

Cartoon
Kirk Anderson

The following cartoon appeared in Ms. magazine in 1993. How commonly do your friends and acquaintances share the attitudes expressed by these characters?

THE INCREDIBLE SHRINKING WOMAN

For Discussion

What is the point of the cartoon's title? What definition of "feminism" is being expressed? Evaluate the effectiveness of the cartoon as persuasion.

A Day without Feminism
Jennifer Baumgardner and Amy Richards

This essay is the prologue to Jennifer Baumgardner and Amy Richard's book Mani-festA: Young Women, Feminism, and the Future *(Farrar, Straus, and Giroux, 2000). Baumgardner and Richards were both born in 1970. Realizing that many women of their generation and younger say they are not feminists, they open their book with a reminder of what life would be like if feminism had never happened.*

We were both born in 1970, the baptismal moment of a decade that would change dramatically the lives of American women. The two of us grew up thousands of miles apart, in entirely different kinds of families, yet we both came of age with the awareness that certain rights had been won by the women's movement. We've never doubted how important feminism is to people's lives — men's and women's. Both of our mothers went to conscious-ness-raising-type groups. Amy's mother raised Amy on her own, and Jen-nifer's mother, questioning the politics of housework, staged laundry strikes.

With the dawn of not just a new century but a new millennium, people are looking back and taking stock of feminism. Do we need new strategies? Is feminism dead? Has society changed so much that the idea of a feminist movement is obsolete? For us, the only way to answer these questions is to imagine what our lives would have been if the women's movement had never happened and the conditions for women had remained as they were in the year of our births.

Imagine that for a day it's still 1970, and women have only the rights they had then. Sly and the Family Stone and Dionne Warwick are on the radio, the kitchen appliances are Harvest Gold, and the name of your Whirlpool gas stove is Mrs. America. What is it like to be female?

Babies born on this day are automatically given their father's name. If no father is listed, "illegitimate" is likely to be typed on the birth certificate. There are virtually no child-care centers, so all preschool children are in the hands of their mothers, a baby-sitter, or an expensive nursery school. In ele-mentary school, girls can't play in Little League and almost all of the teach-ers are female. (The latter is still true.) In a few states, it may be against the law for a male to teach grades lower than the sixth, on the basis that it's unnatural, or that men can't be trusted with young children.

In junior high, girls probably take home ec; boys take shop or small-engine repair. Boys who want to learn how to cook or sew on a button are out of luck, as are girls who want to learn how to fix a car. *Seventeen* maga-zine doesn't run feminist-influenced current columns like "Sex + Body" and "Traumarama." Instead, the magazine encourages girls not to have sex; pleasure isn't part of its vocabulary. Judy Blume's books are just beginning

5

to be published, and *Free to Be . . . You and Me* does not exist. No one reads much about masturbation as a natural activity; nor do they learn that sex is for anything other than procreation. Girls do read mystery stories about Nancy Drew, for whom there is no sex, only her blue roadster and having "luncheon." (The real mystery is how Nancy gets along without a purse and manages to meet only white people.) Boys read about the Hardy Boys, for whom there are no girls.

In high school, the principal is a man. Girls have physical-education class and play half-court basketball, but not soccer, track, or cross country; nor do they have any varsity sports teams. The only prestigious physical activity for girls is cheerleading, or being a drum majorette. Most girls don't take calculus or physics; they plan the dances and decorate the gym. Even when girls get better grades than their male counterparts, they are half as likely to qualify for a National Merit Scholarship because many of the test questions favor boys. Standardized tests refer to males and male experiences much more than to females and their experiences.[1] If a girl "gets herself pregnant," she loses her membership in the National Honor Society (which is still true today) and is expelled.[2]

Girls and young women might have sex while they're unmarried, but they may be ruining their chances of landing a guy full-time, and they're probably getting a bad reputation. If a pregnancy happens, an enterprising gal can get a legal abortion only if she lives in New York or is rich enough to fly there, or to Cuba, London, or Scandinavia. There's also the Chicago-based Jane Collective, an underground abortion-referral service, which can hook you up with an illegal or legal termination. (Any of these options are going to cost you. Illegal abortions average $300 to $500, sometimes as much as $2,000.) To prevent pregnancy, a sexually active woman might go to a doctor to be fitted for a diaphragm, or take the high-dose birth-control pill, but her doctor isn't likely to inform her of the possibility of deadly blood clots. Those who do take the Pill also may have to endure this contraceptive's crappy side effects: migraine headaches, severe weight gain, irregular bleeding, and hair loss (or gain), plus the possibility of an increased risk of breast cancer in the long run. It is unlikely that women or their male partners know much about the clitoris and its role in orgasm unless someone happens to fumble upon it. Instead, the myth that vaginal orgasms from penile penetration are the only "mature" (according to Freud) climaxes prevails.

Lesbians are rarely "out," except in certain bars owned by organized crime (the only businessmen who recognize this untapped market), and if lesbians don't know about the bars, they're less likely to know whether there are any other women like them. Radclyffe Hall's depressing early-twentieth-century novel *The Well of Loneliness* pretty much indicates their fate.

The Miss America Pageant is the biggest source of scholarship money for women.[3] Women can't be students at Dartmouth, Columbia, Harvard,

West Point, Boston College, or the Citadel, among other all-male institutions. Women's colleges are referred to as "girls' schools." There are no Take Back the Night marches to protest women's lack of safety after dark, but that's okay because college girls aren't allowed out much after dark anyway. Curfew is likely to be midnight on Saturday and 9 or 10 p.m. the rest of the week. Guys get to stay out as late as they want. Women tend to major in teaching, home economics, English, or maybe a language — a good skill for translating someone else's words.[4] The women's studies major does not exist, although you can take a women's studies course at six universities, including Cornell and San Diego State College.[5] The absence of women's history, black history, Chicano studies, Asian-American history, queer studies, and Native American history from college curricula implies that they are not worth studying. A student is lucky if he or she learns that women were "given" the vote in 1920, just as Columbus "discovered" America in 1492. They might also learn that Sojourner Truth, Mary Church Terrell, and Fannie Lou Hamer were black abolitionists or civil-rights leaders, but not that they were feminists. There are practically no tenured female professors at any school, and campuses are not racially diverse. Women of color are either not there or they're lonely as hell. There is no nationally recognized Women's History Month or Black History Month. Only 14 percent of doctorates are awarded to women. Only 3.5 percent of MBAs are female.

Only 2 percent of everybody in the military is female, and these 10 women are mostly nurses. There are no female generals in the U.S. Air Force, no female naval pilots, and no Marine brigadier generals. On the religious front, there are no female cantors or rabbis, Episcopal canons, or Catholic priests. (This is still true of Catholic priests.)

Only 44 percent of women are employed outside the home. And those women make, on average, fifty-two cents to the dollar earned by males. Want ads are segregated into "Help Wanted Male" and "Help Wanted Female." The female side is preponderantly for secretaries, domestic workers, and other low-wage service jobs, so if you're a female lawyer you must look under "Help Wanted Male." There are female doctors, but twenty states have only five female gynecologists or fewer. Women workers can be fired or demoted for being pregnant, especially if they are teachers, since the kids they teach aren't supposed to think that women have sex. If a boss demands sex, refers to his female employee exclusively as "Baby," or says he won't pay her unless she gives him a blow job, she either has to quit or succumb [. . .]. Women can't be airline pilots. Flight attendants are "stewardesses" — waitresses in the sky — and necessarily female. Sex appeal is a job requirement, wearing makeup is a rule, and women are fired if they exceed the age or weight deemed sexy. Stewardesses can get married without getting canned, but this is a new development. (In 1968 the Equal Employment Opportunity Commission — EEOC — made it illegal to forcibly retire stewardesses for getting hitched.) Less than 2 percent of dentists are women; 100 percent of dental assistants are women.

The "glass ceiling" that keeps women from moving naturally up the ranks, as well as the sticky floor that keeps them unnaturally down in low-wage work, has not been named, much less challenged.

When a woman gets married, she vows to love, honor, and obey her husband, though he gets off doing just the first two to uphold his end of the bargain. A married woman can't obtain credit without her husband's signature. She doesn't have her own credit rating, legal domicile, or even her own name unless she goes to court to get it back. If she gets a loan with her husband—and she has a job—she may have to sign a "baby letter" swearing that she won't have one and have to leave her job.

Women have been voting for up to fifty years, but their turnout rate is lower than that for men, and they tend to vote right along with their husbands, not with their own interests in mind.[6] The divorce rate is about the same as it is in 2000, contrary to popular fiction's blaming the women's movement for divorce. However, divorce required that one person be at fault, therefore if you just want out of your marriage, you have to lie or blame your spouse. Property division and settlements, too, are based on fault. (And at a time when domestic violence isn't a term, much less a crime, women are legally encouraged to remain in abusive marriages.) If fathers ask for custody of the children, they get it in 60 to 80 percent of the cases. (This is still true.) If a husband or a lover hits his partner, she has no shelter to go to unless she happens to live near the one in northern California or the other in upper Michigan. If a woman is downsized from her role as a housewife (a.k.a. left by her husband), there is no word for being a displaced homemaker. As a divorcée, she may be regarded as a family disgrace or as easy sexual prey. After all, she had sex with one guy, so why not *all* guys?

If a woman is not a Mrs., she's a Miss. A woman without makeup and a hairdo is as suspect as a man with them. Without a male escort she may be refused service in a restaurant or a bar, and a woman alone is hard-pressed to find a landlord who will rent her an apartment. After all, she'll probably be leaving to get married soon, and, if she isn't, the landlord doesn't want to deal with a potential brothel.

Except among the very poor or in very rural areas, babies are born in hospitals. There are no certified midwives, and women are knocked out during birth. Most likely, they are also strapped down and lying down, made to have the baby against gravity for the doctor's convenience. If he has a schedule to keep, the likelihood of a cesarean is also very high. *Our Bodies, Ourselves* doesn't exist, nor does the women's health movement. Women aren't taught how to look at their cervixes, and their bodies are nothing to worry their pretty little heads about; however, they are supposed to worry about keeping their little heads pretty. If a woman goes under the knife to see if she has breast cancer, the surgeon won't wake her up to consult about her options before performing a Halsted mastectomy (a disfiguring radical procedure, in which the breast, the muscle wall, and the nodes

15

under the arm, right down to the bone, are removed). She'll just wake up and find that the choice has been made for her.

Husbands are likely to die eight years earlier than their same-age wives due to the stress of having to support a family and repress an emotional life, and a lot earlier than that if women have followed the custom of marrying older, authoritative, paternal men. The stress of raising kids, managing a household, and being undervalued by society doesn't seem to kill off women at the same rate. Upon a man's death, his beloved gets a portion of his Social Security. Even if she has worked outside the home for her entire adult life, she is probably better off with that portion than with hers in its entirety, because she has earned less and is likely to have taken time out for such unproductive acts as having kids.[7]

Has feminism changed our lives? Was it necessary? After thirty years of feminism, the world we inhabit barely resembles the world we were born into. And there's still a lot left to do.

Notes

1. Phyllis Rosser pioneered the research that named the gender gap in SAT and PSAT scores. She wrote to us as we were finishing the book that in the past couple of years "the gender gap on the PSAT has narrowed from 45 to 20 points (in SAT terms). This means that women will receive about $1,500,000 more in scholarship money in 2000 than in previous years." See Rosser's book, *The SAT Gender Gap: Identifying the Causes,* published by the Center for Women's Policy Studies (1989) for more information.

2. In 1999, the Women's Rights Project of the American Civil Liberties Union (ACLU) won a landmark Title IX case. Two high-school girls from Covington, Kentucky, brought suit against the National Honor Society for ignoring their qualifying GPAs in light of their pregnancy and parental status. The school district argued that the girls weren't denied admission because of their parental status (and implicitly acknowledged that such a practice would be unlawful) but because "they engaged in premarital sex." The school relied solely on pregnancy as proof of sexual activity, though, a determining factor that can apply only to women. (No males had ever been excluded from the school's chapter of the National Honor Society on grounds of having had sex—Title IX prevailed!)

3. Beauty contests are still the largest source of college scholarships for women. For example, the Miss America winner receives upward of $50,000, and the Miss America Organization has given more than $100 million in grants since 1945, when it began awarding scholarships. It remains the largest "scholarship organization" in the world.

4. Anonymous was a woman, as were the translators of most "great" works. For instance, the first English translation of *The Communist Manifesto* was done by a woman, Helen McFarlane. We intend to have any translations of *ManifestA* done by a man.

5. Before 1969, there were no women's studies departments, and very few individual courses. As of 2000, the National Women's Studies Association counted 728 women's studies courses in their database in the United States alone.

6. The McGovern-Nixon election of 1972 marked the emergence of a "gender gap," the first election in which there was a clear difference between men's and women's voting patterns. During the 1980 Carter-Reagan election, the gap had become wide enough for politicians to worry about getting the women's vote. (Only 46 percent of women voted for Reagan, according to the Gallup poll, but 54 percent of men did.)

7. Statistics and facts from "A Day without Feminism" come from a few sources: *The American Woman 1994–95: Where We Stand, Women and Health,* edited by Cynthia Costello and Anne J. Stone for the Women's Research and Education Institute (New York: W. W. Norton, 1994); *The Book of Women's Firsts,* by Phyllis J. Read and Bernard L. Witlieb (New York: Random House, 1992); *Mothers on Trial: The Battle for Children and Custody,* by Phyllis Chesler; *The Reader's Companion to U.S. Women's History;* and the U.S. Bureau of Labor Statistics.

For Discussion

1. Child care in 1970 was seen as the responsibility of the mother. Day care was an option for wealthy women who wanted to pursue careers. How has this situation changed?
2. The authors remind you that girls' sexuality was not acknowledged in 1970. Discuss in what ways women have become the sexual equals of men and in what ways they still have not. What has been the effect of concern over sexually transmitted diseases?
3. Baumgardner and Richards point out that there were few tenured female professors at universities in 1970. Discuss with your instructor what tenure means and what professors must do to acquire it. How many tenured females are on the faculty at your university, and in what departments or disciplines do most of them teach? If you find that women are underrepresented in some departments or the school as a whole, discuss the possible causes of that.
4. Take into consideration all the topics covered by Baumgardner and Richards's day without feminism. Which seem hard to believe from today's perspective? Which seem to linger on in some form even today?
5. Baumgardner and Richards write with an informal style. Find some passages that exemplify a colloquial and/or humorous tone. Discuss their rhetorical effectiveness, given the authors' audience, purpose, and the seriousness of their message.

For Research and Convincing

Do you observe inequality between the genders today in any of these areas: the workplace, the classroom, the playing fields in sports, the household, the church, the political arena—or any other area? If you do, single out one or two related areas, and do more research to confirm or cast doubt on your conclusions about the inequality. Find out what laws or protections already exist with the goal of eliminating the inequality. In an essay, make a case that feminism still has work to do, at least in this area. Or, if you find no real problems in any of these areas, make a case that feminism has completed its work.

For Research and Persuasion

If your library has a copy of Baumgardner and Richards's book, read the epilogue, in which they describe "A Day with Feminism," a day in the future when current inequalities will have been erased. If you cannot get hold of their book, use your own observations and research to determine some inequalities that affect women today—or combine your own observations with some of theirs. Then, write an essay similar to Baumgardner and Richards's description of the year 1970, but describing 2005. You might imagine that you are writing in 2050, to an audience then who would find today's inequalities hard to imagine, perhaps to your own grandchildren.

Mission No Longer Impossible—Or Is It?
Suzanne Fields

Suzanne Fields is a syndicated columnist who comments here on the appearance in the late 1990s of several books by women who decided work outside the home was not as fulfilling as they had believed it would be. Notice that Fields is not actually reviewing these books in any depth but simply informing her readers about this new set of complaints. As you read, decide what her own position is on the issues raised by these books.

Four decades ago Betty Friedan, in her groundbreaking book, *The Feminine Mystique,* wrote about women who suffer "a problem that had no name." They were sick and tired of being sick and tired of having no identity to call their own: "The problem is always being the children's mommy, or the minister's wife, and never being myself." One woman described her situation as living in a "comfortable concentration camp."

There's a new problem without a name now and it's a mare of another color. Women are complaining about work and writing about it. Elizabeth Perle McKenna left a high-powered position in publishing to search for the neglected parts of her life. In writing *When Work Doesn't Work Anymore,* she found lots of baby boomers like herself who had bought into what they call the New Oppression—hard-earned success. The symptoms include burnout, boredom and lack of balance.

The boomers are the polar opposites of Friedan's suburban housewives. Typical then was the mother of four who complained that she'd tried everything—hobbies, gardening, pickling, canning, socializing with neighbors, joining committees, running PTA teas. "I love the kids and Bob and my home," she said. "There's no problem you can even put a name to. But I'm desperate. I begin to feel I have no personality."

How spoiled this woman can sound to a young mother today, who has to work to support her family and who would be thrilled to have the time to garden and can fruits and vegetables. But she sounds no more spoiled than the new whiners who complain that they're undervalued by their bosses, unfulfilled by their careers and enraged by workaholic lives where they must always hide their inner feelings. Who ever said work would be easy? (Certainly not a man.)

"I became the title on my business card," says one woman. "And while it was never a totally comfortable fit, I gauged it to be an essential part of my wardrobe, like panty hose or a brief case." She learned not to protest having to work on Saturday when there was a strategic-planning meeting, instead of taking the kids to a matinee, and never to refuse to work late. She learned to stay cool in the face of office politics and backstabbing.

5

With the hindsight that comes from living with half a loaf, rather than talking about what women want, even Gloria Steinem chastises these boomer women. "If I had a dollar for every time we said you couldn't do it all, I'd be rich," she says. "Look at me, I don't have it all; I never had or wanted children. And I know I couldn't have done what I have with my life if I'd had them." (So that's what she meant when she said "a woman needs a man like a fish needs a bicycle.")

Iris Krasnow, formerly a feature writer for United Press International, who interviewed the rich and the famous and gave it all up to raise a family, tells a different tale. In *Surrendering to Motherhood* (to raise four sons), she writes that she found spiritual fulfillment and deep satisfaction in newly acquired domesticity. As a full-time mother she enjoys "the liberation that comes from the sheer act of living itself."

Friedan has discovered a new "paradigm," too. In her book, *Beyond Gender,* she calls for moving beyond identity politics to reframe family values in the interest of putting children first.

Two boomer ladies, Barbara McFarland and Virginia Watson-Rouslin, agree. They've rediscovered their mothers' wisdom, written about it in a new book called simply, *My Mother Was Right,* and offer this insight: "It is now occurring to us that the person we rebelled against, whom we used as a role model of how we would not like to lead our lives and who upheld outmoded ideas on the place a woman should take in society and how she would behave . . . may not have been entirely wrong."

What goes around comes around.   10

When columnist Hall Lancaster asked his *Wall Street Journal* readers to help him craft a mission statement, referring to ends and goals in life, love and work, more than 200 readers wrote about what sounds like a mission impossible. The tsunami of advice ranged from "obtaining eternal bliss to losing 20 pounds by Christmas" to "the astral projection route." For some readers it was all a matter of business procedures. Others emphasized dreams, visions, values, instincts and purpose. Some suggested he write his own obituary and still others told him to return to the pleasures of childhood.

He finally settled on the two aspects that are most important to him—his writing and his family: "My mission is to enlighten and entertain people through my writing and to help provide a life for my family that is emotionally and financially secure, loving, learning and fun."

So true. Doesn't that sound just like a woman?

For Discussion

1. What is the "mission" that Fields suggests is no longer "impossible"? Does she actually conclude that women as well as men can have it all? Does the man's "mission" statement in paragraph 11 sound like a real possibility for either sex?

2. How can you explain the happiness these women claim to have found in domesticity when the women Friedan interviewed in the 1950s felt so confined by domestic life?

3. A survey conducted for *American Demographics* magazine of young women aged 13–20 found that 56% had mothers who worked full-time outside the home throughout the girls' childhood, and 57% of the young women expect to do the same. Only 9% of these young women believed "a woman's place is in the home" ("Granddaughters"). Consider the advice of Barbara McFarland and Virginia Watson-Rouslin in paragraph 9 of Fields's essay. Discuss how different generations may have different ideas of gender roles depending on the role models they know as they grow up.

4. Of the Fortune 500 companies, only 5% are headed by women. There is still a glass ceiling in the business world. And women now make 76 cents for every dollar earned by men. Are women more likely than men to find the kind of workplace complaints listed in paragraph 4 of Fields's essay?

For Persuasion

Do research about men who have chosen to switch traditional gender roles with their wives and stay at home to take care of the home and children. How do they describe their motivations for doing this? Make an argument to persuade other men who might have considered domesticity to go ahead and take the plunge.

For Inquiry and Convincing

Do research about women who have tried to "do it all." Make a case that it is or is not possible. Be sure to define what you mean by "it." Does "it" include success in a competitive and well-paying job? A successful marriage? A close relationship with their children? Does "it" mean living the exact same life as a family man? You might conclude that doing it all is possible provided that certain conditions exist.

Work Cited

"Granddaughters of Feminism." *American Demographics* 1 Apr. 2000: 43.

Cartoon

B. Smaller

"Sex brought us together, but gender drove us apart."

For Discussion

The speaker is describing a relationship that broke up. Have cultural definitions of gender caused conflict in your own romantic relationships?

Reconstructive Feminism
Joan Williams

Knowing the difference between sex and gender is important in understanding this essay, which is an excerpt from Joan Williams's book Unbending Gender: Why Family and Work Conflict and What to Do About It *(Oxford, 2000).* Sex *refers to biological difference, whereas* gender *and* gender roles *refer to the behavior that is typical for each sex within a culture. Williams, a professor at American University Law School, argues that a gender role system that she calls "domesticity" emerged in the United States around the beginning of the nineteenth century, assigning the role of breadwinner to the male sex and the role of homemaker to the females. Domesticity meant that the worker outside the home was freed from household responsibilities, and that is how the workplace has come to define its ideal workers: people who work at least forty-hour weeks, put in long overtime, travel when the job demands it, and never take personal time off for the demands of family. Williams's argument is that feminism, rather than seeking to change women's roles and lives so that they can participate in this system in a way equal to men, needs to redefine its mission to mean nothing less than changing the system itself. In this excerpt, she describes how Betty Friedan's feminism put women into the impossible predicament of trying to "have it all" as she defines a more family-friendly brand of feminism.*

The traditional feminist strategy for women's equality is for women to work full time, with child care delegated to the market. Economist Barbara Bergmann has christened this the "full-commodification strategy." Its most influential exposition was in Betty Friedan's 1962 book, *The Feminine Mystique.*[1]

This strategy proved extraordinarily effective in starting what Friedan called a "sex-role revolution": Whereas few mothers of young children were in the labor force in the 1960s, most are today. But what is required to start a revolution is often different from what is required to complete it. [. . .]

Friedan defended the full-commodification model by depicting housewifery as virtually a human rights violation, culminating in her famous analogy to a concentration camp.[2] In the popular imagination, feminism still is linked with the glorification of market work and the devaluation of family work. This leaves many women confused once they have children. When they feel the lure and importance of family work, they are left with the sense that feminism has abandoned them.[3] Mothers who frame their lives around caregiving may feel that feminism contributes to their defensiveness at being a part-time real estate agent or "just a housewife."

Another challenge for feminism is the sense that "all feminism ever got us was more work."[4] This reflects the situation that has resulted because the full-commodification model did not go far enough in deconstructing domesticity. This model glossed over the fact that men's market work always has been, and still is, supported by a flow of family work from women. Because women do not enjoy the same flow of family work from men, allowing women to perform as ideal workers means that most must do so without the flow of family work that permits men to be ideal workers. The result is that most women go off to work only to return home to the second shift, leaving many feeling distinctly overburdened and skeptical of feminism.

These forces have exacerbated the unpopularity of feminism among many Americans. "Don't use the word," warned a publisher, "you'll lose half your audience." A 1998 *Time*/CNN survey found that only about one-quarter of U.S. women self-identify as feminists, down from one-third in 1989; just 28 percent of those surveyed saw feminism as relevant to them personally. A common rejoinder is that a "feminist majority" supports programs such as equal pay for equal work. But the sharp disparity between support for feminist programs and support for "feminism" reinforces the sense that feminism is not a beckoning rhetoric.[5]

In part feminism's unpopularity reflects only that it is, inevitably and appropriately, inconsistent with femininity's demands for compliant and reassuring women rather than "strident" and "ball-busting" ones. But the high levels of unpopularity are tied as well to the specific inheritance of the full-commodification model. This chapter explains how and argues for a mid-course correction. Feminists need to abandon the full-commodification model in favor of a reconstructive feminism that pins hopes for women's equality on a restructuring of market work and family entitlements. Instead of defining equality as allowing women into market work on the terms traditionally available to men, we need to redefine equality as changing the relationship of market and family work so that all adults—men as well as women—can meet both family and work ideals. This new strategy holds far greater potential for raising support for feminism by building effective coalitions between women and men, as well as with unions, the "time movement," and children's rights advocates. [. . .]

[. . .] Access to market work was not a key agenda for women's rights advocates in the first half of the nineteenth century. They focused instead on gaining entitlements for women based on their family roles.[6] It was only after the Civil War that feminists began to focus on equal access to market work as the key to women's equality. Indeed, feminists from other countries often have a hard time understanding U.S. feminists' obsession with market work.[7] Why did it take on such profound importance?

Feminists' emphasis on market work reflects the freighted quality of work roles in the twentieth century. In prior eras, privileged women did not need market work to maintain their social position. In the eighteenth century status was tied not to work roles but to class: Privileged women enjoyed high levels of deference and respected social roles by virtue of their membership in the elite. This tradition of social deference gradually ended in the nineteenth century, but by then privileged women had begun to transform their accepted role as the moral beacons of the home into leadership roles within their communities. Women joined clubs, societies, and associations that took active leadership roles in many communities, and engaged in activities that subsequently have turned into consumer, welfare, and environmental activism and social work. Through the female moral reform and temperance movements, women began to challenge traditional male privileges, notably the sexual double standard and the traditional right of a man to "correct" his wife. The "age of association" offered huge numbers of women interesting work and a respected role in their communities.[8]

As the twentieth century progressed, the work formerly performed by married women in associations gradually was professionalized and taken over by men, and the Woman's Christian Temperance Union and like organizations ceased to be sources of status and became objects of derision. People began to place in work the hopes for vocation and self-fulfillment that earlier eras had reserved for religion. With increases in mobility and new patterns of social isolation, work often represented people's chief social role and the center of social life. By midcentury, for all but a tiny group of the very rich, social status was determined by work roles. Arlie Hochschild argues in her [1997] book, *The Time Bind*, that today work has become the center of workers' social and emotional as well as their economic lives.[9] Work also provides the key to most social roles involving authority and responsibility even when those roles do not stem directly from the market.

Friedan's emphasis on market work reflects not only the end of the era of women's associations but also the withering of respect for women's domestic role. *The Feminine Mystique* reflects housewives' lack of status by the 1960s. "What do I do? . . . Why nothing. I'm just a housewife," quotes Friedan. In a world where adult "success" was defined by work, housewives lost a sense of self. "I begin to feel I have no personality. I'm a server of food and a putter-on of pants and a bedmaker, somebody who can be called on when you want something. But who am I?" said one. And another: "I just don't feel alive." Friedan concludes: "A woman who has no purpose of her own in society, a woman who cannot let herself think about the future because she is doing nothing to give herself a real identity in it, will continue to feel a desperation in the present. . . . You can't just deny your intelligent mind; you need to be part of the social scheme." To a nineteenth-century "moral mother," the notion that she played no part in the social scheme would have seemed bizarre.[10]

Meanwhile, increasingly misogynist attacks on housewives at midcentury were linked with the anxiety produced by the changing roles of men. Books such as David Reisman's 1950 *The Lonely Crowd* and William Whyte's 1956 *The Organization Man* reflected widespread fears that men, formerly manly and inner-directed, were becoming feminized and outer-directed by the lockstep of corporate life. Said Reisman, "Some of the occupational and cultural boundaries have broken down which help men rest assured that they are men." Whyte and Reisman painted a picture of "outer-directed" men eager for approval. They reflected men's sense of an imagined past where they had independence and autonomy. Men's sense of loss was exacerbated by their loss of patriarchal authority over children, as a result of the growing importance of peer influence attributable to the rise of mass consumer culture and the spread of secondary schools. Cartoons, films, and studies abounded with imagery of henpecked men unable to stand up to domineering wives.[11] The "moral mother" had become the domineering housewife.

Friedan's belittlement of housewives was an ingenious use of misogynist stereotyping in the cause of women's liberation. She deployed misogynist images of women as evidence that the breadwinner/housewife model hurt not only women but their families as well. She skillfully turned the literature attacking housewives into evidence in favor of the need to eliminate the housewife role. She argued, first, that housewifery frustrated women so much that they made their husbands' lives a misery. To these arguments Friedan added a deadpan public health perspective: "The problem that has no name . . . is taking a far greater toll on the physical and mental health of our country than any known disease."[12]

In summary, the full-commodification strategy arose in a social context where work roles determined social status and personal fulfillment to an extent they never had before. Access to market work seemed particularly important because the only accepted alternative, the housewife role, had lost the cultural power it had enjoyed during the nineteenth century, and had become the object of misogynist attack. Ironically, the cultural devaluation of housewives ultimately came to be associated not with misogyny but with feminism. As we will see later, this stemmed in part from events that occurred after Friedan had ceased to dominate the feminist scene.

Friedan's goal was to start a "sex-role revolution." To accomplish this, she had to downplay the changes necessary to incorporate mothers into market work. First, she minimized the difficulty of finding a responsible job after a period out of the workforce. She pointed to the suburban housewife who found "an excellent job in her old field after only two trips to the city." "In Westchester, on Long Island, in the Philadelphia suburbs," she continued breezily, "women have started mental-health clinics, art centers, day camps. In big cities and small towns, women all the way from New England to California have pioneered new movements in politics and education. Even if this work was not thought of as a 'job' or 'career,' it was often so important that professionals are now being paid for doing it." "Over and over," she continued, "women told me that the crucial step for them was simply to take the first trip to the alumnae employment agency, or to send for the application for teacher certification, or to make appointments with former job contacts in the city." The only thing women had to fear, Friedan implied, was fear itself.[13]

She also minimized the question of who would take care of the children. "There are, of course, a number of practical problems involved in making a serious career commitment. But somehow those problems only seem insurmountable when a woman is still half-submerged in the false dilemmas and guilts of the feminine mystique." Friedan criticized one woman willing to accept only volunteer jobs without deadlines "because she could not count on a cleaning woman. Actually," Friedan tells us, "if she had hired a cleaning woman, which many of her neighbors were doing for much less reason, she would have had to commit herself to the kind of assignments that would have been a real test of her ability." Would a "cleaning woman" really have solved this family's child care problems? Typically they come only once a week.[14]

This was one of the rare moments where Friedan mentioned household help. Her erasure of women's household work was strategic, for she knew full well what was required for a wife and mother to go back to work. When she returned to work in 1955, she hired "a really good mother-substitute—a housekeeper-nurse." But she carefully evaded this threatening issue in *The Feminine Mystique*. It soon returned to haunt women.[15]

Friedan's evasion of these difficult issues was understandable, and probably necessary, at the time she wrote *The Feminine Mystique*. If she had demanded that husbands give up their traditional entitlement to their wives' services, husbands simply would have forbidden their wives to work. If she had admitted the difficult obstacles mothers would face in a work world designed for men, her revolution never would have gotten off the ground. To give Friedan her due, she did reopen each of these questions as soon as she felt she could. By 1973 she was demanding that men share equally in family work, a theme she had mentioned but downplayed eleven years earlier. She also argued that it was "necessary to change the rules of the game to restructure professions, marriage, the family, the home." Finally, in 1981, Friedan picked up a theme she had not stressed twenty years before: that our society devalues work traditionally associated with women. In her controversial *The Second Stage*, Friedan bent over backward to send the message that she was no longer belittling family work, and demanded that work be restructured around its requirements.[16]

But by this time Friedan was no longer in control of the conversation she had helped create. Popular feminism fossilized into the full-commodification strategy and stayed there. Some feminists engaged in frontal attacks on homemaking, as in Jessie Bernard's statement that "being a housewife makes women sick." That statement was repeated almost verbatim a quarter century later in Rosalind C. Barnett and Caryl Rivers's *She Works/He Works*, which asserted in 1996 that "[t]he mommy track can be

15

bad for your health." *She Works/He Works* dramatizes the extent to which popular feminism remains stuck in the full-commodification model. It reports that women are now happy and healthy in the workforce, men are helping at home, and children are better off than ever in day care. It glosses over the pervasive marginalization of mothers, the widespread sense of strain among parents of both sexes, and the central fact that mothers' entrance into the labor force has not been accompanied by fathers' equal participation in family work.[17]

In fact, the drawbacks of the full-commodification model became evident as early as the 1970s. Some drawbacks concern its hidden racial and class dynamics. [. . .] Other dynamics became apparent much earlier. One way to trace the dawning recognition of these drawbacks is through stories in women's magazines in the 1970s through the 1990s. *Glamour* and *McCall's* are most useful for this purpose.

Articles in the 1970s showed great excitement about the prospect of going to work and remind us what a big step it was to take even a part-time job for little money. "I got the check from *Glamour* and bought some schoolmarm clothes. For the first time since we'd been married, I didn't feel guilty spending money on myself," recounted one woman. Another article on the same topic commented, "A very striking conclusion to come out of the questionnaire is that six out of ten women who work believe that what suffers most . . . is the quality of their housekeeping, but their letters are eloquent testimony that their most frequent reaction is, 'So what!'" This article discussed the excitement of market work and the challenges of combining this new role with their existing workload: "I don't think you have to make a choice. I never felt I had to compromise my femininity to continue to work. . . . It makes perfect sense to me to move from one area to another (i.e., home to office). In one day, I pick a fabric for a chair, arrange a party, sign a business deal, pay bills and give rich attention to my husband and children." Other articles are more realistic but still upbeat: "There is a whole generation of liberated young women who are quietly putting the ideals of revolution into practice, combining marriage, motherhood, and a master's degree, cooking and career. . . . Combining the two is far from an easy task. It is not an impossible dream but it takes hard work. The trick is in learning how; the art is in doing it well." This was the era of the Enjoli perfume ad: "I can bring home the bacon, fry it up in a pan. And never, never, never let you forget you're a man." A TV jingle declared:

> I can put the wash on the line,
> feed the kids, get dressed, pass out the kisses
> And get to work by five to nine
> 'Cause I'm a woman.[18]

By 1975 one begins to hear of "casualties." "For more than two years, Ms. Chechik ran her own interior design boutique. Being mother, wife, homemaker and career woman had . . . exhausted her physically and

20

mentally. . . . She explained that by the time she finished all her housework, it was one or two in the morning 'and I was so hyper I couldn't sleep.' When she began breaking out in hives, [she] decided that something had to go: it was the boutique." Men also awoke to the implications of the new trends: "My husband doesn't *mind* my working, but he won't help me. He says when I can't do my own work then I'll have to quit. So naturally I don't ask him to do anything for me." Said one husband, "Now it's all very fine to agree that today's women should have more rights, but whom do they think they are going to get them from? From me, that's who. Well, I don't have enough rights as it is." [19]

Articles in the 1980s show the dawning recognition that entering the workforce without changing the conditions of work resulted in longer working hours for women. The term superwoman was coined in the early 1980s, implicitly blaming the situation on women themselves. The term deflected attention away from the fact that women were forced to do it all because men would not give up their traditional entitlement to women's household work. [. . .]

In the popular imagination, feminism came to be associated with careerists whose model of equality married them to money rather than to caregiving. Thus, to Deborah Fallows, "the feminist movement seemed mainly to celebrate those heroines who had made their mark in business, politics, or the arts; and magazines like *Working Mother* tried to say it was all pointless anyway, since working makes for better mothers and stronger children." Fallows bristled when she heard Gloria Steinem on the radio decrying the "narrow and stifled" lives of women at home. "The feminists may officially say that 'choice' is at the top of their agenda for women. But there are too many hints and innuendos that suggest that this talk comes fairly cheap." [20]

If the first liability of the full-commodification model is its devaluation of family work, the second is its denial that structural changes are necessary in order for women to reach equality. Women's entrance into the workforce without changes to either the structure of market work or the gendered allocation of family work means that women with full-time jobs work much longer hours than women at home. Although it made perfect sense for Friedan to argue in 1962 that women should join the workforce without waiting for changes from their husbands, their employers, or the government, it quickly became apparent that "having it all" under these circumstances often leads to exhausted women doing it all. [21] [. . .]

In "The Superwoman Squeeze" in 1980, *Newsweek* spotted the syndrome Arlie Hochschild named the "second shift" nine years later. [22] That article painted a picture of "an eighteen-hour mother" who works incessantly from sunup to midnight, while her husband "occasionally helps clean up or puts the boys to bed. But for the most part, Jim reads in the living room while Sue vacuums, does late-night grocery shopping, grades papers from 9 P.M. to 11 P.M. and collapses." *Newsweek* documents the "guilt, the goals, and the go-it-alone grind [that] have become achingly

25

familiar to millions of American women." "Now we get the jobs all right," said one woman, "all the jobs: at home, with the kids, and at work."[23]

In her brilliant 1989 book *The Second Shift*, Arlie Hochschild sought to transform work/family conflict from being evidence against feminism into proof of the need for more of it. She argued that men were enjoying the benefits of wives' salaries but refused to share equally in household work. Through carefully constructed narratives, she communicated the message that women's failure to perform as ideal workers was attributable in significant part to their husbands' failure to shoulder their fair share of family work.[24]

Hochschild crystallized an important change. Once husbands lost their felt entitlement to have women do all the housework, the revised standard version of the full-commodification model stressed the need to reallocate household work. This was a shift in focus away from early feminists' reliance on the government, as they envisioned day care centers as being as common, and as free, as public libraries. Thus the solution Hochschild highlighted in the first edition of her bestseller was a redistribution of family work between fathers and mothers (a shift from her path-breaking call nearly twenty years earlier for restructuring of "the clockwork of male careers").[25]

Another element of the full-commodification model was its focus on relatively privileged women. This emphasis was reflected both in the assumption that market work meant high-status, high-paying careers, and in the assumption that child care should be delegated to the market, often without much consideration of what this would mean for women who cannot afford quality child care.[26]

The final assumption of full-commodification feminism was that women should be ready, willing, and able to delegate child care to the same extent male ideal workers do. This proved the most problematic assumption of all.

THE NORM OF PARENTAL CARE

Every day I leave my kids at day care, I think to myself: *What kind of a mother am I?* It's like I'm not raising my own children.[27]

The biggest problem as I see it for both men and women [lawyers] is how to balance children in a large-firm environment. I plan to go part-time when I have a child, and I *hate* the idea. If the firm had a 24-hour day care or nursery, I would not work part-time—I would stay full-time. Obviously, even this is no solution: kids can't grow up in a day care center.[28]

A central assumption of the full-commodification model was that women would feel comfortable delegating family work to the market to the same extent traditional fathers had. Many don't. [. . .]

30

Lillian Rubin comments, "The notion that mom should be there for the children always and without fail, that her primary job is to tend and nurture them, that without her constant ministrations their future is in jeopardy, is deeply embedded in our national psyche." Mothers who do not stay home often find themselves wondering, as did the woman quoted earlier, "What kind of a mother am I?" Sometimes this manifests as explicit gender policing; an extreme example is the hate mail received by the Boston family whose nanny killed their son. "It seems the parents didn't really want a kid," said one caller to a talk show host. "Now they don't have one." Note that the mother "at fault" worked only part time.[29]

[. . . T]wo-thirds of Americans believe it would be best for women to stay home and care for family and children. In significant part, this reflects the paucity of attractive alternatives.[30] In European countries, the shift of mothers into the workforce was supported through government benefits. In Russia and Eastern Europe, programs included maternity leave with guaranteed reemployment, sick leave, and paid time off for child care and housework. In Western Europe, high-quality child care is provided or subsidized by the government. In France, an extensive system of neighborhood child-care centers exists throughout the country, staffed by trained teachers and psychologists, with ready access to medical personnel, so that children's illnesses are both spotted and treated at the center. Parents fight to get their children in, with the sense that being in child care helps children develop social skills. In Belgium and France an estimated 95 percent of nursery-school-age children are in publicly funded child care. Sweden also has a comprehensive system of quality child care.[31]

In the United States, feminists' dream that day care facilities would be as common as public libraries never came true. In 1971, when Congress passed the Comprehensive Child Development Act, President Nixon vetoed it under pressure from an intense lobbying campaign that decried the proposal as "a radical piece of social legislation" designed to deliver children to "communal approaches to child-rearing over and against the family-centered approach." A 1975 proposal was also defeated, decried as an effort to "sovietize the family." As a result, the United States offers less governmental support for child care than does any other industrialized nation. The successful efforts to defeat the kinds of proposals implemented in Europe dramatizes how profoundly U.S. women have been affected by Americans' distinctive lack of solidarity.[32]

As a result, the imagery and the reality of day care are different here than elsewhere. Where child care is prevalent and government-sponsored, it is seen as an expression of social solidarity and national investment in the next generation. In sharp contrast, in the United States, day care is seen as an expression of the market. These perceptions are accurate in part. In countries with significant government support for child care, notably France, child-care workers are well-paid civil servants with steady and respected employment. Child care in the United States, in sharp contrast, suffers from very low wages and very high turnover. One child-care worker of my acquaintance works for Head Start; after fourteen years and several promotions, she now earns about $14,000 a year. At these pay rates, high rates of turnover are not surprising. Nor is it surprising that many Americans have a negative image of day care centers. While many centers are excellent, market realities militate against quality child care.[33]

Day care in the United States also suffers from imagery and symbolism   35 derived from domesticity. Recall the insistent split between home and market. [. . . D]omesticity from the beginning provided very negative images of the market. If economics encapsulates our positive imagery of the market as the benign deliverer of quality goods to satisfied customers, domesticity embeds very different imagery of the market as a selfish and calculating world out of touch with people's needs for genuine intimacy. Throwing child care into this metaphoric maelstrom in a society without a third realm of social solidarity results in a predictable revulsion against market solutions. Some people preserve the negative market imagery for day care centers and contrast it with their chosen form of care. Despite the shift of child care into the market, today most Americans choose child care that is as homelike as they can manage. Keep in mind that one-third of married mothers, and a slightly higher percentage of single ones, are home full-time. Most children not cared for by their mothers are cared for by another relative — care by relatives (typically fathers or grandmothers) accounts for nearly 50 percent of all children in child care. Another 22 percent are cared for by nannies in their own homes, or in the homes of their sitters. All in all, in one-half to one-third of families, mothers are at home. In the remaining families, about 70 percent of children are in care associated with home or family. Only about 30 percent of children in child care are in day care centers.[34] [. . .]

A second major force feeding the resistance to day care as a solution is the sharp increase in the number of hours in the workweek. Juliet Schor, in *The Overworked American,* documented that Americans' average workweek has lengthened in recent years. Increases are concentrated in "good" jobs with a high benefits "load," which include high-paying blue-collar jobs as well as many high-status white-collar jobs. Factory workers in 1994 put in the highest levels of overtime ever registered. Nearly one-fourth of office workers now work forty-nine or more hours a week. A survey of Fortune 500 corporations in the 1970s found that many managers worked sixty hours a week or more, excluding business travel: "They'd leave home at 7:30 A.M. and return home about the same time that evening. They'd also bring home a few hours of work each day." This has not changed much. [. . . O]ne-third of fathers work forty-nine or more hours a week; in high-status white-collar jobs it is closer to 50 percent. Said one forty-one-year-old public relations officer in a major corporation: "I can't imagine having a baby, which I want to do, and still keeping this job. All corporate jobs are like this — you're valued according to the long hours you are willing to put in, and the schedule is so rigid that anyone who wants to do it differently has to leave." Schor notes, "The 5:00 Dads of the 1950s and 1960s (those who were home for dinner and an evening with the family) are becoming an endangered species." The increase in hours means that an ideal worker with a half-hour commute to a "good" job often will be away from home from 8:00 A.M. to 7 P.M. Very few people would consider this an ideal schedule for both parents in a family with children. The result is often that, among people with access to "good" jobs, fathers work overtime while mothers work part-time or on the no-overtime mommy track. Families see little choice.[35]

The forces named thus far—the lack of social solidarity and the sharp increase in working hours—are peculiar to the United States. However, data from Sweden raise intriguing questions about whether the full-commodification model is viable even where these peculiarly American conditions do not exist.

Sweden has implemented the full-commodification model with a level of commitment higher than anyplace else in the world. As a result of a severe labor shortage in a country with no self-consciousness about crafting governmental solutions to social problems, Sweden encouraged workforce participation by mothers by providing child care as well as generous parental leaves available to either parent, accompanied by government efforts to increase men's participation in family work.

The result has not been equality for women. Swedish mothers still suffer marginalization in order to care for children. As of 1986, 43 percent of working women were employed part time. Women continued to do a disproportionate share of family work and took fifty-two days of leave for every day taken by a man. Industrial workers were much less likely to take parental leave than were professional and public employees. Sweden's level of sex segregation is *higher* than even our own very high level: One study concluded that 70 percent of all women would have to change occupations for women to achieve the same occupational distribution as men. Swedish women earn only 37 percent of the country's total wages.[36]

These findings place the full-commodification strategy in a somber light. The Swedish example suggests that many people in advanced industrialized countries feel that having both parents working the ideal-worker schedule is inconsistent with the level and type of parental attention children need. This reflects the fact that children's success in these middle-class societies depends in part on parents' ability to instill the discipline, motivation, and independence necessary to do well in middle-class life.

To say this in a less clinical way, one key to success in life is having your children turn out well: healthy, well-adjusted, secure, successful (in widely varying senses of the word). We are willing to give up a lot to achieve this; often we do. In the face of our dreams for our children, marginalization at work often seems a price worth paying even if it may lead to disappointments or to economic vulnerability later on in life.

40

All this suggests that it is time to acknowledge the *norm of parental care.* Let me say loud and clear that this is not the same as saying that children need full-time mothercare. Domesticity's mother-as-sole-source ideal is not ideal at all. Its most important drawback is that it links caregiving with disempowerment. Not only does this make children vulnerable to impoverishment if their parents divorce; it also means that the adults who know our children best and are most invested in meeting their needs have relatively little power within the household and outside of it. Sociological studies since the 1960s have documented that power within the family generally tracks power outside it.[37] [. . .]

While Friedan was right to reject that model, the time has come to abandon the fiction that both mothers and fathers can perform as ideal workers in a system designed for men supported by a flow of family work from women. We need to open a debate on how much parental care children truly need given the trade-offs between providing money and providing care. A good place to start is with the consensus that children are not best served if both parents are away from home eleven hours a day. This means that the jobs that require fifty-hour workweeks are designed in a way that conflicts with the norm of parental care.

Beyond the fifty-hour week, little consensus exists about how much child care is delegable. However, once feminists name and acknowledge the norm of parental care, discussions of how much delegation is too much will replace conversations in which mothers protest that they "chose" to cut back or quit when further investigation reveals that they did so because they could not find quality child care, or because the father works such long hours that without a marginalized mother the children would rarely see a parent awake.

A formal acknowledgment of the norm of parental care will serve a second important purpose as well: to empower mothers in situations where their partners meet demands for equal contributions to family work by claiming that virtually all child care is delegable. This dynamic does not emerge when mothers marginalize without a fuss; in such cases the conclusion that not all child care is delegable typically is treated as a matter of consensus. But when mothers refuse to follow docilely in domesticity's caregiver role, a game of chicken emerges in which fathers advocate higher levels of delegation than mothers consider appropriate. The classic example is of the high-status father who advocates hiring two sets of nannies to give sixteen hours of coverage so that no one's career is hurt. Or the father who suggested that his wife hire a babysitter to care for the children during a weekend when he had promised to be available so that she could take a long-planned trip. One ambitious father expressed it this way: "Over-involvement with children may operate to discourage many fathers from fully sharing because they do not accept the ideology of close attention to children."[38] Until this "ideology" is formally stated and publicly defended, mothers will have their decision to marginalize cited as evidence of their

45

own personal priorities (for which they should naturally be willing to make trade-offs) rather than as an expression of a societal ideal (for which parents share equal responsibility).

Naming and acknowledging the norm of parental care can help poor women as well as more privileged ones. One central difficulty in the welfare reform debate is the lack of a language in which to defend the right of poor women to stay home with their children, in a society where the child care available to them is often not only unstimulating but downright unsafe. [. . . I]t is hard to defend poor women's right to stay home in a society where a much higher percentage of poor women than of working-class women are homemakers: about 33 percent of poor women are at home, but only about 20 percent of working-class ones. This situation is bound to generate working-class anger. Naming the norm of parental care is not enough to change the dynamics of the welfare debate; that will require a social system where working-class as well as poor children are seen as being entitled to a certain amount of parental care. But acknowledging the existence of a norm of parental care is an important first step.[39]

Defining the norm of parental care starts from an assessment of children's needs, and then splits the resulting responsibilities down the middle. In such a world, mothers' work patterns would look much more similar to fathers'. Consider the following example. Say the parents of elementary-school children decide that one parent needs to be home two days a week, to drive the children to doctor and dentist appointments, to enable them to take lessons not available in the after-school program, to help with homework, to allow for play dates. Then the father and the mother would both work four days each week, and half a day or not at all the fifth. This would be much easier for an employer to accommodate than if the mother comes in alone demanding a three-day week. "They are so unreasonable," a top manager complained to me recently. "A woman came in demanding a three-day schedule. We told her she could either work four days a week and keep her [middle-level] management position, or three days a week in which case she would have to give it up, because things around here just won't run with a three-day-a-week manager. She got angry and quit." If fathers were truly sharing in family work, mothers' demands would be much easier to accommodate. This would end the situation where the only viable alternative a family sees is to have the mother quit or go part-time (making, on average, 40 percent less per hour than a full-time worker), in which case the father has to work overtime to make up for the loss in income. A more equal sharing of market and family work would also avoid the situation where, if the parents divorce, the children are impoverished along with their marginalized mother. We have much to gain from shifting to a strategy of reconstructing both the ideal-worker and marginalized-caregiver roles we have inherited from domesticity. The time has come to abandon the full-commodification strategy in favor of ending the system of providing for children's care by marginalizing their caregivers. This is the agenda of reconstructive feminism.

[. . .] In my view feminism has never been anti-family, but the time has come to point out that feminism is pro-family, in that it advocates changes that will help children as well as women. The system of providing care by marginalizing the caregivers hurts not only children but also the sick and the elderly. The current system rests on the assumption that all people at all times are the full-grown, healthy adults of liberal theory, making the social compact and pursuing citizenship and self-interest within it. This is a very unrealistic view of human life. The time has come to recognize that humanity does not consist only of healthy adults. We have changed from a society that formally delegates to women the care of children, the sick, and the elderly to a society that pretends those groups do not exist. The result, to women's credit, is that women still do the caregiving. But they pay a stiff price for doing so. [. . .]

[. . .] The early feminist vision of two parents working forty-hour weeks did not come to pass; neither did the vision of child-care centers being as common and as respected as public libraries. What we have instead [. . .] is an economy of mothers and others, where many fathers work overtime and a majority of mothers are not ideal workers. This chapter proposes that we abandon the full-commodification strategy in favor of transforming domesticity's norm of mothercare into a template for restructuring the relationship of market work and family work.

If we as a society take seriously children's need for parental care, it is time to stop marginalizing the adults who provide it. The current structure of work is not immutable: it was invented at a particular point in time to suit particular circumstances. Those circumstances have changed. [. . .]

50

Notes

1. Betty Friedan, *The Feminine Mystique* (1962; 1983). Barbara Bergmann, *The Only Ticket to Equality*, 9 J. Contemp. L. Issues 75 (1998).

2. Friedan, *supra* note 4, at 282 *et seq.* (concentration camp).

3. Anna Quindlen, *Let's Anita Hill This*, N.Y. Times, Feb. 28, 1993, at 15 ("At a meeting I attended, one of the women said that the women's movement had been the guiding force in her life until she had children, and then she felt abandoned by feminist rhetoric and concerns.")

4. Steven A. Holmes, *Is This What Women Want?*, N.Y. Times, Dec. 15, 1996, at 1 (quoting Heidi Hartman: "That may be feeding some of the backlash against feminism among some women. People are saying that all feminism ever got us was more work").

5. *See* Ginia Bellafante, *Feminism: It's All About Me!*, Time, June 29, 1998, at 54. The "feminist majority" argument is associated with the Fund for a Feminist Majority, now called the Feminist Majority Foundation.

See <http://www.feminist.org>. *See also* Nancy Levit, *The Gender Line* 123–67 (1998).

6. Reva Siegel, *Home as Work*, 103 Yale L. J. 1073.

7. *See, e.g.*, Paolo Wright-Carozza, *Organic Goods: Legal Understandings of Work, Parenthood, and Gender Equality in Comparative Perspective*, 81 Cal. L. Rev. 531 (1993).

8. *See* Barbara L. Epstein, *The Politics of Domesticity: Women, Evangelism, and Temperance in Nineteenth Century America* (1981). *See generally* Sara Evans, *Born for Liberty: A History of Women in America* 67–143 (1989) (discussing emergence of women's associational activity); *see also* Epstein, *supra* note 10, at 115–51 (1981) (describing growth of Woman's Christian Temperance Union), Evelyn Brooks Higginbotham, *Righteous Discontent: The Women's Movement in the Black Baptist Church, 1880–1920* (1993).

9. Arlie R. Hochschild, *The Time Bind: When Work Becomes Home and Home Becomes Work* (1997).

10. Friedan, *supra* note 1, at 24 (first quote), 21 (second), 22 (third), 343–44 (fourth).

11. *See* Wini Breines, *Young, White, and Miserable: Growing Up Female in the Fifties* 28–29 (1992); *id.* at 32–33 (quoting Reisman).

12. *Id.* at 364. *See* Glenna Matthews, *"Just a Housewife"* 197–200 (1987) (misogynist stereotyping); Friedan, *supra* note 1, at 350, 364.

13. Friedan, *supra* note 1, at 384 (sex-role revolution), 349 (only two trips), 345 ("now being paid"), 349 (last quote).

14. *Id.*

15. Daniel Horowitz, *Rethinking Betty Friedan and* The Feminine Mystique: *Labor Union Radicalism and Feminism in Cold War America*, 48 Am. Q. 1, 20 (1996) (Friedan quote).

16. *See* Friedan, *supra* note 1, at 350, 354, 385; Betty Friedan, *The Second Stage* (1981).

17. Breines, *supra* note 14, at 32–33 (first quote: quoting Jessie Bernard); Rosalind C. Barnett & Carl Rivers, *She Works/He Works: How Two-Income Families Are Happier, Healthier, and Better Off* 32 (1996) (second). *See also* Jessie Bernard, *The Future of Marriage* (1972, reprint 1973).

18. Rivvy Berkman, *The Funny, Searching, Scary, Devastatingly Honest Diary of a Young Woman's Decision to Return to Work*, Glamour, Sept. 1971, at 280 (schoolmarm clothes); Vivian Cadden, *How Women Really Feel About Working*, McCall's, June 1974, at 125 (So what!); Roberta Brandes Gratz & Elizabeth Pochoda, *Women's Lib: So Where Do Men Fit In?*, Glamour, July 1970, at 138 (rich attention; not an impossible dream); Claudia Wallis, *Onward, Women: The Superwoman Is Weary, the Young Are Complacent but Feminism Is Not Dead, and Baby, There's Still a Long Way to Go*, Time, Dec. 4, 1989, at 80, 81 ("fry it up in a pan"); Lynn Langway, *The Superwoman Squeeze*, Newsweek, May 19, 1980, at 256 (TV jingle).

19. Shirley G. Streshin, *The Guilt of the Working Mother,* Glamour, Sept. 1975, at 256 (Mrs. Chechik); Gratz & Pochoda, *supra* note 21, at 138 (not enough rights).

20. Deborah Fallows, *A Mother's Work* 28, 214 (1985) (all three quotes).

21. *See* Joan C. Williams, *Gender Wars: Selfless Women in the Republic of Choice,* 66 N.Y.U.L. Rev. 1559, 1612 (1991).

22. *See* Langway, *supra* note 21. Arlie Hochschild found that, after adding together the time it takes to do home and child care with the time it takes to do a paying job, women work about fifteen hours longer per week than do men. *See* Hochschild, *supra* note 12, at 3.

23. Langway, *supra* note 21, at 72 (all other quotes).

24. *See generally* Hochschild, *supra* note 12, at 110–27.

25. *See id.* at 257–78, Arlie Hochschild, *Inside the Clockwork of Male Careers,* in *Women and the Power to Change* (Florence Howe ed., 1971).

26. *See id.* at 266–70.

27. Lillian Rubin, *Families on the Fault Line* 79 (1994).

28. Emily Couric, *Women in Large Firms: A Higher Price of Admission?,* Nat. L. J., Dec. 11, 1989, at S2, S12.

29. Rubin, *supra* note 32, at 79 (national psyche); Peggy Orenstein, *Almost Equal,* N.Y. Times, Apr. 5, 1998, § 6 (Magazine), at 45 (Boston nanny).

30. *See* Richard Morin & Megan Rosenfeld, *With More Equity, More Sweat; Poll Shows Sexes Agree on Pros and Cons of New Roles,* Wash. Post, Mar. 22, 1998, at A1 (two-thirds).

31. *See* Joan C. Williams, *Privatization as a Gender Issue,* in *A Fourth Way? Privatization, Property, and the Emergence of the New Market Economics* 215 (Gregory S. Alexander & Grazyna Skapka eds., 1994) (Russia and East-Central Europe); Barbara Bergmann, *Saving Our Children from Poverty: What the United States Can Learn from France* (1996) (data on France and Belgium); Marlise Simons, *Child Care Sacred as France Cuts Back the Welfare State,* N.Y. Times, Dec. 31, 1997, at A1 (French parents fight to get children in); Marguerite G. Rosenthal, *Sweden: Promise and Paradox,* in *The Feminization of Poverty: Only in America?* (Gertrude Schaffuel Goldberg & Eleanor Kremen eds., 1990) 129, 137, 144, 147–49 (Sweden).

32. Mary Frances Berry, *The Politics of Parenthood* 137–38, 142 (1993) (Nixon quote; 1975 quote); Jane Rigler, *Analysis and Understanding of the Family and Medical Leave Act of 1993,* 45 Case W. Res. L. Rev. 457 (1995) (less governmental support in United States).

33. *See* Gina C. Adams & Nicole Oxendine Poersch, *Children's Defense Fund, Key Facts About Child Care and Early Education: A Briefing Book,* at B-7 (1997) (low pay and high turnover).

34. Press Release from University of Tennessee News Center, by Dr. Jan Allen, at <http://www.utenn.edu/uwa/vpps/ur/news/may96/kidcare.htm>.

35. *See* Juliet B. Schor, *The Overworked American* 30 tbl. 2.2 (1992) (Hours per Week, Labor Force Participants) (only those fully employed)

(workweek); Peter T. Kilborn, *The Work Week Grows; Tales from the Digital Treadmill,* N.Y. Times, June 3, 1990, § 4 (Week in Review), at 1 (24 percent; managers' hours; first quote); Peter T. Kilborn, *It's Too Much of a Good Thing, G.M. Workers Say in Protesting Overtime,* N.Y. Times, Nov. 22, 1994, at A16 (production workers); Schor, *supra,* at 41 (5:00 dad); Ureta Census Data, *see* note 4 in the introduction (one-third of fathers).

36. *See* Rosenthal, *supra* note 36, at 137, 144, 147–49; Janeen Baxter & Emily W. Kane, *Dependence and Independence: A Cross-National Analysis of Gender Inequality and Gender Attitudes,* 9 Gender & Soc'y 193, 195 (1995) (level of sex segregation).

37. For power studies, see Robert O. Blood & Donald M. Wolfe, *Husbands and Wives: The Dynamics of Married Living.* (1960); Phyllis N. Hallenbeck, *An Analysis of Power Dynamic in Marriage,* 28 J. Marriage & Family 200 (1966); Gerald W. McDonald, *Family Power: The Assessment of a Decade of Theory and Research, 1970–1979,* J. Marriage & Family 841 (1980); Paula England & Barbara Stanek Kilbourne, *Markets, Marriages, and Other Mates: The Problem of Power,* in *Beyond the Market Place: Rethinking Economy and Society* (Roger Friedland & A. F. Robertson eds., 1990).

38. *See* S. M. Miller, *The Making of a Confused, Middle-Aged Husband,* in *Men and Masculinity* 44, 50 (Joseph H. Pleck & Jack Sawyer eds., 1974); Rosenthal, *supra* note 36, at 137, 144, 147–49.

39. Bureau of Labor Statistics, U.S. Department of Labor, Unpublished Marital and Family Tabulations from the Current Population Survey, tbl. 28A (1996) ("Unemployed Persons Not at Work and Persons at Work in Nonagricultural Industries by Actual Hours of Work at All Jobs During Reference Week, Marital Status, Sex, and Age, Annual Average 1995").

For Discussion

1. What is the "full-commodification strategy" version of women's equality with men? What happens to housekeeping and child rearing under the full-commodification strategy?
2. Why does Williams feel that a nationwide, state-supported system of day care is not a solution to the problems of raising children in a society where men and women are equal in the workplace? What reasons and evidence does she offer to show that day care is not a viable solution?
3. In contrast to the commodification strategy and day care, Williams offers the norm of parental care. Explain what she means by this and how it could be achieved.
4. In the preface to her book, Williams cites that working mothers earn 60 cents to every dollar earned by working fathers. Compare this to the average of all women to all men, which was 76 cents to every

dollar as we went to press with this book. What can explain why mothers' salaries are so much lower than fathers'? Look at paragraph 36, which talks about the time commitments of ideal workers in "good" jobs. Do you believe that Williams has made a good case to show that workplace and parenting are in conflict?

5. What evidence does Williams give that in spite of our proclaimed interest in children, our society has put business interests ahead of family interests? What evidence do you observe that corroborates her view? If you feel that you were raised in the "full-commodification" type of household, do you agree or disagree that it hurts children?

For Inquiry

Williams depicts the nationalized day-care system in Sweden as ineffective in helping to bring about equality of the sexes. Look into the results in other countries, such France, that are known for providing high-quality, state-funded day care to determine if they also stop short of helping women achieve equality with men in the workplace.

For Inquiry and Convincing

In the second chapter of her book, Williams suggests some options for management to change the workplace from its traditional "male" norms, which assume a worker has no responsibilities at home. Do further research into businesses that have tried to install more family-friendly policies. Do you find many that truly meet Williams's objections to the model of "domesticity" with its devaluation of all work connected to child rearing and homemaking? What policies encourage a norm of parental involvement? Write an argument to convince your readers that such policies are possible and useful, or if you decide that they are unrealistic and bad for the economy, make a case against changing the status quo.

For Persuasion

If you believe that creating a "norm of parental involvement" would be a good thing for men, women, and children, imagine a society in which such a norm existed, and write a description of this parental "utopia" that would encourage your readers to bring it about.

Cartoon
Garry Trudeau

Doonesbury

Doonesbury © 1987 G. B. Trudeau. Reprinted with permission of Universal Press Syndicate.
All rights reserved.

For Discussion

In the cartoon, two working parents are talking about raising their son. Why
is the mother angry with her husband? What comment does the cartoon
make about the difficulty of escaping from the gender roles our parents
model for us?

The Beauty Myth
Naomi Wolf

Feminist writer Naomi Wolf, a 1984 graduate of Yale, sees a backlash against feminism in our culture's promotion of female beauty. Her controversial book The Beauty Myth: How Images of Beauty Are Used against Women *(1991) charges that as women's material opportunities have expanded, an insidious psychological force has begun to undermine their sense of self-worth. Constantly dissatisfied with their real faces and bodies, women devote inordinate attention, time, and money to pursuing the slender, youthful, unchanging female image dictated by our society as the ideal, some even risking their health to do so through surgery or starvation. Wolf argues that the beauty myth is political, not aesthetic; it is imposed by a society threatened by women's rise in power. The following excerpt is Wolf's introduction to her book. As you read, decide to what extent Wolf seems to be anti-beauty: Does she seem to oppose all efforts to "look good"?*

At last, after a long silence, women took to the streets. In the two decades of radical action that followed the rebirth of feminism in the early 1970s, Western women gained legal and reproductive rights, pursued higher education, entered the trades and the professions, and overturned ancient and revered beliefs about their social role. A generation on, do women feel free?

The affluent, educated, liberated women of the First World, who can enjoy freedoms unavailable to any women ever before, do not feel as free as they want to. And they can no longer restrict to the subconscious their sense that this lack of freedom has something to do with—with apparently frivolous issues, things that really should not matter. Many are ashamed to admit that such trivial concerns—to do with physical appearance, bodies, faces, hair, clothes—matter so much. But in spite of shame, guilt, and denial, more and more women are wondering if it isn't that they are entirely neurotic and alone but rather that something important is indeed at stake that has to do with the relationship between female liberation and female beauty.

The more legal and material hindrances women have broken through, the more strictly and heavily and cruelly images of female beauty have come to weigh upon us. Many women sense that women's collective progress has stalled; compared with the heady momentum of earlier days, there is a dispiriting climate of confusion, division, cynicism, and above all, exhaustion. After years of much struggle and little recognition, many older women feel burned out; after years of taking its light for granted, many younger women show little interest in touching new fire to the torch.

During the past decade, women breached the power structure; meanwhile, eating disorders rose exponentially and cosmetic surgery became the fastest-growing medical specialty. During the past five years, consumer spending doubled, pornography became the main media category, ahead of legitimate films and records combined, and thirty-three thousand American women told researchers that they would rather lose ten to fifteen pounds than achieve any other goal (Wooley and Wooley). More women have more money and power and scope and legal recognition than we have ever had before; but in terms of how we feel about ourselves *physically,* we may actually be worse off than our unliberated grandmothers. Recent research consistently shows that inside the majority of the West's controlled, attractive, successful working women, there is a secret "underlife" poisoning our freedom; infused with notions of beauty, it is a dark vein of self-hatred, physical obsessions, terror of aging, and dread of lost control (Cash et al.).[1]

It is no accident that so many potentially powerful women feel this way. We are in the midst of a violent backlash against feminism that uses images of female beauty as a political weapon against women's advancement: the beauty myth. It is the modern version of a social reflex that has been in force since the Industrial Revolution. As women released themselves from the feminine mystique of domesticity, the beauty myth took over its lost ground, expanding as it waned to carry on its work of social control.

The contemporary backlash is so violent because the ideology of beauty is the last one remaining of the old feminine ideologies that still has the power to control those women whom second wave feminism would have otherwise made relatively uncontrollable: It has grown stronger to take over the work of social coercion that myths about motherhood, domesticity, chastity, and passivity, no longer can manage. It is seeking right now to undo psychologically and covertly all the good things that feminism did for women materially and overtly.

This counterforce is operating to checkmate the inheritance of feminism on every level in the lives of Western women. Feminism gave us laws against job discrimination based on gender; immediately case law evolved in Britain and the United States that institutionalized job discrimination based on women's appearances. Patriarchal religion declined; new religious dogma, using some of the mind-altering techniques of older cults and sects, arose around age and weight to functionally supplant traditional ritual. Feminists, inspired by Friedan, broke the stranglehold on the women's popular press of advertisers for household products, who were promoting the feminine mystique; at once, the diet and skin care industries became the new cultural censors of women's intellectual space, and because of their pressure, the gaunt, youthful model supplanted the happy housewife as the

5

---

[1] Dr. Cash's research shows very little connection between "how attractive women are" and "how attractive they feel themselves to be." All the women he treated were, in his terms, "extremely attractive," but his patients compare themselves only to models, not to other women. [Author's note]

arbiter of successful womanhood. The sexual revolution promoted the discovery of female sexuality; "beauty pornography"—which for the first time
in women's history artificially links a commodified "beauty" directly and
explicitly to sexuality—invaded the mainstream to undermine women's
new and vulnerable sense of sexual self-worth. Reproductive rights gave
Western women control over our own bodies; the weight of fashion models
plummeted to 23 percent below that of ordinary women, eating disorders
rose exponentially, and a mass neurosis was promoted that used food
and weight to strip women of that sense of control. Women insisted on
politicizing health; new technologies of invasive, potentially deadly
"cosmetic" surgeries developed apace to re-exert old forms of medical
control of women.

Every generation since about 1830 has had to fight its version of the
beauty myth. "It is very little to me," said the suffragist Lucy Stone in 1855,
"to have the right to vote, to own property, etcetera, if I may not keep my
body, and its uses, in my absolute right" (qtd. in Dworkin 11). Eighty years
later, after women had won the vote, and the first wave of the organized
women's movement had subsided, Virginia Woolf wrote that it would still
be decades before women could tell the truth about their bodies. In 1962,
Betty Friedan quoted a young woman trapped in the Feminine Mystique:
"Lately, I look in the mirror, and I'm so afraid I'm going to look like my
mother." Eight years after that, heralding the cataclysmic second wave of
feminism, Germaine Greer described "the Stereotype": "To her belongs all
that is beautiful, even the very word beauty itself . . . she is a doll . . .
I'm sick of the masquerade" (55, 60). In spite of the great revolution of the
second wave, we are not exempt. Now we can look out over ruined barri-
cades: A revolution has come upon us and changed everything in its path,
enough time has passed since then for babies to have grown into women,
but there still remains a final right not fully claimed.

The beauty myth tells a story: The quality called "beauty" objectively
and universally exists. Women must want to embody it and men must want
to possess women who embody it. This embodiment is an imperative for
women and not for men, which situation is necessary and natural because
it is biological, sexual, and evolutionary: Strong men battle for beautiful
women, and beautiful women are more reproductively successful. Women's
beauty must correlate to their fertility, and since this system is based on sexual selection, it is inevitable and changeless.

None of this is true. "Beauty" is a currency system like the gold standard.   10
Like any economy, it is determined by politics, and in the modern age in
the West it is the last, best belief system that keeps male dominance intact.
In assigning value to women in a vertical hierarchy according to a culturally
imposed physical standard, it is an expression of power relations in which
women must unnaturally compete for resources that men have appropriated
for themselves.

"Beauty" is not universal or changeless, though the West pretends that all ideals of female beauty stem from one Platonic Ideal Woman; the Maori admire a fat vulva, and the Padung, droopy breasts. Nor is "beauty" a function of evolution: Its ideals change at a pace far more rapid than that of the evolution of species, and Charles Darwin was himself unconvinced by his own explanation that "beauty" resulted from a "sexual selection" that deviated from the rule of natural selection; for women to compete with women through "beauty" is a reversal of the way in which natural selection affects all other mammals.[2] Anthropology has overturned the notion that females must be "beautiful" to be selected to mate: Evelyn Reed, Elaine Morgan, and others have dismissed sociobiological assertions of innate male polygamy and female monogamy. Female higher primates are the sexual initiators; not only do they seek out and enjoy sex with many partners, but "every nonpregnant female takes her turn at being the most desirable of all her troop. And that cycle keeps turning as long as she lives." The inflamed pink sexual organs of primates are often cited by male sociobiologists as analogous to human arrangements relating to female "beauty," when in fact that is a universal, nonhierarchical female primate characteristic.

Nor has the beauty myth always been this way. Though the pairing of the older rich men with young, "beautiful" women is taken to be somehow inevitable, in the matriarchal Goddess religions that dominated the Mediterranean from about 25,000 B.C.E. to about 700 B.C.E., the situation was reversed: "In every culture, the Goddess has many lovers. . . . The clear pattern is of an older woman with a beautiful but expendable youth — Ishtar and Tammuz, Venus and Adonis, Cybele and Attis, Isis and Osiris . . . their only function the service of the divine 'womb'" (Miles 43). Nor is it something only women do and only men watch: Among the Nigerian Wodaabes, the women hold economic power and the tribe is obsessed with

[2] See Cynthia Eagle Russett, "Hairy Men and Beautiful Women," *Sexual Science: The Victorian Construction of Womanhood* (Cambridge: Harvard UP, 1989) 78–103.

On page 84 Russett quotes Darwin: "Man is more powerful in body and mind than woman, and in the savage state he keeps her in a much more abject state of bondage, than does the male of any other animal; therefore it is not surprising that he should have gained the power of selection. . . . As women have long been selected for beauty, it is not surprising that some of their successive variations should have been transmitted exclusively to the same sex; consequently that they should have transmitted beauty in a somewhat higher degree to their female than to their male offspring, and thus have become more beautiful, according to general opinion, than men." Darwin himself noticed the evolutionary inconsistency of this idea that, as Russett puts it, "a funny thing happened on the way up the ladder: Among humans, the female no longer chose but was chosen." This theory "implied an awkward break in evolutionary continuity," she observes: "In Darwin's own terms it marked a rather startling reversal in the trend of evolution."

See also Natalie Angier, "Hard-to-Please Females May Be Neglected Evolutionary Force," *New York Times* 8 May 1990, and Natalie Angier, "Mating for Life? It's Not for the Birds or the Bees," *New York Times* 21 Aug. 1990. [Author's note]

male beauty; Wodaabe men spend hours together in elaborate makeup sessions, and compete—provocatively painted and dressed, with swaying hips and seductive expressions—in beauty contests judged by women (Woodhead). There is no legitimate historical or biological justification for the beauty myth; what it is doing to women today is a result of nothing more exalted than the need of today's power structure, economy, and culture to mount a counteroffensive against women.

If the beauty myth is not based on evolution, sex, gender, aesthetics, or God, on what is it based? It claims to be about intimacy and sex and life, a celebration of women. It is actually composed of emotional distance, politics, finance, and sexual repression. The beauty myth is not about women at all. It is about men's institutions and institutional power.

The qualities that a given period calls beautiful in women are merely symbols of the female behavior that that period considers desirable: *The beauty myth is always actually prescribing behavior and not appearance.* Competition between women has been made part of the myth so that women will be divided from one another. Youth and (until recently) virginity have been "beautiful" in women since they stand for experiential and sexual ignorance. Aging in women is "unbeautiful" since women grow more powerful with time, and since the links between generations of women must always be newly broken: Older women fear young ones, young women fear old, and the beauty myth truncates for all the female life span. Most urgently, women's identity must be premised upon our "beauty" so that we will remain vulnerable to outside approval, carrying the vital sensitive organ of self-esteem exposed to the air.

Though there has, of course, been a beauty myth in some form for as long as there has been patriarchy, the beauty myth in its modern form is a fairly recent invention. The myth flourishes when material constraints on women are dangerously loosened. Before the Industrial Revolution, the average woman could not have had the same feelings about "beauty" that modern women do who experience the myth as continual comparison to a mass-disseminated physical ideal. Before the development of technologies of mass production—daguerreotypes, photographs, etc.—an ordinary woman was exposed to few such images outside the Church. Since the family was a productive unit and women's work complemented men's, the value of women who were not aristocrats or prostitutes lay in their work skills, economic shrewdness, physical strength, and fertility. Physical attraction, obviously, played its part; but "beauty" as we understand it was not, for ordinary women, a serious issue in the marriage marketplace. The beauty myth in its modern form gained ground after the upheavals of industrialization, as the work unit of the family was destroyed, and urbanization and the emerging factory system demanded what social engineers of the time termed the "separate sphere" of domesticity, which supported the new labor category of the "breadwinner" who left home for the workplace during the day. The middle class expanded, the standards of living and of

15

literacy rose, the size of families shrank; a new class of literate, idle women developed, on whose submission to enforced domesticity the evolving system of industrial capitalism depended. Most of our assumptions about the way women have always thought about "beauty" date from no earlier than the 1830s, when the cult of domesticity was first consolidated and the beauty index invented.

For the first time new technologies could reproduce—in fashion plates, daguerreotypes, tintypes, and rotogravures—images of how women should look. In the 1840s the first nude photographs of prostitutes were taken; advertisements using images of "beautiful" women first appeared in midcentury. Copies of classical artworks, postcards of society beauties and royal mistresses, Currier and Ives prints, and porcelain figurines flooded the separate sphere to which middle-class women were confined.

Since the Industrial Revolution, middle-class Western women have been controlled by ideals and stereotypes as much as by material constraints. This situation, unique to this group, means that analyses that trace "cultural conspiracies" are uniquely plausible in relation to them. The rise of the beauty myth was just one of several emerging social fictions that masqueraded as natural components of the feminine sphere, the better to enclose those women inside it. Other such fictions arose contemporaneously: a version of childhood that required continual maternal supervision; a concept of female biology that required middle-class women to act out the roles of hysterics and hypochondriacs; a conviction that respectable women were sexually anesthetic; and a definition of women's work that occupied them with repetitive, time-consuming, and painstaking tasks such as needlepoint and lacemaking. All such Victorian inventions as these served a double function—that is, though they were encouraged as a means to expend female energy and intelligence in harmless ways, women often used them to express genuine creativity and passion.

But in spite of middle-class women's creativity with fashion and embroidery and child rearing, and, a century later, with the role of the suburban housewife that devolved from these social fictions, the fictions' main purpose was served: During a century and a half of unprecedented feminist agitation, they effectively counteracted middle-class women's dangerous new leisure, literacy, and relative freedom from material constraints.

Though these time- and mind-consuming fictions about women's natural role adapted themselves to resurface in the post-war Feminine Mystique, when the second wave of the women's movement took apart what women's magazines had portrayed as the "romance," "science," and "adventure" of homemaking and suburban family life, they temporarily failed. The cloying domestic fiction of "togetherness" lost its meaning and middle-class women walked out of their front doors in masses.

So the fictions simply transformed themselves once more: Since the women's movement had successfully taken apart most other necessary fictions of femininity, all the work of social control once spread out over

20

the whole network of these fictions had to be reassigned to the only strand left intact, which action consequently strengthened it a hundredfold. This reimposed onto liberated women's faces and bodies all the limitations, taboos, and punishments of the repressive laws, religious injunctions, and reproductive enslavement that no longer carried sufficient force. Inexhaustible but ephemeral beauty work took over from inexhaustible but ephemeral housework. As the economy, law, religion, sexual mores, education, and culture were forcibly opened up to include women more fairly, a private reality colonized female consciousness. By using ideas about "beauty," it reconstructed an alternative female world with its own laws, economy, religion, sexuality, education, and culture, each element as repressive as any that had gone before.

Since middle-class Western women can best be weakened psychologically now that we are stronger materially, the beauty myth, as it has resurfaced in the last generation, has had to draw on more technological sophistication and reactionary fervor than ever before. The modern arsenal of the myth is a dissemination of millions of images of the current ideal; although this barrage is generally seen as a collective sexual fantasy, there is in fact little that is sexual about it. It is summoned out of political fear on the part of male-dominated institutions threatened by women's freedom, and it exploits female guilt and apprehension about our own liberation — latent fears that we might be going too far. This frantic aggregation of imagery is a collective reactionary hallucination willed into being by both men and women stunned and disoriented by the rapidity with which gender relations have been transformed: a bulwark of reassurance against the flood of change. The mass depiction of the modern woman as a "beauty" is a contradiction: Where modern women are growing, moving, and expressing their individuality, as the myth has it, "beauty" is by definition inert, timeless, and generic. That this hallucination is necessary and deliberate is evident in the way "beauty" so directly contradicts women's real situation.

And the unconscious hallucination grows ever more influential and pervasive because of what is now conscious market manipulation: powerful industries — the $33-billion-a-year diet industry (O'Neill), the $20-billion cosmetics industry, the $300-million cosmetic surgery industry (*Standard and Poor's*), and the $7-billion pornography industry ("Crackdown") — have arisen from the capital made out of unconscious anxieties, and are in turn able, through their influence on mass culture, to use, stimulate, and reinforce the hallucination in a rising economic spiral.

This is not a conspiracy theory; it doesn't have to be. Societies tell themselves necessary fictions in the same way that individuals and families do. Henrik Ibsen called them "vital lies," and psychologist Daniel Goleman describes them working the same way on the social level that they do within families: "The collusion is maintained by directing attention away from the fearsome fact, or by repackaging its meaning in an acceptable format" (16–17). The costs of these social blind spots, he writes, are de-structive communal illusions. Possibilities for women have become so open-ended that they threaten to destabilize the institutions on which a male-dominated culture has depended, and a collective panic reaction on the part of both sexes has forced a demand for counterimages.

The resulting hallucination materializes, for women, as something all too real. No longer just an idea, it becomes three-dimensional, incorporating within itself how women live and how they do not live: It becomes the Iron Maiden. The original Iron Maiden was a medieval German instrument of torture, a body-shaped casket painted with the limbs and features of a lovely, smiling young woman. The unlucky victim was slowly enclosed inside her; the lid fell shut to immobilize the victim, who died either of starvation or, less cruelly, of the metal spikes embedded in her interior. The modern hallucination in which women are trapped or trap themselves is similarly rigid, cruel, and euphemistically painted. Contemporary culture directs attention to imagery of the Iron Maiden, while censoring real women's faces and bodies.

Why does the social order feel the need to defend itself by evading the   25
fact of real women, our faces and voices and bodies, and reducing the meaning of women to these formulaic and endlessly reproduced "beautiful" images? Though unconscious personal anxieties can be a powerful force in the creation of a vital lie, economic necessity practically guarantees it. An economy that depends on slavery needs to promote images of slaves that "justify" the institution of slavery. Western economies are absolutely dependent now on the continued underpayment of women. An ideology that makes women feel "worth less" was urgently needed to counteract the way feminism had begun to make us feel worth more. This does not require a conspiracy; merely an atmosphere. The contemporary economy depends right now on the representation of women within the beauty myth. Economist John Kenneth Galbraith offers an economic explanation for "the persistence of the view of homemaking as a 'higher calling'": the concept of women as naturally trapped within the Feminine Mystique, he feels, "has been forced on us by popular sociology, by magazines, and by fiction to disguise the fact that woman in her role of consumer has been essential to the development of our industrial society. . . . Behavior that is essential for economic reasons is transformed into a social virtue" (qtd. in Minton). As soon as a woman's primary social value could no longer be defined as the attainment of virtuous domesticity, the beauty myth redefined it as the attainment of virtuous beauty. It did so to substitute both a new consumer imperative and a new justification for economic unfairness in the workplace where the old ones had lost their hold over newly liberated women.

Another hallucination arose to accompany that of the Iron Maiden: The caricature of the Ugly Feminist was resurrected to dog the steps of the women's movement. The caricature is unoriginal; it was coined to ridicule the feminists of the nineteenth century. Lucy Stone herself, whom supporters saw as "a prototype of womanly grace . . . fresh and fair as the morning," was derided by detractors with "the usual report" about Victorian feminists: "a big masculine woman, wearing boots, smoking a cigar, swearing like a trooper" (qtd. in Friedan 79). As Betty Friedan put it presciently in 1960, even before the savage revamping of that old caricature: "The unpleasant image of feminists today resembles less the feminists themselves than the image fostered by the interests who so bitterly opposed the vote for women in state after state" (87). Thirty years on, her conclusion is more true than ever: That resurrected caricature, which sought to punish women for their public acts by going after their private sense of self, became the paradigm for new limits placed on aspiring women everywhere. After the success of the women's movement's second wave, the beauty myth was perfected to checkmate power at every level in individual women's lives. The modern neuroses of life in the female body spread to woman after woman at epidemic rates. The myth is undermining—slowly, imperceptibly, without our being aware of the real forces of erosion—the ground women have gained through long, hard, honorable struggle.

The beauty myth of the present is more insidious than any mystique of femininity yet: A century ago, Nora slammed the door of the doll's house; a generation ago, women turned their backs on the consumer heaven of the isolated multiapplianced home; but where women are trapped today, there is no door to slam. The contemporary ravages of the beauty backlash are destroying women physically and depleting us psychologically. If we are to free ourselves from the dead weight that has once again been made out of femaleness, it is not ballots or lobbyists or placards that women will need first; it is a new way to see.

Works Cited

Cash, Thomas, Diane Cash, and Jonathan Butters. "Mirror-Mirror on the Wall: Contrast Effects and Self-Evaluation of Physical Attractiveness." *Personality and Social Psychology Bulletin* 9.3 (1983).

"Crackdown on Pornography: A No-Win Battle." *U.S. News & World Report* 4 June 1984.

Dworkin, Andrea. *Pornography: Men Possessing Women*. New York: Putnam, 1981.

Friedan, Betty. *The Feminine Mystique*. 1963. London: Penguin, 1982.

Goleman, Daniel. *Vital Lies, Simple Truths: The Psychology of Self-Deception*. New York: Simon, 1983.

Greer, Germaine. *The Female Eunuch*. London: Paladin Grafton, 1970.

Miles, Rosalind. *The Women's History of the World*. London: Paladin Grafton, 1988.

Minton, Michael H., with Jean Libman Block. *What Is a Life Worth?* New York: McGraw, 1984.

Morgan, Elaine. *The Descent of Woman*. New York: Bantam, 1979.

O'Neill, Mollie. "Congress Looking into the Diet Business." *New York Times* 25 July 1988.

Standard and Poor's Industry Survey. New York: Standard and Poor's, 1988.

Reed, Evelyn. *Woman's Evolution: From Matriarchal Clan to Patriarchal Family.* New York: Pathfinder, 1986.

Woodhead, Linda. "Desert Dandies." *The Guardian* July 1988.

Wooley, S. C., and O. W. Wooley. "Obesity and Women: A Closer Look at the Facts." *Women's Studies International Quarterly* 2 (1979): 69–79.

For Discussion

1. Wolf seeks to convince her readers that the beauty myth is just that—a myth. What reasons and evidence does she offer to make them see that beauty is not an aesthetic absolute? Do you find her case convincing?

2. What reasons and evidence does Wolf offer to convince her readers that in creating the beauty myth, society is motivated by politics and economics? (To be sure you understand this part of her argument, write a paraphrase of paragraph 25.) Explain her analogy between the beauty myth and the medieval Iron Maiden (paragraph 24). How does this analogy reinforce Wolf's argument that the myth is politically motivated?

3. Wolf says in paragraph 14, "The qualities that a given period calls beautiful in women are merely symbols of the female behavior that that period considers desirable: *The beauty myth is always actually prescribing behavior and not appearance.*" For example, the quality of thinness might symbolize that our society wants women to deny themselves the pleasures of food, even to exist on the daily calorie rations of a person in the Third World or in a prison camp. What other behavior might the beauty myth prescribe?

4. In a preface to a later edition of *The Beauty Myth*, Wolf wrote that she was misunderstood by many critics as being antibeauty and that she would like to make clear to readers that women should be free to adorn and show off their bodies if they want, celebrating their real beauty. She says it is fine to wear lipstick but not to feel guilty about not conforming to the ideal image of beauty. Do you find any evidence in the excerpt to suggest that Wolf is not against makeup and fashion? Do you find any evidence to suggest that she is against them? Could you write a new first paragraph to introduce Wolf's argument more clearly?

For Convincing

Women know that achieving "beauty" is often painful and expensive, in terms of both time and money. Wolf charges that entire industries have formed to profit from women's anxieties about their appearance. However, a glance at men's magazines in most newsstands shows a proliferation of reading material devoted to men's fashion, grooming, and physique—the "masculine" term for "figure." The advertisements here suggest that a similar industry exists for men. Do men have their own masculine version of the "beauty myth" that causes them to suffer, to spend time and money for the sake of their appearance? If so, how widely is it subscribed to? Do you think any motives other than simple vanity underlie it? Write an argument, perhaps addressed to Naomi Wolf, to make the case that excessive concern for one's appearance is not limited to the female sex. If you don't think this is a significant concern for men, write an argument addressed to women, to convince them that they should or should not be more like men in this respect.

For Research and Persuasion

In "Sex," a later chapter of *The Beauty Myth,* Wolf attempts to persuade her readers that men would prefer women to accept themselves as they are. She writes, "At least one major study proves that men are as exasperated with the beauty myth as women are. 'Preoccupation with her appearance, concern about face and hair' ranked among the top four qualities that most annoyed men about women" (171). However, she does admit that "some men get a sexual charge from a woman's objective beauty," an attraction that is often a form of "exhibitionism" as a man "[imagines] his buddies imagining him doing what he is doing while he does it" (175). You may want to look at the entire chapter in which Wolf discusses love and the beauty myth. Do additional research, both in the field and in the library, to draw some conclusions of your own about how images of "ideal" beauty affect sexual relationships. Depending on your conclusions, write an essay in which you attempt to change the behavior of men, women, or both sexes.

Women's Rights: As the World Turns
Katha Pollitt

Violations of women's rights in countries around the world have drawn increasing attention. Western feminism may not suit all countries and cultures, but an international feminism is developing to address many of the problems Katha Pollitt cites in the reprinted column below. Pollitt writes a regular column for the liberal periodical The Nation; *a collection of her writings, a book titled* Subject to Debate, *was published in 2001 (Modern Library). This column appeared before the fall of the Taliban in Afghanistan, but the other abuses of women's rights continue with little change. Pollitt concludes her argument with a list of excellent Web sites where interested readers can update their knowledge about international women's issues.*

. . . The struggle [for women's rights] in the United States may seem stymied — as if the big shakeup of the seventies were settling into a new, improved, but still sexist, status quo — but abroad all sorts of things are happening, awful and hopeful. We tend to hear more about the former: You probably know about the Italian judge who ruled that women wearing blue jeans can't be raped because it takes two to pull them off — sparking a protest by jeans-wearing female MPs. But did you know that in India the Supreme Court ruled for the first time that mothers, not just fathers, are the legal guardians of their children? Besides rectifying a major insult to women, this ruling has important implications for divorcing women seeking custody and child support. The same court ruled in January that sexual harassment violates women's rights and need not involve actual touching — a particularly interesting verdict, given that sexual harassment, along with legal abortion, is often seen as the obsession of a handful of U.S. feminists.

And speaking of abortion, recently two countries, Poland and El Salvador, made abortion harder to get. El Salvador, indeed, is now one of the only countries to enact in law the official position of the Catholic Church and the platform of the U.S. Republican Party, both of which reject abortion even to save the mother's life. But eight countries — Albania, South Africa, Seychelles, Guyana, Germany, Portugal, Cambodia and Burkina Faso — liberalized their abortion laws. And before you write those letters pointing out that Cambodian and Salvadoran women have bigger problems than abortion, consider that in Nepal, a desperately poor country where abortion is illegal, there are women, including rape victims, serving twenty years in prison for having abortions. Poor women have always needed liberal abortion laws the most, because they are the ones who seek the back alleys or who self-abort, and they are also the ones targeted by the police.

These positive changes—Senegal, Togo and three other African countries have banned clitoridectomy; Spain's Basque region pays battered women a "salary" to encourage them to leave their abusers—flicker like candles in a darkening room. Islamic fanaticism is sending women back to the Middle Ages. In the Taliban's Afghanistan, women are banned from schooling, jobs, healthcare and public life, and are subject to beatings and stonings. The new world disorder of the global economy has thrown millions of women and girls into prostitution, sex slavery and, well, slavery as housebound servants in foreign lands. The Asian economic collapse has caused millions of families to stop their daughters' schooling. War, refugee camps, AIDS, poverty, illiteracy, maternal mortality (one in thirty-eight women in Pakistan) are everyday realities for vast numbers of women. Culturally sanctioned coercion and violence persist—"honor killings," genital mutilation, forced marriage, wife murder (half the murders in India)—sometimes with a weird postmodern twist. In famine-stricken North Korea, women are being sold across the border to Chinese farmers unable to find wives because sex-selective abortion, female infanticide and neglect have produced a demographic disaster: 122 males for every 100 females.

Against these terrible tides, set the movement for women's human rights. Only a decade ago the idea that women's rights are human rights was dismissed as sentimental Western cant: Human rights pertained to state action, not to family, marriage or community norms, however cruel and oppressive. Today, academics—and they usually are academics—who compare clitoridectomy to male circumcision or footbinding to high heels are the ones who seem indifferent to reality. And slowly, as the result of immense effort on the part of millions of women and men, a new set of social and moral paradigms is being articulated.

On International Women's Day, the United Nations opened its first-ever session on violence against women with a teleconference broadcast around the world. "It was something to see," said a friend who attended, "all those heads of state having to listen to women tell them about the harm their laws had done to them."   5

I don't want to make too much of what is at least in part political theater. Behind all the talk about "empowering women," how much really changes? The Cairo conference in 1994 was supposed to overturn the population-control approach to family planning in favor of one that placed women's "empowerment" at the center, but how many clinics in Asia (or the United States) have shifted course? It will take a decade, Barbara Becker of the Center for Reproductive Law and Policy told me, or maybe even two, for practices to change. But little by little a language is developing that did not exist before, one in which new hopes can be voiced and new demands made. It's a language we could learn to speak in the United States as well.

BACKGROUND AND RELATED INFORMATION

The Feminist Majority

<http://www.feminist.org>

The Feminist Majority Foundation online offers a Feminist Internet Gateway, Feminist University Network, Breast Cancer Center and Career Center. Among other topics, they have information on global feminism, current news and events and women's sports. There is a special feature called "Take Action," which helps to advance women's rights through enabling quick response on key issues of the day.

Feminist.com

<http://www.feminist.com>

This site offers a Q&A with Gloria Steinem, the ability to search for women's services by location, weekly news updates, links to pro-feminist men's groups and personal stories of affirmative action. They have an amazing volume of links to other organizations.

Aviva

<http://www.aviva.org>

A huge site for information on international women's issues and current news, including abortion. They have an action alert and a books section.

The United Nations

<http://www.un.org>

The U.N. site can be searched for information on and documents from UNIFEM (United Nations International Development Fund for Women) and UNDP (United Nations Development Program).

For Discussion

1. In paragraph 4, Pollitt describes a change of perspective on women's rights as human rights. What have human rights organizations begun to look at that they had considered off limits before? Which of the abuses described by Pollitt in paragraph 3 are state actions, and which are family and community (cultural) norms?
2. Pollitt names three countries that banned clitoridectomy—the cutting of young girls' genitals. By the end of 2001, Kenya had also

banned this practice. Pollitt mentions that in the United States, some people, especially academics, have defended the practice as part of some cultures' traditions and beliefs. What are the debatable issues on this topic?

3. Pollitt mentions that women's rights abuses often increase in hard economic times. In what countries has economic disorder affected women's rights?

For Exploration and Convincing

Pollitt's column is a brief introduction to the topic of international abuses of women's rights. She is not specific or detailed about the problems she lists. Get specific. Research a particular problem mentioned by Pollitt, for example, the sexual harassment of women workers in Russia or other formerly Communist countries. Or you may be aware of news reports about abuses Pollitt does not mention. In South Africa, rape is not treated as a serious crime, and women who are raped are not given medication to fight possible exposure to AIDS. If your exploration indicates that a violation of human rights exists, write a paper to convince others of the seriousness of the problem.

For Persuasion

Do research to find what organizations are working internationally to fight for women's rights. Write an argument to persuade skeptical Americans who may think that Americans are powerless to correct problems beyond our borders. Or argue that these problems must be addressed by the citizens of the countries in which the abuses occur.

For Further Research and Discussion

1. Research Elizabeth Cady Stanton's nineteenth-century arguments for communal living and child-rearing arrangements. What were her objections to traditional marriage and family?

2. One factor that makes it difficult for American women to have a career and a family is that the United States is one of the few countries that does not have some type of government-supported day care. Look into the arrangements that other countries have made that assist working mothers.

3. Cassandra Langer's account (pages 570–579) stresses the feminist assertion that "the personal is political," but she has omitted from her history a discussion of women's struggle to acquire knowledge and birth control. Reread paragraphs 18 and 19. Look into Margaret Sanger's efforts to win this right for women and the resistance she met from men of her day. How might Langer have used this information in her explanation of sexual politics?

Additional Suggestions for Writing

1. *Convincing.* Those who support same-sex education for girls argue that females achieve more when males are not in the academic environment. Look into the arguments for and against sexually segregated education for women. One argument in favor is that women have different learning styles from men; for example, some proponents say that women learn better in less competitive, more collaborative environments. Recent studies have shown that girls' sense of identity and self-confidence is as strong as that of boys until they reach the age of twelve or thirteen. Do girls become less self-assured as they enter puberty? What theories explain this change? Could anxieties about their femininity be behind the problem? You probably have experiences and observations of your own pertaining to these questions. After you have inquired into the subject, make a case for your position on sexually segregated education.

2. *Persuasion.* After considering the goals of feminism and the possible definitions of "femininity," decide if it is possible to be feminine and a feminist. As you inquire, think about who decides what is feminine — men or women or both sexes? Research the biographies of some leading feminists: Would they serve as examples to support your position? Why do so many people have an image (Naomi Wolf calls it a "hallucination") of the Ugly Feminist? Write a persuasive argument aimed at college women, taking either the position that they can be feminists without losing their femininity *or* the position that, at least in our society today, being a feminist necessarily makes a woman appear less feminine.

3. *Analysis-persuasion.* The consumer culture is very persuasive — toward men, women, and children. Inquire into how advertising might be contributing to some common form of behavior in American society today. Is this behavior in the self-interest of the group targeted by the advertising? Is it in the best interest of society as a whole? Or is it merely in the interest of the business or organization sponsoring the advertisement? Consider how visual images contribute to the persuasion. You might want to look at student Kelly Williams's essay on pages 87–89 to see how one student looked at one advertisement that she believes aimed to make mothers conform to a stereotyped image. Write an essay, with or without graphic support, aimed at persuading the target audience to resist the arguments you have selected.

Chapter 13

Gay and Lesbian Rights: Responding to Homophobia

Homosexuality may not have increased in recent decades, but society's awareness of it certainly has, largely because many gay men and women have become more open about their sexual orientation. Their "coming out" has brought many issues to the public's attention, most notably whether gay people should be protected against discrimination in employment, housing, and insurance and in custody cases and adoption. Indeed, many ask, Why should gay people not be able to marry? In some communities, "domestic partnerships"—both homosexual and heterosexual—have recently been legally recognized as unions similar to marriage, and a small but growing number of employers extend benefits to the partners of homosexual employees.

While many homosexual men and women have decided to become activists, publicly pressing for protection against discrimination, others prefer to stay "in the closet," largely out of fear. According to the National Gay and Lesbian Task Force, over 90% of gay men and lesbians have been victims of some type of violence or harassment. One issue we take up here is *why* some heterosexuals react so strongly to homosexuality and the issues surrounding it. Homophobia is often referred to as "the last acceptable prejudice," because so many heterosexuals think that discriminating against gay people—even exhibiting open hostility toward them—is defensible on moral grounds. Those who call homosexuality immoral usually turn to religion for support. But how strong are these religious arguments? And if homosexuality is judged immoral, what bearing does that judgment have on an individual's constitutional rights?

The causes of homosexuality have been much debated, and so far researchers have yet to agree on an explanation. From the nineteenth century until 1973, the medical community regarded homosexuality as a disease or pathology, something that could be cured using treatments such as aversion and electroshock therapy and neurosurgery—none of which succeeded. Although many still agree with former Vice President Dan Quayle that homosexuality is a choice, current biological research increasingly suggests that it is not. Recent work points to the role of hormones, especially hormones to which the fetus is exposed while in the womb. Research on twins reinforces the view that genetics plays a significant role in sexual orientation.

Why and how people become homosexual, however, is not the primary concern of the public debate over attitudes and policies regarding homosexuals and their rights. Five to ten percent of the American population is gay and lesbian, and because of their minority status, they face discrimination and harassment of one sort or another. The arguments in this chapter address these questions:

> Why do many heterosexual people react so strongly to homosexuality?
> How does homophobia affect American society as a whole? Should people who disapprove of homosexuality be able to discriminate against homosexuals?
> What might both gay and straight people do about homophobia?
> Should sexual orientation be protected by civil rights legislation as race, gender, and religion now are?

The issues raised in these readings are central to the debates about more specific gay rights issues such as the role of homosexuals in the military, the right of homosexuals to marry, and the need for antidiscrimination laws.

Everybody's Threatened by Homophobia
Jeffrey Nickel

Homophobia is a term often used to describe the attitude of those who express hostility toward homosexuals; it suggests a prejudice that is actually rooted in fear. Whatever the cause, the prejudice too often results in acts of violence against gay men and lesbian women. The following argument appeared originally in Christopher Street, a literary magazine whose writers and readers are primarily homosexual. In his essay, Jeffrey Nickel wants to show his readers that they can make a case against homophobia that will appeal to the interests of heterosexuals.

Do I hate my brother because he reminds me of myself, or do I hate my brother because he reminds me of someone who is "not" myself? Whom do I hate; the one who is me, or the one who is anything but me?

—ELIE WIESEL

The answer is both. But knowing that would seem to be of little help. Our brothers *are* hated; sisters, too. We're right to tell America of the horrors that hatred visits upon us; of the humiliation, the isolation, and even the killings perpetuated, all in the name of heterosexual hegemony. These should be enough to convince this country that it's been terribly wrong about who we are. But there's more to the story. We can also tell about what homophobia—perhaps surprisingly—does to *others*; those who are perceived to be gay, those who are afraid they *might* be, and everyone else who clearly isn't but is nevertheless forced to feel bigotry's nasty bite. This is a lot of people—close to everyone, really. If only they could understand *these* things, too; maybe they would see.

As Allen Ginsberg wrote, "They can! They can! They can!" Practically every school child in America knows that a "faggot" is the worst thing they could be. How many wonder to themselves, is that *me*? Kids do have the vague perception that there are people in the world called homosexuals, though that's about all they know. How many boys who don't yet "like" girls think homosexuality is the explanation, when in fact for them, it's not? If gay weren't "bad" in their minds, they would feel no more anguish than that experienced by a child who discovers she's left-handed. But gay *is* bad in the country's consciousness, so children *do* worry a hell of a lot about being it. The "late-bloomer" thinks constantly of what might be "wrong" with him. Because the mere *possibility* that some of our children will be gay isn't even entertained, children who, in a freer society, would be relieved by that plausible conclusion are instead shut off from even *thinking* (much less talking) about it. It is awful that so many young gay people attempt, and often succeed in, killing themselves because of who they are. It's just as awful that so many straight kids try and die for what they mistakenly *think*. How refreshing it would be for young people to be able to discover their sexuality without fear. But right now, that's only a fantasy. Kids in this country must not only be straight; they must make absolutely sure that they are *not* gay. They shouldn't *have* to make sure.

A straight friend of mine whom I came out to when I was seventeen confided in me that he occasionally had gay thoughts and dreams. I told him there was no cause to worry; that virtually all people have same-sex (and other-sex) fantasies to some degree or another. But as enlightened as he truly was about homosexuality, these thoughts *still* bothered him deeply. What would it be like for someone who believed the worst things about homosexuality? I know what it is to be gay and feel the guilt, but I have a hard time imagining what it's like to really be straight and feel it. As a gay person I've had the "coming out process" to sort out all the meanings, but what do straight people have? It doesn't lessen the pain of the gay person's coming-to-terms to admit that these feelings are probably excruciating for many heterosexuals as well. And as is true in our case too, it's all for nothing.

I remember, especially in boyhood, the amazing level of paranoia that surrounded any form of male-to-male physical contact — aside perhaps from sports — as well as any kind of inter-male emotional experience. Males can hardly touch each other in this culture, except, as always, by lashing out. Susan Trausch of the *Boston Globe* put it well when she said that many men (and boys too) are fighting desperately to continue breathing what she called "100 percent pure macho air." They wish to be super-men; super-aggressive, super-obnoxious, and super-ignorant. Their mentality has the dual disadvantage of making automatons of men, and figurines of women. A lot of this mentality is attributable to self- and other-directed homophobia. Men practically have to go to counseling just to be able to talk to each other in real ways. What a pointless chasm we've created, just to make sure that closeness isn't "misconstrued."

I've told before the awful story of what happened to a friend of mine while we were in grade school. This boy hung around another boy so much and so ardently that it seemed he had a crush on him. He probably did. The other kids teased him for it a great deal, as I vaguely recall. But the teacher believed this was so intolerable that she had to do something about it, immediately. It really is unbelievable, but here's what she did: A "trial" was held in the classroom, with all members of the class present, at which this boy had to "defend" his feelings toward the other boy. The teacher herself served as the prosecutor. (He had no real defense.) My understanding is that this boy (now a man) really *isn't* gay. Yet he was totally humiliated in front of all of his peers, in such a way that it took him several years to once again build up any semblance of his lost self-esteem. Dating was impossible for him for quite a long time. Some day, I would like to confront this teacher—whom theretofore I'd adored—and ask her what the hell she thought she was doing. It was child abuse of the worst kind, perpetuated against someone who didn't even possess the "demons" she most loathed.

Although I don't presume to know all of what this anxiety does to women, I imagine that it heightens an already well-inculcated sense that women are supposed to have no sexuality whatsoever. Women are taught to please men. Though they are, in a way, given more latitude to express affection for other women than men are for other men. Because women's sexuality is trivialized, they're often prevented from knowing just what would constitute lesbianism and what would not. If there were no stigma to homosexuality, this stultifying paranoia just wouldn't exist. Prejudice against homosexuality sharply limits how all men and women may acceptably behave, among themselves and with each other.

I hadn't thought much about how homophobia hurts heterosexuals until I saw a piece on the TV show *20/20* about two or three years ago. They had fascinating stories about several straight people who were actually attacked—physically—because others thought they were gay. One heterosexual couple holding hands walking down the street was beaten repeatedly. It seems the woman's short hair made it seem from the back that they were two men. What an awful education in bigotry it must have been for these poor people. It's interesting to contemplate how these bigots reacted to the knowledge that they were pummeling a wife and her husband: "Oh—we're very sorry to have broken your bones, but we mistook you for someone else."

A similar event took place in Lewes, Delaware, just last year. A man walking down the street with his arm around the shoulder of his (male) friend was struck and seriously injured by a pickup truck, after the driver yelled "faggot" at him. A second man in the truck then hit him in the head with a beer bottle. Then, the driver backed the truck over a curb and onto the sidewalk where the man was standing, crushing the man's legs between the rear of the truck and three metal mailboxes. He then put the truck in reverse once again in order to run over this man a second time, apparently in order to finish him off. He was prevented from doing so only because he couldn't gain the necessary momentum in the space available to jump the curb. The man's legs were so severely injured that the doctors had to graft muscles, tendons, and skin from other parts of his body in order to repair them. During the entire incident the men on the sidewalk were pleading with their attackers: "We're just buddies; we're not gay." One of the men attacked was a married, heterosexual father. But it didn't matter.

And this year, three Pensacola teenagers who said they were out to beat up a gay person in order to get beer money, did so with a lead pipe, fatally, to a man named John Braun, who was a married (straight) father of four. It's incredible: Heterosexuals have actually *died* because of homophobia.

For John Braun and many others, it's too late to understand their stake   10
in eliminating prejudice against gay people. It's too late for him to join P-FLAG[1] and march on Gay Pride Day. But for most people, it isn't too late. Before their children kill themselves far from home; before they lie bleeding, mistaken, and prone; before their brothers die slowly alone; if we talk about it, they can understand. They can! They can! They can!

For Discussion

1. Nickel divides his argument into three main sections, each focusing on a different segment of the heterosexual population hurt by homophobia: young people whose sexuality is just developing (paragraphs 2–3), children and adults who do not feel comfortable expressing affection for friends of their own sex (paragraphs 4–6), and men and women who are attacked because they are mistaken for homosexuals (paragraphs 7–9). Which section provides Nickel's strongest reason? Comment on his strategy for arranging and supporting these three reasons.
2. Do you agree that "[p]ractically every school child in America knows that a 'faggot' is the worst thing they could be" (paragraph 2)? If you agree, can you say how our society conveys this idea?
3. What do you think Nickel means when he says that in our society "women's sexuality is trivialized" (paragraph 6)? Do you agree that society gives women "more latitude to express affection" for each other? Could this be related to the idea that their sexuality is not as powerful as that of men?
4. Notice that Nickel wants his readers to feel sympathetic to the problems of heterosexuals. How can you tell that his own sympathies are genuine?
5. What persuasive devices does Nickel use to urge his readers on to action?

For Inquiry

In your writer's notebook, assess the truth of Nickel's argument, based on your own experiences and observations.

---

[1] P-FLAG is an acronym for the national organization Parents–Friends of Lesbians and Gays.

Confessions of a Heterosexual
Pete Hamill

Responding to acts of discrimination and violence, some gay rights activists make a point of displaying their pride and their anger through marches, demonstrations, and civil disobedience. In this selection, Esquire *columnist Pete Hamill argues that some of the protesters have gone too far and are in fact creating a backlash among people who thought they had overcome their prejudices against gay people. As you read, consider whether Hamill is writing to militant homosexuals or to other heterosexuals—and what his purpose is.*

Early one evening in the spring, I left my apartment in Greenwich Village and went out to get a few things from the grocery store. The air was mild, the leaves were bursting from the trees. I paused for a moment on a corner, waiting for a light to change and the kamikaze traffic to come to a halt. Waiting beside me was a gray-haired man with a face the color of boiled ham and the thick, boxy body of an old dockwalloper. Before the light turned green, we heard distant chants, tramping feet, and suddenly, like a scene from a Chaplin movie, a small army of the night turned the corner. They came marching directly at us.

"Bash back!" they chanted. "Bash back!"

One of them looked at me and the other man and screamed: "You're fuckin' *killing* us! And we're not gonna *take it* anymore!"

Most of the members of this particular mob were young. A few were joking around, enjoying the fraternity of the march. But the faces of most of the demonstrators were contorted in fury as they raised clenched fists at the sky. While drivers leaned on auto horns and people came to their windows to watch, one wide-eyed kid spat in our direction and shouted, "Breeder shit!"

"What the hell *is* this?" the man beside me said. "Who *are* they?"   5

One marcher peeled off and explained. They were protesting gay-bashing and its most recent local manifestation, the planting of a bomb inside Uncle Charlie's, one of the more popular homosexual hangouts in the city. The marchers paraded off, and the man beside me said: "Tell ya the truth, I'd like to bash a few of these bastards myself."

With that brutal parting line, he stormed off. But as I watched him go, I felt an odd, uncomfortable solidarity with the man. He was my age, born in the Depression, raised in the '40s and '50s, and though we had probably led different lives, we almost surely came from the same roots. We were both out of the New York working class, children of immigrants, shaped by codes, geographies, and institutions now lost. We had thought the neighborhood triumvirate of church, saloon, and Tammany Hall would last forever; it didn't. We learned from our fathers and the older men (and not

from television) what a man was supposed to do if he was to call himself
a man: put money on the kitchen table, defend wife and children, pay his
debts, refuse to inform, serve his country when called, honor picket lines,
and never quit in a fight. Sexuality was crude and uncomplicated: Men
fucked women. Period. So when my accidental companion had strangers
curse him and spit at him, and above all, when he understood that they
were gay, he reacted out of that virtually forgotten matrix. He wanted to
give them a whack in the head.

But I was alarmed that a milder version of the same dark impulse rose
in me. After all, I know that gay-bashing is real; homosexuals are routinely
injured or murdered every day, all over the world, by people who fear or
hate their version of human sexuality.

Yet what rose in me that night wasn't an instinct to hurt anyone in
some homophobic spasm. It was more than simple irritation, and it was
not new. In some fundamental way, I was bored by the exhibition of the-
atrical rage from the gay movement. I am tired of listening to people who
identify themselves exclusively by what they do with their cocks. And I
don't think I'm alone. Discuss the subject long enough with even the most
liberal straight males of my generation, and you discover that twenty years
of education, lobbying, journalism, and demonstrating by gays have had
only a superficial effect; in some deep, dark pool of the psyche, homosexuals are still seen with a mixture of uneasiness and contempt.

Gay activists, of course, would laugh darkly at the above and think: 10
This is not news. But most of them won't even listen to the reasons for these
prejudices. Sadly, the folklore of the old neighborhood is not the only
cause. Much of this persistent distaste is based on personal experience.
Most males of my generation first encountered homosexuals during adolescence, and those men were not exactly splendid representatives of the gay
community. When I was growing up, there were four known homosexuals
in the neighborhood. All were in their forties. All singled out boys in the
low teens. Two paid for sex, and in a neighborhood where poverty was
common, a few dollars was a lot of money.

By all accounts, gay men, in those darkest years of The Closet, lived more
dangerous and vulnerable lives than they do now. They were subject to
blackmail, murder, beatings, and exposure on a more ferocious scale than today. But nothing so melodramatic seemed to happen in our neighborhood.
Though everybody on the street knew about three of the four gay men, I
don't remember any incidents of gay-bashing. Only one suffered public disgrace. One day, the police came to his door and took him off. A few days later
his weeping wife and baffled children moved away, never to be seen again.

When I understood what these men actually *did,* I was horrified. For an
Irish Catholic kid in those years, sex itself was terrifying enough; the homosexual variety seemed proof of the existence of Satan. Through all my years
of adolescence, I believed that homosexuals were people who preyed
exclusively on the very young, a belief strengthened by later experiences on

subways, in men's rooms, and in the high school that I attended (where I met one of those tortured priests of the Catholic literary tradition). That belief was shared by most of the boys I grew up with, and when we left the neighborhood for the service (the working-class version of going off to college), we saw more of the same.

In the sailor joints of Norfolk or Pensacola, homosexuals were constantly on the prowl, looking for kids who were drunk, lonesome, naive, or broken-hearted over some Dear John letter shoved in their hip pockets. Again, older men taught us the code, demonstrating how Real Men were supposed to react. It was never very pretty: There was often violence, some gay man smashed and battered into the mud outside a tough joint after midnight. There was a lot of swaggering machismo, a triumphant conviction that by stomping such people we were striking a mighty blow against predators and corrupters. I'm still ashamed of some of the things I saw and did in those years.

It never occurred to us that some of these older gay men were actually looking for—and finding—other homosexuals, as driven in their search for love and connection as we were in our pursuit of lush young women. We were all so young that we arrogantly assumed that all of us were straight and they were bent; *we* were healthy, *they* were carriers of some sickness. It took me a while to understand that the world was more complicated than it was in the *Bluejackets' Manual.*[1]

The years passed. I grew up. I worked with homosexuals. I read novels   15
and saw plays written by homosexuals about the specifics of their lives. Gradually, the stereotypes I carried were broken by experience and knowledge. At the same time, I was roaming around as a reporter, seeing riots and wars, too much poverty and too many dead bodies. The ambiguities, masks, and games of human sexuality seemed a minor issue compared with the horrors of the wider world. Even after the gay-liberation movement began, in the wake of the 1969 Stonewall Riot, in New York, the private lives of homosexuals seldom entered my imagination. I didn't care what people did in bed, as long as they didn't wake up in the morning and napalm villages, starve children, or harm the innocent.

Some of my friends "came out" in the years after Stonewall. The process was more difficult for them than it was for me. On more than a few evenings, I found myself listening to a painful account of the dreadful angst that accompanied living in The Closet, and the delirious joy that came with kicking down its door forever. I apologized for any crudities I might have uttered while they were in The Closet; they forgave me. We remained friends.

In the years after Stonewall, I met gay men living in monogamous relationships, gay men of austere moral codes, gay men with great courage. I read interviews with gay cops, soldiers, and football players. I knew that there were thousands of gay men living lives of bourgeois respectability.

---

[1]A bluejacket is an enlisted member of the U.S. Navy.

There were even right-wing gay Republicans. Like many men my age, I thought, What the hell, there's room for everybody.

Then came AIDS.

And for people like me, everything about homosexuals changed once more. Thousands have died from this terrible disease, but for people my age, the gulf between straight and gay seems to be widening instead of closing. I find myself deploring homophobia, like any good liberal, and simultaneously understanding why it seems to be spreading among otherwise decent people. A phobia, after all, is a fear. And AIDS terrifies.

Under the combined pressures of fear and pity, I've been forced to confront my own tangled notions about gays. I cherish my gay friends, and want them to live long and productive lives. But while AIDS has made many millions even more sympathetic to and understanding of gay lives, I find myself struggling with the powerful undertow of the primitive code of my youth. I've lost all patience with much of the paranoid oratory of gay radicals. I can't abide the self-pitying aura of victimhood that permeates so much of their discussion. Their leaders irritate me with their insistence on seeing AIDS as if it were some tragic medieval plague of unknown origin instead of the result of personal behavior.   20

I know that AIDS cases are increasing among heterosexuals, and the virus is spreading wildly among intravenous drug users. For me, this knowledge is not abstract. I know one sweet young woman who died of the disease, picked up from her junkie husband; I was at her christening, and I'm still furious that she's dead. I also know that the rate of infection among homosexuals is down, the result of "safe sex" campaigns, education, and abstinence.

But when the gay militants in ACT UP go to St. Patrick's Cathedral and one of them crushes a Communion Host on the floor as a protest against the Church's traditional policies, I'm revolted. This is cheap blasphemy and even worse politics. I'm angered when the homosexual bedroom police force gays out of The Closet against their will while simultaneously opposing the tracing of AIDS carriers. When gay activists harass doctors, disrupt public meetings, and scream self-righteously about their "rage," my heart hardens.

I'm sure the government isn't doing enough to find a cure for AIDS. But it's also not doing enough to cure lung cancer, which kills 130,000 people every year, or acute alcoholism (57,000 every year), or to avert the ravages of cocaine addiction. Like AIDS (which has killed 81,000 Americans in a decade), these afflictions are spread, or controlled, by personal behavior. I've had more friends die of smoking, drinking, or doing dope than I have friends who died of AIDS. But I don't ever hear about the "rage" of the cigarette addict or the stone drunk or the crackhead, even though none of my stricken friends went gently into that good night. If anything, most current social rage is directed *against* such people, while the diseases continue to kill. And yet in most American cities, if you measured inches of type in newspapers, you might believe that all of the old diseases have been conquered and only AIDS remains.

I'm not among those who believe there is some all-powerful "Homintern" that manipulates the media while filling the museums with Robert Mapplethorpe photographs. But I don't feel I'm lining up with the unspeakable Jesse Helms when I say that I'm also fed up with the ranting of those gays who believe that all straights are part of some Monstrous Conspiracy to end homosexual life. One lie is not countered with another.

Certainly, as gay rhetoric becomes more apocalyptic, the entire public discussion is being reduced to a lurid cartoon, devoid of criticism, irony, nuance, and even common sense. Certainly, there is less room for tolerance. I know a few gay people who resent being told that if they don't follow the party line they are mere "self-hating gays." And as someone outside the group, I don't like being told that I must agree with the latest edition of the established creed or be dismissed as a homophobe. More than anything else, I'm angry with myself when some of the old specters come rising out of the psychic mists of my own generation.

In the face of the AIDS plague, gays and straights should be forging a union by cool reason. Instead, we are presented with cheap pity, romantic bullshit, or the irrational, snarling faces of haters. As in so many areas of our society, divisions are drawn in black and white; there are no shades of gray. Homophobia is countered by heterophobia; the empty answer to gay-bashing is a vow to bash back. There are sadder developments in American life, I suppose, but for the moment, I can't think of one.

For Discussion

1. Using the "folklore" and experiences of his own working-class background, Hamill suggests that there was a connection between homophobia and socioeconomic class when he was growing up in the 1940s and 1950s. Do you think such a connection still exists?
2. Hamill refers to the 1940s and 1950s as "those darkest years of The Closet" (paragraph 11). Can you make any connection between homosexuals' staying in the closet and the experiences Hamill describes in paragraphs 10–13?
3. What made it possible for Hamill to overcome his prejudices? Have you had a similar experience in overcoming any form of prejudice?
4. Hamill defends his own recurring homophobia as a reaction to AIDS and the "ranting" of gay activists. What evidence does he offer to justify his new attitude? Is it all related to AIDS? How does Hamill use language as a tool to persuade readers to see the militant activity as he does?
5. In paragraph 9, Hamill says that "twenty years of education, lobbying, journalism, and demonstrating by gays have had only

a superficial effect" on public perceptions. What solution is he proposing to the problem of homophobia?

For Inquiry and Persuasion

Research any recent demonstrations by gay rights activists, such as those in ACT UP. What are these groups protesting, and what methods are they using? How confrontational are their protests? How often is civil disobedience involved? Why have they taken such a militant approach? Look also at what they are saying, at what kind of language they are using. You might have to turn to periodicals aimed at the gay community, such as *The Advocate* and *Christopher Street*, which are indexed in *InfoTrac*. Your campus may have an organization for gay and lesbian students, which might also be a source for gay rights literature.

After inquiring thoroughly, if you feel Hamill's criticisms are justified, write persuasively to the militants, suggesting a cooler approach. If you think their approach is justified, write to Hamill and others like him who have lost patience with the demonstrations; try to generate understanding and sympathy.

For Mediation

After inquiring into gay rights demonstrations, write a mediatory essay aimed at both militant gays and an audience of men and women who feel as Hamill does. Before you write, create a brief of each side's position and reasons. In your mediatory essay, attempt to get each side to understand the other's emotions and interests. How might militant gays and straights work together to eliminate homophobia?

Cartoon
Garry Trudeau

In one segment of Garry Trudeau's comic strip Doonesbury, *Mike Doonesbury's good friend Mark realizes that he is homosexual.*

Doonesbury

BY GARRY TRUDEAU

Doonesbury © 1993 G. B. Trudeau. Reprinted with permission of Universal Press Syndicate. All rights reserved.

For Discussion

The cartoon makes us laugh at Mike's attitude, a stereotype of heterosexual males' discomfort around homosexuals. But in spite of its humor, the strip raises many issues. Does it suggest that homosexuality is or is not a choice? If sexual preference is innate, not a choice, how could a young man or woman grow up not recognizing gay or lesbian attractions, as happened in the case of the character Mark? Is it possible that American culture, in which heterosexual eroticism pervades our advertising and entertainment, and even the literature that young people read, could lead most everyone to assume that he or she is heterosexual?

Homophobic? Reread Your Bible
Peter J. Gomes

Those who contend that homosexuality is immoral often cite the Bible for support. Although nonbelievers would find these arguments weak, the weight of biblical authority is unquestionable among many Christian audiences. During the crucial election year of 1992, fundamentalist Christians and others called upon Scripture to make their case that homosexuality is immoral and gay rights a threat to "traditional family values"; several gay rights measures were defeated in the process. In the following argument, Peter J. Gomes, a minister and professor of Christian morals at Harvard University, challenges the fundamentalists' interpretation of the Bible.

Opposition to gays' civil rights has become one of the most visible symbols of American civic conflict this year, and religion has become the weapon of choice. The army of the discontented, eager for clear villains and simple solutions and ready for a crusade in which political self-interest and social anxiety can be cloaked in morality, has found hatred of homosexuality to be the last respectable prejudice of the century.

Ballot initiatives in Oregon and Maine would deny homosexuals the protection of civil rights laws. The Pentagon has steadfastly refused to allow gays into the armed forces. Vice President Dan Quayle is crusading for "traditional family values." And Pat Buchanan, who is scheduled to speak at the Republican National Convention this evening, regards homosexuality as a litmus test of moral purity.

Nothing has illuminated this crusade more effectively than a work of fiction, *The Drowning of Stephan Jones,* by Bette Greene. Preparing for her novel, Ms. Greene interviewed more than 400 young men incarcerated for gay-bashing, and scrutinized their case studies. In an interview published in *The Boston Globe* this spring, she said she found that the gay-bashers generally saw nothing wrong in what they did, and, more often than not, said their religious leaders and traditions sanctioned their behavior. One convicted teen-age gay-basher told her that the pastor of his church had said, "Homosexuals represent the devil, Satan," and that the Rev. Jerry Falwell had echoed that charge.

Christians opposed to political and social equality for homosexuals nearly always appeal to the moral injunctions of the Bible, claiming that Scripture is very clear on the matter and citing verses that support their opinion. They accuse others of perverting and distorting texts contrary to their "clear" meaning. They do not, however, necessarily see quite as clear a meaning in biblical passages on economic conduct, the burdens of wealth, and the sin of greed.

Nine biblical citations are customarily invoked as relating to homo-   5
sexuality. Four (Deuteronomy 23:17, I Kings 14:24, I Kings 22:46, and II
Kings 23:7) simply forbid prostitution, by men and women.

Two others (Leviticus 18:19–23 and Leviticus 20:10–16) are part of
what biblical scholars call the Holiness Code. The code explicitly bans homosexual acts. But it also prohibits eating raw meat, planting two different
kinds of seed in the same field, and wearing garments with two different
kinds of yarn. Tattoos, adultery, and sexual intercourse during a woman's
menstrual period are similarly outlawed.

There is no mention of homosexuality in the four Gospels of the
New Testament. The moral teachings of Jesus are not concerned with
the subject.

Three references from St. Paul are frequently cited (Romans 1:26–2:1,
I Corinthians 6:9–11, and I Timothy 1:10). But St. Paul was concerned
with homosexuality only because in Greco-Roman culture it represented a
secular sensuality that was contrary to his Jewish-Christian spiritual idealism. He was against lust and sensuality in anyone, including heterosexuals.
To say that homosexuality is bad because homosexuals are tempted to do
morally doubtful things is to say that heterosexuality is bad because heterosexuals are likewise tempted. For St. Paul, anyone who puts his or her interest ahead of God's is condemned, a verdict that falls equally upon everyone.

And lest we forget Sodom and Gomorrah, recall that the story is not
about sexual perversion and homosexual practice. It is about inhospitality,
according to Luke 10:10–13, and failure to care for the poor, according to
Ezekiel 16:49–50: "Behold, this was the iniquity of thy sister Sodom,
pride, fullness of bread, and abundance of idleness was in her and in her
daughters, neither did she strengthen the hand of the poor and needy." To
suggest that Sodom and Gomorrah is about homosexual sex is an analysis
of about as much worth as suggesting that the story of Jonah and the whale
is a treatise on fishing.

Part of the problem is a question of interpretation. Fundamentalists   10
and literalists, the storm troopers of the religious right, are terrified that
Scripture, "wrongly interpreted," may separate them from their values. That
fear stems from their own recognition that their "values" are not derived
from Scripture, as they publicly claim.

Indeed, it is through the lens of their own prejudices and personal values that they "read" Scripture and cloak their own views in its authority. We
all interpret Scripture: Make no mistake. And no one truly is a literalist,
despite the pious temptation. The questions are, By what principle of
interpretation do we proceed, and by what means do we reconcile "what
it meant then" to "what it means now"?

These matters are far too important to be left to scholars and seminari-
ans alone. Our ability to judge ourselves and others rests on our ability to
interpret Scripture intelligently. The right use of the Bible, an exercise as old

as the church itself, means that we confront our prejudices rather than merely confirm them.

For Christians, the principle by which Scripture is read is nothing less than an appreciation of the work and will of God as revealed in that of Jesus. To recover a liberating and inclusive Christ is to be freed from the semantic bondage that makes us curators of a dead culture rather than creatures of a new creation.

Religious fundamentalism is dangerous because it cannot accept ambiguity and diversity and is therefore inherently intolerant. Such intolerance, in the name of virtue, is ruthless and uses political power to destroy what it cannot convert.

It is dangerous, especially in America, because it is anti-democratic and is suspicious of "the other," in whatever form that "other" might appear. To maintain itself, fundamentalism must always define "the other" as deviant.

But the chief reason that fundamentalism is dangerous is that, at the hands of the Rev. Pat Robertson, the Rev. Jerry Falwell, and hundreds of lesser-known but equally worrisome clerics, preachers, and pundits, it uses Scripture and the Christian practice to encourage ordinarily good people to act upon their fears rather than their virtues.

Fortunately, those who speak for the religious right do not speak for all American Christians, and the Bible is not theirs alone to interpret. The same Bible that the advocates of slavery used to protect their wicked self-interests is the Bible that inspired slaves to revolt and their liberators to action.

The same Bible that the predecessors of Mr. Falwell and Mr. Robertson used to keep white churches white is the source of the inspiration of the Rev. Martin Luther King, Jr., and the social reformation of the 1960's.

The same Bible that antifeminists use to keep women silent in the churches is the Bible that preaches liberation to captives and says that in Christ there is neither male nor female, slave nor free.

And the same Bible that on the basis of an archaic social code of ancient Israel and a tortured reading of Paul is used to condemn all homosexuals and homosexual behavior includes metaphors of redemption, renewal, inclusion, and love—principles that invite homosexuals to accept their freedom and responsibility in Christ and demands that their fellow Christians accept them as well.

The political piety of the fundamentalist religious right must not be exercised at the expense of our precious freedoms. And in this summer of our discontent, one of the most precious freedoms for which we must all fight is freedom from this last prejudice.

For Discussion

1. In paragraphs 5–9, Gomes offers his interpretations of the biblical passages usually cited as showing God's condemnation of

homosexuality. How well does Gomes deflate the arguments from Leviticus and from the letters written by St. Paul? To what extent does Gomes's own authority as a minister and Harvard theologian lend force to his view of these passages? (You may want to consult the biblical passages yourself before you respond.)

2. Gomes argues that all reading of Scripture involves interpretation (paragraph 11). What, for him, is the difference between right and wrong interpretation? How is "right" interpretation similar to inquiry, as we describe it on pages 145–146? Must a "right" interpretation be apolitical—that is, influenced by no political viewpoint?

3. What argumentative and stylistic techniques does Gomes use in paragraphs 17–20 to support his point about right and wrong interpretations of the Bible?

4. In his criticism of the rhetorical, or persuasive, strategy of the religious right, Gomes says their use of the Bible "encourage[s] ordinarily good people to act upon their fears rather than their virtues" (paragraph 16). Do you agree? Is it always bad to use fear as an emotional appeal in persuasive argumentation?

5. What other issues can you think of in which people commonly call upon the authority of the Bible for support? Do you think Gomes would argue that any of these misuse Scripture in the way he describes here?

For Analysis and Persuasion

A classic example of persuasive argumentation that calls upon the Bible as a source of authority is "Letter from Birmingham Jail" by Martin Luther King, Jr. (pages 234–246). After you have read King's "Letter" and our analysis of King's audience and purpose (pages 246–247), go back and locate all of King's references to the Bible. Write a paper in which you discuss King's use of the Bible, noting the specific fears or virtues of his audience to which he is appealing.

Degrees of Discomfort
Jonathan Alter

A person who has no tolerance for others of a particular race is a racist. The following argument, originally published in Newsweek, *asks whether homophobia, or prejudice against homosexuals, is equivalent to racism. The question is important because defenders of homosexual rights argue that the two forms of discrimination are comparable, while those who oppose gay rights claim their own right to disapprove of people whose behavior is repugnant or even sinful according to their own moral standards. Note how Jonathan Alter's argument makes the case for civil rights for gay people but not for universal tolerance of homosexuality. Note, too, that Alter wrote his essay in response to an incident in which Martin Luther King III first made and then retracted a statement critical of homosexuals.*

When Andy Rooney got in trouble last month, gay activists complained he was being publicly rebuked for his allegedly racist remarks and not for his gay-bashing.[1] They wanted to know why homophobia was viewed as less serious than racism. The case of Martin Luther King III last week brought the comparison into even sharper relief. After a speech in Poughkeepsie, NY, in which he said "something must be wrong" with homosexuals, the young Atlanta politician met with angry gay leaders and quickly apologized. His father's legacy, King said, was "the struggle to free this country of bigotry and discrimination." In that light, he added, he needed to examine his own attitudes toward homosexuals.

King will need to ask himself this question: Is homophobia the moral equivalent of racism? To answer yes sounds right; it conforms to commendable ideals of tolerance. But it doesn't take account of valid distinctions between the two forms of prejudice. On the other hand, to answer no — to say, homophobia is not like racism for this reason or that — risks rationalizing anti-gay bias.

Discrimination against homose*x*uals is not the same as personal distaste for homose*x*uality. The former is clearly akin to racism. There is no way to explain away the prejudice in this country against gays. People lose jobs, promotions, homes, and friends because of it. Incidents of violence against gays are up sharply in some areas. Hundreds of anti-sodomy laws remain on the books, and gays are shamelessly discriminated against in insurance and inheritance. The fact is, a lot of people are pigheaded enough to judge a person entirely on the basis

---

[1] Rooney, a commentator on *60 Minutes,* was briefly suspended by CBS in 1990 for making remarks that offended blacks but not for comments critical of homosexuality.

of his or her sexuality. Rooney's mail—and that of practically everyone else commenting publicly on this issue—is full of ugly anti-gay invective.

But does that mean that anyone who considers the homosexual sex act sinful or repulsive is the equivalent of a racist? The answer is no. Objecting to it may be narrow-minded and invasive of privacy, but it does not convey the same complete moral vacuity as, say, arguing that blacks are born inferior. There is a defensible middle position. Recall Mario Cuomo's carefully articulated view of abortion: personally opposed, but deeply supportive of a woman's right to choose. That tracks quite closely to polls that show how the majority of Americans approach the subject of homosexuality.

Like all straddles, this one offends people on both sides: straights who consider all homosexuality sinful, and gays who consider a hate-the-sin-but-not-the-sinner argument merely another form of homophobia. Moreover, the "personal opposition" idea rings more hollow on homosexuality than on abortion; after all, there is no third-party fetus—just consenting adults whose private behavior should not be judged by outsiders. Of course there are times when squeamishness is understandable. In coming of age, many gays have made a point of flaunting their sexuality, moving, as one joke puts it, from "the love that dare not speak its name" to "the love that won't shut up." Exhibitionism and promiscuity (less common in the age of AIDS) are behavioral choices that, unlike innate sexual preference, can be controlled. It's perfectly legitimate to condemn such behavior—assuming heterosexuals are held to the same standard.

Simply put, identity and behavior are not synonymous. A bigot hates blacks for what they *are;* a reasonable person can justifiably object to some things homosexuals *do.* The distinction between objecting to who someone is (unfair) and objecting to what someone does (less unfair) must be maintained. The worst comment about gays allegedly made by Rooney was that he would not like to be locked in a room with them. That would be a tolerable sentiment only if the homosexuals were *having sex* in the room. Otherwise, it's a form of bigotry. Who would object to being locked in a room with cigarette smokers if they weren't smoking?

"Acting gay" often involves more than sexual behavior itself. Much of the dislike for homosexuals centers not on who they are or what they do in private, but on so-called affectations—"swishiness" in men, the "butch" look for women—not directly related to the more private sex act. Heterosexuals tend to argue that gays can downplay these characteristics and "pass" more easily in the straight world than blacks can in a white world.

This may be true, but it's also irrelevant. For many gays those traits aren't affectations but part of their identities; attacking the swishiness is the

5

same as attacking *them.* Why the visceral vehemence, particularly among straight men? Richard Isay, a psychiatrist and author of the 1989 book *Being Homosexual,* suggests that homophobia actually has little to do with the sex act itself. "This hatred of homosexuals appears to be secondary in our society to the fear and hatred of what is perceived as being 'feminine' in other men and in oneself."

Such fears, buried deep, are reminiscent of the emotional charge of racial feelings. At its most virulent, this emotion leads to blaming the victim — for AIDS, for instance, or for poverty. In its more modest form, the fear, when recognized, can be helpful in understanding the complexities of both homosexuality and race.

That consciousness is sometimes about language — avoiding "fag" and   10
"nigger." But the interest groups that expend energy insisting that one use "African-American" instead of "black" or "gay and lesbian" instead of "homosexual" are missing the point. Likewise, the distinctions between racism and homophobia eventually shrivel before the larger task at hand, which is simply to look harder at ourselves.

For Discussion

1. In your own words, explain what Alter sees as "a defensible middle position" on the issue of discrimination against homosexuals (paragraph 4). How does he support and defend that position?
2. Evaluate Alter's argument in paragraph 6, which compares homosexuals to cigarette smokers. In context, how valid is this analogy?
3. In paragraphs 7–8, Alter points out that what many straight people call "affected" behavior in gay people is actually part of their identities, something that they may not be able to hide even if they wanted to. Is one's sexual orientation something everyone should try to downplay in public? Should, for example, heterosexual couples be expected to avoid romantic physical contact in public, as most homosexual couples feel they must do?
4. Alter seems to conclude that homophobia, or "personal distaste for homo*sexuality,*" is not as severe a character flaw as racism (paragraphs 3–4). How does he support this point? Do you agree with him?
5. Alter quotes psychiatrist Richard Isay on a possible cause for homophobia (paragraph 8). What do you think of Isay's theory? Look at Pete Hamill's description of how "Real Men were supposed to react" if approached by a homosexual (paragraph 13 in his essay earlier in this chapter). Do you think Isay's

theory might help explain some of the violence committed against gay men?

For Inquiry

Alter acknowledges that his middle position would offend "people on both sides" (paragraph 5). Write a dialogue with Alter in which you examine the truth of his position, posing questions that would represent the viewpoints of both sides. See pages 159–160 for suggestions about what to ask.

Beyond Oppression
Jonathan Rauch

Some writers have claimed that gay men and lesbians are an oppressed class. Jonathan Rauch sets forth what he sees as criteria for claiming oppression, and he argues that gay men and lesbians in the United States do not meet these criteria. What is Rauch's purpose in denying victim status to gay people?

At 10:30 on a weeknight in the spring of 1991, Glenn Cashmore was walking to his car on San Diego's University Avenue. He had just left the Soho coffee house in Hillcrest, a heavily gay neighborhood. He turned down Fourth Street and paused to look at the display in an optician's window. Someone shouted, "Hey, faggot!" He felt pain in his shoulder and turned in time to see a white Nissan speeding away. Someone had shot him, luckily only with a pellet gun. The pellet tore through the shirt and penetrated the skin. He went home and treated the wound with peroxide.

Later that year, on the night of December 13, a 17-year-old named John Wear and two other boys were headed to the Soho on University Avenue when a pair of young men set upon them, calling them "faggots." One boy escaped, another's face was gashed and Wear (who, his family said, was not gay) was stabbed. Cashmore went to the hospital to see him but, on arriving, was met with the news that Wear was dead.

This is life—not all of life, but an aspect of life—for gay people in today's America. Homosexuals are objects of scorn for teenagers and of sympathy or moral fear or hatred for adults. They grow up in confusion and bewilderment as children, then often pass into denial as young adults and sometimes remain frightened even into old age. They are persecuted by the military, are denied the sanctuary of publicly recognized marriage, occasionally are prosecuted outright for making love. If closeted, they live with fear of revelation; if open, they must daily negotiate a hundred delicate tactical issues. (Should I bring it up? Tell my boss? My co-workers? Wear a wedding band? Display my lover's picture?)

There is also AIDS and the stigma attached to it, though AIDS is not uniquely a problem of gay people. And there is the violence. One of my high school friends—an honors student at Brophy Prep, a prestigious Catholic high school in Phoenix—used to boast about his late-night exploits with a baseball bat at the "fag Denny's." I'm sure he was lying, but imagine the horror of being spoken to, and about, in that way.

If you ask gay people in America today whether homosexuals are oppressed, I think most would say yes. If you ask why, they would point to the sorts of facts that I just mentioned. The facts are not blinkable. Yet the oppression diagnosis is, for the most part, wrong.

5

Not wrong in the sense that life for American homosexuals is hunky-dory. It is not. But life is not terrible for most gay people, either, and it is becoming less terrible every year. The experience of gayness and the social status of homosexuals have changed rapidly in the last twenty years, largely owing to the courage of thousands who decided that they had had enough abuse and who demanded better. With change has come the time for a reassessment.

The standard political model sees homosexuals as an oppressed minority who must fight for their liberation through political action. But that model's usefulness is drawing to a close. It is ceasing to serve the interests of ordinary gay people, who ought to begin disengaging from it, even drop it. Otherwise, they will misread their position and lose their way, as too many minority groups have done already.

"Oppression" has become every minority's word for practically everything, a one-size-fits-all political designation used by anyone who feels unequal, aggrieved, or even uncomfortable. I propose a start toward restoring meaning to the notion of oppression by insisting on *objective* evidence. A sense of grievance or discomfort, however real, is not enough.

By now, human beings know a thing or two about oppression. Though it may, indeed, take many forms and work in different ways, there are objective signs you can look for. My own list would emphasize five main items. First, direct legal or governmental discrimination. Second, denial of political franchise — specifically, denial of the right to vote, organize, speak, or lobby. Third — and here we move beyond the strictly political — the systematic denial of education. Fourth, impoverishment relative to the non-oppressed population. And, fifth, a pattern of human rights violations, without recourse.

Any one or two of those five signposts may appear for reasons other than oppression. There are a lot of reasons why a people may be poor, for instance. But where you see a minority that is legally barred from businesses and neighborhoods and jobs, that cannot vote, that is poor and poorly educated, and that lives in physical fear, you are looking at, for instance, the blacks of South Africa, or blacks of the American South until the 1960s; the Jews and homosexuals of Nazi Germany and Vichy France; the untouchable castes of India, the Kurds of Iraq, the women of Saudi Arabia, the women of America 100 years ago; for that matter, the entire population of the former Soviet Union and many Arab and African and Asian countries.

And gay people in America today? Criterion one — direct legal or governmental discrimination — is resoundingly met. Homosexual relations are illegal in twenty-three states, at least seven of which specifically single out acts between persons of the same sex. Gay marriage is not legally recognized anywhere. And the government hounds gay people from the military, not for what they do but for what they are.

10

Criterion two—denial of political franchise—is resoundingly not met. Not only do gay people vote, they are turning themselves into a constituency to be reckoned with and fought for. Otherwise, the Patrick Buchanans of the world would have sounded contemptuous of gay people at the Republican convention last year, rather than panicked by them. If gay votes didn't count, Bill Clinton would not have stuck his neck out on the military issue during the primary season (one of the bravest things any living politician has done).

Criterion three—denial of education—is also resoundingly not met. Overlooked Opinions Inc., a Chicago market-research company, has built a diverse national base of 35,000 gay men and lesbians, two-thirds of whom are either not out of the closet or are only marginally out, and has then randomly sampled them in surveys. It found that homosexuals had an average of 15.7 years of education, as against 12.7 years for the population as a whole. Obviously, the findings may be skewed if college-educated gay people are likelier to take part in surveys (though Overlooked Opinions said that results didn't follow degree of closetedness). Still, any claim that gay people are denied education appears ludicrous.

Criterion four—relative impoverishment—is also not met. In Overlooked Opinions' sample, gay men had an average household income of $51,624 and lesbians $42,755, compared with the national average of $36,800. Again, yuppie homosexuals may be more likely to answer survey questions than blue-collar ones. But, again, to call homosexuals an impoverished class would be silly.

Criterion five—human rights violations without recourse—is also, in the end, not met, though here it's worth taking a moment to see why it is not. The number of gay bashings has probably increased in recent years (though it's hard to know, what with reporting vagaries), and, of course, many gay-bashers either aren't caught or aren't jailed. What too many gay people forget, though, is that these are problems that homosexuals have in common with non-gay Americans. Though many gay-bashers go free, so do many murderers. In the District of Columbia last year, the police identified suspects in fewer than half of all murders, to say nothing of assault cases.

And the fact is that anti-gay violence is just one part of a much broader pattern. Probably not coincidentally, the killing of John Wear happened in the context of a year, 1991, that broke San Diego's all-time homicide record (1992 was runner-up). Since 1965 the homicide rate in America has doubled, the violent crime arrest rate for juveniles has more than tripled; people now kill you to get your car, they kill you to get your shoes or your potato chips, they kill you because they can do it. A particularly ghastly fact is that homicide due to gunshot is now the second leading cause of death in high school–age kids, after car crashes. No surprise, then, that gay people are afraid. So is everyone else.

Chances are, indeed, that gay people's social class makes them safer, on average, than other urban minorities. Certainly their problem is small compared with what blacks face in inner-city Los Angeles or Chicago, where young black males are likelier to be killed than a U.S. soldier was in a tour of duty in Vietnam.

If any problem unites gay people with non-gay people, it is crime. If any issue does not call for special-interest pleading, this is it. Minority advocates, including gay ones, have blundered insensitively by trying to carve out hate-crime statutes and other special-interest crime laws instead of focusing on tougher measures against violence of all kinds. In trying to sensitize people to crimes aimed specifically at minorities, they are inadvertently desensitizing them to the vastly greater threat of crime against everyone. They contribute to the routinization of murder, which has now reached the point where news of a black girl spray-painted white makes the front pages, but news of a black girl murdered runs in a round-up on page D-6 ("Oh, another killing"). Yes, gay-bashing is a problem. But, no, it isn't oppression. It is, rather, an obscenely ordinary feature of the American experience.

Of course, homosexuals face unhappiness, discrimination, and hatred. But for everyone with a horror story to tell, there are others like an academic I know, a tenured professor who is married to his lover of fourteen years in every way but legally, who owns a split-level condo in Los Angeles, drives a Miata, enjoys prestige and success and love that would be the envy of millions of straight Americans. These things did not fall in his lap. He fought personal and professional battles, was passed over for jobs and left the closet when that was much riskier than it is today. Asked if he is oppressed, he says, "You're damn straight." But a mark of oppression is that most of its victims are not allowed to succeed; they are allowed only to fail. And this man is no mere token. He is one of a growing multitude of openly gay people who have overcome the past and, in doing so, changed the present.

"I'm a gay person, so I don't live in a free country," one highly successful gay writer said recently, "and I don't think most straight people really sit down and realize that for gay people this is basically a totalitarian society in which we're barely tolerated." The reason straight people don't realize this is because it obviously isn't true. As more and more homosexuals come out of hiding, the reality of gay economic and political and educational achievement becomes more evident. And as that happens, gay people who insist they are oppressed will increasingly, and not always unfairly, come off as yuppie whiners, "victims" with $50,000 incomes and vacations in Europe. They may feel they are oppressed, but they will have a harder and harder time convincing the public.

They will distort their politics, too, twisting it into strained and impotent shapes. Scouring for oppressions with which to identify, activists are driven further and further afield. They grab fistfuls of random political demands and stuff them in their pockets. The original platform for April's

20

March on Washington[1] called for, among other things, enforced bilingual education, "an end to genocide of all the indigenous peoples and their cultures," defense budget cuts, universal health care, a national needle exchange program, free substance-abuse treatment on demand, safe and affordable abortion, more money for breast cancer "and other cancers particular to women," "unrestricted, safe and affordable alternative insemination," health care for the "differently-abled and physically challenged," and "an end to poverty." Here was the oppression-entitlement mentality gone haywire.

Worst of all, oppression politics distorts the face of gay America itself. It encourages people to forget that homosexuality isn't hell. As the AIDS crisis has so movingly shown, gay people have built the kind of community that evaporated for many non-gay Americans decades ago. You don't see straight volunteers queuing up to change cancer patients' bedpans and deliver their groceries. Gay people — and unmarried people generally — are at a disadvantage in the top echelons of corporate America, but, on the other hand, they have achieved dazzlingly in culture and business and much else. They lead lives of richness and competence and infinite variety, lives that are not miserable or squashed.

The insistence that gay people are oppressed is most damaging, in the end, because it implies that to be gay is to suffer. It affirms what so many straight people, even sympathetic ones, believe in their hearts: that homosexuals are pitiable. That alone is reason to junk the oppression model, preferably sooner instead of later.

If the oppression model is failing, what is the right model? Not that of an oppressed people seeking redemption through political action; rather, that of an ostracized people seeking redemption through personal action. What do you do about misguided ostracism? The most important thing is what Glenn Cashmore did. After John Wear's murder, he came out of the closet. He wrote an article in the *Los Angeles Times* denouncing his own years of silence. He stepped into the circle of people who are what used to be called known homosexuals.

This makes a difference. The *New York Times* conducted a poll on homosexuals this year and found that people who had a gay family member or close friend "were much more tolerant and accepting." Whereas oppression politics fails because it denies reality, positive personal example works because it demonstrates reality. "We're here, we're queer, get used to it," Queer Nation's chant,[2] is not only a brilliant slogan. It is a strategy. It is, in some ways, *the* strategy. To move away from oppression politics is not to sit quietly. It is often to hold hands in public or take a lover

25

---

[1] A major gay rights demonstration was held in Washington, D.C., on April 25, 1993.
[2] Queer Nation is a gay political organization — many members of which are in their twenties — that advocates a highly visible gay presence in society.

to the company Christmas party, sometimes to stage kiss-ins, always to be unashamed. It is to make of honesty a kind of activism.

Gay Americans should emulate Jewish Americans, who have it about right. Jews recognize that to many Americans we will always seem different (and we are, in some ways, different). We grow up being fed "their" culture in school, in daily life, even in the calendar. It never stops. For a full month of every year, every radio program and shop window reminds you that this is, culturally, a Christian nation (no, not Judeo-Christian). Jews could resent this, but most of us choose not to, because, by way of compensation, we think hard, we work hard, we are cohesive, we are interesting. We recognize that minorities will always face special burdens of adjustment, but we also understand that with those burdens come rewards of community and spirit and struggle. We recognize that there will always be a minority of Americans who hate us, but we also understand that, so long as we stay watchful, this hateful minority is more pathetic than threatening. We watch it; we fight it when it lashes out; but we do not organize our personal and political lives around it.

Gay people's main weapons are ones we already possess. In America, our main enemies are superstition and hate. Superstition is extinguished by public criticism and by the power of moral example. Political activists always underestimate the power of criticism and moral example to change people's minds, and they always overestimate the power of law and force. As for hate, the way to fight it is with love. And that we have in abundance.

For Discussion

1. Rauch acknowledges the opposition's arguments in paragraphs 1–4, but he denies that any of the examples constitute "*objective evidence*" of oppression (paragraph 8). Would you agree?
2. Does Rauch offer enough evidence to show that homosexuals meet only one of his criteria for claiming oppression? Could you raise any questions about the five criteria he sets up? Can you think of additional criteria?
3. In paragraph 24, Rauch argues that gay people work on the model that they are ostracized, not oppressed. What is the difference?
4. Rauch suggests that gay people can improve their situation through personal rather than political action. What is he advocating? Do you think his plan will work?

For Convincing

Many of the arguments in this chapter suggest or deny that parallels exist between racism and discrimination against homosexuals. Make your own case for or against such parallels, using some of the readings here as well as additional sources and evidence.

For Further Research and Discussion

1. One large area of debate related to homosexual rights involves marriage, or the legal benefits of marriage: tax breaks, employer-sponsored insurance coverage for spouses, inheritance rights, even the right not to be forced to testify in court against one's mate. There is, further, the symbolic statement that marriage makes about a couple's commitment to each other. In 1967, the Supreme Court called marriage "one of the basic civil rights of man." Inquire into this issue, and be ready to report to the class on the range of opinions about marriage and domestic partnerships. (Gay people themselves are divided on the question.)

2. Inquire into the latest research on the causes of homosexuality. What interpretation do most gay people seem to accept on this matter? If a clear case could be made for biological causation, your class might want to discuss how such a conclusion would influence any of the arguments about homophobia and gay rights.

Additional Suggestions for Writing

1. *Inquiry and convincing.* Based on your inquiry into the views on gay marriage, write an exploratory essay in which you discuss areas of agreement and disagreement. Conclude with a statement of your own position on this issue, indicating which reasons uncovered in your research best support your position. Then go on to draft and revise a case for an opposing audience.

2. *Persuasion.* In this chapter's first selection, Jeffrey Nickel points out that homophobia is something children learn at an early age in our society. Some school districts have devised curriculums aimed at encouraging greater tolerance of homosexuals through, for example, the use of storybooks that depict children who have "two mommies" or "two daddies." This aspect of New York City's "Rainbow Curriculum" was quite controversial.

   Do research into educational curriculums that deal with homosexuality. Find out where such curriculums have been tried and what the pro and con arguments are. If you decide such curriculums would not be effective in reducing homophobia or that reducing homophobia should not be a function of the schools, write a persuasive argument against instituting such curriculums. If you decide that they are a good idea, make a persuasive argument for some specific course of action.

3. *Mediation.* The AIDS epidemic has focused public attention on questions of rights and responsibilities. Some gay advocates argue that it is the responsibility of the government and the medical community to find a vaccine to prevent AIDS so that people need not live in terror if they fail to follow all the guidelines for safe sex. At the other extreme,

people argue that because AIDS is a preventable disease, it is the responsibility of each adult to see that he or she is not exposed through risky behavior and that the government and medical community ought to give their full attention to life-threatening diseases that strike at random. Investigate these arguments about AIDS research and spending and the range of viewpoints in between. Write a mediatory essay that suggests a position all sides could find reasonable.

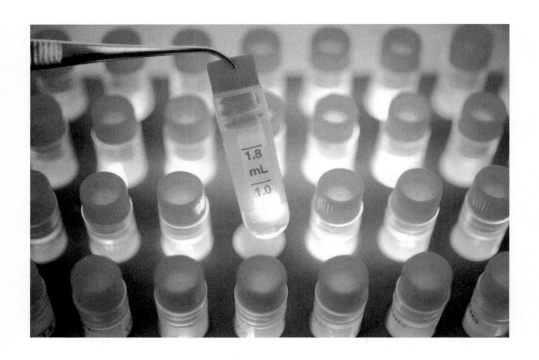

Chapter 14

Genetics and Enhancement: Better Than Human?

Human beings have always found ways to enhance life by improving on what nature provides. That's what technology is all about, from the first primitive stone tools to today's computers and cell phones. Now technology can improve not just how we live but also who we are through genetic engineering. The question is *How far should we go in using genetics to enhance human life?*

Some people object entirely to gene manipulation on the grounds that it's unnatural or playing God. But human beings aren't natural. Other species live in environments; we create our own. Our lives are artificial in the sense of *artifice*—we depend on things we've made. The alternative is naked existence in caves. As for "playing God": That happens every time a doctor cures a disease that would otherwise kill someone. It happens when a couple unable to conceive a child through intercourse opts for artificial insemination. It happens when desperately ill people are placed on or removed from life support. "Playing God" is an everyday occurrence, not something to object to universally unless you're prepared to reject all of medical science.

We should get beyond any simplified version of the "against nature" and "against God" arguments. We should also get beyond popular fantasies. Genetic engineering is not the haunt of mad scientists. Nor is it magic that will give us the perfect world. We are not about to prevent aging or eliminate death. Genetic engineering can do amazing things already and will do things in the near future we can hardly imagine, but our world will remain far from our wisest desires.

So, is genetic engineering just another human artifice, another technology? Is it any different fundamentally from all the other ways we enhance ourselves? To see why genetic engineering is controversial and what the serious objections to it might be, let's compare it to a widely accepted technology, plastic surgery.

When someone gets a "nose job," for instance, only the person with the nose he or she doesn't like is directly affected. Because genetics can alter germ cells, human sperm and eggs, it's possible to alter not only one person but also his or her children, the children's children, and so on. With a nose job, the person knows or should know the possible outcomes that may be less than ideal. Because genes interact with other genes in ways too complex for complete understanding or prediction, it's hard to know exactly what the outcome might be. We might change a person's genes to eliminate, say, colon cancer that runs in her or his family but, in doing so, increase the person's likelihood of contracting some other deadly disease. But the side effect may not turn up for years, maybe not for several generations.

Clearly, then, genetic enhancement is very different from plastic surgery. Its power to transform is far greater. Genetic engineering has the potential to cure devastating diseases, like the Alzheimer's that afflicted President Reagan, and to repair tissue damaged in accidents that otherwise won't regenerate. People like the late Christopher Reeve, wheelchair-bound from spinal cord injuries, could perhaps have walked again. Stem cells, which have the unique capacity to develop into any tissue in the body, might well be used to repair a diseased brain or restore damaged nerves in a spinal cord.

But stem cells are harvested either from aborted fetuses or from embryos created in laboratories for that purpose. This disturbs enough people that President Bush has severely restricted stem cell research. He also formed the President's Council on Bioethics to advise him on all matters relating to genetic engineering.

The ethical problems are hardly limited to what we have mentioned so far. If we can prevent or cure a disease, we might also learn how to raise a child's IQ or make the child more outgoing. In other words, instead of accepting the children that, depending on our beliefs, nature or God gave us, we could select the traits we wanted our children to have. We already can screen embryos to give a couple a boy rather than a girl, or vice versa—why not a child who is unusually pretty or handsome, gifted athletically or musically, and so on and so on? All of this sounds wonderful—why play the genetic lottery if we don't have to? But do we really want to go to such a level? Do we want to be *responsible* for what our children are to a degree that far exceeds the obligation to raise them as best we can?

Even if some of us are willing and able to take the responsibility, others won't have the chance. The analogy with plastic surgery becomes relevant again. It's very expensive. The great majority of people can't afford it and so generally only relatively well-off people get plastic surgery for cosmetic reasons. Similarly, the cost of genetic enhancement will likely restrict it to the wealthy, who can afford to design their children if they want to. What might this lead to over many generations? Two distinct races? Perhaps even distinct species? In any case, the rich will enjoy yet more advantages than they already have. What will genetic enhancement do to us in the long run? Decrease human diversity? Make a democratic society impossible to maintain even in theory?

We've only just touched here on the extraordinary potential of genetic enhancement and the equally extraordinary ethical problems it raises. The articles in this section will take us further and deeper. We need to examine the issues because, like the physics of the atom and the digital revolution, genetic engineering is a major development that must be confronted squarely. Most of the crucial decisions have yet to be made. We need to be prepared to help make them. Nothing less than the meaning of "being human" is at stake.

Stem Cell Stumping
Anne Applebaum

This article reminds us of some basic points we must keep in mind as we read all the selections about genetic enhancement: that politics is not separate from but in the middle of the controversy; that, consequently, to gain political advantage, extravagant and simplistic claims are made both for and against genetic engineering; that, to see clearly past all the hype, what we need most is a solid grasp of the facts. These facts include both knowledge about genetic science in general and the current state of national policy regarding genetic research.

Applebaum is a political columnist for The Washington Post *and a frequent contributor to such journals as* The Spectator *and* The New Statesman *(1996). Her book,* Gulag, *won the 2004 Pulitzer Prize for general nonfiction.*

"We also—we also need to lift the ban on stem cell research—(cheers, applause) and find cures that will help millions of Americans (applause continues)."

Applause continues. That's a direct quote from the transcript of the speech that Sen. Hillary Rodham Clinton gave at the Democratic convention last week. Unexpectedly, the applause continued all week long, for anyone who spoke about stem cell research. Sen. John Kerry got some for asking, "What if we have a president who believes in science, so we can unleash the wonders of discovery—like stem cell research—and treat illness for millions of lives?" Ron Reagan, son of the late president, who mistakenly imagined he was being cheered merely for what he said rather than who his father was, hit an even higher rhetorical note: "Sound like magic? Welcome to the future of medicine."

Listening to all these speeches, you might have come away with the impression that stem cell research is illegal in this country, and that if our recalcitrant, medieval, anti-science fundamentalist president would only "lift the ban," or lose the election, there would be "magic" cures for old people with Alzheimer's and children with diabetes. By coincidence, the quadriplegic actor Christopher Reeve told CNN last weekend that he would walk again "in the next three to five years" with the help of stem cell research. He spoke of the obstacles to that goal as political rather than merely medical. The message: President Bush has grounded Superman.

As it happens, I do think we should liberalize our national policy on stem cell research. But before we do that, it's important to be pretty clear about what that national policy actually is, and how it got to be that way. Stem cell research is not, in fact, either illegal or unfunded: The federal budget in 2003 included $24.8 million for human embryonic stem cell research—up from zero in 2000. Private funding of stem cell research, which is unlimited, runs into the tens and possibly hundreds of millions of dollars. The current, admittedly hairsplitting policy came about because Congress in 1995 passed a ban on federal (but not private) funding for any form of research that involved the destruction of human embryos, because it is a form of research many American voters dislike and don't want to pay for. After some important (privately funded) breakthroughs, the Clinton administration began looking for legal ways to bypass the ban, but never got around to paying for any actual research.

The Bush administration thought about it, too, and came up with a solution: Federal funding could be used for research on stem cell lines already in existence. In practice, this means scientists who get their funding from the government are restricted in which materials they can use. Although this compromise will soon become a real obstacle to research, for the moment the irritant is largely philosophical. "What hampers people is the concept that there is a lack of freedom to operate," one scientist told me.

If all of that sounds a little long-winded and complicated, that's because it is. The question now is whether we want, as a nation, to continue to have long-winded and complicated debates about complicated issues, or whether we want to resort to slogans such as "lift the ban" and "unleash the wonders of discovery." The question is also whether Americans and their political representatives are allowed to think twice about the implications of brand-new science—a prerequisite for public support, one would think—or whether the patients' groups and pollsters behind last week's rhetoric always get the last word.

At some point we also need to make some distinction between science and "magic." It is true that funneling more money into biological research will produce more breakthroughs and more cures. It is also true that even with unlimited funding, Reeve might never walk again. This is research, not abracadabra. Talk of "magic" doesn't do much to reverse widespread scientific illiteracy either, which remains a far greater obstacle to scientific progress than the president.

But simplifying the argument must work as a political tactic or the Kerry campaign wouldn't have let so many people do it. Perhaps it's because "stem cell research" makes a more attractive cultural buzzword than "abortion," and a more unifying cultural issue than gay marriage. Perhaps it's because it is so easy to use personal anecdotes—Ron Reagan spoke of a 13-year-old girl who decorates her insulin pump with rhinestones—to turn a dry scientific subject into an emotional one. Or perhaps it's because the discussion taps into an old and familiar metaphor—Galileo vs. the pope, Voltaire vs. the clerics, progress vs. religion—which helps people feel more comfortable about choosing sides. Call me antediluvian, but I'd still like it better if debates about science began with facts.

5

For Discussion

1. In paragraph 4, Applebaum tells us about the current state of national policy on and funding of stem cell research. Summarize what she says. What didn't you know before reading this essay? What seems most important to you? Why?

2. We all know how politics tends to turn complex issues into simple slogans. But is it realistic to expect "long-winded and complicated debates about complicated issues" (paragraph 6) in the context of political campaigns? What works against such debates? In what contexts and circumstances should such debates go on?

3. Applebaum points to "widespread scientific illiteracy" (paragraph 7) as the "obstacle to scientific progress." Since genetics, like modern physics and digital technology, is difficult for even most well-educated people to understand, how can the scientific community best overcome this obstacle?

For Research and Convincing

Stem cell research is only one aspect of genetic enhancement, but a good place to begin overcoming lack of basic knowledge. As a class project, collect articles and book chapters about it that concentrate on "the facts," current knowledge about stem cells and possible therapies based on it. What do the facts imply about the potential of stem cell research? Make this question the center of class discussion.

Write an essay taking a stance on how much money and talent should be devoted to stem cell research. That is: in your view, how important is it as one among many avenues for scientific research? Conceive your essay as an opinion piece for your campus or local newspaper.

All for the Good: Why Genetic Engineering Must Soldier On

James D. Watson

It's fitting to hear from James Watson: He and Francis Crick won the Nobel Prize for Medicine in 1953 for discovering the double-helix structure of DNA, the foundation of everything that's happened in genetics since. The following article appeared in Time *magazine in 1999.*

His position is summed up in the principle "never postpone experiments that have clearly defined future benefits for fear of dangers that can't be quantified." He points to the lack of harm to humans from genetic work so far and contends the technology will be used to "change a death sentence into a life verdict" by preventing disease. He clearly believes that we do have the wisdom to use this powerful technology to benefit humankind.

There is lots of zip in DNA-based biology today. With each passing year it incorporates an ever increasing fraction of the life sciences, ranging from single-cell organisms, like bacteria and yeast, to the complexities of the human brain. All this wonderful biological frenzy was unimaginable when I first entered the world of genetics. In 1948, biology was an all too descriptive discipline near the bottom of science's totem pole, with physics at its top. By then Einstein's turn-of-the-century ideas about the interconversion of matter and energy had been transformed into the powers of the atom. If not held in check, the weapons they made possible might well destroy the very fabric of civilized human life. So physicists of the late 1940s were simultaneously revered for making atoms relevant to society and feared for what their toys could do if they were to fall into the hands of evil.

Such ambivalent feelings are now widely held toward biology. The double-helical structure of DNA, initially admired for its intellectual simplicity, today represents to many a double-edged sword that can be used for evil as well as good. No sooner had scientists at Stanford University in 1973 begun rearranging DNA molecules in test tubes (and, equally important, reinserting the novel DNA segments back into living cells) than critics began likening these "recombinant" DNA procedures to the physicist's power to break apart atoms. Might not some of the test-tube-rearranged DNA molecules impart to their host cells disease-causing capacities that, like nuclear weapons, are capable of seriously disrupting human civilization? Soon there were cries from both scientists and nonscientists that such research might best be ruled by stringent regulations—if not laws.

As a result, several years were to pass before the full power of recombinant-DNA technology got into the hands of working scientists, who by then were itching to explore previously unattainable secrets of life. Happily, the proposals to control recombinant-DNA research through legislation never got close to enactment. And when anti-DNA doomsday scenarios failed to materialize, even the modestly restrictive governmental regulations began to wither away. In retrospect, recombinant-DNA may rank as the safest revolutionary technology ever developed. To my knowledge, not one fatality, much less illness, has been caused by a genetically manipulated organism.

The moral I draw from this painful episode is this: Never postpone experiments that have clearly defined future benefits for fear of dangers that can't be quantified. Though it may sound at first uncaring, we can react rationally only to real (as opposed to hypothetical) risks. Yet for several years we postponed important experiments on the genetic basis of cancer, for example, because we took much too seriously spurious arguments that the genes at the root of human cancer might themselves be dangerous to work with.

Though most forms of DNA manipulation are now effectively unregu-   5
lated, one important potential goal remains blocked. Experiments aimed at learning how to insert functional genetic material into human germ cells—sperm and eggs—remain off limits to most of the world's scientists. No governmental body wants to take responsibility for initiating steps that might help redirect the course of future human evolution. These decisions reflect widespread concerns that we, as humans, may not have the wisdom to modify the most precious of all human treasures—our chromosomal "instruction books." Dare we be entrusted with improving upon the results of the several million years of Darwinian natural selection? [. . .]

Unlike many of my peers, I'm reluctant to accept such reasoning, again using the argument that you should never put off doing something useful for fear of evil that may never arrive. The first germ-line gene manipulations are unlikely to be attempted for frivolous reasons. Nor does the state of today's science provide the knowledge that would be needed to generate "superpersons" whose far-ranging talents would make those who are genetically unmodified feel redundant and unwanted. Such creations will remain denizens of science fiction, not the real world, far into the future. When they are finally attempted, germ-line genetic manipulations will probably be done to change a death sentence into a life verdict—by creating children who are resistant to a deadly virus, for example, much the way we can already protect plants from viruses by inserting antiviral DNA segments into their genomes.

If appropriate go-ahead signals come, the first resulting gene-bettered children will in no sense threaten human civilization. They will be seen as special only by those in their immediate circles, and are likely to pass as unnoticed in later life as the now grownup "test-tube baby" Louise Brown does today. If they grow up healthily gene-bettered, more such children will follow, and they and those whose lives are enriched by their existence will rejoice that science has again improved human life. If, however, the added genetic material fails to work, better procedures must be developed before more couples commit their psyches toward such inherently unsettling pathways to producing healthy children.

Moving forward will not be for the faint of heart. But if the next century witnesses failure, let it be because our science is not yet up to the job, not because we don't have the courage to make less random the sometimes most unfair courses of human evolution.

For Discussion

1. "We'll cross that bridge when we get to it" is a folk wisdom cliché. Applied to genetic manipulation it means: Don't act to prevent problems that may never arise; act only when actual problems do arise. Do you agree with this general approach to gene enhancement? Why or why not?

2. Watson admits that "[m]oving forward will not be for the faint of heart" (paragraph 8). As with any experimental procedure, what Watson calls "gene-bettered" children must be tried before we can know whether it works and what side effects might result. He's clearly concerned that excessive caution and regulation could retard or prevent progress. Does he have a point? We use clinical trials to test virtually all new medicines and surgical procedures. Should genetic manipulation be treated any differently? If so, in what ways?

3. Watson also points to the sometimes irrational fear that surrounds technological innovation, noting that "test-tube babies," once viewed as unnatural and even grotesque, are now commonly accepted. In your estimation, how much of the anxiety connected with "designer babies" can be attributed to irrational fear?

For Inquiry and Discussion

Sometimes genetic engineering is sharply contrasted with the natural process of evolution, as if human beings, prior to the development of recombinant-DNA technology, had never altered life forms before. Such a notion is obviously false. Many new varieties of plants are created every year by processes like grafting. The modern dog, with breeds in the hundreds, developed from the wolf by the same process that produced all the varieties of farm and ranch animals. The fact is that we have been indirectly manipulating the genes of animals and plants for a long time. What's different now is that we can manipulate them directly.

Viewed in this way, is there any good reason to take the new technology as *fundamentally different* from, say, improving one's cattle by artificial insemination, using only semen collected from a prize-winning bull? In humans, is there any difference between a woman going to a sperm bank and selecting sperm from a man with characteristics she likes as opposed to germ-cell manipulations that would alter the sperm and eggs of a couple in ways both desire?

Think carefully about recombinant technology in the context of selective breeding. Then discuss this comparison in class.

In Defense of Nature, Human and Non-Human

Francis Fukuyama

In recent decades we've gained a renewed respect for nature's blind, trial-and-error approach to genetic diversity, the process we call evolution. We've also learned to appreciate the intricate interactions of life forms in ecosystems and how easily rain forests and coral reefs can be damaged and destroyed by human interventions.

Francis Fukuyama, author of the influential best-seller Our Posthuman Future, *appeals to ecology to argue for strict regulation of bioengineering. He fears, as many people do, that our compulsion to control and manipulate natural processes, including the human genome, will ultimately undermine nature itself.*

Fukuyama is a professor at the Johns Hopkins School of Advanced International Studies. His article appeared in World Watch *(July-August 2002).*

People who have not been paying close attention to the debate on human biotechnology might think that the chief issue in this debate is about abortion, since the most outspoken opponents of cloning to date have been right-to-lifers who oppose the destruction of embryos. But there are important reasons why cloning and the genetic technologies that will follow upon it should be of concern to all people, religious or secular, and above all to those who are concerned with protecting the natural environment. For the attempt to master human nature through biotechnology will be even more dangerous and consequential than the efforts of industrial societies to master non-human nature through earlier generations of technology.

If there is one thing that the environmental movement has taught us in the past couple of generations, it is that nature is a complex whole. The different parts of an ecosystem are mutually interdependent in ways that we often fail to understand; human efforts to manipulate certain parts of it will produce a host of unintended consequences that will come back to haunt us.

Watching one of the movies made in the 1930s about the construction of Hoover Dam or the Tennessee Valley Authority is today a strange experience: the films are at the same time naive and vaguely Stalinist, celebrating the human conquest of nature and boasting of the replacement of natural spaces with steel, concrete, and electricity. This victory over nature was short-lived: in the past generation, no developed country has undertaken a new large hydroelectric project, precisely because we now understand the devastating ecological and social consequences that such undertakings produce. Indeed, the environmental movement has been active in trying to persuade China to desist from pursuing the enormously destructive Three Gorges Dam.

If the problem of unintended consequences is severe in the case of non-human ecosystems, it will be far worse in the realm of human genetics. The human genome has in fact been likened to an ecosystem in the complex way that genes interact and influence one another. It is now estimated that there are only about 30,000 genes in the human genome, far fewer than the 100,000 believed to exist until recently. This is not terribly many more than the 14,000 in a fruitfly or the 19,000 in a nematode, and indicates that many higher human capabilities and behaviors are controlled by the complex interworking of multiple genes. A single gene will have multiple effects, while in other cases several genes need to work together to produce a single effect, along causal pathways that will be extremely difficult to untangle.

The first targets of genetic therapy will be relatively simple single gene disorders like Huntington's disease or Tay Sachs disease. Many geneticists believe that the genetic causality of higher-order behaviors and characteristics like personality, intelligence, or even height is so complex that we will never be able to manipulate it. But this is precisely where the danger lies: we will be constantly tempted to think that we understand this causality better than we really do, and will face even nastier surprises than we did when we tried to conquer the non-human natural environment. In this case, the victim of a failed experiment will not be an ecosystem, but a human child whose parents, seeking to give her greater intelligence, will saddle her with a greater propensity for cancer, or prolonged debility in old age, or some other completely unexpected side effect that may emerge only after the experimenters have passed from the scene.

Listening to people in the biotech industry talk about the opportunities opening up with the completion of the sequencing of the human genome is eerily like watching those propaganda films about Hoover Dam: there is a hubristic confidence that biotechnology and scientific cleverness will correct the defects of human nature, abolish disease, and perhaps even allow human beings to achieve immortality some day. We will come out the other end a superior species because we understand how imperfect and limited our nature is.

I believe that human beings are, to an even greater degree than ecosystems, complex, coherent natural wholes, whose evolutionary provenance we do not even begin to understand. More than that, we possess human rights because of that specifically human nature: as Thomas Jefferson said at the end of his life, Americans enjoy equal political rights because nature has not arranged for certain human beings to be born with saddles on their backs, ready to be ridden by their betters. A biotechnology that seeks to manipulate human nature not only risks unforeseen consequences, but can undermine the very basis of equal democratic rights as well.

So how do we defend human nature? The tools are essentially the same as in the case of protecting non-human nature: we try to shape norms through discussion and dialogue, and we use the power of the state to regulate the way in which technology is developed and deployed by the private sector and the scientific research community. Biomedicine is, of course, heavily regulated today, but there are huge gaps in the jurisdiction of those federal agencies with authority over biotechnology. The U.S. Food and Drug Administration can only regulate food, drugs, and medical products on the basis of safety and efficacy. It is enjoined from making decisions on the basis of ethical considerations, and it has weak to nonexistent jurisdiction over medical procedures like cloning, preimplantation genetic diagnosis (where embryos are screened for genetic characteristics before being implanted in a womb), and germline engineering (where an embryo's genes are manipulated in ways that are inherited by future generations). The National Institutes of Health (NIH) make numerous rules covering human experimentation and other aspects of scientific research, but their authority extends only to federally funded research and leaves unregulated the private biotech industry. The latter, in U.S. biotech firms alone, spends over $10 billion annually on research, and employs some 150,000 people.

Other countries are striving to put legislation in place to regulate human biotechnology. One of the oldest legislative arrangements is that of Britain, which established the Human Fertilisation and Embryology Agency more than ten years ago to regulate experimentation with embryos. Twenty-four countries have banned reproductive cloning, including Germany, France, India, Japan, Argentina, Brazil, South Africa, and the United Kingdom. In 1998, the Council of Europe approved an Additional Protocol to its Convention on Human Rights and Dignity With Regard to Biomedicine banning human reproductive cloning, a document that has been signed by 24 of the council's 43 member states. Germany and France have proposed that the United Nations draft a global convention to ban reproductive cloning. [. . .]

Anyone who feels strongly about defending non-human nature from technological manipulation should feel equally strongly about defending human nature as well. In Europe, the environmental movement is more firmly opposed to biotechnology than is its counterpart in the United States, and has managed to stop the proliferation of genetically modified foods there dead in its tracks. But genetically modified organisms are ultimately only an opening shot in a longer revolution, and far less consequential than the human biotechnologies now coming on line. Some people believe that, given the depredations of humans on non-human nature, the latter deserves more vigilant protection. But in the end, they are part of the same whole. Altering the genes of plants affects only what we eat and grow; altering our own genes affects who we are. Nature—both the natural environment around us, and our own—deserves an approach based on respect and stewardship, not domination and mastery.

For Discussion

1. Fukuyama's point of view relies on a simile: the human genome is like an ecosystem. In what ways does the comparison seem to hold? In what ways does it not?

2. Although some religious viewpoints deny it, much evidence indicates that human beings did evolve from other life forms. But we also developed culture, on which we depend at least as much as on nature. What does the vast influence of culture do to Fukuyama's contention that human beings are "complex, coherent natural wholes"?

3. Fukuyama cites Thomas Jefferson's statement that equal rights depend on people "[not] be[ing] born with saddles on their backs." There's a deep irony here, for Jefferson was a slave owner, a system that depended on the proposition that some people were born "to be ridden by their betters." Do equal rights really depend on the natural equality of human beings? If not, from what does the notion of equality derive?

4. Fukuyama points at the end of his article to Europe's success in preventing the growth of genetically modified foods. So far, however, no demonstrable harm has come to humans who consume such food items—and we need to remember that almost everything we eat has been modified by developing strains and breeds through, for example, selective breeding. In your opinion, does Fukuyama offer any evidence that further regulation of bioengineering is justified?

For Research and Convincing

Fukuyama points to the largely unregulated private biotech industry in the United States, which he says "spends over $10 billion annually on research, and employs some 150,000 people." Find out more about such firms. What are they researching? How are they doing it? What practical applications have resulted? What possible applications are on the way in the near future? Do you see any reason to impose federal regulation on private biotech firms? Write an essay arguing for or against federal oversight. If you support regulation, be sure to indicate what you think ought to be controlled.

For Research and Persuasion

Probably no other country in the world has restricted genetic engineering as applied to humans as much as Germany has. A major motivator has been the ugly memory of Nazi eugenics, ghastly experiments carried out on people Hitler considered less than human—Jews, of course, but also notably the Slavic peoples (for example, Russians). Find out as much as you can about the present German stance on bioengineering of humans. Find out as much as you can about what happened during the Nazi era. Then write an essay discussing whether Nazi eugenics should influence current attitudes toward genetic engineering of humans.

Choosing Our Genes
Gregory Stock

Gregory Stock is director of the Program on Medicine, Technology, and Society at UCLA and author of the best-seller Redesigning Humans. *In his book and the following article from* The Futurist *(July-August 2002), he offers a detailed discussion of what's likely to happen soon in applying genetics to enhance human beings. The heart of his argument is that people will demand the advantages genetic engineering offers. Consequently, banning research of certain kinds or heavy-handed regulation will not prevent the technology from being developed and applied—somebody somewhere will do it. He wants it done here, in the United States, and in other liberal democracies where ethical standards are high and the potential for abuse is low. Unlike some advocates, Stock does not paint a uniformly rosy picture of the impact of genetic engineering, nor does he dodge problems it will create. His view, therefore, has special value and interest.*

Technologies giving us control over our genetic destiny will be developed, whether they are banned or not. But clumsy regulatory efforts could greatly impede our progress toward improving the future health and well-being of our descendants.

What is causing all the fuss are technologies that will give parents the ability to make conscious choices about the genetics and traits of their children. For the foreseeable future, genetically altering adults is not in the cards, other than for treating a handful of specific diseases like cystic fibrosis. Changing the genes of an adult is far too daunting, and there are simpler, safer, and more effective ways of intervening to restore or enhance adult function.

Germinal choice technology refers to a whole realm of technologies by which parents influence the genetic constitutions of their children at the time of their conception. The simplest such intervention would be to correct genes. It is not a particularly radical departure, since it would have exactly the same effect as could be accomplished by screening multiple embryos and picking one with the desired genes. In fact, such embryo screening is being done now in preimplantation genetic diagnosis. Such technology has been in use for more than a decade, but what can be tested for is going to become increasingly sophisticated in the next 5 to 10 years. And as these technologies mature, the kinds of decisions that parents can make will become much more complex.

Farther into the future will be germline interventions—alterations to the egg, sperm, or more likely the first cell of an embryo. These procedures are being done already in animal systems, but using approaches that don't have the safety or reliability that would be required in human beings.

One approach that might bring the greater reliability needed for   5
humans is the use of an artificial chromosome. That technology sounds like
flimsy science fiction, but it is already in use in animal systems. Artificial
chromosomes have been added to rats and passed to several successive
generations. They have also been used in human cell cultures and remained
stable for hundreds of cell divisions. Thus, they could provide a stable
"platform" that could be used for the insertion of whole modules of
genes. [. . .]

GOALS OF GERMINAL CHOICE

The prevention of disease will likely be the initial goal of germinal choice.
And the possibilities may soon move well beyond the correction of aberrant genes. Recent studies suggest, for example, that children who have
Down syndrome have close to a 90% reduction in the incidence of many
cancers. It is possible that trisomy 21—i.e., having a third copy of chromosome 21, with increased gene expression levels that lead to the retardation
and other symptoms of Down syndrome—may be protective against cancer. What if we could identify which of the genes on that chromosome are
responsible for this protection from cancer? Geneticists might take a set of
those genes and place them on an artificial chromosome, then add it to
an embryo to reduce the incidence of cancer to the levels seen with Down
syndrome, but without all the problems brought by the duplication of the
other genes on chromosome 21. Many other similar possibilities will no
doubt emerge, and some will almost certainly prove beneficial.

The use of artificial chromosomes might work quite well, particularly
because the chromosomes themselves could be tested within the laboratory
environment before any human use. They could be tested on animals, vali-
dated, and used in humans in essentially the same state they were tested in.
Today, each gene therapy is done anew, so it is impossible to gain that kind
of reliability. [. . .]

[. . .] All sorts of ideas will occur to future gene therapists, who will
then test them out to see if they are possible. If they are, then we will not
forgo them. Reducing the incidence of cancer and heart disease, for example, or retarding aging are health enhancements that will be seen as very,
very desirable.

GENETICALLY EXTENDING LIFESPANS

Antiaging will be an especially significant area of research because such
interventions seem so plausible and are so strongly desired by large numbers
of people. If it turns out that there are interventions that could—through
our unraveling of the underlying process of aging—allow us to develop

pharmaceutical and other interventions that are effective in adults, then that
is what everybody would want [. . .].

But embryo engineering will likely be easier and more effective than   10
gene therapy in an adult. This is because genes placed in an embryo are
copied into every single cell in the body and could be given tissue-specific
control elements. So there may well be interventions to an embryo that are
infeasible in an adult. And in this case, parents will likely look at conception as their one chance to give their child significant health advantages —
a chance that will never again be available.

A "cure for aging" might be greatly accelerated by an infusion of funds
into research on the biology of aging. Right now, the area is rather under-
funded. Much more money is being spent to find treatments for diseases
of aging than to understand the underlying process that may be responsible
for a wide variety of age-related diseases, such as cancer, heart disease,
Alzheimer's, arthritis, and diabetes. [. . .]

Antiaging — offering one's children longer lifespans — will probably be
a key goal of germline interventions, but not the only one. To do what is
best for our children is a very human response. In fact, international polls
have shown that in every country polled there is at least a significant
minority who are interested in enhancing the physical or mental well-being
of their children. They are thinking not of simple therapy to avoid particular diseases, but interventions aimed at actually improving (at least in their
eyes) a child's beauty, intelligence, strength, altruism, and other qualities.

AN UNWELCOME CHOICE?

Society may not welcome some parents' choices. Sex selection is legal in
the United States, but illegal in Britain and a number of other countries.
And quite a few people think the procedure should be illegal in the
United States as well, despite the fact that in the West, where no serious
gender imbalances arise, it is hard to see who is injured by such choices.
Another immediate decision will be whether parents screen for broad numbers of genetic diseases, some of which may not be terribly serious. And
soon, parents will likely be able to make choices about the height or IQ
of their children, or other aspects of temperament and personality —
predispositions and vulnerabilities that may soon be rather obvious in
each of our genetic readouts.

The first wave of possibilities from germinal choice technology will be
in genetic testing and screening, choosing one embryo instead of another.
Initially, it will be very difficult for a lot of people to accept this, but it
will be almost impossible to regulate, since any such embryo could have
arrived completely naturally. These choices may prove agonizing, but they
won't be dangerous, and I suspect they will be bring us more benefits
than problems.

Some people worry about a loss of diversity, but I think a more wrench-   15
ing issue may be parents who decide to specifically select an embryo that
would result in a child with a serious health condition. Should parents be
allowed to make such choices?

In the deaf community, for instance, there is a whole movement that is
very opposed to the use of cochlear implants, because it hurts deaf culture
and treats deafness like a disability. This is exactly the way most hearing
people view it. And there are deaf parents who say that they would use germinal choice technology to ensure that their children were deaf. That is not
to say they would take an embryo and damage it, but they would select an
embryo that would develop into a deaf child.

That becomes a real issue for society when, for example, such health
problems have medical costs that society must bear. If we feel that parents
do have the right to make such choices and that there is no reason to value
the birth of a healthy individual any more than someone with serious
health challenges, then we won't regulate such choices. But if we decide
there is a problem, and really want to come to grips with it, we may find it
very challenging.

FRIGHTENING OURSELVES TO DEATH

Shortly after reports were heard of the first pregnancy resulting from a
human cloning program (reports that most scientists believe are a total
fabrication), U.S. President George W. Bush voiced his support for a Senate
bill that would outlaw all forms of human cloning, including biomedical
research aimed at creating embryonic stem cells that would not be rejected
when transplanted, so-called therapeutic cloning.

I believe such a ban is premature, futile, extremely misguided, and just
plain wrong. It would not significantly delay the arrival of reproductive
cloning, which in my view is almost certain to occur within this decade
somewhere in the world. It would inject politics, religion, and philosophy
into the workings of basic research and inquiry, which would be a dangerous precedent. It would legislate greater concern for a microscopic dot of
cells than for real people with real diseases and real suffering. And it would
threaten embryo researchers with criminal penalties so extreme (10 years in
prison) that they are almost unbelievable in the United States, a country
where women during their first trimester have the right to an abortion for
any reason whatsoever.

U.S. restraints on embryo research have already had an impact on the   20
development of biomedical technologies directed toward regenerative
medicine. Those restraints have slowed progress in this realm in the
United States, which has the most powerful biomedical research effort in
the world. Such research has now moved to Britain and other countries,
such as Singapore, which is funding a huge program to explore embryonic

stem cells. But such delays are very unfortunate because of the might-have-beens that still are not. For most people, a delay of a decade or two is not a big problem, but this is not so for people like actor Michael J. Fox and others who are undergoing progressive decline from serious diseases like Parkinson's or Alzheimer's.

People's fears are often influenced by the strangeness of various reproductive possibilities. But this strangeness is a poor basis for public policy, and such attitudes can change surprisingly quickly. In-vitro fertilization was shocking 25 years ago, and these children were labeled test-tube babies. Today we see that they are just like any other kids, and the procedure seems the obvious choice for tens of thousands of childless couples. [. . .]

No matter how much it disturbs us, human germinal choice is inevitable. Embryo selection is already here, cloning is on the way, and even direct germline engineering in humans will arrive. Such technology is inevitable because many people see it as beneficial, because it will be feasible in thousands of labs all over the world, and, most importantly, because it will be a mere spin-off of mainstream biomedical research to decipher our biology. [. . .]

A DEMOCRATIZING TECHNOLOGY?

The effort to block these new reproductive technologies renders them extremely divisive socially, because it will guarantee that they are only available to the wealthy who are able to circumvent any kinds of restrictions rather easily, either by traveling to other locations or by simply paying money to get black-market services.

At their core, germinal choice technologies—if handled properly—could be very democratizing, because the kinds of interventions that will be available initially are going to compensate for deficits. It will be much easier to lift someone with an IQ of 70 up to 100 (the population average) than to raise someone's IQ from 150 (the top fraction of a percent of the population) up to 160. And the same will be true in selecting the predispositions of future children. [. . .]

[. . .] The genetic lottery can be very, very cruel. Ask anybody who is very slow or has a genetic disease of one sort or another. They don't believe in some abstract principle of how wonderful the genetic lottery is. They would like to be healthier or have more talent in one way or another. The broad availability of these technologies would thus level the playing field in many ways, because it would give opportunities to those who otherwise would be genetically disadvantaged. 25

Another point is that these technologies, as do any technologies, evolve rather rapidly. The differences will not so much be between the wealthy and the poor in one generation (although obviously there will be more things available to those who have more resources), but between one generation and the next. Today, even a Bill Gates could not obtain the genetic enhancements or services for his child that will seem primitive compared with what any middle-class person is going to have access to in 25 years. [. . .]

LOSING OUR HUMANITY—OR CONTROLLING IT?

Another misplaced fear is that, by tampering with our biology, we risk losing our humanity. But does "humanity" have to do with very narrow aspects of our biology, or does it have to do with the whole process of engaging the world and with our interactions with one another? For instance, if our lifespan were to double, would that make us "not human" in some sense? It would certainly change the trajectory of our lives, the way we interact with one another, our institutions, our sense of family, and our attitudes about education. But we would still be human, and I daresay we would soon adjust to these changes and wonder how we could ever have lived without them. [. . .]

Humans now are just in the very early stages of their evolution — early adolescence at most. A thousand years from now, when future humans look back at this era, they're going to see it as a primitive, difficult, and challenging time. They will also see it as an extraordinary, rather glorious moment when we laid down the foundations of their lives. It is hard to imagine what human life will be like even a hundred years from now, but I suspect that the reworking of our own biology will figure heavily in our future.

For Discussion

1. According to Stock, why is genetic alteration of adults "not in the cards" for the most part?
2. "Correcting genes" in embryos would not be, Stock claims, "a particularly radical departure" from current practices used in in-vitro fertilization. Why does he say this? How does it differ from what he calls "preimplantation genetic diagnosis"?
3. Stock points to an interesting "side effect" of Down syndrome — that children afflicted by it also "have close to a 90% reduction in the incidence of many cancers" (paragraph 6). How does he propose that such knowledge could be used to reduce cancer in the general population?
4. "Society may not welcome some parents' choices," Stock admits. He points out that some deaf parents will want deaf children as an example. What other choices might society find troubling?
5. Stock argues that genetic manipulation of human embryos could be a democratizing technology. What does he offer to support his view?

Compare his argument to Fukuyama's, which takes exactly the opposite position. Who makes the better case?

6. How does Stock view the question of what makes human beings human? Do you agree that gene manipulation will not fundamentally change what it means to be human?

For Research and Discussion

"The genetic lottery can be very, very cruel," Stock observes, and to verify that all you need to do is visit the cancer ward at a children's hospital or encounter an example or two of other congenital diseases. It's difficult to extol natural processes when about 2% of all live births result in genetically impaired children.

Compile a list of diseases linked to genetic defects. Individually or in groups, select a disease, then find out about symptoms and current, non-genetic treatment, including what it costs. Give a short, informative presentation about each disease.

Then discuss this question in class: Can there be any reasonable objection to genetic research designed to prevent such diseases either through screening embryos or through altering germ cells that produce or can produce genetic illnesses?

For Convincing

Stock points to the area of greatest controversy where applications of genetic knowledge are concerned — enhancing human traits a culture considers desirable. It's one thing to cure disease, the common argument goes, quite another to extend lifetimes or raise IQs or design children to be more attractive or less susceptible to depression.

Suppose that we have the knowledge and the means to select the traits our children will have. Suppose also that it's affordable and that conception would be the result of sexual intercourse only — no petri dishes and artificial means of insemination. In a short essay, make a case for using or not using that technology.

The Clone Wars
Francis Fukuyama and Gregory Stock

The following is a selection from an online debate that took place in March 2002 between bioethicist Francis Fukuyama and Gregory Stock. It appeared in Reason *(June 2002). According to the editor, "each participant respond[ed] within hours of the other's posting," which implies that the exchange has something of the spontaneous interaction of face-to-face debate.*

As with any debate, the natural human concern is who won. After you decide, study the exchanges to see what points both make that aren't addressed by the opponent—or that you think aren't addressed adequately. How would you respond if you had the chance?

"GO AHEAD AND CLONE"

Gregory Stock

There has been a lot of hand wringing recently about cloning. Considering that not a single viable cloned human embryo has yet been created, that the arrival of a clinical procedure to do so seems quite distant, and that having a delayed identical twin (which is, after all, what a clone is) has limited appeal, why all the fuss?

The fuss arises because cloning has become a proxy for broader fears about the new technologies emerging from our unraveling of human biology. Critics like Francis Fukuyama imagine that if we can stop cloning we can head off possibilities like human enhancement, but they're dreaming. As we decipher our biology and learn to modify it, we are learning to modify ourselves—and we will do so. No laws will stop this.

Embryo selection, for example, is a mere spin-off from widely supported medical research of a sort that leaves no trail and is feasible in thousands of labs throughout the world. Any serious attempt to block such research will simply increase the potential dangers of upcoming technologies by driving the work out of sight, blinding us to early indications of any medical or social problems.

The best reason not to curb interventions that many people see as safe and beneficial, however, is not that such a ban would be dangerous but that it would be wrong. A ban would prevent people from making choices aimed at improving their lives that would hurt no one. Such choices should be allowed. It is hard for me to see how a society that pushes us to stay healthy and vital could justify, for instance, trying to stop people from undergoing a genetic therapy or consuming a drug cocktail aimed at retarding aging. Imposing such a ban requires far more compelling logic than the assertion that we should not play God or that, as Fukuyama has suggested, it is wrong to try to transcend a "natural" human life span.

What's more, a serious effort to block beneficial technologies that   5
might change our natures would require policies so harsh and intrusive that they would cause far greater harm than is feared from the technologies themselves. If the War on Drugs, with its vast resources and sad results, has been unable to block people's access to deleterious substances, the government has no hope of withholding access to technologies that many regard as beneficial. It would be a huge mistake to start down this path, because even without aggressive enforcement, such bans would effectively reserve the technologies for the affluent and privileged. When abortion was illegal in various states, the rich did not suffer; they just traveled to more-permissive locales.

Restricting emerging technologies for screening embryos would feed deep class divisions. Laboratories can now screen a six-cell human embryo by teasing out a single cell, reading its genes, and letting parents use the results to decide whether to implant or discard the embryo. In Germany such screening is criminal. But this doesn't deny the technology to affluent Germans who want it: They take a trip to Brussels or London, where it is legal. As such screenings become easier and more informative, genetic disease could be gradually relegated to society's disadvantaged. We need to start thinking about how to make the tests more, not less, accessible.

But let's cut to the chase. If parents can easily and safely choose embryos, won't they pick ones with predispositions toward various talents and temperaments, or even enhanced performance? Of course. It is too intrusive to have the government second-guessing such decisions. British prohibitions of innocuous choices like the sex of a child are a good example of undesirable government intrusion. Letting parents who strongly desire a girl (or boy) be sure to have one neither injures the resulting child nor causes gender imbalances in Western countries.

Sure, a few interventions will arise that virtually everyone would find troubling, but we can wait until actual problems appear before moving to control them. These coming reproductive technologies are not like nuclear weapons, which can suddenly vaporize large numbers of innocent bystanders. We have the luxury of feeling our way forward, seeing what problems develop, and carefully responding to them. [. . .]

SENSIBLE RESTRICTIONS

Francis Fukuyama

Gregory stock offers two sets of arguments against restricting future biotechnologies: first, that such rules are unnecessary as long as reproductive choices are being made by individual parents rather than states, and second, that they cannot be enforced and will be ineffective even if they were to be enacted. Let me respond to each in turn.

While genetic choices made by parents (either in the short run, via pre-implantation genetic diagnosis, or in the more distant future, through germline engineering) are on the whole likely to be better than those made by coercive states, there are several grounds for not letting individuals have complete freedom of choice in this regard.

The first two are utilitarian. When we get into human germline engineering, in which modifications will be passed on to successive generations, safety problems will multiply exponentially over what we today experience with drug approval. Genetic causation is highly complex, with multiple genes interacting to create one outcome or behavior and single genes having multiple effects. When a long-term genetic effect may not show up for decades after the procedure is administered, parents will risk a multitude of unintended and largely irreversible consequences for their children. This would seem to be a situation calling for strict regulation.

A second utilitarian concern has to do with possible negative externalities, which is the classic ground for state regulation, accepted by even the most orthodox free market economists. An example is sex selection. Today in Asia, as a result of cheap sonograms and abortion, cohorts are being born with extremely lopsided sex ratios—117 boys for every 100 girls in China and at one point 122 boys for every 100 girls in Korea. Sex selection is rational from the standpoint of individual parents, but it imposes costs on society as a whole in terms of the social disruption that a large number of unattached and unmarriageable young males can produce. Similar negative externalities can arise from individual choices to, for example, prolong life at the cost of a lower level of cognitive and physical functioning.

A further set of concerns about the ability to "design" our children has to do with the ambiguity of what constitutes improvement of a human being, particularly when we get into personality traits and emotional makeup. [. . .] Would an African American's child be "improved" if we could genetically eliminate his or her skin pigmentation?

The final issue concerns human nature itself. Human rights are ultimately derived from human nature. That is, we assign political rights to ourselves based on our understanding of the ways members of our species are similar to one another and different from other species. We are fortunate to be a relatively homogenous species. [. . .] The final chapter of Greg Stock's book opens up the prospect of a future world in which this human homogeneity splinters, under the impact of genetic engineering, into competing human biological kinds. What kind of politics do we imagine such a splintering will produce? The idea that our present-day tolerant, liberal, democratic order will survive such changes is farfetched. [. . .]

Stock's second set of arguments is based on his belief that no one can stop this technology. He is certainly right that if some future biotechnology proves safe, cheap, effective, and highly desirable, government would not be able to stop it and probably should not try. What I am calling for, how-ever, is not a ban on wide swaths of future technology but rather their strict regulation in light of the dangers outlined above.

Today we regulate biomedical technology all the time. People can argue whether that technology is properly regulated and where exactly to draw various regulatory lines. But the argument that procedures that will be as potentially unsafe and ethically questionable as, say, germline engineering for enhancement purposes cannot in principle be regulated has no basis in past experience.

We slow the progress of science today for all sorts of ethical reasons. Biomedicine could advance much faster if we abolished our rules on human experimentation in clinical trials, as Nazi researchers did, and allowed doctors to deliberately inject infectious substances into their sub-jects. Today we enforce rules permitting the therapeutic use of drugs like Ritalin, while prohibiting their use for enhancement or entertainment.

The argument that these technologies will simply move to more favor-able jurisdictions if they are banned in any one country may or may not carry weight; it all depends on what they are and what the purpose of the regulation is. I regard a ban on reproductive cloning to be analogous to cur-rent legislation banning incest, which is based on a similar mix of safety and ethical considerations. The purpose of such a ban would not be under-mined if a few rich people could get themselves cloned outside the country. In any event, the world seems to be moving rather rapidly toward a global ban on reproductive cloning. The fact that the Chinese may not be on board shouldn't carry much weight; the Chinese also involuntarily harvest organs from executed prisoners and are hardly an example we would want to emulate. [. . .]

BIOTECH TYRANNY

Gregory Stock

I have no problem with attempts to address serious externalities that arise from otherwise harmless personal activities. But if government does not bear a heavy burden of proof when justifying such intrusions into our lives, it can employ vague arguments about social harm to take away our basic freedoms. Francis Fukuyama would push us toward just such intrusions by erecting a powerful regulatory structure charged with ensuring the ethical and social desirability of future technologies.

Fukuyama is so suspicious of change in general and new technology   20
in particular that he won't even acknowledge the desirability of allowing people to use safe and beneficial interventions that would almost certainly improve their lives. He will admit only that if a technology is "safe, cheap, effective, and highly desirable," government "*probably* [my emphasis]

should not try" to stop it. If he won't even embrace technologies that meet this high threshold, he would never allow the far more problematic possibilities of the real world. But facing such possibilities is precisely what has improved our health and raised our standard of living so greatly during the last century.

Fukuyama speaks of safety, but his reluctance about even safe and highly desirable technologies suggests that his major concern is neither safety nor aberrant misuse. Moreover, he admits that these dangers are well covered by existing agencies and institutions. He makes his primary focus explicit in his book when he complains that the Food and Drug Administration is charged only with establishing "safety and efficacy," while we need institutions that can look at ethical consequences.

For the most part, Fukuyama is vague when it comes to precisely what we should prevent. This may be good strategy, because notions of safety, caution, and minimized externalities are so appealing. But it is deceptive because it is in the details that the rubber meets the road.

In fairness, Fukuyama is specific about banning human cloning, which in today's climate is about as risky as coming out for motherhood. His reasoning here is faulty, however. To liken a blanket ban on reproductive cloning to a ban on incest is not even fathomable if one considers the cloning of a deceased child or someone other than the parent. But as I said, cloning is a sideshow.

A more interesting situation is sex selection. I argued that in the U.S. such selection—which can be done by sorting sperm, so that no embryos are destroyed—is innocuous. Sex selection does not harm children; indeed, it likely benefits them when a child of the "wrong" sex would seriously disappoint his or her parents. Fukuyama brings up the lopsided sex ratio in China, but this does not justify regulating the practice here, where such imbalances do not arise from the practice. Moreover, the problem in China is hardly an argument for government regulation, since sex selection there has long been illegal. Indeed, government regulation in China—namely, its one-child policy—exacerbates the problem of gender balance by pushing parents who want a boy toward aborting a girl, since they can't try again. Fukuyama opposes sex selection here and has proposed the formation of a review board like the one in Britain that has barred this procedure. But does he have anything better to offer than a fear that the practice would be a step down a slippery slope? If he sees a serious externality to sex selection in the U.S., it would be worth hearing about.

In response to my comments about the obvious appeal and benefit of future anti-aging medications, Fukuyama points out that "negative externalities can arise from individual choices to . . . prolong life at the cost of a lower level of cognitive and physical functioning." This is true, but it is a frightening basis for legislation (as opposed to decisions regarding government funding). I shudder to think about regulatory boards tasked with balancing the additional years that an individual seeks against the social cost of those years. To see the peril, we need only apply Fukuyama's logic to medicine generally.

If he does not want to allow interventions to slow the onset of aging and bring longer lives of relative health (though presumably not matching the vitality of youth), then why not block all treatments for the aged and debilitated? Their extra years are a net cost, and withholding medical treatment for those over 65 would work wonders for our ailing Social Security system. It isn't much of a step to go even further and block medical interventions that save accident victims who suffer crippling injuries.

Fukuyama no doubt feels that a sharp line between therapy and enhancement will avoid such perversions, but this distinction does not stand up to scrutiny. This line will increasingly blur in the years ahead. Anti-aging interventions, for example, fall in a large realm that is best labeled therapeutic enhancement. If we could gain an extra decade by strengthening our immune system or our anti-oxidation and cellular repair mechanisms, this would clearly be a human enhancement. But it would also be a preventive therapy, because it would delay cardiovascular disease, senile dementia, cancer, and other illnesses of aging, which we spend billions trying to treat. [. . .]

UPLOADING NORMS

Francis Fukuyama

I think Greg Stock has misunderstood a couple of the points I was trying to make in my initial response. The issue with regard to sex selection is not that it would be a serious problem in this country; it's possible now, after all, but not widely practiced. The point is that individual choice coupled with the spread of cheap biomedical technologies can quickly produce population-level effects with serious social consequences. In other words, the problem with eugenics is not simply that it is state-sponsored and coercive; if practiced by enough individuals, it can also have negative consequences for the broader society.

I suspect that if the U.S. ever gets into something like this in the future, it will have to do with potential "enhancement" targets other than sex. One I speculate about in my book is sexual preference: It seems pretty clear to me that if parents, including ones who are perfectly accepting of gays today, had the choice, they would select against their children being gay, if for no other reason than their desire to have grandchildren. (Contrary to Stock, by the way, gays can't reproduce, so I'm not quite sure how they'd do germ-line intervention to produce gay children.) The proportion of gays in the population could drop quite dramatically, and I'm not at all sure that society as a whole (let alone gays as a persecuted minority) would be enhanced as a result.

Governments can intervene successfully to correct individual choices like these. The severe sex-ratio imbalance in Korea that emerged in the early

30

1990s was noticed, and the government took measures to enforce existing laws against sex selection so that today the ratio is much closer to 50-50. If the government of a young democracy like Korea can do this, I don't see why we can't.

The reason I noted that life extension coupled with diminished capability can create negative externalities was not to suggest that we should ban or regulate such procedures. Stock is perfectly right that we already have adopted a lot of medical innovations that produce this tradeoff, and that we can't stop future advances for this reason. The reason this is an important issue is that in contemporary debates over stem cells and cloning there is an unquestioned assumption that anything that will prolong life or cure disease is obviously desirable and automatically trumps other ethical concerns.

This is not obvious to me. Anyone who has walked around a nursing home recently (as I have) can see that past advances in biomedicine have created a horrible situation for many elderly people who can't function at anything close to the levels they'd like but who also can't die. Of course, new advances in biotechnology may provide cures for degenerative, age-related diseases such as Alzheimer's or Parkinson's, but the research community is in effect just cleaning up the mess it created. So when we are balancing near-term rights and wrongs, the argument that more medical advance is necessarily good needs to be treated with some skepticism. [. . .]

Stock is correct in saying that much of my interest in having new regulatory institutions in place has to do with ethical and social consequences of new technology and not simply safety. States intervene all the time to shape norms and produce certain social outcomes. Incest is an example, and it seems to me a very apt analogy to reproductive cloning. Of course, you can find sympathetic situations where an individual might want to clone, say, a dead child. [. . .]

[. . .] The possible benefits of cloning need to be balanced against social harms. Consider the following scenario: A wife decides to clone herself because a couple cannot otherwise have children. As their daughter grows up to be a teenager, the husband will find his wife growing older and less sexually attractive. In the meantime, his daughter, who will be a physical duplicate of her mother, will blossom into sexual maturity and increasingly come to resemble the younger woman the husband fell in love with and married. It is hard to see how this situation would not produce an extremely unhealthy situation within the family; in a certain number of cases, it would lead to incest.

Stock is using a rhetorical ploy in suggesting that I am recommending new, tyrannical government intrusion into private lives. Rather, I am recommending an extension of existing institutions to take account of the new possibilities that will be put before us as a result of technological advance. [. . .]

35

CLONES, GAYS, AND THE ELDERLY

Gregory Stock

I'm glad Francis Fukuyama agrees that sex selection here poses no serious threat. To me, this means it should not be regulated. Moreover, we should also hold off on passing legislative protections against other such technologies until actual problems show up. [. . .]

Outlawing a whole realm of benefits not injurious to others — namely enhancements — would be tyranny. Potent regulatory structures that pass judgment on the morality and social cost of future technologies would move us in this direction. [. . .]

Consider Fukuyama's argument about cloning. It is one thing to worry about the obvious medical dangers of so unproven a technology, another to justify a complete ban with stories about a future father's possible sexual attraction for his wife's budding clone-daughter. Kids hardly need to resemble a parent to inspire incest, as many adoptees and stepchildren can no doubt confirm. If we start regulating families on the basis of hypothetical sexual attractions and perversions — and we can conjure ones more lurid and likely than Fukuyama's clone love — we will ultimately damage rather than protect the family. We have laws governing child abuse; let's content ourselves with enforcing them.

As to gays, if there are fewer in the future because of people's choices about the genetics or rearing of their kids, so be it. But I am not at all convinced it would play out that way. Fukuyama asserts that gays can't reproduce, but they do so all the time using donor eggs or sperm, surrogate mothers, and partners of the opposite sex. Moreover, such reproduction will get ever easier. If we want to be sure to maintain our gay population, additional AIDS research would accomplish more than bans on embryo screening.

I'm glad to hear that Fukuyama doesn't oppose anti-aging interventions; I've previously heard him say only that government would be unable to block such enhancements. He is right, of course, that advances in health care bring many challenges, and that the needless prolongation of a dying loved one's pain and decrepitude is nothing to boast about. But my reaction is not to deny the value of the good added years that modern medicine has brought so many of us, but to recognize that we must find better ways for individuals to reach death with dignity when it draws near. Why must so many of our elderly try to squirrel away a stash of lethal drugs in case they might be captured by a medical system that would torture them for their final few weeks or months? The issue of cloning pales alongside this cruelty.

Fukuyama says he is urging only a harmless extension of existing institutions. I disagree. The relegation of decisions about human reproduction to a political process typically driven by impassioned zealots on either side would invite disaster. New agencies with the power to project abstract

40

philosophy, social theory, and even religious dogma into family life would be a frightening development. And when lawmakers on Capital Hill start telling medical researchers not to do certain types of embryonic stem cell research because adult stem cells will work just as well, something is very wrong. These legislators are micromanaging a realm they do not understand, assaulting our freedom of inquiry, and ignoring the entreaties of those afflicted with serious diseases. These steps are not small.

For Discussion

1. Since scientists in Britain cloned the sheep they named Dolly, there's been much ink spilled over cloning, especially the possibility of cloning humans. Why is cloning of people not likely and therefore a distraction from the real issues surrounding human genetic manipulation?

2. Stock argues that nothing can be done to halt the development of beneficial technologies developed from genetic science. Can you think of possibly beneficial technologies that have been controlled through banning or regulation successfully? If he thinks genetic engineering of humans is unstoppable, why does he bother to argue so strongly against governmental intervention?

3. Fukuyama makes a vital point: That we must consider what constitutes "improvement" in human beings. He asks, "Would an African American's child be 'improved' if we could genetically eliminate his or her skin pigmentation?" What doubtful "improvements" might parents opt for if they could?

4. Stock and Fukuyama seem to agree on one thing—techniques for genetic modification must be safe. But the fact is that many widely used medical technologies aren't entirely safe. Surgery has obvious hazards. Many medicines have bad side effects for most people who take them, and nearly all can produce even fatal allergic reactions in a few patients. Vaccines can cause illness, death, or permanent disability for a tiny percentage of people. What level of safety would you say is realistic for genetic modification?

5. It seems likely that we will learn how to retard the aging process and therefore extend the average human life. Stock sees this possibility as irresistibly appealing. Based on your experience with older people, is it? Fukuyama points to the negative externalities of life extension—for example, how shall we support so many people for so long, after their working years are over? Can we afford to ignore such considerations?

6. In the final analysis, the point of contention between Stock and Fukuyama seems to be whether the latter wants "only a harmless extension of existing institutions," as Stock phrases it. In your view,

is Fukuyama proposing that we regulate genetic engineering of humans in ways that are significantly different from our regulation, for instance, of new drugs?

For Convincing

The Stock-Fukuyama debate turns on two strongly contrasting basic attitudes or approaches to human affairs. One is libertarian: Let free individual choices and free enterprise sort things out. This is Stock's approach. The other emphasizes the need for governmental intervention to prevent or reduce the sometimes bad results of free choice and free enterprise—so we have laws requiring people to buckle up in their cars and laws that check the development of monopolies. This is Fukuyama's approach.

Write an essay advocating one of these approaches as better suited to dealing with genetic engineering of humans. Remember that you can be libertarian and favor minimally necessary government intervention; you can favor stronger regulation while still leaving much to individual choice and free enterprise. The choices are not absolute but rather a matter of emphasis.

For Research and Class Discussion

We need to know what controls are in place for all scientific research requiring human testing. For example, genetic research is very expensive. It has to be funded with either government money or private funds. The competition for funding is intense—only the most promising research gets support. Another example: Clinical trials of all new medical interventions are tightly controlled by peer review of methods and results. Find out all you can about these and other "checks and balances" in the system.

Then explore this question: Do we need anything else but the existing system to handle genetic modification? If so, what additional steps or procedures might be warranted?

Why Designer Babies Won't Happen Soon
Steven Pinker

Steven Pinker is a cognitive scientist at Harvard and best-selling author of many books, most recently The Blank Slate. *The following selection came from a talk before the President's Council on Bioethics, "Human Nature and Its Future," delivered March 6, 2003. We have taken a section from Pinker's much longer talk and assigned the title above to it.*

   Sometimes concern about the impact of new technologies becomes overheated, losing touch with common sense and practical realities. If that's happened with genetic enhancement, Pinker's reasoning should cool things down and permit calmer thinking.

I'm going to talk about the ability to change human nature that's of [. . .] direct interest to the members of this committee [President's Council on Bioethics,] namely, voluntary genetic engineering, popularly known as designer babies, and that will be the topic of the rest of my presentation.

   I don't have to remind you that this is ethically fraught, and there are vociferous voices arguing that this would be a bad thing or that it would be a good thing. I'm going to address a common assumption both of people who are alarmed and people who welcome genetic enhancement.

   The assumption [is] that this is inevitable, that science has reached the point where it's only a matter of time before genetic enhancement is routine and possibly the human species will change unless we intervene and regulate the science and practice now.

   I'm going to present a skeptical argument about designer babies to give you an overview. I'm going to suggest that genetic enhancement of human nature is not inevitable. Indeed, I would be willing to venture that it's highly unlikely in our lifetimes.

   Why? First of all, because of the fallibility of predictions about complex technology in general.

   Secondly, impediments to genetic enhancement from what we know about the human behavioral genetics.

   And, third, impediments from human nature itself.

   Well, let me begin with the frailty of technological predictions in general. There's a wonderful book called *The Experts Speak* by Victor Navasky and Christopher Cerf, which has some delicious quotations about what is inevitable in our future, such as the following one. "Fifty years hence we shall escape the absurdity of growing a whole chicken in order to eat the breast or wing by growing these parts separately under a suitable medium"— Winston Churchill in 1932. That should have happened by 1982, and we're still waiting.

   Nuclear-powered vacuum cleaners will probably be a reality within ten years, a prediction made in 1955 by a manufacturer of vacuum cleaners.

A few other predictions that I remember from my childhood, and in fact, from newspapers of just a few years ago. Dome cities, jet pack commuting, mile-high buildings, routine artificial organs, routine consumer space flights, such as the Pan Am shuttle to the moon featured in 2001, interactive television, the paperless office, and the dot-com revolution and the end of bricks-and-mortar retail. All of these predictions we know to be false, and a number of them [. . .] we can say with a fair amount of confidence never will happen.

We're not going to have domed cities, at least not in the future that's   10
worth worrying about.

Now, why are technological predictions so often wrong? First, there's a habit of assuming that technological progress can be linearly extrapolated. If there's a little bit of progress now, there will be proportional progress as we multiply the number of years out.

Engineers sometimes refer to this as the fallacy of thinking that we can get to the moon by climbing trees. A little bit of progress now can be extended indefinitely.

Secondly, there's a tendency to underestimate the number of things that have to go exactly right for a given scenario to take place. Most technological changes don't depend on a single discovery, but rather on an enormous number of factors, scores or even hundreds, all of which have to fall into place exactly right. [. . .]

Third, there's a widespread failure of futurologists to consider the costs of new technologies, as well as the benefits, whereas in reality the actual users faced with a particular technology consider both the benefits and the costs.

Finally, there is an incentive structure to futurology. Someone who   15
predicts a future that's radically different from our own, either to hype it or to raise an alarm against it, will get the attention of the press and the public. The chances are the *New York Times* won't call you up if you say either that the future is going to be pretty similar to the present or we haven't a clue as to what the future will be.

The second part of my talk, reasons for skepticism about designer babies, is that there's a considerably bracing splash of cold water on the possibility of designer babies from what we know about behavioral genetics and neural development today. There's a widespread assumption that we have discovered or soon will discover individual genes for talents such as mathematical giftedness, musical talent, athletic prowess, and so on.

But the reality is considerably different, and I think an Achilles' heel of genetic enhancement will be the rarity of single genes with consistent beneficial psychological effects. I think there's a myth that such genes have been discovered or inevitably will be discovered, but it isn't necessarily so.

Indeed, I would say that the science of behavioral genetics at present faces something of a paradox. We know that tens of thousands of genes working together have a large effect on the mind. We know that from twin studies that show that identical twins are far more similar than fraternal twins who, in turn, are more similar than unrelated individuals, and from adoption studies that show that children resemble their biological parents more than their adopted parents.

But these are effects of sharing an entire genome or half of a genome or a quarter of a genome. It's very different from the existence of single genes that have a consistent effect on the mind, which have been few and far between.

Anyone who has kept up with the literature on behavioral genetics has noticed that there's been a widespread failure to find single genes for schizophrenia, autism, obsessive-compulsive disorder, and so on. And those, by the way, are the areas where we're most likely to find a single gene simply because it's easier to disrupt a complex system with a single defective part than it is to install an entire complex ability with a single gene. The failure to find a gene with consistent effect on, say, schizophrenia means that it's even less likely that we will find a gene for something as complex as musical talent or likability. [20]

And though there have been highly publicized discoveries of single genes for syndromes such as bipolar illness, sexual orientation, or in perhaps the most promising case, a gene that appeared to correlate with four IQ points in gifted individuals; all of those discoveries have been withdrawn in recent years, including the four-point IQ gene withdrawn just last month.

Now, it's really not such a paradox when you think about what we know about biological development in general. The human brain is not a bag of traits with one gene for each trait. That's just not the way genetics works.

Neural development is a staggeringly complex process which we are only beginning to get the first clues about. It involves many genes interacting in complex feedback loops. [. . .]

The pattern of expression of genes is often as important as which genes are present, and therefore, it's a good idea not to hold your breath for the discovery of the musical talent gene or any other single gene or small number of genes with a large, consistent effect on cognitive functioning or personality. [. . .]

I think there are other genetic impediments to the possibility of genetic enhancement. One is that the genes, even acting across an entire genome, have effects that are, at best, probabilistic. A sobering discovery is that monozygotic twins reared together who share all of their genes and most of their environment are imperfectly correlated. When it comes to personality measures, such as extroversion or neuroticism, correlations are in the range of .5. [25]

Now, that's much, much bigger than correlations among non-identical twins or, let alone, unrelated individuals, but it's much less than one, and

what that tells us is that there is an enormous and generally unacknowledged role for chance in the development of a human being.

Secondly, [. . .] most genes have multiple effects, and in general,
evolution selects for the best compromise among the positive and negative
effects that come from an individual gene.

A vivid example of this is [. . .] the [. . .] mice reported two years ago
that were given extra MNDA receptors, receptors that are critical to learning
and memory. These were artificially engineered mice that had an enhanced
ability to learn mazes.

[But] it was later discovered that these mice were hypersensitive to
inflammatory pain. So a genetic change had both positive and negative
effects.

Because of this, [. . .] there are ethical impediments to research on   30
human enhancement, namely, how can you get there from here? Are there
experiments that a typical human subjects committee would approve of,
given the likelihood that any given gene will have negative effects on a
child, in addition to the positive ones?

Finally, most human traits are desirable at intermediate values. Wallace
Simpson famously said that you can't be too rich or too thin, and it may be
true that you can't be too smart, but for most other traits, you really can
have too much of a good thing.

Most parents don't want their child to be not assertive enough, to be a
punching bag or a door mat. [However], most parents would also not want
their child to be Jack the Ripper.

You want your child to have some degree of risk taking, not to sit at
home cowering out of fear of negative consequences. [But] you don't want
a self-destructive maniac either.

So if a given gene, even if it did have as its effect an enhancement, say,
of risk taking, put it in a child and you'll have ten extra points on the risk
taking scale; the crucial question is: what are the other 29,999 genes doing?
Would they be placing your child on the left-hand side of the Bell curve, in
which case an extra dose of assertiveness would be a good thing, or have
they already put your child on the right-hand side of the Bell curve so that
an extra dose of assertiveness is the last thing that you would want?

The third part of the argument is I think there are impediments in   35
human nature to enhancing human nature. Now, one feature of parental
psychology that is often invoked in these discussions is the desire of parents
to give their children whatever boost is possible, and lurking in all of these
discussions is the stereotype of the Yuppie parent who plays Mozart to the
mother's belly while the mother is pregnant, bombards the baby with
flash cards, has them taking violin lessons at the age of three, and so on.
And the assumption is that parents would stop at nothing to enhance their
children's ability, including genetic engineering.

Well, that obviously is a feature of parental psychology, but there's a
second feature of parental psychology that also has to be factored in,

namely, the aversion to harm your children. Most parents know that even if they are not sure whether playing Mozart to a pregnant woman's belly will help their child, they have reasonable belief that it couldn't harm the child. Likewise the flash cards, the violin lessons, and so on.

If it came to genetic enhancement where this was unknown, it's not so clear that parents would opt for the risk of doing their children genuine harm for the promise of a possibility of doing them good.

Also, one ubiquitous feature of human nature is intuitions about naturalness and contamination, sometimes referred to by cognitive psychologists as psychological essentialism, the folk belief that living things have an essence which can be contaminated by pollutants from without.

This has been an impediment to the acceptance of other technologies. Famous examples are nuclear power, which is notoriously aversive to large segments of the population. As you all know, there hasn't been a new nuclear power plant built in this country for several decades, despite the possibility that it could be an effective solution to global warming.

In Europe and in large segments of this country, there is a widespread repugnance to genetically modified foods for reasons that are probably more irrational than rational, but nonetheless cannot be gainsaid. If people have a horror about genetically modified soybeans, it's not so clear that they would rush to welcome genetically modified children. 40

Finally, anyone who knows someone who has undergone IVF knows that this is a traumatic, painful, and rather unpleasant procedure, especially in comparison to sex. [. . .] There is reason to believe that this would not necessarily catch on in the population as a whole.

So the choice that parents would face in a hypothetical future [. . .] would not be the one that's popularly portrayed, namely, would you opt for a procedure that would give you a happier and more talented child?

When you put it like that, well, who would say no to that question?

More realistically, the question that parents would face would be something like this. Would you opt for a traumatic and expensive procedure that might give you a very slightly happier and more talented child, might give you a less happy, less talented child, might give you a deformed child, and probably would do nothing?

We don't know the probabilities of those four outcomes. I think this is a more realistic way of thinking about the choices that parents might face. 45

For genetic enhancement to change human nature or to lead to a post human future, not a few, but billions of people would have to answer yes to this question.

So, to sum up, changing human nature by a voluntary genetic enhancement [. . .] is not inevitable because [of] the complexity of neural development and the rarity or absence of single genes with large, consistent, beneficial effects, and because of the tradeoff of risks and benefits enhancement that will inevitably be faced by researchers and by parents.

The conclusions that I would draw are the following. I am not arguing that genetic enhancement will never happen. If there's anything more foolish than saying that some technological development is inevitable, it's saying that some technological development is impossible.

And corresponding to the silly predictions about the inevitable future of domed cities and jet packed commuters, one can find equally silly quotes from people who said things like we will never reach the moon.

So it's not that I am arguing that genetic enhancement is impossible. 50 Rather, it's an argument that bioethics policy should acknowledge the frailty of long-term technological predictions which have a very spotty track record at best. The bioethics policy should be based on fact, not fantasy. Both our positive and our negative fantasies are unlikely to come true, and that policies predicated on the inevitability of genetic enhancement should be rethought.

For Discussion

1. Like Fukuyama, Pinker emphasizes the complex interaction of genes, each of which may have multiple functions in relation to other genes. But whereas Fukuyama takes the extreme complexity of genetics as warning number one about how genetic alterations can go wrong, Pinker sees it as a good reason to doubt that designer babies will happen in the next few decades or so. Whose view seems more convincing? Why?

2. Pinker emphasizes a point no other author in this section seems to be aware of—that "genes . . . have effects that are, at best, probabilistic." That is, even identical twins, who share exactly the same genetic makeup, do not behave in exactly the same way. It would seem that somehow environment or chance is playing a big role beyond the behavioral impact of genes. What does this mean for the likelihood that engineered children will happen soon?

3. Pinker admits that some parents can go to extraordinary lengths to enhance their children's development and chances for success in life, but he pits this against another parental motivation, "the aversion to harm your children." Think about nongenetic means of enhancement you've seen parents resort to. Did they do any harm? Was the potential for harm understood and did it play a role in choosing and pursuing the enhancement sought? Based on your experience, which motive seems the stronger, the desire to enhance or the desire to not cause harm?

4. Pinker makes the amusing point that not many couples will prefer the joy of IVF (in vitro fertilization) to the joy of sex as a way of conceiving children. This is good common sense. What then would have to happen to make designer babies a practical option?

For Persuasion

Pinker throws cold water on Stock's vision of human genetic enhancement. However, they agree on one crucial point: "The bioethics policy should be based on fact, not fantasy." In other words, both take the position that we should not regulate until genuine problems emerge—facts we must confront, not hypotheticals that may never materialize.

After studying carefully the arguments of Stock and Pinker, write an essay addressed to your senator or congressperson arguing that genetic engineering should not be regulated until demonstrated dangers or irresponsible use of the technology emerge. Urge oversight but not government action.

Making Babies?
Sondra Wheeler

Sondra Wheeler is a professor of Christian ethics at Wesley Theological Seminary, Washington, D.C. The following article appeared in Sojourners *(May 1999).*

   Science and religion have always had, to put it mildly, an uneasy relationship. But the fact is that ethics does matter in scientific research and in technological applications of scientific knowledge. Ethics in turn cannot be divorced from religion, and so science and religion will continue to dance somewhat awkwardly together in human affairs.

   Sondra Wheeler's exploration of genetic reproductive technology is thoughtful and free of dogma, raising issues that even the non- or anti-religious must consider. It reminds us that far more is at stake than how safe and reliable genetic enhancement might be.

One of the obvious but decisive facts about parenting is that prior to embarking upon the relationship, we don't know who is coming. We receive and live out our responsibilities toward our children, whoever they turn out to be, simply because they are ours and we are theirs, and most of the time that is enough to bring us to welcome and cherish and protect them. We do it whether they are beautiful or homely, brilliant or ordinary, cheerful or fretful. Even when they grow into adolescents with strange haircuts who, it seems, can hardly stand us, by and large and with varying degrees of struggle, we continue to welcome and cherish and care for them. Parenting is the most routine and the most socially essential form of welcoming the stranger.

   It is this unreserved and uncalculated commitment to accept and love the children we are given that makes the relationship between parent and child so central a metaphor for our relation to God, who welcomes and receives and cares for us, whoever we are. In this most fundamental and natural of all social relationships, we see the nearest analogue for the divine charity which loves each of us in her or his particularity, but universally and without conditions.

   It now seems likely, due to certain recent advances in scientific technique, that soon we will develop the capacity to make changes in the genetic makeup of human beings, including changes that they will pass to their descendants. The challenge this presents is, how much should we try to determine about our offspring?

   The possibilities go all the way from that offered by cloning—which would allow us to select a complete genome (the total complement of chromosomes of a species) as long as we had an existing "template" to reproduce—to much more modest alterations in a single gene designed to prevent the development and transmission of a particular genetic disease.

Among the myriad questions forming around these technologies is a   5
fairly broad and basic one: What will it mean if we move from a social
practice of welcoming the children who are born to us to a practice of
selecting them and their characteristics, either by cloning or by modifying
the genome in vitro before implantation? In particular, it is important to
address what for Christians and Jews (at least) defines and limits the senses
in which human beings may be said to belong to each other, and what this
suggests about the terms on which we ought to intervene in the genetic
makeup of another human being.

What all this highlights is the very different moral posture between that
of simply accepting the child we are given vs. a decision to engineer the
genetic endowment of a child to replicate a desired genome or to select for
personally desired or culturally valued characteristics. What will it mean
to us, and to our children, if we embrace practices that make a child so
decisively the project of its parents' will?

Certainly to seek such control involves abandoning a certain kind of
reservation grounded in the fellow-humanity of our children, a respect
based in religious awe for the child as a creature whose source and destiny
are in God and who does not ultimately belong to us. It means shifting
from a position in which we discover and foster the nature and flourishing
of the children we receive, to one in which we determine the nature of
the children whom we will accept. It is a kind of embodiment of all those
corruptions of parenting in which the child is viewed primarily as the
means of the parents' fulfillment and forcefully created in the image of
their will.

There are, of course, many much more serious and compelling reasons
to seek the power to intervene in the genetic makeup of human beings.
About 2 percent of all live births are of children with genetic disorders,
some of them imposing severe suffering and early death. To have the power
to prevent such misery or to heal its effects is indeed a worthy goal, and an
appropriate exercise of human powers to intervene. But it is not too soon
to begin asking whether we can even hope to exercise so vast a power with
the caution and deep self-scrutiny that wisdom would demand.

For Discussion

1. "We don't know who is coming," Wheeler says, meaning by that
   something undeniable — every child has his or her own peculiar
   combination of genes, environment, and chance in self-formation,
   much of which parents cannot control. Will genetic manipulation
   do away with the need to accept our children, "simply because
   they are ours and we are theirs," as Wheeler phrases it?
2. One way to think about the ethics of a new technology is to ponder
   the ethics of existing ones in common use. We have ultrasound

and amniocentesis, tools for assessing the condition of the unborn. Sometimes abnormalities are detected, which can result in abortion or in surgical procedures designed to correct the problem. What is your view of such technologies? How different are they from selecting an embryo based on genetic screening, done now in in vitro fertilization? How different are they from germ-line manipulations, which may be common years from now?

3. Wheeler takes genetic enhancement as an "embodiment of all those corruptions of parenting in which the child is viewed primarily as the means of their parents' fulfillment and forcefully created in the image of their will" (paragraph 7). What might she have in mind by the phrase "all those corruptions of parenting"? Does the existence of such corruptions *prior to* our ability to alter children genetically indicate that our real concern should be the ethics of parenting rather than the ethics of a technology, which, like all technologies, can be used for good or ill?

4. Wheeler obviously has serious reservations about genetic manipulation, except to prevent or correct genetic disorders. If we permit, say, germ-line interventions for this reason, can we raise ethical objections to, for instance, interventions to reduce the likelihood of depression? to increase intelligence? Is there any place where the proverbial line in the sand can be drawn and the warning posted, "Do not cross"?

For Inquiry

Wheeler says that "it is important to address what for Christians and Jews (at least) defines and limits the senses in which human beings may be said to belong to each other." Clearly "the senses in which human beings . . . belong to one another" are important for any religion and indeed for people who profess no religion. *It ought to be a fundamental ethical notion for everyone.* The problem is that, at best, most people observe it only in relation to family and friends—beyond the intimate circle it seems to have little force.

What role or roles might such an idea play in applications of genetic knowledge to human beings? Write an essay exploring the possibilities. What does it suggest for how and in what circumstances genetic engineering should be used?

The Tyranny of Happiness
Carl Elliott

Carl Elliott teaches philosophy and bioethics at the University of Minnesota. The following selection comes from the last chapter of his most recent book, Better Than Well: American Medicine Meets the American Dream *(W. W. Norton, 2003).*

   Elliott is concerned not with bioengineering as such but with the American passion for—some would say "compulsion toward"—enhancement of all kinds. He analyzes its motives and traces it to self-fulfillment as the goal of happiness. The problem is that such a notion of the good lacks social connection and eludes definition and assessment. How can we know what fulfills us? How can we know when we are fulfilled?

In America I have seen the freest and best educated of men in circumstances the happiest to be found in the world, yet it seemed to me that a cloud habitually hung on their brow, and they seemed serious and almost sad even in their pleasures.

—ALEXIS DE TOCQUEVILLE

Thirty-five years ago, at the beginning of a twelve-year Senate inquiry into the drug industry, Senator Gaylord Nelson opened the session on psychotropic drugs by comparing them to the drugs in *Brave New World.* "When Aldous Huxley wrote his fantasy concept of the world of the future in the now classic *Brave New World,* he created an uncomfortable, emotionless culture of escapism dependent on tiny tablets of tranquility called soma."[1] Thirty-five years later, *Brave New World* is still invoked, time and again, as a warning against the dangers that await us if we embark on new enhancement technologies. News stories about psychotropic drugs, stem cells, reproductive technologies, or genetic engineering inevitably appear with headlines reading Brave New Medicine, Brave New Babies, Brave New Minds, or Brave New People. It is as if we have no other metaphors for these technologies, no competing visions of possible futures. Whatever the new technology of the moment happens to be, we hear the same cautionary tale: it will lead us to a totalitarian society where generic workers are slotted into castes and anesthetized into bliss. The people in these totalitarian societies are not so much unhappy as they are ignorant of what true happiness is, because they have been drugged and engineered to want nothing more than that which their station allows them.

   We keep returning to this story, I suspect, partly because we like stories of individuals battling the forces of authority, and partly because it allows both teller and listener to collude in the shared sense that we, unlike our neighbors and coworkers and maybe even our family members, have figured out what is really bad about a technology that looks so good. This story says, "Our neighbors may have been sold a bill of goods, they may think that they have found happiness in a Prozac tablet and a Botox injection, but you and I know it's a crock. You and I are too smart to believe the cosmetic surgery Web sites, the drug companies peddling Sarafem and Paxil, and the psychiatrists who tell us we have adult ADHD." Yet as much as we like the *Brave New World* story, as many times as we read it and repeat it and write high school essays about it, somehow it never seems to apply to us. For men, the story of enhancement technologies is about the vanity of women; for women, it is about the sexual gaze of men; for Europeans and Canadians, it is about shallowness of American values; for Americans, it is about "other" Americans — the ones who are either too crooked or deluded to acknowledge what is really going on. If we blame anyone for the ill effects of enhancement technologies, it is either someone in power (the FDA, the media, Big Pharma, "the culture") or the poor suckers who have allowed themselves to be duped (Miss America contestants, neurotic New Yorkers, Michael Jackson). We imagine second-rate TV stars lining up for liposuction and anxious middle managers asking their family doctors for Paxil, and we just shake our heads and laugh. "Why can't they learn to accept themselves as they are?" we ask. Then we are asked to sing a solo in the church choir and can't sleep for a week, or our daughter starts getting teased at school for her buck teeth, and the joke doesn't seem so funny anymore.

We all like to moralize about enhancement technologies, except for the ones we use ourselves. Those technologies never seem quite so bad, because our view of them comes not from television or magazines but from personal experience, or the shared confidences of our troubled friends. There is often striking contrast between private conversation about enhancement technologies and the broader public discussion. In public, for example, everyone seems to be officially anti-Prozac. Feminists ask me why doctors prescribe Prozac more often for women than for men. Undergraduates worry that Prozac might give their classmates a competitive edge. Philosophy professors argue that Prozac would make people shallow and uncreative. Germans object that Prozac is not a natural substance. Americans say that Prozac is a crutch. Most people seem to feel that Prozac is creating some version of what historian David Rothman called, in a *New Republic* cover story, "shiny, happy people."

In private, though, people have started to seek me out and tell me their Prozac stories. They have tried Prozac and hated it; they have tried Prozac and it changed their life; they have tried Prozac and can't see what the big deal is. It has begun to seem as if everyone I know is on Prozac, has been on Prozac, or is considering taking Prozac, and all of them want to get my opinion. Most of all, they want me to try Prozac myself. "How can you write about it if you've never even tried it?" I can see their point. Still, it strikes me as a strange way to talk about a prescription drug. These people are oddly insistent. It was as if we were back in high school, and they were trying to get me to smoke a joint.

People who look at America from abroad often marvel at the enthusi-   5
asm with which Americans use enhancement technologies. I can see why. It is a jolt to discover the rates at which Americans use Ritalin or Prozac or Botox. But "enthusiasm" is probably the wrong word to describe the way Americans feel about enhancement technologies. If this is enthusiasm, it is the enthusiasm of a diver on the high platform, who has to talk himself into taking the plunge. [. . .] I don't think Americans expect happiness in a handful of tablets. We take the tablets, but we brood about it. We try to hide the tablets from our friends. We worry that taking them is a sign of weakness. We try to convince our friends to take them too. We fret that if we don't take them, others will outshine us. We take the tablets, but they leave a bitter taste in our mouths.

Why? Perhaps because in those tablets is a mix of all the American wishes, lusts, and fears: the drive to self-improvement, the search for fulfill-ment, the desire to show that there are second acts in American lives; yet a mix diluted by nagging anxieties about social conformity, about getting too much too easily, about phoniness and self-deception and shallow pleasure. This is not a story from *Brave New World*. It is not even a story of enhance-ment. [. . .] It is less a story about trying to get ahead than about the terror of being left behind, and the humiliation of crossing the finish line dead last, while the crowd points at you and laughs. You can still refuse to use enhancement technologies, of course—you might be the last woman in America who does not dye her gray hair, the last man who refuses to work out at the gym—but even that publicly announces something to other Americans about who you are and what you value. This is all part of the logic of consumer culture. You cannot simply opt out of the system and expect nobody to notice how much you weigh.

Why here, why now? On one level, the answer seems obvious: because the technology has arrived. If you are anxious and lonely and a drug can fix it, why stay anxious and lonely? If you are unhappy with your body and surgery can fix it, why stay unhappy? The market moves to fill a demand for happiness as efficiently as it moves to fill a demand for spark plugs or home computers. It is on a deeper level that the question of enhancement technologies becomes more puzzling. What has made the ground for these technologies so fertile? The sheer variety of technologies on display is re-markable. [. . .] Black folks rub themselves with cream to make their skin lighter, while white folks broil in tanning parlors to make their skin darker. Bashful men get ETS surgery to reduce blood flow above the neck, while elderly men take Viagra to increase blood flow below the belt. Each tech-nology has its own rationale, its own cultural niche, a distinct popula-tion of users, and an appeal that often waxes or wanes with changes in fashion or the state of scientific knowledge. But do they have anything in common? Is there anything about the way we live now that helps explain their popularity?

The "self that struggles to realize itself," as philosopher Michael Walzer puts it, has become a familiar notion to most people living in the West today.[2] We tend to see ourselves as the managers of life projects that we map out, organize, make choices about, perhaps compare with other possible projects, and ultimately live out to completion. From late adolescence onward, we are expected to make important decisions about what to do for a living, where to live, whether to marry and have children, all with the sense that these decisions will contribute to the success or failure of our projects. Yet as Walzer points out, there is nothing natural or inevitable about this way of conceptualizing a life. Not everyone in the West today will think of their lives as planned projects, and most people at most times in history have probably thought of their lives differently. Marriages are arranged; educational choices are fixed; gods are tyrannical or absent. A life might be spontaneous, rather than planned; its shape might be given to us, rather than created. The shapes of lives can be determined not by the demands of personal values or self-fulfillment, but by those of God, family, social station, caste, or one's ancestors.

This notion of life as a project suggests both individual responsibility and moral uncertainty. If I am the planner and manager of my life, then I am at least partly responsible for its success or failure. Thus the lure of enhancement technologies: as tools to produce a better, more successful project. Yet if my life is a project, what exactly is the purpose of the project? How do I tell a successful project from a failure? Aristotle (for example) could write confidently about the good life for human beings because he was confident about what the purpose of being a human being was. Just as a knife has a purpose, so human beings have a purpose; just as the qualities that make for a good knife are those that help the knife slice, whittle, and chop, the qualities that make a human being better are those that help us better fulfill our purpose as human beings.

Our problem, of course, is that most of us don't have Aristotle's confidence about the purpose of human life. Good knives cut, that much we can see, but what does a good human being do, and how will we know when we are doing it? Is there even such a thing as a single, universal human purpose? Not if we believe what we are told by the culture that surrounds us. From philosophy courses and therapy sessions to magazines and movies, we are told that questions of purpose vary from one person to the next; that, in fact, a large part of our life project is to discover our own individual purpose and develop it to its fullest. This leaves us with unanswered questions not just about what kinds of lives are better or worse, but also about the criteria by which such judgments are made. Is it better to be a successful bail bondsman or a second-rate novelist? On what yardstick do we compare the lives of Reform Jews, high-church Episcopalians, and California Wiccans? Where exactly should the choices we make about our lives be anchored?

10

Many people today believe that the success or failure of a life has something to do with the idea of self-fulfillment. We may not know exactly what
a successful life is, but we have a pretty good suspicion that it has something to do with being fulfilled—or at the very least, that an unfulfilled life
runs the risk of failure. In the name of fulfillment people quit their jobs in
human resources and real estate to become poets and potters, leave their
dermatology practices to do medical mission work in Bangladesh, even
divorce their husbands or wives (the marriage was adequate, but it was not
fulfilling). Women leave their children in day care because they believe that
they will be more fulfilled with a career; they leave their jobs because they
believe that it will be more fulfilling to stay home with the kids. Fulfillment
has a strong moral strand to it—many people feel that they *ought* to pursue
a career, that they *ought* to leave a loveless marriage—but its parameters are
vague and indeterminate. How exactly do I know if I am fulfilled? Fulfillment looks a little like being in love, a little like a successful spiritual quest;
it is a state centered largely on individual psychic well-being. If I am alienated, depressed, or anxious, I can't be completely fulfilled.

If I am not fulfilled, I am missing out on what life can offer. Life is a
short, sweet ride, and I am spending it all in the station. The problem is that
there is no great, overarching metric for self-fulfillment, no master schedule
that we can look up at and say, "Yes, I've missed the train." So we look desperately to experts for instructions—counselors, psychiatrists, advice columnists, self-help writers, life coaches, even professional ethicists. We read the
ads on the wall for cosmetic dentistry, and we look nervously at the people
standing next to us in line. Does she know something that I don't? Is she
more fulfilled? How does my psychic well-being compare to hers? [. . .]

In other times and places, success or failure in a life might have been
determined by fixed and agreed-upon standards. You displeased the ancestors; you shamed your family; you did not accept Jesus Christ as your personal savior. You arrived late to the station, and the train left without you.
But our situation today is different—not for everyone, of course, but for
many of us. We have gotten on the train, but we don't know who is driving
it, or where, some point off in the far distance, the tracks are leading. The
other passengers are smiling, they look happy, yet underneath this facade of
good cheer and philosophical certainty, a demon keeps whispering in our
ears: "What if I have gotten it all wrong? What if I have boarded the wrong
train?"

Tocqueville hinted at this worry over 150 years ago when he wrote
about American "restlessness in the midst of abundance." Behind all the
admirable energy of American life, Tocqueville saw a kind of grim relent-
lessness. We build houses to pass our old age, Tocqueville wrote, then sell
them before the roof is on; we clear fields, then leave it to others to gather
the harvest; we take up a profession, then leave it to take up another one
or go into politics. Americans frantically pursue prosperity, and when we
finally get it, we are tormented by the worry that we might have gotten it

quicker. An American on vacation, Tocqueville marveled, "will travel five hundred miles in a few days as a distraction from his happiness."[3]

Tocqueville may well have been right about American restlessness, but it took another Frenchman, surrealist painter Phillipe Soupault, to put his finger on the form that it has taken today. According to Soupault, Americans see the pursuit of happiness not just as a right, as the Declaration of Independence states, but as a strange sort of duty. In the United States, he wrote, "one is always in danger of entrapment by what appears on the surface to be a happy civilization. There is a sort of obligation to be happy." Humans are born to be happy, and if they are not, something has gone wrong. As Soupault puts it, "Whoever is unhappy is suspect."[4] Substitute self-fulfillment for happiness and you get something of the ethic that motivates the desire for enhancement technologies. Once self-fulfillment is hitched to the success of a human life, it comes perilously close to an obligation—not an obligation to God, country, or family, but an obligation to the self. We are compelled to pursue fulfillment through enhancement technologies not in order to get ahead of others, but to make sure that we have lived our lives to the fullest. The train has left the station and we don't know where it is going. The least we can do is be sure it is making good time.

15

Notes

1. Mickey Smith, *A Social History of the Minor Tranquilizers: The Quest for Small Comfort in an Age of Anxiety* (New York: Praeger, 1989) 178.

2. Michael Walzer, *Thick and Thin: Moral Argument at Home and Abroad* (South Bend: Notre Dame UP, 1994) 23–24.

3. Alexis de Tocqueville, *Democracy in America*, trans. George Lawrence, ed. J. P. Mayer (New York: Harper and Row, 1988) 536.

4. Philippe Soupault, "Introduction to Mademoiselle Coeur Brise (Miss Lonely-hearts)," *Nathanael West: A Collection of Critical Essays*, ed. Jay Martin (Englewood Cliffs: Prentice-Hall, 1971) 112–13.

For Discussion

1. According to Elliott, why do people appeal so often to Huxley's novel, *Brave New World*, when enhancement technologies, especially new ones, are discussed? Why does he consider the connection essentially misleading?

2. Elliott claims that American culture and values emphasize "life as a project"—hence, "the lure of enhancement technologies: as tools to produce a better, more successful project." Do you see this as the drive behind such popular TV shows as *Changing Spaces, What Not to Wear,* and *Extreme Makeover?*

3. "If I am alienated, depressed, or anxious, I can't be completely fulfilled," Elliott says, and the solution becomes a pill, plastic surgery, occupational change, divorce—something that will "fix" the prob-

lem. But are there circumstances when people ought to feel alienated, depressed, or anxious? Can such feelings be positive and productive rather than negative and counterproductive?
4. Elliott cites the French surrealist painter Phillipe Soupault, who claims that in the United States "there is a sort of obligation to be happy. . . . Whoever is unhappy is suspect." Thus, according to Elliott, the pursuit of happiness is not a right but rather "a strange sort of duty . . . an obligation to the self." Do you find this diagnosis persuasive? What, according to Elliott, makes such an understanding of the pursuit of happiness unsatisfying and ultimately self-defeating?

For Persuasion

"Our problem," Elliott claims, "is that most of us don't have Aristotle's confidence about the purpose of human life. . . . [W]hat does a good human being do, and how will we know when we are doing it?"

Are we Americans so much in doubt about what we ought to be doing as Elliott claims? Write an essay arguing against his assertion of complete relativity where our notion of the good is concerned. Support it by referring to popular culture—to movies and TV dramas, for instance—which often reflect our values and sometimes expose them for reflection.

Additional Suggestions for Writing

1. As you might imagine, many proposals exist for controlling human bioengineering, some of them advanced by researchers in the field. Collect three or four of these proposals and study them. On what do they agree? Exactly how do they differ? Take what you consider the most promising aspects of each proposal and write an essay attempting to put them together in a coherent and satisfying view. At the end of the essay, indicate what you would regulate most carefully and why.
2. Some bioengineering researchers fear allowing ethical considerations to enter the picture where human genetic manipulation is concerned. They think that only issues of safety, effectiveness, and reliability ought to be considered. Their fear arises from the possibility that, for example, ethical objections to abortion might result in closing off stem cell research altogether. They point to religious and moral objections that have impeded scientific progress before.

   Find out more about efforts to regulate stem cell research in the United States and elsewhere. Then ask, Can we limit our thinking about stem cell research and the applications of such knowledge to objective measures of safety, reliability, and effectiveness? In other words, a new drug is approved if it works as its manufacturer claims, with risks specified. Is that standard adequate for stem cell therapies? Write an essay that either supports such a limitation or argues that "truth in advertising" is not enough.

Chapter 15

Liberal Education and Contemporary Culture: What Should Undergraduates Learn?

No institution in the United States receives more attention than our educational system. Studies of it abound, and new ones seem to appear almost weekly. It is rare not to hear or read something about education in the news every day, while scholarly articles and books about it proliferate beyond anyone's ability to read them all.

Why are we so obsessed with this topic? Most Americans believe that education is the route to a better life, the foundation of democracy, and the key to a strong economy, a competitive workforce, and social and moral progress. "Better education" becomes the magic solution to so many questions concerning the nation's problems. We are obsessed with it, then, because our perceived stake in it is so high. That's why the press covers it extensively and why politicians push the issue toward the top of their campaigns for office and their legislative agendas.

With ideals and expectations so high, we should not be surprised that the educational system often disappoints enough to be called "failing" or "a failure." Until the past decade or so, however, almost all the criticism was directed at the public schools, especially high schools, while our universities and colleges were extolled as among the best in the world. Now higher education comes in for as much criticism as the public schools. As the cost of a college education continues to soar, rising much faster than the rate of inflation, more and more people wonder whether we are getting our money's worth, especially when a degree may no longer lead as often as it once did to a desired first job. Industry spends millions educating their employees after college, in part because many lack even basic communication skills, and businesses increasingly resort to hiring people whose degrees were earned in other countries. There is much talk that we are losing our competitive edge and that college graduates are no longer well-informed citizens, able to provide moral and intellectual leadership. In short, whereas once it was always the public schools that were failing, now many also apply the label to higher education, public and private.

The focus of concern is undergraduate education, especially the first two years, when students traditionally receive broad exposure to the liberal arts (literature, history, philosophy, and so on) prior to concentrating on their majors. The notion of "liberal arts" comes to us from ancient Athens and Rome, where *liberal* meant "free" in the sense of not being a slave: male citizens were educated in the liberal arts, slaves in the manual or practical arts. Liberal arts education still has strong identifications with social class: Virtually all of our most prestigious (that is, selective and usually expensive) universities claim to offer a liberal arts education, as contrasted with technical and vocational schools, which supposedly do not. One problem the liberal arts face in the United States is the association with privilege in a democratic culture uneasy with class distinctions. We want to say the liberal arts are for everyone. But are they?

Another problem is that university faculties cannot agree about what an "educated person" should know and therefore what a liberal arts education should be. The typical result is a laundry list of courses that satisfy what we call "basic requirements" but that do not constitute either a coherent course of study or a shared body of knowledge required for all students. Perhaps we should resign ourselves to such disagreements in a diverse culture with universities offering courses in virtually all fields of knowledge. Who's to say what an "educated person" should know? But if we can't answer this question, does the ideal of a liberal arts education have any substance, any meaning? Or is it merely an empty ideal we cling to out of habit?

Liberal arts education faces many other problems, none of which have easy solutions. For example, the traditional liberal arts education is limited to the West, primarily to the heritage of Greece and Rome as transmitted through later European culture to those parts of the world colonized by European powers. We live, however, in a world of global commerce, communication, and politics, where knowledge of the West alone is insufficient and can foster a destructive cultural arrogance. How inclusive can a liberal arts education become without losing focus and character? Can an essentially Western educational ideal function in a global context?

No matter how we answer the questions posed thus far—and even if we think, as many critics do, that liberal arts education is dead—we should ponder this: Fundamentally, the liberal arts are the study of human achievements, cultures, and institutions. Because nothing human can be created or studied without language, the liberal arts also include English, foreign languages, and mathematics. Clearly, education wouldn't amount to much without humanistic study and couldn't go on at all without knowledge of the various symbol systems that enable all study. As long as we invest in education, we'll be investing in the liberal arts.

But if there is something permanent about the liberal arts, dealing as they do with human culture, they must be responsive to the times, to cultural change and pressures. All the selections in this chapter deal with contemporary American culture. "Collegiate Life: An Obituary" offers a sketch of the undergraduate student and college life based on extensive empirical research. The two articles "on the uses of a liberal education" offer sharply contrasting personal narratives, one by a professor at the University of Virginia, whose students are relatively privileged, and the other by a researcher into poverty, who created a liberal arts course for ghetto students in New York City. For the first writer, a liberal arts education is too often "lite entertainment for bored college students," and for the second, "a weapon in the hands of the restless poor"—a forceful reminder that the cultural situation in which liberal arts are taught has everything to do with what they are and how they function.

No inquiry into liberal education and contemporary culture can afford to ignore university culture itself, exclusive of students—in other words, the institutional structure. Our final reading, John Tagg's "The Decline of the Knowledge Factory," exposes this structure well en route to explaining why reforming liberal arts education is so difficult.

Above all, as we think about liberal arts education and contemporary culture, we must always remember how closely tied together they are. Physics may be physics regardless of where it's taught and to whom, but literature and philosophy, to mention only two important liberal arts, assuredly are not. No curriculum will work if it is out of touch with its culture, and a culture divorced from the liberal arts will be thin and puerile. Getting them to dance together more or less harmoniously while preserving the rigor and discipline of higher education is probably the major challenge we face.

Collegiate Life: An Obituary
Arthur Levine and Jeanette S. Cureton

Arthur Levine is president of Teacher's College at Columbia University; Jeanette Cureton was an educational researcher at Harvard during their collaboration. Their book, When Hopes and Fears Collide: A Portrait of Today's College Student *(1998), presents the results of five years (1992–1997) of research involving many universities and colleges and including extensive conversations with students and student affairs officers. This article from the journal* Change *summarizes their conclusions.*

> *Our institutions of higher education are almost unimaginably diverse, each having its own unique history, character, and student profile. Any discussion of general trends or treatment of the "typical" or "average" student, therefore, may only imperfectly reflect your own experience. Yet we think you will recognize the portrait and find it helpful in understanding and articulating what's happening on college campuses today.*

In 1858, John Henry Cardinal Newman wrote *The Idea of a University.* His ideal was a residential community of students and teachers devoted to the intellect. To him, a college was "an alma mater, knowing her children one by one, not a foundry, or a mint, or a treadmill." Given a choice between an institution that dispensed with "residence and tutorial superintendence and gave its degrees to any person who passed an examination in a wide range of subjects" or "a university which . . . merely brought a number of young men together for three or four years," he chose the latter.

Newman's ideal was so appealing that it has been embraced regularly over the years by higher education luminaries from Robert Hutchins and Paul Goodman to Alexander Meiklejohn and Mortimer Adler. Belief in it remains a staple of nearly every college curriculum committee in the country.

But that ideal is moribund today. Except for a relatively small number of residential liberal arts colleges, institutions of higher education and their students are moving away from it at an accelerating pace. The notion of a living-learning community is dead or dying on most campuses today.

This is a principal finding of several studies we conducted between 1992 and 1997, which involved our surveying a representative sample of 9,100 undergraduate students and 270 chief student affairs officers, as well as holding focus groups on 28 campuses. [. . .]

DEMOGRAPHICS

A major reason for the changes we describe is simply demographic. In comparison with their counterparts of the 1960s and 1970s, undergraduates today are more racially diverse and, on average, considerably older.

5

In fact, since 1980, the lion's share of college enrollment growth has come from students who might be described as nontraditional. By 1993, 24 percent of all college students were working full-time, according to our Undergraduate Survey; at two-year colleges, this figure had reached 39 percent.

By 1995, 44 percent of all college students were over 25 years old; 54 percent were working; 56 percent were female; and 43 percent were attending part-time. Currently, fewer than one in six of all undergraduates fit the traditional stereotype of the American college student attending full-time, being 18 to 22 years of age, and living on campus (see U.S. Department of Education, in Resources).

What this means is that higher education is not as central to the lives of today's undergraduates as it was to previous generations. Increasingly, college is just one of a multiplicity of activities in which they are engaged every day. For many, it is not even the most important of these activities; work and family often overshadow it.

As a consequence, older, part-time, and working students — especially those with children — often told us in our surveys that they wanted a different type of relationship with their colleges from the one undergraduates historically have had. They preferred a relationship like those they already enjoyed with their bank, the telephone company, and the supermarket.

WHAT STUDENTS WANT

Think about what you want from your bank. We know what we want: an ATM on every corner. And when we get to the ATM, we want there to be no line. We also would like a parking spot right in front of the ATM, and to have our checks deposited the moment they arrive at the bank, or perhaps the day before! And we want no mistakes in processing — unless they are in our favor. We also know what we do not want from our banks. We do not want them to provide us with softball leagues, religious counseling, or health services. We can arrange all of these things for ourselves and don't wish to pay extra fees for the bank to offer them.

Students are asking roughly the same thing from their colleges. They want their colleges to be nearby and to operate at the hours most useful to them — preferably around the clock. They want convenience: easy, accessible parking (at the classroom door would not be bad); no lines; and a polite, helpful, efficient staff. They also want high-quality education but are eager for low costs. For the most part, they are willing to comparison shop, and they place a premium on time and money. They do not want to pay for activities and programs they do not use.

In short, students increasingly are bringing to higher education exactly the same consumer expectations they have for every other commercial

10

establishment with which they deal. Their focus is on convenience, quality, service, and cost.

They believe that since they are paying for their education, faculty should give them the education they want; they make larger demands on faculty than past students ever have. They are also the target audience for alternatives to traditional higher education. They are likely to be drawn to distance education, which offers the convenience of instruction at home or the office.

They are prime candidates for stripped-down versions of college, located in the suburbs and business districts of our cities, that offer low-cost instruction made possible by heavy faculty teaching loads, mostly part-time faculties, limited selections of majors, and few electives. Proprietary institutions of this type are springing up around the country.

On campus, students are behaving like consumers, too. More than 9 out of 10 chief student affairs officers told us in last year's Student Affairs Survey that student power in college governance has increased during the 1990s (or at least has remained the same), but that undergraduates are less interested in being involved in campus governance than in the past.

A small minority of undergraduates continue to want voting power or control over admissions decisions, faculty appointments, bachelor's degree requirements, and the content of courses; however, a decreasing percentage desire similar roles in residential regulations and undergraduate discipline, areas in which students would seem most likely to want control. Overall, the proportion of students who want voting or controlling roles in institutional governance is at its lowest level in a quarter century, according to comparisons between our 1993 Undergraduate Survey and the 1969 and 1976 Carnegie Council surveys.

15

This is precisely the same attitude most of us hold with regard to the commercial enterprises we patronize. We don't want to be bothered with running the bank or the supermarket; we simply want them to do their jobs and do them well — to give us what we need without hassles or headaches. That is, help the consumers and don't get in their way. Students today are saying precisely the same things about their colleges.

SOCIAL LIFE

From a personal perspective, students are coming to college overwhelmed and more damaged than in the past. Chief student affairs officers in 1997 reported rises in eating disorders (on 58 percent of campuses), classroom disruption (on 44 percent), drug abuse (on 42 percent), alcohol abuse (on 35 percent), gambling (on 25 percent), and suicide attempts (on 23 percent).

As a consequence, academic institutions are being forced to expand their psychological counseling services. Three out of five colleges and universities reported last year that the use of counseling services had increased. Not only are counselors seeing students in record numbers, but the severity of the students' problems and the length of time needed to treat them are greater than in the past.

Students tell us they are frightened. They're afraid of deteriorating social and environmental conditions, international conflicts and terrorism, multiculturalism and their personal relationships, financing their education and getting jobs, and the future they will face. Nearly one-third of all college freshmen (30 percent) grew up with one or no parent (see Sax et al., in Resources). As one dean of students we talked with concluded, "Students expect the [college] community to respond to their needs—to make right their personal problems and those of society at large."

The effect of these accumulated fears and hurts is to divide students and isolate them from one another. Students also fear intimacy in relationships; withdrawal is easier and less dangerous than engagement.   20

Traditional dating is largely dead on college campuses. At institutions all over the country, students told us, in the words of a University of Colorado undergraduate, "There is no such thing as dating here." Two-person dating has been replaced by group dating, in which men and women travel in unpartnered packs. It's a practice that provides protection from deeper involvement and intimacy for a generation that regularly told us in focus group interviews that they had never witnessed a successful adult romantic relationship.

Romantic relationships are seen as a burden, as a drag or potential anchor in a difficult world. Yet sexual relationships have not declined, even in the age of AIDS. Student descriptions of sexual activity are devoid of emotional content; they use words such as "scoping," "clocking," "hooking," "scamming," "scrumping," "mashing," and "shacking" to describe intimate relations.

In general, with increasing pressures on students, collegiate social life occupies a smaller part of their lives. In the words of an undergraduate at the University of the District of Columbia, "Life is just work, school, and home." In fact, one-fifth of those queried on our campus site visits (21 percent) defined their social lives in terms of studying; for another 11 percent, sleeping was all they cared about. When we asked students at the University of Colorado for the best adjective to describe this generation, the most common choice was "tired."

But not all of the retreat from social life is time-based. Chief student affairs officers describe students as loners more often now than in the past. Requests for single rooms in residence halls have skyrocketed. The thought of having a roommate is less appealing than it once was.

Similarly, group activities that once connected students on college   25
campuses are losing their appeal and are becoming more individualized. For instance, the venue for television watching has moved from the lounge to the dorm room. Film viewing has shifted from the theater to

the home VCR. With student rooms a virtual menagerie of electronic and food-preparation equipment, students are living their lives in ways that allow them to avoid venturing out if they so choose.

STUDENT ORGANIZATIONAL MITOSIS

None of this is to say that collegiate social life is dead, but its profile and location have changed. On campus, there is probably a greater diversity of activities available than ever before, but each activity — in the words of the chief student affairs officer of the University of Southern Mississippi — "appeals to smaller pockets of students."

This is, in many respects, the consequence of student organizational mitosis and the proliferation of the divides between undergraduates. For instance, the business club on one college campus divided into more than a dozen groups — including women's; black; Hispanic; gay, lesbian, and bisexual; and Asian and Filipino business clubs.

Deans of students regularly told us last year that "there is less larger-group socializing" and that "more people are doing things individually and in separate groups than campus-wide." In contrast to the Carnegie Council's 1979 study, current students describe themselves in terms of their differences, not their commonalities. Increasingly, they say they associate with people who are like themselves rather than different.

In the main, when students do take time to have fun, they are leaving campus to do so. Our Campus Site Visits study indicated that drinking is the primary form of recreation for 63 percent of students, followed closely by going to clubs and bars (59 percent) and simply getting off campus (52 percent). By contrast, the latter two activities were not mentioned in the Carnegie Council's 1979 study.

Drinking was not a surprise. It was the first choice in our earlier study, but there is more binge drinking today. Drinking to get drunk has become the great escape for undergraduates.

30

Escaping from campus is a trend that goes hand in hand with the high numbers of students living in off-campus housing — more than triple the percentage in the late 1960s. Only 30 percent of students we surveyed reported living on campus. Add to this the fact that students are also spending less time on campus because of jobs and part-time attendance, and the result is that increasingly campuses are places in which instruction is the principal activity. Living and social life occur elsewhere.

MULTICULTURALISM

Campuses are more deeply divided along lines of race, gender, ethnicity, sexuality, and other differences today than in the past. A majority of deans at four-year colleges told us last year that the climate on campus can be described as politically correct (60 percent), civility has declined (57 percent), students of different racial and ethnic groups often do not socialize together (56 percent), reports of sexual harassment have increased (55 percent), and students feel uncomfortable expressing unpopular or controversial opinions (54 percent).

Multiculturalism is a painful topic for many students. The dirty words on college campuses now are no longer four letters: they are six-letter words like "racist" and "sexist"—and "homophobic," which is even longer. Students don't want to discuss the topic. In focus group interviews, students were more willing to tell us intimate details of their sex lives than to discuss diversity on campus.

Tension regarding diversity and difference runs high all across college life. Students talked about friction in the classroom; in the residence halls; in reactions to posters placed on campus or to visiting speakers; in campus activities and the social pursuits of the day; in hiring practices; in testing; in the dining room, library, bookstore, and sports facilities; in every aspect of their campus lives. In this sense, the campus in the 1990s is a less hospitable place for all undergraduates, regardless of background, than it once was.

ACADEMICS

Although instruction remains the principal on-campus activity that brings undergraduates together, the academic arena is experiencing its own form of student disengagement. Pursuit of academic goals is clearly utilitarian. It's as if students have struck a bargain with their colleges. They're going to class all right, but they're going by the book: they're doing what's necessary to fulfill degree requirements and gain skills for a job, but then they're out the door. They're focused and career-oriented, and see college as instrumental in leading to a lucrative career. "Task-oriented students who focus on jobs" is how a Georgia Tech student affairs official labeled them.

Although students do not believe that a college education provides a money-back guarantee of future success, they feel that without one, a good job—much less a lucrative or prestigious job—is impossible to obtain. At the very least, it's a kind of insurance policy to hedge bets against the future. As a student at Portland (Oregon) Community College put it, "College is the difference between white-collar and blue-collar work." Fifty-seven percent of undergraduates we surveyed in 1993 believed that the chief benefit of a college education is increasing one's earning power—an 11 percentage-point increase since 1976.

By contrast, the value placed on nonmaterial goals (that is, learning to get along with people and formulating the values and goals of one's life) has plummeted since the late 1960s, dropping from 71 and 76 percent respectively to 50 and 47 percent. Whereas in 1969 these personal and

35

philosophic goals were cited by students as the primary reasons for attending college, in 1993, students placed them at the bottom of the list.

Although a great number of students are focused and intent on pursuing career goals, many also face a variety of academic hurdles. They are coming to college less well prepared academically. Nearly three-fourths (73 percent) of deans in 1997 reported an increase within the last decade in the proportion of students requiring remedial or developmental education at two-year (81 percent) and four-year (64 percent) colleges.

Nearly one-third (32 percent) of all undergraduates surveyed reported having taken a basic skills or remedial course in reading, writing, or math, up from 29 percent in 1976. Despite high aspirations, a rising percentage of students simply are not prepared for the rigors of academe.

Another academic hurdle for students is a growing gap between how   40
students learn best and how faculty teach. According to research by Charles Schroeder of the University of Missouri–Columbia, published in the September/October 1993 *Change*, more than half of today's students perform best in a learning situation characterized by "direct, concrete experience, moderate-to-high degrees of structure, and a linear approach to learning. They value the practical and the immediate, and the focus of their perception is primarily on the physical world." According to Schroeder, three-quarters of faculty, on the other hand, "prefer the global to the particular; are stimulated by the realm of concepts, ideas, and abstractions; and assume that students, like themselves, need a high degree of autonomy in their work."

Small wonder, then, that frustration results and that every year faculty believe students are less well prepared, while students increasingly think their classes are incomprehensible. On the faculty side, this is certainly the case. The 1997 Student Affairs Survey revealed that at 74 percent of campuses, faculty complaints about students are on the rise. One result is that students and faculty are spending less time on campus together. With work and part-time attendance, students increasingly are coming to campus just for their classes.

This explains, in part, why students are taking longer to complete college. Fewer than two out of five are able to graduate in four years (see Astin et al., in Resources). Twenty-eight percent now require a fifth year to earn a baccalaureate, according to U.S. Department of Education statistics from 1996. In reality, obtaining the baccalaureate degree in four years is an anomaly today, particularly at public and less selective institutions.

THE FUTURE

The overwhelming majority of college students believe they will be successful. But their fears about relationships, romance, and their future happiness were continuing themes in every focus group. Their concerns about finances were overwhelming. There was not one focus group in which students did not ask whether they would be able to repay their student loans, afford to complete college, get a good job, or avoid moving home with Mom and Dad.

The college graduate driving a cab or working at the Gap was a universal anecdote. There was more mythology here than there were concrete examples, however. College graduates being forced to drive taxis is one of the great American legends, rivaled only by the tale of George Washington and the cherry tree.

Finances were a constant topic of discussion. Students told us of the need to drop out, stop out, and attend college part-time because of tuition costs. They told us of the lengths they had to go to pay tuition — even giving blood. More than one in five (21 percent) who participated in the Undergraduate Survey said that someone who helped pay their tuition had been out of work while they attended college.

At heart, undergraduates are worried about whether we can make it as a society, and whether they can actually make it personally. In our surveys, the majority did say they expected to do better than their parents. But in our focus groups, students regularly told us, "We're going to be the first generation that doesn't surpass our parents in making more money." "How will I buy a house?" "How will I send my kids to college?"

This is a generation of students desperately clinging to the American Dream. Nearly nine out of 10 (88 percent) students are optimistic about their personal futures, but their hope, though broadly professed, is fragile and gossamer-like. Their lives are being challenged at every turn: in their families, their communities, their nation, and their world. This is a generation where hope and fear collide.

CONCLUSION

In sum, these changes in America's undergraduates add up to a requiem for historic notions of collegiate life — the ivory tower, the living-learning community, the residential college, and all the rest. But the changes are not sudden; they began even before Cardinal Newman wrote his classic. Most are a natural consequence of the democratization of higher education. This is what happens when 65 percent of all high school graduates go on to college and higher education is open to the nation's population across the lifespan. Four years of living in residence becomes a luxury few can afford.

So how should higher education respond? Dismissing the present or recalling a golden era lost are not particularly helpful — for the most part the changes are permanent. But there are a few things colleges can do.

The first is to focus. Most colleges have less time with their students on campus than in the past. They need to be very clear about what they want to accomplish with students and dramatically reduce the laundry lists of values and goals that constitute the typical mission statement.

The second is to use all opportunities available to educate students. Required events, such as orientation, should be used to educate rather than to deal with logistics. The awards a college gives should represent the values it most wants to teach. The same is true for speakers. The in-house newsletter can be used to educate. And of course, maybe the best advice is that almost any event can be used for educational purposes if the food and music are good enough.

Third, build on the strengths unique to every generation of students. For instance, current undergraduates, as part of their off-campus activities, are involved in public service—an astounding 64 percent of them, according to the Undergraduate Survey. Service learning, then, becomes an excellent vehicle to build into the curriculum and cocurriculum of most colleges.

Fourth, work to eliminate the forces that push students off campus unnecessarily. For example, most colleges talk a great deal about multiculturalism, but in general have not translated the rhetoric into a climate that will make the campus more hospitable to current students.

In like manner, using financial aid more to meet need than to reward merit would lessen the necessity for students to work while attending college. These are steps any college with the will and commitment can take. Both campus life and our students would benefit greatly.

Resources

Astin, A. W., L. Tsui, and J. Avalos. *Degree Attainment Rates at American Colleges and Universities: Effects of Race, Gender, and Institutional Type.* Los Angeles: Higher Education Research Institute, UCLA, 1996.

Sax, L. J., A. W. Astin, W. S. Korn, and K. M. Mahoney. *The American Freshman: National Norms for Fall 1997.* Los Angeles: Higher Education Research Institute, UCLA, 1997.

U.S. Department of Education. National Center for Education Statistics. *Condition of Education, 1996* (NCES 96304). Washington: GPO, 1996.

---. National Center for Education Statistics. *Digest of Education Statistics, 1997* (NCES 98–015). Washington: GPO, 1997.

For Discussion

1. The article opens by recalling Newman's 144-year-old *Idea of a University,* an ideal grounded in "a residential community of students and teachers devoted to the intellect." By definition, ideals do not correspond to realities, but do you find the ideal of *alma mater* (Latin, "bountiful mother") appealing? If so, in what ways exactly? Why?

2. Which of the demographic trends delineated in paragraphs 4–6 seem most incompatible with the survival and vitality of the residential college?
3. As the subtitle of the article, "an obituary," would suggest, its view of student culture is gloomy and largely negative: Students are said to be afraid and tired, anxious about money, burdened with personal problems, inclined toward escapism, overly demanding of teachers and college services, socially alienated and fragmented, and so on. Would you say the sketch is accurate? fair? balanced? How much do the attitudes and behaviors described reflect American culture in general rather than student culture in particular? How different are they from the attitudes and behaviors of your parents and their parents?
4. Current college students are described routinely as taking an instrumental view of college, seeing it as only a means to an end, not as an end in itself. That is, "task-oriented students who focus on jobs" *is* the common view "we" take of "you." What intrinsic value might college have? How could it be an end in itself? Have your classes so far helped you detect and appreciate the intrinsic value of learning and the overall college experience?

For Analysis and Convincing

If we are feeling charitable, we might describe the authors' suggestions at the end of the article as too general and obvious; if we are feeling less charitable, as vague and unhelpful. Can we do better?

Write an essay offering your own portrait of your generation of students or an essay that assesses the image offered here. Your portrait should reflect the demographics and other characteristics of your school. Then, working from the situation as you depict it, offer more concrete and detailed suggestions for coping with student problems and for improving campus life at your school. Address your essay to your school's student governing body.

For Inquiry and Dialogue

If the residential college is dying or dead, as these authors claim and as a good deal of independent evidence supports, what model might replace it? Could we, for example, build a sense of student community and interaction between students and teachers via the electronic media, especially computers, as some have suggested? If student groups are fragmenting into smaller and smaller communities, how can we get these groups back together and engaged in useful dialogue? In short, a key question to think about and discuss is, How can we recapture something of the values represented by the residential college in an environment that does not lend itself to a closely knit community of students and teachers?

Photograph
Lois Bernstein

When the University of Chicago was founded in the late nineteenth century, its trustees chose for its original buildings the English Gothic architectural style of Oxford University rather than a more contemporary design. The photograph below accompanied a New York Times *article about the university's refusal to soften its rigorous academic standards and requirements in order to attract more applicants. The students are sitting in Hutchinson Commons, the main dining hall, which was constructed in 1901.*

For Discussion

Architecture is a form of visual rhetoric, similar to public sculpture. The style of the buildings at a college or university makes an argument about the education offered there: its purpose, origins, and values. How do you read the argument implied by the interior of this college dining hall? Discuss the architecture of your own school's campus. Is it all in one style? A mix of styles and periods? Do different buildings seem to make different arguments? Consider these arguments in the context of changing ideas about liberal arts education, as discussed in the readings in this chapter.

On the Uses of Liberal Education:
As Lite Entertainment for Bored College Students
Mark Edmundson

This essay and the next one by Earl Shorris appeared together in the September 1997 issue of Harper's. *Each can stand alone as an argument about the liberal arts and culture, but they are far more interesting read together as contrasting perspectives. Mark Edmundson is a professor at the prestigious University of Virginia and thus teaches relatively privileged students of traditional college age, while Shorris, a poverty researcher, discusses an experimental liberal arts program he developed for older, disadvantaged students in New York City. As one might expect, the view from "the top" is radically different from the view at "the bottom." Yet, at a deeper level, the essays connect and illuminate each other in provocative ways.*

Edmundson wrote for people of his age, the sixties generation, not for college students. If you wonder about how professors see you, this essay may enlighten and perhaps irritate. Of course, his view does not represent all professors, nor do University of Virginia students typify the current population. But we think most professors and students will see something of themselves and their institutions in what Edmundson has to say. Furthermore, the issues he raises surely relate to higher education generally.

Today is evaluation day in my Freud class, and everything has changed. The class meets twice a week, late in the afternoon, and the clientele, about fifty undergraduates, tends to drag in and slump, looking disconsolate and a little lost, waiting for a jump start. To get the discussion moving, they usually require a joke, an anecdote, an off-the-wall question—When you were a kid, were your Halloween getups ego costumes, id costumes, or superego costumes? That sort of thing. But today, as soon as I flourish the forms, a buzz rises in the room. Today they write their assessments of the course, their assessments of me, and they are without a doubt wide-awake. "What is your evaluation of the instructor?" asks question number eight, entreating them to circle a number between five (excellent) and one (poor, poor). Whatever interpretive subtlety they've acquired during the term is now out the window. Edmundson: one to five, stand and shoot.

And they do. As I retreat through the door—I never stay around for this phase of the ritual—I look over my shoulder and see them toiling away like the devil's auditors. They're pitched into high writing gear, even the ones who struggle to squeeze out their journal entries word by word, stoked on a procedure they have by now supremely mastered. They're playing the informed consumer, letting the provider know where he's come through and where he's not quite up to snuff.

But why am I so distressed, bolting like a refugee out of my own classroom, where I usually hold easy sway? Chances are the evaluations will be much like what they've been in the past—they'll be just fine. It's likely that

I'll be commended for being "interesting" (and I am commended, many times over), that I'll be cited for my relaxed and tolerant ways (that happens, too), that my sense of humor and capacity to connect the arcana of the subject matter with current culture will come in for some praise (yup). I've been hassled this term, finishing a manuscript, and so haven't given their journals the attention I should have, and for that I'm called — quite civilly, though — to account. Overall, I get off pretty well.

Yet I have to admit that I do not much like the image of myself that emerges from these forms, the image of knowledgeable, humorous detachment and bland tolerance. I do not like the forms themselves, with their number ratings, reminiscent of the sheets circulated after the TV pilot has just played to its sample audience in Burbank. Most of all I dislike the attitude of calm consumer expertise that pervades the responses. I'm disturbed by the serene belief that my function — and, more important, Freud's, or Shakespeare's, or Blake's — is to divert, entertain, and interest. Observes one respondent, not at all unrepresentative: "Edmundson has done a fantastic job of presenting this difficult, important & controversial material in an enjoyable and approachable way."

Thanks but no thanks. I don't teach to amuse, to divert, or even, for   5
that matter, to be merely interesting. When someone says she "enjoyed" the course — and that word crops up again and again in my evaluations — somewhere at the edge of my immediate complacency I feel encroaching self-dislike. That is not at all what I had in mind. The off-the-wall questions and the sidebar jokes are meant as lead-ins to stronger stuff — in the case of the Freud course, to a complexly tragic view of life. But the affability and the one-liners often seem to be all that land with the students; their journals and evaluations leave me little doubt.

I want some of them to say that they've been changed by the course. I want them to measure themselves against what they've read. It's said that some time ago a Columbia University instructor used to issue a harsh two-part question. One: What book did you most dislike in the course? Two: What intellectual or characterological flaws in you does that dislike point to? The hand that framed that question was surely heavy. But at least it compels one to see intellectual work as a confrontation between two people, student and author, where the stakes matter. Those Columbia students were being asked to relate the quality of an encounter, not rate the action as though it had unfolded on the big screen.

Why are my students describing the Oedipus complex and the death drive as being interesting and enjoyable to contemplate? And why am I coming across as an urbane, mildly ironic, endlessly affable guide to this intellectual territory, operating without intensity, generous, funny, and loose?

Because that's what works. On evaluation day, I reap the rewards of my partial compliance with the culture of my students and, too, with the culture of the university as it now operates. It's a culture that's gotten little exploration. Current critics tend to think that liberal-arts education is in crisis because universities have been invaded by professors with peculiar ideas: deconstruction, Lacanianism, feminism, queer theory. They believe that genius and tradition are out and that P.C., multiculturalism, and identity politics are in because of an invasion by tribes of tenured radicals, the late millennial equivalents of the Visigoth hordes that cracked Rome's walls.

But mulling over my evaluations and then trying to take a hard, extended look at campus life both here at the University of Virginia and around the country eventually led me to some different conclusions. To me, liberal-arts education is as ineffective as it is now not chiefly because there are a lot of strange theories in the air. (Used well, those theories can be illuminating.) Rather, it's that university culture, like American culture writ large, is, to put it crudely, ever more devoted to consumption and entertainment, to the using and using up of goods and images. For someone growing up in America now, there are few available alternatives to the cool consumer worldview. My students didn't ask for that view, much less create it, but they bring a consumer [worldview] to school, where it exerts a powerful, and largely unacknowledged, influence. If we want to understand current universities, with their multiple woes, we might try leaving the realms of expert debate and fine ideas and turning to the classrooms and campuses, where a new kind of weather is gathering.

From time to time I bump into a colleague in the corridor and we have 10 what I've come to think of as a Joon Lee fest. Joon Lee is one of the best students I've taught. He's endlessly curious, has read a small library's worth, seen every movie, and knows all about showbiz and entertainment. For a class of mine he wrote an essay using Nietzsche's Apollo and Dionysus to analyze the pop group The Supremes. A trite, cultural-studies bonbon? Not at all. He said striking things about conceptions of race in America and about how they shape our ideas of beauty. When I talk with one of his other teachers, we run on about the general splendors of his work and presence. But what inevitably follows a JL fest is a mournful reprise about the divide that separates him and a few other remarkable students from their contemporaries. It's not that some aren't nearly as bright — in terms of intellectual ability, my students are all that I could ask for. Instead, it's that Joon Lee has decided to follow his interests and let them make him into a singular and rather eccentric man; in his charming way, he doesn't mind being at odds with most anyone.

It's his capacity for enthusiasm that sets Joon apart from what I've come to think of as the reigning generational style. Whether the students are sorority/fraternity types, grunge aficionados, piercer/tattooers, black or white, rich or middle class (alas, I teach almost no students from truly poor backgrounds), they are, nearly across the board, very, very self-contained. On good days they display a light, appealing glow; on bad days, shuffling disgruntlement. But there's little fire, little passion to be found. [. . .]

How did my students reach this peculiar state in which all passion seems to be spent? I think that many of them have imbibed their sense of self from consumer culture in general and from the tube in particular. They're the progeny of 100 cable channels and omnipresent Blockbuster outlets. TV, Marshall McLuhan famously said, is a cool medium. Those who play best on it are low-key and nonassertive; they blend in. Enthusiasm, à la Joon Lee, quickly looks absurd. The form of character that's most appealing on TV is calmly self-interested though never greedy, attuned to the conventions, and ironic. Judicious timing is preferred to sudden self-assertion. The TV medium is inhospitable to inspiration, improvisation, failures, slipups. All must run perfectly.

Naturally, a cool youth culture is a marketing bonanza for producers of the right products, who do all they can to enlarge that culture and keep it grinding. The Internet, TV, and magazines now teem with what I call persona ads, ads for Nikes and Reeboks and Jeeps and Blazers that don't so much endorse the capacities of the product per se as show you what sort of person you will be once you've acquired it. The Jeep ad that features hip, outdoorsy kids whipping a Frisbee from mountaintop to mountaintop isn't so much about what jeeps can do as it is about the kind of people who own them. Buy a Jeep and be one with them. The ad is of little consequence in itself, but expand its message exponentially and you have the central thrust of current consumer culture—buy in order to be.

Most of my students seem desperate to blend in, to look right, not to make a spectacle of themselves. [. . .] The specter of the uncool creates a subtle tyranny. It's apparently an easy standard to subscribe to, this Letterman-like, Tarantino-like cool, but once committed to it, you discover that matters are rather different. You're inhibited, except on ordained occasions, from showing emotion, stifled from trying to achieve anything original. You're made to feel that even the slightest departure from the reigning code will get you genially ostracized. This is a culture tensely committed to a laid-back norm.

Am I coming off like something of a crank here? Maybe. Oscar Wilde, who is almost never wrong, suggested that it is perilous to promiscuously contradict people who are much younger than yourself. Point taken. But one of the lessons that consumer hype tries to insinuate is that we must never rebel against the new, never even question it. If it's new—a new need, a new product, a new show, a new style, a new generation—it must be good. So maybe, even at the risk of winning the withered, brown laurels of crankdom, it pays to resist newness-worship and cast a colder eye.

15

Praise for my students? I have some of that too. What my students are, at their best, is decent. They are potent believers in equality. They help out at the soup kitchen and volunteer to tutor poor kids to get a stripe on their resumes, sure. But they also want other people to have a fair shot. And in their commitment to fairness they are discerning; there you see them at their intellectual best. If I were on trial and innocent, I'd want them on the jury.

What they will not generally do, though, is indict the current system. They won't talk about how the exigencies of capitalism lead to a reserve army of the unemployed and nearly inevitable misery. That would be getting too loud, too brash. For the pervading view is the cool consumer perspective, where passion and strong admiration are forbidden. "To stand in awe of nothing, Numicus, is perhaps the one and only thing that can make a man happy and keep him so," says Horace in the Epistles, and I fear that his lines ought to hang as a motto over the university in this era of high consumer capitalism.

It's easy to mount one's high horse and blame the students for this state of affairs. But they didn't create the present culture of consumption. (It was largely my own generation, that of the Sixties, that let the counterculture search for pleasure devolve into a quest for commodities.) And they weren't the ones responsible, when they were six and seven and eight years old, for unplugging the TV set from time to time or for hauling off and kicking a hole through it. It's my generation of parents who sheltered these students, kept them away from the hard knocks of everyday life, making them cautious and overfragile, who demanded that their teachers, from grade school on, flatter them endlessly so that the kids are shocked if their college profs don't reflexively suck up to them.

Of course, the current generational style isn't simply derived from culture and environment. It's also about dollars. Students worry that taking too many chances with their educations will sabotage their future prospects. They're aware of the fact that a drop that looks more and more like one wall of the Grand Canyon separates the top economic tenth from the rest of the population. There's a sentiment currently abroad that if you step aside for a moment, to write, to travel, to fall too hard in love, you might lose position permanently. We may be on a conveyor belt, but it's worse down there on the filth-strewn floor. So don't sound off, don't blow your chance. [. . .]

From the start, the contemporary university's relationship with students   20 has a solicitous, nearly servile tone. As soon as someone enters his junior year in high school, and especially if he's living in a prosperous zip code, the informational material—the advertising—comes flooding in. Pictures, testimonials, videocassettes, and CD-ROMs (some bidden, some not) arrive at the door from colleges across the country, all trying to capture the student and his tuition cash. The freshman-to-be sees photos of well-appointed dorm rooms; of elaborate phys-ed facilities; of fine dining rooms; of expertly kept sports fields; of orchestras and drama troupes; of students working alone (no overbearing grown-ups in range), peering with high seriousness into computers and microscopes; or of students arrayed outdoors in attractive conversational garlands.

Occasionally—but only occasionally, for we usually photograph rather badly; in appearance we tend at best to be styleless—there's a professor teaching a class. (The college catalogues I received, by my request only, in the late Sixties were austere affairs full of professors' credentials and course descriptions; it was clear on whose terms the enterprise was going to unfold.) A college financial officer recently put matters to me in concise, if slightly melodramatic, terms: "Colleges don't have admissions offices anymore, they have marketing departments." Is it surprising that someone who has been approached with photos and tapes, bells and whistles, might come in thinking that the Freud and Shakespeare she had signed up to study were also going to be agreeable treats?

How did we reach this point? In part the answer is a matter of demographics and (surprise) of money. Aided by the G.I. bill, the college-going population in America dramatically increased after the Second World War. Then came the baby boomers, and to accommodate them, schools continued to grow. Universities expand easily enough, but with tenure locking faculty in for lifetime jobs, and with the general reluctance of administrators to eliminate their own slots, it's not easy for a university to contract. So after the baby boomers had passed through — like a fat meal digested by a boa constrictor — the colleges turned to energetic promotional strategies to fill the empty chairs. And suddenly college became a buyer's market. What students and their parents wanted had to be taken more and more into account. That usually meant creating more comfortable, less challenging environments, places where almost no one failed, everything was enjoyable, and everyone was nice.

Just as universities must compete with one another for students, so must the individual departments. At a time of rank economic anxiety, the English and history majors have to contend for students against the more success-insuring branches, such as the sciences and the commerce school. In 1968, more than 21 percent of all the bachelor's degrees conferred in America were in the humanities; by 1993, that number had fallen to about 13 percent. The humanities now must struggle to attract students, many of whose parents devoutly wish they would study something else.

One of the ways we've tried to stay attractive is by loosening up. We grade much more softly than our colleagues in science. In English, we don't give many Ds, or Cs for that matter. (The rigors of Chem 101 create almost as many English majors per year as do the splendors of Shakespeare.) A professor at Stanford recently explained grade inflation in the humanities by observing that the undergraduates were getting smarter every year; the higher grades simply recorded how much better they were than their predecessors. Sure.

Along with softening the grades, many humanities departments have   25
relaxed major requirements. There are some good reasons for introducing more choice into curricula and requiring fewer standard courses. But the move, like many others in the university now, jibes with a tendency to serve — and not challenge — the students. Students can also float in and out of classes during the first two weeks of each term without making any commitment. The common name for this time span — shopping

period—speaks volumes about the consumer mentality that's now in play. Usually, too, the kids can drop courses up until the last month with only an innocuous "W" on their transcripts. Does a course look too challenging? No problem. Take it pass-fail. A happy consumer is, by definition, one with multiple options, one who can always have what he wants. And since a course is something the students and their parents have bought and paid for, why can't they do with it pretty much as they please?

A sure result of the university's widening elective leeway is to give students more power over their teachers. Those who don't like you can simply avoid you. If the clientele dislikes you en masse, you can be left without students, period. My first term teaching I walked into my introduction to poetry course and found it inhabited by one student, the gloriously named Bambi Lynn Dean. Bambi and I chatted amiably awhile, but for all that she and the pleasure of her name could offer, I was fast on the way to meltdown. It was all a mistake, luckily, a problem with the scheduling book. Everyone was waiting for me next door. But in a dozen years of teaching I haven't forgotten that feeling of being ignominiously marooned. For it happens to others, and not always because of scheduling glitches. I've seen older colleagues go through hot embarrassment at not having enough students sign up for their courses: they graded too hard, demanded too much, had beliefs too far out of keeping with the existing disposition. It takes only a few such instances to draw other members of the professoriat further into line. [. . .]

How does one prosper with the present clientele? Many of the most successful professors now are the ones who have "decentered" their classrooms. There's a new emphasis on group projects and on computer-generated exchanges among the students. What they seem to want most is to talk to one another. A classroom now is frequently an "environment," a place highly conducive to the exchange of existing ideas, the students' ideas. Listening to one another, students sometimes change their opinions. But what they generally can't do is acquire a new vocabulary, a new perspective, that will cast issues in a fresh light.

The Socratic method—the animated, sometimes impolite give-and-take between student and teacher—seems too jagged for current sensibilities. Students frequently come to my office to tell me how intimidated they feel in class; the thought of being embarrassed in front of the group fills them with dread. I remember a student telling me how humiliating it was to be corrected by the teacher, by me. So I asked the logical question: "Should I let a major factual error go by so as to save discomfort?" The student—a good student, smart and earnest—said that was a tough question. He'd need to think about it.

Disturbing? Sure. But I wonder, are we really getting students ready for Socratic exchange with professors when we push them off into vast lecture rooms, two and three hundred to a class, sometimes face them with only grad students until their third year, and signal in our myriad professorial ways that we often have much better things to do than sit in our offices and talk with them? How bad will the student–faculty ratios have to become, how teeming the lecture courses, before we hear students righteously complaining, as they did thirty years ago, about the impersonality of their schools, about their decline into knowledge factories? "This is a firm," said Mario Savio at Berkeley during the Free Speech protests of the Sixties, "and if the Board of Regents are the board of directors, . . . then . . . the faculty are a bunch of employees and we're the raw material. But we're a bunch of raw material that don't mean . . . to be made into any product."

Teachers who really do confront students, who provide significant   30
challenges to what they believe, can be very successful, granted. But sometimes such professors generate more than a little trouble for themselves. A controversial teacher can send students hurrying to the deans and the counselors, claiming to have been offended. ("Offensive" is the preferred term of repugnance today, just as "enjoyable" is the summit of praise.) Colleges have brought in hordes of counselors and deans to make sure that everything is smooth, serene, unflustered, that everyone has a good time. To the counselor, to the dean, and to the university legal squad, that which is normal, healthy, and prudent is best. [. . .]

Then how do those who at least occasionally promote genius and high literary ideals look to current students? How do we appear, those of us who take teaching to be something of a performance art and who imagine that if you give yourself over completely to your subject you'll be rewarded with insight beyond what you individually command?

I'm reminded of an old piece of newsreel footage I saw once. The speaker (perhaps it was Lenin, maybe Trotsky) was haranguing a large crowd. He was expostulating, arm waving, carrying on. Whether it was flawed technology or the man himself, I'm not sure, but the orator looked like an intricate mechanical device that had sprung into fast-forward. To my students, who mistrust enthusiasm in every form, that's me when I start riffing about Freud or Blake. But more and more, as my evaluations showed, I've been replacing enthusiasm and intellectual animation with stand-up routines, keeping it all at arm's length, praising under the cover of irony.

It's too bad that the idea of genius has been denigrated so far, because it actually offers a live alternative to the demoralizing culture of hip in which most of my students are mired. By embracing the works and lives of extraordinary people, you can adapt new ideals to revise those that came courtesy of your parents, your neighborhood, your clan—or the tube. The aim of a good liberal-arts education was once, to adapt an observation by the scholar Walter Jackson Bate, to see that "we need not be the passive victims of what we deterministically call 'circumstances' (social, cultural, or reductively psychological-personal), but that by linking ourselves through what Keats calls an 'immortal free-masonry' with the great we can become freer—freer to be ourselves, to be what we most want and value."

But genius isn't just a personal standard; genius can also have political effect. To me, one of the best things about democratic thinking is the conviction that genius can spring up anywhere. Walt Whitman is born into the working class and thirty-six years later we have a poetic image of America that gives a passionate dimension to the legalistic brilliance of the Constitution. A democracy needs to constantly develop, and to do so it requires the most powerful visionary minds to interpret the present and to propose possible shapes for the future. By continuing to notice and praise genius, we create a culture in which the kind of poetic gamble that Whitman made—a gamble in which failure would have entailed rank humiliation, depression, maybe suicide—still takes place. By rebelling against established ways of seeing and saying things, genius helps us to apprehend how malleable the present is and how promising and fraught with danger is the future. If we teachers do not endorse genius and self-overcoming, can we be surprised when our students find their ideal images in TV's latest persona ads?

A world uninterested in genius is a despondent place, whose sad denizens drift from coffee bar to Prozac dispensary, unfired by ideals, by the glowing image of the self that one might become. As Northrop Frye says in a beautiful and now dramatically unfashionable sentence, "The artist who uses the same energy and genius that Homer and Isaiah had will find that he not only lives in the same palace of art as Homer and Isaiah, but lives in it at the same time." We ought not to deny the existence of such a place simply because we, or those we care for, find the demands it makes intimidating, the rent too high.

35

What happens if we keep trudging along this bleak course? What happens if our most intelligent students never learn to strive to overcome what they are? What if genius, and the imitation of genius, become silly, outmoded ideas? What you're likely to get are more and more one-dimensional men and women. These will be people who live for easy pleasures, for comfort and prosperity, who think of money first, then second, and third, who hug the status quo; people who believe in God as a sort of insurance policy (cover your bets); people who are never surprised. They will be people so pleased with themselves (when they're not in despair at the general pointlessness of their lives) that they cannot imagine humanity could do better. They'll think it their highest duty to clone themselves as frequently as possible. They'll claim to be happy, and they'll live a long time.

It is probably time now to offer a spate of inspiring solutions. Here ought to come a list of reforms, with due notations about a core curriculum and various requirements. What the traditionalists who offer such solutions miss is that no matter what our current students are given to read, many of them will simply translate it into melodrama, with flat characters and predictable morals. (The unabated capitalist culture that conservative critics so often endorse has put students in a position to do little else.) One can't simply wave a curricular wand and reverse acculturation.

Perhaps it would be a good idea to try firing the counselors and sending half the deans back into their classrooms, dismantling the football team and making the stadium into a playground for local kids, emptying the fraternities, and boarding up the student-activities office. Such measures would convey the message that American colleges are not northern outposts of Club Med. A willingness on the part of the faculty to defy student conviction and affront them occasionally—to be usefully offensive—also might not be a bad thing. We professors talk a lot about subversion, which generally means subverting the views of people who never hear us talk or read our work. But to subvert the views of our students, our customers, that would be something else again.

Ultimately, though, it is up to individuals—and individual students in particular—to make their own way against the current sludgy tide. There's still the library, still the museum, there's still the occasional teacher who lives to find things greater than herself to admire. There are still fellow students who have not been cowed. Universities are inefficient, cluttered, archaic places, with many unguarded corners where one can open a book or gaze out onto the larger world and construe it freely. Those who do as much, trusting themselves against the weight of current opinion, will have contributed something to bringing this sad dispensation to an end. As for myself, I'm canning my low-key one-liners; when the kids' TV-based tastes come to the fore, I'll aim and shoot. And when it's time to praise genius, I'll try to do it in the right style, full-out, with faith that finer artistic spirits (maybe not Homer and Isaiah quite, but close, close), still alive somewhere in the ether, will help me out when my invention flags, the students doze, or the dean mutters into the phone. I'm getting back to a more exuberant style; I'll be expostulating and arm waving straight into the millennium, yes I will.

For Discussion

1. This essay links with the previous one in at least one important way: both see a "consumer mentality" in contemporary students and both are critical of it. But to what extent is it *appropriate* to view colleges and universities as vendors, selling a service in demand, much like any other business? To what extent is this economic understanding limited?

2. The sixties generation is often described as anticommercial and antibusiness, an attitude clearly present in this essay's negative comments on capitalism. To what extent is Edmundson's view a continuation of the rebellions of the sixties or perhaps guilt-ridden compensation for his obviously becoming part of "the system"? If we "read" him this way, must we also dismiss what he has to say? Is his critique any less valid?

3. The more or less conscious cultivation of "cool" or "laid back" extends beyond the sixties to at least "the beats" of the fifties, and arguably further, and thus provides some common ground for half a century or more of young adult experience. Such an attitude has always been vulnerable to Edmundson's charge of lacking "passion and strong admiration." To what extent is "cool" an appropriate and functional way of coping with modern society? Is passion necessary for a meaningful life? If we should have "strong admirations," for what or whom should we have them? Should these commitments be unqualified and uncritical—that is, total?

4. In a part of his essay not printed here, Edmundson contends that "some measure of self-dislike, or self-discontent . . . [is] a prerequisite for getting an education that matters" and that "my students . . . usually lack the confidence to acknowledge . . . their ignorance." What is "an education that matters"? What does self-discontent have to do with it? Is his charge true? Are you and your friends too content with yourselves and too insecure to admit ignorance?

For Analysis and Persuasion

Edmundson claims to want his students to be "changed by [his] course," to "measure themselves against what they've read." As he goes on to explain, "intellectual work [should be] a *confrontation* between two people, student and author, where the stakes matter" (our emphasis).

If he is right, most education is wrong, for very little of it changes us, takes our measure, or confronts us with anything whose stakes are higher than meeting a requirement. But there are exceptions. In an essay, describe a course, a work, or a teacher (or all three) that did ignite the fire Edmundson admires, that did change you. Then analyze the experience: What was it, exactly, that made the difference?

In the second part of your essay, which you can think of as an "open letter" to college teachers, advocate whatever it was that made the difference so that professors themselves might be moved to alter their attitudes and approaches. Be tactful—don't make your essay merely an indictment of teachers. And be thoughtful—perhaps what worked for you won't work all the time or in all classes or subjects.

For Inquiry

The unifying theme of Edmundson's essay is power—the power of money and of economic forces generally, the power of the media to shape culture, the power of students over professors, and so on. The last he may exaggerate, because student evaluations alone almost never make or break a professor's career. But in any case, professors must be evaluated as teachers somehow, and part of this process nearly everywhere are student evaluations.

Secure a copy of the current instrument or instruments used at your school. Consider it/them carefully. Are they as blunt and unsubtle as Edmundson depicts them? Do they encourage professors to entertain rather than instruct? Based on your analysis, explore ways to improve teacher evaluations. If you know or can find out what committees charged with designing evaluations have considered, ponder their ideas and approaches as well. Then consider how the evaluations are used. Can they be applied more constructively? If so, what are the options? What are the "up" and "down" sides of each?

Design your inquiry as an independent report to whatever committee or committees are charged with creating and assessing student evaluations.

On the Uses of Liberal Education:
As a Weapon in the Hands of the Restless Poor
Earl Shorris

Earl Shorris was several years into research for a book on poverty and thought he had heard it all—until he met a remarkable young woman, a prison inmate, who gave him the idea for an experimental curriculum in the liberal arts for poor people. The lengthy story of how he developed his idea and found modest financial support for it we have left out, the better to highlight what counts most—attitudes, course content, the students, teaching methods, and results, all of which he reports with disarming honesty, in an account of genuine power.

We agree with Shorris that his course of study cannot reach everyone nor solve by itself the massive and complicated problem of poverty in the United States. But its success is worth pondering, especially when we consider the billions we spend on poverty every year, money that brings relief but no solution. Perhaps the big question implicit in this essay is one we need to address: Do Americans really want to empower the poor, give them weapons to resist their condition, make them more personally and socially effective? If so, what role can a liberal arts education play?

Next month [in 1997] I will publish a book about poverty in America, but not the book I intended. The world took me by surprise—not once, but again and again. The poor themselves led me in directions I could not have imagined, especially the one that came out of a conversation in a maximum-security prison for women that is set, incongruously, in a lush Westchester suburb fifty miles north of New York City.

I had been working on the book for about three years when I went to the Bedford Hills Correctional Facility for the first time. The staff and inmates had developed a program to deal with family violence, and I wanted to see how their ideas fit with what I had learned about poverty.

Numerous forces—hunger, isolation, illness, landlords, police, abuse, neighbors, drugs, criminals, and racism, among many others—exert themselves on the poor at all times and enclose them, making up a "surround of force" from which, it seems, they cannot escape. I had come to understand that this was what kept the poor from being political and that the absence of politics in their lives was what kept them poor. I don't mean "political" in the sense of voting in an election but in the way Thucydides used the word: to mean activity with other people at every level, from the family to the neighborhood to the broader community to the city-state.

By the time I got to Bedford Hills, I had listened to more than six hundred people, some of them over the course of two or three years. Although my method is that of the bricoleur, the tinkerer who assembles a thesis of the bric-a-brac he finds in the world, I did not think there would be any more surprises. But I had not counted on what Viniece Walker was to say.

[. . .] Viniece Walker came to Bedford Hills when she was twenty years   5
old, a high school dropout who read at the level of a college sophomore,
a graduate of crackhouses, the streets of Harlem, and a long alliance with
a brutal man. On the surface Viniece has remained as tough as she was on
the street. She speaks bluntly, and even though she is HIV positive and the
virus has progressed during her time in prison, she still swaggers as she
walks down the long prison corridors. While in prison, Niecie, as she is
known to her friends, completed her high school requirements and began
to pursue a college degree (psychology is the only major offered at Bedford
Hills, but Niecie also took a special interest in philosophy). She became a
counselor to women with a history of family violence and a comforter to
those with AIDS.

She became counselor to women with a history of family violence and a comforter to those with AIDS.

Only the deaths of other women cause her to stumble in the midst
of her swaggering step, to spend days alone with the remorse that drives
her to seek redemption. She goes through life as if she had been imagined
by Dostoevsky, but even more complex than his fictions, alive, a person, a
fair-skinned and freckled African-American woman, and in prison. It was
she who responded to my sudden question, "Why do you think people
are poor?"

We had never met before. The conversation around us focused on the
abuse of women. Niecie's eyes were perfectly opaque—hostile, prison eyes.
Her mouth was set in the beginning of a sneer.

"You got to begin with the children," she said, speaking rapidly, clipping
out the street sounds as they came into her speech.

She paused long enough to let the change of direction take effect, then
resumed the rapid, rhythmless speech. "You've got to teach the moral life of
downtown to the children. And the way you do that, Earl, is by taking them
downtown to plays, museums, concerts, lectures, where they can learn the
moral life of downtown."

I smiled at her, misunderstanding, thinking I was indulging her. "And   10
then they won't be poor anymore?"

She read every nuance of my response, and answered angrily, "And they
won't be poor no more."

"What you mean is—"

"What I mean is what I said—a moral alternative to the street."

She didn't speak of jobs or money. In that, she was like the others I had
listened to. No one had spoken of jobs or money. But how could the
"moral life of downtown" lead anyone out from the surround of force?
How could a museum push poverty away? Who can dress in statues or eat
the past? And what of the political life? Had Niecie skipped a step or failed
to take a step? The way out of poverty was politics, not the "moral life of
downtown." But to enter the public world, to practice the political life, the
poor had first to learn to reflect. That was what Niecie meant by the "moral
life of downtown." She did not make the error of divorcing ethics from

politics. Niecie had simply said, in a kind of shorthand, that no one could step out of the panicking circumstance of poverty directly into the public world.

Although she did not say so, I was sure that when she spoke of the "moral life of downtown" she meant something that had happened to her. With no job and no money, a prisoner, she had undergone a radical transformation. She had followed the same path that led to the invention of politics in ancient Greece. She had learned to reflect. In further conversation it became clear that when she spoke of "the moral life of downtown" she meant the humanities, the study of human constructs and concerns, which has been the source of reflection for the secular world since the Greeks first stepped back from nature to experience wonder at what they beheld. If the political life was the way out of poverty, the humanities provided an entrance to reflection and the political life. The poor did not need anyone to release them; an escape route existed. But to open this avenue to reflection and politics a major distinction between the preparation for the life of the rich and the life of the poor had to be eliminated.

Once Niecie had challenged me with her theory, the comforts of tinkering came to an end; I could no longer make an homage to the happenstance world and rest. To test Niecie's theory, students, faculty, and facilities were required. Quantitative measures would have to be developed; anecdotal information would also be useful. And the ethics of the experiment had to be considered: I resolved to do no harm. There was no need for the course to have a "sink or swim" character; it could aim to keep as many afloat as possible. [. . .]

On an early evening that same week, about twenty prospective students were scheduled to meet in a classroom. [. . .] Most of them came late. Those who arrived first slumped in their chairs, staring at the floor or greeting me with sullen glances. A few ate candy or what appeared to be the remnants of a meal. The students were mostly black and Latino, one was Asian, and five were white; two of the whites were immigrants who had severe problems with English. When I introduced myself, several of the students would not shake my hand, two or three refused even to look at me, one girl giggled, and the last person to volunteer his name, a young man dressed in a Tommy Hilfiger sweatshirt and wearing a cap turned sideways, drawled, "Henry Jones, but they call me Sleepy, because I got these sleepy eyes —."

"In our class, we'll call you Mr. Jones."

He smiled and slid down in his chair so that his back was parallel to the floor.

Before I finished attempting to shake hands with the prospective students, a waiflike Asian girl with her mouth half-full of cake said, "Can we get on with it? I'm bored."

I liked the group immediately.

15

20

[. . .] "You've been cheated," I said. "Rich people learn the humanities; you didn't. The humanities are a foundation for getting along in the world, for thinking, for learning to reflect on the world instead of just reacting to whatever force is turned against you. I think the humanities are one of the ways to become political, and I don't mean political in the sense of voting in an election but in the broad sense." I told them Thucydides' definition of politics.

"Rich people know politics in that sense. They know how to negotiate instead of using force. They know how to use politics to get along, to get power. It doesn't mean that rich people are good and poor people are bad. It simply means that rich people know a more effective method for living in this society.

"Do all rich people, or people who are in the middle, know the humanities? Not a chance. But some do. And it helps. It helps to live better and enjoy life more. Will the humanities make you rich? Yes. Absolutely. But not in terms of money. In terms of life.

"Rich people learn the humanities in private schools and expensive   25
universities. And that's one of the ways in which they learn the political life. I think that is the real difference between the haves and have-nots in this country. If you want real power, legitimate power, the kind that comes from the people and belongs to the people, you must understand politics. The humanities will help.

"Here's how it works: We'll pay your subway fare; take care of your children, if you have them; give you a snack or a sandwich; provide you with books and any other materials you need. But we'll make you think harder, use your mind more fully, than you ever have before. You'll have to read and think about the same kinds of ideas you would encounter in a first-year course at Harvard or Yale or Oxford.

"You'll have to come to class in the snow and the rain and the cold and the dark. No one will coddle you, no one will slow down for you. There will be tests to take, papers to write. And I can't promise you anything but a certificate of completion at the end of the course. I'll be talking to colleges about giving credit for the course, but I can't promise anything. [. . .] You must do it because you want to study the humanities, because you want a certain kind of life, a richness of mind and spirit. That's all I offer you: philosophy, poetry, art history, logic, rhetoric, and American history.

"Your teachers will all be people of accomplishment in their fields," I said, and I spoke a little about each teacher. "That's the course. October through May, with a two-week break at Christmas. It is generally accepted in America that the liberal arts and the humanities in particular belong to the elites. I think you're the elites."

The young Asian woman said, "What are you getting out of this?"

"This is a demonstration project. I'm writing a book. This will be proof,   30
I hope, of my idea about the humanities. Whether it succeeds or fails will be up to the teachers and you."

All but one of the prospective students applied for admission to the course. [. . .]

Of the fifty prospective students who showed up [. . .] for personal interviews [to gain admission to the course], a few were too rich (a postal supervisor's son, a fellow who claimed his father owned a factory in Nigeria that employed sixty people) and more than a few could not read. Two home-care workers from Local 1199 could not arrange their hours to enable them to take the course. Some of the applicants were too young: a thirteen-year-old and two who had just turned sixteen. [. . .]

Some of those who came for interviews were too poor. I did not think that was possible when we began, and I would like not to believe it now, but it was true. There is a point at which the level of forces that surround the poor can become insurmountable, when there is no time or energy left to be anything but poor. Most often I could not recruit such people for the course; when I did, they soon dropped out.

Over the days of interviewing, a class slowly assembled. I could not then imagine who would last the year and who would not. One young woman submitted a neatly typed essay that said, "I was homeless once, then I lived for some time in a shelter. Right now, I have got my own space granted by the Partnership for the Homeless. Right now, I am living alone, with very limited means. Financially I am overwhelmed by debts. I cannot afford all the food I need. . . ."

A brother and sister, refugees from Tashkent, lived with their parents in the farthest reaches of Queens, far beyond the end of the subway line. They had no money, and they had been refused admission by every school to which they had applied. I had not intended to accept immigrants or people who had difficulty with the English language, but I took them into the class.

I also took four who had been in prison, three who were homeless, three who were pregnant, one who lived in a drugged dream-state in which she was abused, and one whom I had known for a long time and who was dying of AIDS. As I listened to them, I wondered how the course would affect them. They had no public life, no place; they lived within the surround of force, moving as fast as they could, driven by necessity, without a moment to reflect. Why should they care about fourteenth-century Italian painting or truth tables or the death of Socrates?

Between the end of recruiting and the orientation session that would open the course, I made a visit to Bedford Hills to talk with Niecie Walker. It was hot, and the drive up from the city had been unpleasant. I didn't yet know Niecie very well. She didn't trust me, and I didn't know what to make of her. While we talked, she held a huge white pill in her hand. "For AIDS," she said.

"Are you sick?"

"My T-cell count is down. But that's neither here nor there. Tell me about the course, Earl. What are you going to teach?"

35

"Moral philosophy."   40

"And what does that include?"

She had turned the visit into an interrogation. I didn't mind. At the end
of the conversation I would be going out into "the free world"; if she wanted
our meeting to be an interrogation, I was not about to argue. I said, "We'll
begin with Plato: the *Apology,* a little of the *Crito,* a few pages of the *Phaedo*
so that they'll know what happened to Socrates. Then we'll read Aristotle's
Nicomachean Ethics. I also want them to read Thucydides, particularly Peri-
cles' Funeral Oration in order to make the connection between ethics and
politics, to lead them in the direction I hope the course will take them.
Then we'll end with *Antigone,* but read as moral and political philosophy
as well as drama."

"There's something missing," she said, leaning back in her chair, taking
on an air of superiority.

The drive had been long, the day was hot, the air in the room was dead
and damp. "Oh, yeah," I said, "and what's that?"

"Plato's Allegory of the Cave. How can you teach philosophy to poor   45
people without the Allegory of the Cave? The ghetto is the cave. Education
is the light. Poor people can understand that."

At the beginning of the orientation at the Clemente Center a week later,
each teacher spoke for a minute or two. Dr. Inclan and his research assistant, Patricia Vargas, administered the questionnaire he had devised to
measure, as best he could, the role of force and the amount of reflection in
the lives of the students. I explained that each class was going to be video-
taped as another way of documenting the project. Then I gave out the first
assignment: "In preparation for our next meeting, I would like you to read
a brief selection from Plato's *Republic:* the Allegory of the Cave."

I tried to guess how many students would return for the first class. I
hoped for twenty, expected fifteen, and feared ten. [My wife] Sylvia, who had
agreed to share the administrative tasks of the course, and I prepared coffee
and cookies for twenty-five. We had a plastic container filled with subway
tokens. Thanks to Starling Lawrence, we had thirty copies of Bernard Knox's
Norton Book of Classical Literature, which contained all of the texts for the
philosophy section except the *Republic* and the *Nicomachean Ethics.*

At six o'clock there were only ten students seated around the long table,
but by six-fifteen the number had doubled, and a few minutes later two
more straggled in out of the dusk. I had written a time line on the blackboard, showing them the temporal progress of thinking—from the role of
myth in Neolithic societies to The Gilgamesh Epic and forward to the Old
Testament, Confucius, the Greeks, the New Testament, the Koran, the Epic
of Son-Jara, and ending with Nahuatl and Maya poems, which took us up
to the contact between Europe and America, where the history course began. The time line served as context and geography as well as history: no
race, no major culture was ignored. "Let's agree," I told them, "that we are
all human, whatever our origins. And now let's go into Plato's cave."

I told them that there would be no lectures in the philosophy section of the course; we would use the Socratic method, which is called maieutic dialogue. "'Maieutic' comes from the Greek word for midwifery. I'll take the role of midwife in our dialogue. Now, what do I mean by that? What does a midwife do?"

It was the beginning of a love affair, the first moment of their infatuation with Socrates. Later, Abel Lomas would characterize that moment in his no-nonsense fashion, saying that it was the first time anyone had ever paid attention to their opinions.

50

Grace Glueck began the art history class in a darkened room lit with slides of the Lascaux caves and next turned the students' attention to Egypt, arranging for them to visit the Metropolitan Museum of Art to see the Temple of Dendur and the Egyptian Galleries. They arrived at the museum on a Friday evening. Darlene Codd brought her two-year-old son. Pearl Lau was late, as usual. One of the students, who had told me how much he was looking forward to the museum visit, didn't show up, which surprised me. Later I learned that he had been arrested for jumping a turnstile in a subway station on his way to the museum and was being held in a prison cell under the Brooklyn criminal courthouse. In the Temple of Dendur, Samantha Smoot asked questions of Felicia Blum, a museum lecturer. Samantha was the student who had burst out with the news, in one of the first sessions of the course, that people in her neighborhood believed it "wasn't no use goin' to school because the white man wouldn't let you up no matter what." But in a hall where the statuary was of half-human, half-animal female figures, it was Samantha who asked what the glyphs meant, encouraging Felicia Blum to read them aloud, to translate them into English. Toward the end of the evening, Grace led the students out of the halls of antiquities into the Rockefeller Wing, where she told them of the connections of culture and art in Mali, Benin, and the Pacific Islands. When the students had collected their coats and stood together near the entrance to the museum, preparing to leave, Samantha stood apart, a tall, slim young woman, dressed in a deerstalker cap and a dark blue peacoat. She made an exaggerated farewell wave at us and returned to Egypt—her ancient mirror.

Charles Simmons began the poetry class with poems as puzzles and laughs. His plan was to surprise the class, and he did. At first he read the poems aloud to them, interrupting himself with footnotes to bring them along. He showed them poems of love and of seduction, and satiric commentaries on those poems by later poets. "Let us read," the students demanded, but Charles refused. He tantalized them with the opportunity to read poems aloud. A tug-of-war began between him and the students, and the standoff was ended not by Charles directly but by Hector Anderson. When Charles asked if anyone in the class wrote poetry, Hector raised his hand.

"Can you recite one of your poems for us?" Charles said.

Until that moment, Hector had never volunteered a comment, though he had spoken well and intelligently when asked. He preferred to slouch in his chair, dressed in full camouflage gear, wearing a nylon stocking over his hair and eating slices of fresh cantaloupe or honeydew melon.

In response to Charles's question, Hector slid up to a sitting position. "If you turn that camera off," he said. "I don't want anybody using my lyrics." When he was sure the red light of the video camera was off, Hector stood and recited verse after verse of a poem that belonged somewhere in the triangle formed by Ginsberg's *Howl*, the Book of Lamentations, and hip-hop. When Charles and the students finished applauding, they asked Hector to say the poem again, and he did. Later Charles told me, "That kid is the real thing." Hector's discomfort with Sylvia and me turned to ease. He came to our house for a small Christmas party and at other times. We talked on the telephone about a scholarship program and about what steps he should take next in his education. I came to know his parents. As a student, he began quietly, almost secretly, to surpass many of his classmates.

Timothy Koranda was the most professorial of the professors. He arrived precisely on time, wearing a hat of many styles — part fedora, part Borsalino, part Stetson, and at least one-half World War I campaign hat. He taught logic during class hours, filling the blackboard from floor to ceiling, wall to wall, drawing the intersections of sets here and truth tables there and a great square of oppositions in the middle of it all. After class, he walked with students to the subway, chatting about Zen or logic or Heisenberg.

On one of the coldest nights of the winter, he introduced the students to logic problems stated in ordinary language that they could solve by reducing the phrases to symbols. He passed out copies of a problem, two pages long, then wrote out some of the key phrases on the blackboard. "Take this home with you," he said, "and at our next meeting we shall see who has solved it. I shall also attempt to find the answer."

By the time he finished writing out the key phrases, however, David Iskhakov raised his hand. Although they listened attentively, neither David nor his sister Susana spoke often in class. She was shy, and he was embarrassed at his inability to speak perfect English.

"May I go to blackboard?" David said. "And will see if I have found correct answer to zis problem."

Together Tim and David erased the blackboard, then David began covering it with signs and symbols. "If first man is earning this money, and second man is closer to this town . . . ," he said, carefully laying out the conditions. After five minutes or so, he said, "And the answer is: B will get first to Cleveland!"

Samantha Smoot shouted, "That's not the answer. The mistake you made is in the first part there, where it says who earns more money."

Tim folded his arms across his chest, happy. "I shall let you all take the problem home," he said.

When Sylvia and I left the Clemente Center that night, a knot of students was gathered outside, huddled against the wind. Snow had begun to fall, a slippery powder on the gray ice that covered all but a narrow

55

60

space down the center of the sidewalk. Samantha and David stood in the middle of the group, still arguing over the answer to the problem. I leaned in for a moment to catch the character of the argument. It was even more polite than it had been in the classroom, because now they govern themselves.

One Saturday morning in January, David Howell telephoned me at home. "Mr. Shores," he said, Anglicizing my name, as many of the students did.

"Mr. Howell," I responded, recognizing his voice.   65

"How you doin', Mr. Shores?"

"I'm fine. How are you?"

"I had a little problem at work."

Uh-oh, I thought, bad news was coming. David is a big man, generally good-humored but with a quick temper. According to his mother, he had a history of violent behavior. In the classroom he had been one of the best students, a steady man, twenty-four years old, who always did the reading assignments and who often made interesting connections between the humanities and daily life. "What happened?"

"Mr. Shores, there's a woman at my job, she said some things to me   70
and I said some things to her. And she told my supervisor I had said things to her, and he called me in about it. She's forty years old and she don't have no social life, and I have a good social life, and she's jealous of me."

"And then what happened?" The tone of his voice and the timing of the call did not portend good news.

"Mr. Shores, she made me so mad, I wanted to smack her up against the wall. I tried to talk to some friends to calm myself down a little, but nobody was around."

"And what did you do?" I asked, fearing this was his one telephone call from the city jail.

"Mr. Shores, I asked myself, 'What would Socrates do?'"

David Howell had reasoned that his co-worker's envy was not his   75
problem after all, and he had dropped his rage.

One evening, in the American history section, I was telling the students about Gordon Wood's ideas in *The Radicalism of the American Revolution.* We were talking about the revolt by some intellectuals against classical learning at the turn of the eighteenth century, including Benjamin Franklin's late-life change of heart, when Henry Jones raised his hand.

"If the Founders loved the humanities so much, how come they treated the natives so badly?"

I didn't know how to answer this question. There were confounding explanations to offer about changing attitudes toward Native Americans, vaguely useful references to views of Rousseau and James Fenimore Cooper. For a moment I wondered if I should tell them about Heidegger's Nazi past. Then I saw Abel Lomas's raised hand at the far end of the table. "Mr. Lomas," I said.

Abel said, "That's what Aristotle means by incontinence, when you know what's morally right but you don't do it, because you're overcome by your passions."

The other students nodded. They were all inheritors of wounds caused by the incontinence of educated men; now they had an ally in Aristotle, who had given them a way to analyze the actions of their antagonists. 80

Those who appreciate ancient history understand the radical character of the humanities. They know that politics did not begin in a perfect world but in a society even more flawed than ours: one that embraced slavery, denied the rights of women, practiced a form of homosexuality that verged on pedophilia, and endured the intrigues and corruption of its leaders. The genius of that society originated in man's re-creation of himself through the recognition of his humanness as expressed in art, literature, rhetoric, philosophy, and the unique notion of freedom. At that moment, the isolation of the private life ended and politics began.

The winners in the game of modern society, and even those whose fortune falls in the middle, have other means to power: they are included at birth. They know this. And they know exactly what to do to protect their place in the economic and social hierarchy. As Allan Bloom, author of the nationally best-selling tract in defense of elitism, *The Closing of the American Mind,* put it, they direct the study of the humanities exclusively at those young people who "have been raised in comfort and with the expectation of ever increasing comfort."

In the last meeting before graduation, the Clemente students answered the same set of questions they'd answered at orientation. Between October and May, students had fallen to AIDS, pregnancy, job opportunities, pernicious anemia, clinical depression, a schizophrenic child, and other forces, but of the thirty students admitted to the course, sixteen had completed it, and fourteen had earned credit from Bard College. Dr. Inclan found that the students' self-esteem and their abilities to divine and solve problems had significantly increased; their use of verbal aggression as a tactic for resolving conflicts had significantly decreased. And they all had notably more appreciation for the concepts of benevolence, spirituality, universalism, and collectivism.

It cost about $2,000 for a student to attend the Clemente Course. Compared with unemployment, welfare, or prison, the humanities are a bargain. But coming into possession of the faculty of reflection and the skills of politics leads to a choice for the poor—and whatever they choose, they will be dangerous: they may use politics to get along in a society based on the game, to escape from the surround of force into a gentler life, to behave as citizens, and nothing more; or they may choose to oppose the game itself. No one can predict the effect of politics, although we all would like to think that wisdom goes our way. That is why the poor are so often mobilized and so rarely politicized. The possibility that they will adopt a moral view other than that of their mentors can never be discounted. And who wants to run that risk? . . .

On May 14, 1997, Viniece Walker came up for parole for the second time. She had served more than ten years of her sentence, and she had been the best of prisoners. In a version of the Clemente Course held at the prison, she had been my teaching assistant. After a brief hearing, her request for parole was denied. She will serve two more years before the parole board will reconsider her case.

A year after graduation, ten of the first sixteen Clemente Course graduates were attending four-year colleges or going to nursing school; four of them had received full scholarships to Bard College. The other graduates were attending community college or working full-time. Except for one: she had been fired from her job in a fast-food restaurant for trying to start a union.

85

For Discussion

1. This essay requires us to think about familiar terms in unfamiliar ways. What does Shorris mean by "the political"? How does this relate to the "moral life of downtown," also called the "moral alternative to the street"? How do most college students know about the political in Shorris's sense? What prevents most poor people from knowing?

2. "You've been cheated," Shorris tells his prospective students, denied an education in the humanities, and therefore "a foundation . . . for learning to reflect on the world instead of just reacting to whatever force is turned against you" (paragraph 22). What does "reflect" mean here? What sort of practical consequences can it have? To what extent has your education encouraged reflection?

3. One interesting feature of Shorris's course on moral philosophy is his concentration on classical Greece, on major works by Plato, Aristotle, the historian Thucydides, and the playwright Sophocles. Does this focus surprise you? What might justify it? Should the classics be part of your curriculum?

4. How would you characterize the attitudes, approaches, and methods used by the professors? How important a role did they play in the success of the courses? Compare them to your high school instruction and what you've encountered so far in college. Are they comparable? If so, in what ways? If not, how do you explain the differences?

5. Near the end of the essay, Shorris reports how the class handled a thorny question: "If the Founders [of the United States] loved the humanities so much, how come they treated the natives so badly?" (paragraph 77). Is Abel's answer adequate? What's the point of

Shorris's commentary on the culture in which ancient Greek thought and art arose? How do you respond to what he says?

6. Read carefully the last four paragraphs and note the details about what happened to the students. How successful would you say the curriculum was? What are its limitations? On what does its long-term impact depend? What measures might be taken to improve the odds of more students completing the course?

For Inquiry and Persuasion

It is not hard to imagine what Shorris's critics will say. In teaching his students how to "get along" with European white culture, some will say, he is only encouraging acquiescence to the system, trying to make white people out of people of color, and devaluing by neglect the cultures to which his students belong. Others will say that most poor people do not need a liberal arts education but rather basic literacy skills, the ability to read and write, coupled with training in some marketable skill, such as data processing.

List on the board these and any other criticisms that occur to you. After extensive class discussion, write an essay either supporting Shorris's program as part of what poor people need for self-improvement or advocating something else. Direct your essay to public school systems whose student populations include people from backgrounds similar to Shorris's group. As preparation for your paper, you may wish to visit such schools and/or talk to members of the faculty.

For Inquiry

As a class, select one or two of the works Shorris had his students study in his moral philosophy course. Read them and, paying special attention to their moral and political "lessons," discuss what we can learn from them about how to live better.

Do they have the virtues Shorris believes they have? Understanding them is more difficult than understanding works written closer to our place and time, works that are not necessarily less insightful or profound. Is the struggle with the classics worth it? Did you gain as much from them as some of Shorris's students apparently did? Why or why not?

For Inquiry and Convincing

Anyone who reads Shorris's essay together with the previous one, by Edmundson, is likely to detect an apparent paradox, which can be expressed in at least two ways. The liberal arts were created by the privileged classes and largely taught to the privileged for the past 2,500 years. So, why do they serve now as at best only "lite entertainment" for the very class of student who belongs to the tradition of privilege? Put another way, both Edmundson and Shorris want their courses to change their students, transforming how they understand the world and how they behave in it, but only Shorris believes that change has actually occurred. Edmundson should have the easier time. Why doesn't he?

Write an essay in which you render this paradox less paradoxical. Tie your explanation to your own experiences with the liberal arts, to your background, to the way your classes have been taught. At the end, make a case for how the liberal arts might be taught better. Or, if you believe the paradox has little or nothing to do with teaching, make a case for what must change to reenergize the liberal arts.

The Decline of the Knowledge Factory:
Why Our Colleges Must Change
John Tagg

In the 1960s, "the system" was often a topic of discussion. Many of the conversations were not especially helpful, but implicit in all of them was an insight we must not forget: Often, what's wrong with society has little to do with particular individuals or the roles they play, with philosophies, or with cultural gaps between generations; rather, the problems may be traced to the way a society is structured in general and to an institution's organization in particular. Individuals may or may not like "the system," but they are caught up in it anyway and realize the powerful forces invested in maintaining the status quo. Understandably, they turn to the practical business of getting the system to pay off for them rather than trying to change it. And so change itself becomes difficult and for many people beyond imagining. It's just "the way things are."

In this article from the journal World and I *(June 1998), educator John Tagg depicts "the system" at most of our colleges and universities well. We must understand it to grasp why things are as they are and what impedes all proposals for change that go beyond mere tinkering. Whether Tagg's own proposals amount to tinkering or represent meaningful change to "the system" is a question we should keep in mind as we read.*

DO COLLEGES WORK?

[. . .] In 1991, Ernest Pascarella of the University of Illinois, Chicago, and Patrick Terenzini of the Center for the Study of Higher Education at Pennsylvania State University published a massive volume, *How College Affects Students: Findings and Insights from Twenty Years of Research.* Their assessments are carefully weighted and qualified, and they find, not surprisingly, that college students learn a good deal while in college and change in many ways. College does make a difference. But perhaps their most striking conclusion is that while attending college makes a difference, the particular college one attends makes hardly any predictable difference at all.

One of the foundational assumptions that guides parents, students, alumni, and taxpayers in thinking about colleges is that a greater investment in human and economic resources produces a better product in terms of educational outcome. Conventional thinking holds that those who run these institutions have some coherent conception of quality, and that this conception of quality is embodied in the best colleges, which others seek to emulate. Parents pay the breathtaking tuition charged by Ivy League institutions, and legislators invest public money in enormous state universities, because they believe quality is worth paying for—and because they believe that while they may not be able to define just what that quality consists of, those professionals who govern higher education can define it and, given adequate resources, create it.

> But Pascarella and Terenzini found that there is little consistent evidence to indicate that college selectivity, prestige, or educational resources have any important net impact on students in such areas as learning, cognitive and intellectual development, other psychosocial changes, the development of principled moral reasoning, or shifts in other attitudes and values. Nearly all of the variance in learning and cognitive outcomes is attributable to individual aptitude differences among students attending different colleges. Only a small and perhaps trivial part is uniquely due to the quality of the college attended.

In other words, if colleges know what quality is in undergraduate education, they apparently do not know how to produce it.

In 1993 Alexander Astin, director of the Higher Education Research Institute at UCLA, published a new study: *What Matters in College: Four Critical Years Revisited.* Astin attempted to assess the effects of college using longitudinal studies of students at many varied institutions and finding correlations between the institutions' characteristics and selected student outcomes. His research, like Pascarella and Terenzini's, leaves us with a disappointing picture, a picture of colleges that attend least to what matters most and often act in ways that seem almost designed to assure they fail at their avowed mission.

Astin's research reveals that what colleges actually do bears little resemblance to what we would be likely to extract from college catalogs or commencement speeches. This probably should not surprise us. Harvard organizational theorist Chris Argyris has demonstrated that the way people say they act in business organizations—their "espoused theory," Argyris calls it—has little relationship with their "theory-in-use," which governs how they actually behave. Astin has discovered essentially the same thing in American colleges:

> Institutions espouse high-sounding values, of course, in their mission statements, college catalogues, and public pronouncements by institutional leaders. The problem is that the explicitly stated values—which always include a strong commitment to undergraduate education—are often at variance with the actual values that drive our decisions and policies.

For an outsider—and for not a few insiders—the first barrier to realistically assessing baccalaureate education is simply finding it in the morass of muddled missions that make up the contemporary multiversity. Astin quotes "one of our leading higher education scholars" as dismissing research about undergraduate learning with the remark, "The modern

5

American university is not a residential liberal arts college." Indeed.
Astin responds that

> all types of institutions claim to be engaged in the same enterprise: the liberal
> education of the undergraduate student. While it is true that certain kinds of
> institutions also do other things — research, vocational education, and graduate
> education, to name just a few — does having multiple functions "give permis-
> sion" to an institution to offer baccalaureate education programs that are
> second-rate? Does engaging in research and graduate education justify short-
> changing undergraduate education? Does engaging in vocational education
> justify offering mediocre transfer education?

The answer to that question today is, for all practical purposes, "yes."
A multiplicity of functions does justify mediocrity and incoherence in
undergraduate education, at least to the not very exacting standards of
most of our colleges.

WHAT HAPPENED?

Why are our colleges failing? Because they have substituted standardized
processes for educational substance. They have become bureaucratized assembly lines for academic credit and have largely ceased, at the institutional
level, to know or care what their students learn.

If we look at higher education as it exists today, what we see is
counterintuitive. In a nation with over thirty-five hundred colleges serving
more than fourteen million students, we find an amazing homogeneity.
Despite the vast number of colleges, they display more sameness than
difference. Why?

Today's system of higher education is a product of the postwar world.
With the impetus of the GI Bill of Rights, rapid economic growth, and the
baby boom, the college population surged after World War II. Between
1950 and 1970 college enrollment more than tripled. The percentage of
Americans over twenty-five who completed a bachelor's degree doubled
between the end of the war and 1970 and nearly doubled again by 1993.
And the most dramatic growth has taken place in public colleges. In 1947
less than half of the nation's college students attended public institutions.
By 1993 nearly 80 percent did.

Today's colleges have developed as part of a nationwide system of
higher education, and hence they have become nearly interchangeable. In
such a system, colleges, especially public colleges, have been able to thrive
only by growing. Thus their operations have become standardized and
focused on providing more of their product to more students. The mission
of colleges in this system is to offer classes. My colleague Robert Barr
has labeled the governing set of assumptions, attitudes, and rules that
define colleges in this system — the theory-in-use of most colleges — the

Instruction Paradigm. In the Instruction Paradigm, the product of colleges is classes; colleges exist for the purpose of offering more instruction to more students in more classes.

In this system, the "atom" of the educational universe is the one-hour block of lecture and the "molecule" is the three-unit course. The parts of the educational experience have transferrable value only in the form of completed credit hours. For almost any student at nearly any college today, the essential meaning of "being a student" is accumulating credit hours.

A credit hour is a measurement of time spent in class. I do not mean to suggest that credit is automatic for students who merely show up. They must, of course, pass the course. But the amount of credit, the weight of the course in the transcript, is based on the length of time the student sits in a room. What the student does in the room, what the teacher does in the room, what they think after they leave the room—these things are irrelevant to academic credit. The qualifications and experience and attitudes of the teacher are irrelevant to academic credit—three units from a creative scholar passionately interested in her subject and her students are equal to three units from a bored grad student who finds teaching a largely avoidable irritation. The attitude and involvement of the student are irrelevant to academic credit—three units earned by a committed and involved student who finds a whole new way of thinking and a life-changing body of ideas in a course are equal to three units earned by a student who thinks about the course only long enough to fake temporary knowledge with borrowed notes.

Public funding mechanisms in most states reward colleges for offering courses, credit hours. Not for grades, not for course completion, and certainly not for learning. States pay colleges for students sitting in classrooms. You get what you pay for.

THE KNOWLEDGE FACTORY

The Instruction Paradigm college of the postwar period is a knowledge factory: The student passes through an assembly line of courses. As the students pass by, each faculty member affixes a specialized part of knowledge. Then the students move on down the assembly line to the next instructor, who bolts on another fragment of knowledge. The assembly line moves at a steady pace. Each instructor has exactly one semester or quarter to do the same job for every student, who is assumed to be as like every other as the chassis of a given model of car. The workers on this line tend to view their jobs narrowly, as defined by the part of knowledge that it is their business to affix. No one has the job of quality control for the finished product.

In the college as knowledge factory, students learn that the only value recognized by the system, the only fungible good that counts toward success, is the grade on the transcript. It is a fractured system dedicated to the production of parts, of three-unit classes. The reason colleges fail is that the parts don't fit together. They don't add up to a coherent whole. They add up to a transcript but not an education.

Most of the lower division, the first two years of college, is dominated   15
by general education requirements. These requirements at most colleges consist of lists of classes — in a variety of categories such as the humanities, social science, and physical science — from which the student may choose. William Schaefer, emeritus professor of English and former executive vice chancellor at UCLA, describes general education as "a conglomeration of unrelated courses dedicated to the proposition that one's reach should never exceed one's grasp."

The incoherence of the curriculum flows from the internal organizational dynamic of the knowledge factory. Required classes are shaped by the dominant organizational unit of college faculties: academic departments. At nearly all colleges, the fundamental duty and allegiance of the faculty is to their home departments. Most academic departments hire their own faculty. Most faculty members literally owe their jobs not to the college as an institution but to their departments. Most of the crucial decisions about a faculty member's workload and duties are primarily departmental decisions. As Schaefer notes, "Departments have a life of their own — insular, defensive, self-governing, compelled to protect their interests because the faculty positions as well as the courses that justify funding those positions are located therein."

Departments become large by bolting more of their distinctive parts onto more student chassis in the educational assembly line, by offering those bread-and-butter required general education courses that garner large guaranteed enrollments. But these are often just the kinds of innocuous survey courses that faculty prefer not to teach. And the highest rewards in most universities are reserved not for those who teach undergraduates but for those who are recognized for their research contributions to their academic disciplines. Academic departments have achieved the "best" of both worlds by hiring large numbers of graduate students or part-time instructors, at low salaries and often with no benefits, to teach undergraduate courses, while freeing up senior faculty for research activities.

Our great research universities have for many years subsidized their research programs and graduate schools at the expense of undergraduate programs. They have, in effect, pawned their undergraduate colleges to buy faculty the jewel of research time. There is no penalty to pay for this transaction, because undergraduate programs are funded based on seat time; learning doesn't count; the failure of students to learn exacts no cost to the department or the institution.

Academic departments are ostensibly organized in the service of "disciplines" — coherent and discrete bodies of knowledge or methods of study. While many of the academic disciplines that make up the sciences and humanities are of ancient and proud lineage, their configuration in the modern university is largely a product of academic politics. And their trajectory in the development and deployment of general education courses is almost entirely a product of competition between departments for campus resources. On the academic assembly line of the knowledge factory, each part must be different, so the incentive is to emphasize what makes a discipline unlike others and to shape all knowledge into these highly differentiated disciplines.

Even skills of universal relevance to virtually everything we do in life have become the property of one department or another. Thus, writing in the student's native language becomes the concern of the Department of English; speaking the student's native language is relegated to the Department of Communication. Quantitative reasoning belongs to the Department of Mathematics. The atomized curriculum has taken an increasingly conspicuous toll: the inability of students to think globally or to transfer methods of analysis from one subject or problem to another. The evidence mounts that what students learn in one course they do not retain and transfer to their experience in other courses or to their lives and their work. The fragments never fit together. This has led to a growing demand for the teaching of "critical thinking." But even the subject of thought itself becomes in the knowledge factory an object of competitive bidding among academic departments. Adam Sweeting, director of the Writing Program at the Massachusetts School of Law at Andover, warns that "if we are not careful, the teaching of critical thinking skills will become the responsibility of one university department, a prospect that is at odds with the very idea of a university."

But then much about the modern university is at odds with the very idea of a university. The competition between "academic disciplines" for institutional turf generates a bundle of fragments, a mass of shards, and no coherent whole at all. It lacks precisely that quality of discipline that provided the rationale for the enterprise from the beginning. It creates a metacurriculum in which students learn that college is a sequence of disconnected parts, valuable only as credits earned. And what comes off the assembly line of the knowledge factory in the end is an "education" that might have been designed by Rube Goldberg, with marketing advice from the Edsel team.

The result is an institution that satisfies nobody. College faculties complain bitterly, often about the administration, but most often about the students. History and philosophy professors complain that students can't write. English professors complain that students know little about history and culture. Science professors complain that students have only a rudimentary grasp of mathematics. And everyone complains that students can't think. Yet grades have never been higher. The mean grade point average of all college graduates in 1994 was 3.0 on a scale of 4. It seems unfair to penalize students with poor grades for deficiencies that really fall outside the scope of the course, deficiencies that could not possibly be

20

addressed in a three-unit, one-semester class. So the professors blame the students or the administration and fight pitched battles in the faculty senate. Yet nothing seems to work, because the deficiencies that plague students are almost by definition problems that cannot be addressed in any three-unit class. But three-unit classes are all there are; they are what the college is made of.

Perhaps least satisfied with the knowledge factory are the students. Those students who come to college from high school today come hoping for something better, but with no framework of educational value to bring to the experience themselves. For many of them, the defining experience of college becomes drunkenness. While some colleges have begun belatedly to recognize the costs of the culture of irresponsibility that has grown up on many campuses, it remains the case that substance abuse is one of the few measurable outcomes of a college education. A commission chaired by former Health, Education, and Welfare Secretary Joseph Califano Jr. reported in 1994 that a third of college students are binge drinkers and that the number of college women who reported that they drink in order to get drunk had tripled since 1973, now matching the rate for men.

William Willimon, dean of the chapel at Duke University, and Thomas Naylor, emeritus professor of economics at Duke, have characterized the chaos and aimlessness that college is for many students in their book *The Abandoned Generation: Rethinking Higher Education.* They offer an especially telling statement of the experience of the knowledge factory from a University of Michigan senior:

> So you get here and they start asking you, "What do you think you want to major in?" "Have you thought about what courses you want to take?" And you get the impression that that's what it's all about—courses, majors. So you take the courses. You get your card punched. You try a little this and a little that. Then comes GRADUATION. And you wake up and you look at this bunch of courses and then it hits you: They don't add up to anything. It's just a bunch of courses. It doesn't mean a thing.

DO COLLEGES HAVE A FUTURE?

The knowledge factory is breaking down as we approach the twenty-first century. The transformation to the knowledge society means that the demand for higher education will increase both in quantity and quality: More students will require more sophisticated knowledge and skills. But this transformation has also brought into existence something new on the higher education landscape: competition.

Competition has emerged for two reasons. First, private employers who need skilled employees have found that the graduates of conventional

25

colleges are poorly prepared to do the work they need to do. Many corporations have either established their own "universities" or sought the support of outside vendors to provide educational services. The second reason competition has burgeoned is that contemporary information technology has made possible immediate access to educational services from anywhere. Education is no longer bound to the campus. Hence many providers can compete to serve students who were formerly too distant. The competition is real. Stan Davis and Jim Botkin—in *The Monster under the Bed,* their book about the growing imperative for corporate education—offer little hope to the conventional college: "Employee education is not growing 100 percent faster than academe, but 100 times—or 10,000 percent—faster."

In the face of such competition, if conventional colleges hold fast to the Instruction Paradigm and continue to grant degrees on seat time, many of those colleges will wither and die—going down, we can hardly doubt, in a blaze of acrimony as the nation's great minds fulminate in faculty senates across the land. If colleges are to thrive, and in some cases if they are even to survive, they must change.

Colleges need to make a paradigm shift, to set aside a whole body of assumptions and implicit rules and adopt a fundamentally different perspective, a new theory-in-use. They must recognize that the Instruction Paradigm mistakes a means for an end, confuses offering classes with producing learning. To put that end in its proper place would be to embrace what Barr calls "the Learning Paradigm." From the perspective of the Learning Paradigm, the central defining functions of the knowledge factory are trivial. What counts is what students learn. That the mission of colleges is to produce learning should be fairly noncontroversial, since it is consistent with what nearly all college faculty and administrators already say in public.

The problem is that most colleges do not assess in any meaningful way what students have learned. They can tell you what classes their students have taken but not what their graduates know or what they can do. The shift to the Learning Paradigm would require that colleges begin to take learning seriously, to assess and measure it, and to take responsibility for producing it.

A large and growing number of faculty and administrators have 30 seen that major changes in the way colleges do business are both desirable and inevitable. The prestigious California Higher Education Policy Center, in a 1996 report, urged that "colleges and universities . . . begin a transition toward making student learning, not the time spent on courses taken, the principal basis on which degrees and certificates are rewarded."

Excellent models of such colleges exist. Alverno College in Milwaukee has for decades been developing "assessment-as-learning," an approach that seeks to both monitor and guide students' development toward the mastery of a set of core competencies that define a liberal education. The new Western Governors' University will reward students with credit only when they have established through rigorous assessment that they have mastered the required skills. According to Alan Guskin, chancellor of Antioch University, more than two hundred colleges across the country are seriously discussing major restructuring.

Nonetheless, if we contrast the glacial rate at which colleges and universities seem inclined to change with the lightning speed with which the society they serve is transforming itself, we must be disturbed by the contrast. Many believe that undergraduate colleges cannot meet the challenge of the knowledge society. Davis and Botkin, for example, foresee that "corporations will continue to need traditional universities to carry out basic education and research. Nevertheless they will increasingly take on teaching themselves." Drucker predicts: "Thirty years from now the big university campuses will be relics. Universities won't survive. . . . Such totally uncontrollable expenditures, without any visible improvement in either the content or the quality of education, means that the system is rapidly becoming untenable. Higher education is in deep crisis."

Should we, after all, care? What matter if many of our colleges pass away or diminish into support institutions for market-driven forces that can adapt more flexibly to the needs of a changing world? What would be lost? Perhaps not much. Perhaps a great deal. For colleges hold a place in American society that no other institution is likely to fill. They hold the place of liberal education, of education for liberty, of the kind of experience through which children grow into citizens, through which men and women learn the exercise of the freedom that is tempered by choosing responsibility. I say that colleges "hold the place" of liberal education today because I cannot say that they serve the function. But they remain the institutional focus of the ideal, which survives as an ideal. [. . .]

Changing the governing paradigm, becoming learning-driven institutions, may seem a daunting task for today's knowledge factories. It seems a little like asking the post office to become a church. Yet the reason that the ideal of liberal education survives in our cultural imagination is that it addresses an ongoing need, the need to nurture in the young the development of both heart and mind, the need to set young people on a course that offers not just facility but maturity, not just cleverness but wisdom. . . .

For Discussion

1. The first article in this chapter, "College Life: An Obituary," strongly supports the remark that Tagg quotes with evident disapproval — that "the modern American university is not a residential liberal arts

college" (paragraph 5). The cold facts — demographic data — back up this contention so that how we *feel* about the diminishing role of the traditional college is one thing and well-documented trends another. Read or reread the first article. How does it "speak to" Tagg's argument? What considerations does it raise for his proposals he does not address?

2. Tagg is right, of course, to say that "the 'atom' of the educational universe is the one-hour block of lecture and the 'molecule' is the three-unit course" and that therefore "the essential meaning of 'being a student' is accumulating credit hours" (paragraph 10). But would his proposed shift from the Instructional Paradigm to the Learning Paradigm necessarily change this situation? Why or why not?

3. "The evidence mounts," Tagg alleges, "that what students learn in one course they do not retain and transfer to their experience in other courses or to their lives and work" (paragraph 20). Is this true? Do you see connections among the courses you're taking? Do you see applications to your life and work? Tagg blames this problem on the "atomized curriculum." Do you agree? That is, would a more coherent curriculum *necessarily* result in more connection and application? Is the problem structural, or does it somehow involve more than how "the system" is organized?

4. What is the relation between knowledge and learning? Is knowing a lot about some subject the same thing as understanding it? If not, what's the difference? What sort of educational structure and approach to teaching would best promote both?

For Research, Inquiry, and Convincing

All shrewd people know the difference between an organization's "espoused theory" and its "theory-in-use" — the difference between public relations and reality, between what we say we are doing and what we are actually doing. There's always a gap because we want to present ourselves to the world in the best possible light while also coping with realities within the organization that may be known only to insiders and that may be discomforting or embarrassing.

Problems arise when the gap becomes too great — when the official rhetoric no longer represents merely a favorable spin but rather becomes an outright lie. The result is cynicism and eventual loss of organizational cohesion, pride, and spirit.

Investigate the distinction by examining the official rhetoric of your school. Collect a representative body of it and, as a class, analyze what it says, implies, and promises, paying special attention to the image or character of the school it tries to project. Compare the image with the reality — what you have experienced, what your classmates think is going on—and, if possible, with the impressions of older students, your professors, and the administration.

Then write a paper addressed to your fellow students or prospective students assessing some aspect of the official rhetoric. How honest is it? Is there a tolerably good match between the said and the done? If not, how could it change and still present your school positively?

Additional Suggestions for Writing

1. *Persuasion.* With the exception of Shorris's, all the selections in this chapter have a negative view of present practices in higher education and of current college students. In this sense they tend to be one-sided, mainly "gloom and doom," as we say. But matters are rarely this simple. For example, the decline of the residential college is matched by greater educational opportunity for more students, who can live at home more cheaply and attend school part-time while holding down a job. Loss of coherence in the curriculum has produced fewer required courses and more options to meet requirements—more freedom of choice. Consumerism has forced colleges to listen more to their students and respond to their needs better, including greater regard for how well professors "reach" students. And so on. We do not have to be Pollyannas, "all sunshine and light," to see that what is bad from one perspective can be good, or at least not so bad, from another.

   Write a response to any one of the negative articles or to some significant part of one. Conceive of it in the genre of a letter to the editor of a journal, but direct it to the readership the essay tried to reach. Argue for the "up" side of the negative points the author raised, and try to persuade your readers that things are not as bad as the author contends.

2. *Exploration.* One of the best remedies for confusion is to return again and again to basic questions. So far as higher education and the college experience are concerned, perhaps the basic question is what *you* want from it—not what the college or some "expert" says you should want or what your parents say they want or even what you think you should want, but rather what you are actually here for.

   Over a period of perhaps a week or two, take time to record in your writer's notebook everything you have done, and ponder it from the standpoint of both apparent motives and deeper or hidden ones. Why are you doing what you're doing? What do your choices say about your real motivations?

Write an essay exploring your genuine motives. Good, bad, or indifferent, what are they exactly? Where do they come from? What motives do you admire that you wish you had? Compare your thoughts with those of your classmates. In class discussion, address this question: Will our motives likely change over the next few years? In what specific ways? Why?

Chapter 16

Race and Class: Examining Social Inequality

P*rejudice*—in its root meaning "prejudge, to evaluate someone or something before knowing the facts, in advance of a particular encounter with the individual thing or person that provokes judgment"—is a more subtle and difficult concept than most people realize. We want to say that prejudice is simply wrong and shameful—for instance, the history of black people in the United States certainly proves that prejudice can be wrong and shameful. We could point also to the treatment of Native Americans, Chinese and Japanese immigrants, Hispanics, and many others whose skin color and cultures marked them as different from the white majority. Hence, we hope to end prejudice and overcome prejudice in ourselves and our institutions. "You're prejudiced" becomes one of the worst of accusations, something that we fear as much as past generations feared steps to undo prejudice, such as integration.

We fear the accusation because most of us know we're guilty. When we encounter anyone for the first time, we don't see that person as an individual. Rather, we see classes of attributes: the person is male or female; is young, middle-aged, or old; dresses this way or that; speaks with a certain accent; and so on, through a host of categories through which we *discriminate*—that is, perceive—*all* people we meet. The problem is that each of the categories carries certain cultural expectations. If the person is female, for example, we expect her to be more or less conventionally feminine, and we are likely to judge her negatively to the degree she doesn't act the part. Of course, not all prejudices result in negative evaluations. When Americans hear a cultivated, upper-class British accent, for example, many will associate the speaker with high intelligence and sophistication, investing that person with all sorts of "positives" he or she may not actually have.

The point is that prejudice and the tendency to discriminate are as inevitable as breathing. We can and should eliminate or reduce some kinds of prejudice, but we can't cease to prejudge things and people and remain human. Simply by living in a society and speaking a language whose words carry positive and negative associations, we will necessarily have prejudices and discriminate. Nor is discrimination always bad. For instance, as a juror in a criminal case, we may be asked to decide whether the accused is legally sane. We can and should make such judgments—indeed, the law says we must.

This chapter is about prejudice in the wrong and shameful sense. What exactly makes some kinds of prejudice wrong and shameful? We would not criticize a home loan company for denying the application of a person whose financial condition should exclude them from moving into an exclusive neighborhood he or she can't afford. But if a person can qualify and is denied simply because he or she is black and the neighborhood is "exclusive" in the sense of all white, that would be not only wrong but also actionable, justification for a lawsuit. The difference is clear: a person's finances are relevant to a loan application; skin color is not. Accordingly, prejudice is justified in the first case and entirely without justification in the second.

Similarly, colleges discriminate among applicants routinely, and no one blames a school for rejecting a student because grades and test scores don't measure up. But sometimes, of course, students get in because, say, a parent has "pull"—there is money in the family and significant contributions have been made or promised. This is wrong, as is favoring students who come from prosperous neighborhoods, because just as race should have nothing to do with loan qualifications, so wealth should have no bearing on qualifications for college admission.

The preceding are examples of racism and classism, prejudice based on skin color and socioeconomic background or standing. The articles in this chapter are about both—as well as about how one can merge with or substitute for the other and how both tend to overlap with other kinds of unwarranted bias, such as ethnic or cultural favoritism. Inevitably, the articles emphasize the black-white division, which has plagued us for about 400 years now, since the beginning of the slave trade and long before there was a United States. We cannot forget this dreadful history, but here we focus on what many have called the "new racism," subtler kinds of discrimination and animosity that progress in civil rights and integration have not as yet touched. We also wanted to bring class issues into the picture because Americans generally resist acknowledging the harsh realities of class-based prejudices. We need to recognize, confront, and understand them better.

Among the issues raised by the readings in this chapter are the following: First, what is the future of class and race-oriented prejudice? Are we headed toward a society of "beige and black," in which skin color differences are less discernible and may well cease to matter? Second, what is "equal opportunity," the core value of most American thinking on issues of social justice and equity? To what extent does equal opportunity exist? Is it an adequate response to the dehumanizing effects of present and past discrimination? Finally, is there a new racism? If so, what forms does it take? How exactly does it differ from older practices? What strategies will reduce prejudice and help victims cope better?

These and other key questions must concern us as we struggle with an old problem that now often takes unfamiliar, confusing, and complicated routes in (and out) of our awareness. One thing we can be sure of as we explore the territory: We have not and will not escape prejudging everything and everybody we encounter. And so we must examine our prejudices carefully and honestly, discarding those that hurt and harm and cultivating those that promote tolerance and understanding.

Photograph
Bruce Roberts

Before the civil rights era of the 1960s, it was common to see blatant discrimination, especially in the South. This photograph of segregated restrooms reveals a great deal about the prejudices of an earlier time. The photograph was taken in South Carolina in 1965.

For Discussion

Rhetorically, the doors are an argument, made by the white majority to members of both white and black races. Discuss the argument in terms of rhetorical context as described on pages 22–23.

Is Class an Identity?
Richard Ohmann

Identity refers to what we are. Many factors go into making an individual's sense of self: age, gender, race, religion, where she or he was raised and by whom, work and his or her attitude toward it, relations with friends and loved ones, and so on. Ohmann wants us to recognize that class is a major factor in making us what we are—that such differences as "white collar" versus "blue collar" matter. As he says, class "is a script you act out daily, a bundle of habits and feelings and ways of relating lodged deep in your psyche and broadcast by your talk and conduct."

Ohmann is a professor at Wesleyan University. The following essay appeared in Radical Teacher *(Winter 2003).*

In my section of Introduction to Literature, we were discussing Jane Austen's *Emma.* I knew from experience that a lot of students would have silently rejected the premise of the plot—indeed, of almost all those 19th-century plots: that whom one marries is really important, where "whom" refers less to any unique individual (Mr. or Miss Right) than to a social status and the conduct that is supposed to enact it in public. [. . .]

Most students could understand the historical and symbolic serious-ness of marriage within and across classes, and even see how such issues got tangled up in the emotions of individual lovers. But along with this grudging acknowledgement went an almost palpable sense of condescen-sion, and of relief that our own civilization had left such superficialities behind [. . .]. I decided, one year, to challenge the assumption:

"Well, hypothetically; if you were ever to get married" (I had to put it that way to get past their quite proper unwillingness to leave lesbian and gay people out of the conversation and their perhaps less proper revulsion against marriage as an arrangement even for straight couples) "if you were to get married, would class lines be no barrier?"

"Certainly not"—general agreement; "it's love that counts."

"You would be as free to marry a 7-11 clerk as a medical student?"   5

"Of course; we'd be less likely to meet and get to know the clerk, but it's the person, not the job or the money, that matters."

"What about differences in education or taste?"

"No, the 7-11 worker could read the same books and like the same mu-sic that we do." (I hear strains of "My Fair Lady.")

"And how would your parents react to news of your plans?" Hmmm: that turns out to be a quite different story. To translate their response into my own words: the parents didn't shell out $25,000 a year or otherwise support and strive and sacrifice, in order to have their kids marry straight down and out of the professional-managerial class (hereafter, PMC). The parents, though maybe nice enough, are old fashioned, bound by antique social rigidities; they are something called "classist." If only we could get rid of classism, along with sexism and heterosexism and racism, people would be unhampered individuals at last, free to love where the heart sings, perhaps even to marry; and the ghost of Jane Austen could rest in her grave.

Now let me acknowledge the narrow reach of this anecdote. Wesleyan   10
University is selective and expensive. Over half of the students have some kind of financial aid, but even many of those come from PMC families. The rest have, with help from parents, striven to join that class. Many of those are minorities. All have come to a college that, like many similar ones, advertises its diversity as an attraction. The ethos is liberal, respectful, what its enemies like to call "politically correct." Most students hate prejudice and inequality; they accept the goal of a small utopia in Middletown CT, at whose threshold you check all invidiousness, distinction, and privilege based on color or gender or sexuality or ethnicity. (I think that's one meaning of the disappearance of family names from social interaction, so that it's almost rude to ask, "Jason what?" after an introduction.)

But if this analysis is right, the anecdote may after all have something to teach about class and identity. These students have entered a college world that is supposedly without hierarchy. Living for a while in such a "diverse" world is a PMC initiation ritual; living in a classless world is, paradoxically, a manifestation of class privilege. To notice or make a fuss about class would, then, spoil the illusion; it would remind all that they came to a selective college in part to preserve or upgrade their class standing. It would call into question their individuality, uniqueness, and freedom. So they enact class without allowing its reality—at least now, at least in this society, at least for enlightened Wesleyan students.

Granted, the students are reasonably self-aware. They can mock the ideology. Gags about "diversity" abound: "Wesleyan is so diverse that you can meet people here from almost every neighborhood in Manhattan." The students make their way through the world with sensitive compasses and gyroscopes that tell them also which neighborhoods in Brooklyn are homelike to them and which parts of Boston; which places have nothing to do with their lives (e.g., Staten Island and Paterson); where are the places to go after college (New York, San Francisco, Seattle, Boston, Washington); where they might spend summers; what styles and fashions signify; [. . .] and—yes—whom to marry, should it come to such a pass. Their political causes are numerous and sincere. They know there are rich and poor people. But many are reluctant to decode all of this intuitive knowledge, and much else, in terms of class.

Is class an identity? I think yes. It is a complex and powerful identity, a script you act out daily, a bundle of habits and feelings and ways of relating lodged deep in your psyche and broadcast by your talk and conduct. It is not instantly visible like race and gender.

But neither is it easy to revise or conceal—much harder than suggested by those ads for tapes you can listen to while commuting, which will soon have you speaking as well as Henry Higgins, thus shielding yourself from harsh inferences about your background.

But most people don't so readily identify themselves by class as by   15
gender or race, and perhaps don't even feel being working class or PMC the way they feel being white or male of straight or, especially, being Latino or black or female or gay — except of course when they are way out of their usual class habitat: a mechanic plunked down in the Century Club, say, or an English Professor at the Elks.

And even such misadventures are not likely to endanger the displaced person, the way women and African Americans and gay men and others risk insult or violence in many venues. Class is not so insistent, not so turbulent an identity as these others. Famously, a large majority of our fellow citizens place themselves in the vague and commodious middle class — just as our rulers would have them do, in order to preserve this supposedly classless and harmonious society. [. . .]

I have much less experience of other class locations in U.S. education, but I wonder if these generalizations mightn't apply, at least partially, in settings very different from Wesleyan. The students I taught a couple of times at our local community college knew where they came from and where they were, and they knew it wasn't Harvard. But except for a couple of trade unionists, they were reluctant to think of the difference in terms of class. First generation college students, they had a big stake in believing anyone could make it in this country. Class seemed an artificial barrier and a rebuke to their hopes of rising. [. . .]

For Discussion

1. We Americans acknowledge differences like gender and race more readily than class. Class bothers us enough that we often want to deny either its reality or its significance. Why is that? How do you explain our reluctance to confront class differences squarely and honestly? Ohmann says that to "make a fuss about class" would "question [his students'] individuality, uniqueness, and freedom." What does he mean? Does this alone explain our reluctance to discuss class differences?

2. Ohmann claims that class is not "instantly visible like race and gender." In what ways is it visible? That is, how do you know a person's class even if you don't know that person and haven't talked with him or her? What are the signs of class?

3. Ohmann acknowledges that Wesleyan is not representative of most colleges and universities in the United States. How class plays out at Wesleyan may be different from your school. How does it work where you are? What are the important class differences and what effect do they have on social interaction?

For Inquiry

Regardless of the nature of the college or university you attend, the students come from varied class backgrounds; partly because of these different class backgrounds, but also for other reasons, class differences take shape on campus as well.

In class discussion, try to describe the class structure among the students at your college or university. Then come up with ways to investigate these differences. You could interview people whose friendships and/or love relationships cross class barriers, for instance. Or you could visit campus organizations identified with the various class groupings — or invite representatives to class for friendly discussions. Yet another way is just to observe the way students behave in some more or less neutral environment — the student center, for instance.

Write a paper assessing how important class is on your campus. Do you see it as a significant barrier to free student interaction either in or out of the classroom? If yes, in what ways? If not, why not?

The Beige and the Black
Michael Lind

We may hope for mutual understanding among the races and toleration of racial differences, but nothing indicates the actual breakdown of old racial tensions more clearly and profoundly than large numbers of racially mixed couples. Hence, many respond favorably to The Cosmic Race, *Jose Vasconcellos's 1924 book, which predicted the end of race through interracial marriage.*

Perhaps the cosmic race will eventually emerge; however, as this article argues, the next fifty years will likely see only part of the vision realized. Americans of European, Hispanic, Asian, and Native American ancestry are intermarrying at significant and increasing rates. African-Americans intermarry as well but at much lower percentages. Thus, even as the old racial divide between white and black weakens, a new line may form separating "the beige"—"a white-Asian-Hispanic . . . majority"—from "the black," especially from impoverished African-Americans segregated in our inner cities.

Michael Lind is the Washington editor of Harper's. *This article appeared originally in the* New York Times Magazine *(August 16, 1998).*

Just when you think you're ready for 21st-century America, it changes on you yet again. A few years ago, predictions that whites would eventually become a minority group in the United States galvanized the multicultural left—and horrified the nativist right. More recently, news of the growing number of mixed-race Americans has inspired the political center with a vision of a true racial melting pot, one in which white and black alike will blend into a universal brown. But a closer look at demographic trends suggests that neither of these futures—a nonwhite majority, a uniformly "beige" society—will very likely come to pass. Instead, shifting patterns of racial intermarriage suggest that the next century may see the replacement of the historic white-black dichotomy in America with a troubling new division, one between beige and black.

Racial intermarriage has long been a source of anxiety in America. After World War II, Senator Theodore G. Bilbo of Mississippi defended white supremacy in a book titled *Take Your Choice: Separation or Mongrelization*. Like other racists of his era, Bilbo believed that an inevitable result of dismantling segregation would be the amalgamation of the races through intermarriage. He was right: since the U.S. Supreme Court, in *Loving v. Virginia* (1967), struck down the last antimiscegenation laws of the states, marriage across racial lines has grown at a remarkable rate.

Between 1960 and 1990, interracial marriages in this country skyrocketed by more than 800 percent. Roughly 1 in 25 American married couples today are interracial. In fact, there are at least three million children of mixed-race parentage in the United States—and this figure doesn't even include the millions of Hispanic mestizos and black Americans who have European and Indian ancestors. Perhaps the best-known multiracial American is Tiger Woods, who has described himself as "Cablinasian": a mix of Caucasian, black, Native American and Asian.

Oddly, the U.S. Census Bureau has yet to account properly for the presence of mixed-race Americans. As a result, many of its projections are off target. For example, the bureau has famously predicted that in 2050, whites will make up 52.7 percent of the U.S. population. (In 1990, it was 75.7 percent.) Hispanics will account for 21.1 percent of the population; blacks, 15 percent, and Asians, 10.1 percent. Presumably, 2050 will be white America's last stand. But this projection is dubious, because it assumes that for the next half-century there will be absolutely no inter-marriage among the four major conventionally defined racial groups in the United States: whites, blacks, Hispanics and Asians. Each group is supposed to somehow expand—or decline—in hermetic isolation.

But according to an analysis of the 1990 U.S. Census data for persons aged 25–34 by Reynolds Farley, a demographer with the Russell Sage Foundation, 31.6 percent of native-born Hispanic husbands and 31.4 percent of native-born Hispanic wives had white spouses. The figures were even higher for Asians: 36 percent for native-born Asian husbands and 45.2 percent for native-born Asian wives. (In fact, Asian wives were as likely to marry white Americans as they were to marry Asian-Americans.) The highest intermarriage rates are those of American Indians. Majorities of American Indian men (52.9 percent) and American Indian women (53.9 percent) married whites rather than American Indians (40.3 percent and 37.2 percent, respectively). And these figures, which themselves document the creolization of America, undoubtedly understate the extent of racial intermarriage that the 2000 Census will reveal.

Of course intermarriage rates vary by region. White men in California in 1990 were more than six times as likely as Midwestern white men to marry outside their race. Overall, interracial marriages are more than twice as common in California (1 in 10 new couples) as in the rest of the country (1 in 25). According to the magazine *Interrace*, San Jose, San Diego and Oakland are among the Top 10 cities for interracial couples. America's racial complexion, then, will change more quickly on the coasts than in the heartland.

Nevertheless, the overall increase in intermarriage means that both multicultural liberals and nativist conservatives have misunderstood the major demographic trends in this country. There is not going to be a nonwhite majority in the 21st century. Rather, there is going to be a mostly white mixed-race majority. The only way to stop this is to force all Hispanic and Asian-Americans from now on to marry within their officially defined groups. And that is not going to happen.

Thus, the old duality between whites and nonwhites is finally breaking down. But don't cheer just yet. For what seems to be emerging in the

United States is a new dichotomy between blacks and nonblacks. Increasingly, whites, Asians and Hispanics are creating a broad community from which black Americans may be excluded.

Disparities in interracial marriages underline this problem. Black-white marriages have risen from a reported 51,000 in 1960 (when they were still illegal in many states) to 311,000 in 1997. Marriages between white men and black women, though still uncommon, rose from 27,000 in 1980 to 122,000 in 1995. Although black out-marriage rates have risen, they remain much lower than out-marriage rates for Hispanics, Asians and American Indians. For the 25–34 age group, only 8 percent of black men marry outside their race. Less than 4 percent of black women do so.

While many blacks frown upon marriage by blacks to members of other groups—such relationships are viewed by some as disloyal—it seems very unlikely that such conservative attitudes are more pronounced among black Americans than among whites or Hispanic or Asian immigrants. The major cause of low black out-marriage rates may well be antiblack prejudice—the most enduring feature of the eroding American caste system. Furthermore, antiblack prejudice is often picked up by immigrants, when it is not brought with them from their countries of origin. 10

In the past, the existence of an "untouchable" caste of blacks may have made it easier for Anglo-Americans to fuse with more recent European immigrants in an all-encompassing "white" community. Without blacks as a common "other," the differences between Anglo-Americans, German-Americans, Irish-Americans and Italian-Americans might have seemed much more important. Could this be occurring again? A Knight-Ridder poll taken in May 1997 showed that while respondents were generally comfortable with intermarriage, a full 3 in 10 respondents opposed marriage between blacks and whites.

In the 21st century, then, the U.S. population is not likely to be crisply divided among whites, blacks, Hispanics, Asians and American Indians. Nor is it likely to be split two ways, between whites and non-whites. Rather, we are most likely to see something more complicated: a white-Asian-Hispanic melting-pot majority—a hard-to-differentiate group of beige Americans—offset by a minority consisting of blacks who have been left out of the melting pot once again.

The political implications of this new racial landscape have not yet been considered. On the positive side, the melting away of racial barriers between Asians, Latinos and whites will prevent a complete Balkanization of American society into tiny ethnic groups. On the negative side, the division between an enormous, mixed-race majority and a black minority might be equally unhealthy. The new mixed-race majority, even if it were predominantly European in ancestry, probably would not be moved by appeals to white guilt. Some of the new multiracial Americans might disingenuously invoke an Asian or Hispanic grandparent to include themselves among the victims rather than the victimizers. Nor would black Americans find many partners for a "rainbow coalition" politics, except perhaps among recent immigrants.

One political response to a beige-and-black America might be a movement to institutionalize binationalism. In Canada, Anglophones and Francophones have been declared the country's two "founding nations." Blacks, as a quasi-permanent minority, might insist upon a status different from that of voluntary immigrants who merge with the majority in a few generations. Such compromises, however, are difficult to maintain. If most immigrants blend into one of the two founding nations—the Anglophone majority in Canada, the mixed-race majority in the U.S.—then working out a stable modus vivendi between the expanding community and the shrinking community becomes almost impossible.

The other possibility is that black Americans will, in time, participate   15 in the melting pot at rates comparable with other groups. Such a result cannot and should not be the aim of public policy—how can you legislate romance?—but it may be an incidental result of greater social mobility and economic equality. The evidence suggests that the association of people as equals erodes even the oldest and deepest prejudice in American life.

According to the 1990 census, white men 25–34 in the U.S. military were 2.3 times as likely to marry nonwhite women as civilians. And white women in the same age group who served in the military in the 1980s were seven times as likely as their civilian counterparts to have black husbands. Indeed, for all groups except for Asian men, military service makes out-marriage much more likely. The reason for this is clear: the U.S. military is the most integrated institution in American society because it is the most egalitarian and meritocratic. It is also—not coincidentally—the least libertarian and least tolerant of subcultural diversity. It may be that in the nation as a whole, as in the military, the integration of individuals can be achieved only at the price of the sacrifice of lesser differences to a powerful common identity.

In the end, racial intermarriage is a result, not a cause, of racial integration. Racial integration, in turn, is a result of social equality. The civil rights revolution abolished racial segregation by law, but not racial segregation by class. Ending racial segregation by class might—just might—bring about an end to race itself in America. It is certainly worth a try.

For Discussion

1. "Intermarriage rates vary by region," Lind notes. There are far more mixed-race couples on both U.S. coasts than in the heartland, the interior regions of the country. Does this matter? If so, in what ways?

2. Intermarriage is also more common in big cities than in small towns or rural communities. Does this matter? If so, in what ways?
3. How do you explain the lower rate of out-marriage for black women as opposed to that for black men?
4. According to a 1997 Knight-Ridder poll Lind cites, 30% of Americans continue to oppose marriage between whites and blacks. How do you account for the opposition?
5. In the next-to-last paragraph, Lind discusses the military and intermarriage. How does he interpret the data? What implications do you see for American society in general?

For Inquiry

"[R]acial intermarriage is a result, not a cause, of racial integration. Racial integration, in turn, is a result of social equality." So Lind claims in the last paragraph, and his logic seems compelling.

Investigate his assertions in the context of interracial dating. If you have had experience with it, examine your relationship(s). Talk with classmates and/or with friends who also have had experience with it. If you feel comfortable approaching interracial couples on campus you don't know or don't know well, get their input, too.

How much does integration have to do with interracial dating? Are the people involved always social equals — that is, do they come from the same socioeconomic class and share other similarities in background? Are such factors as important in dating as they are in marriage? Why or why not?

In a short essay, discuss the conclusions you've reached, and compare them with those of other class members.

White Poverty: The Politics of Invisibility
bell hooks

The way we see or fail to see the poor among us has everything to do with our own class background — and so also with how we understand poverty and the attitudes we have about it. This author has an interesting story to tell — raised poor and black, she was an outstanding student who became a prominent social critic — indeed, one of the most celebrated writers on gender, race, and class in the United States. She knows race and class from the inside, from experience with both the underprivileged and the privileged. The following selection comes from her book Where We Stand: Class Matters *(Routledge, 2000).*

One of the most persistent fallacies in the United States is to equate poverty with skin color, especially black. The fact is that the large majority of poor people are white. Why, then, do we tend to equate poor with black? This essay addresses this and other key questions connected with power, race, and class.

In the southern world of racial apartheid I grew up in, no racialized class division was as intense or as fraught with bitter conflict as the one between poor whites and black folks. All black people knew that white skin gave any southern "cracker or peckerwood" (ethnic slurs reserved for the white poor) more power and privilege than even the wealthiest of black folks. However, these slurs were not the product of black vernacular slang, they were the terms white folks with class privilege invented to separate themselves from what they called poor "white trash." On the surface, at least, it made the lives of racist poor white people better to have a group they could lord it over, and the only group they could lord it over were black people. Assailed and assaulted by privileged white folks, they transferred their rage and class hatred onto the bodies of black people.

Unlike the stereotypes projected by the dominant culture about poor black folks, class stereotypes claimed poor whites were supposedly easily spotted by skin ailments, bad dental hygiene, and hair texture. All these things are affected by diet. While poor southern black folks often had no money, they usually had homegrown food to eat. Poor whites often suffered from malnutrition. Living under racial apartheid, black children learned to fear poor whites more than other whites simply because they were known to express their racism by cruel and brutal acts of violence. And even when white folks with class privilege condemned this violence, they could never openly oppose it, for to do so they would have had to take the word of black folks over those of white folks, thus being disloyal to white supremacy. A white person of privilege opposing violence against blacks perpetuated by poor whites might easily ruin their reputation and risk being seen as a "nigger lover."

When I was a small child we lived in the hills without neighbors nearby. Our closest neighbors were "white trash," as distinct from poor whites. White trash were different because they flaunted their poverty, reveled in it, and were not ashamed. Poor whites, like poor blacks, were committed to trying to find work and lay claim to respectability—they were law abiding and patriotic. White trash saw themselves as above the law and as a consequence they were dangerous. White trash were folks who, as our neighbors were fond of saying, "did not give a good goddamn." They were not afraid to take the Lord's name in vain. Most poor white folks did not want to live anywhere near black folks. White trash lived anywhere. Writing in the anthology *White Trash: Race and Class in America*, Constance Penly comments in "Crackers and Whackers": "A Southern white child is required to learn that white trash folks are the lowest of the low because socially and economically they have sunk so far that they might as well be black. As such, they are seen to have lost all self-respect. So it is particularly unseemly when they appear to shamefully flaunt their trashiness, which, after all, is nothing but an aggressively in-your-face reminder of stark class difference. . . ." Privileged-class southern white folks sometimes saw white trash as more disgusting than black folks, but at the end of the day they lived by the creed that white stands with white and white makes it right.

Our "hillbilly white trash" neighbors lived by their own codes and rules. We did not call them names, because we knew the pain of slurs. Mama made it clear that they were people just like us and were to be shown respect. While they did not bother us and we did not bother them, we feared them. I never felt that they feared us. [. . .]

Desegregation led to the closing of all black schools. Busing took us out of our all-black neighborhoods into worlds of whiteness we did not know. It was in high school that I first began to understand class separation between whites. Poor white kids kept to themselves. And many of their well-to-do white peers would rather be seen talking to a black person than speaking to the white poor, or worse, to white trash. There was no danger that the black person they were talking to would want to come and hang out at their home or go to a movie. Racial lines were not crossed outside school. There could be no expectation of a reciprocal friendship. A privileged white person might confuse the issue if they showed attention to an underprivileged white peer. Class boundaries had to remain intact so that no one got the wrong idea. Between black and white there was no chance of a wrong idea: the two simply did not meet or mix.

Since some folks saw mama's family as backwoods, as black hillbillies, she was always quick to punish any act of aggression on our part toward an underdog group. We were not allowed to ridicule poor whites—not even if they were taunting us. When we began to ride the bus across town to the white school, it was a shock to my sensibilities to interact with black children who were scornful of the misfortune of others. In those days it was

5

a mark of pride for poor whites not to take the bus. That would have placed them in a context where black folks were in the majority. Now the white trash children of single mothers had to take the bus or walk.

To this day I have sad memories of the way Wilma, the white girl who was in my class, was treated by aggressive black children on the bus. Their daily taunts reminded her that she was poor white trash, the lowest of the low, that she smelled bad, that she wore the same dress day after day. In loud mean talk they warned her not to sit next to them. She often stood when there was an empty seat. A big girl with dark hair and unusually fair skin, she endured all the taunts with a knowing smirk. When she was pushed too far she fought back. She knew that with the exception of her ten minutes on that predominately black bus, white power ruled the day. And no matter how poor she was, she would always be white.

Academics writing about class often make light of the racial privilege of the white poor. They make it seem as though it is merely symbolic prestige. This is especially true of northerners. They have no intimate knowledge of the way southern poor whites terrorize and harass black folks in everyday life. My mother's mother lived across town in a big old house in a white section. She could live there because she was surrounded by the homes of poor whites. When we, her grandchildren, were sent to see her, we feared our walk through the poor white neighborhoods. We feared the white folks who sat on their porches making fun of us or calling to us to "come there." We had been told to keep our eyes straight ahead and keep on walking. In the apartheid south, as in most northern neighborhoods, white was always right. Poor whites knew the power race privilege gave them and they used it. Describing her background growing up in Oklahoma, Roxanne Dunbar writes of poor whites: "In the end the only advantage for most has been the color of their skin and white supremacy, particularly toward African-Americans. . . ." Race privilege has consistently offered poor whites the chance of living a better life in the midst of poverty than their black counterparts.

The white poor make up the vast majority of the poor in this society. Whereas mass migration of poor blacks from southern states to northern cities created a huge urban poor population, the white poor continue to live in isolated rural and suburban areas. Now and then they live hidden in the midst of white affluence. From their invention to the present day, the world of trailer park homes has been the territory of the white poor. While marking class boundaries, trailer park communities do not carry the stigma of degradation and deprivation commonly associated with the "ghetto"—a term first used to identify poor white urban immigrant communities. Indeed, in the not so distant past the psychological and economic self-esteem of the white working class and the white poor has been significantly bolstered by the class politics of white supremacy. Currently, we are witnessing a resurgence of white supremacist thinking among disenfranchised classes of white people. These extremist groups respond to misinformation circulated by privileged whites that suggests that black people are getting ahead financially because of government policies like affirmative action, and they are taught to blame black folks for their plight.

While anti-black racism has intensified among whites of all classes in recent years as part of civil rights backlash, overall the white underprivileged are less inclined to blame black folks for their economic plight than in the past. They are far more likely to see immigrants as the group taking needed jobs. Their racism toward nonwhite immigrants who are perceived to be taking jobs by virtue of their willingness to work for less mirrors that of black workers who blame immigrants. More and more the white and black poor recognize that ruling class greed ensures their continued exploitation and oppression.

These changes in the way the poor think are a direct result of racial integration. In many parts of the United States, desegregation led to greater contact between the black and white poor. Housing projects that had been at one time racially segregated were integrated. Greater societal acceptance of interracial bonding created the social context for white and black poor to mingle in ways unheard of at previous moments in our nation. Of course, in many areas, especially northern white cities, it was precisely this disruption of the conventional racial boundaries that led to reentrenchment along racial lines. New York and Boston ethnic white neighborhoods, where there is a class mix, remain race-segregated because racial discrimination in housing, work, etc., continues to be a norm. [. . .]

More and more Americans of all colors are entering the ranks of the poor. And that includes white Americans. The evidence is in the numbers. In the essay "Trash-O-Nomics," Doug Henwood states what should be obvious but often is not: "Of course, the average white person is better off than the average non-white person, those of Asian origin excepted, and black people are disproportionally poor. But that sort of formula hides as much as it reveals: most officially poor people are white, and these days, a white household should consider itself lucky if its income is only stagnant rather than in outright decline." [. . .]

Today, most folks who comment on class acknowledge that poverty is seen as having a black face, but they rarely point to the fact that this representation has been created and sustained by mass media. Concurrently, reports using statistics that show a huge percentage of black folks in the ranks of the poor compared to a small percentage of whites make it seem that blacks are the majority group in the ranks of the poor. Rarely do these reports emphasize that these percentages are based on population size. The reality they mask is that blacks are a small percentage of the population. While black folks disproportionate to our numbers are among the poor, the vast majority of the poor continue to be white. The hidden face of poverty in the United States is the untold stories of millions of poor white people.

Better to have poor and working-class white folks believe white supremacy is still giving them a meaningful edge than to broadcast the reality that the poor of any race no longer have an edge in this society, or that downsizing daily drags previously economically sound white households into the ranks of the poor. [. . .]

Ruling class interests have a stake in reinforcing a politics of white supremacy, which continues to try to socialize white working-class and poor people to blame their economic plight on black people or people of color globally. Since anti-black racism has never been eliminated in the culture, it does not take much [. . .] to brainwash poor whites to believe that it is black folks who stand in the way of their academic advancement. [. . .]

No doubt ruling class groups will succeed in new efforts to divide and conquer, but the white poor will no longer direct its class rage solely at black people, for the white poor is divided within its ranks. Just as there are many poor whites who are racist, there are a substantial group of poor whites who refuse to buy into white supremacist politics, who understand the economic forces that are crippling the American working class. Progressive white poor and working-class people understand the dynamics of capitalism. All over the United States class unrest is mounting. Since there is no collective resistance the future of class struggle is not clear.

Ending welfare will mean that more white women than ever before in our nation's history will enter the ranks of the underclass. Like their black counterparts, many of them will be young. Workfare programs, which pay subsistence wages without the backdrop of free housing, will not enhance their lives. As the future "poorest of the poor" they are far less likely to be duped into believing their enemies are other economically disadvantaged groups than their predecessors. Since they are the products of a consumer-oriented culture of narcissism, they are also more inclined to be indifferent to their neighbors' plight. Constant deprivation creates stress, anxiety, along with material woes. But their desire to ease their pain can change indifference into awareness and awareness into resistance.

Given that today's culture is one where the white and black working class and poor have more to say to one another, there is a context for building solidarity that did not exist in the past. That solidarity cannot be expressed solely through shared critique of the privileged. It must be rooted in a politics of resistance that is fundamentally anti-racist, one that recognizes that the experiences of underprivileged white folks are as important as those of people of color. The class segregation that historically divided the white poor from their more privileged counterparts did not exist in predominately black communities. And while generations of white families have historically remained poor, a host of black folks pulled themselves out of poverty into privilege. In solidarity these folks have historically been strong advocates for the black poor even though that too is changing. More often than not they did not encourage solidarity with the

15

white poor because of persistent anti-black racism. Now they must become advocates for the white and black poor, overcoming their anti-white prejudices. Concurrently, the black and white poor must do the work of building solidarity by learning more about one another, about what brings them together and what tears them apart. We need to hear more from all of us who have bridged the gap between white and black poor and working-class experience. [. . .]

For Discussion

1. How do you explain the way Wilma was treated on the bus by "aggressive black children"? Why would this not happen within the school itself or elsewhere in the world where bell hooks grew up? Why didn't the author participate in harassing the "white trash" girl?
2. Hooks points to "a resurgence of white supremacist thinking among disenfranchised classes of white people" (paragraph 9), anger directed as much or more at recent immigrants of color than at black Americans. How does she explain this resurgence? Do you agree with her explanation? Why or why not?
3. As never before, hooks sees the potential for greater solidarity between poor blacks and whites. Why does she think this possibility exists? She points also to the lack of "collective resistance," organized political activity, among the roughly 40 million poor in America. Why haven't they become a significant political force?

For Research and Convincing

Hooks is a socialist and takes the standard leftist view of why poverty exists: because capitalism permits—indeed, sanctions—vast disparities in income level. What she calls the "ruling class," the rich and powerful, have their status because many people are poor and powerless. The poor are exploited to make rich people rich. Consequently, the wealthy use their power to keep poor people poor.

Do research on poverty in the United States. What groups of poor people do poverty researchers distinguish? Is poverty the same thing for all groups? What causes some people to be poor all their lives? What causes others to fall into poverty? Who climbs out of it and why?

After assessing the information, write an essay taking a stance on hooks's view of poverty. How adequate is the standard socialist view of poverty? Is the "ruling class" to blame? Can poverty be eliminated simply by redistributing income?

Photograph

A. Ramey

In 1998, when California's Proposition 209 went into effect, ending affirmative action programs in public employment and at public colleges and universities, students on many California campuses demonstrated against the law and their schools' compliance with it. The intense moment captured in the photograph below shows police barring the doors of a building on UCLA's campus as students attempted to occupy it.

For Discussion

The photograph raises many issues for discussion. Most obviously, the policy of affirmative action is still under debate, as voters in other states have attempted to introduce legislation similar to California's. Look into the effects of Proposition 209 and the Hopwood court decision in Texas. What has been the effect on minority enrollment at schools there? The essay in this chapter by Linda Darling-Hammond addresses the question of whether equal education opportunity already exists.

Unequal Opportunity: Race and Education
Linda Darling-Hammond

The key principle of social justice in the thinking of most Americans is equal opportunity, as contrasted with equal results. That is, we favor a fair chance for all but believe that outcomes should be different based on individual talent and drive. This article argues that, so far as funding for our school systems is concerned, there is no equity and therefore no genuinely fair chance for all children to get a good education.

Linda Darling-Hammond is an educational researcher at Columbia University Teacher's College and author of The Right to Learn *(1997). This essay appeared in the* Brookings Review *(Spring 1998).*

W. E. B. Du Bois was right about the problem of the 21st century. The color line divides us still. In recent years, the most visible evidence of this in the public policy arena has been the persistent attack on affirmative action in higher education and employment. From the perspective of many Americans who believe that the vestiges of discrimination have disappeared, affirmative action now provides an unfair advantage to minorities. From the perspective of others who daily experience the consequences of ongoing discrimination, affirmative action is needed to protect opportunities likely to evaporate if an affirmative obligation to act fairly does not exist. And for Americans of all backgrounds, the allocation of opportunity in a society that is becoming ever more dependent on knowledge and education is a source of great anxiety and concern.

At the center of these debates are interpretations of the gaps in educational achievement between white and non-Asian minority students as measured by standardized test scores. The presumption that guides much of the conversation is that equal opportunity now exists; therefore, continued low levels of achievement on the part of minority students must be a function of genes, culture, or a lack of effort and will (see, for example, Richard Herrnstein and Charles Murray's *The Bell Curve* and Stephan and Abigail Thernstrom's *America in Black and White*).

The assumptions that undergird this debate miss an important reality: educational outcomes for minority children are much more a function of their unequal access to key educational resources, including skilled teachers and quality curriculum, than they are a function of race. In fact, the U.S. educational system is one of the most unequal in the industrialized world, and students routinely receive dramatically different learning opportunities based on their social status. In contrast to European and Asian nations that fund schools centrally and equally, the wealthiest 10 percent of U.S. school districts spend nearly 10 times more than the poorest 10 percent, and spending ratios of 3 to 1 are common within states. Despite stark differences in funding, teacher quality, curriculum, and class sizes, the prevailing view is that if students do not achieve, it is their own fault. If we are ever to get beyond the problem of the color line, we must confront and address these inequalities.

THE NATURE OF EDUCATIONAL INEQUALITY

Americans often forget that as late as the 1960s most African-American, Latino, and Native American students were educated in wholly segregated schools funded at rates many times lower than those serving whites and were excluded from many higher education institutions entirely. The end of legal segregation followed by efforts to equalize spending since 1970 has made a substantial difference for student achievement. On every major national test, including the National Assessment of Educational Progress, the gap in minority and white students' test scores narrowed substantially between 1970 and 1990, especially for elementary school students. On the Scholastic Aptitude Test (SAT), the scores of African-American students climbed 54 points between 1976 and 1994, while those of white students remained stable.

Even so, educational experiences for minority students have continued   5
to be substantially separate and unequal. Two-thirds of minority students still attend schools that are predominantly minority, most of them located in central cities and funded well below those in neighboring suburban districts. Recent analyses of data prepared for school finance cases in Alabama, New Jersey, New York, Louisiana, and Texas have found that on every tangible measure—from qualified teachers to curriculum offering—schools serving greater numbers of students of color had significantly fewer resources than schools serving mostly white students. As William L. Taylor and Dianne Piche noted in a 1991 report to Congress:

> Inequitable systems of school finance inflict disproportionate harm on minority and economically disadvantaged students. On an inter-state basis, such students are concentrated in states, primarily in the South, that have the lowest capacities to finance public education. On an intra-state basis, many of the states with the widest disparities in educational expenditures are large industrial states. In these states, many minorities and economically disadvantaged students are located in property-poor urban districts which fare the worst in educational expenditures . . . [or] in rural districts which suffer from fiscal inequity.

Jonathan Kozol's 1991 *Savage Inequalities* described the striking differences between public schools serving students of color in urban settings and their suburban counterparts, which typically spend twice as much per student for populations with many fewer special needs. Contrast MacKenzie High School in Detroit, where word processing courses are taught without word processors because the school cannot afford them, or East St. Louis Senior High School, whose biology lab has no laboratory tables or usable dissecting kits, with nearby suburban schools where children enjoy a computer hookup to Dow Jones to study stock transactions and science laboratories that rival those in some industries. Or contrast Paterson, New Jersey, which could not afford the qualified teachers needed to offer foreign language courses to most high school students, with Princeton, where foreign languages begin in elementary school.

Even within urban school districts, schools with high concentrations of low-income and minority students receive fewer instructional resources than others. And tracking systems exacerbate these inequalities by segregating many low-income and minority students within schools. In combination, these policies leave minority students with fewer and lower-quality books, curriculum materials, laboratories, and computers; significantly larger class sizes; less qualified and experienced teachers; and less access to high-quality curriculum. Many schools serving low-income and minority students do not even offer the math and science courses needed for college, and they provide lower-quality teaching in the classes they do offer. It all adds up.

WHAT DIFFERENCE DOES IT MAKE?

Since the 1966 Coleman report, *Equality of Educational Opportunity,* another debate has raged as to whether money makes a difference to educational outcomes. It is certainly possible to spend money ineffectively; however, studies that have developed more sophisticated measures of schooling show how money, properly spent, makes a difference. Over the past 30 years, a large body of research has shown that four factors consistently influence student achievement: all else equal, students perform better if they are educated in smaller schools where they are well known (300 to 500 students is optimal), have smaller class sizes (especially at the elementary level), receive a challenging curriculum, and have more highly qualified teachers.

Minority students are much less likely than white children to have any of these resources. In predominantly minority schools, which most students of color attend, schools are large (on average, more than twice as large as predominantly white schools and reaching 3,000 students or more in most cities); on average, class sizes are 15 percent larger overall (80 percent larger for non-special education classes); curriculum offerings and materials are lower in quality; and teachers are much less qualified in terms of levels of education, certification, and training in the fields they teach. And in integrated schools, as UCLA professor Jeannie Oakes described in the 1980s and Harvard professor Gary Orfield's research has recently confirmed, most minority students are segregated in lower-track classes with larger class sizes, less qualified teachers, and lower-quality curriculum.

Research shows that teachers' preparation makes a tremendous difference to children's learning. In an analysis of 900 Texas school districts,
Harvard economist Ronald Ferguson found that teachers' expertise — as
measured by scores on a licensing examination, master's degrees, and experience — was the single most important determinant of student achievement,
accounting for roughly 40 percent of the measured variance in students'
reading and math achievement gains in grades 1–12. After controlling for
socioeconomic status, the large disparities in achievement between black
and white students were almost entirely due to differences in the qualifications of their teachers. In combination, differences in teacher expertise and
class sizes accounted for as much of the measured variance in achievement
as did student and family background.

Ferguson and Duke economist Helen Ladd repeated this analysis in
Alabama and again found sizable influences of teacher qualifications and
smaller class sizes on achievement gains in math and reading. They found
that more of the difference between the high- and low-scoring districts
was explained by teacher qualifications and class sizes than by poverty,
race, and parent education.

Meanwhile, a Tennessee study found that elementary school students
who are assigned to ineffective teachers for three years in a row score nearly
50 percentile points lower on achievement tests than those assigned to
highly effective teachers over the same period. Strikingly, minority students
are about half as likely to be assigned to the most effective teachers and
twice as likely to be assigned to the least effective.

Minority students are put at greatest risk by the American tradition of
allowing enormous variation in the qualifications of teachers. The National
Commission on Teaching and America's Future found that new teachers
hired without meeting certification standards (25 percent of all new teachers) are usually assigned to teach the most disadvantaged students in low-
income and high-minority schools, while the most highly educated new
teachers are hired largely by wealthier schools. Students in poor or predominantly minority schools are much less likely to have teachers who are fully
qualified or hold higher-level degrees. In schools with the highest minority
enrollments, for example, students have less than a 50 percent chance of
getting a math or science teacher with a license and a degree in the field. In
1994, fully one-third of teachers in high-poverty schools taught without a
minor in their main field and nearly 70 percent taught without a minor in
their secondary teaching field.

Studies of underprepared teachers consistently find that they are less
effective with students and that they have difficulty with curriculum development, classroom management, student motivation, and teaching strategies. With little knowledge about how children grow, learn, and develop,
or about what to do to support their learning, these teachers are less likely
to understand students' learning styles and differences, to anticipate
students' knowledge and potential difficulties, or to plan and redirect

instruction to meet students' needs. Nor are they likely to see it as their job to do so, often blaming the students if their teaching is not successful.

Teacher expertise and curriculum quality are interrelated, because a challenging curriculum requires an expert teacher. Research has found that both students and teachers are tracked: that is, the most expert teachers teach the most demanding courses to the most advantaged students, while lower-track students assigned to less able teachers receive lower-quality teaching and less demanding material. Assignment to tracks is also related to race: even when grades and test scores are comparable, black students are more likely to be assigned to lower-track, nonacademic classes.

WHEN OPPORTUNITY IS MORE EQUAL

What happens when students of color do get access to more equal opportunities? Studies find that curriculum quality and teacher skill make more difference to educational outcomes than the initial test scores or racial backgrounds of students. Analyses of national data from both the High School and Beyond Surveys and the National Educational Longitudinal Surveys have demonstrated that, while there are dramatic differences among students of various racial and ethnic groups in course-taking in such areas as math, science, and foreign language, for students with similar course-taking records, achievement test score differences by race or ethnicity narrow substantially.

Robert Dreeben and colleagues at the University of Chicago conducted a long line of studies documenting both the relationship between educational opportunities and student performance and minority students' access to those opportunities. In a comparative study of 300 Chicago first graders, for example, Dreeben found that African-American and white students who had comparable instruction achieved comparable levels of reading skill. But he also found that the quality of instruction given African-American students was, on average, much lower than that given white students, thus creating a racial gap in aggregate achievement at the end of first grade. In fact, the highest-ability group in Dreeben's sample was in a school in a low-income African-American neighborhood. These children, though, learned less during first grade than their white counterparts because their teacher was unable to provide the challenging instruction they deserved.

When schools have radically different teaching forces, the effects can be profound. For example, when Eleanor Armour-Thomas and colleagues compared a group of exceptionally effective elementary schools with a group of low-achieving schools with similar demographic characteristics in New York City, roughly 90 percent of the variance in student reading and mathematics scores at grades 3, 6, and 8 was a function of differences in teacher qualifications. The schools with highly qualified teachers serving large numbers of minority and low-income students performed as well as much more advantaged schools.

Most studies have estimated effects statistically. However, an experiment that randomly assigned seventh grade "at-risk" students to remedial, average, and honors mathematics classes found that the at-risk students who took the honors class offering a pre-algebra curriculum ultimately outperformed all other students of similar backgrounds. Another study compared African-American high school youth randomly placed in public housing in the Chicago suburbs with city-placed peers of equivalent income and initial academic attainment and found that the suburban students, who attended largely white and better-funded schools, were substantially more likely to take challenging courses, perform well academically, graduate on time, attend college, and find good jobs.

WHAT CAN BE DONE?

[. . .] Last year the National Commission on Teaching and America's Future   20
issued a blueprint for a comprehensive set of policies to ensure a "caring, competent, and qualified teacher for every child," as well as schools organized to support student success. Twelve states are now working directly with the commission on this agenda, and others are set to join this year. Several pending bills to overhaul the federal Higher Education Act would ensure that highly qualified teachers are recruited and prepared for students in all schools. Federal policymakers can develop incentives, as they have in medicine, to guarantee well-prepared teachers in shortage fields and high-need locations. States can equalize education spending, enforce higher teaching standards, and reduce teacher shortages, as Connecticut, Kentucky, Minnesota, and North Carolina have already done. School districts can reallocate resources from administrative superstructures and special add-on programs to support better-educated teachers who offer a challenging curriculum in smaller schools and classes, as restructured schools as far apart as New York and San Diego have done. These schools, in communities where children are normally written off to lives of poverty, welfare dependency, or incarceration, already produce much higher levels of achievement for students of color, sending more than 90 percent of their students to college. Focusing on what matters most can make a real difference in what children have the opportunity to learn. This, in turn, makes a difference in what communities can accomplish.

AN ENTITLEMENT TO GOOD TEACHING

The common presumption about educational inequality—that it resides primarily in those students who come to school with inadequate capacities to benefit from what the school has to offer—continues to hold wide currency because the extent of inequality in opportunities to learn is largely unknown. We do not currently operate schools on the presumption that students might be entitled to decent teaching and schooling as a matter of course. In fact, some state and local defendants have countered school finance and desegregation cases with assertions that such remedies are not required unless it can be proven that they will produce equal outcomes. Such arguments against equalizing opportunities to learn have made good on Du Bois's prediction that the problem of the 20th century would be the problem of the color line.

But education resources do make a difference, particularly when funds are used to purchase well-qualified teachers and high-quality curriculum and to create personalized learning communities in which children are well known. In all of the current sturm und drang about affirmative action, "special treatment," and the other high-volatility buzzwords for race and class politics in this nation, I would offer a simple starting point for the next century's efforts: no special programs, just equal educational opportunity.

For Discussion

1. Darling-Hammond provides much evidence of funding inequities in our school systems. How does the funding system work? What social and political forces operate to keep it in place?
2. Darling-Hammond mentions that many modern, industrialized nations fund their schools centrally—that is, by the equivalent of our federal government. How do you respond to the idea of Washington handling the funding of our schools? Would such an approach work in the United States?
3. According to Darling-Hammond, what makes the greatest difference in student learning and achievement? How exactly is the level of funding related to this difference?
4. How would you define a "prepared teacher"? Is preparation the same thing as effectiveness?

For Research and Convincing

Investigate school funding in the city and state where your university is located or in a neighboring city or state. Are there inequities? How great are they? Do the inequities correlate with educational achievement? By what measures?

Write a paper assessing the school system's (or systems') success in providing equal opportunity. If reform is needed, indicate what should be done. Address your essay to an appropriate authority, such as a state legislator or education agency.

The Recoloring of Campus Life
Shelby Steele

The following personal and reflective essay centers on what the author calls "concentrated micro-societies," our college campuses. In recent years, there has been much discussion of a "new racism" on campuses across the country. Shelby Steele, a professor of English at San Jose State University who attended college in the 1960s, argues that today's campus racism is indeed new; he tries to explain why it exists and how it works. His essay appeared originally in 1989 in Harper's, *an eclectic monthly magazine offering essays on various current topics. Much discussed and often reprinted, "The Recoloring of Campus Life" may well be a contemporary classic.*

In the past few years, we have witnessed what the National Institute Against Prejudice and Violence calls a "proliferation" of racial incidents on college campuses around the country. Incidents of on-campus "intergroup conflict" have occurred at more than 160 colleges in the last three years, according to the institute. The nature of these incidents has ranged from open racial violence — most notoriously, the October 1986 beating of a black student at the University of Massachusetts at Amherst after an argument about the World Series turned into a racial bashing, with a crowd of up to 3,000 whites chasing twenty blacks — to the harassment of minority students, to acts of racial or ethnic insensitivity, with by far the greatest number falling in the last two categories. At Dartmouth College, three editors of the *Dartmouth Review,* the off-campus right-wing student weekly, were suspended last winter for harassing a black professor in his lecture hall. At Yale University last year a swastika and the words "white power" were painted on the school's Afro-American cultural center. Racist jokes were aired not long ago on a campus radio station at the University of Michigan. And at the University of Wisconsin at Madison, members of the Zeta Beta Tau fraternity held a mock slave auction in which pledges painted their faces black and wore Afro wigs. Two weeks after the president of Stanford University informed the incoming freshman class last fall that "bigotry is out, and I mean it," two freshmen defaced a poster of Beethoven — gave the image thick lips — and hung it on a black student's door.

In response, black students around the country have rediscovered the militant protest strategies of the Sixties. At the University of Massachusetts at Amherst, Williams College, Penn State University, UC Berkeley, UCLA, Stanford, and countless other campuses, black students have sat in, marched, and rallied. But much of what they were marching and rallying about seemed less a response to specific racial incidents than a call for broader action on the part of the colleges and universities they were attending. Black students have demanded everything from more black faculty members and new courses on racism to the addition of "ethnic" foods in the cafeteria. There is the sense in these demands that racism runs deep.

Of course, universities are not where racial problems tend to arise. When I went to college in the mid-Sixties, colleges were oases of calm and understanding in a racially tense society; campus life—with its traditions of tolerance and fairness, its very distance from the "real" world—imposed a degree of broadmindedness on even the most provincial students. If I met whites who were not anxious to be friends with blacks, most were at least vaguely friendly to the cause of our freedom. In any case, there was no guerrilla activity against our presence, no "mine field of racism" (as one black student at Berkeley recently put it) to negotiate. I wouldn't say that the phrase "campus racism" is a contradiction in terms, but until recently it certainly seemed an incongruence.

But a greater incongruence is the generational timing of this new problem on the campuses. Today's undergraduates were born after the passage of the 1964 Civil Rights Act. They grew up in an age when racial equality was for the first time enforceable by law. This too was a time when blacks suddenly appeared on television, as mayors of big cities, as icons of popular culture, as teachers, and in some cases even as neighbors. Today's black and white college students, veterans of *Sesame Street* and often of integrated grammar and high schools, have had more opportunities to know each other—whites and blacks—than any previous generation in American history. Not enough opportunities, perhaps, but enough to make the notion of racial tension on campus something of a mystery, at least to me.

To try to unravel this mystery I left my own campus, where there have been few signs of racial tension, and talked with black and white students at California schools where racial incidents had occurred: Stanford, UCLA, Berkeley. I spoke with black and white students—and not with Asians and Hispanics—because, as always, blacks and whites represent the deepest lines of division, and because I hesitate to wander onto the complex territory of other minority groups. A phrase by William H. Gass—"the hidden internality of things"—describes with maybe a little too much grandeur what I hoped to find. But it *is* what I wanted to find, for this is the kind of problem that makes a black person nervous, which is not to say that it doesn't unnerve whites as well. Once every six months or so someone yells "nigger" at me from a passing car. I don't like to think that these solo artists might soon make up a chorus or, worse, that this chorus might one day soon sing to me from the paths of my own campus.

I have long believed that trouble between the races is seldom what it appears to be. It was not hard to see after my first talks with students that racial tension on campus is a problem that misrepresents itself. It has the same look, the archetypal pattern, of America's timeless racial conflict—white racism and black protest. And I think part of our concern over it comes from the fact that it has the feel of a relapse, illness gone and come again. But if we are seeing the same symptoms, I don't believe we are dealing with the same illness. For one thing, I think racial tension on campus is the result more of racial equality than inequality.

How to live with racial difference has been America's profound social problem. For the first 100 years or so following emancipation it was controlled by a legally sanctioned inequality that acted as a buffer between the races. No longer is this the case. On campuses today, as throughout society, blacks enjoy equality under the law—a profound social advancement. No student may be kept out of a class or a dormitory or an extracurricular activity because of his or her race. But there is a paradox here: On a campus where members of all races are gathered, mixed together in the classroom as well as socially, differences are more exposed than ever. And this is where the trouble starts. For members of each race—young adults coming into their own, often away from home for the first time—bring to this site of freedom, exploration, and now, today, equality very deep fears and anxieties, inchoate feelings of racial shame, anger, and guilt. These feelings could lie dormant in the home, in familiar neighborhoods, in simpler days of childhood. But the college campus, with its structures of interaction and adult-level competition—the big exam, the dorm, the "mixer"—is another matter. I think campus racism is born of the rub between racial difference and a setting, the campus itself, devoted to interaction and equality. On our campuses, such concentrated micro-societies, all that remains unresolved between blacks and whites, all the old wounds and shames that have never been addressed, present themselves for attention—and present our youth with pressures they cannot always handle.

I have mentioned one paradox: racial fears and anxieties among blacks and whites bubbling up in an era of racial equality under the law, in settings that are among the freest and fairest in society. And there is another, related paradox, stemming from the notion of—and practice of—affirmative action. Under the provisions of the Equal Employment Opportunity Act of 1972, all state governments and institutions (including universities) were forced to initiate plans to increase the proportion of minority and women employees—in the case of universities, of students too. Affirmative action plans that establish racial quotas were ruled unconstitutional more than ten years ago in *University of California Regents v. Bakke.*[1] But quotas are only the most controversial aspect of affirmative action; the principle of

---

[1] Allan Bakke, a white applicant turned down for admission by a California State University medical school, sued the California system, claiming discrimination because the school's policy of maintaining a 16% minority enrollment meant that minority applicants with lower grade point averages were admitted instead of him. The case was settled in 1978, when a divided U.S. Supreme Court ruled that specific quotas such as those in effect in the California system were not permissible; Bakke was subsequently admitted to the program. However, the Court ruling also stated that race could be considered by college administrators in an effort to achieve a diverse student body. The full legal implications of the ruling have thus been ambiguous.

affirmative action is reflected in various university programs aimed at redressing and overcoming past patterns of discrimination. Of course, to be conscious of patterns of discrimination — the fact, say, that public schools in the black inner cities are more crowded and employ fewer top-notch teachers than white suburban public schools, and that this is a factor in student performance — is only reasonable. However, in doing this we also call attention quite obviously to difference: in the case of blacks and whites, racial difference. What has emerged on campus in recent years — as a result of the new equality and affirmative action, in a sense, as a result of progress — is a *politics of difference,* a troubling, volatile politics in which each group justifies itself, its sense of worth and its pursuit of power, through difference alone.

In this context, racial, ethnic, and gender differences become forms of sovereignty, campuses become balkanized, and each group fights with whatever means are available. No doubt there are many factors that have contributed to the rise of racial tension on campus: What has been the role of fraternities, which have returned to campus with their inclusions and exclusions? What role has the heightened notion of college as some first step to personal, financial success played in increasing competition, and thus tension? Mostly what I sense, though, is that in interactive settings, while fighting the fights of "difference," old ghosts are stirred, and haunt again. Black and white Americans simply have the power to make each other feel shame and guilt. In the "real" world, we may be able to deny these feelings, keep them at bay. But these feelings are likely to surface on college campuses, where young people are groping for identity and power, and where difference is made to matter so greatly. In a way, racial tension on campus in the Eighties might have been inevitable.

I would like, first, to discuss black students, their anxieties and vulner- 10
abilities. The accusation that black Americans have always lived with is that they are inferior — inferior simply because they are black. And this accusation has been too uniform, too ingrained in cultural imagery, too enforced by law, custom, and every form of power not to have left a mark. Black inferiority was a precept accepted by the founders of this nation; it was a principle of social organization that relegated blacks to the sidelines of American life. So when today's young black students find themselves on white campuses, surrounded by those who historically have claimed superiority, they are also surrounded by the myth of their inferiority.

Of course it is true that many young people come to college with some anxiety about not being good enough. But only blacks come wearing a color that is still, in the minds of some, a sign of inferiority. Poles, Jews, Hispanics, and other groups also endure degrading stereotypes. But two things make the myth of black inferiority a far heavier burden — the broadness of its scope and its incarnation in color. There are not only more stereotypes of blacks than of other groups, but these stereotypes are also more dehumanizing, more focused on the most despised of human traits—stupidity, laziness, sexual immorality, dirtiness, and so on. In America's racial and ethnic hierarchy, blacks have clearly been relegated to the lowest level—have been burdened with an ambiguous, animalistic humanity. Moreover, this is made unavoidable for blacks by the sheer visibility of black skin, a skin that evokes the myth of inferiority on sight. And today this myth is sadly reinforced for many black students by affirmative action programs, under which blacks may often enter college with lower test scores and high-school grade point averages than whites. "They see me as an affirmative action case," one black student told me at UCLA.

So when a black student enters college, the myth of inferiority compounds the normal anxiousness over whether he or she will be good enough. This anxiety is not only personal but also racial. The families of these students will have pounded into them the fact that blacks are not inferior. And probably more than anything, it is this pounding that finally leaves a mark. If I am not inferior, why the need to say so?

This myth of inferiority constitutes a very sharp and ongoing anxiety for young blacks, the nature of which is very precise: It is the terror that somehow, through one's actions or by virtue of some "proof" (a poor grade, a flubbed response in class), one's fear of inferiority—inculcated in ways large and small by society—will be confirmed as real. On a university campus, where intelligence itself is the ultimate measure, this anxiety is bound to be triggered.

A black student I met at UCLA was disturbed a little when I asked him if he ever felt vulnerable—anxious about "black inferiority"—as a black student. But after a long pause, he finally said, "I think I do." The example he gave was of a large lecture class he'd taken with more than 300 students. Fifty or so black students sat in the back of the lecture hall and "acted out every stereotype in the book." They were loud, ate food, came in late—and generally got lower grades than the whites in the class. "I knew I would be seen like them, and I didn't like it. I never sat by them." Seen like what? I asked, though we both knew the answer. "As lazy, ignorant, and stupid," he said sadly.

Had the group at the back been white fraternity brothers, they would not have been seen as dumb *whites*, of course. And a frat brother who worried about his grades would not worry that he would be seen "like them." The terror in this situation for the student I spoke with was that his own deeply buried anxiety would be given credence, that the myth would be verified, and that he would feel shame and humiliation not because of who he was but simply because he was black. In this lecture hall his race, quite apart from his performance, might subject him to four unendurable feelings—diminishment, accountability to the preconceptions of whites, a powerlessness to change those preconceptions, and, finally, shame. These are the feelings that make up his racial anxiety, and that of all blacks on any campus. On a white campus a black is never far from these feelings, and even his unconscious knowledge that he is subject to them can undermine his self-esteem. There are blacks on every campus who are not up to doing good college-level work. Certain black students may not be happy or motivated or in the appropriate field of study—*just like whites*. (Let us not forget that many white students get poor grades, fail, drop out.) Moreover, many more blacks than whites are not quite prepared for college, may have to catch up, owing to factors beyond their control: poor previous schooling, for example. But the white who has to catch up will not be anxious that his being behind is a matter of his whiteness, of his being *racially* inferior. The black student may well have such a fear.

This, I believe, is one reason why black colleges in America turn out 34 percent of all black college graduates, though they enroll only 17 percent of black college students. Without whites around on campus the myth of inferiority is in abeyance and, along with it, a great reservoir of culturally imposed self-doubt. On black campuses feelings of inferiority are personal; on campuses with a white majority, a black's problems have a way of becoming a "black" problem.

But this feeling of vulnerability a black may feel in itself is not as serious a problem as what he or she does with it. To admit that one is made anxious in integrated situations about the myth of racial inferiority is difficult for young blacks. It seems like admitting that one *is* racially inferior. And so, most often, the student will deny harboring those feelings. This is where some of the pangs of racial tension begin, because denial always involves distortion.

In order to deny a problem we must tell ourselves that the problem is something different than what it really is. A black student at Berkeley told me that he felt defensive every time he walked into a class and saw mostly white faces. When I asked why, he said, "Because I know they're all racists. They think blacks are stupid." Of course it may be true that some whites feel this way, but the singular focus on white racism allows this student to obscure his own underlying racial anxiety. He can now say that his problem—facing a class full of white faces, *fearing* that they think he is dumb—is entirely the result of certifiable white racism and has nothing to do with his own anxieties, or even that this particular academic subject may not be his best. Now all the terror of his anxiety, its powerful energy, is devoted to simply *seeing* racism. Whatever evidence of racism he finds—and looking this hard, he will no doubt find some—can be brought in to buttress his distorted view of the problem, while his actual deep-seated anxiety goes unseen.

Denial, and the distortion that results, places the problem *outside* the self and in the world. It is not that I have any inferiority anxiety because of my race; it is that I am going to school with people who don't like blacks. This is the shift in thinking that allows black students to reenact the protest pattern of the Sixties. Denied racial anxiety-distortion-reenactment is the process by which feelings of inferiority are transformed into an exaggerated white menace—which is then protested against with the techniques of the past. Under the sway of this process, black students believe that history is repeating itself, that it's just like the Sixties, or Fifties. In fact, it is the not yet healed wounds from the past, rather than the inequality that created the wounds, that is the real problem.

This process generates an unconscious need to exaggerate the level of racism on campus—to make it a matter of the system, not just a handful of students. Racism is the avenue away from the true inner anxiety. How many students demonstrating for a black "theme house"—demonstrating in the style of the Sixties, when the battle was to win for blacks a place on campus—might be better off spending their time reading and studying? Black students have the highest dropout rate and lowest grade point average of any group in American universities. This need not be so. And it is not the result of not having black theme houses.   20

It was my very good fortune to go to college in 1964, when the question of black "inferiority" was openly talked about among blacks. The summer before I left for college I heard Martin Luther King, Jr., speak in Chicago, and he laid it on the line for black students everywhere. "When you are behind in a footrace, the only way to get ahead is to run faster than the man in front of you. So when your white roommate says he's tired and goes to sleep, you stay up and burn the midnight oil." His statement that we were "behind in a footrace" acknowledged that because of history, of few opportunities, of racism, we were, in a sense, "inferior." But this had to do with what had been done to our parents and their parents, not with inherent inferiority. And because it was acknowledged, it was presented to us as a challenge rather than a mark of shame.

Of the eighteen black students (in a student body of 1,000) who were on campus in my freshman year, all graduated, though a number of us were not from the middle class. At the university where I currently teach, the dropout rate for black students is 72 percent, despite the presence of several academic-support programs; a counseling center with black counselors; an Afro-American studies department; black faculty, administrators, and staff; a general education curriculum that emphasizes "cultural pluralism"; an Educational Opportunities Program; a mentor program; a black faculty and staff association; and an administration and faculty that often announce the need to do more for black students.

It may be unfair to compare my generation with the current one. Parents do this compulsively and to little end but self-congratulation. But I don't congratulate my generation. I think we were advantaged. We came along at a time when racial integration was held in high esteem. And integration was a very challenging social concept for both blacks and whites. We were remaking ourselves—that's what one did at college—and making history. We had something to prove. This was a profound advantage; it gave us clarity and a challenge. Achievement in the American mainstream was the goal of integration, and the best thing about this challenge was its secondary message—that we *could* achieve.

There is much irony in the fact that black power would come along in the late Sixties and change all this. Black power was a movement of uplift and pride, and yet it also delivered the weight of pride—a weight that would burden black students from then on. Black power "nationalized" the black identity, made blackness itself an object of celebration and allegiance. But if it transformed a mark of shame into a mark of pride, it also, in the name of pride, required the denial of racial anxiety. Without a frank account of one's anxieties, there is no clear direction, no concrete challenge. Black students today do not get as clear a message from their racial identity as my generation got. They are not filled with the same urgency to prove themselves, because black pride has said, You're already proven, already equal, as good as anybody.

The "black identity" shaped by black power most powerfully contributes to racial tensions on campuses by basing entitlement more on race than on constitutional rights and standards of merit. With integration, black entitlement was derived from constitutional principles of fairness. Black power changed this by skewing the formula from rights to color—if you were black, you were entitled. Thus, the United Coalition Against Racism (UCAR) at the University of Michigan could "demand" two years ago that all black professors be given immediate tenure, that there be special pay incentives for black professors, and that money be provided for an all-black student union. In this formula, black becomes the very color of entitlement, an extra right in itself, and a very dangerous grandiosity is promoted in which blackness amounts to specialness.

Race is, by any standard, an unprincipled source of power. And on campuses the use of racial power by one group makes racial or ethnic or gender *difference* a currency of power for all groups. When I make my difference into power, other groups must seize upon their difference to contain my power and maintain their position relative to me. Very quickly a kind of politics of difference emerges in which racial, ethnic, and gender groups are forced to assert their entitlement and vie for power based on the single quality that makes them different from one another.

On many campuses today academic departments and programs are established on the basis of difference—black studies, women's studies, Asian studies, and so on—despite the fact that there is nothing in these "difference" departments that cannot be studied within traditional academic disciplines. If their rationale truly is past exclusion from the mainstream curriculum, shouldn't the goal now be complete inclusion rather than separateness? I think this logic is overlooked because these groups are too interested in the power their difference can bring, and they insist on separate departments and programs as a tribute to that power.

This politics of difference makes everyone on campus a member of a minority group. It also makes racial tensions inevitable. To highlight one's difference as a source of advantage is also, indirectly, to inspire the enemies of that difference. When blackness (and femaleness) becomes power,

25

then white maleness is also sanctioned as power. A white male student at Stanford told me, "One of my friends said the other day that we should get together and start up a white student union and come up with a list of demands."

It is certainly true that white maleness has long been an unfair source of power. But the sin of white male power is precisely its use of race and gender as a source of entitlement. When minorities and women use their race, ethnicity, and gender in the same way, they not only commit the same sin but also, indirectly, sanction the very form of power that oppressed them in the first place. The politics of difference is based on a tit-for-tat sort of logic in which every victory only calls one's enemies to arms.

This elevation of difference undermines the communal impulse by   30
making each group foreign and inaccessible to others. When difference is celebrated rather than remarked, people must think in terms of difference, they must find meaning in difference, and this meaning comes from an endless process of contrasting one's group with other groups. Blacks use whites to define themselves as different, women use men, Hispanics use whites and blacks, and on it goes. And in the process each group mythologizes and mystifies its difference, puts it beyond the full comprehension of outsiders. Difference becomes an inaccessible preciousness toward which outsiders are expected to be simply and uncomprehendingly reverential. But beware: In this world, even the insulated world of the college campus, preciousness is a balloon asking for a needle. At Smith College, graffiti appears: "Niggers, Spics, and Chinks quit complaining or get out."

Most of the white students I talked with spoke as if from under a faint cloud of accusation. There was always a ring of defensiveness in their complaints about blacks. A white student I spoke with at UCLA told me: "Most white students on this campus think the black student leadership here is made up of oversensitive crybabies who spend all their time looking for things to kick up a ruckus about." A white student at Stanford said: "Blacks do nothing but complain and ask for sympathy when everyone really knows they don't do well because they don't try. If they worked harder, they could do as well as everyone else."

That these students felt accused was most obvious in their compulsion to assure me that they were not racists. Oblique versions of some-of-my-best-friends-are stories came ritualistically before or after critiques of black students. Some said flatly, "I am not a racist, but . . . ." Of course, we all deny being racists, but we only do this compulsively, I think, when we are working against an accusation of bias. I think it was the color of my skin, itself, that accused them.

This was the meta-message that surrounded these conversations like an aura, and in it, I believe, is the core of white American racial anxiety. My skin not only accused them, it judged them. And this judgment was a sad gift of history that brought them to account whether they deserved such an accounting or not. It said that wherever and whenever blacks were concerned, they had reason to feel guilt. And whether it was earned or unearned, I think it was guilt that set off the compulsion in these students to disclaim. I believe it is true that in America black people make white people feel guilty.

Guilt is the essence of white anxiety, just as inferiority is the essence of black anxiety. And the terror that it carries for whites is the terror of discovering that one has reason to feel guilt where blacks are concerned — not so much because of what blacks might think but because of what guilt can say about oneself. If the darkest fear of blacks is inferiority, the darkest fear of whites is that their better lot in life is at least partially the result of their capacity for evil — their capacity to dehumanize an entire people for their own benefit, and then to be indifferent to the devastation their dehumanization has wrought on successive generations of their victims. This is the terror that whites are vulnerable to regarding blacks. And the mere fact of being white is sufficient to feel it, since even whites with hearts clean of racism benefit from being white — benefit at the expense of blacks. This is a conditional guilt having nothing to do with individual intentions or actions. And it makes for a very powerful anxiety because it threatens whites with a view of themselves as inhuman, just as inferiority threatens blacks with a similar view of themselves. At the dark core of both anxieties is a suspicion of incomplete humanity.

So the white students I met were not just meeting me; they were also 35 meeting the possibility of their own inhumanity. And this, I think, is what explains how some young white college students in the late Eighties can so frankly take part in racially insensitive and outright racist acts. They were expected to be cleaner of racism than any previous generation — they were born into the Great Society. But this expectation overlooks the fact that, for them, color is still an accusation and judgment. In black faces there is a discomforting reflection of white collective shame. Blacks remind them that their racial innocence is questionable, that they are the beneficiaries of past and present racism, and that the sins of the father may well have been visited on the children.

And yet young whites tell themselves that they had nothing to do with the oppression of black people. They have a stronger belief in their racial innocence than any previous generation of whites, and a natural hostility toward anyone who would challenge that innocence. So (with a great deal of individual variation) they can end up in the paradoxical position of being hostile to blacks as a way of defending their own racial innocence.

I think this is what the young white editors of the *Dartmouth Review* were doing when they shamelessly harassed William Cole, a black music professor. Weren't they saying, in effect, I am so free of racial guilt that I can afford to ruthlessly attack blacks and still be racially innocent? The ruthlessness of that attack was a form of denial, a badge of innocence. The more they were charged with racism, the more ugly and confrontational their harassment became. Racism became a means of rejecting racial guilt, a way of showing that they were not ultimately racists.

The politics of difference sets up a struggle for innocence among all groups. When difference is the currency of power, each group must fight for the innocence that entitles it to power. Blacks sting whites with guilt, remind them of their racist past, accuse them of new and more subtle forms of racism. One way whites retrieve their innocence is to discredit blacks and deny their difficulties, for in this denial is the denial of their own guilt. To blacks this denial looks like racism, a racism that feeds black innocence and encourages them to throw more guilt at whites. And so the cycle continues. The politics of difference leads each group to pick at the sore spots of the other.

Men and women who run universities—whites, mostly—also participate in the politics of difference, although they handle their guilt differently than many of their students. They don't deny it, but still they don't want to *feel* it. And to avoid this *feeling* of guilt they have tended to go along with whatever blacks put on the table rather than work with them to assess their real needs. University administrators have too often been afraid of their own guilt and have relied on negotiation and capitulation more to appease that guilt than to help blacks and other minorities. Administrators would never give white students a racial theme house where they could be "more comfortable with people of their own kind," yet more and more universities are doing this for black students, thus fostering a kind of voluntary segregation. To avoid the anxieties of integrated situations, blacks ask for theme houses; to avoid guilt, white administrators give them theme houses.

When everyone is on the run from his anxieties about race, race relations on campus can be reduced to the negotiation of avoidances. A pattern of demand and concession develops in which each side uses the other to escape itself. Black studies departments, black deans of student affairs, black counseling programs, Afro houses, black theme houses, black homecoming dances and graduation ceremonies—black students and white administrators have slowly engineered a machinery of separatism that, in the name of sacred difference, redraws the ugly lines of segregation. 40

Black students have not sufficiently helped themselves, and universities, despite all their concessions, have not really done much for blacks. If both faced their anxieties, I think they would see the same thing: Academic parity with all other groups should be the overriding mission of black students, and it should also be the first goal that universities have for their black students. Blacks can only *know* they are as good as others when they are, in fact, as good—when their grades are higher and their dropout rate lower. Nothing under the sun will substitute for this, and no amount of concessions will bring it about.

Universities and colleges can never be free of guilt until they truly help black students, which means leading and challenging them rather than negotiating and capitulating. It means inspiring them to achieve academic parity, nothing less, and helping them see their own weaknesses as their greatest challenge. It also means dismantling the machinery of separatism, breaking the link between difference and power, and skewing the formula for entitlement away from race and gender and back to constitutional rights.

As for the young white students who have rediscovered swastikas and the word "nigger," I think they suffer from an exaggerated sense of their own innocence, as if they were incapable of evil and beyond the reach of guilt. But it is also true that the politics of difference creates an environment which threatens their innocence and makes them defensive. White students are not invited to the negotiating table from which they see blacks and others walk away with concessions. The presumption is that they do not deserve to be there because they are white. So they can only be defensive, and the less mature among them will be aggressive. Guerrilla activity will ensue. Of course this is wrong, but it is also a reflection of an environment where difference carries power and where whites have the wrong "difference."

I think universities should emphasize commonality as a higher value than "diversity" and "pluralism"—buzzwords for the politics of difference. Difference that does not rest on a clearly delineated foundation of commonality not only is inaccessible to those who are not part of the ethnic or racial group but is antagonistic to them. Difference can enrich only the common ground.

Integration has become an abstract term today, having to do with little   45
more than numbers and racial balances. But it once stood for a high and admirable set of values. It made difference second to commonality, and it asked members of all races to face whatever fears they inspired in each other. I doubt the word will have a new vogue, but the values, under whatever name, are worth working for.

For Discussion

1. Steele claims that "racial tension on campus [now] is the result more of racial equality than inequality" (paragraph 6). How does he support this contention? Do you find it convincing? Why or why not? Test his assertion against what you see around you. Are blacks and other minorities treated equally on your campus?

2. Steele has much to say about what he calls a "politics of difference" (paragraph 8) on college campuses. How exactly does he depict it? In paragraphs 26–30, he presents an argument against it. What reasons make up the case? Judging from what you know of American history, is this politics of difference new? Is it restricted to college campuses?

3. How does Steele view the influence of black power? Do you find it persuasive? Why or why not?
4. How does Steele explain the anxieties of black and white students? Do you agree that "[a]t the dark core of both anxieties is a suspicion of incomplete humanity" (paragraph 34)? How might this diagnosis apply to women on campus? to gay men and lesbians? to minority races other than blacks?

For Research, Discussion, and Convincing

Conduct research as Steele did—by interviewing students. (Chapter 5 provides guidelines for conducting interviews.) Talk to members of all races and significant ethnic groups on your campus. Pose the kind of questions Steele did, along with any questions his conclusions suggest to you. Record or take careful notes about what your interviewees say. Then meet as a class and discuss how to interpret and explain the responses.

Finally, write an essay about some aspect of difference on your campus— it need not be black versus white. Attempt, as Steele does, to get to "the hidden internality of things" (paragraph 5), the deeper sources of tension and anxiety. Propose ways to cope better with the aspect of difference you isolate for analysis.

The Distribution of Distress
Patricia J. Williams

The previous selection explored the "new racism" on campus; this one takes us from the campus to society at large and explores prejudice of several kinds, some of it masked so well that we do not recognize it as prejudice. Chief among these is classism, *prejudice based not on skin color or ethnic origin but on socioeconomic differences. If, as the American social critic H. L. Mencken contended, class is the "dirty little secret" of American life, this author tells it eloquently and memorably.*

Patricia Williams is a law professor, columnist for The Nation, *and author of* Seeing a Color-Blind Future: The Paradox of Race *(1997), from which the following selection comes.*

Many years ago, I was standing in a so-called juice bar in Berkeley, California. A young man came in whom I had often seen begging in the neighborhood. A more bruised-looking human one could not imagine: he was missing several teeth, his clothes were in rags, his blond hair was matted, his eyes red-rimmed, his nails long and black and broken. On this particular morning he came into the juice bar and ordered some sort of protein drink from the well-scrubbed, patchouli-scented young woman behind the counter. It was obvious that his presence disturbed her, and when he took his drink and mumbled, "Thanks, little lady," she exploded.

"Don't you dare call me 'little lady'!" she snarled with a ferocity that turned heads. "I'm a *woman* and you'd better learn the difference!"

"Sorry," he whispered with his head bowed, like a dog that had been kicked, and he quite literally limped out of the store.

"Good riddance," the woman called after him.

This took place some fifteen years ago, but I have always remembered the interchange because it taught me a lot about the not so subliminal messages that can be wrapped in the expression of Virtue Aggrieved, in which antibias of one sort is used to further the agenda of bias of another kind.

In an abstract sense, I understood the resentment for girlish diminutives. Too often as a lawyer I have been in courtroom situations where coy terms of endearment were employed in such a way that "the little lady, God-bless-her" became a marginalizing condescension, a precise condensation of "She thinks she's a lawyer, poor thing." Yet in this instance, gender power was clearly not the issue, but rather the emotional venting of a revulsion at this man's dirty and bedraggled presence. It wasn't just that he had called her a little lady; she seemed angry that he had dared address her at all.

If, upon occasion, the ploughshare of feminism can be beaten into a sword of class prejudice, no less can there be other examples of what I call battling biases, in which the impulse to antidiscrimination is defeated by the intrusion or substitution of a different object of enmity. This revolving door of revulsions is one of the trickiest mechanisms contributing to the enduring nature of prejudice; it is at heart, I suppose, a kind of traumatic reiteration of injurious encounters, preserving even as it transforms the overall history of rage.

I was in England several years ago when a young Asian man was severely beaten in East London by a young white man. I was gratified to see the immediate renunciation of racism that ensued in the media. It was a somewhat more sophisticated and heartfelt collective self-examination than sometimes occurs in the United States in the wake of such incidents, where, I fear, we are much more jaded about all forms of violence. Nevertheless, what intrigued me most about the media coverage of this assault was the unfortunate way in which class bias became a tool for the denunciation of racism.

"Racial, Ethnic, or Religious Prejudice Is Repugnant," screamed the headlines.

Hooray, I thought.

And then the full text: "It is repugnant, *particularly*"—and I'm embellishing here—"when committed by a miserable low-class cockney whose bestial nature knows no plummeted depth, etc. etc."

Oh dear, I thought.

In other words, the media not only defined anti-Asian and anti-immigrant animus as ignorance, as surely it is, but went on to define that ignorance as the property of a class, of "the" lower classes, implying even that a good Oxbridge education inevitably lifts one above that sort of thing. As surely it does not.

And therein lies a problem, I think. If race or ethnicity is not a synonym for either ignorance or foreignness, then neither should class be an explanatory trashbin for racial prejudice, domestic incivility, and a host of other social ills. If the last fifty years have taught us nothing else, it is that our "isms" are no less insidious when beautifully polished and terribly refined.

None of us is beyond some such pitfalls, and in certain contexts typecasting can even be a necessary and helpful way of explaining the social world. The hard task is to untangle the instances where the categoric helps us predict and prepare for the world from those instances where it verges on scapegoating, projection, and prejudice.

To restate the problem, I think that the persistence of racism, ethnic and religious intolerance, as well as gender and class bias, is dependent upon recirculating images in which the general and the particular duel each other endlessly.

"*En garde*, you heathenish son of an inferior category!"

"Brute!" comes the response. "I am inalienably endowed with the unique luminosity of my rational individualism; it is you who are the guttural eruption of an unspeakable subclassification. . . ."

Thrust and parry, on and on, the play of race versus ethnicity versus class versus blood feud. One sword may be sharper or quicker, but neither's wound is ever healed.

Too often these tensions are resolved simply by concluding that stereotyping is just our lot as humans so let the consequences fall where they may. But stereotyping operates as habit not immutable trait, a fluid project that rather too easily flows across the shifting ecology of human relations. And racism is a very old, very bad habit.

This malleability of prejudice is underscored by a little cultural comparison. If class bias has skewed discussions of racism in the British examples I have just described, it is rather more common in the United States for race to consume discussions of class altogether. While I don't want to overstate the cultural differences between the United States and the United Kingdom—there is enough similarity to conclude that race and class present a generally interlocking set of problems in both nations—the United States does deem itself classless with almost the same degree of self-congratulation that the United Kingdom prides itself on being largely free of a history of racial bias. Certainly these are good impulses and desirable civic sentiments, but I am always one to look closely at what is deemed beyond the pale. *It will never happen here.* [. . .] The noblest denials are at least as interesting study as the highest ideals.

Consider: for a supposedly classless society, the United States nevertheless suffers the greatest gap of any industrialized nation between its richest and poorest citizens. And there can be no more dramatic and ironic class consciousness than the Dickensian characteristics ascribed to those in the so-called underclass, as opposed to the rest—what are we to call them, the *over*class? Those who are deemed to have class versus those who are so far beneath the usual indicia of even lower class that they are deemed to have no class at all.

If this is not viewed by most Americans as a problem of class stasis, it is perhaps because class denominations are so uniformly understood to be stand-ins for race. The very term *underclass* is a *euphemism* for blackness, class operating as euphemism in that we Americans are an upbeat kind of people and class is usually thought to be an easier problem than race.

Middle-classness, on the other hand, is so persistently a euphemism for whiteness, that middle-class black people are sometimes described as "honorary whites" or as those who have been deracinated in some vaguely political sense. More often than I like to remember, I have been told that my opinion about this or that couldn't possibly be relevant to "real," "authentic" black people. Why? Simply because I don't sound like a Hollywood stereotype of the way black people are "supposed" to talk. "Speaking white" or "Talking black." No in-between. Speaking as a black person while sounding like a white person has, I have found, engendered some complicated sense of betrayal. *"You're* not black! You're not *white!"* No one seems particularly interested in the substantive ideas being expressed; but

20

everyone is caught up with the question of whether anyone should have to listen to a white-voiced black person.

It is in this way that we often talk about class and race such that we   25
sometimes end up talking about neither, because we insist on talking about race as though it were class and class as though it were race, and it's hard to see very clearly when the waters are so muddied with all that simile and metaphor.

By the same token, America is usually deemed a society in which the accent with which one speaks Does Not Matter. That is largely true, but it is not so where black accents are concerned. While there is much made of regional variations—New Yorkers, Minnesotans, and Southerners are the butts of a certain level of cheap satire—an accent deemed "black" is the one with some substantial risk of evoking outright discrimination. In fact, the speech of real black people ranges from true dialects to myriad patois, to regional accents, to specific syntactical twists or usages of vocabulary. Yet language identified as black is habitually flattened into some singularized entity that in turn becomes synonymous with ignorance, slang, big lips and sloppy tongues, incoherent ideas, and very bad—terribly unruly!—linguistic acts. Black speech becomes a cipher for all the other stereotypes associated with racial discrimination; the refusal to understand becomes rationalized by the assumption of incomprehensibility.

My colleague Professor Mari Matsuda has studied cases involving accent discrimination. She writes of lawsuits whose transcripts revealed an interesting paradox. One case featured a speaker whose accent had been declared incomprehensible by his employer. Nevertheless, his recorded testimony, copied down with no difficulty by the court reporter, revealed a parlance more grammatically accurate, substantively coherent, and syntactically graceful than any other speaker in the courtroom, including the judge. This paradox has always been the subject of some interest among linguists and sociolinguists, the degree to which language is understood in a way that is intimately linked to relations among speakers.

"Good day," I say to you. Do you see me as a genial neighbor, as part of your day? If so, you may be generously disposed to return the geniality with a hearty "Hale fellow, well met."

"Good day," I say. Do you see me as an impudent upstart the very sound of whose voice is an unwelcome intrusion upon your good day? If so, the greeting becomes an act of aggression; woe betide the cheerful, innocent upstart.

"Shall we consider race?" I say to you. If you are disposed to like me,   30
you might hear this as an invitation to a kind of conversation we have not shared before, a leap of faith into knowing more about each other.

"Shall we consider race?" I say. *Not* "Shall I batter you with guilt before we riot in the streets?" But only: "Shall we *consider* race?" Yet if I am that same upstart, the blood will have boiled up in your ears by now, and very shortly you will start to have tremors from the unreasonable audacity of my meddlesome presumption. Nothing I actually say will matter, for what matters is that I am out of place. [. . .]

This dynamic, this vital ingredient of the willingness to hear, is apparent in the contradiction of lower-status speech being simultaneously understood yet not understood. Why is the sound of black voices, the shape of black bodies so overwhelmingly agreeable, so colorfully comprehensible in some contexts, particularly in the sports and entertainment industries, yet deemed so utterly incapable of effective communication or acceptable presence when it comes to finding a job as a construction worker?

This is an odd conundrum, to find the sight and the sound of oneself a red flag. And it is a kind of banner, one's face and one's tongue, a banner of family and affiliation—that rhythm and stress, the buoyance of one's mother's tongue; that plane of jaw, that prominence of brow, the property of one's father's face. What to make of those social pressures that would push the region of the body underground in order to allow the purity of one's inner soul to be more fully seen? When Martin Luther King, Jr., urged that we be judged by the content of our character, surely he meant that what we looked like should not matter. Yet just as surely that enterprise did not involve having to deny the entirely complicated symbolic character of one's physical manifestation. This is a hard point, I confess, and one fraught with risk of misunderstanding. The color of one's skin is a part of ourselves. It does not matter. It is precious, and yet it should not matter; it is important and yet it must not matter. It is simultaneously our greatest vanity and anxiety, and I am of the opinion, like Martin Luther King, that none of this should matter.

Yet let me consider the question of self-erasure. I've written elsewhere about my concern that various forms of biotechnological engineering have been turned to such purposes—from skin lighteners to cosmetic surgery to the market for sperm with blond hair and eggs with high IQs. Consider the boy I read about who had started some sort of computer magazine for children. A young man of eleven, celebrated as a computer whiz, whose family had emigrated from Puerto Rico, now living in New York. The article recounted how much he loved computers because, he said, nobody judged him for what he looked like, and he could speak without an accent. What to make of this freedom as disembodiment, this technologically purified mental communion as escape from the society of others, as neutralized social space. What a delicate project, this looking at each other, seeing yet not staring. Would we look so hard, judge so hard, be so hard—what would we look like?—if we existed unself-consciously in our bodies—sagging, gray-haired, young, old, black, white, balding and content?

Let me offer a more layered illustration of the way in which these issues of race and class interact, the markers of class distinction and bias in the United Kingdom emerging also in the United States as overlapping substantially with the category of race. A few years ago, I purchased a house.   35

Because the house was in a different state than where I was located at the time, I obtained my mortgage by telephone. I am a prudent little squirrel when it comes to things financial, always tucking away sufficient stores of nuts for the winter, and so I meet all the criteria of a quite good credit risk. My loan was approved almost immediately.

A short time after, the contract came in the mail. Among the papers the bank forwarded were forms documenting compliance with what is called the Fair Housing Act. It is against the law to discriminate against black people in the housing market, and one of the pieces of legislation to that effect is the Fair Housing Act, a law that monitors lending practices to prevent banks from doing what is called "red-lining." Red-lining is a phenomenon whereby banks circle certain neighborhoods on the map and refuse to lend in those areas for reasons based on race. There are a number of variations on the theme. Black people cannot get loans to purchase homes in white areas; or black people cannot get start-up money for small businesses in black areas. The Fair Housing Act thus tracks the race of all banking customers to prevent such discrimination. Unfortunately, some banks also use the racial information disclosed on the Fair Housing forms to engage in precisely the discrimination the law seeks to prevent.

I should repeat that to this point my entire mortgage transaction had been conducted by telephone. I should also say that I speak what is considered in the States a very Received-Standard-English, regionally northeastern perhaps, but not marked as black. With my credit history, with my job as a law professor, and no doubt with my accent, I am not only middle-class but match the cultural stereotype of a good white person. It is thus perhaps that the loan officer of this bank, whom I had never met in person, had checked off a box on the Fair Housing form indicating that I *was* "white."

Race shouldn't matter, I suppose, but it seemed to in this case, and so I took a deep breath, crossed out "white," checked the box marked "black," and sent the contract back to the bank. That will teach them to presume too much, I thought. A done deal, I assumed.

Suddenly said deal came to a screeching halt. The bank wanted more money as a down payment, they wanted me to pay more points, they wanted to raise the rate of interest. Suddenly I found myself facing great resistance and much more debt.

What was most interesting about all this was that the reason the bank   40
gave for its newfound recalcitrance was not race, heaven forbid—racism doesn't exist anymore, hadn't I heard? No, the reason they gave was that property values in that neighborhood were suddenly falling. They wanted more money to cover the increased risk.

Initially, I was surprised, confused. The house was in a neighborhood that was extremely stable; prices in the area had not gone down since World War II, only slowly, steadily up. I am an extremely careful shopper and I had uncovered absolutely no indication that prices were falling at all.

It took my real estate agent to make me see the light. "Don't you get it," he sighed. "This is what they always do."

And even though I work with this sort of thing all the time, I really hadn't gotten it: for of course, *I* was the reason the prices were in peril.

The bank was proceeding according to demographic data that show any time black people move into a neighborhood in the States, whites are overwhelmingly likely to move out. In droves. In panic. In concert. Pulling every imaginable resource with them, from school funding to garbage collection to social workers who don't want to work in black neighborhoods to police whose too frequent relation to black communities is a corrupted one of containment rather than protection.

It's called a tipping point, this thing that happens when black people move into white neighborhoods. The imagery is awfully catchy you must admit: the neighborhood just tipping right on over like a terrible accident, whoops! Like a pitcher I suppose. All that nice fresh wholesome milk spilling out, running away [. . .] leaving the dark, echoing, upended urn of the inner city.   45

This immense fear of "the black" next door is one reason the United States is so densely segregated. Only two percent of white people have a black neighbor, even though black people constitute approximately thirteen percent of the population. White people fear black people in big ways, in small ways, in financial ways, in utterly incomprehensible ways.

As for my mortgage, I threatened to sue and eventually procured the loan on the original terms. But what was fascinating to me about this whole incident was the way in which it so exemplified the new problems of the new rhetoric of racism. For starters, the new rhetoric of racism never mentions race. It wasn't race but risk with which the bank was concerned. Second, since financial risk is all about economics, my exclusion got reclassified as just a consideration of class, and there's no law against class discrimination, after all, for that would present a restraint on one of our most precious liberties, the freedom to contract or not. If public schools, trains, buses, swimming pools, and neighborhoods remain segregated, it's no longer a racial problem if someone who just happens to be white keeps hiking the price for someone who just accidentally and purely by the way happens to be black. White people set higher prices for the "right," the "choice" of self-segregation. If black people don't move in, it's just that they can't *afford* to. Black people pay higher prices for the attempt to integrate, even as the integration of oneself is a threat to one's investment by lowering its value.

By this measure of mortgage worthiness, the ingredient of blackness is cast not just as a social toll but as an actual tax. A fee, an extra contribution at the door, an admission charge for the higher costs of handling my dangerous propensities, my inherently unsavory properties. I was not judged based on my independent attributes or individual financial worth as a client; nor even was I judged by statistical profiles of what my group actually do. (For, in fact, anxiety-stricken, middle-class black people make grovelingly good cake-baking neighbors when not made to feel defensive by the unfortunate, historical welcome strategies of bombs, burnings, or abandon.)

Rather, I was being evaluated based on what an abstraction of White Society writ large thinks we — or I — do, and that imagined "doing" was treated and thus established as a self-fulfilling prophecy.

However rationalized, this form of discrimination is a burden: one's   50
very existence becomes a lonely vacuum when so many in society not only devalue *me*, but devalue *themselves* and their homes for having me as part of the landscaped view from the quiet of their breakfast nook.

I know, I know, I exist in the world on my own terms surely. I am an individual and all that. But if I carry the bank's logic out with my individuality rather than my collectively imagined effect on property values as the subject of this type of irrational economic computation, then *I*, the charming and delightful Patricia J. Williams, become a bit like a car wash in your backyard. Only much worse in real price terms. I am more than a mere violation of the nice residential comfort zone in question; my blackness can rezone altogether by the mere fortuity of my relocation.

"Dumping district," cringes the nice, clean actuarial family next door; "there goes the neighborhood . . ." as whole geographic tracts slide into the chasm of impecuniousness and disgust. I am the economic equivalent of a medical waste disposal site, a toxic heap-o'-home.

In my brand-new house, I hover behind my brand-new kitchen curtains, wondering whether the very appearance of my self will endanger my collateral yet further. When Benetton ran an advertisement that darkened Queen Elizabeth II's skin to a nice rich brown, the *Sun* newspaper ran an article observing that this "obviously cheapens the monarchy." Will the presentation of my self so disperse the value of my own, my ownership, my property?

This is madness, I am sure, as I draw the curtain like a veil across my nose. In what order of things is it *rational* to thus hide and skulk?

It is an intolerable logic. An investment in my property compels a   55
selling of myself.

I grew up in a white neighborhood where my mother's family had been the only black people for about fifty years. In the 1960s, Boston began to feel the effects of the great migration of Southern blacks to the north that came about as a result of the Civil Rights Movement. Two more black families moved into the neighborhood. There was a sudden churning, a chemical response, a collective roiling with streams of froth and jets of steam. We children heard all about it on the playground. The neighborhood was under siege. The blacks were coming. My schoolmates' parents were moving out *en masse*.

It was remarkable. The neighborhood was entirely black within about a year.

I am a risk pool. I am a car wash.

I was affected, I suppose, growing up with those children who frightened themselves by imagining what it would be like to touch black bodies, to kiss those wide unkissable lips, to draw the pure breath of life through that crude and forbidden expanse of nose; is it really possible that a gentle God — their God, dear God — would let a *human* heart reside within the wet charred thickness of black skin?

I am, they told me, a jumble of discarded parts: low-browed monkey bones and infected, softly pungent flesh.

60

In fact, my price on the market is a variable affair. If I were crushed and sorted into common elements, my salt and juice and calcinated bits are worth approximately five English pounds. Fresh from the kill, in contrast, my body parts, my lungs and liver, heart and healthy arteries, would fetch some forty thousand. There is no demand for the fruit of my womb, however; eggs fresh from their warm dark sanctuary are worthless on the open market. "Irish Egg Donor Sought," reads an ad in the little weekly newspaper that serves New York City's parent population. And in the weird economy of bloodlines, and with the insidious variability of prejudice, "Irish eggs" command a price of upwards of five thousand pounds.

This silent market in black worth is pervasive. When a certain brand of hiking boots became popular among young people in Harlem, the manufacturer pulled the product from inner-city stores, fearing that such a trend would "ruin" the image of their boot among the larger market of whites.

It's funny . . . even shoes.

Last year I had a funny experience in a shoe store. The salesman would bring me only one shoe, not two.

"I can't try on a pair?" I asked in disbelief.

65

"When you pay for a pair," he retorted. "What if there were a hundred of you," he continued. "How would we keep track?"

I was the only customer in the store, but there were a hundred of me in his head.

In our Anglo-American jurisprudence there is a general constraint limiting the right to sue to cases and controversies affecting the individual. As an individual, I could go to the great and ridiculous effort of suing for the minuscule amount at stake in waiting for the other shoe to drop from his hand; but as for the real claim, the group claim, the larger defamation to all those other hundreds of me . . . well, that will be a considerably tougher row to hoe.

I am one, I am many.

I am amiable, orderly, extremely honest, and a very good neighbor indeed. I am suspect profile, market cluster, actuarial monster, statistical being.

70

My particulars battle the generals.

"Typecasting!" I protest.
"Predictive indicator," assert the keepers of the gate.
"Prejudice!" I say.
"Precaution," they reply.   75
Hundreds, even thousands, of me hover in the breach.

For Discussion

1. Williams opens her essay with two examples of what she calls "battling biases," one kind of enmity substituting for another. Have you witnessed "this revolving door of revulsions" yourself? When? Under what circumstances? Did you recognize the prejudice of the person resisting prejudice or not?

2. "[I]n certain contexts," Williams says, "typecasting can be a necessary and helpful way of explaining the social world." What contexts? Can you offer examples of when typecasting was necessary and useful? When does typecasting verge "on scapegoating, projection, and prejudice"?

3. Williams alleges that, in contrast to Britain, a very class-conscious society, in the United States "it is rather more common . . . for race to consume discussions of class altogether." Do you see her point in your own experience? Why might class prejudice mask itself as race prejudice in the United States?

4. Williams says that accent prejudice — judging people based on their speech, which often reveals regional and class origins — is more a problem for blacks than for other races. Can you think of examples of stereotyping based on speech differences involving other races? How did the stereotypes affect your behavior?

For Research and Inquiry

Much has been written in recent years about the problems of the black middle class, the forty percent or so of African-Americans whom most would say are relatively well off. Williams gives us some insight into the tensions and conflicts of black middle-class life, but let's find out more by reading some of the literature and discussing these problems openly with students from all racial and social backgrounds.

What does the literature identify as sources of problems? Are the difficulties serious? Are they essentially different from the struggles of the white majority or from other minorities? If so, how exactly? Are the problems temporary, or are they likely to remain problems for many years to come? What strategies do blacks use to cope with their situation? Does the rest of middle-class America need to be aware of the resentments of black members of their class? Would awareness by itself be helpful?

Compare what the literature says with your own experience or the experiences of classmates whose backgrounds might provide special insight into the issue and questions.

After full class discussion, write an essay offering a tentative "reading"— that is, interpretation — of black middle-class consciousness. Consider especially the future: Will race/class problems be different from those faced by your parents?

For Further Research and Discussion

1. For most of U.S. history, racial conflict stemmed from the unequal balance of power between white Europeans on the one hand and Native Americans, blacks, and Hispanics on the other. But more recently, racial tensions have been complicated by the influx of many new racial and ethnic minorities. Who are they? What do you know about them?

   Divide the class into groups, and with your group do intensive research on one of the United States' new minorities; summarize the results of your group research to the rest of the class. Then ask, How do the background and conditions of these new minorities resemble those of the older ones? How are they unique?

2. Much has been written about the breakdown of the American family — especially the black family. Find out as much as you can about what is happening to the black family and why. How much of our present racial problems can be traced to the virtual disappearance of the traditional family, especially in urban ghettos?

Additional Suggestions for Writing

1. *Persuading.* Much has been written about so-called voluntary segregation, such as the black theme houses Steele mentions. Write an essay for your school paper or some other suitable publication arguing for or against such theme houses.

2. *Inquiry.* Examine yourself for traces of racism, new or old. In what ways and to what degree are you guilty of race stereotyping, avoiding people of other races, and so forth? Do you sometimes feel the "racial anxiety" that Steele found in both black and white students? Where did you acquire whatever residual racism you have? What can you do to overcome it? What should universities do to help students and professors recognize and cope with latent racism?

Appendix

A Short Guide to Editing and Proofreading

Editing and proofreading are the final steps in creating a finished piece of writing. Too often, however, these steps are rushed as writers race to meet a deadline. Ideally, you should distinguish between the acts of revising, editing, and proofreading. Because each step requires that you pay attention to something different, you cannot reasonably expect to do them well if you try to do them all at once.

www.mhhe. com/crusius

For a wealth of editing resources, go to:
Editing

Our suggestions for revising appear in each of Chapters 6–9 on the aims of argument. *Revising* means shaping and developing the whole argument with an eye to audience and purpose; when you revise, you are ensuring that you have accomplished your aim. *Editing,* on the other hand, means making smaller changes within paragraphs and sentences. When you edit, you are thinking about whether your prose will be a pleasure to read. Editing improves the sound and rhythm of your voice. It makes complicated ideas more accessible to readers and usually makes your writing more concise. Finally, *proofreading* means eliminating errors. When you proofread, you correct everything you find that will annoy readers, such as misspellings, punctuation mistakes, and faulty grammar.

In this appendix, we offer some basic advice on what to look for when editing and proofreading. For more detailed help, consult a handbook on grammar and punctuation and a good book on style, such as Joseph Williams's *Ten Lessons in Clarity and Grace* or Richard Lanham's *Revising Prose.* Both of these texts guided our thinking in the advice that follows.

EDITING

Most ideas can be phrased in a number of ways, each of which gives the idea a slightly distinctive twist. Consider the following examples:

www.mhhe. com/crusiu

To take a diagnostic test covering editing skills, go to:
Editing >
Diagnostic Test

In New York City, about 74,000 people die each year.

In New York City, death comes to one in a hundred people each year.

Death comes to one in a hundred New Yorkers each year.

A1

To begin an article on what becomes of the unknown and unclaimed dead in New York, Edward Conlon wrote the final of these three sentences. We can only speculate about the possible variations he considered, but because openings are so crucial, he almost certainly cast these words quite deliberately.

For most writers, such deliberation over matters of style occurs during editing. In this late stage of the writing process, writers examine choices made earlier, perhaps unconsciously, while drafting and revising. They listen to how sentences sound, to patterns of rhythm both within and among sentences. Editing is like an art or craft; it can provide you the satisfaction of knowing you've said something gracefully and effectively. To focus on language this closely, you will need to set aside enough time following the revision step.

In this section, we discuss some things to look for when editing your own writing. Don't forget, though, that editing does not always mean looking for weaknesses. You should also recognize passages that work well just as you wrote them, that you can leave alone or play up more by editing passages that surround them.

Editing for Clarity and Conciseness

Even drafts revised several times may have wordy and awkward passages; these are often places where a writer struggled with uncertainty or felt less than confident about the point being made. Introductions often contain such passages. In editing, you have one more opportunity to clarify and sharpen your ideas.

Express Main Ideas Forcefully

Emphasize the main idea of a sentence by stating it as directly as possible, using the two key sentence parts (*subject* and *verb*) to convey the two key parts of the idea (*agent* and *act*).

As you edit, first look for sentences that state ideas indirectly rather than directly; such sentences may include (1) overuse of the verb *to be* in its various forms (*is, was, will have been,* and so forth), (2) the opening words "There is . . ." or "It is . . . ," (3) strings of prepositional phrases, or (4) many vague nouns. Then ask, "What is my true subject here, and what is that subject's action?" Here is an example of a weak, indirect sentence:

> It is a fact that the effects of pollution are more evident in lower-class neighborhoods than in middle-class ones.

The writer's subject is pollution. What is the pollution's action? Limply, the sentence tells us its "effects" are "evident." The following edited version makes pollution the agent that performs the action of a livelier verb, "fouls." The edited sentence is more specific—without being longer.

> *Pollution* more frequently *fouls* the air, soil, and water of lower-class neighborhoods than of middle-class ones.

Editing Practice   The following passage about a plan for creating low-income housing contains two weak sentences. In this case, the weakness results from wordiness. (Note the overuse of vague nouns and prepositional phrases.) Decide what the true subject is for each sentence, and make that word the subject of the verb. Your edited version should be much shorter.

> As in every program, there will be the presence of a few who abuse the system. However, as in other social programs, the numbers would not be sufficient to justify the rejection of the program on the basis that one person in a thousand will try to cheat.

Choose Carefully between Active and Passive Voice

Active voice and passive voice indicate different relationships between subjects and verbs. As we have noted, ideas are usually clearest when the writer's true subject is also the subject of the verb in the sentence — that is, when it is the agent of the action. In the passive voice, however, the agent of the action appears in the predicate or not at all. Rather than acting as agent, the subject of the sentence *receives* the action of the verb.

www.mhhe.com/**crusius**

For more coverage of voice, go to: Editing > Verb and Voice Shifts

The following sentence is in the passive voice:

> The air of poor neighborhoods is often fouled by pollution.

There is nothing incorrect about the use of the passive voice in this sentence, and in the context of a whole paragraph, passive voice can be the most emphatic way to make a point. (Here, for example, it allows the word *pollution* to fall at the end of the sentence, a strong position.) But, often, use of the passive voice is not a deliberate choice at all; rather, it's a vague and unspecific way of stating a point.

Consider the following sentences, in which the main verbs have no agents:

> It *is believed* that dumping garbage at sea is not as harmful to the environment as *was* once *thought.*
>
> Ronald Reagan *was considered* the "Great Communicator."

Who thinks such dumping is not so harmful? environmental scientists? industrial producers? Who considered former president Reagan a great communicator? speech professors? news commentators? Such sentences are clearer when they are written in the active voice:

> Some environmentalists believe that dumping garbage at sea is not as harmful to the environment as they used to think.
>
> Media commentators considered Ronald Reagan the "Great Communicator."

In editing for the passive voice, look over your verbs. Passive voice is easily recognized because it always contains (1) some form of *to be* as a helping verb and (2) the main verb in its past participle form (which ends in -ed, -d, -t, -en, or -n, or in some cases may be irregular: *drunk, sung, lain,* and so on).

When you find a sentence phrased in the passive voice, decide who or what is performing the action; the agent may appear after the verb or not at all. Then decide if changing the sentence to the active voice will improve the sentence as well as the surrounding passage.

Editing Practice

1. The following paragraph from a student's argument needs to be edited for emphasis. It is choking with excess nouns and forms of the verb *to be*, some as part of passive constructions. You need not eliminate all passive voice, but do look for wording that is vague and ineffective. Your edited version should be not only stronger but shorter as well.

   > Although emergency shelters are needed in some cases (for example, a mother fleeing domestic violence), they are an inefficient means of dealing with the massive numbers of people they are bombarded with each day. The members of a homeless family are in need of a home, not a temporary shelter into which they and others like them are herded, only to be shuffled out when their thirty-day stay is over to make room for the next incoming herd. Emergency shelters would be sufficient if we did not have a low-income housing shortage, but what is needed most at present is an increase in availability of affordable housing for the poor.

2. Select a paragraph of your own writing to edit; focus on using strong verbs and subjects to carry the main idea of your sentences.

Editing for Emphasis

When you edit for emphasis, you make sure that your main ideas stand out so that your reader will take notice. Following are some suggestions to help.

Emphasize Main Ideas by Subordinating Less Important Ones

Subordination refers to distinctions in rank or order of importance. Think of the chain of command at an office: the boss is at the top of the ladder, the middle management is on a lower (subordinate) rung, the support staff is at an even lower rung, and so on.

In writing, subordination means placing less important ideas in less important positions in sentences in order to emphasize the main ideas that should stand out. Writing that lacks subordination treats all ideas equally; each idea may consist of a sentence of its own or may be joined to another idea by a coordinator (*and, but,* and *or*). Such a passage follows with its sentences numbered for reference purposes.

> (1) It has been over a century since slavery was abolished and a few decades since lawful, systematic segregation came to an unwilling halt. (2) Truly, blacks

have come a long way from the darker days that lasted for more than three centuries. (3) Many blacks have entered the mainstream, and there is a proportionately large contingent of middle-class blacks. (4) Yet an even greater percentage of blacks are immersed in truly pathetic conditions. (5) The inner-city black poor are enmeshed in devastating socioeconomic problems. (6) Unemployment among inner-city black youths has become much worse than it was even five years ago.

Three main ideas are important here—that blacks have been free for some time, that some have made economic progress, and that others are trapped in poverty—and of these three, the last is probably intended to be the most important. Yet, as we read the passage, these key ideas do not stand out. In fact, each point receives equal emphasis and sounds about the same, with the repeated subject-verb-object syntax. The result seems monotonous, even apathetic, though the writer is probably truly disturbed about the subject. The following edited version, which subordinates some of the points, is more emphatic. We have italicized the main points.

> *Blacks have come a long way* in the century since slavery was abolished and in the decades since lawful, systematic segregation came to an unwilling halt. Yet, although many blacks have entered the mainstream and the middle class, *an even greater percentage is immersed in truly pathetic conditions.* To give just one example of these devastating socioeconomic problems, *unemployment among inner-city black youths is much worse now than it was even five years ago.*

Although different editing choices are possible, this version plays down sentences 1, 3, and 5 in the original so that sentences 2, 4, and 6 stand out.

As you edit, look for passages that sound wordy and flat because all the ideas are expressed with equal weight in the same subject-verb-object pattern. Then single out your most important points, and try out some options for subordinating the less important ones. The key is to put main ideas in main clauses and modifying ideas in modifying clauses or phrases.

Modifying Clauses   Like simple sentences, modifying clauses contain a subject and verb. They are formed in two ways: (1) with relative pronouns and (2) with subordinating conjunctions.

Relative pronouns introduce clauses that modify nouns, with the relative pronoun relating the clause to the noun it modifies. There are five relative pronouns: *that, which, who, whose,* and *whom.* The following sentence contains a relative clause:

> Alcohol advertisers are trying to sell a product *that is by its very nature harmful to users.*
>
> —JASON RATH (student)

Relative pronouns may also be implied:

> I have returned the library book [that] *you loaned me.*

Relative pronouns may also be preceded by prepositions, such as *on, in, to,* or *during:*

> Drug hysteria has created an atmosphere *in which civil rights are disregarded.*

Subordinating conjunctions show relationships among ideas. It is impossible to provide a complete list of subordinating conjunctions in this short space, but here are the most common and the kinds of modifying roles they perform:

> To show time: *after, as, before, since, until, when, while*
>
> To show place: *where, wherever*
>
> To show contrast: *although, though, whereas, while*
>
> To show cause and effect: *because, since, so that*
>
> To show condition: *if, unless, whether, provided that*
>
> To show manner: *how, as though*

By introducing it with a subordinating conjunction, you can convert one sentence into a dependent clause that can modify another sentence. Consider the following two versions of the same idea:

> Pain is a state of consciousness, a "mental event." It can never be directly observed.

> *Since pain is a state of consciousness, a "mental event,"* it can never be directly observed.
>
> —Peter Singer, "Animal Liberation"

Modifying Phrases   Unlike clauses, phrases do not have a subject and a verb. Prepositional phrases and infinitive phrases are most likely already in your repertoire of modifiers. (Consult a handbook if you need to review these.) Here, we remind you of two other useful types of phrases: (1) participial phrases and (2) appositives.

Participial phrases modify nouns. Participles are created from verbs, so it is not surprising that the two varieties represent two verb tenses. The first is present participles ending in *-ing:*

> *Hoping to eliminate harassment on campus,* many universities have tried to institute codes for speech and behavior.

> The desperate Haitians fled here in boats, *risking all.*
>
> —Carmen Hazan-Cohen (student)

The second is past participles ending in *-ed, -en, -d, -t,* or *-n:*

> Women themselves became a resource, *acquired by men much as the land was acquired by men.*
>
> —Gerda Lerner

Linked more to the Third World and Asia than to the Europe of America's racial and cultural roots, Los Angeles and Southern California will enter the 21st century as a multi-racial and multicultural society.

—Ryszard Kapuscinski

Notice that modifying phrases should immediately precede the nouns they modify.

An *appositive* is a noun or noun phrase that restates another noun, usually in a more specific way. Appositives can be highly emphatic, but more often they are tucked into the middle of a sentence or added to the end, allowing a subordinate idea to be slipped in. When used like this, appositives are usually set off with commas:

Rick Halperin, *a professor at Southern Methodist University,* noted that Ted Bundy's execution cost Florida taxpayers over six million dollars.

—Diane Miller (student)

Editing Practice

1. Edit the following passage as needed for emphasis, clarity, and conciseness, using subordinate clauses, relative clauses, participial phrases, appositives, and any other options that occur to you. If some parts are effective as they are, leave them alone.

> The monetary implications of drug legalization are not the only reason it is worth consideration. There is reason to believe that the United States would be a safer place to live if drugs were legalized. A large amount of what the media has named "drug-related" violence is really prohibition-related violence. Included in this are random shootings and murders associated with black-market transactions. Estimates indicate that at least 40 percent of all property crime in the United States is committed by drug users so they can maintain their habits. That amounts to a total of 4 million crimes per year and $7.5 billion in stolen property. Legalizing drugs would be a step toward reducing this wave of crime.

2. Edit a paragraph of your own writing with an eye to subordinating less important ideas through the use of modifying phrases and clauses.

Vary Sentence Length and Pattern

Even when read silently, your writing has a sound. If your sentences are all about the same length (typically fifteen to twenty words) and all structured according to a subject-verb-object pattern, they will roll along with the monotonous rhythm of an assembly line. Obviously, one solution to this problem is to open some of your sentences with modifying phrases and clauses, as we discuss in the previous section. Here we offer some other strategies, all of which add emphasis by introducing something unexpected.

1. Use a short sentence after several long ones.

   [A] population's general mortality is affected by a great many factors over which doctors and hospitals have little influence. For those diseases and injuries for which modern medicine can affect the outcome, however, which country the patient lives in really matters. Life expectancy is not the same among developed countries for premature babies, for children born with spina bifida, or for people who have cancer, a brain tumor, heart disease, or chronic renal failure. *Their chances of survival are best in the United States.*

   —JOHN GOODMAN

2. Interrupt a sentence.

   The position of women in that hippie counterculture was, *as a young black male leader preached succinctly,* "prone."

   —BETTY FRIEDAN

   Symbols and myths —*when emerging uncorrupted from human experience*— are precious. Then it is the poetic voice and vision that informs and infuses —*the poet-warrior's, the prophet-seer's, the dreamer's*— reassuring us that truth is as real as falsehood. And ultimately stronger.

   —OSSIE DAVIS

3. Use an intentional sentence fragment. The concluding fragment in the previous passage by Ossie Davis is a good example.
4. Invert the order of subject-verb-object.

   Further complicating negotiations is the difficulty of obtaining relevant financial statements.

   —REGINA HERZLINGER

   This creature, with scarcely two thirds of man's cranial capacity, was a fire user. Of what it meant to him beyond warmth and shelter, we know nothing; with what rites, ghastly or benighted, it was struck or maintained, no word remains.

   —LOREN EISELEY

Use Special Effects for Emphasis

Especially in persuasive argumentation, you will want to make some of your points in deliberately dramatic ways. Remember that just as the crescendos stand out in music because the surrounding passages are less intense, so the special effects work best in rhetoric when you use them sparingly.

Repetition Deliberately repeating words, phrases, or sentence patterns has the effect of building up to a climactic point. In Chapter 8, we noted how Martin Luther King, Jr., in the emotional high point of his "Letter from Birmingham Jail," used repeated subordinate clauses beginning with the phrase "when you" to build up to his main point: ". . . then you will understand why we find it difficult to wait" (paragraph 14, page 237). Here is another example, from the conclusion of an argument linking women's rights with environmental reforms:

> Environmental justice goes much further than environmental protection, a passive and paternalistic phrase. *Justice requires that* industrial nations pay back the environmental debt incurred in building their wealth by using less of nature's resources. *Justice prescribes that* governments stop siting hazardous waste facilities in cash-poor rural and urban neighborhoods and now in the developing world. *Justice insists that* the subordination of women and nature by men is not only a hazard; it is a crime. *Justice reminds us that* the Earth does not belong to us; even when we "own" a piece of it, we belong to the Earth.
>
> —H. Patricia Hynes

Paired Coordinators   Coordinators are conjunctions that pair words, word groups, and sentences in a way that gives them equal emphasis and that also shows a relationship between them, such as contrast, consequence, or addition. In grade school, you may have learned the coordinators through the mnemonic *FANBOYS*, standing for *for, and, nor, but, or, yet, so.*

Paired coordinators emphasize the relationship between coordinated elements; the first coordinator signals that a corresponding coordinator will follow. Some paired coordinators are:

both _____ and _____

not _____ but _____

not only _____ but also _____

either _____ or _____

neither _____ nor _____

The key to effective paired coordination is to keep the words that follow the marker words as grammatically similar as possible. Pair nouns with nouns, verbs with verbs, prepositional phrases with prepositional phrases, and whole sentences with whole sentences. (Think of paired coordination as a variation on repetition.) Here are some examples:

> Feminist anger, or any form of social outrage, is dismissed breezily—*not* because it lacks substance *but* because it lacks "style."
>
> —Susan Faludi

> Alcohol ads that emphasize "success" in the business and social worlds are useful examples *not only* of how advertisers appeal to people's envy *but also* of how ads perpetuate gender stereotypes.
>
> —Jason Rath (student)

Emphatic Appositives   While an appositive (a noun or noun phrase that re-states another noun) can subordinate an idea, it can also emphasize an idea if it is placed at the beginning or the end of a sentence, where it will command attention. Here are some examples:

> *The poorest nation in the Western hemisphere,* Haiti is populated by six million people, many of whom cannot obtain adequate food, water, or shelter.
>
> — SNEED B. COLLARD III

> [Feminists] made a simple, though serious, ideological error when they applied the same political rhetoric to their own situation as women versus men: *too literal an analogy with class warfare, racial oppression.*
>
> — BETTY FRIEDAN

Note that at the end of a sentence, an appositive may be set off with a colon or a dash.

Emphatic Word Order   The opening and closing positions of a sentence are high-profile spots, not to be wasted on weak words. The following sentence, for example, begins weakly with the filler phrase "there are":

> *There are* several distinctions, all of them false, that are commonly made between rape and date rape.

A better version would read:

> My opponents make several distinctions between rape and date rape; all of these are false.

Even more important are the final words of every paragraph and the opening and closing of the entire argument.

Editing Practice

1. Select one or two paragraphs from a piece of published writing you have recently read and admired. Be ready to share it with the class, explaining how the writer has crafted the passage to make it work.
2. Take a paragraph or two from one of your previous essays, perhaps even an essay from another course, and edit it to improve clarity, conciseness, and emphasis.

Editing for Coherence

Coherence refers to what some people call the "flow" of writing; writing flows when the ideas connect smoothly, one to the next. In contrast, when writing is incoherent, the reader must work to see how ideas connect and must infer points that the writer, for whatever reason, has left unstated.

Incoherence is a particular problem with writing that contains an abundance of direct or indirect quotations. In using sources, be careful always to lead into the quotation with some words of your own, showing clearly how this new idea connects with what has come before.

Because finding incoherent passages in your own writing can be difficult, ask a friend to read your draft to look for gaps in the presentation of ideas. Here are some additional suggestions for improving coherence.

Move from Old Information to New Information

Coherent writing is easy to follow because the connections between old information and new information are clear. Sentences refer back to previously introduced information and set up reader expectations for new information to come. Notice how every sentence fulfills your expectations in the following excerpts from an argument on animal rights by Steven Zak.

> The credibility of the animal-rights viewpoint . . . need not stand or fall with the "marginal human beings" argument.

Next, you would expect to hear why animals do not have to be classed as "marginal human beings"—and you do:

> Lives don't have to be qualitatively the same to be worthy of equal respect.

At this point you might ask upon what else we should base our respect. Zak answers this question in the next sentence:

> One's perception that another life has value comes as much from an appreciation of its uniqueness as from the recognition that it has characteristics that are shared by one's own life.

Not only do these sentences fulfill reader expectations, but each also makes a clear connection by referring specifically to the key idea in the sentence before it, forming an unbroken chain of thought. We have italicized the words that accomplish this linkage and connected them with arrows.

> The credibility of the animal-rights viewpoint . . . need not stand or fall with the *"marginal human beings"* argument.
>
> Lives don't have to be *qualitatively the same* to be worthy of *equal respect.*
>
> One's perception that *another life has value* comes as much from an *appreciation of its uniqueness* as from the recognition that it has characteristics that are shared by one's own life.
>
> One can imagine that the lives of various kinds of animals *differ radically.* . . .

In the following paragraph, reader expectations are not so well fulfilled:

> We are presently witness to the greatest number of homeless families since the Great Depression of the 1930s. The cause of this phenomenon is a shortage of low-income housing. Mothers with children as young as two weeks are forced to live on the street because there is no room for them in homeless shelters.

While these sentences are all on the subject of homelessness, the second leads us to expect that the third will take up the topic of shortages of low-income housing. Instead, it takes us back to the subject of the first sentence and offers a different cause—no room in the shelters.

Looking for ways to link old information with new information will help you find problems of coherence in your own writing.

Editing Practice

1. In the following paragraph, underline the words or phrases that make the connections back to the previous sentence and forward to the next, as we did earlier with the passage from Zak.

   The affluent, educated, liberated women of the First World, who can enjoy freedoms unavailable to any women ever before, do not feel as free as they want to. And they can no longer restrict to the subconscious their sense that this lack of freedom has something to do with—with apparently frivolous issues, things that really should not matter. Many are ashamed to admit that such trivial concerns—to do with physical appearance, bodies, faces, hair, clothes—matter so much. But in spite of shame, guilt, and denial, more and more women are wondering if it isn't that they are entirely neurotic alone but rather that something important is indeed at stake that has to do with the relationship between female liberation and female beauty.

   —Naomi Wolf

2. The following student paragraph lacks coherence. Read through it, and put a slash (/) between sentences expressing unconnected ideas. You may try to rewrite the paragraph, rearranging sentences and adding ideas to make the connections tighter.

   Students may know what AIDS is and how it is transmitted, but most are not concerned about AIDS and do not perceive themselves to be at risk. But college-age heterosexuals are the number-one high-risk group for this disease (Gray and Sacarino 258). "Students already know about AIDS. Condom distribution, public or not, is not going to help. It just butts into my personal life," said one student surveyed. College is a time for exploration and that includes the discovery of sexual freedom. Students, away from home and free to make their own decisions for maybe the first time in their lives, have a "bigger than life" attitude. The thought of dying is the farthest from their minds. Yet at this point in their lives, they are most in need of this information.

Use Transitions to Show Relationships between Ideas

Coherence has to be built into a piece of writing; as we discussed earlier, the ideas between sentences must first cohere. However, sometimes readers need help in making the transition from one idea to the next, so you must provide signposts to help them see the connections more readily. For example, a transitional word like *however* can prepare readers for an idea in contrast to the one before it, as in the second sentence in this paragraph. Transitional words can also highlight the structure of an argument ("These data will show three things: first . . . , second . . . , and third . . ."), almost forming a verbal path for the reader to follow. Following are examples of transitional words and phrases and their purposes:

> To show order: *first, second, next, then, last, finally*
> To show contrast: *however, yet, but, nevertheless*
> To show cause and effect: *therefore, consequently, as a result, then*
> To show importance: *moreover, significantly*
> To show an added point: *as well, also, too*
> To show an example: *for example, for instance*
> To show concession: *admittedly*
> To show conclusion: *in sum, in conclusion*

The key to using transitional words is similar to the key to using special effects for emphasis: Don't overdo it. To avoid choking your writing with these words, anticipate where your reader will genuinely need them, and limit their use to these instances.

Editing Practice

Underline the transitional words and phrases in the following passage of published writing:

> When people believe that their problems can be solved, they tend to get busy solving them.
>   On the other hand, when people believe that their problems are beyond solution, they tend to position themselves so as to avoid blame. Take the woeful inadequacy of education in the predominantly black central cities. Does the black leadership see the ascendancy of black teachers, school administrators, and politicians as an asset to be used in improving those dreadful schools? Rarely. You are more likely to hear charges of white abandonment, white resistance to integration, conspiracies to isolate black children, even when the schools are officially desegregated. In short, white people are accused of being responsible for the problem. But if the youngsters manage to survive those awful school systems and achieve success, leaders want to claim credit. They don't hesitate to attribute that success to the glorious Civil Rights movement.
>
> —William Raspberry

PROOFREADING

Proofreading is truly the final step in writing a paper. After proofreading, you ought to be able to print your paper out one more time; but if you do not have time, most instructors will be perfectly happy to see the necessary corrections done neatly in ink on the final draft.

Following are some suggestions for proofreading.

Spelling Errors

www.mhhe.
com/**crusius**

For some advice
and practice
related to
spelling, go to:

Editing >
Spelling

If you have used a word processor, you may have a program that will check your spelling. If not, you will have to check your spelling by reading through again carefully with a dictionary at hand. Consult the dictionary whenever you feel uncertain. You might consider devoting a special part of your writer's notebook to your habitual spelling errors: some students always misspell *athlete,* for example, whereas others leave the second *n* out of *environment.*

Omissions and Jumbled Passages

Read your paper out loud. Physically shaping your lips around the words can help locate missing words, typos (*saw* instead of *was*), or the remnants of some earlier version of a sentence that did not get fully deleted. Place a caret (∧) in the sentence and write the correction or addition above the line, or draw a line through unnecessary text.

Punctuation Problems

Apostrophes and commas give writers the most trouble. If you have habitual problems with these, you should record your errors in your writer's notebook.

Apostrophes

www.mhhe.
com/**crusius**

For some
additional help
using apostrophes,
go to:

Editing >
Apostrophes

Apostrophe problems usually occur in forming possessives, not contractions, so here we discuss only the former. If you have problems with possessives, you may also want to consult a good handbook or seek a private tutorial with your instructor or your school's writing center.

Here are the basic principles to remember.

1. Possessive pronouns—*his, hers, yours, theirs, its*—never take an apostrophe.
2. Singular nouns become possessive by adding *-'s.*

   A single parent's life is hard.

   A society's values change.

   Do you like Mr. Voss's new car?

3. Plural nouns ending in *-s* become possessive by simply adding an apostrophe.

   Her parents' marriage is faltering.

   Many cities' air is badly polluted.

   The Joneses' house is up for sale.

4. Plural nouns that do not end in *-s* become possessive by adding *-'s.*

   Show me the women's (men's) room.

   The people's voice was heard.

If you err by using apostrophes where they don't belong in nonpossessive words ending in *-s*, remember that a possessive will always have a noun after it, not some other part of speech such as a verb or a preposition. You may even need to read each line of print with a ruler under it to help you focus more intently on each word.

Commas

Because commas indicate a pause, reading your paper aloud is a good way to decide where to add or delete them. A good handbook will elaborate on the following basic principles. The example sentences have been adapted from an argument by Mary Meehan, who opposes abortion.

www.mhhe.
com/**crusius**

For some
additional
coverage of
comma use,
go to:
Editing >
Commas

1. Use a comma when you join two or more main clauses with a coordinating conjunction.

    Main clause, conjunction (and, but, or, nor, so, yet) *main clause.*

    Feminists want to have men participate more in the care of children, but abortion allows a man to shift total responsibility to the woman.

2. Use a comma after an introductory phrase or dependent clause.

    Introductory phrase or clause, main clause.

    To save the smallest children, the Left should speak out against abortion.

3. Use commas around modifiers such as relative clauses and appositives unless they are essential to the noun's meaning. Be sure to put the comma at both ends of the modifier.

    _____ , *appositive,* _____

    _____ , *relative clause,* _____

    One member of the 1972 Presidential commission on population growth was Graciela Olivarez, a Chicana who was active in civil rights and anti-poverty work. Olivarez, who later was named to head the Federal Government's Community Services Administration, had known poverty in her youth in the Southwest.

4. Use commas with a series.

    _____x_____ , _____y_____ , and _____z_____ ,

    The traditional mark of the Left has been its protection of the underdog, the weak, and the poor.

Semicolons

Think of a semicolon as a strong comma. It has two main uses.

www.mhhe.
com/**crusius**

For more
coverage of
semicolons,
go to:
Editing >
Semicolons

1. Use a semicolon to join two main clauses when you choose not to use a conjunction. This works well when the two main clauses are closely related or parallel in structure.

Main clause; main clause.

Pro-life activists did not want abortion to be a class issue; they wanted to end abortion everywhere, for all classes.

As a variation, you may wish to add a transitional adverb to the second main clause. The adverb indicates the relationship between the main clauses, but it is not a conjunction, so a comma preceding it would not be correct.

Main clause; transitional adverb (however, therefore, thus, moreover, consequently), *main clause.*

When speaking with counselors at the abortion clinic, many women change their minds and decide against abortion; however, a woman who is accompanied by a husband or boyfriend often does not feel free to talk with the counselor.

2. Use semicolons between items in a series if any of the items themselves contain commas.

_____ , _____ ; _____ , _____ ; _____ , _____

A few liberals who have spoken out against abortion are Jesse Jackson, a Civil Rights leader; Richard Neuhaus, a theologian; the comedian Dick Gregory; and politicians Mark Hatfield and Mary Rose Oakar.

Colons

 www.mhhe. com/**crusius**

For some additional help using colons, go to:

Editing > Colons

The colon has two common uses.

1. Use a colon to introduce a quotation when both your own lead-in and the words quoted are complete sentences that can stand alone. (See the section in Chapter 5 entitled "Incorporating and Documenting Source Material in the Text of Your Argument" for more on introducing quotations.)

Main clause in your words: "Quoted sentence(s)."

Mary Meehan criticizes liberals who have been silent on abortion: "If much of the leadership of the pro-life movement is right-wing, that is due largely to the default of the Left."

2. Use a colon before an appositive that comes dramatically at the end of a sentence, especially if the appositive contains more than one item.

Main clause: appositive, appositive, and appositive.

Meehan argues that many pro-choice advocates see abortion as a way to hold down the population of certain minorities: blacks, Puerto Ricans, and other Latins.

Grammatical Errors

Grammatical mistakes can be hard to find, but once again we suggest reading aloud as one method of proofing for them; grammatical errors tend not to "sound right" even if they look like good prose. Another suggestion is to recognize your habitual errors and then look for particular grammatical structures that lead you into error.

Introductory Participial Phrases

Constructions such as these often lead writers to create dangling modifiers. To avoid this pitfall, see the discussion of participial phrases earlier in this appendix. Remember that an introductory phrase dangles if it is not immediately followed by the noun it modifies.

> *Incorrect:* Using her conscience as a guide, our society has granted each woman the right to decide if a fetus is truly a "person" with rights equal to her own.

(Notice that the implied subject of the participial phrase is "each woman," when in fact the subject of the main clause is "our society"; thus, the participial phrase does not modify the subject.)

> *Corrected:* Using her conscience as a guide, each woman in our society has the right to decide if a fetus is truly a "person" with rights equal to her own.

Paired Coordinators

If the words that follow each of the coordinators are not of the same grammatical structure, then an error known as nonparallelism has occurred. To correct this error, line up the paired items one over the other. You will see that the correction often involves simply adding a word or two to, or deleting some words from, one side of the paired coordinators.

> not only _____ but also _____

> *Incorrect:* Legal abortion not only protects women's lives, but also their health.

> *Corrected:* Legal abortion protects not only women's lives but also their health.

Split Subjects and Verbs

If the subject of a sentence contains long modifying phrases or clauses, by the time you get to the verb you may make an error in agreement (using a plural verb, for example, when the subject is singular) or even in logic (for example, having a subject that is not capable of being the agent that performs the action of the verb). Following are some typical errors:

www.mhhe. com/crusius

For additional coverage of agreement, go to:

Editing > Subject Verb Agreement

> The *goal* of the courses grouped under the rubric of "Encountering Non-Western Cultures" *are* . . .

Here the writer forgot that *goal*, the subject, is singular.

> During 1992, *the Refugee Act of 1980,* with the help of President Bush and Congress, *accepted* 114,000 immigrants into our nation.

The writer here should have realized that the agent doing the accepting would have to be the Bush administration, not the Refugee Act. A better version would read:

> During 1992, the Bush administration accepted 114,000 immigrants into our nation under the terms of the Refugee Act of 1980.

Proofreading Practice

Proofread the following passage for errors of grammar and punctuation.

> The citizens of Zurich, Switzerland tired of problems associated with drug abuse, experimented with legalization. The plan was to open a central park, Platzspitz, where drugs and drug use would be permitted. Many European experts felt, that it was the illegal drug business rather than the actual use of drugs that had caused many of the cities problems. While the citizens had hoped to isolate the drug problem, foster rehabilitation, and curb the AIDS epidemic, the actual outcome of the Platzspitz experiment did not create the desired results. Instead, violence increased. Drug-related deaths doubled. And drug users were drawn from not only all over Switzerland, but from all over Europe as well. With thousands of discarded syringe packets lying around, one can only speculate as to whether the spread of AIDS was curbed. The park itself was ruined and finally on February 10, 1992, it was barred up and closed. After studying the Swiss peoples' experience with Platzspitz, it is hard to believe that some advocates of drug legalization in the United States are urging us to participate in the same kind of experiment.

Glossary

agent-action: Technical term for a sentence in "who-does-what" form.

alliteration: The repetition of consonant sounds.

allusion: Reference to a person, event, or text, usually not explained.

annotation: A brief critical commentary on a text or section of text.

apologia: An effort to explain and justify what one has done, or chosen not to do, in the face of condemnation or at least widespread disapproval or misunderstanding.

argument: Mature reasoning; a considered opinion backed by a reason or reasons.

bibliography: A list of works on a particular topic.

brief: Outline of a case, including thesis, reasons, and evidence.

case strategy: The moves a writer makes to shape a particular argument, including selecting reasons, ordering them, developing evidence, and linking the sections of the argument for maximum impact.

case structure: A flexible plan for making any argument to any audience; it consists of one or more theses, each of which is supported by one or more reasons, each of which is supported by evidence. See also *brief.*

claim: In argument, what the author wants the audience to believe or to do.

connotation: What a word implies or what we associate it with; see also *denotation.*

conviction: An earned opinion achieved through careful thought, research, and discussion.

convincing: One of the four aims of argument; to use reasoning to secure the assent of people who do not share the author's conviction.

critical reading: A close reading involving analyzing and evaluating a text.

denotation: A word's literal meaning; see also *connotation.*

dialectic: Dialogue or serious conversation; the ancient Greeks' term for argument as inquiry.

graphics: Visual supplements to a longer text such as an essay, article, or manual.

identification: A strong linking of the readers' interests and values with an image, which represents something desired or potentially desirable.

implied question: A question that is inherent in an argument but not explicitly stated; all statements of opinion are answers to questions, usually implied ones.

inquiry: One of the four aims of argument; to use reasoning to determine the best position on an issue.

issue: An aspect of a topic that presents a problem, the solution to which people disagree about.

mediation: One of the four aims of argument; using reason and understanding to bring about consensus among disagreeing parties or positions.

middle style: A style of persuasive writing that is neither stiff and formal nor chatty and familiar.

paraphrase: To restate someone else's writing or speech in one's own words.

persuasion: One of the four aims of argument; persuasion uses both rational and emotional appeals to influence not just thinking but also behavior.

plagiarism: The act of presenting someone else's words and/or ideas as one's own, without acknowledging the source.

position: An overall, summarizing attitude or judgment about some issue.

rhetoric: The art of argument as mature reasoning.

rhetorical context: The circumstances surrounding the text as an act of communication: the time and place in which it was written; its place of publication; its author and his or her values; the ongoing, historical debate to which it contributes.

rhetorical prospectus: A plan for proposed writing that includes a statement of the thesis, aim, audience, speaker's persona, subject matter, and organizational plan.

sampling: A fast, superficial, not necessarily sequential reading of a text, not to learn all that a text has to say but to get a feeling for the territory it covers.

thesis: In argumentation, a very specific position statement that is strategically designed to appeal to readers and to be consistent with available evidence.

topic: A subject or aspect of a subject; see also *issue*.

visual rhetoric: The use of images, sometimes coupled with sound or appeals to the other senses, to make an argument or persuade one's audience to act as the image-maker would have them act.

Credits

Text Credits

DIANE ACKERMAN, "The Medieval Contribution to Love." Published as "Courtly Love," from *A Natural History of Love* by Diane Ackerman. Copyright © 1994 by Diane Ackerman. Used by permission of Random House, Inc.

YONAH ALEXANDER, "Terrorism in the Name of God." *World & I,* October 2002, pp. 38–42. Reprinted with permission.

JONATHAN ALTER (Moderator), "Moving beyond the Blame Game." From *Newsweek,* May 17, 1999, © 1999 Newsweek, Inc. All rights reserved. Reprinted by permission.

THE AMERICAN HERITAGE DICTIONARY OF THE ENGLISH LANGUAGE, definitions of *mature* and *critical.* Copyright © 2000 by Houghton Mifflin Company. Adapted and reproduced by permission from *The American Heritage Dictionary of the English Language,* Fourth Edition.

NATALIE ANGIER, "Gray Matter of Love: Interview with Geoffrey Miller." Natalie Angier. *The New York Times* (May 30, 2000) F2. Copyright © 2000 by The New York Times Co. Reprinted with permission.

ANNE APPLEBAUM, "Stem Cell Stumping." *Washington Post,* August 4, 2004, p. A19. © 2004, The Washington Post, reprinted with permission.

JOHN ARMSTRONG, "The Perfect Union." From *Conditions of Love: The Philosophy of Intimacy* by John Armstrong. Copyright © 2002 by John Armstrong. Used by permission of W. W. Norton & Company, Inc., and by permission of Penguin Books, Ltd.

RUSSELL A. BARKLEY, "Attention-Deficit Hyperactivity Disorder." From *Scientific American,* September 1998. Reprinted with permission. Copyright © 1998 by Scientific American, Inc. All rights reserved.

JENNIFER BAUMGARDNER AND AMY RICHARDS, "A Day without Feminism." Reprinted by permission of Farrar, Straus and Giroux, LLC: "A Day Without Feminism" from *Manifesta: Young Women, Feminism and the Future* by Jennifer Baumgardner and Amy Richards. Copyright © 2000 by Jennifer Baumgardner and Amy Richards.

EILEEN BERRINGTON, "Representations of Terror in the Legitimation of War." From *Beyond September 11: An Anthology of Dissent,* Phil Scraton, ed. London: Pluto Press, 2002. Reprinted with permission.

SISSELA BOK, "Media Literacy." From *Mayhem: Violence as Public Entertainment* by Sissela Bok. Copyright © 1998 by Sissela Bok. Reprinted by permission of Perseus Books PLC, a member of Perseus Books, L.L.C.

FRANCE BOREL, "The Decorated Body." From "Le Vêtement incarné—Les Métamorphoses du corps" by France Borel © Editions Calmann-Lévy, 1992. Reprinted with permission.

LEO BRAUDY, "Terrorism as a Gender War." In *From Chivalry to Terrorism* by Leo Braudy. Copyright © 2003 by Leo Braudy. Used by permission of Alfred A. Knopf, a division of Random House, Inc.

DAVID M. BUSS, "What Women Want" and "Men Want Something Else." From *The Evolution of Desire* by David M. Buss. Copyright © 1994 by David M. Buss. Reprinted by permission of Basic Books, a member of Perseus Books, L.L.C.

NOAM CHOMSKY, "One Man's World." As found in *New Statesman* (1996), Nov. 17, 2003, pp. 16–19. Excerpt from *Hegemony or Survival: America's Quest for Global Dominance* by Noam Chomsky. Copyright © 2003 Aviva Chomsky, Diane Chomsky, and Harry Chomsky. Reprinted by permission from Henry Holt and Company, L.L.C.

Health of Marriage in America, 2001." The Rutgers National Marriage Project, July, 2001. http://marriage.rutgers.edu/Publications/SOOU/ NMPAR2001.pdf. Reprinted with permission.

PAUL WILKINSON, "Analysis of Terrorist Weapons." From *Terrorism Versus Democracy.* Copyright © 2001 Frank Cass Publishers. Reprinted with permission from Taylor and Francis Books, Ltd (Frank Cass).

JOAN WILLIAMS, "Full Commodification to Reconstructive Feminism." From *Unbending Gender* by Joan Williams. Copyright © 1999 by Oxford University Press, Inc. Used by permission of Oxford University Press, Inc.

PATRICIA J. WILLIAMS, "The Distribution of Distress." Reprinted by permission of Farrar, Straus and Giroux, L.L.C.: "The Distribution of Distress" from *Seeing a Color-Blind Future: The Paradox of Race* by Patricia Williams. Copyright © 1997 by Patricia J. Williams.

NAOMI WOLF, "The Beauty Myth." From *The Beauty Myth* by Naomi Wolf. Copyright © 1991 by Naomi Wolf. Reprinted by permission of HarperCollins Publishers, Inc. William Morrow.

KATE ZERNIKE, "Just Saying No to the Dating Industry." Kate Zernike. (*The New York Times,* Nov. 39, 2003.) Copyright © 2003 by The New York Times Co. Reprinted with permission.

STEPHEN ZUNES, "10 Things to Know About the Middle East." *AlterNet,* October 1, 2001. Reprinted with the permission of www.alternet.org.

Photo Credits

Page 5: The J. Paul Getty Museum, Malibu, California; **25:** Bill Aron/PhotoEdit; **Color Section:** (C-1) Thomas & Perkins Advertising, (C-2) AP Photo/U.S. Postal Service, (C-3) Holzman & Kaplan Worldwide, Bret Wills – Photographer, (C-4) By permission of Volkswagen of America, Inc., (C-5) www.comstock.com, (C-6) Reuters/Gregg Newton Archive Photos, (C-7) By permission of Leagas Delaney, Inc., for Adidas. Adidas has not authorized, sponsored, endorsed, or approved this publication and is not responsible for its content; **68:** Courtesy of the Department of Defense; **69:** (top) Barbara Alper/Stock Boston, (bottom) Richard Pasley/Stock Boston; **70:** Bruce Young/Corbis; **75:** By permission of Yan Nascimbene; **79:** © 2005 Terese Winslow; **83:** (all) Stephen Rose/Liaison/Getty Images; **193:** Kathy Willens/AP Photo/Wide World Photos; **232:** Gene Herrick/AP Photo/Wide World Photos; **309:** Patrick Sison/AP Photo/Wide World Photos; **310:** AFP/Corbis; **311:** Cheryl Diaz Meyer/Dallas Morning Star News; **312:** (clockwise from top) Ali Haider/AP/Wide World Photos, HO/AFP/Getty Images, Cheryl Diaz Meyer/Dallas Morning Star News; **313:** Davor Kovacevic/AP/Wide World Photos; **418:** (top) Camerique/American Stock Photography, (bottom) ©HBO/Everett Collection; **419:** (top) Kimberly White/Reuters/Corbis, (bottom) Robert Doisneau/Rapho; **420:** Courtesy of eHarmony.com; **566:** Susan Ragan/AP Photo/Wide World Photos; **628:** Larry Kolvoord/The Image Works; **658:** Peter Macdiarmid/Reuters/Corbis; **706:** Steve Raymer/Corbis; **720:** Lois Bernstein; **758:** (top) Robert Crandall/The Image Works, (bottom) Kathy McLaughlin/The Image Works; **762:** Bruce Roberts/Photo Researchers, Inc.; **778:** A.Ramey/PhotoEdit

Index

Pages on which a term is defined are boldfaced.